HOLL

an Ofsted outstanding and DfE designated teaching school

A place of scholarship; determinedly academic with outstanding A level and GCSE results.

A place of ambition, endeavour, drive and creativity, with outstanding success in placing students in top flight universities.

A place of self-effacing confidence.

A place to find oneself and hear the still small voice.

A place where the potency of academic prowess embraces the human beating heart.

A place which believes that lives and futures can be altered and that chance can be marginalised.

HEAD: Colin Hall

ACADEMY HEAD: David Chappell

AIRLIE GARDENS, LONDON W8 7AF

www.hollandparkschool.co.uk

admissions@hollandparkschool.co.uk

THE GOOD SCHOOLS GUIDE

London North

www.goodschoolsguide.co.uk

Seventh Edition published 2021 by Lucas Publishing Ltd
The Good Schools Guide, 4/4a Bloomsbury Square, London WC1A 2RP
www.goodschoolsguide.co.uk
ISBN 978-1-909963-25-2 The Good Schools Guide London North seventh edition
A CIP catalogue record for this book is available from the British Library

Printed by Cambrian Printers Ltd

Acknowledgements

Writers

Amanda Lynch
Alison Pope
Bernadette John
Beth Noakes
Camilla Smiley
Catherine Goldwater
Charlotte Phillips
David Hargreaves
Emma Jones
Emma Vickers
Grace Moody-Stuart
Imogen McEvedy
Jane Devoy
Judith French
Jackie Lixenberg
Kate Hilpern
Kate Vick
Lisa Freedman
Mary Ann Smillie
Mary Langford
Mary Pegler
Melanie Sanderson
Phoebe Bentinck
Susan Bailes
Susan Hamlyn

Design: David Preston

Typesetting: Theresa Hare, Optima Information Design

Editorial review: Janita Clamp and team: Simon Coury, Kate Hilpern, Melanie Sanderson, Kathryn Berger, Amanda Perkins, Marijke Doldersum

Advertising sales: Charlotte Hollingshead, assisted by Jo Dodds, Publishing Matters

Project management: Skye O'Neill

Everything held together by: Shari Lord

Thanks to Junior League of London for excerpts from *Living in London: A Practical Guide*

Photography: Thanks to all the schools who supplied photographs.

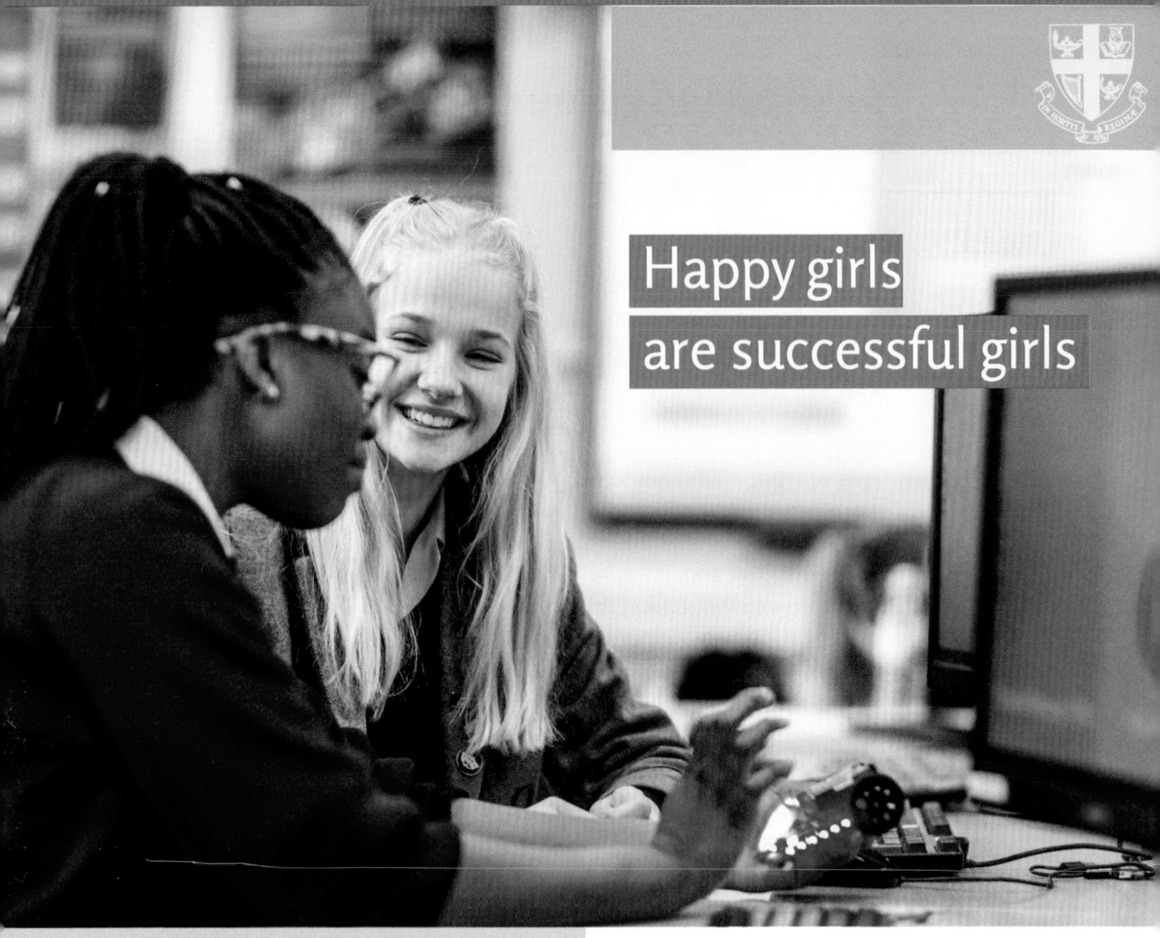

The Good Schools Guide

Choosing a school for your child can be a difficult and time-consuming experience. Our aim is to furnish parents with as much information as possible, including the kind which they won't find in schools' prospectuses or on their websites. Our focus is not on lists of facilities or even league table positions (although these and exam results are always covered in our reviews); we're interested in the culture, ethos and unique personality of a school. We uncover what it's like to be a pupil there and the things, positive and negative, that parents really want to know.

Our writers are given unfettered access not only to head teachers – spending at least an hour in a face to face interview – but also to other members of the senior leadership team. We are privileged to be allowed unsupervised conversations with current pupils and their parents to ensure that the portrait we paint for our readers is a wholly accurate one. No corner is left unscrutinised, no school lunch (always eaten with pupils) left untasted.

We pride ourselves on maintaining a critical distance from the schools we review; we are totally independent and separation of commercial and editorial content is absolute. Schools do not pay, and cannot choose, to be included in (or excluded from) the Guide. We cover our costs by selling advertising space in our books and on our website, as well as licences to allow schools to link to and reprint their reviews. Only schools that we have chosen to cover in the Guide are allowed to advertise with us and whether a school chooses to take advertising or not has no bearing on its inclusion nor on the content of its review.

Our mission is to inform, enlighten and entertain our readers. We hope you enjoy reading our school reviews as much as we, collectively, enjoy writing them.

The Good Schools Guide

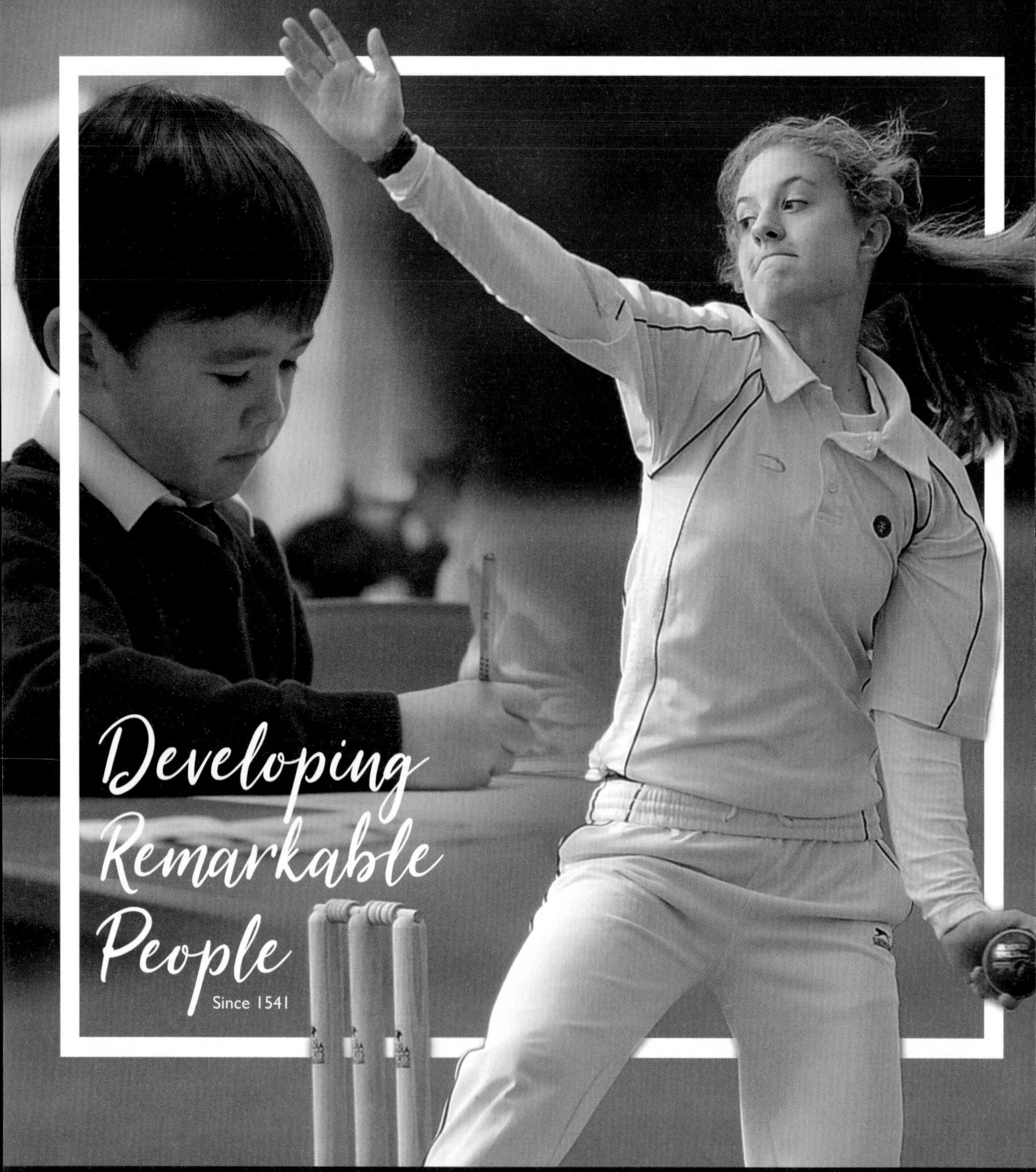

Contents

Key to symbols

The age range of a school is shown by the colour of the title bar.

Junior School

Senior School

Girls' school

Church of England school

Boys' school

Jewish school

Co-ed school

Roman Catholic school

Boys' school with co-ed sixth form

Girls' school with co-ed sixth form

Co-ed pre-prep, then boys only

Co-ed pre-prep, then girls only

Boarding available

London North map

Essex
REDBRIDGE
HAVERING
BARKING &
DAGENHAM
Kent

Foreword

Welcome to the seventh edition of The Good Schools Guide to London North. As we go to press, the nation's children have only just returned to school having been in and out of lockdown for almost a year.

London continues to be a mecca for world class education, attracting a clientele that is both local and global and this year we have seen the best of its schools in both the state and independent sectors rise magnificently and swiftly to the huge and unexpected challenges of a pandemic. In addition to maintaining academic provision most have somehow kept almost all other activities going remotely through lockdown and have proved their mettle in terms of pastoral support. Moreover, proactive initiatives such as the design and manufacturing of PPE for the NHS in DT labs by a conglomerate of schools spanning the capital, and widespread charitable service to communities facing hardship, cannot have failed to influence and mould pupils' outlooks and aspirations for adulthood.

Although public examinations didn't take place, London's independent and state schools retained the lion's share of top spots in the 2020 A level and GCSE league tables. And academic results are only part of the picture; they excel across the board, with the best offering an extraordinary range of artistic, sporting and co-curricular opportunities.

Our writers, used to covering thousands of miles a year by car, train, tube and on foot around vast school campuses (sensible shoes a prerequisite) have, like our schools, seamlessly transferred their activities online to enable us to offer the most up to date reviews available. We have continued to interview head teachers and parents on video calls and tirelessly drilled down beneath the clever gloss of virtual school tours to provide readers with our knowledge, inside information, experience and opinions on the capital's best schools north of the Thames.

We have also used the last year to reflect on how we can adapt and evolve to meet the needs of modern parents and as a result have added new sections to our reviews. Latest exam results can be seen at a glance and we now cover SEN, inclusivity and diversity separately – more important than ever for preparing young people to be tolerant and open-minded adults in the modern world.

Competition for places in London's schools seems to become ever fiercer year on year. For parents choosing a new school for their child advance planning is crucial and gathering accurate and relevant information has never been more important – or more challenging. In an era of virtual open days we hope that this Guide will prove to be the next best thing to an in-person visit.

We aim for our reviews to answer parents' most burning questions about a school. As they move into new territory with the ability to switch between in-school and home learning, however, what should you be looking for in a school right now? If you have the opportunity, ask whether pupils felt supported while they were learning at home. Were they able to ask for academic help if they needed it? Were the lessons well planned and creatively delivered and how did schools help pupils move away from their screens whilst keeping them on task during the course of the school day? Did the school help keep pupils active and were co-curricular options offered? Which elements of remote teaching methods are being retained to further enrich teaching methods?

If you need further guidance our team of expert consultants can help – see page 52 for more details.

We wish you and your family all the best on your educational journey.

The Good Schools Guide Team

The English school system

London has an abundance of good schools – state and private. Many families mix and match, and may have a child or two in each system at different stages of their schooling. A choice of school may depend on logistics as much as ideology. But for those not familiar with English schooling the systems can seem baffling.

State schools

Many families head for London hoping for a place in a good local state school. There are huge advantages: at primary level in particular, your child's friends will almost all be local. You will soon feel part of the local community. You won't spend hours in a car trying to navigate London traffic or have to squeeze onto a rush hour tube or bus. In central London especially, many are used to young children arriving without fluent English and have systems in place to help. And of course they are free.

Primary schools

Primary schools start at 3 (if they have a nursery class) or 4 and most run through to 11, though there are some infants' schools (3-7) and junior schools (7-11), often but not always linked with automatic entry from one to the other. Increasing numbers of senior schools are opening linked primary schools, and will eventually become all-through schools.

The cut-off date by age is 31 August in both state and private schools in England (though some private schools may be more flexible). This means that if your child's birthday is on 31 August they will start in the reception class when just 4, whilst a child with a 1 September birthday will actually be just 5 when they start.

Virtually all British state primary schools are co-ed and non-selective academically (the exception is the London

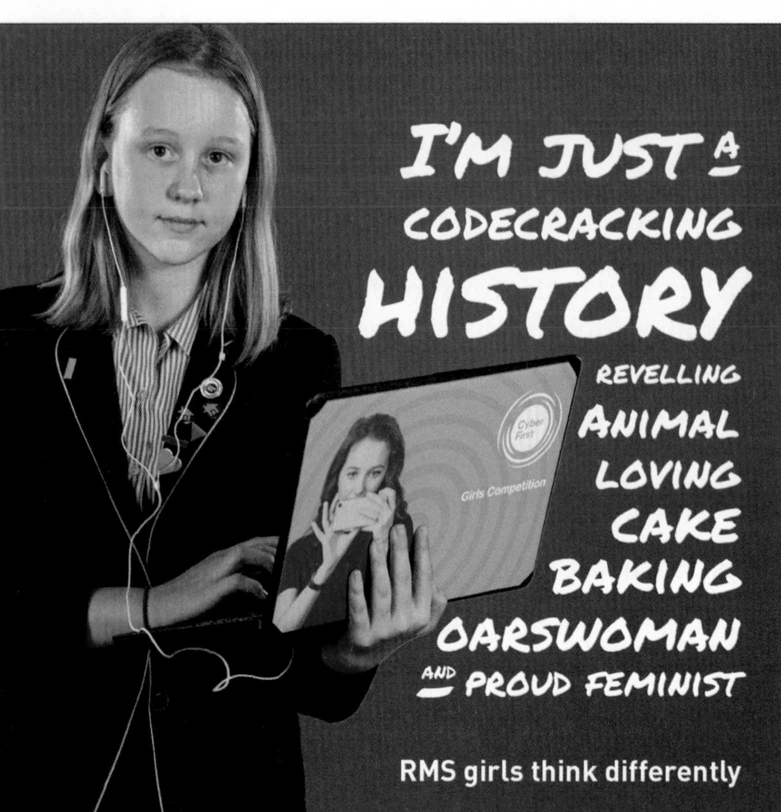

Ages 2-18
Boarding from age 8
(full, weekly and flexi)

Learn more at
RMSforgirls.com

The Royal Masonic School
for Girls, Rickmansworth,
Hertfordshire, WD3 4HF
01923 773168
rmsforgirls.com

BEDE'S
EXTRAORDINARY

Imogen
Lower Sixth

HMC - Day, weekly and full boarding
Boys and girls 13 to 18

For a personal visit please contact
admissions@bedes.org
T 01323 843252 or online at **bedes.org**

Bede's Senior School
Upper Dicker
East Sussex BN27 3QH

Oratory Junior House, which takes only boys – and tests for academic and musical aptitude), though faith schools mostly select by church attendance.

State primary schools may not have the specialist teachers, small class sizes or facilities enjoyed by private prep schools but the quality of teaching shouldn't be inferior. If you're lucky enough to live close to a good primary school and have a good state comprehensive down the road then your children's education is sorted. However, state primaries don't prepare children for 11+ entrance exams, so if you are aiming at a selective secondary school you will probably have to rope in a tutor in year 5 or so (see Tutors and Tutoring, page 805).

Secondary schools

There is a much greater variety of state secondary schools: single sex and co-ed, selective and non-selective, plus those that select a proportion of students for academic, music or dance prowess

The vast majority of London secondary schools are non-selective, but a few academically selective grammar schools remain, in areas such as Kingston, Sutton and Barnet. The BRIT school in south London for 14-19 year olds is the only state performing arts school in the country, with entry by audition.

State primaries may not have the small class sizes, but the teaching shouldn't be inferior

Some students move on after GCSEs to a sixth form college for 16-18 year olds. These tend to offer a wide range of subjects and to have an atmosphere more akin to a college than a school. Some are academically selective, others offer vocational courses to those with a more practical bent. East London Arts and Music is a sixth form for students aiming for a career in music, games design or film and TV.

Academies and free schools

Increasing numbers of state schools – particularly secondary schools – are becoming academies. These are state funded but often run by academy chains, and the current government is encouraging all schools to become academies over the next few years.

Free schools were originally intended to be set up by groups of parents and some of the early ones were, though many were set up by religious groups, and now most have academy chain backers.

Both of these types of school are outside local authority control, can decide on their own admissions criteria (though they should abide by the national code), do not have to teach the national curriculum and may employ unqualified teachers.

Private schools

Families moving to London may find it logistically easier to apply for private school places because, unlike state schools, they do not require you to have a local address before you make your application.

Prep schools

Many areas of London are well-equipped with prep schools (boys', girls' and co-ed). They are likely to have small classes, specialist teachers and a relatively biddable intake – if not the sports facilities you will find in a country school. Don't assume the teaching will be better than at a state school – both sectors include those who would be better off in a different profession.

They are likely to start at 3 or 4 and go through to 11 or 13 – historically, girls have moved on at 11 and boys at 13, though increasing numbers of boys' and co-ed senior schools now have a main intake at 11. Some are divided into pre-preps

(3-7) and preps (7-13), though usually with a fairly seamless transition between the two; others don't start till 7.

As the name suggests, prep schools prepare your child for entrance exams to secondary schools, and advise on which are likely to be most suitable. A prep school is judged at least partly by its leavers' destinations, so it will do its best to ensure your child moves on to a decent secondary school, even if it has to dampen down your expectations.

> *Independent senior schools range from the ferociously selective to those that provide a gentle haven*

A stand alone pre-prep, that goes from 3 or so to 7 years, may be a good bet if you are arriving in London at short notice. Some of the children who join at 3 may move on at 4 or 5, so places do come up. The disadvantage is that they are, inevitably, obliged to spend quite a part of the upper years preparing children for 7+ or 8+ entrance exams.

Senior schools

Independent senior schools range from the ferociously selective such as Westminster and St Paul's to those that provide a gentle haven from hothousing or social integration – with admissions policies to match. A glance at the league tables will give a clue as to the degree of selection they operate.

Historically, girls' independent secondaries have started at 11 and boys' at 13, but increasing numbers – especially boys only schools that have turned co-ed – are switching their main intake to 11, with shrinking numbers of 13+ places. Thirteen plus schools with linked junior schools will often offer 11+ places in their junior schools with guaranteed transfer to the senior school, mostly aimed at state school pupils and those whose prep school finishes at 11.

Some independent schools go all the way through from 3 or 4 to 18, which can provide welcome continuity and

freedom from 11+ or 13+ selection tests. However, few guarantee that a child who is struggling academically will be able to stay on with their peers, and teenagers may well decide at 16 (particularly if they have been in the same single sex school since 4) that the grass looks greener elsewhere.

Independent sixth form colleges

Independent sixth form colleges, sometimes called crammers, were originally set up to prepare students for university entrance, particularly Oxbridge. They still specialise in this field, generally offering a variety of routes that include full two year A levels and shorter courses for those who need to improve on past grades. Some also offer one or two year GCSE courses. Classes are small, the focus is on exam practice and extracurricular options are limited. They are useful for those arriving in London at short notice and students who have rethought their options or need to boost their results.

Applying to a state school

It can be nerve-racking deciding where you would like your child to take their first steps into school, or spend their teenage years.

The primary schools you are considering are likely to be very local. The main admissions criteria for non-faith schools are generally siblings and then distance – which can be less than a few hundred metres for the popular ones.

Secondary schools are far more varied in their character and in their admissions criteria. These may also include academic selection and/or auditions for performing arts aptitude. You may be able to apply under more than one of these.

Timing

Applications are made through your local authority in the autumn of the year before your child starts school or moves on to secondary school. The cut-off date for secondary admissions is 31 October of year 6. For primary schools it is 15 January before the September start date.

If the primary school has a nursery class for 3-year-olds you apply direct to the school when your child is 2; however, you will still need to reapply for a reception (4-year-old) place via the local authority.

Academically selective grammar schools, and some that partially select by aptitude for eg music, now do their admissions tests/auditions in the summer term of year 5 or the September of year 6, so that they can give out initial results before the October closing date for applications. This will usually involve registering with the school during the year 5 summer term – so check dates carefully.

It can be nerve-racking deciding where you would like your child to take their first steps into school

How do state schools offer places?

There are some general rules that most schools adhere to.

- Education, Health and Care plan naming the school. These children come first in line and must be given a place.
- Looked after/previously looked after children. These generally come next.
- Siblings. These often, but not always, come third. Check before you move house after your first-born has got a place.
- Exceptional medical or social need. This generally involves a letter from a doctor or social worker explaining why St Cake's is the only school that will cope with your child's needs. Very few children get a place by this route.
- Distance. Generally as the crow flies, but sometimes by the shortest walking route. Sometimes faith schools designate parishes; other schools may designate particular areas as their catchment. Some have specific feeder primary schools. Some grammar schools limit the distance applicants may travel to school by eg giving preference to those from specified postcodes. Your local authority should have information on how close you probably have to live to any individual school (except faith schools) to be in with a chance of a place.

However, London has a plethora of different types of school with different – and sometimes multiple – entrance criteria.

Grammar schools

These are academically selective by entrance exam (usually some combination of maths, English and reasoning tests). Increasing numbers give preference to children who live relatively locally; some also prioritise a certain number of students on pupil premium. You will be told if your child has reached the qualifying standard before the closing date for applications, but not if he will actually be offered a place.

Faith schools

These may demand that you baptised your child before she was 6 months old and have attended a specific church weekly for the past five years. They are no longer allowed to give points for eg brass polishing and flower arranging, felt to advantage middle class applicants.

Free schools and academies

These may set their own entrance criteria, though they should abide by the national admissions code. They, like most faith schools, also decide which applicants to accept (local authorities make that decision for community schools) and thus are vulnerable to accusations of cherry picking easy-to-teach pupils.

Aptitude

Some schools select part of their intake by aptitude for eg music, dance, technology or languages.

Fair banding

An increasing number of non-selective schools use fair banding to divide applicants into ability bands, taking an equal number from each band via other criteria eg distance. This generally involves computer-based reasoning tests and is not pass/fail.

Filling in the form

You can list six choices of schools in London and we recommend using all of your choices. It's vital to include at least one where you are more-or-less sure of getting a place – even if it isn't your first choice. If you don't, you may only be offered an undersubscribed school some distance away. For faith schools, you will probably have to fill in a supplementary application form and get it signed by your religious leader. If a new free school is opening in your area, you will quite likely in its first year be able to apply direct to the school in addition to your six other choices.

NB Put your school choices in order of preference – if you qualify for a place at more than one, you will only be offered the school highest on your list. The schools don't know where else you have applied, and don't know if you have put them first or last – only the local authority knows that.

Moving to London

As long as you have a right of abode in England, you can apply for a state school place here. However, you can't apply till you have an address in the country and are living here (except for forces/diplomatic families and those applying to state boarding schools).

If you are applying for a school place not at normal admissions times – ie reception or year 7 – admissions will probably be handled by individual schools, though you will have to complete the in-year admissions form. Your local authority should be able to give your information on which schools have spaces, but it's worth contacting schools direct too.

Don't want the school you are offered?

You can appeal for a place at a school you prefer, but do it quickly. In the meantime, accept the school you have been offered (otherwise the local authority is under no obligation to find you a school at all). Ensure you are on the waiting list for any schools you would be happy with. And do visit the school you have been offered: you may find that contrary to local reputation, it is up and coming and will suit your child very well.

Independent school admissions

Prep schools

London prep schools have never been more popular. Their fearsome reputation for preparing children for entry to London senior schools with a champion's regime of revision, tests and extension work may well suit the bright, robust child but can cause others to flounder.

If a school particularly interests you, request a private visit and make sure it includes time to see the head and watch the school at work. Try to get a balanced view of the school – chat to pupils, staff, other parents and don't allow the marketing manager to dominate your visit. Before (and after), browse the website, prospectus and marketing literature – they'll all be glossy with happy, smiley faces, but do you like the tone and the events they put centre stage? Same old faces, same old names or a good smattering of faces, across the ages? Some preps are very traditional – blazers and boaters are often a clue; others more relaxed – sweatshirts could be a signal. You can probably tell without visiting whether or not your family ethos is likely to be a good fit.

Entry requirements at 3 or 4 vary considerably from 'first-come, first-served' (which may mean name down at birth) to mini-assessment days complete with interview and observations to see just how well Harriet integrates with her peers and playmates. Few will expect children to read and write on entry but such is the pressure for places at favoured schools that, to the dismay of many heads, parents have been known to enlist the help of tutors for their 3-year-olds. In general the play and learning that goes on at home or nursery school should be adequate preparation. At 7 or 8, nearly every prep school operates a formal assessment process, and for many London day schools, the pressure is on.

They'll all be glossy with happy smiley faces, but do you like the tone and events they put centre stage?

As their name suggests, the main aim of 'preparatory schools', or prep schools, is to prepare children for entry to fee-paying senior schools at 11 or 13. Traditionally, pre-preps take children from 3 or 4 and prepare them for moving on to preps at 7 or 8. There are fewer stand-alone pre-preps than there used to be as their main market, the boarding prep, has declined in numbers. Today, many pre-preps and preps are linked schools, with a more-or-less seamless transition between them and sometimes their senior school too. In London, with fierce competition for 7+ places at top prep schools, quite a few stand-alone pre-preps survive. Their raison d'être is preparing children for these competitive exams, which can mean the pressure starts in year 1 with regular practice papers. Some, whilst having linked prep schools, also send large numbers of children elsewhere.

Preps tend to stand or fall by their senior school destinations. Parents, whether they are aiming to get their 3- or 4-year-old into the pre-prep of a chosen all-through school, or their 8-year-old into a prep that sends many of its pupils to the top day or boarding schools, are generally looking ahead. Yet all-through selective schools rarely guarantee that children they take in at 3 or 4 or even 7 will have a seamless transfer upwards. If your child is felt to be struggling, you may well be advised to look elsewhere. Equally, a child who fails to gain a place at the pre-prep stage may well have developed sufficiently to sail in there or elsewhere later on. So a school that helps your child to become a happy and confident learner is the best investment.

Senior schools

If your child is already at a prep school then the process of selecting and applying to the 'right' senior school should mainly be taken care of – it's a large part of what you're paying them to do.

It used to be the case that parents rarely challenged a prep's advice about which senior school would best suit their son or daughter, but heads tell us that 'managing parental expectations' is now a significant part of their job. A prep school's reputation stands or falls on the destinations of its pupils at 11 and/or 13; prep school heads spend a large part of their time visiting senior schools and getting to know their pupil profiles. Experienced heads can spot which children should be aiming for which senior schools fairly early on and if this conflicts with parental ambitions then he or she will advise accordingly. No school will 'under sell' an able child, so if you disagree with the advice you have been given you should be able to have a frank discussion about the reasons behind it. The decision about which senior school to apply for should be at least as much about where a child would fit in and be happy as it is about academic ability.

Many prep school heads are concerned that pre-tests don't suit late developers who may not have come into their own academically

State primary to independent senior

Plenty of children from state primary schools do move on to independent secondaries, often with scholarships or bursaries. It is not the state primary school's job to prepare children for independent school entrance exams, so most parents take on a tutor for a year or so to ensure their children are used to, say, writing a story in half an hour, and timing their answers. Neither can you expect a primary school head to advise on likely senior schools, so you will need to make your own judgement on which schools are likely to be suitable for your child.

Applying from abroad

The first step is often an online UKiset test which measures academic English language skills. Most schools will also ask overseas applicants to sit their own entrance test, and are generally happy to send tests abroad, though they may ask applicants to attend interviews in person.

Pre-tests

An increasing number of senior schools offer provisional or definite places based on the results of 'pre-tests' taken in year 6 or 7 (age 10 or 11). Senior schools use these tests as a filter and to give an early indication of demand for places. Many prep school heads are concerned that pre-tests don't suit late developers (often boys) who may not come into their own academically this early.

Pre-tests are age-standardised and include multiple-choice tests in maths, English, verbal and non-verbal reasoning. If your son or daughter is offered a place after completing these tests, he or she may be required to sit the common entrance examinations in year 8 – though some top schools, including Westminster and St Paul's, are abandoning the CE in favour of prep school assurances of 'continued good conduct and academic progress'.

11+ and 13+ tests

The 11+ test is taken in year 6 for entry in year 7 and comprises papers in English, maths and sometimes reasoning. Many London schools set their own papers, though the London 11+ Consortium of 12 girls' schools

Parents feel more responsible for their child's social presentation than their ability to do long division

sets one common exam – a 75 minute cognitive ability test – and shares results.

The 13+ common entrance – a set of exams common to many independent schools – is taken in year 8. Core subjects are English, maths and science and candidates may also sit papers in history, geography, modern foreign languages, Mandarin, ancient Greek and Latin. Tests are taken at the candidate's own school and are marked by the school to which they are applying. Some independent schools set their own tests for candidates (perhaps from abroad) who have not been prepared for common entrance.

Most London independent girls' and co-ed day schools accept pupils from age 11, as do increasing numbers of boys' schools. There are still some traditional boys' schools such as Westminster and St Paul's and boarding schools such as Eton and Harrow that start at 13+. Thirteen plus schools with linked junior schools will often offer 11+ places in their junior schools with guaranteed transfer to the senior school, mostly aimed at state school pupils and those whose prep school finishes at 11.

Interviews

While state schools are prohibited from interviewing any but potential sixth form (or boarding) students, the interview is an integral part of nearly every private school admissions process, and tends to send the applicant's parents, rather than the actual applicant, into a spin. Parents feel considerably more responsible for their child's social presentation than for his or her ability to do long division or conjugate French verbs. And, while a school may breezily describe the interview as 'just a chance to get to know the child better', this hardly quells fears about sending young

Daniel or Daniella into the lion's den.

Oversubscribed at every point, the selective London independent school tends to concentrate on the academic. The majority usually only meet the child after a written exam (generally used as a first edit), and the interview itself will probably contain a significant component of maths, comprehension or reasoning. The aim here is to probe intellectual strengths and weaknesses in order to select from the central bulk of candidates or to pick scholarship material. Finding out a little about a child's character is only of secondary importance.

Even the most academic schools, however, are not necessarily just looking for those guaranteed to deliver a stream of A*s. Some use interviews as an opportunity to create as balanced a community as possible:

'I didn't want all extroverts or all eggheads,' said one ex-junior school head. 'Most children who sat our exam scored between 40 and 65 per cent in the written paper, so I was looking for an individual spark. At the age of 7, particularly, the interview is a crucial counterbalance to the exam. Those born between September and December always scored higher marks in the written paper. At interview we would go back to the list and bring in some younger children.'

'I always tell parents if they're paying to coach 3-year-olds they might as well burn £20 notes,' said a school head with the task of selecting 40 4-year-olds

Parents, stand back!

Concerned parents often do their best to control the outcome of the interview, but professional preparation is seen as a waste of time, both by those who interview and by teachers. 'I always tell parents if they're paying to coach 3-year-olds, they might as well burn £20 notes,' said a junior school head who

has the daunting task of selecting 40 4-year-olds from 200 applicants in a two-tier interview. 'The only useful preparation is to talk to them, play with them and read them stories.'

Further up the system, the advice is equally non-prescriptive. The head of a west London pre-prep does her best to relax the 7-year-olds she sends to prep school interviews by providing them with as much factual information as she can beforehand. 'I try to prepare them for what they'll find. I usually describe the head – because I'm a smallish woman they might expect all heads to be like me – and I'll tell them what the school looks like. Beyond that I just say, "Look them in the eye, answer carefully and be honest." Children sell themselves.'

Some pre-preps and prep schools provide mock interviews, some will carefully guide children on what books or hobbies might show them to best advantage, but most interviewers say they always know when a child has been coached, and honesty – at least in theory – is the quality they're looking for. 'I tell children,' says one private tutor who prepares children for 11 plus, 'to say what's in their heart, not what their teacher told them to say.'

'I am looking for sparkly eyes and interest. If a child sits there like a pudding, you usually don't take them'

Parents, step forward

Although the school interview is nominally about the child, the school is also interviewing parents and it's they who may need a little preparation while their child can happily be him or herself. A balance between steady, respectful (schools are ever keen to avoid the parent from hell) and interesting (but nor do they like dull ones) is best.

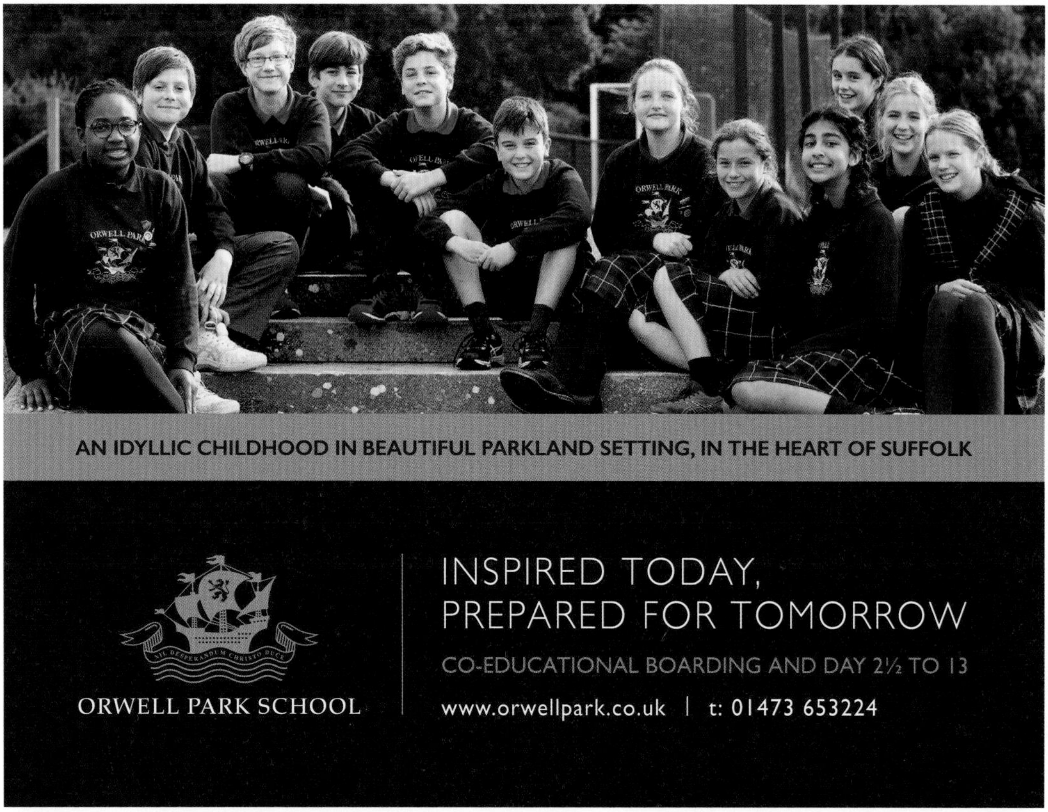
AN IDYLLIC CHILDHOOD IN BEAUTIFUL PARKLAND SETTING, IN THE HEART OF SUFFOLK
NIL DESPERANDUM CHRISTO DUCE
ORWELL PARK SCHOOL
INSPIRED TODAY,
PREPARED FOR TOMORROW
CO-EDUCATIONAL BOARDING AND DAY 2½ TO 13
www.orwellpark.co.uk | t: 01473 653224

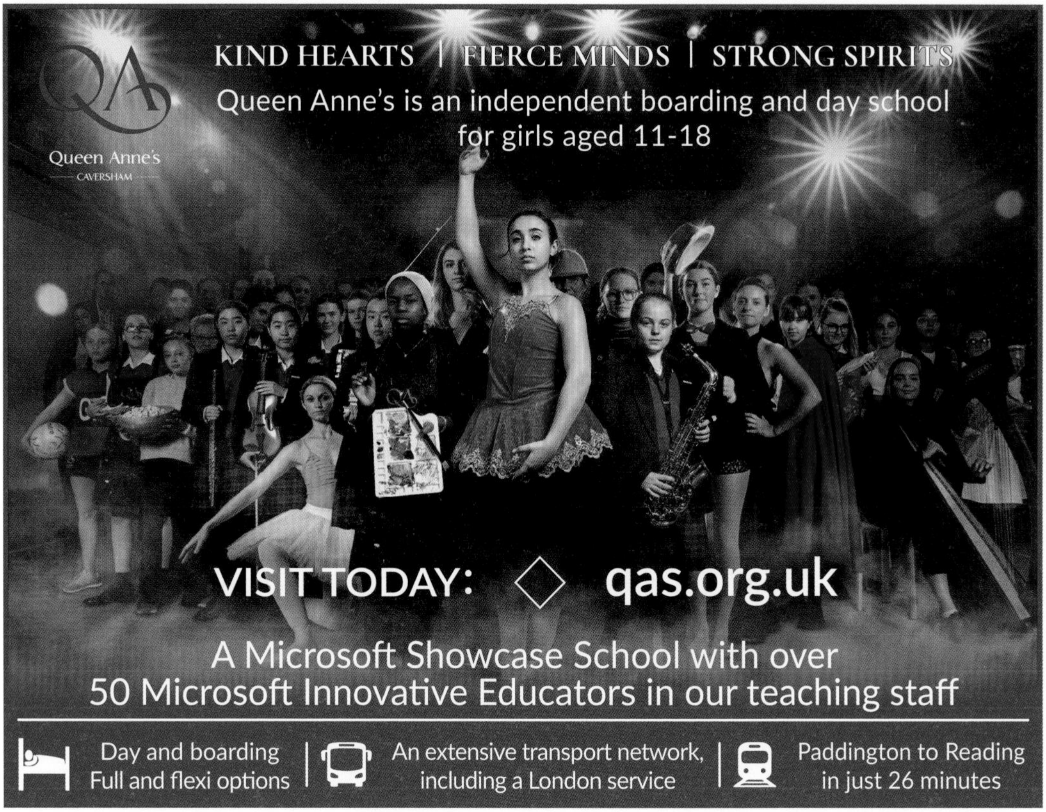
QA
Queen Anne's
CAVERSHAM
KIND HEARTS | FIERCE MINDS | STRONG SPIRITS
Queen Anne's is an independent boarding and day school
for girls aged 11-18
VISIT TODAY: ◇ qas.org.uk
A Microsoft Showcase School with over
50 Microsoft Innovative Educators in our teaching staff
Day and boarding
Full and flexi options
An extensive transport network,
including a London service
Paddington to Reading
in just 26 minutes

Is it fair?

Personality, of course, will always be the most variable aspect of any interview and all interviewers have a personal bias. They may hate boastful children, or those who say their favourite leisure activity is computer games; they may prefer Arsenal fans to Tottenham supporters; but some schools do make a strenuous attempt to counteract the sense of one adult sitting in judgement on one child. One senior school sees candidates individually before sending them off to a lesson where they can be observed by another teacher as they work in a group.

The best interviewers can and do overcome the limitations both of the written examination and of the child. 'Children, even very shy ones, like to talk about themselves, their friends, their families and their pets. I get them to describe what they did on Sunday, or I turn my back and ask them to describe something in the room. Sometimes I even get a child to sing or dance. I am looking for sparkly eyes and interest. If a child just sits there like a pudding, you usually don't take them.' Some schools get over the 'what to talk about' dilemma by asking children to bring along a favourite object. If, however, the child pitches up with a copy of Proust or boasts a collection of Roman ceramics, parents shouldn't be surprised if the interviewer is somewhat sceptical.

Although most heads are honest in their report about a child – after all, their reputation depends on it – the interview can also benefit them. 'Occasionally, a prep school head knows perfectly well that a child is not suited to our school, but the parents just won't listen. Coming from us it doesn't sour the relationship with the school.'

ADMISSIONS
AT YEAR 5,
YEAR 7 &
SIXTH FORM

How to judge a new school

Start a normal business and you can begin with baby footsteps, holding fire on major investment in resources and employees until you are confident you're on to a winner.

Founders of new schools, however, don't have that luxury. In addition to substantial premises, other chunky overheads include a head, senior management team (possibly compatible, possibly not), a full pack of teachers (ditto), not to mention the pupils.

With such a potent cocktail, the scope for fast track failure even in an apparently well set up new school is almost limitless. So why should prospective parents be prepared to take the risk? And how can they judge whether it will be worth it?

Talented team?

How confidence-inspiring is the head? With a massive extra workload and just one shot at getting things right, 'he'll do' or 'give her a try' just aren't enough. If you doubt the head's ability, give the school a miss. But bear in mind that some of the best heads aren't charismatic orators: their most important attributes are appointing able teaching staff and keeping them happily on board.

Check out the teachers. A good new school will thrive on teamwork. Do they radiate inspiration? And when you talk to them, do you wish you had been taught by them? Teachers in free schools and academies don't have to be qualified. Unqualified ones may be fabulous – or they may just be cheap to employ.

Great governors?

In an established school, all parents need know about the governors is that they are happy with the head – and vice

versa. In a new school, however, the governing body's ability to choose a talented senior team, help get over inevitable initial difficulties and, most important of all, replace people fast if they have made the wrong choices, is vital.

You are looking for governors who are good as individuals and even stronger as a team, leading from the front and putting in the time to observe, listen (to you) and learn. Invisibility on open days or other school presentations is a serious warning sign that all is not well.

If your school has an academy sponsor, they will be involved in the governance. Some, like ARK, have stellar reputations. Others are close to disaster areas. Check out not just your school but the others they run. Their Ofsted reports may say more about them as a group than an individual prospectus ever can.

Parent power?

Is drop off time a turn off because of the attitudes and behaviour of other parents or their children? As a group, you are all important in working together to set the school on the right course. It takes extra energy and commitment and you need to know that other parents will chip in. Are they people you could work with? And are their children proud to be there?

Premises

Many new free schools open in uninspiring 'temporary' buildings, with the promise of a move to a fabulous purpose built (but often unspecified) site in a year or two. If the year or two is stretching out indefinitely with no sign of building work finishing (or even starting), beware.

Do your homework

Read the prospectus and study the school website very carefully. The latter should have the most up-to-date information and links to policies on matters such as admissions, discipline, child protection, SEN. How geared up is the school to deal with 'a touch' of dyslexia? Do the less co-ordinated ever get picked for matches? What happens if it becomes successful and oversubscribed and its catchment area shrinks? Will your second child still qualify for a place or will you, and similar other pioneers, be penalised? If you still have questions, ask the school directly or talk to other parents.

Now read on...

For the altruistic, enjoying the inner glow that comes with helping improve education in your local area may be enough. For others, the hope that a brand new school will do your child proud is a more tangible benefit. Whatever your reasons, good luck.

Independent Catholic day and boarding school for boys and girls aged 2 to 13

Situated within 65 acres of beautiful grounds in an area of outstanding natural beauty and within easy reach of London

The Oratory Preparatory School,
Goring Heath, Reading RG8 7SF

0118 984 4511

www.oratoryprep.co.uk

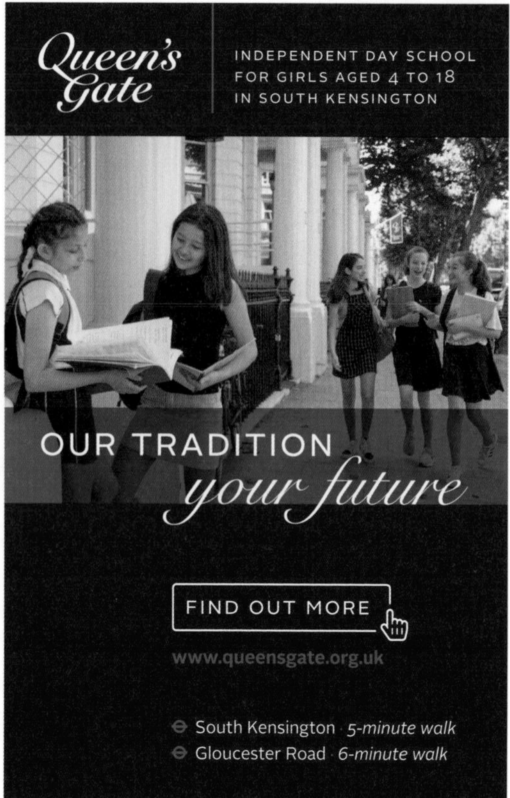

ALDRO
EST. 1898
An independent day and boarding school for boys and girls aged 7-13 in the heart of rural surrey
Daily Aldro bus from Wimbledon
www.aldro.org
WELCOMING GIRLS FROM SEPTEMBER 2021

DWIGHT SCHOOL LONDON
Igniting the spark of genius in every child
"Both Dwight and the IB have helped me prepare for the independent learning required at university."
-- Alysia, Dwight alumna
Dwight School providing a world-class education in London
The International Baccalaureate a pathway to top universities in the UK and abroad
Join us at an information event to learn more: dwightlondon.org/open
London | New York | Seoul | Shanghai | Dubai | Global Online

HAMPTON COURT HOUSE
An independent, co-educational school for children aged 3-18 years
Ranked 2nd on the Independent Schools Council's list of 'Small Independent Schools 2019'
To book our next open event, contact our Head of Admissions and External Relations:
020 8614 0857 or book a place online:
www.hamptoncourthouse.co.uk/admissions

Hawkesdown House School
&
The Walnut Tree Nursery
For girls & boys from 2 years
27 Edge Street, Kensington, London W8 7PN
Telephone: 0207 727 9090
Email: admin@hawkesdown.co.uk
www.hawkesdown.co.uk

The Good Schools Guide Education Consultants

The Good Schools Guide has been trusted by generations of parents to provide expert, honest and unbiased information about schools. Our education consultancy provides the same high standards of expertise, independence and professional integrity to individual families.

Every day our highly-experienced consultants successfully help clients from all over the world to find the right schools for their children. However urgent the deadline, however complex the circumstances, call 0203 286 6824 (UK) or +44 203 286 6824 (international) to find out how we can solve your educational dilemmas.

Our consultants

Our consultants have personally visited and reviewed countless schools for our website and publications; many have professional backgrounds or specialist qualifications in education. Between them they have direct experience of every aspect of both the British and international education systems, not to mention invaluable local knowledge about schools in London and all areas of the UK. Our team includes experts in SEN, school appeals, scholarships and bursaries, grammar schools and relocation to the UK from abroad.

Consultancy built around your needs

Our consultancy packages range from a telephone consultation to a fully bespoke service tailored to meet complex, urgent or other specific circumstances. Additional services include accompanied school visits, providing translators and educational assessments and arranging specialist tuition. Our main consultancy services are outlined overleaf; for full details please visit www. goodschoolsguide. co.uk.

Classic School Search; Premier Schools Consultancy; Premier Plus Schools Consultancy

Our schools' search services are designed to provide tailored individual advice and support to parents. Our consultants will first take the time to understand fully your individual requirements and will then, depending on the amount of hands-on support you need, will ensure that your child is placed in a school that suits him/her and works for the rest of the family.

State School Service

This service, run by the GSG expert in state education, is for parents who are interested in state schools only. It can give advice on admissions criteria, catchment areas and grammar schools.

Special Educational Needs

Our team of SEN experts is unique. We have specialists in eg dyslexia, autism, speech and language difficulties and we have extensive knowledge of both mainstream and special schools which cater for children with these difficulties.

Academic assessments

If you are not sure what academic level your child is at, particularly if you are coming from overseas, we can arrange academic assessments.

Scholarships and bursaries

We have amassed information on scholarships and bursaries to create a unique central resource, with information on the fee assistance available at hundreds of independent schools.

Contact us

Phone us on +44 (0)203 286 6824 or send a brief email to: consultants@goodschoolsguide.co.uk outlining what you need. Tell us the age of your child and where you live plus your contact details. We will contact you within 48 hours, discuss how best to help you and ensure we match you with the right consultant. Consultations can be by phone, email or face to face, and we can find a consultant to speak to you within an hour if necessary.

How much?

Ours is one of the most competitively priced tailor-made education consultancy services in the UK. Check our website for current fees.

Our guarantee

The Good Schools Guide has an international reputation for providing unbiased, independent advice on educational matters. We have no commercial links whatsoever with any school. This gives our education consultants the freedom to consider a huge range of schools in order to find the best one for you. You can have complete confidence that if our consultants recommend a school it is because, and only because, they consider it to be suitable for your child. You can also be assured that we maintain the highest possible standards of privacy and all dealings with clients are completely confidential.

Central

Camden
City of London
Hackney
Islington
Westminster

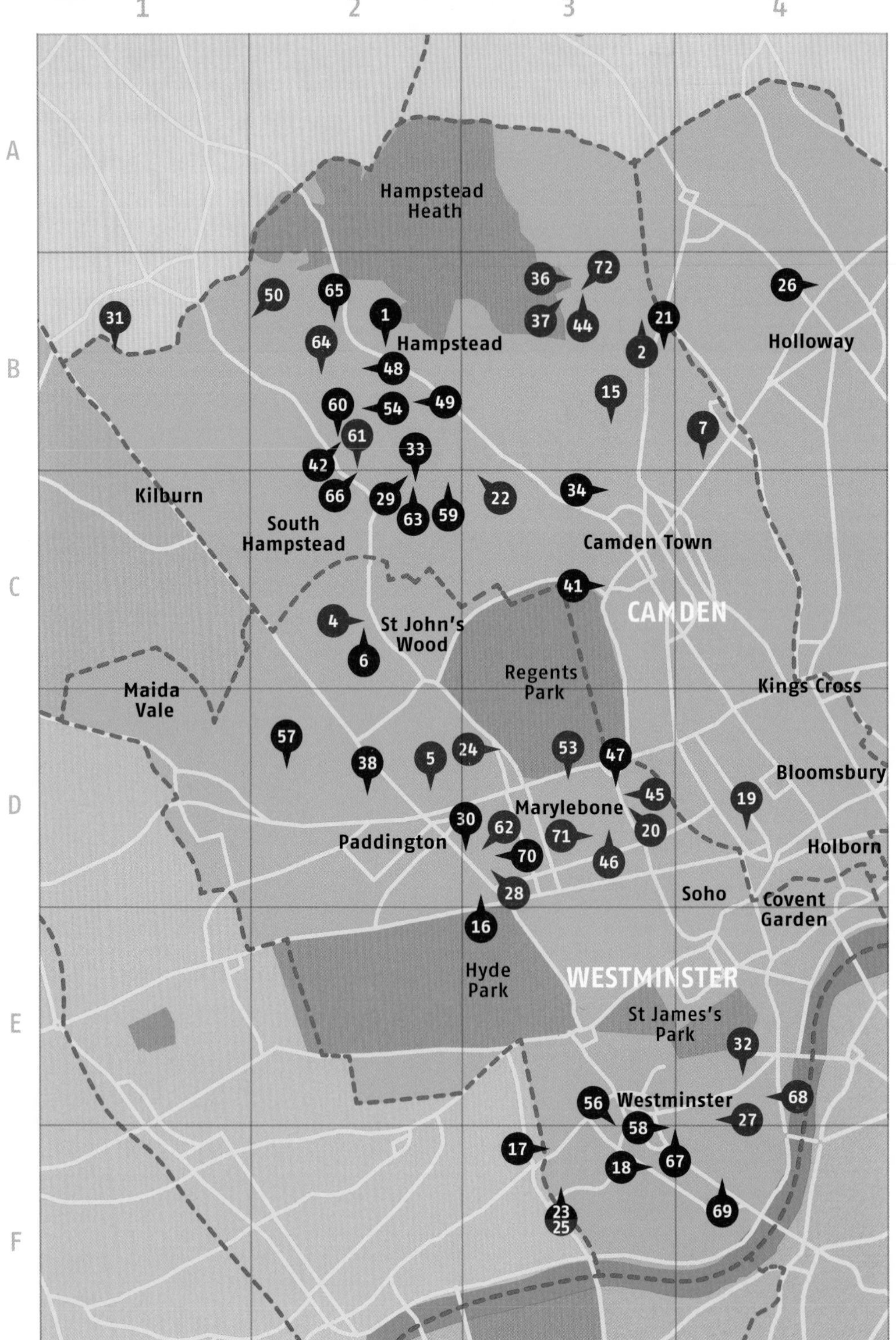
1
2
3
4
A
B
C
D
E
F
Hampstead Heath
Hampstead
Holloway
Kilburn
South Hampstead
Camden Town
CAMDEN
St John's Wood
Regents Park
Kings Cross
Maida Vale
Bloomsbury
Marylebone
Paddington
Holborn
Soho
Covent Garden
Hyde Park
WESTMINSTER
St James's Park
Westminster
1
2
4
5
6
7
15
16
17
18
19
20
21
22
23
24
25
26
27
28
29
30
31
32
33
34
36
37
38
41
42
44
45
46
47
48
49
50
53
54
56
57
58
59
60
61
62
63
64
65
66
67
68
69
70
71
72

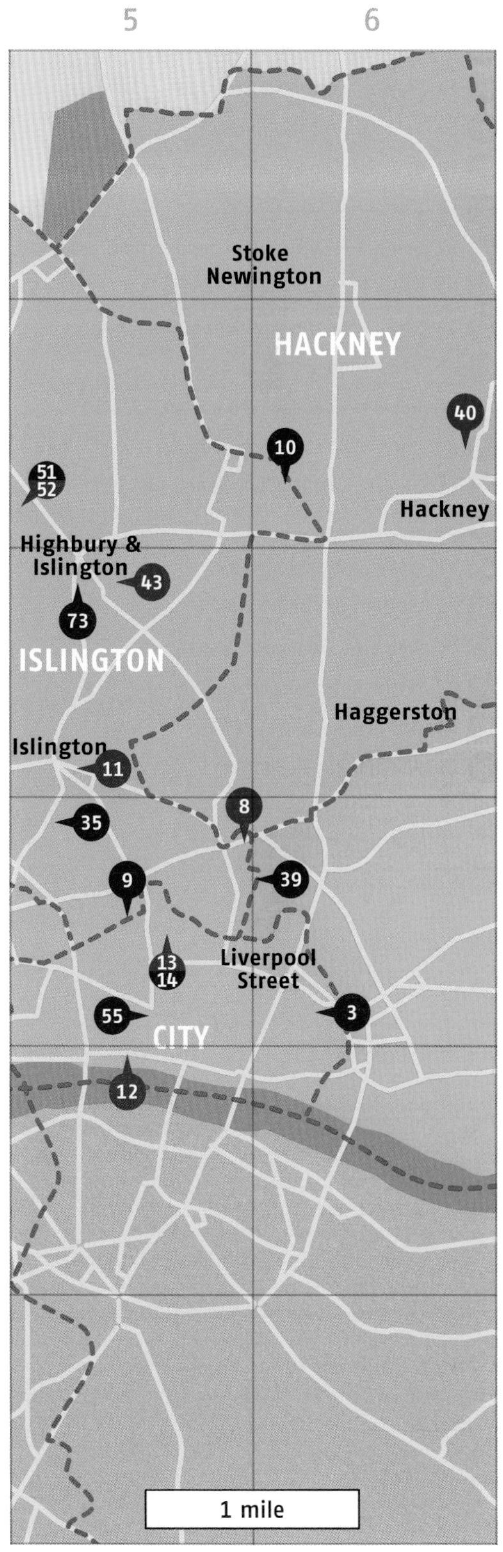
5
6
Stoke Newington
HACKNEY
Hackney
Highbury & Islington
ISLINGTON
Haggerston
Islington
Liverpool Street
CITY
1 mile
10
40
51
52
43
73
11
8
35
9
39
13
14
3
55
12

CENTRAL

Central London and its state schools

Camden

Camden stretches from the mansion blocks of Holborn and Bloomsbury to Hampstead Heath, with its wooded walks and swimming ponds, and from the council estates of Somerstown to the mansions of Hampstead – which, with its winding, hilly streets, exclusive boutiques and streetside cafés (plus plenty of estate agents) has the ambience of an affluent village.

Camden has long been known to have a good local authority education department – and, most likely in consequence, none of its schools have converted into academies. The only academy in the borough at time of writing is the newish and very popular UCL Academy at Swiss Cottage, which was shocked to receive a tepid judgement from Ofsted in its first report, but is now rated good, has achieved creditable GCSE and A level results and has seven applicants for every place.

The most famous and popular secondary school is Camden School for Girls qv (which takes boys in the sixth form). It uses banding to select pupils of a range of abilities, and offers are generally confined to those living within a mile (apart from a few music aptitude places). Girls are also well served by Parliament Hill School qv and La Sainte Union qv, the latter with a strictly Catholic intake. These two are part of a sixth form consortium, LaSWAP qv, with William Ellis boys' school qv (on the up after some rocky years) and co-ed Acland Burghley qv (which received a shock downgrading from Ofsted but is on the up under a dynamic head teacher). Hampstead School qv on the western edge of the borough is popular too. WAC Arts College is a newish free school in Belsize Park, offering a creative curriculum to disengaged 14-19 year olds.

A good range of primary schools, though very much weighted on the faith side – Christ Church CofE, Hampstead Parochial, St Paul's CofE, Kentish Town CofE, Emmanuel, Holy

Trinity and St Silas qv and The Rosary are amongst the most popular, alongside the free school St Luke's in Hampstead. A secular free school, Abacus Belsize primary, opened in 2013 after much lobbying by parents who wanted to redress the balance, and is rated outstanding. Currently at the Jubilee Waterside Centre in Camley Street, it should eventually move into a vacated police station on Rosslyn Hill though there is no timeline as yet. King's Cross Academy opened in 2015 as part of the regeneration of the land behind King's Cross station. Non-church-goers may also want to consider Eleanor Palmer qv, New End, Torriano, Gospel Oak, Fleet, Brookfield, Kingsgate or Christopher Hatton further south.

City of London

City of London, the original Roman settlement that still makes up the square mile or so of one of the world's financial centres, includes the Barbican, some of the Inns of Court and many financial institutions. Its relatively few inhabitants live amongst medieval street layouts, Wren churches and 21st century skyscrapers, and it throngs with suited and high heeled City workers hulking in packs outside the packed pubs on Friday afternoons, and no place for coffee or a crust of bread on weekends. It has several independent schools, senior and junior, but no state secondary schools – though the corporation does sponsor city academies in Islington, Hackney and Southwark. Its only state primary school, The Aldgate School qv, is an excellent, multi-ethnic CofE school, giving priority to regular church-goers.

Hackney

Just north of the City of London and east of Islington, Hackney is an inner city borough that includes trendy Shoreditch and Hoxton as well as the Hackney Marshes and

Lea Valley (home of the 2012 Olympic canoeing and kayaking competitions). Once a rural retreat for the capital's wealthy merchants, Clapton has Georgian and Victorian terraces alongside social housing estates. Shoreditch, on the north east edge of the City, has mazes of small streets, thundering arteries, art galleries, clubs and bars packed with City workers and revellers from across the capital.

Hackney's educational landscape is characterised by a high proportion of state and independent schools for the ultra orthodox Jewish community in Stamford Hill. It also has a Muslim free school, the Olive. Its best known – and very sought-after – secondary school is Mossbourne Community Academy qv, whose founding principal was Sir Michael Wilshaw, who went on to be chief inspector of schools. It has complicated admissions criteria involving fair banding and inner and outer zones. The Mossbourne Victoria Park Academy opened in 2014. Clapton Girls' Academy (places allocated by fair banding and distance) is also successful. City Academy Hackney, which opened in 2009, has business and financial specialisms and is rated outstanding; City of London Academy Shoreditch Park opened in 2017. Hackney New School, which opened in 2013 and overlooks a canal basin, has a focus on music and every pupil may learn an instrument free of charge.

Popular primary schools include Lauriston, London Fields, Grazebrook, William Patten, Northwold, Queensbridge, Orchard and Jubilee. Mossbourne has opened its own primary school, Mossbourne Riverside Academy, and Mossbourne Parkside Academy (formerly Brook Primary) is also part of the Mossbourne Federation. At Hackney New Primary, like the senior school, everyone may learn to play an instrument.

Islington

Islington is uncompromisingly urban, with little green space but Georgian squares, trendy converted warehouses, Arsenal football club, canal-side walks and street markets, thick on the ground with City workers escaping for lunch or window shopping the antique shops of Camden Passage.

It used to have the reputation of being a black hole for good state schools, with parents commuting en masse to Hampstead or Haringey, but times are a-changing. Highbury Fields is an up-and-coming comprehensive; once popular Highbury Grove sank in Ofsted's estimation and was converted into City of London Academy Highbury Grove in 2017 and St Mary Magdalene qv a good all-through school that no longer offers the IB in the sixth form but still has an international ethos. Central Foundation Boys qv is viewed as a 'hidden gem right in the heart of London'. City and Islington Sixth Form College qv has links with some of the top universities and often transforms the prospects of students who arrived with uninspiring GCSE results.

The City of London Academy, a relative newcomer, is sponsored by the City of London Corporation and City University, whilst the newest kid on the block is the London Screen Academy, a sixth form specialising in film, which opened in September 2019.

Primary schools to move house for include William Tyndale qv, Hugh Myddelton qv, Yerbury, Grafton and Gillespie, with St John's Highbury Vale C of E, St Joseph's RC and St Peter and St Paul RC attracting parental bums onto pews.

Westminster

Westminster includes Buckingham Palace and the Houses of Parliament, Mayfair and Belgravia (with its streets of garden squares and creamy white stucco terraced houses, painted in the Cadogan colour code of magnolia). It includes Little Venice, the area of large stucco houses round the Grand Union Canal; Soho, famous for its sex industry venues but rapidly undergoing gentrification; the massively redeveloped

Paddington Waterside area. Also in Westminster are parts of Knightsbridge, with some streets lined with distinctive and imposing six storey red-brick Queen Anne-style townhouses with Dutch and Flemish gables, between high-sided canyons of commercial exuberance. Westminster also includes shabby social housing estates and some very ethnically mixed communities.

It has two of the most popular girls' comprehensives in London, both faith schools with various associated admissions hoops: St Marylebone qv and Grey Coat Hospital qv. St Marylebone has some performing arts places, and Grey Coat Hospital gives some places to girls with a talent for languages; both give a large proportion of places to regular church-goers. Marylebone Boys', now in its permanent home in Paddington Basin, is linked to St Marylebone School and with a similar ethos, but without faith places. All of these schools use 'fair banding' to offer places to children from a full range of abilities. Several academies are doing well: Westminster Academy, King Solomon Academy qv (an all-through school) and Pimlico Academy are all rated as outstanding. A newish sixth form college, Harris Westminster qv, a collaboration between Westminster School and Harris Federation, opened in 2014 at a cost of £45 million, much to the chagrin of other state sixth forms that have suffered massive budget cuts. Students share some lessons with Westminster School sixth formers and it aims to offer a similar level of education.

The church schools tend to be the most sought-after primaries (and the most numerous – more than half are faith schools): Hampden Gurney qv, St Peter's Eaton Square qv, St Saviour's CofE qv, St Joseph's RC and St Vincent de Paul RC qv. Non-church Millbank (beloved of MPs' families), Gateway and Barrow Hill are also well thought of.

The Academy School

3 Pilgrims Place, Rosslyn Hill, London NW3 1NG

020 7435 6621 | office@academyhampstead.com | www.academyschoolhampstead.com

Independent | Ages: 6–13 | Pupils: 95 | Fees: £20,556 pa

Principals: Garth Evans BA (late 50s) and Chloe Sandars LRAM Prof Cert FTCL (early 50s) founded the school in 1997. Garth, whose hoary appearance and wry sense of humour bears more than a passing resemblance to Bill Murray, was born and brought up in London. Educated at Westminster and Queen Mary University London, where he read English. Garth's sugar hair, large frame and intent look lend him an aura of wisdom and experience. He enjoys telling the tale of his great grandfather who was part of Scott's expedition to the Antarctic. Married to Bee, who is responsible for admissions, teaches geography and is the school nurse. The couple divide their time between London and the south coast near where their (now grown up) children were educated at Sevenoaks.

Garth is charismatic, coming across as a maverick. He sees the big picture and values the important things in life. 'Education is about finding what's your thing, whether that's a maths thing or a guitar thing,' he says. 'The aim is to achieve excellence but dare to have fun while you're doing it.' Although he is the disciplinarian in this establishment, the children remark on his kindness and empathy as well as his intellectual rigour: 'He notices when you aren't happy and makes you feel better,' commented one 10-year-old. He started his career teaching English and now teaches maths: 'much better to teach a subject which doesn't come naturally,' he twinkles. He has the older children doing trigonometry and going far beyond what is expected of them – the key thing here is not the grades and 'getting into' a particular school, but instilling a love of learning.

Garth and Chloe met while they were both teaching at Trevor-Roberts, and tutoring too. They decided there was a need for the kind of education the Academy so effectively provides and set up the school in 1997. Chloe, educated at Oxford High School, the Royal Academy of Music and Trinity College of Music, is engaging, thoughtful and thorough. She is passionate about teaching maths, which she does brilliantly, by all accounts, to years 5 and 6. 'It's vital to engage the girls, to make it interesting for them, to show the patterns and make the connections. Many girls switch off maths, and think that they're no good.' Married to Andrew, who left his job in the City to become part of the team, they have two daughters, both educated at St Paul's Girls'. Andrew, educated at Magdalen College School and Cambridge University, deals with the data and the detail (he prefers to describe it as 'the financial, management and regulatory aspects of the school'). He also teaches history. With Andrew's and Bee's support, Garth and Chloe have the time and space to do the things they love, teaching, inspiring and nurturing the children. Each of the four individuals are key corners of this very stable leadership team.

Entrance: Entrance into year 2 (though very occasionally they will take someone, a sibling for example, who is in year 1, typically at the beginning of the summer term). This is essentially a school that begins at 6 and they need to be ready for specialist subject teaching from the word go. The school will entertain applications at any time from then on and is refreshingly welcoming and willing to see if they can make it work. Parents and children come in to meet the principals and the children will be assessed while spending some of the day with their peers. Do they fit in, can they keep up? 'We're happy to work with the very strong as well as the weak,' says Chloe; the important thing is to make sure it's the right fit. Maximum of 95 pupils in total (space is at a premium).

Exit: To a range of London day schools, hardly any to board. Deft management of parental expectation. 'We are very transparent,' says Chloe. Parents sent not only the results of practice papers, but the papers themselves as well as the marks (without the names) of the other children in the class so that they can see where their child sits in relation to others. Most get their first choice of school – recently popular are Merchant Taylor's and Mill Hill. Others to Haberdashers' Aske's, St Paul's, Westminster, North London Collegiate, Channing, City of London, UCS, Highgate, North Bridge House, Francis Holland or South Hampstead. Parents here tend to be sensible and listen to the advice of the experts who really do know where their children will thrive.

Our view: An intimate, small co-ed Hampstead prep school, tucked into the grounds of a church off the lower end of chic Hampstead High Street, the Academy is not well known but most of those who discover it are delighted. Ofsted, in its recent inspection, was bowled over, awarding it an outstanding in every category, not an easy achievement these days. Chloe, referencing the report, smiles: 'Just because we are relaxed I wouldn't want people to think we are lax.'

Everyone is on first name terms, no Sir or Miss here. Rules are kept to a minimum. The uniform is a low key navy tracksuit, there is no ornate reception area filled with flowers, no grand office where parents can meet the principals in private to discuss their children. The fabric of the building, charming though it is, could definitely do with a lick of paint, yet the informality belies a rigour in the classroom that is less easy to perceive on a brief visit. Expectations here are high, there is an attitude of genuine scholarship, children are taught thoroughly and no one slips through the net. 'We know who the 10 weakest readers are and they will get extra individual reading every day,' says Chloe. The aim is to inspire the children. Subject specialist teachers from the start, who really know their subject, imbue their pupils with a love for their it. Parents remarked on how committed the staff are and how skilful at navigating between different abilities, particularly in the early years.

The chapel building lies at the heart of the school. 'We love curling up next to the radiators in there in the winter,' said one child. 'It's such a comfortable space'

Not a school for a child with serious special needs, however, but they can cope and do an excellent job with pupils with mild dyslexia or dyspraxia. No specialist teaching but rather one-to-one work out of class. One part-time SENCo sees only a handful of individuals on a regular basis. Behaviour here is good: 'The discipline is imaginative and creative rather than heavy handed,' commented one parent. 'They look for the positive all the time and treat the child as an individual – a complete person – which is enormously productive.'

Class sizes are small. The child-centred approach extends to making sure that an artificial date such as a birthday doesn't impede or impair progress. As they move up the school the pupils are set for maths and English, but this is done with a great deal of care and tact and there is plenty of movement between the sets. An absence of IT generally, whiteboards and computers particularly, is noticeable. Teaching here is old style, and effectively so.

Parents remark on how nurturing the school is but some expressed surprise at the amount of homework and the focus on academics. 'I thought it was relaxed,' said one mother, 'but actually they have very high expectations and the pace is fast.' This is tempered by a warmth and focused attention that is unusual in most busy London preps. Not only do all the teachers know each child but Sally, a therapist, visits on a regular basis and spends time with individual children who need emotional support for whatever reason, whether for problems at home, difficult friendships at school, or a bereavement. There is a room full of paints and toys where the children can feel completely safe.

The chapel building lies at the heart of the school and is used for anything from whole school theatrical productions and concerts to lessons and even table tennis in break. 'We love curling up next to the radiators in there in the winter,' said one child. 'It's such a warm and comfortable space.' Classrooms occupy the rooms that line the edge of the chapel and when we visited, a class was being taught geography in one corner, while a younger class did classics in another. The central courtyard between the chapel and the main building is reminiscent of an Italian villa – elegant borders, small angular grassy lawns, wrought iron fences, tasteful paving and a few plants sown by the children for good measure. Tucked behind the main building down a narrow path, past the vicar's house, is the hall where they can run around playing team building games like dodgeball or capture the flag. At break time, out come the skipping ropes and hoops. Some heat their packed lunches (brought from home or ordered from the local organic café) in microwave ovens in rooms adjoining the hall and there is a comfortable room with sofas and chairs where children can read and talk.

With the exception of the lavatories, which you might be forgiven for expecting to find in a (grand) house rather than a school, the rooms are small. The library is not much larger than a box room; when we visited, books were scattered untidily on the floor and piled round the edges. However the children love coming in here, curling up on the piles of cuddly toys and choosing the books from the carefully compiled coloured, spotted index. Art takes place in several different rooms at the top of the school; we saw some Picasso influenced self portraits, a collage project based on Matisse and some papier mâché balloons as well as wire sculptures and an impressive array of random clay figures soon to be fired in the kiln.

It would be a mistake to judge the school too much on the premises, however, as they are just part of the picture. The school makes creative use of whole of London, whether it's regular hikes to the Heath for fresh air and exercise, walks to the Royal Free sports hall for team sports, or cultural trips to theatres and museums. Unusually, from the age of 10 the children can go to designated local cafés to buy their own lunch on a Friday.

The big annual event is the musical production. Recently the whole school was involved in a production of Oliver! performed in the chapel. Every child is involved and 'for several weeks everything revolves about making it splendid, which it is,' observed a parent. Although there are not a lot of concerts, productions and whole school events, when there is one it tends to be exceptional. Music is popular, and of a high standard – Chloe's interest and talent are important influences. One enthusiastic pupil relayed how she loved making up a music poem using different sounds from household objects, whether with a water bottle, a table or a saucepan. The talent contest at the end of the year is another hugely successful whole school event. Everyone gets to shine, whether by dancing, gymnastics, reciting poetry or singing a song.

There are games – cricket, tennis, badminton, football, handball, table tennis and netball etc – every day, and a double games lesson every Thursday at the Royal Free Sports Hall. They have qualified sports coaches and play matches against other schools, but a parent observed that the number and quality of competitive matches is disappointing, feeling that sport here is more about getting exercise and having fun than anything else. School disagrees and says 'our children… make very considerable progress in sport'.

When we visited the school had just celebrated its 20th birthday and it's come a long way since the tiny number of pupils it started with. It's still small: the numbers have consistently remained at around 90 for the past five years. This is how they mean to keep it – in a school this size, 'you can properly know every single child,' says Chloe. Shaped like a fish, the school tends to start small (in years 2-4), increases in number in the middle, creating a bulge between years 4 and 6, and then slims down again for the final two years when there tends to be very few girls and about 12 boys.

No organised, structured parents' meetings, PTA, class reps or coffee mornings and very few emails. The school is small enough for things to be conducted more fluidly and informally. If there is a problem the door is open for parents to come and discuss it and 'you can always call Garth on his mobile,' said one mother, 'as can my child if he is having a problem with his maths.' One parent expressed relief that she isn't bombarded by emails here as she has been by other schools, while another observed that it can appear disorganised when they are asked for their consent at the final hour for a rock climbing trip. Parents appreciate the regular updates on progress, together with lists to show where their child ranks in the class.

Parents here are an eclectic mix. Plenty of professionals, doctors, and lawyers as well as academics and scientists, most are local but some originate from all corners of the world, from Scandinavia to China. The one thing they all have in common is they want their children to be happy and to reach their potential. Reams of grateful letters when their children leave, demonstrating again the positive relationships that families form with the quadrumvirate.

The last word: The diverse mix of families all contribute to making the Academy, despite its focus on scholarship, far less of a pressure cooker than many schools of its kind in north London and beyond, though don't underestimate its earnest approach to the work they do.

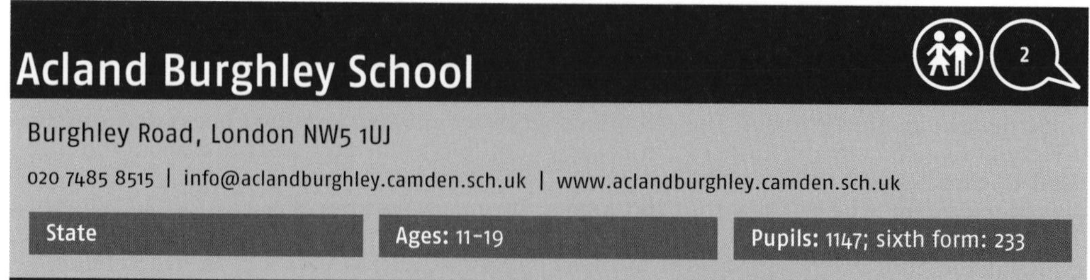

Headteacher: Since 2015, Nicholas John (40s). Read classics at Oxford, followed by a PGCE at Canterbury Christ Church University College and then a NPQH. His first teaching job was at Springwood High School, a mixed comprehensive in King's Lynn, Norfolk, followed by a post as second in the English department at Rosemary Muskar High School, and then head of faculty at Great Yarmouth High School for the next five years. In 2009 he got his first senior leadership position as deputy head of St Paul's Way Trust School in Tower Hamlets, where he helped the school rise in the Ofsted ranks from 'inadequate' to 'outstanding' in less than four years. GCSE results also improved significantly. During this time he also did some consultancy work for struggling schools in Brent and Greenwich.

We were slightly in awe even before meeting this head. We had read much about Nicholas John, who had been employed by the powers that be to transform – or, as he says, 'reinvent' – Acland Burghley after a pretty disastrous Ofsted report in 2013. Amongst the many things the report criticised was the school's poor student behaviour and poor exam results, and called on 'scruffy' teachers to have more pride in their 'personal presentation'. It prompted the resignation of the then head teacher.

It seems Nicholas John was (is) the man for the job, and in the past four years he has taken the school from 'requires improvement' to 'good', with the best yet to come (we believe). He applied for the post attracted largely by the school's diversity, which he says is quite extraordinary: 'I'm very excited about the enormous potential here. Camden has so many outstanding primary schools that can feed into Acland Burghley. I've never taught in an area like it.'

He has always worked in the comprehensive sector which, he says, was not a 'conscious decision, it's just where I've ended up.' However he does say that he has 'a very fierce sense of community coherence and feels very strongly about lack of equality and opportunity.' He himself had a completely different educational experience at Ampleforth College, a Catholic private school famed for its strictness.

Pupils and parents are full of praise for this head who, we are told, is an extremely visible presence around the school, 'even eats in the canteen with the pupils'. Others say how accessible he is to parents and wants to know 'absolutely everything that is going on'. He stands most days after school at the very busy Tufnell Park junction to ensure the safety of his pupils. He is also present at most of the evening performances at school. One extremely satisfied parent summed him up by saying: 'Mr John ticks all the boxes for things that I would want in a head teacher.'

A big Norwich City fan (season ticket holder) – any spare time is spent reading widely, and socialising with family and friends.

Entrance: Heavily oversubscribed, with a catchment area of just over half a mile, but as the head's reputation spreads, this is sure to shrink. First preference to those with a statement of special education needs, then siblings, then proximity.

'If your son doesn't want to dance, this isn't the school for him,' one parent told us. 'No room for alpha males,' said another. Any budding Billy Elliot will be at home here

Some 20 families moved into the area after local resident Damien Lewis switched on a laser show to celebrate the school's 50th anniversary, we were told.

Exit: Around half go on to the sixth form, part of LaSWAP consortium. Of these, most to university, including to art college. Overall an excellent record on destinations, with students moving on to a wide range of universities, vocational training and employers. A quarter of university places are Russell group. Often a few to Oxbridge, though none in the last couple of yeras. One medic in 2020.

Latest results: In 2020, 28 per cent 9-7 at GCSE; 67 per cent 9-4 in both maths and English. At A level, 21 per cent A*/A and 55 per cent A*-B. In 2019 (the last year when exams took place), 20 per cent 9-7 at GCSE; 47 per cent 9-5 in both maths and English. At A level, 12 per cent A*/A and 44 per cent A*-B.

Teaching and learning: A genuinely comprehensive school, with no selection by ability or specialist places. It has a wide ability range, including more than its fair share of students with EHC plans and special education needs. The school sank to its lowest ebb before Mr John joined – however, under his 'dynamic and inspirational leadership' it is bouncing back to form.

A good crop of the very top grade in science at GCSE. One parent told us, 'Maths has had a tricky time at the school, but the quality of teaching is definitely improving.' English has always fared well, and languages in general are their best performing subjects. Ofsted praised the 'broad and balanced curriculum'.

At A level, good results in many subjects with sociology, English and dance doing particularly well. The sixth form is part of the LaSWAP consortium, which comprises four local sixth forms that all work together to create 'a distinctive campus feel'.

The head has worked tirelessly to raise the game of both his staff and his pupils. When he arrived, he immediately set about creating a clear set of expectations which included improving the quality of teaching by assessing leaders and managers and restructuring the staff team; intensifying the school's actions to reduce persistent absence rates and maintain overall attendance; and improving the effectiveness of the 16-19 programme.

The improvements have led to positive changes and teaching is now 'highly effective and so staff morale is extremely high', and the pupils enjoy their learning because their teachers 'make it worthwhile and fun' (Ofsted). 'Tons' of extra revision classes laid on for GCSE students including during holidays and weekends: 'A massively supportive feeling from staff,' one parent said.

Learning support and SEN: Excellent learning support department with effective SEN and EAL teaching – and a good range of vocational courses including skills for life, art and design and business studies.

The Base is impressive – a dedicated space on the lower ground floor for children with autism and other pupils on the SEN register. It includes a couple of bright classrooms, sensory rooms, a small gym room, kitchen area and a lovely outdoor space. It is also used as a 'time out' facility. Given that nearly 20 per cent of pupils are on the SEN register, this wonderful resource shouldn't come as a surprise, yet this is the first of its kind we have seen. The head says: 'This facility attracts a large cohort to the school.' And he doesn't shy away from that fact, unlike other heads we have met.

The arts and extracurricular: This school is artistic on every level. 'If your son doesn't want to dance, this isn't the school for him,' one parent told us. 'No room for alpha males here,' said another. Any budding Billy Elliot will be at home here, without feeling marginalised or embarrassed – and even if dance isn't your thing, it is taught to such a high standard and held in such regard that few make a fuss. Classes for 7-9 use a 'wide range of styles, professional works and choreographers'. A dance enrichment programme runs at lunchtimes and after school. Two wonderful, large dance studios can combine to become one huge performance space.

Drama, too, is pretty high end with a broad and varied curriculum that ranges from ancient Greek theatre and WW2 evacuees to exploring issues such as oppression, business ethics and social exclusion, and bringing to life broad range of writers from Shakespeare to Willy Russell. The school even has a small amphitheatre for summer productions (great for those Greek tragedies).

Art is ingrained in the DNA, visible down the long corridors, around corners, above classroom doors. Where there is space there is art

Art is quite simply off the scale here: 'It's the best school for art in the world,' said one pupil, and judging by the quality and quantity of artwork displayed, we would be hard pushed to disagree. Art is everywhere in the school – ingrained in the DNA, visible down the long corridors, around corners, above classroom doors. In fact where there is space there is art – colourful and engaging. It is no wonder that Turner Prize-winning artist Mark Wallinger (who filled the empty plinth in Trafalgar Square) has chosen this school to become its artist-in-residence. He says: 'Creativity should be at the heart of education... the arts are all about finding out about yourself and Acland Burghley is a great example of that.'

To mark his arrival to the school, Acland Burghley held a special art auction to raise funds towards transforming the assembly hall into a first class exhibition and performance space. It featured pieces by Mark Wallinger and some of his famous friends, including sculptor Anish Kapoor, Great British Bake-Off host Noel Fielding, broadcaster Dame Joan Bakewell and film director Ken Loach.

Music has come a very long way since our last review and is now one of the more popular GCSE subjects at the school, with outstanding results. A dedicated music block, with well equipped studios, a music tech room and various extracurricular band ensembles on offer including School of Rock, classical guitar, music tech and percussion. During our visit, we listened to a GCSE student singing jazz, and were simply blown away.

Lots of trips on offer including creative writing in Oxford, dance performances at Sadler's Wells, bonding trips at the start of year 7 and residential trips to the Isle of Wight, a biology field course, yearly ski trips (last year to Arosa), French and Spanish exchanges and LaSWAP trips to help with their development project in Uganda.

Sport: PE is very good. There's plenty of outdoor space, including a newly laid Astroturf and fantastic indoor sports facilities including two very large indoor gyms, large sports hall and basketball area and a rooftop tarmac football pitch – all courtesy of a large cash injection from Arsenal in the Community. Students also use Tufnell Park playing fields, the Michael Sobell sports centre and Leaside canoeing centre. Girls' sport has particularly shone over the last few years, and they have performed exceptionally well in the Camden Shield competitions, particularly at dodgeball, basketball and football.

Ethos and heritage: Rarely out of the press for one reason or other; we weren't sure what to expect on our arrival. A very urban school, situated in the side streets of Tufnell Park – once gritty, but nowadays showing a hint of Camden cool with its trendy pubs, chic vegetarian restaurants and rocketing property prices.

Slightly underwhelming on first appearance, Burghley, as it is affectionately known, is a sprawling concrete 1960s building. Yet in March 2016, after a complete internal refurbishment, this Brutalist style Camden school became a grade 2 listed building because of its architectural significance. It is the only school designed by the iconic architectural practice Howard, Killick, Partridge and Amis (HKPA) – which also designed the Young Vic theatre and several colleges at Oxford and Cambridge Universities – and it appears in the TV series Killing Eve.

A smart walkway takes you through the glass doors to the main entrance and a vast amount of space, which we would find very difficult to navigate without the help of our lovely, enthusiastic student guides: 'Just think of it as a loop with a tail,' said one. Luckily it has been divided into three coloured blocks: red block for humanities and languages, yellow for history and English, and green for maths and drama. Bright and cheerful classrooms, including a £900,000 learning resource centre stocked with computers, CD-ROMs and books, and staffed from 8am-5.30pm.

Extremely impressive outdoor space, too, for an urban school. Lots of benches and seating areas, a wonderful wooden climbing structure for all ages, several table tennis tables, and lovely large wooden pods filled with plants, cultivated by parent gardeners. There is a real sense of pride in the school.

We had a fun tour, with quite possibly the most confident and engaging pupils we have come across. We were worried on occasion that we would be a disruption to the classes at work – such was the level of chatter between the pupils and ourselves. Individuality oozed from every pore of these Burghley-ites. A non-uniform school and quite frankly we couldn't imagine it any other way.

Although two-thirds of pupils are boys, this didn't seem to bother any of the parents of girls we spoke to. One mum said: 'I don't think either of my daughters have had an issue with being outnumbered. They have both said that it's not a big deal and you wouldn't notice, other than for the fact that people are always asking them! I also think that they have actually benefited from being in the slight minority as they feel special and are noticed by teachers.' Another parent said: 'I think that academically the mix is good as it means that the teaching has to cater for different styles of learning, which benefits everyone – and socially my girls are very relaxed and comfortable around boys as well as girls. There is no silliness or need to impress.'

Pastoral care, inclusivity and discipline: A forward-thinking school – refreshingly alternative in its approach: 'I am much more into outcomes than structures,' the head told us. And whilst many other heads may take a much more disciplined stance on mobile phones, for example, this one believes you cannot be overly prescriptive and have a blanket rule as one size doesn't fit all. Mr John says: 'If you don't personalise the issue, you end up making rules that fit nobody.' (That said, any electronic devices spotted being used on the premises will be confiscated.)

Confident and engaging pupils. Individuality oozed from every pore of these Burghley-ites. A non-uniform school and quite frankly we couldn't imagine it any other way

This approach has been highly commended by the parents, who feel that Mr John understands the culture of the school and didn't try and adapt an alien culture – he worked within its remit. One parent said: 'A school should always reflect the local area. Burghley has a history of being arty, with a large contingent of parents who embrace individuality.' Another told us that this head has the complete opposite of a draconian response to bad behaviour: 'Whilst Mr John is very clear about the behavioural code, he also believes it should make sense to the students.'

He recently implemented a 'reparation' scheme for low level misdemeanours, which gives misbehaving pupils the opportunity to have a five minute chat with teachers after a class to resolve the situation. One parent, whose son was at the receiving end of this reparation, believes they are a good thing: 'This is a really important life skill for teaching pupils how to build relationships. They can maybe discuss in confidence something that is going on with them.'

The school is renowned for its caring, inclusive approach. Pupils are trained to support others who are having difficulties, and they have close links with local primary schools. Attendance and punctuality still an ongoing problem, although slowly improving. 'A London problem and not exclusive to Acland Burghley,' says the head. 'What is important is to give the young people a sense of purpose and to provide a good quality of provision. We now keep the library open over the weekend for those who perhaps have nowhere quiet to work.' Lots of incentives for good attendance include trips, prizes and certificates.

A safe school with good security measures, bearing in mind its close proximity to Camden Town. School has a close alliance with the local police and with Camden Youth Safety Task Force, who work with the young people and talk about drugs and safeguarding. The head says: 'County Lines is a national thing. We have a good sense at the school that pupils will tell us if there is a problem.'

Excellent communication with weekly bulletins and termly newsletters. Each year has a team leader, a non-teaching head of year and a student progress leader, so pupils and parents have plenty of contacts for seeking and offering advice.

Pupils and parents: A huge social mix, with plenty of children from the tough local estates and those from liberal middle-class families who have chosen Acland Burghley for its relaxed, co-ed atmosphere. Popular with TV and media types. Around a quarter of pupils speak English as a second language and just under half are eligible for free school meals – well above the national average. The thriving parents' association runs murder mystery evenings, quiz nights and other social events.

Alumni include Eddie Grant and Lee Thompson of Madness, Ms Dynamite and Sarah Brown (charity executive and wife of former PM Gordon Brown).

The last word: An inner-city comprehensive that achieves creditable exam results from its very mixed intake. Remarkable for its art and dance and for providing a child with a really well-rounded education both academically and socially. 'A lot of heart,' one parent said. 'There's a real feeling that if you want to do something, you can,' said another.

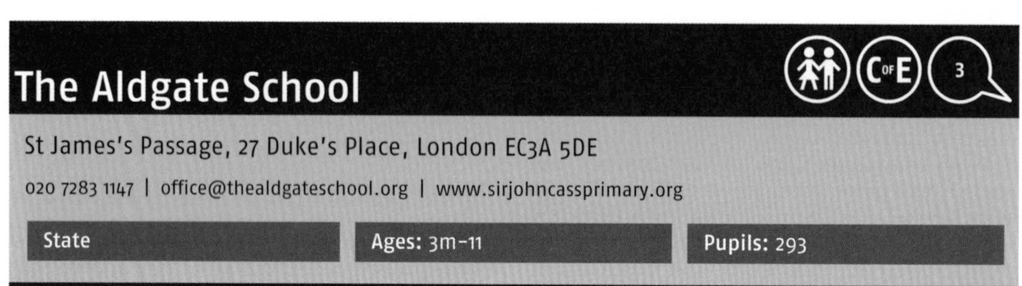

The Aldgate School

St James's Passage, 27 Duke's Place, London EC3A 5DE

020 7283 1147 | office@thealdgateschool.org | www.sirjohncassprimary.org

State | Ages: 3m–11 | Pupils: 293

Headteacher: Since September 2018, Alex Allan (Miss), previously deputy head, head of the school's Children's Centre and SENCo. She has also headed a primary school in NW London and been acting principal in Hong Kong. A historian, she has a PGCE from Newcastle and a postgrad diploma in SEN from the Institute of Education.

Entrance: The only state school in the Square Mile, the Aldgate School is one-form entry. Historically, about 100 apply for the 30 places on offer, with priority given to those who worship regularly at St Botolph's, Aldgate. Desk space decided thereafter by a mixture of church attendance and distance from the gates. The school also runs the Cass Child and Family Centre, an attached children's centre with full provision from 3 months.

Exit: To a wide range of secondary schools, north, south, east and west, notably to City of London's sponsored academies (where City-dwellers gain some preference), selective state schools, and leading faith schools across London. One or two annually to the independent sector. (Has recently started working with City of London School for Girls to help prepare pupils for 11+ testing, and supports children to apply for scholarship and bursary entry at City and other fee-paying schools.) Recent popular destinations include Mulberry School for Girls, Haggerston School, Central Foundation School for Boys, the Crypt School, Walthamstow School for Girls, Anglo European School, Haberdashers' Aske's Borough Academy and Seven Kings School.

Our view: The Aldgate School traces its roots back to the school established by the alderman by the name of John Cass (the original name of the school) in the churchyard of St Botolph's by Aldgate in 1710. The current gracious grade 2*

listed building – described by Pevsner as 'neo-Baroque-neo-Hampton Court' – dates from 1908. It formerly housed a secondary school, with all the benefits that implies, including broad corridors, large classrooms and a generous assembly hall. Its listing also relates to its 'boardroom', a glorious panelled reconstruction of a merchant's home dating from 1669, with a plaster ceiling and 17th century hand-painted panels, where lucky members of the student council enjoy regular meetings. 'It's quite a big building,' said a parent, 'but it still has a very intimate, personal quality. It really feels like a family, not corporate in any way.' As well as recent and ongoing refurbishment, there are plans for a £5m extension and modernisation, and local building works will ultimately give the school access to a leafy square.

Academically, the school has long been recognised as one of the country's best primary schools. Despite the fact that many of its pupils come in with well below average attainment, virtually every child here reaches the expected government benchmark and an exceptionally high proportion soar well beyond it. Success for all is guaranteed through excellent, experienced teaching and, often, by high levels of staffing, which enables children to be taught in small groups when small groups are most needed. (Two teachers, for example, work with reception and year 6.) 'The teachers are incredible,' said one parent. 'They give lots of extra support for whatever kids require.'

Huge emphasis is put on reading from the outset. ('We're less about children catching up than getting it right from the start.') Each classroom has a designated quiet space for private study, and pupils get plenty of extra support, both from City volunteers, who come in to hear children read, and parents, who are encouraged to make nightly reading as customary as tooth brushing. Good, well-stocked library, with full-time library coordinator, and year 6s are furnished with take-home Kindles to embed the literary habit. Regular – but not crippling – amounts of homework. Years 4,5 and 6 use laptops in class, but this is not a place which believes that technology is always the answer. 'Four-year-olds need to interact with each other and the natural environment'; no whiteboards in the nursery classroom.

A fully qualified native speaker teaches French. (The class we visited seemed encouragingly well beyond bonjour and merci.) Art, too, now has a refurbished studio and expert teaching three days a week, with several nascent Picassos reaching the finals of a recent Diocese of London art competition.

Music a celebrated strength, with a long-established Strings Programme giving all children in years 4-6 a weekly music class and a smaller group session to concentrate on technique. Performance developed further at Christmas and summer concerts, and star performers (who often achieve grades 4/5) invited to study at specialist music colleges and play at the Guildhall. Outstanding choir, under legendary choirmaster, has also made plenty of public appearances (including on the Queen's Christmas speech). African drumming and dancing recently introduced in year 2. Performing arts group meets twice weekly to study drumming, dance, drama and vocal techniques, all taught by specialists. 'Performance makes pupils more confident and articulate,' says school.

Outstanding choir, under legendary choirmaster, has made plenty of public appearances (including Queen's Christmas speech). African drumming recently introduced

Sport goes well beyond the statutory minimum, with a recently recruited sports coach developing skills in rugby, hockey and multi-sport in the expansive school gym as well as swimming at several local pools. Unsurprisingly, the school generally represents the City of London in inter-borough competitions for tag rugby, cross-country and swimming.

A significant proportion of children here receive the pupil premium and/or come from families whose native language is not English, and additional needs are taken seriously. The attached nursery is very much seen as the foothills of primary, with children encouraged to get muddy and explore materials. Special needs lead is aided by number of teaching assistants specialising in English as an additional language. A Tavistock-trained counsellor also attends weekly.

Lavish menu of trips, both in London (Buckingham Palace, Natural History Museum, Regent's Park) and beyond, which 'help pin down history and geography'. Out-of-London jaunts include a week-long stay at the Hampshire and Cass Centre in the beautiful Brecon Beacons, and a country-town mouse exchange to Caunton Dean Hole in Nottinghamshire, where urbanites can get up close to cows, fresh air and pond dipping. Lunch-hour and after-school clubs include chess and Lego, football and art, as well as inexpensive breakfast and after-school care.

Behaviour throughout is exemplary, with classrooms quiet, orderly and attentive (misdemeanours generally confined to coats not hung up properly on pegs). 'All the children get along.

There are no dominant groups, no cliques.' One tiny child came up and gave the head a big hug, another waved as we entered the classroom.

As a voluntary aided Christian foundation, the school has a strong, traditional Christian focus, with a bible corner in each classroom, Christian assemblies and regular church attendance. Whatever their views, parents welcome the faith structure. 'My family are not religious, but I really value the fact that my kids learn about religion with children of all backgrounds,' said one mother.

School lunch eaten by virtually all with appetising food cooked daily on site and crudités laid out (and consumed) on all tables. City Gardeners work with pupils on a well-tended roof garden, so children can eat what they have grown, and a project with Leith's cookery school ensures everyone leaves with a repertoire of 12 dishes in their personal recipe book.

About 30 per cent of families are City residents, the rest are from adjoining boroughs. Though number on free school meals has diminished as more professional families move into the City, the school remains unusually diverse. The school has worked hard on developing the PTA, bringing everyone together.

The last word: There's not much you can't celebrate here – academics, sport, music, behaviour, the lot. And it's diverse too. 'The school really represents London,' said one mother. 'It's very open-minded, very inclusive. For me, it's like a dream.'

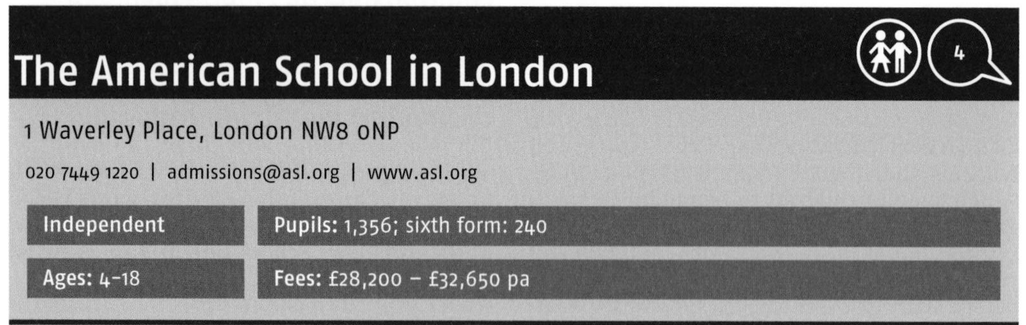

Head of school: Since 2017, Robin Appleby; has a degree in English from Dartmouth College as well as two masters degrees. She taught in the States (Ohio and then New York) before joining the American School of The Hague and stayed in international education as well as being a trustee on the Council of International Schools. The two previous heads at ASL had long tenures and she is rather hoping to do the same, though she is from a different mould to the last head and 'may bring a new style to the previous head, though it is early days,' according to parents.

She aspires to a progressive approach to learning and wants ASL to represent 'best practice in US' with the child at the centre of the process. She believes in 'learning by doing', which very much fits with the long existing ethos and curriculum in the school, with emphasis on understanding concepts, not learning by rote or for exams. She was attracted to the 'sense of tradition at ASL... a highly functioning school'. She is hoping to increase diversity as well as 'make innovative changes that will help prepare pupils for future opportunities'. Robin feels her challenges include ensuring pupils get the best from technology without losing social skills, and developing their emotional quotient alongside their intelligence quotient.

She is accountable to a very active board (around 20 members) who 'are supportive of change but protective of ASL'. They are involved in strategy while she is left to manage the school 'democratically'. She also has an articulate parent body. Staff say that she is 'marvellous' and 'really intelligent' and parents told us 'she is receptive and doesn't hide in her office – we think she is going to get a lot of stuff done!'

Entrance: The million dollar question – how to get in? 'We are looking for pupils with a passion, who like to learn and will thrive and be independent.' 'Parents have offered gifts to get their pupils in but they are not accepted.' Families of younger applicants will all be invited to visit: 'We need to know that we can work with the family, that we have common aspirations.' Higher up the school, applicants need to explain their motivation and interests and school reports will be scrutinised. More families are staying on (only a 10 per cent annual turnover) though even this can be difficult for pupils. 'My kids find the fact that staff and pupils often move quite difficult. Perhaps it is an inevitable downside of a school with an international community.' This is 'an academically challenging school' and pupils need to be able to keep up.

Exit: Most pupils go on to university in the USA, including University of Pennsylvania, Yale University, University of Chicago, Brown University, Dartmouth and Georgetown. Far fewer but increasing numbers go to UK universities: King's College London, UCL, Edinburgh, Imperial and Exeter. UCAS accepts pupils' AP (Advanced Placement), SAT/ACT and Subject Test results. Recently pupils have attended university in Ireland, Canada, Italy, the Netherlands, Spain and Australia.

Latest results: School provides an American curriculum and offers Advanced Placement (AP) exams. In May 2020, during the COVID-19 school closure, 273 students took 738 exams in 30 subject areas online, at home, with 97 per cent receiving scores of 3 or higher.

Teaching and learning: Not only the brightest of pupils but also the most motivated come to ASL for an American education. 'Pupils here need to have passion,' according to students, 'and they can't be bystanders.' They 'need to be advocates for themselves with teachers'. Totally American curriculum with an emphasis on critical thinking, collaborative working, questioning and listening. Classes average 20 pupils. Parents told us that 'the instruction is outstanding'.

Lower school has specialist teachers and well equipped classrooms (though lower school playground needs some enhancing). Space to learn outside, both in plant filled courtyards and the playground and at the learning centre at the school's 21-acre playing fields in Canon's Park. Some phonics in youngest years but emphasis on 'word awareness' and use of 'whole language', with reading schemes, lots of experimenting and learning through play. By grade 1, iPads and technology integrated in learning, with document cameras in all classrooms and pupils being taught coding and touch typing. Spanish taught from the youngest classes. Team planning for mixed ability classes.

Each year group has a central hub, promoting camaraderie between classes. Huge lower school library has seating pods like sailors' bunk beds as well as soft floor cushions. Weekly library lessons particularly useful for project work. Science room with specialist teachers and parent volunteers allows for experiential learning. Colourful displays of work and motivational messages all around the school rather than neat, copied stories, which gives an indication of priorities – all about what they have understood, with plenty of discussion. 'They teach them to think and be inquisitive,' say parents. No homework is given in the lower school – though pupils are expected to read daily and seem to do projects on subjects that interest them. This 'home learning' has taken a while to be accepted, but parents on the whole appreciate the lack of pressure and believe that 'they take ownership of their own learning.'

Middle school starts in grade 5 (year 6). Laptops given to pupils in grades 7 and 8 and then in high school it is 'bring your own device'. Language learning expanded in middle school to choice of Spanish, French or Mandarin, but little in terms of maintaining mother tongue languages, though the library has foreign language books. Science rooms for each year group mean that experiments can be left out. The Make, Innovate, Learn Lab (MILL) does what it says on the tin – it is used for robotics, designing and making, and plans to 'revolutionise teaching and student learning at ASL by inspiring student to explore, innovate, collaborate, and to change the world'. An indication of the aspirational thinking that fills the school. No streaming but parents spoke of their pupils being extended and supported. Middle school pupils praised 'supportive teachers' and explained that 'they were slow at marking sometimes, but that is because they have a life too, you know'. They said, 'ASL respects what you are comfortable doing and you are not pressured but encouraged.'

Recent developments continue to make this inner London school a veritable Tardis – there is a large swimming pool under the newly raised and improved playground

High school pupils an articulate and motivated lot – with good results to boot. One parent said that 'high school is where things become more challenging and purposeful'. Enormous range of classes on offer each semester, from game design to macroeconomics, from Russian literature to computational circuits, from sport leadership to advanced dance performance. Languages taught as in middle school with the addition of Arabic. Separate biology, physics and chemistry labs. English taught round oval tables with discussion-based learning only (and each lesson is mapped to show how the discussion moved around and who spoke). Journalism encouraged with guest speakers and pupils producing the school magazine. (Impressive recent magazine dedicated to gun crime.) No external exams until AP in upper school, but progress mapped with grade level outcomes. Pupils told us that they have very full timetables as well as a big involvement in sport – they might get three or four hours' homework if they are taking a large number of AP classes. 'Teachers stay behind school and are always available to help you – even if they are not your actual teacher.' They suggested that 'math has a good reputation, and social studies and history are good'.

Learning support and SEN: The head believes that 'we have an ethical and moral responsibility to those who need support' and the learning support department tests and teaches pupils both in the classroom and out. Parents we spoke to were highly impressed with the support their children had – 'they gave her study skills she uses all the time' and 'they recognised a need and acted on it to support her'. Special mention by parents on the way the learning support department liaises well with both parents and teachers. Non-English speakers taken in up to grade 3.

The arts and extracurricular: Drama has the advantage of a professionally equipped theatre seating 450. Fairly full-on productions at all ages. The theatre also used for concerts – everyone takes music, with youngest pupils learning recorder and then moving on to ukulele with an enthusiastic and experienced specialist music teacher, then in middle school each pupil gets given an instrument and music lessons as well as belonging to a choir. This appears to pay off because even in the high school, where music is a free choice, 120 pupils sing in the high school choir and go on music tours. Two jazz bands, ensembles, quartets, orchestras – plenty of opportunities for music making.

Pupils here know that they can be heard and instigate change. Pupils say, 'You can't be a bystander, you have to speak out for what is right'

Specialist art rooms with pupils being creative in the widest sense – designing, engineering, building as well as painting, sculpting and drawing. Higher up the school, there is a photography lab and dark room, video classes, ceramics and kilns, textiles, banks of computers for design work, and a light filled art gallery to display work.

Endless clubs – 'we can create a club if we have an idea, we make an application for resources and get given a grant,' pupils told us. A board advertising large numbers of societies included Amnesty, autism awareness, robotics, south Asia, magic, creative writing, computer science, fitness, dance, textiles – the list of clubs worthy of a university freshers' week.

High school pupils expected to be involved in community projects too ('service learning'). Staff members (not just teachers) take groups to local homework clubs, care homes, community centres, gardening projects, community projects, where they help on a regular basis. 'It is the highlight of my week,' said one staff member.

Sport: 'The school is dominated by sport,' according to parents. It's an integral part of school life, running alongside and with at least equal importance to academics. Lower school has its own gym and own specialist PE teachers. Pupils excited by interestingly named 'spy training' (circuit training). Two full-size gyms, a fitness centre and sport rooms for middle and high school, with playing fields out at Canons Park, a half-hour drive away. Wide range of sports during the year – boxing training, fitness suites, gymnastics, athletics, swimming, basketball and of course football. Tournaments against other international schools in London and abroad. 'We like it that our kids get to stay with families when they go on tournaments.' All the students get swimming lessons in school and can use the pool for training as well as competitions. Families can use the pool and the gym facilities outside school hours.

Ethos and heritage: Started in 1951, and originally designed with open learning areas, it has now adapted these to individual year classes. The theatre has been renovated and there's a new art building and fitness suite. Most recent developments continue to make this inner London school a veritable Tardis – there is a large swimming pool under the newly raised and improved playground. The school has a strong sense of identity and stability and pupils said they felt 'safe'. 'The security guard checks if I am getting a taxi and makes sure he knows who I am getting in the car with.' Not least thanks to the extensive security that surrounds a school with some very influential and/or wealthy parents – no access without an ID or appointment, with several guards and a bollarded entrance.

The hub of the school is the meeting area outside the theatre – used by parents, pupils and teachers. The canteen is large and spotlessly clean with a generous selection suiting all dietary requirements. Handy snack bar for eating outside meal times – useful for those staying on for practice or sport or activities. Pupils in grades 5 and 6 don't like the fact that some days they

'There is an awesome social environment, but you have to get involved, you get your social group through common interests'

have assigned seating (but it 'helps avoid cliques and ensures new friendship groups can develop'). Parents considered that 'it is not a tidy or fussy school and it has a warm environment'. Not a formal atmosphere, but highly respectful (one of the school's core values – along with kindness, responsibility, integrity and the ability to act). 'Teachers truly care,' say parents. 'They feel they owe it to these children to find out what works for them.' Pupils said, 'There is an awesome social environment, but you have to get involved, you get your social group through common interests.'

Pastoral care, inclusivity and discipline: Emphasis on being emotionally articulate from very early on – 'ways we can show kindness' in kindergarten, and drawings of 'what is in my head' to encourage thinking about feelings. From an early age the pupils are taught conflict resolution. We saw two 7-year-olds sitting outside a classroom discussing what had gone wrong in the playground – 'Did you even listen to me?' 'I heard you but I must have misunderstood you.' 'Well, now I am telling you again' – and then later we saw them working together in the PE lesson. Conflict resolved!

Middle year pupils told us, 'this is not a good school if you are rebellious (you go on behaviour report and if you get three of those you might be suspended)'. So a clear discipline policy understood by all. They told us 'counsellors are there to give emotional support if you need it'. They were completely unanimous in saying that 'we feel safe at school'. Many of the pupils are very well travelled and streetwise, but quite a mix in terms of life experience.

School counsellors, well-being classes; 'excellent orientation activities really helped me when we first started,' said pupils, and they in turn become student ambassadors. This school is used to helping at transition points. 'There is always a teacher to speak to,' according to pupils, 'or you can speak to your class representative to take it up in council meetings.' 'Everyone is very accepting here – people are all treated the same,' according to middle school pupils, though older pupils told us 'you have to be proactive here'.

School fees are among the highest in London and pupils are privileged to have a raft of highly motivated and professional teachers in a school with seemingly endless resources and excellent facilities. 'Families have good values and no sense of entitlement,' according to one parent – hard to believe it to be true of all families. 'This is an entitled group of young people, with hired limousines to the prom and branded trainers. I was not comfortable with the fancy cars and the party scene,' another parent said. Teachers are dedicated and motivated, with plenty of professional development training to keep their educational practice cutting edge. Teachers tend to stay and if they are prepared to work for demanding pupils and parents, then being in London in such an innovative, dynamic school surely has much to attract.

Pupils and parents: Articulate beyond their years, these pupils are constantly encouraged to 'speak out', and are expected to be involved at all stages. They are taught to explain their feelings – 'the social emotional side is encouraged,' according to parents – and 'to advocate for themselves to teachers and to others'. Active school council. Pupils here know that they can be heard and instigate change. Pupils say, 'You can't be a bystander, you have to speak out for what is right.' 'We think that integrity is important – you have to do the right thing.' Clearly the school's message about core values including respect, integrity and the courage to act (written large throughout the school) has been fully absorbed.

Parent evenings sometimes involve student-led portfolio conferences – showing the work they have done, which in the younger years can include videos and talking about their work. We didn't come across students who were arrogant or self-satisfied – 'you have to be accepting of other people,' students told us.

Parents are involved at every level – making cakes, helping teach science, attending sports matches, hosting visiting international students, volunteering in the library, fundraising and giving money. International Community Committee provides weekly activities to help parents bond and get to know London. All parents we spoke to mentioned the 'welcoming community' that exists at ASL.

Parents largely from the financial sector, though diplomats, journalists, entrepreneurs also represented. Not all American parents, plenty of 'third culture kids' with parents from different countries. The admissions page comes in nine different languages as there are applications from around the world. A few British pupils: 'I wanted a school that had a curriculum that was freer and not focused on one or two subjects,' one English pupil told us.

Money matters: A big priority is to increase diversity in this exclusive school. Parental giving is in the culture (and prominent on the website, where they say 'annual giving is a tradition') and there is an annual £4m fund for bursaries. School very proud of the fact that 12 per cent of pupils on some amount of financial aid. The financial stability and strength is evident in the buildings, extraordinary resources and the 'efficient, extremely professional administration'.

The last word: The grande dame of international schools in London, it has plenty to be proud of and yet continues to expand and develop, both in terms of the buildings and educational methodology. The school encourages both inward looking questioning (how to plan and study, how to think through and achieve goals, what is your passion, what motivates you) and outward looking involvement in the world (conflict resolution, what we can offer to others, how to work and plan in a team, world issues). 'You cross that threshold and you enter little America' but it has huge resources and extraordinary facilities, and a dynamic learning atmosphere in a central London campus, so you can see why there is huge competition to get in and staff and families stay loyal.

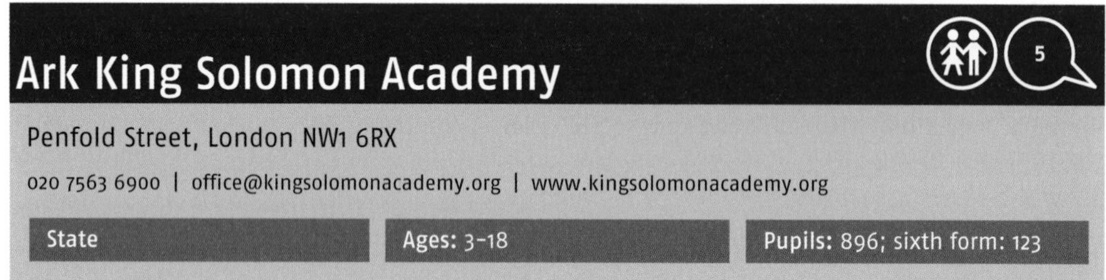

Principal: Since 2008, Max Haimendorf MA Oxon (40s). One of the first generation of super-bright heads to swop a City job for teaching. He graduated from St Hugh's College, Oxford, in biological sciences and joined the first cohort of Teach First. As part of his on-the-job training, taught science at Uxbridge High School, then worked as the scheme's PR. A period with management consultants Oliver Wyman clarified his career goals: 'Teaching seemed so different from the usual conveyor belt that takes Oxbridge graduates to the City,' he told the Guardian soon after his appointment – when still in his 20s – as the youngest head in England.

At King Solomon, he has taken the core problem ('the endemic issue of educational disadvantage') and addressed it with a Wyman-like mixture of 'creative enterprise and analytical rigour'. Still boyish in looks and enthusiasm, he is much admired by those in the sector. 'From the beginning, he was impossible to intimidate, full of integrity and had a "whatever it takes" and beyond approach to the care and outcome of pupils,' said one fan. Married to fellow Teach First evangelist Rebecca Cramer (co-founder of Reach Academy, Feltham).

Entrance: Working along the lines of 'give me a child by the age of 7', King Solomon is very much intended to be an all-through school taking pupils from reception to Freshers' Fair. Non-denom and non-selective, after the usual specialist categories (including children of staff, where priority is given to those who teach subjects 'where there is a demonstrable skill shortage'), siblings and distance from the gates are given priority. More than three times oversubscribed at 4, with the furthest successful applicant living less than half a mile away. Don't hold your breath for a place in year 7: all year 6s transfer automatically at this point and the school does not expand (so no new openings at all last year). Sixth form, on the other hand, may have spots available. School also operates its own nursery, with 60 places on offer.

Exit: King's Solomon's raison d'être is to guide first-generation university goers on the straight and narrow to higher education, a goal now being fully realised with ex-pupils off to study the full range of subject options (from chemical engineering and law to creative writing and psychology). Warwick and London universities popular. Around a third to Russell Group. Offers specialist preparation for Oxbridge and medicine – in 2020, one to Oxbridge.

Latest results: In 2019, 37 per cent 9-7 at GCSE; 56 per cent 9-4 in both English and maths. At A level, 27 per cent A*/A (53 per cent A*-B).

Teaching and learning: The school's slogan is 'Climbing the Mountain to University' (an image perhaps more suggestive of blood, sweat and tears than joy in learning), and progress from base camp in 2007 has undoubtedly been exceptional. One of the top-performing state schools in the country. (And KSA doesn't do 'soft', so about half the pupils garner the full sweep of the EBacc, passing English, maths, science, a modern foreign language and a humanity.) A solid performance, too, at A level.

The approach to peak performance here is specific (and inspired by international example, such as the US Charter Schools). KSA keeps a tight control on numbers, never going beyond the 60 that start in reception, making its secondary school, at about 400, exceptionally small. A longer school day allows for deeper immersion, with English and maths the central plank of learning up to year 11. 'We believe that without mastery of English and mathematics, success in academic study beyond GCSEs is impossible,' says the head.

Many pupils start primary with well below average skills but make outstanding progress in literacy and numeracy in the early years, and the emphasis doesn't let up thereafter. Those in year 7 spend a chunky 12 hours a week studying English language and lit plus a further five hours reading (in and out of school). Pupils are expected to notch up 30 'ambitious' new words every term and timetabled book clubs encourage 'challenging' discussions about what is read. No dumbing down outside the classroom, with years 7 and 8 performing, designing and marketing their own unabridged Shakespeare production. Mathematicians, too, stretched both at school and in the public arena (with individuals and teams entering the UK Maths Challenge, Ark Maths Challenge, Times Tables Rock Stars and more).

A focus on the 3Rs, however, does not mean other subjects are neglected. In primary, two hours a week are devoted to science, expanded to four at GCSE, when a truly remarkable 75 per cent of students take triple science (a statistic to make many independent schools blush). Here again, a wide range of related extracurricular underpins the main menu (Curie-ous Club, Year 8 Science Fair, Dissection Club, Journal Review Club, Open Labs). French taught for a committed hour-and-a-half each week in primary and nearly all go on to take a GCSE in French or Spanish. Highly structured homework programme from year 7 helps embed it all.

The school has embraced the theory of 'cognitive overload', so the secondary curriculum is kept deliberately narrow and teaching style is traditional, with teacher-directed lessons and pupils spending a significant amount of time working in silence. All agree that teaching is outstanding (made so by weekly coaching on professional development). 'We tell our teachers we are going to help them become better teachers,' says the head. 'It means very talented people want to work with us.'

Post-GCSE only 16 subjects on offer though economics, politics, psychology and business studies are added to the range. The school only teaches A levels (plus one BTec in business studies), believing that 'these are the best preparation for university study'.

Learning support and SEN: About 12 per cent on the SEN register and SEN well supported with three SENCos, on-site speech-and-language therapist, and regular tutorial sessions to help staff with teaching and learning strategies. Aid given both in and outside the classroom, including by Westminster-supplied specialists. Lift for those with mobility difficulties.

The arts and extracurricular: Music is heavily embedded in the curriculum, taught for its 'cognitive benefits, moral, social and cultural understanding and potential to build effective teamwork' – plus, no doubt, its advantages on the well-honed UCAS form. All supplied with a cello, violin or viola from year 3 and taught to read music, with regular whole-class lessons and small-group instrumental sessions. Compulsory participation in the school orchestra, which is timetabled from year 7 to GCSE. Popular annual summer orchestra tour abroad for older pupils.

The school has embraced the theory of 'cognitive overload', so the secondary curriculum is kept deliberately narrow and teaching style is traditional

Elsewhere, extracurricular heavily entwined with curricular goals. After-school clubs focus on English (with all invited to participate in a year-long creative-writing programme), languages (including Latin), maths, music, and sport. Debating (entries in national competitions) enhances public-speaking and contributions to the school magazine – The King's Speech – train up potential broadsheet talent. Trips, too, are intended to stretch, so local outings to the Imperial War Museum, British Library, Houses of Parliament and LSE public lectures, and residential adventures include living on a farm, visiting Paris or camping – experiences which are, as the website points out, 'in many schools... the privilege of those whose parents can afford them'.

Art pursued earnestly (with skills tracked, targets set and 'key words embedded'). If creativity still manages to make it through, enthusiasts can develop 'new techniques' as part of the out-of-class enrichment programme.

Sport: PE every week and offered as a BTec; other sports (girls' and boys' football, basketball, cricket, dance, martial arts, badminton, table tennis) available in after-school clubs, played in the spacious, well-maintained playground. School fields football and basketball teams, which compete in Westminster and Ark competitions, and are 'working towards' a netball and a rugby team.

Ethos and heritage: KSA is a leading light of the 35-strong chain of academies run by Ark (Absolute Return For Kids), a charitable trust founded by hedge-fund financiers intended to improve the life chances of children by creating high returns on philanthropic investment. The USP of Ark Schools, set up in 2004, is closing the achievement gap between children from disadvantaged and more affluent backgrounds and the charity aims to apply sound business disciplines to all its programmes, with a strong emphasis on target-setting, monitoring and evaluation.

The school aims, in Manichean fashion, to create a light and dark culture. 'We make it normal, expected and visible that the majority do the right thing'

King Solomon operates very much within the brand with all energies directed to the end game of making 'a university education something which is accessible, exciting and aspirational'. The curriculum is 'planned backwards' with that goal in view. Sights are constantly focused by add-ons such as the Odysseus Project (in partnership with OxFizz), which provides free tutoring courtesy of volunteers from Slaughter and May, McKinsey, the Telegraph, Barclays, Accenture and the Cabinet Office. Societies for medics and Oxbridge offer specialist advice.

An all-through education is, of course, a key part of the strategy ('The disruptive effect of the transition from primary to secondary can often affect confidence, behaviour and academic attainment,' says the head), while the scale is critical. 'We create a community where there are no strangers and no pupil will be left behind.' The school as family is another leitmotif. But this is not simply an exercise in Victorian paternalism distancing children from undesirable influences beyond the school gates: the modern way is to solidify home-school links and educate the birth family, so the head pays a visit to welcome both parent and child into the community and mum and dad are encouraged to participate (including handy Positive Parenting workshops).

Built as Rutherford School for Boys in the late 1950s as part of London County Council's secondary school building programme. The grade 2* listed building with its distinctive roofline, Carrara-marbled foyer and varnished concrete and tiled surfaces was designed by Leonard Manasseh at a high point in the development of post-war school design.

Pastoral care, inclusivity and discipline: The disciplinary style is a further integral strand of the approach. Again, objectives are clear: 'We are responsible for teaching the children in our care how to work hard, and how to be good people.' The school aims, in Manichean fashion, 'to create a light and dark culture'. 'We make it normal, expected and visible that the majority of the group do the right thing.' Everything is explained ('We never ask children to do things... "because I said so") but after that 100 per cent compliance is expected.

Praise is an important part of the package, with daily 'shout outs' to identify who and what has been done well, as well as class (to celebrate 'the successes of the team') and individual rewards ('to rejoice in personal choices, growth and successes'). Good behaviour is also rewarded financially (at least, notionally). An elaborate 'payslip' system gives pupils an (imaginary) sum for turning up. Those in credit at the end of the week are allowed to take part in Friday enrichment, while big earners win an annual bonus – attendance at a week-long residential course at a leading university.

Those – and, alas, there will always be sinners – who for whatever reason do not make the correct decision are given the chance 'to reflect on the choice they made and what different choice they can make in the future to achieve a better outcome'. To facilitate this, a 'follow-up conversation' with families is also sometimes necessary. Persistent offenders are taught in isolation.

Behaviour in immaculately ordered classrooms is (perhaps unsurprisingly) impeccable, off-task chatting virtually unknown. Silence – gained by clapping out a quick rhythm – is also expected elsewhere, including in the corridors in years 7-9, with a (slightly) more liberal regime thereafter. Some have described the silence as 'disturbing', including one visiting head. Parents are, however, delighted with the outcome. 'The school has given my daughter a great start in life,' said one. 'Every day she becomes more confident.'

Pupils and parents: Surrounded by streets full of some of the sterner remnants of turn-of-the-century local authority housing, the school sits in one of London's most deprived wards and its intake reflects its locality, with 58 per cent on free school meals, 75 per cent on pupil premium. Top 20 per cent in the country, too, for ethnic diversity, with over half speaking English as an additional language.

Money matters: Being part of the Ark chain of academies brings considerable financial benefits, and after-school clubs (from £5 a term) and trips (including the annual music tour abroad) are heavily subsidised. Ark bursaries also available to underwrite university fees for high achievers.

The last word: Teaching is inspirational and results significantly better than many schools in affluent suburbs. Some find the approach a bit 'cult-like', but who can argue with the outcome? 'What is being achieved at King Solomon is extraordinary,' remarked an observer. There's no doubt that KSA pupils are safe, happy, secure and also successful.

Arnold House School

1 Loudoun Road, London NW8 0LH

020 7266 4840 | registrar@arnoldhouse.co.uk | www.arnoldhouse.co.uk

Independent | Ages: 5-13 | Pupils: 270 | Fees: £20,346 pa

Headmaster: Since 2006, Viv Thomas BEd MA. Previously deputy and head of maths here, then head of Keble Prep, Winchmore Hill; has also taught at University College School. Read PE and history at St Luke's, Exeter. Married to Rowena. 'Very kind,' according to one boy we spoke to, recently cheered up by him when his beloved football team lost. Another described him as 'chatty and easy to talk to. In assembly, he is always finding stories from the newspaper that are interesting.' A very able sportsman in his youth. When asked about his free time, he explained, 'I play golf and a bit of tennis, and I try to hook up with my buddies to catch a rugby match at Twickenham. I like walking and have travelled a lot. It sounds really dull. I've got to get a grip!' Parents like and respect him, with one commenting, 'He does not try to curry favour with parents.' Another felt he was 'friendly and sociable, but authoritative. He certainly knows the boys and what makes them tick.' Universal approval from parents and pupils we spoke to.

Leaving September 2021. To be replaced by Giles Tollit, currently head of Horris Hill School. During his decade long tenure, he was been instrumental in developing both pastoral and academic excellence.

Entrance: Register before second birthday, for entrance at 5. No reception class, partly for logistical reasons. Head believes that what they have at the moment is 'something rather special and cohesive' and that would be changed if it became diluted onto two sites. 'The age range really works.' Some parents irritated that they have to find another school to fill the gap between nursery and year 1, but others felt it worked well. Sibling priority. Sons of old boys also favoured. Massively oversubscribed with approximately 200 applicants chasing 40 places. Individual meeting with head, in which parents are checked out as much as the boys. Probably best to avoid comments such as 'I want my son to go from Arnold House to Westminster to Oxford' if you want young Freddie to gain a place. 'Parents who make comments like this are missing the point,' explains head. 'What I am looking for, from our "getting to know you" session, is whether he looks like a nice little boy to teach.' School is looking for boys who will get on with people, have good manners, try their hand at a variety of things and who will join in enthusiastically. Nursery report required. Offers made 17 months before entrance.

Exit: Mr Thomas knows his onions regarding senior schools and parents rave about his knowledge of both day and boarding schools and which ones would best suit their sons. Majority depart at 13 to London day, including perennial favourites City of London, Mill Hill, St Paul's, UCS, Westminster, Bradfield, Eton, Harrow, Marlborough, Radley, Rugby, Tonbridge and Winchester. Roughly a third to boarding. The odd boy might disappear off to Highgate at 11 and a trickle leave at end of juniors to board in the country, though certainly no mass exodus. One scholarship in 2020 – to Harrow.

Our view: Founded in 1905 by Miss Hanson, who used to borrow a carriage so she could be seen driving around St John's Wood by prospective parents. Insisted upon all boys calling her 'sir'. Named after Dr Arnold of Rugby. Motto: Conquer We Shall. Traditional school. Boasts its own coat of arms, which references all four houses (Wellington, Brunel, Nelson and Pitt) and the founder herself. Boys are immensely proud of their school, its alumni and its history.

An academic boys' school, though without the hothouse hysteria that often accompanies schooling in this part of London. Head feels one of his jobs is to take the heat out of this over-charged London atmosphere. Some of the boys told us they had plenty of exam practice in the run up to 13+ but the school does not expect or want manic revision. This sensible approach pervades the school.

Two parallel classes averaging 17 boys, which are regularly rejigged to encourage a social shake-up. Setting from year 3 for maths (into three sets) and English, year 6 for Latin, and French and science in year 8. Boys assured us that there was fluidity within sets and no stigma attached to being in a lower set. No scholarship class per se. French from day one, Latin from year 5 and Greek by invitation from year 7. Mandarin introduced as a club, but it failed to take off.

Academically very sound, though repeated mutterings from parents about 'the weakness of science all the way through'. One mother complained about a 'conveyor belt of teachers, so my son had to start the syllabus from scratch with a tutor'. Another disagreed, saying school is now on top of this, that the boys love science and being in the sparkling new lab. Other parents said that tutoring went on, particularly with the middling boys, though this is hardly headline news for a smart London prep.

School instils a love of reading from early on, encouraged by the highly knowledgeable librarian. One pupil explained, 'She knows exactly what kind of book would suit you. She has even written a book guide that has been published.' Numerous visiting authors such as Robert Muchamore, Anthony Horowitz and Caroline Lawrence.

Arnold House celebrates success on all levels, not just academic. All boys win a prize at the end of year 4 and all win a cup (or three) at the end of year 8. Head explains, 'When I came here, the currency was "Are you clever?" If you weren't going to Westminster or St Paul's, were you a bit of a disappointment? I don't know. That needed some subtle changing. Boys now know there is as much value in playing your cello or saxophone well as there is in excelling in Latin. We now reward across the board.'

Founded in 1905 and named after Dr Arnold of Rugby. Motto: Conquer We Shall. Traditional school. Boasts its own coat of arms

School can support boys at the milder end of the autistic spectrum, dyslexia and dyspraxia. Every pupil is screened for dyslexia in year 2. Roughly 10 per cent receiving extra support from teachers and TAs with some having specialist one-to-one learning support, for which an extra charge is made. Probably not the place for a boy in a wheelchair, as no lift, but school will bend over backwards to accommodate physical disabilities.

Sport has taken off on Mr Thomas's watch. On-site gym, cricket nets, basketball courts and short tennis courts. School also owns a seven-acre sports ground and activity centre in Canons Park, a 30-minute bus ride away. Boys describe it as 'incredible' as it offers cricket, tennis, football, rugby, athletics, cross-country and hockey. Though Arnold House does not pride itself on one sport above others, boys say 'gym is very competitive' with squads often making national finals. Close ties with Lord's Cricket ground, on the doorstep. School fields A-E teams, so even the most athletically-challenged boys play in inter-house or inter-school matches. 'We hold our own against larger prep schools,' commented one parent. 'They learn the value of teamwork,' said another.

Cracking music provision with mega amounts on offer. Over 20 different ensembles, including chapel choir, senior orchestra, rock group, jazz combo, Yamaha sax and Hendrix guitars. Vast majority learns an instrument. Well-used music suite, and older boys enthused about the digital music provision. Annual winter and summer concerts. Boys told us, 'You actually have to be able to sing for chapel choir', though for other choirs the standard is slightly less stellar.

High-profile art. One large, collaborative exhibition annually, with informal open studio events scattered throughout the year. Extensive Visiting Art programme, involving artists, designers and illustrators coming into school to work with boys. Some of the most impressive art displays we have seen in a prep school. Original stuff. The boys who showed us round were bowled over by their classmates' work. 'I can't get over that one. When you look closely, you can see it took so much effort!' raved one boy.

Drama is sound but perhaps a little less starry. Traditional fare of harvest festival assemblies, summer plays and nativity in years 1 and 2. At the top end, boys have staged Romeo and Juliet and

Macbeth at National Shakespeare Schools Festival. Recent younger boys' shows include Charlie and the Chocolate Factory and Aesop's Fables. Head admits an onsite drama studio would be a welcome addition, though the theatre at Canons Park is used for rehearsals and productions.

Good spread of clubs, including Formula 1, scrabble, mad scientists, Marvel superheroes, poetry, Roman model building and war drawing. Knitting currently very popular with the older boys who find it helps them to relax. Dodgeball a perennial favourite. Boys encouraged to set up their own clubs.

Residential trips from year 5 upwards, to Devon, Dorset, Rome and Paris. All staff go on trips of some sort. Year 8 has a week of total immersion prior to CE at Maison Claire Fontaine in Burgundy. School is ideally located for day trips to British Museum, the zoo and Tower of London.

Excellent, well-structured pastoral care. No school counsellor. Head explains, 'I am not a fan of counsellors, as then the pastoral responsibilities of the staff are diminished. I want every adult in the building to care for the boys pastorally. The boys think the world of their teachers and that is a wonderful resource – don't diminish that. Counsellors cannot be as invested in this place as the teachers are.' Teachers and parents work together, and only after that do clinical partners and outside agencies get involved. Mindfulness is explored. One boy explained, 'We are taught how to express feelings and emotions and how we should not judge others. It is really helpful.' Arnold, the school goldendoodle, has been introduced to enhance the family ethos and strengthen the pastoral provision. Boys sometimes read to this four-legged member of staff. He is certainly a well-stroked and greatly adored addition.

The boys are nurtured. Head aware that it is 'easy for little boys to lose confidence. They compare themselves to the others.' Schools aims to build up their confidence and fosters public speaking and independent thinking skills. Not everyone here is loud and exuberant, though some certainly are. Shy boys are gently coaxed out of their shells when they are ready. One mother explained, 'My son is quiet, but they let children be who they are.' Everybody has a voice here. Head explains, 'The quiet ones need to know we are happy with them.' Boys very polite and kind. One mother commented that 'the younger ones soften the older boys. There are lots of brothers and this creates a truly family atmosphere.'

Punishments are fair but firm. Boys will be boys and head is keen to give those who have strayed from the path of righteousness the benefit of the doubt. Once in a while, persistent offenders are told that they are not welcome in school for a few days. Head has never had to resort to expulsion. 'It is a stain on a boy's character. Boys can get in a tangle socially. We need to help them untangle it.'

Staff need to be, and are, fully committed to the school. 'Little boys need to know that teachers like them and are interested in them. Just being a subject teacher is not enough in a prep school. I have appointed all-round prep school staff.' Healthy mixture of new recruits and long servers. Half male, half female. No shortage of good role models here.

Mindfulness is explored. One boy explained, 'We are taught how to express feelings and emotions and how we should not judge others. It is really helpful'

Most pupils hail from St John's Wood, Islington, Highgate, Hampstead and Regent's Park. Many live within walking or scootering distance, and all within a five-mile radius. On the morning we visited, boys were dashing along the pavement, dying to get into the school as soon as possible. Without exception, all were beaming and excited about the day ahead. Professional families, some dual income, mostly from UK, Europe and Asia. Arnold House Parents' Association is 'a friend-raising committee rather than a fundraising committee, which organises school-wide social events.' Parents throw themselves into the life of the school. Strong sense of community. 'When we get together, we have a very jolly time, with plenty of laughter and chat,' commented one mother. As another parent put it, 'The families here are all just working hard to do their best for their kids.'

Money matters: Unusually for a prep school, there is a bursary scheme introduced by current head. Huge amounts of fundraising by boys and parents (including galas, fun runs and auctions of artwork) to build up the bursary fund. Old boys are generous donors. Boys entering in years 5, 6 and 7 (mostly from state primaries) are eligible for these means-tested bursaries of up to full fees including uniform and extras. Bursary boys must be bright enough to keep up academically; they aim to have up to eight at any one time. Head explains, 'We make sure they get into their senior schools with bursaries, to places like Harrow, Mill Hill, Rugby, City and Dulwich. I need to be confident with that. We help them with that process. I can't have them going back into the state sector when they leave here.'

The last word: Arnold House is a special place, run with great warmth and dedication. The perfect school for your son if you want him to be inspired, well-balanced and happy. Everything about this school is wholesome. The boys we met were decent, lively and articulate – well on their way to becoming delightful young men.

The Camden School for Girls

Sandall Road, London NW5 2DB

020 7485 3414 | csg@csg.school | www.camdengirls.camden.sch.uk

State | Ages: 11-19 | Pupils: 1,054; sixth form: 443 (151 boys)

Headteacher: Since 2010, Elizabeth Kitcatt BA MA (Institute of Education), previously deputy head here and English teacher ('I still do a tiny bit of that'). Completed her probationary year at Walworth School in Southwark in the mid 80s where typical leavers' destinations were professional boxing or market stalls ('I learned to teach English without ever turning my back on the class,' she told the Association of State Girls' Schools.) First taste of leadership at the Archbishop Michael Ramsay school nearby, before moving north of the river as head of English at Parliament Hill School, where she 'immediately loved the pervading optimism about girls' potential and the sense that it was OK to be a feminist'.

'Not a natural extrovert,' commented a longstanding parent, 'and I think isn't comfortable in public settings or interviews.' (Indeed, she refused to meet the Guide, and most of her open day speech detailed the intricacies of the entrance procedures.) 'But she is grappling pretty well with real constraints on the budget.'

'Businesslike, very committed to the school's success,' said another parent. 'My girls like her but don't feel they know her.'

Entrance: At 11, everyone sits an assessment test which places them in one of four bands – 28 admitted from each band. Preference within this to those with an EHC plan naming the school; then looked after children; then siblings; then those with exceptional medical or social need. Eight music places: three offered to those scoring highest in musical aptitude test; next 50 invited back for a five minute instrumental performance audition to compete for other five places ('we're after a certain amount of technical fluency but musicality is more important'). Distance the tie-break for the remaining places – generally rather less than half a mile. CSG is definitely a school which people move (or pretend to move) house for. If that's your plan, living within a few feet of the gates is your only sensible course of action.

In the sixth form, Camden goes co-ed, admitting a further 150-170 new pupils (from about 1,000 applicants), no more than half of whom can be boys. Once again siblings are given precedence (but only if the sibling is still at the school on the date the applicant starts). Other places are dependent on distance from the gates, whether there's space in their chosen subjects, academic references and GCSE grades, predicted and actual (documentary proof required). Grade 6s essential in at least five subjects, including maths and English language. At this point, a further 15 music places on offer to those who play 'an orchestral instrument to a high standard'.

Exit: Quite a number leave at 16, either because they don't make the grade or because they prefer a sixth form college, apprenticeship or employment. Vast majority of leavers at 18 to university, three-quarters to Russell Group and a third to study STEM courses. In 2020, 18 to Oxbridge, and six medics. Bristol currently the most popular university, followed by Manchester, Sussex and Leeds. Some to art colleges and music schools.

Latest results: In 2020, 54 per cent 9-7 at GCSE; 97 per cent 9-4 in both English and maths. At A level, 58 per cent A*/A (87 per cent A*-B). In 2019 (the last year when exams took place), 46 per cent 9-7 at GCSE; 75 per cent 9-5 in both English and maths. At A level, 45 per cent A*/A (78 per cent A*-B grades).

Teaching and learning: Successful applicants generally feel they have won the golden ticket. 'The teaching has been really impressive,' said a parent whose daughter had attended a private junior school. 'We didn't take the decision [to move her to a state school] lightly but we have no regrets.'

In the top two per cent of comprehensives for both attainment and progress. No pretence here that exam results don't matter: posters extolling the latest successes were conspicuous at the open morning. 'Our very optimistic motto is Onwards and Upwards,' says the head. 'Education for all is still at the heart of what we do.'

French and Spanish for everyone in the first term of year 7; they choose one to continue from the spring term onwards. Classics in year 8, with options to study Latin or classical civilisation in year 9. Classical Greek is a twilight option (its continuation amidst budget cuts enabled by crowdfunding amongst parents). More vocational offerings at KS4 include health and social care and hairdressing and beauty therapy.

The main school intake is selected only by banding to achieve a balanced ability range. Some setting for maths from year 7, science and languages from year 8. 'They can move up or down so they know there's something at stake,' said a parent. At KS4 there's a small English group for those who need extra help.

Music has always been high profile here. 'The teachers are fantastic,' said a parent. 'I'm often in tears at concerts because it's so moving what these girls can do'

'Years 7 and 8 were challenging in some ways,' a parent commented, 'but one of the things that impressed me the most was how well they integrate them and maintain a strong atmosphere of academic success and girl power.' 'I never felt she was held back,' said another. 'On the contrary, they were pushing her hard. They find a way of encouraging people at different levels.' 'I'm impressed with the education my daughters are getting and pleasantly surprised with the level of academic enquiry,' said a mother.

The sixth form is the jewel in the crown, with entry requirements to match for both internal and external applicants (a minimum of several grade 6s at GCSE) and a large external intake of boys and girls, many from independent schools. A largely traditional academic subject offering with a definite popularity bias towards the humanities, English and history attracting large numbers, though a good take up for maths too. Most take three A levels, though high flyers with mostly 7+ grades at GCSE may take four.

Detailed individual higher education and careers advice for sixth formers, including those applying post-A levels. 'I got so much help from the UCAS officer and teachers, including what books to read, even though I applied to Cambridge after I'd left,' said an ex-student.

Very low staff turnover – 'It is important to me that they could have the same teacher in year 7 and year 10,' said the head – and all maths and science teachers have a degree in their specialism, which is by no means a given nowadays.

Learning support and SEN: Support for those with SEN may consist of individual help in class or small group withdrawal for eg help with literacy, numeracy or settling in to year 7. 'Get in touch with our SENCo,' said head at open day. 'She will consult on whether we can meet your daughter's needs. We're very welcoming to a wide range of SENs – we do our best to be inclusive.' There's a range of lunchtime homework clubs with teachers available to lend a hand to anyone who feels the need for extra support.

The arts and extracurricular: Music has always been high profile here, bolstered by those who come in on music places at year 7 and year 12. 'The teachers are fantastic,' said a parent. 'I'm often in tears at concerts because it's so moving what these girls can do.' Two orchestras, three choirs, chamber groups and a wind band have performance opportunities throughout the year, ranging from a chamber concert to the choral society and orchestra performing works such as Brahms's Requiem or Haydn's Creation.

Drama is rather less in the spotlight, available as an A level but not a GCSE option, with public performances largely confined to the annual sixth form play and end of year whole school musical ('really impressive,' a parent commented). However, 'They encourage performance and speaking out loud,' said a pupil. 'By the end of year 7 or 8 most of us are quite confident, even those who were very shy when they joined.'

Art 'brilliant', with most candidates getting A*/A at A level and many off to study art related courses. Eclectic and intriguing work displayed through the school. 'They know how to help you improve in your own way,' said an ex-student. The art displays, in a parent view, 'are more interesting than those at Central St Martins.' Photography an A level option, and a twilight course in the main school. DT includes textiles and resistant materials.

Sporty year 8s and 9s are invited to spend a long weekend in Devon climbing and abseiling, raft building, wading through bogs. Other school trips range from year 7s to the British Museum to GCSE geographers off to Iceland, linguists to Madrid and musicians to Italy.

Particular opportunities to broaden horizons at the top of the school. Weekly sixth form assemblies host speakers on 'current and divisive

Hampstead School

issues'. Tempting sixth form masterclasses have included Tamsin Greig on Shakespeare's Twelfth Night, Robert Peston discussing Why Brexit, Why Trump?, John Mullen on Charles Dickens and Jonathan Freedland asking Can you be a liberal and a Zionist? Year 12s are offered enrichment classes which range from football to debating to the history of ideas. 'We discussed really interesting things,' enthused a student. 'Anything from Dante's Divine Comedy to Israel and Palestine.'

Sport: Not historically a sporty school, but a parent reported it is much improved – 'they've realised that sport is important.' Netball court and gym on site, but most sport takes place at the Cantelowes sports ground just across the road, where there's a floodlit Astro and a skateboard park where year 7s have lessons. Trampolining, netball, handball and basketball are all on the curriculum and teams compete in borough-wide competitions ranging from football (with an Arsenal team coach) to rounders and dodgeball, for the coveted Camden Shield. Professional dance tuition for year 7s, who put together a performance piece for the Borough Showcase; school-wide CSG Dance Company is by audition. There's a cross-country team and lots go running on Hampstead Heath with the Highgate Harriers.

Ethos and heritage: Founded in 1871 by renowned educationalist and suffragist Frances Mary Buss in her mother's home in Camden Street, as an affordable alternative to her other school, North London Collegiate. NLCS moved from Sandall Road out to Edgware in 1938; the Camden site was bombed during the second world war, and it was 1956 before CSG moved into the rebuilt school. Once a grammar school, it turned comprehensive in the late 1970s.

Compact site off the busy Camden Road with a motley collection of buildings, from the high-ceilinged, large-windowed Victoriana through 50s red-brick and 60s concrete and glass to the most recent redevelopment, the light and bright extended foyer and dining room. Outside – amidst the separate sixth form centre, music cottage, netball court and gym – includes grassy areas with benches where, say pupils, 'we eat lunch with our friends'.

No uniform (writer Fiona Millar remembers voting to abolish the bottle green uniform soon after she joined the school in the late 60s), liberal and progressive ethos, with all students encouraged to be politically aware and engaged in community action and activities. Influential school council organises events such as Pink Day (breast cancer awareness), International Women's Day and charity fundraising. 'They really do want you to get involved,' commented a parent. 'People feel very connected with the school and define themselves in terms of it.'

Alumnae include Ellie Rowsell (lead singer/guitarist of Mercury Prize winning Wolf Alice), Emma Thompson, Georgia Gould (leader of Camden Council), Arabella Weir, Tamsin Greig, Julia Hobsbawn and Julia Donaldson.

Pastoral care, inclusivity and discipline: Transition for new year 7s aided by a team-building trip to an outdoor activities centre. They often keep the same form tutor and head of year through the main school so can build strong relationships with them. Parents generally feel the school is proactive on pastoral care. One, whose daughter had had friendship problems in the early years, commented, 'they were really onto it – they'd chatted to the girls and had suggestions for me on helping her move forward. I was really glad they were on top of that and kept me in touch with what was going on with my daughter.' A pupil commented: 'There are cliques, but people will always help you even if you wouldn't hang out together.'

Liberal and progressive ethos. No uniform (writer Fiona Millar remembers voting to abolish the bottle green uniform soon after she joined the school in the late 60s)

Broad range of leadership opportunities: alongside a sixth form leadership team that includes a head girl and boy plus senior prefects, there's a main school (year 11) head girl and her deputies, with a 'quick chat and a Kitkat' on offer to anyone who would like advice from a fellow student. Undoubtedly, some do struggle with anorexia and self harming, others with exam pressure, which the school does its best to counter (school counsellor and therapist available). 'We had a meeting with the head of year whose message was don't stress out – keep doing your hobbies and going on trips,' said a year 11 parent. 'We left the meeting feeling so much better.' Sixth form head is 'superb – progressive, warm, nothing is too much trouble,' say parents, with an open door policy 'if there's any hint of a problem'. 'It gives you a freedom that most high achieving schools don't,' said a student, 'but there's a real backbone of support.'

Pupils and parents: The sixth form may be, as one parent said, 'more like a private school', but the main school is hugely diverse ethnically and socially, including many middle class families who did a tactical move to the area during the late primary school years, plus large numbers who speak eg Bengali, Greek or Somali at home (the school has a Bengali liaison colleague). Some 30 home languages and around 40 per cent disadvantage figure (pupils eligible for free school meals during the last six years). Parents see this mix as one of the great advantages of the school. 'It made her so comfortable with every sort of religion and background.' 'I like the variety of it – it's a microcosm of the world... She's learning about privileges and gratitude and that's one reason why we put her into this school.'

Benefits from supportive and high flying parent body, characterised by the local left-leaning media and political classes plus 'glittering alumnae'. They all add 'huge cultural capital' as speakers, mentors and fundraisers, with anyone from Alastair Campbell to Natalie Haynes to Caroline Criado Perez dropping in to give a talk. Camden girls – including sixth form boys – tend towards the cool, confident and indie, strongly opinionated and sure of their place in the world.

Parents say: 'Very good for independent minded, critical students... Possibly not a good school for the very shy, who might find it all too overwhelming.' 'I don't know anyone who didn't come up with a good group of friends.' 'An eclectic and interesting group of girls.' 'They go off to extraordinary things,' said a parent.

Money matters: Camden is a voluntary aided school and has to contribute 10 per cent to its building costs. Parents give generously and there is an annual fundraising appeal, with monthly donations from £10. Plenty of further fundraising activities, too, where celebrity watching is the order of the day.

The last word: Pulls off the difficult job of being a hugely popular, high achieving, all ability comprehensive. Benefits from the support of a greater range of well known and inspiring alumnae than most independent schools. As a parent said, 'There's a very special ethos.'

Central Foundation Boys' School

Cowper Street, City Road, London EC2A 4SH

020 7253 3741 | info@cfbs.islington.sch.uk | www.centralfoundationboys.co.uk

State | Ages: 11–18 | Pupils: 780; sixth form: 176 (24 girls)

Head teacher: Since 2010, Jamie Brownhill LLB (40s). Originally a lawyer, he worked as a construction litigator for city law firm Mayer Brown before training as a teacher at CFB in 2000. 'I wouldn't have gone to just any school,' he says. 'It was very much a sense of vocation and moral purpose that leads one from being a city lawyer to such a challenging environment.' And lucky for the school that he did make that choice – after just five years at the top he'd completely turned it around.

Extremely visionary and not one for small talk, he is prone to sounding as if he's permanently giving a speech, making big, sweeping statements ('One needs to have a vision and follow it through'; 'There's a recognition that a head has an incredible impact' etc), which make him an impressive orator. 'Even in the corridors, he has important words of wisdom,' one pupil told us. Parents talk about being 'blown away' by him. One said, 'Our older sons were educated privately and we looked round 15 schools for our youngest, including private, selective and comprehensives – but this one stood out head and shoulders above the rest, largely because of Brownhill. He sets the tone, the culture and the expectations within the school and we love his inclusiveness, his energy, drive and commitment.' Praise indeed. Another commented, 'We love the fact that he's from the outside world – it gives him a much broader perspective than heads who have spent their entire careers within education.'

Rare is the day that pupils don't have some contact with him – he greets them every morning, runs weekly whole-school assemblies, teaches history to the lower years and he's usually out and about during changeover and break times. His office even overlooks the playground. Staff say he has a finger in every pie (which one admitted can be as frustrating as it is helpful), but ultimately they agree it's enabled him to make the school what it is, with the systems he's brought in for the likes of behaviour and targeting being described as 'nothing short of brilliant'.

Entrance: More than 600 boys compete for the 180 places. All applicants take CATs (Cognitive Ability Tests), with students split into four ability cohorts. Within each of these cohorts, the boys closest to the school get in. All sixth form entrants must have 6s at GCSE in the subjects they want to study, including English and maths, as well as getting through a detailed interview. 'The way we see it, we have a short period of time to achieve a lot, so we need to know students have the right character and work ethic,' says the head. Attendance in sixth form is 98 per cent (compared to the average of 85-90 per cent for London) and the head intends to keep it that way. Usually, around 10 of the school's own applicants tend to get turned away, while around 25 new students come in (of whom 10-15 are female).

Exit: Around 60 per cent stay on to sixth form, those who don't have generally having decided to study A levels elsewhere, including the private sector. STEM subjects are commonly studied at university, including medicine, mathematics, chemistry and engineering. Humanities and arts also popular. Recent destinations include UCL, King's College London, Imperial, Warwick, Manchester and Edinburgh. Apprenticeships facilitated by a partnership between the school, the international law firm Slaughter and May, and the Access Project charity.

Latest results: In 2019, 33 per cent 9-7 at GCSE: 63 per cent got 9-5 in both English and maths. At A level, 29 per cent A*/A (52 per cent A*-B).

Teaching and learning: GCSE performance has put this school in the top 10 per cent of schools nationally for added value, while the sixth form results mean the school is in the top 15 per cent of KS5 providers in the country – very impressive for an inner city comprehensive with 65 per cent pupil premium (in fact, it was nearer 80 per cent when the head joined). At GCSE, strongest results in maths, English, science and computing.

French or Spanish from year 7, with after-school classes also available for Mandarin, Arabic and ancient Greek (all of which can also be done at GCSE), though few continue languages to A level. Setting in English, maths, science, languages, geography and history from year 7, with a reassuring amount of movability. Homework in abundance – building up from an hour in year 7 to two hours in year 11 – and woe betide any student who doesn't hand it in on time.

A level subject choices are largely traditional – sciences, maths, economics and computing most popular – but the school is part of the Islington Sixth Form Consortium, meaning there's the opportunity to study the likes of photography, psychology, media studies and a whole wealth of languages at one of the other member schools.

Head believes the school's success is largely down to maximum class sizes of 24, plus the major push on the fundamentals in year 7 and 8, which ensures literacy, maths and learning habits (how you revise; how you organise homework etc) are up to scratch, ready for GCSE learning (unlike at so many other schools, where the overt focus is on years 10 and 11). 'It seems to me that the importance of learning is at the heart of every single piece of communication with the boys,' one parent told us. Perhaps this explains why the boys we spoke to were not only enthused about their studies, but able to directly relate them to their futures.

The visionary head is not one for small talk. 'Even in the corridors, he has important words of wisdom,' one pupil told us. Parents talk about being 'blown away by him'

Lessons, which are all taught by subject specialists (most of whom have firsts or 2:1s in their degrees), are well-planned and, according to students, engaging. 'If you don't respond well to a teacher's learning style, they'll adapt it for you,' one told us, whilst several pointed out that teachers are always available by email or after school to go over anything you don't understand.

Teachers say they are helped by the centralised system for dealing with behaviour (same-day detentions even for small transgressions), along with a painstaking focus on tracking and monitoring, which they say means they can get on with the job in hand. Very few teaching assistants – they tend to be used on a temporary basis for getting a child's behaviour sorted. There's a mixed diet of practical, interactive lessons and heads-down learning. Food tech, for example, always involves cooking, whereas in the maths and languages lessons we witnessed, it was very much a case of chalk and talk.

Learning support and SEN: SEN provision – which covers the usual dyslexia, ASD etc – is almost exclusively classroom based (and helped by those small class sizes, as well as setting) and offers exceptional outcomes for students, evidenced by the results. 'I couldn't have asked for better help throughout my son's education,' said one mother, whose son is dyslexic. 'He's had the "Why me?" moments when he's had to work much harder, but the school keeps him positive, as well as making sure he has attainable goals and extra support and time where he needs it. Dyslexia has certainly never made him feel he can't achieve as much as anyone else.'

The arts and extracurricular: Music is integral to school life. Incredibly, every boy who wants to can borrow an instrument for the duration of his time at the school. We're not just talking recorders, but cellos, saxophones and clarinets. No wonder 150 students are heavily involved with the department. From 7.30am every day, there are rehearsals, whether for the three school choirs, orchestra, bands (including house band and concert band), string quartets, woodwind groups etc. The department's equipment is sophisticated and there's a 10-strong staff team, including two full-time music teachers. Expect to see a raised eyebrow if you use the word 'peripatetic' to describe the visiting teachers – this dedicated team say this is the only school in London they work in where they are considered part of the school community – the result of which is that they are more than willing to put extra time in for the three main performances per year. Parents describe these performances as 'amazing'. 'We nearly all had tears in our eyes at the last one,' one parent told us. External opportunities range from singing in the Royal Albert Hall to providing the musical entertainment for local law firm functions. While many of the musical children are also academic, others aren't – and music gives them a great opportunity to excel.

A delightful art room is home to some serious artistic talent – much of it bold, brave and inspiring. Drama also thriving, with weekly lessons for years 7, 8 and 9 in the two-roomed, carpeted drama studio. There are three main performances per year, providing opportunities for both pupils in the lower and upper years. Debating strong; they were national schools Debate Mate champions recently and were third out 250 schools in a recent competition when we visited.

Day visits to all the usual museums and galleries that this school has on its doorstep, as well as French and Spanish trips (year 9, 10 and 11), an annual ski trip open to all and a rural activity trip for sixth formers. Extracurricular provision focuses on music and sport in the main, with other options ranging from cooking (particularly popular) to arts club and gaming to drama. The school takes full advantage of its location, with excellent links with the City.

Sport: Football and basketball are the top sports, with boys doing CFB proud when it comes to competing against other schools. Cricket is on the up and there's also fencing, boxing, martial arts, table tennis and gym workouts. Whilst the school is good at playing to the boys' strengths (hence winning all those high level competitions), the head is adamant that sport here is for all. 'There's no stereotypical male bravado around sport at this school. In short, you don't get the jocks,' said one parent. On-site facilities include an undercover Astroturf pitch, running track, a couple of gyms and two halls. Off-site, the boys do climbing, swimming and more. 'When a young person leaves here, they really know how to access the community's facilities,' says the head.

Music is integral to school life. Incredibly, every boy who wants to can borrow an instrument for the duration of his time at the school

Ethos and heritage: There could hardly be a more unlikely location for a school – smack in the middle of the City. Squeezed between, and overlooked by, law buildings and financial institutions, you walk in expecting it to be bursting at the seams. But this place is a Tardis, with a roomy outside courtyard (some of which is covered) and Astroturf pitch, along with ample classrooms of various sizes, break-out rooms, labs, halls, library, dining room, sixth form centre, art block, drama and more. The oldest parts date back 150 years and boast beautifully tiled walls and polished wood floors, albeit with a few areas that look in need of a lick of paint. 'The school even smells of tradition,' said one dad – and he's right.

The school originally opened in 1865 by Rev William Rogers (chaplain to Queen Victoria), who recognised the pressing need for more education in the City. Having initially used temporary buildings in Bath Street, the current purpose built school then opened in Cowper Street in 1869 and the Great Hall came four years later, by which time there were over 900 boys. Post-war, it became a grammar, then in 1975 the school returned to being a comprehensive, with various building works having taken place over the decades – the newest and most significant involving a science block and a new reception, followed by a new arts centre, then a four court sports hall – along with some more general landscaping and renovation.

During lesson times, the school is so quiet that you could be forgiven for thinking the place is empty. It's another story at break times, though, when boys inevitably let off steam – and with everyone changing lessons or having breaks simultaneously, it can be loud. 'It's essential, in my view, to avoid interruptions, so when we learn, we all learn and when we move, we all move,' says the head.

Notable former pupils include Anthony Wedgwood Benn (before he became plain old Tony Benn), Kingsley Wood, Jacob Bronowski, Richard Seifert, Ronnie Scott, Martin Kemp, Trevor Nelson and Reggie Yates.

Pastoral care, inclusivity and discipline: Eight form groups of 18 students per year, all with a tutor that stays with them as they rise up the school (with which every student is allocated regular tutorials). Meanwhile, directors of learning (heads of year) do a detailed analysis of each student each term, looking at issues such as attendance (including at after-school clubs), punctuality, learning and behaviour. Then there's a house system, which generates all the usual leadership opportunities and cross-year friendships. There are three student counsellors and a high level of engagement with CAMHS.

No word gets used more by the head than 'community' and it's this ethos, say students and their parents, that ultimately makes the school such a supportive environment – a place that students want to be. Some older students told us bullying used to be a real issue, but that this head's zero tolerance has helped – measures such as teachers in playgrounds, and even bus stops and underground stations, mean there are no longer any hiding places. 'There are instances of bullying,' one boy told us, 'but teachers are good at sorting it out quickly.'

The glass cabinet in the reception area sets the tone for discipline. Displaying beautifully handwritten notes from the headteachers in the 1800s, outlining intricately detailed rules around issues such as not throwing paper and not pulling other boys' hats off, this isn't just a light-hearted look back to harsher times. The message remains crystal clear that boys must not misbehave, even slightly, or else they'll get short, sharp shock – notably an hour's detention. Talking in class, forgetting your PE kit, lacking focus, failing to hand in your homework – all these things will land you in deep water. No wonder Ofsted marked behaviour here as outstanding and we did not see a single boy failing to pay full attention in class. 'There is the odd time when a boy flares up and hits out,' the head told us when asked if there are ever more serious misdemeanours, but it's not like it once was, reflected by the drop from 190 exclusions per year before he joined to just 10 in the academic year we visited.

Boys are expected to dress immaculately both in and outside school. The messiest you'll see is an undone top button. 'I have a room with every piece of uniform in every size, so if a boy forgets something, they can borrow it,' says the head.

Unusually, sixth formers can do paid work in school eg working in the kitchen and doing lunchtime duties in the year 7 play area. 'We don't want the students working every hour at Sainsbury's to earn money, which would get in the way of their work. It means everyone wins,' says the head.

The student council is taken seriously and individual requests are often met too. 'One student in year 7 asked for there to be a skateboarding club and they set it up within a month,' one student told us.

Pupils and parents: There are 35 first languages spoken by students at this truly ethnically diverse school; it's English for 47 per cent of students, then Bengali (16 per cent). Nineteen per cent of students are white British, with other significant numbers being Bangladeshi, Somali, Turkish and Black Caribbean. Because of the banded entry system, some of these students come from neighbouring boroughs, as well as the whole of Islington. The students are a mixed bag socially too – both extremes of wealth and poverty, plus everything in between.

The message is crystal clear that boys must not misbehave, even slightly, or else they'll get short, sharp shock. Ofsted marked behaviour here as outstanding

There's no PA, although parents are seen as key to enabling the boys' learning and there's almost 100 per cent attendance at the two annual parents' evenings and other talks and meetings. We found pupils to be articulate and enthusiastic, even in year 7, and there's already a huge sense of pride.

The last word: This extremely disciplined, well-ordered and highly academic, urban school runs a tight ship, giving boys who are prepared to toe the line a chance to leave with both excellent exam results and a genuine readiness for the modern world in terms of character, moral compass and work ethic. A hidden gem right in the heart of London, it is a school going from strength to strength and has the feel of a grammar, without the selection. 'It's a hugely well-kept secret, with many parents – including me – thinking, "Why don't all local boys apply?"' summed up one parent.

Charterhouse Square School

40 Charterhouse Square, London EC1M 6EA

020 7600 3805 | life@charterhousesquareschool.co.uk | www.charterhousesquareschool.co.uk

Independent	Ages: 3–11	Pupils: 201	Fees: £17,730 pa

Head: Since 2009, Caroline Lloyd (40s). BEd in geography from Exeter University (although her parents had wanted her to do a 'proper' degree). Her first job as an NQT was at Charterhouse Square School in 1994, straight after leaving university: 'I was young, determined and desperate to be a teacher.' Indeed Caroline (as she is known to staff and pupils), knew she wanted to teach from the age of 7 and 'used to line up my teddies, pretending they were in class.' However, she had a very specific idea of the kind of school where she wanted to teach and only five schools matched her criteria – Charterhouse Square being one of them.

During her 15 years at the school and prior to becoming head, Caroline experienced teaching in all year groups from nursery through to year 6. After leaving to start a family she returned six months later on a part-time basis as she 'missed teaching so much'. In 2008, the school was purchased by Cognita and the position of head was advertised. Caroline says: 'It was never my intention to become a head, but I was worried that someone new would come in and not see how special the school was' – so she applied for the post. After so many years at the school her application was seen as a natural progression by both parents and children. One parent told us: 'The school was good before with the previous head, but it's great now. The children have just blossomed under Caroline.' Another praised her for being such a consistently visible presence: 'She knows every pupil by name and is naturally great with children. The school just seems to run seamlessly.'

Tall, attractive and immaculately turned out, she could have been separated at birth from the Middleton sisters and would look quite at home sipping Pimm's at a polo match. Her boundless enthusiasm for both her job and life in general is infectious but don't be fooled, this head is no pushover and knows that some people might go so far as to call her a control freak: 'I'm on the school door every morning and most afternoons. I feel that if communication is strong, we can get things sorted before they escalate out of control.'

One can't imagine too many things getting out of control at this genteel school, which has had no permanent exclusions in its 25+ year history; the head concedes that her main challenge is 'managing over-aspiring parents'. She says: 'I've often had to remind parents that I'm actually on the side of the child, especially when they are being pushed too hard to get in to certain secondary schools.'

Entrance: Completely non-selective, entry is by lottery – unless you have a sibling who already attends. Twenty-six 3+ places offered each year and roughly 70 on the waiting list. No point planning the Caesarian or putting names down at birth, you can register up till the end of June the year before entry and a ballot is drawn on 1 July. Head says this comes as a shock for some parents, 'who have been used to pulling out a cheque book to buy their way in' and concedes that 'It can make me pretty unpopular.' Cheque book will, however, come in handy for £4,000 non-returnable deposit payable when accepting a place.

Exit: Most to high calibre selective London secondaries. Fierce competition for places at both (girls and boys) City of London schools and some pupils even pulled out early at age 7 or 10 by parents who think this will increase their chances of getting in. School says this is a shame and 'can be disruptive'. Other recent popular destinations include Highgate, Alleyn's, Channing, Forest School, Francis Holland Baker Street, Queen's College.

Our view: Charterhouse Square School is located on the south side of historic Charterhouse Square in Smithfield, central London. The square was built on what was the site of a 14th century Carthusian monastery (an almshouse and chapel remain) and also London's largest Black Death plague pit. The five-storey Victorian building occupied by the school, though smart enough, is easily missed among neighbouring offices and apartment blocks, but any lack of character, not to mention green space, is more than made up for by such a central location. This is a City school and parents know exactly what they're buying into when they make the decision to send their children here. One told us: 'I am able to drop my kids off on the way to work, which is one reason I chose this school. The other reason is that I noticed how happy and well-mannered the pupils were when they were out and about. I know some people think it looks more confined than other schools, but it works for us and my children are very happy here.'

Though it wouldn't suit those who like to plan ahead, most parents seem to welcome the diversity and 'range of abilities' that result from school's non-selective, lottery-based entrance procedure. It's an unusual independent school in other ways: there's no uniform and it's first name terms for all teachers, including the head. One parent told us: 'I love this school for being individual with very individual ideas.' Another said: 'Coming from a convent school background I was initially horrified about the idea of first name terms, but I have to say it works very well and makes the teachers far more approachable to the children, without diluting any respect.'

Nursery was having its annual 'animal dress up day' and we were greeted by tigers, bears and monkeys plus a couple of unidentifiable but colourful animals

Head has worked hard to ensure that hers isn't a one size fits all school: 'When I came on board, early years was very formal and a bit of a hothouse. Drama was only every other week and there were no school trips. I think it's about broadening the curriculum so that we can make sure that all pupils can excel at something.' Parents wholeheartedly agree. Teaching described as 'exceptional' and 'instilling a love of learning'. Years 4 and 5 are taught together so that they have the same teacher for two years before the all-important year 6. They work on a two-year curriculum, with the exception of homework, and English and maths textbooks. They are also ability grouped. One parent told us, 'I'm not really sure how it works – but the kids seem to understand it, so that's the main thing.'

Designated SENCo provides one-to-one support and booster groups for children with SEN, which accounts for a handful of the school's intake. The nature of the school building (five flights of stairs) may make it unsuitable for pupils with physical disabilities.

Pastoral care is paramount and school employs a number of highly effective strategies to help pupils feel safe. Older pupils can make use of classroom 'feelings boxes' to share concerns privately with teachers, and the 'buddy' system supports new pupils. Every parent we spoke to raved about this: 'It's a great system as it makes new children feel less intimidated and older children rise to the responsibility of looking after the younger ones.'

Our tour started in the early years foundation stage classes, nursery and reception. Nursery was having its annual 'animal dress up day' and we were greeted by tigers, bears and monkeys plus a couple of unidentifiable but colourful animals. Sweet little add-on area designed for role play was effectively outside, but covered by a canopy and surrounded by a high wall. This, we were told, was to prevent anything landing on the tracks of Barbican station, something that carries a huge fine (on an hourly rate). Thankfully, this has not happened so far.

Small but well stocked library from where children are encouraged to take books home nightly, and a carpeted school hall with beautiful white piano and colourful wall display of ukuleles. Extracurricular activities such as judo and table tennis take place here and all children have the opportunity to learn a musical instrument. 'Informal' Spanish also offered in the early years. One parent said: 'I was amazed when we went on holiday to Spain last year, that my 5-year-old daughter was able to communicate with a local in pidgin Spanish.'

Bright, neat, colourful classrooms were full of interested, happy and very polite children and the atmosphere of the school is extremely warm and friendly. Pupils who were leaving told us how they'll miss Charterhouse 'sooo much', especially the teachers. 'What I really like about the teachers is that they are all so friendly. Also, we are often asked to tick a box privately at the end of a lesson about whether we found the classes easy or difficult. If we are really struggling, we can sometimes get an extra private lesson.'

Despite the limitations of a tall and narrow building ('I often had to walk up five flights of stairs when I was pregnant,' the head told us), children don't seem to lack breathing space and fresh air. During the warmer months they spend their lunch break in the private Charterhouse Square gardens; when it's cold and wet they play in the school's 'jungle' downstairs. Organised sports take place nearby at Coram Fields or the Golden Lane Leisure Centre. Pupils do take part in inter-school sporting events, but no regular fixtures because of the issue of 'bussing children around'. One parent did say that this school is perhaps not the right option for the 'extremely sporty child', although another said that her two boys 'are extremely sporty and it meets their needs'. A highlight in the calendar is sports day: 'It's just such a joy, well handled and fun.'

No school meals prepared on site and no dining room because of limited space so until recently all pupils had to bring in a packed lunch. School has now organised for a company to bring in hot food in thermos containers, if the parents require. The head says: 'This system works very well and the advantage is that parents know what their children like and can order accordingly.' We are told the quality and choice is great, with meatballs, pasta, wraps, soups and stews on offer.

The last word: Lack of space may deter some, but Charterhouse Square is a wonderful option if you live and work in the City. This is a successful school and a happy environment in which pupils of varying abilities thrive and with comments such as: 'My child loves every day of her school life!' Who could ask for more?

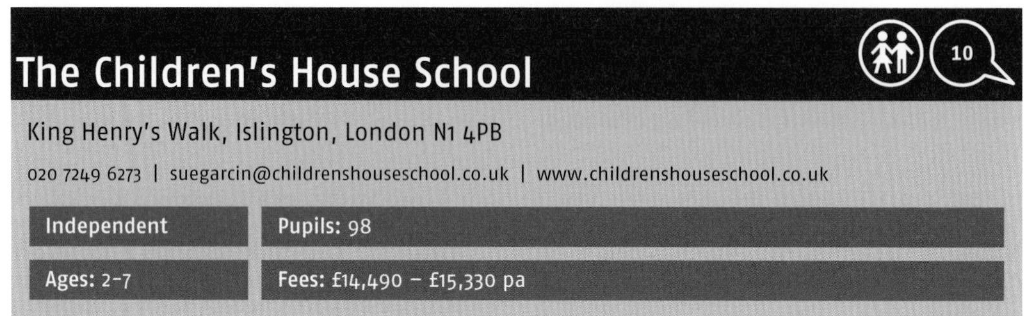

The Children's House School

King Henry's Walk, Islington, London N1 4PB

020 7249 6273 | suegarcin@childrenshouseschool.co.uk | www.childrenshouseschool.co.uk

Independent | Pupils: 98

Ages: 2-7 | Fees: £14,490 – £15,330 pa

Head: Since 2016, Kate Orange Cert Ed (Wellington, New Zealand College of Education) – 60s (not that you would know it) with an interesting background in education. After graduating in New Zealand and working for two years as a teacher there, she moved to the UK, cutting her British teeth working for the Thomas's School group in their first school near Sloane Square. However, after two years and with a yearning to work in France, she moved to a village school in Provence, which she says was the most incredible experience: 'I was a New Zealander and this was my first experience of living in a completely foreign environment.' With her schoolgirl French, she even managed to wow officials (from the Mitterrand government at the time), who were sent to the school to inspect this new foreign teacher: 'I became a national cause célèbre.' She spent her spare time there acting with a Parisian theatre company, performing at the Avignon Festival. Her love affair with France has persisted.

When she returned to London three years later, she worked in knowledge management for a City law firm for four years. After having children, she taught at an Islington school for two years before moving to the Children's House as a class teacher. She took on the role of deputy head in 2005, taking over as head when the long-standing former headteacher retired. 'This school just has a lovely feel to it; it's very child centred, which in turn makes it very family centred,' says Kate (as she is known to all, even the pupils). Indeed, during our visit, her office door burst open on two occasions with pupils desperately wanting to ask 'Kate' something. As one parent said, 'This school very much operates an open-door policy at all times. You can have a chat to Kate whenever you want, and you often see parents popping by her office in the morning. She's also very quick at responding to emails.' Another parent said: 'I've had both heads and they've both been great, but Kate has a real educational rigour to her and the school has a great academic focus without hammering it home.' Others talk about how dedicated she is and how she knows everything about every child in the school.

Married with two grown-up children, one in law, one studying architecture, Kate is a classical music enthusiast and belongs to a small group of people in southern France who facilitate concerts in Provence, where she tries to spend around three months of the year.

Entrance: Register for nursery as soon as possible after birth; nursery children are now guaranteed the offer of a place in reception (£100 registration fee and £2,000 deposit). Places are offered by date of registration and sibling priority. Most places in the pre-prep are filled from the nursery, but 'one or two' spaces might be available in reception, again based on date of registration. Consideration has been given to expansion, but finding suitable premises has been as issue.

Exit: A few leave at at 4 and 5. Twenty-eight children enter reception in two classes of 14, but numbers naturally reduce to a manageable 20 by year 2; 'although this number does vary from year to year – we don't like to turn anyone away who has come through the nursery.'

The vast majority of 4+ and 7+ leavers go to Cavendish and North Bridge House. Others to Forest School and City of London. In previous years, destinations have also included Channing, Highgate, Queen's College etc.

Our view: Founded as a nursery in someone's front room in 1973, when 'there was little in the way of early years provision and nothing in the way of policies and procedures', the nursery is now a fully-formed school in central Islington, housed in a former Hindu Temple, the first of its kind in London: 'Hindu Saints still pilgrimage here, but not during term time,' we are told. Situated a brisk 15 min walk from the pre-prep (although there is flexibility in pick-up times for parents with children on both sites). Two-year-olds upwards enjoy a rich and dynamic offering (including conversational Spanish, dance, yoga and art) taught by fully qualified teachers. 'It's a lovely, friendly place,' said one parent. 'They really care about each child.' At the nursery we were impressed by the large, bright and airy rooms with a plethora of activities to stimulate any child. Although there is no attached outdoor space, children are taken to a nearby garden three times a week and to soft play weekly. Hours increase from mornings only in the nursery to full days for pre-reception children.

The pre-prep came into being when a former parent spotted a school to let in the local newspaper. 'Our nursery parents always felt it was a pity that children had to move on at 4 and 5.' Now they can remain in the fold, housed in a petite and picturesque Victorian school building. The classrooms lead off a lovely sheltered playground. 'It's idyllic, like Enid Blyton,' said one parent.

Very much a 'child-led' school: 'We like them to work collaboratively, one child supporting another.' It's not a hothouse, but with the 7+ ever-present at the end of year 2, children are expected to do homework after school on most days (introduced gently in reception and year 1) and during the summer holidays before entering year 2. 'A fairly challenging environment,' one parent said, but another added: 'Whilst they do take the 7+ very seriously, they do it without panicking parents.' However, as Kate says, 'being a small school, the teachers do get to know the children very well and are quietly assessing their progress on a daily basis. We can then cater for their individual needs and there is a lot of fluidity between ability groups.'

It is a very creative environment in which the arts – music, art and dance – are central to learning. Children might make shoebox interiors as a part of a home topic, create giant tetrahedron mobiles in maths, or paint and embroider textiles in a study of fabric-making. During our visit, the children had just been learning about the Jewish Festival of Succot and had created their very own Succah (a temporary wooden shelter) in the playground.

Specialist teachers extend the core. Spanish is taught from nursery onwards for one lesson a week, and ICT has a dedicated teacher and a full-class supply of laptops throughout. Singing and rhythm are taught by a music teacher, plus a weekly half-hour violin lesson with two professional violinists. 'We could have chosen any instrument, provided the children learned pitch, rhythm and musical notation. Most children play the violin very well by the end of year 2.'

The school prides itself on being very inclusive and an on-site SENCo addresses both minor and significant difficulties. Good support is given to those with English as an additional language, addressing the requirements of an increasing number of bilingual children.

The children had just been learning about the Jewish Festival of Succot and had created their very own Succah (a temporary wooden shelter) in the playground

The children are introduced to team games and specialist ball-skills teachers provide additional PE lessons in one of the two large adjoining church halls. Well-equipped playground: 'We have a lot of play resources and use them to extend children's learning with carefully planned activities' – a fabulous wooden pirate ship was a recent addition. Regular trips to nearby King Henry's Walk Garden provide the opportunity to observe seasonal changes and grow their own vegetables in the allotments.

Plenty of enrichment. 'The school is fantastic at making lovely things happen for the children,' said one parent. Each class has at least two visits a term, always educational and usually entertaining (storytellers, puppeteers, exotic animals, LSO concerts and an African drummer, to name but a few) as well as numerous themed events. During our visit it was the annual Our Wonderful World Week. 'Everyone is invited to take part, from grandparents to aunts and uncles, to share something from their country of origin, which could be food, stories, music etc.'

After-school clubs twice weekly, and activities change termly – everything from sewing, fencing, chess, cookery, science, drumming to football skills could be on the agenda. Homework club 'helps parents and promotes a sense of independence in the child'. Lunchtime clubs include coding, games and puzzle club.

School uniform is minimal and practical (navy and white with specific school sweatshirts and fleeces). The school encourages healthy eating and children bring in lunchboxes, supplemented by a snack with fruit in the morning (provided by the school).

Traditional values of courtesy and consideration are central to the ethos. Kindness is rewarded here, and if you achieve 10 certificates, you get to choose half an hour's 'golden time' for the whole class: 'Being kind is paramount,' said a mother.

Founded by parents, the Children's House remains a parent-driven operation, with active participation from its Parent Committee. All vote for the council of management, which administers the school. Unsurprisingly, the cosmopolitan families (Islington and Hackney media, lawyers, bankers and artisans) form a tight bond both with each other and the school, regularly arriving to read, organising the summer fair, quiz night etc. There is a genuine commitment to community links and charity fundraising. 'We couldn't do it without the parents, who are amazing.'

Money matters: The school offers three fully-funded and some partially funded bursary places.

The last word: One of the things parents like most about the Children's House is its home-away-from-home atmosphere, and 'being made to feel so welcome'. One parent told us: 'Literally, my only criticism of the school is that it doesn't go up to 11. It's such a shame to leave such a happy place.'

City and Islington College

283-309 Goswell Road, London EC1V 7LA

020 7700 9333 | courseinfo@candi.ac.uk | www.candi.ac.uk

State | Ages: 16-19 | Pupils: 1,600

Director: Since September 2020, Kurt Hintz, who is also principal of College of Haringey, Enfield and North East London.

Entrance: Five 4s needed at GCSE to study three A levels, higher grades required to take four subjects, and the college sets its own entrance test for maths. Applicants are encouraged to visit the open day in November and apply before the end of January. Oversubscribed, more than four applicants per place, but interviews 2,500 before making offers. A nucleus of students from Islington and Hackney, and has a partnership with three local schools: Elizabeth Garrett Anderson, Holloway and Islington Arts and Media, which have priority, although current cohort attended 200 different secondary schools. A taster day at the start of July is followed by registration at beginning of autumn term and a last opportunity to finalise courses. A handful of international students, who board with local families.

Exit: The college is rightly proud of the statistics: 70-80 per cent to university, one fifth to the Russell Group. One to Oxbridge in 2019; other recent destinations include King's College London, LSE and Sussex. One off to do a degree apprenticeship in 2019. Several students praised the dynamic careers advice service, which supervises applications.

Latest results: In 2018, 30 per cent A*-B at A level.

Teaching and learning: A sixth form college for A levels, sheltering under broader academic umbrella of City and Islington College and Westminster Kingsway College, has the advantage of offering a wide range of subjects (over 34 on offer when we visited), delivered by A level specialist teachers, in a tailor-made environment for 16-18s. Class sizes are kept to around 20 (22 max) in the popular subjects, supported by over 140 staff and technical assistants; smaller numbers attend the more unusual options, electronics, dance, graphic communication, Turkish. One parent was impressed by the flexibility in the timetable: 'They've been very open minded about changing course.' Mainstream subjects like physics have seen a surge in popularity, boosted by the college's two female physics teachers, while the college has extensive technical back-up for a range of practical options including textiles, photography and media studies, whose students get to show final pieces at nearby Screen on the Green.The college describes the student experience as academically rigorous. Around 60 students take the EPQ, which distinguishes independent learners and researchers. The staff are A level specialists, some with doctorates, some authors of school text books – and unanimously got the thumbs up from parents.

Students who aren't lucky enough to be visiting the Supreme Court or meeting a Nobel Prize-winning astrophysicist can enjoy more earthly activities, including football

Re latest Ofsted inspectors' tour: 'Overwhelmingly they were grade 1 lessons; we didn't have to hide anyone from them, there are no bad teachers here.' The management team described as 'fantastic' and 'sparky'; the parents' verdict: 'interconnect well as a team'. The college's mission to create links with industry and academia has a two-fold effect. Aspiring medics get to sit alongside UCL students at the Royal Free Hospital; 'It is stimulating for the staff, and that comes back into the classroom.'

Students with issues knew how to contact their tutor, and met with them every week in the normal way to discuss progress. They were in no doubt how to seek out help in applying for university from the full time careers officers; 'They are always telling us who to go to,' said one. The higher education department offers advice on UCAS applications, explains personal statements, carries out interview practice using former members of staff and even helps plan gap years. They run a dazzling timetable of tutorials, eg applying for Oxbridge, medicine, teaching, nursing or apprenticeships, along with a range of informative talks (STEM work experience for Girls caught our eye) in addition to masterclasses in work-related skills such as online IT courses and young drivers' workshops. Staff talk to universities all the time, which explains the respectable number of offers to competitive courses, though it was disappointing to find a capital-centric attitude in the students we met, who appear content to study close to home.

Learning support and SEN: An inclusion co-ordinator supports a full range of special needs, from mild dyslexia to ASD, with one-to-one support in class or in separate smaller rooms, depending on the level of need. The user-friendly building, complete with lifts, accommodates physical disabilities too.

The arts and extracurricular: As part of Wednesday enrichment, there's an in-house dance troupe and theatre shows, including an annual talent show and a Christmas production, which take place in the drama studio or at Islington's Almeida Theatre. Students from both music and music tech courses join with others in a combo band, though numbers don't allow for a choir or orchestra. The walls of the corridors display lively posters for a wide choice of clubs: history club, talking religion, talking politics, geo-justice, robot club, as well as political debates about local elections and the London mayor. Teachers make the most of the graphic design students in promoting courses: 'Why learn a language?' asked one eye-catching poster and 'Congratulations on completing your coursework' cheered another message. Trips out include London museums and Tate Modern; residentials for geographers to Derbyshire, while the RS class gets to visit a Buddhist retreat in Scotland.

Sport: Wednesday afternoons are for enrichment. Students who aren't lucky enough to be visiting the Supreme Court or meeting a Nobel Prize-winning astrophysicist can enjoy more earthly activities, including football, basketball, netball, boxercise and gym, co-ordinated by a sports youth worker, off site.

Ethos and heritage: In an area that Dickens refers to as where 'London began in earnest', the college site at Angel stands at a confluence of the metropolis's business and residential life. To the south and east it touches the City with its commercial and banking quarters, to the north it embraces the mixed residential areas of Highbury, Finsbury and Holloway and the buzzing shops and bars of Upper Street. The college's sparkling glass, steel and chrome structure catches the eye, with its grey themed interior and a city garden. Past the turnstiles and uniformed security checks, the visitor is greeted by a large canteen/hall/chilling area on the ground floor, labelled 'a thriving hub' by one mum. Beyond this is the library, with its purple and grey colour scheme, and shelves of journals. Many of the rooms are convertible to smaller meeting rooms, with soft dividers and screens; an adjacent IT suite houses computers as far as the eye can see.

A tour up the glass stairwell, with Barbara Hepworth-style holes, takes us to the classrooms and workshops above. Textiles, photography, and visual arts studios look out over the many cranes and offices of the cityscape, while film studies are found further along the corridor they call Media Street. Disappointingly little to see of the students' artwork in the designer building, and one mum felt the art and design department could be more inspiring. However, a room full of recording equipment run by dedicated techies provides support for the many and successful media students (alumni include singer Paloma Faith; actor David Oyelowo OBE; TV presenter Reggie Yates; and news reporter Symeon Brown). Humanities and languages classrooms have a floor to themselves, with seven science labs below, fully equipped with the latest kit and a flock of white coats and goggles; 'It seems to be very well resourced,' commented one parent. A vibrant hub on the first floor, full of upholstered chairs and scarlet beanbags, houses the careers advice centre.

Past the turnstiles and uniformed security checks, the visitor is greeted by a large canteen/hall/chilling area on the ground floor, labelled 'a thriving hub' by one mum

A lone horse chestnut tree on a patch of green breaks up the austere landscape of the grounds (this is EC1 real estate) while an all-weather court on the roof of the science building next door allows for floodlit matches. Students can take a break between classes at brutalist picnic tables or work up an urban sweat at a game of garden ping pong.

Pastoral care, inclusivity and discipline: Dress is teen-casual and it's first-name terms for teachers. The relationship relies on mutual respect; 'we are trying to turn them into young adults,' and students we spoke to were aware of the journey. 'It's preparing me for life after,' said one. The young adults recognised the school's high expectations: three warnings for misconduct or poor work, followed by a 'cause for concern' notice. One parent reported that the tutor had been quick to notice when her daughter's new-found freedom had gone too far, and called a meeting; 'we all three of us got her back on track.' No bullying, except the occasional modern menace of cyber-bullying. A more serious misdemeanour involves discussion with the parents. Serious alcohol or drugs issues are rare and accountable to a disciplinary panel. A mum praised the pastoral tutor system, for 'quite closely monitoring' a particularly shy daughter. The college is conscious that its population is at a fragile stage of adolescence, so employs a full-time counsellor, alongside others including a mental health and well-being worker. 'As a society we are more enlightened. In the past people got on with it or sunk.'

Pupils and parents: Starting afresh in a new sixth form, rather than staying at their secondary school, gives the students a real chance to reinvent themselves, and the ones we spoke to described a variety of reasons for choosing the college: 'it gives you more independence'; 'looking for somewhere you are doing things by yourself'; 'it's more diverse'; 'more subjects'; 'closest to home'. One parent commented about her daughter, 'She hadn't had a good experience, and had a lot of catching up to do with feeling good about learning... it's a place that gives inspiration to the students.' More girls than boys (60:40) and a typical urban cultural diversity: 'The ethnic mix is a real mix; 30 per cent Asian; 30 per cent Afro-Caribbean; 30 per cent white,' says the college, plus a few international students who 'want to have a London experience'. With huge numbers of students, the variety of ambition was also evident: the high achievers gain scholarships with banking or legal companies, others apply for vocational courses, while some are content to munch cookies in the canteen. 'The scale allows the range,' explains the school.

Parents commented on the study body as 'a mixed bag of individuals... from far and wide' and 'it's very diverse'. They meet the teachers at the annual parent evenings, or at individual sessions with the tutor or course leader, if requested. Surprisingly for such a large cohort, the parents all felt involved, and emails and phone calls were answered promptly. The school sends out a termly newsletter, though no-one we spoke to had read it.

Money matters: Centrally funded by Education Funding Agency; international students self-fund. Dedicated college advisor supports applications for a host of bursaries, sponsorships and additional expenses, including travel. Parents pay towards school trips.

The last word: City and Islington College offers students a new beginning with a wealth of courses and great facilities. The students are encouraged to take advantage of their position in the heart of London to forge connections with the world of work and academia. Throw in supportive staff, a savvy head and a blessed central location at Angel and no wonder they are off to a flying start.

City of London School

Queen Victoria Street, London EC4V 3AL

020 3680 6300 | admissions@cityoflondonschool.org.uk | www.cityoflondonschool.org.uk

Independent	Pupils: 950; sixth form: 250
Ages: 10–18	Fees: £18,939 pa

Head: Since January 2018, Alan Bird (40s). First headship. Original childhood ambition to be a high flyer – as a pilot – has been amply, if differently, fulfilled. After reading economics at Cambridge (it was that or music as a degree), decided on education as a career after teaching at his old school between completing his degree and taking his masters. Manages to have 'a hinterland' – enjoys travel, skiing and is a bit of a foodie, as well as retaining an abiding interest in politics.

Started at Tonbridge School in 2002 as an economics and politics teacher, was promoted to head of politics in 2004, also taking in roles as an assistant housemaster and school magazine editor as well as coordinating Oxbridge admissions for arts and humanities and looking after bursaries programme. Moved to Brighton College as head of sixth form in 2010, where he was promoted to deputy head three and a half years in.

School's ethos really chimes. 'It's very down to earth, we don't stand on ceremony.' The sort of pupils who thrive here may be hugely diverse when it comes to wealth, background, religion and location. What they share is desire to throw themselves into everything the school offers and do well on their own merits. The result is 'a vibrant atmosphere that makes it a really rewarding place to work.'

Mr Bird is clever, thoughtful and popular. Staff think he's great. 'A delight,' said one. 'I genuinely don't see how he could have been a better fit – obvious that he loves the school and the job.'

Parents who've met him describe him as friendly, nice. 'He feels like he's invested, he cares,' said one. Pupils rate him. 'He's maintained the level of the school,' pronounced one. He's youthful (some parents rumoured to know him as 'baby Bird'), which helps. 'Feels quite refreshing,' said one. In addition to teaching (year 12 economics and year 8 PSHE), he's inviting small groups of youngest and oldest boys to chat to him over pizza. 'Being chatted to on their level feels like much more of a connection with someone who could feel quite out of reach,' said parent. Pupils' questions have been varied. 'At 10 and 11 they have no inhibitions,' says Mr Bird. 'I've been asked everything from opening times for the sports entrance to how I got the job and what school inspectors are looking for.'

From the view from his office across the Thames to the Tate (better in winter when attention-seeking tree, slap bang in front of office window, loses its leaves) to the school's raison d'être, there's nothing about the role he doesn't enjoy. He exudes the air of someone who's almost pinching himself that he's here.

Entrance: Highly competitive – and, in keeping with mood of frankness, school makes no bones about it. 'Every year we turn down hundreds of candidates who are top of their class at their current school,' warns admissions booklet. Message – don't be disappointed if your son is one of them – and certainly don't let them feel they've failed. 'It just means that CLS is not the right school for him.'

Any hopefuls need to be well read with a wide vocab (pays to work way through classic texts – abridgers name checked over original authors: useful to explain that Charles Dickens, rather than Kathleen Olmstead, wrote Oliver Twist...). School suggests prepping with age-appropriate resources to start with, then moving up the age groups 'to refine his skills'. Parents should get going early 'in case you need to do the paper first to get the answers'. So fun for the whole family.

Apply September of previous year for 10+ (44 places) and 11+ (55 places); October of previous year for 16+ (around 15 places) and three years in advance for 13+ (45 places).

At 10+ VR, maths and multiple choice comprehension English requiring skills (and practice) to rule out the obvious answer and 'leave time to focus and ponder...' NVR added for the 11+. ISEB pre-test for 13+ candidates, best candidates interviewed and sit further tests.

They're also frank about tutoring. It happens, and would be 'naïve' to pretend otherwise. 'Where used to support and consolidate', it has its place – 'but if child is going to need support throughout school career he just won't get the most out of time here,' thinks school. Parents should 'reflect honestly' and in any case, says school, can normally spot the over-prepared child when shortlisted candidates (at 10+ and 11+) are interviewed.

Learning needs welcomed (including GAD – general anxiety disorder) as long as reports provided in advance and candidates pass the entrance tests.

Exit: Almost everyone to Russell Group – first or second choice. In 2019, 29 to Oxbridge. Vanishingly rare for anyone to leave after GCSEs except by choice. In theory might happen if don't get the grades but 'would have been flagged a long way in advance,' says school.

Latest results: School won't release 2020 results as it believes 'they cannot be used in any rigorous manner as a basis for comparison of performance across schools.' In 2019 (the last year when exams took place), 94 per cent 9-7 at GCSE; 75 per cent A*/A at A level or Pre-U equivalent.

Teaching and learning: 'Unashamedly academic,' says school. It's taken as read. 'We don't talk about it a lot at open days,' says Mr Bird. But wait: there's more – much more – that will help pupils get the most out their time here, including a 'passion for intellectual exploration', a desire to 'challenge, query, question and argue…' so they're 'engaged and excited and ready for undergraduate life at university.'

Pupils share a desire to throw themselves into everything the school offers and do well on their own merits. The result is 'a really rewarding place to work'

'Does feel like they're thinking not just about the academic side of things but ultimately producing more rounded men,' said parent.

Whole form learning most of the way through, with limited 'loose' setting in maths (most able can take an additional level 3 maths qualification on top of GCSE) and French. Year 6 pupils ('Old Grammar' here) have a lesson a week on getting themselves sorted (everything from time management to touch typing). Plenty of academic support all the way through. 'If struggling in any subject we can approach teachers who organise sessions,' said pupil.

Exam results do them proud. Most take 10 GCSEs in year 11 which could – unusually – include five modern and classical languages, with some sitting a couple of music and languages a year early.

Languages are very ambitious. There's Latin, French and Mandarin from first form (OG study classics and linguistics). Essential grounding, says the school, which points out that Mandarin can't be covered from a standing start in year 10, unlike eg Russian, though it's dropped by quite a few pupils in third year.

Results in A levels/Pre-U equivalent also impressive – the latter taught in nine subjects, mainly modern languages and some humanities. STEM enthusiasts dominate – maths, economics, chemistry, physics and further maths account for around 60 per cent of total A level entries.

But while numbers taking English, art, drama and Latin are currently well below horde levels, they're rising, says the school, while parents confirm that bright boys whose interests lie outside STEM aren't made to feel like second class citizens. 'Any boy should be able to do any A level and feel [equally well] supported,' agrees Mr Bird.

In a similar vein, lower maths sets are allocated top quality teachers, whose confidence boosting powers can be transformative. 'Has turned things round because he's starting to learn at his own pace,' said parent. 'It's a credit to the school that they've made it something that he enjoyed. Certainly hasn't felt that you're dismissed if you're not naturally good at maths.'

School also good at celebrating all achievements. 'Not just the boys who got into Oxbridge and no one else counts,' said parent. Mr Bird's goal is for boys to be comfortable in their own skin. 'If that means 140 different outcomes for 140 leavers, it's fine by me.'

Amount of homework (which attracts a 'diversity' of opinion, says Mr Bird, diplomatically) is chunky (there's a big step up from year 8, thought a parent). Good organisational skills are a definite bonus, though teachers felt to be really aware of what boys are doing – 'have a really good handle on the balance they have,' said parent – and to adjust deadlines if needed.

We like the evident pride school takes in 'our boys' talents', as do the inspectors. Pupils are 'exceptionally well educated,' they say. No doubt, like us, they took in the stretch curriculum with boys entering essay competitions (Erasmus, John Locke, Peterhouse, Juvenes Translatores, Trinity), Olympiad competitions in maths and sciences, and recently 'excelling' in the International Genetically Engineered Machines (synthetic biology, apparently). Parents agree. 'I feel his outlook on the world is growing, he'll suddenly be able to discuss things I didn't think he knew anything about. There's a confidence that they have in themselves that they will get them through the journey,' said one.

Some tutoring is inevitable but pressure, here, reckoned to come from the boys rather than the school. 'The school has a trust in its own ability, it doesn't so far seem to be obviously pushy and demanding,' said mother. 'If my son gets frustrated it's when he compares himself to his peers, not because his teachers have made him feel like that.' Pupils agree. 'You see your friends do well and want to do everything you can do to get yourself there,' said one.

Even daily form time is a cut above the norm – a 'dynamic 20 minute period [with] fast paced games of chess, poetry competitions, fierce debate about newspaper articles, and discussions ranging from football to sexual identity and consent,' according to school policy.

Makes the most of world class organisations at their fingertips – hosts regular science conference at the Guildhall (well, when you can partner with the City of London Corporation and its academies, would be rude not to). Speakers range from Alastair Campbell (delivering 'frank' talk about Trump and Brexit) to AC Grayling on human nature and the inevitability of warfare (jolly).

Equally wide-ranging trips also offered, with school ensuring that costs don't put them out of reach for less affluent families (all boys on busaries will have one funded overseas trip during school career). Any curriculum-fulfilling essential trips funded by school. Others, like taking a night train in Vietnam, or riding a camel in India, won't be. 'Not all those who wander are lost,' says school website, though normal extensive risk assessment probably also helps.

The arts and extracurricular: Good range, from LAMDA qualifications to Model United Nations. Plenty of prodigies, including chess and table tennis stars, while 'sporting teams continue to secure silverware against stiff opposition,' writes the alliteratively agile head (try repeating that 20 times wearing a gumshield).

Visual arts impressive, thought-provoking, technically accomplished, performing arts ditto. Many productions, from senior school production with girls' school – small cast but lots of backstage opps too – to one-offs. One pupil wrote and co-directed 'N1' about homeless/rough sleepers as his EPQ project – script based on interviews... 'met my character,' said one of actors. 'Enough to go round so that everyone who wants to get involved,' said pupil. 'Recently did Chess. Ambitious but we absolutely nailed it.'

Music toe-tappingly good. Jazz band rehearsal – Take the A Train – underway on day of visit, just one of the many ensembles, vocal and instrumental, on offer. Bottom two years get to try out a range of instruments, free to start with, advanced taking top level grade exams. One parent felt that given the range of talent, could perhaps sparkle even more. 'Should be extraordinary.'

Fundraising is incredibly successful (bringing in over £80,000 a year), with pupil-run events including cake sales and an annual bake off (winner praised for 'his lovely lemon macaroons,') as well as a semi-staged production of The Magic Flute to raise money for charity, organised from scratch by two sixth formers. Lots of outreach, and support for good causes.

Speakers range from Alastair Campbell (delivering 'frank' talk about Trump and Brexit) to AC Grayling on human nature and the inevitability of warfare (jolly)

Parents delighted, though one thought that community service 'should be compulsory' as it's currently losing out to CCF when pupils make a choice in third year. Head doesn't plan major shake up, but given that many boys, he says, contribute to local communities rather than via the school, plans greater recognition for CSO activity overall.

Staff have forged excellent links with local state schools, with pupils coming in (to use sports facilities and science labs), and English, French, PE and science teachers going out to share specialist knowledge.

For any time left over, there are 48 clubs – run consistently and well. They range from delightful rambles through the predictable (astronomy, debating, running) to the hobbyist (model railways, birdwatching) to robotics (we listened to erudite explanations of how to programme a cart to negotiate a maze – sonic sensors that, bat-like, measure sound waves are the answer...) to the distinctly niche, like the cheese-tasting society. 'Wensleydale, Stilton and crackers,' said pupil, rolling eyes to indicate sheer heaven of the experience.

Staff keep an eye on levels of activity, think parents. 'Have a good handle on the balance and if they feel they could be doing more to broaden their horizons, they'll be encouraged to do so.' Only improvement mentioned – ensuring that everyone knows club locations – can be confusing as 'so many options and so many societies,' said parent.

Sport: No question of which sport dominates – 31 football teams ('really strong,' said a parent), 10 water polo – courtesy of attractive heated pool that's also used, gratis, by pupils at local primary. Cricket has nine teams, basketball five. Also futsal (one team) and unofficial cricket in the courtyard (blue rubbish bins mark bowling/batting ends). Weekly sessions on superb games fields – downside the 35-40 minute journey, though 'coach journey is something to look forward to,' said pupil.

Plenty of successes – footie first and second 11s were doing well. Fixtures and wins tend to reduce among the sixth, seventh or eighth teams, not helped by limited weekend match culture. Pupils we spoke to weren't fussed – felt that anyone playing in less than elite teams had plenty of other interests to keep them occupied.

Ethos and heritage: Ancient school, originally founded in 1442 with money left by John Carpenter – whose statue presides over the atrium – to raise four deserving local children through to adulthood. Unusually, welcomed all comers: '…Jews and Gentile – all will be admitted to the same advantages.'

Diversity has endured to this day, as has educational innovation. Unlike other schools which moved out of central London, this one stayed put and 'aligned itself to … the industrial world,' most tangible manifestation its early adoption of science and other commercially-related subjects at a time when the classics dominated the curriculum elsewhere.

Current site is its third. Managed by the City of London Corporation (which still appoints the governors – nitty gritty of relationship best not attempted without a Venn diagram expert and a clear head), opened in 1837 in Milk Street, moved to larger buildings on Victoria Embankment in 1882 and – after evacuation to Marlborough College during WW2 – opened in current location in 1986.

The red-brick, almost symmetrical frontage is a 1980s take on a traditional mansion with wings, vaguely ecclesiastical-looking towers and the main entrance, accessorised by London pigeons perched on the railings, doing their best to add atmosphere (and droppings).

Cheerfully unpretentious, website featuring plenty of impressively ungussied up images of smiling, cheerful boys with ties adrift, blazer with the odd grubby patch and hands in pockets. We even went back and double checked that we'd clicked on the right school (we had). 'Scruffy but happy,' agreed a parent. 'Don't have to be polishing shoes till see face in them. Certainly not an emphasis on being manicured.'

Site is shaped either like an H (according to pupils) or an F (reckoned teacher) and there's no ground floor (starts at level one). Go up, along and down (like a complex crossword clue) when there's no through route and finding your way round will be a doddle, especially when you've got features like the Concourse and Great Hall to navigate by.

'Day-to-day chivvying should be the main way staff try to change inappropriate behaviour,' says school handbook

Artefacts from school's history pop up all over the place, from panels of Victorian stained glass in the dining hall (and elsewhere), each representing a City livery hall or benefactor, to Roman steps left over from excavation work. Even the organ ('second most expensive thing in the school,' according to tour guide. The first? 'The boiler') is the original, transported from previous school and reconfigured.

Plenty of the newer features pack just as much of a punch, particularly the new library (officially the Levene Learning Centre but 'who says, "I'm just off to the learning centre"?' says teacher) is appealingly light, offering an 'endless supply of books,' said pupil, and some fascinating extras. Displays, on shelves running round its inner walls, cry out to be looked at – currently work includes pupil-designed Ausopoly – a version of Monopoly featuring WW2 (and with Hitler very definitely in jail).

Similar museum-quality exhibitions make other corridors places to linger, sciences especially, with row upon row of vintage equipment (stroboscope, Butchard balance); antique glass chemical bottles and jars of different life forms – sponges to vertebrates – by the yard, all the work of the school's team of dedicated technicians (think house elves but with total autonomy) with an exceptional sense of order and desire to label, name and cross-reference. Even vintage wooden lab benches in one of the biology labs gleam. 'Technicians come in, sand them down and polish them each holiday,' says teacher. Pupils' own work – haemloglobin realised in painted plaster of Paris and a neuron intricately fashioned out of playdough by year 7s of an equally high standard.

Practical aspects get similar attention to detail. There's a school shop that's also evolved from single cell tuck shop to more sophisticated form – sells everything from house badges and pens to combs ('A real bargain for 45p,' says tour guide). While common rooms aren't available to all year groups, sixth formers' version is divided into games area (pool table cues only allowed after morning break) and quiet zone. Highlight is industrial roll-on, roll-off toaster, wall-to-wall loaves of bread and catering pack of jam. Ganneted by end of morning break, crumbs and the empty wrappers all that remains. (No rota, say boys. 'Fortunate to have cleaners and porters to clear it up,' commented one.) Not entirely accurate, clarifies the school: there's certainly an expectation – though not formalised – that boys will keep the place clean and tidy, and generally they do.

Old Citizens is the name for former pupils and they're a busy lot. In addition to the organisation of jolly social events and reunions everywhere from the House of Lords to the Olde Cheshire Cheese, they host networking events and each year are involved in hosting careers events for the boys.

Pastoral care, inclusivity and discipline: School's latest strategic vision talks about being kind, ready, and aware (helpfully interlinked on a Venn diagram) as well as 'cherish[ing] individuality' and 'shun[ning] stereotypes'.

School's goal, felt parent, is to produce 'rounded, emotionally intelligent boys' and not just high flyers. Normal temptations apply but no expulsions while Mr Bird has been in post. Zero tolerance to drugs on site, though for other offences, 'may be times when alternatives to disciplinary approaches are required,' he says.

There are pleasantly old-fashioned rewards, ranging from distinctions for 'truly exceptional work', which are recorded in the leather-bound Head's Book, to the award of a CLS bookmark (highly valued, according to one recipient) or Parker pen, to boys who 'have made a significant contribution to school life'.

For anyone who hasn't, 'Day-to-day chivvying should be the main way staff try to change inappropriate behaviour,' says school handbook, with escalating detentions rising to suspensions and imaginative ways of getting the message across – anti-bullying month featured a 'cool to be kind' competition where boys had to be caught doing something nice. 'No good deed went unnoticed,' reckons the school.

In addition to the very well rated head of pastoral care who's 'approachable' and 'on top of issues', as well as 'brilliant' and 'kind', there are good heads of year, who work closely together. Also two counsellors – pupils can either self-refer or be referred. Translates into effective action when boys need it, with anxiety-related disorders 'a pastoral priority,' says the school.

Pupils and parents: Microcosm of London at its eclectic best. 'Massive mix is one of the most special things about the school...you don't feel you're drowning in a sea of wealth. Son will have friends who run the gamut from single mum right through to the Russian oligarch.' Bright pupils from all over, half from minority ethnicities, 40 different nationalities, a quarter getting some form of financial support, just under 100 paying no fees at all.

One of the few schools in London where, thinks Mr Bird, not a single boy is driven to school by his parents. Means almost total absence of school gate contact, while sons are confident users of tubes and buses from the age of 10, sense of independence highly valued. Security, says school, is something they do well. Hence, 'I'm surprised by how little I get asked about [it] at open mornings,' says Mr Bird.

Niche clubs include the cheese-tasting society. 'Wensleydale, Stilton and crackers,' said pupil, rolling eyes to indicate sheer heaven of the experience

'Liked the instant independence I got,' said pupil, though older pupils will keep an eye out for the youngest (tube users tend to spill out of same carriage closest to the exit each morning). 'On first day... sixth former came up and said "how's your first day?" – and that was the moment I felt really welcomed,' said one.

Social events for parents range from quiz and curry night (where parents and teachers 'compete in a friendly manner' – phew) to Sunday afternoon City walk with professional guide.

Money matters: Full and partial bursaries at 11+ and 16+, ranging from 25 to 100 per cent. Will need income of under £75K to qualify, limited assets ('unlikely' to qualify with six figure income, large house or second property...). Scholarships (academic, music and sport) – awarded at 10+, 11+, 13+ and (minus sport) at 16+. Worth £250 so honour and glory variety, though sports and music scholars also receive some additional funding. School also educates choristers from Chapel Royal, St James's Palace and the Temple Church, who get a partial discount all the way through to GCSEs. For Chapel Royal, boys must pass entrance exam and be a pupil at the school to stay in choir past probationary period – each year, some don't make the cut.

The last word: Hard to see how independently minded, intellectually curious boys could fail to to thrive in this happy, busy, fast-paced school where everyone – up to and including the head – feels privileged to be here.

City of London School for Girls

13

St Giles' Terrace, London EC2Y 8BB

020 7847 5500 | admissions@clsg.org.uk | www.clsg.org.uk

Independent	Pupils: 770; sixth form: 166
Ages: 11–18	Fees: £19,212 pa

Linked school: City of London School for Girls – Prep, 104

Headmistress: Since September 2019, Jenny Brown, previously head of St Albans High School for Girls. Educated at North London Collegiate before reading English at Oxford. With both parents English teachers 'it was the very last thing I wanted to do,' she says, instead taking a job at Robert Maxwell's publishing house (thankfully too young to invest in pensions) – 'the last word in really dull jobs'. Escaped to teach English at Cranleigh ('like coming home'), followed by Highgate School, South Hampstead High, Channing and St Paul's Girls where she was director of senior school. Still adores the 'sheer joy' of teaching.

One half of the Good Schools Guide's first set of identical twin head teachers – her sister, Jane, is head at Wimbledon High ('it's lovely to be able to share ideas'). Lives in Highgate with playwright husband, Ben, and enjoys theatre, literature (muses 'who would I head towards first in heaven – Shakespeare or Donne?') and a weekly swim in Hampstead Ponds. Writes poetry 'when creative space allows'. Two children.

Entrance: Numbers of applicants, as at other academically selective London schools, now hitting heights of absurdity and severely straining schools' resources, especially here, where physical space needed on assessment days is limited. School is no longer part of the London 11+ Consortium so sets own exams in English and maths and what is graphically described as 'an interview with teeth'. Twenty-five from own prep plus around 850 now applying for the 75 additional places at 11+. NB acceptances on a first-come-first-served basis, with offers withdrawn when the 75 places are filled (usually within days). Around 70 applicants for the 10-15 places at sixth form. Sixth form places conditional on school's own exams taken in potential A level subjects and on 9-7s at GCSE in all subjects. During COVID, there's a socially distanced one-hour computer-based test, assessing numerical, verbal and non-verbal skills, plu school reference then advanced interview session.

Exit: Around 15-25 leave post-GCSE to board or go co-ed or to sixth form colleges. Early warning given if sixth form standards likely to be a problem. Some parental criticism of the less than gentle manner in which this has taken place in the past but this has become a rare occurrence, though the criterion for staying – ie eight grade 7s at GCSE – remains in force.

Sixth form leavers are starry – 16 to Oxbridge in 2020, and four overseas to Harvard, Stanford, Barnard College and University of Chicago. The London University colleges also take a good number. Great range of serious courses – nearly a third STEM and number of linguists now rising.

Latest results: The school isn't releasing 2020 GCSE results, but at A level, it was 82 per cent A*/A. In 2019 (the last year when exams took place), 94 per cent 9-7 at GCSE; 79 per cent A*/A at A level.

Teaching and learning: Maths rules. As elsewhere with clever students, this has become the most popular – and successful – A level subject, and recent takers outnumbered the entire languages cohort. 'The girls are strategic, and they know that if they take a language they are less likely to get an A*/A than if they take maths.' The girls say: 'People really like maths – they see the use of it.' Other popular subjects – in an, admittedly, conservative range – are history, chemistry and English. Mandarin, after a very successful course to GCSE, now offered at Pre-U, and should markedly boost the number of language takers, which has increased anyway recently.

Although the impressive results are obviously a key factor in the school's success, the school itself puts the emphasis elsewhere – on, for example, independent learning and thinking. Lots of computers and library has a bank of borrowable laptops. Librarian seen as 'wonderful', though library itself, possibly, not the most impressive feature – we were bemused by some strange cataloguing and location of books and it felt a bit tired.

Learning support and SEN: Although a third of the pupils speak a language other than English at home, almost none need EAL help. Around 12 per cent with a mild SEN of some kind, all supported as needed on an 'as and when' basis but no-one with major learning difficulties here. School not easy for those with mobility difficulties.

The arts and extracurricular: Art is, according to all, wonderful. We saw some terrific painting and the results at A level and GCSE are phenomenal. Good hall for display of work and three studios, all richly and messily busy – the colour and variety of the top floor a refreshing relief. DT taken by all years 7-9 in good sized studio with everything you'd expect, including inventive year 7 torches.

Lots of music – individual, large and small groups, pursued with excellence and enthusiasm. Two good sized teaching rooms at top of the building plus numerous practice rooms. Drama in huge hall and Black Box Theatre at the top of the building. Well-designed literature for shows is evidence of classy production values throughout. Draughty outdoor theatre a splendidly imaginative recent innovation – a bit like a Greek theatre, only colder.

But perhaps the most exciting aspect of the extracurricular offering is London itself. There are all the galleries and museums – 'they are so easy to go to from here, you can get there in a double art lesson'. 'It's one of the reasons I came here,' typifies the response. Young Enterprise, likewise, outside speakers, visits, lectures at UCL, the Royal Institution etc, trips and tours – all add to the avid seizing of a rich variety of opportunities here.

Sport: Games, remarkably, mostly take place on site – planners found flat spaces, inside and out, for two tennis courts, a large Astro pitch, various other spaces for a gym, 25 yard pool, table tennis and newish dance studio. Outside space overlooked by flats – the girls must get used to it. Non-selective approach to some teams gives all enthusiasts opportunities and it works. They do cross-country round the high level walkways. Many representatives in borough games and several notable individual successes on local and grander levels.

Ethos and heritage: The original school began life in 1894. William Ward, who believed in giving girls a broad and liberal education with an emphasis on scholarship, left a third of his fortune – £20,000 – to the City of London Corporation for the foundation of a girls' school. Livery companies, banks and city firms continue to give financial support; the Corporation still administers this and the board of governors is appointed by the Court of Common Council. The Corporation has an education strategy and its portfolio of schools gives rise to mutually beneficial links between City Girls' and state primaries, eg sixth form community service.

One of the more surprising school locations in the UK. Navigating the Barbican complex is notoriously tricky, but if you negotiate the grey concrete and glass mini-village to its heart, following brick-paved walkways, you will find the school. It sits between the ancient church of St Giles, Cripplegate (glass office blocks behind) and the Guildhall Conservatory, the Barbican arts venue and city flats with their valiant window boxes – with a large, flagged and lilied, ornamental pond between. Also surprising the eye and breaking up the harshness are the gallant trees and the improbable wodge of ancient London wall which squats defiantly opposite the school's main entrance.

Perhaps the most exciting aspect of the extracurricular offering is London itself. The galleries and museums are so close, 'you can get there in a double art lesson'

The school opened here in 1969 – the first, pretty much, of the reincarnations of venerable educational institutions needing new and purpose-built homes. A bold conception and it wears well. The inside is as stark and work-full as Gradgrind could have wished, though lively displays and lots of big windows help relieve the Spartan architecture. Sixth form centre cleverly bolted on. You go in and out a lot – rain and shine – as you negotiate the five storeys. Good-sized dining hall and jolly good menu – Wok Theatre, Italian/Indian Fusion and Big Bowl Salad looked tempting.

Famously diverse mix of pupils and staff as befits the school's situation in the heart of the city. 'Diversity' is a word you hear a lot here, in numerous contexts. Not least the effect of coalescing people from so huge an area. Likewise, we heard 'exciting' a lot. The girls say, 'It's always busy here – but in a good way, and being in the Barbican is so exciting!' Pupils are bright-faced, smiley, articulate and confident – with no trace of arrogance. They have a sense of their responsibilities to the wider world alongside their own personal ambitions.

Notable former pupils include Claire Rayner, Hermione Lee, Alison Weir, Elizabeth Emanuel, Romola Garai, Winklemans – Claudia and Sophie – and Daisy Christodoulou. Also Anna Blundy and Dido Armstrong, who both did their sixth forms at Westminster.

Pastoral care, inclusivity and discipline: Light but 'tightly run' discipline. 'The teachers really care that the girls are happy,' a parent told us, and 'they deal quickly with problems.' 'No-one gets thrown out if they haven't had loads of warnings first,' girls told us. 'They bring in parents. It's mostly just poor behaviour over a long period but it hardly ever happens.' And most pay tribute to the excellence of pastoral care and their 'lovely' teachers.

Pupils and parents: They come from a vast circumference around the city – Chigwell to the north east, Harrow to the north, Shepherd's Bush and Fulham to the west – even as far away as Cambridge. 'It's helped me become a lot more independent and the school gives us "travel buddies" when we join so that we can get used to the journey with someone experienced.' Parents say: 'The mix of girls is wonderful. They're not a flashy lot and they're not tarted-up either.'

Money matters: Around 25 per cent on some kind of fee assistance. Bursaries from 25 per cent to 100 per cent. Unusually no academic scholarships, but music, drama and art scholarships of up to £1,500 a year at 11+ and 16+, and an 11+ sports scholarship.

The last word: By any standards, a top school for girls, with an edge of excitement, modernity and realism. Makes the most of what it is, where it is. Said a parent: 'My daughter is incredibly happy there. She has blossomed. Her friends are amazing. I've only ever heard good things.'

City of London School for Girls – Prep

14

St Giles' Terrace, Barbican, London EC2Y 8BB

020 7847 5500 | admissions@clsg.org.uk | www.clsg.org.uk

Independent | Ages: 7–11 | Pupils: 96 | Fees: £19,212 pa

Linked school: City of London School for Girls, 102

Head: Since 2017, Rachel Hadfield BA. Two school-age sons. Mother was a teacher so education was 'in the blood' – put up a brief fight not to follow in her footsteps, though given that uni dissertation (Durham) was on the geography of film and children's perception, was always a lost cause.

After graduating, spent three years in Japan, employed by a small town to teach English to everyone – toddlers, farmers, senior citizens. 'A wonderful experience,' she says. Returned to train as a teacher in 2006, working in state primary schools in London, specialising as an ethnic minorities achievement teacher. Experience of seeing nursery pupils unable to communicate was a defining moment in recognising importance of education in 'levelling life chances'. Joined failing school (Foxhill Primary) in 2014, first as lead practitioner, then as assistant head teacher (promoted 2016). In just 15 months became fifth school in the country to go from special measures straight to outstanding. 'Taught me a lot about society… gave me fire in my belly,' she says.

Move to current post in 2017 prompted by desire for challenge and to see education from a different angle, though stresses there's considerable diversity here (cultural rather than economic). 'Just as complicated an organism as a bustling primary in Woolwich.'

Energetic. Marathon runner (regularly runs to school from home in south London – and back again). Other interests include yoga and barre training. Mindfulness qualified – means that when has visitors, devotes her full attention to them (including this lucky GSG reviewer).

Though works with head of senior school and 'very active' board of governors, has considerable autonomy. A shaker upper but purposefully so. Goal, she says, was 'to aim for 50 per cent consistency, 50 per cent change. People appreciate the things that make the school the school.'

She's a stickler for clarity. 'Should be able to walk into a room and know what the topic is. The first question is "Why are we learning this?",' she says. Similar passion for aesthetically pleasing displays in and out of the classroom. Nothing is printed – it's all in best handwriting (including teachers') – a richer, warmer medium – and an integral part of the teaching process, from beautifully illustrated sticky flipchart pages in one classroom that take you through the process of creating a purse to pastel-coloured self-portraits, all with ambitious words – and definitions – to describe how subjects are feeling: 'sumptuous: adjective – splendid and expensive-looking.'

Parental confidence high now they've got to know her and she's much liked. Approachable, friendly and – a relative rarity in the serious world of education – has a sense of humour. 'Girls adore her,' said parent. 'Makes science interesting when she teaches us,' confirmed one.

Best thing about the job? The girls who are 'an absolute delight, so life-giving with their endless curiosity'.

Entrance: Massive competition for the 24 places on offer in year 3 each year. They're looking for candidates at the top end of the ability range who also have 'curiosity and wonder about the world'. Shy girls will be encouraged to blossom during the process (and very often do).

High levels of empathy and the ability to interact with others won't go amiss either. Need to be able to cope with fast paced life so entrance process will 'stress test' candidates, says head. Tutoring isn't encouraged: 'Do not wish for girls to endure hours of extra tuition,' says school (but inevitably, many will).

Urge all potential families to attend open event before registration. Assessments take place November in the year before entry – reading a simple story, writing with 'good spelling', maths paper. Cap at 150 entrants. Little in the way of SEN – though open to supporting pupils, usually with mild dyslexia or needing support with organisational skills, working with senior school learning support team.

After written exams, about 50-60 shortlisted candidates will be invited back for practical activities such as a science enquiry. Some borderline cases interviewed and Mrs Hadfield may also speak to current schools. Whole entrance process completed and offer letters posted within two weeks – impressively cutting down on agony of waiting process.

Exit: Almost everyone to senior school. No longer have to sit 11+ exam, however. Instead, entrance to senior school based on head's letter of recommendation in year 5.

No guaranteed places. The odds are good – in most years, every child in year 6 who wants to go on to the senior school will do so – but it's not a given. 'Majority will be ready… but children do evolve and change and needs might become apparent,' says the head. Normally two or so departures in year 6, usually because of offers from even more selective senior schools, eg St Paul's, but parents needing to prepare for entrance exams would have to make own arrangements. Occasionally move to more local school if daily commute is just too much.

Our view: With the exception of a short spell in Yorkshire during WW2, the City of London School for Girls, established by a bequest to educate girls in a way that 'would correspond, as near as may be, to the City of London School', has been a fixture in the area since the 1890s (though confidence levels weren't exactly flattering – original building in Carmelite Street was future proofed so it could be converted back into offices if school didn't work out).

School's energetic head is a marathon runner and mindfulness qualified, meaning that when she has visitors, she devotes her full attention to them

Lack of space prompted move to the Barbican in the 1960s and school has been here ever since, the prep occupying a wing of the senior building, classrooms all running off single long 'corridor of power'.

City location has its drawbacks – space is very limited and prep library in particular is cosy but tiny – but also enriching. 'We want the girls to be socially aware and able to deal with tomorrow's problems so do use our City of London contacts,' says head. Girls help to run Guildhall Art Gallery, attend Lord Mayor's tea party, visit different livery halls and sing as part of Beating of the Bounds event. Also lend premises (after hours) to City of London Police – hide money in the prep corridor which trainee sniffer dogs have to find.

With just one class in each year group, you're going to feel pretty special just to be here. It's a place that suits thinkers – 'girls who have a love of learning and are up for challenges,' felt a parent – and helps to arrive in year 3 with 'lots of determination to make most of time there'. One pupil, who was 'a feminist because this is an all-girls school', praised school's efforts to encourage pupils to 'take jobs that men mainly do'.

May be a small school but life is full-on, with many lessons taking place out of their classrooms – so need to be comfortable with plenty of change during the school day. To make the most of time

here, thought year 5 pupils, 'you need to be quite passionate about the things you like so you can take them seriously and enjoy them.' Being organised a definite plus. 'With homework, you need to know where it is and make sure it can be presented neatly.'

Could so easily translate into uncomfortable atmosphere, with alpha kids jostling for position. Certainly a bit of that around with the inevitable friendship issues, but school does its best to ensure that doesn't turn into bullying by lowering the temperature. Girls aren't, for example, ranked with others, subduing the competitive instinct, at least to some extent. 'Parents get termly reports but we see no value in [...] competition, it's not encouraging,' says Mrs Hadfield. Girls are aware of progress, achievement and next steps, all communicated 'little and often' so in theory are competing only with themselves. Hotly contested house sports help release pent up ambition, confirms pupil. 'Quite a few people are competitive but in a good way – you do a lot of sport to channel it.'

School's values founded on three Rs – respect, responsibility and resilience. Underpinned by sensible organisation – prep fees include all school lunches and snacks, school houses are arranged by postcode, for example. While could scarcely be closer to London's money-making heart, school is extremely diverse with 'children from everywhere' – furthest lives close to Chelmsford.

Parents – many City workers, some in high profile jobs – are generally low key. Usually rushing off to work, so there's limited school gate banter but, said mother, they're 'very straightforward and relaxed – no hierarchy. They can be a CEO but they don't boast; when they arrive they're just a parent.'

After-school club runs till 6pm, very reasonable flat charge (a fiver). Fun doesn't currently appear to be the goal, starting with its official title – 'evening supervision'. After all homework is completed (non-negotiable), girls 'will be permitted to play educational games or read'. Woo hoo.

Collect after 6pm and there'll be a further charge and if parents prove hard to contact, policy states that 'we may need to contact the police or social services,' though head stresses that this has never happened. 'Makes us sound a lot more draconian than we are.'

Mrs Hadfield is softening the edges, wheeling a piano from year 3 classroom so girls can do their daily practising. Violins allowed, too. Not exactly a house of high jinks, but it's a start.

Teaching generally reckoned to be good – 'stimulating and interesting,' thought a parent – buoyed by school-funded incentives for staff that include opportunity to take on research projects or have sabbaticals (though rarely taken up). Range from the brand new (includes recently qualified former TA) to several who are well into their second decades.

Retail expert – one of many external speakers – recently delivered eye-opening session on how punters are persuaded to part with their money in shops

English felt to be stand out subject (but lots of competition), girls 'enjoying the learning and finding out about things', helped by critical thinking sessions that inform other areas. Retail expert – one of many external speakers, some current parents or alumni – recently delivered eye-opening session on how punters are persuaded to part with their money in shops. 'When go into shop will think about the techniques being used,' thinks head.

Core curriculum includes DT, computer science and a big focus on languages – learn one a year. Will have covered Spanish, French, German and Chinese, as well as some Latin and classics, by year 6. Pack in three science lessons a week as well as weekly swimming, gym, dance and games. Older girls have opportunity to be involved in research projects with senior teachers, eg metacognition – does articulating how you're learning help you to learn better?

While there are some specialists, class teachers tend to cover many subjects, particularly in first year or two. Homework is on the manageable side (school has light touch approach), essential given that some girls don't get home until 7.30pm each night – though there's the inevitable division between parents who'd like more and others who feel it's just right. Trips include learning about Anglo Saxons in Dorset and sleeping overnight on a WW2 destroyer. (School could consider funding for anyone struggling to pay for these.)

Subject-focused weeks give teachers the opportunity for some in-depth inspiration. On the day of our visit, the whole school is engaged in cross-curricular science day – talks followed by series of practical experiments, with all four year groups working together.

Some are making triangle towers and testing their load-bearing capacity, others making a trumpet, shaping a proper reed out of a straw and then adding the horn end to amplify the sound – and defining amplification accurately along the way (definitely no infantalisation). Most popular of all is chance to make slime, displaying impressive understanding of the science behind the process. Viscosity? Why, it's 'when the molecules link to make a chain,' says year 4 child (pay attention at the back). 'We've got the polymer, what we do is add colorant and then the saline.'

Even mufti days have cherries on the top (perhaps literally so, if they decide to come, say, as a metaphor…). In addition to World Book Day, devoted to classics – where characters of choice include 'Aphrodite – from the Iliad', there's the chance to dress up for science day. 'I'm coming as a solid,' announced one pupil. She isn't, you know, she's going to come in all three states, confirms Mrs H – liquid and gas as well. Staff also dress up. Possibly as Higgs bosun particles, to scale, or existing in two states simultaneously.

Sense of proving yourself is fairly strong when it comes to sports. Gym and swim squads stars can be felt to be the popular ones. 'They're top of the tree,' though a parent. 'Sport is valued here.' Here, too, parents think that Mrs Hadfield is softening this aspect of school culture, with plenty of positive messages about participation, not just coming first, being transmitted in eg assemblies. 'Have confidence that she'll change this.'

Drama 'incredible' – even with a relatively small number to cast from. Unabridged Shakespeare (eg year 5s taking on Hamlet) daunting enough at any age. Here girls take it in their stride – all down to 'incredible' teacher with total faith in young cast. 'Not infantalised,' says Mrs Hadfield, with considerable understatement.

Music equally ambitious with pupils encouraged to try a range of instruments before committing to serious study. Department is keen to encourage endangered species – offers free loans of French horns and bassoons, while there's also viola club for anyone who's achieved grade 5 or above on the violin. Every prep pupil is also in the choir. Put on an opera in the summer term and take on classics year round (Handel's Gloria and all sorts).

Active minds keep on going after school, with impressive range of after-school clubs from sport (includes gymnastics, fencing, cricket) to robotics, coding, online publishing, school of rock (music, rather than geology, though could be either…). Here, they're called 'challenges', happening in last lesson period four days a week (except Mondays, when there's staff training and a 3.35pm finish), each with scheme of work, goals and regular reviews, though no formal assessment. Year 3 pupils have term and a half to catch their breath, then expected to make a long term commitment. Arts and crafts popular and oversubscribed, though 'name a second choice and you'll get it,' said year 5 pupil.

Pupils' wish list isn't a very long one. Would like more playground equipment – 'have things and they disappear' – and more snacks (currently one for all – bananas on day of visit). Also school dog (Mrs Hadfield also keen) and permission to wear shorts in the summer term (can opt for trousers instead of pinafore or skirt in year 6, with crimson cardigan).

Money matters: No bursaries offered at this stage (though watch this space – goal, if some way off, is to end up with needs-blind admissions).

The last word: A lovely school with quietly confident pupils who clearly relish the banquet of opportunities they get here. Is it worth all that effort to secure a place for four years without the cast-iron guarantee of a place in the senior school at the end of it? It's a judgement call only parents can make.

Collège Français Bilingue de Londres

15

87 Holmes Road, London NW5 3AX

020 7993 7400 | info@cfbl.org.uk | www.cfbl.org.uk

Independent	Pupils: 700
Ages: 3-16	Fees: £10,940 – £11,980 pa

Headteacher: Since September 2019, Denis Bittman, previously head of the Lycée Français de Jérusalem. He started his career as a primary school teacher in Strasbourg in 1983, and went on to teach in various countries, becoming founding headteacher of École Européenne de Strasbourg, and heading a school in Marrakech before joining the Lycée in Jerusalem.

Deputy head for primary is David Gassian, and deputy head for secondary is Cécile Denais.

Entrance: Due to the recent opening of new French schools in London, not as oversubscribed as previously. We hear that a maximum of 30 per cent of the places are allocated to children whose parents work for the consortium of French companies that helped to secure the school building. The list of partner companies is available for inspection if required.

Admissions priorities are: siblings (both primary and secondary), children from another official French school (local or abroad), including students following the CNED (the French distance-learning programme), then any miscellany of Francophones fortunate enough to get in. It seems there are some last minute surprises. The nearby La Petite École is a popular feeder, while others opt for local British independent schools while they wait for the coveted place at CFBL. School welcomes beginners in French up to year 7, and beginners in English at all levels.

Nursery and reception opened for 2020/21.

Exit: Most move on to a French Lycée in London (mainly the Lycée International Winston Churchill, but also the Lycée Charles de Gaulle) or another school in France or overseas. Some students continue in the English educational system (some families find the fees an issue, though remarkably good value when compared to most London independent schools). Students who are less confident about their French language skills may leave after quatrième to do GCSEs in the local British sector, although the English section at the Lycée Charles de Gaulle is an option for them.

Latest results: GCSEs are not taken. In 2019, of the 70 that took and passed the DNBI (see below), 50 got 'very good', 10 'good' and nine 'quite good'.

Teaching and learning: The French primary model has two divisions – maternelle (from nursery to year 1) and primaire (years 2 to 6). At the junior section of the CFBL 50 per cent of children have French and English language instruction and 50 per cent follow the French national curriculum. Half the staff are UK qualified and half are French. The teachers are timetabled in such a way that when classes are being taught by French teachers, the English-speaking staff are freed up to support students whose English language skills need bolstering and to ensure that English literacy standards are of a high level.

There are two forms of 25 students each for the youngest classes, 30 per class from the age of 7+. Classes are of mixed ability but the combination of French and English teachers means that they are able to differentiate the curriculum. English and French as a foreign language taught up to four times per week. Other specialists include teachers of PE, music and ICT (interactive whiteboards in all classrooms), while the bilingual French librarian works closely with the teachers in developing the literacy scheme and creating class libraries.

The French secondary model has two divisions – collège (years 7 to 10) and lycée (years 11 to 13). CFBL offers the collège division, following on from the school's primary section. According to the new norms of the French educational system, all students in secondary school are taught English for five hours a week and begin a third language (German or Spanish). They are also taught music, sport, IT and art in English.

Students (already working in French and English) have the option to join the international section of the DNB (Diplôme National du Brevet) where 45 per cent of the curriculum is taught in English, preparing them nicely for the new international diploma (DNBI). They are taught history and geography two hours a week in English.

CFBL is working to win over the hearts and minds of locals. Part of the charm offensive was the introduction of French language classes for the local community

Parents have mixed views – some feel the bilingual programme gives their (French-speaking) children lots of good exposure and immersion in English while others say the level of English is not as challenging as they'd like and that it's essentially French with a few English classes. Bilingual school models are never straightforward, with different perceptions about what exactly they mean. IT is taught weekly – some parents would like to see a bit more, but concede that with the extra time already devoted to languages, this would be challenging.

The pupils work long hours (approximately 30 per week) – the additional English language means more hours than usual – so parents should be clear on this before they enrol their children. This is in addition to the homework load. The French educational system is regarded as one of the best in the world and academic standards are not an issue here. It's deciding if you want to do this with the added challenge of a bilingual or trilingual programme. School was rated outstanding by Ofsted in 2018.

Learning support and SEN: No specialist SEN support but class teachers are able to provide some support and there is a part-time educational psychologist too. Parents pay for diagnostic testing. A speech therapist is available.

The arts and extracurricular: Though extracurricular activities don't traditionally loom large on the French educational landscape, they do make a great effort at CFBL. The school is working on launching a choir and developing interest in instrumental music activities. Sixième students (first year secondary) go on a residential trip with outdoor pursuits activities aimed at integrating new students and team building.

CFBL has an exchange programme with schools in Uruguay, Valence and Berlin for students studying Spanish or German, and strong links with a school in Spain. Mandarin club recently introduced. The college hopes that these experiences will help students and parents value the importance of learning languages and about other cultures.

Sport: More sports on tap here than is the norm for French schools – the football team practises locally and took part in an international tournament. Netball is popular with girls.

Ethos and heritage: The Collège Français Bilingue de Londres was born out of a previous French ambassador's call for increased capacity to meet the growing demand for French education in London. With funding from the French government and from French companies (we're guessing banks and perhaps Eurostar, whose London base is conveniently nearby), who formed a charity to acquire the school property, the school's mission is to offer a French curriculum in a bilingual context to 700 students. The school was at one time known as L'Île aux Enfants and located in a nearby building that now houses La Petite École, a feeder primary school.

The French educational system is regarded as one of the best in the world and academic standards are not an issue here

Housed in a Victorian school building in Kentish Town. The college is aware of the impact that the mass arrival of a French community in the heart of this traditionally working-class area of north London has had and is working to win over the hearts and minds of locals. Most families living in the area were attracted to the Victorian terraced properties and the 'gentrification' of the area is thought to be partly thanks to the school

The brilliant refurbishment takes full advantage of the high Victorian ceilings and large windows, while incorporating modern touches

(as well, of course, as the long-standing local Camden School for Girls). Part of the neighbourhood charm offensive was the introduction of French language classes for the local community.

The school backs on to some picturesque residential streets, though it fronts onto a street that is less so, and a bit of planting and tidying of the outside pavements and garden patches would improve the first impression. Step inside, however, and it's another story. The refurbishment is brilliant, taking full advantage of the Victorian features, with high ceilings, large windows drawing in masses of light, brick and glazed tile walls and parquet wooden floors, while incorporating modern touches. The upper school library – with high ceilings and huge windows – is fully equipped with impressive French and English collections, loads of computers and armchairs. Cosy primary library in its own little building on the playground – most of the resources are French, although they are developing the English language collection.

A small portion of the central playground has been forfeited to create a bright and airy cafeteria. Lunches compulsory, with meat and fish served daily and vegetarian options available for those observing kosher or halal diets.

The school has recently acquired an outdoor space a five-minute walk away which features a massive inflatable structure for sports and other activities and is available to the local community too.

Part of the AEFE (Agency for Teaching of French Education Abroad), CFBL is one of an international network of schools directed by the French ministry of education. The school is managed by a 12-member board – six representing the companies that helped fund the acquisition of the building and six elected by the parents. Its goals are to provide continuity of education to the French expat community in London, but also to prepare students to go to the best French universities. In fact 80 per cent of students who graduate from the Lycée Charles de Gaulle head to British or US universities. The head feels that the internationally-minded, multilingual emphasis of the school serves to provide good preparation for these options later on.

Pastoral care, inclusivity and discipline: Parents are very pleased with the school, many jumping through hoops to secure places. A parent of a child with SEN described it as particularly caring and attentive to her child. Classes are smaller than most French schools – a maximum of 30 in a class, with a two or three form intake. Discipline is not a worry for parents – one parent speculated that the presence of more UK-trained teachers (there to deliver the bilingual programme) strengthens the pastoral care perspective of the teaching faculty (not always as high on the French teachers' radar). The school runs careers counselling through a jobs forum that parents help to organise. The school employs a full time nurse as well as a part time speech therapist and child psychologist.

Pupils and parents: The community is a blend of expat corporate types on international assignments and more permanent French families who have found themselves in London for other reasons, including entrepreneurs, local business owners and French nationals whose marriages have created bi-cultural families. Parents suggest that the socio-economic atmosphere at CFBL is less 'rarified' than one finds in the more salubrious environs of the Lycée Charles de Gaulle in South Ken. While some end up at CFBL by default (no room at the Lycée), others prefer this school. The size is another factor – even with its capacity of 700, it is much smaller than the Lycée. French families who find the Eurostar terminal at St Pancras convenient are increasingly moving into neighbourhoods that are handy for the train journey through the tunnel to France and for the school.

The community is about two-thirds French. Some parents feel the school is less international than they would like, while others who come from France find it very international by comparison. There is obviously an underlying French cultural and educational foundation, but it seems that with a school community consisting of many dual national families, they seek to honour all cultures and traditions. Parents are happy that the children integrate easily, although some say teachers don't make as much of this diversity as they might. A parents' association provides lots of volunteer opportunities for those who want to get involved.

Money matters: The fees at CFBL are reasonable by London independent school standards (although CFBL fees are marginally higher than the Lycée Charles de Gaulle). As a charity, school engages in some fundraising activity – such as its annual gala event.

The last word: A sparkling little gem in the heart of Kentish Town, it is a bilingual environment with a truly international mindset.

Connaught House School

16

47 Connaught Square, London W2 2HL

020 7262 8830 | office@connaughthouseschool.co.uk | www.connaughthouseschool.co.uk

Independent	Pupils: 76 (46 girls, 30 boys)
Ages: 4–11	Fees: £17,160 – £18,855 pa

Principal: Since 2017, Victoria Hampton, 40s. A former ice-skating champion, who joined the British Olympic team at 14, Mrs Hampton was educated mainly at Queen's Gate School. After injury curtailed her career, however, she took an early years foundation degree and Montessori diploma, before launching her own nursery school at just 24. The mother of three – two currently at the school – she initially joined family-run Connaught House at her in-laws' invitation, starting as a head of early years and spending four years as assistant principal, before taking over on her mother-in-law's retirement. 'I felt I really understood what the school was about.' As well as continuing the tradition of 'knowing the families inside out', her own focus is on language, enrichment and, particularly, well-being – 'I want it to be a fun, calm place, a pocket of peace where you can learn.' Positive evolution is also a priority. 'I want to ask, "is this the best way to go forward?"' Her first major departure was to appoint a head teacher. 'My parents-in-law ran the school together, and I felt I needed a teammate.' Together, in Ofsted's opinion, the principal and the head 'have high expectations and are uncompromising in their ambition for pupils'.

Head since 2017 is Ellie Grunewald, BA (Liverpool), PGCE (Kingston), MA (UEL). Educated in north London, Ms Grunewald studied history and psychology at Liverpool University, before taking a PGCE and masters in a psychoanalytic observational approach to education (outside her school commitments, she works as both a life coach and mindfulness coach). Gained widespread experience in the state sector before a long-term appointment at North Bridge House School, where she taught up to common entrance, specialising in English and RE. Arrived at Connaught House as academic co-ordinator, and now works very closely with Mrs Hampton, even sharing a desk. Pupil well-being is central to both and much appreciated by parents. 'They are a dynamic duo,' said one.

Entrance: A tiny school, which fills up quickly. No registration before birth, but don't linger long thereafter. Siblings and children of former pupils given precedence, and the school has also developed a 'priority pathway' with a smooth route from local nurseries with a similar ethos (Paint Pots Montessori, Great Beginnings Montessori). Those from elsewhere take a brief assessment. 'There's a lot of chat and games, a little bit of colouring and construction,' says Mrs Hampton. 'They don't need to know their letters.' Occasional vacancies further up the school.

Exit: Close, established link with local independent secondary Kensington Park School, which offers priority places at 11 (after written assessments and interviews in year 5) and about a third go on there. Other popular destinations include: Francis Holland NW1 and SW1, Queen's College, Godolphin & Latymer and South Hampstead High. A few to St Paul's Girls' and City of London School, plus a sprinkling to board. Traditionally, boys have left at 7 and 8 to a broad spread of prep schools, including Westminster Under, Dulwich College, UCS, Latymer Upper, Wetherby and Sussex House. Boys can now remain till 11, though the school will continue to support an earlier transfer. 'We appreciate some may still will want to move for more sport or a bigger social pond.' Whatever the age of departure, in-depth consultation goes on with parents well beforehand and appropriate guidance is given for testing and interviews.

Our view: A traditional academic school, taking in a reasonably broad spectrum of children and providing the opportunity for all to excel. 'There's an impressive standard of work without any hothouse vibe,' said one parent. National curriculum followed in a general way, with plenty of stimulating enrichment and bespoke tailoring beyond. 'We're passionate about individual learning and each child is differentiated,' says the principal. Tiny classes (maximum 16) allow experienced teachers to implement the strategy with enthusiasm. Basic diet enlivened with French, thinking skills and philosophy. ('Is democracy a good idea?' was the puzzler year 6 was addressing during our visit.) More able are enticed well beyond the curriculum, with lateral thinking and mathematical skills often not encountered till secondary.

Basic diet enlivened with French, thinking skills and philosophy. 'Is democracy a good idea?' was the puzzler year 6 was addressing during our visit

Reading is central to the offering. Reading record every day and reading for pleasure promoted with well-stocked library ('There are lots of good quality books in the library; I am so pleased my children are encouraged to read books I loved as a child,' commented a parent), 'reading ambassadors', regular book fairs and visits to local bookshops. Annual poetry competition assessed by an external judge inspires younger children to write their own, juniors to learn their chosen verse by heart.

Not an IT-obsessed school, but providing a balanced, up-to-date approach in the form of whiteboards, iPads, DoodleMaths tracking app, etc, with digital portfolios of work now being rolled out.

Thoroughly metropolitan intake means 30 per cent speak English as a second language, and the school has also happily welcomed new arrivals with limited English. 'We assess how receptive they are to language,' says the principal. SENCo visits several times a week implementing appropriate strategies for those with learning difficulties (dyslexia, dyspraxia, dyscalculia, speech and language). No lift, so not the ideal environment for those who would struggle with the abundance of stairs.

Parent-school communication unusually strong. Younger years' families receive a weekly email about what's being covered in class, and school telephones all parents regularly to update about progress. Parents also encouraged to get in touch – 'If it takes more than half a page to write, we suggest they ring,' says Mrs Hampton – and principal on prominent display at drop off. 'We see parents every morning, so can share news and concerns.' Regular reports, termly parents' evening, and annual open day for parents to see work in situ complement an open-door policy. Parents appreciate the approach. 'The school really listens to both parents and pupils,' said one.

Founded in 1952 by Nancy Keane, a former actress, the school remains on its original site in what was once a large private house near Marble Arch, the domestic interior providing bright, cheerful classrooms, but no outside space. Children pay a daily visit to Hyde Park – just across the road – for fresh air, quick cricket and free play, and travel to local centres for swimming, athletics, tennis, dance and drama. FIFA-trained head of sport oversees two hours of sports tuition weekly, and after-school clubs increase the range with dance and yoga.

Music unusually strong for such as small school, with a dynamic and ambitious dedicated head of music. Most take instrumental lessons; all get the opportunity to study a wind, string and percussion instrument (recorder, ukulele, glockenspiel) and, from year 4, participate in the school orchestra. Singing, too, a forte, with participants in the National Youth Choir and local chamber choir. Art, again headed by a specialist, is equally vigorous, with colourful work on display and frequent scholarships at 11. Extended day (till 4.30pm) on Wednesdays provides a kaleidoscope of 'enrichment', from cake baking to coding, further widened in daily after-school clubs.

A non-denominational school with an ecumenical outlook on high days and holy days. 'We mark as many cultural festivals as possible.' The annual carol concert, for example, includes Chanukah songs alongside French and German carols. Assemblies focus on mindfulness, music and good works. A strong sense of community encouraged both outside the school and within. The principal sits with pupils at lunch to ensure all are eating. 'If no-one is monitoring what they've eaten, it can result in a bad afternoon.' Children are encouraged to try all that is put before them, with fussy eaters motivated by house points to consume their five a day. Behaviour is excellent, with polite chiming of 'Good Afternoon' on the entrance of visitors.

Parents mainly live or work locally but originate from all over the world. Due to the scale of the school, many get to know each other well. 'If you have a good class,' said one parent, 'you end up doing lots together.' Most are down to earth, prioritising what's best for their children over scholarship glory.

Money matters: Not a wealthy school, but does offer a number of bursaries from 10 per cent to full.

The last word: 'What I love about the school is that it has a cosy, old-fashioned feel with an emphasis on the traditional aspects of education,' said one parent, which sums it up well.

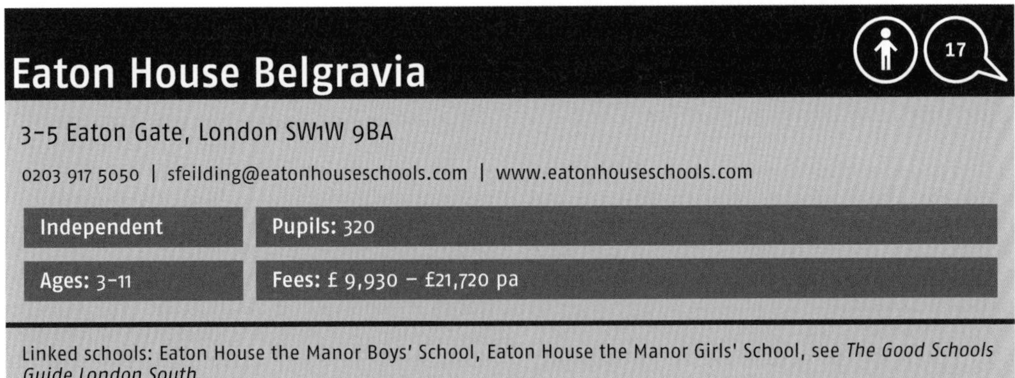

Eaton House Belgravia

17

3-5 Eaton Gate, London SW1W 9BA

0203 917 5050 | sfeilding@eatonhouseschools.com | www.eatonhouseschools.com

Independent	**Pupils:** 320
Ages: 3-11	**Fees:** £ 9,930 – £21,720 pa

Linked schools: Eaton House the Manor Boys' School, Eaton House the Manor Girls' School, see *The Good Schools Guide London South*

Head: Since 2017, Huw May (late 40s) MA Ed, NPQH, advanced diploma Royal Welsh College of Music, BMus, previously head of Eaton House the Manor Pre-Prep. Earlier experience in headships include Sydenham Junior School, Roedean Junior School and St Aubyn's pre-prep. A professional singer for several years before taking up teaching, he is a trained ISI inspector.

Mr May lives over the school during the week, returning to his home in Sussex at weekends. Gardening, classic cars (MGs and older Mercedes) and walking his dog Harvey – boy-approved relaxations. He has quickly gained the respect and trust of parents who find him 'approachable' and 'a good listener'. They especially value the fact that he has 'the boys' well-being and interests at heart'. Ambitious for his school, shows vision and is full of enthusiasm for developing each boy's all-round potential, emotionally as well as academically. A parent commented: 'We really value the immersive approach to learning and the school's entrepreneurial spirit; for example, Mr May has set up a partnership with the Science Museum'.

Mr May's arrival, after a brief tenure by respected long term deputy Annabel Abbott, coincided with a change to school organisation plans (see below). He speedily got a grip, emphasising individual learning plans for each boy, and the school seems as good as ever, with excellent results.

Entrance: Genuinely non-selective (but this is Belgravia). Main entry is at 4+ into kindergarten with, on average, 70 places. Places are allocated on a first come first served basis, with priority given to siblings, so it is important to put your name down early. Large deposit payable on accepting a place. For entry further up the school, the occasional places are subject to an assessment to see if the applicant will fit into the year group. Entry at 8+ is possible, now that the prep is open, but has yet to develop in any volume. Eaton House Schools Group is happy to let it develop at an organic rate.

EHB offers a very particular brand of boy-friendly teaching. Boys work hard in short bursts in the morning; in the afternoon games are followed by clubs and other activities

Boys come from a wide range of Belgravia nurseries plus Victoria, Pimlico, Fulham and Battersea, with a few from as far away as the City. The majority of pupils have British or part-British nationality (60 per cent) with the remainder mostly European.

Exit: About 40 per cent leave at 7+ although boys now able to stay until 11 (and could travel to Eaton House the Manor in Clapham for years 7 and 8). Mr May is clear and direct in advising parents on which schools they should aim for. Main senior schools are Westminster and St Paul's (19 offers for these two in 2020). Others to Haberdashers' Aske's, Latymer Prep, Westminster Under, Thomas's Battersea, Wetherby Prep.

Our view: Eaton House Belgravia is part of the Eaton House group of schools. The principal Hilary Harper and her husband took over Eaton House Belgravia in 1978 and developed the school into the group it is today. On retirement in the summer of 2016, she sold a majority stake in the group to private equity group Sovereign Capital, though her daughter, chief executive Luchie Cawood, has a significant stake and is thoroughly involved in the schools.

Parents who choose EHB want a traditional pre-prep/prep experience and the school delivers with a 3Rs curriculum, academic rigour and plenty of extras. In particular they value 'the excellent, nurturing male and female teaching staff who ensure they know their boys and care for them'. Classes are small with so far only informal sets for maths and English from year 2 upwards, so that the boys gain a full understanding in all maths and English topics.

EHB offers a very particular brand of boy-friendly teaching. Boys work hard in short bursts in the morning; in the afternoon games are followed by clubs and activities such as football, cookery, coding and Spanish. The extensive list of clubs changes regularly. They are supposed to enjoy the work and to have a riotous time in extras and 'run around after school and relax in supervised activities'. Some parents suggest that 'this would not be the right school for a slow developer, as the boys work at a fast pace and it becomes demanding in year 2 with plenty of homework.' Some teaching talk & chalk (albeit on interactive whiteboards these days), but much based on doing something physical, thinking through what you have done, and then applying it to a problem.

Individual provision ('differentiation') involves weekly consideration of how to support each child: all will at times be taken off into a side room for one-to-one. Not just academic/SEN support: there's Move Fit, run by physiotherapists for anyone who needs to improve coordination, and occupational therapy, for example handwriting and touch typing. In the kindergarten, Lego groups help develop social skills.

Communication between home and school is frequent and well coordinated. The original plans to grow Eaton House Belgravia Prep organically on its south Kensington site changed in 2018 to expand Eaton House Belgravia pre-prep up to 11 years on its own site. The school is comprised of two immense, linked cream town houses on several levels. The basement houses the kitchen, dining rooms, staff room, some individual music lesson rooms and a well-used science lab where boys enthusiastically carry out experiments and make discoveries. On the ground floor there is a well-stocked, light library and classrooms. The top two floors of the No 3 building, previously administrative offices and living accommodation, have been converted into learning enrichment classrooms, art and languages rooms for the new prep school. More recently, a new science lab took the place of the old kitchen, with a DT classroom in the old science lab. Boys care about their food, and now this is freshly prepared on the premises, but some parents still believe there is further scope for improvement – school says that with the old kitchen moved closer to the dining room, there is now 'more space [for] a wider range of freshly prepared and tasty meals to be produced onsite'.

Boys enjoy their art and we saw some house competition inventive illustrations for selected poems, as well as arresting year 1 wild west T shirts for a forthcoming fashion show. We spotted an attractive watercolour crab on our tour and evidence of interesting artwork in topic lessons throughout the school.

Mr May is clearly going to add zest to an already excellent musical provision (inter alia he has commissioned an opera for the school). Music takes place in the hall and is timetabled for all. Boys perform in fortnightly music assemblies and termly concerts and take part in competitions and charity events. Parents say that the head of music nurtures and encourages all ages to take up an instrument – drums, piano, singing, trumpet, guitar and violin all taught – with those who are fearful of performing offered strategies to gain self-confidence. The school has a dedicated ICT room, touch typing and coding are encouraged in the curriculum and classrooms have touch interactive boards and now tablets.

There is only one tiny outdoor space, but planning permission has been submitted for a sizeable outdoor learning centre. The fairly small hall/gymnasium is tightly packed when the whole school assembles. By necessity the days are very structured. The school council suggestion of Five a Day interruptions of five minute physical activities by desks is popular and beneficial. Boys are bussed to Hyde or Battersea parks every day to let off steam and play sports. Staff ensure boys are not taken out of sports and bemoan the time spent sitting in traffic. Swimming takes place at the Queen Mother's sports centre. Parents comment approvingly of the sport and 'the diverse clubs on offer including optional weekend activities, so there is lots to do'. A number of football clubs operate outside school hours. The boys enjoy their fixtures, stating that 'If we lose against the Manor, who are bigger than we are, we beat them at chess.'

The house system underpins all areas of the school and is very effective. It supports a culture of positive reinforcement regarding behaviour and respect, whilst enabling the boys to interact and enjoy the healthy competition on which they thrive. There is real engagement and an understanding of responsibility: 'Boys don't want to let their house down and captains write prayers for assembly.' Good manners are encouraged and one special feature we observed was the practice of one boy in every class shaking our hand, making eye contact and welcoming us to the class. The boys learn to make presentations and recite poetry confidently in public. 'I want them [the boys] to develop skills for life including adaptability, resilience, and determination and learn to listen and articulate their opinions confidently,' says Mr May.

Boys enjoy their art. We saw some inventive illustrations for selected poems, as well as arresting year 1 wild west T-shirts for a forthcoming fashion show

The majority of pupils live within walking distance, with some international families and many parents working in the City as lawyers or bankers, and most are very ambitious for their sons. 'We don't mind taking a round boy in a square hole' and parents agree that the school happily accommodates boys 'with different personalities and backgrounds, providing a really good real experience'. School advises, 'EHB is probably not the right school for you if you want your son in bubblewrap' and parents agree that the boys 'are not coddled and must be able to cope with academic rigours'. All boys wear uniform shorts and long socks whatever the weather. The pace is fast and there is an expectation that everyone will join in and accept challenges; excellent preparation for the top academic prep schools they are aiming for. 'We are slightly quirky' and the school is not purpose-built or manicured but full of energetic, interesting boys. Boys and staff muck in and this works a treat, as the boys are clearly happy. Staff are always on hand to advise parents about a suitable choice of prep schools where their engaging personalities and good manners will be an asset.

Money matters: There is no financial help on offer.

The last word: This school has nailed it with boy-friendly teaching – lots of wiggle room in and between classes and afternoons packed with activities outside the classroom. But this aspirational school is not for the faint hearted, with the academic rigour best suited to boys who can cope with a demanding syllabus.

Eaton Square School

18

55–57 Eccleston Square, 79 Eccleston Square, London SW1V 1PH

02079 319 469 | admissions@eatonsquareschool.com | www.eatonsquareschool.com

Independent	Pupils: 330
Ages: 4–11	Fees: £18,165 – £22,665 pa

Principal: Since 2019, Sebastian Hepher BEd (early 50s), who joined as headteacher in 2010. Educated at Alleyn's and University of Greenwich. Began teaching career in state sector, at Hurstmere Boys' in Kent, followed by the London Nautical School. Joined Eaton House Pre-Prep in 1990, before being asked to lead Eaton House The Manor in 1993. Under his headship, the school grew from the initial embryonic phase to a thriving prep school. Married, with four children currently at four different schools, with the youngest here. Swims in his local lido every day of the year, come rain or shine. Avid reader of Russian literature. Warm and charismatic, with a good sense of humour. Every parent we spoke to described him in glowing terms. 'He is the reason people gravitate towards the school,' according to one mother. Teaches reasoning.

Headmistress of the prep school is Patricia Watt, previously deputy head at Eaton Square Kensington, which has merged with Eaton Square School. She has an English degree from Brunel followed by a PGCE. Two children; enjoys travelling, hot yoga and spending time with her family.

Entrance: Main intake is at 4+ via assessment. The school runs several nurseries for children from 2 to 4 and these pupils are assessed by head of nurseries and head of pre-prep. They are given priority over other candidates and make up well over half the intake. 'It's not automatic but very rare not to accept a child from one of our nurseries,' explains head. Assessments, in November for external candidates, involve phonic and numerical activities, as well as colouring, cutting and talking to teachers. Between 100 and 150 external applications for 30 places. Sibling policy.

Occasional vacancies further up the school are quickly filled from the school's waiting list, after the child has successfully completed a series of online tests and spent a day at the school in a classroom setting.

Exit: Pupils progress onto a wide range of senior schools, both boarding and day. In 2020, 54 per cent to Eaton Square Senior School. Others to eg Wetherby Senior School, Queen's College, Westminster, Roedean, Godolphin & Latymer. Dialogue about senior schools starts in year 5, with parents often encouraged to look at boarding too even if previously dismissed out of hand by international clientele. Numbers of boys heading to boarding has increased noticeably and is 'beginning to bubble for the girls'.

Our view: Founded in 1981. Recently became part of the Minerva Education Group. Teething problems have left some parents feeling a little raw. One mother we spoke to said, 'The transition to the new ownership has been pretty bumpy, especially as it coincided with an escalation in fees.' Head feels some parental perception has been inaccurate and that school fees have not actually increased more than usual. Indeed, the second year of ownership saw a reduction to the usual increase. On the positive side, Minerva has bought a new building just down the road from the original Eccleston Square site to accommodate the expansion as staff and pupils from Eaton Square Kensington all move here. Everyone up to year 4 is housed in the new stucco buildings, with years 5 and 6 staying in the original site with specialist art and science buildings. Minerva has also enabled funded a building on Piccadilly overlooking Green Park for the new senior school, Eaton Square Upper School, which will eventually go up to 16.

Current principal is credited with having pulled the school up by its bootstraps academically. It has grown both in size and standing on his watch. One parent commented, 'It used to just be a sweet, local school before Mr Hepher took over. He is much more ambitious and has taken it to another level.' Pupils now follow a more academically rigorous and broader curriculum. Excellent language provision.

Principal abhors the culture of tutoring and believes 'we need to educate parents'. He has addressed the matter of intense competition for senior places with intelligence and worries that increasing number of schools using pre-tests works against late developers. Pupils are placed in sets for maths and English at start of year 2 but these are fluid, with 'plenty of room for manoeuvre'.

Parents feel pupils are well prepared for transition to senior school, partly because the curriculum is kept broad throughout. From the start, all pupils are encouraged to be articulate and confident citizens. Principal believes that good manners are essential. Each class has its own official greeter who comes to the front, shakes hands firmly and welcomes visitors on behalf of the rest of the class. A charming touch.

Thriving pre-prep department. Vibrant, colourful classrooms where emphasis is on practical work, consolidated by written work. 'It's hands on, creative learning here.' Impressive writing on display up the stairs. Everything is beautifully presented, from the work crafted by the children to displays produced by teachers.

As school is non-selective, there is a huge ability range. Full-time SENCo, supported by highly experienced learning enrichment team. Approximately 30 pupils currently having SEN support (mostly dyslexia, dyspraxia and dyscalculia), either one-to-one or small group sessions. Two children with EHC plans. More able pupils extended through challenging extracurricular activities.

Pastoral care is well structured. Principal worries about life being stressful for these children. 'We have a duty of care to shield children from excessive pressure which London and the system place on them. Parents who are anxious tend to pass that on to their children. I worry that we're causing a very anxious society. We want to make sure that children are happy when they are here.' Whole school comes together once a week for a reflective and celebratory assembly at St Michael's Church, Chester Square. Charity is an important part of school life. Huge amounts raised by parents and children.

Teachers mostly in late 20s and early 30s; some 10 members of staff have been here a decade. One parent described them as being 'friendly, energetic and good at communicating with the parents. Just what you want.' 'We haven't had a bad teacher yet!' said another, whose children are currently in the middle of the school.

Sensational drama. Huge annual musical performed by year 5 and 6 children at Unicorn theatre in the West End. Professional theatre director hired for the occasion. Younger children perform on stage twice a year. Music also a central part of the school with over 100 pupils learning an instrument. Performances in abundance, from carol services to rock concerts. Art taught to a high standard. Extra scholarship classes offered to the most artistic; the standard of portfolios is considered exceptional.

Despite its lack of outside space, school takes sport very seriously and coaching is excellent. Mainstream sports all offered as well as ballet, climbing, fencing and kayaking on the Thames. Pupils compete strongly in prep school ski-ing championships, recently bringing back a clutch of gold medals. Legendary swimming squad currently on a four-year unbeaten streak. Unusually, pupils swim here from day one. Football also strong, with plenty of practice taking place in Battersea Park. All children make a team of some description. 'The problem is finding enough other schools who can field C and D teams,' laments head.

Extracurricular activity viewed as important. Sensational residential trips. Year 3 heads off to Sussex for a four-day adventure. Years 4 and 5 go on a skiing and cultural trip to France where pupils practise speaking the language in context and also have daily French lessons. Snowball fights with the teachers apparently one of the highlights. One mother was delighted that the children were made to 'carry their own skis and make their own beds'. A novel experience for some, apparently. Pupils in year 6 go on a classical tour of Rome and Naples.

Each class has its own official greeter who comes to the front, shakes hands firmly and welcomes visitors on behalf of the rest of the class. A charming touch

Pupil composition is predominantly expat. Americans, Australians, Italians, French, Spanish mostly, with a sprinkling from Germany, Russia and Asia. One mother observed that there had been 'a thick crust of oligarchs' children in the past, but not any more'. Currently 14 per cent of pupils require targeted EAL lessons, which are intended to 'help speed up the process of full inclusion in the classroom'. Rare for mothers to work. A sea of nannies at the school gate on the day we visited. Pupils mainly come from local area. School bus service in operation to and from west and south-west London for those who live further afield.

Parents are encouraged to become involved, from hearing children read to giving career talks. Strong sense of community here and very active PTA. 'When you go into the school, there is a smile on the staff's faces. It's not the sort of school where you drop your child at the door and never get to venture across the threshold,' explained one mother. Principal feels parent body is caring and empathetic: 'Parents who come here are quite open, as they have often changed city and country themselves. You need to be outward looking to do that and this feeds into their children. It creates a lovely atmosphere.'

The last word: Heady mix of traditional British education with an international flavour. Children are happy here as they have the freedom to be themselves. Judging by stampede to get into the building at the start of the day, Eaton Square offers its pupils a joyful start in life.

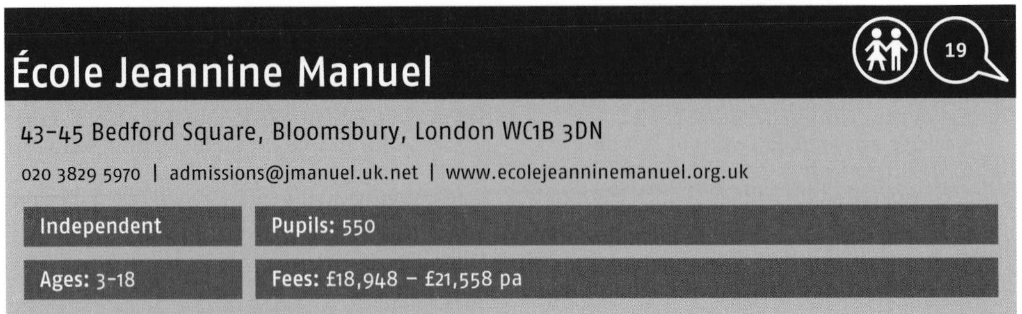

École Jeannine Manuel

19

43-45 Bedford Square, Bloomsbury, London WC1B 3DN

020 3829 5970 | admissions@jmanuel.uk.net | www.ecolejeanninemanuel.org.uk

Independent	Pupils: 550
Ages: 3-18	Fees: £18,948 – £21,558 pa

Head: Since the school opened in 2015, Pauline Prévot (40s). Degree in biology and science education from Versailles and Saint Quentin University and a DESS, or masters, in computer science. Her first job was with École Jeannine Manuel in Paris where she taught for 12 years, joining the maths department then becoming science and maths lead and head of computing. She developed a Jeannine Manuel maths curriculum that is about critical thinking and working maths out in an experimental and experiential manner, and was thrilled by the opportunity to move to the brand new site in London, which she loves. Her husband is the financial director at the school, her two children are pupils here and they live five minutes away. She is hoping to stay for some time to come.

They are building a senior leadership team, but with the school so new and pupil numbers growing so quickly, staff will need to grow and settle. Parents said the head was approachable and accessible but they mostly speak to one of the separate heads of the junior or senior school. They said she was 'fantastic', 'deeply committed to teaching' and 'a passionate educator' and 'very animated when giving workshops to parents on the maths method'. The school has a strong board of trustees, including the dynamic and impressive head of the Paris schools, who comes over regularly, speaking at open days. Ms Prévot 'won us over completely and gave us confidence,' said one parent.

Entrance: Unlike the Paris branch, there are not (yet) long waiting lists for this school. One form nursery, then two classes per year. Selection of pupils very 'light touch' – a simple test of language and maths. Mostly they are looking for parental commitment to the school's ethos. 'You have to believe that the school will do the educating but they need the family to support their ethos.' 'It is an inversion of normal entry requirements,' said one parent. 'They interviewed us for over an hour, wanting to know about our backgrounds and education and aspirations. They hardly tested our child at all!' The joy of not having to sit through 7+ or 11+ entrance exams is enough to tempt many parents, one imagines, as well as the absence of working towards exams generally. Beginners in French accepted at all levels, beginners in English up to year 7.

Exit: Currently, leavers only when families move country; otherwise, pupils seem to be staying on and so the school is growing with them and creating ever more years, with now a fledgling sixth form. Hard to know where these pupils will go to, though the École Jeannine Manuel in Paris sends three-quarters of its pupils to universities outside France, almost half to UK universities – and of those 90 per cent to Russell Group universities. With IB accreditation plus the French bacc it is certainly well equipped to do well in London too, with current cohort of determined, mature, well-educated pupils from aspirational families. No home tutoring goes on that we could find out about, little homework and little pressure, just a set of enquiring minds and high expectations.

Teaching and learning: This is bilingual teaching done well – English pupils are challenged to raise their standard and French pupils not allowed to coast in French lessons, but are pushed to improve too. 'We chose this school because we wanted both languages and cultures taught and didn't want to lose one or the other. Our children were happy the moment they walked in and we were no longer paying for schools where our kids sat bored in French classes.' It follows the French national curriculum except for English, science and Mandarin, where it has developed its own.

EYFS includes a one form nursery, with space to play inside and outside, reasonably well equipped with dressing up and play areas and plenty of art, rest time with kids lying down after lunch with blankets from home and quiet music – a safe, calm environment. Reception and year 1 start basic phonics and lots of coordination work in preparation for writing, but this being the French system, reading and writing proper waits until they are in year 2, with EYFS given to memory, poetry learning, speech and physical coordination.

Junior school classes of up to 20 pupils, with teaching shared between a French native speaker and an English native speaking teacher. Day books show work in neat French handwriting, maths with cuisenaire blocks, writing marked at pupils' own levels – each one expected to challenge themselves from whatever level they start at. They start to learn reading and writing in French (fewer graphemes make it easier to learn to read and spell in than English) and once they have mastered French reading and writing, they can then start English in little groups, working at their own level until they are all bilingual. Parents said that by about 8 years old all the kids are fluent in both. Maths very practical 'and at a higher level than my nieces and nephews in English schools'. Joint sciences, plenty of humanities (no RE in the French system) taught by both French and English teachers, art, music.

'Children get a tailored education – each of my kids has been pushed and developed in different ways.' 'Teachers don't have kids comparing to each other, they need to show progress at their level and they are expected to be ambitious for themselves.' 'Grading is based on effort and achievement and they need to show improvement,' explained one junior school parent. There is a no homework policy until senior school, though junior pupils said they sometimes have to do reading or learn a poem. Older pupils not overwhelmed with the hour or so homework they are expected to do.

Senior school has pupils using lockers and moving between rooms, half the subjects in English and half in French. Only humanities taught in both French and English under a curriculum that shows historical events from two different perspectives. The battle of Waterloo seen from both the winners' and losers' point of view – pupils see how to question the source and look at cultural context. 'It allows pupils to think about what is truth and to question fake news.' All lessons include collaborative, participative working.

Interactive whiteboards allow group work done on iPads to be shared by the class in real time. We saw groups collecting references from a text and uploading it to a shared table of references so they could all learn from each other's research. English enhanced with outings to theatres, workshops and some challenging teaching. 'I was blown away by the depth of understanding and analysis my child showed when explaining a Jekyll and Hyde text.' A French student won an English playwriting competition run by National Theatre with hundreds of entrants. Total bilingualism noted by parents – 'They flip from one language to the other and you can't tell what is their mother tongue language.' 'There is an organic mixing of pupils and exchanges take place in both languages.' This is achieved by intensive language teaching in 'petits groupes' so that by the time they are 7 or 8 they are all at the same level; higher up the school, new pupils are given intense language support so they can integrate. Late joiners who have insufficient French to learn maths under the school curriculum can do maths IGCSE. Maths gets special mention by parents who believe 'that it is at a higher level than comparative French or English schools'.

The curriculum shows historical events from two different perspectives. The battle of Waterloo is studied from both the winners' and losers' point of view

Extra tutoring or language learning takes place in years 7 and 8 during the 45 minute daily Drop Everything And Read (DEAR) period while most pupils lie out on giant cushions and read from the English or French reading list.

Parents mentioned appreciating the 'incredibly nuanced report cards that assess both effort and achievement and show that teachers know each child's strengths and weakness'. Well as teachers know their pupils, there are no external examinations before IB except for language exams, so pupils are tested with internal exams and results matched to École Jeannine Manuel in Paris and Lille to check for progress. Currently the small classes, motivated pupils and teachers, are showing better results even than the Paris pupils. New sixth form offers the IB and the French baccalaureate.

Learning support and SEN: Dyslexic pupils or those who need help from speech and language therapists get extra support if needed without missing other lessons. No special needs teaching but parents said that 'this is not a one-size fits all curriculum, but there are customised classes to boost pupils. Because that is happening all the time, 'no-one notices the dyslexic child who has specialised activities, since they are all rotating and doing work at their own level'. The school won't take a pupil it is not equipped to support, but everyone is used to therapists coming in. Most classrooms are wheelchair accessible and school is happy to adapt room timetables if needed.

The arts and extracurricular: DofE provides opportunities for learning to map read, big hikes and volunteering, and they are making volunteering opportunities within school for the younger kids.

Lunch is very French – a protein, a vegetable and a carbohydrate, as much as they want to eat, but no choices and no hot dogs. A proper shared mealtime

Art taught in classrooms (very fine Picasso portraits being done in year 3 the day we visited), and we saw critical thinking demonstrated as pupils explained and discussed the thinking behind a gilded shopping trolley artwork. Continuous opportunities to express ideas orally and to get used to public presentations.

No individual music lessons, but juniors can try out instruments in class, while senior pupils go up to music room to hear and learn to appreciate different types of music as well as playing and composing.

Talent show very inclusive and diverse – a Rubik's cube champion, yoyo tricks, a rap done by two students in both English and French – comparing Shakespeare and Molière. Not your everyday talent show from a London school.

Clubs at lunchtime and after school, for juniors while they wait for senior school to finish (eg drama, storytelling, fencing, chess, choir, parkour, arts and crafts) and for seniors (eg robotics, debating, gymnastics, choir, street dance, basketball).

Sport: Very little outdoor space – each balcony and terrace used to the utmost with little ones using climbing blocks and playhouses, and older ones using the basketball nets. Longer playtimes involve donning wellington boots and going into Bedford Square, or older students to Coram Fields, with footballs and rackets. Junior kids do go out every day and there are big efforts to provide sport despite there being no playground; older pupils are allowed out at breaktime. They have a contract with the YMCA sports centre for gym and indoor courts, and with University College EnergyBase for more gym space and basketball. Some fixtures against other French schools, but pupils said that 'it wouldn't suit a child who was very sporty' and parents said, 'it allows them to explore different sports but won't make champions'. Having no homework in junior school allows them 'time to explore their own interests,' according to parents.

Ethos and heritage: Jeannine Manuel spent some time in London during the war as part of the resistance and believed in the need to create understanding between nations, and the importance of language in learning about other people and their culture. To this end she opened a school and developed a pedagogy based on collaborative working and critical thinking. The Paris École Jeannine Manuel has 2,400 pupils and the Lille branch 800, and École Jeannine Manuel is now an education 'brand' with a reputation for high academic standards and exciting teaching that means it has long waiting lists. Jeannine Manuel's son Bernard, a passionate educationist, worked to ensure funds from the Fondation Jeannine Manuel were set aside to open a school in London as a tribute to his mother's love of London and to make bilingualism a reality.

Three very fine Georgian buildings built in 1770 by Robert Palmer (fine enough to be included in the architectural Open House weekends) have been joined sympathetically and are now both elegant and functional. They face Bedford Square and are next to the British Museum and a minute away from Tottenham Court Road station, so could hardly be more central London. The Bedford Square building has room for up to 500 pupils and another building in Russell Square houses senior years as they move up to IB.

High ceilinged, carpeted rooms, with fine stucco architraves, neat modern furniture and lockers for pupils. Two particularly large rooms with tables and benches that open out from wall storage allow all pupils to eat school lunches or packed lunches in several sittings. Lunch is very French – a protein, a vegetable and a carbohydrate, as much as they want to eat, but no choices and no hot dogs. Set lunchtimes means not only do they all eat the same food, but that they all eat it together. A proper shared mealtime.

Polite, calm atmosphere, youthful teachers and purposeful collaborative teaching methodology. We didn't see any pupils daydreaming – too much going on and classes too small for that.

Pastoral care, inclusivity and discipline: Pupils said that if they had any concerns or issues they could and would speak to teachers at any time, and believed it would be dealt with. A well-being curriculum carried out in all years may have something to do with this. None we spoke to said there was bullying or roughness, though some admitted to social issues between friends. One parent said, 'minor things are dealt with efficiently at school, by caring teachers, with little parental involvement.' 'Pupils were told to go away and think about it and come back to resolve the problem – which they did.' We were told that 'pastoral care is excellent' and 'there is a nurturing environment', but it would seem that it happens simply because of caring teachers rather than strict systems or policies.

Pupils and parents: Most of 185 pupils who joined in the first year they opened were Parisians who knew of the École Jeannine Manuel Paris reputation, as well as French families who hadn't been able to get into any of the other French schools in London. The current pupils are from a much more mixed demographic – lots of third culture kids whose passports and backgrounds are very international. Lebanese, French Canadian, Hong Kong, Irish, increasing numbers of British families who, according to the school, are looking to 'maintain some European culture – the Brexit effect'. Parents are bankers, lawyers, doctors. Pupils were surprisingly unsophisticated for such a well travelled lot – worldly, travelled, educated, but no designer trainers to be seen. Parents we spoke to said kids were 'gentle', 'no bling', 'allowed to be kids'. Pupils move at 11 from other French junior schools or from British primary schools 'if they are looking for a small, centrally placed private school with an emphasis on critical thinking'. French pupils' parents want them to keep their French up and keep links to their roots when the French schools which are subsidised by the French government are full, or they may be seeking an alternative to schools that are totally French in language and pedagogical style. School buses go north to Swiss Cottage, west to Kensington and Shepherds Bush via Paddington and Marylebone, and to Fulham and Chelsea.

Money matters: London private school level fees as no French government subsidies. Extra for lunch, for clubs and for trips. The school was supported by French École Jeannine Manuel for first couple of years, but is now fully self sufficient with annual accounts healthy enough to develop the new Russell Square building and plans for a third local site to allow for more growth in pupil numbers. Currently student numbers increasing by up to 30 per cent a year and no reason to see that diminishing for a little while yet. Bursaries available for all year groups.

The last word: Ideal for a mixed heritage family where both French and English languages and cultures are of equal importance, and heaven for a child who wants to be encouraged to think and discuss and experiment rather than regurgitate facts. Not good if you need the reassurance of endless public exams and certainly no preparation for 11+, 13+ or GCSEs (except English lang and lit). Not a sporty school or a competitive school. Each child challenged to improve from their own baseline and they all seem to want to rise to the challenge, making the most of London, of each other and of themselves.

EIFA International School

36 Portland Place, Marylebone, London W1B 1LS

020 7637 5351 | registrar@eifaschool.com | www.eifaschool.com

Independent	Pupils: 279
Ages: 2–18	Fees: £20,850 – £23,700 pa

Head of school: Since September 2018, Françoise Zurbach, who has been teacher, pedagogical counsellor, and head of school in France and London for more than 20 years. With a French father and English mother, she spent her first 10 years at an English school in Montreal, moving to France and continuing her education in the French system. She spent 20 years teaching in a small French primary school, moving to head Wix primary in London in 2013.

Entrance: This young school, which has only recently opened a secondary department, does not yet have waiting lists for the senior school. It is currently relatively non-selective, with admission is based on completing a straightforward application form and providing school reports. Does not require fluency in English or French for entry up to year 8.

Exit: Parents say that some families who aspire to the French Bacc opt to move at 11 to the bilingual school in Kentish Town or one of the Lycées, and some, particularly those whose parents are not French speakers, transfer to British independent schools, but an increasing number of families are choosing to stay on for senior school for IGCSEs. Around half leave after GCSEs.

Latest results: In 2020, 80 per cent 9-7 at IGCSE. In 2019 (the last year when exams took place), 71 per cent 9-7 at IGCSE.

Teaching and learning: A bilingual school from nursery (21 months) to 18-years-old. Nursery children in Little EIFA follow the EYFS, taught in French and English; therefore children learn literacy and reading at an earlier age than would be the case in a traditional French setting. Little EIFA offers flexible part-time hours. Primary students follow the French national curriculum using a bilingual French-English model. Each year group (two form entry in most years) has a Francophone (and French-qualified) teacher as well as a native-speaking English qualified teacher, who plan jointly and teach different parts of the programme in both languages, creating a completely bilingual learning environment for every year group.

Each year group has a Francophone teacher as well as a native-speaking English qualified teacher, who plan jointly and teach different parts of the programme

In the senior school, years 7-9 continue with French curriculum (taught in both languages). In year 10 students may take the diplôme national du brevet as well as follow the IGCSE subjects now that the school has been authorised by Cambridge Exams and Edexcel.

Senior school staff bring solid international school experience and a good overall understanding of the various curricula – English national curriculum, international curricula and French programmes. School benchmarks student learning via French standardised tests and is inspected by both Ofsted and the IEN (Inspecteur de l'Education Nationale Française).

As the school has 'homologue' status with the French Education Ministry, French and English teachers must be qualified and hold recognised credentials. One parent of a very bright child was effusive about the way he is challenged academically.

The school now offers its students the opportunity to follow the International Baccalaureate diploma programme.

Year 2 pupils were very proud to be the winners of a recent European film competition for the animated movie they created

Learning support and SEN: School engages specialist teachers for children with learning challenges for those who need additional support; there is no cost to the parents for this. Students who are not yet fluent in English or French may also be expected to take lessons with language teachers.

The arts and extracurricular: More on offer than in a typical French school. After-school activities are offered by teachers with a special talent or interest, as well as external providers. A range of musical instruments and ensembles including rock bands; activities such as rugby, football, ballet, yoga, language clubs, IT coding; a few parents mentioned a creative writing course and one teenage boy refreshingly told us it is his favourite activity; homework club every day. Some parents see it as a way to extend their children's exposure to French or English. Year 2 pupils were very proud to be the winners of a recent European film competition for the animated movie they created.

Early morning drop-off and after-school care till 6pm are available for Little EIFA children; this is convenient for working parents, but also those whose older children may stay after school for club activities. Extracurricular activities incur additional fees but no one we spoke to grumbled about that: they were very happy with the range of activities on offer. Parents told us of a trip to Brussels where the students had a hand in crafting an EU law on the environment.

Sport: There are opportunities to take part in sports competitions and tournaments with other French and international schools in London.

Ethos and heritage: The co-founders, plus their fellow investors who form the governing board, have had good support from the local Howard de Walden Estate – major landowners in London W1 – who were keen to see EIFA on the menu of international schools available to the local Marylebone gentry. The combination of the strategic planning and foresight of the founders and this collaborative partnership with HdW Estates has enabled this school to secure two impressive buildings for their prep and senior schools. Originally conceived as a prep/primary school in 2013, but parents wanted their children to continue to be educated bilingually, and so a senior school opened and moved into its own premises in 2016.

Little EIFA and the prep school are in a large late Georgian building in Portland Place. Little EIFA is based in a well-organised maze of rooms in the basement level with enclosed outdoor space exclusively for the youngest children. On the ground floor are the reception children and the library, stocked with 5,000 books – half French, half English (on the day we visited full of relaxed but fully engaged children with their noses in books), in bright rooms with original period features such as lofty Wedgwood-blue painted ceilings decorated with crown moulding and fireplaces. Other primary classes perch higher up on top floors with large windows that brighten the rooms year round.

The senior school is a short walk away on quiet side street with a nicely refurbished building that contains bright classrooms fully equipped with all the requisites – science lab, study hub, an amazing large art studio with walls of windows on two sides, and an inviting canteen that serves as a multi-purpose space. This room features a huge painting of a London cityscape with silhouettes of children in the foreground, donated by a parent and painted by South American artist Walter Blanco as part of a school event. Children's work gets equal prominence, and there is also a collage of maps of all the countries the children come from featured on another wall. There is a clean, uncluttered feel despite the ample careful displays of student work and art. Daily recreation and breaks take place at nearby Regent's Park. Students use the library at the prep school or visit nearby Marylebone Library.

EIFA is an urban school; parents say that some families come expecting more, but what makes it all worthwhile is the positive EIFA school culture – that is the major draw for families we spoke to.

Pastoral care, inclusivity and discipline: Parents tell us that EIFA has a strong sense of community and this is part of the attraction. The diversity of families helps to create an ambiance where acceptance and respect are the norm. The school is young, and there is a definite 'pioneer spirit' among those families who joined in the early years and who speak with pride about what the school community has created. Communications are good and parents feel well informed and able to approach the school teachers or administration whenever needed. Senior and junior school parents describe the teachers as versatile, devoted, nurturing and impressive. The kids we saw in the classrooms, study hubs and library looked happy and were welcoming and at ease with their visitor. Some parents attribute the good behaviour to the school's small size. No uniforms except for PE and games classes. Active parents' association regarded as refreshing by many who find this parent engagement a welcome change from the norm at other French schools. It's also an important support that can help to integrate parents new to London. Meeting minutes and photos of activities are on the website.

The inviting canteen features a huge painting of a London cityscape with silhouettes of children in the foreground, donated by a parent and painted by South American artist Walter Blanco

Pupils and parents: The increasing number of French-medium schools on offer in London has enlarged parental choice; those selecting EIFA want what it says on the tin – an international school with a French bilingual programme. Over 40 nationalities; the French, Americans and Canadians are the main groups but there are many bicultural, bilingual families of mixed nationalities; some local residents, others expats. A few French families seeking the dream life in 'France's sixth city – London' (with perhaps one parent commuting to France for work). Though some of these families have returned to France, the school has not yet seen the impact of Brexit and continues to grow. In many respects a 'neighbourhood school' and many children walk or ride their scooters, but some travel longer distances – the school's outsourced school bus service covers Highgate and Hampstead to the north, Notting Hill to the west, and Fulham to the south west. Parents do not seem to mind having play dates scattered across London.

Money matters: International school prices are to be expected here. The school has needs-assessed financial aid. Low student-teacher ratio (6-1), and since extras such as English or French language support and special needs support are not extra, the fees are competitive with those of other international schools. Lunch is included in the school fees and is compulsory unless the child has dietary restrictions. It is prepared by outsourced caterers, and is tasty by all accounts (and our own sampling).

The last word: This is a niche school with high aspirations that ticks the right boxes for families who appreciate a certain discipline associated with French education (we saw lots of immaculate handwriting), and the opportunity to acquire or maintain French language fluency, but who at the same time like the quirkiness of an international school that draws on global themes and topics to enhance the students' learning and world view. The principal was quick to say, 'EIFA is not a French school, it is a bilingual (French/English) international school.' The rich displays of African masks made in art classes, green Irish shamrocks to celebrate St Patrick's Day, student rehearsals for Wizard of Oz, beautifully written essays on Macbeth and even stir-fry chicken noodles for lunch serve to illustrate her point. Worth a look.

Eleanor Palmer Primary School

21

Lupton Street, London NW5 2JA

020 7485 2155 | admin@eleanorpalmer.camden.sch.uk | www.eleanorpalmer.camden.sch.uk

State | Ages: 3-11 | Pupils: 236

Head: Since 2003, Kate Frood MA,OBE (50s). Knew she wanted to be a teacher from the age of 8 and started her career doing just that at nearby Fleet Primary in 1983. Aside from a four-year stint as a maths consultant to Islington Council, has taught in Camden ever since. Trained when child-centred learning (as opposed to testing) was the focus, and this has remained fundamental to her approach. In order 'to keep her hand in and share ideas', continues to teach year 6 maths. 'She really knows what kids can do and – more importantly – what they can't,' said a mother. 'She makes sure every child is well-prepared for secondary.' Liked and respected by parents. 'She's a brilliant head, incredibly good behind the scenes and incredibly forward thinking,' said one. 'Problems are dealt with before they turn into problems.' Awarded the OBE for 'services to education' in 2014. One daughter who attended Camden School for Girls.

Entrance: Hugely oversubscribed, with about eight applicants per place for a single reception class of 30. Proximity is key and there's been much tut-tutting about families renting to squeeze through the gates. (Camden now scrutinises applicants carefully, particularly looking for those who own or let another address locally.) Full-time Camden-funded nursery of 26, but bagging a place here does not guarantee admission into reception (children have been rejected in the past).

Exit: Pupils here tend to go on to local community secondaries, generally the cluster round Dartmouth Park – William Ellis, Acland Burghley and Parliament Hill – plus some to Camden School for Girls. A few, too, to selective state schools, and a further sprinkling to independents. By and large, however, this is a parent body committed to state schooling.

Our view: Housed in a medley of low-built mid-20th-century buildings on a reasonably spacious, but very urban, site, the school has well-cared for and imaginatively used grounds, including an adventure playground and colourful entrance ornamented with art, fish, running water – and a prominent plaque declaring 'racism is unacceptable'.

Academically, the school falls firmly into the Outstanding category, with high standards in the core and a rich offering well beyond. Heavily committed to topic-based study, with themes such as World War 2 or Victorian childhood taught using imaginative links between history, geography, art and literacy. 'We see learning as an adventure,' says the head, an adventure explored through plenty out-of-school visits and and in-house contributions from storytellers, artists and experts.

The school has both a national reputation for maths teaching and a highly-praised literacy strategy. Children read daily for half an hour and end every afternoon with a class story. Great emphasis, too, placed on the best children's

Effort and persistence are what count, so no star charts, no ability sets; each child is encouraged to achieve their personal best

literature, with new titles added regularly and a handy booklet of recommendations. Year 5 studies and performs a Shakespeare play. French for all from year 3, taught by the classroom teacher. Homework (including daily reading and times tables) from the start, and ICT well embedded, with access to a myriad of laptops and iPads.

Eleanor Palmer is a 'teaching school' – one of just 350 in the country – teaching teachers how to teach. This, according to parents, can have both its upside and its down. 'It means,' said one mother, 'the staff are young and hugely energetic, willing to work after school and at weekends, but some are also pretty inexperienced.' Head, however, tends to restrict the rawest recruits to the younger years.

The ethos of the school has been shaped by the work of Carol Dweck – whose perspective is that effort and persistence are what really count. 'This teaches children to see mistakes and failures as positives and makes for a very energetic and inclusive culture,' says the head. So, no star charts, no ability sets; instead, each child is encouraged to achieve their personal best, with marking emphasising steps forward rather than what's gone wrong.

Special needs is led by the head, aided, in school, by support teachers and learning support assistants, and, out of it, by an educational psychologist and occupational therapist. Parents feel the SEN offering has improved in recent years. 'The head is very responsive and things like touch typing are now standard.'

Two hours of PE weekly, with a dedicated sports co-ordinator mentoring both those who struggle and those who excel, as well as arranging participation for all in out-of-school tournaments. Plenty of alternatives, too, to conventional team sports, with dance and skipping workshops, fencing and taekwondo sessions. The school is also 'very committed' to walking. Nearby Parliament Hill used for class activities and sports days.

Specialist music teacher visits twice weekly, overseeing a 'strings programme', which provides all pupils from the age of 8 with (free) group tuition by a specialist in violin or cello. Multiple opportunities to perform in concerts and musicals.

Head very much of the '50 things to do before' philosophy, and her objective is that all leavers should have completed a substantial tick list of activities, from growing their own vegetables to visiting a farm. Trips, trips, trips make the most of the wealth of galleries and museums a bus ride away, as well as of opportunities further afield (everyone gets four residential stays, ranging from camping in Epping Forest to a year 7 week at a Michael Morpurgo's Farm for City Children.)

As the leader of a 'multi-cultural community', the head has taken up the option to skip the daily act of Christian worship. Instead, the red-letter days of all the major religions are covered in assemblies and younger pupils are taught philosophy by trained philosophy teachers. The school is also a level 2 Unicef 'rights respecting' school, which entails listening to children's views and including them in such decisions as the fairness of team selection. Every class draws up a charter based on agreed rights, and then lists how adults and children will respect these. 'Once behaviour is seen in this way there is little need for rules,' says the head. Local councillors, politicians and lawyers, too, are invited in to teach pupils about their rights and responsibilities as citizens. Charity link to school in Sierra Leone.

Kentish Town is more affluent than formerly, particularly after a recent influx of French émigrés, and the popularity of the school means the sharp elbowed have gained ground in recent years, but you'll still find a good cross section of traditional locals and recent refugees alongside the organic set. About 20 per cent receive free school meals, a national average, but well below what might be expected for the location. As the head concedes, this can be a positive, as those from more affluent backgrounds provide 'a critical mass of high-achieving, motivated, liberal, middle class kids – so all my working class or refuge kids get caught up.' Parents, too, feel the balance works ('I think it still has that community school feeling,' said one) and are full of praise for its warm and nurturing atmosphere.

The school grounds include an adventure playground and colourful entrance ornamented with art, fish, running water – and a plaque declaring 'racism is unacceptable'

The last word: The growth mindset, very high standards of teaching and innovative topic based study all combine to make this a terrific place for children to learn. 'Our children have been extremely happy here – and very well educated,' summed up a parent.

Fine Arts College Hampstead

22

Centre Studios 41-43 Englands Lane, London NW3 4YD

020 7586 0312 | mail@hampsteadfinearts.com | www.hampsteadfinearts.com

Independent	Pupils: 212; sixth form: 175
Ages: 13-19	Fees: £22,560 pa

Principal: Candida Cave (50s). Elegant, quietly spoken, compassionate and creative, a lovely lady. Attended Ruskin School of Art, Oxford, then started teaching art and art history when a flatmate fell in love with an Italian racing driver and needed someone to take on her tutees. Quickly discovered she had a flair for teaching, and soon had 20 more students. Set up Fine Arts College as a part-time concern in 1978 with artist and co-founder Nicholas Cochrane in rented rooms at the YMCA in Great Russell Street; then in 1982 took the plunge and opened a full-time school in a house in Belsize Park. School moved to its present site in 2002.

Until very recently she was still actively involved in teaching at the school, and still teaches on study trips and lectures. Painting is her passion, and she has exhibited in various galleries in London and elsewhere. Also a keen theatre and concert goer. Married to Stephen, a historian and writer, she has a grown up son and daughter (the latter now head).

Attributes success of school to its founding ethos: 'We wanted to have the sort of college that we ourselves would have liked. We wanted a holistic education, where the arts were as important as academic subjects. We wanted a co-operative, self-motivated style of learning. And we wanted to know everyone's name.' Parents agree. 'I have nothing but praise for Candida, and the atmosphere she creates in the school is so positive,' commented one.

Her daughter, Emmy Schwieters, has been head of the college since 2019. Read English and history of art at Leeds, and worked in the hospitality industry before joining Fine Arts in 2003, taking on the roles of head of the history of art department and director of studies.

Entrance: Entry points at year 9, year 10 and year 12, and school admits around 12 annually to each of these year groups. Reference from current school is required, but no testing. All applicants are interviewed personally by Candida Cave for at least an hour; she looks for a sense that they've clicked with the school and what it has to offer – 'they have to want to be educated here.' If she's unsure, she'll ask another member of staff to interview them as well. School is happy to admit at any point in the academic year.

At 16+, school looks for a minimum of five GCSEs at grade 4 or above, but doesn't make the offer of a place contingent upon this. 'If they don't have maths or English GCSE they must take fewer A levels and get these done.'

Exit: Around 15 per cent leave after GCSEs. The remainder move on after A levels to a wide range of destinations, including Camberwell College of Arts, Met Film School, Ravensbourne University and London College of Fashion. A trickle of Oxbridge successes – three in 2020. The occasional student off overseas – two in 2020, to Berklee College of Music in New York and California Institute of the Arts. Popular courses include history of art, art foundation and fine arts.

Latest results: For 2020, school has only provided A*/C at A level – 68 per cent. In 2019, 27 per cent 9-7 at GCSE; 17 per cent A*/A at A level (48 per cent A*-B).

Teaching and learning: Biology and maths are offered at A level, but as you'd expect, the arts and humanities dominate, along with economics and business studies and an excellent range of languages (take-up for Italian is high). Teaching groups are small, allowing for a seminar-style delivery of the course. The approach relies for its success on students' chattiness and willingness to participate, but that's clearly not a problem here. We dropped in on a delightfully lively and sparky year 13 politics lesson where the students were all very ready to speak up, and the standard of contributions was informed and thoughtful. Nearly 30 subjects on offer to sixth formers, and it's possible to do entirely art-based options: we met a student who was revelling in being able to study fine art, graphic design, photography and fashion/textile design. 'My previous school could only offer me art. This is brilliant!' Most students still take four subjects and drop one after year 12. EPQ also available. School also offers a one-year A level course, often taken by those who have done a year of the IB and decided it's not for them.

Since 1994 school has taken students into years 10 and 11 in response to parent demand. It provides both a conventional two-year and an intensive one-year GCSE course, the latter offering a lifeline to able students who have nonetheless struggled in more academically pressurised environments. In September 2018 the first year 9s joined the school: just one small cohort of 10 pupils when we visited. The lessons we saw were very quiet, reflecting perhaps the kind of children that at this age would prefer this eccentric and artsy little school, but pupils said they appreciated the very high level of individual attention they received and seemed glad to be here. At GCSE most students do eight or nine GCSEs, including three arts subjects and one science, biology, which is now taught in purpose built lab (rather than an ordinary classroom).

Photography is thriving here, and we were relieved to see the dark room still very much in use – 'For the students, it's not nostalgia, it's a new thing'

Drama is very popular and taught in the school's 'big space' – which, truthfully, isn't that big – and is extremely popular at all levels, and it's probably no coincidence that the school has as many successful performing alumni as artistic ones. Music and music technology taught in purpose built room that pulses with purpose. But naturally it's the art rooms that really impress. Light, peaceful, littered with classical busts, the creativity here wafts over you like a Mozart aria. Even the skeleton used for teaching purposes was in the throes of ecstasy instead of the normal demure pose. We paused to admire a sculpture of Laocoön fighting off the serpents that students were copying in order to produce a monochrome portrait, using tone rather than colour to create a 3D look. 'You can't do a bad drawing of it, really,' mused the officiating teacher, drifting over in paint-splattered smock, tea in hand. Small class of students bent over their work, completely absorbed, and we were much struck by the atmosphere of focused and calm artistry.

Big emphasis on classical antiquity and ancient history is such a pleasure to see. But the modern world is also very much in evidence throughout the curriculum. Excellent graphics classroom was full of punchy, inventive work by the students, and film studies and media also very successful. Photography is thriving here, and we were relieved to see the dark room still very much in use – 'For the students, it's not nostalgia, it's a new thing.' Textiles room an absolute treasure trove of fabrics, buttons and bows, inviting budding fashion creatives to dive right in.

We didn't get the chance to speak to anyone from the lower school, but the sixth formers here are clearly very happy. They relish the freedom to think and develop for themselves and the emphasis laid on a collaborative approach, describing the sixth form experience as a 'proper step between school and university'. 'You force yourself to do a lot of work – and you end up accomplishing more.' 'The creative range here is unparalleled.' 'If you aren't motivated to do work in your own time, you'll fall behind. But if you have that drive, they'll help you 100 per cent. In fact, they'll help you anyway.' 'We're expected to be creative and think differently. The teachers here are open to discussion and challenge, and they're always willing to stay behind and help you.'

Learning support and SEN: SEN provision is strong, and students told us they felt very well supported here. 'The teachers are just great, and really helpful, and needing help isn't an issue here.' 'We try and support in the most subtle way possible,' says Candida. 'If a student has dyslexia, then their personal tutor will be a dyslexia specialist.' School keen to emphasise, however, that it isn't a special school and can't support one-to-one teaching throughout the curriculum.

The arts and extracurricular: LAMDA extremely popular and successful, and each crop of exam results brings plenty of distinctions at grade 8. Peripatetic music lessons also available throughout the school – 'I can actually sing now!' said a grateful student after commencing singing lessons here. Frequent trips to exhibitions and to places of beauty and culture both at home and abroad, as well as to theatres and musical events. Students encouraged to initiate projects if they wish to, and there have been a number of charitable and fundraising events of this kind.

On the whole, though, young people here are engaged full time in what at other schools is usually peripheral – film, fashion, music, art, drama – so there isn't the demand for off-timetable activity that you'd find elsewhere. As one student put it, 'There aren't that many extracurricular subjects, because most people here want to focus on their A levels.' Those seeking a full-on, UCAS-form-busting programme of opportunities

Queen's College London

should look elsewhere; the students we spoke to here were happy with the balance.

Sport: Lower school does a range of sports every week including team games such as football and netball, although the emphasis is on enjoyment and fitness rather than competitive fixtures. Yoga also offered.

Ethos and heritage: Once the school was a sixth form college almost exclusively offering specialist arts teaching. Over the decades it's evolved into a more general provider of non-selective education at 13+ with a particular emphasis on the visual arts. It is not, nor does it aim to be, the fine arts equivalent of a specialist music school, and students are not selected on their artistic ability.

Now in its 40th year, the school is spread over multiple sites, all within a few minutes' walk of each other. The main building in Englands Lane is a former Victorian dairy: still flanked on all sides by grey and beige brickwork, its interior is a honeycomb of small corridors and classrooms. The cobbled main courtyard is the first thing people see, and it really is rather special. Beautifully adorned with shrubs, trees, potted flowers and wooden benches, the impression on a summer's morning was one of shade and sunshine in a Tuscan village. The students make full use of it in the warmer months and say it's amazing. 'I fell in love with the school as soon as I saw it!'

Since 2015, the school has been owned by Dukes Education, which has enabled it to purchase a nearby former stables for turning into additional classrooms, but space remains an issue here. There's no library, for instance – students use local public libraries instead – and sixth formers would love a common room of their own. But these privations haven't made a dent in the atmosphere here, which is buzzy and cheerful. 'We use the local cafés instead, and that pushes us to be more sociable,' said one student. 'The feeling at Fine Arts College is always welcoming, and I'm really loving being here,' was another comment.

Alumni include artist Robert Fry, actors Orlando Bloom and Helena Bonham-Carter, and guitarist and singer Johnny Borrell.

Pastoral care, inclusivity and discipline: Everyone is given a code of conduct to sign – which includes not making a mess, rather endearingly for an art school – so expectations are clear, but in the main there are few rules and no cause to break them. The school is run on mutual respect, and Candida Cave is proud of how well the students respond to this. 'We haven't had to exclude or suspend anyone for 10 years.' Those who arrive exhausted and discouraged from different school environments quickly find their feet. Parents and children alike told us that this was a kind and accepting place. 'Bullying is non-existent here.'

Teachers are addressed by their first names, and there's no uniform for any of the year groups. Dress code is casual, with the only requirement being that the students must be decently and inoffensively attired. Prettily appliquéd sweaters and fashionably motifed sweatshirts abound, and there's no shortage of pierced ears and noses. Nonetheless, anyone expecting to find the place a pushover will be quickly disabused. Students' progress, both academic and pastoral, is comprehensively tracked. Everyone has a personal tutor whom they see every week for at least an hour. There are fortnightly reports so students can see how well they're doing, and consistently low effort grades will swiftly result in interventions, including (for sixth formers) being made to drop a subject if they're clearly not trying at it. Anyone who is more than 10 minutes late for a lesson isn't allowed to join it until they've made the work up in a study space outside the classroom, 'so I'm never late!' commented a student; 'it's been really effective for me.' Said another, 'It's a good idea, because after all, it is distracting when people are late.'

The art rooms really impress. The creativity here wafts over you like a Mozart aria. Even the skeleton used for teaching purposes was in the throes of ecstasy instead of the normal demure pose

The college will admit school refusers and home-schooled if it believes they would benefit from what it has to offer, but does so on a trial basis and tracks their progress particularly closely; no term's notice is required by the school from parents, but school also has the right to ask them to leave after half a term if it's patently not going to work.

No school lunches. Students bring their own, or eat at local cafés (some of whom offer a discount to FAC students) with parental permission, and Englands Lane is patrolled by staff members throughout lunch break. 'But quite a few celebrities' children go there, so the paparazzi can be out in force when the students are coming and going,' warned one mother. Students themselves unfazed by this, and just enjoy the independence. 'It's 100 per cent better than my last school – there's no ordering about, just freedom and an ethos of mutual respect.'

Pupils and parents: Mostly, but not exclusively, British students, drawn mainly from a local radius, but some coming from as far away as south London, Essex and Watford. Many are seeking an alternative to boarding, selectivity or just the conformity required at a large school. Parents are relieved and grateful that they've found the place. 'My child is really happy there, and enjoying life so much more.' Some international students, particularly post-GCSE.

Money matters: Each year either one 100 per cent scholarship or two 50 per cent scholarships to existing Fine Arts College students who demonstrate outstanding achievement in academic, artistic or musical fields of study, as well as exceptional commitment and exemplary behaviour. Limited number of bursaries available to students who have previously been educated in the state system who would not otherwise be able to afford private education.

The last word: A haven of culture, creativity and kindness amidst the tumult of north London selective schools, and a route to success for those who have been disheartened hitherto. 'I've had a really good time here, and I'll be sad to leave,' said a year 13 girl, and of the boys added, 'It's a really nice community. I actually don't mind getting up in the mornings and going to school. And I've never said that before.'

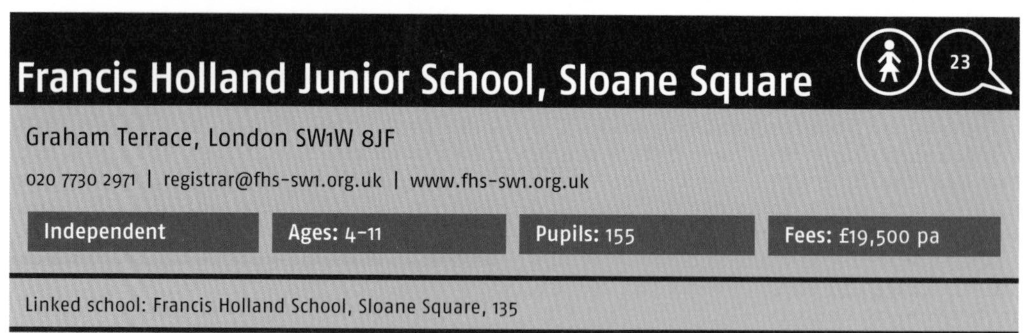

Francis Holland Junior School, Sloane Square

23

Graham Terrace, London SW1W 8JF

020 7730 2971 | registrar@fhs-sw1.org.uk | www.fhs-sw1.org.uk

Independent | Ages: 4–11 | Pupils: 155 | Fees: £19,500 pa

Linked school: Francis Holland School, Sloane Square, 135

Head of juniors: Since September 2019, Suzy Dixon MA. Previously acting headteacher for the school, after which she took a 10-month break from school leadership to focus on educational research and consultancy work. Before that, she was deputy head and head of English at Daneshill Prep and she has also held leadership roles at Highfield & Brookham Prep (while studying for her masters in educational management at King's College London), Downe House and Gateways School. Studied her BA in English and literature at Leeds and her PGCE at York. Enthusiasm and kindness are at her core – her ethos being that a happy school is the best starting point for high expectations. Considers these 'exciting times for education, particularly in London'.

Entrance: At 4+ are looking for social and intellectual readiness. 'Don't expect them to write their names, do expect them to listen to a story and tell you what it's about,' says the school. Want girls who can grasp opportunities and 'have a go'. Now involve SEN team as little differences in age can mean big developmental differences. Deadline for admission is now 31st October.

Some pupils have EAL and may need support (assessment is held only in English). Dyslexia is the biggest learning need supported here though also some with ASD and ADHD, often undiagnosed when first start here. Pride themselves on early interventions, not necessarily seeking labels but 'just supporting them'. Will go 'way beyond reasonable adjustments,' says the school. Offer one-to-one and in-class/small group support. There's also a disabled loo. Currently one pupil with EHCP.

Exit: Start having discussions on future schools in year 5 or in year 4 if learning needs are involved. Junior pupils compete with external candidates for senior school places – no longer automatic entry, which devalued senior school by positioning it as the safe back up if nothing else worked out.

Today, senior school is seen as a positive choice with about a third of the pupils going there, a third to other day schools – Alleyn's, JAGS, St Paul's Girls, City of London Girls, rest to boarding schools like Wycombe Abbey and Downe House. Normally a few to specialist dance and performing arts schools.

Our view: School you can fall for – literally in our case, thanks to sudden step down into reception. 'Don't worry, everyone does it,' reassures welcoming PA. (For the sake of balance, we stumbled over a door stop in the senior building later on.)

Normally, when a junior school is so entwined/embedded with the seniors – on the same site and sharing some facilities with senior school (from playground and games fields to science and art) – The Good Schools Guide would amalgamate the two in single review.

But with no expectation that everyone (or even the majority) of the junior pupils will go on to senior school, and with much teaching in top years devoted to preparation for other top senior schools (back-of-the hand-knowledge of every leading senior central London day school out there and a fair few boarding schools besides) this remains, philosophically if not physically, a separate school.

Not as selective as progress and results would suggest. No setting, either – it's all down to terrific well-differentiated teaching (not easy to do well so a real tribute to staff and leadership) 'Don't want to cap expectations,' says school. Still manages to give reception to year 2 a half day every Friday.

The downside is an assumption that girls move out of necessity. 'Other schools still tend to assume that our girls are leaving because senior school isn't up to standard,' says school. Was true once but not since senior school raised standards and ditched juniors' automatic entry.

Our tour guides agree that year 6 is a tough old year, with weekly tests in autumn term in the run up to the 11+. However, 'teachers try to make it enjoyable' and there are plenty of them – even in top years (5 and 6) might be three adults in the class. Pupils praise marking that doesn't overdo the congratulations or caveats but makes it easy to know how to improve work for next time – 'will use a green pen to add a little extra question'.

Plenty of feedback to parents, from open classrooms (every half term) to termly written reports. Teachers also have consultations with pupils to look at progress and set targets.

Lessons designed to boost thinking even from an early age, with philosophy on the menu and debating a form-based activity. Religion also part and parcel of the school day. All helps girls question everything and not be fazed if things don't go their way to start with, developing gift of gab from the start.

The mega focus is on literacy and numeracy, with class teachers still delivering significant proportion of lessons. Geography, history and science added in years 1 and 2 with PE, music teaching taught by specialists, ditto and ballet (on the curriculum for all – dance teacher legendary) and computing languages introduced year 3, when pupils also start to work with juniors' own STEM specialist.

Power of positive thinking impressively reinforced by numerous references to growth mindset in teaching and displays. No mere jargon-fest – pupils' understanding was impressive. 'If you think you can't do it, you say that you can't do it – yet,' said one (school's most important three letter word).

No doubt helps boost appetite for extra activities – some pupils have a club every day, pottery among the top favourites – school has changed homework policy so girls have two days to complete homework (used to be next day), and no weekend homework. Achievements, in and out of school, recognised in assembly and on notice board, photographs updated weekly, with house points geeing up sense of competition to varying degrees, sports day when feelings approach fever pitch. (Can also pick up extra points for eg picking up litter at breaktime.)

If things do all get too much (academically or otherwise) there's a Place2Be counsellor on hand to help (requests via special mailbox, appointment arranged and teacher notified in advance so pupils can slip out of lessons without fuss). 'Can be confidential if you don't want to tell a teacher or a parent,' said pupil (unless any safeguarding issues involved). Dodge some of the inevitable friendship issues by moving classes round. 'Have a new seat quite regularly.'

Pictures of pupils as Roman legionnaires appealed, though not as much as excellent pre-execution speeches by Anne Boleyn, crying out to be performed – 'I was glad – glad to be leaving this cruel world...'

School's layout is basically straightforward – takes up most of one side of quadrangle that bounds the playground (juniors shortly to have separate break times), with senior school additions (and extra floors) that can make pinpointing location feel like complex equation – juniors' second floor = seniors' mezzanine, for example – but undoubtedly add to the charm, along with the slam lid desks in some classrooms (change to more mobile, lighter variety in top two years, with lockers that close but don't lock – avoids stress of lost keys – for everyone).

Classrooms are large, bright treasure troves of colourful work ('Everyone's work goes up,' says teacher). Run out of wall space, say pupils, so 'have to hang things from the ceiling'. Pictures of pupils as Roman legionnaires appealed, though not as much as excellent pre-execution speeches by Anne Boleyn, all crying out (if not sobbing, in period costume) to be performed – 'I was glad – glad to be leaving this cruel world...'

Amazing that teachers manage to fit in any actual teaching but they do, and plenty of it. There are creative STEM sessions (plenty of problem-solving activities to inspire girls early), everything from building moving cars or working catapults (fires mini marshmallows – prize for distance), to coding the Grinch to jump over reindeer.

While not necessarily the school for cut-throat sporting competitive types (they come, they play but they don't always conquer), performing arts magically good.

Drama excellent – 'has seen a massive improvement,' said parent. Music could perhaps do with a few more bands and activities by comparison, though school feels this is out of date – options have 'increased considerably'. Ambitious production every year (Mary Poppins and Lion King have both featured recently). Ballet, compulsory in first three years, is run by legendary teacher who knows everyone – 'Darcey Bussell comes to our performances,' says pupil guide (not quite accurate, says school – instead has 'her ballet shoes as a prize') – and sends several girls on to specialist schools most years (Tring and Royal Ballet School all feature regularly). Watching year 3 pupils execute complex-looking sequence in lunchtime club (all so involved that nobody turned to look at the visitors), we weren't surprised.

Bar slightly underwhelmed reaction when quizzed about school food, traced by us to 'fish that has black skin on the back', everyone was delighted with life here. 'I love it here,' said one. 'There's a variety of lessons and it's not all English and maths, there are plays and concerts – and mufti days.' Who would it suit? 'Any bright pupils and even if they're not bright, the school will do its best to help,' reckoned another.

The last word: A hardworking school with a heart. Academically, it's really going places, with innovative teaching and that all important focus on maths and English but room for much more besides. These girls grow up really believing in themselves, and so they should.

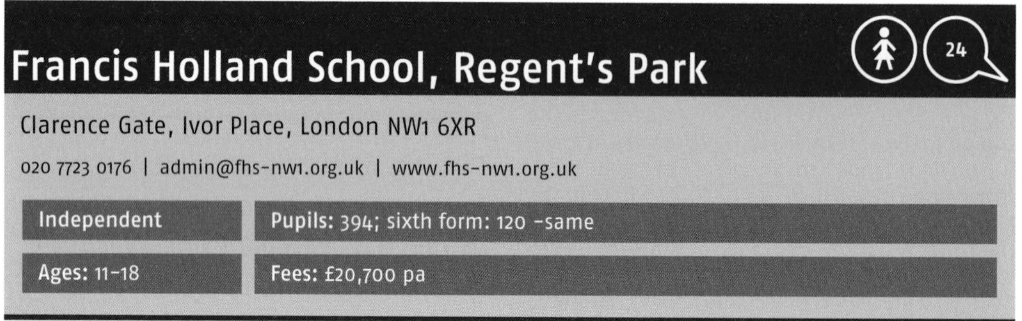

Francis Holland School, Regent's Park

Clarence Gate, Ivor Place, London NW1 6XR

020 7723 0176 | admin@fhs-nw1.org.uk | www.fhs-nw1.org.uk

Independent	Pupils: 394; sixth form: 120 -same
Ages: 11-18	Fees: £20,700 pa

Head: Since January 2016, Mr Charles Fillingham (early 40s). Urbane and very approachable, he exudes a calm pleasure in his role and the school. A modern linguist, with degrees from University of Wales, Bristol and King's London. His career has been spent between maintained schools and independent – he had a spell at the Grey Coat Hospital and was deputy at City of London School for Boys. He commutes from Surrey each day and spends what free time he can rescue with his wife and two young children, 'though I try still to read French literature'. Like so many other heads, a marathon runner. His three deputies are women: 'They are all in position entirely on merit – but it also really matters for the girls to have outstanding female role models.' Much liked by parents who were particularly wowed by his deftness and approachability in an Q&A session led by pupils very early in his tenure: 'he was easy, natural, and played fair.'

Entrance: At year 7, some 600 girls apply for just 75 places. Prospective parents are encouraged to come to an open morning during their daughter's year 5 or at the start of year 6. The school tries hard to make the essentially heartless business of selection as humane as it can. As part of the London 11+ Consortium, the process now consists of a cognitive ability test (rather than maths and English exams) with great emphasis on the interview. At sixth form, candidates are tested in their probable A level subjects as well as interviewed. At this point, there are usually around 20 places and about six successful applicants (but numbers are expanding in 2020).

Exit: Girls arrive from a whole range of feeders – 45 schools last year supplied 75 girls. Some two-thirds of the girls come from prep schools, the others from primaries or international schools abroad. Once they're in, Francis Holland sees it as an article of faith to stick by them, come what may, until A levels. In other words, indifferent performance at GCSE debars nobody from the sixth form: 'The gain in trust and goodwill outweighs any hit you may take in the league tables,' opines the head. Nearly all to Russell Group universities, including Durham and Bristol, plus several off to study art or drama. In 2020, 15 to Oxbridge and six medics. Others to a range of overseas destinations including University of British Columbia, Canada University of Pennsylvania USA, University of Notre Dame USA, NYU USA, Northeastern USA, McGill Canada, KU Leuven Belgium, Georgetown USA, Cornell USA, Dartmouth College USA, Amsterdam. 'The calibre of advice for those seeking entrance to US colleges is superb,' said one parent (though none off there this year): this is very often a source of grievance in independent schools, so – praise indeed.

Latest results: In 2020, 86 per cent 9/7 at GCSE: 63 per cent A*/A at A level (89 per cent A*/B). In 2019, 83 per cent 9-7 at GCSE: 53 per cent of A level grades at A*/A.

Teaching and learning: Punching in many ways well above its weight. Given that entrance is not nearly as academically selective as many, they're doing extremely well and across the full range of subjects. This wasn't always the case – a recent big hike in a couple of STEM subjects.

Mr Fillingham, not surprisingly, takes particular pleasure in the immense value-added over which the school presides. Many girls are outperforming their own expectations of themselves, and he's in no doubt why: 'Small classes, immensely hard-working and well-qualified teachers.' This sounds too good to be true, but parents back up the claims: 'totally committed teachers'; 'wonderful care when my daughter needed to work from home' etc. There's no arguing with results. There would appear to be a slight tilt towards the arts and humanities in terms of subjects being studied, but two girls went off to Imperial recently, six to study medicine and another dentistry. These successes have elicited pride and pleasure from both staff and pupils.

Equally telling, the school seems not to suffer from the level of attrition which has led bright and ambitious girls to move to chic co-ed sixth forms after GCSEs, with some 80 per cent staying on. 'We don't begrudge a girl her deserved success when she wins a place at another school,' says Mr Fillingham equably. 'We will miss her and wish her well.'

Modern languages are thriving in the school – everyone takes at least one for GCSE, and Mr Fillingham is now busily fundraising for the school to buy a house in France as a study centre.

The sensitive integration of pupils from a range of cultural backgrounds is part of the explanation for the school's academic success, which has undoubtedly been assisted by a high degree of staff retention. 'We're losing one member of staff after 42 years this summer,' says head, 'and will be the poorer for it.' He insists that his experience of older colleagues has been only positive and uplifting and that their diligence and enthusiasm has benefited staff as well as students.

This is an intensely musical school. On our walk round the school we passed a brass ensemble and a string trio, and as well as three orchestras and a jazz group

Learning support and SEN: The school's strengths in the classroom owe a good deal to unobtrusive but effective early intervention. There are three teachers dealing with pupils' special needs – often related to dyslexia and dyspraxia. 'All the girls who come here are pretty clever,' says the head, 'and so we ought to be able to help them manage these problems.' Although a number of girls don't speak English at home, the school has not had to make special provision for EAL.

The arts and extracurricular: This is an intensely musical school. On our walk round the school we passed a brass ensemble and a string trio, and as well as three orchestras and jazz group, there are also innumerable chamber groups and five choirs. Recent tours to Russia and the USA testify to music's popularity and another is now planned to China. The head is particularly pleased that the two Francis Holland schools (including the one in Sloane Square) recently shared a platform for a splendid concert, fruit of the work of both schools, to mark the founder's birthday. About two-thirds of the girls have instrumental or singing lessons – hence, the most recent big school production (The Sound of Music) seems to have a particular resonance. Photographs adorn the walls, and the memory is clearly fresh for all those lucky enough to participate or attend. Drama is also lively and very strong, with interform competitions for all years, and a dizzying array of short plays.

Masses of clubs ('and they actually meet,' said one parent): touring the school, it was easy to spot how easily and cheerfully engaged pupils seemed in all they were doing. The two art studios conveyed a special joie de vivre – lots of lunchtime and after-school activity goes on here as well – and pupils' work exhibits, in addition to drawing skills, plenty of exposure to different materials and textures.

'We have this mantra about being kind,' says Mr Fillingham, 'and it has to reflect a reality.' All sixth formers do volunteer work – sometimes at local primary schools or in local charity shops – and there is an annual Francis Holland Summer Camp in which pupils spend a residential week with other local children in the Westminster borough. Duke of Edinburgh Award is popular with many girls, and several continue it right through to gold. There's also music and reading with elderly people and with Swiss Cottage School, and a series of links with children's centres in Sri Lanka and Tanzania. A host of activities are also anchored around wider fundraising: the Help Fund raised £17,000 recently. 'There's a big spirit of giving back,' a parent said. 'It's made the school a much bigger deal in my eyes.'

Sport: Despite being located a stone's throw from Baker Street, the school takes sport seriously – and it shows: the place abounds with buzzy girls who exude the kind of energy which comes from plenty of exercise. It may help that Regent's Park is just across the road, and this allows pupils to make full use of the fact that central London is still full of green spaces.

There's a splendid swimming pool in the basement, which perhaps explains the fact that there is so much competitive swimming and water polo

'The sport is good, but not desperately competitive,' said one parent, 'which has been great for my daughter. She has got into teams which, at certain other schools, wouldn't have happened. And that was great for her.' Tennis and rounders are both flourishing and the netball and hockey teams went on a tour to South Africa last year. Hockey takes place a five-minute coach journey away at Paddington Recreation Ground and, for those of an equestrian bent, there are trips to the stables at Hyde Park. There's also a splendid swimming pool in the basement (the head has just extended opening hours) which perhaps explains the fact there is so much competitive swimming and water polo. The school also has a fitness suite and a gymnasium, and gymnastics is big news.

Ethos and heritage: The school was founded by Rev Francis Holland in 1878 and endowed with an uplifting motto, taken from Psalm 144, 'That our daughters may be as the polished corner of the temple'. There's a definite patina of that ecclesiastical temper in the building into which it moved in 1915, although nowadays, of course, everything is bright and lively. Still, architecture tells a story and it maintains close links with St Cyprian's Church across the way and still holds many concerts and services there.

The school's pride in confident and ambitious education is palpable, and the most important way this manifests itself is in an atmosphere which is effervescent and unstoppably cheerful. We're not talking about manic high spirits, but something purposeful and upbeat.

The environment supports this – and, in addition to its aesthetic advantages, the place looks intelligently cared for. There was no litter or graffiti (God forbid) and scarcely any mess, even in the sixth form common room. But everywhere buzzed and, while the place felt busy, we divined no sense of tension or crowding. Girls up to GCSE have a uniform – it's worn easily and properly, and the effect is reassuring rather than pompous. Sixth form girls dress 'as for their workplace' and seem to accept this without the need for too many standoffs. Rumours of gripes following a ban on wearing black trainers at school shows among some younger girls, but – in the words of the parent of an indignant daughter – 'that's all good growing-up stuff'.

'I think it's very telling,' another parent said, 'that the staff get along with each other so well. They work late; they turn up to watch plays and concerts; they compete at school quizzes. It's a community which functions.'

Pastoral care, inclusivity and discipline: There are thoughtful systems in place to harness the abundant goodwill one sees. Every girl has a form tutor who is in turn supported by a deputy, and any concerns are fed through to a head of year and to the pastoral deputy head. There are no houses – formal competition within the school tends to be inter-form. Like most schools which aren't too large, they capitalise on the strength that virtually every pupil is well known to several teachers, and anxieties and inconsistencies are usually quickly picked up. A counsellor also visits on three days a week to provide collateral support. There are a range of opportunities for pupils to shine, starting with a head girl and a small cohort of deputies, as well as a school council. One of the head's recent innovations has been arranging for senior girls to read routine announcements at assembly ('quite empowering, actually,' he reflected).

Parents welcome the clarity of the system and the commitment offered by staff as well. 'London girls can be quite feisty,' one parent reflected, 'and the school offers early and thoughtful engagement when there are problems.' Although there is a system of detentions in place (usually for lateness), the head is emphatic that the girls are sympathetic company and very reasonable. There have been no exclusions, temporary or otherwise, in recent times

Pupils and parents: Lots of communication with parents. There are six sets of reports a year, which sounds like overkill, but the head believes that 'calm, regular, communication serves everyone best', and there is also at least one parents' evening annually per year group. 'Very often, both parents do demanding jobs, so the feedback is essential,' he adds.

Francis Holland attracts what, if poorly managed, could be a challenging constituency of parents, in which the elite professions (lawyers and bankers in profusion) are generously represented. The head insists: 'We enjoy the loyalty of all, and we try to return it in willingly – and even-handedly.' And that loyalty seems to extend to one of the school's most famous alumna, Joan Collins.

Money matters: Fees are mid-range relative to London, and the school tries hard to ensure there are as few extras as possible. Special trips are billed separately, as are music, yoga and speech and drama lessons. A recent change has been to ensure no extra charge is made for books ('a useful discipline for all of us,' comments the head). Lunch, about which we received glowing opinions, is also part of the package. There are a good range of scholarships at 11+ and 16+ for academic, musical and artistic excellence. There are also a number of bursaries, depending on individual needs and circumstances.

The last word: A distinguished school which communicates sanity, high standards and sterling example. Teachers and pupils talk easily in classrooms and in corridors – men and women alike – and seem to enjoy one another. Mr Fillingham evidently relishes his work: 'Frankly, I find the people with whom I work – staff, pupils and parents – easy to like and impossible not to admire.'

Francis Holland School, Sloane Square

25

39 Graham Terrace, London SW1W 8JF

020 7730 2971 | registrar@fhs-sw1.org.uk | www.fhs-sw1.org.uk

Independent | Pupils: 559; sixth form: 93

Ages: 11-18 | Fees: £21,600 pa

Linked school: Francis Holland Junior School, Sloane Square, 130

Headmistress: Since 2012, Lucy Elphinstone MEd PGCE FRSA (50s). Previously five years as head of sixth form at Downe House. Unlike her daughter, who wanted to be a unicorn when she grew up (now a successful children's author), Mrs E's dream was to be a poet 'and sit in a romantic cottage.' Hadn't expected to end up teaching in central London but parents thank their lucky stars she did. No sign of contemplative existence so far but seems to have packed in at least four lives in the time most of us take to work through just one.

As role models go, her ability to take what life throws at her and flourish triumphantly could hardly be bettered. Read English at Cambridge, went into book trade straight from university in the 80s, first in publishing and then book sales.

Married life in an ice cold house in Scotland followed. Entertaining the hunting and fishing crowd – 'was an expert on lice on salmon' – wasn't quite enough ('a girl needs a little more') so took up ghost writing, notching up six books and four babies in the 1990s and simultaneously running a B&B. Educational career kickstarted by friend's invitation to take over Montessori nursery. Sold it to a prep school, staying on and completing teaching training after its successful integration, and was invited to join Scottish Schools Council to advise others on how to do the same.

After rapid promotion at the prep (head of English, director of studies) moved to St Michael's School near Barnstaple in 2000 as director of studies, then to Fettes in 2001 (English teacher and director of drama), head of English at King's College, Taunton in 2003 and Downe House in 2007, before being invited to apply for the post here, attracted by school's reputation for happiness and kindness as well as religious dimension – her faith is very important to her.

Universally reckoned by parents to be the force behind school's rise in popularity. She's 'inspirational'. 'Empowering.' 'The most impressive thing [about the school].' 'Has an amazing energy, she literally crackles as she walks.' (Generally felt to be highly energising for all, similar energy levels probably a must-have to avoid feeling overpowered.)

What's she looking for when considering a new pupil? Parents like the way that don't have to conform to a type here. 'Lucy Elphinstone encourages the girls to be themselves and as a group they embrace that, and I like that very much,' said mother.

The headmistress 'truly, truly cares about the girls – fantastic ethos that girls can be anything, do anything and go anywhere as long as they give it a go'

Ethos has totally changed under her watch. 'Way she runs it is completely different.' 'Truly, truly cares about the girls – fantastic ethos that girls can be anything, do anything and go anywhere as long as they give it a go.' Results, applications and mood are all up. Numbers have grown. 'About as many as we can fit in – just don't open any cupboards,' says the head.

She's also a firm believer in approach advocated in Educating Ruby, which calls for a rethink of teaching and emphasis on creativity and collaboration needed to prepare for future world (has given all staff a copy).

Whatever the future throws at these pupils, initiatives from impressive entrepreneurship scheme to DIY sessions run by the maintenance team in what would have been the boiler room (small groups of girls are learning to fix taps, unblock pipes and wire lamps – parents and staff petitioning for own classes) are designed to give them the skills (and, more importantly, the right mindset) to succeed.

Staff, to a man and woman notably (and sometimes unstoppably) enthusiastic about the school, appeared to be thriving under snap, crackle and pop of Mrs E's leadership. She, in turn, praises a senior leadership team 'to die for'. 'Girls can't be happy unless the staff are,' she says.

What was she like to work for, we asked her? 'Tiring,' she said, without missing a beat. 'But it's such fun here.'

Entrance: Results suggest ultra selectivity. Not so, says the school, which prides itself on mixed intake, fab teaching and excellent value added. Now scaling up the facilities to accommodate extra numbers in style. At 11+ takes around a third from own prep school (unusually, given that prep is on the premises, remains a stepping off point for majority of 11-year-olds). Numbers joining the sixth form rising steadily – now up to 17. 'We wanted to grow sixth form,' says head.

Looking for child who is curious, not crammed, has love of learning and sense of fun, but shy and confident children will flourish. Shy child 'will find love and be encouraged to be braver than they feel.'

Exit: In past years, around half would leave post-16. Now down to about five. If pupils 'throw themselves into it' school will tailor workload (might reduce GCSEs – currently need at least six GCSEs with top grades to make the sixth form). University destinations mostly Russell Group/redbrick, with occasional Oxbridge (four in 2020). Durham, Edinburgh, Exeter, Hull, KCL, Oxford, Royal Holloway UCL, University of West of England and Bristol recently popular. Four medics in 2020, plus several overseas – Chapman University, Duke University, Georgetown University and Sciences Pro (Paris).

Latest results: In 2020, 89 per cent 9/7 at GCSE; 63 per cent A*/A (87 per cent A*/B). In 2019, 89 per cent 9-7 at GCSE; 48 per cent A*/A at A level (75 per cent A*-B).

Teaching and learning: In the past, prep school pupils were guaranteed automatic entrance to seniors, something that, says school, did nothing to boost either standards or reputation. 'Meant we were simply seen as the safe bet,' says school. Now, just about everything in the garden is whizzy.

Value added is excellent – 1.5 GCSE grades, 'far higher than you'd expect from a school like ours,' though head stresses that 'we don't want academic sausages – should have love of learning and sense of fun.'

Have accordingly reduced GCSEs to nine (do fewer, better and have more time left over for everything else), bringing financial awareness, DIY, self-defence and first aid into years 10 and 11.

Most girls – normal exceptions for medic hopefuls and further maths enthusiasts – take maximum of three A levels plus EPQ and enrichment programme. 'One hundred per cent better,' says sixth former. 'New A levels are harder and stressful – course has just got bigger.'

From a year 10 geography lesson with girls memorably considering glacier action as akin to eyebrow shaping ('scree... moving down the valley and plucking') – to supportive drama lesson – year 8 pupils quick to praise effort as well as achievements of others ('Really good, you created a really emotional atmosphere') – engagement in learning is impressive.

Aided by tutor system (ratio one to 12 pupils in lower and upper schools, eight to one in sixth form) plus director of studies who is accessible and 'makes a big effort,' said parent, as do mainly highly regarded teachers, supplemented by plenty of trips, German to Cologne, history of art to Venice.

STEM in particular is going great guns, with much to enhance the appeal, from own magazine to lively science notice boards. There's Yogi Bear as you've never seen him before, digestive system bared to the world (but still smiling); gory looking science safety instructions – girl clutching blood-bespattered bandaged eye, 'always wear safety glasses' (we probably will after this...). A stand out subject, said parent. 'Haven't had a bad teacher.'

Highlight in one of older labs (most thoroughly modernised with sci-fi style high gloss units splashed with primary colours) is animal corner, featuring gerbils, Fluffy the chinchilla, Bobby the tortoise and a corn snake.

Parents generally delighted, only query relating to dips in maths staffing (school's most popular subject) – down to promotions elsewhere (one headship, one deputy) and some staff illness, says head.

We flagged up parents' feedback about widespread tutoring, something that – surely – must undo school's positive messages about building confidence and learning independence. 'I'd say we're in the minority [in not having a tutor],' said one mother who wondered how – if so widespread – it affected the school's exam results.

While head cites supports academic mentoring, which helps girls 'to understand how brains work' and can reinforce learning, sees long term tutoring as 'completely unnecessary and dispiriting – we talk about it constantly.' School's approach is to 'develop strong children, so parents don't feel they need tutors'.

Learning support and SEN: Reasonable number of pupils have SEN – around 90, with 52 receiving extra support. Needs include autism (one gifted pupil airlifted from state school and currently working two years ahead) and specific learning difficulties (particular interest of head's – has first hand experience of dyslexia as a parent). Bottom line is that though have upped the support team (to approval of inspectors), have finite resources so 'will take as many pupils as have staff for'.

The arts and extracurricular: When Mrs E first arrived, there were three clubs: pottery, chess and needlework; now 114. Only niggle here is occasional last-minute communications – parents can suddenly receive an email on Thursday or Friday announcing meeting on a Monday about new activity. 'Have got better but still happens,' said parent. 'Not everybody is not at work.'

School's commitment to entrepreneurship is impressive – and unmissable. It's compulsory in the sixth form where 'every single girl sets up a business and works on real life industry problems,' says school, which recently appointed its own director of creative enterprise.

STEM is going great guns, with lively science notice boards. There's Yogi Bear as you've never seen him before, digestive system bared to the world (but still smiling)

His palpable enthusiasm is infectious; pupils' ideas for new businesses range from dog pods (safe haven/spa while owner goes shopping – ideal for SW1, possibly limited appeal elsewhere) to ethical, plastic-free makeup range – creator impressively committed to launch. Can also spark thinking that goes far, far, beyond Knightsbridge – girls recently won international competition to design lunar settlement.

Excellent opportunities to be involved in music and drama. Teachers are of the quirky enthusiast variety and hugely respected for devoting large chunk of their free time to making things happen. 'Phenomenal' music department 'give up so much of their own time to do extra stuff with the pupils,' said parent. Talented singers could end up performing at St Paul's Cathedral, Windsor Castle or Oxbridge College with the choir. Single minded head of drama expects everyone to share commitment. 'As far as he's concerned, drama is what they're there for and nothing else.'

Sport: Most sports played in Battersea Park and while it's an important part of school life, 'more of a have-a-go mindset,' thought pupil, upside is that everyone gets a game – 'We're happy with getting the occasional win' – while it can mean more, not fewer sporting opportunities as more girls are likely to be selected for teams. 'Daughter is an avid netball player and I feel gets more play than perhaps she would in a bigger school,' said parent. School describes sport as a huge strength. 'We are highly competitive and have repeatedly been regional champions in netball, hockey and swimming,' says head.

Numerous sports tours (netball to Barbados and South Africa). Most of top sports players notch up achievements out of school. Elite squad, with own noticeboard, includes swimming, fencing and ice skating stars – all well supported. 'Allowed to miss school for events; can replace school sport for training.' said sixth former.

Otherwise, sixth formers have one sports session a week, from team games (netball) to popular self-defence, pilates and fitness suite/gym. PE, unsurprisingly, a popular GCSE.

Ethos and heritage: Perhaps appropriately for a school that espouses resilience (has faced closure threats several times over its official history), it is called 'The school that refused to die'.

Though bears the name of Francis Holland, Canon of Canterbury Cathedral, school owes existence to his wife Sibylla. Opened 1881 in what become Eaton Terrace and moved to current site three years later, when added co-ed kindergarten (attended by both Laurence Olivier and Tony Benn). Progressive – started entering girls for public exams in 1882.

After a couple of building moves, settled in current premises (and still has the original doorbell to prove it). Now a 'bigger, grander school than it was when we started here,' said parent – though retains Church of England values. Worries about size tend to disappear once daughters start here. 'Small, intimate natur ... suits her,' said parent, who had thought that scale might be just too diminutive.

School recently expanded, with new sixth form centre to open in November 2020. (Expansion has been achieved with commendably little effect on day-to-day life. 'Managed very well... doesn't seem to have impacted at all,' said parent.)

Not half as bijou as surroundings – pretty (and pricey) little houses just round the back of Sloane Square – might suggest. Most senior and junior school buildings, some double layered and cunningly extended (creates odd anomaly where stay on same level but move to different floor when cross from junior to senior buildings) form rectangle round decent sized playground, and every facility is full sized – nothing cut down and many generous as to space and number. Art particularly impressive – runs to four rooms, including one for photography, results uniformly impressive, from introspective self-portraits to textiles beautifully printed with tile-inspired patterns.

Site spick and span bar odd pre-lunch drop and run pile of school bags. Girls very smart in their blue uniform – delighted that request to wear trousers was heard. No dress code for sixth formers online – assumed will make appropriate choices, and they do. Can also use main school entrance – 'much quicker' – and have lunch in common room, part of attractively refurbished building that includes a work room.

Size of school means 'no one goes under the radar,' head says. There's 'a culture of support, care and love – pupils do look out for one another and come and tell us'

Newly completed wavy and wonderful building (tipped to win design awards) is not a library with extras but a centre of creative learning, though full of books and places to perch and read. Librarian, who appears to be a centre of creativity all on her own and has fund of fabulous anecdotes (ask about the owl that made 2am bid for freedom on Harry Potter sleepover night), stresses that will remain a library in her eyes.

Location, though wonderful in many respects, can be a disadvantage when it comes to links with other schools. 'Girls are a little isolated socially,' said mother. 'It's normal and healthy at this stage and wish my daughter had a bit more of it.' Work in progress, says school. Recently had two boys who auditioned for school play but pulled out. 'Think we may frighten them,' says head.

Only other slight difference of opinion was over the school lunches. Website stresses that all food prepared on site and highlights 'legendary' cookies, though not all parents are currently feeling the love. 'Daughter hates it,' said one. Girls we spoke to were polite without gushing. School's view is that all delicious but a tad on the sophisticated side (salmon, quinoa and giant couscous feature) for palates in training.

Pastoral care, inclusivity and discipline: Care for older girls (school felt to be slightly over preoccupied with makeup and skirt length in younger years – 'don't feel they have emphasis in the right place,' thought parent) is excellent. Led by a two-strong team who are 'both wonderful,' said parent. Deputy head comes in for biggest plaudits. 'Can't praise him enough.'

School emphasises 'growth mindset – trying to see that getting things wrong is a way of learning,' said pupil, with Mrs Elphinstone setting a cracking example by regularly discussing her own failures. 'I'm a perfectionist,' said senior pupil. 'In year 7, would stress if I got something wrong. Now if I do badly in a chemistry test, I'll know it's because I didn't do enough work.'

Bullying does happen – inevitable, reckon parents – though there is a counsellor, and attitude of the girls goes a long way towards helping to sort things out. 'Girls are not angels but the vast majority are very nice and supportive of each other,' said parent. 'Tend to self-police in my daughter's year.'

Counselling via Place2Be (one of very few senior independents to use it) focuses on early identification and early intervention to stop girls reaching 'terribly dark place,' says head. Have had experience of eating disorders, some pupils hospitalised, 'now thriving'. Sympathetic to transgender pupils – though 'not greatly affected so far,' says the head. Size of school means 'no one goes under the radar,' she says. There's 'a culture of support, care and love – pupils do look out for one another and come and tell us.'

Support includes just-added therapy dog (allergy friendly) and training for teachers so they can support parents, who can be in denial. 'Still a stigma about mental illness,' says head. Girls trained as mentors but – most importantly – encouraged to look out for each other, and do, say parents. 'Teachers really know you – much closer community,' said pupil previously at highly selective school who felt far more at home here.

Head so far has suspended one girl but not asked anyone to leave and no-one would get the heave ho for poor academic performance as long as effort, punctuality and attendance all line up.

Pupils and parents: Mistake to assume that this is entitlement central. Location inevitably attracts strong cohort of Belgravians but parents stress that other areas are represented and postcode doesn't equate to overweening sense of privilege. Some parents are involved with the church, there's a thriving bursary programme, support for charities for needy locals in Westminster and Lambeth (we're steering well clear of any jokes involving politicians or senior religious figures) and a big enough percentage of pupils come in from surrounding areas including Wimbledon and Twickenham.

Admittedly, we're not talking substantial social deprivation – 'Even the cost of the uniform is fairly significant, so the chances are that they will come from a relatively affluent background,' said parent – but it's 'not as Belgravia as you might think,' and it's a friendly place to be, not just for pupils but for parents, too. Tradition tends to dominate – dads go off to work, mums lead the socialising.

Pupils 'make lovely friends. There are some slightly spoiled girls around as there are in all central London private schools in my opinion but it has never been an issue for us.'

One mother felt school was far more convivial than daughter's prep school had ever been. 'Have made some very good friends that will stay in touch with when she leaves.'

Sense of community summed up during our visit by team of gardening enthustiasts (one the mother of a teacher) planting out first of many trenches at the playground at lunchtime. Hours later, they'd were still going strong. 'We're the eco-warriors,' said one.

The last word: Increasingly a first-choice school for parents in search of approach that's caring but not cushioned, arts and creativity focused but also academically rigorous. Girls can even put your flat pack furniture together. Who could possibly want more?

Grafton Primary School

26

Eburne Road, Holloway, London N7 6AR

020 7272 3284 | graftonschool@grafton.islington.sch.uk | www.graftonschool.co.uk

State | Ages: 3-11 | Pupils: 488

Head: Since 1993, Mrs Nitsa Sergides OBE (awarded in 2012 for services to education), 60s. Qualified as a teacher in 1973, followed by 19 years of teaching at another local school. Became deputy head of Grafton Primary in 1991, and head two years later.

Cypriot born Nitsa (as everyone calls her) is the embodiment of Mediterranean warmth. Her pupils adore her, 'lovely to all of us, talks to us like family.' Her teachers are loyal and parents marvel at her dedication: 'She's quite amazing, her enthusiasm never wanes and she genuinely wants the best for everybody.' 'She is truly exceptional. Apart from her incredibly nurturing side, she has a gift of being able to get hold of every resource going for the school.' An iron fist inside the glove, we are told.

Nitsa came to the UK at the age of 13 with teaching firmly on her radar; 'I think I was 7 when I realised that's what I wanted to be.' Now in her third decade at Grafton School ('they'll have to wheel me out') – she still wants to make a difference. 'I believe that children must be given every chance to succeed regardless of background or ethnicity. We try to create opportunities some pupils may not otherwise have.' This could be a yearly trip to the coast (which for some pupils is their first experience of the sea), or the chance to learn a musical instrument.

One of Nitsa's proudest achievements is that she hasn't had to exclude a child for 20 years, 'I always believe more in preventative measures rather than reactive measures.' She also believes that, given the correct guidance, inner-city schools can be as good as any: 'My three children were all products of Islington comprehensives. My son is now a neurosurgeon and both my daughters were barristers.'

Married for 46 years to an engineer, 'my bouncing board', she loves visiting art galleries and museums and spending time with her grandchildren. Such is her infectious enthusiasm and witty comments like: 'As I said to the Queen...' (referring to when she received her OBE). We left her office grinning (and stuffed from all the pastries plied on us!)

Entrance: Standard local authority criteria of siblings, proximity to school and children in care etc. Competition for places is fierce – roughly 354 applicants for 60 places yearly with more than 100 on the waiting list. As word spreads about this school there is concern about wealthier parents buying property in now trendy Holloway to get their kids a place, with predictable consequences for Grafton's diversity.

Exit: Mixed bag on offer for secondary schools in the Islington area. Most go on to Acland Burghley (if they live close enough), Highbury Fields, Highbury Grove, Mount Carmel school for girls, St Mary Magdalene or others including AMSI, Central Foundation Boys' School, Camden School for Girls, Highgate Wood, Parliament Hill, Beacon High and William Ellis. A few try for grammars like Latymer or Dame Alice Owen or independents such as City of London.

Our view: A tricky one to find, Grafton Primary sits adjacent to the Holloway Road, off Seven Sisters Road, accessible by car via a tiny slip road. Most pupils walk to school thereby avoiding the perils of Holloway's one-way system.

Pupils told us they have friends from many different cultures and it's like 'one big family'. Definitely a sense of unity and loyalty as well as pride in this school

We were expecting great things and we weren't disappointed. Rated outstanding by Ofsted for the past 15 years and awarded the title of Beacon School, Grafton defies its demographics. A staggering 55-60 per cent of its pupils would qualify for free school meals (although in Islington, these are fully funded for all pupils), 35 per cent of children have SEN, 13 per cent of whom have an ECHP. One parent we spoke to said that the support her son receives for his special needs is amazing: 'the dedicated SENco person is wonderful, super responsive and very dedicated. My son loves going to school.' The school even created a sensory room last year in response to the needs of a particular child and is now used for a number of children with sensory needs throughout the school.

Grafton is genuinely inclusive – big on equal opps for pupils with disabilities and a vast ethnic mix. It is a school that doesn't shy away from the difficult cases and there is a real focus on the individual need. 'We don't discard children. If they are out, they are at risk,' says the head.

Grafton is a teaching school, meaning that it trains teachers and support staff from other primaries. It is also one of only a few pioneering schools to have been chosen to introduce the CAME maths programme (Cognitive Acceleration through Mathematics Education). Maths is already a very strong subject at Grafton with, most recently, a pass rate of 83 per cent, well above the national average of 79 per cent.

On entering, one is immediately struck by the spectacularly colourful lobby. Rarely have we seen so much artwork, sculpture, ceiling displays (including a wonderful tree of life installation which ran the length of the lobby and through the school's office). Artsmark commented that 'it is evident that creatives are at the heart of the school.' Grafton has partnerships with art professionals, a specialist art and design teacher and an artist in residence, believing that time given to creative subjects helps children achieve in other areas.

The interior of the school is charming, if a little cramped (could be because every inch of space is covered with student displays). The Victorian building is DDA compliant and has a lift for wheelchair users. A £3.5m refurb means all classrooms are now up to spec and there is a relatively new sports hall and reception play area.

Outside is an oasis of calm – amazing, considering proximity to the very urban and not very pretty Seven Sisters Road. Grounds are fairly large for an inner-city school and in addition to the playground there is a quiet, formal garden with benches for students to have lunch and read and a wildlife garden. This mini ecosystem with pond and bug hotel feels a million miles from the city. At the end of the wildlife garden is a wonderful new outhouse building (in its final touches during our visit) which will be used as dedicated space for art, science and music. Fully insulated and equipped with toilet and cooking facilities too.

Plans are also underway for a new 'green wall' to be installed near the entrance to the school, which will be two vertical fences with various climbers growing in-between, in a bid to combat pollution from the Seven Sisters Road. The school is also in discussion with the local authority, to prevent cars from driving near the school apart from one hour in the morning and one at the end of the day.

In the assembly hall we were treated to a music assembly in Swahili, just one of the 34 languages spoken here. On site translators assist parents from the three main non-English speaking groups – Somalian, Turkish and Bangladeshi, and the school told us, 'We do what we can to make parents from all sectors of society feel included.'

The pupils we met were a highly articulate bunch – happy, confident and engaging. They loved their school and the opportunities it offered. One told us, 'England cricket captain Eoin Morgan came to talk to us and author Rob Lloyd Jones has done writing workshops with us which were amazing and inspiring.' 'Even Sadiq Kahn visited!' It seems that a lot of good will is poured into this school.

Pupils also told us how they have friends from many different cultures and it's like 'one big family'. Others praised the cricket and football at the school. A few negative comments about the lunches (free for all pupils) and for some the only cooked meal they'll get in a day.

A parent told us, 'The school is amazing at being proactive, especially with day trips. If they're not hopping on the bus to St Paul's Cathedral, visiting the zoo or going to art galleries and museums, they're doing a walking tour around London. That's the benefit of being so inner city with free bus travel.'

The quality of teaching came in for particular praise. One mother told us: 'My older children go to private schools and I know that the teaching my youngest is getting here is better than they received at her age.' Another said 'a high ratio of staff to pupils, as good, if not better than at some independent schools.' Very low turnover of staff which is unusual for a London school – and those who do leave often come back. 'One big family,' we are told, and there is definitely a sense of unity and loyalty as well as pride in this school.

The last word: Parents are extremely happy with this inclusive, aspirational and caring school. One parent did mention that she would like more sporting activities within the school day as opposed to just afternoon clubs, but added that the Grafton school day is such a busy one, she's not sure where they would fit it in anyway.

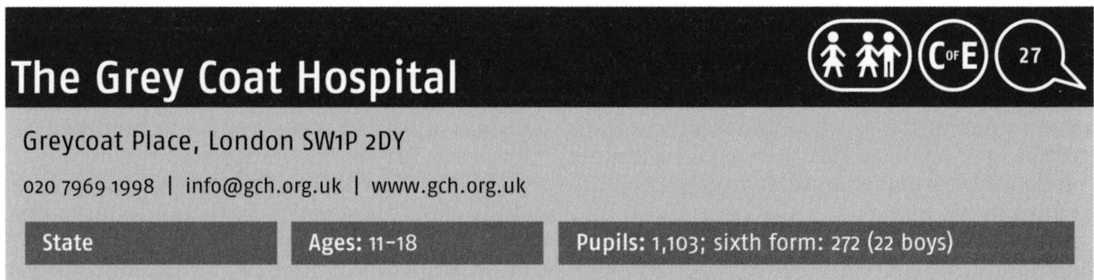

Headteacher: Since January 2020, Susanne Staab. Previously head at Norton Knatchbull School in Kent since 2010, followed by a sabbatical. Subject specialisms are history and politics, both subjects that she still teaches. She has 24 years of teaching and leadership experience spanning the selective, non-selective and independent sectors and is also a trained OFSTED inspector.

Entrance: Huge catchment area from the dioceses of London and Southwark. Pupils travel from as far away as Essex and Kent and are rarely local.

Total of 151 places offered in year 7. Fifteen language places (following an aptitude test which 450 sit); 88 CofE places; 28 other church places; 20 open places.

Priority given to looked-after children, then siblings, church attendance for church places and a distance tie-breaker. The comprehensive intake is placed into bands following an assessment test – 25 per cent places to band 1, 50 per cent places to band 2 and 25 per cent to band 3.

Relatively little movement of pupils. 'We are a very stable population,' says the bursar. Once pupils are here, they tend to stay put, even if it means travelling long distances. In-year admissions are dealt with by the local authority. A few boys in sixth form, all 'charming', according to one member of staff.

Exit: Around a third leave after GCSEs, usually for schools closer to home or offering subjects not available here. Their places are taken by a fresh intake. Around 90 per cent go on to higher education. School encourages pupils to aim for top universities and some 40 per cent go to Russell Group universities as well as art colleges. Popular destinations include Oxbridge (nine places in 2020), Exeter, St Andrews, Leeds, Durham, Nottingham, Bristol and Manchester. Popular subjects include medicine (four medics in 2020), sciences, maths, English, religious studies and classics. Art foundation courses and apprenticeships also popular.

Latest results: In 2020, 57 per cent 9-7 at GCSE; 92 per cent 9-4 in both maths and English. At A level, 50 per cent A*/A (76 per cent A*-B). In 2019 (the last year when exams took place), 45 per cent 9-7 at GCSE; 73 per cent 9-5 in both English and maths. At A level, 36 per cent A*/A (36 per cent A*-B).

Teaching and learning: School is regularly rated outstanding by Ofsted. Also regularly receives congratulatory letters from schools minister praising pupils and staff for attainment and progress as one of the top 100 non-selective state schools in the country. Has also won local awards for the success and value-added progress of its disadvantaged pupils.

Good range of subjects on offer to GCSE, including Latin and business studies and Pre-U offered in Latin, Greek and art history, all of which are taught at neighbouring Westminster School. Girls take between nine and 11 GCSEs. 'The pupils love their lessons at Westminster,' says school. A level subjects include film studies and sociology as well as more traditional fare. Biology, chemistry, maths, English, history, psychology and religious studies currently very popular. EPQ is becoming increasingly fashionable.

Grey Coat is a specialist language college and has an outward-looking, global focus. 'We encourage an international outlook as well as strong grades,' says school. 'It is important for our students to gain an understanding of other countries and cultures and to have an open and inclusive approach, as well as to develop their linguistic skills.' All students study Spanish and a second modern language (French or German). Many continue with two foreign languages to GCSE. Opportunities to study Japanese out of school hours. Japanese exchange offered to girls in year 10; longest standing exchange trip to Germany in the country since 1952 and very successful exchange trip to Spain.

International May Fair for younger pupils is an annual highlight. Students are encouraged to represent a country – through fashion, food, dance, ecology and culture. The competition is judged by staff and the prize, awarded to the most impressive tutor group, is a trip to an outdoor activity centre. School is excellent at offering incentives to pupils; girls are encouraged to be competitive. Pupils regularly win local and national science and maths competitions.

A specialist language college with an outward-looking, global focus. 'We encourage an international outlook as well as strong grades,' says school

Average class size is 27, with a maximum of 30. No setting in year 7. Year 8 pupils set for English, maths, science and languages.

Learning support and SEN: Grey Coat prides itself on being an inclusive school. SEND pupils make good progress academically and are fully involved in school life. All year 7 girls are screened for learning difficulties on entry to school. Small support groups for literacy, numeracy and social skills run at lunchtime for younger girls. Five per cent have a statement of special educational needs. Gifted and talented extension programmes in place for more able.

The arts and extracurricular: Creative subjects taken seriously. Excellent facilities in art and design; these remain very popular subjects and the quality of art displays is very high. 'The standard of art work is mind-blowing,' according to one parent. Music and drama both strong.

The American School in London

Instrumental and singing lessons are subsidised by school's foundation. Good range of choirs, bands, string and jazz groups and orchestra. Several concerts every year. Successful gospel choir recently reached semi-finals of BBC's School Choir of the Year competition.

Roughly 15 pupils a year achieve DofE gold award. Good spread of clubs, including maths challenge, debating, football, trampolining and creative writing. External inspirational speakers come in regularly to motivate and encourage the girls. Workshops led by outsiders a regular feature of the education offered here. School takes part in BBC News School Report, enabling pupils to make their own news reports for a live audience. Students develop their journalistic skills and have a ball.

School occupies two fabulous buildings in the heart of Westminster. Strikingly beautiful building in Greycoat Place, freshly painted and polished

Lots of time for fun here too. Talent show at the end of the Easter term is eagerly anticipated while staff pantomime is apparently 'the best day' of the school year. 'It's absolutely hilarious watching the teachers,' said one pupil. Post-GCSE celebration for year 11s includes a fashion show of their textiles work.

Sport: Good level of participation in wide variety of sport. 'We are the Westminster sports champions in practically everything and we provide a rich variety of sports,' we were told. Opportunities for fencing, squash, indoor rowing and athletics as well as team sports. Currently Westminster netball champions. 'We've struggled a bit with athletics as we have to bus the pupils over to Battersea Park,' admits bursar. Massive sports hall at Regency Street site. Annual gym and dance display.

Ethos and heritage: Originally founded for boys in 1698. In 1706, Queen Anne granted the Grey Coat Hospital Foundation a royal charter and her portrait hangs in pride of place in the Great Hall. Original wooden boards detailing the names and donations of 18th century benefactors line the stairs. In 1874 Grey Coat Hospital became a girls' school, under church management.

A CofE school, Christian values play a key part at Grey Coat. Church services held each term either in Westminster Abbey or St Margaret's, including a July celebration to which new pupils (and their parents) are invited. 'It's a lovely event – beautifully done,' said a parent. Confirmation services take place at Westminster Abbey and school has its own chaplain.

School occupies two fabulous buildings in the heart of Westminster, huge quantity of traffic and people encircling it on the streets outside. Strikingly beautiful building in Greycoat Place, freshly painted and polished. Statuettes of Grey Coat boy and girl adorn the front façade of the school. Wonderful entrance hall, glistening with trophies and artwork. School celebrates the achievements of the girls at every opportunity.

Original building at Greycoat Place is used by the younger pupils (years 7 to 9) but lots of coming and going of pupils from one site to another. Fantastic new arts wing includes swish drama studios where recent productions have included The Tempest and The Winter's Tale. 'Drama is a subject that is taken very seriously at Grey Coat and the performances are very professional,' we were told. Facilities hired out to National Youth Theatre in holidays.

Welcoming staff. Healthy female/male ratio and mix of long-servers and newly qualified teachers. Variable staff turnover.

Symbiotic relationship with Westminster School. Grey Coats go there for lectures, some lessons and Oxbridge preparation, while graduate trainee teachers from Westminster come here to gain experience of teaching in a state school. 'It's wonderful for our students that they have these opportunities and they seize every opportunity,' says school.

Old Greys include MP Dr Rosena Allin-Khan, TV presenter Sarah Greene and Tamsin Dunwoody. A more recent leaver is Ebony-Jewel Rainford-Brent, the first Black female cricketer to play for the England team (she presented awards at a recent prize-giving). Many old girls remain loyal to the school and return to the annual school celebration service in Westminster Abbey each year and to the year 12 orientation day.

Pastoral care, inclusivity and discipline: Pastoral care is a major strength of the school. Each girl is part of a tutor group family and a year group family. Strict code of conduct, but relatively few behavioural issues here. Older girls are given plenty of responsibility, with 40 prefects in final year. Girls can become ambassadors for their year group in years 9 and 11, having successfully explained at interview why they should be chosen. 'There is a strong sense of community here,' says school. 'We have ambassadors, peer counsellors, and older students working with younger pupils. It's about creating a sense that we're all in this together.' It certainly seems to

Staff pantomime is apparently 'the best day' of the school year. 'It's absolutely hilarious watching the teachers,' said one pupil

be working well. A learning mentor is on hand to help girls organise themselves if needed, as well as a drop-in school nurse.

Girls start off in smaller, lower school – helps them cope better with the progression to upper school. 'It's rare to hear of anyone being miserable here,' a parent told us. 'The school keeps a close eye on its pupils and intervenes quickly if things are going awry.'

Food thought to be 'very good, with lots of choice,' according to one pupil. Vast quantities of pizzas being eaten at break on the day we visited. Oyster card system in place so girls don't need to carry money and the canteen is open from breakfast onwards. School is confident that 'we'd know if a girl wasn't eating.'

School is justifiably proud of the excellent attendance record of 98 per cent throughout the year – rating it the third highest in the UK. 'All our pupils came in when the recent tube strike was on.' Pupils with 100 per cent attendance and punctuality for a year get a trip to the theatre.

Pupils and parents: 'A real mix,' we were told. Twenty-eight per cent of pupils eligible for pupil premium. Two-thirds from minority ethnic groups. A third whose first language is not English – more than 50 languages spoken at home, including Yoruba, Swahili, Spanish, French and Dutch.

Big inner-city blend of families, including daughters of politicians and education professionals. School recently hit the headlines with the news that prominent politicians are sending their daughters here.

Money matters: Parents' Guild raises money each year for both the school and charity. Recently paid for a beautiful stained-glass window by Michael Coles. Parents are asked to contribute a small amount of money on a monthly or annual basis.

The last word: A sensational mix of high academic standards strongly supported by caring and devoted staff. No wonder they are prepared to travel for hours each day to be part of this buzzing school. The girls we met were charming, articulate, interesting and purposeful. Their pride in the school was striking. Not only are they ambitious and successful but they're also happy. On the day we visited, groups of girls were sitting cross-legged on the tarmac playground at break time, chatting and laughing as though they didn't have a care in the world.

Halcyon London International School

28

33 Seymour Place, London W1H 5AU

020 7258 1169 | join@halcyonschool.com | www.halcyonschool.com

Independent	Pupils: 158; sixth form: 58
Ages: 11–18	Fees: £26,961– £27,486 pa

Director: Since 2015, Barry Mansfield (50s); studied history at Nottingham and did his PGCE at UEA (history and English). His first teaching job was in an international school in Athens, followed by Nairobi, then Dubai, becoming head of English and learning about IB schools. He worked in Sofia Antipolis in France, then Jeddah, where he set up the diploma programme, before teaching in Bern International School in Switzerland (and setting up the MYP) while simultaneously doing an MA (Open University) in educational leadership.

All that IB experience fits very firmly with his commitment to the ideology of students as active learners. He believes that learning has a social, interactive component with enquiry based, collaborative learning at the heart of Halcyon. He is 'quietly spoken and has a calming, steadying presence' and 'whilst he sets rules and guidelines, his is not a dictatorial role, which allows others to have a voice,' according to parents. 'He listens, thinks things through and comes up with a solution'; 'I have never met a head who listens like that.' An egalitarian who shares an open plan space with colleagues. He has one son who went through the IB programme.

Entrance: 'Holistic approach to admissions' which involves parent and pupil interviews with admissions team and the head, two years' school reports and two teacher references for younger pupils, three of each for older pupils. They need an academic profile of average or above and good enough English to access the very full-on IB diploma. 'Families are as important to us as the students': they are looking for those who will engage and are not expecting a focus on scores and data, and who will 'embrace the digital learning style'. Pupils told us it works for pupils who are motivated and curious, and that the admissions team were 'interested in my education and me and not only in talking to and selling the school to my parents'.

Exit: Early days for the school still, but popular UK destinations include LSE and King's College London, plus UCL, Royal Holloway, SOAS, Westminster and Central St Martins. Others to Manchester, Sussex and Dundee. Recent overseas destinations include Maastricht University, Delft, University, Design Academy Eindhoven, Leiden University (all Netherlands). Also Parson New School of Design, Minerva Schools at the Keck Graduate Institute (USA), American University in Paris (France), University of Granada (Spain) and College of International Management (Japan).

Latest results: In 2020, IB results averaged 35 points. IB results in 2019 averaged 31 points.

Teaching and learning: Teachers are passionate about their subject, which they discuss with students and other staff. Middle years programme followed for first five years, which involves enquiry-based learning – as much of it student-led as possible. Pupils like the fact that there is plenty of independent work. Modern, neat, floodlit classrooms – we saw students working on their laptops on beanbags creating, researching and preparing for tests with other students. Subjects all taught within a global context and in a cross-curricular way to encourage what parents referred to as 'soft skills like public speaking, discussing and learning to bridge differences and work together'. This leads to the IB Personal Projects which they present to the community at the end of grade 10 (year 11). Huge numbers of oral presentations, videos, multimedia work in addition to essays. Very few text books as the school provides students and parents access to countless online curriculum resources.

The IB diploma range means they all do, for example, maths and a second language (Spanish, Mandarin or private tutoring of mother tongue languages). To further broaden the school's offerings, students explained that they could take online Pamoja courses in eg IT, psychology, economics, business management and film, with the support of the school coordinator.

Outdoor learning day an example of the creative teaching with all lessons in Hyde Park: some used iPad apps to paint, some did pencil drawings of trees; others acted in a Shakespearean play; some tested pollutants in the Serpentine

Science in well-equipped labs. Interactivity means that students can share their research results with the class by airplaying to large screens in each classroom. Outdoor learning day an example of the creative teaching with all lessons happening in Hyde Park: students measured respiration for science and exercise; some used iPad apps to paint and others did pencil drawings of trees; others acted in a Shakespearean play or wrote poetry; some tested pollutants in the Serpentine.

Clear assessment criteria and feedback. Both pupils and parents spoke about the close monitoring and watching possible in small classes: 'kids get pushed, they don't get lost or coast; when they need more, they get more because the teachers are very good at differentiating.'

Learning support and SEN: New SENCo because none in place when Ofsted visited (and judged the school outstanding in all categories). Whilst all the technology is helpful for a child with dyslexia, and the small classes and self-initiated work allow each pupil to go at their own pace, there is no specific support for SEN and the school will only take children with learning differences if they are sure they can match needs and can accommodate them within the classroom. No pupils with EHC plans. English Plus programme offered to support students with more limited language skills – integrated fully into the classroom.

The arts and extracurricular: Art room displays oil pastels, 3D model making, sculpture and papier mâché masks, mosaics, installation art and fabric printing. Two enthusiastic specialist art teachers and a DT teacher extend the popularity of these subjects.

Music is a challenge in a small school but noise limitations overcome by using electronic instruments and headphones, and the music room has a good supply of electronic keyboards for composing and playing. Some bands – ensemble, contemporary band, small choir. Soloists get to play in assemblies and at graduation. Plenty of drama in school with students acting, directing and stage managing.

A number of extracurricular activities are generated by students themselves – eg Model United Nations conferences which students organise entirely, and they work hard to include students from local state schools as well as other private international schools, plus Global Issues Network, charity fairs, school trips, student driven assemblies. New explorations classes (choice of three taster classes that run for the term) now also on offer for grade 10, including ice skating, rock climbing, forensics, astronomy, mindfulness and some sporting options. Emphasis on pupils taking responsibility and leadership roles as often as possible.

Grades 6-11 attend a one week residential team-building trip each September. Work and achievements shared and celebrated in class and assemblies and on the school website.

Sport: PE twice weekly compulsory up to grade 10 (year 11) then optional in the sixth form. Table tennis in school and some gymnastics and plenty of dance, otherwise swimming, football, basketball and other sports at local leisure centre or in Hyde Park. Too small for many team sports but has a running club, table tennis and football teams (mixed training, separate fixtures). So not the right school if you want competitive sports.

Ethos and heritage: The school opened in 2013; buildings that are in part grand and old, as the landlord is the neighbouring synagogue, but renovated and extended to provide a number of state-of-the-art classrooms, art room and super hi-tech labs. Meeting room and large assembly hall. The location could hardly be more central, and pupils say they 'use London as a classroom'. Strong commitment to sustainability with a vegetarian canteen and a virtually paperless operation.

Pastoral care, inclusivity and discipline: Well-being coordinator runs mentoring system with some pupils trained in conflict resolution and mediating. The aim is to make pupils feel that they are 'recognised and have a voice'. Pupils all spoke of the amount of interaction they have with teachers, who 'know you really well and are almost like friends' and 'are interested in what I have to say'. The staff are there to 'advocate for students all the time'. The school uses 'guiding principles not rules'. Assemblies and discussions about bullying, but students from all over the world are very supportive of each other – and they laughed when we asked about stealing, which they couldn't imagine in their school: 'we respect each other and our possessions'. High security but pupils not mollycoddled: they may visit increasingly wider areas outside at lunchtimes as they go up the school.

Pupils and parents: About one third from US, and second largest number are British, with a good mix from other nationalities, so a real third culture kids atmosphere. Parents said they wanted an international rather than American environment, and liked the fact that kids learned so much from each other's different cultures and backgrounds. They also liked the central position – that is why they had moved to London, they said, to make the most of the city. Small year groups but pupils make friends through multi-age courses and activities in school, as well as outside clubs and from inter-school connections. Articulate and inquisitive pupils said school is 'welcoming and friendly, you speak to everyone – and students who leave come back to visit and join in'. Active involvement by parents – careers talks, cake baking, trips, twice-termly meetings of class reps with the head.

Students are from all over the world. They laughed when we asked about stealing, which they couldn't imagine in their school: 'we respect each other and our possessions'

Money matters: An expensive option and no green fields or grand library buildings to show for it, but this is a charity and all the money is being invested back into the school as well as gradually repaying backers.Teachers are well paid and unrushed, with the calm that comes from having time to do the job properly. Bottomless resources in terms of technology – laptops, iPads, large screens, video recording, electronic instruments etc. Spotlessly clean. Excellent administration so good, clear communication.

The last word: Advanced, not only in terms of digital technology but also in attitude. The school focuses on the pupils and listens to them, making sure they are happy and learning at their own individual speed, with no pupil left behind or slipping. Well-being a priority, proactive and central to learning, which is rare in pressurised London. A friendly school that not only cares and supports but also energises pupils to strive, self-motivate and learn.

The Hall School

29

23 Crossfield Road, London NW3 4NU

020 7722 1700 | admissions@hallschool.co.uk | www.hallschool.co.uk

Independent	Pupils: 460
Ages: 4–13	Fees: £20,229 – £20,844 pa

Headmaster: Since 2013, Christopher Godwin, previously head of Bedford Prep. Read geography at Loughborough, then masters in Middle Eastern studies at Durham. Joined Bedford in 1993 as second master and director of studies before taking over the headship four years later. With no experience of London schools, his post came as a surprise to some parents, although he quickly won hearts and minds with his keenness to maintain the ethos and values of the school, along with his gentle and unassuming nature and fresh pair of eyes. 'There's a track record of people taking this job who are greying and in their early 50s,' he laughs, 'but I hope I've brought a new energy to the school.' Parents and pupils praise his emphasis on 'positive psychology rather than rules, rules and more rules,' as one parent put it. 'There's a strong pastoral element to his thinking,' said another.

Sees the next phase as making the school even more responsive to 'the world we now live in', with a growing focus on preparing boys for what their next schools require and embedding ever more IT into an already technology-heavy curriculum. Known for being open and available to parents and a great team builder among staff. Often seen out and about in school and is not precious about his office, whose conference table is often used by boys themselves. Teaches current affairs to year 5s upwards and frequently reads stories in junior school. Heavily involved in the assessment of boys. Keen and active sportsman, particularly rugby – now as coach rather than player.

Entrance: This is the top north London boys' prep school for those looking towards the country's top academic secondary schools, so competition for entrance is hotter than hot, with applications restricted to those registering before their first birthday – and even so, the school is three times oversubscribed. A recent decision to only offer entry into reception from September 2020 (rather than offering a choice to parents of entry at 4+ or 5+) has been warmly received by parents, says head. All applicants are invited in for a 'play-date' in the spring term before entry for an hour of games, construction activities and stories. Teachers are looking for curiosity, willingness to have a go, social skills and learning readiness.

Favours siblings, but no guarantees and many haven't got places in recent years. Occasional places arise higher up the school, with a formal registration process for the waiting list. 'They do a good job of picking the right boys,' said one parent.

Exit: Most pupils to St Paul's (14 places in 2020), others to Westminster, City of London and Mill Hill. In ones and twos to Eton, Wetherby, Haileybury, Harrow, Magdalen College, Sevenoaks and Tonbridge. In other years, Highgate and UCS have also featured. Exceptional guidance in secondary school choices. 'We encourage parents of boys in year 4 upwards to start looking widely. We don't leave it with a year to go,' says head. The match is made by a meticulously planned programme of assessments, which include annual verbal and non-verbal reasoning and day-to-day performance, and which are all tracked on a graph for each boy. Scholarship form in year 8 for those completing the demanding exams of Eton and Westminster, but not all scholarships derive from this form.

Our view: From September 2020, three classes of 18 in reception. By year 8, four classes of 12 to 14, with a scholarship form and three fast common entrance forms. Staff are a broad age range, and have notable experience and enthusiasm. 'They're strict, but you can have a real joke with them too,' said one boy, and we certainly found humour abundant in the classrooms and corridors, with a refreshing ease of communication between pupils and staff.

Specialist French, science, music, sport and ICT more or less from the word go. Latin added in year 5, Greek in year 7 for scholarship candidates. Setting in core subjects from year 5 and Latin from year 6 – no stigma for lower sets, say pupils. Three sciences, taught in a more combined way than in the past. ICT provision has long been outstanding, with digital learning embedded into just about every subject. Advanced coding and programming is praised, as is the collaborative work using shared computer files. No Sats but exams taken very seriously, with all subjects examined twice yearly in the upper forms. 'The teaching is so good that you actually don't need to revise for exams,' said one boy, 'although most of us do anyway.' Does well in national competitions, such as the Townsend Warner History Prize and national Maths Challenges.

The school itself is divided up, with junior school (reception to year 3), middle (years 4 and 5) and senior school (years 6-8) on separate sites all within a short walk of this upmarket residential area. Junior school (substantially refurbished) is made up of two well-ordered Victorian buildings, with the head living in a flat above. Middle school is a 1970s building that was probably cutting-edge at the time, but could do with a rethink in terms of use of good space now. Senior school is the original red-brick school building, with lots of quirky design features, including split level classrooms, which make for a cosy learning environment.

Classrooms generally on the small side, especially in the middle school, but well ordered, and many are innovatively designed (especially the history room, with its very own upstairs library and historically decorated walls). Even the DT room, where boys were making splurge guns ready for their production of Bugsy Malone when we visited, is carpeted. Lovely, bright art room, with separate pottery room. Wathen Hall, which is the main hall, feels a bit past its use-by date. Well-stocked, two-storey library. Stand-out common room, known as the Pit, with a focal snooker table and split level, contemporary and airy environment.

Like most north London preps, outside space is limited, although the junior school has a colourful and imaginative playground, while the older boys use one all-weather pitch, which school admits 'can get crowded' at playtimes. Sport, however, is prioritised, with £2m recently invested in the sports field at East Finchley, to which the boys are transported by coach two afternoons a week, and where they play football, rugby, hockey, cricket and tennis. Gymnastics and fencing in Wathen Hall. Every boy gets a chance to represent the school at some point in a team game (nine football teams) and the school is currently looking to extend its fixture list outside London. Some parents concerned that sport generally favours the best boys, however. 'If the boys aren't sporty, they're not really bothered with them,' said one. County and national representatives at chess, fencing, skiing and tennis. Annual skiing trips to France and biannual cricket tour of Sri Lanka. 'We competed against teams that got 1,000 runs in 10 games in the last tour. The quality of cricket was amazing,' said one boy.

Over 80 per cent of boys play an instrument (often three), with an army of peripatetic teachers. Plenty of encouragement to join the large orchestra, string quartets, jazz group and choir, all of which regularly win music awards. 'You get to sing in some amazing places if you're in the choir,' said one boy. Drama taken seriously, with boys of all ages encouraged to perform in plays, concerts, public speaking and most notably debating. Huge range of clubs, including cookery, model making, computer maths games etc. Lots of links with the local community – boys join forces with other schools to do everything from enrichment maths to drumming workshops, and boys are also encouraged to help out at the community centre 100 yards away.

This is the top north London boys' prep for those looking towards top academic secondary schools, so competition for entrance is hot, with applications restricted to those registering before their first birthday

School accommodates all the usual SENs, provided the underlying intellect is there. 'My son is dyslexic and the school just took it in their stride, which had a hugely positive effect on his confidence,' said one parent. Learning support department, which is run by a full-time staff member (BEd and certificate in dyslexia), brings in outside expertise where necessary. Only one child with an EHCP when we visited.

A strong reputation persists that the focus on academics is at the cost of emotional support. But we heard convincing arguments from parents and pupils that problems are nipped in the bud, with good pastoral care from teachers, two matrons and the part-time school counsellor, who has links with the Tavistock Clinic. In consultation with parents, the school undertakes a pastoral review every three years. Far less bullying under the current head, say parents.

Expectations (many of which are dotted on posters around the school) favoured over rules, but boys say punishment can be inconsistent. 'You can wind up with a worse punishment for running to pass a boy a book in the corridor than being really rude,' said one.

This isn't the kind of school where every boy knows each other (not helped by the lack of single campus) but school encourages peer support and cross-year activities. Lively school council. Boys say the atmosphere is supportive and friendly.

Parents mostly high-flyers – bankers, media types, lawyers etc – many with extremely high aspirations for their boys. Mainly local, but some travel from Notting Hill, Holland Park and Islington. Some said to be cliquey, with very strong personalities; active PA.

Money matters: Offers means-tested bursaries of up to 100 per cent for year 4 and 5 entry via report from current school and maths, English and cognitive ability tests plus interview. At any one time there are 10 bursary holders in the school.

The last word: Prep schools don't come more ambitious than this. Catering to the needs of boys who are intellectually curious, academic and highly motivated, this is a school that stretches them in every direction.

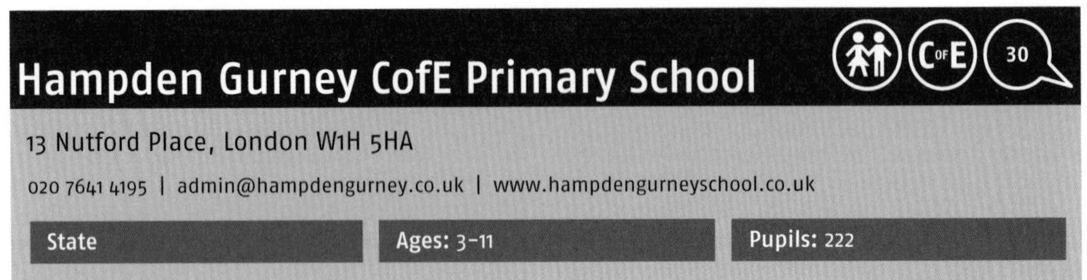

Hampden Gurney CofE Primary School

13 Nutford Place, London W1H 5HA

020 7641 4195 | admin@hampdengurney.co.uk | www.hampdengurneyschool.co.uk

State | Ages: 3–11 | Pupils: 222

Headteacher: Since 1997, Evelyn Chua (50s). Born in a small town in Malaysia, Mrs Chua came to England to do her A levels at boarding school, before proceeding to study piano at the Royal Academy of Music. After a postgraduate degree in music education in the US and a brief stint as a classroom teacher, she took on her first headship at Hampden Gurney, when it had the lowest attendance of any primary in Westminster. The school is now one of the borough's most oversubscribed, and Mrs Chua's super-head status been widely recognised both by parents ('She's like the leader of a ship, you can approach her with any problem') and her professional colleagues (she received a Teaching Awards' Leadership Trust Award for School Leadership). Strongly motivated by her faith, she's focused, dedicated and slightly formidable. ('The children are not scared of her, but they don't want to go up to her office.') Married with two children, she sees the school as her second home. 'Everything about it has her stamp,' said one mother. 'She could easily rest on her laurels,' said another, 'but she doesn't, year after year after year.'

Entrance: Open mornings held in the autumn term. The school is affiliated to the High Anglican Church of the Annunciation in Bryanston Street near Marble Arch, and gives firm priority to long-term churchgoers. (Alternatives venues for worship include St John's Hyde Park, St Mary's, Our Lady of the Rosary.) Hugely oversubscribed with 150+ applying for 30 places.

Exit: Outstanding advice and preparation given for secondary school transfer, with early information meetings in year 4 and one-to-one talks with the head further along the line. About 60 per cent to independents (including four each to St Paul's girls and boys in 2019, two to Godolphin & Latymer and one each to NLCS, King's Wimbledon and City boys), many on scholarships and bursaries. Also to top-flight faith schools (St Marylebone CofE, Grey Coat Hospital, the London Oratory and Twyford CofE). About 50 per cent of year 6 apply for scholarships and bursaries, aided by a team of support assistants in the lead up to exams: 'Because of the amount of pressure they're under they need mentoring,' says the head. Parents definitely see the benefit. 'The school is amazing at preparing them,' said one grateful mother. 'It was definitely one of my reasons for going there. You know your kids are going to be given a choice.'

Our view: By any measure, Hampden Gurney is an 'outstanding' primary school, lauded not only by Ofsted, but by numerous external bodies (Primary School of the Year, Outstanding Progress Achievement, National Association for Able Children in Education Challenge Award). Teaching – it goes without saying – is a strength. 'The head recruits really well,' said one parent. 'She's brilliant at finding enthusiastic young teachers, who bring in new ideas, and the staff are very committed to getting the best out of children.' Early years comes in for particular praise. 'They manage to get everyone reading very quickly, while being very nurturing.'

Pupils test their writing skills in out-of-school challenges, such as the Sunday Times Goosebumps story-writing competition

Broad curriculum includes timetabled Spanish, creative writing and humanities. Two hours a week of science as a separate subject from year 1 (helped by a small roof garden with a pond and greenhouse, and regular outings to science attractions, such as the Science Museum). Computer suite with dedicated hour-long weekly lesson, plus whole class set of laptops. Well-stocked library – one of the best children's libraries in the borough – central to promoting enthusiasm for reading, and pupils test their writing skills in out-of-school challenges, such as the Sunday Times Goosebumps story-writing competition.

All undergo a thorough-going programme of aspiration raising. 'We inspire the children because we accept that every child has got ability somewhere and can achieve,' says the head. Loads of positive reinforcement plus Building Learning Power programme to instil resilience, perseverance, concentration, and organisation. Infants given extra help through a buddy system which matches them with older pupils. 'It's someone away from class to whom the children can express themselves.' After-school clubs maintain the focus and set sights high. Design club, for example, is intended for 'future engineers, architects and artists', while journalism club lays the ground for the next generation of Fleet Street's finest. The home-school relationship is critical to the mix, and parents meet teachers at the beginning of the year for a briefing on curriculum, expectations and homework (from year 1). 'There's quite a lot of homework and it's encouraged to be done,' said one mother approvingly.

Special educational needs well supported. Dedicated SENCo and learning mentor work closely with classroom teachers (who are given specialist training) and parents. Outside experts called upon when required. School celebrated, too, for its gifted and talented approach ('Our policy starts with the expectation that there are gifted and talented learners in every year group,' says the head). Early identification then monitored by a full-time specialist, who develops reasoning and creative thinking through after-school clubs, visits, masterclasses and summer schools (at St Paul's, City of London School for Girls and Oxford University). 'It's OK to be a geek,' said one parent. 'It may not be precisely cool to be clever, but you're not penalised by your peer group for wanting to do well.' Head works personally both with those who struggle and those who excel and all acknowledge her talent as a teacher. 'If you're not improving or not where she expects, she will focus on this. She cares deeply about the success of every child and can really inspire children.'

Arts taken seriously. In-class tuition in theory of music and composition (including electronic works), plus the chance to learn either ukulele or recorder. Weekly music club run by professional musicians and links with both the Royal Academy of Music and Royal College of Music for projects and workshops. Individual lessons in piano, saxophone, clarinet and violin at a reasonable cost. Children's choir performs at mass and elsewhere (the Royal Albert Hall, for example, with the BBC singers). Dedicated art teacher. Dance club, taught by qualified dance instructor. Despite its tight urban location, the school manages a good range of games (netball, basketball, tag rugby and football), athletics and gymnastics. Swimming from year 1 at nearby pool. Plenty of sports clubs (some run by year 6) during and after school, on site and in the nearby park. Some inter-school competition, where the school performs with credit ('They often win because the school teaches them not to give up; you can do it, you will succeed'), but, for the very sporty, out-of-school options may be required. Stimulating range of clubs (girls' football, musical theatre, chess, origami, cooking, martial arts) and trips, both local and more wide-ranging (year 6 residential trip to the rolling Surrey hills).

In inter-school sports competition, the school performs with credit. They often win because the school teaches them not to give up; you can do it, you will succeed

Established in 1863 in memory of the Reverend John Hampden Gurney, rector of St Mary's Bryanston Square, the school's ethos is still strongly High Anglican, with compulsory attendance at weekly sung eucharist. (Parents, too, invited into school for weekly prayer group.) Termly visit to the church in Bryanston Square and year 6s take positions of responsibility as servers at mass. Order and discipline underpin it all. Firm emphasis on attendance and punctuality. Escalating punishment system (warning, missing play time, time out, Mrs Chua), but these are well-behaved children. 'Everyone comments on it if you go out on a school trip. They sit there and listen and all ask questions,' said a parent. 'It's a joy.' Wide-ranging pastoral strategy. House system – with houses named for local heroes Alexander Fleming, John Wesley, Michael Faraday, Florence Nightingale – develops cross-year bonding, and gentle competition (with certificates for academic prowess and good behaviour). 'The house system encourages everyone to work as a team.' Motivational speakers (Colin Jackson, Cherie Blair) invited in to teach about rejection and reflection. Strong, too, on promoting British values with hands-on experience of democracy, through school council, mock elections, voted-upon school prefects (including head boy and girl) plus visits to parliament and local council. 'They're taught to ask thought-provoking questions about life,' said one father. Smart red-and-blue uniform, with separate PE kit.

If Hampden Gurney didn't stand out in so many other ways, it would still be distinguished by its building. Opened in 2002, it was described by the RIBA as 'innovative, bold and dynamic'. Admirers refer to it as 'the beehive', the less well-inclined 'the car park'. Whatever your perspective, it's a clever solution to a tight urban site, offering covered outside play playgrounds on each of its three floors, and identical plans for each age group to proceed from nursery at ground level to top-of-the-school and top of the world in year 6.

Parents, who mainly live close by, are a healthy mix of those who could afford to go private and the just-about-managing. Overall a fairly cosmopolitan lot, often European (western and eastern, so German, French, Russian, Polish), almost all practising Christians. ('If you really didn't believe in God it might be a problem,' said one mother.) Strong community feel. 'It's a small school and everyone knows everyone. We all see each other at church, in the park, on weekends.'

Money matters: Energetic PTA, which raises more than £20,000 a year 'for all the softer stuff' such as arts and music provision. Voluntary subsidy of £40 per pupil contributes to school maintenance.

The last word: Most parents are delighted with the school ('My children have enjoyed themselves from day 1. The school really makes learning fun'), praising its well-structured discipline and high aspirations ('There's pressure, but within reason; it's certainly not excessive'). That said, some acknowledge the approach might not be ideal for all. 'You have to be a well-disciplined child who likes learning. If you're a wonderfully creative, dreamy child, it might not be the right place for you.'

Hampstead School

31

Westbere Road, London NW2 3RT

020 7794 8133 | enquiries@hampsteadschool.org.uk | www.hampsteadschool.org.uk

State | **Ages:** 11-19 | **Pupils:** 1,340; sixth form: 290

Head: Since 2020, Matthew Sadler BA PGCE (30s). Newcastle born and bred. Started here as a newly qualified teacher in 2010 (the same day as previous head). Was an assistant head at a school in Chiswick and deputy head at a school in Sutton before returning to the fold. Attended his local comp, Kenton School; history degree from Cambridge; PGCE from IoE. Teaching 'sort of' in the blood as both parents were teachers, albeit for a short time. Grounded, benevolent and surprisingly mellow given his extreme efficiency. Big on social justice and closing education gaps for those with disadvantaged backgrounds, he loves nothing more than the idea of a 'proper comp with a genuinely comprehensive intake', making him the perfect fit. Also refuses to run 'an exclusive sixth form that isn't geared towards the school's cohort,' with school offering a growing number of vocational courses so students don't feel shunted towards local colleges. Hear hear to that. Top three things in his inbox? Enhancing the school's offering for so-called 'high potential learners' (that's gifted and talented in old money); widening enrichment to run right through the sixth form; and engaging more with the local community eg relaunching PTA, engaging with alumni, looking at fundraising with local businesses.

Lives locally with his wife and three young children (one still a babe in arms). Runs when he can – 'a big stress reliever.' Also continues to 'try and live out my dream as a five a side footballer.'

Entrance: Totally non-selective and open to all, as befits the head's ideology. From over 70 primary schools across three boroughs – Camden, Brent and Barnet (admissions managed by Camden). No named feeders. Oversubscribed in every year group; hard to believe the poor reputation it once had, though that was many moons ago now. Around 40 external applicants join for sixth form (and some in year 13 who are disillusioned with their current place of learning), with entry requirements varying according to the level of course, but at least a grade 6 in subjects to be studied.

Exit: Around 20 per cent leaves after GCSEs, mainly to other sixth forms or colleges or straight into employment, some into an apprenticeship scheme. A further 20 per cent leaves after year 12, mainly due to the high number of one-year courses available. Eighty per cent of year 13s head off to university (a quarter to Russell Group), with an overwhelming lean towards maths and science based subjects (three medics in 2020), although many also into humanities, arts etc. Most to London universities (King's, Imperial and UCL all popular) 'because they can't afford to move away'. But some go slightly further afield to the likes of Sussex, Herts and Surrey. Often a few to Oxbridge, though none in 2020.

Latest results: In 2020, 13 per cent 9/7 at GCSE; 51 per cent 9-5 in both English and maths. At A level, 35 per cent A*/A (56 per cent A*/B). In 2019, 12 per cent 9-7 at GCSE: 63 per cent achieved 9-5 in both English and maths. At A level, 15 per cent A*/A (30 per cent A*-B).

Teaching and learning: Wowzers results when you consider that nearly half the pupils are bilingual (over 60 different nationalities), nearly half are on pupil premium and five per cent have EHCPs. 'Think big, work hard, be kind,' is – lest the students forget – plastered across banners, appears on student resources and uttered by most teachers in most lessons. By and large, the message gets through, with high participation rates in class and really good questioning in particular a two way street. Teachers here don't just go to the students with their hands up – mini whiteboards, group conversations and good sequenced activities are just some of the ways they get everyone's brains working at full throttle.

Students are tracked from the moment they arrive (well, the summer before, actually). But that no longer means a seemingly endless stream of tests (although they are well prepared for exams), with more qualitative in-class assessment providing the data the school needs to make sure nobody slips through the net. Makes for a much happier student body, we can tell you. Interventions range from one-to-one support to subject clinics for those who need it, and they don't seem to be afraid to ask. And for 'high potential learners' (top of the head's inbox, remember), there are more deep thinking challenges that run alongside lessons; these students are also invited to eg Model United Nations, debating club, university mentoring etc. French and Spanish from year 7, plus opportunities to learn community languages. Setting from year 7 in maths and science, but it's fluid and reviewed annually; interestingly, they've found English results rose after setting was dropped. Homework levels 'reasonably high' but 'fair' and 'not unmanageable,' report students, and there are opportunities for after-school homework sessions – great for those lacking a quiet study space at home or for the particularly dedicated.

'Think big, work hard, be kind,' is – lest the students forget – plastered across banners, appears on student resources and uttered by most teachers in most lessons

STEAM a big focus – students can't get enough of the modern, spacious science labs that are often literally alight with whizzes and bangs. Given half a chance, we'd have grabbed the nearest white coat and got stuck in too. Around a third take triple science. In the top 20 UK state schools for continuing into science A levels. Maths also strong; school is very involved in maths challenges and maths mastery has taken off big time. The school offers free Saturday school maths masterclasses for gifted mathematicians from years 5 and 6 of local primary schools. Other popular subjects at GCSE (of which students take between nine and 11) are psychology and economics, testament to the wide range on offer. Virtually no subject is offered at GCSE level which can't be carried through to A level, of which students take three or four. EPQ available. Vocational qualifications on the up, including in criminology and sport, plus BTecs in eg catering and hospitality – with multiple exit points for flexibility.

Learning support and SEN: Really strong and well-resourced SEN department – this is a school that walks the walk when it comes to inclusion. More EHCPs than average, with intricately personalised plans to support these students. Regular meetings to talk through needs – often includes teachers eg over breakfast or lunch. For all learning needs – diagnosed or not – support is available both in and outside the classroom. 'My son is a completely different child, thanks to this school – when he left junior school, he was introverted and didn't have friends and had the reading age of a 9-year-old,' one parent told us. 'Now, he loves reading, is at the level he should be and has a really nice mix of friends. Between the SENCo, head of year and his form tutor, they've completely nurtured him and given him all the support he needs while never overwhelming him.' The department shone throughout COVID due to their early adoption of tailored remote learning.

'We're not a marching in silence in hallways kind of school,' students told us, 'but you know what the school rules are and what happens if you don't follow them'

The bilingual department is the go-to place for EAL support – again, well-resourced with highly experience members of staff providing support in and outside class and even online, with significant progress shown in most cases.

Wheelchair access throughout – the school is completely DDA compliant. There is a disability resource which can cater for up to seven students with complex needs, complete with washrooms. These students are fully integrated into mainstream lessons.

The arts and extracurricular: Fizzes with activity. Music is popular and heavy investment in this department has meant that each of the school's 1,300 students is offered the opportunity to learn a musical instrument. Around 100 students have periplectic music lessons and a large number get involved in musical activities, including senior or junior orchestra, guitar orchestra, a very popular jazz band, junior choir and many more. The onsite replica fringe theatre has partnerships with the Hampstead Theatre, Royal Court and The Kiln – all helps to inspire budding thespians and, as one student noted, 'we get the opportunity to do things like professional lighting too.' Performances most terms. Art has an outward lens that's lacking in so many schools, with masses of outside partnerships to keep things fresh (and competitive). Currently working with local artists around mural projects, with a theme of survival techniques during COVID. No wonder they have a platinum award from Arts Council of England.

Commendable efforts to involve the outside world in other areas too, with lots of local partnerships and charity work. Enrichment days three times a year – with examples including year 9 trip to the coast, year 7 maths puzzles with experts, and business studies students visiting Brent Cross for an Apprentice-style activity. Annual trips to eg Berlin and battlefields. School 'really takes advantage of our setting in London too.' Most students do at least one club – the school tracks this, so it knows, but few need persuading. From poetry to rugby and aikido to dance, there's something for everyone.

Sport: High participation rates, with a 'sport for life' ethos really shining through. Kids here really enjoy PE, and there's lots of opportunity for sports leadership too. Facilities, ever on the up, include a four-court sports hall, dance hall with sprung floor, fitness suite, multi-use Astrourf and basketball/netball courts, which joined the existing on-site indoor pool. Not much to speak of by way of playing fields but, hey, this is London. Football is the clear winner both in terms of trophies and thumbs up among students – basketball and athletics also do well. Dance is taking off, largely thanks to the hard work of some much praised specialist dance teachers – it's popular right up to year 11 and the school is currently looking at ways to include it more in sixth form too (along with other sports – they are currently looking into developing a dance and basketball academy).

Ethos and heritage: Hampstead Schmampstead – this school is no more in Hampstead than Arsenal (FC) is in Arsenal. Situated in between colourful but definitely not posh Cricklewood, Kilburn and semi-posh West Hampstead, you can see the flag before you see the school. Red and emblazoned with the school logo, it waves proudly high above this impressive large red-brick building. The main building – formerly the old Haberdashers' Boys' school – was built in 1908, while the rest of the school is unrecognisable from even a decade ago, with nearly £20m spent on bright, light, carpeted modern class rooms and vast science labs that make you want to grab the nearest white coat and get stuck in. There are lovely wide squeaky-clean corridors to get from A to B and a refurbished and roomy library – 'there is nothing you can't access in here,' said our guide proudly, although the number of books isn't anything to write home about. Dining and outdoor recreation areas have had an upgrade, as has the large assembly hall and aforementioned sports facilities. A well-equipped ICT and catering block is home to industrial spec kitchens, complete with TVs for cooking demos – we half expected Jamie Oliver to jump out to present one of his programmes. And back in the main building, there's a good sixth form centre with huge common room overlooking the central atrium. Students' pride in their school is evident in the total lack of graffiti, vandalism and litter.

No 'them and us' culture, with students speaking proudly of their school as 'we,' and their sense of ownership in the school means they aren't afraid to speak out. So while in many other schools the best that student councils do is get new fountains brought in, students here recently helped bring about a complete overhaul of the whole detention and reward system and new in-house catering ('the food is all cooked onsite now and it's so good,' one student told us).

Former pupils include Sadie Frost, Rachel Yankey, ex-MP Julia Drown, Alec Bogdanovic, Jake Lensen, Tobias Hill, Zadie Smith.

Pastoral care, inclusivity and discipline: If punctuality and attendance ain't your bag, this ain't your school. Students that show up even one minute late risk landing themselves in deep water. The senior management team, head included, are at the gates to greet pupils from 8.40am, after which sluggards have to report individually. (Early risers' club offered from 7.30am onwards.) Other rules similarly stringent, though pupils largely take it in their stride – 'We're not a marching in silence in hallways kind of school, but you know what the school rules are, why they're there and what happens if you don't follow them,' said one. Noticeably less punitive since our last visit, however, with fixed term exclusions – once numbering around 50 a year – now down to about 30. School attributes this to two changes. First, the new student support centre which has three trained counsellors (far greater than most schools), with programmes for everything from anger management to confidence building. And second, a greater emphasis on restorative conversations – both generally and as part of every detention. All coupled with lots of buddying and mentoring, as well as non-teaching pastoral heads of year who are available to both students and parents. One or two permanent exclusions a year. Clear phone policy – students can have them, but they can't be seen or heard. Good on bullying – different ties denote whether or not a student has been trained in HABZ (Hampstead anti-bullying zone, a model that has since been rolled out across other schools), and any student feeling vulnerable can approach those who have one – extremely popular among students. Good level of security – brings to bear the stark reality that you are in an inner-city school.

An appreciation of the diversity of the school is prevalent – Black History Month, gay/transgender month, trips to Auschwitz etc, and we saw posters for a forthcoming Irish night (Cricklewood has many families of Irish descent), to name a few. No shying away from big celebrations around Christmas, Easter and Eid, as at some other diverse urban schools.

Pupils and parents: From barristers earning £2m a year in moneyed West Hampstead to recent refugees in temporary housing, the demographic is hugely diverse – all the more admirable when you consider how far the school has come. One pupil told us: 'There are no cliques according to how wealthy your family is or their ethnicity – everyone mixes.' Under 20 per cent are white British, rest a melting pot of pretty much everywhere you can think of. Communications from school praised by parents – 'that goes for general information to conversations about your own child,' said one. We found the students – who come from Kilburn, West Hampstead, Willesden and Cricklewood (and further still if they've moved during their time at the school or enter at sixth form) – polite, chatty, comfortable in themselves and ambitious.

The last word: We think this is what all urban comprehensive schools should look like. Ambitious and inclusive, it's a school that opens its doors to all and gives them an enjoyable, vibrant education that can – if they want it – safely see them through to 18. Once ultra-strict, it's now more carrot, less stick – and more outward looking too.

Harris Westminster Sixth Form

32

Steel House, 11 Tothill Street, Westminster, London SW1H 9LH

020 3772 4555 | enquiries@harriswestminstersixthform.org.uk | www.harriswestminstersixthform.org.uk

State | **Ages:** 16–19 | **Pupils:** 568

Principal: Since 2014, when the school started, James Handscombe BA (Oxon) MA (Harvard) mathematics PGCE NPQH (early 40s). Previously deputy head at Bexley grammar school, Mr Handscombe started his career in what was perhaps his most formative experience, as a maths teacher at

Tonypandy comprehensive school in south Wales. Youthful, purposeful, wholly unaffected but intimidatingly intelligent, he is relishing running the innovative and above all scholarly sixth form he is leading here at HWSF. Married with two school age daughters, he met his wife as a student in Oxford. A truly vocational teacher, Mr Handscombe could have done almost anything with his brilliance and brains, but the children he teaches are the lucky beneficiaries of his calling. Educated at a comprehensive in Sheffield, he went on to achieve a top first in maths at Merton College Oxford followed by a masters at Harvard.

His students admire him as a 'well rounded intellectual'. He is 'not boring or plain but has real cross-curricular knowledge,' one told us. He confided to us that he likes to see himself as a polymath. A regular tweeter, his 140 characters tend to be about an array of subjects from U2 lyrics to mathematical juggling. He described to us, as well as to the world at large on the HWSF website, his insecurity and lack of confidence when he arrived as a very young man at two of the best and most prestigious universities in the world. However he concludes that 'it doesn't matter where you come from: the only thing that matters is how interesting you are to talk to.' The three nouns, ambition, perseverance and legacy, emblazoned across the HWSF website and elsewhere lie at the heart of his journey as well as those of his students. It is ambition that propelled him, perseverance that enabled him doggedly to pursue that difficult path, and finally produced the legacy that he is now bequeathing to his students and with which, he hopes, they in turn will imbue generations to come.

Entrance: Students choose to be tested in the two favourite subjects that they want to study for A level. Some 80 per cent take maths exams. There is a mixture of translating and writing for languages, and essays in the humanities and English. Physics exams consist of standard science questions with a focus on problem solving. The content is relatively basic (year 10 standard) but the questions harder than GCSE standard. Promising candidates can choose the subject they would like to be interviewed in – 'We want to see how clever they are – we're interested in their teachability, enthusiasm, aptitude, speed of learning and ownership of learning,' says Mr Handscombe.

A maximum 650 are interviewed from (in the recent intake) over 1,500 applications for 300 places, with priority to those on pupil premium who reach the required standard.

Exit: Over half to Russell Group. Recent popular destinations include Bristol, Manchester, Nottingham, UCL and Queen Mary. In the fourth batch of leavers (2019), 25 students secured places at Oxbridge, 18 went off to study medicine, two to dentistry and four to US (including Princeton). They choose a wide range of courses, with popular ones including economics, law, physics and biomedical sciences. Some seepage at the end of year 12, with around 10 per cent likely to trip over the requirement to achieve at least four Ds in end of year 12 exams.

Latest results: In 2019 – the fourth set of A level results – 48 per cent of grades were A*/A and 75 per cent were A*-B grades.

Teaching and learning: This is a highly academic school. It takes the brightest and best students from all over London and the suburbs. Its continuing association with Westminster School is influential in setting the tenor of scholarship and creating high expectations among the students. Its aim, it states, is 'to nurture a community of scholars'. Its A level subjects are the 'facilitating subjects', those most valued by the top universities. Most popular subject by some margin is maths. The department is very strong with high calibre teachers who excel in their field. French, Spanish and German offered. Classics, history of art, drama and German are all taught at Westminster School. Music, art, politics and economics are also taught alongside the sciences and the humanities.

The nouns, ambition, perseverance and legacy, emblazoned across the HWSF website, lie at the heart of the head's journey as well as those of his students

HWSF follows the Westminster School timetable as well as the curriculum, right down to Saturday morning lessons. 'A real shock' to many students (and teachers) when they first arrive, observes Mr Handscombe, but they start to enjoy the quieter commute on a Saturday and the opportunity to become immersed in their academic study. As at Westminster, students here have set exeats each term when school is closed on Saturday. 'The core of Westminster School is threaded all the way through HSWF,' says Mr Handscombe. 'There are links at every level.' Teachers share schemes of work, the senior teams meet regularly, they share the same chair of governors, the two heads meet regularly and there is lots of mentoring as well as lesson observations.

The same 'loyal dissent' that has characterised intellectual debate and classroom discussion at Westminster for generations is being fostered in its sapling.

Teachers here are young, energetic, and ambitious for their pupils. 'Learning is amazing' is a phrase you hear frequently and it is written all over the place, even on the cushions in Mr Handscombe's study. All pupils take four A levels, some more.

Results are strong. Students take the more challenging Pre-U in a number of subjects including English literature, modern languages, Latin, art and design and art history. High percentages of students achieved a distinction in these subjects (in most subjects well over 50 per cent). 'Our students work hard at hard work,' says Mr Handscombe. The results are a by product of this, not the main end game.

Learning support and SEN: Although there are a few people with mild dyslexia, Asperger's etc, they are all high performers and have to be able to keep up. 'Provision for students with exceptional needs is via the student support coordinator and the Harris Federation SENCo,' says Mr Handscombe.

The arts and extracurricular: An idiosyncratic feature of extracurricular provision at HWSF is the Tuesday afternoon 'Lab' – a time for scholarly work, collaboration, one-to-one sessions with teachers, and an important building block on the path to entering the country's top universities. On the same afternoon 'Lab lectures' take place. Stimulating speakers at the top of their field come to the school to lecture, whether it be on human rights, politics, climate change or science. A select number of students are invited to principal's tea with them afterwards for the opportunity to network and discuss thoughts and ideas in a more intimate setting.

Cultural perspectives – courses not part of their A level study – form part of the timetable. For eight weeks students study three from a wide range of colourful and intellectually stimulating cross-curricular courses. These include beginners' Mandarin, business start ups, the Other in literature, gender trouble from Freud to Beyoncé and introduction to grand opera. Designed to widen cultural horizons, inform the debate and prepare for interview, the programme also helps with the schools' challenge 'to convince them that learning is amazing'.

Students also become members of a weekly subject society. A president is elected to run the society and to chair discussions and debates. In addition there is a wide range of extracurricular societies from the hugely popular Afro-Caribbean Society (ACS, which boasts over 100 members) and the Intersectional Feminist Society (the IFS, in which there are plenty of young men as well as women) to Diplomacy (a highly competitive and mind-bending board game).

A short walk from Westminster Abbey and the Houses of Parliament, you can't escape the sense of purpose and excitement of being in a historic part of London

Art is offered as a Pre-U and each year a few do go on to do foundation courses, to study fashion or history of art at eg the Courtauld, or to train as architects. The art room is on the seventh floor: bright, busy and creatively chaotic. Music, also on the top floor, is offered as an A level – a few take it each year – and there are individual music rooms and instruments (guitars, electric and acoustic, pianos and drum kit) for recreational purposes. Carols at Christmas, a spring concert at St Margaret's on Parliament Square, as well as a few informal performances each year, either in the classroom or in the hall on the ground floor.

The library, on the ground floor, is like a magnet. Well stocked with books (generously donated by the Wigoder family foundation) as well as with very hardworking and focused students, it is always busy. It opens at 7.30am and closes at 6.30pm, yet at the senate meeting we attended, one of the requests from the student body was that the library hours be extended.

Sport: All students are encouraged to play sport on Thursday afternoons ('it's part of our ethos to be fit and healthy,' says the website) at venues across London. Football and netball are co-ed, athletics buoyant. HWSF students are the reigning athletics champions in the borough of Westminster. They also do a wide range of minor sports from archery and fencing to trampolining and table tennis. Debating society and bridge club for those who would prefer not to do sport, but they are no less competitive.

Ethos and heritage: Founded in 2014, HWSF, as it is known, forms part of the Harris chain of academies, or MAT (multi-academy trust). The school building is essentially an office block spanning eight floors (good for fitness though you can qualify for a lift pass if you can prove a need for one). Grey, functional, clean lines, minimal decoration; if it weren't for the unmistakable buzz of young bright people you would think there was not much of an atmosphere. However, a stone's throw from St James's Park tube and a short walk from Westminster Abbey and the Houses of Parliament, you can't escape the sense of purpose and excitement of being in a historic part of London where things are made to happen.

Despite its relatively short history, tradition is important here, and we were lucky enough to be present at the leavers' ceremony for the upper sixth. It was held in the splendid Westminster Abbey, and the young students filed in below the flying buttresses, bright eyed and full of optimistic confidence to listen to the various speeches and thanks of their principal and heads of house. Humorous and erudite, the speeches reflected the intelligence and acuity of this cohort. James Handscombe's final words were significant: 'You are the brightest and the best and I hope you will remember that learning is amazing, and that one day some of you will become teachers... give me a call if you do.' There is a barely veiled intention that some of the students will return one day and take on the mantle, whether by contributing financially or becoming part of the teaching team.

Assemblies are held in Westminster Abbey once a month, and in St Margaret's once a week. As part of the intention to create a sense of history and ethos in the school Mr Handscombe and his team, and the wider Harris MAT, have set out to instil longevity in the institution, a place that will have a dramatic and lasting impact on these young people's lives.

What these pupils have in common is a love of learning and thirst for intellectual rigour. One pupil admitted, 'I didn't know what scholar meant before I came here'

The main aim is that the students are taught to think for themselves and become the kind of students universities are looking for. So far the work is bearing fruit in terms of both the results they get and also how former students are faring at university. The school keeps in touch with its alumni and a key part of their work is to track their progress and development beyond their time here.

This is an institution that is not just run by the staff. The senate (student council), its president and two vice presidents (the proud wearers of yellow lanyards, setting them apart from the rest) also play a key role, as well as the house captains. Students and teachers are given equal weight in the voting process. The process is rigorous. Of the 40 who apply for membership, 20 will be interviewed and 10 appointed. The president we met could run for office, at a national level, tomorrow. Seriously impressive.

What is striking about the students here at HWSF is that their passion for learning and for scholarship is nakedly evident. Whereas their cool cousins at Westminster School might be paddling madly underneath but floating serenely on the surface, all the paddling is laid bare here, and proudly so.

Pastoral care, inclusivity and discipline: These are highly intelligent, high functioning young adults, who are knitted together by a shared thirst for scholarship and who are generally held in high esteem by their teachers. They respect themselves and the institution. They look smart (dress code is suits but there is some flexibility). Behaviour is generally good. 'The most common transgression is bunking off a lesson to do other work,' says Mr Handscombe. He hopes he will never have to permanently exclude anyone, and hasn't so far; 'it will be a sign that we've failed. The secret of behaviour management is to give them learning, intellectual stimulation. They know that they have to manage themselves, and if I have to step in, we've got a problem... it's a deal, we give them excellent teaching, stimulating assemblies and talks, and they work hard and behave well.'

Pupils and parents: Looking over the sea of 250 pupils in year 12, the immediate impression is the racial mix. No one culture, religion or skin colour dominates. For many, English is their second language and some need support with their English. Some 40 per cent of pupils are on pupil premium. They come from schools all over London and some from as far as Essex and Kingston, Bromley and Barnet. One of our stunningly intelligent and articulate guides said with complete poise, 'A lot of students go out to get their lunch; I always eat in the canteen though as I am pupil premium.'

The largest proportions currently come from Lewisham, Westminster and Croydon. No-one knows anyone else when they arrive, however. There are no large swathes of pupils from a particular school or area. What these pupils have in common is a love of learning and thirst for intellectual rigour. 'It's the scholarly engagement that is key to the melting pot,' says Handscombe, 'and we will fight to preserve that'. One pupil admitted, 'I didn't know what scholar meant before I came here.'

We often found it difficult to distinguish pupils from teachers. Many teachers are young, most pupils mature, confident, assertive but relaxed. Students here are polite, but not overly deferential. They look you in the eye and politely disagree.

The last word: A melting pot of the brightest and best pupils from all over London. HWSF is a genuinely stimulating and scholarly environment in which to study. The end game isn't to get into top universities, though that is what most students do, but to instil a love of learning and breadth of knowledge that will serve these students well throughout their lives. Students feel fortunate to be there. The staff feel privileged to teach them. A stunning combination.

Hereward House School

14 Strathray Gardens, London NW3 4NY

020 7794 4820 | office@herewardhouse.co.uk | www.herewardhouse.co.uk

Independent	Pupils: 165
Ages: 4–13	Fees: £17,520 – £17,970 pa

Headmaster: Since 2014, Pascal Evans (40s), formerly at Westminster Under and Colet Court. Gentle, reflective, low-key – but do not be deceived: Mr Evans has a very supple mind (with a law degree from Oxford) and is a man of wide-ranging talents and interests – passionately interested in football, and a serious runner who still puts in some 40 miles a week. 'I like the thinking time,' he says. 'Most of the knottier problems can be untangled in the course of a longish run'. Married with a Japanese wife and two teenage daughters – both trilingual.

Entrance: Most boys arrive in the September following their 4th birthday. As one might expect of a relatively small school which lies in the heart of Belsize Park, it's heavily oversubscribed. But Mr Evans and his colleagues are emphatic that they want an entrance process which is humane, conducted according to a criteria that is rational and democratic. Parents need to try to get their sons' names down by 2, but the testing is very gentle and every effort is made to take siblings of existing pupils. The emphasis is to identify families who can share the school's values and ethos and enable them to work for the best interests of the child. 'As the boys grow older it's always reassuring if one spots a child who, say, loves music, or sport,' says the head, 'quite as much as a potential scholar. But we're also looking to see if we can help them to taste or become immersed in new experiences.'

Obviously, there are a lot of Hampstead children here, but the reach goes further than that – lots from Islington as well as others from central London. There's some busy school bussing, but lots of tube and bus rides, as well – inevitably – as journeying on foot and by car.

Exit: Destinations testify to the school's ability to cater handsomely for the upper as well as less lofty academic echelons. 'Unstinting time spent on individual children,' said a parent, 'and an equal commitment to the needs of different children are having a big impact on selection.' When pre-testing was introduced by many top senior schools, a range of good prep schools found some pupils unexpectedly short of offers. There were indications that Hereward House was, briefly, among them – but, if so, it certainly wised up very quickly. Westminster, St Paul's, City of London, UCS and Eton all popular destinations in 2020. Head says, 'pastoral boarding at its best can be transformative for some boys'. This kind of 'catholicity' used to be typical of London prep schools, but vaulting parental ambition of the last two decades can all too easily leave children and parents feeling second best. It is much to the credit of Mr Evans and his staff that they want no part of that.

Our view: One of the charms of Hereward House is that it is small enough to be intimate – people know one another. The youngest children are carefully nurtured in basic social skills and helped towards physical literacy. Music and games, play and art and drama are all given due emphasis. Of course, all the time this is going on they are receiving a careful grounding in the rudiments of reading and writing and numeracy, which serves as an excellent springboard for the time when they gradually gravitate away from the form teacher to subject specialists.

Because of the size, systems here can be low-key. There are fewer than 20 staff members, but they tend to be versatile as well as highly capable. Obviously, the need for expertise is understood: there are two permanent special needs teachers and extra assistants brought in as required. But the culture supports turning one's hand to come-what-may: the headmaster teaches a decent number of lessons and views marking prep, setting classes and carrying chairs up and downstairs as a natural and perfectly appropriate task. The supremely capable director of music is also head of classics. In a modest-sized school, everyone pitches into the drama – the majority of senior boys were heavily involved in the recent production of The Sound of Music. 'Staff here,' says the head admiringly, 'just knuckle down. I find their example continually reassuring and admirable.' In the words of one parent: 'The teaching my son is receiving is of the highest calibre – the delivery is sympathetic and often original, and the substance is challenging.'

There's been a surge of popularity in chess, which is a lesson in forms 2 and 3. 'It's a great activity,' says the head, 'and a powerful education in its own right'

The potential downside of 'smallness', of course, could be the lack of choice. The 2016 ISI report, while mainly very complimentary, did suggest that the extracurricular activities lacked an element of range as well as some ICT provision. The school has since invested heavily in both hardware and systems management, and the results are welcomed by all parties, although the school website feels mundane and clearly needs some love. Philosophy and Mandarin have also been introduced and new clubs have appeared – coding, Greek and LAMDA all have their own enthusiastic followers. 'He has more after-school clubs from which to choose than he can ever manage,' said a parent, 'and he comes home enthused.'

Above all, there is no trade-off in terms of quality. Because the school is on a relatively small site, there may be a patronising assumption on the part of bigger preps that their own standards are higher. Yet the academics and music at Hereward House are outstanding and the drama and the sport are excellent. Given the number of pupils, it doesn't field the endless numbers of teams of the bigger prep schools, but plays excellent football, cricket and cross-country and uses local facilities (whether it's Primrose Hill for the youngest children or Brondesbury Cricket Club for the older ones) to best advantage. Nor has it sacrificed choice – judo, basketball, hockey and tennis are among other sports played to a high standard. Results hold up well and – admittedly it's not yet a premier league sport – the school's five-a-side soccer players can hold up their heads with the very best.

The school's biennial music concert may not be held in a state-of-the-art 21st century acoustically-perfect concert hall in school grounds, but it's a powerful expression of school-wide dedication and there are ensemble concerts every term which draw in roughly half the school ('and there are many, many other boys doing excellent music in addition to these,' says the head.) 'Outstanding,' said one parent with a very musical child. 'How they bring off this range of talent and dedication in a small school defies all probability.' It's unsurprising, then, that Hereward House pupils have won top musical awards to Eton and Westminster in the past two years. There's also been a surge of popularity in recent times in chess, which is a lesson in forms 2 and 3. 'It's a great activity,' says the head, 'and a powerful education in its own right. I'm glad some of our boys are proving highly successful at it, but what I really value is that it's reaching out to all levels here.'

In the 2016 ISI report, inspectors raised an eyebrow at a system of governance. It isn't hard to see why: the founding head (and still proprietor) is chair of governors. Her grandson is the bursar, and the previous head (who departed at the end of 2014) sits on the governing body. And yet, like all quasi-family schools, the potential downsides are nullified when relationships between the key players are strong, and a former senior school head has recently become a governor. Mr Evans exudes calm and satisfaction, and demonstrably believes he has the latitude to function effectively while benefiting from the support of those who have known the school longest of all.

There's lots of good interaction with the local community, enacted through fundraising initiatives, fun runs, a carol service at the local church and links with the Simon Community for the homeless. Facilities are good (a lab had just been upgraded and the playground relaid when we came round) but there's an eye to what's practical and reasonable, rather than lavish – and therein lies a clue to the underlying ethos of the school. It wants its pupils to give their best in every area of school life and, perhaps above all, to find ways to be themselves while always behaving generously to others. To execute that vision, in the heart of one of the most affluent and challenging parental constituencies in the prep school world, demands clarity of vision and steadfastness of purpose. The head's low-key manner, and his gentle appreciation of his staff, pupils and parents, speaks not just well of him and of them, but also suggests the governors who appointed him know their school as well as their man.

The last word: We saw impressively relaxed and happy staff and children, and this – given the constraints of space – suggests that every aspect of pupils' lives has been thoughtfully and effectively considered. 'In six years as a parent,' said one mother, 'there's never been a day when either of mine haven't wanted to go to school. I don't take that for granted.'

Holy Trinity & St Silas

Hartland Road, London NW1 8DE

020 7267 0771 | admin@holytrinitynw1.camden.sch.uk | www.holytrinitynw1.camden.sch.uk

State | Ages: 4–11 | Pupils: 210

Head: Since 2013, Lorraine Dolan (40s) BEd and masters in education, both from the University of North London. Her first job as an NQT in 1996 was at Holy Trinity and St Silas; 'My plan was never to stay at the same school for long but to have an open mind.' She stayed for 14 years, however, moving to become deputy head at St Paul's Catholic school in Wood Green, returning here when the headship came up.

Tall, with waist-long fair hair, Ms Dolan looks on first impression like someone who might be in the world of media rather than a primary school head teacher. Although softly spoken and friendly, this ex-convent school girl is definitely no pushover and hides a steely determination. It is a prerequisite for this job. Any weaker souls would not survive the legacy of the former head teacher, Anne Williams, who changed the fortunes of a not particularly good school to an 'exceptional school' (in the words of Ofsted) and was a woman who had edited the word 'compromise' from her vocabulary. Ms Dolan says, 'Annie was a force to be reckoned with.' Ms Dolan offers a more 'open door policy' than her predecessor and welcomes parent inclusion in the school. One pupil told us, 'she's very approachable and a great role model.'

She has been described by a parent as being 'very old school, in a good way'. She is very intent on bringing traditional values back into the school and has particularly clamped down on the school uniform, which was a bit hit and miss prior to her headship. As she points out, 'You either have a uniform policy or you don't; you can't have a bit of a uniform.' Another parent told us, 'She is around most of the time and is often chatting to parents in the playground.'

Ms Dolan has a grown up son, whom she had in her early 20s, and who, she says, 'has been the making of me in many ways'. The product of Irish Catholic parents, Ms Dolan went to a convent school, where she says she was 'often challenging the system'. Her son forced her to be responsible, and although she wasn't thinking of a career in education at that time, was accepted onto a Montessori teaching course, 'which was perfect as I could take my son with me and leave him at the nursery'. Little did she suspect then where that first rung up the ladder would eventually lead. She and her long-term partner are both members of a cycling club, and she also enjoys running: 'Keeping fit is a great outlet for stress.'

Entrance: After the customary priority for looked-after children, the primary admissions criterion is church attendance, either at the Most Holy Trinity Church across the road or at St Silas the Martyr in Kentish Town. Approx 60 per cent come via this route; the remaining 40 per cent of admissions are catchment based. Once very much bottom of the parental-choice agenda, the school's intake has altered and now gets more professional parents – particularly in creative and media related fields. Not too many, school hopes – 'we have a good social mix and want to keep it that way'. At the moment, remains a class and ethnic melting pot, with the largest minority being Bangladeshi.

Exit: Mainly to the local comprehensives – Haverstock, William Ellis, Parliament Hill, St Marylebone and Camden School for Girls – but school has also developed a relationship with The Hall, one of north London's leading prep schools, and some year 6 boys go there with bursaries before proceeding to leading London independent day schools.

Our view: Housed in a typical Victorian schoolhouse, a meander from tourist-packed Camden Lock; one has to enter two heavy-duty doors to reach the main reception – the first to the playground and the second to the main building: 'We qualified for extra security,' the head told us (part of their recent funding programme). However, once inside with its pristine, soothing interior, you'd never guess where you were – fresh flowers, polished parquet and a big red school bell are all from another era.

We were particularly struck by an astonishing ceiling display of famous London landmarks – the London Eye, St Paul's Cathedral etc, all made from papier mâché

Teaching at the school is strong; a number of parents have pointed this out and cited a couple of exceptional teachers, one of whom held the school together after the previous head's departure and is described by parents as 'simply the most exceptional, passionate teacher – the cornerstone of the school'. Ms Dolan herself has been very successful in turning the maths results around – something she has been working hard to address. When she first came on board, results had been dipping, but her close monitoring seems to have worked – more or less everyone at least reaches expectations at KS2 Sats, with around two-thirds now exceeding them.

The teaching staff are generally well qualified, with two MAs, one law degree, three teachers who speak fluent French (so French is taught convincingly from reception to year 2), and a couple of graduate teaching assistants who, according to Ms Dolan, arrived with 'passion and drive'. The excellent teaching is partly the legacy of Ms Williams, who had said: 'I'm very snobbish about teachers – they have to have been to a good university and to have travelled. It gives them a cultural understanding', and partly due to the current head who adds: 'All the teachers are clear about my expectations. It's not OK for one child to slip through the net.'

Despite the fact that the majority of pupils arrive at Holy Trinity with well below average attainment, the school is at the pinnacle of the league tables, with results in English in the top one per cent nationally. Literacy is taught for two hours a day, primarily through poetry and prose. This again, we are told, is largely down to another inspirational teacher – a specialist drama teacher who teaches English and drama from reception to year 6, through the works of Shakespeare. Every year the school puts on a whole-school Shakespeare play, including every pupil and member of staff, and has now helped found a borough-wide Shakespeare festival with five neighbouring primaries. Hardly surprising then that, according to Ofsted: 'Pupils' empathy with the works of Shakespeare is quite remarkable.'

All the arts are fundamental to the curriculum. Music is central to the school and one parent told us that music largely formed her decision to send her daughter there: 'The school just feels amazing when you walk in. There is the sound of laughter and always someone playing the piano or another instrument.' Pupils can choose to join the jazz band or one of two choirs, or learn an instrument from a long list of specialist music teachers. However, drop-ins on any of the music groups have been abolished in favour of auditioning for them, as the head firmly believes, 'if you make that sort of commitment, you need to stick to it.'

Art is equally important, and despite limited square footage, has its own department; pupils' work is hung boldly throughout the building. Painting even spills out into the large urban playground (underneath the rattling of the Camden overground train), where one inner-city wall has been reborn as a rural, summer scene (with a 3D vegetable plot to extend the experience). We were particularly struck by an astonishing ceiling display in the upper school hall of famous London landmarks – the London Eye, St Paul's Cathedral etc, all made from papier mâché. The idea for this came from a walk around London with year 6 pupils, who were learning about architecture (from a parent architect) inspired by the imminent development works to the school. One parent told us: 'We're so lucky at this school, there is such a pool of talented and creative parents who can come in and share their skills.' Trips are very much part of the education. Visits to the theatre, opera, ballet and museums are planned on a regular basis.

Though about 40 per cent of pupils are not Anglicans, the Christian message is strong, with a thoroughly involved parish priest (Father Graham), regular church attendance and class mass held half-termly. Grace is said before lunch. Lunch itself is entirely healthy, and mealtimes, too, are considered a development opportunity. Music is played and, on Fridays, tablecloths laid. A firm emphasis on good manners. The 'golden rules' dictate: don't talk with your mouth full; learn to use your knife and fork correctly. Rules elsewhere are equally clear cut. Attentive good behaviour is the norm, but for those who stray, the first offence means displacement to another class; further disruption means an encounter with the head.

Although standards may be firmly upheld, one parent complained that the pastoral care system is not great and there isn't much of a structure in place. However, the head says that whilst historically issues were not dealt with, she 'has worked very hard to get parents to trust that when they raise a concern about their child, whether emotional or academic, it will be dealt with and monitored.' The children are supported by the class teachers. They have weekly circle time sessions and are encouraged to share their concerns as well as develop their understanding about relationships with their peers.

The school takes a proactive approach to its parents, and offers core subject curriculum evenings to support parents with home learning. Parents respond with energetic fundraising – the PTA raises on average £4,000-£5,000 a year which goes towards buying new computers. Ms Williams herself was no ingénue when it came to fundraising and won considerable support from charities – a legacy continued after her death, with the Annie Williams Education Trust, set up by her husband, which has received many donations.

Plans are currently under way to expand the school building and make it more accessible, the school being one of 10 schools in Camden identified as in need of updating. This will include a three-storey extension at the side to house a new office, reception area and staff room and will allow the hall downstairs to be opened up into a large performance space. Classrooms will be increased in size (as they are rather on the snug side) and a lift will be installed, as this old Victorian building is currently unsuitable for anyone with a disability.

The last word: 'Superb' is Ofsted's summary of the Holy Trinity and St Silas experience, and pupils agree: 'We love it here, we don't want to leave,' said one year 6 pupil. And a parent added: 'I just love the mixed demographic and the fact that everyone talks to everyone. I once saw David Miliband [a former parent] in the playground chatting to a mother in flip flops and pyjama bottoms, about the best pirate parties for boys.'

Hugh Myddelton Primary School

35

Myddelton Street, London EC1R 1YJ

020 7278 6075 | admin@humydd.islington.sch.uk | www.hughmyddeltonschool.org.uk

State | Ages: 2-11 | Pupils: 500

Executive Head: Since 2013, Nathalie Parker, BMus (King's College, London), PGCE (Goldsmiths), BSc psychology (Birkbeck). After various posts in south London including deputy head at an all-through academy, glamorous, smoky-eyed Ms Parker (40s) arrived at what, unexpectedly for her, turned out to be a school in difficulties. 'Its Ofsted and data suggested it was a good school, so when it was immediately put on warning notice it came as a shock.' Even so, she took the challenge in her stride, turning around the culture of the school in a matter of months and recently earning from Ofsted the most outstanding of outstanding reports. Charming and persuasive, she is lavished with praise by inspectors and parents. 'Inspirational,' say the former; 'visionary,' chorused a parent. 'She's very good at team building and organising, and is completely non-ideological in the best possible sense. She's prepared to use what works.'

Head of school is Tim Barber, BA history (King's College, London), PGCE (Manchester). Now that Ms Parker is spreading her expertise across the local authority, Mr Barber is responsible for the school on a daily basis. After work at primaries in the north of England and north London, he started at Hugh Myddelton as a year 2 teacher in 2011, and has since done virtually every job going. 'It been quite fast moving,' he notes with understatement. Down-to-earth, friendly and enthusiastic, he's also immensely hard working and committed. 'The two make an extraordinarily dynamic duo,' commented a parent.

Entrance: After an understandable dip in applications, word of improvement has now spread and queues are starting to form. This is a community primary so, once the usual reserved categories have been addressed, siblings and distance from the gates are next in line.

Exit: Strenuous efforts are made to ensure every pupil finds the right secondary, whether that's at a local comp (City of London Academy, Highbury Fields), selective state (Dame Alice Owen's, Queen Elizabeth Barnet), or independent (Highgate, City of London boys and girls, Christ's Hospital).

Eleven plus preparation given for entrance tests and interviews, and high flying year 5 girls encouraged to attend City of London School for Girls summer school.

Our view: What's extraordinary about Hugh Myddelton is the rapidity of its progress from floundering to fantastic, moving from 'causing concern' to 'can't-say-a-word-against-it' in just three years. (Nowadays, it sits in the top three per cent of all schools in England for pupils' progress in reading, writing and maths, and most whizz comfortably beyond the national norm.) The formula for its success lies in excellent teaching, exceptional teamwork and a relentless focus on the needs of every child, starting with incoming 2-year-olds, who are given a speech-and-language fillip to ensure they're reception ready. Reading taught as early as possible, through phonics, corridor walls decorated with common words, and a 'talk-for-writing' strategy (originally introduced for those on the foothills of English, now working well for all).

Teachers consult daily to ensure each child is receiving what they require, and subject-specialist teams work across the age groups. 'In the English team, for example, all the teachers will look at each book, identifying what's being done well, what's needed to improve.' The overall approach is 'keep up, not catch up', supported through tailored work and one-to-one tuition where necessary. Once reading, everyone is given challenging texts, and writing standards are truly impressive. Year 5 and 6 benefit from an additional teacher, bringing class numbers down to 18-20, ensuring everybody gets added focus in these critical final years.

One mother said that her 6-year-old son came home the other day and said 'I'll get you some money from my money box because women don't earn as much as men'

Special needs particularly well supported, with two internal teachers, a speech-and-language specialist and Ms Parker's psychology-informed background. Teaching assistants given specific training, too, and external experts called on as needed. Those who arrive with little English well catered for ('When my daughter started, she was groping for words,' said one parent. 'Now she loves English.') as are the gifted and talented – the school works with the National Association for Able Children (NACE). 'They're completely aware of who the kids are and are very good at getting everyone to learn without making them feel like losers or driving them to distraction,' said one father. 'They stretch them, but never push them too far.' Homework is made fun with six-week topic-based projects, produced with teacher and parent help, and displayed in the dedicated 'homework gallery'.

Virtually every child reaches the government targets in national tests, but tests are certainly not the main objective of the education here and the curriculum is broad and stimulating ('exciting,' say the inspectors). All taught Spanish by a native speaker ('Though we're thinking of moving to Mandarin,' says the head). Expansive new science and technology room allows hands-on experience of everything from cooking to stargazing. Well stocked library is the venue for book club and a welcoming place for older pupils to listen to younger ones read. Technology well supported with a plethora of chrome books and iPads, but personal mobiles locked safely away every morning on arrival.

Ms Parker, a composer by training, came to the school with the brief of improving the arts and sport, and, alongside her multitude of other achievements, these goals have been fully realised. A music specialist now works with classroom teachers, all learn recorder in year 3, keyboard skills in year 5, and singing thrives with junior and senior choirs. Free clarinet and brass tuition put into practice in school band. Music made real, too, with visits to orchestras at the Barbican and Royal Festival Hall. The visual arts also well supported by Islington Arts Factory, and the school has partnered with neighbouring Sadler's Wells Theatre, bringing subsidised tickets and opportunities to perform.

Generous, well kept grounds, Astroturf pitch and well-equipped gym are all put to good use, with a specialist sports coach teaching hockey, tennis and multi-sports. Basketball and football on offer before school, and after-school clubs include karate, gymnastics and street dance. All interests catered for, however, with clubs for Gutsy Girls (to encourage female leadership), archaeology and debate (with pupils excelling in Debate Mate primary-school league.). Much-enjoyed forest school ('Forest school is number one,' said a pupil) takes place in Abney Park in Stoke Newington, developing appreciation of the natural world alongside confidence and independence. High aspirations fostered, too, by 'spotlight days', when pupils visit City University and talk to students about law, computer science, engineering and psychology. Breakfast and after-school club are a boon for working parents.

Named for Hugh Myddelton, royal jeweller to James I, the school was originally founded in the 1850s, but moved to its current building – a

Expansive new science and technology room allows hands-on experience of everything from cooking to stargazing

mid-century gem by Julian Sofaer – in the 1960s. A dazzling new extension added in 2009 was opened by former pupil Yusuf Islam (Cat Stevens). The composite provides a luminous and harmonious backdrop to the calm, well organised and purposeful atmosphere within. Classrooms and corridors are spacious and bright, outside space, blessed by an electronic noticeboard and covered picnic tables, an oasis of green in a gritty urban world.

Behaviour, once something of an issue, is now acknowledged by Ofsted to be 'impeccable'. 'Children won't accept poor behaviour,' says the head. 'They're horrified if someone doesn't open a door.' The 'manners curriculum' focuses on topics such as 'meeting and greeting' and 'how to disagree politely', within an overall culture where the dominant motif is praise rather than blame (with parents regularly alerted to the positive through electronic ClassDojo system).

Pupils given plenty of responsibility – on the school council, as head boy and girl, as anti-bullying champions (the school belongs to the Anti-Bullying Alliance and bullying is a rarity). The message 'Be reflective, responsible and respectful' is also regularly addressed in assemblies, which explore big world issues (gun law, Brexit, equal pay, etc) in 'thought for the week'. 'I'm so impressed by their general knowledge,' said one mother; while another admired the empathy this instils. 'My 6-year-old son came home the other day and said "I'll get you some money from my money box because women don't earn as much as men".' Community engagement also firmly emphasised, and pupils recently won a competition with the bright idea of exchanging their own technical expertise with gardening help from the elderly.

About 60 per cent of pupils are in receipt of free school meals, but local professionals are increasingly in evidence. What's more, parental attitudes throughout have changed. 'When we started,' says the head, 'there was a sense of apathy, even hostility, a real sense of them and us.' That's definitely a thing of the past. Wide ethnic mix, with no dominant group, and kids mix well in school and out. 'The kids love each other and spend a lot of time together. There's a real sense of community.'

Money matters: Though money, as always, is tight, the head has been clever at tapping in to local resources, such as the Worshipful Company of Water Conservators and Thames Water, who helped fund the science room, and Foyles, who contributed to the library. Nearby City University provides volunteer students for extra tuition.

The last word: What a journey this school has been on. 'Everything about this school is fantastic,' exclaimed one parent. 'My kids complain when it's the holidays,' said another. A year 6 who's gone through the revolution agrees with both: 'It's now an exciting place to come to school.'

La Sainte Union

Highgate Road, London NW5 1RP

020 7428 4600 | admissions@lsu.camden.sch.uk | www.lasainteunion.org.uk

State | Ages: 11–18 | Pupils: 1,032; sixth form: 198 (25 boys)

Linked school: LaSWAP Sixth Form Consortium, 169

Headteacher: Since September 2017, Sophie Fegan, 40s. Frenchwoman Mrs Fegan (who retains a slight accent) began at the school teaching French in 2008. Since then, she's moved up the ranks from (popular) teacher, to head of year, then deputy head, so no radical changes expected now she's in the top spot. (Though consultations are taking place with girls on ways to improve the school – and tartan trousers could, one day, be an option.) Smartly suited, earnest, evidently devout, she sees the school's mission as promoting 'gospel values so that girls can go on to lead good Christian lives'.

Hugh Myddelton Primary School

Entrance: Oversubscribed with admissions criteria that don't admit much leeway on the faith front, so realistically only thoroughly practising Catholics need apply. That said, living next to the school gates is not essential, and girls come from north, south, east and west (though a reasonable number worship at Our Lady, Help of Christians, Kentish Town, St Joseph's, Highgate, and St Gabriel of Our Lady of Sorrows, Archway). Siblings given priority and 18 places also awarded annually for musical aptitude, with tests held in November of year 6 and Catholics given priority. Faith criteria not applicable to sixth form entrance, when boys and non-believers may apply to LaSWAP, a four-school consortium formed when LSU unites with neighbouring comprehensives Parliament Hill, William Ellis and Acland Burghley.

Exit: Reasonably large exodus post-GCSE, with about half departing for other RC schools (such as Cardinal Vaughan and the London Oratory) or local FE colleges (City and Islington and Westminster Kingsway). At 18, everywhere and anywhere, with top performers proceeding to Russell Group. Bristol, Manchester, Edinburgh, Bath, Queen Mary and Leicester among recent destinations; the vocationally inclined to apprenticeships. None to Oxbridge in 2019 or 2020.

Latest results: In 2020, 36 per cent 9/7 at GCSE; 84 per cent 9/4 in both English and maths. At A level, 58 per cent A*/B. In 2019 (the last year when exams took place), 29 per cent 9/7 at GCSE; 81 per cent 9/4 in both English and maths.

Teaching and learning: The head is emphatic that this is a 'traditional school offering a traditional curriculum with "no short cuts"': 'We aim to nurture a love of learning, engaging with difficult things and exposing learners to high culture.' (So, year 9 study the work of Bertolt Brecht and Arthur Miller, as well as French poet Lamartine.) Teaching, too, on traditional lines (ie silent, orderly and attentive), with classrooms staffed by the bright-eyed, enthusiastic and energetic. ('Teachers are kind and they help you learn,' said one girl; 'We really trust the teachers,' said another.) Work appropriately challenging and fast paced (a forest of 12-year-old hands, for example, was raised to define the meaning of 'variegated'). GCSE results are strong, particularly in English; RS also noticeably (if, perhaps, unsurprisingly) buoyant. Inspectors, however, have voiced concern about the relative weakness of science and maths, and there was a dip in maths recently, though results seem to be on the up. Here, as elsewhere, the impression is very much that the school is on the case. Post-GCSE, membership of LaSWAP sixth form consortium allows a wide choice of courses (over 30 A levels, from further maths to film studies, plus numerous vocational qualifications) either on site or at one of the sister schools, and sixth formers are given very good support.

Pupils, many joining from Catholic primaries, typically start out strong and just get stronger. Testing carried out in year 7 to assess 'needs', then broad banding applied, but no setting. Instead, the school uses carefully considered 'strategies' to address the requirements of its wide ability range. 'We don't say: you're bright, you're not bright. We teach them how to get where they want through hard work and love of learning.' Progress, as the head notes, is 'phenomenal' (significantly above the national average).

Gracious period buildings and spacious grounds, including a beautiful, peaceful garden (plus orchard), hidden behind its elegant 19th-century frontage

Facilities generally good and up to date but, at least in some subjects, a distinctly old-world mood prevails. In DT, for example, the priority is for girls to 'make sure they can make their own clothes', with the advice that the best preparation for starting at the school is knowing how to thread a sewing machine! (First efforts – a small dress – are then sent to an orphanage in Tanzania.)

Learning support and SEN: Those requiring additional assistance are quickly identified, monitored by a senior member of staff, dedicated SENDCo, learning support assistants and SEN governor, and aided by small classes for English and maths, literacy and numeracy catch-up groups, and external help where needed.

The arts and extracurricular: Impressive extracurricular, with a stimulating range of activities available before and after school and at lunchtime. (Everything from Afro culture to manga, feminist committee to cheerleading, gardening to first aid.) All the arts flourish ('We want students to have access to cultural capital'), but music a notable strength with instrumental lessons in everything from violin to bassoon, and plenty of opportunity to put skills into practice (school orchestra, soul/jazz group, gospel choir, chapel choir, regular concerts, chapel music tour). Annual art competition, poetry workshops, cross-school drama production (most recently The Crucible) encourage creativity, plus good use made of what London has to offer, with the curriculum abandoned several times a year for outings to the National Gallery, etc. Trips further afield, both nationally (geography to the Lake District) and internationally (Spain).

School council (operating at all levels) gives pupils leadership opportunities, as does Duke of Edinburgh bronze. Mass participation (50 girls) in Jack Petchey Speak Out develops public speaking and political awareness (as do visits from politicians). Outward-looking approach also evidenced by the recent acquisition of the British Council's International School Award.

Sport: Sport well catered for with own courts and gym providing scope for basketball, netball, handball, athletics, rounders, trampolining and rugby (with one girl recently selected for Middlesex County). Girls compete regularly in Camden competitions (rounders, athletics, basketball), frequently emerging triumphant, particularly in basketball.

Ethos and heritage: Founded in 1861 by the sisters of La Sainte Union, a French order of nuns, for much of its history LSU was an independent Catholic boarding school, before becoming an all-girls comprehensive in the 1970s. Boys have been admitted into the sixth form since 1995; LaSWAP consortium includes nearby schools William Ellis, Acland Burghley and Parliament Hill.

Punishment, when necessary, is quick and clean, with same-day detention, 'so they know they're forgiven and can start the next day afresh'

Located in the heart of affluent Dartmouth Park directly opposite Hampstead Heath, its convent background has left it with gracious period buildings and spacious grounds, including a beautiful, peaceful garden (plus orchard), hidden behind its elegant 19th-century frontage. This cloistered mood permeates the daily routine, with prayers held every morning (inspired by the school's motto, Each for All and All for God, emblazoned on a banner across the assembly hall), compulsory attendance at weekly mass in the school chapel (sixth form non-believers are allowed to sit in silent reflection), and about 10 per cent of lesson time up to GCSE devoted to RE (five per cent thereafter). Charity and social justice both highlighted, and energetic fundraising undertaken for the LSU Tanzania project, North London Citizens' Project, and various local and national causes, with pupils taking a leading role through the house system in deciding when and which charities to support. Regular cake sales and other activities raise significant sums.

Pastoral care, inclusivity and discipline: A safe and pleasant place to go to school, with attendance and behaviour both exemplary. Girls in tartan pleats and forest-green blazers are generally orderly and well brushed. 'When they enter and leave, they're appropriately dressed. Paying attention to the small details means other things are right as well.' Between 11 and 16, pupils kept on site during the school day, with a keen eye kept out for unhappiness or unkindness, particularly in year 7, when the school runs an effective mentoring scheme with year 10. 'It's the biggest change in their education other than going to university,' says a teacher. 'It's exciting and exhilarating, but it can also be exhausting and a bit daunting.' The home-school bond unusually strong. The online Firefly system documents progress and shares behaviour with parents, who are also aided by workshops on issues such as mental health. Discipline here means instilling good habits: 'We teach children to self-discipline and always know right and wrong. We talk with them and sort them out.' Punishment, when necessary, is quick and clean, with same-day detention, 'so they know they're forgiven and can start the next day afresh'. Plenty of leadership roles for senior students, who act as heads and deputy heads of houses (named for patron saints).

Pupils and parents: Over 90 per cent baptised Catholics, but culturally and socially diverse, united by an atmosphere of respect and cooperation. Pupils – quite often the daughters of old girls – are generally co-operative and industrious. 'There are a lot of studious girls who work hard and get good results,' said one mother. 'If your daughter is that kind of child, she should be able to find like-minded friends.' Parents choose the school for its safe environment and academic focus ('My parents were impressed by its academic success,' said one high achiever) and for the articulate and responsible girls it turns out.

Money matters: Not a rich school by any means either in terms of its students (about a third in receipt of pupil premium) or endowments, but no one seems to suffer the lack. Active Parents and Friends Association raises funds to subsidise school trips, buy computer equipment and refurbish accommodation (such as the sixth form common room).

The last word: A safe, calm and orderly place to go to school, with a strong spiritual core, providing a rich all-round education and producing industrious, articulate, responsible girls.

LaSWAP Sixth Form Consortium

William Ellis School, Highgate Road, London NW5 1RL

020 7692 4157 | laswap@williamellis.camden.sch.uk | www.laswap.camden.sch.uk

State | Ages: 16-19 | Pupils: 1,000

Linked schools: La Sainte Union, 165; Parliament Hill School, 189; William Ellis School, 269

Directors: Since September 2019, Ella Schlesinger and Mayo Ogunlabi are the co-directors. They have their job cut out as working across four schools is complicated. Ensuring consistency across four large comprehensive sixth forms is, in particular, no mean feat, especially when the well-being of roughly 1,000 students is in question – a job made all the trickier by LaSWAP's free flowing arrangement, whereby students could have lessons in any one of the four schools that make up the consortium (La Sainte Union, William Ellis, Acland Burghley and Parliament Hill). To help manage this transient system, school has recently introduced a consortium-wide web based system called e-Tutor, which is available to every tutor in the four schools, and a way of keeping tabs on each student and updating records. New LaSWAP office is at the front of William Ellis School and Parliament Hill School.

Entrance: LaSWAP has some 1,000 pupils. The number has slightly declined over the past few years because of other closer to home schools across London who have opened sixth forms. New entrants make up approximately 40 per cent of year 12. The entrance procedure is intricate, and careful attention must be paid to every step and date. First step is to register interest online. Then, armed with a ticket and a parent, prospective candidates attend the open evening in November. Applications must be submitted by post or by hand in early December – those who miss the deadline are put on the waiting list. All applicants who meet the deadline are offered a meeting at LaSWAP in February or March to discuss subject choice and given offers conditional on GCSE grades. Those with offers are invited to attend the one-day taster sessions held before the start of the summer holidays, when summer assignments are set. Post GCSE results, further enrolment appointments and places are confirmed. Now asks for at least five grade 6s at GCSE (rather than grade 4s, as previously) to study A levels. Pathways other than A levels ensure that individual needs are met.

Exit: Destinations are 'outstanding', and LaSWAP has a significantly above national average success rates to university in general, and Russell Group specifically – the most popular choices are Sussex and London universities, but across a wide range of degree courses: eg international relations, marketing, philosophy, politics, economics and business. Virtually all of their level 2 vocational learners go on to advanced further education, apprenticeships or employment – a third returning to LaSWAP for advanced applied courses. Three to Oxbridge and one medic in 2019.

Latest results: In 2019, 17 per cent A*/A and 44 per cent A*-B at A level.

Teaching and learning: These four comprehensives, geographically within a few hundred metres of each other, created an amalgamated sixth form to provide the widest possible subject variety and range of qualifications. Lucky sixth formers here have a choice of a remarkable 41 A levels, as well as BTecs, NVQs, a choice of six vocational subjects, the new 'flagship' post-16 advanced maths studies, and post-16 GCSEs (for those who need to gain a grade 4/5 in maths or English) About 80 per cent of students follow a purely academic course, the rest take vocational courses, but those who want to can mix and match. IThe consortium's strengths lie in the visual arts (with consistently outstanding results) and arts subjects, like RE, film and media studies and English. Languages tend to perform well, but not many students take them up.

With such a wide and varied intake of sixth form students, we can't help wondering how the recent government move of abolishing most AS levels in favour of linear A levels will impact on future results. School isn't overly concerned – in fact it welcomes the opportunity for students to learn subjects in a bit more depth: 'Students will learn how to learn more deeply and apply this. At the moment, many students acquire the knowledge for the exam, have the exam and then forget it.'

Some criticism for not always taking into account the wide range of ability in this relatively unselective sixth form, but not all would agree – 'In my classes, some people have 10 grade 8s and others mainly 4s, but I haven't found that a problem,' said one boy. A LaSWAP student, we were told, is one who wants to pursue 'more than just academic excellence, with its broad and innovative curriculum'. Teaching (with over 200 'highly experienced' sixth form teachers) is enthusiastic, knowledgeable and well prepared. 'Teachers are good, inspiring and they listen to you', one student told us, but another one grumbled that 'they enforce too much discipline here.'

When a student starts LaSWAP sixth form, they are given a detailed and colourful planner, which includes a mine of information – worth enrolling at LaSWAP for

All students are allocated a base school, depending on the subjects they choose or where they took GCSEs, but most study on a number of sites. Some subjects are taught on all the sites, the more rarefied – music technology, textiles and dance, for example – on only one. Each student is given target grades on entry based on GCSE results and is carefully tracked thereafter, with good exam preparation and help with study skills, as well as thrice yearly reports. 'The communication with home is excellent,' said one parent. 'If my son has done something well they email me. Equally, if he's not doing his homework, they'll let me know.' The academic side is clearly complex, but well organised. 'I wanted to change one of my subjects early on,' said a student. 'I went to see the head of year and it was sorted by the end of lunch hour.'

The arts and extracurricular: The extracurricular here is a significant part of what LaSWAP has to offer, being as varied and extensive as the academic range. The activities, which largely take place on Wednesday and Thursday afternoons, provide 35 options, from ballet and debating to theatrical make-up, DJ-ing and maths masterclasses. Off-site sports include sailing and climbing. The programme is not compulsory, but everyone is encouraged to have a go, regardless of previous knowledge or expertise.

Students also benefit from a wide enrichment programme of visiting speakers and volunteering opportunities that 'stimulate debate and interest in current affairs and the wider community'.

Sport: Sport is a biggie here and students with an interest in sports coaching and working with young people can enrol on the sports education and training programme which consists of level 1, 2 and 3 qualifications. If successful, students can progress until they achieve the advanced level 3 diploma in sports development, which leads on to university and/or employment. This takes place at the nearby Talacre Community Sports Centre.

Ethos and heritage: The four schools (La Sainte Union, an all-girls Catholic school, William Ellis, an all-boys former grammar school, Acland Burghley, a co-ed comprehensive, and Parliament Hill, an all-girls comprehensive) decided to unite their sixth form offering nearly 40 years ago. Each school retains its distinctive ethos and students generally enjoy the change of pace. 'I really like the different atmosphere in each school,' said one. Students can enjoy the plush new common room that Acland Burghley has to offer – or the beautiful and serene gardens of La Sainte Union. However, the free usage of all the various facilities that are not a student's base school has caused a bit of controversy with some students. One told us, 'I thought I'd be able to use the facilities of the other schools, but the reality is I would be asked to leave if I was in the common room of Acland Burghley after school, being a La Sainte Union pupil. It really is for lessons only.' The school says that this is because all students have to be monitored and safeguarded by their head of sixth form, which would be too difficult off site.

And surely even the most disgruntled of students can find somewhere to hang out during lunchtimes, as the location of these schools would be hard to match. Whilst Acland Burghley is a short walk from bustling Kentish Town with its plethora of restaurants, cafés and quirky shops, both William Ellis and Parliament Hill back on to Hampstead Heath.

Parliament Hill and William Ellis combine to form a joint co-ed sixth form, the other schools retain the pupils they take in at 11, and each has its own director of sixth form and heads of year.

One great plus of the model is the halfway house it offers between school and sixth-form college. 'My daughter originally wanted to leave and go to college,' said one mother, 'but once she'd started at LaSWAP, she found the teachers treated her with more respect and she was given much more responsibility for her assignments.' The advantage for students who opt for continuity is that they remain in familiar surroundings while meeting new people and conquering new horizons. 'In the earlier years, my daughter's friends were all local,' said one parent. 'In the sixth form, she suddenly had a whole new set of friends from all over London.' New students, however, don't

The location is hard to match. Even the most disgruntled of students can find somewhere to hang out at lunchtime

feel excluded – 'I felt everybody was in the same position as I was,' said one. 'People had friends from their original school, but they didn't know anyone from the other schools.'

LaSWAP is careful about taking both existing students and recent arrivals to a more independent level of study, with a well-planned induction programme, including a thorough briefing on the outline of each course and relevant dates and department procedures. Students like the friendly, laid-back but organised approach and strong sense of community.

Pastoral care, inclusivity and discipline: All students register at their base school, where they take most of their lessons. Here they have a head of year and a tutor who monitors their work and well-being, with regular interviews to discuss problems and set appropriate targets. Also a confidential professional counselling service and regular PSHE, with outside speakers, group work and discussions. School is also in the process of setting up a sixth form peer advising system around e-safety and well-being. 'Sadly, as we know, there is more self-harming these days, or at least more people are talking about it. We want to train willing sixth form students to signpost professional support services to their student peers around mental well-being and mindfulness.' Students are also offered the opportunity regularly to access the services of two dedicated higher education advisors.

When a student starts LaSWAP sixth form, they are given a detailed planner (which is a colourful diary-like book), which includes a mine of information. Everything from planning one's workload to code of conduct and even evacuation points at the four schools. There is also a Who's Who list at each of the base sites including who is the child protection officer etc. (For this fantastic planner alone we thought it was worth enrolling at LaSWAP…)

Dress code is smart casual, and at enrolment the consortium will stress the importance of having at least five outfits which fit this description. However, Georgina says that they don't like to tell students exactly what to wear, but instead she suggests that 'perhaps they look at people who go to work – either from magazines or commuters – and get ideas from that, so as to prepare them for the eventual workplace.'

Pupils and parents: Students from a huge range of ethnic and social backgrounds apply from a vast swathe of north London. Despite the consortium's leafy surroundings on the eastern edge of Hampstead Heath, all four schools are inner-city comprehensives with a socio-economic intake reflective of the term. Generally, pupils are confident and mature and get on well.

The last word: A good compromise between school and a sixth form college, with an extraordinary range of subjects on offer. Tends to suit the motivated and the self starter, but not ideal for those who will be distracted by studying on a number of sites or who require the disciplined parameters of a school sixth form to function at their peak.

L'École Bilingue Élémentaire

38

St David's Welsh Church, St Mary's Terrace, London W2 1SJ

0207 224 8427 | admin@lecolebilingue.com | www.lecolebilingue.com

Independent	Ages: 3–11	Pupils: 120	Fees: £11,760 pa

Headteacher: Since its opening in 2004, Veronique Ferreira, who studied biochemistry at the University of Paris, and after obtaining her teaching licence in 1999 began her career as a primary school teacher in the suburbs of Paris, working with children with behavioural and academic difficulties. This gave her a lot of insights into the different learning styles of children, something that has shaped a lot of the teaching approach she has established at L'École Bilingue. Moving to London, she started in a French nursery school, but as parents continued to speak of their interest in a more bilingual programme, she pondered on how she might introduce a different sort of

French primary school model in London. She focused on child development theories, looking at Canadian, UK (including EYFS) and French Breton bilingual educational models.

Youthful yet wise beyond her years, her confidence is drawn from her solid foundation in pedagogical studies and the popularity of the school which was her brainchild. Her partner and the father of her daughter, Franck Laurans (head of administration), has provided the business knowledge needed to help her realise her vision for a school that is small, personalised and less rigid that the traditional French models where her students can 'find pleasure in learning'.

Curriculum is bilingual. Children move between English and French classrooms so that they are immersed in the relevant language for that part of the day

Entrance: L'École Bilingue is non-selective, but with only 15 places at the 3-year-old entry class, places are highly sought-after. Parents like the fact that, unlike other French schools, this is a transparent process. Priority is given to siblings (which can take up three-quarters of spaces), but after that it is first-come, first-served, so sign up early – from birth if you wish. (Nationality/passport are not a factor as in other French homologue schools.) Vacancies for children older than 3 are subject to space; worth a call but most classes are wait-listed, so as soon as someone leaves (and with many expats, children do leave) there is someone to fill the spot. Note that if you miss out on the first round you need to proactively let them know you remain interested.

Exit: The head meets parents individually to discuss the options, and some non-native French speakers may at this point opt for 11+ exams (a very few leave at age 7 or 8) and a move away from the French system. Recent examples include Kew House and Holland Park. As the school is part of the AEFE agency for French education abroad, year 6 pupils have automatic access to French secondary schools such as the two Lycées (South Kensington and Wembley) or the Collège Français Bilingue in Kentish Town, which follows the bilingual mode, and most go on to one of these. Others to Winston Churchill, Wetherby Senior School and Queen's Gate. While moving from L'École to the ginormous French Lycée is a big change, the Lycée tries to place two L'École students in the same year form group, so that helps a bit. The school has noted that French students repatriating to Paris often seek out bilingual schools there to keep their English language strong.

Our view: The curriculum is bilingual French and English, and although the French curriculum model is predominant, the head says that she has looked in depth at other curricula, including the national curriculum, the IB primary years and the international primary curriculum, and drawn on elements of all these. Some subjects are taught in French (French, maths, history), some in English (science, English, geography) and some are taught in both languages simultaneously (arts, ICT, drama, music). Children move between English and French medium classrooms so that they are immersed in the relevant language for that part of the day.

Though a small school, the limited space is used to good effect and is immaculately tidy. The compact library is brimming with French and English children's books, a cheerful space where we saw some one-to-one learning taking place; walls lined with colourful boards neatly display creative work by students of all ages; we noticed some tailors' mannequins with student-designed fashions – part of a broader project including all the London French homologue schools in celebration of the centenary of the Lycée Charles de Gaulle. Some special needs support (French and English) available; some children with EHC plans in the school receive individual support either in-class or on a withdrawal basis. Teachers (19 in total, average age early 30s) are a mixture of French and English, all suitably trained and qualified. Staff turnover is higher amongst the French teachers than the English as they may be here as accompanying spouses or may move on to other French-medium schools in London or abroad.

By all accounts, the pupils are busy and engaged in a wide range of activities. They are especially proud to have been invited – by recommendation of the French education inspector – to participate in the French Parlement des Enfants (a sort of 'junior parliament'). This event has influenced some of the themes and topics that have been studied by pupils in all the year groups. Other academic extras sometimes include a French mathematics competition for French schools in the north of Europe. French assessments are given in year 3 and year 6 to measure attainment against French standards; the school is inspected by Ofsted as well as the IEN French Inspector for the northern European region.

Year 3 goes to Brighton for two nights, year 5 spends three days in East Sussex and year 6 goes to Brittany for a week. The music programme is strong and some children do extra Suzuki violin and piano. Parents sang the praises (no pun intended) of the innovative music teacher who

Parents sang the praises (no pun intended) of the innovative music teacher who had recently done a 'bilingual Beatles' unit

had recently done a 'bilingual Beatles' unit. As with other London French schools, many of the extracurricular activities are organised by the parents' association, and parents run some of the clubs, which include fencing, dance, art, choir and football. There are no competitive sports on offer; they use the local sports centre – where many students do taekwondo after school; from year 2 they swim at Imperial College pool. There are two major shows – the annual Christmas carol service and an end-of-year show. We saw the former in final rehearsal – joyful voices, silver tinsel halos and red Santa hats.

Though the school is secular, some of the ecclesiastical architectural features in the former Welsh church nestled in a quiet back street in Maida Vale have been put to effective use, making this a most unusual school building. An enclosed garden behind the school features a vegetable garden for pupils, an eco-pond (with resident creepy crawlies), and an area for messy hands-on learning with sand and water. There is an outdoor play area at the front of the school. A small multi-purpose hall is used for assemblies. Four-course lunches (optional) are prepared and served at school by cooks who know each child by name, chivvy those with picky palates to eat their vegetables and then report to parents on how many ate their carrots. Too much chatter is discouraged during lunches to encourage eating; an adult may read stories aloud instead.

There is a big emphasis on developing the 'soft skills' and the small size means that there is no anonymity in the school. Everyone contributes; everyone has a role to play. The appeal, parents say, is that at l'École they have found a near-perfect balance of strong (French) academic foundations in a very caring environment where everyone knows everyone. The intimacy of the school ensures that behaviour standards are high, and parents subtly suggest that the presence of several English teachers means that discipline is managed differently than in traditional French schools. Parents describe the children as 'kind' and very welcoming of new students. It's also highly inclusive. 'Birthday parties usually involve all of the siblings.'

Parents are big fans of this school, so much so that when they heard of the Good Schools Guide interest in meeting them, they organised a coffee morning (mostly mums, though one dad came) to share frankly their opinions about the school. The small size is an attraction – 'it's digestible for young children'. Another said, 'It's like comparing a mom and pop shop with B&Q.' One recent arrival accustomed to French schools voiced a concern that l'École may lack rigour; others from elsewhere in Europe and the US were delighted with the academic standards. Despite its small size, it appears that communication is patchy; some people seem to be in the know; others (particularly those new to the school) felt they were out of the loop. The school gate is definitely the place to find out what's happening. It seems that parents who are not fluent French speakers can find other parents willing to help and explain things.

Some 40 per cent of families are French (expat and local), 25 per cent are dual French/other nationals, 18 per cent are French/British, and some eight per cent represent other nationalities (including French-speaking north Africans, Canadians and others). Some international families also speak Arabic, Spanish, Italian, etc. Most families live nearby and walk to school, though some are drawn from as far as Fulham, Kentish Town, South Kensington and Hampstead. Because of the school's South Kensington origins, a bus that comes from the Brompton Road area serves families who joined the school in the early days.

Four-course lunches are prepared and served by cooks who know each child by name and report to parents on how many ate their carrots. Too much chatter is discouraged

The school is owned by founders Franck Laurans and Veronique Ferreira. Parents like the fact that this couple, who 'live above the shop', are firmly at the helm; they feel they provide continuity and sustainable leadership that secures the school's future – at least for the time being.

Money matters: Some subsidies come from the French government for French national students.

The last word: Described by one parent as small, friendly 'village' school that draws on the best of French academics and English pastoral education, this bite-size school in the centre of London is worth a visit by parents who want something a bit different.

The Lyceum School

65 Worship Street, London EC2A 2DU

020 7247 1588 | registrar@lyceumschool.co.uk | www.lyceumschool.co.uk

Independent	Ages: 3–11	Pupils: 145	Fees: £17,655 pa

Headteacher: Since January 2019, Hilary Wyatt, previously head of Eaton Square Kensington (once called Hyde Park School), also owned by Dukes Education. Masters in education, NPQH and is an ISI inspector. She has also been head of pre-prep at Durston House, and has taught pupils from nursery to A level during her nearly 30-year career.

Entrance: Via assessment and taster session 'to ensure that the school is able to meet the physical, social and learning needs of the child'. Children wanting to join from year 4 upwards are asked to take small online GL assessment in maths and English during their 'taster' morning.

Exit: In 2020, leavers to Channing, Eaton Square Upper School, Francis Holland (Regent's Park), James Allen's Girls' School (JAGS), More House, Portland Place and South Hampstead High. The school explicitly sets itself to teach to 11+ entry, although they will try to support and guide families who are looking to have their children prepared for 7+ and 10+. There are clear expectations that all pupils, bar the very youngest, will have a little homework, but care is taken to ensure that it leads on from what has being gone that day in school, and is never burdensome.

Our view: The school began life in 1997 in what was once the Radio Times production building in Paul Street, largely at basement level. Has now moved to a new five-storey building with its own playground plus yoga studio and dedicated science/arts room (with a professional artist coming in). It communicates an unpretentious cheerfulness which is both attractive and impressive, and a strong sensitivity to performing and visual arts. The classrooms tumble over with happy children – a lot of quite concentration was apparent when we visited, and the teachers seemed calmly and gently immersed in the children and in what they were doing.

There is a 7.30am breakfast club for early arrivals but parents are welcome to be around until shortly before 9am – coming to assemblies, meeting teachers and so forth, and now joining in Tuesday yoga lessons. Then it's school time and parents go off (many work in the City, of course, which makes dropping off and collection of children a great deal easier). Now has its own dining room with hot organic lunches served. School is finished by 4pm but there are after-school clubs until 5pm, generally managed by the teaching assistants. For some children, whose parents work late, there is a homework clubs until 5.45pm. It's a long day for a young child, but staff pace everything with a view to offering reassurance and, when the moment suggests itself, relaxation.

There's a lively and happy nursery department (with newly renovated classroom), with some pupils attending part time and some doing the full five days. 'We did a trial period,' said one parent, 'but very soon there was no doubt in anyone's mind. We'd picked a winner.' There's plenty of learning even here, but evidently gently calibrated to allow the children's days to be full of interest and excitement. By reception, there is more time and focus being given to the rudiments of reading and writing and counting, and the journey obviously picks up pace between years 1 and 6.

The ethos of the school is avowedly traditional, but mainly in the sense of celebrating ageless good manners – being mindful of others and of their feelings

One singularity of the Lyceum is the emphasis it places on a topic approach – that is, picking up on a subject or theme which will allow the children to experience it through a host of media and disciplines. 'For me,' said a parent who has had two children go through the school, 'this way of learning has been decisive. It allows the children to get immersed and excited in a way which feels very natural and gives them all a reference point. It really impacts on their experience of school and of each other and spills over into home.' The aim is to stimulate and channel artistic and creative energies, and use these to help reinforce their excellence in traditional subject areas. The library is generously provisioned and clearly a favourite spot for many.

Pupils with special needs are able to draw off a specialist teacher who comes in several days each week. In addition to the qualified teachers, there is also a battery of teaching assistants, and full-time support staff in the nursery and reception years. The most recent two deputies have gone on to their own headships.

Theatre and music are at the heart of each pupil's experience. All children learn the recorder and most at least one or two instruments – and, of course, they sing. There is a full-time music teacher and a plethora of instrumental teachers. There's at least one big production each term and a big band, an orchestra and a chamber choir – impressive in a school of around 100 pupils, all of whom leave by the age of 11. They are particularly proud of their summer term concert – the so-called 'summer pudding'. There are endless other concerts and performances besides: a Christmas concert at the Wesley Chapel, a chamber choir concert at St Giles. That's in addition to termly performances for most year groups, often tied in with the particular topics they've been studying during the term.

Both before and after school, clubs flourish: chess, dance of all kinds, French, Spanish, Latin, Chinese – the list goes on and on. There are also visiting speakers and the children seem completely unfazed by visitors and happy to engage with them. Twice a year every pupil from year 3 and year 4 goes away on week-long residentials, with years 5 and 6 going away three times a year. These are designed to extend academic learning (often that which features within pupils' topics), and also offer cultural, social and artistic enrichment. Most are in the UK, but recent year 6 destinations have included Paris, Amsterdam and Rome.

Sport becoming a real strength with teams competing regularly against other schools. One afternoon is spent each week at the Royal Artillery Ground, football training is now under way at Finsbury Park, and they swim at the Golden Lane pool on Friday afternoons. Sports day is at Mile End Stadium, featuring track and field events, with more than 40 competing in the latest parents' race. Links have opened up with local community groups – the chamber choir recently went along to sing to a group of local elderly people, and there's much energetic fundraising for good causes, also for elderly people and also for Great Ormond Street Hospital.

The ethos of the school is avowedly traditional, but mainly in the sense of celebrating ageless good manners – being mindful of others and of their feelings. There's no hint of stuffiness and, while it styles itself Christian, it embraces children of all faiths and of none. 'I find the children unusually empathic,' one mother told us. 'They're extraordinarily supportive of each other. Not my experience in other schools!'

One singularity of the Lyceum is the emphasis it places on a topic approach – that is, picking up on a subject or theme that allows the children to experience it through a host of media and disciplines

Children wear a simple but appealing uniform – navy duffel coats are a nicely archaic touch, as are the girls' hats (felt in winter and a very smart boater in summer). They look confident and upbeat as they go about their days. At no point did we glean anyone taking on airs and graces – a great tribute to the school and its families.

As the school is located in the middle of a transport hub, most pupils travel by tube with their parents. Many parents use the time between 8am and 9am to ensure they are in close contact with form teachers, who are the first port of call. There are also written reports twice a year and a two week slot at the end of each term during which parents can book to meet teachers for a full half hour. No parents' evenings as such.

A cosmopolitan feel – many Europeans and Asians – as befits somewhere in the financial heartland of London. Parents are industrious, unpretentious and seem very grounded. They want their children to have a happy and effective start to their schooling. With just over 100 pupils, the Lyceum has one form per year and, for the moment, seems happy to keep it that way.

Money matters: Fees are mid-range and an effort is made to keep down extras. Nursery vouchers are also accepted.

The last word: This is a happy school, calmly and competently working on bringing out the very best in their youngsters, and laudably unprecious. 'This is real education,' said one parent. 'The children are happy and mindful of one another. It's not greedy, it's not pushy, and people care.' The smooth transition they make to next-stage schooling seems to bear all that out, and is a huge recommendation.

Mossbourne Community Academy

100 Downs Park Road, London E5 8JY

020 8525 5200 | enquiries@mca.mossbourne.org | www.mca.mossbourne.org

State | Ages: 11–18 | Pupils: 1,322; sixth form: 289

Principal: Since 2017, Rebecca Warren.

Entrance: Some 1,500 apply for the 216 places, making it one of the country's most oversubscribed schools. The school is looking for a balanced intake: 'We want a comprehensive – we don't want a secondary modern.' Applicants sit cognitive ability tests to divide into four equal ability bands. Fifty per cent of places in each band are given to those who live within the inner zone (up to 1km from the gates); 30 per cent of places go to those in the middle zone (1-2km) and 20 per cent to those in the outer zone (2-3km). Priority is given to looked-after children, those with a child protection plan, siblings, those with medical needs and children of staff. Further places by lottery, which school says prevents parents from buying their way into the school by moving into a property nearby, although some parents say the inevitable consequence of the gentrification of Hackney is that this feels less of a community school than in the past. Offers an additional 20 year 9 places to those with the potential to become elite rowers (zoning does not apply to this group).

The lower sixth form has 200 places. Applicants must meet the demanding criteria of seven 9-4 GCSEs including English and maths, with priority given to pupils already at the school – around 100 of whom generally secure places. All candidates, including those already at the school, must also meet the subject specific entrance criteria in their chosen A level subjects. Whilst successful external candidates used to come mostly from other Hackney comprehensives, they are increasingly applying from further afield, utilising the quick and easy train route from Liverpool Street.

Exit: Those who leave at GSCE leave mainly do so to do vocational qualifications or go straight into work. After sixth form, 90 per cent to universities, nearly half of those to Russell Group universities (a wide mix). Thirteen to Oxbridge in 2019. Broad array of subjects studied, including music, maths, physics, engineering, law, communications; six medics and one dentist in 2019. Remaining 10 per cent mainly into apprenticeships, with around 4-10 students taking a gap year.

Latest results: In 2020, 39 per cent A*/A at A level. In 2019 (the last year when exams took place), 40 per cent 9/7 at GCSE; 69 per cent got 9-5 in both maths and English. At A level, 33 per cent of grades were A*/A in 2019.

Teaching and learning: Exceptional results. Not only are these some of the best state school results in the capital, they are also all the more extraordinary when you consider that some of the pupils arrive in year 7 hardly able to read. That said, Hackney is experiencing a rise in the quality of students leaving its primary (and secondary, for that matter) schools, making Mossbourne a less steep learning curve for students than it once was.

School has remained in the top one per cent in the country for value added ever since it opened, a feat it puts down to several factors. First, they've created an environment with a 'can do' attitude, where it's cool to learn. Second, there are exceptionally strong structures in place, with a strict uniform policy, ferocious discipline and meticulous monitoring with weekly target setting. The 'personalised learning agenda' is certainly not just government jargon at this school. Third, young and eager teaching staff provide top quality teaching, helped by great facilities. 'Three things are expected of the teaching staff here – giving high quality feedback; providing nurture and care; and being accountable for their results. The rest is up to them,' says school. Although some teachers are inevitably better than others, they generally do whatever it takes to help kids grasp the subject and are nearly always prepared to go the extra mile, say parents. 'Whatever support you need, they'll give it,' said one.

The banded intake is set on entry in all the main curriculum subjects (English, maths, science, humanities, ICT and modern languages), with significantly smaller class sizes for lower sets and considerable movement between sets. Music, drama, dance, PE, art and design technology are not setted. Three modern languages on offer at GCSE – French, German, Spanish – as part of the core curriculum, and students also have the opportunity to take public exams in Turkish (large take-up), Latin (significant take-up), Bengali, Swedish, Italian. 'We meet the requirements of parents,' says school, 'so if they speak a certain language at home, but want their son or daughter to learn it in a more formalised way here, we can accommodate that.'

Traditional academic sixth form, offering around 25 A level subjects, the most popular of which are maths (around two-thirds take this), English (around half choose this), history, psychology and the three sciences. Also on offer are Latin and classical civilisation, plus creative options such as music, art and drama.

Plenty of computers throughout, many built into the modern white desks – technology is embedded into learning here. Homework is set in abundance, but a 4.20pm finish for all means students can spend the last period of the school day either doing homework, preparation for the next lesson or revision – especially good for students lacking a quiet space to work at home. This period can also be used for some of the 30 activities on offer – from bicycle maintenance to table tennis and from journalism to debating club – although only if the student commits to doing their homework later on those days. Saturday morning school not compulsory, but provides a safe place to do weekend activities such as the City explorers' club, revision lessons, Mandarin and other optional classes (including English for non-native speakers) and, of course, sports.

Learning support and SEN: Outstanding autistic spectrum disorder provision via its own well-resourced teaching centre and well-qualified specialists. 'We take three children per year under this provision, which continues in sixth form and beyond, through the transition into college or work,' says school. 'Everyone is fully integrated into mainstream school life here.' Parents are impressed. 'The help they've given my son around his dyslexia has changed his life. He went from struggling to write a paragraph in year 7 to writing reams of pages within months, and his growing confidence led to him moving up his sets too,' said one parent.

The arts and extracurricular: Music is a specialism, with over 250 pupils having subsidised instrumental lessons. Junior and senior choirs and bands, along with an orchestra, all perform in regular concerts and performances. Music scholars programme enables selected students to perform in public at the likes of the Jazz Café and Tower of London, and these students are also expected to share their learning back at school to help develop other students. 'My children had never done music before Mossbourne and I now have a leading guitar playing, violin playing child,' one parent told us.

Drama practice mainly takes place in the modern and well-equipped auditorium and lecture theatres, culminating in regular performances and an annual whole-school production, with recent examples including Charlie and the Chocolate Factory, Romeo and Juliet and Little Shop of Horrors.

Not only some of the best state school results in the capital, but all the more extraordinary when you consider that some of the pupils arrive in year 7 hardly able to read

Plenty of examples of skilled and creative artwork showcasing strong artistic talent across fine art, clay, screenprinting and more. A dedicated A level art studio means students never have to compromise on space and time to work. 'I always think art is one of the unsung successes of Mossbourne,' one student told us.

Trips to Edinburgh, Belgium, the Isle of Wight, language trips to Spain and Germany; Spanish play, poetry competition, debating, links with London College of Fashion. Lots of careers advice. 'My son talks about his future a lot – he has high aspirations,' said one parent.

Sport: Sports include football, netball, basketball, cricket and 'best in Hackney' for athletics. Rowing is big and continues growing, with links to the London Youth Rowing and London Regatta Centre, opposite City airport – originally a training centre for the Olympics and still a world-class training facility for the school's rowers, of whom the elite may train 12 times a week. Rowing is part of the PE timetable in years 7-9; recent medals at British championships and European and world indoor event. Impressive sports facilities include a full-size sports hall and rowing gym, while all grass sports take place on Hackney Downs. Latest on the building agenda is a performance pavilion, a dedicated space designed by Rogers Stirk Harbour + Partners, where students can train on-site for rowing, as well as providing extra sensory provision for the school's autistic intake and enhancing the school's already notable music provision.

Ethos and heritage: Founded on the site of Hackney Downs School, once a successful local grammar school, whose alumnae include Sir

Michael Caine and Harold Pinter. By the 1990s, however, it had become notorious as 'the worst in Britain' and was eventually demolished. Mossbourne was rebuilt on the same site, a tricky triangle bounded on two sides by railway lines. Founding principal Sir Michael Wilshaw worked alongside architects, Richard Rogers and Partners, to design a school (costing £32.5 million) which met his requirements. Now one of the largest wooden structures in England (known locally for looking like an IKEA, not least because it's huge and blue on the outside), it was created in a V shape, which holds in its arms a welcoming triangular social area, complete with tables and benches, basketball areas, table tennis tables etc.

'If you sweat the small stuff, the big stuff takes care of itself,' says the school. 'The most serious offence I've ever seen here is talking in class,' said a student

Wilshaw believed that pupils need to be kept under constant observation, so the head's office and the classrooms all overlook the grounds. No corridors – hidey-holes for bullying – and no staffroom, since Wilshaw felt teachers need to be involved at break times and after school, when most trouble occurs. Inside (where the IKEA comparison still feels apt, such is the emphasis on modern, innovative and fresh interiors) the triple-height space is light and airy and learning takes place in 'learning areas', which are split into themes of sport, history, music etc – including one specifically for year 7s, whose transition is a major area of focus. Glittering new sixth form centre.

In each glass-walled classroom – all of which have an open-door policy – all students begin lessons by reciting the Mossbourne reflection: 'Throughout this lesson I aspire to maintain an inquiring mind, a calm disposition and an attentive ear, so that in this class and in all classes I can fulfil my true potential.' Sure enough, the students we saw did look attentive and interested.

Active school council and peer mentoring scheme for core subjects. Prefects in year 13. No house system. Pupils we spoke to were articulate, polite and delightful – oozing pride about their school. We were also wowed by the set-up here. It's bright, contemporary and spotless, with superb facilities and seemingly endless examples of attention to detail, including language booths and a huge amount of space for private study.

Pastoral care, inclusivity and discipline: Woe betide students who don't toe the line here, with staff giving out detentions for things like keeping a watch on during PE, untidy uniform and being more than 10 seconds late when the morning whistle goes at 8.40am. 'We work on the principle that if you sweat the small stuff, the big stuff takes care of itself,' says the school. 'Nothing ever escalates into anything more serious,' agreed one student. 'The most serious offence I've ever seen here is talking in class.'

Among parents, it tends to be the middle-class liberals who struggle, with some thinking teachers can be overzealous. There was also a feeling among some parents we spoke to that new teachers are particularly extreme. 'There's a joke that new teachers here don't smile until Christmas,' one told us. 'My son got a detention for writing his homework on the wrong page – I mean, come on,' said another. But most approve, saying the heavy-handedness has made their child very driven.

No physical contact between students is allowed ('If a boy has his arm around a girl, how do we know it's not making her uncomfortable, but she's too embarrassed to say, for example?' explains school) and no more than six people in a single group in the playground. Staff always on hand, with stairwells manned between lessons and students monitored after school.

Pre-GCSE pupils wear smart grey and red school blazers and neatly knotted ties, sixth formers graduate to business-like suits and skirts (at or below the knee). Mobiles banned and students not allowed to enter shops on their way home or loiter outside the gates in groups. Racism a non-issue, and the same can be said for truancy, with a 96 per cent attendance rate.

Pastoral care exceptional. Everything is geared towards students feeling safe and comfortable so they are ready to learn, with as much access as they need to school counsellors, who come in as and when they're required (the school works with a private company), plus plenty of senior teaching staff (including the deputy head) whose sole responsibility outside teaching is pastoral care. Few personal problems go unnoticed, whether self-harm or being picked on. At the first sign, parents are invited to come and speak to the staff, with two dedicated meeting rooms available. 'We very much believe parents are our partners and are fundamental to the success of the school,' says school. Bullying extremely rare and when discovered, it's dealt with swiftly and seriously. 'My daughter told me about a boy who came out in year 8 and there was no nastiness about it at all, with everyone being really accepting – that would have been unheard of in Hackney in the past,' one parent told us.

Pupils and parents: A large percentage of the intake comes from the adjacent Pembury estate, an urban sprawl which tends to hit the headlines for its shootings and drugs rather than its high educational aspirations. Two-thirds of pupils are from minority ethnic groups (many Turkish Kurds), two-fifths speak English as a second language, 50 per cent are on free school meals. But also a fair number of clued-up, middle-class parents – the kind who used to go private or bus their children out of the borough – who fight from a great distance to get their children the superb education the school offers.

Money matters: Money not a problem at this well-resourced school – everything from the buildings to the technology is of the highest standard and whatever the head wants to get done he has the means to achieve.

The last word: If ever there was a school proving that the right ethos, leadership and sufficient resources can provide not just a good education but a great one, in the most deprived of areas, this is it. Everything about it is geared around the concept of passive supervision and students feeling safe, nurtured and ultimately ready to learn. This, together with the combination of high-quality teaching, excellent facilities and strong discipline and pastoral care, means it's hardly any wonder that results are outstanding and that parents fight hard to get their kids in.

North Bridge House Preparatory School

41

1 Gloucester Avenue, London NW1 7AB

020 7267 6266 | prep.reception@northbridgehouse.com | www.northbridgehouse.com/prep-school-regents-park

Independent	Ages: 7-13	Pupils: 465	Fees: £19,275 pa

Linked schools: North Bridge House Pre-Prep School, 181; North Bridge House Senior Canonbury, 185

Headteacher: Since January 2019, James Stenning, previously head of sixth form and deputy head academic at North Bridge House Canonbury. Educated at a prep school in Kenya then Downside school, with an economics degree from Swansea, a PGCE and a masters in education leadership from Buckingham. Began his career teaching economics at St Olave's grammar, then head of economics and head of extracurricular at Highgate (where economics became one of the most popular A levels, and he was heavily involved in DofE and outdoor education). Joined NBH Canonbury in 2014. Married to Tom, a group account director for an advertising agency. Very keen runner, often taking part in marathons in far flung corners of the globe such as North Korea, Sierra Leone and Nairobi.

Entrance: Entrance into year 3; most move seamlessly from the pre-prep but around 20 places remain for external applicants. Assessments in English, maths and reasoning taken in the January of year 2. Open mornings held throughout the year. Occasional places arise throughout the school so always worth a call.

Exit: Practically all aim for London day schools (the odd one each year may board at eg Downe House, Sevenoaks or Haileybury), with Channing, South Hampstead, Francis Holland and Immanuel College most popular currently amongst girls, Mill Hill and City of London amongst boys. All girls leave at the end of year 6 (although they no longer have to, they do still leave). Most boys stay until the end of year 8. Some parents of boys who leave at the end of year 6 expressed concern that their sons didn't get the required support – 'school not geared up to boys leaving at 11'.

Our view: Situated on the corner of Gloucester Avenue where Primrose Hill meets Camden Town, North Bridge House Prep School is a big and busy school on a big and busy road. Cramped outside but spacious inside, but there are plans afoot to renovate the playground to make it 'a more green and friendly space'. School compensates by sending the children to Regent's Park, a five minute walk away, where they can kick a ball and let off steam. A feature of all Cognita schools, security is thorough, tight and unforgiving. Everyone is vetted at the door, lanyards flow from reception. The timing of our visit was not long after the terrorist attack on Westminster Bridge, so with year 8 boys going out on daily trips in central London (part of the post common entrance curriculum) security issues were very high on the agenda. There are regular security drills and all the staff given guidance on how to talk the children about these issues. Everyone here is conscious of the importance of balancing safety with the need to take risks, but acknowledge that it is not an easy balance to strike in this climate.

The school has moved into its 80th decade, and it's over 30 years that it has been on this site, and nearly 15 years since it was bought by Cognita. Now under the leadership of corporate dynamo, Chris Jansen, Cognita has had a chequered history. Signs suggest this is soon to change, though change in education is slower than the pace of change Jansen is used to achieving. North Bridge House Prep has always been one of the more successful schools in its stable, but the streamlining, management, sharing of resources and marketing are clear for all to see. Data, tracking the performance of pupils and staff, is an important tool and is used very effectively here. The SIMS system paints a profile of the whole child. The staff are in control and parents feel safe and assured that their child is not lost in the system. There is mutual support and sharing of resources between the heads across the Cognita schools, particularly all four North Bridge House schools.

High praise from parents for the quality of teachers, particularly class teachers. While many said the school feels a bit like a machine – in a good way – they all said that the class teachers brought a very personal feel. SEN support is given primarily in the classroom. However there is flexibility, and occasionally your child may be given one-to-one lessons at the expense of a language if necessary. Range of conditions from ADHD and autism to dyscalculia and dyspraxia. Strong SEN team, says school, and concurred by parents, and it would only turn away a child it felt it couldn't support. There is a 'well-being officer' as well as a school counsellor (available at additional cost).

Children study both French and Spanish as well as Latin from year 6 and some take up ancient Greek. Academics are solid, sometimes inspiring. Ofsted says outstanding. Setted for maths from year 5. Girls and boys are also taught separately from year 6, the intention to prepare them more thoroughly for their respective exams. In years 7 and 8 there is a top, scholarship stream and three other classes. Technology woven into the curriculum; there are laptops and iPads available on each corridor for use in any lesson. Two imaginatively decorated science labs with planets hanging from the ceiling, and molecule diagrams. Classrooms are high ceilinged, spacious and well equipped. Corridors wide with highly polished floors and well kept carpets.

Lots of co-curricular. Music, drama and sport all thrive here. Plenty of informal concerts in the local church as well as the large summer and Christmas concerts. You don't have to be a maestro to perform. Art room at the top of the school among the roof beams. An inspiring space and we saw cubist self-portraits inspired by Braque. Each child is given an art sketchbook that they use all year. Year 8s were out and about on a street art tour of Brick Lane. Drama productions take place in the 'chapel' (lunch and talks also happen here). Everyone gets involved; recent productions include Matilda and Canterbury Tales. Lots of adventurous trips – PGL and bushcraft, as well as to France, China and Morocco, and post common entrance sailing for year 8 after their intensive trips around London. Football and cricket for the boys, netball and rounders for the girls. Good use is made of Regent's Park and the Astro at Talacre sports centre in Kentish Town. Sports day is a huge event: around 350 parents and spectators attend the event at the Saracens sports ground in Barnet Copthall. There is a lot of focus on chess, taught by external specialists, and the pupils win competitions – national as well as local and within the school. A number of talks from outside speakers – engineers, journalists, army officers and others (parent contacts come in useful here and school recently started an alumni network). Topics range from the building of the channel tunnel to recycling and international affairs. Disappointing library, surprising in a school with such a strong focus on learning.

There is a lot of focus on chess, taught by external specialists, and the pupils win competitions – national as well as local and within the school

Discipline is strong. System of house points (four houses: Guinevere, Merlin etc) encourages children to try harder and behave well. From year 6 they can get demerits as well as merits. Lots of positions of responsibility from head boy and girl (though a slight mismatch here as girls are in year 6 and boys in year 8), to heads of houses and sports captains. All traditional prep school stuff that provides the glue and grit that make the system work. Parents a real mixture of busy professionals (in a high proportion of families both parents are working hard), mostly English and based in north London, but there are some European nationals, and other overseas parents from further afield – US, Canada, China and Japan.

Lots are in the media and the arts, and and there is a smattering of celebrities and a number of first time buyers. With little playground space to congregate in it can take time to find your milieu but most do and speak warmly of their fellow parents.

The last word: A large, bustling, well-oiled machine of a school that – almost always – matches expectations. Children here are busy, happy and safe. A good choice for your all rounder who isn't likely to get fazed and is ready to seize the many opportunities on offer.

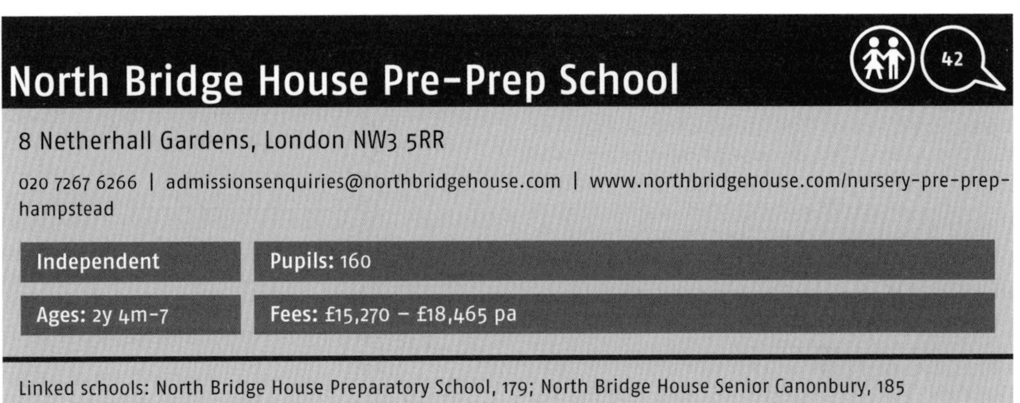

North Bridge House Pre-Prep School

8 Netherhall Gardens, London NW3 5RR

020 7267 6266 | admissionsenquiries@northbridgehouse.com | www.northbridgehouse.com/nursery-pre-prep-hampstead

Independent	Pupils: 160
Ages: 2y 4m-7	Fees: £15,270 – £18,465 pa

Linked schools: North Bridge House Preparatory School, 179; North Bridge House Senior Canonbury, 185

Head: Since 2015, Christine McLelland BEd (40s). Previously deputy head at St Nicholas Prep in Kensington (also a Cognita school), and before that worked in the state sector in both secondary and primary schools. She has been a class teacher for all year groups from reception to year 6 and held various senior leadership positions. Married to a teacher, an early years leader, Mrs McLelland particularly enjoys teaching ICT and maths, the latter because she didn't enjoy it at school and is determined that it should be taught better now. Like many heads we meet she loved school and is proud to report that 98 per cent of her pupils say maths and problem-solving are their favourite subjects. She doesn't teach as much as she would like to now, but can teach anything and does what she can: 'it's good for the soul, there are some children who always cheer you up. Spending time with the children is the highlight of my day.'

Started here as interim head in July 2015, following her predecessor's brief tenure and early departure for 'sad personal reasons'. The ship needed steadying. An SIS report in February 2016 identified a number of problems, particularly with the quality of the teaching. Inspectors nonetheless described Mrs McLelland's leadership as 'determined and effective, she is an excellent communicator who takes decisive action.' Parents describe her as 'smart, confident with good communication and marketing skills'. 'Takes a bit of warming up. A bit defensive,' said another, 'but she came in at a tough time on the back of a worrying SIS inspection report and very weak leadership from the previous head.' McLelland describes herself as 'stubborn by nature, I enjoy turning a challenge into a motivation.' We would agree but might add 'with a manner that is a touch brittle'. However, when we met her she seemed to be feeling on the back foot and we were impressed by her fighting spirit. The conclusions of the inspectors 'did not come as a shock,' she asserted and 'a huge amount of work has been done since.'

Full of praise and gratitude for the support and expertise given to her by the Cognita management, Christine McLelland is a woman who isn't afraid to ask for help and seems to work well as part of a larger organisation. We noted that once or twice her vocabulary drifted away from the language of education as she started to refer to 'the product' and 'if you've got a good product the rest of it looks after itself'. Not words that fall naturally from her lips and we detect the influence of private equity backed management. Perhaps not surprisingly, there was a high turnover of staff soon after she took over – 'some had a problem with planning lessons,' she says candidly, 'and were just recycling.' Fresh blood has been easy to recruit, however. Many come from the state sector like McLelland herself and she is proud of her high performing team. She loves the children here: 'they are very, very normal,' she says, 'not snobbish or rude but polite, kind and generous.'

Entrance: Children automatically filter through to the pre-prep from the nursery school at the age of 5, so fewer external places at this stage. Families are invited in to meet the head – who heads both the nursery and pre-prep schools – prior to admission and places are allocated at her discretion, with priority given to siblings and children of past pupils.

Exit: Children automatically progress to the prep school in year 3 – about 75 choose to do so. Close liaison with the head of prep to ensure the transition is as smooth as possible.

Some still take the 7+ to eg UCS, South Hampstead, Highgate, North London Collegiate, Haberdashers', Belmont, Devonshire House or Westminster Under. The school is focused on journey for your child from 2-18 so while it will respect parents' wishes, you would be naïve to rely on your child getting into a competitive school from here at 7 without external support. Lots of tutoring in years 1 and 2, say parents, an unsurprising consequence but something that is nonetheless bemoaned by both the prep and the pre-prep.

Our view: The pre-prep (years 1 and 2) is housed in a five-storey red-brick Victorian building in a leafy Hampstead cul de sac. The nursery (nursery, pre-reception and reception) is round the corner in Fitzjohn's Avenue in a similar building with big open spaces for play, exploration and exercise.

This is the base camp of the North Bridge House group of co-ed schools which are scattered around north London. The prep, a 7-13 (years 3-8) school, is in Camden Town, and there are two senior schools, one in Hampstead and the other in Canonbury, Islington. In theory your child could put down roots here and continue seamlessly through the NBH schools to 18, however to find a pupil who has been all the way through from the start continues to be rare.

Inspectors described Mrs McLelland's leadership as 'determined and effective'. Parents describe her as 'smart, confident with good communication and marketing skills'

Some of the infrastructure of the pre-prep in Fitzjohn Avenue seems to be a little tired and worn, from the broken tap in the visitors' lavatory to the uninspiring, sparse and functional head's office. A stark contrast to the classrooms, which were bursting with decoration, displays and colour when we visited. Wide staircases and corridors with high ceilings and large, well-proportioned classrooms create a sense of space and room to grow.

Wide staircases and corridors with high ceilings and large, well-proportioned classrooms create a sense of space and room to grow

Fresh air and exercise is important here; pupils play outside at least twice a day. Wonderful space with an Astroturf playground, complete with slides and climbing frame, and chicken coop at the back. Pupils queue up to take responsibility for collecting the eggs and feeding the chickens – even during the holidays. Fresh food is prepared on site and eaten in a wood cabin in the playground which doubles up as a dining and assembly room.

Specialist teachers in music, art, PE and games. Music is a strength and time is made for performances, lessons and groups. The whole school learns percussion, singing and composition, peripatetic teachers also teach guitar, violin and piano, and lessons can continue into the prep. Plenty of opportunities to perform in assemblies as well as in one of the big shows per term (recently Charlie and the Chocolate Factory). LAMDA classes also popular.

Art is particularly impressive, and the lack of designated art room does not appear to have an adverse effect. Each class in the school annually produces a particular themed canvas, in the style of William Morris for example, which parents can then bid for in a private auction. An art exhibition is held at the end of each year and we were lucky enough to see this in the final stages of preparation. A rich collection of work influenced by Monet's water lilies, Kandinsky and sketches of corgi dogs reminiscent of Hockney's sausage dogs, reflect the topic Kings and Queens.

One hour of dedicated IT each week but otherwise use of computers and technology is embedded in the curriculum. These 21st century children are already deft in the art of managing a device and mini iPads and laptops are used across the school.

Safeguarding is an absolute priority in all Cognita schools and the pre-prep is no exception. Rigorous vetting and checking at the door for all visitors, who are issued with a set of rules and banned from using their mobile phones. We were even accompanied to the WC. Strong pastoral care: tabs are kept on the welfare of the children, assisted by a worry box in each in classroom into which the children can place slips and then follow up with the head of pastoral care. An effective system that is used and not just there for show, which is often the case. We saw it in action.

Sarum Hall School

Children split into 10 classes (five in year 2, five in year 1), named after trees (Katsura, Beech, Hazel), one of the many innovations from Mrs McLelland: a move to trees from the birds creates more of an impression of growth, development and strength and can be less easily misinterpreted. Children now mixed into separate house groups too for sport and music competitions etc. Co-ed and inclusive, the school is nonetheless boy heavy. 'There is more competition from other girls' schools in the area,' observed one parent. Many move at the end of nursery to other schools, but on the whole parents are supportive of the school.

Majority of families live in the Hampstead area, within two miles of the school. Some with strong connections to the school – they may be alumni themselves or have other relatives who started their school days here. Eclectic mix of nationalities, with 27 languages spoken. Mix of educated professionals – fair few bankers and lawyers, as well as GPs, PR executives etc. Plenty of working mothers. Fewer big name celebrities than at similar schools.

Provision for EAL support is disappointing, we were told by more than one parent. Surprising for a school which proclaims to be all-inclusive and non-selective and which attracts a number of applicants from non-English-speaking families. 'Best to make sure your daughter's level of English is secure before she arrives,' warned one parent. However, school assures us that EAL support for children is provided by learning support assistants across the school and insists that children with little or no English make progress and can catch up with their English-speaking peers.

A ceremony, full of pomp and mortar boards, is held to celebrate the reception class graduation to year 1 and there's an even grander one for the end of year 2

We received similarly confused reports about SEN provision. There are two full-time SENCos and Mrs McLelland assured us that they wouldn't turn down a child with specific language difficulty or because of their English; 'we would look at their attention and ability to focus,' she says. Yet parents we spoke to warned that school can only really support mild special needs. There were no children with ASD on the school roll when we visited. This is clearly an area that is benefiting from Mrs McLelland's eagle attention, however. A follow-up report from SIS in November 2017 observed that pupils identified as having SEN and disabilities, including those with an EHC plan, make good progress because of very good provision and their needs are met 'with great sensitivity and care'. Pupils with EAL make very good progress because they receive 'very effective support'.

Mrs McLelland has been firmly focused on the academic side of things. In 2018 the pupils' attainment in maths put the school in the top five per cent in the country. Mrs McLelland attributes this in large part to excellent teaching from staff who are at the top of their game. CPD and sharing of best practice is high on her agenda. The improvement is acknowledged by the Inspectors. SIS, in November 2017, marked the quality of education as 'good' – a step up from their report in 2016, but probably not good enough for Mrs McLelland, her bosses at Cognita nor the parents. Leadership, management and governance also still fall short of an outstanding grade. We are not usually ones to pay overmuch attention to inspection reports, but Cognita has had a chequered history, is keen to raise standards and, we feel, needs to be called to account.

On the plus side, there has been a gear change in recent months: 'expectations have changed,' says Ms McLelland. Plenty of good, full time teachers with six or seven years behind them, including a relatively high number of male teachers, and we don't often see that for this age group. A native speaker teaches French. Italian has recently been added to the curriculum; ditto for forest school.

Lots of attention is paid to encouraging the children to achieve academically. A ceremony, full of pomp and mortar boards, is held to celebrate the reception class graduation to year 1. An even grander one for the end of year 2, complete with 'graduation day' prizes, video montage and speeches.

Heartening ethos of 'giving back' – different charities are supported each year. Chosen by the children and the parents, these have included Diabetes UK and Little Village Camden, provides clothing and equipment for disadvantaged women and families.

The last word: A school with heart, although it is not always easy to feel the beat of it, on account of its impersonal systems and sometimes mechanical, rather than personal, communication. Schools that are a part of a large commercial organisation can often fall foul of the personal touch, but this suggestion is vehemently denied by the school. They have found just the right person in Christine McLelland to marry these contradictions and we are confident that as she continues to find her stride the school can only get stronger.

North Bridge House Senior Canonbury

6-9 Canonbury Place, Islington, London N1 2NQ

020 7267 6266 | canonbury@northbridgehouse.com | www.northbridgehouse.com

Independent	Pupils: 223
Ages: 11-18	Fees: £19,230 - £20,400 pa

Linked Schools: North Bridge House Preparatory School, 179; North Bridge House Pre-Prep School, 181

Executive head teacher: Brendan Pavey, BSc, PGCE, MA (mid-40s). Has only ever worked as teacher and with over 20 years' experience maintains that being a parent has been best qualification for job. Smartly dressed, well-cut suit and tie, and open, relaxed manner, he exudes quiet low-key authority. A father of four, holds impressive academic credentials: Geography BSc from Durham and further degrees courtesy of London's prestigious Institute of Education. Originally geography and games teacher, journey as head started in 2013 at Long Close School, a co-ed independent in Slough and, like North Bridge, a Cognita school. Next step was North Bridge House Hampstead in 2017, and in an unusual move, the role was expanded to include North Bridge House Canonbury couple of years later. Parents weren't initially thrilled: 'Bit nervous when Mr Pavey was appointed as head of both' confessed one 'but I have always been able to get hold of him and he has always been receptive to concerns'. To head's credit 'dubious' parents have been won over and in remarkable show of stamina he combines constant travel between sites with teaching Canonbury geography set. 'It seems to work out ok' agrees one father 'he's definitely on it'. 'Very impressive' according to another. Also popular with students we grilled: 'lovely' was received verdict. One parent claimed to simply not know this unassuming but empathetic head very well, 'I just talk to the deputy' but all agreed that school is extremely well run: 'There is a real dialogue between leadership, staff and parents which is very special' explains appreciative parent and one mum spoke of 'flawless communications'.

Head keen to accentuate positive role of Cognita, proponents of 'great learning based on best practice'. The organisation, which once garnered bad press, now has a portfolio of 70+ schools worldwide and is under new leadership. Founded in 2004 by former chief inspector of schools, the late Sir Chris Woodhead, its aim was to make private schooling 'affordable'. Fees today are in keeping with any other independent and Cognita was sold at enormous profit to Swiss Investment company at end of 2018 in reported £2 billion deal.

Mr Pavey, clearly a team player, says he is always grateful to draw on experience of Cognita community, which was invaluable during Covid lockdown: schools in Asia were already established online, before Canonbury was forced to follow suit. Also keen to endorse 'personalised teaching', a Cognita cornerstone, with reliance on metrics to track progress: 'There is no hiding place' and adds 'just the start of a conversation'. Parents definitely on board: 'They have an educational philosophy' and school ethos is 'all about personal best rather than being pushed to attain a certain standard'.

He's a firm evangelist for mixed ability teaching and celebration of diversity: 'It's easy to forget that a good school can cater equally for Oxbridge and pupil who wants to become a chef'. His own four children, he tells us, are all very different and at different stages in education: two at university and two at secondary school. As a parent he confesses there have been challenges and he is clearly no stranger to ups and downs of adolescent life. He met his wife as a teenager, married at 23 and became a father at 27. He describes himself as 'a family man' and 'rugby fanatic'. Admits to playing more golf these days but going to watch live rugby remains a great family day out.

Entrance: Although academically non-selective, involves maths and English test (years 7-10) to 'assess match for academic curriculum'. Admissions 'fairly open-minded' and reference from past school and interview equally important. Sixth form: interviews with head of departments and minimum five GCSE grade 6s, to include English and maths. Main entry point is year 7 or 12 but applications accepted throughout school year. Impressive online teaching attracted newbies jumping ship during Covid pandemic.

One boy turned down places at super selective schools: 'He just didn't feel at home there' his mum explained and 'from first visit onwards, Canonbury was the school he really wanted to join'. Another pupil (and parents) delighted to have conversation with staff about finding spark of genius and making something of it: 'Only tour we did with element of individual caring'.

Exit: Minority after GCSEs: popular non-fee paying sixth forms like Camden School for Girls and Marylebone beckon; others head north to prestigious Highgate, UCS or Forest. Leavers usually ready to swim in larger pond and exit well qualified and well primed to make move. Nascent sixth form, currently around 30, attracts new arrivals too (often traffic decamping from same schools that have attracted Canonbury students). Post A level: majority to Russell Group universities including Oxbridge (two in 2020) with significant numbers to art school and occasional places at musical conservatoire.

Latest results: In 2020, 66 per cent 9-7 at GCSE; 68 per cent A*/A at A level. In 2019, 62 per cent 9-7 at GCSE; 34 per cent A*/A at A level.

Teaching and learning: Impressive results considering diverse abilities of intake, with upwards trend. Double or triple science available at GCSE but choice of either French or Spanish made at start of year 7. Mandarin, Latin, drama, music, computing and PE add breadth to usual GCSE range. Three or four A levels norm (with or without EPQ) and more choice: government and politics, photography, psychology now added to traditional mix. No Btecs on offer but head shared that growing popularity of sixth form could necessitate move to dedicated site, with potential scope for variety of qualifications. Odd parental grumble regarding options but outnumbered by positives and school efforts to facilitate classes even with just a couple of students at A level. 'Quality of teaching is really impressive – in everything' says happy parent but maths certainly has strong A level show, and Mandarin, drama, art, English, music, history all subject of special distinction in our feedback.

Arrival of new head coincided with a lot of staff changes, according to parents, but personnel have settled and teaching is source of great praise. One mother notes: 'School clearly puts a lot of effort into recruiting top level teachers' and another echoed: 'Teachers are super - very enthusiastic, caring and knowledgeable'. Parents especially appreciate personalised nature of learning: 'I feel they [teachers] have adapted their teaching to my son's particular strengths and weaknesses' and also 'there is a real desire to get best from each child and support where they struggle'. Use of data collection widely acclaimed: 'We were stuck by thoroughness of tracking and detailed feedback'. One father delighted in son's top GCSE maths result: 'At his prep school he always struggled' and believes success due to 'absolutely sensational experience' at North Bridge.

Canonbury success is sum of parts: small school (223 roll), small classes (around 14 up to GCSE / five at A level), late start Wednesdays for all, 'couldn't cope without' said one pupil (9.50am every day for sixth form), differentiated and hi-tech teaching delivered by sympathetic teachers who 'don't overload us with stress'. Parent says: 'vibe is positive rather than scholarly' and while one mother wondered if her son was being 'pushed enough', most agreed students were challenged 'within acceptable parameters'.

Pupils say they 'are never bored' and we confess to reluctance at leaving fascinating maths class on equations: clever use of white boards (two) and central screen hooked up to computer generated presentation allowed romp through world's most famous equations like: E=mc2 on one hand and brush up of GCSE essentials on other. Some students encouraged to opine on theory of relativity whilst others coaxed to recall calculation for area of triangle. Whole class fully engaged and encouraged by teacher's repeated assurances that we all knew more than we realised.

Head is a firm evangelist for mixed ability teaching and celebration of diversity: 'A good school can cater equally for Oxbridge and a pupil who wants to become a chef'

GCSE Mandarin class we checked into was fast paced, interactive and lively. Skill set already way beyond GCSE level and trusting rapport between teacher and pupils striking: no one was afraid to speak up or make a mistake - perfect language learning dynamics.

Chemistry next: pupil laptops out and linked up with screen in middle of white boards - all used to demonstrate chemical reactions and equations: portrayed for these teenagers as game of attractions where one suitor could be supplanted/ displaced by 'stronger' bond with another. Cartoon characters flashed up to personify chemical elements and fun of joining together (or not) began. Video footage allowed students to predict and then enjoy drama of explosive reactions in safety. Enthusiasm levels high and this animated year 8 group of 20 students (never more in class according to head) subject to teacher's firm but multiple kindly prompts to refocus.

Well-integrated and sophisticated use of tech is stand out and lessons are creative, ambitious and fun. Pupil laptops omnipresent and school clearly at ease with all things electronic. Music lesson, an example and memorable: greeted by silence but welcomed by head of music who explained that headphone clad students transfixed at computer screens were composing alternative soundtracks to tv ads. Mastery of music software an absorbing and appealing task well chosen for young teens.

Parents also invited online and academic progress, school news and messages shared electronically via Firefly platform.

Learning support and SEN: Full-time SENCo and 60+ pupils currently registered: majority for exam accommodations with mild to moderate cases of dyslexia or dyscalculia. Around 20 students require external support and/or SENCo help and one EHCP for autism. Inclusive and open to supporting students with complex needs, potentially even one-to-one assistance but usually differentiation within classroom teaching is norm. School heavily invested in admissions process: 'Right match creates successful outcomes' and 'we could never encourage someone who wouldn't manage'. After mutual agreement one student recently left as school no longer considered 'best fit'.

'Nurturing environment can have huge positive impact' according to SENCo and school encourages understanding that 'all needs are everyone's responsibility': example given was discreet group support for student suffering panic attacks.

Classrooms tucked away in warren of corridors and winding staircases so tricky challenge for anyone with mobility issues.

The arts and extracurricular: Drama, music, art? 'More please' was unanimous verdict from group of students we consulted and one budding thespian declared 'Drama is best thing ever!' School productions universally praised and much anticipated. Teaching acclaimed as 'exceptional' but also versatile as school play transitioned seamlessly into school film - all made in compliance with social distancing rules. Strong uptake for GCSE drama and LAMDA along with regular forays into West End's theatreland (as many as 10 shows a year) making drama a hot ticket. Popular with parents too who are invited along to accompany their children.

Thriving music department, and like drama, commended for rich programme on offer and dedication of energetic staff. Music also v inclusive: ' My son has been able to participate in whatever he wanted at this school' commented parent but another spoke of 'very small orchestra' and 'limited ensembles'. Committed musicians after big band experience should look to supplement elsewhere. Choir popular after-school activity and another showcase for devoted artistes. Canonbury lacks dedicated performance space but King Edward's Hall (formerly home to Tower Theatre Company) is pressed into daily service, seamlessly transforming from dining room to exam/assembly hall or theatre/concert venue as required.

Drama, music, art? More, please! One budding thespian declared 'Drama is best thing ever!' School productions universally praised and much anticipated

'Art is brilliant and a big plus for school' declares admiring parent and again high option uptake tells own story. Our visit coincided with reorganisation of art room and walls were bare but eye-catching and accomplished self-portraits were on display around the school.

Duke of Edinburgh award scheme available and optional lecture programme throughout year with outside speakers, as well as timetabled enrichment sessions from creative writing to environmental issues. Extra-curricular activities (and sports clubs) open to all ages as consequence of small student body.

Thumbs up for school outings, 'an amazing breadth of visits' declares impressed mum: regular ski jaunts abroad, memorable 'cultural' expeditions to Vienna and Berlin and days out at museums and gardens.

Sport: Beware: next to no sports facilities on site and outside space is scarce - a few all weather table-tennis spots and courtyard just about big enough for restrained kick-around for football enthusiasts. Consensus is that school 'tries extra hard' but we were rather taken aback to hear, 'sports are amazing here' from recent newcomer. Central location allows easy access to local amenities: outdoor spaces of Highbury Fields a walk away and Regent's Park and Sobell Leisure Centre a short bus ride. Climbing, sailing and trampolining as well as more usual staples like tennis, squash, swimming, and football rotate every half term. Sports are always mixed, apart from girls-only netball and after school clubs run daily. Super sporty types might lament limited numbers when it comes to fielding competitive teams although swimmers have found success. Expect in-house games and just occasional 'friendlies' with other schools rather than weekends chasing league glory and silverware.

Ethos and heritage: Founded in 2014, North Bridge House Senior Canonbury is first and only independent secondary in Islington. Surrounded by elegant Georgian townhouses, school is tucked away in genteel corner of London where writer George Orwell first settled into family life in the 1940s. Quiet leafy streets still attract families and initially there was local concern when plans for new school emerged. Cognita was keen to expand thriving North Bridge House family of schools with first sixth form and additional senior to complement Hampstead provision and Regent's Park prep. Acquisition of two empty listed historical buildings in Canonbury conservation area was starting point: extensive and considered refurb project began and result is stylish makeover with sensitive restoration of 16th century features. Effect is warm and non-institutional. Ornate plasterwork, winding staircases, chimney places and beamed ceilings returned to former glory which 'feels very Harry Potter' according to year 7 student. School has integrated well into surrounding community and support of local charities favourably received.

The head chided a sixth former for not wearing a tie during our visit but 'there's lots of respect here,' say pupils and another summed up: 'everyone is chill'

Size repeatedly viewed as 'biggest strength': 'My child knows everyone in school and multi age sports and mixed teams mean looking out for younger groups, as well as each other.' Pupils enjoy friendships across year groups and 'treat one another as part of "big" family'. Parents agree: 'a deeply happy school' with 'lovely relationships between boys and girls' remarked one. Students divided into three houses and enthusiastically compete for good behaviour merits with visits en masse to movies or local pizzeria as prize. Academics also deserving of merit points and joy of past house celebrations together palpable. 'Lots of fun and camaraderie' affirmed parent and another with two children at school summed up: 'There is strong sense of nurture and community'. Head described Canonbury as 'low pressure high support model' and size is significant: more village primary than urban secondary. Thoughtful parent reflected: 'Kids are sheltered here from full force - it's a quiet corner'. Cheery newbie's verdict: 'This is just the nicest school ever'.

Pastoral care, inclusivity and discipline: 'It's refreshing,' states parent 'a place where pupils matter as individuals, and differences are celebrated'. Students we consulted all nodded in agreement when one affirmed: 'Trans, gay, queer - we're all equal'. Also relief from another to have left last school: 'Biggest difference is that no-one hates anyone here'.

In 2018 Cognita rolled out software programme to track student wellbeing being across its schools. Questionnaires assess how safe and secure students feel and if there is someone they can discuss worries with. Confidential feedback used to flag concerns and facilitate early interventions. Parents appreciative of 'emphasis on good mental health and resilience' and describe pastoral care as 'excellent' and 'major strength' of school. Head resolute: 'Young teenagers need ability to talk about mental health issues' and as one parent points out: '[with] generous number of staff to kids on site they have the numbers to do it'. One mother grateful for 'real understanding of pressures on us as a family' as result of daughter's health issues.

Parents who took a 'leap of faith' moving daughter mid-way through GCSEs delighted with Canonbury welcome: 'supported and encouraged in every way with a well-matched student buddy to help her find her feet'. Parents of incoming sixth former noticed how 'quality of attention [was] enabling academic progress and increasing levels of confidence and maturity' for their child. Approachable and inclusive school's individualised approach 'makes kids feel special' and as parent confessed: 'I absolutely love the fact that my son can get such personal attention'.

Discipline definitely of light touch variety but we were reliably told 'strict when it needs to be'. Head chided sixth former bereft of tie during our visit but 'lots of respect here' say pupils and another summed up: 'everyone is chill'.

Pupils and parents: More boys than girls with current ratio at 60:40. Less culturally diverse than usual London smorgasbord but almost all local to area, including staff. Most will either walk to school or catch bus together. Popular PTA and relaxed parents who are 'more happy that our son has found a lovely group of friends' than just hitting top scores. 'Some kids get A*s and some don't – and that's okay' said another who believed 'kids tend to have spiky profiles' excelling in some areas and struggling in others.

Uniform appears to encompass variety of imaginative combinations with recent demise of school hoodie mourned by students. Sixth formers switch to business attire (with tie) and have small common room space with access to garden.

Definite parental fear that school might overload on capacity front (maximum roll is 300): already full in early years and 20 in class definitely a squeeze in some rooms.

Money matters: Hardship bursaries for existing families and five scholarships on offer in years 7 and 12. Academic scholarships subject to further assessment and available in maths and English as single award (20 per cent fee remission) and one double award for maths and English combined (50 per cent remission). Performing arts and art both single awards and audition/portfolio required. Scholarship for exceptional sixth form candidate possible with 100 per cent fee remission.

The last word: In north London, where super selective independents reign, this is a welcome alternative with a gentler pace and fewer sharp elbows. The focus is on personal challenge with tailored teaching in a nurturing and attractive setting: a safe haven for developing teens.

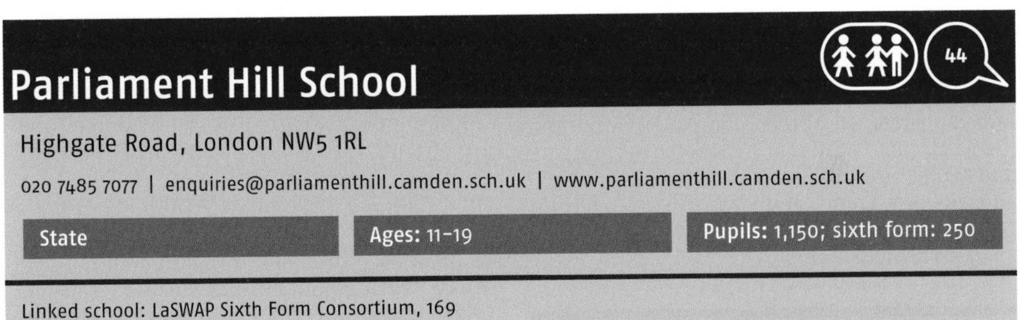

Headteacher: Since 2017, Sarah Creasey BA PGCE, NPQH (late 40s). Spent 25 years working in London secondary schools, starting out in a single-sex school in Wimbledon, followed by a decade at Preston Manor, a mixed all-through school in Brent, where she headed the English department and rose to assistant head.

Arrived at Parliament Hill in 2012 to become part of a tight-knit senior leadership team, first as associate head, then as deputy. Her mission is clear: to deliver on the school's motto, 'happiness and high achievement for all', and she addresses the complex requirements of the school's broad-ranging community with calm dedication. Girls warm to her: 'She's very nice and understanding,' said one; parents consider her relatable and down to earth: 'I was surprised on parents' evening to find her sitting in front of me at one of the desks; she seemed to know my daughter well,' said one mother. 'What you want in a head is a firm hand and a kind heart, and she has that,' said another.

Entrance: About 600 apply for 180 year 7 places. Applicants are accepted under the usual community comprehensive criteria (exceptional social and medical need, looked-after children, siblings, etc) with no banding or other ability edit. After that, it's a generous 1.5 miles (ish) from the gates, giving it one of the largest catchments of any Camden secondary.

Exit: About two-thirds continue to LaSWAP, the sixth form consortium which unites four local comps (Parliament Hill, William Ellis, La Sainte Union and Acland Burghley). The rest either wave goodbye to education for good or transfer to other popular local sixth forms, such as Camden School for Girls, Woodhouse College, City and Islington and Westminster Kingsway. About a quarter of those who complete year 13 qualifications – and there are certainly drop-outs – continue to Russell Group universities. One to Oxbridge in 2020, plus two medics. Sussex, Chelsea Art College, UCL, Brighton Medical College, Edinburgh, Manchester Bristol all popular. National apprenticeship week introduces a range of practical training on offer, and good numbers continue to vocational courses.

Latest results: In 2020, 43 per cent 9-7 at GCSE; 77 per cent 9-4 in both English and maths. In 2019 (the least year when exams took place), 41 per cent 9-7 at GCSE; 58 per cent 9-5 in both English and maths. At A level in 2019, 28 per cent A*/A.

Teaching and learning: Academically, 'Parli''s strength undoubtedly lies in its GCSE years, where it takes in a broad range of girls and delivers success for all, achieving results that put it in the top 10 per cent of non-selective schools nationally, the top five in many subjects.

At this stage, it exceeds every government benchmark, with a well above average value added score; ditto for uptake of the EBacc (over half). Results at the top end are particularly pleasing.

English is notably strong, while maths (until recently a weak spot) has, with the replacement of staff, careful nurturing and thoughtful embedding across the curriculum (film studies students, for example, deconstruct box-office takings, art pupils measure geometric forms), seen a marked improvement, with about a third now achieving 9-7. Parli also places a strong emphasis on 'non-girly' science – those taking all three do particularly well and good numbers go on to study sciences at A level.

On average students gain nine GCSES, and the broad curriculum is designed to provide something for everyone, with popular options including music, food tech, computer science and media studies. Vocational choices too in child care and health and social care. Limited range of languages – only French and Spanish – though Latin can be studied to GCSE (as can photography) in an extracurricular club.

Parli places a strong emphasis on 'non-girly' science – those taking all three at GCSE do particularly well and good numbers go on to study sciences at A level

Teaching generally strong, albeit somewhat more uneven in the sixth form, with well-planned lessons and well-honed exam technique delivered by knowledgeable, well-qualified staff. 'Teaching is usually good, sometimes inspirational,' said one parent. 'They're good at differentiating work and setting creative, interesting homework in manageable quantities. It's definitely not a hothouse.' Teachers also good at recognising appropriate pace. 'My daughter was struggling a bit in one subject, and she was transferred to a class working slightly more slowly, making her much happier.'

The LaSWAP sixth form is one of the largest in the UK, with over 1500 pupils, allowing it to offer a vast range of qualifications – 40 A levels, plus AS levels, the EPQ and BTecs – in almost any combination. Those who start out at Parli continue at Parli for core subjects, allowing staff to build on existing appreciation of strengths and weaknesses, but freeing pupils to study elsewhere for more rarefied options like further maths. Every pupil passed at A level, with a significant number achieving well above their target grades in both A levels and vocational courses.

The school does very well by the struggling – for academic, emotional or financial reasons, and there are plenty – with thoughtful and consistent intervention from year 7. All new entrants are assessed to ensure appropriate support is given from the start, with carefully monitored tailor-made strategies that range from mentoring to intensive behavioural intervention, from buying a first bra to financial support for trips and extracurricular activities.

Parli is also noted for its out-of-the-ordinary efforts to identify and encourage potential. High flyers are spotted early – 'They quickly recognised where my daughter excelled,' said one year 7 parent – then cheerled through the system with a raft of support, from workshops for parents (important for those who may not have finished school) to involvement with the independent charity, the National Association for Gifted Children. In 2018, the school was the first in the UK to achieve the charity's gold award for its 'inspirational' out-of-class activities, such as the Brilliant Club, Students as Researchers and Great Minds Think Again, led by a teacher with a doctorate in astrophysics. Maths masterclasses and science week seminars further embed the message that women can and do succeed in science by highlighting female role models (black women mathematicians, for example, who worked at NASA). 'Girls who have the potential are incentivised to aim very high indeed,' said one parent. 'All the evidence suggests that those who have the capacity to get top grades do as well at Parli as they do anywhere else, with plenty of girls achieving strings of A*s.' Not, however, at the expense of the comprehensive ethos. 'Teachers know to push them more, but they're not in separate groups, which would not be nice for the other kids.'

Learning support and SEN: Impressive, tailored help for SEND. Parents (or carers) of girls with a SEND profile have their own go-to member of the 'Inclusion' team at parents' evenings.

The arts and extracurricular: Many Parli pupils come from homes where 'cultural capital' is in short supply, and the school makes every effort to compensate, aided by specialist facilities for art, media and performing arts. 'We're about opening doors to every student by making sure they have as many opportunities as possible,' says head. Music is taught in rotation with dance and drama in the early years, with scope to perform in concerts (year 7 singing, LaSWAP Winter concert, soloists' concert), bands, choirs and orchestras (junior brass band, jazz band, pop choir, chamber choir). Plenty of drama too, both as a popular

Head is a strong believer in the potential of single sex education. 'Girls are always centre stage in a girls' school,' she says

and successful GCSE and after-school club. Art is taken seriously with dedicated space for graphics, textiles, photography and design, and budding artists are taken to Hampstead Heath for observational drawing and encouraged to contribute work for outside exhibitions, such as Unicef's Rights Respecting Schools. All the arts brought together in annual musical with as many as 200 involved.

Clubs also provide the entrée to everything from debating and Model United Nations, to coding and Explore the Bible, while the school's energetic climate change action group fights the good fight with its schemes for crisp packet recycling, clothes swapping and meat-free days. Plenty of trips – almost all in London – are used to enrich the curriculum and raise aspirations, and recent outings include attendance at Women in Jazz day, Black History month workshops, and visits to the supreme court, Channel 4 and a large-scale property developer. Year 8 bond on a residential trip.

Sport: The new building, opened in 2019, has added a large sports hall with four indoor courts, enhancing what is already a successful offering. Rich PE curriculum (rugby, rounders, athletics, fitness, swimming and dance), some carried out on neighbouring Hampstead Heath, is supplemented by an extensive array of in-lunch and after-school sports clubs (football, basketball, table tennis and cross country). Sights are set high through activities such as Young Women in Sports day, and Parli girls are definitely of the go, fight, win variety, competing hotly in the cross-borough Camden Shield, with regular triumphs in table tennis, dodgeball and cross country. 'Because it's an all-girls school,' said one parent, 'boys don't take over, and if you're sporty, you're able to be incredibly sporty.'

Dance – unusually offered as a GCSE with its own studio – is particularly popular, and girls participate both in school (with clubs for elite dancers, choreography, contemporary and street dance), and outside, in competitions and festivals.

Ethos and heritage: Having originally opened in 1906 as the Community School for Girls, Parli sits on an attractive site on the south east corner of Hampstead Heath, providing it with a leafy aspect and bright interiors. At its core is the original, gracious red-brick Edwardian building but in 2019 it was catapulted into the 21st century by the addition of a striking, streamlined £30m extension, providing new classrooms for maths, English and science. This has been accompanied by a facelift for existing space, and the launch of a deluxe stand-alone sixth form centre (for all LaSWAP students), ecologically enfolded in a living green wall. 'The rebuild was very disruptive, but it's been money well spent,' said one year 11 parent. 'The new building is fantastic. It helps everyone's self-esteem.'

Parli is a member of the Association of State Girls' Schools and the head is a strong believer in the potential of single sex education to transform lives. 'Girls are always centre stage in a girls' school,' she says, and pupils here are encouraged to take on roles of responsibility, sit on student interview panels, co-plan lessons, and gain confidence in public speaking, through debating and competitions such as Jack Petchey's Speak Out. 'What people often say is that our students are really articulate, confident and know their own minds,' says the head. 'They have strong opinions and we're developing them as leaders.' Aiming high in the world of work is also encouraged through partnerships with leading employers, such as Matrix Chambers, Deloitte, Sky and the British Library, as well as through university visits and mentoring schemes. 'My daughter wanted to go to an all-girls school,' said one parent, 'because she wanted somewhere that would focus on her. It's been very good for her, particularly in science, and she's now thinking of taking Physics for A Level.' 'They're very pro women,' said another. 'I've learnt from my daughter in that respect.'

Parents overall are positive about the package. 'Parli has a lovely buzzy, creative atmosphere,' said one. 'It's a mixed intake, so you do have to acquire a degree of self-motivation – you get out of it what you put in – but it's always true to the ethos of a liberal comprehensive education, rather in defiance of the spirit of the times.'

Former pupils – Chelsea FC manager Emma Hayes, entrepreneur Rosie Pope, BBC journalist Laura Trevelyan, and singer Dua Lipa – attest to the positive outcome.

Pastoral care, inclusivity and discipline: School takes its motto seriously and the emphasis here is as much on the happy as the high achieving. 'We know girls won't achieve unless they're happy and safe,' says the head.

High protective gates and high standards of behaviour, both inside and outside the classroom, ensure a safe and secure environment, and the head has reduced the rate of exclusions by half. 'They're thoughtful in how they apply discipline,' said one parent. 'It's the antithesis of zero tolerance, detention-for-breathing-wrong kind of policy. And the girls respond well to it as far as I can tell.'

Outside the gates, things can be slightly more turbulent, eg on the day we visited two boys from the adjoining boys' school were having a blood-drawing fist fight with no teachers in sight. The benefits of proximity, however, become clearer in the sixth form, when the consortium provides a campus-like bridge between school and university.

Care overall considered excellent. 'Pastoral care is very, very good,' said one new parent. 'At our first parents' evening, my daughter's form tutor knew exactly who she was hanging out with and what extracurricular clubs she was taking.' Another agreed. 'You think you know your daughter, but they nailed it. It felt like they'd known her for years.' Feedback is equally good for those who've faced challenges at home. 'They're very good at working with the triangle – school, home, child. When we told them about problems we were having with our daughter, they really stepped up to the plate.' Parents appreciate, too, that they can 'always get hold of someone when they need to'.

Bullying rare and promptly dealt with. 'My daughter, who's quite quirky, was picked on at primary school, but has blossomed at Parli. It seems to be fine to just be who you are.' Indeed, the school prides itself on its open-armed attitude to difference. 'We're a really diverse community,' says the head, 'and encourage our students to appreciate individuality.' An approach underlined in the non-uniform dress code, dedicated citizenship lessons and events like the celebration of LGBT history month.

Wellbeing and mental health also a strength – commended in an award from Challenge Partners. A wellbeing manager, supported by art therapists and counsellors, runs a drop-in service four days a week; Wellbeing week teaches relaxation and stress management; and regular workshops provide parents and students with guidance on friendships and teenage anxiety. Free breakfast club undoubtedly a boon.

Pupils and parents: Pupils from challenging backgrounds (60 per cent are pupil premium, including numerous refugees) blend happily with well-spoken girls from the affluent, liberal left homes that abut the gates. Parents very supportive of the school's ideals and approach. 'It's a good mix of students, and my daughter is very happy there. She gets in an hour early to hang out with her friends and never has a bad feeling about going to school,' said one.

Money matters: Not a rich school, but well supported by Camden, which underwrote its recent modernisation. Some partnerships too – with the Worshipful Company of Butchers, for example – which provide bursaries for activities such as DofE. Those who can afford it are given the option to add their mite through the Parent Pay app. 'But you don't get the feeling that money is an issue,' said one.

The last word: A truly comprehensive comp, with outstanding pastoral care, sparkling modern facilities and a positive atmosphere, addressing the needs of everyone from the local affluent middle class to the latest refugee. Particularly good at raising aspirations and making sure girls recognise they can be anything they aim to be.

Head: Since 2017, David Bradbury, 50, BSc MSc PGCE (all from Keele) plus an MA in education from the Open University. A Yorkshireman who came to teaching by accident but is not regretting it over 25 years later. He describes his time teaching in Bangkok as 'an incredible experience of living and working in a wholly different culture' and once back in the UK, rose through the teaching ranks to be assistant head at Alleyne's High School and deputy head of South Hampstead High before speedily saying yes to the headship of Portland Place.

On meeting him, it was easy to understand why he had told us that he 'immediately felt at home here' because he fits both comfortably and confidently into his role, answering all our questions in a relaxed, straightforward way. He came here as the third head in as many terms (never a great starting point for this job), believing that this was a school with 'huge potential and some of the most interesting students I have ever worked with' and parents say that he is someone they can always talk to: 'I really like him, firm but fair, I could chat to him about anything.'

Entrance: The natural entry point is in year 7 but there is one form entry at year 6, designed for parents who do not want to put their children through 11+ or have recently moved to London and don't want a double move. Whilst prepared to accept a wider range of ability than a large number of senior schools in London, they require baseline testing and an interview and say that they place great importance on references/recommendations from entrants' previous schools.

Exit: Students continue their education at eg CATS Canterbury, Brampton College, Wycliffe College, Ashbourne College, DLD College London, Albemarle and Marianopolis College in Canada.

Latest results: In 2020, 46 per cent 9-7 at GCSE; 95 per cent 9-4 in both maths and English. At A level, 38 per cent A*/A (72 per cent A*-B). In 2019 (the last year when exams took place) 27 per cent 9-7 at GCSE.

Teaching and learning: More than one of the parents we spoke to felt that the school's image of an also-ran, compared to some of the fiercely competitive academic alternatives, was unfair. One stated, 'Every parent feels that their child deserves to get the best results that they can and this is what the school delivers.' The head confirms this opinion by remarking with total conviction, 'What we do is get the best academic outcome for that particular student.' However, they take a wider range of abilities than is usual in private London schools and concentrate on value added (in the top 15 per cent nationally for the last three years) rather than just the starry results achieved by the academic high-flyers.

Small classes are commonplace and all are capped at 16. When we looked in on lessons the pupil count was often in single figures. Some setting in maths in year 6, apparently a particularly bright bunch this year, with science and English added in year 7. Teachers came in for high praise from a parent: 'some of the lessons sound fantastic and they carry a theme across the entire curriculum'.

We were particularly impressed by the Strive Programme, an initiative leading to extremely well-designed and appealing brochures packed with clear, imaginative ideas on how to expand your knowledge outside the classroom. This was definitely the work of a dedicated teaching staff and the ones that we met laughed at the idea that they might leave when the sixth form closes in 2020. DB has changed the faculty structure for a clearer model that parents seem contented with and all the teachers were sparky and positive: 'I just love it here, I'm not going anywhere.'

Rehearsals for Bugsy Malone were in full swing and the excitement was palpable, with about a third of the school involved either on stage, behind it or in the orchestra pit

A big push to increase IT with iPads on the way for all in years 6-9, a homework app and an aim to achieve Apple Distinguished School status. All take core GCSEs and double science (a few take triple) but the creative arts, along with business, computer science and media, tend to feature in the top five choices, unsurprising given the creative remit of the school. Not as many takers for languages as the school would like but the head of faculty is hoping that new extracurricular clubs for Arabic, Japanese, Mandarin and Russian will pique the interest of potential candidates, and a fifth of students are already involved.

Results show that students make tremendous progress from their starting points.

Learning support and SEN: They enrol a larger proportion of students identified with SEND than many independent schools, mainly mild to moderate problems (dyslexia or similar), but who still need to be able to operate in a mainstream environment. Having said that, the SEND team has four members and they also have a dedicated EAL teacher for support when students first join. Learning Lab (timetabled) is there to provide help, but one parent told us that the attitude was 'it's almost a badge of honour to have challenges, but it's not true that children are held back if they don't.'

The arts and extracurricular: 'Art is brilliant at PP, he's loving it,' enthused a parent, and we felt very at home in the art department at the top of the stairs. Articulate teachers were imaginatively combining learning technique – 'we don't want them to realise that's what they're doing at the start' – with a non-tramline approach to the story of art evolution, and making full use of some of the world's greatest museums and galleries nearly next door. There is also a new design space in the basement, enthusiastically praised – by both the girls, at work on sewing machines, and their teacher – as a great improvement on the previous poky spaces.

Great efforts to get everyone on board musically and they now offer Symphonfree to all year 7 pupils, supplying them with a free musical instrument and lessons for a year. There are choirs, some needing auditions, and they can rustle up almost any form of musical group, barring a full orchestra, for their concerts at RADA studios.

Rehearsals for Bugsy Malone were in full swing all over the school and the excitement was palpable, with about a third of the school involved either on stage, behind it or in the orchestra pit. Few opportunities to bring the surrounding cultural riches into the curriculum are wasted and there are regular outings to the Globe and Unicorn Theatre, as well as visits to BAFTA, the Met Film School, Wigmore Hall and the Royal Opera House.

Pupils are encouraged to join clubs that take place before, during and after school, and they try to offer the options usually only available in larger set-ups. For instance, they have gone ahead with DofE awards despite only the minimum number signing up, where other schools might have made excuses.

Sport: For a school whose outside space would seem cramped for a cat, and whose numbers mean that putting teams together for the myriad sporting activities available is sometimes a struggle, they do remarkably well at sport, with students succeeding at both county and national level in athletics, women's football, baseball and netball, as well as one boy qualifying for junior Wimbledon. Some form of sport happens four times a week including swimming up to year 10, the only slight moan expressed by a parent: 'They work really hard at offering sport but it is a bit of a pain that they can spend half the lesson in the bus on the way to Queen's Park.'

Ethos and heritage: A new kid on the block compared to more established rivals, it is part of the 20-strong Alpha Plus group. This affiliation means that after the closure of the sixth form families can remain inside the group by sending their offspring to Alpha's sixth form college, DLD, now housed in a brand new building.

Portland Place itself is a stately dowager calmly parading in this elegant bit of town between the charms of Regent's Park and the fumes of the West End, watched over by embassies and professional institutions. The opposite of purpose-built and not the smartest in decorative terms, even a bit scruffy, the school operates out of three buildings. Inside the imposing house fronting onto Portland Place, an elegant library on the ground floor is topped by classrooms and attics, now given over to music, whilst the rest of the school operates out of two locations in the parallel street.

School concentrates on value added (in the top 15 per cent nationally for the last three years) rather than just the starry results achieved by the academic high-flyers

This is not an ideal layout but will be improved once they have replaced the sixth form classrooms in Great Portland Street with a canteen and a multifunctional performance area. A new studio for graphics, photography, film and media has already been finished and the lack of outside areas for letting off steam will continue to be more than compensated for by the number of stairs.

We found that parents were taking a pragmatic attitude to the closure of the sixth form, their remarks ranging from 'it's a shame but unsurprising given the small numbers' to 'it would have been so easy to take the soft option, now I'll have to work harder at the next stage'. But it is definitely not undermining their confidence in the school, which is proactively encouraging students to look at every possible option open to them and not railroading them down the A levels route.

Pastoral care, inclusivity and discipline: Always known for the close relationship between staff and pupils, its slightly informal atmosphere compared to some London schools feels comfortable rather than chaotic. With 20 per cent of pupils being bilingual and a sensitive attitude to teenagers, this can never be a conveyor belt school, and the impression that they really dig down to understand each child is unmistakable.

As in all London schools, the spectre of drug use is ever present. The school adopts a zero-tolerance policy to drugs and enforces an uncrossable red-line policy of expelling anyone who brings drugs into the school. The head was admirably open and honest about the potential problem; it would be naive to ignore the reality that drugs are readily available and indeed, in his first year in charge, he had to handle a situation in which two students were implicated in drug use (not on school premises). He made the point that they always do their best to find a way to support teenagers with problems, and one parent's verdict was 'it is a particularly safe atmosphere... they provide a rock, it seems to come naturally.'

External speakers talk to both parents and children on internet safety, citizenship and the current dangers for children growing up in a global city, and the school seems to be fully aware of the need to communicate with families. 'It is an easy school to deal with.'

Pupils and parents: The head classifies the school as a 'London school' not a 'local school', despite one pupil living practically next door, but most of the pupils come from north and west London with an increasing number from Hackney and Shoreditch and the odd one from much farther afield. There are several tube stations within easy reach so travelling from almost any part of London is fairly hassle free.

Parents tend to be professionals in law, finance, creatives, media and business owners with a fair number of working mums and a healthy mix of old hands in the private sector and first timers. As in all London schools, students are drawn from all over the world and PP has a fair number of pupils who do not have two parents born in this country. On average, 12-15 per cent of families in each year are in London for a temporary stay, although they tend to be on multi-year postings.

Several of the children have come here after unsatisfactory experiences at other schools, with happy results, one parent telling us that her son 'jumps out of bed to go to school' now and the unpressurised environment leads to a lot of noticeably unstressed teenagers.

Money matters: As part of the Alpha Plus group, they have the back-up of a well-resourced operation as well as benefiting from the economies of scale, and there appears to be a detailed plan to make improvements to the school spaces. Eleven scholarships are available at year 7 entry: one discretionary academic and the remainder for music, drama, art and sport.

The last word: A lot of trendy, 'on message', pedagogic phrases are bandied about whenever we visit schools but, in this case, we were entirely convinced that Portland Place really does try to understand each individual pupil and help them find the best possible outcome for their abilities and skills. This is a place that genuinely seems to resist academic snobbery when it comes to guiding their charges onto the next step and parents back their attitude up with enthusiasm.

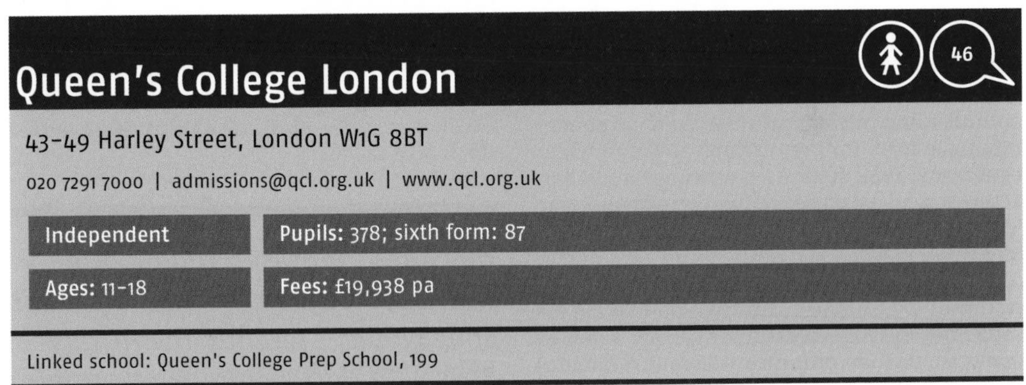

Queen's College London

46

43-49 Harley Street, London W1G 8BT

020 7291 7000 | admissions@qcl.org.uk | www.qcl.org.uk

Independent | Pupils: 378; sixth form: 87

Ages: 11-18 | Fees: £19,938 pa

Linked school: Queen's College Prep School, 199

Principal: Since September 2017, Richard Tillett (40s), former deputy head at Harrogate Ladies' College. Degree in modern languages and history from Cambridge. Driven by altruism from a young age, says he knew from the get-go the City or corporate life wasn't for him, so eschewed the milk round corporates and joined the health service training scheme, specialising in mental health. Disillusioned by bureaucracy, gained his PGCE from Sussex and hasn't looked back. Taught history and politics at King Edward VI Grammar and was housemaster and history teacher at the Leys before joining Harrogate Ladies' in 2010 as head of sixth form.

Wife and daughter remain in North Yorkshire, from where he commutes weekly. So what drew him to QCL from so far afield for his first headship? 'Just a brilliant fit,' he says. 'I was struck by its extraordinary history and values – it's a school where the default position is to be kind.' Says pastoral care is 'absolutely the most important thing', and parents concur that this key cornerstone of Queen's hasn't wavered on his watch. Fans of former head (even the 'sexist' ones hoping for another strong female role model) have not been disappointed with his arrival, describing him in a flurry of superlatives: 'amazing', 'fantastic' and 'such a character'. Keeps his hand in teaching A level politics and has seized his predecessor's baton of believing that 'girls are able to do anything'. Had to manoeuvre his way through some awkward and unpleasant situations with some troublesome junior pupils early in his tenure, a situation that resulted in a handful of departures, but parents on the inside tell us 'things were dealt with pretty quickly' and the ship has mostly stabilised now, though we do still hear of some fall-out. Has made some major positive strides in changing sixth form curriculum to bring it in line with his vision: 'to prepare Queen's girls for the uncertainty of the future.' This on top of a whole-school assembly to kick off every week and the introduction of a new house system. Next up will be to face the challenge of stabilising a formerly high staff turnover – we'll watch with interest. Mastermind specialist subject would be either Russian history (he's a Russian speaker) or Arsenal FC. Avid follower of football and cricket, cellist and lover of travel, good food and hill walking.

Entrance: No automatic entrance from Queen's College Prep but a good percentage come from there. Otherwise over 40 different feeder schools, with up to a quarter from local state primaries. Mainly into year 7 via the London 11+ Consortium (formerly the North London Girls' Schools Consortium). Now a bespoke cognitive ability test (maths, VR and NVR), an 'imaginative interview experience' to explore candidates' skills, aptitudes and intellectual acuity and a common reference form for prep schools to detail wider contextual information on attitudes and character as well as academic performance. Some 500 applicants for 60 places. Unusually, everyone is interviewed before the exam. 'We like to form a picture of the child without seeing her test results.' Genuinely selective and looking for someone who is going to enjoy getting involved and seize the opportunities available. A handful join into sixth form; requirements are minimum of grades 6 or 7 in chosen A level subjects (although some subjects have own criteria) plus minimum grade 5 in maths and English and reference from current school.

Exit: Some 30 per cent leave after GCSEs, mostly to board or move into the state system. It isn't usual for girls to be asked to leave if GCSEs aren't up to scratch but school doesn't offer 'soft options' at A level so occasionally pupils do depart for this reason. Post A level leavers to a range of universities and colleges (Birmingham, Leeds, Warwick, UCL, Exeter currently popular) to read a vast array of subjects, from the trad academics to business-related degrees in fashion or music. Russell Group universities feature heavily in the leavers' list, along with new universities, arts colleges and some overseas (there is a dedicated international university counsellor). In 2020, one Oxbridge, no medics and two overseas, both to study liberal arts – one at Georgetown University and the other at University of San Diego.

Latest results: In 2019 (the last year when exams took place), 77 per cent 9-7 at GCSES; 45 per cent A*/A at A level (79 per cent A*-B).

Teaching and learning: Not top of the academic heap in the London girls' day school scene but on the up and now giving local rivals Channing, South Hampstead High and Francis Holland a real run for their money – matching or outperforming them on results day. 'Academics are now largely where we want them to be,' says head. Head has axed girls taking a fourth or half A level (apart from in exceptional cases or for those taking further maths) in favour of a standard three A levels plus EPQ and work experience for all. Broad range of subjects at A level with 'totally flexible' timetabling making unusual combinations possible. English takes the popularity prize followed closely by history and religious studies, all with top results. Sciences and further maths less so, particularly physics, and stellar grades less prevalent in these departments. Languages also niche at A level despite strong provision in KS3 with Mandarin, Spanish, French and Italian all offered in year 7. Top Latin set introduced to ancient Greek in year 9 – also available at GCSE with a small take up.

There are chances to collaborate with boys' schools on their dramatic endeavours – recently The History Boys with Harrow and Frankenstein with Wetherby

Don't expect your year 7 daughter to be thrust into an academic frenzy on arrival – those at the top of their prep school might find themselves freewheeling at first. The approach is 'softly softly', say parents, with academic focus gently ramping up as girls progress through the school. Ten GCSEs is the default, with respectable results. Girls now take the robust IGCSE in almost all academic subjects (exceptions are Latin, RS and Italian), with no obvious areas of weakness. Computing GCSE newly introduced.

'Results are going up precisely because we are not a robotic exam factory,' says head, and girls concur, reporting the secret of their most recent exam success (aside from the 'unstuffy' teachers who are 'very generous' with their time) as 'being there for each other'. Parents 'not surprised' by good results pouring out of 'an environment with such a tremendous amount of respect that makes girls feel so comfortable'.

Three-form entry into year 7 with a maximum of 22 per form makes for an intimate feel where 'all staff know who your child is'. We heard mutters, but only from one or two parents, about a 'lack of focus' on reading. Newly appointed director of teaching and learning now facilitates good practice and innovation amongst teaching staff. New Firefly platform not only allows staff to set online homework but also provides access to class materials and enrichment activities for pupils as well as showcasing best examples of work.

Learning support and SEN: One 'talented' SENCo in situ and there are some 65 girls with diagnosed SpLD on the register as well as another 25 or so with undiagnosed needs. Approach to support is absolutely 'can do' and 'totally inclusive' with minimal withdrawal from classes – never from curriculum subjects. Most is included in fees and there's a collaborative approach with the pastoral team. School has experience dealing with dyslexia, dyspraxia and dyscalculia plus ADHD/ADD, visual impairment and anxiety disorders; 'girls who might be isolated in other schools are not, here'. Some of site is wheelchair accessible and, if necessary, timetabling would be managed to cater for pupils with mobility issues. No EAL students at the time of our visit but we were assured it was all doable.

The arts and extracurricular: On curriculum to year 9 and available at both GCSE and A level, with good take up at both levels, drama 'massively ramped up' following arrival of another new, buzzy departmental head. Tons of opportunities to perform: at the time of our visit productions in rehearsal included Jane Eyre, Cinderella (panto version) and various pieces for the approaching house drama competition. There's also an academic drama showcase each year, up to 40 girls taking the Trinity Board certificates, a plethora of lunchtime clubs to cater for thespian inclinations plus chances to collaborate with boys' schools on their dramatic endeavours – recently The History Boys with Harrow and Frankenstein with Wetherby. Music also flying high and yes, you guessed it, there's a super new director of music (with a passion for jazz) at the helm. Ensembles and choirs galore perform everything from classical and jazz to pop at the major concerts at the end of each term and informal half termly performances. School orchestra comprises pupils from grade 3 to diploma level, with sixth formers happily presiding over rehearsals if needed. School is well connected to both Wigmore Hall and the Royal Albert Hall to see professionals at work and there are applications most years to both the Royal Academy and Royal College of Music. Carols take place at All Souls Church in Langham Place, jazz musicians join their male counterparts as part of Harrow's big hand and there are plans to stage a collaborative performance with the Royal Philharmonic Orchestra at Cadogan Hall to celebrate QCL's 170th anniversary.

Sixth formers wear their own clothes and fashion statements such as blue or pink hair are allowed and not unusual. 'Girls are allowed to be eccentric,' say parents

Over 80 clubs each week ranging from boxing to manga. Many are student led, eg a pupil founded the Yokosos Club (Japanese mindfulness, apparently). Plus LGBTQueen's, run by sixth formers.

Sport: With its central London location, tiny (albeit charming) outdoor courtyard and subterranean gymnasium, we wondered whether Queen's could possibly be a good fit for super sporty girls. Parents of girls in upper years say 'definitely not', but since the recent appointment of a 'wonderful' new head of sport and the decision to stop marching girls to substandard facilities in Regent's Park and instead transport them by 'nice warm coach' to the all-singing, all-dancing Paddington Rec, we think it's worth a second look. Thanks to access to these facilities, hockey and athletics are now available, as well as netball, football (coached by a former pro), tag rugby, lacrosse and cricket, played at nearby Lord's; school assures us that new pupils are 'assured an amazing sporting experience'. PE teachers run clubs almost every evening and there are fixtures aplenty for those that want them, with A and B teams plus a development squad for all sports – although success depends on the year group ('it's work in progress,' says school). Sixth formers now have compulsory games sessions with broader options and are able to use the gym at Paddington. Their Wednesday afternoons are spent either taking part in work experience or charity initiatives in the local community.

Dance, on curriculum in years 7 to 9, has been 'revolutionised' by 'amazing' new hires who are inspiring girls with Fosse, African and tap in addition to more traditional dance forms. The annual dance show is 'on another level', say parents. Swimming takes place at Marshall Street Leisure Centre.

Ethos and heritage: Founded in 1848 and given a royal charter in 1853, the first institution in Great Britain to give academic qualifications to girls. Still on its original site spanning four elegant, well-proportioned Georgian houses – and so discreet you barely notice it amongst the neighbouring smart doctors' consulting rooms – it has been altered through the years to provide a well-equipped, modern learning environment whilst maintaining its historic charm. The William Morris wallpaper decorating the ground floor corridor – tastefully toning in with the teal sweaters worn by girls in 'the school' (years 7-9) – together with the high ceilings, large windows and sweeping staircases, speaks volumes about the school's style. A warren of charming nooks, crannies and staircases hang all the facilities together; charming oak panelled libraries with light streaming in cater for different age groups and we loved the 'fish bowl' IT suite with its incongruously futuristic feel. Classrooms not the largest or most modern we've seen and the labs could certainly do with a facelift (although the lessons we observed were lively, interactive and looked huge fun), but they all do the job adequately. The multi-purpose school hall ticks all the boxes with its smart lighting rig, and an unexpected delight is the beautiful, modern sixth form centre – a largely glazed roof extension – reached via a lift that whisks the eldest girls up to a serene sanctuary of their own.

The overall vibe is one of intimacy and acceptance and although it no longer has the 'wild west' vibe of its past, there's definitely more than a sniff of freedom. Pupils of all age groups smile and greet one another in the hallways, there's certainly no feeling of social boundaries hampered by hierarchy and 'community' is a word that comes up time and again in conversations, the oldest girls saying that they are seeking out the same feeling in their university destination choices. Individuality is a theme too; the uniform – although under scrutiny by new head who is keen to keep things smart(ish) – is pretty casual; girls in years 10 and 11 (junior college) wear school white shirt and blue jumper but can choose their own bottom half (apparently brightly coloured and patterned trousers are in, black leggings are out). Sixth formers are free to wear their own clothes, and fashion statements such as blue or pink hair are allowed and not

The William Morris wallpaper decorating the ground floor corridor – tastefully toning in with the teal sweaters worn by girls in 'the school' (years 7-9) – speaks volumes about the school's style

unusual; 'girls are allowed to be eccentric,' say parents. Different sexualities and gender identities are embraced and supported. Parents say there's 'quite a feminist' culture – 'it's all about finding out what you're into and encouraging it'. Former pupils include Amber Rudd and Emma Freud.

Pastoral care, inclusivity and discipline: Pastoral care a key strength of school, parents uniformly telling us it's 'really kind' and 'feels like a family'. Pupils love the 'cosiness' and 'old-fashioned nature' of the school, with many telling us it was love at first sight when they walked through the doors on their first visit and describing it as 'relaxed' and 'non-judgemental'. Year heads and form tutors oversee the development of each girl with a head of section above them to step in on major issues as required. 'Staff talk to each other and join the dots,' parents told us. New school counsellor available by appointment one day a week. Disciplinary issues seem to be few and far between – perhaps because of the relatively relaxed vibe, there's no need to push boundaries with silly transgressions.

'Big sister, little sister' scheme has been enhanced to add a 'middle sister' so the younger party doesn't feel bereft when the eldest leaves the school. Years 10 and 11 are trained to mentor younger girls in relation to responsible internet use: 'they're the experts,' says school. Pupils feel very well supported and the ethos is very much about helping them overcome mistakes within a safe environment. Even bullying is dealt with in the most humane way possible – despite zero tolerance policy, we were told that 'a happy child doesn't bully, so we give them support too'. New house system seems to be a good addition (although head admits it hasn't all been plain sailing) and girls, although initially reluctant to throw themselves into house events and competitions, admit to enjoying them all. Years 7 to 9 hand phones in when they arrive at school in the morning.

School has recently launched its Thrive programme – includes an anti-bullying ambassador programme, which has been so successful that the Diana Award invited Queen's to host 'Anti-Bullying Ambassador' training for 20+ other schools across the south-east.

Pupils and parents: Tiger mums move along please – Queen's parents describe their girls as 'happy go lucky… perhaps that's why they do well'. Head says parents 'trust us to get on with it', although parents say school does like them to be involved, not that they need much enticing into school, with information meetings generally turning into jolly social occasions. We are assured that 'wealthy, spoilt girls are few and far between' these days and we felt no sense of entitlement amongst the sincere, ambitious and personable young women we met on our visit. 'Really varied' parent body according to head – plenty in academia as well as the creative industries and almost never flashy. Reflective of modern central London, many have international backgrounds and although the majority were born in the UK, around 40 different languages are spoken at home. Majority from quite nearby – Notting Hill, Belsize Park and St John's Wood – although we also met girls from as far afield as Harrow and Hackney. With such excellent transport links the majority travel to and from school by tube. 'Queen's girls are interesting people,' say parents.

Money matters: Several means-tested bursaries available at 11+ and 16+, funded by the Old Queen's bursary trust fund – around 15 full and eight partial bursaries at the time of our visit. Academic, music and art scholarships, for up to 25 per cent of fees, for both internal and external candidates. In 2019, school launched a new bursary appeal to widen access to girls from disadvantaged backgrounds – the aim is to have at least 10 per cent of pupils on full bursaries by the school's 175th anniversary in 2023.

The last word: Head is possibly the first we've met who claims to have drawn career inspiration from lavatory graffiti (albeit at Cambridge): 'work hard and be nice to people,' it said, and to us that sums up Queen's. Proof that you don't have to be in a pressure cooker to get good results; solid academics, the arts, sport and tip top pastoral: 'it's all here for the taking,' say parents. Dynamic newish head and staff are moving things up a notch – we hope they all stay put. One to watch.

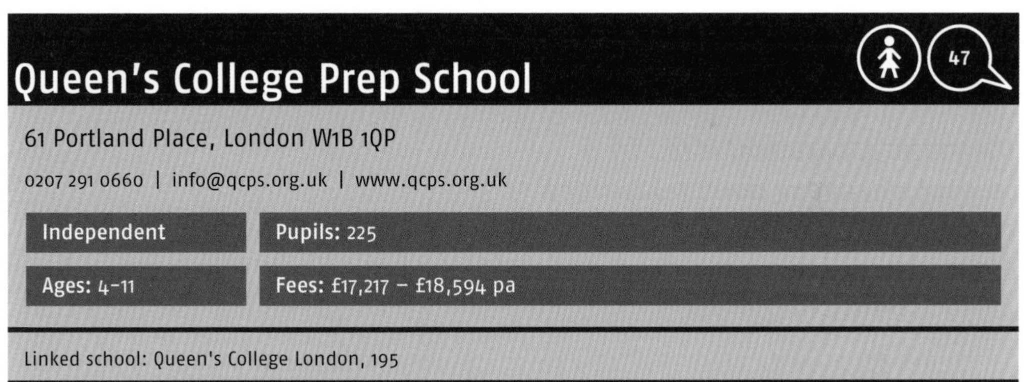

Headmistress: Since September 2020, Laura Hall, formerly deputy head at City of London School for Girls. After completing a degree in history of art at Bristol, she spent two years travelling the seas on cruise ships, giving lectures on 19th century American and European art. When an opportunity popped up at the primary school she attended as a child on the Isle of Mull, she was inspired to move into teaching, leading her to do a PGCE and later an MA in education at the University of Hertfordshire.

Entrance: More put down at birth now for two classes in reception and although there is no active sibling policy, the head is confident that younger girls naturally follow their elders. The few occasional places higher up the school, almost all due to globetrotting parents, are in high demand. This is a genuinely international school with parents who come from, literally, all over the world. A large percentage of parents work in the professions. Most of the girls live nearby, or at least north of Oxford Street, but a few come from Kensington or the City.

Exit: In the main, parents choose the usual London academic (often single sex) senior schools. In 2020, 14 to the linked senior school (four with scholarships), Queen's College, and four to Francis Holland Regent's Park. Others in ones and twos to American School, Belmont, City of London Girls', Francis Holland Sloane Square, Godolphin & Latymer, Highgate, Latymer Upper, Northbridge House, South Hampstead High School, Wycombe Abbey and Queenswood.

Our view: Past the pointy hat of All Souls, Langham Place and the sexy art deco glamour of the BBC, you turn the corner into more sedate Portland Place, framing the distant trees of Regent's Park. Here, QCPS has some unlikely neighbours, including the decidedly odd couple of the People's Republic of China embassy and the openly hedonistic Quintessentially concierge company.

The hall is covered in imaginative artwork and you are immediately aware that you are in a busy school, even if some of the years are out on trips. The layout, spread over two original houses, is slightly confusing to an outsider as they are not joined on every floor but girls, scurrying purposefully, prove that it is no worry to them. The 19th century houses were designed for entertaining so the ceilings are high and the windows are large, at least until you reach the attic, but even there the seductively colourful and popular art room and the classrooms for year 6 are bright and airy. The dining room in the basement does strike chords of the 'downstairs' element of Upstairs, Downstairs but the classroom at the back escapes any gloom by opening onto an interior garden.

The music department is led by a teacher whom one parent described as 'magnificent' and, as he is South African, there is even the chance to play his native marimbas

The tour de force is the brand new STEM lab, paid for by parents, full of exciting labelled drawers and bins for pipettes and goggles as well as a row of startlingly clean, white lab coats embellished with the green school logo. Any budding scientist would have a field day in here and the head's enthusiasm suggests that she would love to join them, given half a chance.

Plenty of opportunity too for outdoor learning, including forest school, which has become a big focus for the school – mostly, as you'd expect, in Regent's Park.

The school was described by a parent as 'not a sausage factory', but it is still keen to ensure that the academic standards attained by the girls gives them the widest choice of secondary education. They are particularly keen on maths and the sciences taking an equal place in the curriculum,

The new STEM lab is full of labelled drawers and bins for pipettes and goggles as well as a row of startlingly clean, white lab coats

along with the subjects more traditionally taught to girls: 'We want to encourage them to build bridges in ballet shoes.' The sciences are condensed into two and a half of the three terms yearly higher up the school, allowing the pupils time to conduct an experimental project (not 100 per cent successful in the case of the irrigation of the vertical gardens on show).

School's enthusiasm for STEM has not allowed it to neglect other subjects, with English teaching being praised as well as the introduction of Mandarin, Spanish and Italian as extracurricular options alongside French. The fact that none of the teaching staff left at the end of her first year is proof that they are all happy with the new hierarchies that have been established and certainly, on our visit, there were nothing but smiley faces. A 'fab head of learning support' has been appointed, we heard, and staff appear to handle the challenge of teaching a child with no English on arrival (provided it is at the lower end of the school) with absolutely no fuss and great success.

A major play for the creative arts is made at QCPS and Miss Rosy's Dance Academy plays a large part, with grateful London parents, casting around to entertain their children, remarking on how brilliant it is that she also runs holiday classes. The music department under the roof is noisy and enthusiastic, led by a teacher whom one parent described as 'magnificent' and, as he is South African, there is even the chance to play his native marimbas. As well as the slightly unconventional percussion-playing opportunities, there are the more usual events such as the harvest festival and nativity plays (a camel-based offering last year) in All Souls church, and annual musicals.

One of the school's targets is to increase the sports provision, in particular competitive sports. School has appointed a new head of sport and the offering is going to be widened to include current favourites such as cricket, now that scoring a century at Lord's is open to all. Unfortunately, all inner London schools suffer from having little outside space and QCPS is no exception, the girls having to walk to the gardens at the end of the street to let off steam outside on non-sporting days.

At the beginning of the day an Early Birds breakfast club helps out overstretched parents, and after school ends, teachers run a variety of additional activities. External help is also summoned and your daughter can choose from a selection including coding, cooking, gardening, sign language and yoga. The food is alone in being given a low rating, despite a new catering manager and an attempt to move away from 'nursery food'.

The last word: Parents say 'the school has a more modern, professional feel' and that it is aiming to be 'a platinum brand in a competitive market'. This sounds as if the school's charm might be at risk, but we were persuaded that the head is simply trying to make it fit with the aspirations of modern London families.

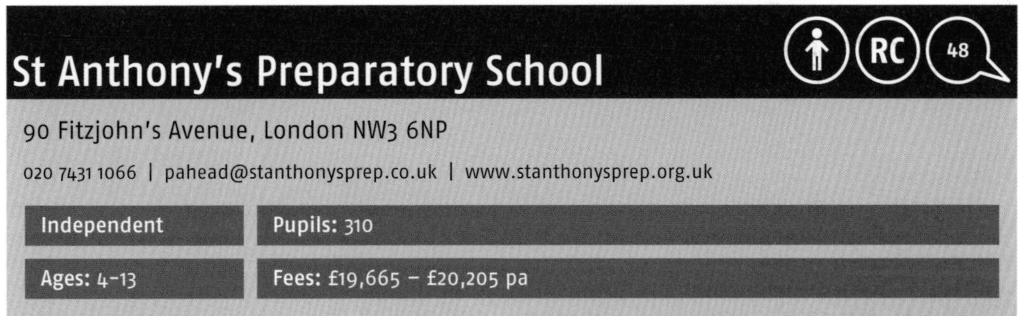

St Anthony's Preparatory School

90 Fitzjohn's Avenue, London NW3 6NP

020 7431 1066 | pahead@stanthonysprep.co.uk | www.stanthonysprep.org.uk

Independent	Pupils: 310
Ages: 4–13	Fees: £19,665 – £20,205 pa

Headmaster: Since September 2020, Richard Berlie, formerly vice principal of MPW London and before that head of upper school at Dulwich College. A practising Catholic, he attended the Salesian College, Battersea and read history at Cambridge (Magdalene College), where he stayed on for his PGCE. Kicked off his teaching career at Wymondham College, moving on to Ampleforth, where he was also an assistant housemaster and the scholars' tutor. Thence back to London to Emanuel School, Wandsworth where he was later promoted to head of humanities and politics and where he also ran the able, gifted and talented programme.

Entrance: For the past few years, main entry point has been at reception, where there is now a two form entry. Boys come from about 25 different feeder nurseries: Catholic pupils have typically been at either St Mary's down the road or St Christina's in St John's Wood. Although the school is keen to maintain a strong constituency of Catholic pupils, everyone has to go through the assessment procedure. 'Given that most of the children are only 3 or 4,' explains the head, 'we try to make it feel like a play day as far as possible, and to identify those most likely to respond to our style of teaching and learning.' Occasional spots for boys coming in at other times, but the general rule is to take a tour and then, as early as possible, register.

Exit: Leavers' destinations showcase how adept the school has become at nurturing a whole range of interests and appetites – including some boarding schools. In 2020, City of London, Merchant Taylors', Mill Hill and Wetherby Senior were the most popular. The odd one or two to Eton, Westminster, UCS etc.

Like so many London prep schools, St Anthony's has had to adapt to a ruthless and rapidly changing world in which many pupils are under pressure to join junior departments of their senior schools aged 11, rather than hold off until 13. For many pupils, years 5 and 6 leading up to the 11+ is the time of maximum pressure. 'The heyday of common entrance feels quite distant at times,' says the head. 'But for those staying all the way, we make sure these last two years are the most enriched: to release the full academic potential of youngsters, and spice it up with the individuality which St Anthony's has always sought to foster.'

Our view: Taking children mainly at reception, the aim is to offer at once a broad and balanced curriculum. 'English and maths open up a whole world of learning,' says the head, 'and we want our pupils exploring all of it.' Science and ICT are there right at the start, but from year 1 there is French and Mandarin as well as everything else one would expect – history and geography, art and DT. Religious studies is also taught – but with an eye and an ear for pupils of all faiths and of none.

By the time pupils are 10 and have moved to the senior school, everybody studies Latin and there are after-school opportunities to do ancient Greek and Arabic as well. There's a specially equipped classroom for DT, as well as lashings of art, music and drama. 'We don't want any part in

the reductionism in the curriculum one sometimes hears about,' says the head. 'Creativity is at the heart of the school.' There are also a host of out-of-school hobby and discussion groups – philosophy and chess among them alongside the arts. 'My son has been given masses of opportunity to find his voice,' said one parent. Another added: 'The staff have a genuine love of learning, and are superb at communicating it.'

Limited play areas (it is in the middle of Hampstead), but does have its own rather splendid swimming pool ('Thank God,' said one parent)

Because testing, in all its iterations, has become such a big feature of life for prep school children from the age of 10 or 11, St Anthony's deploys a range of tests (such as CAT4, PIPS and MiDYis) to acclimatise pupils. 'They are useful visitors,' says the head, 'but life here is dictated, first and last, by what we believe to be enriching in its own right. Dedicated study skills department – one full time teacher and one part time, and two of the TAs have special training. There are regular diagnostic assessments to identify anyone needing extra input.

All qualified teachers at St Anthony's – from the half dozen or so who have been there for over 20 years to the young Turks. Five TAs have recently studied for their PGCEs while working full time at the school. 'They are astonishingly dedicated,' says the head, 'and many are already academically highly qualified.' One parent, whose son had won a scholarship to a famous school, said what he liked most was that his son had felt 'inspired, rather than under pressure'.

Limited play areas (it is in the middle of Hampstead, after all), although it does have its own rather splendid swimming pool ('Thank God,' said one parent). Normal games see pupils take a 10-minute coach ride to Brondesbury playing fields. 'There's the odd day when traffic is a nightmare,' said a father. 'But they do well at getting them out at break and into the fresh air.' Since we last visited, a quiet revolution has taken place in the profile of sport, perhaps not unconnected with the appointment of outstanding sports teachers. Recent pupils include a boy who went on to captain the first XV at a major rugby-playing senior school, and two members of the Lawn Tennis Association. The main staples are football, rugby and hockey in winter and cricket and athletics in summer, but efforts are made to offer reasonable choice. Cross-country is enjoying a surge of popularity: 15 teachers ran a half marathon recently and another is an elite marathon runner. 'This level of commitment,' says the head, 'rather rubs off on the pupils.'

The school is explicit that it wants all pupils physically literate, and there are competitive fixtures with other schools from year 4. 'They have to be fit enough to cope with life's assorted pressures,' says the head. Inevitably, 'some have to learn they are not always the best in the pack, but the idea is that everyone who wants to represent the school at sport can do so.' There is a clear underlying message here – for parents as much as for children: emotional resilience is all-important, and teamwork and games can, or should be, a significant part of the learning.

As always, masses of drama, music and art, with regular visits to museums, theatres and galleries. One of the head's early moves was to triple the number of music lessons, and the fact that the school also acquired a grand piano and built a new music studio left no doubt that he and the governors were dead set on protecting the school's reputation as a bastion of the creative arts. There's a full orchestra and a jazz orchestra, and the head of music allegedly claimed that every boy who finished his time at St Anthony's could take grade 5 theory in music – quite an achievement, if true.

'We don't want any part in the reductionism in the curriculum one sometimes hears about,' says the head. 'Creativity is at the heart of the school'

Plays are performed annually – every pupil takes part in a play for their year group each Christmas and summer, and there are myriad further opportunities for performance – in designated school assemblies and so forth. There's also a major Shakespeare production every year – the most recent ('a triumph,' said one parent) was Macbeth. Art is every bit as strong – a raft of student work has recently been gracing the Saatchi Gallery, and the walls of the school are filled with pupils' latest creative output.

Founded in Victorian times, the school moved from Eastbourne to Hampstead in 1952, and was a family affair until recently – indeed, the present bursar is one of the founding family. It has long enjoyed the reputation for being ever-so-slightly alternative. 'Terms like "wacky" and "bohemian" fall too easily from the lips,' chuckled Mr Keyte. 'Schools always spawn myths, and one myth is that it always used to be wackier than it is now – now being 30 years ago, 10 years ago, or here today.' One parent said, 'The place fosters individuality, but they also foster awareness of others. My sons' friends at the school were all lovely kids.'

In fact, there is strong continuity: it's less academically assertive than some of its competitors, and continues to invest huge time, as well as significant resources, in its arts and mixed curriculum. What is gently shifting is the extent to which it can compete, on all fronts, with the best. The plant is hugely impressive, there is a long waiting list and the staff are evidently completely committed. Taken over by Alpha Plus in 2009. 'They've offered massive support – moral and material,' says the head, 'and through the links they offer to other schools. In academic, pastoral and administrative terms, we are part of a powerful shared network of understanding and best practice.'

'Pupils have to be fit enough to cope with life's pressures,' says head. 'The idea is that everyone who wants to represent the school at sport can do so'

Good local community links and endeavour, and energetic and impassioned fundraising. A particular charity to which the school has attached itself – Mary's Meals – seeks to provide food for the neediest children all over the world, and pupils raised over £58,000 for the key school charities recently. 'Not bad,' says the head, 'and it came from the heart, I assure you.'

The prevailing atmosphere is of calm – children always generate a degree of noise, but the motif is jolly rather than manic, and there was a laudable absence of rush around the classrooms and in the school canteen (the food is widely regarded as excellent). It may be a boys' school, but it is blessedly short of that testy laddishness which serves to exclude rather than embrace. There is also a strong and experienced senior leadership team – of whom the bursar, head of junior school and academic deputy head are all women.

High ceilings and shrewdly-adapted Victorian buildings have managed to foster a sense of space and light. A school for all-comers, all types, and for all seasons. The sense of children at ease around the place is emphasised by the way they wear their uniform – a green and grey affair, which sits comfortably on them. The effect is to suggest an identity, and it's easy to see it's worn with pride – but, mercifully, without swagger. A big emphasis on kindness and tolerance. We heard teachers talking to classes and individual pupils, quite unaware that anyone was around, and the tenor was consistently one of calm benevolence. The payoff is obvious – the children seem remarkably patient and tolerant of one another. Very strong sense that the care of the children is anchored by affection and good sense.

A high-powered staffroom – Oxbridge and doctorates all over the place – but school culture fosters collegiality among staff, and old hands willingly share best practice with newbies. Form tutors are the first point of contact for parents, and share concerns with senior teachers as well as with the pastoral deputy head. Stout denials from all parties that parents are anything other than strongly supportive. 'We aim at prevention,' said one long-serving teacher. 'We encourage anyone – child or parent – to tell us if they're worried or doubtful about something. It breeds trust, and it usually means stuff gets sorted out before it gets difficult.' It seems to work too – the previous headmaster, in his ten years here, invoked the sanction of detention precisely twice.

Reports get sent home twice a year, and there are two annual parents' evenings, as well as a lot of informal meetings. 'We aim to be around,' says the head. 'A lot of goodwill is built up, and a great deal of information exchanged, simply by teachers being around – not least at the school gates.'

Pupil constituency is noticeably more European than many other schools of its kind – hardly surprising given that St Anthony's is the only all-boys Catholic prep school in north London, and hence a favoured destination for the many Spanish, French and Italians who live around here. It also won a string of 'outstanding' commendations in its recent diocesan inspection, which helped to cement its credentials with this particular parent body. On the other hand, it's also a mainstream Hampstead prep school, with lots of parents drawn from the professions, the media and the City. Some remarkable old alumni – David Suchet and Antony Gormley among the older generation; a more recent luminary is Jack Steadman of the indie band Bombay Bicycle Club.

The last word: A very likeable school. Conscious of its individuality, but not in thrall to it. 'A nice balance of informality and old school,' said a parent. Smack in the middle of north London, it is championing values more abiding than merely those of fame and fortune. It achieves considerable success, but not by stepping over the bodies of others. The affection with which St Anthony's is viewed by parents and staff seems to suggest they, like the pupils, are only too glad to have bought into this wisdom.

St Christopher's School

32 Belsize Lane, London NW3 5AE

020 7435 1521 | admissions@stchristophers.london | www.stchristophers.london

Independent | Ages: 4–11 | Pupils: 247 | Fees: £15,750 pa

Head: Since September 2020, Sandrine Paillasse, previously deputy head and director of pastoral care at St Paul's Girls' School. Has over 20 years of experience in education, including senior positions at various girls' independent schools including Queen's College and South Hampstead High School, where she was acting head for a term. Sandrine is also a qualified and practising psychotherapist.

Entrance: St Christopher's is one of London's highest-achieving academic prep schools, with results at 11 the envy of many of its neighbours. This, however, is a school which selects primarily on ability, with places offered on outcome of 4+ and 5+ assessments held each January. 'It is not an academic assessment. We observe how they play together and how they interact with other children.' The school operates a split entry and although all are assessed at the same time, girls with September to February birthdays will generally join in reception, whilst March to August birthdays join in year 1. Test dates and results are co-ordinated with other leading selective north London prep schools. Early registration is essential (as near birth as possible) for those already resident in London. Entry lists are closed at about 300 to be assessed for 38 available places. The school, however, is always willing to be flexible for those who've just arrived. Siblings are given an automatic offer, unless it is considered 'they will not flourish'. Not flourishing, however, is fairly loosely interpreted. 'If you have two clever daughters and the third is not as bright, some parents think she'll upset the exit poll, but that's not the way we work.' Parents confirm that year groups cover a (relatively) wide spread of ability. Occasional vacancies after entry.

Exit: This is generally a school of bright sparks and ambitious parents and the majority proceed to the highest performing London day schools and a handful to high performing state secondaries. In 2020, destinations included Camden School for Girls, Channing, City of London School for Girls, Forest School, Francis Holland, Godolphin & Latymer, Haberdashers', Highgate, Immanuel College, North London Collegiate School, North Bridge House, Northwood College, Queen's College, South Hampstead High School, St Paul's Girls' School, Henrietta Barnett and Wycombe Abbey.

Our view: St Christopher's was founded in 1883 by two local literary lesbians but established in its current form in 1950 by the writer Rosemary Manning. It became a charitable trust in the 1970s. Housed in a large Victorian family house (with modern additions) in fashionable Belsize Park, this is a top-flight prep school for top-flight north London parents and the ethos and atmosphere are reflective of that. The education the pupils receive here is thoughtful and exciting. It concentrates on the fundamentals, but only after the fundamentals have been carefully considered. 'We have to ask the question "what are we educating children for?" It's a world we know nothing about, a world very different from our own.' The school has carefully analysed the impact of technology. 'The girls think technologically and it can be much more difficult to get them to listen to a story and concentrate.' The issue is addressed by concentrated focus on the task of reading and understanding and girls read aloud every day from reception to year 3 and regularly thereafter. 'If you can't read, you can't do maths.' No concessions are made when it comes to literature ('We don't use abridged texts') and Dickens and Lewis Carroll are digested in the original. An excellent library underlines the school's priorities.

No concessions are made when it comes to literature: Dickens and Lewis Carroll are digested in the original

Much of the timetable follows the national curriculum ('It would be foolish not to – there are some very interesting things – but we cut away the trivia. We don't reject it, we tweak it') and the approach is based on 'child-initiated learning' with pupils taught to question and take responsibility for what they learn. Work is then tailored to the needs of each pupil, with maths books, for example, customised to the age and stage. (Though those in need of learning support are in the minority – mainly younger siblings – parents consider this tailoring, too, to be strong.) Spanish ('one of the most widely spoken languages in the world') is taught throughout, Latin from year 5 and French as a club from year 3. Specialist subject teaching from year 4, with drama added to the curricular mix, joined by history of art in year 5. Flexibility of mind is encouraged by the inclusion of chess. ('It's a brilliant thinking exercise.')

Hard-working, well-qualified staff, particularly in the final two years. 'I cannot imagine better teachers than the maths and English teachers in years 5 and 6,' said one parent. 'They are really transformative.'

Despite the school's outstanding scholarship record, there is no scholarship class and no setting, except in maths in the final two years. Nor is this a school that crams for exams; preparation lasts just one term, when practice papers are given weekly. 'They're not missing core subjects from year 5, they still have time for all the extracurricular, they're not pressured and processed.' The approach here is enriching and the school believes there is as much value in creativity as in the core subjects.

The message that banking is as worthwhile a career for girls as nursing is instilled with visits to the Bank of England

Music is generally considered strong and enthusiastic, with two music classes plus a singing class each week. What's learnt here is put into practice with a junior orchestra, a wind group, a string group, piano club, junior and senior choirs and a chamber choir. This is media-land, too, and there is also a thriving film club, where girls learn to make their own. Cultural outings are very much part of the offering, with regular visits to theatres and museums and a young writers' workshop.

Sport is perhaps less important than it might be elsewhere (some parents complain that unless you're in a team, this can be a rather neglected area). Netball court and gym on site and regular matches against other schools in netball and rounders. Short tennis is also taught in the summer term and senior girls play lacrosse. Swimming lessons only in year 3 at nearby Swiss Cottage baths, sports day held at Hampstead Cricket Club. Though the outdoor space here is not unduly extensive, it is used very effectively, with an outdoor classroom, an Alice Garden and a science-themed garden. 'Children today have a very boring existence, chauffeured here and there, and we wanted to create an environment where they were allowed to be imaginative.' Indeed, the thread that runs throughout St Christopher's is that a good education is stimulating, interesting and exciting. The extracurricular is therefore addressed as energetically, with everything from public speaking to self-defence and Indian dance and, while there may be a Florence Nightingale workshop, the message that banking is as worthwhile a career for girls as nursing is instilled with visits to the Bank of England and a mock Dragons' Den. All staff are required to run two clubs a year and the offering is extensive.

Four houses – Brontë, Nightingale, North and Pankhurst – provide the basis for inter-house competition. The school has a strong family feel, sheltered and relaxed. There are no school rules ('We just ask for respect in the classroom and for them to be polite to teachers'). Good behaviour is instilled by discussion. ('Why did you do that? How do you imagine that would look?') Occasionally parents feel that emotional difficulties are not picked up as quickly as they might be. ('If you mention a problem, they take it seriously, but it's not always spotted,' said one.) Assembly every Friday is non-denominational. School meals exclude pork, shellfish, ham and nuts in order to cater for all. The facilities here have been brought thoroughly up to date, too, with a smart extension providing additional classrooms and impressive IT. The uniform of green Aertex shirts and blue trousers is practical and durable.

Over a third of pupils live within walking distance and the rest travel from affluent nearby postcodes like St John's Wood, Maida Vale, Islington and Highgate. Demographic is diverse in terms of race and religion – representative of the local area. Parents are often intellectual and professional. Occasionally celebrities. 'They are interesting and incredibly well informed. They are very involved and desperately keen to support their children's education.' ('Sometimes too keenly involved,' remarked one father. 'There are a lot of non-working mothers who once had high-powered careers and are now directing their energies on their children.') Occasionally expectations have to be gently adjusted.

Money matters: One 100 per cent means-tested scholarship available per annum and other support available as necessary.

The last word: A high-octane education producing confident, well-informed and articulate girls. 'The nice thing about St Christopher's is that it provides an excellent education without trying to breed a master race,' said one happy customer.

St Margaret's School (London)

50

18 Kidderpore Gardens, London NW3 7SR

020 7435 2439 | enquiry@st-margarets.co.uk | www.st-margarets.co.uk

Independent	Pupils: 171
Ages: 4–16	Fees: £13,473 – £15,609 pa

Principal: Since 2008, Mark Webster BSc (50s). Educated at Highgate School and University College London (where he read psychology), PGCE at Cambridge. Spent 15 years at the Royal School, Hampstead (first in primary, then IT, psychology and maths, before becoming deputy and acting head). Never planned to become a teacher – 'If you'd asked me early on what job I wanted to do, I'd have said teaching was 999th out of 1000'. A chance encounter changed his mind. 'I was working in publishing, when I met someone who said their job in teaching was fantastic. I'd never met anyone who felt that way about work.' Now equally enthusiastic about his chosen profession, Mr Webster continues to be hands-on in his approach and still teaches mathematics.

We were initially struck by Mr Webster's bold shirt of candy coloured stripes, which belies his very calm manner. He is not extrovert by any means (as his shirt may imply), but is calm, thoughtful and extremely warm and friendly. He takes the time to consider our questions, and responds diplomatically and graciously. Parents unanimously agree that he is a 'brilliant head teacher and a real leader'. During our meeting there are a number of students who pop into the head's office for a variety of reasons ranging from charity fundraising questions to other Christmas related issues. Clearly students feel he is very approachable, and whilst in common with some other heads he does operate an open door policy, unlike with many other heads, students actually take him up on this.

He says one of the benefits of working in a small school is that 'I have the privilege of knowing every student.' He enjoys the proximity and seeing the children grow up: 'You feel you can make a significant difference.' Unlike, he says, a much larger school, where perhaps you don't have the hands-on input: 'I can sleep well at night as I know I've done my very best.' Fundamental to his approach is the view that education is about instilling a sense of curiosity – 'Qualifications are a passport to the next stage, but if you remain curious you will never be bored.'

He himself retains a passionate interest in art, history and reading. Also plays football for Highgate Old Boys. A tactful, sympathetic enthusiast, Webster is a good fit for this family-like school. Possibly slightly unusual to have a male head teacher in an all-girls school, but that doesn't seem to bother the parents. 'He is wonderful, we are so very lucky.' Married to a teacher; they have two young sons.

Entrance: 'Loosely selective.' From reception to year 2 assessment involves girls coming in for the morning and working with the class teacher. A handful of places offered from year 3 upwards and potential candidates take a standard set of English and maths assessments. Guaranteed transition from within at 11. 'Once we've made the commitment, unless there are particular special needs we can't support, we stick to it.' Now part of the London 11+ Consortium and external candidates take its cognitive ability test. They do operate a basic sibling policy: 'We're not über selective, but we have rejected siblings if we don't feel the school is right for them.'

Exit: About 70 per cent of junior school girls stay on to the senior school, though a small number move to more selective senior schools such as Henrietta Barnett or South Hampstead High School. There's no intention of opening a sixth form, despite parental requests: 'One of the things about being a small school is that you are aware of the things you can't offer, in terms of space and subjects, which is why we will never have a sixth form.' However, by then most parents agree it is time to move on.

Notably successful with applications at 16. Most popular choices at that point are local co-ed sixth forms such as UCS and Highgate, more selective schools such as Henrietta Barnett, and similar atmosphere girls' schools such as Channing. A reasonable number goes to the state sector – Woodhouse College is particularly popular. Good guidance on offer at both 11 and 16 – 'It's really important to make an informed choice.

Not every school will suit every girl and they are used to being supported here.' School also works with them on interview practice and personal statements. One parent told us: 'Prior to looking around a few schools, I was advised to by Mr Webster to look out for things which would never have otherwise occurred to me – like to not be swayed by all the high tech stuff.' St Margaret's girls generally get their first-choice sixth form.

Latest results: In 2020, 82 per cent of GCSEs were graded 9-7. In 2019 (the last year when exams took place), 58 per cent 9-7 at GCSE.

Teaching and learning: Results are impressive when you consider that the school is relatively non-selective and the ability range always includes the very able and those with more modest aspirations. One parent told us: 'I was a bit worried as I do have a very academic daughter and I thought she might not reach her full potential, but the luxury of a school this size is that teachers can cater for each individual in a mixed-ability class.'

GCSE options include Spanish, French, art ('which is amazing,' one student told us), psychology and drama alongside the compulsory subjects. All girls are required to take the science trilogy (taught in a compact, but efficient lab) and the vast majority go on to do at least one science A level. A modern language is compulsory.

Setting introduced when necessary but, with limited space, teaching is usually differentiated rather than physically separated. Extremely low turnover of staff (the French teacher has been there for 25 years) – 'I've only had to write one reference in eight years,' the head told us. This is largely because most departments are very small 'so teachers can actually make the role their own and achieve what they actually came into the profession to achieve'. This consistency can only be a good thing for the wellbeing and academic progress of the students.

Learning support and SEN: School does cater for pupils with mild SEN, but 'we don't have the depth of resources for learning support that a larger school would have,' says the head. Two SENCo support plus a couple of teachers trained in dyslexia and dyscalculia, but the main support comes from classroom teachers. All abilities equally well catered for – 'We aren't results-driven and we try to exhaust every avenue.'

The arts and extracurricular: The head's view is that education is a 'can-do, must try' matter, and is inspired by the celebrated art historian Sir Ernst Gombrich's attitude: 'You don't have to like it, but it's important to understand why other people do. We compel them to try lots of things. They may moan, but we make them give it a go.' Drama is taken seriously and there's a lovely new space for it. Shakespeare is now a biggie here. 'Our drama teacher has a big pedigree in Shakespeare.' From year 7, pupils have a non-Shakespeare year where they are encouraged to devise their own pieces to perform. The head says: 'We want to encourage them to devise their own roles by exploring situations.' Other productions have included Matilda and Wind in the Willows.

The head believes that education is about instilling a sense of curiosity – 'Qualifications are a passport to the next stage, but if you remain curious you will never be bored'

Music, too, is important with a variety of traditional and less traditional extra-lesson options – anyone who wants to can join the ukulele club: 'It's a very egalitarian and upbeat instrument.' A number of choirs, plus a junior school orchestra. At least half of girls have private instrument lessons at the school. Art immensely popular, with excellent results at GCSE: two studios, one reasonably spacious, the other definitely petite. Dance popular too.

Plenty of extracurricular going on: street dance, choir, theatre, cookery, cheerleading, philosophy, orchestra, chess, tennis and origami. Trips local and international, from walks on Hampstead Heath to Tuscany and Iceland.

An unusual incentive which the head introduced is '125' (a tribute to the school's 125th anniversary), which provides pupils with a list of activities to attempt before they leave the school: 'To complement the academic, performing and sporting curriculum we offer, the girls undertake activities throughout the year as part of the school's Skills Grid. The range includes the practical, the cultural and the altruistic: everything from touch-typing, learning a magic trick or "doing something nice for someone who can do nothing in return".'

Sport: Outside space is relatively restricted, with a largish garden transformed into an Astroturf playground. A local hall is used for gym and the school now has a sports area for netball, tennis and other sports two minutes' walk away. Minibus takes girls to Hampstead Heath for rounders or running, to Hendon Leisure Centre for aerobics, rock climbing and badminton and the Welsh Harp for rowing. Inter-house and inter-school matches from year 4 upwards. In David and Goliath mode, the school is unafraid to compete with much larger north London schools like Channing, despite the fact that 'we often lose'. One parent told us: 'For the super sporty, this school may not be your first choice.'

Ethos and heritage: Founded in 1884 and one of the oldest schools in Hampstead, it moved to its present site in a quiet, suburban Hampstead road in 1943. A large, elegant red-brick house accommodates 155+ girls and the head says, 'The house element has become a pivotal cornerstone of how I think about the school. Everything emanates from it being a house – the relationships, the attitudes etc. We've spent quite a lot of money on knocking down a lot of walls.' We believe he meant that both literally and metaphorically.

Fairly recent building work has completely altered the layout of the ground and lower ground floors to incorporate a new school hall. The idea was also to open up the ground floor as much as possible to give the house a much more open-plan feel, thereby creating more light and space. Everything is transparent – even the head's office. The school has also added a pretty roof terrace to encourage reading and quiet study for the upper years.

On entering the building we were treated to the melodic voices of a few girls doing choir practice. We watched for a few minutes entranced. It all added to the warm and cosy atmosphere of the St Margaret's experience (it helped that it was nearly Christmas at the time of our visit). We were struck by how deceptively big the school seems on the inside. Yes, there are areas which are exceedingly tight and narrow, and would definitely not suit any physically impaired student, but the floors upwards seemed endless and the corridors often led into quaint hidden areas. Although classrooms were snug, they were adequate for the number of students in each class (no more than 20). None of the students we met or chatted to seemed particularly fazed about the spatial issue. As one parent said, 'They don't know any better, as some have been here since infants and go all the way through.'

We were charmed by the lovely reading area for the juniors and the loft-style library. It definitely felt as if we had entered a bygone era – not a conventional school by any means (think the Brontës). This, it seems, is what some parents most love about the school. One told us: 'Both the head and the school are very unusual in education and sadly part of a dying breed – not caught up in the madness of it all, but eminently sensible.'

The girls who showed us around were happy, polite and totally unpretentious. We were taken aback by one student who openly admitted she had had 'difficulties' in some areas, but unlike other schools she had been to, everyone at St Margaret's was 'friendly and caring'. (Again, another of the school's many charms is that it didn't select one of its obvious 'stars' to show us around the school and do the whole PR number.)

Senior and junior schools both occupy the same building and have the same head, with different uniforms but little separation between them. Uniforms are smart – red and white in the junior school, black and white in the senior. The uniform was changed a few years back for the seniors as they didn't like it. Girls are listened to here. There are two 'agony aunts' (senior students) available at all times for confidential chats, and a school council. One pupil told us: 'We voted for a tuck shop at the school council and now we have one. We can choose what is sold.' The school has three houses and pupils of all ages work together to raise funds for charities of their own choice and compete at sports.

In David and Goliath mode, the school is unafraid to compete with much larger north London schools like Channing, despite the fact that 'we often lose'

The small, friendly and homely atmosphere 'allows the girls to achieve whatever they can – but in a safe, non-confrontational environment,' said one parent.

Daphne du Maurier was a pupil.

Pastoral care, inclusivity and discipline: Discipline not a significant issue. Though head insists this is not the garden of Eden, disciplinary issues tend to be confined to infringements of uniform – 'We can live with earrings if there's no drink or drugs.' Bullying – 'We get a case every year' – is dealt with promptly. Detentions, it seems, are an alien notion: 'We haven't needed to give one since 2011.' One parent who is a teacher herself working in an inner city school told us: 'I have to laugh sometimes when my daughter comes home and says "OMG! One of the girls threw a pen in class".' Girls generally very well behaved and extremely supportive of one another – 'an extended family,' one said. Another told us: 'My daughter went through a very difficult time one year because of social media. I was alerted to this by her form tutor, who in turn had found out from three of her close friends, who were very concerned. She was closely monitored and supported throughout and got through it.'

Parents, too, tend to be very supportive; they are known to choose the school for its caring environment: 'You get ups and downs with some of the girls, but if you ever get a problem it's dealt with straight away,' said one. Most parents feel one of the school's greatest strengths is its pastoral side, allowing girls to fulfil their potential and know exactly who they are. One parent told us: 'This school allows every girl to flourish. It formed my daughter into the happy, caring girl she is today.' Another told us: 'What struck me about this school when I first looked around, and what still remains true five years later, is that the girls all seem to have that wonderful, quiet confidence. Not that brash sense of entitlement that some wealthy kids can have.'

The school has its own head of pastoral care but also relies on a school counsellor when needed and proactively encourages bonding with a variety of trips. 'The girls mix across the years and are often close to girls in the year above and below,' said a parent.

Pupils and parents: Nice, well-behaved, confident girls from a cosmopolitan range of backgrounds reflecting the school's north London location – a large chunk of second-generation French and Italians. A fair number come from within walking distance, then in an arc stretching from Wembley to Islington (school minibus on offer for those who require it). Very much a family school in every sense – 45 per cent of pupils are sisters or relatives of current or ex-pupils. 'A lot of people like the sense of support and nurturing.' The school rarely advertises and most newcomers hear about it by word of mouth and favourable newspaper coverage. The internet has slightly altered the traditional intake, as it is accessible worldwide. One parent told us: 'What I like most about the parents who send their girls to St Margaret's is that they defy the Daily Mail stereotype of bling parents.'

> *One parent told us: 'What I like about the people who send their girls here is that they defy the Daily Mail stereotype of bling parents'*

Money matters: Not an expensive school by any means, though a number of girls receive bursaries to cover all or part of their school fees: 'A reasonable proportion on some sort of financial help.'

The last word: A gentle, nurturing school with a strong and secure family atmosphere providing a stimulating, tailor-made education. 'A little gem,' to quote one parent, though possibly not the ideal venue for the child who needs plenty of space to run around or one who requires the challenge of a big stage.

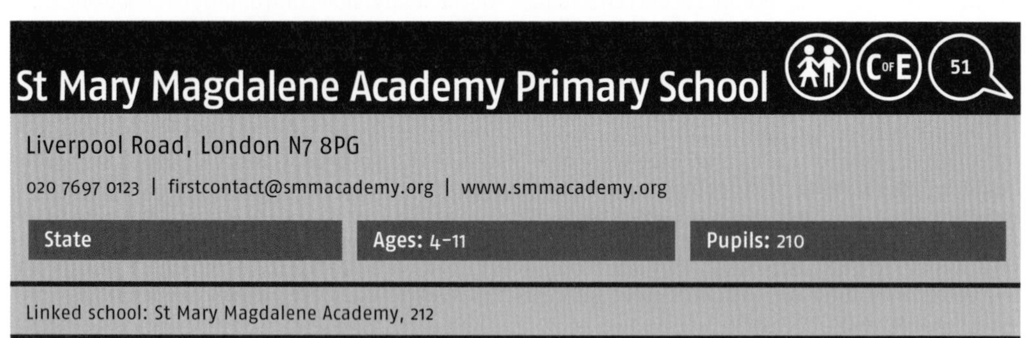

Headteacher: Since 2016, Ruth Luzmore (30s) has brought enthusiasm, warmth, appreciation and energy to this small primary school. Memories of a very happy primary education led her to teaching. She studied in the evenings at Birkbeck College for a degree in politics, philosophy and history whilst earning a living in the daytime. She has continued working days and studying evenings since, gaining a masters in leadership at the Institute of Education whilst working as deputy head in another Islington primary school and now, as head of St Mary Magdalene Academy (SMMA) Primary, she is working towards a PhD in enquiry-based professional development. She says, 'It is good to have a life outside the job, which otherwise can be all-consuming.'

Her commitment to working hard and the importance of education for social change can be seen – involving teachers with an active senior leadership team, engaging parents through the parent-teacher association, good email and newsletter communications. The school also gives a voice to pupils, who say 'teachers listen to you' and 'you can talk to Ms Luzmore or teachers about any issues'. Teachers 'are open to change and we are evolving policy together'. Many of the TAs have been at SMMA for years – some taught parents of current pupils – and their monitoring in the playground means that 'the care continues from the classroom into the playground and they can be aware of pupils' issues'. 'I like being part of the academy group because it means I run a small, friendly school but can look outwards too, to the senior school.'

Entrance: Priority to looked-after children, then those who regularly attend one of the three local churches – St Mary Magdalene, St Luke's or St David's – then residents of Islington who attend another church, then siblings (some years as many as half the reception class is made up of siblings), then distance from the school (has been as local as within 0.3 of a mile). Heavily oversubscribed.

Exit: Almost all go on to the secondary school of SMMA, though a few to Dame Alice Owen, Highbury Fields, City of London boys and girls.

Our view: Having a previous literacy coordinator as head ensures literacy is a backbone of the school: 'They need to leave not only reading but enjoying reading for pleasure.' Phonics taught formally (Sounds Write system) but then a wide range of strategies – topic based, class readers, buddy reading, reading road maps – to lead pupils through age-appropriate books. Writing in evidence on the walls and in neatly marked homework with the emphasis on self-expression. 'Enough homework to please parents but not so much kids spend all the weekend working,' according to one parent.

Maths coordinator makes sure that whilst they cover the national curriculum, maths is included in topics and in practical ways (eg visiting fruit snack bar run by sixth formers, raising money for charity – 'generating money is empowering for the children and helps them to realise money needs to be earned'). No setting in maths – 'we don't want to put limits on anyone's ability'; extra tutoring groups by deputy head extend or support pupils. Booster classes after school which, according to pupils, are 'really fun and help with your learning'. Pupils said, 'there are different levels of work and you can choose your challenge'.

Mandarin or Spanish taught from reception. Child-led, topic-based learning leads to 'intellectual conversations around themes, so that the year 6 conflict module started with Middle Ages and battles and moved right on to Trump and Kim Jong Un'. Parents said that 'kids become obsessed with the theme for six or seven weeks; we prepare it during the holidays, discuss it over meal times – they are always thinking about it. It gives them a chance to really get into a subject in depth.' Year 1s were learning about people's jobs – a lovely set of dressing up clothes and equipment for role play. Pupils said, 'teachers are not too strict, they give us chances, listen to us and are fair'.

Good results at KS2, above national average in all subjects. However, it is the ability to discuss and articulate ideas that makes this school shine – pupils are used to developing ideas and backing them up. After Sats in year 6, pupils create an 'exhibition where they present a poster with their opinions and collected thoughts which they explain to visiting parents and teachers – a sort of conference' (PhD students in the making?). Topics have included 'How terrorism affects society', 'How do we work for political honesty?' and 'The influence of government on health care around the world'. Mentor teachers work to support these mini presentations.

Topic-based learning: year 6 conflict module started with Middle Ages and battles and moved right on to Trump and Kim Jong Un. Mandarin or Spanish taught from reception

Music taught by inspirational and dedicated teacher – 'the four-part harmony put goosebumps on my skin, it was so impressive'. Peripatetic music teachers for some 10 different instruments. Pupils enthusiastic about the music, acting and dance. And they, plus parents and teachers, all look forward to the annual Shakespeare production involving the whole school acting and dancing the play.

One afternoon PE per week with specialist teachers ('really good,' according to pupils we spoke to). Also specialist are the language teachers and the dance teacher, who comes in for at least a term each year to help prepare for Shakespeare production. Swimming in years 3 and 4. Recent win at the London Schools Football Championship particularly impressive for a one form entry school and a cause of great delight. Girls' football well coached, according to pupils. The fact that there are a good number of male staff ensures regular break-time football practice. Playground spacious – pitch, table tennis, outside learning area, outside toilets etc, but money currently being raised to improve the amenities and make more use of flat roofs outside classrooms. Reception shares really well-equipped Astroturf playground with neighbouring Islington nursery.

School lunches cooked on the premises and eaten from china plates in older years. 'Younger years get to the salad bar so there is less left for us,' bemoaned older pupils, who also said, 'You have to eat vegetables, which makes you get used to healthy eating, but we wish older children could get seconds.' 'Bring a parent to lunch' scheme allows parents to see lunch at school and parents say school is receptive to feedback.

Pastoral care a highlight thanks to the full-time school chaplain. American by birth, upbeat, leopard-print wearing and totally involved in the school and the pupils. She runs one of the mid-morning assemblies and helps ensure that Christian knowledge and ethos is embedded in the school. One pupil said, 'We don't just talk about values, we use them too.' They said that 'problems are sorted out straight away and you can talk to teachers about every issue, even things at home'. 'We learn about bullying and are trained as mini-mentors.' There are 'worry boxes' in the classroom for anonymous concerns.

SEN supported by academy SENCo, and several pupils had individual TAs. 'We have helped a few pupils acquire an EHC plan' and there are some 20 on the SEN register for medical or educational needs, though 'if I had a child with additional needs I wouldn't probably send them to SMMA,' said a parent, unsure if there is sufficient extra support. Pupil premium used in part to pay for extra helper in reception: 'We focus on reception because if we invest lower down the pupils have a solid knowledge to carry up the school, so we aren't trying to catch up in year 6.'

The school shares a governing body with the senior school. Parents very involved – invited to help with trips, raising money, running clubs, attending Friday coffee morning, at the welcome BBQ and the inclusive and community spirited Christmas fair. 'We are raising money for the school but we want everything to be as affordable as possible for everyone.'

The last word: Everyone knows everyone in this small, friendly school with different year groups playing together and parents who are involved. A really solid, well-planned education with plenty of extracurricular clubs and activities. Creates articulate, thinking pupils who have been encouraged to engage in, and have meaningful conversations about, all their learning.

St Mary Magdalene Academy

C of E 52

Liverpool Road, London N7 8PG

020 7697 0123 | firstcontact@smmacademy.org | www.smmacademy.org

State | **Ages:** 11–18 | **Pupils:** 1,210; sixth form: 225

Linked school: St Mary Magdalene Academy Primary School, 210

Head: Since 2012, Vicky Linsley (late 40s): she joined the school as deputy head in 2008 and credit must go to her for the transformation of this school to a highly oversubscribed 'extremely well run' school with fantastic results. She was a scholarship child who studied history at Nottingham and then to Oxford for a masters degree and her teaching qualification.

Youthful, energetic and pragmatic; pupils call her 'inspiring' and 'really, really nice'. Very present around the school, she is generous with her praise of pupils and her pride in the school. An eloquent speaker, which helps her to build partnerships with businesses (Deloitte, Virgin Trains, local businesses). Teachers find her 'approachable, she always has five minutes for us, even for small matters'. She has nurtured many and entrusted them with responsibilities, maintaining a surprisingly stable staff body – no staffing vacancies when we visited and, unusually for any school, no shortage of maths or science teachers. She is an Ofsted inspector – 'an opportunity to learn what works and what doesn't in bringing about change' – and works as a consultant with schools looking to improve.

Entrance: Of the 210 places in year 7, 30 come from SMMA primary school, then preference to children in care and siblings of pupils in the school. Ten per cent selective on language aptitude (400 children sat for those 18 places recently). Remaining places are 30 per cent Islington Church of England primary school pupils (catchment area around one mile) and

70 per cent on distance from school (currently about a half a mile from the school). A further 18 admitted in year 9 via language aptitude test. At sixth form, top third stay on to create half of the selective sixth form (no automatic transfer). Usual entry requirement is at least seven GCSEs at 4+ including English and maths, with 6+ in proposed A level subjects – 7 for maths and 8 for further maths.

Exit: The 60 per cent or so that leave after GCSEs go to eg Woodhouse, Camden Girls or City and Islington College. But 'why would I go somewhere less good than here just to have a change?' Some 40 per cent of sixth formers go to Russell Group universities. Popular destinations include Imperial, UCL, King's, Durham, York, Warwick, SOAS, Bristol, Nottingham, Southampton, Queens Belfast, Leeds and the Courtauld Institute. Sixth formers get work experience with one of the partnership firms together with exposure to other worlds through the masterclasses and visits, as well as a paid for visit to a university, which all helps with personal statements for university applications.

Latest results: In 2020, 32 per cent 9-7 at GCSE; 86 per cent 9-4 in both maths and English at GCSE. At A level, 44 per cent A*/A; 81 per cent A*-B. In 2019 (the last year when exams took place), 30 per cent 9-7 at GCSE; 60 per cent 9-5 in both maths and English. At A level, 30 per cent A*/A (60 per cent A*-B).

Teaching and learning: The school has no qualms about saying that it has 'a clear focus on academic achievement' and it works to develop 'globally-minded citizens who are happy and successful'. For financial reasons it has stopped teaching the IB, but the IB ethos has strongly influenced the curriculum and teaching – encouraging independent and team learning, keeping timetables very full and having the equivalent of creativity, activity and service through the Inspire Programme.

The results have been rising and are impressive for a primarily non-selective school. The sciences are especially strong with almost all pupils getting grades 9-6. Also strong emphasis on languages, resulting in 100 per cent top marks in Mandarin, with Spanish and French also successful. Religious studies (unsurprisingly for this church school) get excellent results. 'Good results thanks to a really excellent work ethos built up over time in the school' and 'not stressful thanks to three-year GCSE programme and the school culture'.

Some streaming in lessons from year 7. The pupils who have got into the school on the language aptitude test are expected to take Mandarin enrichment classes as well as a European language taken by other pupils; those who join the Mandarin Excellence Programme have four hours' Mandarin each week. The school has an extra three full-time Mandarin teachers from China, who also teach Chinese culture.

Parents say the school has 'nailed the curriculum and ensures the kids get the results they want'. No-one was dreaming or looking out of windows when we visited

Year 9 pupils start their GCSE curriculum and class size drops to 25: 'having three years gives us time to teach more than just the content of the curriculum' and also allows for more outings in year 10, helping to 'raise aspirations and give a sense of purpose for exams'. 'We aim to give a broad and balanced curriculum so kids really enjoy learning, and they want to learn more because we have more time for content.' Generous selection of subjects, but core subjects given priority. Pupils said that 'teachers have our interests at heart and know what we like' and 'teachers care about you'. And parents raved about the youthful vitality, energy and enthusiasm of teaching staff.

Library used for English lessons and weekly library lessons and for book clubs after school; the school is clearly almost as busy before and after school hours as during. Parents say the school has 'nailed the curriculum and ensures the kids get the results they want'. Certainly, no-one dreaming or looking out of windows when we visited.

Sixth form completely selective by GCSE results, and students get a very full timetable of lessons, extracurricular activities, exercise and a real commitment to enrichment, with many collaborative projects – encouraging leadership and entrepreneurship. Pupils appreciated 'plenty of choice at A levels, but if you reconsider your subjects, you can change – the timetable seems to work for you to be able to take any subject combination you want'. 'Our teachers are organised and knowledgeable and enthusiastic.' 'They make it applicable to real life and raise ethical questions, not just teaching to get grades,' according to sixth form students. 'They get us involved; lessons are really interactive.' Maximum of 15 pupils per A level class. Not a huge amount of dedicated space for sixth form. Full-time graduates supervise study areas, help with essays and 'keep work going generally'. This type of subtle mentoring works to raise expectation and graduates are also available to help with UCAS forms and encourage the idea of going to university. Every student in sixth form taken to visit a university (some now lucky enough to go first class on train with a parent or friend thanks to a partnership with Virgin Rail).

Learning support and SEN: Special needs supported by SENCo with ASD specialism and part-time dyslexia specialist; all pupils screened before joining school. Some 13 pupils in school with EHCPs, and 70 accessing support in or outside school. Those who just need an extra bit of help can have tutoring sessions with maths and English graduates in the main hall. Parents say 'they don't give up on anyone' and that thanks to target tracking they are 'on it like a car bonnet if they slip'.

The arts and extracurricular: School is open from 7.30am when children can be found in the chess club, martial arts training, extra lessons, or just coming in for the £1 breakfast. The day often ends late, so plenty of time for clubs before, during and after school.

Students from China, Indonesia, Korea and even Kazakhstan attend school for a term as part of 'global citizenship', which is a founding principle of the academy

Arts rooms aplenty – sixth formers have own studio so are able to leave artwork out. Textile, pottery, art and tech GCSEs enhanced by equipment like 3D printers and laser cutters. You don't have to be doing tech GCSE to be involved in Formula E club, building an electric car and then racing it at Goodwood racing track. Proper, spacious cooking facilities for both food tech and popular after-school clubs and enrichment programme. Music a growing part of school life (with new facilities from September 2020), partly thanks to MiSST (Music in Secondary School Trust), with every new pupil being lent an orchestral instrument and having small group lessons, as well as individual music lessons ('excellent peripatetic teachers,' according to some parents) for those who continue with their instrument. So 300 music lessons timetabled in somehow as well as orchestra, rock band, string groups and then the annual huge musical – 'a semi-professional experience for the kids with lighting, costumes, musicians'. 'My shy child just came out of herself through the school musical production.' For some 20 pupils the highlight of their year is going to a music residential to Radley School.

Inspire programme includes masterclasses (talks by Jeremy Corbyn and Nick Robinson recently, and the Grayson Perry talk was a sell-out), workshops (Deloitte Consulting sent their chef to give classes, the RSC brought in a group to work on Hamlet) and City trips – not only to offices but also to British Film Institute and theatre outings (local Almeida theatre generous with free tickets). Pupils join competitions and get onto programmes such as STEM courses, Oxford Girls' Maths Conference and Women in Leadership conferences, and to go for visits or internships at City firms they have partnerships with – RBS, Cushman Wakefield, Société Générale, UBS.

Students every year from China, Indonesia, Korea and even Kazakhstan attend school for a term as part of 'global citizenship', which is a founding principle of the academy. Once the students leave, friendship and global citizenship encouraged as pupils become email penpals. 'With the job market changing so fast, we prepare our children to have flexibility, interests, skills and ideas, rather than just careers.'

Sport: Games in huge soundproofed state-of-the-art gym – no whistles or shouting needed to get classes playing team sports (basketball, hockey, dance, trampoline, cricket, badminton) for weekly two hours' PE. Astroturf on the roof for football and other sport and Finsbury Park for athletics. This is an urban environment and so the playground is not large, however a mad keen footballer we met said that he gets to play 'all the time' – and has plenty of matches against other schools too. Girls' teams encouraged and included – no sense that anyone is second class here – and the year 7 and year 8/9 teams recently triumphed in a borough girls' football tournament. Recognition for effort or achievement for sportspeople given at weekly assembly.

Ethos and heritage: This is a London Diocese sponsored school and the motto (James 3:13) 'show by a good life that your works are done by gentleness born of wisdom' sets the tone. A sense of kindness and action and learning emanates. RIBA awards for this purpose-built school which one parent called a 'Tardis, a building that flows nicely and does not feel cramped'. Built around a closed atrium with all classes looking inwards to the central library and chapel built on stilts over the canteen. Windows onto the corridors, open study areas and flow of the building give a feeling of transparency and openness. Pale wood, excellent acoustic management, curved edges, large windows, glass-topped atrium all help to soften the edges of an otherwise totally urban and closed-in school off a fairly main road. Pupils said 'there are no hidden corners or blind spots', 'we are really safe here'. We were struck by the calm and quiet in such a vibrant and active school – there are no bells in between lessons and playtime is managed well with room for activities in the playground without impeding each other.

Early establishment of ground rules about behaviour and study skills ('the SMMA way'). 'They have to learn to self regulate – we have 1,300 pupils and they need to learn about manners and being polite.' Christian ethos with teachers and pupils treating each other with respect (everyone on first-name terms). Engaged and open-minded students listened and spoke kindly of each other when we met them. Teachers don't interrupt each other or the pupils. Mealtimes are a pleasantly calm and orderly event with pupils and teachers sharing food, space and conversation. The canteen is in the centre of the school, like a kitchen being the heart of the home, busy and used (from breakfast club to after-school snacks via the feeding of the 1,300 at lunchtime) and spotlessly clean. Pupils called food 'healthy and tasty' but of course raved about Friday chips.

Pastoral care, inclusivity and discipline: Spiritual, moral, social and cultural education embedded in the school through curriculum lessons as well as assemblies and activities and in form time. Full-time chaplain for guidance and support. 'Reverend April is my son's favourite person in the school because she is such a kind, generous presence, comes to cheer at basketball matches, and may well be the heart of the school in her eyrie in the centrally placed chapel.' A part-time psychotherapist (appointment by self-referral or suggested by staff). Pupils said there was 'no bullying, but if you see something you can go straight to a teacher or report it anonymously on school website anti-bullying page'. Teachers spoke of restorative justice meetings – how would you feel, how would the other person be feeling. The need to be 'kind' is the leading principle.

Tutors work with Guardian Groups of pupils in the same house but across all year groups. 'It means we know older pupils and they tell us how to do things and we say hello to them round school.' It also means the older ones look out for the younger ones. The 'academy guardian' acts as first port of call for any issues as the group meets each day. The system seems to create a 'close and small community and allows us to get to know them really well and they trust us,' say the guardians. Pupils also said they liked having the same pastoral group throughout their school life because it 'is like my family away from home'.

The deputy head for expectations and standards meets heads of year, the SENCo and chaplain every fortnight to ensure pupil well-being. They work on the premise of 'what would a good parent do?' in all dealings with pupils and he leads assemblies about humanity, compassion and expectations in order to ensure happy, and therefore successful, children.

Music is a growing part of school life. Every new pupil is lent an orchestral instrument and has small group lessons. So 300 music lessons timetabled in somehow as well as orchestra, rock band, string groups and the annual huge musical

Discipline from detentions set by teacher, heads of year and if necessary involvement of parents. 'Certainty of consequence more important than severity of consequences' – so pupils not intimidated or fearful. Parents appreciate the fact that they get phone calls not only if there is a problem but also if there is something to celebrate when their child has excelled.

Pupils and parents: The school is mostly non-selective and reflects the diversity of the area well. 'We chose it over an independent school because there is no sense of entitlement here, and our child has really polite, kind friendships with kids he would never have met at a north London independent school.' Around half on free school meals and eight looked-after pupils. Parents told us that the school has high expectations and everyone is expected to comply – strict uniform policy evident, tight punctuality enforced, and serious work ethic encouraged. The curriculum guide given at the beginning of each year includes 'practical ways to reinforce your child's learning', 'how you can help' and 'resources for pupils and parents to support learning'. Learning is clearly expected to be a whole family endeavour. Parents said that they felt listened to – suggestions by staff, pupils or parents are heard and responded to positively.

The last word: A shining example of an excellent school. Parents and pupils are aware that they have picked the golden ticket if they can get an education here – the results are evidence of top quality teaching, and pupils' involvement and happiness are enhanced by the wide enrichment programme, whilst the pastoral care provides a tight safety net. If you want a top notch inclusive comprehensive education, this is the place to go.

The St Marylebone C of E School

64 Marylebone High Street, London W1U 5BA

020 7935 4704 | info@stmaryleboneschool.com | www.stmarylebone.school

State | Ages: 11–18 | Pupils: 1,155; sixth form: 338 (71 boys)

Headteacher: Since 2014, Kathryn Pugh MA (Cantab) PGCE NPQH (early 40s). A Cambridge graduate with first class honours in English, she joined St Marylebone in 2005 as an English teacher and learning co-ordinator, and was promoted to assistant head in 2008, before succeeding the long-serving and legendary Elizabeth Phillips OBE. This is only the second school she has worked at. She arrived here after cutting her teeth (as she puts it) at Riddlesdown Collegiate, a large co-ed comprehensive in Surrey, where she taught English and drama. Straight after leaving Cambridge she spent four years working in business and media, and then in theatre and communication for 18 months in Malawi, as well as for the Teacher Support Network, an educational charity.

Tall and willowy, Ms Pugh looks more like a Chanel model than headmistress. She cycles to work each day and is described by her pupils as 'inspirational', 'accessible', and 'empathetic'. We were regaled with tales of her contorting herself into yogic positions during English lessons as well as her passionate encouragement of 'complete randomness in lessons'. Said to be a fruitarian, she is described as looking strikingly beautiful in her red cape, while standing in the midst of girls in green cartwheeling and cavorting. She 'mucks in – not afraid to get her hands dirty during the fairs'; and 'She's so dynamic,' enthused one parent, 'everyone wants to do their best for her, both her pupils and her staff…the school is lucky that it has so many years of someone so ambitious and committed.'

We spoke to her surrounded by her senior management team. This is a woman who clearly prefers to see herself as prima inter pares. Her predecessor was a great delegator, and responsibility continues to be very much shared. She wants to talk about the school and its achievements and defer to her colleagues. She is deeply uncomfortable when the questions focus on her. Appreciative of a strong and supportive team, Ms Pugh is doing sterling work channelling the goodwill of both her staff and a diverse parent body.

Entrance: As maddeningly oversubscribed as you would expect – something like 1,000 applicants for 168 places. Looked-after children and those with statements have priority. Sixty per cent CofE places, 40 per cent 'open', with distance the only criterion. Fourteen places annually given to those with outstanding aptitude in an aspect of performing arts (music, choral, dance or drama). Applicants divided into four ability bands with equal numbers accepted from each band. Tiebreaker of how near to the school you live. In the sixth, 330 places – priority to existing students, though they have to fulfil requirements (minimum of five 9-6 GCSEs, with at least grade 5 in maths and English). Boys are taken into the sixth and, again, more apply than there are places for. Performing arts and maths/ICT scholarships for sixth formers. School receives five applications a week for occasional places.

Exit: Up to 40 per cent leave after GCSE and go to further education colleges, the independents, eg Latymer Upper, or other state schools, eg Camden, largely for a greater range of A level subjects or more vocational courses. Most stay, though entrance to the school's own sixth form is not a given, even for their own. Sixth form leavers to good universities and a range of courses including arts, humanities, business, social sciences, classical civilisation, engineering, sciences, maths, ICT and computing and medicine. In 2020 65% went to Russell Group universities six to Oxbridge, one to study medicine. One to study in the US. A few each year to read music, usually several to art foundation, dance foundation and drama school – immediately or after a gap year. Others into apprenticeships and employment.

Latest results: In 2020, 61% 9-7 at GCSE; 90% 9-4 in both maths and English. At A level, 52% A/A*, 83% A-B. In 2019 (the last year when exams took place), 47 per cent 9-7 at GCSE; 86 per cent 9-4 in both maths and English. At A level, 38 per cent A*/A.

Teaching and learning: Results are excellent. School keen to point out that girls who take further maths and chemistry perform brilliantly. While English, maths, art and politics are the most popular subjects, school does have 10 STEM ambassadors, and offers two sixth form maths/ICT scholarships to students likely to go on to study STEM subjects at university. Psychology, sociology and economics among the options – the first much the favourite, with a spread of results. German now phased out in favour of Spanish. High take-up; French and Spanish students achieved excellent results with a high percentage of top grades – a great improvement since our last visit. Supervised study periods during year 12 help the less-disciplined with their homework. Relatively good teacher:pupil ratio, with setting from the start, and school invests in retaining good staff. Our student guides were keen to tell us how many of their teachers had doctorates and were specialists in their fields.

Offers a good choice of subject options – 'an amazing variety,' enthused one parent. A future skills award and child development have replaced health & social care; dance, Latin and business studies canter alongside the frontrunners at GCSE and all are in the ribbons. RS results are knockout and the curriculum is praised for its earnest inclusiveness. The Englishes are good, so are the single sciences. One full class takes triple science each year, though most take the double award. Maths more than respectable. School does, after all, have a maths and computing specialism as well as performing arts. All students study both French and Spanish in key stage 3 and over 75 per cent take at least one language at GCSE. Art, geography and history strong and popular. School has policy of taking some subjects – ICT, RS – early to excellent effect.

A future skills award and child development have replaced health and social care; dance, Latin and business studies canter alongside the frontrunners at GCSE

Gifted and talented programme now called Aspiration and Challenge, with the idea of achieving excellence for everyone. High achievers' programme for those with high academic ability; scholarship programmes those talented at dance, music or drama.

Learning support and SEN: Two SENCos, a full-time SEN teacher, learning support assistants and specialist centres for students with learning difficulties. It is a centre of excellence for severe emotional and behavioural difficulties. Can provide for moderate physical difficulties too. EAL is an important area also (about half of the cohort speaks a language other than English at home) and this department plays a vibrant part in celebrating cultural diversity.

The arts and extracurricular: Dance, drama and music are outstanding and production values are high – with 16 places awarded to those talented in these specialisms. 'The girls take huge pride in their performances,' we were told, 'even if not everyone can take part. It is inspirational.' The inspiration is further fuelled by the innovative and outstanding three-storey building that incorporates the visual and performing arts space, with dance studio and gym in the basement. This makes a huge difference – not least to the amount of space it frees for other curricular activities. In all respects the arts reign here. You can make everything from jewellery to ceramics and print your own photos. Up-to-date laser cutters in the well-equipped DT workshops. Graphics also well regarded. Debating, dance and musical performance of all kinds thrive. Scholars' concert happens in the Wigmore Hall; some musicals, eg sixth form production of Chicago, performed at the Rudolf Steiner Theatre; whole-school production of Grease in the old-fashioned, polished-wood-smelling school hall.

Some disagreement among parents as to whether there is an opportunity for everyone to get involved in these productions and performances. Grumblings in some quarters that only the best are given roles – and here, there are a lot of girls considered to be glittering. So your aspiring Milly who doesn't quite make the grade may well end up sitting on the sidelines for much of her school years. School quick to point out that over 150 pupils across the school took part in whole-school production at Christmas. We, like Ofsted, were impressed with range of other co-curricular activities which don't necessarily require high-confidence performance skills: book clubs, green committee, Young Entrepreneurs, Fair Trade group etc. However, opportunities like GCSE photography work in the highly professional Metro Studios only available to the three or four girls whose applications to take the course are considered sufficiently impressive. This is the reality of a state-funded school, but it must be trying for the also-rans and would-bes.

Sport: School has a performing arts specialism, so it is perhaps not surprising that sport has a lower profile. That is not to say that there are not opportunities available, and there are a surprising number of athletically ambitious girls. Our guide was a pentathlete, excelling at high jump, long jump, shot put, 800 metres and hurdles, participating in clubs both in and out of school. Cross-country is also popular. Grey Coat Hospital School is the big rival at netball; they also play Portland Place and Holland Park. Plenty of inter-house sports competitions too (five houses across the year groups – Hardwick, Dickens, Barrett, Nightingale and Wesley). Annual sports day at Willesden Green. Other sports on offer include football, trampolining, rugby and tennis as well as DofE. They have managed to fit an underground sports hall into this already overfilled space and have a seven metre climbing wall. Sport very much available even if not always enthusiastically taken up.

Ethos and heritage: Tucked between Princess Grace Hospital and Marylebone High Street and close to the teeming runway that is the Marylebone Road, the school is a leafy, contained oasis of calm and purpose. St Marylebone Parish Church is a focus point and contributes to the peacefulness. This is where assemblies and concerts happen as well as religious services. A closely-knit jungle of buildings from red-brick Victorian, complete with heavily green gloss painted corridors, to modern glass and concrete are packed onto this one compact site. Further down the High Street on Blandford Street is the sixth form building, which is modern, purpose-built, and feels more like a tiny university campus than a school.

Zero tolerance approach means that your child may well end up with detention just from talking in class. The bar is high, girls feel lucky to be here and want to behave well

Five forms per year; St Marylebone is a relatively small inner London comprehensive – and this shows. As intimate as it can be, spread over two sites, it is an unintimidating place, with plenty of smiles and polite greetings between staff and pupils as well as between the pupils themselves. No space for lockers, so girls have to learn to be adept at carting their lives around with them and being organised about what they need for each lesson. Lunch is eaten in form rooms, though year 10 examinees and upwards are mercifully allowed out to settle in the numerous cafés round about at lunchtime. Sixth formers have their own canteen in Blandford Street.

Pastoral care, inclusivity and discipline: Pastoral care is very strong, affirm several parents. As well as there being systems of support in place among the staff and pupils, there is a strong mentoring facility between the older and younger pupils. This is an intense time of life for any teenager, but one senses that in this school the experience can perhaps become more intense than elsewhere. School says that the intensity is 'offset by a very caring community feeling which identifies and helps deal with problems' – and denies that this is a school of 'precious princesses'. Maybe it is part of the performing arts culture.

Girls, on the whole, very supportive of each other, though there is a lot of competition and this has to be managed. Behaviour is good. Cases of bullying rare, we were told. A smell of smoke doesn't linger in lavatories here, and a zero tolerance approach means that your child may well end up with detention just from talking in class. The bar is high, girls feel lucky to be here and want to behave well. Parents commend the fluid communication lines whenever a problem arrives. Lots of positive feedback when a struggling girl starts to perform well, as well as the more obvious commending of high performance. Much appreciated are the proper, old-fashioned termly reports which don't just parrot at you what the class has done but actually talk about your own daughter. Good, realistic and collaborative target-setting also works.

Pupils and parents: Broad social mix, made up of the heady variety of backgrounds and cultures that you would expect in an inner London comprehensive. Much more middle class than many of its kind, however, because this is the golden apple if you are after an excellent education for your creative daughter who also likes to perform. A higher proportion than usual of parents are actors, barristers, artists and, yes, even bankers, than you would find at just any ordinary central London comprehensive, many of whom have been privately educated themselves.

The gritty detail is that approximately 65 per cent are from ethnic minority backgrounds and from 90 different countries. Over 50 per cent of pupils are bilingual. More than 60 languages spoken at home. Sixty per cent CofE members; the largest second religious group is Muslim. School clearly tries hard to integrate the social mix – has an annual World Culture Day among many other initiatives – and attracts fierce loyalty. Girls travel some distances to get here – from as far as Hackney in the east to Ealing and Shepherds Bush in the west, Kilburn, Kentish Town and Islington in the north, as well as Wandsworth and Southwark in the south.

Money matters: National funding programmes largely cut so bidding for extra money from various sources takes up a lot of time. The result, however, is a school that is well staffed and well equipped, if not to lavish private school standards.

The last word: If your daughter is outgoing, confident and creative this is an excellent choice. St Marylebone is an exceptional school. It has the benefits of the moral ethos of a Church of England school but is ethnically diverse and serves many different communities. With a bright young head at the helm, its future looks as rosy as its history.

St Mary's School, Hampstead

47 Fitzjohn's Avenue, London NW3 6PG

020 7435 1868 | enquiries@stmh.co.uk | www.stmh.co.uk

Independent | Ages: 2–11 | Pupils: 300 | Fees: £15,945 pa

Headmistress: Since 2016, Harriet Connor-Earl BA (RE – from Brighton). In her late 30s, she is young for a head teacher – but definitely not green. She has been in the teaching profession for many years, starting off her career at a state secondary school in Haywards Heath before a stint in New York teaching at St Columbia Elementary School: 'I taught grade 8, but a lot of the expectation was teaching to test, so you couldn't be creative.' She still enjoyed it and benefited from the experience. When she came back to the UK, she worked for two years at Chapter School for Girls in Kent, followed by four years at Warden Park School. Subsequently she became director of studies and boarding housemistress at Ardingly College Prep School, Sussex, before being offered the post of head at St Mary's: 'The minute I walked in the chapel, I fell in love with it and the school… and the girls were the kindest and happiest I'd ever met.'

Children, she says 'are wonderful and curious and the best bit about humans'. She simply loves working with them and her career in teaching was preordained, from when she used to line up her teddies in her pretend classroom to having a mum and two aunts who are all teachers. We liked this head almost instantly (the aroma of the warm pain au chocolate and coffee we were offered did nothing to change our mind). With her wonderfully posh name, Mrs Connor-Earl is all the things you would hope the head of a cosy independent girls' school to be – understated and elegant, straight up but with a twinkle or two. Her girls would probably like to be her one day, and the parents would secretly like to be her mate.

She didn't have an easy task, following in the footsteps of her much-respected predecessor. One parent told us: 'I loved Ms Rawlinson so much I was determined not to like Ms Connor-Earl, but actually that changed pretty quickly.' Most parents agree that Ms Connor-Earl is a lovely, approachable and welcoming head with bags of energy and a tough job of putting her mark on a school where some parents don't like change. One parent said: 'She has injected fresh ideas into a slightly tired school, which although well regarded for its pastoral side, was less so for its academic achievements. She now runs a much tighter ship and her enthusiasm and experience have brought about positive changes.'

A committed Catholic, she is married and has one son. Enjoys family skiing holidays, cooking and renovating her house in Brittany. She has successfully completed the 110km London to Brighton cycle challenge and raised over £3,000 for charity.

Entrance: School will be all-girls from September 2022 and as such, they are no longer accepting applications from boys (only a handful remain in nursery).

All year groups are oversubscribed and prospective parents are encouraged to register as early as possible. Non-selective academically. Places go first to siblings, then to Catholics. Family-orientated ethos means that other faiths and cultures are also warmly welcomed. Nursery arrangements are particularly parent-friendly. Children are admitted from 2 years 9 months and can stay to lunch or all afternoon with minimum notice. A few further places often become available in year 3.

Exit: Plenty of offers from leading academic secondary schools, with several scholarships. Most popular destinations are Francis Holland Regent's Park, South Hampstead High, Queenswood, Queen's College London and Channing. Secondary school advice is a strength, starting with individual parent meetings in year 5. 'Parents trust us and listen to what we recommend,' says the school. Boys leave by the age of 6, many to neighbouring

Catholic prep, St Anthony's, others to Devonshire House, UCS, Hereward House, Habs, Highgate or The Hall.

Our view: Founded in 1871 by the Congregation of Jesus, the school moved in 1926 to its present site, a spacious turn-of-the-century building with polished mosaic floors and vast country-like gardens. In 1992, when there were too few teaching nuns to manage the school, a charitable trust was formed to continue the good work under lay management.

Year 5 book club with the head in her tranquil office and freshly baked cookies sounds so wonderfully Enid Blyton, we hope it's accompanied by lashings of ginger beer

Against the gracious period backdrop, facilities are thoroughly up to date, with a large, bright assembly hall, a well-stocked library and a super new global learning centre with a cutting edge engineering and robotics lab, virtual reality launch pad, art and design studio and green room. Significant recent investment in IT: new iPads and laptops in every classroom and MacBooks in the music department to help pupils create digital music.

Teaching (as described in their most recent ISI report) is 'excellent' – sharp, lively and very pupil focused: 'The teacher worked out my daughter in three minutes,' said one parent, and 'communication with the staff is excellent,' said another. Results are achieved by encouragement and risk taking, rather than a hothousing ethos. The head says: 'I don't believe that children should be assessed at 3 and 4 years old, and I also won't choose one girl from a family and not her sibling. Yes, it means I won't have 32 girls going to St Paul's, but I will have 32 girls going to the right school for them.'

The head has introduced an assessment programme, with pupils monitored from year 1 so they get used to the process and gain the experience: 'By the time they get to year 6, they are used to exams and we can pretty much safely say what they will achieve academically.' She has also introduced the four Rs into the school's ethos (Risk-taking, Resilience, Respect, Reflection). One parent told us: 'Mrs Connor-Earl encourages girls to take risks and leave their comfort zone. They are rewarded for challenging themselves and making mistakes, to help them achieve more academic progress and build their self confidence.'

The brightest are stretched through a curriculum enriched with plenty of arts-related activities and sport. 'We wanted to make teaching more relevant and incorporate risk-taking and thinking independently.' Interesting extra work for those who need stretching (lunchtime puzzle club, for example, is a big hit). Fluid ability grouping throughout, then setting in maths and English in year 6 in the run up to 11 plus.

Excellent support is available, with one full-time SENCo and various special needs teachers – depending on cohort – providing help in class and out of it (in lovely, bright teaching spaces). 'We would never turn anyone away. We try and cater as much as we can for all children – we assess them on a case by case basis.' One parent told us: 'You really feel they care about every single girl.'

Strong sport (new Astroturf) with a double court for netball and a well-equipped gym. All the usual team games: rounders, netball, hockey, football, plus swimming at Swiss Cottage baths (for years 3 to 6) and athletics in Regent's Park. Gymnastics particularly popular, with pupils competing at regional and national level. High achievement too in music and excellent dance and drama (including an all-encompassing production in year 6).

Heaps of extracurricular going on with everything from spy club, illustration, knitting, origami, gardening, cooking, yoga, various music clubs and chess etc to a wealth of languages including Mandarin, Latin and Spanish. We particularly loved the idea of year 5 book club with the head herself in her lovely, tranquil office accompanied by freshly baked cookies (it sounds so wonderfully Enid Blyton; we hope it's accompanied by lashings of ginger beer).

An after-school club until 6pm every day supports working families, with emergency places bookable on the same day. It includes a quiet area where children can complete their homework or read with a teacher.

Plenty of trips too. For year 4s it's their first residential trip with a night away, for year 5s an activity week in Devon and for year 6s there is a trip to the Alps post-exams and a trip to France to meet penpals and make croissants. Little ones go to a safari park or the seaside. Ex-pupils are also invited back once a year to enjoy a pizza and DVD night with the year 6s. Cake concerts are popular, with gluten-free brownies on offer. One year 6 pupil told us, 'There's a lot to like here and I'll be completely upset to leave.'

Boys are well integrated in the nursery and given appropriate scope in the Big Boys' Club, where they play football and let off steam on imaginary motorbikes. 'It lets them be boys in this all-girls environment,' said one mother.

About 70 per cent Catholic families. 'I think one of the most wonderful things about it is that the Catholic ethos permeates every aspect of the children's life,' said one parent. Those who wish can be prepared for first holy communion by much-loved Father Chris on his twice-weekly visits to the school chapel. Pupils take part in mass and study Catholic Christianity. 'Many of our parents have had a Catholic education themselves and want that for their children' – but even those who haven't feel included. 'As a non-Catholic,' said one parent, 'I was quite concerned at the outset, but Father Chris is so lovely and gives such interesting talks. They really teach the children how to be good and loving members of the community.'

Pupils are smiley and notably well behaved. They have a certain girlish innocence which is often so sadly lacking in today's techno age. Our two lovely guides giggled conspiratorially when we asked if they ever had the need to confess anything to Father Chris, to which one replied: 'Well, I did once borrow my brother's toy without asking and so did confess.' Everything here is geared towards doing things 'the St Mary's way'; those who slip up are gently reminded of 'expectations'. 'We want pupils to do their best.' Most pupils adore the school ('my daughter can't wait to get back after the holidays') and parents are equally appreciative: 'I can't say a bad word about this place. I have had three daughters come through this school, and I almost want another one just so she can come here.'

Mostly professional families from Hampstead and the surrounding areas, with a wide range of backgrounds (Europe, the US, Asia and the Far East). About half speak at least one other language at home (with good in-school support for newcomers on the foothills of English).

Money matters: Some full bursaries available.

The last word: A non-selective school, this (very Catholic) school still manages to pull off high-flying results at 11. Ticks all the boxes for extracurricular too. Very welcoming, report parents, 'which can be unusual, especially in the London private school bubble. But here they are grounded and down to earth.' Despite its Hampstead location, it is surprisingly understated.

St Paul's Cathedral School

2 New Change, London EC4M 9AD

020 7248 5156 | admissions@spcs.london.sch.uk | www.spcslondon.com

Independent	Pupils: 241; Boarders: 25 (boy choristers)
Ages: 4–13	Fees: £14,733 – £15,861 pa; Boarding choristers £8,911 pa

Headmaster: Since 2016, Simon Larter-Evans, previously head of boarding, housemaster and head of English at the Yehudi Menuhin School. He studied ballet at the Rambert Academy, then spent four years as principal dancer, performing in the UK and abroad. After 15 years working in commercial management, publishing and IT industries, he gained a first class degree as a mature student in English literature, drama, theatre and performance from the University of Surrey, and a PGCE from the Institute of Education. He has been a teacher of English and head of year 9 at St Edward's School, Oxford, and a teacher of English and drama at Pangbourne College. He is married to Dawn, a director at Accenture, and they live 'over the shop' in a house within the school.

Friendly and approachable, he has quickly won over the SPCS community. 'He has a great manner with both parents, teachers and staff,' wrote one parent. 'Really lovely!' enthused another. 'Open to new ideas,' was another comment. A general feeling that the school, already good, can only get better with him at the helm. Interests include photography, gardening, cooking, cycling and writing. His study is lined with an erudite collection of books, and he is currently doing a PhD on psychological development in young musicians and dancers.

Entrance: Register early – school is massively oversubscribed. Recently increased intake at 4+ from September 2021 – 80 children to be assessed for 34 places. First list is closed, then there's a reserve list. After that, the school keeps names and addresses but doesn't charge a registration fee. Informal style assessment – number games, drawing pictures, telling stories, etc. Staff look for children who are able and who will get on well within the school. Preference is given to siblings as long as they're able to access the curriculum.

Year 3 entry of a further 12 pupils. School doesn't follow any kind of formal 7+ assessment programme, but children are tested in English and maths 'just to see where they are'. A few join at year 7, as others leave and places become available.

Choristers (boys only) can join at any time, including mid-year, but are unlikely to be accepted after year 5. The school takes around six per year. Auditions are held by Andrew Carwood, director of music at St Paul's Cathedral, who looks for a desire for music, an innate openness of the voice, and the ability to hold a tune.

Exit: Diverse destinations, reflecting the intake: King's Canterbury, Oundle, Rugby, UCs, Westminster, Forest School, City of London School, Queen's College, Highgate, South Hampstead High School all featured in 2020.

For senior choristers, autumn term finishes at 4pm on Christmas Day, but for those who can cut it, the musical training is unrivalled

Majority of girls leave after year 6 for London day schools. The few who stay on go to mixed schools with a 13+ entry eg City of London Freemen's. Excellent track record of scholarships, both academic and specialist. Choristers do very well, often winning music awards to top senior schools, eg Eton, Winchester, King's Canterbury, Uppingham.

Our view: The choir school dates from around 1123, when eight boys in need of alms were provided with a home and education in return for singing the cathedral office. It wasn't a particularly child-friendly place, however, and by the early 19th century the stipend paid for the boys' upkeep was so inadequate that they were usually dismissed to roam the streets once service was over. Victorian philanthropist Maria Hackett, shocked by their predicament, campaigned tirelessly for 60 years to get them something better, and the present school was eventually founded in 1874 in Carter Lane. Threatened with demolition in the 1960s, it moved to its present brutalist modernist site in New Change. Originally for choristers only, it became a day school in the 1980s, and co-ed in the 1990s. The swimming pool that once occupied the basement is now the English department; needs must.

It is, to modern sensibilities, a very ugly building, but it's a truly lovely place to go to school, sheltering under the lofty and awe-inspiring splendour of St Paul's Cathedral, and flanked by St Paul's Cross, with its inscription that recalls 'such scenes of good and evil as make up human affairs'. The original roll of eight pupils has grown to 250+, spanning reception to year 8.

Not a school for those seeking flashy facilities, although school has recently ploughed money into play and teaching spaces, as well as dining room, and ongoing building works improve and expand both residential and teaching spaces, plus enable important outreach work. For now, however, the building remains a homely rabbit-warren of rooms, many of them low-ceilinged and endearingly scuffed. Pupils allude happily to the 'garden', the school's outdoor space, but it isn't very green, and the school's biggest space isn't that big. On the other hand, weekly assembly is held in the quire of the cathedral itself, affectionately referred to as 'the school chapel', and how many schools can say that? Tell Out Your Soul was sung full-throatedly by children clustered four to a hymn book – not enough to go round, rather charmingly, in this most august of settings. Worship was friendly and child-centred but still assembly as we used to love it: a good sing, a bit of pi-jaw, a few notices, then off to the strains of the organ. Except that it's the St Paul's grand organ, and visiting tourists were agape.

They teach the International Primary Curriculum here; both head and staff like its theme-based approach. They're certainly doing something right. Everywhere we looked, we saw children who were confident, articulate, comfortable with wider learning. In a year 7 English lesson students had come up with their own scholarly questions about Shakespeare that they wanted to research: 'Did he copy work from Christopher Marlowe?' 'What was the political landscape when he was writing?' 'Who did Shakespeare take inspiration from?' and, bluntly, 'Are any of his plays not considered to be any good?' Year 5 maths lesson invited similarly independent thinking: children worked in pairs to 'mark' each other's (anonymous) mistakes on a recent exam paper, and embraced the task with relish, although the gleeful written comments may not have been quite what the teacher had in mind – 'What do you think you're doing?' 'You haven't put the units in, you idiot!' and, more generously, 'Don't forget to wright [sic] the answer.' The only modern language taught is French, but the children also do Latin, and Greek is offered for those who stay on to year 7. Pleasant and well-stocked library is used enthusiatically by the whole school. After a

Queen's College Prep School

morning on the go teachers are still cordial and full of vim, and the standard of work on display is extremely high – we loved the year 3 postcards from Ariadne to Theseus, complaining about being dumped on a desert island. Science taught in dedicated science lab.

It was assembly as we used to love it: a good sing, a bit of pi-jaw, a few notices, then off to the strains of the organ. Except that it's the St Paul's grand organ; tourists were agape

Full-time qualified SENCo delivers integrated learning support in lessons, aided by team of assistants. School is able to cater for mild dyslexia, dyspraxia, etc and doesn't see it as a barrier. At the other end of the spectrum, however, several parents contacted us to express concern about the teaching lacking stretch and challenge for the most able pupils, particularly in the middle years. 'They do differentiate in most lessons but they don't really challenge the most able with extension activities,' wrote one who seemed to speak for several. 'There are several gifted children in both maths and English for whom this is the case, and those parents are quite frustrated.' School strongly contests this. 'Extension materials are available in classrooms, and children are directed to them, or can elect to do them. The puzzle wall outside the maths room contains sums which are fiendishly difficult. But it it's true that we are not a hothouse, and we work hard not to make school a misery.'

Sport described as 'very inclusive and energetic' by parents, and boys and girls are equally encouraged to play all sports. Team games are played in nearby Coram Fields and Victoria Park, and the school has its own training playground on site. Swimming down the road in the pool at City of London boys'.

Drama is 'inspirational, exciting and contemporary,' according to one parent, and recent shows have included Dr Jekyll and Mr Hyde performed by the year 8s and A Midsummer Night's Dream by the year 5s. Lots of clubs after school, and trips to all sorts of museums and galleries, both in London and further afield – the year 3 camping trip in Essex was 'the most fun ever,' according to pupils.

However, the stand-out activity, as you'd expect, is music, described by a mother as 'Superb! Very uplifting and of a fantastic standard.' Twenty visiting teachers deliver 450 individual music lessons weekly. Senior and junior orchestra, three choirs and an abundance of ensembles including early music group. Outstanding ABRSM exam results, with merits and distinctions at grade 8 common – all the more remarkable given that no child here is older than 13. Music-making here is inclusive – 'It is the norm to sing in a choir or play instruments,' confirmed one mother – but raised above the ordinary by the choristers, whose musicality pervades the entire school community.

Choristers' cathedral life happens before and after school, but their day school life is the same as the other children's. 'The school does a fabulous job of keeping the choristers integrated into the wider school,' wrote a grateful mother, 'but also manages to build a close sense of community and support amongst the boys.' For those who can cut it (for senior choristers, autumn term finishes at 4pm on Christmas Day), the musical training is unrivalled. 'I think the whole chorister experience is rather magical and has probably fundamentally changed my son's life and attitude to life for the better,' marvelled a parent. 'It has given him a love of music, a real sense of confidence, calm and an ability to slow down and relax.' 'It's busy, but in the best way, and it's become such a big part of my life,' confirmed a year 7 treble, before delivering a stunning rendition of Take, O Take Those Lips Away that left us open-mouthed with admiration.

Behaviour is lively but generally impeccable throughout the school. House points system not unlike Hogwarts, with points won and lost for your house through good or bad behaviour. 'The sanction of removing house points is extraordinarily potent here,' remarked the head, and detentions are rare. Achievement and good behaviour rewarded through commendations, gold certificates, etc.

SPCS families are professionals from all walks of life – 'comfortable, but not super-rich,' according to school, which aims to keep its fees as low as possible. Strong international contingent – at least a dozen languages spoken here. A SPCS mother wrote, 'The school tends to attract interesting families from a wide mix of backgrounds.' Alumni include England cricket captain Sir Alastair Cook, Walter de la Mare, Charles Groves and Sir Simon Russell Beale.

Boarding: There are usually around 30 choristers and they all have to board. (They can also be of any faith – the school has no issue with this.) Boarding house is a little sparse, but welcoming: L-shaped common room offers books, board games, DVDs, sofas, a Wii, and the ever-popular Lego and K-Nex. Bedrooms were, we thought, rather cramped by modern standards, with up to eight boys to a room, but new accommodation is under construction for 2020. Run by a mix of male and female staff. 'The boarding team are responsive and have endless patience for worried or slightly disorganised parents. The communication is very good and open,' wrote one mother. Parents can visit them in the evenings to help with homework, etc. There's time off on Saturday afternoons and boys can also go home on Sunday night, 'which really helps, because obviously we miss him!' according to a parent.

Money matters: A few bursaries, funded directly out of fee income and limited to children in year 3 and above. The only scholarships available are for choristers, whose education is paid for by the cathedral.

The last word: This is a kind, nurturing, but exciting place to learn and to grow up. 'Overall, it is a fantastic school. Caring, and academic without being too pushy,' was one parent's verdict. 'I'm delighted my children have been educated there. It's been a special time in their lives and they've all benefited from it in different ways.'

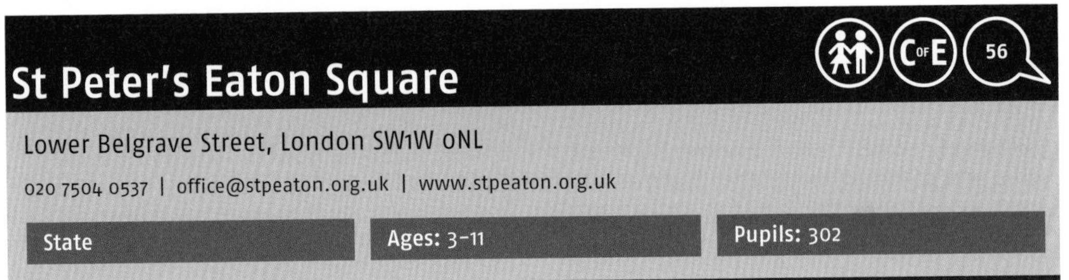

St Peter's Eaton Square

Lower Belgrave Street, London SW1W 0NL

020 7504 0537 | office@stpeaton.org.uk | www.stpeaton.org.uk

State | Ages: 3–11 | Pupils: 302

Acting Head: Since January 2020, Sarah Shayler, previously assistant head teacher and SENDCo.

Entrance: Admission by Westminster LA criteria: priority given to looked-after children, those baptised at St Peter's Eaton Square church, siblings, children of staff, baptised children who attend the affiliated church and then other CofE churches. Most of the 10 children from their own nursery gain a place, but have to apply. Oversubscribed three to one, until top years, when some filter off to local prep schools. Catchment area is mostly Westminster, but some from Lambeth and Wandsworth

Exit: About 50 per cent go to state secondaries, recently including Holyport College, Chestnut Grove, Lady Margaret School, Marylebone Boys' School, Pimlico Academy, St Marylebone and Grey Coat Hospital. Some success with independent day schools, including Latymer Upper, Queen's College and City of London, with one or two applying to board at eg Pilgrims ('not without tutoring,' one parent murmured). Exit at age 7 or 8 discouraged.

Our view: Academically up with the front-runners, with well above national average results in Sats. Parents praised the maths teaching, which adopts the Shanghai Approach, learned from visiting Chinese teachers. Literacy was also mentioned: 'My son started off uninterested in reading and is now one of the best in the class.' We saw formal grammar being taught in year 2, while junior cruciverbalists were compiling their own word-search. Latin is taught from year 3. Class sizes are kept at 25 with two classes per year group, except at the top of the school, due to (mostly) boys leaving early.

The class teacher is often supported by a TA and year 6s volunteer to read to younger children. London turnover of staff (or, as one child put it, 'Teachers leave very often'). We heard about Science Day, when students become science detectives; 'We made slime with borax and PVA glue and food colouring.' No homework policy though we heard replacing traditional homework with school-supported home learning had upset some parents. SENCo supports some with learning difficulties, Down's, ASD and complex needs; 'we would never say no,' remarks the school. One mum of a girl with cerebral palsy described a general readiness among staff to manage her medical needs and frequent outpatient appointments. 'They treat her like a normal child. They administer medication at lunchtime and have never complained.'

Music is abundant across all years and from year 4 in the form of group violin lessons. 'There's lots of research about how learning a musical instrument gives you extra brainpower,' says school. One mum criticised the lack of variety of instrument teaching: 'They made things so hard for the peripatetic teachers that they all quit… it was interfering with core subjects.' All children participate in singing and drama, performing in house singing competitions, at the church and local concerts, including in Victoria Station and Trafalgar Square at Christmas. Nativity plays for infants, and year 6 leavers raise the roof in a full production, the likes of Pirates of the Currybean; 'they are spectacular,' commented a teacher. Proximity to the West End shows enables easy access to museums and theatres on school trips.

Artwork was prolific; we particularly liked the pop art self-portraits and models of revolving stages, inspired by a visit to Cirque de Soleil. A termly magazine, SPARK, sponsored by an international publisher, showcases the children's activities in glossy magazine form, as well as providing a platform for aspiring writers and advice from young agony aunts. No sports fields; only a tiny green soft surface playground and basement hall, used by a specialist PE coach. The youngest children take yoga, while others start the day with Shake and Wake dance moves. Sports day takes place in Battersea Park and year 6s walk to Hyde Park for outdoor pursuits. Swimming at the nearby Queen Mother sports centre, from year 2. Parents run an after-school football club in Battersea Park. One mum lamented the lack of space for sports: 'shame there isn't more space to run and get energy out of themselves'. Year 6 enjoys a residential at Sayers Croft, which introduces caving, pond dipping and orienteering – all without screen time; 'it was really easy,' said one boy.

The termly SPARK showcases the children's activities in glossy magazine form, as well as providing a platform for aspiring writers and advice from young agony aunts

A Christian school in ethos, with regular visits to the high CofE Romanesque church in Eaton Square. Christian values are visible, from the motto 'Together, we will realise the potential God has given us', to daily hymns at assembly. The Saint Peter's Way code of conduct, with its four simple principles, is familiar to each child. 'It works,' says school, which has had emails from the public praising the children's behaviour. As for bullying, 'We teach the child to understand the difference between teasing and bullying.' We saw charts of traffic light warnings in each class and incentives in the form of house points. A celebration assembly rewards good conduct with 'star of the week' and the four houses (named after the gospels) compete for house points. One mum commented it was 'very Hogwartsish' and reported that the thrill of winning the house competition was so great there was no need to supply a prize.

Founded in 1815 by the parish of St Peter's at the east end of Eaton Square, the school started in Eccleston Place, before moving to its present site in Lower Belgrave Street, 'practically in Victoria Station,' laughed one mum. A Victorian red-brick frontage, with imposing square tower and large round windows, squeezed between office buildings and mansion flats, with original front-yard style playground, all within earshot of the London-Brighton line. Teaching space is chiselled out of every available corner, from the attic storey, where high ceilings give a gothic feel, down to the basement nursery. Red-painted doors outside and spidery fire escapes lead to blue doors and creamy paintwork inside, with original artwork by Axel Sheffler on the walls. Fortunately, our guides knew where they were going, as we were quickly disorientated by the internal layout, recently redesigned, with plenty of small tuition areas.

The older years occupy the top floor, with banners of spelling words draped across the ceiling and an international map woven into the rug. Two-person desks facing the front in year 6, while further down the school we saw four to six children to a work table and in the youngest classes the bright picture carpets were used for group times. Most rooms have a touchscreen board ('like a massive iPad,' suggested the children). A separate computing suite with desktops and an iPad chariot provide enough computers for a whole class. New library. If you stare closely in the reception class you will glimpse the pet snails. The kitchens on the ground floor serve up lunch on long tables in the adjacent hall; jolly, illustrated menus announce a diet of school favourites, as well as Meat Free Monday. Lasagne and chocolate cake were voted tops.

As one parent put it, 'the playground is the thing you notice more than anything' due to the restricted size, lack of climbing equipment, and, when crammed with whooping children, the intense noise. Another parent mitigated, 'it's so not a reason not to send your child there'. The children, however, don't appear fazed by the lack of outside space. Our guides personified the St Peter's Way dictum, in being kind, polite, and articulate. 'The children always show you round,' said one mum. 'What better advert can you have?' We agreed. They led the way in trim blue and yellow uniform, complete with stripy ties. 'I would rather wear my own clothes, but I can understand why there is a school uniform,' said one. Another informed us the clothes were available to buy at 'John Lewis slash Peter Jones'.

Parents, we heard, were 'driven, aspirational with a disproportionate number of barristers, lawyers etc, to whom standards are important… a real cross-section of that part of London'. A school council ensures the children have their say too. Many families walk or use the bus or tube to get to school; the head is on a mission to reduce idlers in four-by-fours at the school gate.

The new PTA has a talent for fundraising; recent initiatives include a Burns night supper. There are clubs before, during and after school, including breakfast, debating, drawing, yoga and French, the extended day clubs now run by Fit for Sport. Parents are satisfied with communication, via the 'very nice reception staff', who filter emails 'to stop the teachers from being harassed'. 'I've never had an issue in almost 10 years with teacher access,' said one mum.

The last word: A top scoring school which provides an all-round education with a Christian soul. Ethical values underpin the direction and modern teaching methods provide a firm grounding for the school's metropolitan population. As one parent put it, 'It offers what a private school might be without the price tag.' Good things come in small parcels.

St Saviour's CofE Primary School

Shirland Road, Maida Vale, London W9 2JD

020 7641 6414 | office@stsavioursprimary.co.uk | www.stsavioursprimary.co.uk

State | Ages: 3-11 | Pupils: 240

Headteacher: Since 1994, Lindsey Woodford, BA in education from London University. A warm, humorous, approachable woman with none of the lofty airs that waft around some heads. 'She's fun and she's ballsy, but she's strict. It's a winning combination.' Happy to muck in, she even joined a team of parents in a sponsored swim to raise £12k to Astroturf the playground. 'I don't know many other headteachers who'd don a wetsuit and swim 3.5km in the Thames. She's pretty game.' Her office, far from being a scary place, is crammed with 100-200 soft toys which have colonised every available surface. She is ably assisted by Ripley, her border terrier, who is adored by the children. Pupils who have done well (or are perhaps just feeling a bit glum) are occasionally awarded Ripley Time, which means being allowed to sit in her office for a supervised stroking session.

In her spare time Ms Woodford enjoys embroidery, crime novels, antiques and baking. We can vouch for her excellent homemade biscuits (gooey peanut butter flavour the day we visited). Very much hands on – small children approach her for a hug as we walk through the playground (and you can't fake that). Previously deputy head at St Michael's in Highgate, following stints at schools in Bucks, Brent, Haringey and Ealing, so oodles of experience. A local girl, she was born at nearby St Mary's Hospital and attended Parliament Hill School in north London. She is married to the contractor who created the nursery in 2000. The ultimate accolade comes from a grateful mother. 'I'm proud of how my daughters have turned out and I feel they have been formed by Ms Woodford as much as they have by me. I owe her a lot.'

Entrance: Heavily oversubscribed one-form entry school. Over 90 applicants for nursery and 140 for 30 reception places. Nursery is mornings only, though afternoons are available for a fee. No catchment area; pupils come from as far afield as Camden, Kentish Town, Kensal Rise and Harlesden. After the customary preference given to looked-after children, admission boils down to enthusiastic worship at one of two affiliated churches, St Saviour's and St Mary on Paddington Green. This means 'at least three Sundays every month for at least a year before application'. Prospective parents might want to reconsider that sneaky lie-in every fourth Sunday, as admission is uncompromisingly awarded to the 'most frequent worshippers'. And don't even think of slacking off once you've got your foot in the door as progress from nursery to reception depends on continued regular worship – a rule that is enforced. 'We hate to lose children but it does happen,' admits the head.

Admission for siblings languishes way down at no. 8 on the list of criteria, though occasional places in later years are well worth applying for as later places are awarded 'on need'.

Exit: Pupils progress to a wide variety of schools. Favourite state schools include Grey Coat Hospital, St Marylebone and Twyford High School, plus Paddington Academy, Holland Park and St George's. The head is also very open to the independent sector ('We love a good badge') with pupils winning places at Highgate, St Paul's Girls', Latymer Upper, City of London, UCS, Merchant Taylors', Channing, plus boarding schools like Christ's Hospital and Wycombe Abbey. It's enough to turn an expensive prep school head green with envy. 'For the last two years we've got a child into St Paul's Juniors at 11 plus. We're very proud of that.'

Secondary transfer meeting in September where both state and independent school admissions are explained and various bursaries and scholarship options discussed. 'It's never too early to come and talk to me.' Parents who are considering the independent sector are given advice from year 2 onwards, plus suggestions for specific tutors. Ms Woodford is brutally honest about a child's chances of success. 'I don't mind where children go on to as long as it's the right school for that child.'

Our view: Nestling in a quiet side street amongst the tall wedding cake mansions of Maida Vale, this Ofsted outstanding state primary has won more awards than you can shake a stick at. But, despite the wealthy area, this is no middle class ghetto school.

'It's truly comprehensive,' said one parent. 'You've got people who live in million pound houses and families who live in local authority housing by the canal. Everybody just gets on with it and befriends each other.'

Progress from nursery to reception depends on continued regular worship – a rule that is enforced. 'We hate to lose children but it does happen,' admits the head

Broad international mix with 35 languages spoken (the largest groups being white British, followed by Eritrean and other African). A tranche of bankers, diplomats and media types alongside a large number of low-income families just above the free meals threshold. Twenty-four children on free school meals (approx 10 per cent) when we visited, though the number waxes and wanes. Winner of Mayor's Gold Club Award for succeeding against the odds in improving pupils' achievements. 'It doesn't matter to us that we get a badge for it, what matters is our free school meal pupils do at least as well, if not better, than other pupils. We buck the trend,' says the head.

The socially and culturally diverse mix makes the school's outstanding results all the more impressive. Over 60 per cent of pupils regularly achieve above expectations in Sats. 'They really encourage each child to discover something they can excel in, whether it's art, English, maths or anything else,' said one happy parent. 'It's not just about sitting exams, it's about becoming a well rounded, caring, bright little person who wants to learn.'

Our immediate impression was that St Saviour's is an exceptionally smiley school. We got eye contact and a friendly grin from pupils and adults alike as we waited in reception, and the smiles kept on coming throughout our tour. In an age when so many children look down and mumble when addressed by an adult, the confidence of these pupils shines out. Clearly, the social graces are given the same importance at this state primary as they are in the private sector.

Bog-standard Victorian school building, but preferable to the cramped conditions so often seen in converted premises used by some London independents. Here the classrooms are large and light-drenched with walls of vast windows. Trad architecture could feel forbidding in dark stairwells, but they've done their best to create a bright, cosy and well cared-for learning space. Walls covered in excellent artwork. Comfortable sofas, toys and a multi-sensory room in the early years section. Pupil loos are clean and colourful (no smells) and only one wet tissue apologetically stuck to the ceiling.

Separate junior and senior playgrounds. Outside space is limited, typical of most inner city primaries, but they've made the most of what could have been a rather dank concrete area. Good range of outdoor toys including space hoppers, a climbing wall and some rather grand-looking trees in pots. Small side garden growing potatoes, rhubarb and herbs and we even spotted the head's mum who had popped in to tend the plants. Truly a family-oriented school.

Setting starts in reception, with four groups per class. Some groups might have just two pupils, while others are much larger, depending on the needs of each individual year group. Teaching assistants work with higher ability as well as lower ability pupils. 'We focus on what each child needs.' Weekly Spanish lessons from reception onwards with a linguist Star of the Week award.

Regular pupil progress meetings to identify and keep track of underperforming pupils. Each child on the SEN register has a target sheet so progress can be tracked in lessons and support groups, and to ensure no child slips through the net. A qualified SEN specialist working part time is ably supported by battalions of TAs trained in many different types of strategies and interventions. Success of the school's support safety net self-evident in outstanding results for all pupils,

In Maths Week every class pitches a business idea to Ms Woodford and she decides whether to 'lend' them £20. The class must turn a profit and pay her back, plus one per cent interest. Pupils have fun and grasp the idea of profit, loss and interest

regardless of background. 'I have a dyslexic daughter and they are very clever with their thinking,' said one mother. 'If you can't learn your times tables they'll come up with another way to teach them to you. They teach each individual child, rather than sticking to a formula.'

Provision in sports and the arts is a huge strength at St Saviour's. Thriving PTA holds monthly fundraisers to generate over £65k a year, most of which is used to fund three specialist teachers for art, music and sport. This means, in addition to the standard PE hour with class teachers, all pupils have a weekly session with a professional sports coach. There are also dance lessons with a West End choreographer, covering fun stuff like Bollywood, musicals and Strictly Come Dancing. Then there's swimming in year 4, cycle training in year 5 and the year 6 pupils do a course of horse riding lessons in Hyde Park. Opportunities to try tennis, golf, cricket and tag-rugby and to compete in teams against other schools.

Art is taken seriously here and is of a high standard. The PTA-funded artist in residence works with each year group on a project relating to subjects they are studying in class, for example year 3 pupils made a giant sarcophagus when they were studying the Egyptians. We saw excellent William Morris designs done by year 5 while studying the Victorians, screen prints of the Tudors by year 4, and some awesome studies of real fish done by gifted and talented pupils. Pupils identified as G&T in art are given additional opportunities to work on projects with visiting artists (such as designing the 3D climbing wall), plus there are regular drama and music workshops run by outside experts.

For working parents there's an (oversubscribed) wrap-around care scheme running up to 6pm and a two week summer holiday camp. All staff members (including the headteacher) are responsible for an extracurricular club running from 3.30-4.30pm. Pupils can choose from horticulture, ICT, arts and crafts, media, football, website, cooking, construction, choir and many other options. More innovatively, there's a coding club, and coding is also taught as part of the curriculum in years 3 and 4. 'Coding is a big buzz in education at the moment and we're right at the forefront of that,' says Ms Woodford.

'What we do here is we don't say no,' says head. 'We consider all ideas and are willing to try new things.' STEAMco was a concept some parents had seen at a festival. It's now an annual day when lessons are suspended and every corner of the school is given over to different creative activities such 3D printing, learning the ukulele, an apothecary's garden, dance, sculpture, making furniture out of newspaper, launching home-made rockets, cooking and much more. Pupils are free to browse at will – some try everything, others stick with one experience all day. Year 6 pupils built an electric goblin eco-car designed to spark an interest in engineering, which they subsequently raced at Goodwood. Then there's Maths Week. Every class pitches a business idea to Ms Woodford and she decides whether to 'lend' them £20. The class must turn a profit and pay her back, plus one per cent interest, by the end of the week. Business pitches mostly involve making and selling various sweets and cakes but pupils have fun and grasp the idea of profit, loss and interest.

Pastoral provision is outstanding. Each child selects two staff 'listening partners' that they can talk to about any fears or worries. Some staff members are chosen by 20 children, others just a handful, but even the catering staff and site manager have their listenees. Then there is a buddy system in which each year 6 pupil is paired up with a reception 'buddy'. The buddies read and play together, go on trips and can be invited to tea by the respective parents. There is a daytime 'sleepover' where pupils bring a pillow, toy and sleeping bag and lie in the art room reading stories to each other.

Few behavioural problems. A general policy of positive behavioural reinforcement, high expectations and aspiration seems to work well. Much ado is made of the Star of the Week system, with postcards sent home, a mention in the newsletter and announcements at school. Four houses (named after planets) and team points awarded for a variety of endeavours. 'The school is strict and that's what I love about it. They will not tolerate any bullying and they don't like cliques either. Pupils are encouraged to be friends with everyone, so nobody is left out,' said a satisfied parent.

The last word: What sets St Saviour's apart is the head's boundless enthusiasm and creativity. She is inclusive, forward-thinking and compassionate and the ripple effects are wide. We're not a bit surprised that pupils and parents adore it.

St Vincent de Paul RC Primary School

RC 58

Morpeth Terrace, London SW1P 1EP

020 33515990 | office@svpschool.co.uk | www.svpcatholicprimary.org

State | Ages: 3-11 | Pupils: 180

Head: Since 2015, Nathaniel Scott Cree BA (early 40s). Also executive head of Westminster Cathedral Primary School. Teaching degree from Roehampton Institute of Higher Education, followed by a masters in Catholic school leadership from St Mary's Twickenham. Originally from the Surrey/Sussex borders, his first job was at St Osmund's School in Barnes, followed by a complete contrast in locality – Brixton – where he taught for six years at Corpus Christi School. He says: 'It was a very well run school. Parents moved to put children in there.' He left to become deputy head at St Vincent's Primary School in Marylebone, where he stayed for the next six years before being offered this headship. He has always taught in Catholic schools, which he says is his 'personal preference', and is 'very committed to them'.

Mr Scott Cree is young in terms of head teachers: 'not the youngest,' he says, but he clearly has a wise head on his youthful shoulders plus bucketloads of dry wit. His straightforward, honest and no spin approach instantly endears him to us. It was his dad who initially suggested teaching to him as being a 'good option' and he also felt committed to doing a job which makes a difference: 'I wanted to help improve children's chances in life and I believe that to be through education.'

His commitment to the job is evident in the changes he's brought to the school: the new house system; tighter security (more about those later); changes to the syllabus; better communication between the school and parents – and he's even teaching himself Latin in order to teach it to his students. He says: 'When I started here I decided to continue with Latin and run with it. I now teach two lessons a week in Latin for years 4 and 5.' He is liked and respected by both pupils and parents, who tell us 'he's really blended in well with the school.'

Married to a deputy headteacher at another school, Mr Scott Cree has three children of his own, and although he wouldn't dissuade any of them from a path of education ('if they believe it to be their true vocation etc etc'), he would point out the difficulty of teaching nowadays and all the bureaucracy around it: 'I probably wouldn't cut the mustard if I was entering the profession now,' he says drily. We beg to differ. Any spare time he has he mostly enjoys 'doing nothing', he says jokingly, but other than that he enjoys reading, listening to music and watching a good film.

Entrance: Always oversubscribed. Nursery children are not guaranteed entry into the main school at 4+. Priority given to practising Roman Catholics, with distance from the school used as a tiebreaker. First priority goes to looked-after Catholic children, then baptised, practising siblings, then baptised Catholics. A waiting list is kept for occasional places.

Exit: Most pupils get their first choice secondary school. For most girls it is Grey Coat Hospital (if it's good enough for the former prime minister's daughter…); other popular choices for boys and girls include Sacred Heart, London Oratory, Cardinal Vaughan and St Thomas More as well as independents including Westminster Cathedral Choir School.

Our view: School was founded in 1859 by the Sisters of Charity of St Vincent de Paul to enable them to work with the poor of Westminster. Moved to current premises in the shadows of Westminster Cathedral, conveniently next door to St Paul's bookshop, in 1974. For a young and impressionable soul eager to soak up all London has to offer, fewer locations could beat this school in the heart of London.

It is hardly surprising that pupils come from a wide variety of countries and backgrounds. Around three-quarters speak English as an additional language. Indeed most of the parents we spoke to, although fluent in English, spoke it as a second language. Many parents choose the school for its diversity, but mainly for its strong Catholic ethos. One parent told us: 'As Roman Catholics ourselves, this school has a great reputation locally for its strong ethos of upholding values, discipline and academia, but also being a loving and caring environment.'

This is a Catholic school foremost and whilst pupils are taught to understand other faiths and cultures (Judaism and Islam weeks etc) there is a strong Christian ethos to adhere to. The head says: 'The behaviour at SVP is outstanding, but it is naive to say that incidents don't happen from time to time. However we do instil in pupils to love one another as I love you.' Chaplain Father Brian leads assembly ever Wednesday, and there is a collective worship every morning. One parent told us: 'I have sat in assembly for one hour and nobody moves. They are so engrossed and well behaved.' Good behaviour, thinking of others and cooperation go without saying.

Pupils are monitored regularly to assess their progress and there are plenty of parents' evenings, giving everyone the opportunity to discuss their children. Parents comment on how approachable the head is and that you can pop by his office without an appointment. Mr Scott Cree has also introduced a small letterbox outside his office, where pupils can write down any concerns they may have either anonymously or as something they wish to share (and confessionals with Father Brian are also offered).

A parent told us, 'This school has a great reputation locally for its strong ethos of upholding values, discipline and academia, but also being a loving and caring environment'

When we entered the school at the start of our tour, we were immediately stuck by the double-door entry and security systems put in place. Sadly quite pertinent in light of the recent Westminster attack, which happened a week after our visit and only a few minutes away. The head says: 'At the end of the day, I'm responsible for these pupils if something goes wrong. Where we are located there are a few unsavoury characters around, and whilst I don't want the school to be a prison, I want it to be as safe as possible.' And one parent added: 'Before Mr Scott Cree was head, you could just walk in, which is incredible really if you think about it. I feel so much happier now that it's more secure and I feel my child is safer.'

Fairly compact site – outdoor space has been redeveloped to create three separate play areas for nursery children, infants and juniors. Cleverly designed, with lots of greenery and modern play equipment. Plus who could tire of seeing the majestic Byzantine structure of the neighbouring Westminster Cathedral, which almost borders the playground? Pupils also use the playgrounds and local facilities for team sports and have a dedicated sports coach for all PE lessons. Inside, school is light, modern and well designed but has the very nostalgic feel of a primary school from yesteryear. Peaceful chapel is very much at the heart of this friendly and well-disciplined school.

Large, multi-purpose hall where children practise for termly concerts and plays and musical performances. School is part of the Westminster Cathedral Choir School outreach programme and the choir performs at Westminster Cathedral as well as singing regularly at family masses. Well-stocked music room with an impressive selection of instruments – from glockenspiels to bongo drums. All have singing and music lessons, provided by a dedicated music teacher. Pupils talk excitedly about how they are encouraged to create their own music. Small charge is made for individual lessons on a wide range of instruments. (No formal library, but that is up for discussion: 'it's a space issue.')

Alongside the national curriculum, pupils benefit from being taught Spanish from the age of 7 (a good chunk of Spanish speakers already at the school). Latin is introduced in year 4. Academic results are exceptional. Staff have high expectations and have created a good learning ethos. The SENCo coordinates additional needs and runs a Units of Sound online literacy development programme for dyslexics.

Polite, engaging and kind pupils were what we witnessed during our time at the school (lots of opening doors for us). It struck us how unspoilt many of these children were: 'I went to Wagamama for the first time,' said one excited 9 year old (as part of a food workshop which included a trip to the restaurant). Other trips have included London Zoo, Legoland and various museum outings. Years 5 and 6 do trips to forest schools and Sayers Croft outdoor centre.

Sports quite big on the agenda and the school has fared admirably (given its size and on-site facilities) at football, swimming and athletics, 'and we have even been to the Olympic Copper Box Arena,' one proud pupil told us. Sports now all the more competitive since Mr Scott Cree introduced the new house system named after saints: St Theresa, St Joseph, St Francis and St Bernadette. One parent said: 'The introduction of the house system has added a healthy competitiveness to the school. My daughter is now desperate to earn house points.'

Yearly nativity plays are performed actually in Westminster Cathedral, with full costumes and music. (We'd be hard pushed to imagine anything more spiritual.) There are two other occasions in the year when they join the parish of Westminster Cathedral for mass. We are told that some parents choose the school for this reason. Sixth formers from neighbouring Westminster School work as volunteers, acting as classroom assistants and helping to run school clubs. ICT room doubles up as a cinema for film club.

Not a place for those who wish to sit on their laurels. Energetic PTA meets regularly to discuss the organisation of numerous fundraising events for the school. Each family is asked to make a small annual contribution towards the maintenance and building fund – for the benefit of the present community and to ensure continuation for future generations. Pupils are active fundraisers and run regular charity events. The school also works with Mission Together, a charity that encourages children to care about mission through prayer, learning and fundraising.

School was downgraded by Ofsted in 2015 to 'requires improvement', but was upgraded again in 2016 to 'good'. The head says, 'The issues that had affected the school have been addressed and lots of support has been put in place to get it back on track.' However, he adds that the report was limited in its judgment to one particular area, which can have a big impact, and we were left in no doubt as to how much parents rate the school.

The last word: Parents praise the school to the rafters and pupils say they look forward to going to school. One parent added that 'SVP starts with the assumption that there's something great about you and let's work on that.'

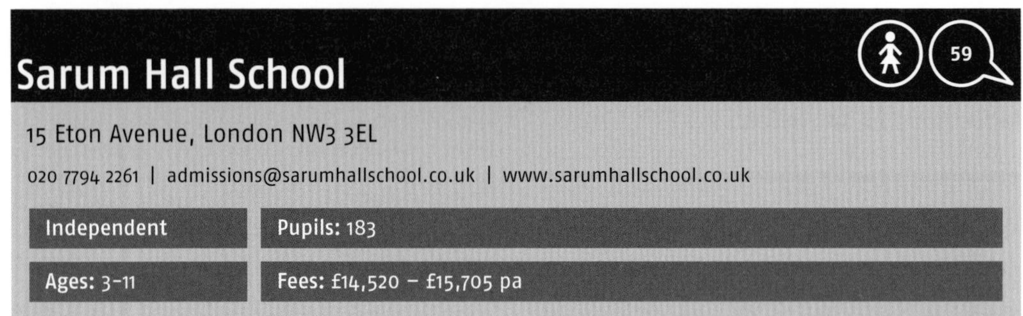

Sarum Hall School

15 Eton Avenue, London NW3 3EL

020 7794 2261 | admissions@sarumhallschool.co.uk | www.sarumhallschool.co.uk

Independent | Pupils: 183

Ages: 3-11 | Fees: £14,520 – £15,705 pa

Headmistress: Since September 2019, Victoria Savage, previously deputy head at Newland House School. She read music at Edinburgh, where she was in demand as a musical director, accompanist and organist. She was musical director at a local church, president at the university Footlights Society and directed the studio opera Dido and Aeneas at the Fringe. Leaving university garlanded with numerous prizes, she studied piano accompanying at the Royal Academy of Music and performed in concerts across the country.

She has taught at Eton, Falkner House and Lambrook, been director of music at Garden House and then the Dragon School. As deputy head at Newland House, she taught English, history and French, as was appointed acting head in her final term.

Entrance: Main intake in September after 3rd birthday. Parents are advised to register their child as soon after birth as possible (non-refundable fee of £100), visit the school on a working day two years before said child is due to start and then confirm their continued interest in writing. Non-selective, although priority given to siblings and children and grandchildren of former pupils (of whom there are many). The rest of the 23-24 nursery places are based on the decision of the head, who meets all parents and is 'looking for those who understand that the arts, and indeed play, are as important as academic learning for children's development', although presumably that's all of them, unless they failed to research the school before applying. It's all a bit vague for our liking; we feel that fitting in probably plays a vital part.

Exit: Almost all to their first choice of school at 11: Francis Holland, Regent's Park, North London Collegiate, Queen's College, Downe House, City of London School for Girls, Channing, Godolphin & Latymer, Queen's Gate, South Hampstead High, St Marylebone, St Paul's Girls', Sylvia Young. Unusually for a north London prep, a fair number go on to board too, at the likes of Cheltenham, Queenswood and Wycombe Abbey. Recommendations as to the next school have so far been very much the head's own.

Our view: Nestling among the opulent period homes of this leafy north London street is a contemporary, RIBA-lauded, purpose-built building, with no fewer than three secured doors to get inside the learning environment ('Safeguarding means a lot to our girls' parents'). Inside the building, which was completed in 1995 (although the

No fewer than three secured doors to get inside the learning environment. 'Safeguarding means a lot to our girls' parents'

school itself dates back to 1928), the combination of high design standards, light oak floors, high ceilings, masses of natural light and (recently) air conditioning makes for a welcoming, airy space in which to work, move about and play. White walls are tastefully decorated with displays of the girls' work from across the curriculum but it's the pink (there's lots of it) that really sets the mood of the school, which parents repeatedly refer to as turning out 'very well-mannered young ladies'.

National curriculum forms the cornerstone of learning, but without the dreaded Sats and with embellishment of other subjects, including French from reception, Mandarin in years 4 and 5 and Spanish for one term in year 6. Specialist subject teaching in music, IT and French from nursery, science from year 3, English, maths and humanities in years 5 and 6. Some setting in maths. Big emphasis on cross-curricular teaching, with girls preparing for a performance of Frozen when we visited, having made the characters (art), in preparation to perform the play (drama) in French (languages). Great attention to tailored learning, with plenty of classroom assistance and additional work, for instance, for those sitting boarding school entrance exams. Great preparation for 11+, according to parents.

Music, art and drama all thriving, with pleasant learning spaces. Majority of girls study one or more instruments after year 2, with plenty of opportunity to perform in assemblies, recital evenings and frequent concerts. Junior and senior choirs, open to everyone. 'My daughter does eight music-related things a week including choir, music theory, music lessons and two instruments,' lauded one parent.

Drama performances generally involve double year groups, and English Speaking Board exams (and LAMDA if requested) are available to build up communication skills. Fabulous high-ceilinged studio art room, with girls studying sculpture, textiles, woodwork and more. New food studio where all pupils learn to cook healthy meals. Plenty of outings to exhibitions, including the Royal Academy, with which the school has close links.

IT suite organised in round tables. Well-equipped science lab, with a teacher having introduced sustainability in a big way to the school. Sunlit, well-stocked and welcoming library, with visits from authors, such as Helen Peters and James Mayhew. Nursery and reception areas nurturing, including an (again pink) indoor wigwam and free-flow outdoor space on the balcony, with two stylish 'SH' embossed canopies to keep the sun off young skin. Plenty of mingling with older girls, thanks to buddying and monitor opportunities, along with a shared play time once every half term.

Outdoor space had been recently refurbished when we visited. It's not big, but is exceptionally well planned, with a new two-storey playhouse and colourful beach huts, where you can do anything from arts and crafts to borrowing sports equipment. Surrounding this and the adjacent sports court are wormeries, raised beds and an environmental pond, allowing children grow vegetables and herbs and do gardening club, all of which have helped the school achieve Green Flag status. Pupil voice much improved in recent years. Big on charitable fundraising.

Daily sport (netball, hockey, rounders, soccer, cricket and tennis) takes place on the court or in the assembly hall, which doubles as a gym for both dance and gymnastics, and triples as a theatre. Swimming once more part of the curriculum, at nearby Swiss Cottage Baths from year 4. Cross-country at Primrose Hill. Annual sports day becoming more competitive, after parents complained it was too gentle.

Breakfast club from 7.30am, and homework club until 4.30pm, included at no extra cost. Over 40 after-school clubs (photography, chess and draughts, yoga, board games among them), also included in the fees, unless outside staff need to be brought in. Outings to London museums and galleries. Residential trips to Norfolk for year 5 and a château in France for year 6.

'My daughter does eight music-related things a week including choir, music theory, music lessons and two instruments,' lauded one parent

The girls themselves 'aren't the most savvy and streetwise,' as one parent put it – but they seem to like it that way. 'It can make the transition to senior school a bigger deal, but having nice, polite girls is a good trade-off,' said one. Behavioural problems minimal.

Great food (all clean plates when we visited and we cleared our own too) prepared daily on site and served on long tables with pastel spotty tablecloths, where staff eat with girls (after grace has been said).

Parents and pupils reasonably multicultural, but mainly affluent, white, middle-class. Plenty of bankers, lawyers and barristers. Many girls have brothers at The Hall or Arnold House (and school tries to coordinate term dates). Bursary fund, which is means-tested. One girl on it when we visited, with another about to join. Many of the governors have a connection to the school and have been there for many years, with (unusually) no set system of election or removal.

Learning support unit has one dedicated member of staff (trained to RSA level 7) who comes in four days a week. Copes with mild dyslexia, dyspraxia (five children in total when we visited) and the 'gifted and talented' at no extra cost. Support is mainly in the large dedicated room, but some classroom assistance too. Two deaf children when we visited ('The school has been incredible with meeting her additional needs and going the extra mile,' said the parent of one) and one child with a visual impairment had just been offered a place. But while school is well laid out for wheelchair access, no child who uses one has ever attended. Won't take children with serious behavioural difficulties, although never had to turn anyone away or asked a child to leave. Outside help brought in for speech and language when required. School nurse recently brought in, who doubles up as school counsellor. 'Both my kids were flagged as needing extra help,' said one parent. 'The school kept me informed, we had meetings and they made innovative suggestions, all of which has meant the children are now on the right path. I can't fault it.'

The last word: This is a small, intimate, highly structured and extremely traditional girls' prep in a stunning modern setting that gets children of a broad range of ability to reach their full potential, without too much pressure. Its emphasis on the arts and play, alongside academic learning, means it's not for the tiger parent and its preciousness, emphasis on authority and very high expectations around manners means it's probably not for the non-conformist child either.

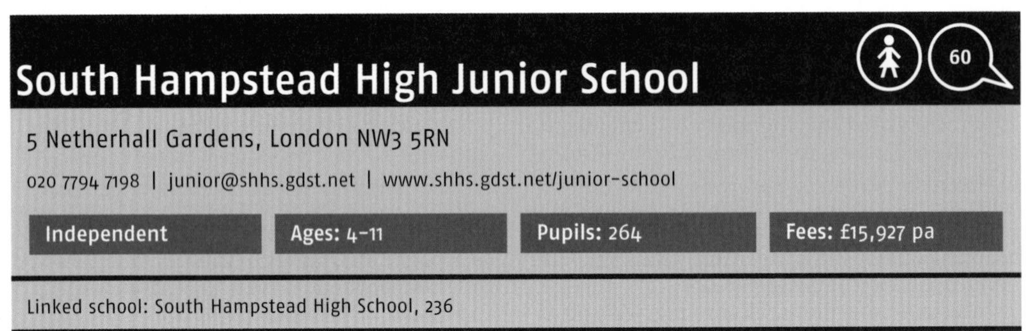

South Hampstead High Junior School

5 Netherhall Gardens, London NW3 5RN

020 7794 7198 | junior@shhs.gdst.net | www.shhs.gdst.net/junior-school

Independent | Ages: 4-11 | Pupils: 264 | Fees: £15,927 pa

Linked school: South Hampstead High School, 236

Headmistress of junior school: Since September 2019, Caroline Spencer, previously head of Francis Holland Junior School.

Entrance: At 4+, some 250 apply, at least a year before start date, for the 24 reception places. At 7+ around 130 apply for 24 more places in year 3 (applications close in the November of the year before entry).

Reception assessment is play-based, in the November prior to entry, in similar age groups of 12-13 girls with four or five staff observing and interacting. 'We're looking for signs that they will benefit from the academic education we have to offer – for their ability to notice, examine, explain.' A hundred of the 250 return in January in smaller groups when the school 'looks for a range of personality types' and aims at a balanced year group. No barrier against those with summer birthdays – 'we expect a little less of them'.

Year 3 applicants are tested in maths, English and non-verbal reasoning, with high performers invited back for interview and small group activities. At this point 'we are looking at what they can do', but hoping to see past tutoring to potential, and 'the small group assessments are the most useful in making final judgements.'

Inevitably the assessments are not an exact science, and though nearly all of those accepted do, indeed, thrive, the school is aware that there are plenty more suitable candidates than they have room for in both age groups.

Exit: Nearly always 100 per cent to the senior school, round the corner. 'Our job is to assess them properly and help them achieve what they need. If a child works hard we can usually get them to the right standard.' Occasional leavers to eg Henrietta Barnett. Six scholarships in 2020.

Our view: Happily, staff do not have to cram their charges through the 11+ and thus can oversee an education outside of the box. The previous head introduced the concept of the Growth Mindset ('I can do it…' proclaim posters in each classroom), to encourage girls to take risks, challenge themselves and learn from mistakes. 'Self-assessment – what did I do well and what do I need to improve? – can counteract girls' tendency to be "people pleasers".'

Junior and senior school heads believe that resilience is one of the most important qualities schools can inculcate in girls. Pupils are encouraged to speak up – they have 'talk partners' with whom to share ideas in class, they perform in assembly from the youngest years, talk about their work, debate, recite poetry, perform in plays. By year 6 even the most naturally reticent are confident enough to show parents around the school.

Our extremely self-assured and chatty guides showed us how topic work encompasses a range of subjects. Reception children were painting pictures of jungles to decorate their role play area. We saw pictures of the year 2 (Raging Rivers) trip to the River and Rowing Museum; we viewed year 5's Chinese pottery vases, dropped in on their Mandarin class and heard about their impromptu trip to Liverpool to see the Terracotta Army exhibition – 'you have to grab these opportunities'. Year 4s sculpt Viking chessmen and have a residential trip to York ('really, really fun'). Year 6s were enthused by their visit to France (which took in a chocolate factory and a goat farm).

Our guides were keen to tell us about Open Homework. 'You're given a word and you can do anything with it, from art to baking'; 'I made a board game'; 'I made 100 paper aeroplanes'; 'I painted a picture.' We liked the display board showing a reasoned discussion on whether girls would prefer to live in London or in a village in Africa.

Parents approve of the SHHS emphasis on inspirational and powerful women, which begins in the junior school. Year 5s learn about the Suffragettes (a then staff member spent time in Holloway prison), about Rebel Girls and significant Women Through Time. 'It makes the curriculum meaningful to them.'

No setting or grades in the junior school. 'We focus on what they did well and how they can improve.' A few have dyslexia, dyspraxia or are on the autism spectrum, but 'all are academically able. They may need support at different stages and in different ways, and we want to get in quickly with help. We have a wonderful SENCo.'

Sport rapidly improving, and girls use the senior school sports hall and playing fields as well as their own games area. They now play football alongside netball – hurray – and have jettisoned rounders for cricket. Year 5 were off to Sydenham High when we visited to be coached by an England cricketer. Even the youngest ran a mile for Sports Relief recently. Cross-country, yoga, fencing and dance all popular. Year 5s and 6s compete against other schools, with A-D teams, and PE clubs are open to all. 'We want them to love sport and enjoy being physical.'

Year 5s learn about the Suffragettes (a then staff member spent time in Holloway prison), Rebel Girls and significant Women Through Time – it makes the curriculum relevant

Plenty of inter-GDST school competitions. Displayed in the entrance hall we saw awards for cross-country and quiz competitions, and for young choir of the year. The relatively recent house system – with houses named after Bronte, Curie, Parks and Pavlova – provides more gentle opportunities to compete.

There's a good musical grounding with all year 1s learning the violin or cello and all year 2s playing the recorder, and orchestras, ensembles and choirs for those who would like to progress further. Drama performances start early and year 4s were away at the senior school rehearsing for their production of Pirates of the Currybean when we visited. We heard about workshops on architecture and dance, robots and forensic science. Waterlow Hall, a new state-of-the-art performance space for debating, drama and concerts, opened in 2020.

A big party celebrated the 60th anniversary of the junior school's move from Waterlow House on the senior school site to its own red-brick building round the corner in Netherhall Gardens in 1957. Pupils also dressed up in 50s clothes and listened to guests talk about their junior school days in that era – 'we heard about the great smog and how hard it was to get to school'.

This building now houses reception to year 4, plus the science lab (home to skeletons Bob and Bob Junior, where 'we do lots of experiments, so we can see what happens, not just hear about it') plus the art room full of clay sculptures. There's a bright and comfortable library where classes spend half an hour a week ('Really nice. You get to sit and read!') and there are 'star reads' suggested for each year group by previous years. A second building across the road, purchased in 1993 to cope with increasing numbers, houses classrooms for years 5 and 6 plus the music room, another library and the DT room.

Outside space is limited at both sites but reception has its own outdoor classroom with Wendy house, and a row of scooters indicated how many local girls get to school. They also manage to fit in a mini sports pitch and playgrounds with climbing frames. 'At least half of our girls can be seen running up and noisily at play time. There's space to run, jump, climb and throw balls.'

The last word: A creative and liberal start to education where girls are encouraged to speak out and challenge themselves inside and outside the classroom.

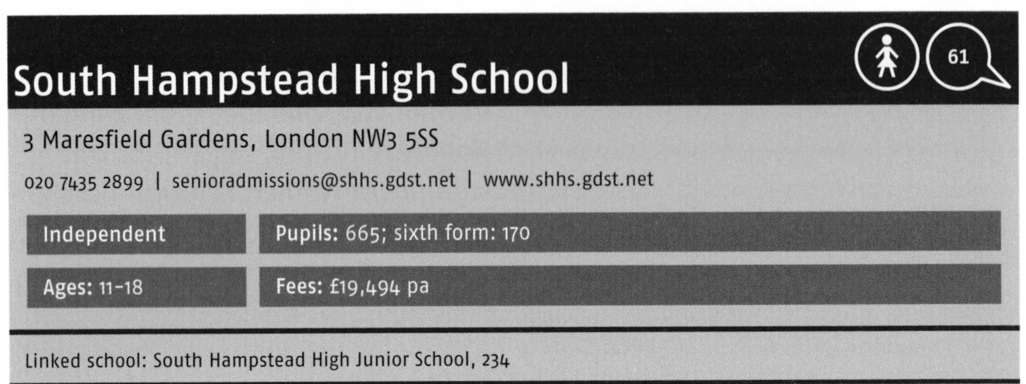

South Hampstead High School

3 Maresfield Gardens, London NW3 5SS

020 7435 2899 | senioradmissions@shhs.gdst.net | www.shhs.gdst.net

Independent | Pupils: 665; sixth form: 170

Ages: 11–18 | Fees: £19,494 pa

Linked school: South Hampstead High Junior School, 234

Headmistress: Since January 2017, Vicky Bingham (40), previously deputy head at Guildford High. Educated at the European School in Brussels – her father worked for the EU; classics MA from Oxford; PGCE in classics from Cambridge. Started her career teaching classics at Guildford High; off to St Catherine's Bramley as head of classics, before returning to Guildford as deputy head in 2010. 'I didn't always want to teach, but during my final year at Oxford I realised that by the time I retired I wanted to have filled my head with something worthwhile and I felt that teaching classics is important to humanity.' She 'fell into' working at girls' schools and has found them 'unpretentious, unstuffy, moving with the times'. With an international upbringing, she feels at home amidst the cosmopolitan buzz of SHHS. 'In many families at least one parent comes from overseas.'

We found her energetic, enthusiastic, full of ideas. Sees developing resilience as a vital part of girls' education, via a well-rounded, holistic curriculum. 'The more activities there are outside the classroom, the more chances they have to shine in something.' Very keen on debating and public speaking: 'I won an international public speaking event that gave me confidence and I want the girls to have that chance.' Also passionate about improving school's sporting offering, of which more later.

A big thumbs-up from parents and pupils, who have experienced a rapid turnover of heads over the past few years, and fervently hope she is here for the long term. 'She's very focused on the girls,' said a father. 'I'm a big fan,' said another. 'The girls respect her, she's on their wavelength, she's a big hit at the school.'

A keen walker (with her dog, Max), she took up running at 34 and was first lady in her first race. 'Sport wasn't valued at my own school and I felt it was a waste of my 20s that I hadn't realised I was good at this.' She has gone public with her views on the British values curriculum ('somewhat jingoistic') and tutoring ('it robs children of the critical ability to surmount problems themselves'). The day we visited she hit headlines for her criticism of women who insist on micromanaging the domestic sphere as well as holding down demanding jobs. 'What kind of blueprint are some of us providing for our daughters by infantilising men?'

Her daughter is at the junior school here.

Entrance: Nearly all junior school girls (around 46) move up to the senior school without taking the entrance exam. They are joined by some 55 girls from approaching 600 applicants from outside, about 20 per cent from state primary schools.

The 11+ assessment for entry now consists of a 75-minute cognitive ability test (rather than maths and English exams) with great emphasis on the interview. The intention is to make the tests as tutor-proof as possible and to cut down on the prep school culture of 'endless practice papers'. An aim of the interview is to find 'children who can think for themselves when they encounter academic obstacles'. 'No silver bullet but we are doing something address the problems' of the advantages given to the tutored and prepped under the current system. Forty per cent increase in applicants recently.

At 16+ by exams in three A level subjects plus general paper, interview and predicted GCSE grades.

Exit: Around 20 per cent leave after GCSEs. A few to state sixth forms such as Camden School for Girls and Marylebone, and a few more to join their brothers at UCS up the road or to Westminster, one or two off to board. Sixth form leavers off to study eg art history at UCL, business and sustainable global development at Warwick, geography at Nottingham and linguistics at Cambridge. A good handful now to international universities (three in 2020 – Harvard, Yale and Indiana) and to Oxbridge (15 in 2020). Several medics (five in 2020).

Latest results: School won't disclose 2020 exam results. In 2019, 92 per cent 9-7 at GCSE; 77 per cent A*/A at A level (91 per cent A*-B).

Teaching and learning: Results at GCSE hard to beat. Good showing in languages – everyone studies one MFL in year 7 plus Latin (a choice of French, Spanish, German and Mandarin) and two in year 8, taking at least one to GCSE – and a fair few continue to A level. Maths taken by about two-thirds of sixth formers with impressive results; psychology, history and economics all popular; generally good numbers taking science A level, though physics less popular (the department, we were told, has 'now stabilised', and indeed a physics teacher was shortlisted for a global £3m 'world's best teacher' prize).

Everyone studies four subjects in year 12, many dropping to three in year 13: some parents voiced a feeling that taking three subjects throughout would lead to less stress and more time for enrichment. The first term in year 12 sees a Friday afternoon Great Ideas course which is a springboard to an EPQ (increasing take-up with strong results), and students are encouraged to enter for national essay writing competitions, Olympiads, engineering scholarships etc, with some great successes. The Futures Programme, preparing for life beyond school, taps into the GDST Alumnae Network of over 75,000 members. Journalists, vets, psychiatrists, charity executives come back to talk about their work. In the younger years, the new This Is Me project encourages girls to talk proudly about themselves and their achievements in an interview-style situation.

'I want us to do more than chase exam results and prizes,' says head, who believes that they get results 'without an insane amount of pressure'. 'I thought it might be hothousy and too pushy, but it really hasn't been,' said a parent. General agreement that any hothouse atmosphere is created by ambitious families rather than by the school.

Universal praise for staff. 'They're well supported by very able teachers.' 'When my daughter struggled with maths, the teacher went to endless trouble to help her understand it. And they're all like that.'

Learning support and SEN: The SEN department here is not rushed off its feet, but there's always a proportion of pupils with specific needs such as dyslexia or dyspraxia, some of which don't come to light until the sixth form. 'Because they're so bright they tend to be able to work with strategies we give them.' Support given unstintingly: one-to-one when needed, but most within lessons. 'A good lesson for a dyslexic child is a good lesson for everyone.' Laptops provided to all those that need them.

The arts and extracurricular: Music a strong point with numerous opportunities at all levels ('My daughter is a fairly average player but has plenty of chances to perform'), ambitious concerts and recitals large and small. And amongst the lunchtime and teatime recitals, choral and orchestral concerts, a ukulele ensemble, the Big Band and jazz groups provide a jaunty air, with the summer Jazz Night a showcase for saxophonists and their ilk.

FemSoc discusses problems with the patriarchy; Womanities Soc examines the less-than-well-behaved women who have shaped history, created art or literature

Art as popular as at most highly academic schools where many parents push their daughters towards more 'academic' subjects. Small but perfectly formed A level groups produce some impressive work in 'relaxing and enjoyable' top floor sixth form art and sculpture rooms. Visits to local galleries and far-flung exhibitions: Vienna, Kyoto, New York. DT product design available to A level but take-up tends to be bijou at this level.

Recent production of Made in Dagenham – based on the 1968 sewing machinists' strike for equal pay at the Ford factory in Dagenham – 'very impressive' and there are plenty of musicals and classical plays, recently Euripides' Trojan Women. However, drama's not generally amongst the high flying subjects at GCSE, few take theatre studies at A level and we heard about some thespians moving to sixth forms elsewhere for this reason. Plenty of opportunities to speak up, though, with debating increasingly popular and compulsory public speaking competitions from years 7-10.

Huge range of speakers drop in, from Dame Stella Rimmington, Olympic hockey players and Angela Saini (Inferior: How Science Got Women Wrong) to Michael Gove (who apparently provoked intense questioning on Brexit). Those invited by year 13s have included Laura Bates (founder of the Everyday Sexism Project).

Clubs for cheerleaders and comedians, Shakespeare and Dr Who devotees, fashionistas and philosophers. FemSoc discusses problems with the patriarchy; Womanities Soc examines the less-than-well-behaved women who have shaped history, created art or literature; the popular LGBTQ+ discussion group is now known as PRIDE. DofE hugely popular: 'nearly all my daughter's group seem to be doing it'.

Sport: Historically, South Hampstead 'has never been a sporty school,' say students, and indeed many parents we talked to cited sport as the weakest link. However, head – who 'sees sport as a cornerstone of pastoral life,' said a colleague – is overseeing a transformation. 'Playing as part of a team gives you a sense of pride,' she says, and there are now A-E netball teams in year 7, with increased competition feeding gradually up the school. Lots more competitive matches against other schools and over 20 sports now available thanks to recently expanded PE dept from athletics and badminton to yoga and zumba. Two netball teams recently reached the Middlesex finals, football is increasingly popular, with external coaching, and they have dropped rounders in favour of cricket as a key summer sport with coaching from ex-England players. Years 7-9 now get a full afternoon a week at the four-acre sports ground, a 10-minute walk away, as well as PE lessons in the new sports hall deep in the bowels of the reconstructed school building. Sixth formers talked enthusiastically of the 'very competitive' staff v students netball match.

Ethos and heritage: Opened in 1876 as St John's Wood High School at Swiss Cottage with 27 pupils, changing its name to South Hampstead High in 1887 and moving to a purpose-built site in Maresfield Gardens with 300 pupils. And there it stayed, in the same red-brick building with the odd acquisition or two: Waterlow House, bought in 1921, originally home to the junior school, and rebuilt in 1988; and Oakwood, bought in 1991 as the new sixth form centre.

In 2014, after a major £35m reconstruction, the 600 pupils moved back from temporary premises on the Lymington Road sports ground to the multi-storey glass and red-brick home, full of light and air, that rises from an underground sports hall to a rooftop garden, with panoramic views of north London from its upper floors.

The walls are alive with murals and artwork, including the abstract Hampstead Mural panels by the late Gillian Ayres, commissioned in 1957 for the school's then dining room, now joined by five new paintings donated by the artist to celebrate the new building, and which form the school's modern art collection.

Waterlow Hall, lined with honours boards, is the site for assemblies and performances. Currently it is underwhelming from an acoustic point of view and fundraising is underway to transform it into a worthy setting for concerts, plays and speakers.

The current head has turned end of year assemblies into a celebration of the life of the school. 'I cry every time we sing the school song,' said a sixth former unapologetically

Oakwood House, the sixth form's own, is more reminiscent of a wood-panelled grammar school of yore. Sixth formers love the rooftop garden and ground floor grassy area with picnic tables and Mira Cinnamon statue. They have an agreeably informal common room with slouchy sofas and table football and, with staff's rooms nearby, the head of sixth form is 'very available'.

The previous head, perhaps with the aim of giving the school a more pronounced individual identity, commissioned a variety of blue and yellow penguins with water bottles on their backs, carrying the message of water conservation, which dot the school. The girls, somewhat bemused, have taken the name Penguin for their own magazine, 'the voice of satire and quirkiness'. The current head is 'keen to tap into new traditions' and has turned end of year assemblies into a celebration of the life of the school. 'I cry every time we sing the school song,' said a sixth former unapologetically.

A tradition of celebrating girls' education and empowerment, with a suffrage week of events to mark the centenary of women gaining the vote. 'You learn early on about the value of women,' said a sixth former. 'Virtually all the girls here would say they're a feminist.' 'A good place for a girl to learn – not too precious,' added a parent.

Pastoral care, inclusivity and discipline: The usual pastoral scaffolding, including one-to-one chats

Westminster School

with a tutor on a regular basis, also features a life coach and a counsellor. The counsellor, a child psychotherapist, 'makes herself approachable by coming into assemblies,' and even girls without specific problems go along for a chat and a biscuit, said a parent. 'She's brilliant. They've nailed it.' The life coach is there to help on a practical level – 'perhaps with specific things a girl would like to change about her behaviour. Some have recurring themes and we encourage them to think about what would work better.' 'My daughter finds her very useful,' said a parent. 'If you are struggling academically, she reorganises your life,' said a sixth former (which sounds fabulous; can we all have one?). 'There will always be a teacher you can speak to,' she added, mentioning how much care she had seen a teacher take with a pupil who became upset in her class.

As a highly selective all-girls school, South Hampstead might seem a likely candidate for widespread anorexia and the like, but no-one we spoke to – parents, girls or staff – felt it was a pressing issue. 'They keep a good watch on the girls,' said a parent. A deputy head confirmed: 'We keep a close eye if we think anything is emerging that suggests an eating disorder. We do have the usual gamut of teenage issues, but the girls are very supportive of each other – they will come and tell us if they feel someone needs help.' Staff are well aware of the dangers of modern communication modes. 'We're constantly talking about screen time, the pitfalls of Instagram reality, of trying to have a thick skin in relation to social media.'

'My daughter struggled socially when she first joined,' said a parent, 'and they were really onto it, very supportive.' Girls agree: 'There's a very warm atmosphere here. Very nurturing.'

This is liberal Hampstead, where being right on and tolerant is more or less a given. So how would the school cope with transgender issues? 'Fundamentally, we are proud to be a girls' school,' says the head. 'But if one of our pupils transitioned we would make kind, considerate, sensitive adjustments to make it possible for them to stay. We're ready for it. Our uniform includes trousers and could easily be unisex.'

Pupils and parents: Characterised by members of the north London liberal intelligentsia, with a good ethnic mix. The bulk of the intake from Camden and the surrounding boroughs, including many international families, with increasing applicants from further west. South Hampstead girls are 'diligent but flexible and creative about their thinking,' says head. They are 'great social campaigners – they like things with edge'. Parents are 'really supportive, like to have an open dialogue, like to give advice; they like us to be honest and transparent'.

Notable old girls include Helena Bonham-Carter (who opened the new school building), Lynne Featherstone MP, Suzy Klein, Angela Lansbury, Joanna McGregor, Rabbi Julia Neuberger, the late Lynsey de Paul, Fay Weldon, Olivia Williams, Naomi Alderman.

Money matters: Academic and music scholarships, plus means-tested bursaries of up to 100 per cent, available at 11+ and 16+. Art and drama scholarships also available at 16+ and sport scholarships at 11+.

The last word: A busy, buzzy school regaining its pre-eminence in northwest London under an energetic head who is determined to empower her pupils. Said a satisfied parent: 'They really do care about the girls and giving them a broad education.'

Sylvia Young Theatre School

62

1 Nutford Place, London W1H 5YZ

020 7258 2330 | info@syts.co.uk | www.syts.co.uk

Independent	Pupils: 235; Boarders: 6 (with host families)
Ages: 10–16	Fees: £14,310 – £14,550 pa

Principal: Since 1981, Sylvia Young OBE (70s), founding principal and true trailblazer. An East End girl, she trained part-time as an actress at Mountview but realised that a performing career wasn't for her. Married, and working as a part-time librarian, when her daughters' primary school asked her to teach some holiday drama classes, and a star was born. In 1972 she started an evening school, enlisting friends from Mountview to help with the teaching and charging pupils 10p a class to cover the hire of the church hall. She started the full-time school in 1981, because all the part-time students kept asking for one.

Decades later, the school is one of the most highly regarded names in arts education for under-18s, testament to its founder's revolutionary drive (rumour has it she can trace her ancestry back to Leon Trotsky), vision and simple humanity. 'I find it difficult to accept how well known the school's become,' she confided. Parents are more forthright in their praise. 'Sylvia is incredibly inspirational for the children, she is amazing with them,' wrote one. 'We have found Sylvia to be exceptionally supportive. Her culture runs right through the school and we have found it to be a strong and positive one,' said another. Given an OBE in 2005 for her services to the arts.

She and husband Norman still live in their flat on the top floor of the school building. Their two daughters, Alison, a theatrical agent who now works alongside her mother at the school, and Tony-award-winning actress Frances Ruffelle, are both grown up and mothers themselves – pop singer Eliza Doolittle is one of the grandchildren.

Since 2005 Frances Chave BSc PGCE (50s) has been the academic and pastoral head. Ms Chave read maths at Exeter University, did her teacher training at Southampton, then taught at two large comprehensives (Cranford Community College and Feltham Community College), before helping to set up a third, Overton Grange School in Sutton, where she was deputy head. Came to SYTS because she wanted a change and the school wanted her hand on the academic tiller. Both provision and results have risen under her care, and she loves it here: 'It's a fabulous place!' she told us. 'Being in a school where every single student wants to be there is very special.' Valued by parents and students alike – 'Very welcoming and approachable; she encourages the parents to contact her… always around the school and not locked away in her office,' was a typical comment. Not a performer herself, but loves theatre. Likes walking and cycling in her spare time.

Entrance: Around 350 apply each year – school takes between 30 and 40. One-form entry into year 6, two-form into year 7. Capacity for up to 26 in each class, but in practice the forms are rarely this big – 'We don't take children just to fill up places – they have to be good.' Thereafter students can join at any point other than year 11, although rarely at year 10 because GCSE preparation begins towards the end of year 9. Auditions are held throughout the year, and children can start mid-year if need be.

At all ages, applicants have to audition before a panel: they perform two acting pieces supplied by the school, plus a song and dance of the child's choice. 'We're looking for potential in at least one of the vocational areas,' said Sylvia, 'a student we feel we could train.' They also have to sit tests in maths and English, but these are diagnostic, and to check that a child can cope with doing in three days the academic study that other schools would do in five.

Parents are forthright in their praise of Sylvia Young. 'Her culture runs right through the school and we have found it to be a strong and positive one,' said one

The school assesses progress regularly, but doesn't make a practice of assessing out. 'We wouldn't ask a student to leave if they're working to their best ability. We find that children develop at different times, and we know that all our students will leave us with a good level of attainment.'

Exit: No sixth form. At 16, around 50 per cent to dance schools – Bird's, Laine's, Urdang. Others to performing arts schools such as Tring Park, Arts Ed, ELAM, the Brit School, BIMM, LIPA. Some to independent sixth form colleges, eg Hurtwood House, Ashbourne, often on full scholarships.

Not an obvious Russell Group route, but the odd student does go off to do A levels at the likes of Westminster School and Wimbledon High. 'I'm always thrilled when I hear of our students who've gone into law, medicine, forensic science…' remarked Sylvia with pardonable pride.

Latest results: In 2020, 39 per cent 9-7 at GCSE. In 2019 (the last year when exams took place), 26 per cent 9-7 at GCSE.

Teaching and learning: Not stellar GCSE results, but very respectable given the school's totally non-academically selective intake. One parent expressed disquiet about the academic provision, claiming it was uneven, but the overwhelming majority were extremely positive. 'The standard of the education and the teachers' dedication to the children is second to none.' 'We have been impressed with the academic provision. The teachers mostly seem dedicated and fair.' 'Our experience has been that the academics are strong – they have an excellent set of teachers on the whole and they care, teach well and motivate the children.'

SYTS still adheres to the weekly curriculum model it first adopted out of necessity: three days of academic education followed by two days' vocational training. Housed in wonderfully spacious surroundings since 2010, there's no longer a need to push the desks back on Wednesday night and convert classrooms into studios, but, says Ms Chave, 'it really works. From Monday to Wednesday there's a complete focus on academics – it's quite a different atmosphere from the vocational days, and they're not always running off to get changed.' Students love it: 'It's good that they have the academics first, because then you're really ready to get going on the vocational side.' 'It's a really effective use of time, and you don't have to carry around so much.' 'The vocational days are the carrot they hold out to us, and it makes you work really hard on Monday, Tuesday and Wednesday.' A parent commented, 'An initial concern was that the three day/two day split could mean that the academic side could suffer, but this does not seem to be the case.'

SYTS still adheres to the weekly curriculum model it first adopted out of necessity: three days of academic education followed by two days' vocational training

Parents also praised the school's insistence that professional work shouldn't compromise the children's academic attainment. Every week the staff post online what needs to be completed and see that it's done, and when a child is absent longer-term eg on tour, SYTS staff liaise with the child's appointed tutors. One mother commented, 'My son has worked consistently over the past two years and has always had help keeping up with his academics, as the school takes this very seriously.' Another wrote proudly, 'My daughter is a working child and the school fully supports working children, but they do expect them to maintain their grades and work very hard.'

Pushed into three days, the curriculum is necessarily compact. For key stage 3 the core subjects English, maths and science are taught alongside the humanities, art, ICT and Spanish (the only language offered here). Music study is taught as part of the vocational curriculum. At key stage 4, students take eight or nine GCSEs: everyone does drama, English lang & lit, maths and double or triple science, plus two options from music, art, media studies, history and Spanish. As one student remarked, 'There are subjects we can't do. But the ones we do are really well taught.' The lessons we observed were professional and lively, delivered by cheerful, upbeat teachers with excellent communication skills. Students are vocal, attentive, diligent, very keen to get things right.

Learning support and SEN: SENCo is in school on the academic days, aided by a SEN support teacher. The main needs here are mild to moderate dyslexia and some dyscalculia, and children are helped in class or with weekly individual sessions.

The arts and extracurricular: Performing arts are, of course, the school's raison d'être. Thursdays and Fridays are devoted to vocational training in acting, singing and dancing and everyone has to do all three. This was a huge plus for the young folks we spoke to: a boy who had previously attended another performing arts school switched to SYTS because 'at my last school you had to choose a pathway, either dance or drama, whereas I wanted to specialise in everything!' Lots of nodding at this.

Students are taught ballet, jazz, contemporary and tap; speech, characterisation, improvisation, stagecraft and audition technique; singing, aural awareness and technological awareness. The buzz in all these classes is palpable, and the students achieve great things, coached by top-notch industry professionals for whom they clearly have the utmost respect. 'The vocational training is amazing, second to none!' was a very typical comment. We saw the head of music – brusque, scary and taking no prisoners – coax an amazing performance of The Impossible Dream out of the year 10s. 'That should give me a tingle, I haven't had a tingle yet!' he admonished towards the end of verse 3, but we certainly got that tingle ourselves. 'Oh, he brings it out of you, I don't know how!' exclaimed a young alumnus who was also watching. 'He's so professional! I didn't have confidence in singing when I came here, and now I'm a singer. This school sets you up for a career in this industry.' Parents have regular opportunities to watch their child perform, and every December the children sing at the Actors' Church in Covent Garden. LAMDA exams taken by virtually everyone, and very high standards achieved. The Lab, an experimental drama club, meets after school and prepares plays for workshop performance.

Sylvia Young began her famous agency in the spare room of her house in 1972 armed with a scrapbook of primary school portrait photos, with the aim of creating some extra performance opportunities for her young charges. A young advertising chap called Saatchi liked her style, and it went on from there. Today the agency is located on the ground floor of the school and manned by up to seven staff. All full-time SYTS pupils are automatically members. At any point in the day children might be told they have an audition, whereat the school will chaperone them there and back. If successful, the agency deals with all the paperwork and licences. Some of the children become very successful indeed, playing principal roles in West End shows and on tour – one of our tour guides had just extended his contract as young Harry in Harry Potter and the Cursed Child – and you might expect there to be an overly competitive atmosphere as a result, but there really doesn't seem to be. 'It's friendly competition!' insisted the students. 'When we come here we know it's going to be competitive; it's what we signed up for.' Students also learn a mature and resilient approach to the inevitable rejections. 'If they don't get a part, it's not them or their talent that's being rejected, it's that they're not what the director sees for that role,' insisted the principal. 'We teach them that NO stands for Next Opportunity.'

Sport: The year 6 pupils go swimming once a week, but otherwise there are no sports; the timetable doesn't allow for it, and the children keep super-fit with all that dance. Would the students like sports, we asked? 'No!' was the unanimous answer. Acrobatics offered as an extracurricular, but not much else: the children work hard both on and off the premises and it's not unknown for them to commute daily from eg Birmingham – so they're not looking to stay after school for the Philately Club.

Boarding: Because children come from such a wide radius, some board with host families found by the school. SYTS is inspected as a boarding school and adheres to the national standards. 'We live overseas, and my daughter boards; she has been with the same family throughout her time at the school,' wrote the mother of a year 10 pupil. 'She is happy and well cared for there.' Some other students lodge with their own relatives or friends. For those living at home, journeys of at least an hour each way are common.

Ethos and heritage: 'I was determined to call it a theatre school,' explained Sylvia Young, 'because I was from a drama background. At the time, the others were all called stage schools, and to me that meant little chorus girls with their hair in bunches.'

Initially housed in the Gainsford Club for amateur boxers in Drury Lane – now long gone, a casualty of the Covent Garden gentrification. The lease expired in 1983 and the school had to find new premises in a hurry, alighting on a derelict school in Rossmore Road, Marylebone. 'The building was full of dead pigeons,' Sylvia reminisced, 'so the staff and I went down to Church Street market to buy mops and buckets.' It was a happy move, however, and the school stayed there for 27 years, with each leaver inscribing their name on a brick in the attic walls – a lovely photo-montage in the school's current site shows all the bricks and reads like a Who's Who of British popular entertainment. In 2008, with the school's success continuing to grow, Sylvia put in an offer on a disused Church of Christ Scientist in Marble Arch – Ginger Rogers used to worship there – and here the school is now, housed in air-conditioned space and splendour following a two-year programme of gutting and total refurbishment. The school boasts 10 purpose-built studios, two computer rooms, two science labs, two art rooms, various academic classrooms, a library, and a large and airy canteen. There are even two small outdoor courtyards where students can let off a small amount of steam. School is proud of these central London rarities, but one rueful parent did comment, 'If I have a criticism, it is the lack of outside space in which to run around, especially on academic days,' adding, 'however, I do think that is a small price to pay for the extra benefits of SYTS.'

At any point children might be told they have an audition, whereat the school will chaperone them there and back. If successful, the agency deals with all the paperwork

The school began all those years ago as a community initiative, and its priorities remain the nurturing of children and the family atmosphere, something which everyone we spoke to agreed was one of its best aspects. Students work hard, develop professionalism, make friends and are overjoyed to be here. 'I only have praise for SYTS and feel it was the best decision to send my son there,' wrote a parent. 'He can't wait to get there each day, and is the happiest he's ever been in a school.' 'The kids are immensely supportive of each other and very close,' commented another, 'and there is lots of fun and laughter.'

Alumni include Billie Piper, Keeley Hawes, Nicholas Hoult, Matt Di Angelo, Denise van Outen, Matt Willis, Rita Ora and Amy Winehouse.

Pastoral care, inclusivity and discipline: School is 'very strict' about the everyday things – no chewing gum, neat appearance, punctuality, attendance. 'They HAVE to be respectful to each other and to teachers,' said Sylvia, forcefully. A parent wrote, 'One headmaster from a major public school told us that he always prefers to take ex-Sylvia pupils as they are so much better behaved than from any other school.'

Pupils are very presentable, smartly turned out in traditional red and black uniform on academic days, black movement clothes on vocational days. Refreshing emphasis on common sense, eg 'We got rid of the pink ballet shoes because it was so much kerfuffle changing.' Girls now wear black ballet shoes and can move from class to class in them. Hair is neatly tied back, even on academic days.

Children work to achieve a place here, and discipline problems of the mainstream kind are rare. Reprimands and detentions are usually all that's necessary, and there's a strong culture of rewarding academic achievement. The students we spoke to couldn't think of any recent episodes of bullying – in fact, they were clear that bullying was something they'd left behind at their previous schools – but insisted that staff were approachable and that they had confidence to speak out if anything arose. However, there was a consensus that a school counsellor would be welcome – 'I know that counsellors can't talk to other teachers, whereas here you're worried that what you've said might not be private,' was a comment that had everyone murmuring agreement.

Pupils and parents: Children come from 'absolutely everywhere', some from affluent families, others from poorer backgrounds where the extended family is working to put them through the school. Girls outnumber the boys two to one, but the boys are unfazed – 'We've been doing the performing arts before coming here, and we're used to it.' 'And the boys here are really lovely!' cried a year 8 girl. Some pupils from showbiz backgrounds, but by no means all.

Everyone is united by a common love of performing. 'Our son has a wide and varied friendship group. They're all there for the same purpose, so there is a stronger bond between them,' said a father.

Money matters: Fees are extremely reasonable for an independent school in central London, remarkably so given all the top-quality specialist tuition students receive. Lots of children here on some form of financial assistance – equivalent of some £350k a year in bursaries. Children's agency earnings can be put towards the fees.

The last word: Not a school simply for children who like to have fun on stage. Standards are extremely high, the discipline is exacting, the work hard and the hours long. Children need to have genuine talent, passion, and focus. 'If they don't have all this, then re-think!' advised several parents. But if they do, this is a fantastic school, combining sound academics with first-rate vocational training, and producing confident, happy, polished and likeable young people.

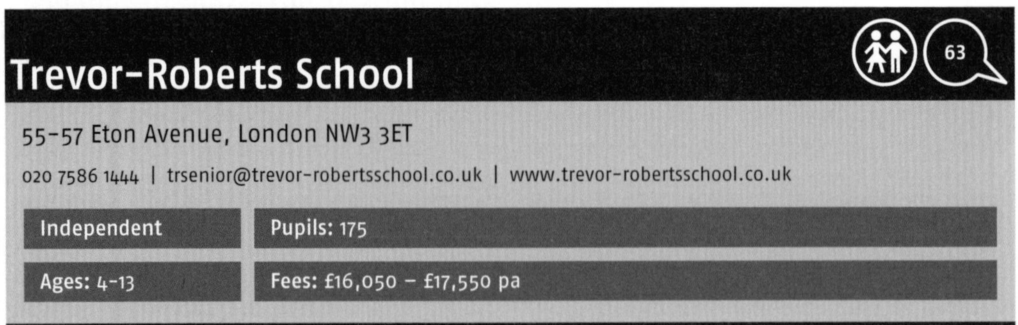

Headmaster: Since 1999, Simon Trevor-Roberts BA (50s). Son of the founder, Trevor-Roberts studied at Westminster School before reading English at Aberystwyth. In 1983, he joined his father Christopher in the family firm, where he learnt his trade by example. (He has since been joined by his sister Amanda, who heads up the junior school.) Mild mannered and reflective, he has a very clear sense of what the school is about: 'We try to get children to enjoy the process of learning.' Continues to teach maths to the 13+ candidates, because he's found he, too, now has the knack of putting things across clearly. 'I shadowed my father for a long time and learnt how to do it by osmosis.' Parents find him immensely approachable and engaged. 'You always have complete access to the head and he knows all the kids incredibly well.' Married with two grown children, both of whom attended the school.

Entrance: Register as soon after birth as possible. School assesses the first 50 children on their list in the September prior to the calendar year in which they turn 5. 'We're not expecting any preparation, but we want to make sure it will be a happy transition,' says the registrar. 'We're looking for inquisitive children who want to learn. Getting that is more a dark art than a science.' The school generally tries to give priority to siblings, 'but only if it's the right school'. Often takes in one or two more in year 4, when the year group divides into two classes.

Exit: Girls mostly – though not exclusively – at 11, generally to Francis Holland NW1, South Hampstead and other north London favourites. Most boys (and some girls) at 13, to regular placements including City of London, Eton, Harrow, Highgate, Latymer Upper, Wetherby Senior, Merchant Taylors', UCS and Westminster. 'The head is very good at managing parental expectations,' said one former parent.

Our view: This is a family-run school with a very distinctive ethos, deriving in large part from its origins. Founded by the current heads' father in the 1950s with just 14 boys, it was originally seen as a refuge for the 'unteachable'. 'My father had a reputation for taking those whom other schools had given up on and getting them through entrance exams to leading public schools,' says head.

Today, the school can take its pick of north London's brightest, but continues to select a mixed-ability (now co-educational) intake and provide a tailor-made education for all. 'They want every child to work to his or her potential and really do treat every child as an individual,' said one parent.

Children start in year 1 in a class grouped according to the calendar year of their birth. In year 4, this is rearranged to allow everyone to be in place for secondary school entrance. One class of 16-18 in the early years, two classes in years 4 to 6, then a single form again for the final two years. 'We like to move children around so they're not in the same group for eight years. It gives us the flexibility to allow those who require it a bit more time and accelerate those who need it.' Parents confirm this is skilfully managed. 'They're constantly readjusting their approach for different levels of learning, but not in a way that disturbs the children.'

Specialist subject teaching from the word go, with a classroom teacher for the core subjects, but music, history, geography, science and art all taught in their own space. 'It keeps the week fresh.'

Plenty of imaginative teaching by intelligent (including many Oxbridge), though not always qualified, staff. French from year 1, Latin from year 5, some Greek in year 8, Mandarin taught as a club. Special needs addressed by weekly sessions with the learning support coordinator and outside specialists.

Everyone staying for the final two years sits common entrance. 'We take it very seriously. Eleven plus is about flexible problem solving; by 13, it's more structure on the page.'

'We insist that children use a pen rather than touch type. If you have to write an essay under exam conditions, you have to be able to discipline your thoughts'

Very good at ensuring the basics are in place. 'Sometimes you have to be a bit tough. We insist that children use a pen rather than touch type. If you have to write an essay under exam conditions, you have to be able to discipline your thoughts.' No truck with overly formalised exam training. 'Non-verbal reasoning is not a subject,' he says crisply.

Formal homework from year 3, starting out with 20 minutes in English or maths ('It shows them how to work by themselves and for themselves'), up to two hours a night for the top forms. 'They do work very hard, but the atmosphere still manages to be reasonably relaxed,' said one mother.

Good relationships with staff are fundamental ('The teacher is not someone they're trying to hoodwink,' says the head), as is the view that effort should be lauded over achievement. 'Children are perfectly aware there's competition elsewhere, they don't need it reinforced. We want them to be in competition with themselves.'

Breadth well beyond the exam curriculum is given enormous emphasis. Outstanding music – 'We love music' – with a dynamic head, numerous ensembles (brass, jazz, string, woodwind, chamber choir, rock band) and much external participation (at the Royal Festival Hall, St John's Smith Square, etc). Twice weekly art lessons (one in year 7) in a bright art department at the top of school, with its own kiln. Extra art and DT on offer for enthusiasts on Wednesday afternoons.

Cultural values that have largely been submerged elsewhere – 'Everyone is encouraged to have a novel on the go' – with half an hour of silent reading daily after lunch. Poetry and drama matter and prove great confidence builders. 'My son almost died of nerves the first time he had to read out a poem,' said one mother, 'but now he loves drama and performing.' 'The plays are unbelievable,' said another.

Plenty of fresh air and exercise, with a good-sized, well-equipped playground, including popular table tennis, miniature railway and chicken coop ('the chickens are a great comfort to quieter, shyer children'). Primrose Hill, a few hundred yards from the door, enables twice-weekly games. Definitely not a school, however, where 'go-fight-win' is on the agenda. 'Children love sport, but I don't want a First Eleven ethos, with the captain of games strutting around,' says the head. 'We do play matches against other schools, but everyone has a go.'

The senior school building, a fine example of arts and crafts, was the founder's own home and still offers delightful domestic interiors with William Morris wallpaper in the front hall and mid-century classic tables used instead of desks in the top forms. The juniors are housed in their own building with a separate dining room and science lab.

The atmosphere is civilised but structured ('It's a nice mix of the very strict and the nurturing and kind – teachers are always willing to talk things through'). Everyone has a hot lunch, served through an open hatch, 'so they can see where it is made'. Staff share the dining hall with pupils.

'Children love sport, but I don't want a First Eleven ethos, with the captain of games strutting around,' says the head

'Eating is socialising.' Food is freshly prepared on site using local produce.

Manners and uniform are both reasonably relaxed. Light blue polo shirt for younger children, dark blue for older ones. Trousers and skirts, 'something reasonable'. 'Jeans are fine, jeans hanging off the hips are not.'

Mainly local, some from Notting Hill, Queen's Park, Islington. The head feels 'there's no typical child, but I've heard people say our children are very kind.'

The last word: Often the school of choice for the liberal, media intelligentsia (including some famous names), the type of parent who genuinely believes in the well-rounded education, not the rush to the top of the league tables. (Competition here, though it undoubtedly exists, tends to be on the level of how many operas your child has seen rather than where the family went skiing.)

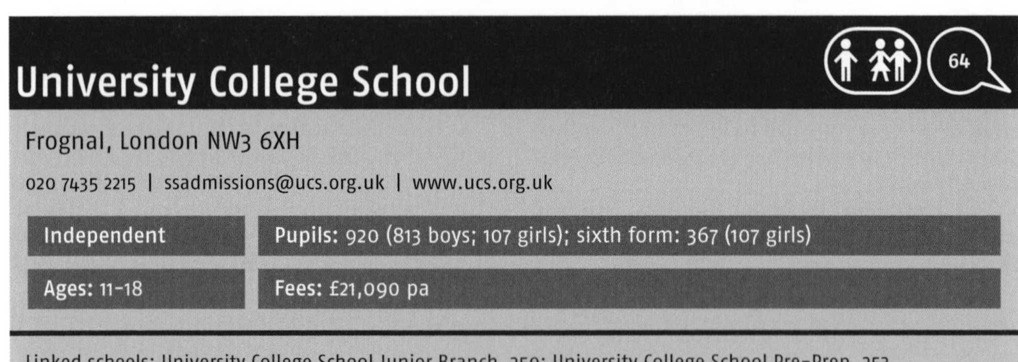

University College School

Frognal, London NW3 6XH

020 7435 2215 | ssadmissions@ucs.org.uk | www.ucs.org.uk

Independent	Pupils: 920 (813 boys; 107 girls); sixth form: 367 (107 girls)
Ages: 11-18	Fees: £21,090 pa

Linked schools: University College School Junior Branch, 250; University College School Pre-Prep, 253

Headmaster: Since 2013, Mark Beard BSc MEd (40s), a chemist. Previously at Brighton College where he'd been deputy head with a period as acting head between the redoubtable Seldon and the remarkable Cairns – a good place to cut headmagisterial teeth and during which he was credited for dramatically improving Oxbridge numbers. Relished his own government assisted place at Whitgift, 'especially the positive relationships with teachers', but it was being thrown in at the deep end as a gappie to teach science in another language in Kuala Lumpur that clinched his decision to go into teaching after his degree at Oxford. Began his career at King Edward's School, Birmingham, thence to St Paul's School as head of chemistry, where he did his MEd.

'He'll do interesting things over time,' predicted a parent when we last visited and this thoroughly likeable, laid-back, receptive and forward-looking head has not disappointed. First off, he tightened things up on the uniform, manners and punctuality front ('A liberal school this may be, but it had got too relaxed about protocols,' noted a parent). Second, he focused on community links and outreach work, everything from sixth formers mentoring in local primaries to sharing governors with other schools. And third, he broadened the curriculum ('We are entirely focused on the individual and so allocating a full menu of choices must be part of that') – Mandarin, history of art and psychology now available as A levels, Italian and computer studies at GCSE and PPE with a link to anthropology is taught in lower school, while dance has been added to the curriculum 'to help grow confidence'. Building planning and refurb also high on his agenda which includes stunning new, multi-space library designed in partnership with Cambridge University, with the same architects set to be involved in the exciting new (2021) sixth form centre. His study – a colossal oak-panelled space with chic mix of handsome antiques and vibrant velvet seating – is among the nicest we've been in.

Students praise the time he puts into getting to know them ('We all get an invite to his study on our birthday'), his subtle but unswerving wit ('you never get an assembly without him injecting quite a bit of humour') and soft touch authority ('He's definitely not an "I'm the head so you better be on high alert when I'm around" sort'). A widower, he has two children, both in the senior school. Enjoys squash, reading and ancient history.

Entrance: At 11+, about two-thirds come from the junior branch in Holly Hill – they don't take an entrance exam. For everyone else entering year 7 there's hot competition, with 350+ boys, mostly from local primaries, trying for 40 places. Exams in maths and English in January of year 6. Around 40 per cent of applicants invited back for interview. No entry point at 13+. At 16+, some 200 apply for around 60 places – mostly girls who come from eg City of London, Francis Holland, North London Collegiate, Channing, South Hampstead, Highgate School, St Marylebone School, Hampstead School and William Ellis. Selection via November assessment (an objective test of thinking, reasoning and problem-solving) with around half invited back for interview. Applicants need an average of 6.5 at GCSE and a 7 in the subjects (or related) they want to study.

Exit: Hardly anyone leaves after GCSE and post A levels everyone goes off to a good university to read a proper subject. Sixth form has been restructured to better facilitate university entry advice, and careers advice in tandem – 'it feels like it's available 24/7, which is amazing,' said one student. London University is a favourite; many also to Bristol, Edinburgh and Manchester. Most years see 20+ to Oxbridge (25 in 2020). Four medics in 2020, though there are usually more. University overseas is increasingly popular, including Harvard, Stanford, NYU and UPenn. The vast range of subjects they pursue is testament to the individuality fostered here.

Latest results: In 2020, 96 per cent 9-7 at GCSE. At A level, 79 per cent A*/A at A levels/Pre-Us (95 per cent A*-B). In 2019 (the last year when exams took place), 92 per cent 9-7 at GCSE. At A level, 75 per cent of A*/A at A levels/Pre-Us (93 per cent A*-B).

Teaching and learning: School was already on a strong footing academically and has now upped the ante even further, with recent results among the best in the school's history. Impressive even when taking into account that it's selective (although worth noting that at sixth form, entry requirements are lower than some nearby state schools). What's more, there are no weaker subjects.

In the lessons we saw hands popped up left, right and centre to ask penetrating and articulate questions – woe betide any unprepared teachers

Independent thinking is the name of the game here and this, believe many parents, is the UCS secret weapon: 'In stark contrast to more prescriptive schools, there's a lot of opinion exchange here.' 'They really do think outside the box – it's incredible to experience.' In the lessons we saw hands popped up left, right and centre to ask penetrating and articulate questions – woe betide any unprepared teachers (we didn't spot any – one was even prepared to doubt a piece of information in the set textbook). 'Lessons are never a bore,' a student told us. Regular tracking, thorough reports and plenty of clinics also credited. Class sizes around 20, dropping to between five and 15 in sixth form.

Lots of opportunity to follow your dreams, rather than feeling you have to slot yourself – as is the case at so many schools – into straightjacketed choices; this includes no blinkered (in our view) insistence on three separate sciences at GCSE. 'If you don't like science, why not spend your time doing something more interesting?' says head. Quite. No silly numbers of GCSEs, with most taking 10. Music and drama consistently popular, so is computer science. Sixth formers all start with four A levels (out of 22 options), with the option to drop one at the end of the first year, with popularity evenly split across social sciences, STEM and humanities. Around a third do EPQ.

All boys expected to take at least one language GCSE. French taught from year 7; Spanish and German from year 8; Italian and Mandarin are options in year 9. Gets top results in the country for German. Greek and/or Latin also available. Setting only in maths at GCSE. Teaching praised across all subjects, with lots of material tailor-made by school's own staff – that's proper teaching. Also one of the most thorough teacher recruitment processes we've come across (took the head a good few minutes to outline and includes detailed student input and several interviews). 'My son has been genuinely inspired right across the board,' remarked a parent, although another commented, 'Not every teacher is brilliant and we experienced some patchiness in the lower years, but on the whole – and certainly higher up the school – all departments are very strong with really varied teaching' (school insists a recent parent survey revealed very strong teaching throughout).

Learning support and SEN: At under five per cent, the number on the SEN register is small and all cases are mild. A full-time learning support specialist arms teachers accordingly, with one-to-one support also available by withdrawal or classes before and after school. Ditto for EAL. But SEN is no add-on here, with school claiming that 'all children need learning support so bespoke study skills are therefore offered to everyone', an ethos that parents told us works: 'They've gone above and beyond with us to chat through our son's challenges and to integrate him in such a way that he doesn't feel the odd one out.'

The arts and extracurricular: Our first taster of the spine-tingling standard of music was an informal pop-up lunchtime concert (of which there are several a term) in the Great Hall, a thoroughfare where students can (and many did) sit down to watch a solo violinist followed by a funk quartet, both mesmerising (there was also a baritone singer but we missed that). The full list of ensembles available would have taken up several pages in our notebooks – symphony orchestra, chamber orchestra, several chamber groups, umpteen bands of all kinds including jazz and swing and excellent choirs. 'I'm always amazed at the high level,' remarked a parent and although another felt 'the focus is still too classical', it's fair to say that rock has come a long way in the last few years, with every year group now having a rock band that performs in the regular rock concerts; moreover, alternative music at the school has a fine tradition (Bombay Bicycle Club were former UCS pupils). But it's not just a showcase school, insisted a student. 'If you're interested, there's a place for you. They use the music scholars to keep the standard high and then bring everyone else in.'

This ethos spills over into art, where everyone is encouraged to go to town with materials and techniques to experiment, create and express themselves through a wide range of genres. The dept has more the air of an art college and we saw many students lost in their own worlds producing the kind of eye-catching creations displayed throughout the school, many of them literally off the wall (yet which somehow fit through the hoops of the exam board – and if they don't, the school simply requests a senior moderator to return – 'usually gets the just result'). DT equally stimulating – we loved the woodwork including a fabulous curved chair with shelving in the seat.

At a pop-up lunchtime concert in the Great Hall, a thoroughfare where students can sit down to watch, a violinist was followed by a funk quartet, both mesmerising

There are lower, middle and upper school drama productions, along with whole-school one – Sweeney Todd a recent favourite, in which the acting, choreography, singing, stage crew and music were all acclaimed. They even borrowed the original barber's chair from the West End production. Students write and direct their own plays to a high standard and our guide got equally excited about lighting – 'you do it as part of your GCSE'. Many take LAMDA exams to high levels. Dance is expanding and two shows (one by year 12s and one by year 13s) are performed for a week at the Edinburgh Fringe Festival every year.

Over 150 clubs, virtually all student led. Beekeeping club, physics breakfast, pyrotechnics club and gender politics were all examples we'd gladly have signed up to. 'The students love promoting them in assembly – you might get a sixth former coming up to the podium to talk about a new politics society, followed by an 11-year-old pulling the microphone down to plug his Dr Who Society and the best thing is they're all supportive and respectful of each other,' reports head. Friday afternoons are given over to sixth form enrichment with pupils choosing courses which broaden their appreciation of a subject they are considering studying at university. Applicants for medicine follow a tailor-made support programme. Houses are called 'demes' (short for democracy) and matter to students, but not so much that things get tribal.

Sport: In some schools, sport is about the winning, in others it's the taking part. 'Call me greedy but I like both!' says head. 'Liberal doesn't mean you don't do your homework and the same goes for trying to beat your opponent at sport.' Parents told us sport is much more aspirational and there is far greater emphasis on performance than in the past, with regular Saturday fixtures for up to 18 teams (including C and D) and masses of extracurricular. The 1st rugby XV had a 72 per cent win rate in the season we visited and the girls don't miss out, with a 40 strong netball team and a decent track record in hockey and football. Individual triumphs too – they have county/academy ruby players, hockey players, cricketers and tennis players very high in the national rankings, as well as international swimmers. Excellent rowers, sailors and fencers come and go, such is the random nature of the student cohort. New dazzling £10m facilities nearby (15 min walk; 5 minutes in a minibus) much appreciated by students – the 28 acre playing field site in West Hampstead includes new double pavilion (UEFA are using the fields for their European Championships 2020 – gives you a sense of the standard). In sixth form, say students, you get carte blanche to do pretty much anything – yoga, gym, team sports, 'whatever floats your boat'.

Ethos and heritage: An unusual history that begins in 1830, a time when civil liberty was felt by growing numbers to be at risk due to excessive control of government, church and education. Various interested liberal intellectuals created London's University College to challenge what was felt to be a narrow and dogmatic view of education, and later added an associated school. There was no form of communal worship (unique at the time), no corporal punishment and no boarding. Its earliest incarnation was in Gower Street, hence alumni being known as Old Gowers. So, from the off it was regarded as 'liberal', and the tradition has been proudly maintained. What does that mean? 'No petty rules,' ventured one student, and that's at least part of it. 'A spirit of exploration, curiosity and free thinking,' reckoned a parent (remember those lessons we observed), again important. 'Focusing on the championing of the individual,' added another – 'you can be as quirky as you like here and it will be celebrated.' A sixth form girl agreed: 'At my last school you might be laughed at for going along to certain clubs, let alone starting one up, but here that's celebrated – that pretty much sums up this school to me.'

The environment lends itself to such ideals. The main buildings, dating back to 1907 and perching on the southern slopes of the Hampstead hill, look magnificent from both the front and back. And although a terrible fire in 1978 destroyed the huge Great Hall, the rebuilt version is almost overwhelming in its size and gravitas – wood panelling, stucco ceiling, huge organ and brass chandeliers. More recent buildings include the sports centre with large pool (where we saw year 10s have a jolly good splash around – 'usually, lessons are much more serious,' assured our guide) and gym (lots of pumping of iron going on) – also used by the local community. There's the Lund theatre, a fabulous blacked out space with huge backstage and masses of seating, and the spectacular new library – 'shame it closes at 5.30pm, though,' grumbled a student. The social sciences centre and creative learning centre provide further flexible areas. Could do with more outdoor space, but they still manage to squeeze in three Astro pitches/courts, a fabulous vegetable garden (also used by juniors), beehives (the honey is delicious), war memorial (taken very seriously) and a few nooks to sit and relax. Everyone eats in the panelled refectory with its dark long benches and walls – all very monastic. Food is excellent – 'something we all appreciate as it wasn't always the way,' said a student. Some of the original classrooms need a lick of paint (on the rolling refurb programme, says school). New sixth form centre opening 2021.

Girls arrived in the sixth form in 2008 (initially doing better than the boys, but now both on a par) and make up a third of the cohort, allocated equally across the houses. 'They're a critical mass, so not weird anomalies floating around the school,' says head, although girls we met said they'd prefer a 50/50 split. School likes that the girls tend to be feisty, vibrant and settle well – 'Because they self-select, they tend to be the confident characters,' we heard.

The school has always been regarded as 'liberal', a tradition that has been proudly maintained. 'You can be as quirky as you like here and it will be celebrated'

Uniform is smarter than it used to be and by and large the boys are a presentable lot. But the head is keen not to make it a battleground so while the odd boy had his shirt untucked or button undone, he 'won't start conversations on a negative footing – relationships are important here'. A school best suited to fired-up self-starters, students reckon (although school says they teach that to those that aren't). 'You have to be quite independent because they're not "on you" and they do encourage us to have a life outside academics.' 'Almost like a university setting where you're your own worst enemy if you don't do your bit,' thought a parent.

Notable Old Gowers include: Tristram Hunt, actors Hugh Dennis, David McCallum and Bertie Carvel; journalists Ian Katz, Jonathan Freedland and Paul Dacre; composer Thomas Adès; cancer specialist Professor Justin Stebbing; climber Chris Bonnington, four-minute miler Roger Bannister and members of Bombay Bicycle Club.

Pastoral care, inclusivity and discipline: Friendly, informal feel all round. Noticeably warm relationships between staff and students, and with each other. Parents too are welcome to email teachers. Light touch on discipline for most ('They don't sweat the small stuff and they're not hung up on rules,' said parent). But school won't hesitate to sanction for bigger misdemeanours, with up to 10 suspensions a year and one permanent exclusion a year (usually for inappropriate online behaviour outside school). Hard-ish line on drugs. Deal them or bring them into school and you're out; try them out of school and they take a more pastoral approach coupled with final warning and random drugs testing regime. 'We work hard to walk forward with students who seriously mess up, with a stick in one hand as the disciplinary measure but trying to be pastoral with the other. Why did this happen? Is your self-esteem low? Have you mixed with some dodgy guys round the corner?' The code of conduct is merely a few lines and about what you can do rather than what you can't. Very little bullying – tends to be lack of understanding, as part of immaturity, rather than anything deliberate.

Pupils and parents: Despite Hampstead itself outpricing most mere mortals as an area in which to lay your hat, it's extremely well connected by transport links. Upshot is that while not many families come from south of the river, there is otherwise a broad spread from a 180-degree swathe with most student journey times comfortably under an hour. Parents are achievers, ambitious, cultured, moneyed – for the most part – and involved. 'Very friendly, especially to me as a newcomer,' said one. Students are as diverse as the capital itself. We found them articulate and considerate, though some not quite as comfortable in their own skin as we'd have anticipated.

Money matters: Rare is the year in which fewer than fifty-something students are on 100 per cent bursaries (54 when we visited), one of the most generous provisions in the country. In total, £1.2m a year goes on students who would not otherwise be able to afford UCS, most of which comes from letting of school facilities to the community, charitable work and donations. No academic scholarships but music schols worth up to 25 per cent.

The last word: This inclusive, broad-minded school is one of the leaders of the pack in the north London bubble. Its distinctive approach encourages boys (and girls in sixth form) to reach their potential by steering them on a personal journey to discover their skills, passions and abilities both in and outside the classroom. An enriched education, with all the trimmings.

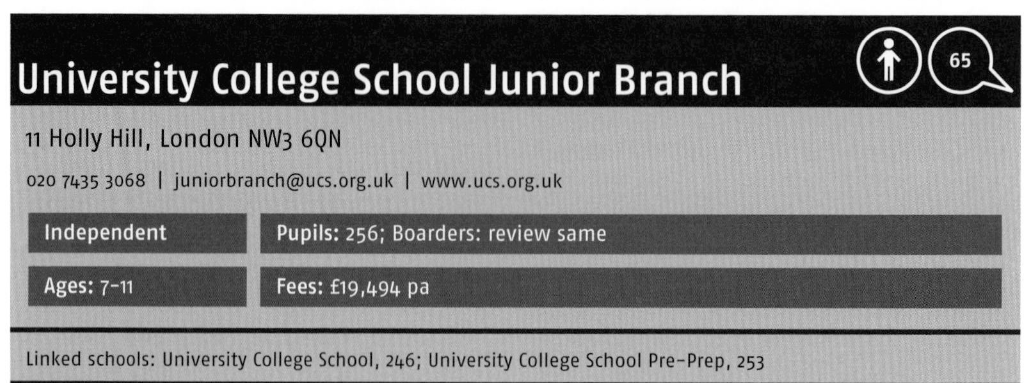

University College School Junior Branch

65

11 Holly Hill, London NW3 6QN

020 7435 3068 | juniorbranch@ucs.org.uk | www.ucs.org.uk

Independent | **Pupils:** 256; Boarders: review same

Ages: 7–11 | **Fees:** £19,494 pa

Linked schools: University College School, 246; University College School Pre-Prep, 253

Headmaster of Junior: Since 2014, Lewis Hayward MA Oxon MA ed management (OU) PCGE, a classicist (40s). An interesting former life – he began his teaching life in EFL in Nairobi and Saudi. Thence to the relative quiet of Holmewood House and Highfield preps' classics depts until he left for Highgate School in 2009, where he became deputy principal.

Plan A was to become an author; chose teaching because he thought there would be enough spare time for the writing. Surprised himself by taking to the world of education like a duck to water, although happily does 'manage a bit of writing too' – though we're not sure when given that he's up at 4.50am every day, running nine miles as part of his commute from south London before arriving at school by 6.30am to avoid the crowds and making a head start on the day. Energetic and dedicated, he doesn't miss a trick (knows all pupils' names and many of the parents' too) and has plenty of backbone ('he won't be pushed by the pushy parents,' one mother told us). 'Stretching without cramming' is his academic credo – one that parents appreciate. 'Gets involved,' we heard from many – 'not just there for the glory moments, but attends every meeting and every play and we were all touched that he ran with the boys on a charity run for Great Ormond Street,' said one. Still keeps a hand in teaching, mainly English and PSHE. 'Universally popular,' we heard, although 'can be quite serious – not sure if he's ex-army.' Children concur – 'he's really fun but you don't cross the line'. One parent was particularly touched by his attitude on 7+ test day: 'It was a freezing cold January day, yet he stood there and shook the hands of each and every family – believe me that doesn't happen in other schools round here.'

A keen sportsman and environmentalist, he has two children – a grown-up daughter who is a highly acclaimed ballet dancer and actress (most recently, the lead in Cats the movie) and a teenage autistic son.

Entrance: At 7+, 60 boys are selected from the 200-odd applicants to join those who transfer from the pre-prep. Two-part assessment comprises a series of concentration and listening exercises and a formal exam including comprehension, maths and NVR. Newbies join from other local preps eg Hampstead Hill, Golders Hill, Mulberry House. School is more sibling friendly than most and makes a concerted effort to keep families together but all siblings must go through the same process as other applicants.

Exit: Almost all to UCS senior school, except (almost unheard of) if a child isn't cutting it – in which case, parents can expect conversations around year 4, with head helping to them into gentler, more appropriate, schools elsewhere.

Our view: Located in the heart of gorgeous Hampstead village, the purpose-built main house – which dates back to 1928 – is functional rather than beautiful, but works well. Supplemented by a small science block and smaller arts block, the school covers pretty much all indoor needs on site. Outside there's a terrace with table football, table tennis tables and outdoor chess, plus the 'cage' for ballgames although there are plans afoot to re-jig it and get rid of staff parking ('there should be no need for any cars,' says head) to create a bigger more innovative area including adventure play space. When we arrived, at school drop off time, we were met with a sea of red and black striped blazers making a beeline for the entrance – we were left in no doubt as to these boys' eagerness to start their day.

'It was a freezing cold January day, yet the head stood there and shook the hands of each and every family – believe me that doesn't happen in other schools round here'

Academic excellence is a given, and the children here are sponges who mop up everything intellectual, cultural, esoteric, thrown at them. Staff (described as 'cool', 'fun' and 'with great energy') tend to stay for the long haul – even the so-called newbies have been here four or five years. Parents are impressed – 'their CVs are all Oxbridge, Exeter, Bristol and so on and a really vibrant mix of characters,' said one. 'Of course, lessons can't be entirely individualised in a school but you really do feel they are,' remarked another. Curriculum recently tweaked to fit more in, and the school day is now longer with lessons from 8.30am to 3.30pm (many stay later for clubs and school is looking into introducing wrap-around care). But a pressure cooker this is not. 'It's a very academic school, but once you're in it doesn't feel like that – the teaching is much quirkier than at other schools, with a sense of fun always providing the backdrop,' felt one parent. Homework is kept to a minimum and much of the work is project based – if they're learning about diseases in science, for example, it will probably be woven into history and quite possibly English.

We hung around an English lesson where boys were learning about car pollution through creative writing (you'd never get in a car again if you'd heard the reading we did); in ICT they were editing a 1960s style film they'd made. No hanging back or bashfulness in sight. Reading underpins everything, with a reading scheme that's punctuated by quizzes to track progress. Reading mums are usually to be found somewhere or other – crammed in like sardines with their young charges in the upstairs corridor when we visited. Good-sized labs in the science block (more sizzles than bangs, report pupils) – also home to a corn snake, tarantula, African bullfrog and some startling tropical fish (our guide informed us, rather alarmingly, that 'unfortunately our scorpion died because the family who had it over the holidays forgot to feed it').

Average class size 22. All start with French, replaced by Spanish in years 5 and 6. No setting but some 'extension within lessons' (sitting at different booster tables) for maths and English in the older years. 'Not a school with lots of testing, but they have all sorts of algorithms to predict and measure abilities and put in the relevant targets,' said one parent, although another felt 'feedback could be improved, including at the parents' evening – they tell you where your child is academically but I'd love to know more about the areas of improvement and the resources parents could use.' Another felt there could be more explanation in the homework diary 'as a lot gets lost in translation'.

There are lots of bi- and trilingual boys here and the few who need EAL help are supported by the SENCo, as are the five or so per cent with mild learning difficulties – all closely monitored. The specialist trained TA, who is on hand to help in or out of lessons, is qualified in emotional intelligence and there are also booster clubs.

For a cramped London prep, the extracurricular offering is astonishing. Before school, at lunchtimes and after school there are clubs galore, with boys encouraged to set up their own ('although some ideas are really futile,' said one). Split into three categories, they are academic (eg G&T – open to all – in maths, English, coding etc, plus debating, German, Mandarin etc), sports based (head does a running club over Hampstead Heath and there's boxing, fitness, table tennis, fencing, football to name a few) and hobby related (we heard about art, drama, Viking chess, birdwatching and even 'randoms', 'where we choose what we'll do on the day – last time it was football predictions,' explained a boy).

Our guide informed us, rather alarmingly, that 'unfortunately our scorpion died because the family who had it over the holidays forgot to feed it'

Small art block, located across the playground somehow manages to accommodate both a studio and DT room, with classes split between the two so they never feel overcrowded. We'd have loved to join the boys making clay pictures based on the work of Hundertwasser, while the vivid corridor displays in the main school reveal the breadth of genres studied in drawing and painting. Downstairs we saw boys learning how to use an automatic drill (there's also a laser cutter, 3D printer etc) to assist them in creating 1920s wooden racing cars. 'Make the wheels really smooth,' recommended our tour guides to their younger peers – 'there's a big race of all the cars at the end and if you beat the teacher, which nobody ever has, you get a prize.' Super kitchen, where year 6 boys cook a three course meal for staff and parents and they even learn how to make sushi (well, this is Hampstead).

We saw boys learning how to use an automatic drill to assist them in creating 1920s wooden racing cars. 'There's a big race of all the cars and if you beat the teacher, which nobody ever has, you get a prize'

Longstanding and much praised drama teacher ensures every boy performs, rather than just a few auditioning. In years 3 and 4, the focus is on delivery and speech; by years 5 and 6, boys engage in more ambitious projects, including black box theatre – often Shakespeare ('When my son came home with the Julius Caesar script, I thought, "Really? But you're 9!" but actually he loved it,' said a parent). Plays are taken seriously here, often planned a year in advance and with real attention to detail – a West End theatre asked to pinch their home-made trench from a year 6 War Horse production. 'Drama here has really brought my quiet child out of himself,' reported a parent.

All the boys we met scrape or blow something; those that don't are apparently a tiny minority. From very young, they are encouraged to join one of the many ensembles, orchestra or big band and all boys perform in at least one group or other at the autumn concert in the senior school. Compliments also abound for the two oversubscribed choirs: 'It's unusual to have boys fighting to get into the choirs – it's really motivational,' thought a parent. 'I think it helps that the music is modern – pop songs more than dusty old hymn books.'

Sport onsite is limited to dance, football, boxing fitness, karate, fencing and table tennis. But school uses facilities including swimming pool and tennis courts at the big brother school a five minute walk down the hill, plus recently redeveloped 27 acres of nearby fields. In autumn term, it's rugby or hockey on curriculum, in spring it's football or hockey and for the summer term boys do cricket, athletics or gymnastics (and a handful even do golf). Pupils grateful for the choice, with one telling us, 'If you don't want to be thrown around in the mud, nobody minds – you just do another sport instead.' For years 3 and 4, it's one afternoon a week, while the upper years get two. Does well in fixtures – remained unbeaten in rugby the season we visited. Individual successes too – some boys play academy rugby and football and school boasts a regional fencing champion. 'But it's not a sporting school as such – I wouldn't choose it for the sport,' said a parent.

Kindness and good manners are rewarded. 'When was the last time you went out of your way to do something for someone else?' is the kind of question that's embedded into the culture, rather than mere tokenism. Discipline is more traditional, and less light touch, than in the senior school but nothing draconian and self-discipline is prioritised over rules. Pupils told us they like the small size of the school – 'means you know every face'. 'Not particularly strict on uniform,' said pupils, and we liked seeing a few wacky-ish haircuts.

Alumni include Sir Roger Bannister, Julian Lloyd Webber, Hugh Dennis, Ian Katz.

Most families live within two miles, three tops – prizes (literally) for those who use public transport and better still, walk (40 per cent car-use reduction in 18 months as a result). Parents, mainly well-heeled but increasingly dual income, are a close-knit bunch and involved – that includes dads who are invited on a big football trip with their sons to Spain. Not a school for helicopter parents, reckoned one – 'You absolutely don't do your kids' homework and I've never packed my son's sports bag, for instance.'

The last word: Less single-minded than some of its more pressurised neighbours, this school turns bright children into independent thinkers and doers. They work hard and play hard but feel free to be themselves. A sound preparation for the more liberal senior school.

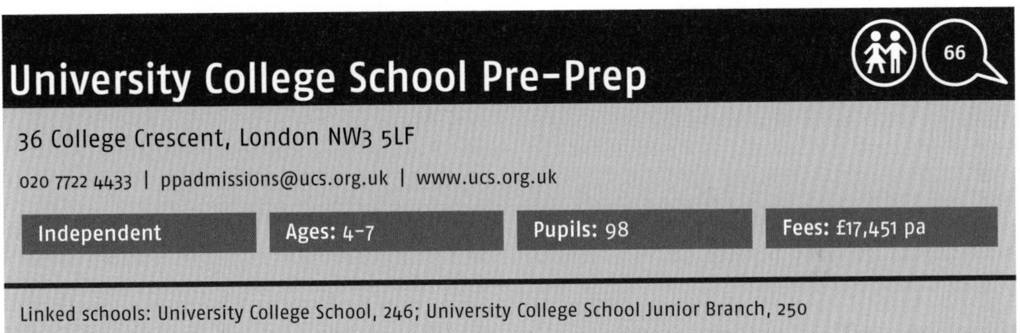

University College School Pre-Prep

36 College Crescent, London NW3 5LF

020 7722 4433 | ppadmissions@ucs.org.uk | www.ucs.org.uk

Independent | Ages: 4-7 | Pupils: 98 | Fees: £17,451 pa

Linked schools: University College School, 246; University College School Junior Branch, 250

Headmistress: Since 2015, Zoe Dunn BEd PhD NPHQ (early 40s), an Eng lit specialist with an impressive pedigree, fitting for this neck of the woods. Schooled at a Kent grammar, she did her degree at Homerton, Cambridge and continued to teach reception children throughout her postgrad, admitting with a chuckle that 'sometimes I found the 5-year-olds more mature than the undergraduates.' After five years at The Hall, down the road, she went to the Royal School – up the hill, and now taken over by North Bridge House Senior – first as deputy head and latterly as head of its junior school. After a sabbatical travelling across Alaska, Sweden and some of the States to study how they approach social and emotional learning in schools, she founded and then led a local faith free school – the Rimon Jewish Free Primary School – down the far side of the hill for four terms before taking maternity leave. Deliberated giving it all up for motherhood, but it turns out you can't tear her away from school leadership and one imagines there was no way she was going to let this post pass her by.

Parents are besotted and it's not hard to see why. Super-bright and warm-hearted, she sparkles and charms and has the enviable combo of the energy of a politician coupled with the temperament of a psychotherapist. 'She was the reason we chose the school,' gushed parent after parent, who particularly appreciate her 'genuineness and kindness', 'the fact that she's a parent herself – it means she gets it from both sides', and that 'what she doesn't know about child development isn't worth knowing'. Something of a mentor too, it seems, with one parent enthusing how she 'empowers us to look at ourselves and what we project to our children – she has taught me such a lot.' In the words of one happy customer, 'a wonder woman'.

Big on STEAM (more of which later), outdoor learning, sustainability and cross-curricular learning, she is also keen to enhance emotional resilience among her charges, plus (unusually and we like this) she has a special interest in speech and language, having recently tasked one enthusiastic staff member to do a research project on oracy with the Institute of Education. Definitely not from the let's-get-rid-of-prizes-at-sports-day brigade, she is adamant that boys thrive on collaborative competition and has introduced four houses, with boys now competing over everything from pancake flipping to daffodil growing – 'You can't beat a bit of shared success and shared disappointment for learning how to thrive in life,' she says.

Definitely not from the let's-get-rid-of-prizes-at-sports-day brigade, the head is adamant that boys thrive on collaborative competition and has introduced four houses

Lives locally with her criminal barrister husband whom she met at uni and their young son, though it is her kitten that seeks the most attention. A lover of reading, she is a sucker for the classics (is currently reading North and South) and any educational musings she can get her mitts on. With friends all over the world, she takes advantages of summer holidays to visit as many of them as she can.

Entrance: Boys only for 4+ entry. Registration any time from birth, with over 300 applying for 32 places. Boys in the same birth month are observed for an hour playing, chatting, listening to stories etc and those that pass muster are invited back for another hour's play. School looks for 'engaged, curious, resourceful boys who are able to relate to teachers' and is at pains to point out that all birth months are represented in every class. Siblings get no preference, going through the same entry process as anyone else, but as with the junior school they aim to keep them together. Occasional 5+ and 6+ places.

Exit: Virtually all to UCS Junior Branch, as the name-change to UCS Pre-Prep suggests. But school is at pains to point out that transfer is not automatic and UCS Pre-Prep boys sit 7+ entry assessments in line with all external candidates. As much notice as possible is given where it looks like a boy won't make it through.

Our view: Tucked away down a surprisingly quiet side street off the thunderous Finchley Road and in the shadow of the imposing brick and glass grandeur that is South Hampstead High School, UCS Pre-Prep is something of a hidden gem. Big and flashy it most certainly isn't but what it lacks in architectural splendour, it gains in warmth and friendliness and – evidenced by the fact that it's almost unheard of for these bright young sparks not to make it into the junior school – academic robustness. Parents (many of whom start off torn between The Hall and here) tell us they chose it because 'it has such soul', 'every boy is treated as an individual' and (surely the jewel in the crown) it offers a 4-18 trajectory through one of London's best schools.

With morning (and after-school) clubs getting such high acclaim from (especially grateful working) parents, we decided to join the furore at 8am where we were met – as are the boys – by Dr Dunn ready with a big smile and firm handshake. We hope she has a warm coat ready for colder mornings as she continues to welcome in these tinies, dressed in their smart maroon ties and grey pullovers (or tracksuits on PE days), until 8.40am when lessons start. We noticed that for every boy that leapt eagerly down the stairs into the main reception area that doubles up as a cosy library, another was accompanied by Mum or Dad to help them with their coat and grab a reassuring kiss goodbye. Parents need not concern themselves with being missed for long, however – in choir club, boys were far too busy singing and/or swaying to Abba, while in Lego club they were scrambling over plastic pieces to create and recreate. Shrieks of delight could be heard from construction club where boys watched their paper helicopters circling dramatically to the ground; for more lively endeavours boys pick the popular playball.

Once a co-ed pre-prep and nursery, the school (purpose built in the late 1800s, with a rather less attractive but arguably more functional 1960s add-on) has now phased out both girls and 3 year-olds. Downstairs, the library – with its thoughtfully displayed books and beanbags – leads to two classrooms each for reception and ditto for year 1, along with an arts and science space in the previous nursery's domain. Upstairs (with loos en route) is home to two year 2 classrooms, an IT room/extra library and room for more physical activities (it would be disingenuous to call it a hall, though it's just about big enough for an elbows-tucked-in assembly). Outside space is very limited but enthusiastically used, especially the playtower and tunnel slide over the safe surface flooring, and there's been some imaginative thinking around an outdoor area in the middle of the school – though postage stamp in size, it's now a vibrant green eco-garden. The boys make

'Bella Mama! Bella Mama!' sang the head of music and drama beautifully as we entered her class and by the time we left, she'd got half the boys singing in one pitch and the other overlapping in another – wowsers to that, we say

good use of the junior and senior facilities too, especially for theatre and sport and there's forest school and an allotment and beehive – Dr Dunn told us they'd been eating home-grown courgettes for 16 weeks; we couldn't work out whether she was delighted or long suffering.

Class names all follow the bird theme (school was previously called the Phoenix), eg Kingfisher, Barn Owl, Robin etc and parents report a 'real family feel throughout' – 'teachers know your siblings' names, your pets, interests, the lot'. Staff (including three males when we visited) too describe themselves like kin – one told us she'd worked there through five heads and considered 'the other staff like my children and the boys like my grandchildren'. No shortage of specialist teachers, including for music, drama, PE (lots), French, food tech and science and all classes (most with 16 boys, but 18 max) have both a teacher and TA. We were impressed with how naturally they got down to the boys' level, as well their ability to ensure nobody slipped through the net – in one maths lesson we we observed that the teacher wouldn't get going on an assigned task until she was absolutely sure every boy understood (though we wondered if she started to regret it as one daydreamer held things up). A joy to see the boys learning through touching, feeling, moving about and trying out – boxes of colourful plastic shapes for maths, boys soaring about like aeroplanes following the theme of a story about Amy Johnson they'd just heard, one boy leading the class with his whiteboard pen with help from classmates when he got it wrong etc. Everyone dresses up for eg Ancient Greek day and they build trenches in the classroom as part of a World War One day ('My son hasn't stopped begging me for books about WWI ever since,' said one parent). As for STEAM activities, we reckon this school would give the Science Museum a run for its money – we watched one class of boys making a phantom projector, designing a maze for an electronic ball and playing a range of interactive engineering games. Overall, a fun packed, fast paced day that parents say 'never feels pressured' and with homework levels that are 'kept sensible'.

Learning support given in small groups or one-to-one, though numbers are small for SEN at around 10 per cent and similar for those who need support for EAL (20 per cent speak another language at home, but for half their English isn't affected). School unusually mindful of the prevalence of colour blindness in boys, seeking to address it through eg lack of colour coded questions.

'Bella Mama! Bella Mama!' sang the head of music and drama beautifully as we entered her class and by the time we left, she'd got half the boys singing in one pitch and the other overlapping in another – wowsers to that, we say. Stockpile the paracetamol, though, as all boys learn the recorder from year 2; many others learn either the violin or piano via peripatetic teachers. Plays are written in house (with – get this – the music written especially) and performed twice a year in the senior school auditorium. Wigs and dressing up all part of the fun. 'The kids skip their way there, singing all the way,' reported one parent, while another told us, 'Every child gets a part and a line – absolutely no bored wriggling at the back.'

Art is a properly taught subject, with everything from ancient Greek theatre masks to colourful dog drawings adorning the walls and the whole place was practically taken over with an array of fabulous sustainable sky scrapers when we visited, following a visit from an eco-minded architect (but was the one made out of plastic straws meant to be ironic, we wonder).

Senior school facilities used for sport and team games including football, rugby, cricket and hockey to gymnastics, athletics and even cosmic yoga. Swimming taken seriously too, with every boy leaving the pre-prep able to swim a length of the pool.

There was a time when it would have been a pretty safe bet to ask another boy's father whether he worked in finance or law, but things are getting more diverse these days, with parents also from eg the creative industries and the professions – and more mums work too. Mainly from the NWs, some Ns and the odd W postcode although families occasionally stretch as far as Highgate and Edgware. Sixteen home languages spoken at the time of our visit and all cultures celebrated. Parents told us of 'the odd pushy parent', but mainly there seems to be huge trust in the school – 'anyone with any sense realises Dr Dunn knows exactly what she's doing,' reported one.

The two big hiccups in otherwise universal parental acclaim for the school are the Great Hot Lunch Controversy ('such a shame to have to make a packed lunch every day') and the limited space ('it almost put me off'), although most eventually come round on both points – realising that (a) a dining hall would come at the cost of one of the existing spaces and that (b), as one put it, 'actually the boys swan around thinking they are big fish in a small pool and the confidence and happiness that come with that is lovely'.

The last word: A small school with a big heart that gets pupils ready for the next stage of their UCS journey and which is going from strength to strength under dynamic leadership.

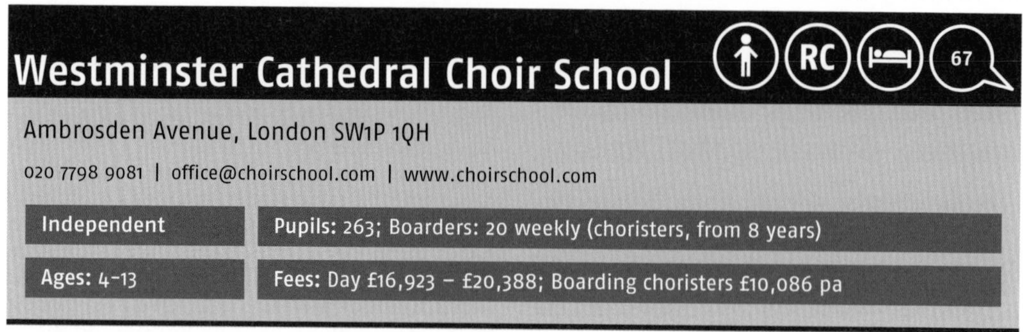

Westminster Cathedral Choir School

RC 67

Ambrosden Avenue, London SW1P 1QH

020 7798 9081 | office@choirschool.com | www.choirschool.com

Independent	**Pupils:** 263; Boarders: 20 weekly (choristers, from 8 years)
Ages: 4-13	**Fees:** Day £16,923 – £20,388; Boarding choristers £10,086 pa

Headmaster: Since 2007, Neil McLaughlan (40s). For a man with a truly Catholic background (large C), a Catholic boarding school and posts in all the obvious schools, including Stonyhurst, Worth and Downside (only Ampleforth missing), he is engagingly undoctrinaire and also extremely good company. On our last visit he told us that he hopes to be here 'for the duration' and there's no change here, in fact it would be hard to imagine the school without him, he does literally appear to be part of the fabric. Parents are equally convinced: 'he picks up on everything'; 'totally approachable'; 'understands my son'; in fact it's lucky that he loves living in London and is definitely not heading out the door any time soon. Prodded over any further ambitions for his hugely successful school, he admitted that only a lack of cash was stopping his dream of a senior branch of WCCS turning into a reality and we hope that help from above may solve this problem for him.

Entrance: Reception class of 30 boys joins via an assessment, described as 'very relaxed' by a parent, in groups for an hour to find out how they interact and respond. Entry at 7+ (16 places) and 8+ (12 places) is heavily oversubscribed with three to five boys trying for each place. Tests in maths, comprehension and composition, punctuation and spelling in the January before September entry.

Satisfying the Master of Music's accurate ear is only the first step for choristers who also have to make the same academic grades as the day boys.

Exit: Today's parents (almost all major players in the financial and legal world) set their sights on the internationally famous English public schools, with Eton firmly at the head of the boarding wish list and St Paul's, Westminster, Dulwich and City of London the main choices in London. All going to plan: 2020 saw seven boys going to Eton, four to Dulwich, three to St Paul's and two to Winchester. The choristers also tend to head in the same directions, nearly always with music scholarships.

Our view: WCCS is as close to being a school inside a church as is physically possible: only a Westminster version of the Bridge of Sighs (thankfully, a happier outcome for its occupants) separates the school building from the cathedral's interior. In contrast to the solemnity of the surroundings, there is a wondrous space outside with an Astro pitch and running tracks as well as room for all the off-letting of steam.

Music is part of life here for everyone, not just for the choristers: if you can hold a tune you can sing in non-chorister choirs

Luckily, they found a building for the pre-prep just across the playground. Deeply suitable, having been home to Franciscans amongst its various incarnations, it is an architecturally surprising building, reminiscent of a galleon, with a rather sad St Francis serving as an off-centre figurehead. This unusual, one-room-deep layout has been sensitively turned into a great teaching space, with light classrooms, a playground and a tempting covered porch for rainy days. The teaching is 'pacy' even at this level and the competition (using numbering fans) was fierce to be number one fan of tables. Music is already part of school life and one tiny violinist was spotted concentrating hard on his individual lesson.

The prep itself is unflamboyant inside (in contrast to the stripy brick exterior), the colour provided almost entirely by the cherry red of the boys' blazers and the occasional sparkly shoes of a female teacher. The corridors are lined with red and blue lockers, more than usual due to the number of instruments, and music stands replace works of art on the walls. Darth Vader appears, in poster form, offering an unlikely exhortation to earn points towards stars, described by our extremely articulate guide as 'an unlikely paradox'. These stars are serious stuff: they don't just stop at gold as in most other schools but also have an exalted platinum and diamond level – 'everyone gets gold but the others are quite hard'.

The curriculum, 'begged, scraped and borrowed from every possible source', according to the head, is 'not fogeyish in any way' despite its structured feel. There is obviously an extremely successful attempt to marry the 'grammar – logic – rhetoric' classical approach to a more modern, integrated way of learning. This is proper joined-up teaching and the combination of art/RE teacher who starts each RE lesson with a religious painting is typical of their modus operandi. Very little streaming is necessary because, as they explain, there is a narrow range of ability here, but there is a SENCo available to offer one-to-one or group sessions to anyone struggling, and also the odd boy with educational needs. However, it is made very clear that it is essential for everyone to be able to handle the speed of the teaching.

The art teacher explains that her life is made far easier by the fact that she has a large number of the most exciting galleries in the world on her doorstep, which eases the task of embedding art into the school's curriculum, and there is a kiln and a printing press to extend her creative options. Naturally, music is part of life here but not just for the choristers: one day boy told us that if you can hold a tune you can sing in non-chorister choirs and even perform outside the school. The choristers all play the piano and one other instrument, but the majority of boys also have individual music lessons and there are several orchestras of differing abilities (if all rather better than average).

The number of names signed up for football on the tidy noticeboard says it all and they have been winners of the Thomas's five-a-side tournament at both U10 and U13, but the size of the school makes it less sporty than some of its competitors (one boy wrinkled his nose when questioned on their cricketing prowess) – still, two sports scholarships recently (one to Winchester) is pretty impressive. Lots of alternatives to football on the clubs list with the boys responsible for suggesting magic, mad science and even British military fitness, all of which have takers.

WCCS is as close to being a school inside a church as is physically possible: only a Westminster version of the Bridge of Sighs (thankfully, a happier outcome for its occupants) separates the school building from the cathedral's interior

WCCS families have changed over recent years and there is now a much higher percentage of Catholics amongst the day boys (up from 50 per cent to over 80) but there are Anglicans and several non-Christian families. We felt convinced by both parents and head that the spiritual element was an addition rather than a handicap and was not forced down the boys' throats: instead they got a buzz out of their connection to the cathedral and its faith.

Boarding: The top two floors are home to the chorister boarders and it's a pretty good sanctuary for such incredibly hard-working boys, who have to combine their full-on musical life (singing in the cathedral on a daily basis and honing their skills) with a packed academic timetable. The head says that their welfare is his 'biggest single headache' and that sometimes he has to tell them to take time out 'when they are bushed'. Anyway, the dorms, whilst not exciting and amazingly tidy, have a cosy feel and apparently the matrons and cleaning staff make sure that 'Teddy is on the right bed'. A big common room is equipped with pool and football tables and a chorister assured us that there was plenty to do at weekends – the most popular pastime being 'ripstiking' (a form of skateboarding) which looked extremely difficult when demonstrated and that was minus cassock… However, full boarding has given way to weekly, with boys returning home from Friday evenings to 9am on Sundays, which will preclude families who live further afield.

The last word: Last time we wrote a review, we concluded by saying 'this is just about as near perfect as it gets' and we would endorse that sentiment today with only one caveat; this is now a school for seriously bright boys and it would be wrong for any parent to overestimate their son's academic ability when considering putting him up for the entrance exam.

Westminster School

17 Dean's Yard, London SW1P 3PB

020 7963 1003 | registrar@westminster.org.uk | www.westminster.org.uk

Independent	Pupils: 760: 137 girls/623 boys; sixth form: 402; Boarders: 49 full, 131 weekly
Ages: 13–18	Fees: Day: £28,809 pa; Boarding: £41,607 pa

Linked school: Westminster Under School, 261

Head Master: Since September 2020, Dr Gary Savage, formerly headmaster of Alleyn's School. Previously head of history and master-in-college at Eton and before that under master at Westminster. Grew up in Suffolk and read history at Cambridge, taking a double first before doing a PhD on the political culture and foreign policy of later 18th-century France. Married to Natalie and enjoys history, the arts, studying German, walking his two Jack Russell terriers and following the fortunes of Ipswich Town FC.

Entrance: Register by the end of year 5 for 13+ entry (boys at state primary and other schools that finish at 11 may apply to Westminster Under School). Computer pre-tests in English, maths and reasoning in year 6; high performers who also have a good report from current school called for interview, which includes short maths and English tests. Those with conditional places sit either the Challenge scholarship exam or CE (pass mark 70 per cent) in year 8. Entry from 2021 onwards will not depend on passing the CE but on 'continued good conduct and academic progress at their existing prep school, including an unreserved reference of support from their school in year 8'.

For 16+ places, register between summer and October of the year before entry. Applicants – boys and girls – take exams in their four most likely A level subjects, and are interviewed.

Exit: Excellent and detailed preparation not only for Oxbridge but also for US colleges, with school trips to visit east coast universities. 'The school has been very supportive from an early age,' said a student, 'keeping us up to date with when to take subject tests and when to visit colleges.' Good preparation too for medicine, which is amongst the most popular degree subjects alongside liberal arts.

Up to half of sixth formers do, indeed, go to Oxbridge (60 in 2020). Also in 2020, 16 medics. Many overseas universities including Harvard, Yale, Stanford and Princeton; most of the rest to London universities, Edinburgh, Durham or Bristol.

Latest results: School is not releasing 2020 results. In 2019 (the last year when exams took place), 98 per cent 9-7 at GCSE; 83 per cent A*/A at A level/Pre-U (93 per cent A*-B).

Teaching and learning: With these very bright pupils, 'you can teach for the love of the subject and focus on the exam when need be,' says head. 'It's a breath of fresh air,' said a parent. 'Intellectual risk taking is encouraged. They're never not challenged.' Many of the teachers are experts in their fields, encouraged to follow their interests. 'I cannot believe there is a more stimulating place to teach in the country,' said a teacher. 'It is so much more liberal than at my previous school,' said a sixth form student. 'It's not constrained by the syllabus – it's learning for the sake of learning. It really allows you to get a proper understanding outside the exam baselines.' Pupils tend to internalise that love of learning. 'They read and they question and they challenge,' says the head. 'In my first lesson one asked me, "Where is the evidence?" I'd never been asked that before.'

Everyone encouraged to include a practical subject like art, electronics, drama or music at GCSE. Huge range of languages includes Dutch, Arabic and Portuguese. Several parents commented that inspirational teachers had sparked their sons' interest in subjects they had previously hated. 'He'd always been a bit of a maths boy but now he is flying at English and languages too. They've understood how to teach in a way that suits him.'

Top exam results are, nonetheless, part of the package. Thinking skills course – designed as a more challenging alternative to critical thinking A level – introduces sixth formers to the elements of informal logic, and helps prepare for university entrance skills tests such as the Oxbridge Thinking Skills Assessment.

Links with local state schools Grey Coat Hospital and Harris Westminster Sixth Form – the latter sponsored by Westminster School – see sixth formers from these schools joining in German, Latin, art history and drama lessons. 'They've done a really good job at integrating us,' said a Westminster sixth former. 'I'm as good friends with students from outside as anyone else in the class.' Joint senior management meetings with Harris Westminster staff: 'We are going to learn from each other.'

Learning support and SEN: High academic ability is obviously a prerequisite, but study skills coordinator works with all those who need support for mild dyslexia, dyspraxia or Asperger's or just lack of organisation, helping them with the skills needed to cope with learning at different levels as they move up the school.

The arts and extracurricular: An almost overwhelming range of extracurricular opportunities. Societies often stem from the particular passions of both staff and students, ranging from feminist to secular to geography. English society may see Simon Russell Beale answering questions on playing King Lear at the National, whilst Piyush Goyal, national treasurer of the Indian Bharatiya Janata Party (BJP) party, tells the political society about Indian public affairs. 'I set up a society and had an ambassador from Panama come to talk,' said one student. 'Staff are really supportive when you want to set up new things.' Huge range of journalists and politicians, scientists and thinkers drop in to give talks; poet in residence inspires creativity. Trips everywhere: climbing in Cataluña, Beijing exchange, art history in Venice. Years 9-11 go off for a week's climbing, sailing, hill walking or camping at home or abroad.

'They read and they question and they challenge,' says the head. 'In my first lesson one asked me, "Where is the evidence?" I'd never been asked that before'

'Phenomenal' music, with professional standard orchestral concerts at St John's Smith Square and the Barbican, carol service in Westminster Abbey, masterclasses, eminent musicians from Nicola Benedetti to Ian Bostridge giving evening concerts. One parent felt that 'unless you are excellent you won't get a look in', whilst staff point out there are house concerts and ensembles for the less stratospherically talented. 'We like to think there is room for everyone.' Drama equally high performing – Guys and Dolls a recent sell-out but much cerebral fare too, plus house drama and GCSE/A level pieces – and again huge talent required to bag a role in the large-scale school productions.

Art, too, 'wonderful', with much emphasis on traditional drawing and painting skills, life classes, film making facilities and a darkroom. Plus, of course, easy access to all of London's galleries and museums. 'My son had no artistic ambition when he arrived, but is now doing art A level. They have totally inspired him,' said one parent, whilst another commented: 'They let these academic boys be so creative – they feel free to explore.'

Volunteering taking on increasing importance with head's passion for outreach, with nearly all Westminsters teaching music or setting up debating societies in local primary schools, working on Hampstead Heath or learning sign language to communicate with deaf children. 'People are really involved and really making a difference,' said a student. 'Staff have the time, passion and faith in us to let us get on with things.' Phab week – where year 12 Westminster students host young people with physical and/or mental challenges, taking part in creative activities and seeing London together – is a 'life-changing experience'.

Old Westminsters span the centuries and the professions: the massive list ranges from Ben Jonson, John Dryden, Robert Hooke, Lord Lucan, Kim Philby, AA Milne, John Gielgud, Tony Benn, Corin Redgrave, Helena Bonham-Carter and Imogen Stubbs to Dido and Mika.

Sport: Sports – known as 'Station' – take place on Tuesday and Thursday afternoons, mostly on the enviably large playing fields in nearby St Vincent Square plus adjacent sports centre (in a previous life one of the Royal Horticultural Halls). In Westminster liberal fashion, no particular sport is compulsory, with a huge range of choices from sailing to judo to golf to girls' football. 'You wouldn't send a very sporty boy to Westminster,' thought a parent, who was grateful that her keen but not-particularly-athletic son had been in teams which he would have been unlikely to make at a more overtly sporty school. However, particularly successful at rowing (and was basking in the glow of recent success at National Schools' Regatta when we visited), fields nine football teams with 'at least respectable' results, and 'we do very well at niche sports such as rock climbing and fencing'. Often dominates the London School Cross-Country Championships and the

Westminster Secondary Schools Swimming Gala, with pupils representing Westminster in the London Youth Games, and is successful at fives and real tennis. 'You are encouraged to try lots of things and find something you are passionate about,' said a student.

Boarding: The last Anglican monastery in London now houses Purcell's, a girls' boarding and boys' day house with attached chapel. Five other boarding houses, all in or near Little Dean's Yard and all of which include some day pupils. Many rooms surprisingly spacious; younger boys in College, the scholars' house, in dorms of up to eight, whilst upper years have their own rooms and those in between may share with one other. 'Because these are all old buildings, the room arrangements can be random, and sometimes we have to improvise.' All boarders are cared for in relaxed fashion by the housemaster (male or female), some with own family; resident tutor and matron also on site. Breakfast and supper in College Hall, the medieval dining room of Westminster Abbey, which day pupils may also join.

The only full boarders are sixth formers, and Saturday evenings tend to be quiet, though school is increasing organised weekend activities, particularly for the 10 per cent or so of overseas sixth form boarders.

Boarders have supervised prep sessions, and there are evening activities in the sports and music centres after prep, but those after a full-on boarding experience jammed full of organised activities may want to look elsewhere. 'He likes it for the independence and to be with his mates,' said a boarder parent, whilst another said, 'It feels like a convenient B&B. Much better than having to pick him up at late after a rehearsal or lecture.' However, a sixth form boarder commented on the 'serious sense of community you can only get from living with others. The people in your own house become quite special to you.'

Ethos and heritage: Whilst some other great public schools overshadow their environs, Westminster is an integral but discreet part of central London, largely located in the walled precincts of the former medieval monastery of Westminster Abbey. Its main buildings surround the square of Little Dean's Yard, known as Yard, where pupils spill out after lessons to chat or kick a football or practise basketball. The Abbey, next door and with its own private entrance, serves as the school chapel, used for twice weekly services plus carol and other concerts.

Westminster had become a school by 1179, with pupils taught by monks of the Abbey at Westminster. It survived Henry VIII's dissolution of the monasteries in 1540 and has been in continuous existence since the 14th century, with Elizabeth I celebrated as the school's official founder.

'It is an incredibly tolerant and civilised atmosphere,' said a parent. 'Unlike other schools, they don't try to mould pupils into a particular product. They are quite laissez-faire.' Parents of quirky students are relieved to find a school that is very kind and accepting of eccentricities. 'If he was at any other school he'd be toast,' said one. 'Some schools can be so unforgiving: Westminster is the complete opposite.' Another reported that it has 'catered brilliantly' for each of her very different children. 'It's so wonderful to see these kids spark off each other.'

Parents of quirky students are relieved to find a school that is very kind and accepting of eccentricities. 'If he was at any other school he'd be toast,' said one

Has signed an agreement with Hong Kong education company HKMETG to set up six bilingual 3-18 schools in China by 2028, with 10 per cent of places free to less affluent families, and consultancy fees contributing to the Westminster bursary fund.

Pastoral care, inclusivity and discipline: Tutors attached to each house oversee the academic side, whilst housemasters look after all else. One parent felt that both have too many charges to know her son well. 'I feel his well-being is my responsibility, not the school's. I don't think anyone there knows him well in the round.' Others, however, described the pastoral care as 'exceptional', and a student said, 'I have always found the school really responsive. Your housemaster is always there and will take care of everything from not feeling well to having too much work.'

Pupils expected to be proactive, motivated and organised, with very full timetables but no compulsion to take part in organised activities. 'But anything you want to try, there's some way of doing it,' said a student.

Pupils and parents: Westminster families undoubtedly tend to be wealthy, intellectual, metropolitan, cosmopolitan and no doubt demanding, but most parents are extremely supportive of the school. 'It is very hard to withstand this full on praise and delight.' 'I am a real believer.' 'Fantastic on every front.' And from an initial sceptic: 'I am increasingly fond of it.'

Girls entering the sixth form report a much easier ride than they might have expected. 'I had heard rumours about the boys being awful and arrogant – but they weren't,' said one. 'Some would show off in lessons to begin with, but they calmed down pretty quickly.' 'I suspect they look for a certain confidence,' said another. 'If you were insecure you might find it intimidating.' 'It was quite a shock to the system at first,' said a third, 'but we can hold our own.'

'Westminster imbues in you a sense that it is fine to talk to anyone on equal terms,' said an ex-student. 'You have a real feeling of being special.'

Parents – nearly all are Londoners, with even boarders mostly coming from within the M25 – offered a cornucopia of outings to Dulwich Picture Gallery, tours of Westminster Abbey and the Houses of Parliament, plus quiz nights, drinks parties, concerts in the Abbey, and the opportunity to attend expert lectures with their children. 'Parents very friendly and there's a good sense of community and involvement,' said one.

Money matters: A number of means-tested bursaries of up to 100 per cent of fees available at 13+ and 16+; applicants must live in London. Bursaries also available at 11+; boys spend two years at the Under School before moving on automatically to the Great School. Eight Queen's Scholarships awarded at 13+; recipients must board, and the scholarship covers half the boarding fee. This can be topped up by a bursary in case of need. Five exhibitions at this level. Up to eight music scholarships at 13+ worth 10 per cent of day fee and four 16+ music scholarships, plus free instrumental tuition. Four 16+ Queen's Scholarships now available for girls.

The last word: One ex-student commented that Old Westminsters of her acquaintance have gone into a far wider range of careers than those from other schools. 'They seem to be following their passion. Westminster instils a belief that you can do whatever you want to do.'

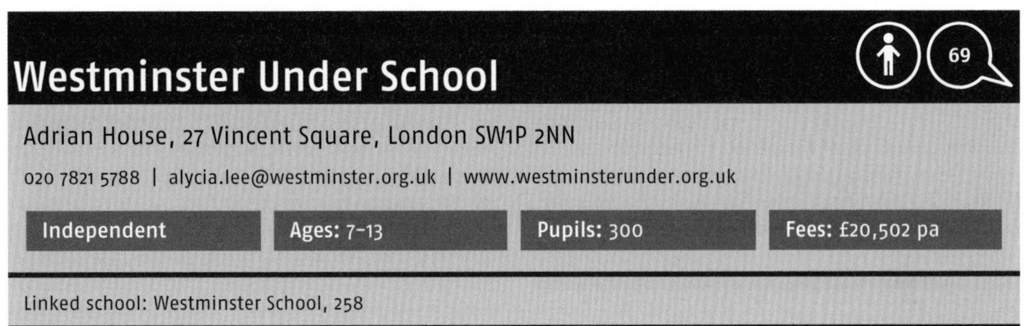

Westminster Under School

69

Adrian House, 27 Vincent Square, London SW1P 2NN

020 7821 5788 | alycia.lee@westminster.org.uk | www.westminsterunder.org.uk

Independent | **Ages:** 7-13 | **Pupils:** 300 | **Fees:** £20,502 pa

Linked school: Westminster School, 258

Interim Head: Since September 2020, Dr Steve Bailey BEd PhD FRSA. Previously headmaster at Twyford for 10 years and before that at Winchester College for 29 years, where he taught history and was housemaster then senior housemaster. Born and raised bilingually in Hong Kong. Educated at Kent College, Canterbury, Southampton University and St Paul's College of Education. A Fellow of the Royal Society for the Arts, research fellow of the International Olympic Committee, author of six books and an international reputation as a historian of sport and the Olympic Games. Played hockey at county and regional levels and enjoys tennis, water polo and surfing.

Entrance: Academically selective (very) at 7, 8 and 11. The school urges prospective parents to take the advice of their children's current school heads on whether pupils are likely candidates – 'they are very experienced and advise parents sensibly'. School stresses that Westminster Under is about breadth – 'sport, extracurricular activities, finding passions as well as being able to cope with the syllabus'. The school offers a comprehensive guide to admissions on its website and says it looks for potential natural ability. 'Our challenge is to find that potential, rather than simply select intensely tutored boys, and whose natural ability will grow with the challenges a Westminster education provides.' It strongly recommends that parents don't cram their sons or tutor them for the entrance exams. 'This can detract from the freshness, spontaneity and eagerness to learn, which are some of the qualities we are looking for,' it says. A parent we spoke to concurred. 'It's definitely a school for boys who are keen to learn,' she said. 'You hear stories of tutoring before the entrance exams but I don't know of anyone being tutored while they're in the school.' No obvious feeder schools, but schools like Garden House, Wetherby and Eaton House are well represented. At 11+, a reasonable number from state primaries.

Boys sitting 7+, 8+ and 11+ entrance assessments take written papers in maths, English, verbal reasoning and non-verbal reasoning and around 50 are invited back for interviews. At 7+ entry, there are around 300 applicants for 22 places. At 8+, 200 boys compete for another 22 places and at 11+ there are usually 500 applicants for 30 places.

Exit: Around 80 to 90 per cent progress to the senior school at 13 (including those who arrive at Westminster Under at 11), often with scholarships. Parents told us that the boys are very well prepared for the transition to Westminster. Others to eg Eton and Dulwich College.

Our view: Founded in 1943 as a class of 17 boys, Westminster Under originally shared the Westminster School site. The school expanded rapidly and moved to Eccleston Square in 1951 and then to its present site in Vincent Square in 1981. The school comprises three buildings – Adrian House, a red-brick Victorian former hospital, is the main one, overlooking London's biggest square. Vincent Square, just a couple of minutes' walk from Vauxhall Bridge Road, is owned by Westminster School and comprises 10 acres, including football pitches, a cricket square, tennis courts and plenty of room for junior boys to run around in. Westminster Under shares its governors and outlook with the senior school (known as the Great School), allowing the same careful planning over future development.

As the school says: 'There aren't many schools where pupils can walk to the Tate Britain, study a world-famous painting and be back in school for the end of a double lesson'

The school is top of the tree academically. Well-qualified, very committed staff provide lively, challenging teaching. One teacher told us: 'It's the happiest school I've ever worked in. It's teaching heaven.' The pupils we met brimmed with energy and enthusiasm too. On the day of our visit the results of the national Townsend-Warner History Prize for prep schools had just arrived and boys flocked round the noticeboard, eager to see how they'd fared. Brilliantly, it turned out – the school scooped the team prize for the third year running and a year 8 boy won the individual award for the second year in succession. The boys are so keen on history that some of the year 8 pupils were reading EH Carr's What Is History?, a book more commonly read at undergraduate level. 'Every department is rigorous, go-ahead and keen to push the boundaries,' said one of the teachers. 'The boys question everything. They don't just accept things.'

English, maths, science, history and geography are taught by form teachers in years 3 and 4 but there's specialist teaching in all subjects from year 5. The teachers are 'really keen', a parent told us. 'My son never says he's bored. It's a fantastic place to learn.' French from the start, classics from year 5, Latin from year 6 and Greek in year 8. Three well-equipped IT rooms, where we spotted a class writing computational algorithms for getting out of bed – very impressive. Lots of digital projectors and interactive whiteboards in classrooms. Laptops and iPads are available if teachers want to use them but textbooks are in constant use as well. No mobile phones for younger boys but year 7 and 8 pupils can bring them in – 'we are in central London after all,' says school. 'But they are not allowed to use them in school.' All year groups have a weekly PSHE lesson. Assessment and monitoring is very thorough, with internal exams twice a year. Clear guidelines on homework, which ranges from 20 minutes a night, plus reading, in year 3 to 100 minutes a night (three subjects) in year 8.

The school is committed to supporting pupils with additional needs, whether it's a disability or medical condition, a learning difficulty such as dyslexia or dyspraxia or help with time management and organisation. Head of learning development works with the pupils, sometimes in small groups or one-to-one. Other help includes daily maths clinics, study skills sessions and a handwriting club.

Boys are encouraged to read widely from the start. Reading lists are updated termly, the annual Readathon raises money for charity and pupils get the chance to learn a piece off by heart and recite it to the rest of their class. Recent choices include poems, Greek myths, Philip Pullman and Miranda Hart.

New arrivals at 11 attend Saturday morning lessons from the moment they're accepted (March to July), so they can get up to speed in French, Latin and other subjects. In the past, new year 7s were put in separate forms to get them used to the pace of learning but now the new boys are integrated with the rest of their year group from the outset. 'It's been a great improvement,' a parent told us.

Despite its location in the heart of the capital there are plenty of opportunities for sport. The boys have two sessions of games a week, a PE lesson and up till the end of year 6 a weekly swimming lesson at the nearby Queen Mother Sports Centre. Main sports are football, hockey, cricket, tennis and basketball but the new director of sport has broadened the sports offering and boys can also opt for land rowing, fives, ultimate frisbee, table tennis and gymnastics. The school uses Westminster School's £5 million multi-level sports hall a short walk away, complete with a movement studio, rowing training suite, fencing pistes, indoor cricket nets, gym and climbing walls. All the boys get the chance to represent the school in matches.

Music is superb. When we arrived a choir rehearsal was in full swing and the boys' singing resonated across the street. Virtually all pupils play at least one instrument (taught by more than 20 visiting music teachers) and there's a plethora of choirs and orchestras to join, as well as a big band called the Pink Panthers. Drama is popular, with three plays a year in the new performing arts theatre (Macbeth rehearsals in progress at the time of our visit). Art is housed in a light and airy double studio – everything from painting, drawing and printing to ceramics, sculpture and digital design. A pupil is chosen as artist of the month and their work is proudly displayed in the school's reception area. Plenty of opportunities to go to museums and art galleries. As the school says: 'There aren't many schools where pupils can walk to the Tate Britain, study a world-famous painting and be back in school for the end of a double lesson.' Lunchtime and after-school clubs galore, including fencing, judo, LAMDA, karate, cookery, parkour, robotics, animation and more. Chess is big – there's chess teaching after school each week and boys have achieved major success in national competitions. Plenty of external speakers and trips in London and further afield, including an annual residential expedition for all.

Alongside their academic achievements the pupils are encouraged to become 'compassionate, contributing citizens'. The school's enterprise programme is divided into three components – fundraising (£50,000 raised every year), community and the environment. Boys take part in a host of community activities, from playing bingo and dominoes at an old people's home around the corner each week to helping year 4s at a local primary school with their maths. The school also runs Platform, working closely with 35 schools across London to identify bright children in year 5 'interested in an academic challenge'. A total of 40 children attend Saturday morning enrichment teaching sessions, where they are taught by Westminster Under teachers. The results of this programme have been impressive – a girl recently won a 100 per cent bursary to Wycombe Abbey and two boys were awarded places at Westminster Under.

The school describes itself as 'very diverse'. Around 70 per cent of boys come from homes where English is not the first language. Parents told us that the school suits 'a particular type of boy'. One said: 'It suits boys who are intellectually curious. It's an academic school so they need to enjoy academic challenges and the thrill of doing a history, science or maths quiz. It challenges them, stretches them and gives them the opportunity to be with other boys like themselves.' The younger boys tend to live more locally and travel to school with their parents by bus, tube and train (many fathers and mothers do the drop-off on the way to work) while year 7s and 8s may live up to 45 minutes away – as far afield as Chislehurst, Dulwich, Elstree and Stratford. Pimlico tube station is 10 minutes' walk in one direction and Victoria station is 10 minutes' walk in the other.

Music is superb. Virtually all pupils play at least one instrument and there's a plethora of choirs and orchestras to join, as well as a big band called the Pink Panthers

Parents praise the school's pastoral care, particularly its six core values of compassion, integrity, resourcefulness, service, diligence and commitment, and say the school is 'very caring and nurturing'. 'They make everybody feel they have something to offer,' said one mother. Each pupil has a form teacher who is the first point of contact when issues arise. A school counsellor visits twice a week to offer confidential counselling to pupils and/or parents in need of advice and support. Lunch is served in three sittings for different age groups – plenty of choice, tasting sessions so boys can try different foods and the option to make their own sandwiches using the school's home-made bread. The school recently invited parents to come in for lunch so they could try the food for themselves.

Discipline isn't an issue here. A parent told us that the pupils 'learn how to behave in a way that allows teachers to teach'. The boys we met were polite (standing up unbidden when visitors entered the room), articulate, sparky and clearly enjoying their learning.

Money matters: The school is keen for boys from disadvantaged backgrounds to apply and now offers fully funded bursaries to 10 year 7 and 8 pupils. 'We are committed to being a needs-blind school,' says the school. At the time of our visit they'd been interviewing prospective bursary pupils and said they'd heard some 'heartrending' stories. 'I asked one boy what he'd done during the summer holidays and he said: "My father took a day off work and took me to the park to play football".'

The last word: An exciting, intellectually demanding education for bright, industrious boys. There's plenty to enthuse, challenge and occupy them here and they relish the opportunities they get.

Wetherby Preparatory School

70

48 Bryanston Square, London W1H 2EA

020 7535 3520 | admin@wetherbyprep.co.uk | www.wetherbyprep.co.uk

Independent | Ages: 8-13 | Pupils: 385 | Fees: £23,475 pa

Linked schools: Wetherby School, 428; Wetherby Senior School, 266

Head: Since 2008, Nick Baker BA PGCE (early 40s). A grammar school boy, he hails from Bucks, and was educated at Dr Challoner's and University College London, where he read geography, before qualifying as a teacher at Newcastle University. He has taught geography in a range of schools, including Holloway Boys comprehensive, head of year at Borehamwood, a former state middle school, and head of geography at Chesham Prep School (where he went as a boy, is now chair of governors, and which his two sons currently attend). He has taught at Wetherby Prep since it first started in 2004, initially as a senior master before becoming deputy head, and he also headed the new Wetherby Senior School from its opening in 2015 until 2017.

Tall, broad-shouldered and youthful, with a reassuring laugh that echoes from his belly, Nick Baker is hugely popular, with parents, pupils and staff as well as colleagues in the wider prep school world. A keen supporter of Watford Football Club, he celebrates their victories at whole-school prizegiving events as well as in his blog and emails, and even the many Chelsea supporters among the families here share in his delight and enthusiasm. Open and affable, his weekly newsletters in Wetherbuzz frequently include anecdotes about his two boys and what his family is getting up to. Hot on values and manners, one of the many 'challenges' he initiated is the Politeness Challenge. 'Much the best news is hearing that Wetherby boys are good house guests,' he says. Parents like the fact that he is so present, both around the school and at the many social events organised for teachers and parents, the Headmaster's Ball, or 'pub nights with dads', for example, as well as the Come Dine with Me event where teachers cook and wait on the parents. The adjectives that we heard most often were 'very professional', 'excellent communicator' and 'very driven and opinionated', but what is most apparent and consistent is that they trust him.

Entrance: At 8 into year 4 (when 200 sit for 40 places). Boys from the pre-prep have automatic entry. Everyone else (including those from other Alpha Plus schools like Chepstow House, but apart from siblings who also enter automatically) sits papers in English and maths during an assessment day at the school and also takes part in group activities.

Exit: An impressive number to top academic schools, especially considering the range of ability in each year. In 2020, eight to Eton, eight to St Paul's, five to Westminster, five to Harrow, four to Winchester, four to Latymer, three to City and three to Dulwich. Others to Charterhouse, King's, Marlborough and St Edward's. Around a quarter to Wetherby Senior School (19 in 2020). Scholarships in 2020 to Eton, Harrow, Dulwich (all academic) and Reed's (sport).

Our view: Wetherby Prep, and its brother, pre-prep Wetherby School, are currently riding high and widely regarded by parents across London as the jewel in the Alpha Plus crown. Slick as a well-oiled machine, Wetherby delivers precisely what its parents demand: high-quality teaching, a broad and extensive choice of activities and sports and exceptional communication. Many of the parents are bankers and Wetherby is the prep school equivalent of a well-resourced City institution. Boys here are polite (everyone stands up when you enter a room – 'our parents like that,' says Mr Baker) but sparkling and not squashed. One occasion which captures the spirit of the school is the prizegiving assembly which takes place every Friday in the Church of Annunciation behind Marble Arch. Parents and children cram into every corner and, after singing a hymn, prizes are distributed. These can be anything from the history prize to the prize for the best joke – let alone for sporting achievements (like running the marathon). Mr Baker conducts the whole occasion with warmth and humour. He clearly knows every child well and there is a lot of boyish banter. A cauldron of competitiveness, when house points are read out there are huge whoops and cheers. These boys really care if their house is ahead – especially if it's about the amount of food waste they are managing to avoid. We also witnessed a charming joy in their peers' achievements. The best kind of competitive spirit. We were most impressed when boys not only moved aside to let us sit down but also folded and cleared our chairs for us amid the chaos of cricket bats, violins, hockey sticks and trumpets at the close of proceedings.

Situated behind Marble Arch in leafy Bryanston Square, the Georgian building is grand and spacious. The signature red painted front door welcomes you into a smart, light, high ceilinged entrance hall, complete with wood panelled, gold leaf scholarship boards and lists of head boys, prefects and house captains of the school. Boys pile past heaving musical instruments and sports equipment, looking smart but tousled in cricket gear, grey and red blazers and caps. A sweeping staircase takes traffic up the several flights, a small back staircase channels them down. All the classrooms are large, light and airy, well-equipped and organised. The basement not only houses a couple of very well-equipped science labs, a fitness suite with rowing and running machines, and the dining room, but also a pet snake which boys can stand and stare at to while away any spare minutes in their busy day. Every boy has his own red locker – no need to lug every book and file around with him the whole time. School laptops seem to be littered at strategic points around the school and are available for anyone to use. School has recently expanded into a building a short distance away in Manchester Street. Even more recently, it has expanded next door to accommodate new ICT suite (where the boys learn coding, touch typing and animation), drama suite and extra classrooms.

From year 4, boys are setted in maths and English and have specialist subject teachers; most other subjects are setted in year 6, when they also start Latin. Three classes per year, with about 20 in each class. With automatic entry for siblings and boys from Wetherby School, alongside selective entry for others, the school is mixed ability but, Mr Baker observes, 'the academic demographic gets stronger year by year. The average CAT score used to be 112 and is now 120.' Full-time SENCo, assisted by one other person, gives support to children with mild learning difficulties, including dyslexia, dyspraxia and mild autism. Support provided ranges from touch-typing to reading groups as well as one-to-one session in maths and literacy outside the classroom. Approximately 16 in the school are getting support at any one time. Lots of prizes and rewards including a meeting with the head – the Headmaster's Good Show – to commend outstanding work. One young 9 year old told us proudly that he was 'very good friends with Mr Baker' as a result of his regular chats with him.

Sport is strong and getting better and better each year, both in terms of what is offered, the facilities and the teams' performances against other schools. The Park Club, in Acton, is now their home ground, and although some parents complain of traffic and the length of time it takes to bus them there, most were very enthusiastic about the excellent facilities, the space and the fact that they no longer need to box and cox in various places around central London. Boys play rugby and football in the winter, athletics, tennis and cricket in the summer. Their annual sports day is a major fixture in the calendar. There are plenty of other sports on offer too – hockey (including roller hockey), horse riding, fencing, rowing, rock climbing and badminton. One gets the impression that when Mr Baker goes to his Alpha Plus governors to ask that the tap be turned on (to make provision for another club, for example), it will be done. Lots of popular 'fathers and staff' fixtures too, in cricket and football.

Boys here are certainly polite, but sparkling and not squashed. Everyone stands up when a visitor enters the room ('our parents like that,' says Mr Baker)

Parents enthuse about the 'excellent' music. 'Despite the fact that my son is sporty, his favourite club is choir,' observed one father. Dynamic head of music has a modern and innovative approach. Plenty of public performances, impromptu as well as more formal. Breakfast concerts happen twice a term, there is a junior and senior school recital and a band as well as an orchestra and a chamber choir. Art is well organised and cross-curricular. We saw lots of lino cuttings and Mac books in the art room as well as impressive pieces of work around the school. In DT they were building clocks, and there is a dark room for photography, but the 'backbone of the department is printing,' we were told. Drama could be better, Mr Baker acknowledges; some parents, more brutally, described it as 'almost non-existent.' They use the Rudolf Steiner theatre up the road for productions, 'but it's so difficult to get good drama teachers/directors,' explains the head.

Parents here are slightly more diverse than those at the pre-prep. The numerous school buses run like clockwork and depart and arrive when they are meant to, enabling many parents to entrust their boys to the school transport, so they come from as far as Islington in the north east to Hammersmith in the west. Lots of well-heeled bankers and lawyers, and a smattering of celebrities – what would you expect in this part of London? – but a refreshing mixture of cultures and backgrounds. Nick Baker's openness and inclusivity – both in the weekly Wetherbuzz newsletters as well as in his public addresses – help to contribute to a real family and community feel.

The last word: An outstanding school, polished and professional, and an excellent foundation for your all-rounder son.

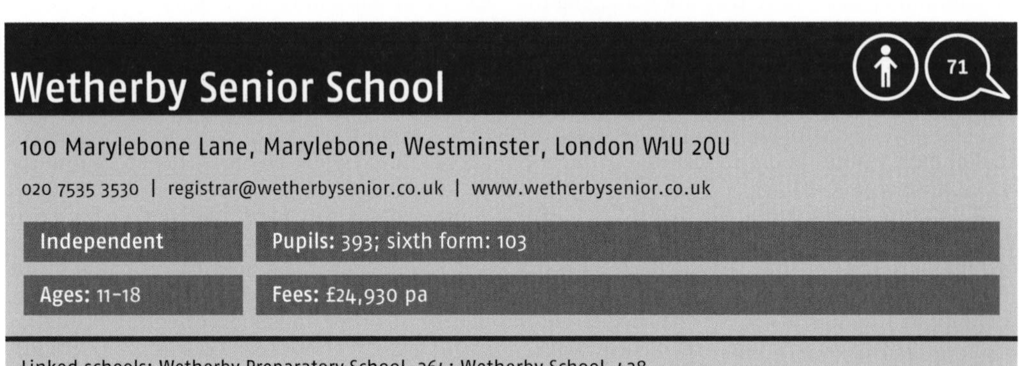

Wetherby Senior School

71

100 Marylebone Lane, Marylebone, Westminster, London W1U 2QU

020 7535 3530 | registrar@wetherbysenior.co.uk | www.wetherbysenior.co.uk

Independent

Pupils: 393; sixth form: 103

Ages: 11-18

Fees: £24,930 pa

Linked schools: Wetherby Preparatory School, 264; Wetherby School, 428

Head: Since September 2017, Seth Bolderow MSt BA, early 40s. Succeeded the much-loved Nick Baker who helped set up the school and ran it alongside the prep school for two years, but it was time to hand over the tiller to refocus on the prep school. Bolderow was regarded by some parents, who felt that they had bought into the 'Nick Baker ticket', with some suspicion initially. Formerly deputy head of Harrow International School in Hong Kong, Bolderow, whose name isn't the only thing that seems to have stepped out of a Thomas Hardy novel, hails from farming stock in Norfolk and was educated at Norwich school, and Exeter University where he studied classics. He was awarded a distinction for his MSt in Greek and Latin languages and literature at St Anne's College Oxford, and was sorely tempted by a life of academia. However, drawn to the camaraderie of the classroom and sports pitches, he commenced his teaching career at Blundell's, then Uppingham and King Edward's School Bath, before taking on head of sixth form at the John Lyon School and then making the move to the Far East with his girlfriend, soon to become wife. They have two young children. His proudest moment, he says, was delivering his son, less than a year old now, as there was a dearth of midwives at the time.

Full of appreciation for the wider network of support and expertise afforded by the Alpha Plus group (a common theme among heads of school groups, we find). Bolderow's functional office is warmed by evidence of his passion. Piles of classical Loebs and ancient Greek and Latin texts line the shelves. Quietly modest and understated, he is not one to play table tennis with the boys, as his predecessor was, and he keeps a respectable distance from the parents. While one wouldn't ascribe to him an urbane charm, he is authentic, a good listener and a man with a clear and defined purpose, and has won the admiration and respect of parents and boys alike.

Entrance: Academically selective at 11, 13 and 16. Tests in English and maths at 11, held in the January of the year of entry, but school will also give equal weight to the reference from his current school and his performance at interview. For 13+ entrance, all boys will sit the Common ISEB pre-test in the autumn of year 6 together with an interview. For 16+ entry, candidates are interviewed and examined in the subjects they want to study for A Level and offers are conditional on GCSE results. Always worth checking for the occasional place. They are looking for boys who will contribute to school life and benefit from the rounded education.

Exit: Fifteen per cent leaves after GCSEs. All boys are prepared for university, and the expectation is that the most academic will go to the top US and UK universities. 'Staff are experienced in supporting applications to UK universities and the school will be working with US university specialists to support boys who are aiming to study further afield.' One to Oxbridge in 2020.

Latest results: At GCSE, 76 per cent 9-7 at GCSEs. First set of A levels in 2020 – 58 per cent A*/A at A level (85 per cent A*-B). In 2019 (the last year when exams took place), 60 per cent 9-7 at GCSE.

Teaching and learning: Third set of GCSE results in 2020; internal data suggests pupils make very good progress, and systems in place to track progress constantly. 'For GCSE boys,' says school, 'projected grades given to boys and parents after year 10 and 11 mocks are tracked against independent baseline data (MidYIS). Using Attainment 8 as an overall measure for each boy, we are adding 0.22 of a grade on average, with 29 per cent of cohort adding more than one grade.' Almost every parent we spoke to praised the quality of the teachers and how impressive both their subject knowledge is and their understanding of the ethos of the school and commitment to it. A blend of experienced and relatively newly qualified, an equal split of men and women, they are recruited from both sectors, state and independent, and while naturally differ in style manage to combine being unpretentious with a traditional approach. 'All of our teachers are really lively,' averred the boys we spoke to.

A traditional academic curriculum includes Latin with German, French and Spanish the choice of modern languages. Native speakers and those who show a particular aptitude will be invited to take the GCSE as early as year 8. Graphic design, no DT. Practical skills are taught, the use of laser cutters etc. An esoteric part of the curriculum is that every pupil to age 16 is taught philosophy and learning skills. The head of philosophy is keen to throw everything at them, from Plato and Aristotle to Kant and Hobbes. The aim, to create independent learners who can think for themselves – qualities top universities are crying out for. Boys setted for maths from year 7 and in English and science from year 9. There are five sets for science. Beginners' sets for German and Spanish in year 9. Class sizes are small, currently 16. Judicious and sensible use of sets and there is movement up as well as down. A healthy broad range of ability when we visited, but as the school fills up, and word spreads, we suspect intake likely to become more and more academic.

First sixth form intake was in September 2018, most moving up from year 11, with a few places for external applicants. The sixth form will grow organically – from an initial 35 – as the larger year groups move up the school.

Learning support and SEN: A specialist SENCo but no one-to-one support in the classroom. Needs of anyone with learning difficulties are met in the classroom through differentiation. A tiny few need EAL support. Lucid Exact software used to screen boys once they're here to spot any difficulties, like dyslexia. School works closely with an educational psychologist who is brought in when there's a problem. They avoid labelling as much as possible, but Mr Bolderow said that around 25 per cent of current pupils are on the SEND register. Whatever their needs, he says, they can all manage in class without individual support.

The arts and extracurricular: Drama is vibrant and everyone gets a chance to be involved. Last year they did a 'promenade' production to great acclaim, as the actors moved round parts of the school performing. This year we witnessed the dress rehearsal for an edgy play set in a prison written by the head of drama. She fizzes with excitement as every head of drama should, and the boys respond positively. Some prefer to do backstage work, whether it be costumes and make-up or lighting and set design. Productions, small and large, throughout the school year, including a Christmas cabaret. LAMDA very popular in years 7, 8 and 9 and the teacher is in school most days

Bolderow's office is functional but the bookshelves reveal evidence of his passion, we saw piles of classical Loebs and ancient Greek and Latin texts

'The head of music is an inspiration,' say the boys. A French horn player, he has a fleet of colourful plastic brass instruments and with his combination of music technology and practical playing gets all the boys involved. There are already a number of groups including a wind ensemble, brass group and rock school plus DJ Buster teaches them to DJ. While the school is still relatively youthful it is hard to get the strength in depth for a whole school orchestra, although there is a chamber orchestra which will expand to full orchestra as the school grows.

Art technician specialises in sculpture and this was evident in the displays. Much use is made of the kiln. We saw a variety of silkscreens, and while there is a separate art and graphic design teacher, there is much crossover in the work produced. Boys' artwork is prominently displayed in the headmaster's office and throughout the school, but there is also a lot of artwork that has not been done by the boys – perhaps to fill the space? A number of exhibitions during the school year; the younger boys exhibited their art and graphic design work at the Saatchi gallery. An additional art studio has recently been added.

Lots of trips: 'they are always off somewhere,' remarked one parent, to Croatia (geography), Barcelona (combined Spanish and football tour), Pompeii (classics) and closer to home. Located in the heart of London, they don't waste the opportunity to take advantage of the museums and theatres on their doorstep.

The chef (God forbid you should refer to her as cook) used to work at Soho House and while the food is delicious, there was a plea from the boys to tone down the sophistication

Activities take place at the end of each day and are built into the timetable. As well as 'academic catch up' clubs in every subject, they can choose from a range of activities, from bridge, to cinema, scientific illustration (an example of their innovative use of cross-curricular expertise) to boxercise.

Mr Bolderow is a governor at Queen's College and already the two schools are forming alliances, whether it be social, musical, Duke of Edinburgh awards or lectures. A relationship is also developing with Francis Holland Regent's Park, so there will be lots of opportunity to experience working alongside girls.

Sport: Traditional sports, rugby, football, cricket, tennis and athletics, with lots of competitive fixtures. Two afternoons a week are timetabled for games and they play matches against leading London secondary day schools including Latymer Upper, Westminster and Kingston Grammar as well as the top two years of the prep schools. The downside, say a number of parents, is the one hour plus round coach trip to the sports ground, which is Trailfinders in Ealing. Some wonder how much time they actually get to play when so much time is taken up travelling. Nonetheless, the U15 football team had an impressive season, reaching the quarter final of the ESFA small schools cup. They are starting to punch above their weight.

The director of sport, an ex-Saracens rugby player and elite RFU referee, is highly praised by colleagues and parents. A 'fantastic sportsman, he is increasingly attracting sporty boys,' say some parents we spoke to. One parent was particularly impressed by his attitude to sport and exercise. It is not just about competition and fixtures but laying down the foundations for a healthy lifestyle and contributing to a mental health. Year 10 boys are linked to gyms and can opt for boxing, spinning etc, and there are a range of minor sports offered from fencing to basketball. Even unenthusiastic sportsman have to do one afternoon of physical activity in the sixth form – other afternoons they can do work in the community or work experience. School recently formed partnership with Ealing Trailfinders – home to a professional rugby union and rugby league club – which provides Astroturf and grass pitches, plus facilities for tennis and cricket.

Ethos and heritage: The last link in the chain of the formidable Wetherby schools, owned and managed by the private equity backed Alpha Plus group, Wetherby Senior School caters for the oldest boys in the group but is the youngest school. Alpha Plus have cleverly given all their Wetherby schools the signature colours – the red and grey, evident from moment you arrive at the brightly painted red front door, to the furnishings throughout the school, and the boys in their smart uniforms – and also through each school runs an ethos of traditional boys' education blended with a modern and global outlook.

The school opened in 2015 with 67 boys in years 7 and 9. There are now over 300 and the maximum number will be 600. 'The size is an essential part of our ethos,' explains Bolderow. 'We will be big enough to be able to compete, have an orchestra, field a number of different team sports, but not so big as to lose the intimacy that we value so highly.' Expectations are high, but boys can be themselves and there is no particular 'Wetherby mould' that they feel they should fit into.

Set in the heart of central London, the main site is in a surprisingly quiet corner of Marylebone Lane, tucked behind the famous haberdashery shop with its colourful array of ribbons. A Victorian mansion block, it has the benefit of being a traditional building with soul, but high ceilings, large classrooms and a sense of space, and a gym in the basement. A second, more newly purchased, similar five-storey building, Hannah House in Manchester Street, is largely the base for the junior years. A flow of boys make the five-minute walk between buildings, as the division of use is largely by department, but timetables are designed to minimise movement for the youngest boys. The new building has a large cafeteria, signature red benches and grey tables and staff eat with the students. Sixth formers can also have lunch and snacks throughout the day in their café in the sixth form centre in Marylebone Lane.

Pastoral care, inclusivity and discipline: One message we received very clearly from parents is that the care taken by all the staff and their sensitive approach to the boys' welfare is remarkable. Whether a response to a particular crisis, or the general awareness of the difficulties of being a teenager in the 21st century, the school takes it seriously and responds professionally but with compassion. They will not hesitate to bring in professional counsellors for support and one mother remarked how pleased she was that her son came home buzzing from a series of talks from 'the good lad initiative', a group of cool young men promoting 'positive masculinity'.

Boys are split into horizontal groups within their year group, known as Tributaries or 'Tribs', and assigned a tutor, who not only sees them every morning for registration but also meets with them for an hour each week. The tutor, overseen by a head of section, is responsible for the welfare of the boys in their care as well as keeping an eye on their academic progress and behaviour. The system works well, was the unanimous verdict of the parents we spoke to, and the communication between tutor and parent is invaluable.

Mr Bolderow sees a different tutor group each Friday to talk about the school. They have about 20 minutes to ask questions and make suggestions. 'This is usually about the food,' admits Bolderow. The chef here (god forbid that you should refer to her as cook) used to work at Soho House and while the food is delicious, there was a plea from the boys to tone down the sophistication of the recipes, since when baked potatoes have been back on the menu. There is a busy school council which consists of representatives from each Trib, and which reports to school in assembly.

A tiny courtyard at the back of the Marylebone Lane building makes it possible for boys to play football, and they do; there are two common rooms here complete with table football, and a Nintendo Wii. A range of lunchtime activities at Hannah House, indoor and out, as well as time in the park. Most of the boys we saw in break were staring at their phones, disappointing but a reflection of the age. A number of parents we spoke to would welcome a more robust approach from the school on the use of mobile phones.

Only sixth formers allowed out to lunch. We happened to see a number of younger boys filing into a local tea shop at the end of the day and were impressed by their deportment in the bustling streets of Marylebone.

Pupils and parents: Wetherby Senior couldn't be more of a reflection of its central London location. Thoroughly multicultural, one parent might be Swiss, the other Swedish. Whilst the majority of the boys are long term residents of the UK, the school is a truly global environment with boys from all over Europe as well as Russia, the Middle East and the USA. Most come from London prep schools.

Boys we met and spoke to were refreshingly individual and polite. They look you in the eye, are confident but not arrogant. This is far from a macho culture. Boys here can be any kind of peg, and will still fit the hole.

The last word: Wetherby Senior could not have arrived at a better time. Parents of boys will be flocking to its red door in this overheated senior school market, in which it is particularly hard to find good schools for boys. If the school continues along the trajectory it has set for itself it will only become ever more popular. A marvellous education for the modern teenage boy.

William Ellis School

72

Highgate Road, London NW5 1RN

020 7267 9346 | info@williamellis.camden.sch.uk | www.williamellis.camden.sch.uk

State	Ages: 11-18	Pupils: 858; sixth form: 253 (69 girls)

Linked school: LaSWAP Sixth Form Consortium, 169

Acting Head: Since September 2020, Izzy Jones, formerly deputy head, having joined the school in 2016 from Parliament Hill School where she was assistant headteacher for teaching and learning.

Entrance: Usual admissions criteria for 130 year 7 places: looked-after children, medical and social need, siblings, up to 12 musical aptitude places, then by distance (usually up to about two miles).

Generally around 300 outside places for LaSWAP sixth form consortium, with an intricate admissions system and a range of entry requirements for different levels of courses.

Exit: Most (around 70 per cent) to LaSWAP sixth form. Some go off to eg Camden School for Girls, Woodhouse College, St Marylebone, Fortismere or FE colleges. After A levels, students go off to a variety of universities, with destinations in 2019 including Brunel, Imperial, Nottingham Trent, Loughborough, Northampton, Bournemouth, Herts and Middlesex to study eg maths, chemistry, product design and law. In 2020, three to Oxbridge; five medics.

Latest results: In 2020, 33 per cent 9-7 at GCSE; 87 per cent 9-4 in both maths and English. At A level, 29 per cent A*/A (55 per cent A*-B). In 2019 (the last year when exams took place), 36 per cent 9-7 at GCSE; 59 per cent of pupils got 9-5 in both English and maths. At A level, 30 per cent A*/A (75 per cent A*-B).

Teaching and learning: Huge ability range, with year 7 reading ages ranging from 8 to 17. Parents report that English, once a weak point, has been turned round by the 'very impressive' HoD; the school now teaches the IGCSE English language.

School uses Future First, set up by old Elysians, to help it keep in touch with alumni and get them involved in giving careers advice, work experience and mentoring

The school has a language specialism, and everyone starts French in year 7, with around half studying it to GCSE. School has links with the nearby Collège Français Bilingue de Londres. Most take up either Spanish or German in year 8 (offered in alternate years), but this is no longer compulsory, and some spend extra time on English fluency instead. Latin and Mandarin are taught in clubs, and fundraising enabled a recent sixth form Mandarin and geography trip to China.

Around a quarter of boys take single sciences to GCSE. Those with a more vocational bent can take OCR science, and choose from various other courses with a large coursework element such as business studies, travel and tourism, and ICT. Some spend a day a week in years 10 and 11 at Westminster Kingsway College studying eg catering, construction or motor mechanics. New food tech facilities.

Fluid grouping rather than setting across the curriculum from year 8 (school hopes to group maths and science from year 7 in future) at the discretion of each faculty head. 'If a set of boys has a particular weakness in a subject we may put them together for a term, but there's plenty of movement.' Some parents would prefer more rigorous setting, but praise the willingness of staff to go the extra mile for boys at all levels. 'They will take time and a lot of patience with those who are bright but not pulling their finger out. I don't feel they are just settling for the easiest way of getting them through exams.'

Parents are mostly optimistic, though one complained about a lack of homework. 'We've found the teaching really good so far,' said another. 'My son is very happy here and seems to be doing well.' 'My son, who is very academic, is being well supported,' said another. 'I had severe reservations about some of the teaching during my son's early years here,' said a long-standing parent, 'but I don't now. I've never felt I had to get a tutor in.'

Joint sixth form with Parliament Hill School, which is part of the LaSWAP consortium that also includes La Sainte Union and Acland Burghley. This enables a wide range of courses including a choice of 41 A levels, as well as BTecs, NVQs, vocationally applied subjects and post-16 GCSEs. Students stay in their base school (which for William Ellis boys will be their own school or Parliament Hill) for the majority of lessons, but may go elsewhere for minority subjects.

As well as working with Camden to provide one-to-one careers advice, school uses Future First, set up by old Elysians, to help it keep in touch with alumni and get them involved in giving careers advice, work experience and mentoring. It organises career sessions here and brings back old boys to talk about their work.

Learning support and SEN: Teaching assistants are increasingly being trained to help with particular subjects, or with behavioural or language difficulties, rather than being velcroed to a particular child. The school uses some of its pupil premium funding (alongside sponsorship) on its City Year team of volunteers, who act as mentors, support teachers in class, run breakfast and homework clubs and supervise in the playground. The funding also helps with small group and one-to-one teaching, particularly in English, as well as counselling and interventions to improve attendance.

The arts and extracurricular: A large trophy on the head's table when we visited is the house cup.

Increasing emphasis on carrots rather than sticks, with boys earning house praise points for good work and good attitudes

Houses (named after local historic buildings: Lauderdale, Burgh, Willow, Keats and Fenton) are run by 'young, enthusiastic staff'. Pupils gain house points by competing at sports and taking part in talent shows, spelling bees, chess, model building, cake sales et al.

Year 7 and year 9 have a week camping at the school's field centre, the Mill, in Surrey. Boys also go on ski trips, language exchanges and field trips. 'The extracurricular activities have improved markedly over the past few years,' said a parent, citing her son's sessions at the Royal College of Music, playwriting with professionals, theatre and concert trips, Model UN.

Light top-floor art rooms display impressive work; a sixth former was recently a finalist in the Camden Art Competition, and students have exhibited their work at the local Lauderdale House. Some parents find the music provision underwhelming, but there are choirs, ensembles and a range of concerts for all, from beginners to advanced musicians, often in conjunction with Parliament Hill School and La Sainte Union, which form a joint orchestra with WE. There are also workshops and masterclasses run by professional musicians. The head of music 'has been very supportive of my son writing and performing his own music,' said a parent, and a school group recently reached the finals of the Roundhouse Band Slam competition. School subsidises instrumental lessons for boys on free school meals.

Not a school that goes in for full-scale musicals, but has recently opened a new music suite and drama studio and there are many smaller drama performances, such as the recent drama club interpretations of The Ancient Mariner and Christmas Eve in the Trenches at the winter concert. Pupils work with outside organisations such as the Donmar Warehouse, and take part in the Shakespeare Schools Festival. 'They do it thoroughly and well,' said a parent.

Sport: Football and basketball are the most popular team sports, but rugby is up and coming – the RFU provides coaching and talented players are encouraged to join local clubs. The eight table tennis tables get enthusiastic use. Takes part in the annual Camden Shield boys' competition, which sees teams from six Camden secondary schools compete in football, table tennis, basketball, badminton, athletics and cricket. Pupils report that team sports peter out in the higher years: 'The teachers do try, but we tend to get a bit lazy in years 10 and 11.' The school has a newish sports hall, with facilities for PE and basketball and a multi-gym, and the playground doubles up as five-a-side football pitches. Sadly, the school cannot afford to hire the field next door, groomed for cricket when we visited, but it does play games on other parts of Parliament Hill Fields and uses the athletics track there. Clubs include cricket, running and trampoline.

Ethos and heritage: William Ellis was a public-spirited businessman who founded several schools in the mid-19th century, believing children should be taught 'useful' subjects such as science and to develop their reasoning faculties, rather than rote-learning religious tracts and ancient languages. William Ellis School, the only one of his schools that still exists, was founded in Gospel Oak in 1862 and recognised as a boys' secondary school in 1889. It moved to its present site, on the edge of Parliament Hill Fields, in 1937. Originally a grammar school, it turned comprehensive in 1978; the red-brick vine-clad buildings still have a grammar school feel. Brand new sixth form study centre.

'My son has had a very happy time here,' said a parent. 'He has a sense of belonging and pride in his school. It fosters a nice attitude and spirit in the boys – confident but not arrogant.'

Old Elysians include Toby Young, Robert Elms, Sean French, Andrew Sachs and Len Deighton.

Pastoral care, inclusivity and discipline: The school's tightening up on discipline and appointment of an effective head of pastoral care have helped to cut down on the low-level disruption that once marred many lessons, and has made boys feel safer inside and out. 'They are much stricter on uniform than they used to be, and you no longer have to hack your way through a posse of boys smoking round the gate,' said a parent. Year 7 has its own quad, with table tennis and picnic tables. The year 7 head has links with most of the feeder primary schools, and boys are invited to summer school before they start.

One parent commented: 'The pastoral care is very good. A few years ago I went through a difficult divorce and they were brilliant at supporting my son.' Another said, 'Whenever I've emailed to ask questions, I've had an immediate and pleased reply. They are extremely responsive to an interested/meddling parent.'

Increasing emphasis on carrots rather than sticks, with boys earning house praise points for good work and good attitudes, from persistence to creativity. 'Relationships can be much more relaxed once ground rules are established,' says school. Deep Learning Days, part of the PHSE curriculum, see timetables dropped for a day in favour of discussions on relationships, including peer pressure and bullying, careers and the world of work, with plenty of outside speakers. 'We try to make it circular – get the boys to present back to their peers what they have learned. Recently 25 year 9 boys did a play for the rest of the school.' One parent commented on her despondency at a lack of creativity in the PHSE teaching, but another said, 'They are very good at raising the boys' social and political awareness. They don't shy away from issues that can be sensitive, such as homophobia and religion.'

Pupils and parents: Huge ethnic mix, with less than a third of pupils from white British background, and others ranging from Irish to Turkish to Somalian. Wide social spread, from the large social housing estates of Gospel Oak to the multimillion pound houses of Dartmouth Park. 'There were cliques lower down the school, but in years 10 and 11 everyone hangs out together and we all get on,' said a pupil. 'The fact that the boys come from a huge range of backgrounds doesn't seem to matter one bit, which is a very impressive trick for a school to pull off,' said a parent.

Money matters: Voluntary aided by the William Ellis and Birkbeck Schools Trust, but otherwise is as hard up as most other state schools.

The last word: Small boys' comprehensive in idyllic situation on the borders of Hampstead Heath, now emerging rapidly from the doldrums under strong, popular and enthusiastic head. 'It can only get better and better,' said a satisfied parent.

Head: Since 2005, Tanya Watson BMus NPQH (50s). She was raised in America (there's still a suspicion of an accent), then trained as a concert pianist at the Royal Academy of Music. While developing her performance career, she started taking pupils, and was so taken with teaching she decided to commit full time. Undoubtedly a good decision for William Tyndale, since, over the past decade or so, she's carefully nurtured this always popular primary into one of the borough's star attractions. Articulate, organised and capable, she's at the gates every day and is widely admired. 'She's a very strong leader and provides a real sense of order and reassurance,' said one parent. 'She's both very approachable and a little bit formidable,' said another. What parents particularly respect about her, however, is her commitment to extending beyond the expected. 'She's filled my children with confidence and given them opportunities I couldn't have anticipated.'

Entrance: Parent tours held twice a year by appointment through the school office. Sixty reception places allocated via Islington Council. After the usual priority categories (including siblings and the children of long-serving staff), entrance is based on distance from the gates (adjudicated by a computerised mapping system). Needless to say, you have to live very, very close (within less than 0.2 miles). The school then operates a waiting list.

Exit: To well over 20 different schools. Popular local choices include Highbury Grove, Highbury Fields, City of London Academy and Stoke Newington, but a sprinkling across the northern reaches of the capital, including to Camden School for Girls and Mossbourne Community Academy. Others to eg Highgate, City of London (boys and girls) and Forest.

Our view: From the outside William Tyndale, which recently celebrated its centenary, seems a bit of a fortress, commanding the playground and lording it over the children below. Recent additions and a carefully modernised interior have softened the tone, with an inviting streamlined entrance, spic-and-span classrooms and up-to-date facilities (including plans for improved science space).

This is a school where the phrase 'every child matters' is definitely not empty rhetoric. Teachers take time to make detailed analysis of progress and, while standards are immutable, the approach

Keen competitors in the Islington Primary School Football League, with both girls' and boys' teams highly successful

to obtaining them is often tailor made. Results – for everyone – speak for themselves, with children, whatever their background, performing well above expected (and national) standards.

Literacy (undoubtedly a strength) is reinforced (and reinforced again) throughout the timetable. Classes named after famous children's authors (Morpurgo, Rosen, Dahl, etc) and class assemblies give plenty of opportunity to explore their namesakes. Lewis class, for example, not only delivered fascinating facts about the author of the Narnia books, but wrote its own wintry poems, did a snowflake dance, and used castles to discuss structures. Lots of learning poetry by heart, and older pupils take part in a school-wide poetry recital. Maths, too, made fun, with activities, such as the (prize-gaining) Multiplication Bee. Sky-high expectations for all, so timetabled Latin (with proper vocab tests, etc) from year 3 because the head believes 'it improves writing across the curriculum, helps pupils understand the nuts and bolts of English and provides a strong cultural base for their understanding of history.'

Other non-standard enrichment includes regular chess. 'The national curriculum can be a bit thin,' said one mother, 'but William Tyndale provides all the extra flourishes.' Dedicated librarian develops library skills. IT facilitated by iPads throughout. Recently relaunched homework strategy now targets individual needs. ('After consulting parents, the school stopped sending home those projects we all used to do. Now we get homework we know is right for our kids.') Outdoor classroom where all pupils work with the school's 'environmental educator', maintaining both a 'wildlife' and 'growing' garden (with fruit and veg contributed to school dinners).

SEND well supported – at both ends of the spectrum. Three specialists help with reading recovery ('Fantastic,' said a beneficiary) and other challenges. Extra tuition provided before school and during breaks so 'everyone has fair access'. One of the top performing schools in the country, too, for boosting the performance of disadvantaged pupils.

William Tyndale is a school where curricular and extracurricular do not operate in separate spheres. Art is 'exceptional', 'inspirational', 'really wonderful', chorused parents. The school has its own recently improved art block and artist in residence, and juniors study art for two hours a week and work with external arts organisations (Stamped Arts, Cubitt Artists) on large-scale projects, such as the chronological history of the school which lines the stairs. Pupils can also gain an Arts Award Explore qualification, by participating in arts activities (for example, the school's film club), attending arts events and keeping a portfolio. Understandably, the school has gained an Arts Council Artsmark gold award.

Music, too, exceptionally strong, with weekly, specialist-taught music lessons in the dedicated music studio. Free recorder lessons for all in year 3, and Hackney Music Hub provides tutors in African dance and drumming in year 4 and samba in year 5. Instrumental lessons (recorder, flute, cello, brass, clarinet) also available. School orchestra plus two choirs (infant and juniors), with regular opportunities to perform in school (musical assemblies, shows, concerts) and outside (Pure Voice, Hackney Music Festival). School won a Sing Up gold award in 2016, and head undoubtedly brings her own expertise to bear. 'After a concert, she will pick out and discuss various themes,' said a parent.

Sport dynamic. Dance, gymnastics, cricket and rounders all on offer, with expert coaches imported for lessons and clubs. ('My daughter was taught by coaches from Arsenal, which she absolutely loved.') Swimming lessons at Highbury Pool. A rare primary school with a third-generation floodlit football pitch (available for hire to aid school's coffers), in constant use for lunch-hour sporting activities and inter-school competitions (mini Olympics, netball and football tournaments). Keen competitors in the Islington Primary School Football League (with both girls' and boys' teams highly successful), and in local hockey matches (with co-ed team), tag rugby and athletics tournaments.

Classes named after famous children's authors (Morpurgo, Rosen, Dahl, etc) and class assemblies give plenty of opportunity to explore their namesakes

Comprehensive programme of London visits (Geffrye Museum, Museum of London, Central Mosque etc), and extensive range of clubs (sports, music, creative writing, book club etc) with debating club notably strong. (Pupils recently won the London Primary Debate Mate Cup, confronting such knotty questions as: 'This house believes that people should break the law to save the environment', and 'This house believes that children should be paid for good exam results'.)

School is relaxed and informal, but not slack. No uniform and reasonably scruffy end-of-day look, but no question of come-as-you-please, so no jewellery, nail varnish or hair dye (to prevent jealousy). Masses of positive reinforcement for pupils (with awards for attendance and punctuality) and praise for parents (for making sure kids stay off playground equipment after school). Parents encouraged, too, to talk to teachers about concerns as they arise rather than bottle it all up until parents' evening. Draconian measures, however, for late pick-up from (privately run) after-school club. (£20 fine, which increases by £1 a minute per child.) Atmosphere widely praised by all. 'It's a lovely community, very friendly, very disciplined,' said one father. 'It's very uncompetitive, and children are encouraged to help each other. I just don't worry about the children once they've gone in. I feel they're in very good hands.'

Parents a broad mix, so the expected chattering-class professionals (overheard in the playground: 'I forgot your smoothie, have you got a banana?'), but also 35 per cent on pupil premium, and wide ethnic range. Dads unusually well represented at after-school collection.

Money matters: Parents here are well organised and generous. The William Tyndale Charitable Trust was set up to raise funds for school improvement, and has helped finance significant capital projects, including the new performance stage and sports pitch (£5,000), playground equipment (£10,000) and stairwell art project (£6,000). Regular money-raising events include the quiz night, summer fair and weekly cake sales.

The last word: Parents overwhelmingly delighted with William Tyndale. 'I feel so lucky. It's completely brilliant. I can't praise it highly enough.'

Central West

Hammersmith & Fulham
Kensington & Chelsea

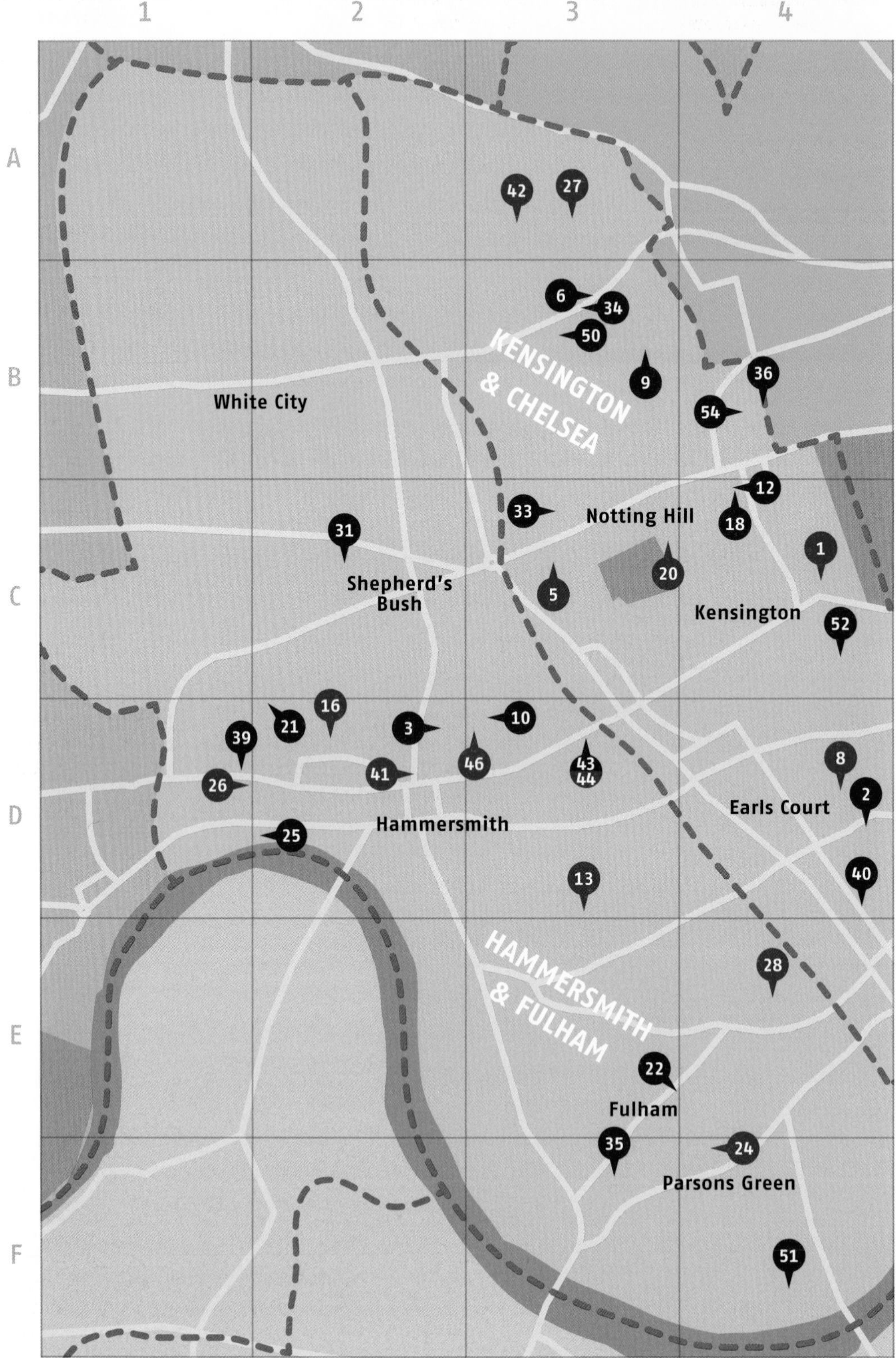
1
2
3
4
A
B
C
D
E
F
42
27
6
34
50
KENSINGTON & CHELSEA
9
36
54
White City
12
33
Notting Hill
18
31
1
20
5
Shepherd's Bush
Kensington
52
16
21
10
39
3
46
43
44
8
41
26
2
Earls Court
25
Hammersmith
13
40
HAMMERSMITH & FULHAM
28
22
Fulham
35
24
Parsons Green
51

5 6

Knightsbridge
Chelsea
1 mile

CENTRAL WEST

Central West London and its state schools

Hammersmith and Fulham

A long borough that travels from north to south, albeit with numerous bus routes linking the two ends. Just west of Chelsea, this is a hard borough to pin down, with Fulham's pockets of large mansion flats near the river and Victorian terraced houses within sound of gentle thwonk of tennis balls at the Queen's Club – cheek by jowl with council housing and some fairly mean streets. But some of the harder areas are on an upward trend, particularly near the recently gentrified Fulham Broadway and in Hammersmith with bustling King Street, ever improving pubs and new development spreading out from the huge Westfield shopping centre.

A high percentage of children used to attend secondary schools outside the borough, but the arrival in 2011 of two very different schools, and in 2014 a third, has changed the face of secondary school provision here. The Hammersmith Academy had a wobbly start in the face of the sudden and fierce competition from the much publicised and popular West London Free School. The latter, with its public-school-like stipulation that Latin be learnt by all and that boys play hockey and rugby, not football, was a London middle class magnet. The WLFS's GCSE results have so far not fallen short of expectation. The Hammersmith Academy is modelled on the highly successful Thomas Telford Academy in the Midlands. It has three hour lessons conducted in its splendid circular premises between the Goldhawk and Uxbridge Roads, and the Mercers (the Guild that is behind St Paul's boys and girls, among others) as sponsors.

At the other end of the borough, the evangelical Christian Fulham Boys has made an impressive start since it opened in 2014. Still waiting to move into permanent premises near Fulham Broadway, its dynamic outspoken Welsh headmaster with his passion for a single sex boys' education (as well as Welsh rugby) has impressed both the boys and their parents. An emphasis on excellence in everything from academics to sport combines with a strong pastoral approach. However its zero tolerance attitude to discipline ignites mutterings about pettiness, and patchy progress among pupils, particularly those in the lower sets, is causing unhappiness among some. A CofE school, it operates 'fair banding' and has 50 per cent faith places.

Burlington Danes Academy, towards North Kensington, is one of the Ark academies, with the associated financial and expert support that comes with that. With a focus on maths and the performing arts, the school plummeted from outstanding to requires improvement in the 2018 Ofsted report. Phoenix Canberra, in Shepherd's Bush, benefitted enormously from the tight control and charismatic headship of Sir William Atkinson. While he has gone now academic performance remains reasonably steady with some improvement. A good choice of vocational subjects as well as academic but probably not the place to sit A levels.

Sacred Heart High qv in Hammersmith is a reason for parents of girls to convert to Catholicism and choose a local Catholic primary school (siblings are quite low on the priority list).

In the south of the borough, Fulham Cross Boys' School (once called Henry Compton) and Fulham College Girls' School (both 11-16 years) are now in federation with the new Fulham Enterprise Studio. This is a vocational studio school for 14-19 year olds, specialising in construction and performing arts (production).

Lady Margaret qv in Parsons Green, an all-girls, Church of England school with over 50 per cent church-goer places, feels more like Wycombe Abbey than a London comprehensive. This end of the borough is also home to the highly prestigious London Oratory qv – the holy grail for Catholic parents with sons, with its own junior house that takes musical boys from age seven. Boys are accepted from across London, the admission requirements stringent, but the lucky parents who have succeeded in jumping through those precarious hoops (including Blairs and Cleggs) are satisfied customers.

Popular primary schools include John Betts qv, traditional and small, lots of parents opining that it reminds them of their own primary school, Brackenbury, Greenside and the West London Free School primary school, with automatic entry to the senior school a definite pull for parents. Burlington Danes Primary, part of the Ark MAT, and a feeder for the secondary school, opened in 2015 and all the signs are that it will perform as impressively as its sister school, The Ark Conway Primary School, in the far north of the borough. The latter is in a relatively deprived area on the borders of East Acton, but in a splendidly characterful building (the old library).

There is a plethora of good church schools, most notably the outstanding St Stephen's on the Uxbridge Road which sends large numbers to Twyford CofE qv high school in Acton as well as the West London Free School (its founder's children go there) and the eternally popular St Peter's in the leafy Hammersmith square of that name off King Street. For the Catholics, Larmenier & Sacred Heart in Brook Green and The Good Shepherd off Askew Road feed boys to Cardinal Vaughan qv and the London Oratory qv, girls to the ever outstanding Sacred Heart.

Kensington and Chelsea

The Royal Borough of Kensington and Chelsea is one of London's smallest boroughs geographically and yet one of the most densely populated areas in Europe. It includes Holland Park, the area named for the eponymous park, which features leafy streets and some of the largest detached and semi-detached houses in London. Notting Hill of Hugh Grant fame is home to the Portobello Market and hosts the largest annual street party and carnival in Europe, held over the August bank holiday weekend.

The borough houses some of London's wealthiest as well as its poorest – including the ex-residents of Grenfell Tower. Half the residents educate their children privately, half of the state school pupils receive free school meals, and half of the borough's children go to secondary school in another borough. It is also, on DfE statistics, the best performing area in England for GCSE results.

Of the six mainstream secondaries only Holland Park qv and the relatively young Kensington Aldridge Academy (started in 2014 near Ladbroke Grove) are community schools. Holland Park is rated outstanding and is hideously oversubscribed, but gives up to 10 per cent of places to students who show an 'aptitude in art and design'. Kensington Aldridge, also judged outstanding by Ofsted, operates its sixth form jointly with Charterhouse qv and Godolphin & Latymer qv.

The rest have a religious requirement as part of the admissions process. Three are Catholic: St Thomas More (co-ed) in SW3, All Saints Catholic College (co-ed), North Kensington and Cardinal Vaughan qv (boys) in Holland Park. Co-ed Chelsea Academy (Fulham) is CofE (50 per cent faith and 50 per cent open places with some preference for children from K&C primary schools).

Cardinal Vaughan is responsible for weighting some of these figures. A school with consistently high results, a rigorous attention to the more challenging subjects and tight discipline, it is the number one choice of school for the children of a number of prominent political figures.

Fox qv, with its tiny catchment tightly focused primarily on and around Kensington Church Street, is a very vibrant and a reliable primary school choice. Half of the 27 primary schools are either Catholic or CofE. St

Barnabas and St Philips and St Mary Abbots – the latter attracting leading lights in parliament – are perhaps the most coveted. Further south towards Chelsea, the Oratory is a popular choice for Catholics (boys get priority admission to the London Oratory school), Christ Church qv for the Anglicans. If you're not religious and live close to a salubrious area that incorporates, inter alia, The Boltons, then Bousfield qv is likely to be your primary school of choice. Other less well known schools that have a good reputation include Barlby and Thomas Jones qv. Kensington Primary Academy, an offshoot of the West London Free School in Hammersmith, opened its new premises on Warwick Road W14 in 2016.

Ashbourne Independent School

17 Old Court Place, London W8 4PL

020 7937 3858 | admin@ashbournecollege.co.uk | www.ashbournecollege.co.uk

Independent	Pupils: 283; sixth form: 283
Ages: 14-19	Fees: £27,750 – £29,250 pa

Principal: Since 1981, Mike Kirby BApSc MSC (60s). Raised and educated in and around Toronto, his second degree was in aerospace engineering and astrophysics. He became a maths teacher because he was 'entirely unsuited to the aerospace engineering profession' and still teaches once a week. An extremely tall, gently ironic man with a slightly lazy sounding Canadian drawl, but with a mind that is not remotely idle. No plans to hand over the reins entirely, as we speak, but has a plan for the succession in place if the mountains of electronic paper, needed by modern legislation, threaten to swamp the pleasure of running his school. His son, Lee, is already in place and is given the 'thumbs up' by parents, particularly in his handling of student interviews and the energy he brings.

Entrance: The school is 'picky' rather than selective, particularly for years 12 and 13, and is looking for at least a grade 4 average at GCSE. The process involves an academic assessment and an interview with either the principal or a senior member of staff. According to one pupil this was 'not scary', but another told us that he was turned down initially and had to work really hard to persuade them to take him (possibly more because of his attitude than his lack of qualifications).

Exit: A quarter left after GCSEs in 2020. Usually over 50 per cent to Russell Group universities with particularly popular destinations including UCL and King's College London. Eight to Oxbridge in 2020. One medic and a dentist in 2020, both studying overseas (Universitat de Valencia); one student to California Lutheran University. Drama students tend to go to university rather than drama school but art students often go straight to art college, some without doing the initial foundation year.

Latest results: In 2020, 50 per cent 9-7 at GCSE; at A level, 51 per cent A*/A (79 per cent A*-B). In 2019 (the last year when exams took place), 32 per cent 9-7 at GCSE; 76 per cent A*-B at A level.

Teaching and learning: Results are up there in the sector. GCSE students only account for some 10-15 per cent of the total roll call but an increase of numbers is on the cards. The range of courses covers the core compulsory subjects plus computer science, graphic design and textiles. As in the rest of the school, the classes are tiny as Ashbourne guarantees that there will be fewer than 10 pupils in a class and they 'will only violate this policy in an emergency'. This rule means that Ashbourne could well be a GCSE slot for a student having trouble finding their feet in the ultra-competitive world of more conventional London schools, or for teenagers who might be happier in a more 'grown-up' environment.

The vast majority of A level students are here for two years, although they still offer one-year courses (for first-time fluffers and very able students) and 18 month courses (a rare bird in London) which can be a life-saver for parents whose lives are suddenly disrupted and for international students who may be on a different timeline at home but want to join the English system to qualify for university entry here.

A top-floor studio with additional textile space feels more like an art school than an art department

Strong maths and science departments (recently renovated labs) unsurprising for the brainchild of a maths teacher, but the school also has a proven A level track record and successful results in English, a wide range of language options, theatre studies and art. They are extremely flexible and will try to construct a timetable that allows for a more unusual course selection than is often available, meaning some subjects only have two or three students in a class. Pupils say that this can lead to some fairly wacky timetabling and you can find yourself working every hour of the school day (9-6) for three days a week and theoretically putting your feet up the rest of the time. However, with mock exams every half term and reports four times a year on everything from grades to punctuality, there's not much latitude given to slackers.

More teachers than is often the case tend to have done time in the outside world before turning to education (although all have professional and academic qualifications), with backgrounds ranging from the civil service to the wine trade.

Probably partly because of the number of international students there is a steady demand for economics and finance courses, and carrying on the original theme there is a specialist engineering programme. Laying the groundwork for Oxbridge entrance and organising legal seminars for law school applicants and preparing them for LNAT tests are also a core part of their offering.

Learning support and SEN: School has recently appointed a specialist teacher to help students on the 'dys' spectrum; however, all successful applicants need to be able to keep up with only a moderate amount of help.

The arts and extracurricular: For the rare students with time on their hands they promote a series of clubs from tango and salsa to meditation and mindfulness, plus an astro particle physics club (seriously impressive). There's an annual visit to a European city but these are, on the whole, a fairly well-travelled bunch anyway.

The music department is an essential component, according to MK, as it 'makes the school round', and they offer scholarships to outstanding students. New practice rooms and all the computer techy stuff necessary for advanced music composition are attracting more students to a place where the synergy between music and maths comes naturally.

Drama (also with many scholarships on offer) is 'absolutely fantastic' according to one ex-student and they take full advantage of being a short bus ride from the theatrical Mecca of the West End. Drama students go to plays regularly and get the full greasepaint experience by producing, directing and acting in theatres hired by the school.

A top-floor studio with an additional textile space feels more like an art school than an art department and the standard of work is correspondingly high. The head reports that art and drama numbers are steady but under pressure as they were not facilitating subjects for Russell Group universities (a term the universities have now dropped).

Once a year, everyone becomes creative and produces the Ashbourne Revue (always oversubscribed), which showcases dance, drama, music and fashion (much helped by the quality of the textile department).

Sport: An atmosphere and ethos that is more university than school and a site just off Kensington High Street makes it understandable that games are not timetabled and the students tend to be the initiators of any new sport. There is a very popular eight-a-side football club, the Ashbourne Allstars (a name chosen perhaps for its alliterative qualities rather than their goal scoring prowess) and students talk of how helpful the school is if they want to start any form of sporting club, down to finding a venue and providing the funds for equipment.

Ethos and heritage: It may have been in the same building for 27 years, but what started as one teacher in one room with two students aiming for better grades has grown into a school with nearly 300 students, and maths, science and economics A levels have been joined by 30 other options.

The classrooms are designed to suit the teaching method, more chairman and board members than teacher and pupils, with everyone sitting round one large table

As one parent commented on the school exterior, 'how it looks is not its most impressive side'. Turning off the High Street, under the stern gaze of two armed officers protecting the back entrance of the Israeli embassy, you follow a steady trickle of casually dressed teenagers (definitely no dress code) heading in through a somewhat scruffy door and up some concrete stairs.

The vibe inside is relaxed modern office rather than school lobby, with the receptionist half-hidden by a bunch of flowers and a library where young people are working on computers or chatting: apparently, a warning shot is fired if the noise level disturbs the workers on the teachers' side of the glass wall. The simple classrooms are designed to suit the teaching method, more chairman and board members than teacher and pupils, with everyone sitting round one large table and plenty of spaces to work around the school when not in class. Decoration is minimal apart from Rothko prints (much appreciated by us) and posters advertising the existence of an LGBTQ club and various other societies.

Across the High Street are the other two buildings, both on the same lines of functional classrooms and science laboratories, although the art room adds a splash of colour. The layout, constrained by its location, is not perfect, and a slightly wistful look comes into MK's eyes when he talks about the possibility of housing his school in a less bitty manner. That said, school has recently expanded its Young Street building to provide space for six new classrooms and an additional library/study facility.

Pastoral care, inclusivity and discipline: The GCSE pupils are under more supervision but everyone has a personal tutor whom they see twice a week, and the school counters its outwardly laid back atmosphere by using a highly sophisticated electronic system which both teachers and parents can access. This not only keeps a close eye on each student's academic progress but also on basics like whether they actually turn up for lessons and hand in their work on time. One parent told us that when her normally dead punctual daughter turned up late 'they were on it in a flash, leaping into action and checking where she lived'. Some 10-20 per cent of the students live away from home, but the responsibility lies with the parents for finding suitable accommodation and ensuring their welfare, although the school will provide advice and hopes to flag up any potential problems through its tutorial system.

This is very much a half-way house between school and university and some of the usual problems can arise, as they do in all London schools. Drugs and alcohol are only too readily available and sometimes the principal has had to exercise his zero tolerance policy and show the offenders straight out the door. Parents support the 'very hard line' and feel that the message he gives is a massive deterrent for the students. We also observed that on the surface everyone appeared to be much more intent on passing their exams than being led astray by London's temptations.

Pupils and parents: MK expresses slight surprise that the ratio of UK to international students over

Everyone appeared to be much more intent on passing their exams than being led astray by London's temptations

the last 10 years has nearly been reversed to 65:35 from the exact opposite, although he doesn't feel that Brexit is playing a part.

Still some students needing improved grades for top universities, but these retakers are less than 10 per cent currently with MK stating that they 'often are able to turn A/B students into confident As'. Most (about 70 per cent) of the English students come from private education and many from schools where they found it 'hard to cope and are looking for a different landscape'. The international cohort are truly global, but this is an environment where your English needs to be fluent as students are encouraged to speak English all the time, not just in school, where it is compulsory. As a result EAL classes (at no extra cost) have fewer takers now, although there are students of more than 40 nationalities.

Money matters: This level of teaching and class sizes never comes cheap in central London but to ease the pain Ashbourne offers some scholarships and bursarial help for exceptionally gifted drama, music, art and academic students.

The last word: For a self-disciplined teenager, who wants to be treated like a grown up, learn to run their own life and concentrate on academics, this could be just the answer. A parent backed this up saying that they 'treat them like adults but the boundaries are still there'.

Bousfield Primary School

2

South Bolton Gardens, Old Brompton Road, London SW5 0DJ

020 7373 6544 | info@bousfield.rbkc.sch.uk | www.bousfieldprimaryschool.co.uk

State | Ages: 3-11 | Pupils: 430

Headteacher: Since 2014, Helen Swain BEd MA, deputy head for previous eight years. Has been in teaching for 26 years and joined Bousfield as a year 6 teacher some 20 years ago.

Entrance: Due to cuts in funding there are now 60 part-time places in the nursery on offer, rather than the previous 30 full-time places. Two parallel classes from reception to year 6, each with

30 pupils. Applications for the nursery are done through the school; applications to the main school via local authority.

No automatic transfer from the nursery to the main school – parents must reapply. Children who are in care or have an EHC plan are considered first, followed by siblings and then proximity to school (currently approximately 0.5 miles and shrinking). Distance measured as the crow flies. Places do become available further up the school due to high mobility rates of pupils, so worth persevering. Hugely oversubscribed. As one current parent put it: 'If you get offered a place here, you'd be mad to turn it down.'

Exit: Most popular secondary schools include Holland Park, Chelsea Academy, Lady Margaret's, Fulham Boys' School and St Thomas More. Over a third go on to independent senior schools, including Latymer Upper, City of London, The Harrodian, Putney High and Francis Holland. No special preparation given for those doing 11+ exams. School knows a large amount of tutoring probably goes on, but says pupils get plenty of exam practice anyway. Much parental advice and support given when it comes to choosing next school.

Our view: Strikingly international, with 41 different first languages currently spoken at home. Sixty per cent have English as an additional language. After English, the most prominent languages are French and Arabic. School sees this cosmopolitan element as a real strength and the high level of harmony being something to celebrate. A significant number arrive with very limited English. It is 'sink or swim, but usually swim.' Much language teaching on offer, including Italian classes laid on by the Italian Consulate and French to all KS2 pupils. Bilingual pupils tend to outperform monolingual ones overall. Much coming and going due to large expat intake. Only about half the class in year 6 has been there from reception.

Superb academic results, particularly given the huge EAL contingent, though school always looking to 'up the ante'. English, maths and science Sats results well above national average. There are plans afoot to introduce some setting for maths and reading in year 6, though lack of space means separating children into groups is challenging. Pupils' progress is tracked carefully.

When we visited, children were beautifully behaved and fully engaged. A sense of calm pervades the school. Manners and presentation clearly high on the agenda. No uniform. Packed lunch or school lunch. Fruit given to the younger years.

One full-time teacher and one teaching assistant in each class, as well as extra support staff for pupils with statements and EAL pupils in the early stages of learning English. A great team of dedicated staff, who 'put the hours in'. Many loyal, long-serving teachers (20 members of staff have been there more than 10 years), as well as newer ones. A strong team – 'no prima donna.'

Bright, vivid displays throughout the school. Some classrooms smallish; every iota of space used. School is a 1950s listed building, with courtyards and coloured panels, which makes expansion and development problematic. Beatrix Potter was born and brought up in a house on the site.

Arts are very strong in the school, though not at the expense of academics. Lots of music, dance and drama going on. School believes performance helps to build children's self-esteem. Pupils are offered a rich curriculum, full of workshops, plays and concerts. More than 90 learn a musical instrument. Guitar and strings ensembles, two choirs but no orchestra. Parents attend practice workshops, so they know what a good music practice at home should involve.

When we visited, children were beautifully behaved and fully engaged. A sense of calm pervades the school. Manners and presentation high on the agenda

Plenty of sport – gym and games as well as after-school clubs offering tennis, football, cricket and even cheerleading. Swimming for years 3 and 4. Pupils take part in borough events (including athletics) in the summer term.

Quantity of homework has been reduced as parents were completing too much of the pupils' project work ('you can always spot the hand of a parent,' we were told) and copious amounts were being downloaded unthinkingly from the internet. Homework now more focused on the basics, with reading, spelling and maths given from early on.

Some children with EHC plans. More on the SEND register, receiving support of some kind. No specially trained teachers but school feels they have strategies and experience to help those in need. Has experience of pupils with Asperger's syndrome, autism, ADHD, emotional/behavioural difficulties and moderate/severe learning difficulties, as well as dyslexia, dyspraxia and hearing and visual impairment. School is not a centre of excellence for all of these – very occasionally pupils move to special schools, either when Bousfield can no longer adequately support them or when they move to secondary school. Staff say

Bousfield is 'an inclusive school' that does its best to accommodate those with difficulties.

Strong parental involvement, with school questionnaires showing overwhelming parental support and high levels of satisfaction. Numerous opportunities for parents to attend curriculum workshops and 'book looks' (when they visit to look at children's books). Parents welcomed in at the beginning of the day.

Some wrap-around care available, albeit not all on-site. Breakfast club on offer and pupils can be escorted to a neighbouring school (with more provision) at the end of the day if required.

Bousfield has close connections with artist Quentin Blake, who attends prize-givings and pops in regularly. All leavers receive a prize at the final assembly and Blake says his spirits are raised as each leaver is celebrated. 'After the ceremony, I go away feeling that at this point in their lives perhaps they really have all won,' he adds.

The last word: A great sense of purpose permeates this thriving school, with pupils bright-eyed and focused, offered a lively, dynamic and interesting education. As one satisfied parent lamented: 'I just wish it could go on into secondary school.'

Bute House Preparatory School for Girls

Luxemburg Gardens, London W6 7EA

020 7603 7381 | mail@butehouse.co.uk | www.butehouse.co.uk

Independent | Ages: 4–11 | Pupils: 318 | Fees: £17,529 pa

Head: Since 2012, Helen Lowe BA Oxford Brookes, LGSM Guildhall School of Music and Drama. Previously drama teacher at St Paul's Girls', curriculum co-ordinator at Lady Eleanor Holles juniors, and head of juniors at King's House, Richmond. Loves being head, stating convincingly that 'it really is the best job in the world, even with all the challenges.' A live wire with a funky appearance to boot: bright pink lipstick, cool glasses and statement hairdo. The girls love her warmth and straight talking. Not intimidated by pushy parents and no favourites among staff. She explains, 'I treat everyone the same and that makes people feel safe.' Fulsome parental praise. One father described her as 'inspiring' – 'She knows the girls incredibly well and really understands them.'

Unsurprisingly for such a ball of energy, free time is chock 'full of socialising, looking after grown-up family, trips to the theatre and reading'. Husband is a management consultant and writer, daughter a teacher and son a political journalist.

Entrance: Two entrance points, at 4+ (non-assessed) and 7+ (assessed). At 4+, ballot is drawn in presence of head, chair of governors, one of the school's accountants and registrar, so grovelling is pointless. Twenty-two girls accepted from a jungle of 400 applicants. Unsuccessful candidates kept on the waiting list for 7+, when another 40 are accepted. The 7+ assessment involves maths investigations, an open-ended discussion requiring critical thinking, an oral comprehension and story writing. School looks at how girls respond and focus. Girls' reactions to school tour also noted. Tutoring is futile, as girls are chosen for their curiosity, sparkle, and willingness to have a go, not on the spouting of accumulated knowledge. School is more delighted by girls who vividly recount their weekend adventures with granny, than those dripping with medals and certificates. No sibling policy at 7+, though roughly 60 per cent of sisters are accepted. This two-tier system is complex and causes considerable headaches for everyone involved but it is here to stay, for now.

Exit: Despite the sharing of some facilities, Bute girls sit 11+ exam for St Paul's Girls' School on same footing as girls from elsewhere. Many Bute girls end up there, as well as Godolphin and Latymer, Francis Holland (south and north), Queen's Gate School, South Hampstead High and Notting Hill and Ealing High. Popular boarding schools include Wycombe Abbey, Downe House and St George's Ascot. Starry results, which are the envy of other preps. Huge numbers awarded scholarships, from academic to ballet, chess, drama, sport and music. Head hates the stress that 11+ puts on families and wishes parents would just 'trust the school when it says that all will be ok.'

The head is a live wire with a funky appearance to boot: bright pink lipstick, cool glasses and statement hairdo

Our view: Named after the marquis of Bute who owned the original Bute House which stood on the site of the current swimming pool. Scottish link remains in the form of jolly Gordon tartan uniform.

Describing the building exterior as a carbuncle is putting it kindly, though the interior is spacious and attractive. Mammoth rebuilding programme means the school now boasts some of the best facilities in town, including a new playground, studio theatre, science lab, art studio, food technology room, library and digital learning space. An added bonus is the outside space attached to younger girls' classrooms. A godsend in the summer term. Reception girls are luckiest of all, with a vast room for their play-based learning incorporating a home corner, sand pit and water area with bubbles galore. Heaven on Earth for four-year-olds.

Non-competitive academic ethos is central to everything in the classroom, and this sets the school apart from other west London hothouses. Mixed ability classes throughout. No streaming, no scholarship sets, no prize giving and no rankings. Teacher feedback given as written comments rather than marks. Girls may be aware of other girls being quicker to pick up concepts, but the emphasis is on every girl running her own best race. Head is determined there should be 'no labelling, as it is very powerful. People tend to live up to their label and the damage is done. If you don't have a label, then you are much freer.' Girls are encouraged to give their own opinions, rather than trying to second-guess what they think the teacher wants to hear. Setbacks are seen as 'I can't do that yet' with the emphasis on 'yet'.

Exciting teaching is the norm, delivered by notably dedicated staff. Barely a textbook in sight. Maths often involves puzzles and investigations. Science might include the dissection of a sheep's heart and lungs. Everything introduced in an engaging way and the girls are genuinely enthusiastic about their learning. On the day we visited, one teacher encouraged her pupils to 'look at how the data tells a story' and another asked 'I wonder what would happen if …' In ICT lessons, lots of coding and graph-creation from the start. Older years get stuck into app design and computer simulation. Head declares, 'You won't find any girls here who don't like maths or technology.' We can well believe it. One pupil told us she wanted to be a doctor, not because she thought it would impress, but because 'there is so much to learn in science. It's just so interesting.' Head describes girls as 'very real' not the slightest bit prim. Modern languages taught with pizazz. French and Spanish from year 1. Emphasis on oral work, enjoyment and gaining confidence. Bi-lingual girls stretched with differentiated work in a specially designated audio-visual area, to the delight of their parents.

Emphatically, and refreshingly, not an exam factory, though from year 5 girls practise sitting formal assessments to prepare for 11+. Bespoke exam practice then offered as head recognises that different schools have individual exam formats and expectations. Calmly considered approach to 11+ exams, so the whole process is less of a circus than elsewhere.

Learning Enrichment department offers group and individual support, both in and out of the classroom from year one onwards. Some require long-term support, others only fleetingly and all intervention covered by the fees. A fluid system that delivers. Extension activities organised for exceptionally able, comprising roughly one third of the school. School enriches every which way. On the day we visited, a year 3 extension group was busy designing eco water bottles and could barely contain their excitement. Another girl was having individual support with decimals and was relishing the quiet lesson tailored to her own pace. Fewer than 20 girls currently have special educational needs, including dyslexia and dyscalculia. However, if learning support is offered but refused by parents, then they must sign a letter to this effect. Pretty draconian. Extra support also offered to girls who have English as an additional language, with areas such as inferential language and idioms. No stigma attached to extra support here, because it is spread over all ability levels, to stretch as much as to reinforce.

Barely a textbook in sight. Maths often involves puzzles and investigations. Science might include the dissection of a sheep's heart and lungs

Homework is not onerous, though daily reading is expected. At the start of term, a home learning menu is distributed, from which girls complete one task per week. By the final two years, daily tasks need completing. Head is averse to tutoring as 'it tends to increase stress and makes the girls more competitive.' She acknowledges that tutoring happens but encourages parents to come in to discuss it, so school can be directly involved.

All sports facilities on site. The envy of other schools where pupils waste endless hours in London traffic. Huge array of sport offered, from cross country to cricket. Bute girls are literal and metaphorical hotshots at netball and have twice cleaned up at national level for gymnastics. Unlike the academic approach, sport is competitive. Lots of chances to stretch growing limbs more informally too in the playground, whether climbing on the timber pirate-ship or bouncing on fluorescent space hoppers.

Fantastic dance and drama studio with a drama-school vibe, including curtains around the stage creating a black box performing space. Swish lights and sound system, and video-editing options. Teacher has a weakness for Stevie Wonder, so her music regularly booms out in dance classes. Drama teacher writes own plays, which are either a twist on other works or chances to explore emotion through performance. Another way this school sets itself apart.

When we asked a pupil what the best thing about Bute was, her answer was not the lively lessons or sensational sport. It was the kindness

Choirs for all year groups. Rock bands, samba schools, string quartets and ensembles of every hue and variety. Around 60 per cent of girls have individual music lessons. Girls encouraged to perform, no matter their level. One breaktime, we discovered two girls quietly practising a complex piece that one of them had composed. No fanfare. No showing off. Just Bute girls cracking on.

Well-equipped art studio, with kiln and heat press. Endless opportunities to be creative, from photography to manipulation of electric-conductive thread to make wrist bands. Specialist DT teacher in addition to art teacher. Recent creations include pets' toys, shawls and mini scooters.

Wraparound care now offered in response to increasing numbers of dual-income families. Clubs galore too, including street dance, cookery, musical theatre and debating. Wednesday afternoon clubs for everyone from year 1, incorporating drama, newspaper production, gardening and even the making of friendship bracelets. Residential trips to Isle of Wight, York and France. Optional trip to NASA, Orlando in year 6.

When we asked a pupil what the best thing about Bute was, her answer was not the lively lessons or sensational sport. It was the kindness. 'If you have any problems or are just having a bad day, there is always someone to help you.' Everyone is nurtured. Counsellor comes in three times a week, offering either drop-in sessions or pre-arranged appointments. 'Learning powers' are adopted wholeheartedly at Bute, as a way to teach life skills including integrity, initiative and risk taking. Pupils think in terms of what powers they will need to overcome daily challenges. Gives girls the language they need.

Younger girls are served lunch while older girls help themselves to canteen options. Lasagne and garlic bread perennial favourites. Sunshine tart, a creation consisting of pastry, syrup and cornflakes is the Bute House signature dish, served up on the school birthday, end of term and other high days. When describing it, one girl fell into a dreamy daze.

English is an additional language for two thirds of pupils, but 'all are in the advanced band'. Over 20 different languages spoken at home, mostly Spanish, French, Russian, Italian and Mandarin, followed by Hindi and German. 'We very much promote and celebrate the fact that we have so many languages spoken here,' says head. School runs an EAL programme for pupils; plans afoot to run a course for non-native speaking parents to help them support their daughters' advanced reading at home.

Parents must buy into whole ethos of school, rather than seeing it as a feeder for St Paul's or Godolphin. As elsewhere in west London, parents are noticeably more demanding and entitled. Some see the school as just another paid service. However, most are overwhelmingly happy and in a recent poll over 40 per cent stated that Bute exceeds their (extremely high) expectations.

Money matters: Up to six means-tested bursaries available at 7+. Roughly twenty applications per year. Some pupils receive 100 per cent reduction, others significantly less. Assets and salary assessed. Often awarded to very bright girls from single-parent families, who may lack adequate extension in the state system. Fundraising galas help source bursary scheme.

The last word: Parents love the school for its high academic standards and because the girls leave with a profound love of learning. They value the sense of empowerment it gives their daughters, reflecting the mantra 'we are the girls who will become the women who make change happen'. Girls adore it because 'every day is fun'. One of the very best preps in the country.

Cameron Vale School

4 The Vale, London SW3 6AH

020 7352 4040 | info@cameronvaleschool.com | www.cameronvaleschool.com

Independent	Ages: 2.5-11	Pupils: 60	Fees: £19,305 pa

Headmistress: Since September 2020 Bridget Saul BA (French with Italian, Uni of London), MA (Education, KCL), PGCE (Oxford). Previously head at Wandsworth Prep. Began her career at Tettenhall College in the West Midlands before moving to Thomas's, Battersea for 13 years where posts included head of French and monitoring and evaluation coordinator. She is a keen cake maker, proficient skier and avid cricket fan, following the progress of her home county team, Sussex.

Head of lower school (including the nursery) since September 2020 is Chloe Dorrington BSc (geography, Durham), MA (Education, Cambridge), PGCE (Cambridge). Previously, class teacher and pastoral leader (reception) at Thomas's School, Clapham, where she completed training in working therapeutically with children, with the charity Place 2 Be. She is a keen runner, with other interests including mindfulness, intergenerational care and baking.

Entrance: One class in reception, which is not about to change. Following the founder's maxim, they are still looking for children who will 'be kind, work hard and have fun'. A large number come by word of mouth, with many from the local nurseries such as Miss Daisy's. Occasional places further up the school, but the head says she will only take children who she believes will fit into the existing class.

Co-ed nursery opened in Sept 2020. The Chelsea Nursery will cater for children aged between 2½ and 4½ years old.

Exit: Definitely not an academic pressure cooker of a school but the children move on satisfactorily to their next destinations. Queen's Gate most popular, followed by Wetherby Senior, Queen's College, More House and Holland Park School. A few off to board. In the last three years there have been a couple of academic and music scholarships, which is a fair haul for such a small school. The founder, Josie Cameron Ashcroft, is also particularly proud that two of her past 'scholars' (paid for by the school's foundation) went on to St Paul's Girls and Godolphin & Latymer and subsequently to Oxbridge.

Our view: The Vale is one of Chelsea's wider and leafier streets due to the London plane trees that line it, but Cameron Vale is brighter than its neighbours, with shiny white windows, burgeoning flowers and a clutch of scooters hung on the railings in neat rows. Inside the front door, you are definitely in a house which happens to be a school, rather than an institutional building, with a frame containing pictures of 'school counsellors', marginally eccentric trophies, a tartan stair carpet and lots of pupils' artwork. Every conceivable inch has been used: teachers pop out of what appear to be cupboards, books are crammed onto walls, hidden by doors (health and safety at work) and the music room is squashed into the corner of a renovated garage. Nevertheless it all works, even if there is a lot of toing and froing on the stairs, controlled by a traffic system which seems to favour the continental approach – ie keep to the right. The outside space is basically a standard Chelsea garden disguised by fake grass, toadstools and hopscotch squares – pint sized but cheerful.

Following the founder's maxim, Cameron Vale is looking for children who will 'be kind, work hard and have fun'

The idea of the assessment process fazed one of the international families but turned out to be less daunting than they'd feared, and most of the parents we spoke to chose to send their child here after putting them through the equivalent scrutiny at alternative schools, a process colourfully described by one as 'a load of Mickey Mouse'. However, a parental statement that 'we looked at many, many schools' is the norm in the smarter enclaves of west London.

The school has spaces at the moment due to a hiccup some two years ago (a previous headmaster left at short notice), and the lack of communication with parents (which may not have been under the school's control) led to some families losing trust in the school. Nevertheless, the great majority of the people that we spoke to felt that they wanted 'to give them a chance because I trust the school and the teachers'. There is also an upside in that there is now a board of governors who provide both a buffer state between the owner and the parents and a source of expertise.

From the children on the ground floor, in a particularly well-decorated classroom with glitzy fish and strings of hot air balloon cut-outs (apparently jellyfish next in the pipeline), to the older ones under the roof, there was an air of happy purposefulness surrounding both pupils and teachers (one for each class plus an assistant up to the end of year 2, and a shared assistant each for 3/4 and 5/6). Lessons are differentiated rather than set and they run a Discovery Club for the lower school and an Explorers' Club for the upper school to stretch children who are showing greater academic ability.

For those who might need an extra boost or who have dyslexia or dyspraxia, there are two learning support teachers who work one-to-one. Both children and parents say there is no awkwardness over this and, indeed, one teacher and child were right out in the open when we visited, squeezed onto a landing, both of them only too happy to explain what they were up to. We remarked on how impressively tidy the writing and diagrams were, proving that if the numbers needed help, the letters certainly did not.

Cameron Vale is brighter than its neighbours, with shiny white windows, burgeoning flowers and a clutch of scooters hung on the railings in neat rows

The top two forms were involved in a practical and enjoyable experiment to see whether they could construct a transporter for an egg so that when it was dropped from the convenient balcony (watched by a crowd including the head) to the pavement below, it would survive the crash. This was a typical example of the obvious rapport between the children and the teachers, several of whom have been here for more than 10 years (and are mothers themselves) but whose ranks also include new faces.

Sport is always difficult for small London schools in adapted buildings but a big step forward has been taken by the intelligent sports directors of local preps (taking up a Cameron Vale suggestion) to form the Chelsea Prep Team, enabling them to make up teams to play larger schools and give the children more opportunities to compete in their own age groups. Sport is timetabled twice weekly with swimming in Chelsea Sports Centre plus games in Battersea Park, and although the school is a minnow in the prep school sporting world, karate has always been taken seriously and there are past and current black belts.

From the children on the ground floor to the older ones under the roof, there was an air of happy purposefulness surrounding both pupils and teachers

Music is intrinsic, with either Little Singers, the upper school choir or even the staff choir kicking off the day. Drama is not on the curriculum but regular school productions at the Kensington Library Theatre allow the older pupils to play the leads and provide lots of parts for the younger ones. There is a specialist art teacher and the results are displayed everywhere.

Clubs are mainly sporting, rugby and netball being particularly popular in the upper school along with karate and fencing and, guess what, lots of girls sign up for ballet. Hoping to give her charges a taste of life beyond Chelsea tractors and glam restaurants, the head is trialling Bushcraft (an opportunity to spend two nights in the relative wilds of Surrey).

Most parents tend to work in the law, finance, design or their own businesses and live locally, and the commute is mainly on foot or scooter. Over half of the mothers work (the head 'gets it because I'm a working mother too'), often for themselves, and there is the usual London international mix with a high proportion of bilingual children. The FoCV (Friends of Cameron Vale) suffered in the upheaval of the previous head's departure, but both parents and head announce that they want to reignite the flames and add to the current social events.

The last word: Cameron Vale appears to be sailing on happily once again under its new captain, but small is still the operative word here. If you have a child needing lots of professional TLC or even just a child that doesn't cry out for a larger environment then you should definitely consider this petite, engaging and competent school.

The Cardinal Vaughan Memorial School

89 Addison Road, London W14 8BZ

020 7603 8478 | mail@cvms.co.uk | www.cvms.co.uk

State	Ages: 11-18	Pupils: 1009; sixth form: 385

Headmaster: Since 2011, Paul Stubbings MA (40s), a classicist. Educated at Worcester Grammar school and Durham University. 'Home grown', having originally joined the school in his teaching practice placement in 1988, becoming classics teacher the following year. Was promoted from deputy head, pastoral, but don't expect soft edges – we've rarely met a head given to so many military comparisons ('sergeant major', 'leading his army of boys' etc), though you'll be hard pushed to find anyone with a bad word to say about him, with parents and pupils absolutely delighted. 'Knows his path and marches down it at full throttle – means we're always well ahead of the game educationally.' 'He's succinct, always to the point and so fast at dealing with any issues.' 'Very driven and absolutely loves the school and the boys.' Etc. All agree he's dynamic, fair and leads by example. Acutely aware of what he calls his 'dizzying responsibility', he is also outward looking – we were left in no doubt as to his insight into the sector as a whole or indeed his disgust at the 'profound strain' that state schools have been put under.

The worst thing about the job? 'That I literally have too much to do to continue teaching.' But he's on the daily lunch queues, when pupils told us he's as quick to have a laugh with them ('he calls me by the football team I support,' chuckled one boy) as to dole out his hierarchy of sanctions for untucked shirts (normal detention for a little bit of shirt, Friday detention for half way out, Saturday detention for fully out). 'I'd feel like Hitler in his bunker if I stayed in here all day,' he said, surveying his hyper-neat office – 'I've got to get out there and deal with Berlin and make sure the Russians aren't invading.' Reckons that, as a direct result, he has some kind of relationship with all of them and knows 80 per cent by name.

Calls the school 'unapologetically traditional' – 'not in the sense of wanting to turn the clock back, but by taking the best of the old and jettisoning the worst of it, then doing the same with the new. In other words, we steer a middle course between stupidly reactionary and crazily progressive.' Adult authority ('kids want it'), gowns ('which point to academic excellence and a badge of authority') and latest evidence based teaching (school is now a teaching school) are in; mute obedience is out.

Lives in the depths of south London with his wife; their son and daughter are both at uni. But doesn't he mind the hour commute? Not a bit: 'I'm like a dad in the adverts, engrossed in my latest book right up until Clapham Junction, then I turn into a different person ready for the day ahead.'

Entrance: Around 950 apply for the 128 year 7 places; pupils come from over 50 schools. School has long been (in)famous for the rigour of its admissions criteria and stories abound of devoted little church-goers being rejected on account of imperfect catechism or knowledge of parables. 'Nonsense!' bellows school. 'It's an urban myth that you have to be hyper-Catholic. If you're baptised, you qualify.' (Although note that weekly attendance at mass, holy communion are all taken for granted in applicants.) As to the other common accusation that the school is socially or academically elitist, 'cherry picking' pupils from privileged backgrounds (some eight per cent of pupils are on free school meals against 21 per cent in the local authority as a whole), school gives equally short shrift. After the 12 music places and priority places have been taken (Catholic children in care, siblings, etc), school says it uses a 'random allocator' for the 70 or so remaining places.

At sixth form, around four for every place – mostly girls, lots from Sacred Heart. To start with five A levels (don't panic – most end up doing four or even more likely, three), applicants need four 8s and two 7s at GCSE. For those that start with four (and usually end up with three), entry criteria is four 7s and two 6s. To kick off with two of your choice (probably dropped to one) plus business and sociology (chosen by school because the value added is huge), it's six 6s to get in and to do the business studies BTec, it's six 5s.

Exit: Nearly a quarter left after GCSEs in 2020 (more than usual) – most to join other schools, a few to employment, another few to other RC colleges. A regular mighty handful to Oxbridge (16 in 2020), most of the rest to heavyweight universities to do heavyweight subjects, many to study architecture and engineering. Popular destinations include Bristol, Leeds, Birmingham, Warwick, King's College London, Queen Mary, Sheffield, Nottingham, Edinburgh and Durham.

Latest results: In 2020, 54 per cent 9-7 at GCSE; 94 per cent 9-4 in both maths and English. At A level, 63 per cent A*/A (88 per cent A*-B). In 2019 (the last year when exams took place), 50 per cent 9-7 grades at GCSE; 94 per cent 9-4 in maths and English. At A level, 46 per cent A*/A (69 per cent A*-B).

Teaching and learning: Out of the 282 boys in the country who got more than seven 9s at GCSE, five were from The Vaughan. And remember this is a comprehensive school. Sunday Times regularly rates it as the highest attaining comprehensive school in the country (last time in 2018) and at A level, they get the second best results in the country for Catholic comprehensives (only recently, much to the head's agitation, being kicked off the top spot). Strongest performers are English, maths and sciences.

The headmaster calls the school unapologetically traditional – 'we steer a middle course between stupidly reactionary and crazily progressive'

No-one could eulogise the school's facilities. These consistently impressive results are instead a result of a one-track aim for academic excellence, which parents put down to 'traditional hothousing', 'high expectations in the classroom' and 'meticulously individualised learning'. 'Right from the start, the school gives you an idea where your son will be by GCSEs – that can come as a bit of a shock when he's only 11, but there's a detailed plan in place and that is all you can really ask for as a parent,' said one.

School believes the magic ingredient is streaming. While in other comps, the children would be in four forms of 32, the Vaughan divides them into five ability-based bands from year 7, with further setting in some subjects. The top three streams are home to the brightest kids, while the rest are a more mixed bunch – some knock on the door of the third stream while others have significant problems accessing the curriculum. So the school splits them into two groups of around 15 each. 'All good schools get clever kids doing well, but great schools ensure progression for all,' says head, who gets some of these boys into Russell Group universities. 'Subjects I really didn't think I'd do well in, I have,' said one, shaking his head as though still in disbelief.

French from year 7, with taster sessions in Spanish; both are available at GCSE. Top two streams also do Latin and those who do the GCSE can also take Greek. Most take 10 GCSEs, a few take 11. RE compulsory. Geography and arts particularly popular. School doesn't do well on EBacc, but head 'couldn't care less – if a boy would rather do art or music than French or geography because he knows he'll do better, then why not?' Huge co-ed sixth form, with largely traditional A levels and one BTec in business. Very little take-up of EPQ.

Learning support and SEN: School takes more than its fair share of children on ECHPs (23 when we visited, most with ASD) and as such, is a beacon of hope for parents of children with significant difficulties. New heavily staffed annexe gives these and other pupils with milder SEN (making up around 10 per cent of the whole school population) access to a whole suite from which they can gain one-to-one support if required, although classroom based interventions are more common. Gifted and talented isn't a term you'll hear – 'that is our raison d'être'.

The arts and extracurricular: Music, under the supervision of the highly regarded director of music, is 'astonishing', according to parents. It all started when the head 40 years ago decided to add to the 'perfectly normal music department' the elite Schola Cantorum. This became the catalyst that elevated the liturgy of the weekly masses – and they now go on regular tours to, most recently, South Africa, plus eg Spain, Greece, Holland, Germany, USA and the grandest places in Rome. They recently filled the Albert Hall and also perform at the likes of Cadogan Hall, St John's Smith Square and Westminster Cathedral. The Schola has its own Songschool – just like in a regular cathedral choir school – in which the choir rehearses: a real boon. Those with a talent for singing also get the opportunity to sing in operas at the Royal Opera House as well as the ENO and it was Vaughan boys that sang in the last Harry Potter film and Life of Pi. For less gifted singers, there's a non-audition choir. School also boasts two full orchestras and all manner of ensembles, plus concert bands and a Big Band which has a regular slot at the Bull's Head in Barnes and occasionally plays at Ronnie Scott's.

There's always a massive drama performance to close the academic year – most recently Kiss Me Kate. 'With so many of the boys classically trained in singing, the quality is superlative,' we heard.

Drama GCSE recently introduced despite government contraction in this area – 'I think it's really good for boys, taking them out of the edifice of themselves,' says head.

A thriving art department displays a good standard of ceramics, sculpture, mobiles, printing et al, plus wood, metal and plastic work from DT. 'There's lots of choice and you're given real freedom of expression,' a boy told us.

Roman Catholic faith permeates the very bones of the school, from the smell of candles in reception to the photographs of pontiffs dotted around the head's office

School runs more trips than all the other schools in the local authority combined – everything from skiing in USA to computer trip to Thorpe Park HQ. Vaughan Foundation means nobody misses out. All the usual clubs and societies available for those that want them, though surprisingly little take-up among the boys we met.

Sport: Vaughan rugby and football teams are not to be messed with and are widely respected by other west London schools. All this despite the boys' having to travel half an hour on the bus to Twickenham to train. In the last four years, the first XI football teams have reached the finals of the QPR league; in rugby, they are regular finalists in the Middlesex plate. There's a strong athletic tradition – the current European U20s high jump champion attends the school. Cricket also played in the summer. Fixtures on Saturday mornings, though if you get a detention you are in danger of being dropped from the team. There is a gymnasium on site and rock climbing, basketball and table tennis are also on offer. Girls in the sixth form can play netball, and some do rock climbing. 'There's real diversity – my son is playing lots of new sports and is really enjoying it,' said a parent.

Ethos and heritage: The school was originally built as a memorial to the third Archbishop of Westminster, Herbert, Cardinal Vaughan. Founded in 1914, it started life as an independent school with 29 pupils but became a grammar school in 1944 and a comprehensive in 1977. Girls started joining the sixth form in 1980 and it's now firmly co-ed and considered by most almost as a separate school. No chance of going co-ed throughout – not enough room. Today the school comprises three main buildings: the 1960s lump known as the New Building (or 'Grange Hill' by the head), the Centenary Building ('that's the LA Hilton') and the original building, Addison Hall ('Hogwarts'). The former two have been added on to over the years, with very little space left outside ('try playing basketball without knocking elbows – literally impossible,' a boy told us and don't get them started about the stampede for the library at wet break). Even inside, some areas are pretty cramped, not to mention bleak, although pupils say they have all the facilities and resources they need and we noted a roomy library, modernised science labs and lovely big art space among the highlights.

Located in well-to-do Holland Park – wide, quiet streets lined by well-appointed Victorian villas and mansion blocks. 'Jeremy Clarkson lives just up there and Simon Cowell had a house here at one point,' said one boy. Shepherd's Bush, on the other side of the monster roundabout seems a world away. Situated in these pricey, leafy avenues, you'd expect an upmarket local school population. But boys told us of classmates travelling up to an hour-and-a-half to get here – from the northernmost reaches of Barnet, Harrow and Hillingdon to Southwark, Merton and Kingston in the south. Here the offspring of a few of the well-heeled 'old' RC families from Kensington learn alongside those of their Filipino, Portuguese or Spanish live-in domestic staff – 'you have to reinvent yourself as we are all equal here,' says head. What they all share is a commitment to the Roman Catholic faith, which permeates the very bones of the school. From the smell of candles in reception to the photographs of pontiffs dotted around the head's office, there is certainly no shortage of visual clues. Meanwhile, religious observance includes year groups going on retreats at Tyburn Convent and at Farm Street and the school day and week are punctuated by regular mass, confession, Benedictus, Angelus and so on. All lessons begin and end with the sign of the cross and some teachers have prayers in each of their lessons – to a degree rare even in RC schools. 'Sometimes it can feel a bit much – the masses, in particular, can really go on,' said one boy, but pupils told us they are encouraged to enquire and debate, with theology, the philosophy of religion and epistemology and ethics all there for the taking. Faith, for those who have it, is expected to spill over to works, eg sixth formers take disabled children on an annual pilgrimage to Lourdes.

The atmosphere is orderly. During lesson time, you could hear a pin drop, not just in the corridors but in many of the classrooms themselves, save for the commanding voices of the teachers. Everything about the pupils – from their posture to their wide eyes – seems ready to learn; they seemed instinctively to know not to even turn to us as we walked in mid-lesson.

Notable former pupils include actors Richard Greene – Robin Hood in earlier days – and Roger Delgado, footballers Bernard Joy of Arsenal and Fulham and the last amateur to represent the England national football team, Paul Parker, Kevin Gallen of QPR and Eddie Newton, novelist Helen Oyeyemi and comedian Dominic Holland. Also WWII flying aces Donald Garland VC and Paddy Finucane DSO and recent Olympic rowing gold medallists Martin Cross and Garry Herbert. Many more seem, however, to have careers in the City.

Pastoral care, inclusivity and discipline: 'You'll smell it as you walk round,' said the head when we asked him about the standard of behaviour – he was right. Discipline couldn't be tighter – 'they don't let you get away with anything and they let you know that from the off, so few transgress,' reported a parent. For the little trouble-shooting that is needed, head's motto is 'firm, fair and fast'. Detention system for low level offences – scruffy uniform, talking over a teacher (this is the newest rule, known as 'TO') etc. Even the 20 or so fixed-term exclusions and one or two permanent exclusions per year (both massively below the national average) are far more likely to be for a build-up of these than for a serious whopper of a school rule violation. Zero tolerance for, and no real problems with, drugs – boys we met had just signed a pledge to never touch them. Nor could they remember the last time they saw a pupil smoking in the street: 'I don't think anyone would be that stupid – remember that even wearing your uniform wrong out of school will get you in trouble,' said one. Complete ban on mobile phones (including on journey to school) universally unpopular with pupils, although felt to have reduced the number of muggings. Minimal bullying – nobody denies some individuals are going to want to lord it over others in a school this size, but the culture of non-acceptance seems to prevent most gaining any real control. Catholic ethos underpins everything and is palpable. Sex ed taught by the RS dept for the moral side and the science dept for the biological details. Four houses – Campion, Fisher, Mayne and More.

Pupils and parents: Around half are from ethnic minority groups – after white British and white European, next biggest group is black African. Some 40 per cent EAL. 'The pan London multiracial aspect has been one of the best things about the school – I love the way our son is growing as an individual among this wonderful diversity,' said a parent.

Money matters: Head spends a quarter of his time asking (never pressurising, say families) parents, former parents, ex-pupils and friends to donate to the Love and Service Fund. The majority donate something, some more, some less, and the odd individual donors are particularly generous. Leads to an annual half-a-million pounds which is gift-aided up – school claims this has prevented teacher redundancies, keeps up smaller classes for less able pupils and provides more A levels. A few instrumental bursaries for sixth form entrants who must have reached at least grade 6 on an orchestral instrument.

The last word: Some see the Vaughan as a 'quasi grammar school' and its cousin in Fulham as a 'quasi public school'. Whatever you label it, we can tell you it's the kind of school parents search high and low for but rarely find. It's a school where everyone (school, parents, pupils) expects a huge amount from everyone else and, in turn, gives a huge amount back. But don't bother unless your son (or daughter in sixth form) won't crumble or rebel under unyielding authority.

Headteacher: Since 2010, Angela Barr BA Ed (50s). Has been head since school started. Previously head of the lower school at Pembridge Hall, another Alpha Plus school. Studied geography and education at Christchurch College, Kent University and then taught in a state school in

Essex before taking off and travelling around Africa for a year, with her husband Simon. 'I loved school and always wanted to be a teacher,' she says with passion.

Marked her 50th birthday celebration with another trip to Africa (Namibia) with her husband – this youthful, warm and attractive head is a spirited and independent character who lives for the moment and is all about the 'doing now.' Indeed, it's not often we come across a head who has zip-wired across the Thames to raise money for charity. One parent told us: 'She really is up for anything.' Another said: 'It was truly amazing and helped raise some much needed money towards the Evelina Trust at St Thomas's. It shows the sort of head she is.'

Teaching, she says, is her hobby – 'I love it so much it doesn't feel like a job' – and she is by all accounts a very hands-on head who personally supports youngest pupils with their reading. 'I am a big believer in getting children reading,' she says. Also works hard to make sure her staff are teaching with all the different learning styles in mind – 'essential in a co-educational school.' Parents have told us she is on the front gate to greet pupils every single morning, and knows every child by name and even their siblings: 'It gives a really personal element to the school and helps the younger ones settle in.' 'Firm but fair' we are told, and whilst she is open to new ideas and welcomes feedback from parents, 'she also won't be led by them, however influential and high powered they are.'

Still ambitious for the school as 'it's still growing' and, more importantly, 2018 saw the first set of (very creditable) 11+ results.

Entrance: Non-selective, so it's a case of registration at or as soon as possible after birth (embryonic stages even better). Current cost £150 – non-refundable if you don't get a place. School allots five definite places a month, and tries to stagger them among children born at the beginning, middle and end of the month, so no advantage in booking your Caesarean for the first of September. Attempts are made to keep an even number of boys and girls and those who drop out are replaced like with like, as far as possible, from the waiting list. That way they don't get a surfeit of, say, boys born in August. Priority given to siblings. The school now includes Little Chepstow Nursery which can accommodate 40 children, all of whom will be guaranteed a place at the school if they have spent the full two years there. Chepstow House has expanded gradually to year 8, with entry points at 7, 8 and 11.

Exit: Pupils can now stay on until 13, with year 6 leavers off to eg Francis Holland NW1 and SW1, South Hampstead, St Paul's, City Boys, Westminster Under and Wetherby. As a result most pupils now continue through, although there is a handful whose parents still opt for the 7+ to gain entrance to schools such as Wetherby, where competition is possibly less rife than at 11+. One parent told us: 'It's a shame Chepstow House doesn't go on until 18.' (We couldn't help feeling that there is no pleasing some.)

Our view: Born into the now well-established stable of Alpha Plus Group schools, this nearly fully matured school has much to live up to – no doubt in part due to the huge demand there is for good schools around the sophisticated area of Notting Hill. However, so far the school has risen to meet that demand with style. It moved to its stunning new home on Lancaster Road in 2014 (bang opposite its rival Notting Hill Prep), into a building formerly known as the Isaac Newton Centre. Tucked away from the hubbub of the Westway, the impressive black wrought gates are the only giveaway that there may be a school around. On entering what looks more like a portcullis than a gated entrance to a school, followed by a short walk through a tunnel, one arrives at the bright, glass-fronted reception.

It's not often we come across a head who has zip-wired across the Thames to raise money for charity. One parent told us: 'She really is up for anything'

Chepstow House is built all on one level… but what a level. The corridors are endless. With red carpet throughout, it feels more like a large, glamorous chalet, than any school we've been to. A very shiny and exquisitely maintained school, where even the teachers – blonde, long limbed, healthy – look as though they have stepped out of their own teachers' version of Tatler (we felt decidedly old and washed out). Children, too, look enchanting in their quaint red berets and jackets, girls in tartan pinafores, boys in red tank tops and grey shorts (some parents worry about their sons getting cold knees in the winter – although they can graduate to corduroy trousers from year 4 upwards).

It does feel very moneyed, but not pretentiously so, quite understated but with a few eye-catching facilities. We particularly liked the main hall, which also doubles up as the dining area and performance space, and is designed with a semi-circular upper level, which parents can stand on and look down to watch their children perform. 'A bit Shakespearean,' one parent said. Colourful mosaics of various animals adorn the walls, 'which most of the children have helped to make.' We were also struck by the imagination of many of the teachers, particularly in the gloriously colourful art room, with an assortment of interesting objects dangling from the ceiling or on the walls. The art teacher was enthusiastically describing her latest art project, which involved recyclables, at the time.

Another thing that caught our eye (and the first time we'd seen this in any school we've been to) was a very realistic looking fully clothed 'dead body' in the science lab, with an exact replica of a cordoned off area as a murder scene (even down to the windows with No Entry tape strips across). The science teacher – who clearly has a great sense of humour – told us that it was the pupils' job to find out how he died, by carrying out a series of forensic investigations. Genius and imaginative, we thought. The drama room, too, was an interesting space with the ceiling swathed in colourful Moroccan-style chiffon material. Much thought had gone into the aesthetics of the school, evidently.

Classes named after birds (get to year 6, and you make Eagle status). With a teacher and teaching assistant in each class the children get lots of support and attention. French and music start from reception. Three sets for maths in year 2 and lots of differentiation in the lower years. Maths Whizz, used from year 3, is a programme which individualises each child's maths programme 'to stop anyone falling through the net'.

Even the teachers – blonde, long limbed, healthy – look as though they have stepped out of their own teachers' version of Tatler

Each child has the use of an iPad – technology skills are learned on the job as well as in a separate lesson devoted to IT. We saw children as young as 4 year using iPads in the nursery. Any learning difficulties are identified quickly, says head. School sets high standards for reading and writing, and tracks development and progress in-house with a reading test as well as SEN assessment. One parent told us that her child is severely dyslexic, and needs a lot of extra support: 'Chepstow House picked up on this really quickly and were really on top of it.' This was echoed by other parents in similar situations.

The sense of purpose is palpable. During our visit, children were focused and interested in their lessons. We were amazed by the quality of writing from children as young as year 1. Gone was the giant, looping, large-spaced scrawl we often see from 5 and 6-year-olds, instead replaced by neat, legible writing kept between the lines. 'We spend a lot of time working on both their gross motor skills and fine motor skills. We even do magic spells with them, where they learn to pick up things with small tweezers.'

Music is vibrant and the pupils are introduced to a number of different genres. A number of pupils have violin, guitar or piano lessons taught by peripatetic teachers. Sport has also been taken up a notch since the school has grown and Chepstow competes successfully with other local independent schools. It's also very inclusive: there is an A and a B team for most fixtures, and everyone has the chance to compete. Sport is on site from reception to year 2 – from year 3 upwards they go off site for sports such as football, cricket and hockey as well as regular swimming and access to a climbing wall. 'I love the sport here; boys get to do netball and girls get to do football,' said one happy pupil. Lots of extracurricular, too, from fencing, dance and martial arts to Spanish, coding club and even skateboarding.

Ofsted was glowing in its report and the only minor criticism was the need for some sort of external covered area for pupils to play in all weathers. This has been addressed, and indeed the outside play areas are some of the nicest we've seen in a city school in terms of space and facilities. Lots to play with and play on, colourful and interesting and all beautifully maintained by the onsite manager and a couple of ex-parents who oversee the 'grow your own' area.

Parents from all over the globe – plenty of Americans, Australians and Canadians, a fair few from Scandinavia, Eastern Europe and Russia, as well as French and Italians. Attracts the less traditional English who prefer co-ed at this stage. Parents are in media, finance, law as well as in the arts. Head makes good use of the parents' experience. One parent arranged for someone from Sky News to give a talk in assembly while another organised expeditions to private art galleries hosted by another parent.

Parents are generally very supportive and enthusiastic. 'It's a tight ship – with high energy,' we were told. A very active parent committee, which managed to raise a gobsmacking £390,000 last year – through galas, fairs and produce selling (together with the head's zip-wire challenge). The school also ran a separate charity appeal for the partner school in Ethiopia, which raised enough money to build an children's home in the grounds: 'It was quite a year last year; I think it'll be a quieter one this year.'

Lots of smiling faces, both parents and children, when they arrive first thing. Kiss and Drop, as it is enchantingly called, is a system for parents who don't want to come into school and hang around until the official start time of 8.30am.

The last word: Head welcomes every child every morning and is proud of school's open door policy. 'We are not hiding anything,' she says. Nor does she have to. These children are very lucky indeed to have such a focused and privileged start to their education. Definitely one to watch if you live in or near this very oversubscribed area of London.

Christ Church Primary School Chelsea

1 Robinson Street, London SW3 4AA

020 7352 5708 | info@ccht.rbkc.sch.uk | www.ccht.rbkc.sch.uk

State | Ages: 4-11 | Pupils: 210

Head: Since 2009, Avis Hawkins, BSc NPQH (40s). Read psychology at Royal Holloway with a view to becoming an educational psychologist, but got the teaching bug while training at the Institute of Education. Started her career in a state primary in Lewisham, then opted for a struggling school for the challenge: 'That made me the teacher I am.' Appointed deputy at Christ Church in 2000 and was the natural choice to step into the role when previous head retired.

Attractive, energetic and disarmingly open, she has both children and parents on her side. 'So personable and friendly,' said one. Another added, 'Not the kind of head who just sits in their office,' though with the white and grey Danish-look furniture, complete with functional teaching table – no leather sofas here – she might be tempted. 'Open door' policy taken literally; pupils appeared in her study and opened up drawers in her desk during our chat. Her wide smile only wanes when lamenting the tight budget. In response, she has created an enrichment assistant, who makes the most of local contacts, invited to talk to hand-picked groups of children. Recent visitors include a fashion designer, artists from the nearby Saatchi Gallery, and volunteers from the Chelsea Physic Garden. 'I am taking experience-based learning and applying it to the curriculum,' she explains. Married with three children, two at the school, her hobbies range from food to DJ-ing. There is no doubt she leads by example.

Entrance: Vastly oversubscribed CofE school, with perennial waiting list. Priority given to siblings and families attending St Luke's or Christ Church, Chelsea; remaining places for other CofE families and locals. Takes from RBKC and Wandsworth, with a few from Hammersmith and Lambeth. Single class intake at reception, with occasional places further up the school. One parent told how 'wealthy families used to take them out at 7', but it appears they have now got wise, and none leave unless through relocation.

Exit: Increasing numbers, 30-50 per cent, to independents, including Godolphin & Latymer, Alleyn's, Dulwich, Westminster; lots bag bursaries and scholarships. Many to top London state schools: Lady Margaret, The Grey Coat Hospital, Chelsea Academy, West London Free School, Holland Park School, The St Marylebone CofE School plus Fulham Boys School. One parent felt more help could be given to parents with bursary and scholarship applications.

Our view: Located in the hushed affluence of a terraced square, in an area of celebrated artists, writers and politicians, this charming Victorian school has an exterior that harks back to a bygone age, when Chelsea was no more than a collection of small parishes, and church, schoolroom and public house all clustered together on one corner. 'A village school in the heart of London' was how one parent described it and the charm lingers on, with lollipop cherry trees and a butcher's boy bike poised to deliver lunches to a nearby nursery.

However, step inside and you have a Narnia experience: the interior has been redesigned to a spacious and functional plan, with chic grey walls, birchwood trimming and rows of navy pillars. Purpose-built in 2005, the main building on the north of Christchurch Street opens out to accommodate an internal playground for reception, with multicoloured apparatus, as well as an open central stairwell and roomy classrooms for years 1-3. Behind doors we found a cookery room, art studio and ICT suite, as well as cosy beanbags in the reading room (emphatically 'not a library') and a multi-use hall with gym and dining tables. As one parent put it, 'Every nook and cranny has to be made useful.'

The buildings are well maintained. The charming neighbourhood is reminiscent of a scene from Mary Poppins; all it lacks is a dancing chimney sweep

Outside and across a wide pavement (or The Piazza) the older years occupy what was the infant school, opened in 1850 by the patron, Earl Cadogan, we are reminded on a stone plaque. Three classrooms here have a more studious feel, with individual desks facing whiteboards, but each has its own corner with plump cushions for bookworm breaks. Opposite stands Christ Church, a Victorian gothic parent building, visited on feast days and Fridays by the school, while at the fourth corner of this tiny crossroads is the playground, discreetly hidden behind a tall wall of ivy. The large play area has been landscaped to accommodate a sports pitch, gardening plots, a pergola and free play areas. 'I would like a bit more playtime,' sighed one child, and we were not surprised. Several parents commented how well maintained the buildings were, and one ventured, 'environment helps behaviour'. The charming neighbourhood is reminiscent of a scene from Mary Poppins; all it lacks is a dancing chimney sweep.

This is a school that claims to take a holistic approach to education, but still hits the spot academically. Class sizes are 30, with a 22:1 student to staff ratio, but with lots of small groups or half-class sessions at specialist subjects. The head assures us, 'if you're looking for a school at the top of the league tables, we're not the school for you', but it is hard not to be impressed by these children's achievements on paper. Numeracy and literacy is managed by the leadership team as a through-school experience, not split into key stages. Verbal reasoning and non-verbal reasoning are taken in year 6; 'We pay lip service to the 11+ exams,' says the head. 'Aspiration is important.' We witnessed a Friday afternoon English class hard at metaphor and metre.

Inclusion is a watchword too, with several SEN children supported within each year group. A range of difficulties, from dyslexia to ASD, are managed by a dedicated department and visiting OT, SLT, nutritionist and school nurse. The head welcomes the differences: 'It makes everyone aware of social behaviours.'

Not surprisingly, the staff profile is 'very static'; several boast 10+ years of loyal service, so the head continually makes waves with professional training programmes. The school forms an alliance with four other local primaries, mutually inspecting and monitoring each other and offering suggestions. The head also has a knack of finding restless retirees and enlisting them into some extracurricular activity: a retired headmaster takes gardening, as a curriculum topic, directing the wheelbarrows, tending the chickens and watering the kale beds. Another ex-teacher runs cricket sessions in morning break, and several volunteers have become student teachers, and later join the staff. As one mum put it: 'They are very good at growing their own.'

There's a daring zing to the curriculum, or, as the head puts it, 'I am trying to make the curriculum wide enough and rich enough so children can find their talents beyond the three Rs.' This is evident in the music teaching: over 50 per cent of the school take up an instrument. Youngsters can pick up a ukulele, trumpet or drums, as well as the more usual options, funded for a term by the school. As an Artsmark school, there's an artist in residence in each year group, who encourages messy creativity in an upstairs studio. Year 1 recently completed a metal-bashing project, while the corridor was arrayed with giant paper planets. A recent leaver went on to star in the West End production of Matilda, a talent no doubt fostered in the ambitious Christmas and Easter shows; productions have included King Lear and Richard III (abridged).

A specialist sports teacher co-ordinates team games in Battersea Park or in the Royal Hospital pitches nearby. There's room for football and netball on the hard court in the playground, dance for boys and girls in the hall, and swimming from year 2 at nearby Chelsea Sports Centre. A mass of after-school clubs include Mandarin, chess, judo, and knitting as well as a kayaking experience up river to Putney. One parent had to pinch herself when faced with the list of clubs, for fear she had confused it with the exclusive school up the road.

Christian values appear modestly within the school, as a poster on the doorway or mosaics of Biblical scenes on the walls. There is daily assembly, led by the head, or a celebratory one each Friday, known by the visiting vicars as 'The Oscars'. Here the children applaud each other's achievements and two Students of the Week are named from each year. Other incentives to good behaviour include an afternoon's golden time, sparingly reduced for poor behaviour. One parent said, 'They are all incredibly well behaved and respectful,' and 'The last thing they would do is exclude a pupil.' The youngest children have a designated 'shepherd' from year 6 to sit with them at lunch. The system looks after the lambs but also instils a sense of responsibility in the older pupils. One mum worried that responsibility was not always shared evenly between the children: 'They could mix up responsible roles, like reading in church.'

Unlike many London prep schools, the pick up was not dominated by hooting 4x4s; instead, parents chatted outside in groups. The school's community spirit was evident: 'Phenomenal at bringing everyone together. Very welcoming,' thrilled one mum. Many meet up crossing the bridges from Battersea. One dad stressed the 'connectivity between teaching staff and parents'. There are parent workshops in maths and English, with crèche, to coach parents in helping with homework. Day to day queries are dealt with by phone or teacher meeting. More than one mum reported how they got an overnight response from the head and an invitation to meet the next day. Children are 'a mix of privilege and none', as the head put it, though all looked equally smart when dressed in the navy and cherry uniforms and stripy ties.

Parents and offspring raved about the improved catering. The kitchen is literally a home-grown affair, using eggs and produce from the school's garden, cooked up into healthy meals by two mums, who have a background in catering, with a sprinkling of advice from the community nutritionist. One of the cooks even delivers carry-outs by bike to a nearby nursery. The result is an education in healthy eating and sustainability. According to the kids, it tastes good too, especially the pizza and apple crumble.

The last word: This is a school that claims to take a holistic approach to education, but still hits the spot academically. The head assures us, 'if you're looking for a school at the top of the league tables, we're not for you', but it is hard not to be impressed by these children's achievements

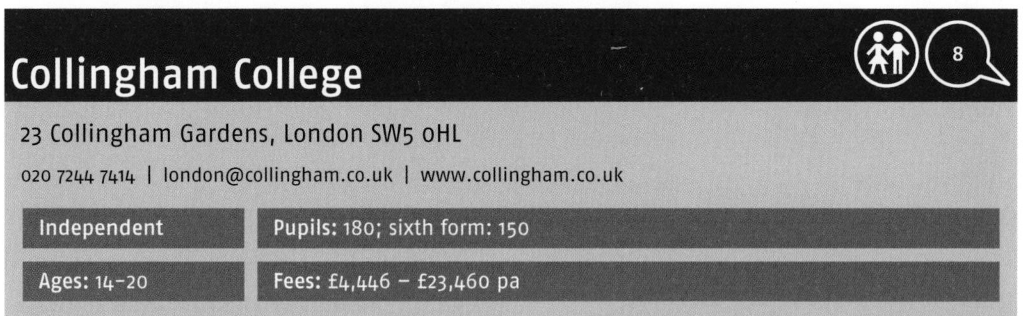

Principal: Since 2012, Dr Sally Powell BA (Royal Holloway), PGCE, MPhil, DPhil (Oxon). Charming and vivacious, she has been at Collingham for two decades and very much sets a tone of calm, welcoming reason. Raised in Guildford, she had an unconventional educational trajectory, beginning her first degree (in English literature) aged 24. 'I worked in bar jobs. It gives you a new perspective, and an understanding there's not just one path.' Her own route then clearly became focused, and after a PGCE from Oxford and a spell teaching in a state school, she returned to the dreaming spires to complete her Master's and PhD. While looking for a permanent academic post, she landed at Collingham. 'I found I was doing university-like teaching with really interesting students and I was hooked.'

Despite a heavy administrative load, she remains passionate about teaching, gets to know every student over tea in their first term, and is widely liked. 'She's very dedicated and hardworking,' said one parent. 'Highly approachable,' said another. A former chair of CIFE (the professional association for independent sixth-form colleges), outside of work she enjoys theatre and art. One daughter, currently at the college.

Entrance: No open days. Instead, prospective students and their parents are invited in for a meeting. 'We want to understand what we can do for them,' says head. 'What we offer has to be right for the student.' This is particularly important as families choose Collingham for a multitude of reasons. 'Some students have struggled elsewhere, some have been bullied or lost time through illness, and the fact that we offer a very flexible timetable means we're also a good option for those involved in sport or the arts at a high level.' Accepts new entrants in year 9 – useful for those who've failed to find a happy berth elsewhere or suddenly arrived from abroad – then generally admits about 10 in year 10, 20

St Paul's Girls' School

in year 11 for one-year GCSEs. The college, however, began as a sixth-form enterprise and the sixth form remains its primary focus. Around 60 new students enter year 12 for the two-year A level course, with an additional 20 signing up in year 13 for a one-year option. Some refugees, too, from the IB – 'We find there's sufficient overlap for them to complete A levels in a year.' No rigid grade benchmarks, but those hoping to study maths, science and languages at A level are encouraged (rather than required) to have grade 6 and above in a related GCSE. Entry possible at any point in the year. 'They're very understanding about sudden arrivals,' said one grateful parent.

Exit: Around a third leaves after GCSEs, usually for schools closer to home or offering subjects not available here. Their places are taken by a fresh intake. Around 90 per cent go on to higher education. School encourages pupils to aim for top universities and some 40 per cent go to Russell Group universities as well as art colleges. Popular destinations include Oxbridge (nine places in 2020), Exeter, St Andrews, Leeds, Durham, Nottingham, Bristol and Manchester. Popular subjects include medicine (four medics in 2020), sciences, maths, English, religious studies and classics. Art foundation courses and apprenticeships also popular.

Latest results: In 2020, 36 per cent 9-7 at GCSE: 48 per cent A*/A at A level (76 per cent A*-B). In 2019 (the last year when exams took place), 25 per cent 9-7 at GCSE; 40 per cent A*/A at A level (59 per cent A*-B).

Teaching and learning: Despite its non-selective intake, results overall are selective-school strong with 'value added' even stronger. At A level, a notable showing in history, economics, physics, religious studies and maths. GCSE results are less stellar, but reflective of pupils often on the foothills of the English language or confronting other difficulties.

At every stage, what distinguishes Collingham is its bespoke approach allowing students to turn the clock back, speed it up, or mix and match. 'Students can do A levels in one year or three, take one A level in one year and the others in two, mix GCSEs with A levels. Everything is honed to the individual.' Thirty-three subjects at A Level, 26 at GCSE and acrobatic timetabling and small classes (maximum eight in the sixth form, nine in years 9-11) allow almost any combination. Most take traditional academic subjects. 'Probably our greatest strength is in the humanities, but we're seeing increasing numbers in science.' Happy, too, to import tutors for less common languages such as Japanese or Portuguese. 'We're in London, so there's a really good tutor base.' Most, but not all, practical subjects – no drama or textiles, for example – and no EPQ. 'It's incredibly time consuming,' says the head, 'and I'm not sure it's worth it.' Instead, sixth formers are given the opportunity to research and write the school's own cross-curricular dissertation. Most take four A levels in year 12, dropping to three in year 13. GCSE pupils generally sit eight or nine, with compulsory maths and English and 'encouragement' to do a science, a humanities subject and at least one modern foreign language. Holiday revision courses available to allow both internal and external students to reinforce exam technique.

At every stage, what distinguishes Collingham is its bespoke approach allowing students to turn the clock back, speed it up, or mix and match

Staff are well qualified (good number of PhDs) and long serving ('I feel like a newcomer,' says the head). Some are practising artists or writers. Teaching qualifications less in evidence. Forty per cent full time, others share their teaching load with a university (such as Imperial College or Queen Mary) or professional commitment. 'They're passionate, energetic and knowledgeable and bring a wonderful wealth of experience to the classroom,' says head. 'We're also careful they can communicate.' Excellent relationships between staff and students, with plenty of positive reinforcement. 'I was incredibly impressed by how encouraging they were,' said one mother. 'Midway through my son's A levels, his results were a disaster, but his teachers engaged with him and were incredibly positive. In the end, he pulled the rabbit out of the hat.' Seminar-style teaching also boosts classroom confidence for those who may have struggled elsewhere. 'One girl told us that at her old school she always felt 20 pairs of eyes were rolling every time she said something; here, she feels everyone knows her well so can speak out.'

Long working day – 9.30-6pm – but years 9 and 10 finish at four and year 11's hours kept as compact as possible. All lessons are two hours long – 'It provides a more focused atmosphere and helps with organisation' – and all classes mixed ability. 'You can do differentiation well if you only have five or six pupils.'

Parents kept firmly in the loop with half-termly reports and termly parents' meetings. 'We have very full communication,' says school. 'It's a small team and parents can speak to teachers immediately about problems.'

Learning support and SEN: The most able are 'stretched' in the 'Electus' programme of visits and lectures, and a permanent SENCo provides good support, mainly outside the classroom, for a range of difficulties – primarily dyslexia, dyspraxia and autism spectrum. Head warns, however, 'You do have to be fairly independent. This is a sixth-form college environment not a school.' EAL well catered for, with eight hours of English instruction a week plus preparation for IELTS.

The arts and extracurricular: Very strong reputation for art – pupils have won top prize in the Royal College of Art Young Artist competition twice – and budding talent is nurtured in a picturesque pitch-roofed studio. Art, film and photography all available and high-quality output ornaments corridors and staircases.

A reasonable range of after-school clubs – chess, film, drama and art – but no orchestra or major school productions, and parents have been known to complain about the range. 'The focus of the college is academic,' says head. 'Everything else is here on the doorstep.' Plenty of outside speakers, debates and discussions, plus theatre, museum and gallery visits and an annual ski trip.

Sport: Some sport, though definitely not the place for those looking for world-beating teams. GCSE pupils play football in adjacent Kensington Gardens, sixth formers travel further afield for football, netball, basketball and gym. The college fields a boys' football team, which plays in a sixth-form college league, but insufficient interest from girls means little in the way of external competition.

Boarding: No boarding option, but the college can sponsor Tier 4 visas and help with homestays.

Ethos and heritage: Founded in 1975 as a private tutorial college, Collingham Tutors, the college has now developed a broader remit, but continues to be a family-owned business, overseen by the sons of the two founders.

Based on two sites half a mile apart, A level students are taught in a grade 2 listed redbrick Victorian house, which originated as a grand private residence and has left it a legacy of a vertiginous sweep of staircase and vast first-floor drawing room (now the study room/exam hall). Facilities up to date but not luxurious. 'If you're looking for an Olympic size swimming pool, you won't find it here,' says head. That said, a space for everything with 20 classrooms, three labs (including sparkly new basement science lab), a dark room (for 'the magic of wet development') and dedicated space for SENCo. Classrooms are master-bedroom size, and all lessons taught in a horseshoe formation. 'It gives a very different relation with the teachers.'

'My daughter felt she fitted in for the first time,' said one mother. 'It's full of cool, slightly wacky kids. She finally felt at home'

Parents and pupils see the scale as a strength: 'My son loves the cosiness of it.'

In January 2020, years 9-11 were relocated to an elegant, double-fronted Georgian building just off Kensington High Street refurbished with soothing Farrow & Ball colours, contemporary art prints and a string of clean, white classrooms, including a large lunch-cum-common room.

Overall numbers are those of the average London prep. 'It's been deliberately kept small,' says school. 'It means we can be light on our feet and make decisions that work for the students.' Traditional but relaxed atmosphere – on our visit a member of staff was asking, 'Shall I put the kettle on?' – and students clearly like the homely feel and supportive, close-knit community. 'My son has made very good friends.' The shift to linear A levels has also given a boost to student-generated activity. 'With no exams in year 12, we now have a lively student council, which organises numerous fund raising activities from a treasure hunt to a 'Bake Off'.

Elaine's basement café opens between 10-5, serving morning pain au chocolat and tasty home-cooked lunches. 'Students are free to go out but when work piles up, we provide everything here.'

Pastoral care, inclusivity and discipline: Little scope to go astray with 20 hours of teaching in year 12, 18 in year 13, plus four hours of closely monitored 'supervised study' (with no music or phones). Each class registered individually and parents immediately contacted if child not in attendance. 'They're given a little bit of freedom, but not too much.' Excellent pastoral care is administered by personal tutors who meet their tutee regularly on a one-to-one basis, providing help and guidance with studies and career decisions. 'My daughter, who couldn't make up her mind about which subject to choose a university, was given endlessly patient support,' said one father.

Outside the timetable, sixth formers are free to come and go – and lunch in local South Kensington venues is popular. Some cluster outside the front door for a less than surreptitious cigarette, but no common room means free moments are often spent sitting in the downstairs hallway under the eye (and feet) of staff. 'There's nowhere to kill time,' says head.

The ethos of the college demands a certain level of maturity. 'It's quite an intensive environment and you have to behave in a grown-up way,' says head. Drink and drugs lead to immediate expulsion, day-to-day misdemeanours addressed through talk. 'Most things are rectified through conversation,' says the head. 'Anything that disrupts learning is not acceptable. If there are those who don't appreciate that, regrettably they have to leave, but it's very unusual for that to be the case.' No formal assemblies and few obvious rules, but atmosphere of tolerance, punctuality, and politeness seeps through and students are courteous, approachable – and happy. 'It's the first time in his entire academic career my son actually looks forward to going to school on Monday morning,' said one parent. A view echoed by others.

Pupils and parents: Mostly domestic, with large numbers from UK independent schools from a wide catchment across London and the surrounding suburbs. About 35 per cent arrive straight from boarding. 'Their parents often welcome two years when they can be at home before going off to university,' says the head. And, of course, for creative types, the siren call of London is irresistible. 'If you're very keen on the arts or music, there's much more on offer than in rural Devon. Here, a teacher can say, "I think we'll walk to the V & A this afternoon".' An eclectic, cosmopolitan mix – 'We don't have a mould; they come to us to find something that fits them' – which pupils and parents recognise and embrace. 'My daughter felt she fit in for the first time,' said one mother. 'It's full of cool, slightly wacky kids. She finally felt at home.' Pupils generally confident and mature, responding positively to the individual approach.

Money matters: Fees depend on numbers of subjects taken. High-performing students from the state sector are sometimes awarded a means-tested bursary, to a maximum 30 per cent fee reduction.

The last word: A bespoke education addressing the needs of individual students in a friendly and nurturing environment, allowing them to flourish and often succeed beyond expectations. 'My son, who stayed for GCSEs and A Levels had the most fantastic teenage years. It really was a tailored education.'

Colville Primary School

9

Lonsdale Road, London W11 2DF

020 7229 6540 | info@colville.rbkc.sch.uk | www.colville.rbkc.sch.uk

State | Ages: 1–11 | Pupils: 480

Head teacher: Since 2011, Jagdeep Birdi BA QTS (40s). Studied history, English and education at Lancaster, then headed for the Big Smoke, where he has since taught across five different London boroughs. For the 11 years before he joined Colville, he was deputy head at Ronald Ross, Wimbledon, then at Sir John Lillie, Fulham.

Despite the school leaping from its place in the bottom 200 schools in the country to one of the top 200 since he joined, he's not one to wax lyrical about vision, strategy and grand plans. In fact, this modest, mild-mannered man even struggled to answer our questions about what makes the school stand out, although you don't have to talk to him for long before his passion and dedication for both education and this school reveal themselves. It is this heartfelt, unaffected and laid-back attitude – in which aspiring for the best is seen as the most natural thing in the world – that staff say sums up his leadership style. He joins the children daily for lunch, as well as doing the meet and greet daily and both children and parents chat to him informally – he knows them all. 'His natural manner is to make us feel as if we're an important part of the school – that our views about the school matter as much as the teachers,' said one parent. Another told us, 'I don't think you could find a more accommodating head.'

His first-floor office – a Big Brother set-up, with floor-to-ceiling glass overlooking the key stage 1 area of the school – seems an unlikely choice for such an unassuming leader. Until, that is, staff explain that actually, it means they can see when he's free to talk to and, perhaps more crucially, it places him firmly at the heart of the school rather than being hidden away in some corner office.

Entrance: After the customary priority for looked-after children and those with special needs, siblings are next on the list. Then it's down to distance, which currently stretches to 0.45 miles, although this is rapidly shrinking, with over 200 applications for the 60 reception places. Even if families move to another part of London, they tend to stay, with some children coming from as far as Hackney and the far side of Barking. Cohort is truly ethnically diverse, with 46 languages spoken and no dominant group among them (even the most common language spoken apart from English only has 18 speakers). 'These children know how to acquire a language – that's a good thing,' says the head, adding that diversity is seen to enrich the school. Seventy per cent of pupils at the older end of the school are on free school meals, although that figure drops to just 10 per cent at the bottom end, telling you all you need to know about the change in reputation of the school.

Though not one to wax lyrical about vision and grand plans, you don't have to talk to him for long before his passion for both education and this school reveal themselves

From September 2020, subject to Ofsted approval, a new school nursery will enrol 54 pupils aged 3 and 4, who will attend 8.50am-3.10pm Monday to Friday. School will also admit up to six children who turn 3 during the term of admission. Priority given to pupils who attended Colville Primary Nursery during 2019-20 and are not of reception age, followed by looked-after children, children of staff, then siblings.

Exit: The largest share – half the pupils – go to the local comprehensive of Holland Park, whilst around a quarter go to Kensington Aldridge Academy. The rest go to a wide range of comprehensives right across London, with a handful per year group now moving into the independent sector.

Our view: 'Let's not beat around the bush – this school used to be appalling when my child, who is now in year 6, joined,' said one parent. 'Colville was the school that nobody really wanted for their child and the one that poor low-income families got lumbered with,' reported another from the same year group. But in the last five years, standards of attainment have shot up, with Colville having received two ministerial congratulations in the last two years – and parents, particularly those of the older kids, can't believe their luck.

Teaching was poor, acknowledges the head, and the school wasn't in a good place. 'A number chose to leave during my first few months. Now we get top-notch teaching staff coming in and the teaching is rigorous, particularly in maths and English.' There are specialist teachers for computing, games, art, music and French, all of whom teach from reception upwards and every teacher we saw in action – bar none – was successfully engaging the children. There's a lot of them too (males as well as females), with some classrooms we visited having four teaching staff for 24 children. Most of the teaching assistants are graduates. These extra adults bods in classrooms also means there's more room for learning-through-doing. In fact, we didn't see one instance of chalk-and-talk during our visit.

Outside, there's a reasonably sized tarmacked playground that's tucked behind the fashionable Portobello Road and overlooked by high-rise flats and town houses. Playtime here does what it says on the tin, with raucous children running around loudly and happily and making full use of the new plush, large wooden climbing structures. There's also a school garden and separate edible garden (with links to Wholefoods in Notting Hill). 'You don't get left out here because we have a playground buddy system,' one pupil told us. A school survey, completed just prior to our visit, found that 99 per cent of children felt the school is a respectful environment, where pupils are respected whatever their background.

Originally, the school opened in 1879 as Buckingham Terrace Primary, when six teachers – poor things – were charged with 550 pupils. During WWII these pupils were evacuated and when they returned after the war in 1945, the school reopened as Colville Primary. The old laundry building (girls were taught laundry back in the day) has now been converted into a modern, welcoming space for reception, while another outdoor building is home to the nursery. The rest of the school is taught in the three-storey main building, where the (mainly) large classrooms boast high ceilings and where there are three school halls, one doubling up as the dining room known as Le Bistro (one pupil told us the one thing she'd change about the school is the food; that said, only 20 or so kids choose to bring in packed lunches).

The well-stocked, spacious library is welcoming, while the art studio/food tech room is huge and light. 'I never thought my son would like art, but he loves it now,' said one parent, who praised the specialist art teacher's links with local galleries, including the Saatchi gallery. Music is taken seriously, with all children given the opportunity to play instruments, with a steady stream of six peripatetic teachers teaching in small groups and individually. There's a school choir (which has performed at the likes of the Royal Albert Hall) and orchestra. Much of the school could do with a lick of paint and it's never going to look state-of-the-art due to the age of the building, but space is used impressively and the £4.5 million refreshment has made some exciting changes.

Sport is fun and inclusive, with all the usual options, some are taught on site, others, including swimming, involve a short walk to the local leisure centre. There are links with major local football clubs and Lord's cricket ground and dedicated coaches regularly visit to teach and enthuse the children. 'Sport is brilliant in comparison to other inner city schools,' one parent told us.

The school's motto, 'Inspiring success', is clearly not an empty phrase here, but something that they aspire to for every child. Part of this involves setting – in phonics and reading from October half-term in reception, and in maths from year 2 – while another area of focus for the school is SEN. With seven statemented children when we visited, and plenty with extra needs ranging from those on the dys spectrum to those who may not have quiet areas to study at home, the school has made sure it is a learning environment where individual support is prioritised and provided both inside and outside the classroom. Without really planning to, the school has also gained something of a reputation for specialising in hearing loss.

Behaviour is generally good, with a traffic light system helping to keep youngsters on the straight and narrow and privilege points to counter them, which can be redeemed for toys out of the special cupboard when they reach increments of 10. 'Ten points will buy you a nice little toy, but if you save up 30 or 40, you can get something like a Bop-it,' said one pupil excitedly.

There is before and after-school provision, plus a breakfast café which parents can come to and 42 before and after-school clubs from breakdancing to violin and ballet to gardening club. School trips a plenty to the capital's museums, Kew Gardens and Holland Park (the latter for forest school), while year 4s upwards get to go on residential trips. Community links are a strength, with children involved with everything from Jamie Oliver's (for cooking sessions) to Salvation Army (where the choir performs to the elderly).

The last word: We found this school refreshing, unpretentious, aspirational and spirited. It is also testament to the fact that, with the right leadership, a poor performing school can become a school of choice within a short space of time – not just for parents

École Française Jacques Prévert

10

59 Brook Green, London W6 7BE

020 7602 6871 | info@ecoleprevert.org.uk | www.ecoleprevert.org.uk

Independent | Pupils: 260

Ages: 4–11 | Fees: £6,756 – £7,563 pa

Director: Since 2016, Delphine Gentil, who was a head for 10 years in a country school in France before applying to the French authorities to be moved to Jacques Prévert. She is in London with her two children, who attend the Lycée Charles de Gaulle, and her husband commutes regularly from France. She is sporty and cycles and swims regularly. Cheerful, enthusiastic and clearly hard-working, she is thrilled to be in London and hopes to extend the minimum three year contract (maximum allowed by the French state is five years).

She is enamoured by the greater freedom she has in England regarding the curriculum, the budget choices and the collaborative work between London's French schools. More pastoral care, more awareness of the need to support pupils with SEN (her special area of interest) and improved English curriculum have been her particular input to the school in her short tenure. Excellent Ofsted report reflects her efforts. Parents say she is 'excellent' and 'respected by staff, parents and teachers', although some parents also bemoaned the turnover of heads imposed by the French department of education and the fact that tenured staff may end up with more power than the short-term head... Parents praised 'the great lengths she goes to, to make sure pupils acquire diverse experiences rather than just learning about things "the French way", including supporting teachers' projects such as going to the opera in Holland Park, going to the Hindu temple in London, getting out to see art and theatre, bringing in experts from other cultures'.

Entrance: Admission at all times of the year, not academically selective, priority given to children from French schools (either in France or abroad). French aptitude test if pupils are not from a French school and are over 6 years old, to ensure they will be able to access the curriculum, though children can join the infant section without knowing any French. Some 80 per cent French pupils and a few British, Turkish, Canadian etc. British families choose it if they live locally and want a reasonably priced small school (all the scooters parked up showed evidence of locally living pupils and a sustainable travel plan). This is a French state school though – so not strictly an independent school. Some parents felt that there is a two tier system with French families given preferential treatment at entrance and in the school.

Exit: Pupils mostly expect to move on to the nearby French Lycée (which remains the parents' main choice with a number of pupils joining the International Section if their English is good enough – all applicants for IS got places recently). It used to be a feeder school to the Lycée, but a secondary school place there is no longer guaranteed. If not, then they might choose the newer Winston Churchill school in Wembley or other French schools. A couple each year to English schools – Francis Holland, for example – though parents aware that they will get little, if any, advice on transfers to to non-French schools. Furthermore, it is not possible to move to another French school without the current school's written permission – this means the school has more power than is usual and parents cannot vote with their feet to move to another French accredited school if they are not happy.

Our view: The school follows the French curriculum entirely; half staff brought in from the French authorities, so they are French 'fonctionnaires', and half the staff are locally employed. The head (on a short-term contract and with little real power) has however managed to bring about some changes – interactive whiteboards and updated classrooms to make the most of the small, awkwardly shaped rooms in the 'charming and historic' redbrick house facing Brook Green in Hammersmith. Parents appreciate the setting, 'leafy and facing the green and in a lovely part of London'. Two sets of stairs (one for going up and one for coming down), a tiny playground, canteen in the basement with good quality (mostly organic) food made from scratch on the premises. Lunch menu published weekly, though kids bring in packed lunch on Wednesday when they all have half day.

The school has been updating its IT provision – 70 new iPads to back up the small suite of computers in the well-stocked basement library. Enthusiastic French librarian brings in guest authors and teaches library skills. Pupils are encouraged to borrow from both the French and the English libraries. Emphasis on rote learning and neatness, with a strict French national curriculum to follow and reading and writing only after year 2. Before then, plenty of work on fine and gross motor skills, language acquisition and memory. Specialist teachers for English and music.

One parent told us that 'at the end of year show you can't hear their English accent or know whose mother tongue is English'

Four hours a week of English work with English teachers, who follow an adapted curriculum with differentiated content and teaching according to pupils' level of English. If a pupil comes in with no French (one of the 20 per cent non French pupils, for example), they are given extra support in French. One parent told us that 'at the end of year show you can't hear their English accent or know whose mother tongue is English'. However, parents pointed out that this is French school, not a bilingual school, so all English teaching is a bonus. Pupils seem to reach a surprisingly high level of English thanks to some inspirational English teaching – quite a few pupils named English as their favourite subject (though science and lunch time followed closely on our straw poll). French parents said that English tends to be the main language in the playground (helped by English speaking playground assistants – 'when they are not on their phones,' complained parents). That, together with PE and science often taught in English, helps their children acquire really fluent English and become truly bilingual; all of the pupils we spoke to slipped easily from one language to another. Parents and the head are aware of the 'challenge of a good level of English instruction in a French school'. The very much improved English teaching and newly developed English curriculum was raised by most of parents as being a real asset now. Parents said 'the quality of instruction is superb', giving as an example the fact that this small school had several pupils who came in the top one per cent of 30,000 French students in an international maths competition.

Lunch playtime either in the small playground or opposite in Brook Green, sports at local centre include swimming as well as rock climbing, ice skating and rugby, alternating between years and terms. Playtimes and classroom assistance run by 'animateurs', not teachers. Littlest ones have gym in school hall. Dedicated music room and teacher who helps pull together end of year show and Christmas choral performance. Some art by class teachers enriched by visiting artists who help on projects and for inspiration. Thanks to increased interest in supporting diversity by the current head, there are pupils on a register with different levels of educational support – some with in school and in class differentiation and awareness, some with outside support, families frequently using French speech and language and other therapists. The odd pupil with a teaching assistant (paid for by parents). Building totally unsuitable for anyone who can't manage the many stairs.

The head is very keen to work on pupils' wellbeing, since she 'can see how pressurised both they and their parents are, living and working in London'. She has introduced workshops looking at mental health and self-esteem, and 'who they are as a group and how to behave in a group', with lectures and training by a psychotherapist who works with pupils, parents and teachers. Pupils are an enthusiastic bunch, wanting to share their love of the school – 'I love everything' repeated by several pupils we spoke to. If they had come from schools in France, they appreciated the art and music and sport, which don't happen much in France. If they had come from English schools, they liked the clear rules and purpose. Working parents also appreciate pre- and post-school care in morning club from 8am onwards ('my child just loves morning club,' said more than one parent) and after school in clubs and then daycare until 5pm.

In many families both parents work, but they are very involved in the school – either on the management committee or in the PTA, or as class representatives, meeting three times a year to discuss class issues. These meetings – or conseil – cover matters raised by parents, though this is vetted first and there are no independent governors or parents at these meetings, so some concern by parents about how to complain and be heard. Parents help to run the many subsidised extracurricular clubs, taking pupils to outside school clubs, organising rotas and finding leaders to teach, for example, coding, football, karate, chess, zumba, art, cooking. The school management board appoints the local staff who are not appointed by the French government. Issues can be raised with the class representative who then may take them to the conseil, but there is only one parent meeting a year, so not the kind of parental inclusion seen in English schools. Parents can see the head informally, as she is at the school gates each morning and evening, or by email or appointment. Head regularly meets with 13 other French curriculum schools in London and they share good practice and joint training.

Many also all raised the fact that most pupils 'feel looked after and loved, in an environment where they are safe and taken care of', though if a child is not happy, there was concern by some parents that the response is very poor.

Money matters: Means-tested bursaries available to French citizens.

Parents all mentioned the 'outstanding value for money' aspect of the school – 'much more reasonably priced than other London private schools, and one of the cheapest French schools in London too'.

The last word: A close-knit and purposeful school that follows the French curriculum. Parents who want to get involved can do and pupils are an eager bunch who tend to lap up all the school has to offer.

Falkner House

19 Brechin Place, London SW7 4QB

020 7373 4501 | office@falknerhouse.co.uk | www.falknerhouse.co.uk

Independent	Pupils: 286
Ages: 3-11	Fees: £10,140 – £20,010 pa

Principal: Anita Griggs (60s). She's the daughter of Flavia Nunes, who set up the girls' school in 1954 to give girls the same educational advantages as boys. She also oversees the boys' school, opened in 2017.

Falkner House is a family business par excellence. Flavia Rogers (40s), headteacher of Falkner House Girls School (a qualified history teacher who taught in New York and at Kingston

Grammar) and Eleanor Dixon MA Cantab (30s), headteacher of Falkner House Boys' School, are Mrs Griggs's daughters. The three form a tight management team. 'You could move any of us into either of these three jobs,' says Mrs Griggs. A third daughter, Marina Wood, works as the registrar of the boys' school.

Individualistic, kind and with just the right amount of firmness, the principal and two heads focus on developing the characters of all children in their care, as well as academic achievement.

Education is 'a gift which nobody can take away from you,' says Mrs Griggs, and 'it should come with no strings attached.' When speaking about the girls' school, she defends a woman's right to be at home as vociferously as her right to work. 'There is sometimes a sense of it being a shame for a well-educated woman to be at home with her children,' says Mrs Griggs. 'But don't tell me that a woman at home looking after an autistic child isn't working as hard or harder than anyone in a job.' Saying that, she estimates about 70 per cent of Falkner House mothers work outside the home.

The heads make a point of not talking about careers to the children, or, for that matter, exam results. 'Each child is cherished for themselves, not because they are good at maths, or cross-country. We nurture them and the exam results are a happy by-product,' says Mrs Rogers, a sentiment echoed by Mrs Dixon, who speaks of 'happy rigour and love of learning'.

The three describe themselves as 'producer consumers' because each was educated at Falkner House and had or has children at the schools.

Entrance: Entry to the co-ed nursery is by date of registration after birth. Entry from 3 years old, two sessions, morning and afternoon, each with up to 24 children.

Education is 'a gift which nobody can take away from you,' says Mrs Griggs, 'and it should come with no strings attached'

Entry to reception to both the girls' and boys' schools is by assessment for which children cannot be prepared. They are looking for children with the ability to remember and use relevant information while in the middle of an activity, as well as demonstrating that they are 'ready to learn' and 'have an ability to listen'. Characteristics like kindness, focus and 'genuine enthusiasm' also count. The heads say that they don't get many 'false positives', and turn down a 'significant' number of children.

There is no guaranteed sibling policy, although siblings are always 'very much given additional consideration'.

Falkner House Girls' has a single form intake of 24. Most families live in Kensington & Chelsea although many also come from further away (eg Hammersmith, Fulham and Barnes).

Falkner House Boys' (in Penywern Road nearby in Earl's Court) also has a single form intake of 24, with a similar catchment area. They opened in 2017 and currently have boys from reception to Y4. In the first year of opening, over 70 boys applied for 24 places, and the school is already oversubscribed. 'We couldn't have done it without the reputation of the girls' school, but we wish also to be judged on our own merits,' says Mrs Dixon.

Exit: In 2020, five boys out of 28 to St Paul's at 7+; one to St Paul's and two to Westminster out of 12 at 8+. For 11+ girls in 2020, two out of 22 to Godolphin & Latymer (including one music scholarship, seven to St Paul's Girls, two to City of London, two to Latymer Upper, one to Fulham Cross, one to Notting Hill & Ealing, one to Queen's Gate, one to Putney High School, one to Benenden, one to St Mary's Ascot (academic scholarship), two to CLC (including one academic scholarship) and one to Wycombe Abbey.

Our view: Falkner House schools pride themselves on the character, as well as the academic achievements, of their children. The aim is for both the girls and boys to go to their next schools 'brimful of confidence', says Mrs Griggs, whose idea of a successful Falkner House child is one who can 'pick up a train at Vladivostok by themselves and take it onto Moscow without being able to speak Russian'.

Parents speak of both schools' emphasis on creating 'impeccably behaved well-rounded children' where 'manners are more important than an A*.'

Falkner House Girls' School – two Victorian houses knocked together in Brechin Place – is demarcated by a collection of scooters hung outside the side door. Falkner House Boys' School is nestled in Earl's Court. Once inside, both schools are spread over four or five floors of brightly lit classrooms, music practice rooms, art rooms, dining rooms (with fresh food prepared each day that has excellent reviews from pupils and staff alike). Each site has a hall where school assembly happens every morning, and at which guest speakers are invited – recently an American astronaut spoke at a whole-school assembly hosted at the boys' school.

Parents report the 11+ as 'stress free' for their children. 'Your child will come out of the 11+ smiling,' said one

Both schools consciously foster a sense of family. In addition to a house system, older girls mentor their little 'sisters' and 'brothers', and four dogs shared across the two sites add to the sense of home. There are portraits and antiques, and, in the girl's school, reminders of the school's founder, Mrs Nunes: some paintings and her collected netsuke. The boys' school is a similar mix of the domestic and academic, with the top floor of Penywern Road now a science lab, and the lower ground will become a creative arts centre in 2020.

Key to the Falkner House ethos of care and nurture is the idea that as well as exploring a syllabus that includes DT, history of art, art, Latin (from Y5), geography, RE and music, children are prepared for exams during school hours. Both schools are vehemently opposed to tutoring, and hope that parents listen to them. Homework is limited and holiday homework is minimal.

The boys are prepared for the 7+ and 8+ in much the same way, with 'a blend of academic prep for exams, with nurture and love of childhood, and never having to choose between either extreme,' says Mrs Dixon. The school seeks to ameliorate any stress at sitting the 7+ and 8+ with 'the best teaching, small group work and sanity'. The head speaks of 'doing right by these boys without damaging them, having seen so much happen to brothers of the girls.'

There's an emphasis on building children's confidence. One parent from the girls' school described a 'dream team' of teachers that see the girls through exams. Parents report the 11+ as 'stress free' for their children, and 'fantastically handled'. 'Your child will come out of the 11+ smiling,' said one.

There is a culture that focuses on encouraging children to be aware of each other and kind, and Mrs Rogers speaks of how 'tolerance' is 'dripped' into everything they do. The children we met at both the girls' and boys' school were articulate, engaged and charming.

Teaching at both schools is praised by the parents as managing pressure for the children while stretching them to achieve their best. Teachers tend to stay for a long time, which fosters a sense of tradition and what Mrs Griggs describes as the 'historic memory'. Teachers are chosen for their experience as well as excellence. Boys in particular 'can be an unforgiving audience,' says Mrs Dixon.

There is a small outside playground at each site which is used a great deal, and four hours of off-site sport a week is timetabled for each group. PE happens in Holland Park and Battersea Park, and Y3 children swim at the Virgin Active in Fulham or the pool on the King's Road.

At both schools, there are specialist PE staff with a traditional gender divide. The girls are taught rounders, netball and ballet, whilst three PE staff oversee the boys' football, rugby and martial arts. Both boys and girls take part in cricket, athletics, swimming and cross-country, with a joint annual cross country, swimming and sports day (which includes Y1 and Y2 running the 400m, and Y3 upwards the 800m).

The schools discourage screen time at home, and pupils are not allowed mobile phones in school or on school trips. The year 5 and 6 curriculum is taught on iPads at the girls' school, and the same will happen at the boys' school. Both schools have a dedicated head of IT.

The curriculum is broad, both traditional and modern, and includes Latin from year 5 and Greek myths and legends from year 3, as well as RE, art, art history, DT, music and computing, plus Spanish instead of French. There is no official SEN provision at either site, and the (very) few learning issues are dealt with by the mainstream staff.

Most of the pupils in Y1 and above learn an instrument and play in chamber groups and orchestra. There is a whole-school drama production every five years (Oliver! in 2019, staged at the Southbank Centre). The wide range of clubs and co-curricular activities includes art, sports skills, chess, cookery and football (boys and girls), as well as netball, street dance, musical theatre and ballet (girls) and rugby, tennis, robotics and drama (boys).

There is no board of trustees, no PTA and no school motto. 'I hate slogans,' says the principal, adding 'Do what you believe to be right and you will carry people with you.'

Parents don't miss the PTA (indeed some find it a relief that there isn't one). They speak of how accessible the principal and the heads are at both sites, and the supportive school-parent relationship. Mrs Griggs, who lives above the school in Brechin Place, will invite parents in for dinner – especially if they are going through troubled times. They have 'never had a child leave for financial reasons,' she says, although there is no formal bursary policy.

Alumnae include Amber Rudd and (appropriately) her daughter journalist Flora Gill.

The last word: Schools often claim to be like a family but this one really is. Turns out polished, confident children with a love of learning and empathy for others.

Fox Primary School

Kensington Place, London W8 7PP

020 7727 7637 | info@fox.rbkc.sch.uk | www.fox.rbkc.sch.uk

State	Ages: 4–11	Pupils: 387

Executive head: Since 2006, Paul Cotter BA PGCE (40s), who is executive head of the federation of Fox Primary and Ashburnham Community School, Chelsea. Previously deputy head at Avondale Park Primary, North Kensington. As successful head of Fox, became acting head of Ashburnham, and oversaw the transformation of the smaller school at World's End. Sees the formal union of the two schools, both with multicultural populations but from different social spheres, as a positive: 'Fox has benefited from the whole experience. We've had to reflect upon our own practices'. Described as 'approachable' by the parents, and visible at the school door every day.

Head of school since 2013, Emma Madden BA (Cantab) MA (IoE); mid 30s. Like Paul Cotter, joined Fox from Avondale Park Primary in 2007, swiftly rose through the ranks of assistant, deputy, then associate head. Married with two children, husband works as an environmental campaigner. To call Ms Madden purposeful is an understatement; more like a human dynamo. She takes great pride in the school's training record, and is at the door every afternoon, keen, committed and capable; but don't expect a relaxing chat over coffee.

Entrance: LA managed, prioritising looked after children, exceptional need, siblings and children of staff. Then by random allocation within priority area, which extends from Chepstow Villas to Kensington High Street, from Kensington Palace Gardens to Holland Park, including more billionaires' basements than you can shake a stick at, and a small local authority housing estate. Some occasional places, but loyalty is encouraged. 'We only want people to come if they intend to stay,' says the head of school, with a nod at the 'state till 8' brigade.

Exit: Roughly half of all leavers go to Holland Park School, a few to Chelsea Academy. Others (with helping hand from a tutor) successful at top London day schools, including St Paul's Juniors, City of London Boys and Girls, Latymer Upper, Godolphin & Latymer. Parents say head makes no judgement about where the child goes, as long as it's the best fit.

Our view: Perfection comes in small packages, and the teaching at Fox Primary is no exception. The small classes (two of 24 per year) and the impressive KS2 Sats results (around half reach above the expected level) have consistently put the school high in the league tables. The key to its success is training good staff, of which they are justifiably proud. 'It has huge respect for teaching as a profession,' a parent remarked. Emma Madden is unashamedly serious about the school's role as a training centre, providing professional development for two London boroughs as well as courses for newly qualified teachers and TAs. In addition the school is a maths hub for central and west London, sharing methods among teachers as far as Shanghai.

Fox publishes its own cookbook, with toothsome photographs by one of the parents (not a turkey twizzler in sight)

We were surprised to hear that, though energetic and youthful-looking, some staff had more than 10 years' experience, and a few up to 20. The best of the newly qualifieds in training at the school are persuaded to join. 'There's a lot of support for young teachers,' said a parent. 'I guess you want that fresh voice, but you want it to be quality.' The school has children with statements supported by the two special needs teachers, one a science specialist, but overall number of SEN children is lower than average. EAL proportions are high. One parent remarked how quickly the class teacher had noticed and dealt with her daughter's reading and maths difficulties. Support came in the form of small group work and individual attention; 'She's flying now,' commented the delighted mum.

Classrooms are high ceilinged, utilitarian design, with steel framed windows, many brightened up by pots of geraniums. The younger years enjoy the ground floor rooms, where round tables in primary colours, a carpeted reading corner and bunting brighten the space. They make the most of their direct access to the rear playground, where netball posts share the tarmac with raised vegetable beds. Upstairs, we met a class of older children, in quiet discussion at a large group table. Another group was colouring the Brazilian flag in a geography lesson, strains of gentle music in the background. We heard from one articulate boy that a parent had visited earlier to teach them some Portuguese in addition to the Spanish, taken in class. On the top floor a music activity had children, grouped in front of the whiteboard, following acoustic patterns by clapping out rhythms. A display of the SS Windrush emblazoned the white walls of the oldest children's room in celebration of black history month. The children we met were unpretentious yet confident, happily engrossed in their work. PE in the hall, involved youngsters shooting hoops in sensible royal blue T shirts and track suits. No uniform otherwise, though Hackett rugby shirts were all the rage.

Fox values are displayed around the school: collaboration, loving learning, independence, creativity. All children learn recorder in year 3, with individual instrument lessons offered further up the school. A school orchestra practises before lessons. Shows are big at Fox, with end of year productions carrying an ethical message (Charlie doesn't just find sweets in his chocolate factory but Fox's moral values too). 'They are really nice events,' said a parent, 'with a lot of real warmth towards the child who stands there.' Other children join the inter-schools' debating team. A makeshift studio in a classroom at the top of the school allows the specialist art technician space to do her thing. We saw satisfying slab pots and displays of paper cutting.

An experienced PE teacher, 'adored by the children', ensures every child in year 6 represents the school in an activity: football, tag-rugby, hockey and netball run alongside judo and athletics in local leagues. Table tennis is a big success, with an all-weather table in the playground, and involves ex-Fox students in national tournaments. With many working parents, clubs after school are popular; one parent told us, 'The day people sign up, parents are queuing into the street'.

Founded in 1842 by a doughty female philanthropist, Caroline Fox (curiously under-celebrated at the school, we thought), when modish Notting Hill was no more than muddy fields. Originally a charity school for the local labouring classes, Fox Primary moved to its present site behind the antique shops of Kensington Church Street in 1935. Since then, the utilitarian architecture has withstood a sea change of bohemian chic in the neighbourhood. Within the high walls surrounding the school, some of the noble intentions of the founder re-emerge in a save the planet philosophy. A children's eco committee rakes out compost, feeds the wormery and monitors rubbish, and has achieved the Green Flag award. Solar panels operate on the roof, while a water butt supplies the gardening teacher with rainwater to cultivate some tasty extras for lunch. The chickens have now given way to beekeeping and two hives produce Fox honey, which is sold for school funds. These city children are not just playing farms, they grow their own lunch and even supply produce for a local restaurant.

Shows are big at Fox, with end of year productions carrying an ethical message (Charlie doesn't just find sweets in his chocolate factory but Fox's moral values too)

Lunches are cooked on site, with meat delivered by Lidgates butchers on three days; the rest of the time it's a meat-free menu. Some choose to bring packed lunches. 'Food's excellent,' said a parent. Favourite dishes included chicken and rice and yogurt fruit compote. Fox publishes its own cookbook, with toothsome photographs by one of the parents (not a turkey twizzler in sight). Trips out have included the Holland Park edible garden and London Wetland Centre, as well as the walkable South Kensington museums.

'We celebrate success a lot,' remarks Emma Madden, both among the four houses (named after species of fox: arctic, desert, silver, red) and at afternoon assembly, timetabled at 3pm, to keep the mornings free for the most concentrated tasks. Children are motivated in class by the chance of becoming 'Star/Speaker/Reader of the week' or by competitions, eg 'Who can invent the healthiest snack?' with a trip to a local café as a reward. Homework is regular but not excessive, numeracy once a week, reading and spelling daily. 'Behaviour is very, very good,' remarks Emma Madden; 'children need to have clear expectations.' Parents' concerns are managed by face-to-face meetings with teachers in the playground each morning, or by email. Despite this, one mum felt notice of school decisions did not always get through. 'I know the information is there, but it's just letting the parents know... it's been a full time job keeping up with it all.' Parents' evenings twice a year bring opportunities to chat to the class teacher, as does the annual international evening, a festival of the multinational flavour of the school.

The parents are a committed lot; 'Fox is fortunate as it is in an affluent area,' said one mum (very low numbers on free school meals). Despite the area being known for its cosmopolitan beau monde, the school's parents include a few past pupils as well as professionals from business, legal and arts spheres. Fundraising by the parents, through summer and winter fairs, aims to create benefits for children from all backgrounds – Caroline Fox would be proud.

The last word: For the fortunate who break through the oversubscribed entry lists and can breach the formidable railings outside, it is a rare find: a quality education with a broad curriculum, led by a staff with vision and commitment. As one mum said, 'It's a brilliant school and we are very, very lucky.'

Heads: Since September 2020, Christopher Cockerill, who grew up in Anchorage, Alaska and Surrey and attended TASIS England and Imperial College (maths). Before joining Fulham, he was director of sixth form at North London Collegiate School. Has also worked in Highgate School and Sevenoaks School. Plenty of experience at pre-university stage, including IB, A levels and American advanced placement courses. Married to Olivia and has two children, Eric and Jonathan.

Head of prep since September 2018, Neill Lunnon BSc (40s). Previously biology teacher, housemaster and master in charge of football at Wellington College 1994-2018, his first post after uni (where he met his wife, now head of Wimbledon High School). Spent three years on secondment at linked prep, Eagle House, as deputy head of strategy, performance and pastoral care. Raved about by parents for, among other highlights, open door policy and dedication – can be found at 7.30am on wet Saturday mornings on match duty. Extends to residential trips. He turned up midway, checked everyone was happy, then drove all the way home again. 'Delightful, chatty, approachable,' says a mother. 'Whenever you email him, he emails straight back, knows all the children's names.' Signed birthday cards to all prep pupils one of the highlights of their time at the school.

Head of pre-prep since 2005, Di Steven BEd. Previously deputy head for two years. Before that, taught in independent girls' school for three years, after 12 years teaching in Scottish state primaries. First teacher in her family. Had originally planned to be an architect but gave in to the lure of the profession at university. Talents now diverted into timetabling (eye for structure essential) and creating wonderful and versatile backdrops. One moment it's a pastoral landscape for summer production, the next a winter wonderland (just add reindeer and cotton wool). Originally saw role as a stepping stone to another role but 'loved the entire feeling and ethos'. Teaches literacy and numeracy (toggles between years 1 and 2). Clearly a fine diplomat – has established excellent relations with neighbours, bonding over recent successful communal effort to make busy road at back one way.

Entrance: Main entry in reception based on date of registration – the earlier the better. Either offered a definite, reserve or waiting list place. Non-selective, aim for balance of genders, birth dates and also give priority to siblings as long as it's felt they'll thrive. Was taking in four forms in each pre-prep year during building works, now back up to five.

All new reception children visited by pre-prep team who speak to keyworker to assess strengths and areas of need. Where child has learning needs, will involve SENCo to see if can make it work – have had children with visual impairment, specific learning difficulties (normally diagnosed at ages 7-9). If needs (like ASD) make environment uncomfortable for pupil, school will work with parents to find an alternative setting where can flourish.

Parents see the school as occupying the middle ground – a relatively unselective place where pupils can be themselves

Smaller intake in years 3 (15 pupils), 7 (25) and 9 (15) – some occasional places available in other years. Mostly automatic entrance to prep and senior school from pre-prep, though will sit assessment.

Largely local intake – nurseries, pre-preps and preps as well as state schools. About 30 per cent from 'all over the world'.

Sixth form opening in September 2021.

Exit: Small numbers to eg Ken Prep at end of year 2 but most carry on until at least year 6 (when 45 leave) or year 8 (35 departures) – so parents looking for a change of scene at 7+ or 8+ are on their own. Instead, thoughtful transition from pre-prep to prep with numerous opportunities to get acquainted for the children to visit the prep school, including full day of lessons in June.

Latest results: First GCSEs will be taken in summer 2020, first sixth form will start in autumn that year, working towards IB.

Teaching and learning: Parents see the school as occupying the middle ground – a relatively unselective place where pupils can be themselves. If you like the approach, great, but accept that it won't be for everyone. 'School is very honest that it's for some children and not others,' says parent. Air also allowed into the curriculum by way of themes that work their way through every subject – an approach that's a much touted feature of many schools, says head, but frequently not done terribly well. Links to philosophy of Inspired, the new education group owner of the school, which extols benefits of 'lateral thinking, comprehension and innovative application of skills and concepts'. Could range from getting each senior year group to create or make something (anything from a party to a play or charity initiative) to a whole-school teaching initiative, where members of staff filter a theme through their own subject. It's also – like other London schools – tapping into the current vogue for building young entrepreneurs, with initiatives like 'Perfect Pitch' – a competition where teams present their business ideas to a panel of judges.

Goals are 'simple' says the school – it's all about diversity of outcome, with children's achievements celebrated in context. Low-ish class sizes (18 in pre-prep and prep, normal max of 22 in senior school) undoubtedly help, ditto the pupil to teacher ratios, best of all for seniors – just 3:1 (compared with eight and six to one in prep and pre-prep respectively). Senior ratio will change as school expands.

Lessons are big on interactivity, delivered by what parent described as 'sensational' teachers (some stalwarts with decades of experience). In pre-prep, child might be singled out for score of 3/10 in spelling that – for them – is exceptional. Displays don't seek to backspace the mistakes. One year 1 pupil's cheeky picture of a big cat was labelled, 'A lion can eat a persn' (sic).

Key in these youngest years is fluid differentiation – no setting – with children moving to different groups for literacy and numeracy and TAs used tactically from year 1, going where they're most needed, adding spot of challenge here, a dollop of support there (while there's no official labelling or comparison children here as so often have a very clear idea about their strengths).

Form teachers (impressively large number of men on the staff) cover much of the ground, but school stresses number of specialist teachers employed (they reckon a school USP). Music, dance and French (from reception); ICT, art and sport from year 1. Science, taught in the lab, big on experiments but low on Bunsen burners (come in at prep stage). Plenty of (chaperoned) movement between lesson venues sows seeds of later independence. Prep adds additional subjects (such as Latin – from year 5) and – from year 5 – specialists in everything.

Inspired, the new education group owner of the school, extols the benefits of 'lateral thinking, comprehension and innovative application of skills and concepts'

Between years 5-8, some pupils stay on, others prepare to leave and new pupils join. School's solution is for everyone to follow the same curriculum, syllabus broadly aligned with Common Entrance and sets (and CE scholarship group) introduced in year 7. Exams become more formal (taken in the school hall from year 5). 'Don't go from zero to 100 but ease their way. The pace they go in year 3 isn't the same as year 5 or year 7 – it's like building a muscle, not throwing into the deep end but allowing them to swim up there,' says parent.

Parents stressed the particular magic that goes into the 11+ and Common Entrance process. Somehow it's de-toxed, they say, so that children genuinely seem to approach exams as a step up rather than a mountain to climb. 'Haven't seen my child or friends exhibit any sense of stress or anxiety,' thought one parent.

Emphatically not a testing, testing and more testing regime (though for all the laid-back vibe, tutoring remains rife, according to parents). Instead, plenty of opportunities for original thinking and attractive addition of gentle humour. To hear year 7s confidently debating the proposition 'Are we born evil?' with a fine line in semantics – one point was dismissed as an opinion, and thus invalid – was an eye opener. Plenty of fun, too. We enjoyed watching some of the younger prep pupils, delighted to be creating a marble run out of cardboard boxes and sellotape.

While numbers going on to senior school are currently small (children who've had almost a decade's worth of the school by year 8 understandably want fresh horizons) parents think it can only grow in popularity. 'Having a senior school that's co-ed and middle of the road and caters for a wider range... [makes it] a fantastic option,' says parent. 'There's a huge need, particularly in this part of London because there just aren't that many options.'

To hear year 7s debating the proposition 'Are we born evil?' with a fine line in semantics – one point was dismissed as an opinion, and thus invalid – was an eye opener

Expectations in senior school are that everyone will take six core subjects at GCSE (English lit and lang, maths, and three sciences) plus four options, including French, Spanish and Latin, art and design, computer science and drama but currently not music or PE. School does its best to be infinitely adaptable. Flexible approach to subjects – if children really aren't keen, potential to drop a subject. Tracking and progress designed to pinpoint where student is and what might be capable of achieving (will soon be compatible with pre-prep and prep tracking system).

Preparation underway for first teaching of the IB programme in September 2021 when the new sixth form opens.

Learning support and SEN: There are regular reports and meetings, not so much to pick holes but fill any gaps, while much praised SEN team offers one-to-one lessons (extra charge, maximum two a week) with dedicated SEN team (two in pre-prep, working four and two days respectively). Also sessions with external OT and SALT who work across other schools.

The arts and extracurricular: Drama and music felt to be most popular synapse boosters and first-class throughout. Lots of choirs (separate for boys and girls) orchestras and ensembles – even a percussion club and school of rock band, while pre-prep pupils enjoy timetabled lessons that include a weekly singalong for each year group together and, from year 2 are introduced to recorder, violin and ukulele. Chamber choir much praised – singing is 'amazing', says parent (an understatement, if final prep rehearsals for Lion King on day of visit were anything to go by). Around 170 pupils take individual music lessons in school (many more outside), achieving up to grade 7.

Residential visits start in year 4 with trip to Flatford Mill learning (among other things) to set humane mammal traps. Also annual ski trip, assorted sports tours (year 5 football – boys and girls – to Gothenburg). All teachers are involved in running lunch time and after school clubs (others bought in at extra cost). Prep pupils are encouraged to choose at least one club each term – homework to hair braiding, jewellery making to mini engineers. Seniors have music ensembles, comedy improvisation, science clubs, debating, coding, singing groups with DofE offered from year 9. Generally good though parents occasionally question value for money. 'Child's end of term karate display consisted of standing up, lifting leg in the air and bowing,' says one.

Sport: Improved sports facilities at King's House Sports Ground in Chiswick, have significantly reduced travel time. 'Encourages every pupil to do something, whether they're good at it or not,' says a parent. And teachers know how to raise flagging spirits after a bad result. 'We lost the semi-finals at football and the teacher got us food from Tesco. They have this way of making people happy,' says prep pupil. Team games – for which school uses nearby sports grounds – dominate until year 10, when there's switch to more individual activities e.g. life-saving, badminton, aerobics. Lots of tours – co-ed football tour to Gothenburg, year 5 rugby in Cornwall, prep and senior girls' netball to Marbella, annual ski trip. Currently just doesn't have the critical mass to field the numbers, and standard of teams that some parents would like to see – in which case tend to move either for bigger co-eds or selective single sex schools. However, as school grows, team choice – and results – both expected to be bigger and better, girls' sports already upweighted.

Ethos and heritage: Surprisingly young, started only in 1996 with a single class by Jane Emmett (still a governor). In 2014, snapped up by Inspired, an international education group which boasts '64 premium schools, 45,000 students, five continents' but has managed to keep this school's identity miraculously intact. Now on three sites with decent amount of outdoor space – soon to be four when new IB sixth form opens. Has new name (was Fulham Prep) though internet has yet to catch up with searches – at time of writing, quite often coming up with newish state boys' school, just down the road, with a very similar name.

Pre-prep on Fulham High Street is a recently renovated 1860s building housing reception over two floors and extending in approximate horseshoe shape out into the playground. It's comfortable, cosy and listed (top floor roof buttresses have welcome padding to protect taller visitors). Second more modern, and recently renovated, building with four floors accommodates remaining year groups, also includes hall with warm lighting, specialist teaching rooms and music room – which is 'beautiful', says the head.

Outdoor spaces – more and prettier than you'd think – are attractively hidden round corners: outdoor play areas for reception, artificial grass, pirate ship playground, astro, plus delightfully unmanicured garden with crops tended to by children (and ex-goldfish tended to by heron).

Closer to west Kensington is the prep school, currently also housing senior school pupils and occupying about an acre. Outside it's slightly on the bare side, though not necessarily the school's fault. There's a token tree – lovingly tended and looks it – and they have recently added a new green surfacing on the playground. Nice touches include water fountains and the odd eccentricity – an old red phone box that's 'just decorative or used as base for hide and seek,' says pupil.

Inside, school has been built up 'into the eaves'. Stairs – 'too many,' says pupil – can get congested, though breaktime noise was well within acceptable limits. Year 9s and 10s currently share premises on top floor with bright, white classrooms, a small shared common room (tour guides slightly embarrassed by cheerful clutter of dumped bags) and thoughtful touches including a notice board with 'Gratitude corner' in printed letters above a blank space (we assume a TBC rather than deficit in thankfulness). Library (with mezzanine treehouse reading space), theatre, science lab, art studio, dance and fitness studio are among the areas recently improved and there's a new music block.

Pastoral care, inclusivity and discipline: School previously had its three Cs – consideration, commitment and courtesy – known by heart by all pupils. Now developed into the Fulham 'core' with input from pupils, designed to (among other things) teach the value of failure; it crops up in initiatives like 'Failsafe' – get your mistakes in early – and as an enterprise goal. Staff won't always leap in to rescue initiatives that aren't working but will encourage children to talk through process and help themselves, an approach that brought recent fashion show, entirely pupil-led initiative, back from the brink. Perhaps accounts for moderate rather than febrile competitive spirit between houses, thought older pupils, reaching apogee on sports day.

Nice touches include water fountains and the odd eccentricity – an old red phone box that's 'just decorative or used as base for hide and seek,' says pupil

Bullying swiftly dealt with, felt parents. One rare incident was posted into the worry box and 'never mentioned again'. School counsellor also on hand, daily meetings with tutor good at flagging up and resolving many of the routine issues.

When things do go right, they're made much of – big and small. Celebration assemblies recognise everything from top academic prizes to lining up awards in pre-prep so low hoverers as well as high fliers get their moment in the sun. But the biggest lure, we reckon, is decision to let year 11s wear own clothes – bound to be a surefire winner.

Prep school food was only area felt to be letting the (buttered) side down though one parent reckoned children are just too fussy. Strenuous efforts now made and children vote with their tokens – if like their grub, post smiley face disc by way of acknowledgement – and there's also a wizard wheeze where all lunch waste is weighed and logged by house. 'Brilliant at encouraging people to eat everything on their plate,' says pupil.

Pupils and parents: Still traditional – more working dads than mums but dual incomes now far more common, says school. Many parents are from the immediate area and paint an idyllic picture of informal out of school socialising in local parks. Happy, relaxed vibe. 'Have made some lifelong friendships,' says one. At senior level, smaller cohort felt by one parent to be 'ideal for those who can excel in small group rather than get lost'. Parents all praise the natural charm of pupils and desire to answer questions (not deliver pre-rehearsed response). 'Sweet and not robotic,' says parent, 'just happy little children, never fails to astound me how normal they are – hold the door open without being told but still chatting with their mates, might have a finger up their nose – it's a real school.' Co-ed but with girls still in the minority – though for most parents it's not an issue, particularly with more girls starting to join in years 7 onwards.

Money matters: Sibling discount of 10 per cent. No bursaries or financial support currently offered – 'programme under development'.

The last word: A warm, popular and well-led school that reaps high praise from its predominantly local parents. Evolution into all-through school is being carefully managed (separate senior school premises – and a few more girls – will undoubtedly help) and could pay off for early adopters. But for prep parents seeking success at 11+ and 13+ – the biggest customers of the lot – it's reassuringly business as usual.

Head: Since September 2020 joint principals are Mr Christian Warland (previously head of boys') and his sibling Mrs Sophie Strafford (previously school's registrar for 25 years).

Head of girls since March 2020 is Emma Studd BSc (psychology from Bristol), PGCE (Roehampton). Initially gained her teaching experienced abroad and in the state-maintained sector before joining the school as a class teacher in 1998, since when she's had a number of positions including head of maths, head of English and co-ordinator for able, gifted and talented.

Head of boys since September 2020 is Dan Jameson, who joined the school in April 2020 to allow an extended handover. Mr Jameson attended St Ambrose College, Cheshire, then gained a First in education from MMU and the University of Granada. Started off in the state sector, later joining Kensington Prep, rising the ranks rapidly to assistant head, a position he held for five years while continuing to teach English, overseeing the curriculum and teaching scholarship pupils. He is married and lives in London.

Head of early years since 2014 is Julia Adlard. Originally employed here in the mid-80s, she is a real pro, who effortlessly demonstrates her understanding of and fondness for small children, and also her knowledge of the skills they need when they move on from the cosy environment of the lower school.

Entrance: All 26 children tend to move up from the nursery and together with the automatic sibling entry policy this means that there are usually only 40-45 places available for external candidates. Most years there are three or four children applying for each space. Admission is by interview and they are looking for both children and parents who will fit into this family school. Occasional places later on due to families relocating.

Exit: Boys to London schools including Sussex House, Wetherby Prep, WCCS, Thomas's and St Paul's Boys', with some heading further afield eg Winchester House, Summer Fields and Ludgrove. By far the most popular London day school for girls is Francis Holland Sloane Square, followed by Francis Holland Regents Park, Godolphin and Latymer, Latymer Upper and Thomas's. Boarding schools for girls include St Mary's Ascot, Heathfield and Cheltenham Ladies College.

Our view: The previous owner, Jillian Oddy, took over the school from the refreshingly unqualified and charmingly named Margery de Brissac, ballet teacher to the offspring of political grandees including Winston Churchill. Margery started the school in 1950 and ran it until she handed over in 1973. Her legacy is obvious with lots of little girls at the barre, although we were told that there are no takers from amongst the boys when ballet stops being compulsory.

The school's home for the last 15 years has been a purpose-built building, bang in the middle of red-brick Sloanedom but with the architectural gem of the Royal Hospital literally round the corner. We walked into a particularly sweet atmosphere as it was Cake Day and the Bratby of John Betjeman (strong as it is) was eclipsed by tables loaded with a kaleidoscope of wildly decorated cupcakes. Fingers pointed proudly at their own creations and one small boy, beaming at us, whispered 'I just ate a volcano' – proof that even cupcakes can be woven into the curriculum.

The nursery lives on the other side of Sloane Square and is long on teachers (six) but definitely short on space with a tiny front yard (although they also share a playground with the school across the road), a wide passage and two classrooms all crammed into the back of Holy Trinity church, so maybe not suited to a very boisterous child. Not entirely cut off, they make the best of their limited area and do gym and ballet in the main school as well as attending assembly there once a week.

From reception upwards the classrooms are in Turks Row, and the meshing of the lives of boys and girls (despite being taught in separate classes) seems to work beautifully. Streaming is kept to the minimum, hardly at all in the boys' school and only for maths in the girls'. The high ratio of teachers to children (1:5) means that they feel able to teach the cohorts together. Neither is technology ignored as there is a well-equipped ICT room and coding and computer programming are both taught, the school's comment being 'we are far more conscious of applied maths these days'.

It was Cake Day and tables were loaded with a kaleidoscope of wildly decorated cupcakes. Fingers pointed proudly at their own creations and one small boy, whispered 'I just ate a volcano' – proof that even cupcakes can be woven into the curriculum

No formality when we entered the classrooms but engaged, cheerful children heads down over their work or, in the case of the little ones, raptly listening to the day's story. The only exception was the classes who had been making Christmas biscuits and were rather endearingly, if inefficiently, trying to clear up the considerable mess before heading off for a swimming lesson. The leavers' destinations prove the success of the academic teaching, but 'we are, definitely, not a hothouse,' said CW.

Lower down the school individual phonics support is available, and later on, if any of the 'dys' or ASD families, are diagnosed they can provide one-to-one support as well as extension classes for the most academically able, but most SEN and EAL needs are handled in the classroom. Well aware of the dangers of the internet they 'put the fear of God' into the parents and make them sign up to a code of practice.

The art room is smaller than some but has a high ceiling above shelves crammed with crates, overflowing with props. The size of the space certainly fails to cramp the imagination of the head of art – in fact she regularly produces art scholars, who are encouraged by an invitation-only after-school club. Everyone has class music lessons with over 80 per cent learning an instrument, leading to plenty of opportunities to take part in concerts and the annual carol service. Drama is part of the weekly curriculum and they experience the real 'theatricals' with the summer show held at the Royal Court.

Sport is less of a problem to organise than some central London schools with the green spaces of Burton Court across the road, and all the traditional sports are on offer, but it is probably not the school for an intensely sporty child unless they show a bent for fencing, which all take from the age of 7. A staggering number of after-school clubs (extra charge) and sport and fitness clubs in the morning for the early birds.

High praise from parents about the handling of the choice and transition to senior school but, with the relatively narrow field of traditional schools, this may be a less daunting task than for some heads. Having said this, the parents here are a demanding lot with serious aspirations for their children, so finding the right spot for each child is a pressurised task. If you are a high achiever earning a substantial salary you expect your chosen school to deliver the goods – and they do.

The last word: There is a great deal to like about this school and we were particularly pleased to have an opportunity to talk to a group of teachers, one of whom shared our enthusiasm for introducing Philosophy for Children (P4C). The only proviso would be that although they undoubtedly do an excellent job for all the very diverse (by nationality) children in their care, it might not be as easy for some parents to fit in if they were unfamiliar with the slightly rarefied world of the Chelsea/Belgravia borders.

Glendower Prep School

87 Queen's Gate, London SW7 5JX

020 7370 1927 | office@glendower.kensington.sch.uk | www.glendowerprep.org

Independent	Ages: 4–11	Pupils: 249	Fees: £20,100 pa

Headmistress: Since September 2019, Nina Kingsmill Moore, previously deputy head of Lambrook School. UK born, she was educated in South Africa, reading education at Edgewood College (University of Natal). She also has a masters in educational leadership from Buckingham. Started her teaching career at the Unicorn School in Kew, moving on to teach at Upton House and then Wetherby pre-prep, where she was deputy head. At Lambrook she has also headed the pre-prep, and teaches maths and geography. She is married to Hugh, who works in finance, and they have three children.

Entrance: Thirty-six places at reception with girls coming from more than 20 different nurseries. No sibling priority. Informal, small group assessments – essentially to see if the girls interact well and can do the basics competently. English fluency matters. As one parent summed up overall, 'Girls are expected to be engaged and interested in their learning.' Unsuccessful applicants for 4+ entry and later applicants placed on a waiting list for consideration. Occasional places do occur with longer assessments to see how they cope and interact with their peers. Unlikely to offer after year 5.

Exit: Very impressive results reflect the school's established excellent academic profile with girls consistently moving on both to top boarding schools and, mostly, to prestigious day schools. Most popular in 2020 were Francis Holland South and Godolphin & Latymer, then Wycombe Abbey (with a scholarship), followed by Kensington Park School, Latymer Upper, Putney High School and St Paul's Girls' School. In previous years, pupils have also gone to St Mary's Ascot, North London Collegiate and City of London. Catering for individual personalities and talents, the team 'really know the children' and, taking account of individual personalities, have widened the range of schools in recent years, which makes excellent sense.

Our view: Founded by two intrepid spinsters, Miss Edith Lloyd and Miss Maud Cornwell, in 1895, Glendower is a charitable trust, and has always been run as a not-for-profit organisation. A nostalgic relief as new profit-making companies pop up throughout the city, establishing expensive schools to meet demand. The school colour purple is all-pervasive; from the helpful website, to the girls in their uniform, sporting natty purple berets, smart winter dresses with purple and white striped blouses, or summer purple and white checked dresses, to their purple bags, folders and playground benches. The year 3s we accompanied to a Shakespeare workshop at nearby Beit Hall looked smart in tailored, velvet-trimmed grey coats with matching tights and neat hairstyles sporting purple clips and ribbons. The school feels like a welcoming grand house with its well-stocked library and airy, panelled entrance hall, carpeted throughout with excellent displays on every staircase. Every classroom is light and well-equipped, sets of iPads regularly employed, with only the science laboratory below ground level. School has recently gained additional space (and wider refurbishment) without increasing the pupil roll. This will provide a smarter entrance, make moving between the two buildings seamless, no longer involving considerable stair climbing, and more rooms will allow staff flexibility for teaching in more groups.

The science department arranged to borrow moon rock samples to celebrate the 50th anniversary of the first landings on the moon

Class sizes of between 16 and 18 with one teacher/assistant to nine girls mean that they receive considerable attention and their strengths and weaknesses are known and acted upon. One parent commented, 'Teachers are engaged on an individual level. We can email them all if we have any worries and they will provide support and are prepared to put themselves out.' The parental portal is well-used and informative. 'They are constantly improving the IT interface with parents to support them.' Not a school for those with serious SENs but school will pick up and support those with mild difficulties and make individual learning plans for those who need them. Between five and 10 per cent of girls are on the SEN register without any stigma, just plenty of support including handwriting club during lunch break and touch-typing practice. Speech therapists and occupational therapists come into school for a few. Some, who have been diagnosed dyscalculaic, receive external support, at Emerson House for example. EFL is given in small groups or one-to-one to the few who need a little extra help.

Well-qualified teaching assistants, all with degrees in upper school, are given opportunities for professional development. We heard excellent French accents during our visit with specialist native speaker from reception upwards. Mandarin is on the curriculum for years 4 and 5 with girls often obtaining full marks in the ISEB tests. Parents are a real international mix – US, Chinese, European – so many girls are bilingual or trilingual, but mostly long-stayers with very little movement. Parents of occasional place pupils praise how well the girls treat newcomers and how welcoming other parents are, arranging coffee mornings and play dates. 'If parents want to be involved they can be but if not, this is accepted, not questioned.'

Specialist teaching in music, drama and PE from reception with most subjects specialist taught from year 4. Girls seem happy, love their school and all it has to offer. They commented, 'Everyone is busy here, there's no lounging about.' They are responsive in lessons and we witnessed their enthusiasm for acting, playing a trumpet, carrying out experiments using microscopes and devising a board game employing algebraic substitutions. The Glendower '6 Rs' (learning habits), including resilience and reflection, underpin everything. The broad curriculum is, parents agree, 'varied and fun' with a wide range of clubs, including football, spy, coding, Spanish, bridge, chess and magazine writing, along with music, art and, extremely popular, drama.

Inspirational speakers have included the local mayor, plus others who have climbed Mount Everest, explored the North Pole and rowed the Atlantic: great role models preparing them for a changing world. We witnessed a whole school initiative to ensure girls understood the importance of recycling and their responsibilities. Much care is taken to provide a post-11+ programme which includes Thames conservation and young enterprise projects, Latin, poetry reciting competitions and balloon debating competitions against other schools. Full advantage is taken of the school's location with trips to museums, galleries and theatres. The science department arranged to borrow moon rock samples to celebrate the 50th anniversary of the first landings on the moon, and one team recently came third in a national science championship. Girls' work has been exhibited at the National Gallery as part of its Take One Picture initiative.

Despite the lack of a sports field on site, Glendower has a reputation for sports with proud reports in the school magazine. It is a serious business; just take a look at the sport selection policy on the website. There are weekend netball workshops involving famous players, year 6s take part in local football tournaments and girls have won IAPS fencing, sailing and triathalon events. 'They enjoy sharing and celebrating one another's achievements.'

The school colour purple is all-pervasive; from the playground benches and helpful website, to the girls sporting natty purple berets, purple bags and purple folders

Music thrives. Around 90 per cent take music lessons, which can include singing (several choirs) and musical theatre. We attended orchestra practice with good trumpet, violin, flute and clarinet players, and there are brass, string and woodwind ensembles. Some are members of the National Youth Orchestra and National Youth Choir. Girls chatted to us about termly productions including year 3's silent movies and parents looked forward to the autumn harvest concert in the local church.

Plenty of leadership roles, from librarians to sports captains.

'They leave with a "can do" approach to life and are well balanced as the staff really care about their mental health just as much as their academic progress,' we were told. As one parent said, 'As parents we worry about the daunting examination system: Glendower makes it as soft and gentle as it can possibly be. It's all about the child, not what exit results look like on paper.'

Money matters: Some bursaries available for needy local girls or those already in the school who fall on hard times.

The last word: This is a happy school, keen not to be seen as a hothouse. 'It achieves a perfect balance between encouraging girls to do their best and reaching high academic standards whilst ensuring they feel supported and have opportunities so they grow up with good values,' said a parent.

Godolphin & Latymer

16

Iffley Road, London W6 0PG

020 8741 1936 | registrar@godolphinandlatymer.com | www.godolphinandlatymer.com

Independent	Pupils: 800; sixth form: 205
Ages: 11-18	Fees: £23,085 pa

Head mistress: Since September 2017, Dr Frances Ramsey, MA PGCE DPhil, 50s. Previously principal of Queen's College, London for eight years. Before that, 17 years at Westminster School where she was director of studies and academic deputy head from 1998 to 2003, when she became the school's first woman master of the Queen's Scholars. (Give it another few hundred years and the title could catch up, too.) A big cheese in the Girls' School Association and HMC (she prefers the more modest 'highly regarded'), she has two children, one at school, one at uni.

Could, like husband, have spent life in academia but recognised that her interest in 'big ideas and movements' would be better served by school teaching. 'I did it and loved it.' Varied days inevitably dominated by meetings of one sort or another. Impressively, still manages to teach each of five year 7 forms for half a term, though 'do it mostly to get to know the girls.' It's important. 'Heads would be missing out if they didn't.'

Quiet, forceful, and an excellent role model for the girls – both super-brainy and poised without being disconcertingly super glam. Rated as nice, authentic. Pupils describe her as an 'approachable, positive authority' and 'normalised', and clearly feel at ease with her – no corridor double-takes when she goes walkabout.

Former pupils who remember the school in its pre-independent, grammar school days are resigned to, if not wholly comfortable with, today's glitz and gloss. Dr Ramsey, however, makes the strong case that the humanity of the old grammar school ethos has been retained – and pupils, and parents, tend to agree.

Goals? Head talks of boosting pupils' resilience and ability to flourish in a rapidly changing society. 'The school is in a really good place. When I talk about where we're going, it's about refinements rather than revolution.' Parents see her as stable force – not trying to change the school but enhance its many good points. 'They strive for high academic results… I think she is pushing that even further.'

Best bit of being a head? 'The opportunity to influence young people's lives and to give them the best possible platform to move into what's quite an uncertain world.' Parents don't dispute this. 'I am very glad about Dr Ramsey,' said one.

Entrance: Around 900 applicants sit for 110 places (five form entry) and that's normally it apart from a small sixth form intake.

Admissions process kept 'as fair as possible', says school, with a quarter of intake coming from state schools. Will offer extra time (with appropriate paperwork) for anyone with SEN but candidates expected to deliver the results. 'If not scoring up with the others when have had the extra time, might not be the right school,' says head.

Now part of London 11+ consortium which sets a 75-minute cognitive ability test (VR and NRV plus maths) in the January prior to September entry. Curiosity, thinking for yourself and ability to enjoy learning here all count; interview (for all) matters – though under review. If more than 900 candidates (and looks as if will be getting there soon) 'might have to look at it,' says registrar. Current school reference also taken into account and there is now an interview too. No sibling policy. At 16+ around 12-15 places available, very keenly competed for. School says it is 'very mindful' of COVID disruption and will adapt the process where required for 2021 entry.

Exit: Around 10 per cent leave after GCSEs, some lured by leading co-ed sixth forms (eg Westminster), a very small number to study subjects – like psychology and DT – not on offer here.

Over 90 per cent go to their first choice university, with normally good numbers to Oxbridge (18 in 2020). Increasing offers from US unis (12 in 2020) including Princeton, Stanford, McGill, Yale, Dartmouth and Duke; school felt to support and prepare very well. Seven medics in 2020.

Latest results: In 2020, 99 per cent 9-7 at GCSE; 89 per cent A*/A at A level. IB average score 41. In 2019

(the last year when exams took place), 96 per cent 9-7 at GCSEs; 77 per cent A*/A at A level. IB score 41.

Teaching and learning: Results matter (of course) but are achieved with a minimum (if not an absence) of stress, something that often becomes apparent when families hear of the more competitive atmosphere that dominates elsewhere.

'Not high achievement at any cost,' says school. 'Want girls to be well-rounded – simply getting that set of top grades is not enough.' Best, though, to see that in context. Dr Ramsey tells of girls' ability to empathise with the very few who recently gained only As (7s), rather than A*s (9-8s) in their chemistry GCSEs. 'In other schools this would have been devastating – but our girls realised that for them it was a real achievement.' This reviewer's B grade coughed politely and left the room.

We were welcomed in every lesson we went into where girls were tackling a variety of tasks with gusto and good manners. From making chocolate chip cookies in food technology (apologetic teacher stressed that this was last lesson treat – emphasis is almost exclusively on healthy eating) to year 10 class studying roles in Kindertransport play, or collaborating in a dear little two-person pod (roofed, though corridor location makes chances of sudden rainfall very slim), sense of mutual respect between teachers and pupils came across strongly.

Best bit of being a head? 'The opportunity to influence young people's lives and to give them the best possible platform to move into what's quite an uncertain world'

It's reflected in parent feedback. No complaints about any subject areas, with classics singled out for particular praise. Tiniest of tiny suggestions in otherwise sparklingly clean bill of health from school inspection before last was incorporation of more IT. Now a certified Google Educator and Apple Regional Training Centre and also offers iPads for all, felt to be well used by all teachers (and reduces number of printed handouts).

Subjects spec has recently expanded to include Mandarin Chinese and computing from year 7 (both available as GCSE and A level). Many study additional maths in year 11.

Choice of A levels or IB in the sixth form. IB remains very much the minority but a growing one. Cohorts now top 30 for IB.

Of the remaining 80+ candidates taking A levels, impressive results. Almost universally blip free (bar single figure Ds or beyond in chemistry, physics and maths – often down, says school, to personal issues). 'Personalised support for pupils who find the sixth form programme challenging,' says the school. Some parents do use tutors. Fine for short term goal, catching up if pupil was previously educated abroad, or to fill in a specific gap, says the school, which urges parents to come clean to avoid pedagogical clashes with school teachers. 'Nothing worse than tutor giving contradictory advice,' says Dr Ramsey.

Plenty of wraparound extras – subject-related clubs and societies with 'amazing' external speakers. School has educational partnership with Kensington Aldridge Academy – shared lessons so pupils there can access wider range of subjects. It's also Ogden Trust's hub school for physics in local state schools.

School's approach felt by parents to be sensible, grown up and intelligible. It's big on cooperation, helped by manageable classes and high teacher to pupil ratio (6.5:1). Inspectors praise teachers not just for knowing subjects inside out but understanding what makes the girls tick. Will stress that 30 minutes of maths homework means just that, whether work is finished or not. No endless striving for unreachable perfection.

Pupils take a very active part in the process, attending – and contributing – to all parent-teacher meetings from year 7, and self-evaluating themselves as learners so teachers know how best to help them. 'We have learner surveys twice a year and teachers do everything they can to find what techniques help you,' said pupil.

Continues as girls move up the school. 'Teachers are really good at tailoring how they teach lessons and how they format them,' said pupil. No shortage of fun, either. 'We got quite bored with writing in geography so we made a music video about deforestation, instead,' said middle school pupil. Homework challenging but do-able – and here, too, teachers will involve girls in timings and allocation.

'Encourage them to take responsibility and embrace challenge,' said parent. Starts small (organise eg own school bags and homework diaries, with minimal reminders to parents), takes in eg public speaking along the way. 'Get very comfortable with taking a risk and speaking in front of the class,' said parent.

Approach designed to help girls cope with difficulty. Everybody makes mistakes – school helps pupils to articulate difficulties and collaborate to resolve them. 'Will say what they feel is challenging… get a group together to work on it and focus on whatever is difficult,' said parent.

'We expect quite a lot of independence from the beginning but are there to support them if it goes wrong. It's not about sink or swim,' says school. 'We explicitly talk to the girls about learning to learn,' says Dr Ramsey. 'We don't assume here that if a teacher says "revise for a test" that pupils will know what is meant by that. Revising for a test is a complex thing and they need to know the best strategies to employ.'

Learning support and SEN: While SEN resources are praised, pupils won't enjoy life here if constantly struggling to keep up. Just under 10 per cent of pupils have some kind of learning needs, says head, and while SEN team is 'very good at finding individual strategies, the need itself shouldn't be a barrier.'

The arts and extracurricular: Even-handed approach to every aspect of school life that ensures that whatever your interests, you'll have the impetus and support to make the most of them. (Ensuring girls' enthusiastic participation is part of staff responsibilities, according to current job ads.)

Masses of activities on the timetable, loads out of it, and if that's not enough, girls are encouraged to grow their own, many groups run by sixth form, some with staff moderators. We saw flyers for open platform club's next meeting – 'Are good people also capable of evil?' – as well as a call for musicians to audition for a mystery new band. One pupil was in the process of setting up a mixed netball tournament involving London children with SEN, for example.

'We explicitly talk to the girls about learning to learn,' says Dr Ramsey. 'We don't assume that if a teacher says "revise for a test" pupils will know what is meant by that'

Most do two to three activities a week (sport participation felt to decline in senior years where girls have multiple interests, or switch to fitness options such as strength and conditioning, and pilates). Generally compatible with academic demands because of understanding teachers who will redistribute homework. 'The fact that almost everyone can keep on top of their homework is really a testament to how well it's tailored,' said pupil. 'If you have a match, teachers will give you an extension.'

Music in profusion from instrumental groups to choirs, all supported by highly qualified peripatetic teachers teaching 600 individual lessons a week. If not to girls' tastes, welcome to set up own vocal groups.

DofE offered all the way to gold and school, understandably, broadcasts the good news about results at every possible opportunity.

Sport: 'Lots of detail in head's speech about sporting achievements, silverware for hockey, cricket, musical and theatre performances,' said (very slightly jaded sounding) former pupil at recent reunion.

Mind you, hard to blame Dr Ramsey, with recent successes including cricket (county and London Youth Games championships for U13s), netball (U14s reached finals of national schools competition) and hockey (where U13 and U15s reached last 16 in independent schools hockey cup). Over 70 girls now row, crews recently gaining gold at national schools' regatta, two girls invited to GB trials. Football, felt by some to be slightly poorer cousin, is played weekly. Currently only enough kit for nine players. 'Not so good when playing 11-a-side,' pointed out supporter.

Otherwise praise that, generally, it's play for everyone where possible, with every team granted some fixtures. Daughter – keen on hockey but not a top player – 'never felt excluded,' said parent.

Ethos and heritage: School is what you might call sector-curious, starting off as independent, becoming a maintained grammar school and moving back into the private sector in the 1970s, where it seems likely to stay. Celebrated its birthday in September (a surprise to more mature old girls, who remember it being 4 May, with a birthday song to go with it).

Make it through initial security vetting to reception and visitors will experience a green treasure of a site in highly urban Hammersmith (easy walk to tube and bus station) – its Victorian buildings with (small) gravel sweep, set in six acres, are bounded by roads on every side. It's also immaculate – we saw two lost pairs of trainers and a sports shirt placed neatly on a bench, awaiting collection,

Though panoramic vistas are inevitably limited, there's plenty of charm to be had. Even the less eye-delighting buildings (such as the new sports hall, a typical example of the genre, with fab features including climbing wall and fitness suite) don't loom over the others. Assorted pitches and courts to the rear have been converted to all-weather surfaces). 'Beautiful,' said parent. 'It all blends in.'

Real grass is confined to a couple of attractive little courtyard areas (girls bring out cushions on fine summer days from the library) and an ecology garden where ducks are hatched and then, we were told, 'retired'.

St Charles Catholic Sixth Form College

Even-handed allocation of facilities is in keeping with a school philosophy designed to ensure that girls feel free to follow their hearts as well as heads when picking the subjects – and activities – that most delight them. 'Really push the girls to open their minds,' said parent. 'Gives them the potential and support to explore whatever area they're interested in.' Spills over into school life: pupils have put on pressure for the school to become plastic free. 'Now have reusable cups in the dining hall though not quite enough of them yet,' said one.

Most subjects are treated with generosity (sciences each have their own floor, for example) though DT – currently offered up to GCSE – could do with a bit more space.

Highly proficient and beautiful art – a popular GCSE and A level choice – fills the corridors and staircases. All technically excellent and varied – from the vaguely hallucinogenic (vast drawing of corset from which crabs were emerging – as they do) above a notice declaring that 'we are not afraid to tackle scale,' to flamboyant knitted insects. Nice to see, however, that house notice boards (six, all named – no surprise – for inspirational women) are curated exclusively by the girls and refreshingly un-manicured.

Infectiously enthusiastic librarians (tracked us down later to ensure we'd got the gist of apparently unlimited online resources) open up early and close late (and would probably work 24/7 if they could). Two floors, one fiction (conversation allowed), one fact (with quiet, quieter and quietest areas). Books approximately arranged by age-appropriateness but decisions arrived at through guidance rather than overt censorship.

Star feature is acquisition of converted church. Previously grime-streaked and deteriorating, it's now a lush performing arts centre linked 'seamlessly' to the music department and its music tech and practice rooms.

Until the currently silent organ gets the multi-million-pound restoration it needs, main attraction is centre's magic floor. Literally a moveable feast, it goes up and down more often than those magnificent men in their flying machines, accommodating orchestra pits to whole school assemblies. The source of great corporate pride (frequently mentioned by staff, less so by girls) appears on own video (will be Vlogging next).

From September 2020, the foundation charity overseeing the school is also running Redcliffe School in Chelsea, although under separate head with no automatic entry.

Pupils go on to huge range of careers, from star-studded (singer/songwriter Sophie Ellis-Bextor) to academia (Baroness Susan Greenfield) and every profession going.

Star feature is acquisition of converted church. Previously grime-streaked and deteriorating, it's now a lush performing arts centre

Pastoral care, inclusivity and discipline: Dr Ramsey's focus is on being 'respectful, courageous and remarkable'. School felt to be supportive when pupils have difficulties related to academic or other difficulties, including mental illness. Have two counsellors, two nurses and part-time doctor.

'Really cared and were there,' said parent, of child who was struggling. Offer peer mentoring, buddy system between older girls and new pupils. (Sixth formers also direct year 7 Christmas play.)

Clear lines where it matters but school doesn't sweat the small stuff if it can be avoided.

School council's campaigning also means that girls can now wear up to three earrings (per ear) 'as long as not massive,' said pupil. Similarly, rules on uniform changed so now allowed to travel to and from the school in sports kit. However, staff are on duty before and after school to ensure that girls are correctly attired – wearing tracksuit bottoms, not skort, for example. (School takes this area very seriously. 'There are... postural, physiological and safety issues to consider when purchasing school shoes...' says school uniform document.)

Not all pupils comply though reasons for rules are carefully explained, said parent. 'Although the girls find it annoying, you do eventually have to have that conversation.'

Some nice touches. We liked the positivity tree in main corridor garnished by fairy lights and cards, themed to 'What makes you smile?' 'Food', 'Having no homework', 'Matt Smith' and 'Alice's dog' among the suggestions.

Challenge Your Limits programme, designed to boost resilience and address fear of failure – which school describes as 'a very significant inhibitor to fulfilling potential' – by 'giving tools to overcome this fear and develop the confidence to pursue their individual hopes and aims.' Described as 'very successful' (though – unusually for school which is generally very good at evaluation – agrees that 'it's quite hard to measure resilience in a metric...').

Girls, who initially had their doubts, say it does have an effect. 'You hear the word "resilience" and everyone goes "here we go again", but it subconsciously goes in,' said one.

Two-way communications generally felt to be excellent. School receptive to feedback (good and bad). It's a 'don't be shy, let us know approach,' said parent. Only reported blip was where mega stress point – a recent A level results day – was felt by some parents not to have been as well handled as it could have been, with (a very few) girls who had just missed out on first choice places not having staff support instantly on hand to remove and comfort.

All the parents we spoke to, however, were generally very pleased with school's approach. 'You're very carefully advised before, during and after,' said a parent. 'I think you would have a heads up about whether you should have a little bit of concern.' Dr Ramsey confirms this. 'We would ensure a pupil got an email at 8am saying that we understand you may be disappointed, and inviting her to come in to the school.'

Pupils and parents: Website can sound a tad unnerving for anyone who's not part of the London super smart set that appears to be organising get-togethers – including cookery sessions for parents. Crab ravioli tutorial, anyone? The reality is a warm and welcoming cosmopolitan and multilingual community (if predominantly white British) that comes across from first contact. Highly active parents organise everything from weekly river walks (dogs welcome) to ladies' poker.

Current pupils who'd visited were instantly struck by tour guides who 'were enjoying showing people round. It was infectious,' said one. 'One tour guide was French, one was Chinese and it was so multicultural and supportive,' agreed another.

Friendly, gently humorous pupils seem notably happy with their lives here, setting high stock on the ability to be themselves. 'There's no stereotypical girl,' said one. 'We can have bookworms in our classes, people who are loud, people who are funny, people who are blatantly not funny. The school allows for any kind of girl. I think we're more carefree and relaxed than other schools.'

For the best time, thought pupils, it helps to be reasonably gregarious. 'There's a big social element to it, you're not going to have the best time if you just stick to your studies,' felt one.

Unlike other schools, sixth formers wear their own clothes and look entirely presentable without being OTT – no pressure to get up early to achieve a reality show level gloss. 'I think it's really positive that I get that extra sleep,' said senior pupil.

New year 7 parents are grouped with others from similar postcodes – makes those initial journeys in a lot less fraught – with events from gala fundraising nights to coffee mornings as well as evening drinks so working parents (especially fathers) aren't left out. 'We buddied up with two other families and it was just great,' said parent.

Results in lifelong friendships between parents and pupils. Even the few who leave at 16 are included in all reunions.

Money matters: No academic scholarships but music (first year) and music and art (sixth form) available (up to 30 per cent of fees), with bursary top up. Otherwise, families can apply for means-tested bursaries (no number given, can vary year by year) either before entry or in cases of hardship once attending the school. Parents have to declare income and 'realisable assets'.

The last word: Parent in earlier review felt that 'to have your daughter offered a place here is a real gift.' Nothing's changed. 'I count myself lucky that we wound up here. It's been absolutely fantastic,' said parent. 'My only wish is that it would be so nice if there was a school like it for boys.'

Headmistress: Since September 2018, Pamela Edmonds BEd MEd EdD, originally qualified as a maths and PE teacher. She enjoyed a globetrotting teaching career whilst bringing up her two daughters, both now grown up and living in London.

Comfortably settled as head of St Cedd's School, in Chelmsford, she uprooted when the

Hampshire School, Chelsea came calling. This was, she admits, a 'wobbly' time for the the Hampshire: staff turnover was high and pupil numbers were dropping.

In her late 50s, neat and precise in manner, she exudes a cool professionalism and quiet authority. Her EdD contained modules on educational management and policy and these are being put to good use. She has a vision for this school – establishing a greater academic focus while not losing its character – and a plan to go with it. The plan, in all its colour-coded glory, was briefly flashed during our visit and has been published to parents.

On taking the job, she did her homework, canvassing the local community, parents and pupils and then began to make changes. She recruited new staff, brought in better pupil record keeping systems, expanded maths provision, joined up to inter-school sports competitions and began developing an ambitious, whole-school 'Pupil Voice Programme'. This included a re-imagining of the standard school council model into six, pupil-led development groups that represent key areas of school life.

Entrance: Looks for what the head calls 'the right fit', with all would-be pupils sitting an entrance assessment to consider their academic potential and, from year 2 upwards, an interview with the head. School body draws on the local multinational community and so the majority of students are multilingual. Ethos is inclusive and support is given within the classroom. Assistance is in place for children who have English as an additional language.

Exit: Pupils go on to a broad range of London schools, mainly day schools but some boarding too. Kensington Park School appeared a popular choice with the year 6 pupils we spoke to, but Francis Holland, Dulwich College, St Paul's School, City of London Boys, Charterhouse, Radley and Emanuel were all named as recent destinations

Our view: Founded in 1928 (by the mother of the actress Susan Hampshire) with a focus on music and dancing, the Hampshire School, Chelsea continues to evolve. In 2004 it was bought by GEMS Education, an organisation primarily invested in independent schools in the Middle East. Whilst still under the GEMS umbrella, in late 2018, a partnership was announced with UK based Bellevue Education. Billed as bringing added 'support' to the leadership team, this latest move has been generally welcomed by the school's loyal parents.

Historically, the school has been split between two school sites but since 2020, pupils from pre-nursery, nursery and reception have joined years 1 to 8 at Manresa Road, just off the King's Road, once housed the Old Chelsea Library. It enjoys an almost palatial entrance, with a sweeping staircase and high ceilings. Inside, a magnificent oak-panelled library, crammed with books, is next to well-equipped classrooms for specialist lessons in art, drama, IT and music. Dance continues to be well represented with ballet on the core curriculum for all up to year 3 provided by the Chelsea Ballet School. One small boy confessed that he preferred rugby to ballet, but in the delightful year 1 class we witnessed boys and girls were equally engaged. Pre-school is located in the spacious lower ground floor with free access to a garden and outdoor classroom; phonics taught in small groups and the introduction of maths mastery has gone down well.

We joined a year 2 class being adeptly guided through a mechanical engineering challenge: how do you make an axle with elastic bands and lollipop sticks?

The Hampshire School, Chelsea caters to a broad range of musical and sporting tastes, ferrying sports to Battersea Park, which is within walking distance, for athletics, netball, tennis, cricket, hockey, rugby and football as well as the local Chelsea swimming pool and Latchmere pool in Battersea. One parent recounted that her daughter, having just joined the school, was 'thrilled' to play tennis and cricket for the first time, but that swimming was still her favourite. Extended day is on offer with a plethora of interesting sporty activities such as jiu-jitsu, fencing, fitness, gymnastics and archery as well as the ubiquitous dramas, LAMDA, Chelsea Young Writers, 11+/13+ booster and homework clubs.

Majority of children have private music lessons at school and parents are regularly invited to concerts. Ukulele, school choir and band are all popular tickets but the school has reared a group of very enthusiastic, talented young drummers and their last concert was deemed 'amazing' by one proud parent. 'We are missing more musical ensembles,' mused another, 'but I believe the new director of music and Dr Edmonds are working on changing that.'

The spacious school hall also comes in useful for theatrical productions, and the year 6 annual play is a favourite. Drama is compulsory throughout the school as well as a popular after-school club. On the day we visited the central school hall was put to good use, doubling up as dance studio, archery range and canteen. This reviewer is happy to confirm the high quality of school lunch on offer: fresh and home cooked on the premises. Our year 6 lunch companions agreed in the main, but the fruit-only dessert (favoured by parents) was not a crowd-pleaser.

Smart-looking science labs and slightly cluttered music rooms, one entirely full of drum kits, are all present and correct. Colourful art on display in classrooms, while plentiful and testament to the creative spirit, seemed a little lacklustre compared to the very talented pencil drawings we witnessed underway in one of the art rooms.

One of the Hampshire School, Chelsea's prime assets, however, must be its generous outdoor playground space with an adventure climbing frame that is surely the envy of other schools in the area.

We dropped in on several classes during our visit and students were impressively well-behaved, fully engaged, calm and relaxed. Respect, patience in taking turns and ability to work well in groups and independently were all in evidence here. There was a fun French class with students playing dress up and describing Le Look for a video camera. We joined a year 2 class being adeptly guided through a mechanical engineering challenge: how do you make an axle with elastic bands and lollipop sticks? We also particularly liked the year 8 class with the school's head of English. Perhaps it was the soothing classical music playing gently in the background, or the small class size, but the scene was one of contented concentration as a handful of students set about their project work. It was an English class with a difference, where for one student, writing on desks was not only allowed but positively encouraged, albeit with a wipeable marker pen. 'It's a poem exploring boundaries,' said the young author as she stepped back to take stock of her handiwork – four desks pulled together were her canvas and words in thick black ink criss-crossed over them – 'and about fitting in.'

This is a friendly school where 'fitting in' is unlikely to be a problem. 'It feels like home,' said one year 6 girl who admitted she would be sad to leave in the summer. Students do seem to wear their smart bottle green and scarlet uniform with pride and without any of the usual customisations one might expect of fledgling teens. Equally the mobile phone ban at the school is accepted with remarkable equanimity despite this reviewer's prodding: 'We just pick them up before going home,' said one patient pupil. Parents who contacted us all agreed that their children were 'very happy'. 'She loves her teacher,' said one, and 'kind' and 'kindness' were keywords that regularly arose in describing the school. One complaint from a working mother that too many school events happened in the middle of the day was offset by the majority, of perhaps non-working mothers, who loved the regular coffee mornings and get togethers. The Parent Association is very active: 'We always try and organise play-dates for newcomers to the school,' said one member, and in the constant flux of London life this is a school that seems able to offer a warm, cosmopolitan welcome to everyone.

The last word: Giving all the signs of a school on a firm, increasingly self-assured footing, the Hampshire School, Chelsea is turning out thoughtful, polite, quietly confident children. 'It's not bling or show off here, everything is low key,' said one satisfied mother who knows the school well, having sent all three of her children there. Dr Edmonds' appointment brings a renewed and sharper academic focus, but tiger mums keen to hothouse their precocious cubs should probably still look elsewhere.

Hawkesdown House

18

27 Edge Street, London W8 7PN

020 7727 9090 | admin@hawkesdown.co.uk | www.hawkesdown.co.uk

Independent

Pupils: 120

Ages: 2-8 (gradually becoming 2-11)

Fees: £17,085 – £20,100 pa

Head: Since 2017, Jenny Mackay, BEd from Westminster College, Oxford. Previously deputy head of juniors at both Lady Eleanor Holles and Streatham and Clapham High. Has also taught at Dulwich College, Eaton Square and in Dubai. Teaches year 3 comprehension and drama.

The day after running the London Marathon, Mrs Mackay took up her role as head. She recalls rehearsing her speech to teachers as she pounded along the Thames. 'I had to take it fairly slowly on the stairs on my first day!' she jokes. Keen theatre-goer and bookworm. Has travelled extensively. Proactive head who enjoys networking and spreading the word about Hawkesdown. As one parent put it, 'By cold calling the heads of local preps, and inviting them in, she literally rebuilt the relationship between Hawkesdown and these schools.' Stands cheerily at the entrance every morning welcoming pupils and parents, aware that minor problems can often be nipped in the bud through a timely word at the door. Married.

Entrance: Names down as soon as possible after birth. Pupils can now join at 2 in the nursery or 4 in reception. Occasional places thereafter. Parents invited into the school two years before starting, to meet head individually. Confirmed or waiting list places offered 12-18 months ahead of start date.

On the day we visited, pupils were busy being explorers on a magic carpet in one class and pouring out gunk into measuring cylinders in another

Nursery is capped at 16, but room for 20 in reception. 'We appreciate that many families may want their children to complete their own local nursery, and so we are happy to take them in reception too.' Sibling priority at every stage.

Gradually becoming co-ed and expanding up to 11: its first girls joined the nursery in 2018 and it will take girls into reception in 2019, with the first year 4 class in 2022.

Exit: Informal chats begin with parents at the end of year 1 to identify possible prep schools. Most boys currently leave at the end of year 3 though sizeable proportion leave after 7+. They head for a mix of boarding and day preps, with most favouring London. In 2020, leavers to St Paul's Junior, Westminster Cathedral Choir School, King's College Junior, Westminster Under, Sussex House, Caldicott, Notting Hill Prep, Summer Fields, St Philip's School. Some boys sit for one or two schools at 7+ or four or five schools at 8+. 'When one leaves depends upon where one is heading. If parents have a clear future school in mind, this will dictate which year they want to sit exams.' From 2022, boys and girls will be able to stay on to 11.

Our view: Founded in 2001 as part of a group of schools that includes Devonshire House and Lyndhurst House. Named by its owner-founders, Mrs F Loveridge and Mr M Loveridge, after Hawkesdown in Devon where there is an ancient fortress. The name chosen reflects the team spirit, hard work and sense of community of those who built it.

Formerly a boys' pre-prep, now taking boys and girls through to 11+. The big change on Mrs Mackay's watch is the expansion of the school to year 6 and the introduction of girls, starting in nursery and filtering up to the top over time. Exciting times ahead. Mrs Mackay's calm professionalism will surely mean Hawkesdown takes it all in its stride. Parents are delighted she is at the helm for this regeneration. No major building modifications needed to house additional pupils. School will become one-form entry, with an occasional bulge year.

School went through a difficult patch when there was an interregnum with deputy head becoming acting head. Shrinkage in numbers enabled school to plan forward. One mother stated, 'It is definitely back on track.' Another commented that 'the school now has a sharpened sense of direction.'

Huge emphasis on literacy and numeracy from the off and many pupils read well by the age of 5. On several occasions, head stressed, 'We are not a hothouse, but we do get the best out of the children.' No setting as small classes allow differentiation and no child is under the radar.

Inspired teaching much in evidence on the day we visited and not a dreary worksheet in sight. Pupils were busy being explorers on a magic carpet in one class and pouring out gunk into measuring cylinders in another. Without exception, the boys were captivated. 'I want the children to have a very creative experience, so they look back on these years with happy memories,' states head.

Homework is equally imaginative, taking the form of a Take Away Menu, with starters, main courses and desserts that allow for various creative activities linked to the term's topic. Pupils complete a meal over the course of the term. The menu of tasks might include learning one's name in sign language, paint blind or create a Florence Nightingale lantern. 'It gives them a chance to choose and be more independent in their learning,' explains head.

Head not in favour of after-school tutoring. She wants her pupils to 'have a life. They need to work hard in school but then have down time, so they are refreshed for the next day. We need to think carefully about what we expose children to.' One parent admitted there is a smattering of tutoring but 'not that much. The parents put in the work, though!'

Experienced SENDCo, on-site four days a week. All pupils screened for dyslexia in year 2. School does what it can to help with physical disabilities but there is no lift and it is not the easiest school to navigate. Some seven boys currently receiving speech and language therapy and one boy weekly one-to-one sessions. EAL support offered.

Non-denom but with a Christian ethos. All newcomers are given a stylish teddy bear, named Jack. Jack is an acronym for school values: joy of learning, all in, confidence and independence, kindness and respect. Children are rewarded with stickers when they demonstrate JACK values. Gold stickers also given for tying ties or shoelaces independently and for demonstrating community spirit.

Pastoral care is a priority. School very aware of mental health issues and accepts that taking prep school entrance exams at the age of 7 or 8 can be hard. Masterclasses and workshops for parents to help alleviate pressure on their offspring. Head has noticed a reduction in families being hellbent on supremely academic schools for their sons at all costs. Mrs Mackay knows that 'if you put pressure on children they crumble, especially if they are getting it from home too.' No such thing as a typical Hawkesdown pupil: 'We have the loud, quiet, quirky, those who struggle to tuck in their shirts, those who want to save the world… we are very much about the individual.'

Children have a say in running the school and boys recently requested to serve themselves at meals. Bedlam on days when rice and corn are served, but generally works well and children feel empowered. Not all child-led initiatives are approved and drinking hot tea at meals was firmly rejected. Hawkesdown pupils do not go hungry. Food includes a sandwich mid-afternoon. Sophisticated home-made vegetarian options include polenta cakes and asparagus tart; rice cakes for snacks.

Located on a pretty road off Kensington Church Street, next door to Fox Primary, so the street is awash with children first thing. Purpose built as a school. Fairly cramped premises with tiny outdoor courtyard but Kensington Gardens is used for daily 'huff and puff'. Not bad as a back garden. PE takes place in school hall, as well as nearby Holland Park. Football, cricket and tag rugby offered, as well as judo and fencing. Tournaments and matches galore. Everyone gets the chance to play in a team. Possibly not the right school for the uber-athletic. Chess taken seriously and is compulsory from year 2 upwards.

About 30 per cent currently learn either the piano or violin. Choir meets regularly and performs at the carol service, Notting Hill Christmas market, harvest festival and summer concert. Annual event singing to elderly at a local residential care home. Parents feel that 'art has taken off recently'. Collages aplenty.

All newcomers are given a stylish teddy bear, named Jack. Jack is an acronym for school values: joy of learning, all in, confidence and independence, kindness and respect. Children are rewarded with stickers when they demonstrate JACK values

After-school clubs mostly run by school staff, but with some outside agencies too. Internal clubs include art, storytelling, cooking, brain benders, board games and cricket. External clubs include chess, Chinese Dragons (Mandarin with some art thrown in) and Relax Kids (mindfulness and yoga). Sport, anything IT related, art and drama are always a hit, but all have respectable numbers attending. Many are free.

Mostly dual-income professional families. Majority British but with sizeable contingents from America, Europe and Russia. About 40 per cent of pupils are fluent in more than one language. Most live within walking distance, and tend to walk, scoot or cycle to school. Most are very involved, but school is not afraid to tell parents to be more visible if they have not been glimpsed for a while. They are encouraged to attend assemblies, concerts and matches, as well as annual prize giving, sports day and carol service, and attendance is very high. Parents and grandparents read to the children twice a term. Parents recently watched delightedly as their children sashayed down the catwalk in eco-friendly outfits, complete with compère.

Money matters: No bursaries but head explains that 'if someone was struggling while already at the school, we would have a discussion and see what we could do. We are a family and people do go through hard times.' No sibling discounts.

The last word: Changes are afoot. The introduction of girls and the extension to year 6 mean that this school is positively buzzing. Hawkesdown nurtures its pupils, encourages fun but also achieves academic success. Happy memories guaranteed.

Hill House International School

19

17 Hans Place, London SW1X 0EP

020 7584 1331 | info@hillhouseschool.co.uk | www.hillhouseschool.co.uk

Independent | Pupils: 622

Ages: 4-13 | Fees: £14,400 – £18,000 pa

Principal: Since 2002, Richard Townend. Grew up sweeping and polishing the floors of Hill House. 'The children think I'm 100,' he quips – and he probably is around mid-70s although spruce, sprightly and remarkably good at remembering pupils' names. Known affectionately as Mr Richard he accepted the head's baton when his father and founder of school, Lt-Col Townend died. Hill House is a proud family affair and his own two sons, Edmund (deputy head) and William (bursar), appear poised in the wings for dynastic succession. Their avuncular father, graduate of Royal College of Music's Conservatoire, originally taught music at Hill House. He continues to lead choirs and plays organ, treating us to an impromptu rendition of the national anthem with school band corralled in support. Anthem a mainstay of weekly assembly ('because we are British') followed by a rousing chorus of Jerusalem, just one of school's quirks.

'Music is for pleasure,' he states, eschewing music exams but admitting that some do grades outside school regardless. 'Parents are more competitive today,' he reflects and confesses to mixing up class names to obscure top set status. Despairing of 11+ tests and pre-tests – 'terrifying' is his verdict – and asserts goal of Hill House is 'happy, smiling children'. Parents are almost all adoring. 'Always enthusiastic and positive.' 'A father-like figure but neither paternalistic nor overbearing.' 'Leads by example.' 'An inspiration.' 'Passionately dedicated'. Just one former parent, not quite so evangelical, resorted to eye rolling at mention of his name, and a lone voice broached 'occasional misunderstandings' caused by 'incoherent' communications. Easy manner with pupils got our vote: a small child handed him an enormous instrument case which he simply took and placed in store without a single word having passed between them.

Entrance: Welcoming and based on 'mutual affinity' after spending morning/afternoon in school. Space permitting, Hill House is open to all between ages of 4-11 and youngest accommodated with several visits as school says 'anyone can have a bad day'. Year 1 onwards, maths and English assessments completed as part of class activity.

Exit: A varied and impressive list of destinations await. Most boys leave at 13+ with around half awarded boarding places at Eton, Harrow, Charterhouse, Winchester College. Fewer girls board and some stay until 13+ before taking up places at Cheltenham Ladies College, St Mary's Ascot, Benenden and Bryanston. Majority leave at 11+ for London day schools: Francis Holland both SW1 and NW1 are popular, as is Queen's Gate, usually at least one to St Paul's Girls' or City of London Girls. Some boys at 11+: Highgate, Latymer Upper, Wetherby Senior but in the main 13+ when the boys head off in droves across the river to St Paul's, also Westminster, Dulwich College and City of London Boys. Around 15-20 scholarship awards every year.

Our view: Originally established in 1949 as a Swiss ski and climbing school, the school upped sticks and expanded two years later to Knightsbridge, which completed the transformation to Hill House International, a pukka prep that has enjoyed royal patronage (HRH Prince Charles attended briefly, aged 8). The Swiss outpost in Glion is still going strong, with popular sojourns for older years, but school life is now mainly confined to annexes dotted across capital's swishiest neighbourhoods. Hans Place, Knightsbridge remains admin HQ, and houses the main school (ages 9-13) in grand style with oak panelled corridors bedecked with sports memorabilia, plus Townend family portraits. 'Just like Hogwarts,' offered one cheery guide before disappearing down winding staircase. Cadogan Gardens, another warren-like conversion of handsome redbrick townhouses, is home to pupils aged 5-9. Reception runs on open plan model, self-contained in a former church hall just off King's Road, with playground and garden. Each annexe has full-time nurse and laundry, as well as a kitchen providing snacks (lots of fruit bowls in evidence), freshly cooked lunches (delicious salmon on day we visited) and sandwich tea for seniors (mountain of cheese sandwiches demolished in seconds). In a triumph of spatial planning, the school – once housing over 1000 pupils – makes room for around 620 on current roll (650 capacity tops now) and remains London's largest prep.

Classrooms are myriad but small-scale, with stair-landings converted into cupboard-like music rooms. General elbow room in short supply, although everyone appears to rub along good naturedly enough. One corridor jammed with coats, not all on hooks, and a bit of black tape covering a worn carpet, made for homely touch in otherwise impressively maintained and well-resourced operation. Principal keen to show off latest acquisition: former Welsh church in Chelsea, lovingly restored with glittery chandeliers from Italy, transformed into music rooms, art studio, large gym plus space for drama, fencing and concerts.

Lt-Col Townend declared, 'We are a school like no other.' 'Most schools are all about keeping parents happy, but Hill House is about keeping pupils happy,' translated a parent. The school has always made its presence felt eg unisex uniform of reddish-brown plus fours and gold cable knit pullovers (because school believes 'grey uniforms equal grey minds') is both distinctive and practical. Daily dose of sports and fresh air manifests visually in endless Hill House crocodiles parading between annexes and sports fields, something that has earned them the sobriquet, 'Knickerbockers of Knightsbridge,' courtesy of BBC documentary.

School believes 'grey uniforms equal grey minds'; unisex uniform of reddish-brown plus fours and gold cable knit pullovers is both distinctive and practical

Tutors (Hill House speak for teachers) are 'characterful and brilliant,' we heard. Some are loyal Hill House veterans of 20 years or more. At least one couple met, married and now have children at school. Teaching is a relaxed but traditional affair, although one pupil said there are 'strict ones'. Mediaeval history class exploring popular pastimes and resulting in game of conkers looked great fun, but Latin class with 'scholarship' group offered drier fare. Brisk and no-nonsense grammar on board with written exercises to reinforce – still impressive for keeping pupils on their toes and focussed at 5.15pm. General resignation to mounting homework and extended days (as late as 6pm) when secondary entrance tests loom: 'Level of preparation is high but not too pushy,' thought one mother – and results, as another pointed out, are 'impeccable'. Class sizes always small, around 12, and subjects set by ability as pupils progress through school. Classrooms all happy, lively, surprisingly chatty places but work-focussed and clearly productive too. Appreciative parent said, 'Teachers go out of their way to bring out the best in every child with a lot of encouragement'. Conventional language offering, despite cosmopolitan pupils and international moniker: compulsory French from reception (taught by native speakers) and Latin option later.

Full time SENCo team of three currently assists 45 children with moderate levels of support and one pupil with EHCP (medical reasons). Specific needs like dyslexia and dyscalculia addressed, but also literacy booster groups and lots of early intervention. Key support mainly provided by tutor in classroom for later years.

Parents rave about sports. Swimming once a week, with kit provided by school (no excuses and no soggy schoolbag). Fencing boasts national titles. Skiing in Switzerland always a winner. Plus all the usual suspects including rugby, tennis, cricket, hockey, football etc. Fleet of mini-buses provide taxi service going further afield and plenty of muddy knees (girls and boys) in evidence (along with one cheerful casualty attached to icepack) on our visit. Annual sports day is a celebratory affair, with one mum confessing, 'It always brings tears to my eyes'. It's modelled as quasi-Olympics, with flag waving encouraged (multi-nationals wave several) and national anthem played (again).

Music integral and over 80 per cent of pupils participate in choir/orchestra or both. Huge store of musical instruments (even mini harps and baby bassoons) is available on loan. One parent told us, 'Children grow musically as they try out different instruments and develop confidence.' Frequent opportunities to channel parental pride with drama and musical showcases and all levels encouraged to perform, whatever the skill set.

Snap poll with handful of seniors revealed art unanimous winner of favourite subject accolade, with talented art-lovers clearly accounting for abundance of stand-out work on display. Early 1pm school finish every Friday and array of popular after-school clubs on offer. Parents grateful for 'creative freedom' Hill House provides, with one mother delighted that her children get a chance 'to try out lots of things and find out what they are really good at and flourish'.

Student council gives pupils taste for debate, as well as having recently launched a kindness campaign. One alumnus did speak of encountering unwanted rough and tumble – and a parent recalled school intervening to split up a clique of girls once – but pupils we met were self-assured, with no difficulty in speaking up for themselves and were respectful when others did so too. School ethos of good manners is 'consistently emphasised,' as one father put it, and valued by parents.

Originally a school for boys only, it has been mixed since 1981 – and although still slightly boy-heavy today, it's worth remembering that numbers are skewed by majority of girls leaving at 11. Families are a smorgasbord of nationalities and lifestyles – many local, but some travel despite Hill House offering no transport. Working parents can utter sigh of relief – no PTA to bake for: school puts on welcome drinks party at start of year and then leaves parents to organise themselves. 'Both children and parents make friends for life,' claimed one parent and pupils we spoke with were incredibly loyal and proud of their school. A current pupil even told his mum, 'My children will all go to Hill House'. School often graced with touch of glamour: as well as being choice of royalty and diplomats, singer Lily Allen attended, as did Jemima and Imran Khan's boys – and politician Jacob Rees-Mogg, a proud alumnus.

Money matters: Fees competitive and can be paid monthly. Hardship bursaries available for current families.

The last word: Don't expect your child to be wrapped in cotton wool, but do expect Hill House to deliver on top class preparation for secondary school. A full-on, broad education with touch of 'Boy's Own' adventure.

Head: Since 2001, Colin Hall BA PGCE (60s). Durham born and bred, he attended Durham Wearside grammar school, thence to Sheffield Uni (history) and Cambridge (teacher training). Spirited, erudite, ambitious and unswerving in his devotion to his vocation, it was never going to take him long to shine, with his first senior positions at Cheney School in Oxford and King Edward VI Morpeth in Northumberland and his first (and only other) headship in Hounslow. Couple these attributes with his fastidious attention to detail, boundless energy and fearlessness in thinking outside the box to ensure students and staff are aspirational and you start to get a picture of this seriously impressive head who has turned this school around from failing urban comp to Ofsted Outstanding and widely celebrated. A dynamo of a man, he is part of an elite band of 'superheads' and, we would argue, a true one-off (something that wasn't lost on former education secretary Michael Gove, who chose to send his younger child here after asking to 'observe' him; John Bercow's three children also attend the school). 'His drive for excellence and to ensure everyone does their job well is astonishing – I haven't come across anything like it ever, even in the army,' said a parent.

'I'm sorry if you missed the 80s,' were the first words we heard him utter as he emerged from the shadows following some stirring clips from the movies Brassed Off and Pride in the morning staff meeting (the vast majority were so youthful that we reckon he could have missed out the 'if'). It was a time, he explained, when things such as the miners' strike defined people forever, just as COVID has since. 'If they could face the impossible then, we can do it again,' was the message. Charismatic and persuasive, he is able to work the room and the money, with the great and the good ranging from Sheila Hancock to Alan Bennett and from Dame Janet Baker to HRH The Duchess of Kent (known here as Katharine Kent – she has her own set of keys) making up the body known as 'the friends of Holland Park'. 'No child is outside our grasp' has been his unfailing mantra and he will do whatever it takes and schmooze whoever he can from the neighbourhood (thank goodness it's Holland Park) to achieve it.

One of the best-paid academy bosses in the country with a salary of £260K, he still finds time to teach English, albeit 'really only so that other teachers can learn from me – I'm a great believer that the headteacher should be one of the best teachers in the school'. But there's humility too – he makes no secret of his reliance on and affection for his trusted loyal advisers, the senior leadership team, most notably his right hand man, David Chappell, academy head. And nobody doubts his big heart, with parents and students describing him as empathetic (although some feel, as one put it, that he is 'more interested in the brightest kids and the ones with family connections').

'Lives and breathes the school – it is literally his baby,' said a parent, and he concurs. 'I go on holiday to north Norfolk once a year, but it's my work that I live for.' Perhaps it's for the best, reckoned one parent – 'I wouldn't want to go on holiday with him just because, in the nicest possible way, he'd be exhausting! He is an extraordinary man.'

Entrance: An ever-shrinking catchment area that now stretches to no more than about half a mile from the school. About 1,600 apply for 240 places, with up to 50 appeals, only a few of which are successful. Siblings get priority and 24 places (10 per cent) are reserved for the specialist 'art aptitude test' (two drawings under exam conditions), with distance no object. Normally about 380 apply, with a waiting list for this test as well as a main waiting list. Most pupils come from local primaries, especially Fox up the road, but there are growing numbers from independent junior schools. Tests for banding take place in the autumn of year 6.

For entry into sixth form, at least seven GCSEs graded 9-6 including English and maths and at least 7s in the subjects you want to study. That goes for existing pupils as well as external applicants, although the former get priority, with proximity to school the decider for the latter.

Exit: Around half leave after GCSE, mainly to colleges to do more vocational courses, other sixth forms to do other subjects or into apprenticeships. Hardly any to the independent sector. After A levels, all but one or two to university. Two-thirds to Russell Group universities. Five to Oxbridge in 2020 and six medics, as well as one overseas to École Polytechnique to study maths and physics. Some years quite high numbers take a gap year, others hardly any. Most popular are the London unis, particularly UCL and King's, but the school is working to drive them further away with recent students off to Warwick, Sheffield, Nottingham, Manchester, Bristol and Durham. Wide range of subjects from engineering to law, to English, classics, architecture and theology. A few go off to art college.

Latest results: In 2019, 69 per cent of pupils got grades 9-4 in both English and maths at GCSE; 43 per cent A*-A/9-7 grades. At A level in 2019, 36 per cent of grades were A*/A; 62 per cent were A*-B. For 2020, 87 per cent of pupils got grades 9-4 in both English and maths at GCSE; 55 per cent A*-A/9-7 grades. At A level in 2020, 55 per cent of grades were A*/A; 96 per cent were A*-B.

Teaching and learning: Lessons are not so much classes as theatre. We saw an RE class with lights dimmed, incense burning and da Vinci's Last Supper lit up as a backdrop to 12 glasses of wine and plates of flatbread on a table with a red velvet tablecloth. We sat in on what we thought must be a food tech lesson only to discover the English teacher was using bowls of ingredients to teach King Lear (Which character is like the plain flour? And which is sickly sweet like sugar? etc). One maths lesson involved complex sums using Celebrations chocolates and we heard how Narnia was to be recreated later that week with bowls of ice, hot chocolate and Turkish delight and even wind and smoke machines. The teachers' performances are packed with pizzazz and the pupils are spellbound.

English and the humanities trump everything else, say both students and parents – 'just because that's the area of interest for the senior leadership team,' reckoned one. 'You only have to watch how many of the Perfect Tense prizes fall into those categories,' said another. This glamorous annual summer event sees star pupils selected by staff for 'outstanding achievement' being celebrated at a star-studded (remember those 'friends' of the school) black tie awards ceremony. The event is a very big deal that acts as a key motivator for students.

This seriously impressive head has turned this school around from failing urban comp to Ofsted Outstanding. A dynamo of a man and a true one-off

All students are streamed into four different groups. Band 1 students are the crème de la crème and are taught Latin (in addition to the French or Spanish that all students learn from year 7 and can add to with the other one from year 9) and taken on day trips to universities, among other things; bands 2, 3 and 4 are 'reasonably mixed'. Within those bands are sets for every subject and the desire by students (and their parents) to move up keeps everyone on their toes, contributing to personal drive and aspiration. They are worked hard from day one and there's tonnes of testing and rigorous monitoring.

Teachers (30 per cent from Oxbridge, all thoroughly committed – they have to be or they don't last) are expected to teach across a range of abilities and year groups ('We don't save our best for the top students') and all are observed and stretched. Their open-ended questions are relentless; oracy and deep analysis matter. 'What do you think, Izzy?' 'Ok, you can't answer – pick a friend to answer for you.' 'Great, now unpack what you said!' 'Oooh yes, but why?' As for exercise books, we've never seen anything quite like it. Not for these students a dogeared, doodle-covered old thing but a heavily branded, beautifully illustrated volume in Farrow & Ball colours including week-by-week map of learning, handy tips such as writing creatively (English), geographical command words (geography), exemplar work complete with red comments, common errors, glossary etc. The lined (or plain for art; grid for maths) pages are filled in with some of the neatest handwriting and most constructive, detailed feedback we've ever come across.

A measure of staff commitment is the (unpaid) Saturday (and occasionally Sunday) morning school, with the school also open for a week during the holidays. For students, it's voluntary but well-attended, with around 200 coming in on Saturdays (when there may well be sports fixtures and practices too) and up to 600 during the Easter holidays. Granted, they don't skip down the pathway, but they (or their parents) appreciate the extra support and teaching.

Every spring term, the leadership team puts on a Shakespeare play (most recently King Lear), a bonding experience for them and great fun for the pupils

GCSE teaching happens in short, sharp bursts – two (chosen by the pupil based on their favourite and strongest) taken in year 9; three in year 10 (to include English language); the rest in year 11. Means all leave with 11 GCSEs. 'Students love it because they grow up knowing exactly what big exams feel like rather than waiting for a spin of panic and the parents don't have to wait for that one big moment of shock or delight,' says head – although some parents told us they feel depends on how motivated your child is and warn of the potential heightened tension lasting three years. 'For some subjects like history, I also think you need to be more mature to get the most out of it,' added another. Results are strong, including for MFL (pupils can take up to three languages, although most do one), although PE and drama let the side down a bit (school says it's because 'the less shiny students tend to choose them – the rest want EBacc'). At A level, 15 'proper' subjects are taught until 12.50pm, the idea being that students do independent study (with interventions where necessary) at school or home in the afternoons. Fewer than 10 take Spanish, French or Latin and a tiny few do music or drama.

Learning support and SEN: SEND, once a weak spot, is now going from strength to strength, with 42 EHCPs and four physically disabled students when we visited. In particular, the school is known for its expertise in high functioning autism. Also caters for milder dyslexia, dyspraxia etc mainly via TAs in the classroom and, where necessary, sessions with Greta, their warm and delightful 80-something ex-SENCo. The full-time SENCo is one of the deputy heads.

The arts and extracurricular: It was a production by staff not students that piqued our curiosity about the drama department. Every spring term, the leadership team puts on an annual Shakespeare play (most recently King Lear), a bonding experience for them and great fun for the pupils (a few of whom get involved – sixth form only). Students perform in an annual large-scale school musical production (most recently Guys and Dolls). There is also a 'drama evening' held in March and annual student Shakespeare performance in November. But a student told us that drama teaching 'can be up and down – the teachers often leave so it all depends who you get.'

The 100-strong (including eight staff members) choir – which is what everyone talks about as soon as you mention music – is something to behold. Large, impressive and growing, we spoke to one student member who had performed in Florence and at Carnegie Hall in New York, as well as in St Paul's, Chichester and Durham. The orchestra plays a wide repertoire of classical and modern music. Plenty of instruments – double basses, guitars etc – available to borrow but only 25 have individual instrumental lessons (plus 12 singing) which you can only do outside the school day. Students rave about the jazz, rock bands etc and there are opportunities for music production too.

Art is exceptional. When you walk into the pristine hotel – sorry, school – reception area (more of that later), you'd be well advised to stop and look. Expect quality over quantity – only two when we visited, but jaw-dropping stuff. One, a self-portrait by a sixth-former, was produced under exam conditions – all the more incredible. Thorpe Lodge, an enchanting building, formerly inhabited by the Bank of England, is home to A level art. Students rave about its bohemian

Ercol tables and chairs in the classrooms as well as the front hall and communal areas; not a hint of mess, clutter or damage

environment and magical gardens, where they are given complete creativity to express themselves. Particularly talented students as young as year 9 have been known to take A level art under supervision by the academy head. DT is well equipped and popular.

Clubs and societies? You name it, they have it: reptile, chess, student leadership, film, theatre etc. 'Some are quite small but we don't mind – passion is more important than numbers,' says head. DofE attracts 400-strong a year.

Sport: Not an obvious choice for families seeking sporting glory. By the school's own admission, it is not 'our biggest priority'. We didn't spot a single trophy on our visit, although we were reassured they do compete impressively in football and basketball against significant locals eg Cardinal Vaughan, Burlington Danes, Chelsea Academy and Latymer Upper. And there are termly house matches and a house sports week. There's certainly no shortage of facilities including lots of outside space, Astro and tarmac for netball, tennis, football and cricket on the doorstep, as well as a new, shiny, well-equipped gym with basketball courts etc in the basement, not to mention the 25m competition swimming pool. Rugby also on offer (although not considered a strength), as well as plenty of minor sports including lacrosse, badminton, table tennis and athletics, and there are netball and football tours as well as a ski trip. But, report parents, the overall quality is patchy, they only do two hours a week PE as part of the curriculum (there are two hours a day available as part of extracurricular too) and there aren't many fixtures. ('As with many London schools, we struggle to find schools to compete against and don't think the benefits of travelling a two hour round trip to play a match is proportionate to the benefits it brings,' explains school.) Dance – which has two studios and several teachers – is popular, both as a mainstream subject and after school.

Ethos and heritage: 'Holland Park School spent £15k on Farrow & Ball paint and £6k on Jo Malone candles,' ran one of many such press headlines in recent years. You certainly don't feel like you're entering an inner city comp when you walk into the shimmering glass building, replete with tasteful furniture, exquisite rugs, beautiful fixtures and fittings ('I know it sounds silly, but I just love the doorknobs,' one student told us) and, yes, the sophisticated fragrance of Jo Malone. 'Why do we do it? Because the students are worth it and because I wanted to put things in place that many of our students don't have at home,' says head, who points out that these extra luxuries are either funded by the 'friends' of the school or given as gifts or non-delegated funding.

It's a far cry from the 1960s monolith that preceded it, although to be fair this particular west London comp has long had glamorous associations. Founded in 1958, it quickly became the school of choice for the liberal left (Tony Benn and Roy Jenkins both moved their sons here from Westminster and Winchester respectively) and with Anjelica Huston among the alumni, the school had a decidedly cool reputation. But 'the socialist Eton', as it became known, later went to the dogs and it is the current head and his leadership team that have wrought a remarkable change not just in terms of behaviour, aspirations and academic results (an Ofsted inspector once called it 'a grammar school for all') but the overall look and feel of the school. There are Ercol tables and chairs in the classrooms as well as the front hall and communal areas, and not a hint of mess, clutter or damage. Everything is immaculate, everything is high-end.

The building itself is all glass and (sun) shine and provides teaching areas for every student. With the exception of A level art, all lessons and activities take place in this one building. Everything is open plan, from the library to the unisex loos, and the spacious passageways are easy to police and regularly patrolled. There is, says the school, nowhere to hide.

Pastoral care, inclusivity and discipline: Pastoral care and behaviour management are two sides of the same coin here, with a behaviour and attitude team made up of non-teaching staff, along with a trained counsellor. 'It's a tough love approach and the fact that they are as forensic with it as they are with the grades means you don't see much rebellion,' said a parent. 'I make no apology for providing clarity and boundaries – children need to feel safe and happy to learn and expectations of good behaviour and rules are part of achieving that,' says head. There is little scope for miscreants. The leadership team ('the men in black,' as some call them, although there are two women; the lack of diversity is not lost on students) is ever present and picks up on everything from attire to skullduggery. The open design of the building means that if you're banished from the classroom for poor behaviour, it's like being sent into a goldfish bowl. Uniform, attendance and behaviour all strictly observed. How else would the delicate Ercol chairs and tables that adorn all the classrooms survive with not one scratch or speck of flicked ink or graffiti? These young adults are taught to take care of their surroundings, of themselves and of others. Nobody we met considered it unfair or punitive – 'It's just common sense. You just read through the rules and don't do them,' said one student. School won't shy away from working with families – parents are involved as soon as their child is excluded from lessons. Internal exclusions are rare and there have been no permanent exclusions in over a decade. Vertical tutor system are praised, and students report a strong student voice, although parents told us they'd like a more formalised system for them to air their views. Inclusivity is in the bones of the school – 'Everyone is accepted for who they are here and there's nothing they shy away from talking about,' said a student.

Pupils and parents: Parents range from self-confessed 'champagne socialists' to high profile conservatives, creative and media types and wealthy entrepreneurs. Many who might otherwise have gone private can't believe their luck to have such a high standard of education, funded by their taxes alone. But just because the school is smack, bang in the middle of one of the most fashionable and expensive corners of London, not everyone here is monied – far from it, with 31 per cent on pupil premium. To put things in perspective, the Grenfell disaster had a huge impact on the school.

Pupils are driven, friendly and courteous. They are articulate and – hurrah to this – teachers work hard to ensure their every other word is not 'like' and 'basically'.

Money matters: Now an academy but retaining its very close links with the Royal Borough of Kensington and Chelsea, it remains the area's flagship comprehensive school. Always well-funded by the Royal Borough, this is now matched by funding from the Education Funding Agency. For a state school, it is exceptionally wealthy, with a head knows only too well how to tap into any available and potential resources.

The last word: We love the idea of these students being mentally transported back to their inner-city comp schooldays not by a whiff of a sweaty gym but by the aroma of a Jo Malone candle. But while the media have had a field day haranguing them for it, we think they're missing the point. The environment, in all its swankiness, is part of a much bigger message this school gives youngsters about being worth investing in on every level and with an attention to detail we have rarely seen. For youngsters who are prepared to toe the line and work hard, this is a dazzler of a school.

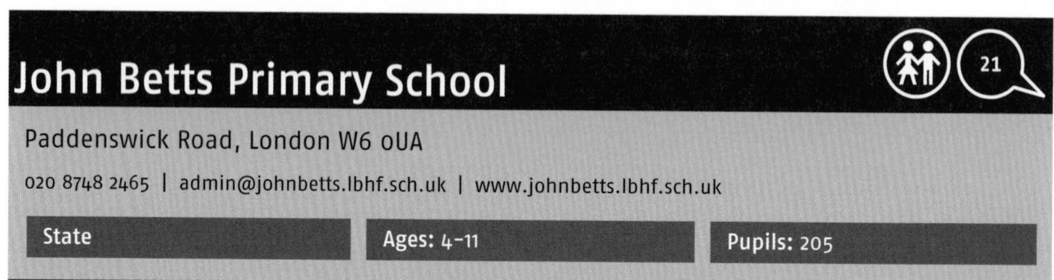

Headteacher: Since 2015, Jessica Mair BA QTS NPQH (late 30s). After a degree in drama and education at Roehampton University, earned her teaching colours at London primaries from World's End to the East End, before spending two years in Argentina, as deputy head of St Andrew's Scots School: 'It was a very good experience, to be immersed in a different culture and way of thinking'. More recently, deputy head at Queen's Manor Primary, where, as head of inclusion, she was responsible for its special needs unit. She describes herself as 'a change agent', which gave her the courage to take up the reins at John Betts after a popular predecessor's 26 year tenure.

Visibly competent and professional in manner, she reveals the secret of her success: 'If you find out what a child is good at and make sure they are happy and settled, they will fly and make progress,' a philosophy she acknowledges that has been handed down from her own headteacher at Queenswood. She and her 'very strong leadership team' have introduced careful changes in the traditional workings of the school, swapping individual desks for work tables, updating the curriculum to reflect a contemporary urban population and starting up an orchestra. Parents appreciated the changes: 'She's modernised us a bit… new staff, new ways to attract the children.' 'Very impressive, very together,' said one mum; also impressively quick up and down the many school staircases. 'I think it's important that children run to school,' she laughs, leading by example.

Entrance: Vastly oversubscribed. Places are allocated by London Borough of Hammersmith and Fulham criteria: priority to looked after children, SEN needs, siblings, then according to catchment area, which in some years is no further than one tenth of a mile.

Exit: Fewer children leave at KS2 than in the old days, as shrewd parents have become more appreciative of the 'bargain' of a John Betts education. At 11, half go to independent schools, half to state secondaries. Recent destinations include West London Free School, Hammersmith Academy, Holland Park, Ibstock, Kew House and Latymer Upper. One scholarship in 2020.

Our view: Eight classes of 30 (one per school year with a 'bulge' year for a double class intake), with a teaching assistant to support each class teacher, as well as learning support staff, for SEN children. The national curriculum is taught in a topic-based approach over two years, so both years 3 and 4 may be studying the same topic, but with differentiated work, to challenge them at the appropriate time. 'Our children are very good at asking significant questions,' comments the head. There is a 'London school turnover' of staff, though some are of nearly 40 years' standing.

The curriculum includes French from year 2, Italian from year 3 and students from nearby independent schools visit in the lunch hour with an introduction to Latin. A feast of extracurricular clubs complement the children's day: chess, coding; as well as yoga, netball, and skittleball. Drama club, we heard, is 'incredibly well attended'. Years 3 and 4 swim at nearby Latymer Upper School and a football team, coached by parents, plays in a local league. One mum described how her son left school with the sports prize, and credited his confidence to the school's ethos: 'I feel he can deal with anything.' There is a tuneful school choir and, since the recent introduction of individual instrument lessons, an orchestra.

John Betts, a Victorian physician and philanthropist, established the school in 1859 and it continues to operate as one of only two voluntary aided non-denominational schools in London. The founder's desk fills the head's office and his portrait on the wall oversees that his original vision continues, as a non-denominational school with Christian values. 'The values that are handed down at John Betts are still here,' a former parent told us. 'My son has been taught to be kind, and tolerant and independent.' Sitting on the edge of Ravenscourt Park, the building is sometimes mistaken for a church, with its stately gabled frontage and marble portico. The local area embraces both community housing and smart stucco villas of Ravenscourt Park, so there is a vibrant cross-section of locals, 'a good reflection of London,' commented the welcoming receptionist. A short bus ride down the road are the business hubs of Hammersmith and Shepherds Bush, but inside the school's sleek new lobby, you are greeted by an oasis of calm and orderliness. We were slightly bewildered by the labyrinthine layout of the school, the three buildings of contrasting age and style interconnecting with stairwells and walkways.

'The values that are handed down at John Betts are still here,' a former parent told us. 'My son has been taught to be kind, and tolerant and independent'

Downstairs the younger children enjoy a low level suite of modern rooms, and an ICT studio, with smoky picture windows, which open directly into the playground. A glass canopy shelters the children walking to and from the adjacent 1980s extension, which houses a year 5 class. As we peek in, groups of six children round work tables are chatting constructively about maths. An old school hand bell marks the boundary with the original Victorian school house with its raftered ceilings and gothic windows, where we find a multipurpose room for music, art and breakfast club as well as an interconnecting classroom for the two bulge classes. The lively displays of work hung from washing lines include rock cycles and ancient Greece, as well as a useful board of speech bubbles, encouraging the children to pipe up confidently with their own ideas: 'I noticed that…' and 'I disagree because…'. The head explains, 'We encourage chat.'

Behind the school, the playground has been given a makeover, thanks to the generous PTA, with an all-sports pitch, climbing equipment, a huge Four-in-a-Row and painted chess boards. Summer sports day is held in the open spaces of Ravenscourt Park.

The hall converts to the dining room, with congenial round tables for lunch, cooked on site by a private catering company, and staff eat with children. Hot lunch is compulsory, to ensure the kitchen is viable, but judging by the aroma of the day's special, Moroccan chicken with apricots, with homemade bread and carrot cake as sides (vegetarian option too), it's quite a treat. Whole school assemblies use the hall every Friday, and British values are promoted, in the form of kindness, tolerance, resilience etc. 'We're not just responsible for preparing them for the next step, but preparing them for the rest of their lives,' explains the head.

Good behaviour is encouraged with gold awards at assembly, and house points for the three houses: Eagle, Falcon, Hawk. Mindfulness and yoga encourage well-being among the students, and if these are too soporific, there's always Wakey Shakey in the playground. No reports of bullying – the school council explores both 'bullying' and 'victim' behaviour patterns, and the police visit to teach 'bystander awareness'. One mum reported, 'My daughter takes part in a little nurture group that is all about exploring emotions in a private space for children to talk.'

Teaching tailored to the individual is conspicuous round the school. One mum explained, 'They craft the lessons to engage everybody.' We visited a year 2 maths class, where the majority of the children were involved in a carpet time activity with the class teacher. Nearby a child with special needs was enjoying independent calculations at the computer, while a cluster of faster learners gathered around a table for extension work with the TA. The sense of industry and enthusiasm was contagious and we were pleased to see 'hands up' was still in favour here. 'They work really hard to differentiate and that takes a lot of work behind the scenes,' explained one parent. NHS therapists and SEN support workers visit the children with additional needs. 'Learning support might be for a more able child', explained the head. Despite this, one parent confided, 'tutoring does happen at the school.'

The staff got the popular vote from the children – 'my son just falls in love with each class teacher,' said one mum – and the 'family feel' of the school is upheld by having several ex-parents as employees; others run school clubs. Head takes advantage of the wealth of experience in the cosmopolitan community.

We heard about the 'very dynamic PTA' whose reps 'do a good job of keeping everyone up to date'. In addition, the head writes a newsletter each week, and there's a policy that all enquiries receive a response in 24 hours. Parents were aware they could have a quick chat to the class teacher after school, or make an appointment for a longer discussion. The head encourages face-to-face or telephone calls and has a firm view on emails: 'written word can be easily misinterpreted, clear communication is key'. Parents help on school trips, popularly to the Kensington museums, Imperial War Museum and even The Royal Opera House, and years 3 and 6 enjoy residentials.

Children looked smart in navy, white and grey uniforms with touches of green and yellow on their stripy ties. 'The school council is not just a name, they are given autonomy,' one mum reported. A head girl and head boy are elected, along with prefects, giving the older children an opportunity to write a job application and undertake an interview, the head explained. 'It gives them exposure to talking to adults and public speaking experience.'

Money matters: Possibly the best bargain in education west of Notting Hill. Extras for school trips made up by parents.

The last word: Dr John Betts must look on with pride from his gilt-edged portrait in the old study to see how the school's original principles of curiosity and compassion are flourishing. Traditional and modern practices enrich the teaching. Add to this mix a dynamic head, a lively modern curriculum and energetic parents, and – local fee-paying institutions beware – this school is a rattling success.

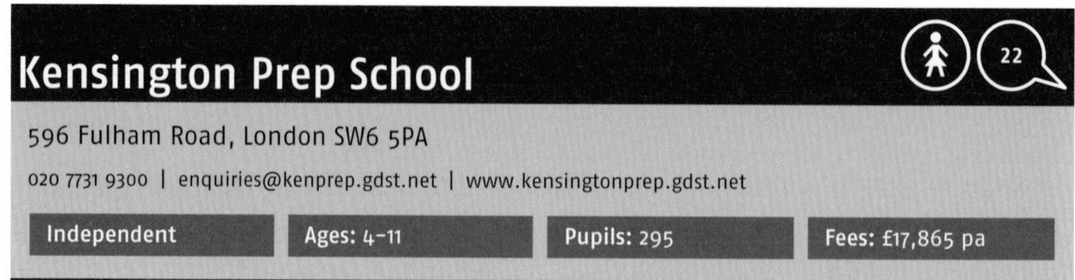

Head: Since September 2018, Caroline Hulme-McKibbin BEd (Homerton College, Cambridge), previously principal since 2009 of the King's School Macclesfield Infants and Juniors. Degree from Homerton College, Cambridge. Taught in state primaries in Trafford then at King's Junior when co-education introduced; became academic head. After a career break to have family returned in 2003 as vice principal; 2005 head of Alderley Edge School for Girls' junior section. Husband a business consultant, two daughters. Interests include netball umpiring, theatre, reading. The previous head, Prudence Lynch, retired after 15 years.

Entrance: Girls come from 40 local nurseries and most live locally, many within walking distance. There are over 200 applicants for 44 places at 4+. Register any time up to September prior to entry the following September, with assessments in January. Girls are seen in groups of five or six and observed during play with every aspect graded. 'I couldn't care if they can recite the three times table. I want to know if they understand the threeness of things in another context.' An understanding of English is important: 'It's no good if they have no basic understanding of what is going on and what adults say to them.' School no longer holds a 7+ entry process but it is always worth trying at this, or other stages, as occasional places do crop up. Girls already registered for the 7+ for 2021 or future years will have their registration automatically transferred to an occasional place registration. Siblings accepted provided they can cope, but this is not automatic.

Exit: A record number of scholarships in 2020: 42 (22 academic, 9 music, 6 sport, 5 art and 1 drama). Destinations include mainly selective, academic girls' day schools. St Paul's School for Girls, Godolphin & Latymer, Latymer Upper, City of London Girls' School and Wimbledon and Putney High Schools GDST all popular. Some to boarding schools including Wycombe Abbey, Benenden and Cheltenham Ladies' College.

Parents we spoke to who had experienced the ruthless competitive examination process commented on how they have complete confidence in the school system, and how well prepared the girls are so that they feel very secure. One recalled that the girls did knitting on a Friday afternoon to keep them calm. The process is carefully managed with plenty of meetings in years 5 and 6 alongside an open door for advice from the head.

Our view: Founded in 1873 in Kensington, it was the first school to be established by the Girls' Day School Trust and today the only stand-alone prep school in the group. In 1997 it moved to its present site, previously a secondary Marist convent in just over an acre of grounds. Clearly values belonging to the GDST, which provides expertise and financial support alongside independence. The trust cares about the ongoing professional development of its leaders and staff. 2016 saw the completion of a £2.7 million building project appropriately titled Creative Spaces for Growing Minds. We saw the multimedia recording studio, and the eco greenhouse which complements the outside garden and pond. We were delighted to see the girls thoroughly enjoying their spacious classrooms with breakout areas and retractable doors, as well as the improved specialist drama, art, science and IT suites and two new lifts making the school thoroughly accessible throughout.

We witnessed a year 2 geography project work on the hi tech 'explore floor'. A carousel of 10 minute activities meant groups of six learnt about the United Kingdom in a stimulating, exciting way. Some learnt to use directions accurately and programmed small robots, others learnt to recognise London landmarks, whilst others learnt the difference between physical and human features. The girls we spoke to 'love the freedom to do what you like in learning. The teachers make maths and science fun.' Perhaps that explains why they do so well, winning the GDST Maths Competition twice recently, and four year 6 girls qualified for the UK MT Maths Challenge designed for years 7 and 8.

Parents we spoke to remarked that the school has a lovely community feeling and right from the start girls know how important it is to be kind and good

The dining room looks inviting with its bright colour scheme, modern lighting and freshly cooked food on the premises, which we sampled and enjoyed. There are a few classrooms with traditional desks but all have plenty of light and space. Accomplished artwork decorates walls, many of which are crammed with questions and ongoing thinking by pupils, not often seen on a school tour. Self-directed, independent and collaborative ways to learn abound, and in such an academic environment, girls need to be robust and willing to participate if they are to thrive.

With two courts on site as well as nearby Fulham pools and King's House Sports Grounds for sports day, girls are given plenty of opportunities to play in fixtures. In truth the games department is eclipsed by the starry music department. Girls perform at Cadogan Hall and there are three choirs, four orchestras, chamber ensembles and a main orchestra with over 100 players. A biennial overseas music tour takes place to Europe, for example to Holland and Venice, with a planned visit to Budapest. An artist in residence works alongside the art teacher as well as providing clubs. There is no pottery but we saw accomplished models. There is an extensive club programme which includes football and trips galore.

The early years section is superbly resourced inside and outside with free flow. The girls we saw were fully engaged in a breadth of activities without realising they were being assessed by experienced staff. One parent shared how 'the girls hear about fairies or the Big Bad Wolf visiting, and in year 2 a fairy lives in the classroom and girls can write to her if they have a concern and receive a reply.' Parents love the fact their daughters are happy and have fun at school. A director of individualised learning and assistant learning support coordinator ensure pupils are given extra support at different levels where necessary. This may be small group support by a teaching assistant or teacher within or outside the classroom. A school counsellor is in school three days a week. The online communication system supports homework with iPads and a learning platform showing how mathematics has been taught in the lesson.

Parents we spoke to remarked, 'The school has a lovely community feeling and right from the start girls know how important it is to be kind and good.' This is a caring but not a cosy school, where girls need to be willing to be challenged.

The last word: Inspectors awarded the school the highest possible grades across the board in the latest report. They rated the quality of pupils' learning and achievements exceptional. This is not a school for the fainthearted, staff or pupils, but it is one where all share the excitement and creativity of learning. KP is the ideal school for a high flyer. The pace is fast and the girls are happy, have fun and are zippy.

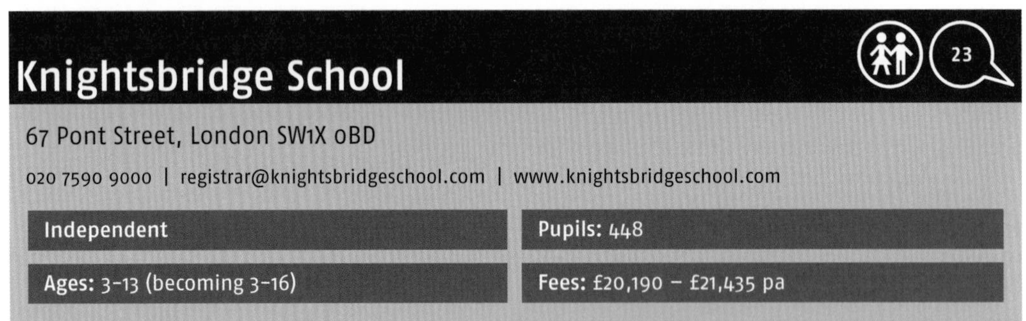

Principal and founder: Since the school opened in 2006, Magoo Giles (50ish), known universally and affectionately as Magoo. Married with two children, one in the school. Via Summer Fields, Eton, the Coldstream Guards and two years as personal equerry to the Queen, he spent six years as head of nearby Garden House Boys' School. If he wasn't a teacher from the off, he should have been – he exudes ebullience, dedication and high educational values. With the backing of 50 friends and family members, he got hold of the building on the corner of Lennox Gardens and Pont Street – formerly home of the Hellenic College – and began to create a dream come true. Magoo is energy, enthusiasm, loquacity and huge fun in pinstripes. He is not out to process children for any particular school but to ensure his school maintains the values, atmosphere and friendliness that make a sound learning environment for all. Parents praise his pastoral care for their children. His school was celebrating its 10th anniversary when we visited. Hard to believe it's not been a fixture for far longer.

Headteacher since 2015, Shona Colaço MA PGCE MSB CBiol (50s), previously head of science, director of studies and, finally, deputy head at Hampton Court House School; a biologist by training. Married and with two children, she has upped the profile of science in the school and has also developed leadership courses for her staff – which can, of course, lead to their leaving to lead elsewhere. 'I am as ambitious for my colleagues as for our pupils.' Parents approve: 'The school needed someone more academic.' If listening to Magoo is like being showered by freshly uncorked champagne, chatting with Shona is a reassuring glass of fine wine. She is calm, efficient, warm and experienced – and just as much fun as Magoo, only quieter. Their rooms adjoin, an open door between them, and you can't avoid thinking 'dream team' when you see – and hear – them working together. A wise and mature appointment for a fast-maturing school.

Entrance: Nursery is just for siblings and most entrants join at reception into which they take four classes with a maximum of 18 children in each. They close the lists at 200 applicants and Magoo sees all candidate parents and children – the child does activities with the head of early years while the grown-ups chat. Occasional places thereafter – younger candidates spend a day with their own age group and older ones sit tests and are interviewed. All is designed to ensure that children will fit in and involve themselves and that school and child will suit each other. Most from local nurseries eg Miss Daisy's, Tadpoles, Chelsea Pre-prep and Pippa Poppins. School has had a year 9 since September 2020 and will grow organically to year 12 by September 2022.

Exit: Most girls leave at 11 and boys at 13; Harrodian currently the most popular at 11, then Francis Holland SW1; Dulwich College and King's Canterbury most popular 13+ destination, with ones and twos to Prior's Field, Uppingham and Charterhouse. Wise approach to children going to the best schools for them. This is not the school for you if you want your sprog spoon-fed for a school with a name you can brag about.

Our view: On the corner of Pont Street and Lennox Gardens in a tall, six storey, once private, house complete with grand, limed oak staircase, back stairs, ballroom, erstwhile kitchens, spacious halls, interesting and large triangular corner rooms and lots of little rooms and passages. Few vestiges of the late lamented Hellenic College and its Grecian legacy can still be found about the place. An upmarket prep was the natural successor to its prior tenant and Knightsbridge School has quickly established itself as the natural school for its local constituency of sophisticated, moneyed and cosmopolitan residents; from 2020 it will cater for them to the end of year 11. Despite its location, the road is extraordinarily quiet much of the day. The school encourages its families to walk to school, in the interests both of health and out of consideration for neighbours.

Quiet learning in every room. Every class has a teacher and an assistant. We have seldom seen such engaged children, at all levels. Bright, young (mostly female and blonde) staff – all smiles and energy. Curriculum trad and sensible, complemented by brand-new Macs and iPads and laptops with in-class charger units and all used with proper educational values rather than for their own sakes. We even spotted some books! Those on school's SEN register are supported in-class, in small groups and individually. Speech and language and occupational therapists come in as needed. Full-time SENCo of whom warm reports. Tribute from one particularly grateful young dyslexic learner: 'Learning support changed everything for me. I don't go to ICT classes, I have one-to-one instead. I'd never have got to Harrow without her help.'

Much enthusiasm for many teachers eg 'he is brilliant!' Parents praise the care and attention given to their children. Rare and only gentle grouse from both parents and children is about a high turnover of staff – especially among the younger ones. To some extent this reflects the school's success in creating new leaders but, as one harder-nosed, parent observed, 'They all want Knightsbridge on their CV.' Also some wise and older staff, so youth and energy are balanced by experience and thoughtfulness. But the hope that a house tutor would stay with a child throughout its KS career seems unlikely to be fulfilled very often. Parental praise for academic support given to those who stay into year 8. Somewhat quieter praise for support given to those who take 11+ entrance tests. 'We need more help with English and maths and less other stuff when the exams are coming.' But this may express perennial parental anxiety more than anything else.

Art room on top floor with pitched ceilings and skylight. Art activities limited by space and resources but what we saw was imaginative and pleasing. Projects on eg 'fish' and 'looking out of the window'. No real DT though some textile work; 3D printer in Mac room. Though the (very well-cared-for) building has its airy spaces, on-site activity space is limited. 'We do miss having a playground.' One good gym in the basement is supplemented by the excellent and capacious facilities at St Columba's church opposite with its huge hall – used by the school for everything that needs real space. Otherwise, buses take children to local parks etc and no-one complains of a lack of exercise – despite the lack of space. Hot days make much of the place airless and stuffy, despite fans and windows.

Parents praise the home-school communications. Teachers in the junior school are Miss, Mrs or Mr plus First Name. On Magoo's door is, simply, Magoo

Much of the ethos is encapsulated in and by the little KS book given to pupils. Its 96 pages include everything from The KS Code and Song ('You're on the winning team all the way at KS/ You get the most from every day'); selective capital cities (no Brazil, Nigeria or Israel but Monaco?); rules of various games including poker; wives of Henry VIII; 12 famous women (one is Coco Chanel); famous speeches; 'thank you' in 24 languages; the periodic table; signs of the zodiac; instructions on how to tie a tie and some predictable hymns. It is quite wonderful, whisks us cheerily back to our grandparents' childhood and we will carry it everywhere.

Parents and children enthuse about the range and variety of activities and clubs on offer – impressive for a prep, especially a day prep. Lots of rewards (Supers) and some demerits (Subs) and a well-understood system for both. Trophies, cups and shields galore. House system which works vertically and horizontally and important for competition in sports, quizzes, arts etc. Effective tutor system clearly trusted by the pupils and especially in moments of anxiety or distress. Also Place2Be – recently won award – a counselling resource with its own room and handled with tact. Parental praise for the home-school communications which are frequent and close. Teachers in the junior school are Miss, Mrs or Mr plus First Name. On Magoo's door is, simply, Magoo. Food looked jolly good to us – especially scrumptious fruit bowls – but a few junior gourmets grumbled about lack of choice.

Most families live in Kensington, Chelsea, Belgravia. A few from such outbacks as Fulham and Battersea. Lots of Americans. But, at time of our visit, around 20 home languages spoken so an interestingly diverse constituency reflecting the neighbourhood. Smallish percentage of pupils need and get EAL help but the staff can muster several languages between them and induction of ESOL pupils is carefully handled. International families love the fact that so many are from overseas, 'so my children don't feel alien like they would in other preps – it's a real melting pot,' said one. Very lively and popular parents' association particularly valued by the recently arrived international families who make friends and quickly involve themselves. Five PA committees and a Knowledge Society which invites guest speakers for parental enlightenment, education and entertainment. Every parent we spoke to stressed how 'super-happy' their offspring were. Lots of involvement in local charities and eco initiatives – a palpable concern not to upset the neighbours, many of whom are current parents – clearly a priority.

Money matters: KS Foundation – largely supported by parents – offers two 100 per cent bursaries annually for children in years 7-9. NB this is an important opportunity, especially for state primary leavers who want to go to senior schools which start at 13+. The commitment can extend to helping bursary-holders into senior schools which will offer continuing significant financial support. Otherwise, no fee assistance lower down the school unless in cases of dire, short-term need.

The last word: A lovable school with a warm and community feel that surprises in such a location. If you have no other reason, it's worth moving to Knightsbridge for.

Headteacher: Since 2015, Elisabeth Stevenson MA PGCE, previously deputy head at Grey Coat Hospital. Degree in medieval history plus later, part time, degree in early modern European history at Birkbeck. Taught history at Rickmansworth School before moving to Grey Coat in 2000 as head of history, then assistant, then deputy head. An excellent training ground for Lady Margaret, with which it has much in common. Although only a year into her tenure when we visited, her leadership, innovations and smiley presence were palpable. Parents and girls seem enchanted by her – 'so involved and visible about the school'; 'she speaks so well'; 'look – her door is open, it always is – that speaks volumes'. And in fact, both doors into her room – to the atrium and to the garden – were wide open: she could hardly be more accessible. Entirely visible around the school, Ms Stevenson is completely invisible on the school website, even if you put her name in Search, which seems a shame.

A practising Anglican, she celebrates the 'Christian values' and the 'centrality of worship' to her school's ethos. 'It frames and shapes the day,' she told us. 'Every assembly begins with lighting a candle and ends with a prayer. And we say grace at the end of each school day.' But she will not rush to embrace the option of admitting 100 per cent of pupils on the basis of a shared faith: 'I think as a Church of England school we should serve everyone in our local community, not just the church community.' She has ideas and principles but is not dogmatic. 'I don't think education is something that happens to you. It's about engaging. Schooling should be characterised by kindness and engagement.' Girls concur: 'She runs a tight ship and is very organised but is so approachable!'

Entrance: Banding via non-verbal reasoning test which tests maths and a piece of independent creative writing. Sixty-seven foundation places reserved for girls who regularly attend CofE services. Fifty-three open places reserved for girls of any other, or no, religion. Applications divided into three ability bands making six categories. For each category, distance measurements are then applied. No priority for those with SEN unless EHC plan submitted naming Lady Margaret. First priority to looked after, or previously looked after, girls, then (up to a third of places to) siblings. In effect, in the year we visited, this meant: 17 girls admitted from each of foundation bands 1 and 3, and 33 from foundation band 2. In the open bands, 13 were admitted from bands 1 and 3 and 27 from band 2. There was no point in living more than 0.3 of a mile away if you applied for an open place, but some foundation entrants lived up to five miles away. Church-going essential for the latter – at least twice a month for previous three years.

Hundreds apply for the 40-50 sixth form places – applicants, like existing pupils, need six 6s at GCSE and between 9-6 for individual A levels. Admissions at this stage recently amended to allow students with EHCP.

Exit: Over a third leave after GCSEs. One of the most impressive leavers' lists we have seen from an academy. Four to Oxford in 2020 and, while Oxbridge isn't the measure of all things, it suggests the school has an ambition for its alumnae that may be lacking elsewhere. Otherwise, a good spread of universities from the newbies to the redbricks and, again, a diverse mix of courses chosen – from IT through midwifery to anthropology. Two medics in 2020, plus one student overseas to study engineering at the University of Chicago.

Latest results: In 2020, 57 per cent 9-7 at GCSE; 96 per cent 9-4 in both maths and English. At A level, 53 per cent A*/A at A level (84 per cent A*-B). In 2019 (the last year when exams took place), 48 per cent 9-7 at GCSE; 83 per cent got 9-4 in both maths and English. At A level, 34 per cent of grades were A*/A (69 per cent A*-B).

Teaching and learning: They are doing something right here. Despite a scrupulously banded intake, the results they produce defy any reasonable expectation. It must be all about aspiration and ambition. Psychology, Eng lit, maths and history the most popular A level options in a range that includes history of art and IT. Fine art – see below – and history the most successful but few subjects saw many grades below C. Everyone takes core GCSEs which here include RS. Equal numbers for French and Spanish – no other languages timetabled. Around three-quarters take all three sciences. RS, perhaps unsurprisingly, the stand-out success. We were interested in the approach here: 'Not all the RS teachers are from the Anglican tradition. They are very open to all religions and always willing to debate and discuss.' We toured the school and witnessed class after class of girls, head down or in earnest collaboration – evidence of the head's claims that 'girls don't have to be ashamed of working hard here... they are ambitious and want to do well – even the naughty ones!'

We witnessed class after class of girls, head down or in earnest collaboration – evidence of head's claims that 'girls don't have to be ashamed of working hard here'

Overwhelmingly positive approach. The school uses the WWW (What Went Well) remark and an EBI (Even Better If) comment on every piece of work. We think this a sound way of keeping teachers up to the mark quite as much as pupils. We enjoyed many features of work and evidence of thinking here eg the What Is Your Favourite Book display board and were intrigued by the choices: lots of Roald Dahl (predictable), one Pride and Prejudice (estimable), one Ulysses (impressive, if implausible) and one 50 Shades of Grey (lamentable).

Learning support and SEN: At the time of our visit, 10 girls had EHC plans and a further 60 received some kind of SEN support. Level of support varies according to need eg differentiated work and resources, LSAs in lessons, withdrawal, small groups and in-class support where needed. SEN department runs homework club, reduced timetables and curriculum support sessions. Also external agencies provide eg additional therapies such as speech and language and drama. School would welcome anyone including those with mild ASD but the site prohibits entry to anyone with complex physical problems. Those who need EAL support also helped by the SEN dept and on a similar basis.

The arts and extracurricular: Art is exceptional. It inhabits six separate studios and rooms including a designated oil painting room. We were delighted by some of the most interesting, careful and creative work in painting and drawing we've seen anywhere; large numbers of fine art A levels are awarded A*s. Lively textiles, food tech lab and a sizeable DT workshop testify to the emphasis placed on head and hand collaboration here. Annual fashion show and competition display girls' own handmade work. Music, likewise, is celebrated here – both in theory (fabulous ICT suite for music) and in practice – lots of lessons, practice rooms, four choirs, ensembles and enthusiasm. Dramatic productions staged with verve and hard work and with impressive results. Until now, drama has not been a 'subject'. However, girls who chafe at the lack of timetabled drama will chafe – and leave for other schools in pursuit of it – no longer. It's now possible to take a GCSE in drama – Ms Stevenson very clear about its usefulness on the timetable in terms of character development, team work and expressiveness.

'Very well-run' DofE programme. 'Fantastic' dance opportunities – street to ballet on offer and parents rave about the choreography and production standards – 'they rehearse so hard!' A sense of trying everything and having a go.

Sport: Energetic sports include rowing at Fulham Reach, games at Eel Brook, five minutes' walk away, or at Barn Elms, by public transport. Tennis in Bishop Park. Lacrosse, badminton, cricket – no shortage of sporting opportunities whatever your thing. And successes, both individual and in teams, across the board.

Ethos and heritage: Parsons Green is a purlieu on the eastern edge of Fulham, in this hip part of London. A three-bed house will set you back more than £1.5m. Facing the triangle of grass shaded by ancient plane and ash trees which is the actual Parsons Green, the school is housed in a row of attractive buildings from several eras. Parsons Green tube station is a convenient two minutes' walk away. The school has an interesting role in the history of women's education. Founded in 1841, Whitelands College was a teacher training college 'to produce a superior class of parochial schoolmistresses'. Whitelands College School followed a year later. In 1917, when the school was threatened with closure, the remarkable second mistress, Enid Moberly Bell, rescued it and reopened it as Lady Margaret later that year. (She also moonlighted as the vice-chair of the Lyceum Club for female artists and writers.) Her life-partner, Anne Lupton, financed the purchase of the school's second building, Elm House, and named the school after Margaret Beaufort, of whom Erasmus, no less, wrote on her tomb: 'Margaret, Countess of Richmond, mother of Henry VII, grandmother of Henry VIII, who donated funds for three monks of this abbey, a grammar school in Wimborne, a preacher in the whole of England, two lecturers in Scripture, one at Oxford, the other at Cambridge, where she also founded two colleges, one dedicated to Christ, and the other to St John, the Evangelist.' The school's transmogrifications since founding reflect the changing times and mores – from a grammar, to a voluntary aided and now an academy.

We saw the head turning down the odd collar and a girl or two pulling down a shorter than average skirt on her approach. She has smartened us up, we were told

The Christian backbone of the school is proudly proclaimed by the 12-foot wooden cross with the Tudor rose ingrained on it which leans against the wall of the most modern of the buildings – a plate glass and marble statement – at one end of the extensive frontage. The two main buildings are handsome Georgian townhouses which retain some elegant features of their former selves and a mass of small rooms, passages and staircases. The school – when you are in it – is far larger than you'd guess from the outside, having accrued buildings, outside space and assorted additions. Most of it is well-maintained and treated with respect. We saw no litter. The girls, too, are well turned-out in their black with red stripe uniform. We witnessed the head turning down the odd collar and a girl or two pulling down a shorter than average skirt on her approach. 'She has smartened us up,' we were told. Sixth formers wear home clothes and treat this privilege with respect.

Excellent library – and one of the best-stocked we've seen, a little cramped but full of girls actually working, something we do not often encounter. Good study areas elsewhere including one 'informal' and one silent one in the sixth form centre. Excellent Busby Auditorium – a real lecture theatre seating 140 – used for talks, rehearsals, presentations etc. Good and tidy displays about the place. One large tarmac playground. School food not seen as irresistible. About half bring lunch from home, most sixth formers go out to get it. But with pasta and salad bars, hot choices and fruit pots, it looked OK to us.

An interestingly diverse list of leavers over recent decades includes Diana Garnham, ex-chief

Christ Church Primary School Chelsea

executive of the Science Council, Nigella and Horatia Lawson, Lady Zoe Barclay, actresses Kelly Hunter, Joanne Adams and Jessie Burton, film director Mahalia Belo, upcoming soprano Louise Alder, Martha Fiennes – oh, and Janet Street-Porter.

Pastoral care, inclusivity and discipline: Well understood pastoral care system. Problems first to form tutor, then head of year. School counsellor around two days a week for support. But girls attest to 'happier' atmosphere under new regime and a new emphasis on self-esteem. 'The head wants us to develop into confident young women.' When girls get into trouble – and in rare cases of exclusion – it is because of persistent behavioural lapses rather than anything else. Social media abuse a persistent hazard here as everywhere. 'We have a very strong community feeling but we do have girls who behave badly on occasions. We deal with it very quickly,' explained the head – this view supported by both parents and girls. Pastoral care described as 'amazing' by parents and school is assiduous in home-school comms. 'We have the numbers of absolutely anyone we might need,' said a parent. Parents also feel involved – 'they do listen to concerns'.

Pupils and parents: About as diverse as it gets. Some from local, affluent families who also apply for the local independents. Many from far less privileged homes. Great mix of backgrounds. Some 18 per cent speak a language other than English at home – a relatively small proportion given the school's location. Very active PTA – lots of drinks dos and other events. A few parents feel a bit pressured to involve themselves and cough up for school appeals but they stress these are, of course, voluntary and some keep away though everyone we spoke to praised the school's sense of community.

Money matters: Parental contribution asked for and willingly donated in most cases.

The last word: Outstanding school for an ambitious, motivated, outward-looking girl. The anxious faces of the parents handing in their applications for next year's places said it all.

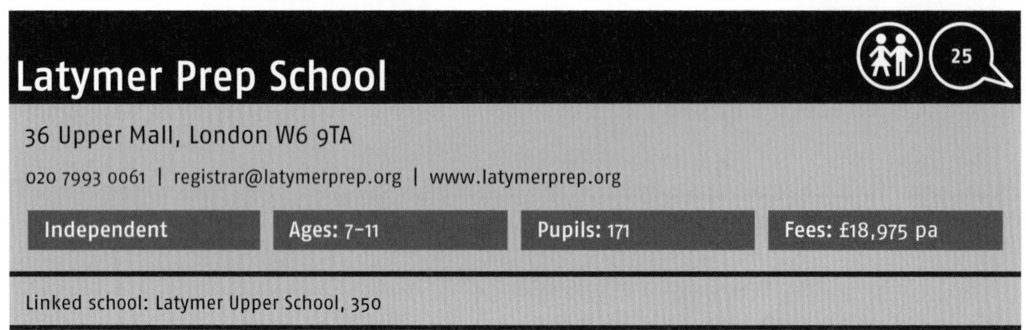

Latymer Prep School

25

36 Upper Mall, London W6 9TA

020 7993 0061 | registrar@latymerprep.org | www.latymerprep.org

Independent | Ages: 7–11 | Pupils: 171 | Fees: £18,975 pa

Linked school: Latymer Upper School, 350

Head: Since September 2017, Andrea Rutterford, previously deputy head at Devonshire House prep in Hampstead. She has also headed year 3 and year 5 at Highgate Junior School.

Entrance: Highly selective, around 220 competing at 7+ for 38-40 places. Exam, after which 50 per cent invited back for science-related activities, team-building exercises and observation. See website for changes to 2021 entry due to COVID. The gender split is about 50/50. Two classes of 20 each year (occasionally 21). Families are mainly local, although the reach of the school has expanded in recent years to stretch as far as Kensington and Notting Hill.

Exit: Now a through school, so automatic entry to senior school. Does not prepare for other senior schools.

Our view: Rivercourt House, an attractive 1800s villa overlooking the Thames, is the main building. Full of light, with an elegant staircase and plenty of original features and creaky floorboards, it has the feel of a well-to-do, kindly aunt's home. Next door, Latymer House accommodates more classrooms, food tech, cookery, IT and art – all very well equipped, with plenty of space. Both use walls and corridors to the max to display children's work. Even a window had lovely artwork draped across when we visited.

Opposite the rather limited outside space is an odd 1930s building, whose outside spiral staircase leads to the Seahorse Drama Studio, with a truly professional feel. Pupils also regularly parade down the underpass under the A4 to Latymer Upper to make use of facilities for sports, music and drama (recent productions including My Fair Lady, Toad of Toad Hall and Peter Pan).

Prep school teachers do regular observations of year 7 teaching to get a feel for standards. All this, agree parents and pupils, makes the transfer into the upper school pretty seamless. 'They don't get scared because they're already familiar with it,' explained one parent.

Expect specialist teaching from day one, so whilst each class has its own form room, pupils go to subject-dedicated rooms to learn. Of particular note is the large, fantastically well-equipped art room at the top of the school, where pupils were busy painting clay pots they'd made, and a delightful, well-stocked library. Delicious baking aromas drifted out of the food tech room when we visited, whilst in the science lab, pupils could hardly have looked more animated.

The curriculum is future-orientated, with all learning Mandarin and Spanish, and technology is genuinely embedded throughout all subjects, with regular use of iPads in class, including art. This is not at the expense of more traditional learning, however. 'We want them to read and write before they can swipe,' says school.

Every child plays a musical instrument and half of them play two, for which one-to-one tuition is timetabled into the curriculum. Big on brass, with lots of children learning the French horn or trombone, whilst the cello also remains popular and there are two main choirs. Music tech also a focal point. 'I was certain my kids had no talent for music and I've been truly shocked what they've brought out in them,' said one parent.

The focus on sport that the upper school is noted for is seen as equally important here, with specialist sports coaches teaching both girls and boys rugby, football, netball, cricket, dance, rounders and – the particular strength of the school – swimming. A £14m sports facility behind the 1930s building has revolutionised facilities. Sport is inclusive. 'Our aim is that every pupil leaves with one sport they like doing. That might not sound very ambitious, but actually girls often fall away from sport because they're not given the opportunity to find something they love. Not here.'

Over 20 school clubs, including zumba, film studies, The Latymerian (school magazine), chess, bridge, drama, coding, Warhammer and karate. Most are free, although a few bought-in ones, such as zumba, do charge. No after-school care, but the prep room remains open until 4.30pm. Plenty of day trips to places including V&A and Kensington Gardens, whilst residential trips include Norfolk (year 5) and Italy (year 6).

This isn't a school that believes in lots of rules. 'There's just a general expectation of respect and being nice,' said one pupil. And with the exception of some year 6s who have passed their 11+ swanking around a bit, it's all pretty low-key, with a genuine feeling of innocence. About the worst behaviour you'll see, say teachers, is children running to the next class, when they should walk.

As for bullying, it's hard to imagine here. 'Of course children sometimes fall out, and there are situations in which children lack empathy or fail to see the implications of what they've done. But there's very little deliberate unkindness. We think that's down to modelling by the staff and the fact that, for the children, the absolute worst thing for them is feeling they've disappointed us. They can't bear it.'

'I was certain my kids had no talent for music and I've been truly shocked by what they've brought out in them,' said one parent

'You learn through trying,' is an unofficial mantra of the school, with the staff encouraging intellectual risk-taking. 'We are constantly reminding the children that the point when you're not quite sure is the point when you learn. Getting to the top therefore isn't the be-all-and-end-all and we encourage them to see that and value the moment when they're not quite sure.'

There are pupils with SEN, including dyslexia and Asperger's, and they've also had students who are registered blind or deaf. 'We delight in being open'; anyone with any kind of learning challenge is encouraged to make full use of the upper school's learning support department (now known as the academic mentoring department to remove stigma), which is run by three specialists. 'They offer unbelievable support,' said one parent.

There's a lively PA, which does all the usual fundraising and organising of school fêtes and social events, along with each class having a 'rep' and 'dep', in close touch with the school. 'If there's ever an issue or misunderstanding, the rep and dep won't encourage parents to write saying, "We all think this or that". It's much more a case of them coming in informally and early to nip it in the bud.' Parents agree this works, and value the relaxed, welcoming and open atmosphere.

We saw relaxed, engaged, happy and confident (but not precocious) children, who are clearly at home and keen to learn. 'You're encouraged to ask questions,' one pupil told us. 'In fact, if we are really interested in a particular area, that can drive the class in a new direction.' 'Teachers always tell us, it's our enthusiasm they want to build on,' explained another. For this reason, comment a couple of parents, it's probably not the best school for shrinking violets. 'I think a really quiet and withdrawn child might feel a bit lost here,' said one.

Unlike in the upper school, there is a house system, all named after birds. 'It gives a sense of healthy competition and gets them out of their year groups,' said one parent. There's also a school council, although it's not particularly active.

The last word: This is a charming prep that children genuinely adore. 'My child is often up at 7am fully dressed and asking when it's time to go,' said one parent, whilst another said, 'The children might not come out looking as neat as they went in, but you know they've had a really lovely time.' Despite the expectation on high academic achievement (which some parents say can be tiring), there's a big emphasis on a rounded education, and above all it's lots of fun, with warm relationships between staff and pupils. As one pupil summed up, 'This school is like one, big warm hug.'

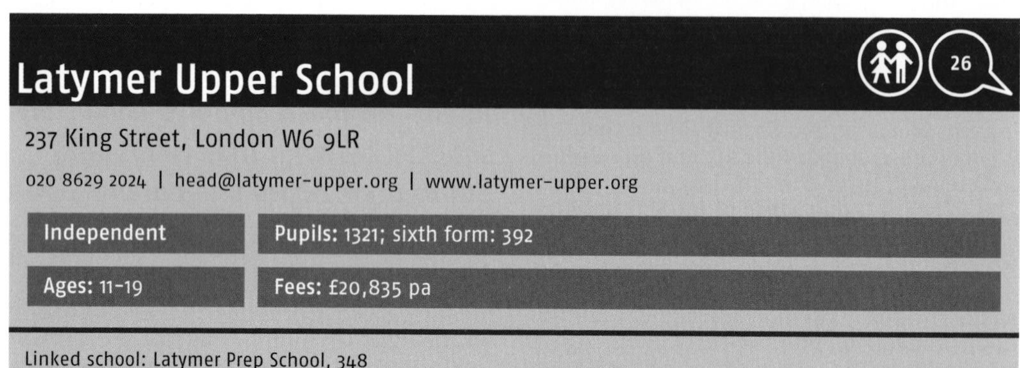

Latymer Upper School

26

237 King Street, London W6 9LR

020 8629 2024 | head@latymer-upper.org | www.latymer-upper.org

Independent

Pupils: 1321; sixth form: 392

Ages: 11-19

Fees: £20,835 pa

Linked school: Latymer Prep School, 348

Head: Since 2012, David Goodhew (MA Oxon), originally a local boy who has now moved 'back home', living 10 minutes down the road with his French wife, Céline, and two young sons. Read classics at Oxford and previously deputy head of Durham School. Spends at least one hour every day walking around the school – visits lessons for a few minutes, which both pupils and parents say sums up his 'hands-on approach' and 'openness to ideas for change'. Not stereotypical headmasterly, parents and pupils describe him as 'very approachable'.

Entrance: Of the 170 places available at 11+, 40 come from the school's own on-site prep. Of the remaining 130, 50 per cent come from local state primaries, with the other half coming from other preps. Some 1,200 candidates altogether. The entrance assessment consists of its own English and maths papers (no longer reasoning, with the aim of creating a more level playing field for the untutored), with successful candidates invited for interview. There's no 13+ entry.

At 16+, over 200 candidates for 30 places. Although attracting a high calibre at this age, entry for sixth form doesn't set a ridiculously high bar, with the school expecting minimum eight or nine GCSEs including maths and English, with 9-7 grades in the subjects they wish to study (or related subjects).

Exit: Hardly any students leave after GCSEs (three per cent in 2020, with 41 new students joining). Careers and university advice considered second to none. In 2020, 29 to Oxbridge and 17 to university overseas including Yale, Brown, Georgetown, NYU, Bocconi, Uni of Melbourne, Delft, Erasmus-Rotterdam. Thirteen medics in 2020.

Latest results: In 2020, 96 per cent 9-7 at GCSE; 80 per cent A*/A at A level (95 per cent A*-B). In 2019 (the last year when exams took place), 92 per cent 9-7 at GCSE; 70 per cent A*/A grades (91 per cent A*-B).

Teaching and learning: Key aspects of the innovative curriculum include the Global Goals course in year 9 that critically examines the 17 sustainability targets set by the UN. This leads nicely into the UCAS-accredited World Perspectives, which has replaced the 11th GCSE in the middle school. Exploring global political issues, pupils love it and parents delight in their children 'watching more news' and 'talking about bigger issues at the dinner table'.

All year 7s learn Mandarin (carried on from the prep school, if they went) and Spanish and all pupils expected to do a modern language at GCSE. IT has been ditched in favour or computing and coding and technology is genuinely embedded into all learning, with all pupils from year 10 upwards given an iPad. 'I do all my essays on it, plus I can do things like surveys,' said one pupil, while one upper sixth pupil has even designed a rowing app that is now used by the GB rowing team.

Majority of teachers hugely admired, with several references to them going the extra mile and being 'very imaginative in their teaching methods'. 'Staff really care, not just academically but in a pastoral way,' summed up one parent. 'I could frankly hug all of them,' said another. 'The teachers try and inspire you – there's no fobbing off of pupils' questions, ever,' remarked a pupil.

Careers and university advice is outstanding, thanks to a knowledgeable and dedicated team, including a careers specialist and international university admissions specialist. The latter post was brought in due to the recent surge in applications to American universities. 'Because of our rounded approach to education, it means our students are often drawn to the American university model of taking seriously areas like sport, music and drama, and the fact that you can delay specialisation,' explains the head.

Learning support and SEN: Parents and pupils rave about the learning support department, which is now known as the 'academic mentoring department' (to remove stigma). Run by three specialist women whom nobody could praise more highly if they tried, pupils can visit for one-to-one sessions any time, whether they have severe dyslexia or just a piece of challenging homework, at no extra cost. The department's peer mentoring scheme is popular, whereby older pupils help younger ones, with benefits to both sides. 'If anything, the department could be bigger, though, as it's always full,' said one pupil, who added that on results day, this is where you'll find students running to give staff a hug. School reckons on around 10 per cent needing some kind of support.

The arts and extracurricular: All pupils take DT, art, music and drama to the end of year 9 and then choose, although we wonder how they decide. Art is outstanding, with talented and impressively free and imaginative artwork in just about every media, displayed everywhere from the head's office to the four good-sized studios. Similarly, DT is fantastically equipped, with an emphasis on creativity. One excited pupil passionately talked us through some of the machines: 'I once asked to build a stomp rocket powered table tennis ball dispenser for a project. I was allowed and it worked!' he added.

Performing arts also taken seriously, with a commendable theatre (plus other studios) and plenty of year group plays, plus an annual all-school one. Meanwhile, each week 800 individual instrumental lessons are taught by 40 visiting music teachers in air-conditioned, soundproofed, purpose-built rooms. Group music lessons focus on getting children enthused with practical work, not simply focusing on theory. Singing takes place across several choirs through to grungy bands, and everything in between. Students even have their own record label, 32 Bit Recordings, with profits from releases going into the school bursary fund. 'The arts aren't considered an alternative to academia here,' said one pupil. 'There's room for people to excel in both.'

Astounding range of extracurriculars on offer, with over 100 clubs, as well as a good range of outside speaker. Trips, it seems, are organised to pretty much every corner of the earth, with the Horizon fund ensuring that no pupil is excluded for financial reasons. The annual 'activities week' causes much excitement, where students do anything from cycling coast-to-coast to building a shelter for teenage mums in Uganda. 'It all comes back to our rounded view of education,' says the head. 'Skills learned in leadership, resilience and teamwork matter every bit as much as academia.'

'Staff really care, not just academically but in a pastoral way,' summed up one parent. 'I could frankly hug all of them,' said another

Sport: Famed throughout the western (London) world for rowing (Henley, National Schools Regatta) and swimming (ESSA, Bath Cup, Otter Medley), these remain some of the school's strengths and are pursued with much enthusiasm and success. In the past a number of parents have complained that girls' sport has been taken less seriously than boys', but there's also notable accomplishment for both in football, hockey and cricket (girl footballers coached by QPR trainers), plus netball and rugby, all of which are taught by professional coaches. Sport is also known for being inclusive, plenty of C, D and E teams, with enjoyment of sport valued as much as sporting prowess. One parent also pointed out how 'my son has been encouraged to try out sports he wouldn't normally opt for, which has been great for him.'

The impressive £14m sports centre – including swimming pool, sports hall and bouldering wall – enables a full programme of sports and fitness activities, including netball and cricket training before school and at lunchtimes whatever the weather, and there are now greater opportunities for teaching more sports simultaneously, as well as enabling classes in fencing, climbing, yoga and pilates. Sports grounds at Wood Lane used by the England rugby team for training.

Ethos and heritage: Located on the banks of the Thames in west London, the grounds occupy a rectangular plot between the main entrance in King Street and the busy A4 into London, under which runs a cunning underpass, through which children parade to the prep school, sports centre, pool and Latymer boat house.

But if you didn't know better, you could be forgiven for thinking the school is a church, since your eye is immediately drawn to the huge stained-glass windows of the gothic, red-brick main hall, which is nestled behind a long, low gothic arched wall. Dating from 1890, the hall now has several smart newer buildings surrounding it, most recently the striking glass-fronted library and science block, while the old car park has been transformed into a charming 'piazza', complete with giant outdoor chess set, which students describe as the hub of the school during nice weather and exam time (although there have been recent improvements to the other outside areas too).

The annual 'activities week' causes much excitement, where students do anything from cycling coast-to-coast to building a shelter for teenage mums in Uganda

Back in the main hall, expect portraits of old heads and war memorial tablets, along with brown glazed tiles on the walls and blue carpets on the floor, which very much set the mood throughout the old building, with its seemingly endless supply of nooks and crannies, hidden staircases and innovative linkages between buildings. 'Pupils can be here five years and still discover new areas,' said one pupil. Wooden lockers, which are dotted around the school, had just been replaced with metal ones when we visited ('so much nicer,' said a pupil), while the mezzanine areas of many classrooms give a nice warmth to many of the teaching areas.

In contrast, lots of light wood and huge windows feature in the newer buildings, the most exceptional of which is the science and library block. The ground-floor library is exemplary and one that many towns would be proud of – well-stocked, not just with books and DVDs but computers, with genuinely studious looking pupils. Meanwhile, the corridors of the three floors of science boast interactive periodical table, television with live newsflashes and even live lizards and fish (not together) behind glass, among other innovative features. 'We're just about to do a class on how much vitamin C exists in fruit drinks,' said one excited teacher as we walked past one of the well-equipped labs. On top is a roof garden, weather station and observatory.

Other areas of note through the school include the huge dining room and the well-used sixth form common room, with plentiful and colourful booths and sofas. Outside, expect inevitable queuing and logjams at changeover times, as a result of 1,400 students in limited space, but nobody seems to really mind.

Originally a boys' school, girls started coming in sixth form in the late 1990s, and it became fully co-ed in 2004. Now 50/50 across every year group, with the head genuinely astounded that anyone could think single sex is preferable. Certainly, nobody could argue that uptake for maths and science among girls isn't strong here. Active school council, which recently put together an initiative for more recycling bins and voted against bringing in a house system.

Incredible list of alumni, including Hugh Grant, Alan Rickman, Christopher Guard, Imogen Poots, Mel Smith, Gus Prew. Also Walter Legge and Raphael Wallfisch, and Pete Townsend's dad, who was expelled. Then there's Kulveer Ranger, Keith Vaz, George Walden, Joshua Rozenberg, Andrew Slaughter, Heston Blumenthal, Dr Hilary Jones and Lily Cole. 'If you're lucky, you get to meet one of them at a prize giving,' said one pupil.

Pastoral care, inclusivity and discipline: There was a perception in the 1980s (and, some argue, rather later) that the school was 'a bit rough', admits the head. 'Not now. The behaviour is excellent.' Parents and pupils concur, putting it down to warm, mutually respectful rapport with staff, as well as pupils knowing exactly what's expected of them.

Head acknowledges that any school would be foolish to believe bullying is non-existent. What matters, he says, is what you do about it on the rare occasions it occurs. 'There's a big focus on encouraging pupils or parents to report it immediately, after which it's dealt with it quickly and sensibly,' concurred one parent. Despite some relatively recent drink and drugs related expulsions, the head says the zero tolerance to drink, smoking and drugs means it's not a problem now (and wasn't a big one then), which parents and pupils agree with.

Teachers genuinely interested in pupils' well-being, and although there's not huge interaction between the different year groups, pupils seem at ease with different ages.

The old car park has been transformed into a charming 'piazza', complete with giant outdoor chess set

Pupils and parents: Around 90 per cent from within a three-mile radius, who arrive by tube, bike or on foot. Diverse population for an independent school, which the school is clearly proud of. 'We attract a real mix from city investors, media types and academics living in leafy streets through to families on the White City estate, which is surely better than just those from a privileged bubble mixing with each other. What life lessons that does that teach you?' explains the head. Parents agree, describing the school as 'grounded'. 'Privileged, yes, but posh, no,' said one. Communication with parents – both via the school and the Parents' Guild – is considered good.

Money matters: Founder Edward Latymer, a wealthy puritan, pledged funds on his deathbed in 1624 to educate and feed 'eight poore boies'. So when the previous head came into post in 2002 and there were just seven free places (even less than Latymer's pledge) he took action.

The school has since raised over £13m specifically for the bursary programme, with around 175 pupils now on means-tested bursaries, the majority 75-100 per cent of fees. The school has just launched its most ambitious fundraising campaign in its history and the aim is for one in four students to receive bursarial support by 2024.

At 11+, academic scholarships (usually a one-off £1,000) and music scholarships (one of 40 per cent, others up to 20 per cent). Sixth form drama (40 per cent), music, art and sports scholarships (nominal amounts).

The last word: Oodles of pupil pride about pretty much every aspect of the school, with only minor niggles from pupils and parents. 'If you're not academic, you'll struggle. But it's not just about the academia as there's this constant focus on being well-rounded,' said one pupil. If you're after a school that encourages academic curiosity and a real passion for life, this is it.

The Lloyd Williamson School

12 Telford Road, London W10 5SH

020 8962 0345 | admin@lws.org.uk | www.lloydwilliamson.co.uk

Independent | Ages: 1-16 | Pupils: 114 | Fees: £14,400 pa

Proprietor and co-principal: Since 1999, Lucy Meyer BSc, MPhil (Cantab). Studied neuro- and developmental psychology at Reading University, before taking an MPhil in psychology and education at Cambridge. Then worked in the City for four years. 'It was a big mistake, but I learnt that teaching is my passion.' Taught for two years in the state system, followed by a stint at Hampstead Hill pre-prep, before deciding to go it alone. 'Both systems taught me what I did and didn't like and I've used elements from both.' The head's passion for the school is evident ('I put my heart and soul into it') and her accessibility ('Lucy is always available to talk') and approach ('She's clever and sympathetic, not too headmistressy') are much appreciated by parents. Has been a senior marker for Sats and written academic books for teachers. Married with one daughter at the school.

Co-principal Aaron Williams BEd MSc (psych) PTSRA MBACP is also a psychotherapist in private practice, and works here part time. Like Lucy, he is considered very available and responsive.

Entrance: Children admitted from six months and any time of year – so a welcome port for those arriving unexpectedly from abroad. 'We don't have a formal exam, we invite children in for a day's interview to see if they fit in.' As a result, the school has a very inclusive, cosmopolitan feel, and Lucy believes is often a good match for 'square pegs'.

Exit: All prepared for 11+ exams – 'Exams are part of life; it's important to get used to the etiquette,' says Lucy – but, as the school continues to 16, there's no pressure to depart. Leavers'

destinations are as broad as the intake, stretching from highly competitive independents like St Paul's and Latymer Upper School to nearby comprehensives (Queen's Park, Holland Park, St Marylebone and Twyford). Population tends to be fluid with comings and goings at all ages.

Latest results: Only one GCSE entrant in 2020, whose percentage of 9-7 grades was 100. No A levels or IB currently offered.

Teaching and learning: Not overly focused on results, but providing both a rich and interesting curriculum and more-or-less tailor-made support for every child. Class size kept very small – ideally, not more than 12, never more than 18 – and well-qualified teachers know pupils well, furthering the school's goal of fostering 'individuality, initiative and a love for learning'. High aspirations for all build self-confidence. 'Children who excel are pushed, and those that struggle aren't made to feel like a reject,' said one parent.

In primary years, follows the national curriculum 'plus' (French and Spanish, for example, from year 1), and, according to Ofsted, pupils make rapid progress. Reading a particular strength, aided by close attention and a well-stocked library.

School is currently transitioning to become a full secondary school. At this level, despite its diminutive size, the school is able to offer a broad range of subjects at IGCSE, supplementing a core of full-time subject teachers in maths, English, the sciences and French with part-time staff who teach everything from sociology to Afrikaans. 'We ask the children what they want and customise what we teach accordingly,' says Lucy. A parent confirms the claim. 'I said my son wanted to study classical Greek and "hey presto", they found a Greek scholar. They're hugely responsive.'

Learning support and SEN: The school copes well with mild (and the head stresses 'mild') learning differences (dyslexia, dyspraxia, cerebral palsy, ADHD) and is quick to spot problems. ('My son had early learning difficulties,' said one parent. 'The school assessed this, communicated regularly with me, and put consistent measures in place to personalise his learning. As a result, he's made excellent progress.') Deputy head is SEN trained, and two SENCos guide on differentiated support in the classroom. School also happy to place a child out of year if they feel it's right.

The arts and extracurricular: On-site studio for dance and drama, which doubles for assemblies. Spacious music room, with large peripatetic music staff and imaginative approach to instruction. 'One boy was bored with the guitar, so I bought a mandolin,' says Lucy. However, doesn't currently tend towards large scale music or drama performances. Art is more concerned with the built environment than drawing and painting.

'We ask the children what they want and customise what we teach accordingly,' says Lucy. A parent confirms the claim. 'My son wanted to study classical Greek and hey presto, they found a Greek scholar'

Attractive on-site playground for early years and tiny allotment, where younger pupils grow vegetables for in-school consumption. Daily clubs provide plenty of extracurricular enrichment from chess and jewellery-making to languages and 'funky dance'. Wide variety of out-of-school activities, too. 'They go on amazingly good outings and are particularly good on Shakespeare, with regular trips to the Globe.' Annual sleep-away trip, too, to the Isle of Wight – 'You go across the ocean, so it feels like going abroad,' says the head. Freshly cooked meals and healthy snacks served in large, bright top-floor dining hall.

Sport: Not a huge amount of on-site outside space and no gym, but pupils taken daily to the local authority-run adventure playground – 'better than most playgrounds', said one parent – which the school has sole use of during the school day. 'They do plenty of exercise, but there's no full-on programme of cricket or team games,' commented another.

Ethos and heritage: Started with just four children in 1998 and named for its principal, the prep remains on its original site – a low-lying 1970s office block, which started life as England's first family-planning clinic – where the school has slowly expanded from a small space to occupy the entire building. In addition, it has established a satellite nursery in Notting Hill, and a new senior school just minutes away.

The senior school (11-16s) is housed in what was once a Catholic working men's club. Still distinguished by various appurtenances of the faith – such as a supersize statue of Mother Theresa – out of hours its dining hall continues to be used by nuns to feed the poor. Above ground level, the freshly spruced-up space now houses plenty of nice, light classrooms – including a good lab – and an ample common room with table football, and walls adorned with photographs of role models, from Rosa Parks to Freddy Mercury. Velvet sofas and patchwork textiles make it cheerful and welcoming. 'I want it to feel like home,' says the head. It currently has some 30 pupils across the senior age range, with plans to expand to around 150.

Strong family feel throughout with staff known by their first names and pupils making friends across the ages. 'My son knows most of the school, from the older kids to the teachers.' Virtually all the senior school pupils have moved up from the juniors.

The school is non-denominational and staff as well as pupils very diverse, with plenty of headscarves on display. The overall ethos is an unusual mix of trad and bohemian. So, smart navy-and-gold uniform, with plenty of competitions and silver cups. 'You have to learn to win,' says the head – but prizes awarded mainly for less than cut-throat activities, such as the World Book Day fancy-dress competition, where this year's winning entrant was a latterday Frida Kahlo.

Parents love its haven-like quality – 'My son had been through a traumatic time and I wanted somewhere he could feel safe and secure; Lloyd Williamson absolutely offered this' – and strong community mood. 'It could be a bit tidier and the admin a bit slicker,' says one, 'but when it comes to the warmth, positivity, academic achievements and support from staff, it's head and shoulders above other schools we considered.'

Pastoral care, inclusivity and discipline: Pastoral care undoubtedly a strength. 'Pupils' personal development is outstanding,' says Ofsted, and 'teachers care deeply about pupils' wellbeing.' Undoubtedly the imperative here is 'putting children first'. 'We're about making children feel good about who they are,' says the head. 'They're not spoon fed, but we're very supportive.'

Prizes awarded mainly for less than cut-throat activities, such as the World Book Day fancy-dress competition, where this year's winner was a latterday Frida Kahlo

Not the place for 'snowflakes', however. The aim is to teach emotional literacy, resilience and how to cope with setbacks. 'We teach them to fail and think again.' The head is definitely not encouraging of helicopter parenting. 'If someone comes to me and says, "Why has my child not got the biggest role in the school play?", the answer will be: "They didn't audition well enough. That's life".' Parents also expected to back up the school's expectations. 'They have to understand that if their child doesn't love a teacher, they still have to do their homework.'

Firm boundaries mean bullying virtually non-existent – 'We indoctrinate children in being kind and being part of a group' – and tolerance is a leitmotif. (The school, for example, is a Stonewall school.) Feel-good factor enhanced by the presence of numerous 'pre-loved animals' – dogs, cats, guinea pigs – and the head tries regularly to do something personal for every child, whether that's bringing in a coin for a coin collector or a special book they might be interested in. 'Everyone benefits from individual attention.' Support further enhanced by staff mentoring and a psychotherapist, who is a part-time member of staff. 'If they're anxious, they don't learn.' As a result, the school is particularly good at addressing the needs of children who may be struggling emotionally elsewhere. 'One boy, for example, came back to us from a large comprehensive where he was required to be very grown up at 12. Here, there's no pressure to grow up.' Overall, a strengthening experience. 'My children left the school with a true sense of themselves and always talk about how lucky they were to be listened to and be able to voice their opinions.'

Children generally well behaved, disciplinary issues minimal. 'I have excluded five children in 20 years,' says the head. Her view is that: 'children do not want to be in trouble; all behaviours have a reason.' Parents' needs, too, well attended to with an open-door policy and wrap-around care from 7.30am to 6pm.

Pupils and parents: Mainly families with two working parents, though the demographic is divided between banker-belt Notting Hill on the Palace Gardens Terrace site and the more boho feel of those attending the Ladbroke Grove school. Plenty of single mums and grandparents funding the fees, plenty of creatives working at the BBC, in design and fashion. A few celebs. Families overall are very international, often here for brief stints while circling the globe, though virtually all speak English fluently. 'It's not at all snobby,' said one local mother. 'Unlike many of the other independent schools in the area, it has a real egalitarian quality, with no veneer of entitlement or privilege.'

Money matters: Fees kept at a reasonable level and paid monthly throughout the year. One 100 per cent bursary available, which can be divvied up and is allocated in the strictest confidence. 'But it won't go to someone doing a house extension.'

The last word: Effective, affordable school, providing an intimate, nurturing environment and positive ethos that inspires children to succeed.

The London Oratory School

Seagrave Road, London SW6 1RX

020 7385 0102 | registrar@los.ac | www.london-oratory.org

State | Ages: 7–18 | Pupils: 1,366; sixth form: 369 (110 girls)

Headmaster: Since January 2018, Daniel Wright MA (40s), previously deputy head of St George's College, Weybridge. History degree from Cambridge; began his teaching career at Gordon's School, moving to Godalming College in 2004 as head of history then director of faculty. Took up his post at St George's in 2015.

'Much more involved than the last one,' said one boy and there's no doubt this is a very visible head, who teaches (currently a self-written course to sixth formers on spiritual direction for teenagers), gives 'inspirational talks' and 'really gets to know us boys'. Pupils say he has 'breathed new life into extracurricular' (including the popular addition of boxing), while behind the scenes he is utilising his previous experience as a curriculum design planner to create a more virtue-based curriculum, in keeping with his greater emphasis on Catholicity – 'I'm big on character formation', he explains, something we saw for ourselves in his uncompromising chapel sermon on temperance.

'An older soul in a young body' is how one parent referred to him, with others agreeing. Although that didn't resonate with us when we first met this personable, dynamic and progressive thinker, his traditionalist, conformist core soon shines through. Added to this – say parents – he is all for 'old-school discipline, including a fastidious attitude to things like timing, haircuts and uniform', for which he makes no apology (and parents seem to approve too). That said, he is recognised (and praised) for making the school a more nurturing environment, as well as involving parents more and holding his hands up (as he did with us) where there's obvious room for improvement.

Married to Michelle, also a teacher, they have a son and a daughter who attend a state school in Surrey where they live. Works long hours ('a 12-hour day is short for me') and as for hobbies, 'theology is my passion'. Honorary fellow at the Jubilee Centre for Character and Virtues and Dominican Tertiary at Blackfriars, Oxford.

Entrance: Admits up to 20 boys at seven into year 3, up to 10 of whom are choristers. All applicants tested for general academic ability and for music aptitude; potential choristers also tested for choral aptitude and suitability. Priority to practising, baptised Catholics who attend mass frequently and siblings. All get automatic entry to the senior school.

Entrance to main school simpler than hitherto, but don't bother applying unless you are a pillar of your local church and known to your priest, who can vouch for your bona fides – both pupil's and family's. Admission process involves completing the school's Supplementary Information Form and a local authority Common Application Form. Over 1,000 apply for the 160 places. The current oversubscription criteria are based upon mass attendance, siblings and attendance at the Oratory Primary School in Chelsea, with a ballot system as tie-break.

'I'm big on character formation,' the head explains, something we saw for ourselves in his uncompromising chapel sermon on temperance

Sixth form (400 pupils in total) also oversubscribed, with 50-70 places attracting 350 applicants. Requirement is grade 6s in six GCSEs and at least a 4 in maths and English, with grade 7s or over in the subject to be studied at A level. Beware the postman if your son looks as if he won't make the standard expected at A level – the school was working on the letters to year 11s warning them to find a place elsewhere when we visited. RC credentials also count at this stage. Girls (around 100 in sixth form altogether) join from, mainly, Sacred Heart, Gumley and the Ursuline Convent.

Exit: All Junior House boys move up to the main school. About three-quarters of pupils stay on after GCSEs. Regularly win Oxbridge places (six in 2020), covering the range of disciplines. Around 70 per cent to Russell Group (high numbers currently to Durham and Bristol); four medics in

2020. Otherwise to good universities everywhere, including overseas. Fairly equal spread of arts, sciences and practical subjects, with classics, music and English popular. Refreshingly few silly subjects pursued – these pupils have been properly taught and sensibly advised.

Latest results: In 2020, 52 per cent 9-7 at GCSEs; 96 per cent 9-4 in both maths and English. At A level, 38 per cent A*/A (68 per cent A*-B). In 2019 (the last year when exams took place), 48 per cent 9-7 at GCSEs; 73 per cent 9-4 in both maths and English. At A level, 36 per cent A*/A (68 per cent A*-B).

Teaching and learning: The Junior House, which incorporates 80 boys (20 in each of years 3-6) chosen for musical aptitude as well as academic ability, enjoys the use of all the senior facilities including recently refurbished science labs and breathtaking library, which all agree makes for enriched learning. However, there is little interaction with senior boys and both playtimes and lunchtimes are organised so as not to coincide with the traffic of burly teenagers. Your junior boy will need to be 'robust for his years', according to one parent, with several telling of these youngsters being regularly pulled out of lessons for their music and expected to catch up independently. 'And there's lots of homework too.' As with the senior boys, there is plenty of testing, but boys seem to take in their stride ('it's there to help show up the areas you need extra help in, after all,' said one), and regular reports are sent home to parents, although there's only one parents' evening a year.

Once in seniors (year 7), boys are streamed in two broad bands, with setting in English and maths, then they are set in all subjects from year 9, although school is currently rethinking this model. Languages are a strength, with French or German from year 7 and boys that show an aptitude for languages can choose to also learn Spanish. Impressively, school will endeavour to facilitate any language if there is a demand, however low the numbers – Russian, Arabic, Chinese, Portuguese and Polish have all been offered at one time or another and a good solid classics department encourages high achievers to take Latin and Greek GCSE. A few go on to A level.

Most boys take nine GCSEs, which include a language and RE, although a number of parents told us the academically able are sometimes encouraged to take 'silly numbers' – 'and they make it very difficult to give any up once you've started,' said one, although school is reconsidering this and has already put a stop to taking subjects early. Large numbers do geography and history, with strong results across the board but particularly in English and physics. At A level, 15 traditional subjects are on offer (plus EPQ), with English, history (strongest results for these two), Latin, maths and physics all popular. Consistently impressive results. Friendly academic rivalry with notable rival, Cardinal Vaughan, and is at pains to point out that their A level results cannot be directly compared as they have a broader range of ability in their sixth form as their entry requirements are lower. With double figures gaining places at Oxbridge most years, the Sutton Trust continues to rank it among the highest performing state schools in the country. Standards here are high and pupils strive to maintain those standards.

The Schola Cantorum is a choir of professional standard and considerable significance: they sing three times a week in school (we heard them – wow)

Good results can partly be attributed to good and committed teaching but must largely stem from an excellent work ethic that is drilled in from the start. Homework is rigorously monitored and it's a detention for repeated failure to produce it. Sixth formers have to work together in the library or study hall (both staffed) during study periods. No lounging around on comfy sofas here.

Learning support and SEN: School attracts standard numbers of SEN, with the usual spread of needs, including ASD – 'They like the order and structure and we do quirky well here,' says head – and some with emotional issues, social and/or communication issues. School can accommodate pupils with cerebral palsy and is wheelchair friendly. Currently around 40 with EHC plans. Parents told us the provision is 'excellent' – 'they do whatever they need to, in or outside the classroom, in a caring way.'

The arts and extracurricular: Lots of sixth involved in community work – helping at local schools and care homes, soup kitchens on Saturdays, the offices of a local charity etc. For juniors, tag rugby is organised against other junior schools and they swim once a week in the school pool, while water polo is a popular after-school club.

Plenty of other after-school clubs for all – including Lego, debating, chess, programming, photography, history and science societies.

Music is remarkable and best of all, it's seen as cool to be involved. Many parents, some of whom themselves are top-notch musicians, choose the school for the music alone. Junior House boys are highly committed, with all playing two instruments – one orchestral, normally supported by the piano. In fact, for potential applicants, who must be of at least average academic ability, musical promise is the only criterion which counts here, once you have demonstrated your Catholic credentials. For those who are picked for the elite Schola, every day kicks off at 8am with an hour's choir practice while Saturday evenings are taken up with singing in the vigil mass at the Brompton Oratory. But while some parents feel 'really disappointed' if their son doesn't get in the Schola, we spoke to one who was 'relieved' because 'it's a lot of extra time and travelling for all the performances'. The remaining boys just follow an instrumental course, playing just about every instrument you can name, under the care of innumerable peripatetic teachers of high quality. They tour, record and give stunning concerts. At senior school, 600+ pupils learn at least one instrument. Bands, including the popular jazz group, choirs and orchestras thrive and play serious pieces (think Bach and Beethoven more than Beastie Boys) to a high standard. The Schola Cantorum is a choir of professional standard and considerable significance in the world of RC – and secular – music: they sing three times a week in school (we heard them – wow), as well as regularly touring overseas, including Rome (and there, the Vatican), and they record for films (eg Lord of the Rings) and TV, as well as their own CDs.

Art is vibrant. At junior level, they learn about eg da Vinci in lessons then put their learning into practical effect in the art room, while in seniors the focus is on fine art, although the head of art told us 'if pupils want to take their work down, say, a textiles or photography route, that would be possible'. Drama and musical productions galore, with recent examples including Animal Farm and Bugsy Malone. School's on-site arts centre is an impressive asset and includes stunning 300-seat galleried theatre, complete with orchestra pit. When we visited, Oliver! was in rehearsal.

Lots of overseas trips in the holidays, whether cultural and historical visits. Rugby tours to far-flung places and singers and instrumental players performing far and wide.

Sport: Rugby fixtures against a huge number of schools including the top public schools, many on a Saturday. Six teams in the first form alone, and more than 20 in total, so plenty of opportunities for everyone to have a go. Boys are bussed to Barn Elms in Barnes for training – a round trip of not much less than an hour. 'We are a school that plays rugby, not a rugby school,' insists head, although boys told us everything else plays second fiddle. 'If you're not a rugby player, the sport isn't great,' said one. 'Hockey and cricket are the other main sports, but we rarely get fixtures compared to rugby,' said another, while a sixth form girl told us sports for females are 'thin on the ground'. Head, who is patently aware (and recently recruited a new head of PE for this very reason), says he's on the case with widening participation. Expect the school's fencing kit to be dusted off in the future and for football to take more centre stage, with other sports added to the mix too. All-weather 4G playing field, 17m pool and planned refurb of huge gym all vote winners among the pupils. Water polo strong, with fixtures against other schools. Also popular is DofE. CCF perhaps the biggest in any state school, both army and RAF – tours, camps and expeditions of all kinds.

'We are a school that plays rugby, not a rugby school,' insists head, although boys told us everything else plays second fiddle

Ethos and heritage: Founded in 1863 by the Oratorian Fathers (with the Junior House added later specifically to enhance the school's musical offering), the school moved to its present site and buildings – in the lee of Chelsea FC's massive stadium – in the 1970s and has worn surprisingly well. Splendid extension and refurbishment of main teaching area was nominated for architectural award. A bright glass central atrium with pods of different sizes round the edge – for smaller groups and lessons away from the main central area, which is the school library (rich with intellectual ambition – many of the books here are university standard). This stunning new development is a modern and dynamic contrast to the more old-fashioned class rooms for years 7 and 8. Everyone eats by house in their 'house rooms' (aka classrooms outside feeding times) with six separate serveries. An unusual system that boys say can lead to 'very clogged up rooms at times'.

The Junior House is a separate wing situated, appropriately, in the heart of the music school with four classrooms, a choir room and several practice rooms. It is one of very few state choir schools, which head points out is 'not a primary school, nor a prep', with his open day talk always used to explain to prospective parents that it's 'just not cricket' to treat it as such. 'You're signing up to the whole nine yards and it would be deeply unfair for someone really wanting a place to be knocked out by middle class elbows using it as a means to getting into another high-flying school,' says head.

The chapel, opened in 1992 by Basil Hume and dedicated to St Philip Neri and St Edward the Confessor, is simple in design and has a warm and gentle feel. Services here are intimate and spiritual – only room for one of the houses each day and for the young boys in Junior House; part of the Schola sings, eg, Faure Requiem. Beautiful. Major ceremonies held in the famous, huge, Italianate Oratory Church in South Kensington. The Catholic ethos underlies all aspects of the school but not obtrusively or obsessively.

Calm, purposeful atmosphere, but reassuring amounts of gusto. But no football or even running ('frustrating as we are boys with a lot of energy', said one) in break and at lunchtime here. Health and safety has stopped that.

Notable former pupils include Simon Callow, rugby union star Michael Swift and Hayley Atwell.

Pastoral care, inclusivity and discipline: Discipline is tight and steely and rules are strict, which doesn't please all the boys although they do deem it a 'fair' school. Complete ban on mobile phones, even for journeys to school. Low level disruption clamped down on as much as uniform and haircuts. We didn't see so much as a whisper during chapel. Anywhere between 10-30 temporary exclusions a year, usually for one-off acts of defiance, never for persistent behaviour. Pupils told us there are 'only about one or two fights a year'. A couple of permanent exclusions a year, most recently for drugs and violence.

Senior house system – there are six houses with 200 pupils in each house – encourages friendships between the year groups and boys in the sixth mentor younger ones. Pastoral system already good and seen to be improved further under current headship, with a three-tiered system now including male mentor, psychotherapists and even psychiatrists. Plus a chaplain. Pupils told us 'teachers are approachable' too and that there is 'very little, if any' bullying. The sixth form girls talk of close relationships across the two year groups.

Pupils and parents: From a vast geographical area, most London boroughs, inner and outer; some leave home before dawn breaks to come here. Over 50 languages spoken at home; serious Roman Catholicism the only common denominator. A lot of boys in Junior House have brothers in the senior school, and parents (many of whom attended the school themselves) have close bonds compared to other secondary schools. Parents talk with an air of exclusivity – the bar is high to get in and they, and the pupils, feel fortunate and proud – but nobody is smug or precious, it's all very down-to-earth. We heard no raised voices, saw few inattentive faces. Sixth form girls are no mere modern import designed to boost results. They date back to a link with a girls' school in the 19th century and were incorporated into the sixth in the 1950s after a merger. Their numbers are small but are seen to add much to the school. Popular among politicians – Tony Blair and Nick Clegg both sent their sons here.

The last word: Junior House is a wonderful start in life for your musical, self-motivated, Catholic little boy, while the senior school also stands out for music, academics and spiritual and emotional development. From refugees fleeing persecution to the sons of peerage, this school is a refreshingly broad church that churns out delightful, hard-working and ambitious young people. But don't even think about it unless they are prepared to conform to strict discipline.

Lycée Français Charles de Gaulle

29

35 Cromwell Road, London SW7 2DG

020 7584 6322 | inscription@lyceefrancais.org.uk | www.lyceefrancais.org.uk

Independent	Pupils: 3,503; sixth form: 546
Ages: 3-19	Fees: £5,990 – £12,532 pa

Proviseur: Since 2018, Didier Devilard (55). Uniquely, M. Devilard, officially a civil servant, has diplomatic status, and reports direct to the French Embassy. The role of proviseur has a limited life span, usually no more than five years: 'No time for revolutions,' he tells us, 'but still enough to make a difference.' One parent who has seen several proviseurs come and go maintains, 'It's a job for bureaucrats' but added, 'at least this one listens.'

A keen rower in his youth and former sports teacher, M. Devilard has headed lycées in Burkina Faso and Senegal. More recently he left Lycée Victor Hugo in Toulouse but shuttles back and forth from London. His wife, Hélène, is a sports teacher there and they have two adult children. The oldest works in London in marketing and the youngest, a student, remains in the family home in Toulouse.

M. Devilard gives the impression of being an extremely busy, dedicated, hard working and thoughtful man who takes his responsibilities very seriously. After all, with a roll call of almost 3,600 pupils, the Lycée is one of the biggest schools in the UK. He is impressed by his teachers, scores of whom have worked at the school for many years: 'They know their job.' Much of his time is spent listening to and talking with parents about their children and he is philosophical about it. Occasionally, he will suggest the Lycée is not the best fit for a child: the pace is tough and there is a steady trickle of students who transfer out, particularly during the first years of primary and secondary.

The refurbishment of the South Kensington site remains a priority: the kitchens are next up. M. Devilard confesses that his own personal wish list would probably include an extra sports hall: 'We might be able to convert a few spare classrooms,' he suggests mischievously.

The small but significant, Brexit-related, drop in student numbers has been welcomed. The Lycée, especially the South Kensington site, has been stuffed to the gills for years and this recent pocket of breathing space is seen as a blessing.

Entrance: Registration takes place online and opens one year before entry. Multiple opportunities to register within the year and strict criteria (all on school website) govern the allocation of places, but note that being French isn't one of them. Exceptions are the bilingual 50-50 streams at primaries Marie d'Orliac and Wix: these can be accessed as a private school, eg via Lycée registration (with fees), or via the local borough authority (without fees). Success going this route is primarily dependent on proximity to the school. One unsuccessful parent said the process was known locally as 'the golden ticket lottery'.

The British Section also welcomes external candidates for GCSEs and A levels, who don't necessarily have to be from bilingual backgrounds. Online registration again but also combined with written tests and interview. 'A more streamlined procedure than the Lycée used to have,' said one veteran 'and there are now official open days to have a look round too.' We would suggest early booking (via website) for open days, currently held in November, as places get snapped up.

Rote learning features heavily in these early years and by the end pupils will have committed large chunks of poetry to memory

Exit: Post-Bac, normally around a third of students will continue their education in France, divided between those going straight into university and others preparing competitive entrance exams for elite schools, the famous Grandes Écoles. For the rest, Russell Group universities are by far and away the most popular destination and impressive numbers regularly go to Imperial College, UCL, Exeter, Bristol and Warwick. Some parents grumble about lack of support, but every year a number of Oxbridge places are usually gained. Recent decision to outsource Oxbridge prep is expected to boost numbers. US colleges are attractive destinations and parents often resort to (expensive) consultants to navigate the application process.

Latest results: In 2020, 82 per cent 9-7 at GCSE; 88 per cent A*/A at A level (70 per cent A*-B). French Baccalaureate results in 2020 were 81 per cent A*-B.

Outcomes are robust with over 60 per cent of grades at 9-7 at GCSE. Dipping later (possibly due to the post-GCSE brain drain), around 50 per cent of A levels are awarded A*/A.

Teaching and learning: The Lycée is part of a network of around 500 schools that bring the French curriculum and a slice of French life to more than 130 countries worldwide. In this display of soft power, the Lycée Français Charles de Gaulle is the jewel in the crown of the Agency for Teaching of French Education Abroad, the AEFE. Every year its students gain enviable academic results and its alumni bag places at some of the world's most prestigious colleges and universities. Following a very precise curriculum from day one, there is a focus that ensures a reliable and consistent education almost anywhere in the world. This isn't lost on the jet-set: Madonna signed her whole brood up and the offspring of the rich and famous are fairly common.

London has four distinct primary schools under the Lycée umbrella. All converge on the South Kensington campus for secondary. From

September 2020, South Kensington Primary offers nursery entry from three years old, following in the footsteps of Marie D'Orliac (Fulham), and André Malraux (Ealing). Wix Primary School in Clapham will continue as before with entry at age four. No Wednesday afternoon school in French primaries and this time traditionally is dedicated to music lessons or sports. Working parents need not be unduly alarmed as Londoners can enrol their 'petits choux' in after-school activities on site, often run by teachers. Early morning drop-offs are also catered for with breakfast clubs.

All the primaries offer a bilingual programme (English Intensive – 3 to 4 hours per week of English) and two sites, Marie d'Orliac and Wix, also offer a bilingual 50-50 programme where pupils spend an equal number of hours in both languages. In the bilingual 50-50 stream, pupils learn to read in reception, whereas in Bilingual Intensive, reading is delayed until year 2 or the beginning of year 3. 'Yes, I know it all sounds mad,' said one veteran mother of Wix, 'but it works.' Another parent concurred: 'The kids all seem to end up bilingual – whichever route they take.'

Rote learning features heavily in these early years ('Primaire') and by the end pupils will have committed large chunks of poetry to memory. 'Children do spend a lot of time mastering handwriting, grammar and spelling,' reflects another parent. Class sizes are big, around 30, and there is no setting. Children of all abilities are taught together (except for English language classes) and discipline is most definitely on the firm side. As one parent put it: 'The teacher is there to teach, not be your friend.' It was all business when we peeked in: desks facing front, heads down and silence.

Early September marks the first parent-teacher get-together across the Lycée when curriculum for the year ahead is outlined. Pupil progress meetings follow in the first term with a dedicated parent-teacher day and termly reports thereafter. In the French system bright sparks can skip a year, maybe two, and until recently stragglers could be held back a year, but this no longer happens at the Lycée. Primary years are rigorous. One father told us that it's all about 'learning self discipline and resilience'.

A particularly beady eye is kept on pupils during these early years. A mother recounted receiving 'endless' phone calls and attending regular meetings in which the behavioural shortcomings of her son were catalogued. A school-home 'carnet' keeps communications flowing. Focus on penmanship means little hands devote many hours to mastering a distinct cursive script. 'Les profs' mark thoroughly, and often copiously, in red, which some might find discouraging. 'Of course, it's not for the faint-hearted, of course it's boring to write out correction after correction, but the kids get used to it, they become tough.' This well-travelled parent, familiar with different educational systems, insisted: 'At primary level, the French model is simply the best.'

Pupils from the four Lycée primary schools are guaranteed a place at the South Kensington campus for Collège, years 7 through to 10. Other students from schools following the French curriculum jostle alongside new arrivals to the capital for the remaining spots.

Collège continues in the spirit of égalité: no setting and classes are re-formed every year to ensure a cross-section of abilities and so a genuine comprehensive style of education. 'Every year, teachers, kids, classes all get mixed up,' said one mum, herself an alumnus 'You might get a so-so teacher one year but an absolutely brilliant one the next – it evens out.'

In the primary schools, pupils are not set in any subject but there is extra support given to those who need it. For newcomers to English, there is a dedicated EAL class at South Kensington and Marie d'Orliac. At Wix and André Malraux, non-English speakers are taken in small groups once or twice a week to boost their level quickly. At entry, the plurilingual or international options dictate the course of study through to and including the Bac. The former allows the study of an additional language from 6ème and is favoured by those keen to add another language in the mix right from the word go. The international option (NB this is not the same as the IB diploma) concentrates more on English and students have to pass a language test to ensure their skills are up to snuff.

The French curriculum ensures a reliable and consistent education almost anywhere in the world. This isn't lost on the jet-set: Madonna signed her whole brood up

Workload now starts to ramp up and the relatively homework-free years of primary become a distant memory. International option is considered most challenging with more teaching hours and more prep. Student class numbers remain high in certain subjects, but there are many areas where the students are split into smaller groups. Days are long: 8.30am starts and 6pm finishes. Parents and students seem to grumble and rhapsodise in equal measure about teachers, but 'les profs' are universally respected. 'They all absolutely know their stuff, but some are better at teaching it than others,' was one student verdict.

Recent building works have focused on increasing accessibility, new lifts recently installed, but still probably some areas tough to navigate with a physical impediment. Great strides forward regarding learning disabilities are reported. One parent, who had felt obliged to move her dyslexic son, acknowledged an entirely different experience for her younger, equally dyslexic daughter: 'She started in Collège last year and is definitely being supported. She adores everything about the school and feels very grown up.'

Parents, students and teachers use a computer system called Pronote in secondary. As a parent you can log on, follow basic lesson content, see student grades and class averages and view homework assignments. There is nowhere to hide; being bottom of the class is not cool. Some feel that children in the 'anonymous middle' could go unnoticed as most attention is directed towards the academically brilliant or the failing. School says that 'regular positive feedback on classroom differentiation is received'. Drama, music, sport and art all start to get squeezed in the timetable and serious arty or sporty types will feel the need for weekend supplementation.

End of Collège is marked with an external French exam called the Brevet, the equivalent of GCSEs. Some two-thirds of the cohort consistently achieve the highest mark possible, a 'Mention Très Bien'.

Over lunch in the staff-only bit of the school canteen, Mr McNaught explains, with a hint of a Gallic shrug, that the British Section is 'unapologetically academic'

Next comes the Bac and a seamless transition from Collège to the upper school, called, confusingly, Lycée. Like A levels, the Bac has recently undergone huge reform and the new exam will be tested for the first time in 2021. Lycée teachers we spoke to were excited about the changes, looking forward to teaching a 'modern' programme with more student choice. Maths, for example, will no longer be compulsory and students can demonstrate 'new' skills like delivering presentations, as well as sitting traditional written exams.

The Bac pathways at the Lycée remain the same and students choose between; Bac L – focusing on literature, Bac ES – Economics and Social Sciences or Bac S – Sciences. Results at this stage are very impressive, especially given the non-selective nature of the school: around 80 per cent of students will achieve 'Mention Bien' or 'Très Bien'. Bac S remains the star of the show with 65 per cent gaining a 'Mention Très Bien' in 2019. This top academic accolade also wins an invitation to the coveted champagne reception thrown next door at the Embassy.

Here we have to say something about tutoring: 'Let me tell you about the taboo of the French Lycée,' chirruped one parent: 'tutoring!' Most parents we spoke to had gone down the tutoring route at some point; one or two had even managed to hire a Lycée teacher for the job. Official line is that tutoring, in moderation and when school and tutor pull together, can be helpful.

Head of the British Section (La Section Brittanique) is Mr Simon McNaught, (BA Hons, PGCE), a former language teacher in his mid-40s. A 'deputy head' within the Lycée hierarchy, his post is not time-limited, unlike the proviseur's. The amiable McNaught worked at inner London state schools before signing up at the Lycée in 2016. He seems very at home here; over a tasty lunch in the staff-only bit of the school canteen, he explains, with a hint of a Gallic shrug, that the British Section is 'unapologetically academic'.

A school within a school, the British Section ('Le British') was founded over half a century ago. Classrooms are set slightly apart from the general brouhaha, leading off an elegant staircase in the relative peace of the Lycée's administration block. With around 220 students, it starts in year 10 with the first year of GCSE preparation and continues through to A level. Most students will be expected to sit four A levels, including French which is obligatory. Leavers mostly head to Russell Group universities.

No music, RE or drama on the timetable but art at both GCSE and A level are well subscribed. British Section art department, accessible via a tiny winding staircase, is a cosy, welcoming oasis and has fantastic rooftop views. Students told us they liked to relax here as well as work. Mr McNaught is constantly reviewing the curriculum and recently added Arabic to its GCSE offer. Maman opinion is broadly supportive, from 'absolutely fantastic' to a more measured 'he's getting there'. The arrival of Mr McNaught has coincided with a recruitment drive opening up places to Lycée newcomers, ability testing at the start of GCSEs to monitor progress, outsourcing of Oxbridge applications to a private company, and an overhaul of the way French is taught and examined.

'Teachers do a phenomenal job getting our kids up to scratch for GCSEs,' one parent declared. Another felt the intensity of the programme and the 8.30am to 6pm day (just like the French side) left little room for home life. Class sizes

Bute House Preparatory School for Girls

vary according to subject area and are taught in mixed abilities, apart from mathematics. Maths and sciences are the most popular and strongest performers, alongside compulsory French, which reliably delivers top grades. Academic results are not as uniformly starry as Bac but still good. Class sizes drop at A level, especially in humanities, and often have just a handful of students. Long school days are punctuated with plenty of private study periods in sixth form. 'I'm glad I didn't leave. I've really had a great time doing my A levels,' says one student who had just finished exams. 'Definitely friendlier and more relaxed and better school trips,' says another who has just started A levels. Science labs, sports facilities, canteen and outdoor spaces are all shared with the French side and some of 'les profs' work between the two schools forming a very tangible 'entente cordiale'.

The arts and extracurricular: Long days mean busy extended lunchtimes with a varied menu of activities and clubs to choose from but little going on after hours. Popular clubs run over a staggered lunch break to satisfy differing schedules and demand. Annual concert at Cadogan Hall showcases a choir and orchestra honed during lunch breaks, the yearly talent contest remains the big crowd-pleaser and the annual fashion show, organised by sixth formers, guarantees French chic. Justice au Coeur charity remains a stalwart of school generosity raising funds for children in need around the world.

Students make good use of all the cultural treasures on their doorstep. Language exchanges for Collègiens with other international Lycées are getting under way and a long-standing exchange with The King's School, Canterbury (a 'traditional English boarding school') is thriving.

Sport: An urban school where playground space doubles up as sports pitch – beware any wayward balls when visiting! No cricket, netball or lacrosse but lots of volleyball, basketball and football. Once a week, Collègiens head out on a 45-minute coach trip to Raynes Park for athletics and green fields. Lycée and British Section students skip this weekly ritual and stick to onsite activities only. Primaires make local arrangements for swimming and Collègiens take the plunge at St Mary's pool in Paddington. Sporting fixtures play out on an international stage, with Lycée teams competing all over the world under the AEFE banner.

Ethos and heritage: Boys and girls were kept apart when the French School of London was founded in Belgravia in 1915. The South Kensington site, acquired in bits and pieces, was renamed Lycée Français Charles de Gaulle in 1980 (De Gaulle commandeered evacuated school buildings during World War II). Ealing and Clapham 'Primaires' came on board in the 1990s and most recently, in 2008, Marie d'Orliac in Fulham was added to the fold.

Food, as expected, is taken extremely seriously. Lunch is always a three-course affair: the Primaire bistro was a delight to behold

The school is sovereign French territory; it houses and teaches children from all corners of the world. Home to a diverse and vibrant community, a school which one parent summed up as 'a lifestyle.' French parents remain keen that their offspring retain their 'French-ness'. Close your eyes for a moment, and La Belle France is alive and well in a Bute Street filled with chic mamans gossiping over coffee after drop-off. Later, their sons and daughters vie for the same seats for their own Java (and often cigarette) break.

Food, as expected, is taken extremely seriously. Lunch is always a three-course affair: the Primaire bistro was a delight to behold. Flanked by Parisian photo views and decorative lampposts, tables were already laid, including napkins, awaiting the day's clientèle. No self-service here, but chefs taking time to talk about and share the pleasure of the food they serve. Forget sugar-free, this is all about healthy balance and enjoyment. Pains au chocolat and croissants are sold (as a parents' association fundraiser) once a week in morning break. Canteen has menus from different regions of France, plus international days. USA day is always eagerly anticipated: hamburgers, ice cream and even Coke. 'It's just once a year,' smiled the head chef. Older students rarely eat at the canteen; courtesy of the school 'carnet' with photo, they are free to eat off site, timetable permitting.

Lycée primary is typically gaily decorated with classroom artwork on display but we noticed sections of some corridors that were bare with sparse notice boards and just an occasional battered poster in view. 'Too many people – anything would just get wrecked,' said a trusted source. When the 'sonnerie' trills for lesson changeover we understand: a sleeping giant has awoken, and a huge noisy multi-coloured caravan is on the move.

Lack of space means no cloakroom or locker provision in secondary, and bags and coats are unceremoniously dumped in vast mounds at breaks and lunchtimes. Girls and boys throughout the school mingle happily in a friendly, demonstrative and relaxed manner, conversing in 'franglais'. No uniform and anything goes, often daringly little for some in the summer months, but jeans and t-shirts generally prevail. South Ken has an enviably large adventure-themed playground for little ones to romp on while older students gather animatedly in their own separate outside space to chat or play ball games during breaks. Mobile phone use is banned during school; although we were told students do get round this, but there were no phones on view when we visited.

Eclectic roll call of former pupils includes Paloma Picasso, Mika, Jacqueline Bisset and Dominic Grieve.

Pastoral care, inclusivity and discipline: Negative marking used for non-submission of homework – it's unpopular but effective. Saturday morning detention is usually only reserved for recidivists: 'My son started to look forward to Saturday school,' confessed one mother ruefully, 'he would get his homework done and liked the help from the surveillants.' The 'surveillants', usually Francophone undergraduates, supervise corridors and maintain order in the school outside the classroom. Rules, especially around punctuality and absences, follow strict protocols but generally this is a remarkably self-regulating school in which students have a voice. Student-elected representatives attend meetings with teachers (and parent association reps) and in the later years of secondary, community-minded pupils run for a seat on the policy-making committee of the school. South Kensington campus is rightly proud of its large, well-resourced sanatorium, complete with full-time doctor.

French parents remain keen that their offspring retain their 'Frenchness'. Close your eyes for a moment, and La Belle France is alive and well in Bute Street

'As long as your marks stay good it's pretty laissez-faire,' said one alumnus. 'It's a very adult experience at secondary,' explained a parent. 'The kids are treated like adults and are expected to take care of themselves.' That's not to say it doesn't take pastoral care very seriously. 'Everyone tried really hard to help [when we had an issue],' said one parent. 'The school couldn't have done more.' Another told of the school quickly intervening and separating students into different classes to stop bullying.

Pupils and parents: Gatherings at the school gates indicate a noisy student body still full of life and fun, even at the end of a long school day. Lycée system of mixing students every year also means that despite its size, many students are at least partially acquainted with one another and some have known each other since nursery. It makes for an easier passage for Lycée newcomers too, who can enter the school at the start of any academic year and join a class which is newly formed. 'Still definite cliques,' says one alumnus, 'just very big fluid ones.' Some pupils do come from extremely wealthy and privileged homes but, aside from the odd designer handbag on display, this is a pretty homogenous crowd. One thing parents agree on is that the Lycée is a happy school.

Like their offspring, parents tend to be multilingual, and families often hold several nationalities. Parents organise an annual careers day where students can talk to them about the work they do. An informal and very popular event, it encompasses many different professions. 'Mamans' generously give their time to the school; running the alumni club, working for the parent association and school charity and altogether harness formidable fundraising power. Parent association is represented at every level within the school and has regular face time with proviseur and deputy heads. Mothers tend to do the morning run and new families will find a supportive network, ready to swing into action with useful intel and connections. 'A Lycée friend is a friend forever – parents as well as pupils,' said one maman. Another parent agreed but added that it can take a while making connections if you don't speak French.

Money matters: Fees have seen a sharp upward trend in recent years but still remain excellent value compared to other London private schools. Welfare grants and bursaries are available; parents association and charity also help. Lycée benefits from a French government subsidy, a point not lost on parents new to London if directed to subsidy-free Collège Bilingue or Lycée Churchill. British Section is also exempt from subsidy and fees reflect this.

The last word: Sophisticated, often well-travelled, and sometimes very well-heeled, Lycée students are a cosmopolitan crowd who enjoy school life. A place reportedly full of contradictions: tough, huge and laissez-faire but also caring, disciplined and friendly. Above all, for those fortunate to secure a place, this is a much-loved, oversubscribed school with a unique window on the world in the heart of South Kensington.

Mander Portman Woodward (MPW)

30

90–92 Queen's Gate, London SW7 5AB

020 7835 1355 | london@mpw.ac.uk | www.mpw.ac.uk

Independent	Pupils: 651; sixth form: 598
Ages: 14–19	Fees: £29,715 pa

Principal: Since 2016, John Southworth, previously a vice principal. Engineering degree from Leicester and MSc in defence technology from the Cranfield Institute of Technology. Has been a major in the army, director of co-curriculum at the Perse, principal of Lansdowne College and vice principal of MPW since 2014.

His army background (20 years) is evident in his no-nonsense, plain-speaking manner – and his cutting to the chase is valued by parents, most of whom don't want the hard sell but to know whether he'll take their child and how they're doing once there. 'You always know exactly where you're at with him and he never lies, unlike at the well-known public school my daughter went to, where they always said she was amazing at everything when she clearly wasn't,' said one. Others praise him for his 'rapport with young people' and his 'academic intellect, but without being conceited, pompous or arrogant in any way.' Doesn't teach ('no chance, I'd be doing students a disservice as I have so much on') but students confirmed his claim that he's both visible and approachable. Doesn't claim to know every student, although don't let on to the students (who describe him as 'friendly' and 'funny') as they think he does – 'he often stops us by name and remembers our subjects and interests,' said one.

Was preparing to move from Cambridge to Hove with his wife Clare and their black lab, Poppy, when we visited. They have two grown-up sons, one a paramedic, the other at university. Loves walking and is a keen sea fisherman and golfer 'to a pretty reasonably standard'. Fine wine also a passion.

Entrance: Non-selective, though applicants must complete a maths and English assessment and most have good middling GCSE grades (three 7s, three 6s, a couple of 4-5s). 'But we don't lay down any particular entry requirement other than needing a positive academic and behavioural reference from their previous school.' If the student isn't keen to go to MPW, doesn't have commitment to their subjects and doesn't understand that 'the price of freedom is behaving like an adult,' forget it. Nor will they consider any student who has been involved in bullying or drugs. All students are interviewed by the head or senior member of staff.

Most GCSE students stay on for A level, even if they arrive with other plans – 'it's not unusual to have 50 per cent predicted to leave and it only winds up being 25 per cent,' says head. 'Once you get hooked into the MPW way, no other school seems very appealing,' said one student. Some join in the second year of A levels after a hiccup elsewhere.

Exit: Around a third leave after GCSEs. Some 95 per cent of A level leavers to university, most to leading universities (particularly in London – Imperial, Kings, UCL and LSE all popular). About 30 per cent annually to professional degrees (medicine, dentistry, veterinary medicine, science and law) and high numbers, too, to leading art colleges. Business finance also a popular course. Specialist preparation for Oxbridge, medics, lawyers, etc; experts also available for uni preparation in America and Europe.

Latest results: In 2019, 43 per cent 9-7 at GCSE: 35 per cent A*/A at A level (56 per cent A*-B).

Teaching and learning: Once well known for being a 'crammer', helping students with short-term goals such as exam retakes or Oxbridge entrance, today MPW cringes at the word – although students told us 'there's still some of that, with the one-year A level and GCSE courses and short retake courses.' But there's no doubt it's changed and MPW is now also a thriving sixth-form college, with 65-70 per cent taking two-year A level courses (typically three subjects); and recently, there has also been an increase in students taking two-year GCSE courses (typically eight topics maximum) from year 10.

What marks it out is the range and flexibility of options on offer, with 27 GCSE subjects and 45 A levels, in any combination (and some do one or two GCSEs alongside starting their A levels). At

GCSE, there's psychology, economics and business along with all the more usual suspects, while at A level offerings include nine modern languages, statistics, ancient Greek, Latin, geology and more art options than you can shake a stick at. A long day (9am-5pm for GCSEs; 6pm for A levels – although students can leave once lessons are over) and 36 classrooms allow a timetable that suits almost all. 'It's incredibly tailored – I honestly don't know how they do it,' a parent told us. Parents say the stand-alone one-year A level programme is great for aspiring medics moving from arts to science or those with weak results wanting to try their hand at something new; and the one-year GCSE is especially appreciated by those recovering from ill health or recently arrived in the UK. Results overall are strong, particularly in light of the wide-ranging intake, and a hefty dollop of star performers deliver top grades. Value added a key strength.

'We love our art here,' enthuses head, whose modern office displays some of the students' prized work that has appeared in the Saatchi Gallery

Without doubt, an exam-oriented place, with a persistent spotlight on the syllabus and exam technique honed by regular timed tests and ample supplies of homework – 'plus a very comprehensive coursebook for every course that's followed to the T,' say students – but it's clearly far more than an exam factory. 'We have some interesting debates around history since my daughter started here – instead of the usual teenage grunting, she shows real care for her subjects,' one parent told us. All pupils get close attention in classes never larger than nine and teaching staff – nearly all of whom have masters degrees and are public examiners and many of whom have published text books – are well-qualified. 'You're never embarrassed to ask a question that might seem obvious and teachers are always willing to give up an extra half-hour with a surgery or one-to-one if you haven't understood something,' one student told us. Walking around the college, there's more a feeling of tutorials than traditional school classes.

EPQ available for all two-year A level students. University of London International Foundation Programme, developed and assessed by LSE for overseas applicants looking to UK universities without the requisite qualifications, also on offer. And because 'accounting A level hasn't been popular' MPW is also trialling the Association of Accounting Technicians (AAT) level 3 advanced diploma in accounting as a more practical alternative – successful graduates achieve professional status as AAT bookkeepers.

Learning support and SEN: Between 20-25 per cent of students have some form of special educational need, mostly dyslexia or dyspraxia, and a few on the autistic spectrum, albeit at the milder end – 'the main thing is they can access the curriculum,' says head; if college can't help, they won't beat around the bush. There's still plenty of opportunity to take resits and for students that have planned a gap year but suddenly find themselves without the grades they'd hoped for, 'there is room for negotiation at interview, so they can still do maybe a ski season or couple of months travel in Thailand. But we provide them with the risks involved and expect them to catch up whatever they miss.'

The arts and extracurricular: Stand-out art, with university-feel studios for ceramics, textiles, graphic design and photography. A levels available in all those subjects, plus general art. 'We love our art here,' enthuses head, whose modern office displays some of the students' prized work that has appeared in the Saatchi Gallery (other impressive artwork to be found throughout the rest of the college). On the longer-term wish list, he says, is to open a separate nearby art school. Music taught as GCSE and A level, but not enough space for orchestras or ensembles. 'You have to take the attitude of, "that's fine, we'll do our music out of school",' said one parent. Drama is available at GSCE and theatre studies at A level, with a nearby drama studio (above a pub) used regularly.

Sport compulsory on Wednesday afternoons for GCSE students, optional thereafter with Wednesday afternoon alternatives for A level students including debating, drama (leading to an annual Christmas performance), beginners' guitar, Mandarin, Spanish and Italian for travel, college magazine, widely attended lecture series, among others. Or you can just opt out and take the time off, which was the preferred option for most of the students we met. 'It's another reason students like MPW – many don't want to be stuck on a sports field in the middle of winter catching a ball or holding a stick,' says head.

Extracurricular on the up, with all the usual add-ons – student council, Duke of Edinburgh (bronze taken by all year 10s) and Bank of England Interest Rate Challenge. Students make full use of local museums and theatres with regular trips – 'and some of us just go there to study,' said one student. Tiny basement canteen provides food, although it looked pretty uninspiring to us – no wonder local eateries are a big draw.

Sport: For those that do sport, a fleet of coaches delivers students to a range of venues ('when it's not cancelled,' grumbled one parent). Well-qualified coaching staff in rugby, football and tennis and the head personally runs the golf lessons. Cricket nets at Lords used regularly. Rugby popular and successful, with matches against leading independents like Dulwich College and Epsom. Football, too, has an enthusiastic following. Those allergic to team sports can enjoy tennis, dance and yoga, and all students have free access to a local gym. But, say parents, quality of sport offering 'still doesn't come close to what's offered in schools'.

Ethos and heritage: Founded in 1973 by three Cambridge graduates who hoped to apply the best bits of the Cambridge tutorial system to a school, providing more choice and less tradition. Now part of the MPW group, with branches in Cambridge and Birmingham, the London HQ is housed in a series of three adjoining high-ceilinged, sympathetically decorated, stucco-fronted Victorian buildings in South Kensington. Be prepared to keep fit – they're all four storeys high (five including basements). Each one is identical, with labs, for instance, on the same floor of each, which, as one student told us, 'makes it easier to navigate, but going to the wrong one will cost you a lot of steps so believe me, you only make that mistake once.'

Co-ed throughout, the vibe is grown-up, academically disciplined, but socially relaxed – no uniform and teachers are called by their first names

No scruffy corners anywhere, computers everywhere (some folding into desks) and excellent, light and airy facilities for the myriad subjects on offer, including fully equipped media suites, computing and film rooms, art studios galore, drama studio, and six science labs. Smart reception areas, deep-pile red carpets throughout and whopping £10,000 spent on fresh flowers annually – 'we want it to feel special.' It couldn't, in other words, feel less like a traditional inner city – or any, for that matter – school, though we couldn't help notice the squeeze as students move around between lessons. It doesn't seem to bother them, though – 'more space would be amazing, but the trade off is being located where we are,' shrugged one.

Co-ed throughout, the vibe is grown-up, academically disciplined, but socially relaxed – no uniform and teachers are called by their first names. 'I like to think of it as a conduit between school and university,' says head. Students have a strong sense of community, with – they say – 'no cliques or bullying; it's just not like that.'

Pastoral care, inclusivity and discipline: Every parent we spoke to, without exception, praised the director of studies system. Each student has one, who acts as the pivot of their personal and academic life. They get to know the student's strengths and weaknesses, help them manage the workload and deal with other aspects of daily life, as well as being the main point of contact for parents (who, by the way, don't get parents' evenings but do get half-termly reports). 'My son worships the ground his director of studies walks on – she gets what drives him and works with that in a non-patronising way.' 'My daughter's director of studies phones or emails me if she wasn't herself in class to ask if everything is ok – that's outstanding service.' And so on. 'If students feel happy and safe, everything else slots into place,' says head. Counsellor also available.

A level students are only required to attend college for actual lessons; ditto with GCSE students, but only with their parents' permission – otherwise, they are supervised between classes and given timetabled library sessions. Behavioural management 'not really an issue,' says head, as boundaries and rules are clear – you have to attend, to behave and to be on time; failure in any one area leads to being 'on report' and 'they don't like that,' says head. Parents very much kept in the loop – 'you never get any surprises as they let you know the moment there are any problems,' said one. A couple of temporary expulsions a year, usually due to lack of work ethic which can rub off on others; and one permanent in the year we visited. Zero tolerance for drugs, with regular random drug testing. Freshers' week type activities help integrate newcomers.

Pupils and parents: We found students mature, sincere, comfortable in their own skin and supportive of each other – 'that's what makes them zing,' says head. At A level, incomers are those looking for greater freedom and informality, or for A level combinations or subjects not offered at their current school. Significant number of refugees from leading independent schools, day and boarding, plus the usual international clientele (which is capped at 30 per cent, but nearer 25 per cent when we visited – mostly Chinese and Russian, but from 60 countries in total). One parent grumbled, 'My child ended up in a class with only Chinese kids, and a Chinese teacher, and because their learning style is different it was geared towards them,' but most happy with the diversity. Families are, in the main, wealthy (you have to be to afford the fees) – everything from Russian oligarchs and celebs down to those whose grandparents and aunts cough up.

Money matters: 'It's expensive, really expensive,' said one parent; others concur. But all consider MPW good value for money, albeit with some moans and groans about added extras – 'I've been told we need extra tuition in one subject and I think they should provide it rather than me being expected to pay for top-ups,' said one parent. Around 20 scholarships a year, with 'very rigorous exams – the top mark we've ever had is 67 per cent.' Plus a 100 per cent scholarship a year for the best at English literature. For those planning 'worthwhile' travel in a gap years or holiday, there are also travel scholarships worth up to a £1,000. No bursaries 'because if you can't afford the fees, then a bursary may not be enough.'

The last word: For those that don't suit (or who want a change from) more traditional schooling, this more liberal and very snazzy urban college is both positive and professionally run, with strong teaching, small class sizes, huge flexibility and outstanding pastoral care.

Miles Coverdale Primary School

31

Coverdale Road, Shepherds Bush, London W12 8JJ

020 8743 5847 | admin@milescoverdale.lbhf.sch.uk | www.milescoverdaleprimary.co.uk

State | Ages: 3–11 | Pupils: 240

Headteacher: Since 2008, Taranum 'Tara' Baig BEd (early 50s). Honours with French, NPQH and PQSI (qualified as an Ofsted inspector). Studied at the Sorbonne – 'a really exciting time studying with foreign students from around the world'. Previously acting head and deputy head of Dairy Meadow Primary, Ealing and acting deputy head at Stanhope Primary, Greenford.

Born in India but moved to London at five years old – her dad was a doctor for the NHS. Describes her childhood as 'privileged', but says it was shaped by her dad being 'a real advocate for the UK state system'. One of the reasons she was drawn to Miles Coverdale Primary School was the fact that she would be dealing with children who may not have the opportunities she had, or the necessary structures at home: 'How inspiring when you see such enjoyment from pupils and how they thrive.' This head is staying with both feet firmly planted in the state system, much as other schools would like to try (and have tried) to poach her.

Conscientious and hard-working, she was recently voted one of London's most influential people in education by the Evening Standard and Citi Group – and it is clear to see why. Apart from the fact that she radiates warmth and genuinely seems to care about the welfare of each student and staff member (encourages staff not to stay too late at school so they can get a healthy work/life balance), pupils score top results despite starting with generally low attainment.

Parents and pupils speak very highly of her. 'Ms Baig is excellent at building a really good team around her with excellent leadership skills,' one parent told us, while a pupil said, 'She makes this school a very happy place.' Gentle sense of humour and self effacing in that she doesn't seem to realise the amazing work she does, but notices it in others. Her assistant head teacher (nominated by Ms Baig) was awarded an MBE for her dedication and commitment to education for many years. If Her Majesty is reading this…

Enjoys travel and tennis in her spare time. Married, no children. Says her vision for the school is best summed up by a quotation of Martin Luther King, 'Intelligence plus character – that is the goal of true education.' Adds, 'irrespective of background'.

Entrance: At three into the nursery. Admissions to the nursery are managed by the school office, but from reception to year 6 they are handled by LA, Hammersmith and Fulham. A place at nursery does not guarantee a place in reception.

Heavily oversubscribed. Roughly 130 applicants apply for 25 places in nursery; 165 applicants for 30 places in reception. One form entry. No plans to expand 'as it would lose part of what makes it so special'.

Exit: Pupils go on to Fulham Cross, Phoenix Academy, Fulham School for Boys, Hammersmith

Academy and Ark Burlington Danes Academy. Some move to schools out of the borough.

Our view: School is named after Miles Coverdale who, in the 16th century, produced the first complete printed translation of the Bible into English. This school has gone from strength to strength on current head's watch. She puts this down to high expectations of pupils and staff 'knowing the data' (school keeps a close eye on anyone falling behind), quality of teaching and an excellent team of governors. 'A combination of delivery and accountability,' she says.

It is year 1's mission statement that we feel best sums up the ethos of the school: 'to respect each other, sing out loud, smile often and work hard'

Housed in a vast red-brick, Edwardian building in the busy heart of Shepherd's Bush. A mixed, multicultural area which is reflected in the ethnic diversity of the pupils. Largest contingent is west African, followed by white British and a rise in eastern European families. Fifty per cent do not have English as a first language.

Languages spoken at home include Somali, Arabic and a variety of eastern European tongues. Twenty-four per cent of pupils eligible for free school meals. Head acknowledges that some pupils come from unsettled backgrounds, so 'we can give them the stability they sometimes lack at home.' A very inclusive school.

Rated outstanding by Ofsted and placed in the top 100 schools nationally for several consecutive years. Awards and commendations seem to be spilling out of the door. Everything from the Jack Petchy 'Academic Achievement Award' to a gold club award for succeeding against the odds in improving pupils' aspirations and achievements, numerous chess awards and previous recipients of most improved school in London.

Academically, each year group performs well above national average. Head confident that pupils can will have excellent results under their belts by the time they leave: 'We maximise potential.' Children fully engaged in their lessons and teachers full of energy on the day we visited. School works hard to narrow the gap between higher and lower attainers. Booster classes given to year 6 before Sats to make sure everyone performs well. A handful achieves well above expectations in maths and in grammar, spelling and punctuation before leaving. Head is delighted that she has been made a National Leader of Education and the school has been designated a National Support School, in recognition of the continued school improvement work with other schools at local, national and international levels (and contributions made to published research for the DfE and HMI). A real feather in her cap.

Currently 36 children with EHCPs. Early targeted support is the order of the day here, with maths and reading intervention groups for those falling behind. Specialist unit offers speech and language classes for children with language impairment (the only one of its kind in the borough); these pupils are very much part of the mainstream school. Wide variety of difficulties catered for, from those who are unable to produce speech sounds to others who find it challenging to recall words. Most pupils then transfer to their local mainstream school at 7 or, if still in need of ongoing help, stay at Miles Coverdale where they receive additional support. A counsellor visits three times weekly to help with children with social and behavioural problems.

Strikingly attractive, immaculately clean and glossy school with a real sense of pride. Most classrooms are huge, bright and colourful, often two rooms knocked into one. Food technology room where all pupils are given the opportunity to cook; large ICT suite. Library is wonderful: comfy sofas, bright murals of book characters and inventive furniture, all of which underline the emphasis on reading within the school. Even the most reluctant readers must be enchanted.

Lots of small rooms dotted around the place for one-to-one support or small group sessions. Two playgrounds, one for each key stage, with plenty of equipment and a quiet area. Separate outside play area for reception pupils, complete with sandpits and water tables. A recent addition to the outside area is 'The Qube' – an attractive wooden pod, which is used for meetings, training and fundraisers.

Very low teacher turnover which is unusual for a school in London. Staff consists of a mix of long servers of more than 20 years and more newly qualified. Head keen on constant training of staff: 'We see ourselves as a learning community. We all need to keep learning.' High pupil/teacher ratio, with two or more assistants in some classes. High morale among the dedicated staff.

'The teachers are close to the parents. They're welcoming and friendly. If you have an issue, they are happy to discuss it,' said a parent. A teacher we spoke to happily gives up his free time to take pupils to events at weekends, such as chess tournaments. The only downside we heard (through the grapevine) about the longevity of staff is that it can be quite frustrating as no one ever leaves, so staff promotion is slow. Head insists that staff talents are maximised and 'additional responsibilities are taken by the majority of the staff.'

Music is a strength, with the music co-ordinator encouraging the children to join musical events going on out of school: 'I keep my eyes open for those with that something extra, then I push them on. I even go to the auditions with the parents.' Dynamic department which uses IT to great effect. Choirs put on performances for elderly in local nursing homes. Drama is also strong. Plays include an annual black history performance ('amazing' we heard), as well as Christmas and year 6 productions. Poetry recitals, debates and presentations also encouraged.

Numerous outings and trips for all age groups including to the Royal Opera House, theatre outings ('Matilda was £10 a ticket,' said one incredulous parent), Harry Potter World and even a private tour of Wimbledon. Frequent workshops too in conjunction with the English National Ballet and maths magicians etc. Children are exposed to a variety of enriching experiences from Shakespeare to street dance. Head says, 'The reason for us arranging these activities is that the core of the children here do not have access to this sort of experience otherwise. I want them to be introduced to the multicultural aspects of Britishness, to British values.'

The school participates in inter-school sport tournaments and much silverware won for chess (if slightly lacking in other sporting fixtures). Coaches come in from nearby QPR football club. Football popular and cricket also offered in the summer. A hugely busy extracurricular timetable. Pupils able to attend up to three clubs a week and all mostly free – current clubs include French, multisports, basketball, dance, chess, gymnastics, debating, music, movement club, top trumps club and fitness sessions for parents and pupils. Homework club also offered as head is aware that some pupils may not have a quiet and conducive space at home.

We experienced confident and happy pupils on our tour and the school has never had to carry out a permanent exclusion: 'That would be a terrible day for me,' says head. High parental satisfaction too. Those we spoke to were very supportive of the school and felt there were plenty of chances to get involved. A number of the parents work here as support staff.

Historically not a school which has had much of a PTA, largely down to language and cultural barriers. However, this is slowly changing and one parent told us that she has now set up a WhatsApp year group to communicate news from the school as this previously 'wasn't one of their strongest points'. Events such as cake sales, cinema nights, Christmas and summer fairs and other fundraisers, are now slowly on the increase.

An outward looking, community-focused school. Teachers work with numerous outside agencies and school provides placements for work experience, teacher training and volunteering. Now has much higher profile within the community and is seen in a positive light by neighbours. 'There is a lot of goodwill poured into this school,' one parent told us.

'We are what we are, we're successful. The results speak for themselves,' says head. But it is year 1's mission statement that we feel best sums up the ethos of the school: 'to respect each other, sing out loud, smile often and work hard.'

The last word: A school that has been transformed from one which had 'a poor attitude and negative feel' to one that is firing on all cylinders. Seriously impressive on every level.

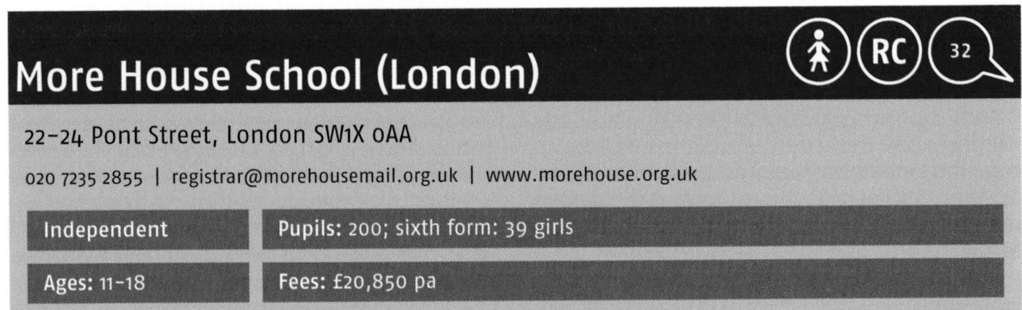

More House School (London)

RC 32

22–24 Pont Street, London SW1X 0AA

020 7235 2855 | registrar@morehousemail.org.uk | www.morehouse.org.uk

Independent | Pupils: 200; sixth form: 39 girls

Ages: 11–18 | Fees: £20,850 pa

Co-heads: Since 2014, Amanda Leach, previously deputy head here for eight years. BSc in sports science from Liverpool and PGCE from Exeter. Has taught at Cranbrook School, Kent, and Uffculme School in Devon. Spent a year teaching EFL in Rome. Joined More House in 1998 as a science teacher and has also taught ICT and PE here. 'Why would I want to leave here? I love it so much,' she enthuses. Married with two daughters; husband is director of sport at Bedales. 'I love being outdoors with my family. My kids are into gymnastics. We are not allowed to sit still for very long at home!' Described by one parent as being 'approachable and down to earth, though we don't see much of her.' Another said, 'I love Mrs Leach. She is breathing new life into the place. She has lots of energy and is a total delight.' Enthusiastic, effervescent and warm. A breath of fresh air. Leaving at the end of spring term 2021.

Since 2017, Michael Keeley BMus. After studying music at Goldsmith's College he completed his teacher training at Birmingham University. In 1990, he became assistant director of music at the Godolphin School in Salisbury, then on to More House as director of music in 1993, promoted to deputy head in 2014 and then co-head. He continues to sing at St Paul's Cathedral as much as his teaching commitments will allow.

Entrance: Open mornings throughout autumn and summer terms and private tours for girls looking to take occasional places in year groups. Part of London 11+ Consortium. The entrance process now consists of a cognitive ability test (rather than maths and English exams) with great emphasis on the interview which takes place during an activities morning that all applicants are invited to. Head always tells girls that they will be able to answer all the questions as they are about themselves, so no need to be nervous. Increasing numbers of applicants every year. Normally 32 places available (two forms of 16) though some bulge years of 48 (three forms). Girls are either offered a definite place or put on the wait-list. Very few turned down completely and when they are it is 'because they are not More House material as they are off the scale at either end. I can't support the very lowest ability or very highest ability, given the cohort I've got. I don't want one girl on her own at the top. If a girl can't be challenged intellectually by peers here, she's better off elsewhere. It would be great for my results to take them on, but I won't do it,' explains head. Occasional vacancies further up the school are filled quickly. Three or four join in sixth form. School is looking for potential as much as performance at each stage. 'I want to find the golden nugget that's hidden somewhere in a girl. I want to watch them blossom.'

Exit: About 60 per cent stay on for sixth form. 'The ones who leave are those who are too cool for school. I'd rather have the ones who want to be here.' Some depart for co-ed establishments or go to local sixth form colleges. Post A level, many go to art college. Others head to universities all over: Exeter, Reading, Queen Mary and Oxford Brookes popular. Subjects include maths, criminology, psychology and classics. One parent felt the school 'isn't striving to get everyone into university. That's not what they are about. They try to support the girl in finding out what is best for them.' Even if a girl is deemed to be Oxbridge material, there is no pressure on her to apply if it's not the right course for her. Usually one girl to Oxbridge every couple of years though none recently. School is now focusing on more careers advice for girls and is aware that it should tap into the expertise of its alumnae more.

Latest results: In 2020, 43 per cent 9-7 at GCSE; 60 per cent A*-B at A level. In 2019 (the last year when exams took place), 30 per cent 9-7 at GCSE; 19 per cent A*/A (41 per cent A*-B) at A level.

Teaching and learning: Wide range of academic ability. As one parent put it, 'There are less intellectually confident girls here who are nurtured, but there are also some very clever girls, whose parents have chosen the school because it is Catholic.' All girls take two modern foreign languages in year 8 with Spanish and German options available and those that are bilingual can take that GCSE early. Maths, science and modern languages are taught in ability sets. Religious studies compulsory for GCSE and many choose to continue with it at A level. Heads favour the philosophy and ethics course as it 'encourages girls to question their spirituality'. Pupils take eight to 11 GCSEs.

Religious studies compulsory but heads favour the philosophy and ethics course as it 'encourages girls to question their spirituality'

Psychology currently popular at A level, though subjects wax and wane, depending upon the cohort. School happy to have only one or two pupils taking a subject at A level and class sizes seldom above four. Polish, Russian and Arabic all fell into this category recently, with no take up for physics or chemistry. Timetable built around what girls want to do and school tries to be flexible. Eighteen different subjects currently taught at A level. EPQ taken by lower sixth.

Head has tightened up on academic rigour, making some significant changes since her appointment. Templates now printed in exercise books to ensure that feedback from teachers is detailed and effective and that there is constant dialogue between staff and pupils. School is also getting better at monitoring girls, with assessment points five times a year to ensure those not making enough progress are quickly identified. Colour-coded boards in staff room help teachers to see when a pupil is falling behind in subjects other than their own and gives a more holistic view of each girl's overall progress. Staff appraisals take place more regularly and twilight sessions help ensure staff are on board with changes being implemented.

Gifted and talented programme for the brightest pupils. 'The top end is identified within three or four weeks of being here. A learning mentor then sits down with them and asks them whether they are being challenged in each subject.' Extension work might include Italian classes for able linguists. School explains, 'It's not just a case of giving them an extra worksheet. It's more undercover than that, but we know who has a special talent or ability. We take notice, but they don't feel pressurised.' Scholars and gifted pupils are invited to join More's Household, which offers lunchtime talks, given by internal and external speakers.

Learning support and SEN: Excellent provision for girls with specific learning difficulties. The department comprises a full-time SENCo, two learning support teachers and part-time speech and language therapist, occupational therapist, school counsellor and educational psychiatrist. EAL girls have extra English support until it is up to scratch. School can support girls with dyslexia, dyscalculia and dyspraxia; currently one or two per year group have quite severe difficulties. About 25-30 girls currently receiving one-to-one support, with others having help with maths and English in small booster groups. Some girls stop support lessons around year 9 and then come back to having support nearer to GCSEs. 'It is flexible. Girls can dip in and out, depending upon their need.' All subjects offer weekly intervention classes for year 11 and above, from October through to start of exams. One parent felt that 'girls have to flag up their need for support themselves, but once the school is aware of it, provision is made pretty quickly'.

The arts and extracurricular: Creative and performing arts at the heart of the school. Deserves its artistic reputation and currently boasts a textiles specialist, a painter and a mixed-media artist. Weekly, after-school life-drawing classes put on for sixth formers. Numerous visits arranged to London galleries.

Three-quarters of girls have individual music lessons. All year 7 girls play an instrument (brass, string or woodwind), bought through PTA fundraising. Strong choral tradition. In the last concert, 130 girls sang alongside staff, parents and alumnae. Annual international music tour. All musical tastes and talents catered for, from chamber choirs to karaoke and geek club, which involves hand-bell ringing for the Christmas concert. 'The music is exceptional. All-inclusive. You don't have to be talented to be allowed to perform,' according to one parent.

All musical tastes and talents catered for, from chamber choirs to karaoke and geek club, which involves hand-bell ringing for the Christmas concert

Drama is another strength of the school. Sold-out drama productions of Little Women and As You Like It. Biennial play and musical which run on a carousel system. Musical is staged in a professional theatre. If a smaller production is put on one year then a junior production is also staged so that as many girls as possible can perform. 'Everyone is given a chance.'

Plenty of early morning and lunchtime clubs, such as a thriving debating club, as well as play-dough modelling and knitting for those who prefer something more sedate. 'We want the girls to keep their childhood as long as possible. We also offer flower pressing. We don't want girls to bypass that lovely age.' Touch-typing compulsory for all in year 7. Most clubs are run by sixth formers and year 11 girls; some are run by professionals. Enviable overseas trips to Europe as well as skiing in America. Year 8 trip to France is a highlight, involving canoeing and camping overnight. Those that cannot afford the trips are subsidised, and alternative trips are also organised in London. 'Always lots going on here. That's why I am such a fan of the school,' said one satisfied parent.

Sport: 'PE is being taken much more seriously than in the past,' according to one delighted parent, and sports department is well led. New PE kit has made a world of difference and hoodies without pockets mean that girls are more likely to catch the rounders ball. For the first three years, all girls participate in netball, rounders, hockey, athletics and dance as well as a healthy active lifestyle programme. Years 10-11 may also do circuit training, fitness classes, spinning and climbing and sixth formers take part in boot camp. Two girls recently selected to represent borough in London Youth Games netball team. Teachers run the London marathon and raise significant amounts for charity in the process. 'The great thing about sport at More House is that everyone participates,' commented one parent. As heads explain, 'We are competing against bigger schools. Sometimes we win, sometimes we lose, but all girls get the chance to play in a team.'

Ethos and heritage: Founded in 1953 by canonesses of St Augustine. Since 1971, the school has been under lay management. Named after Sir Thomas More, the Tudor theologian.

In the heart of Knightsbridge, though not as glamorous as its location might suggest. Described by one parent as being 'essentially two houses in Pont Street with minimal outside space. Pretty scruffy and quite dark.' Much of the school was looking distinctly tired when we visited, but all has been transformed: classrooms ripped out, new furniture installed and redecorating throughout. One delighted mother told us, they have 'been busy tidying up the place, decorating where it was needed and making it more aesthetically pleasing'.

Parents cite the pastoral care as being a main strength of the school, and those we spoke to felt that issues were dealt with efficiently and effectively

Heads determined that the school should 'not be a pressure cooker. We're not waiting for that top to blow off.' This is a very nurturing environment in which girls are constantly encouraged. One mother commented, 'At parents' evening, the teachers always highlight the girls' strengths and are keen to build on these, rather than just dwelling on what they can't do. It boosts the girls' confidence.' Very small classes which do not change from year 7 to GCSEs. 'That's my one gripe about the school. It would be good for everybody if the classes were mixed up regularly,' said one mother. Almost all classes have no more than 16 girls up till GCSE. Sixth form classes range from one pupil to 10 (but mostly many fewer). Family feel to school and all age groups mix well together, partly due to flourishing house system.

Pastoral care, inclusivity and discipline: Catholic heritage and ethos strong, with many crucifixes on display around the school. Currently 40 per cent Catholic, though there are girls of all faiths and none. School has its own chapel and the chaplain takes mass once a week. Girls are prepared for confirmation. 'Catholicism is quite a big deal here,' said one parent. 'We get the balance right between Catholic and non-Catholic,' believes Ms Leach. 'It's part of our foundation, to respect each other and to be kind. I'm not a Catholic, though I went to a convent school and then on to a missionary school, so faith is very much part of me.' Spiritual growth fostered here. Girls also raise decent sums for charity and this is seen an important part of their education.

Parents cite the pastoral care as being a main strength of the school, and those we spoke to felt that issues were dealt with efficiently and effectively. Heads keen that girls should develop a sense of perspective, and they are frequently reminded that 'It's not failure you should worry about. It's how you pick yourselves up. I don't paint a perfect image of myself. We all have ups and downs. It's my duty to help the girls through their difficulties.' Ms Leach stands at the door each morning as the girls file past. She can usually spot when something is amiss with a pupil. Layers of support in place, including tutors, and all 'minis' (year 7s) have a 'big sister' in sixth form. Because it is such a small school, eating disorders and emotional difficulties are spotted quickly. Hard for pupils to hide under the radar here.

Excellent relationships between staff and pupils. Girls see their teachers as approachable. As one parent put it, 'The teachers know the girls so well, that's the beauty of a small school.' Occasional short-term suspensions for rudeness to a member of staff but school is not overly quick to punish girls. 'If a girl has messed up, she's going to get an earful from her parents. I tend to ask them what they'd do differently next time.' Saturday detentions recently introduced for persistent offenders.

Pupils and parents: Roughly 70 per cent British. International contingent from all over, including Spain, France, China, Russia, America and Middle East. 'A mixed bag. Some with lots of money, who are driven in and out by chauffeurs, and others who are struggling. Quite diverse, with a good percentage of different cultures,' according to one mother. Girls travel from all over London.

Parents mostly professional. 'I don't think I have the most demanding parents in London. That's a reflection of the girls who are here. These parents want the best for their daughters. They are not idealistic in terms of what their daughters are capable of. They are realistic and know we're going to do the best job we can for them.' Parents feel the communication is good: 'We are kept fully informed, both with the good and bad. We are kept in the loop.'

Money matters: School offers academic, sport, creative and performing arts scholarships to year 7 and lower sixth. Entry bursaries for those starting the school in year 7, as well as special governors' bursaries offered in response to a particular set of circumstances. Normally only awarded to girls who are already at the school and in examination years.

The last word: If your daughter needs a large, competitive school with plenty of space, this is probably not the place for her. But, as one satisfied customer put it, 'If you're after an all-girls, Catholic school in central London, this is a great choice. It's not for everyone, but if your daughter wants a small, happy and supportive school, this couldn't be better. If I had my time over, I'd send my daughter here again like a shot.' School is aware that many parents do not know about More House yet, but that 'word is getting out as we're getting better and better.' The way things are moving, this school is not going to remain a secret for much longer.

Norland Place School

33

162–166 Holland Park Avenue, London W11 4UH

020 7603 9103 | registrar@norlandplace.com | www.norlandplace.com

Independent | Pupils: 222

Ages: Girls 4–11, boys 4–8 (9 from September 2020) | Fees: £16,911 – £18,795 pa

Headmaster: Since 2002, Patrick Mattar LRAM MA (early 50s). Degrees in music and education management and administration. Educated in Solihull. Came here in 1989, as head of music, straight from the Royal Academy of Music. This was followed by six years at Wetherby, first as director of music then deputy head. Returned here as headmaster in 2002. Married with two teenage sons and laughs that 'parenting does not get any easier!' Wife is director of lower school at Sussex House.

Music is his passion. Performs piano recitals at charity concerts, auctioned off by school. Parents rave about his talent. He admits that practising 'takes up a lot of time but I enjoy it.' A keen cyclist.

Softly spoken, with an infectious laugh. Parents find him approachable, compassionate and hardworking. 'A superb head who has given great stability to the school,' enthused one mother. Another commented that 'the school is jolly lucky to have him'.

Entrance: Non-selective at 4 (48 places at this stage, half boys, half girls). Names down as soon as possible after birth; ideally the form will be dropped off at the school on the way home from the maternity ward. Each month, four definite places are allocated to two boys and two girls, on a first-come, first-served basis, so it helps if your child is born in the first half of the month. Other children placed on waiting list. Head jokes, 'Have your child in December or January when everyone else is too busy thinking about Christmas to register!' Siblings must still register but get wait list priority and school has 'not yet failed to get a sibling in'. Head sees all parents who have places in reception to explain the ethos of school. He considers it important that parents share his philosophy. Head explains, 'We are non-selective, but we are very much part of the London academic environment, so parents need to be aware that their child must be able keep up with the pace.' Nursery heads' advice is invaluable about whether a child would suit the school and vice versa.

Exit: Boys disperse to a range of schools including St Paul's at 7+ and Harrodian, Lambrook, Norland Place, Sussex House, WCCS, Wetherby and Westminster Under at 8+. A few head to country boarding preps, such as Caldicott. Girls' destinations, at 11, include City of London, Downe House, Emanuel, Francis Holland Sloane Square, Godolphin & Latymer, Queen's College, Lady Eleanor Holles, Latymer Upper, Notting Hill & Ealing, Putney High and Wycombe Abbey. A couple of academic and music scholarships every year.

Head is aware that he is 'operating within a tighter academic belt' and that increased competition for London day places is a reality. School still gets similar numbers into same schools as it always has, 'though perhaps they need to work a little harder across the board to get there,' he smiles. Some parents complain about too much homework in the final years. Head is conscious of the 11+ pressure but also notes that 'it's incredible how motivated, rather than battle weary, the children are by year 6. Many of the girls are switched on by the whole process and enjoy it.'

Head believes that 'if a child is struggling here, you have to be very careful about where you send them next. Sometimes boarding can accommodate a richer variety of pupils than London day schools.' Gives as much advice as parents want on the next stage but states 'it's always up to the parents at the end of the day.'

Since September 2020, the school has admitted boys to year 4 into a two-form coeducational model. These forms will rise through the school and in Sept 2022 the school will be fully co-ed.

Our view: Founded in 1876. Situated in the heart of noisy Holland Park Avenue in three large town houses, connected by steep stairs and narrow corridors. Not the most spacious of schools but good use is made of the two smallish playgrounds decorated with murals and climbing wall, so children have the chance to let off steam regularly.

Mainly local families from Notting Hill, Holland Park and Shepherd's Bush. Most walk or come by scooter. Mainly professional families, many of whom are second and third generation Norlanders. Predominantly British, though with significant numbers of bilingual Europeans. Fifty-five currently have EAL requirements, catered for through classroom differentiation and a year one EAL club. Alumnae include George Osborne, Rosalind Franklin and Arthur Bliss.

The school is structured around the fact that the boys scatter at 8 and the girls at 11, but is adapting the school as this changes. For the first three years, pupils are taught in two parallel (but age differentiated) co-ed classes. In year 3, the girls and boys are separated so boys can focus on 8+ exams while girls head down the 11+ route. Effectively, school becomes single sex from start of year 3, though spelling remains co-ed and some mixed classes are re-introduced once the boys' exams are over. Up to 24 per class, down to fewer than 20 in the one remaining class in the final years. We spoke to one parent who wished the school also offered 7+ preparation, but no imminent plans for this.

Lessons are exciting. Inspired science teaching with emphasis on experiments. Recently, year 4 girls have been busy imagining they were water particles. Latin taught by head, post-exams in year 6. He also teaches reasoning to years 3-6 – 'A great way for me to get to know the children.'

Wide range of academic ability. 'As we're non-selective, we don't have a certain type of child. We love the variety we get.' Setting is fluid and discrete. School favours plenty of differentiation from the start (parents consider the most able to be well stretched and the weaker ones are effectively supported). From year 2, maths and English are divided by ability into separate classes and split lessons continue up to year 6. 'In effect, we are streaming pupils, though not for all lessons. What we are aiming for is very small group teaching.' It works well. Children do not fall by the wayside here, as they can do in larger establishments.

Lessons are exciting. Inspired science teaching with emphasis on experiments. Recently, year 4 girls have been busy imagining they were water particles

All children are screened for dyslexia at the start of year 2. Twelve currently have mild specific learning difficulties. School does its best to support those who are struggling but concedes the building lay-out is not ideal for those with physical disabilities. Visiting speech and language therapist. Some have one-to-one (at extra cost) or small group support. Mr Mattar himself has undergone medical training to support a current pupil who requires extra physical help, reflecting the school's consistently caring approach.

No laptops or other devices brought in from home. Small ICT room where computer skills are taught in half classes. Other than researching, homework is not done on the computer. 'Parents support this – they are quite a traditional parent body.' Head is mindful of the fact that senior schools are old-fashioned in terms of entrance exam requirements (cursive handwriting, decent spelling, accurate punctuation and grammar). 'If that changes, we'll change what we do in school too,' he states categorically.

From year 2 upwards, the whole of Thursday afternoon is dedicated to games. Twice weekly PE lessons also taught in the playground or hall, with an emphasis on acquisition of skills. Football and cricket for boys; netball and rounders for girls; swimming for years 2 and 3; tennis, touch rugby and rock climbing. Years 3-6 participate in matches and tournaments with neighbouring schools. Though most children make a team at some point, head thinks it is important that children learn to cope with the harsh reality of team selection. 'It teaches them to persevere and prepares them for disappointment at senior school. We are encouraging, though, and get them to keep trying.' Some parents complain about insufficient sport, especially at the top end of the school, though most believe this has been partly addressed through the wide variety of clubs offered, including 'netball shoot off' and 'catch it' clubs.

Plentiful opportunities for pupils to play music together, from string and woodwind ensembles to recorder and guitar groups. Superb ABRSM results, from grades 1-6. Recently, over a quarter gained distinction. Large music room, chock-full of instruments. Copious choirs. The chance of selection is high – 'that's the strength of a small school. Some are disappointed but that's life,' states head.

Art plays a strong part in the school. Large, airy art room. On the day we visited, there were stacks of clay on every surface and an assortment of mini creatures ready for the kiln. Children can try their hands at a rich variety of art, from weaving to screen-printing T-shirts.

Abundant opportunities for pupils to take to the stage. Children here learn to conquer any fear of public speaking early on and giving each child confidence is an aim of the school. A flamboyant musical in year 3 marks the boys' last year in style, as does the large-scale performance put on by departing year 6 girls.

Parents feel that issues such as bullying are stamped out quickly and effectively. All pupils play together in the playground; 'very inclusive,' according to one parent. Everyone (including head, teachers and pupils) looks after everyone else. Without exception, the teachers we met were bubbly and enthusiastic.

Refreshingly, Norland is not afraid to celebrate individual achievements at weekly assemblies and termly prize-giving. Each Friday there is a 'sports person', 'musician' and 'art duck' of the week. Three head girls selected, one per term, in the final year. Ample opportunities for leadership.

Parents are welcomed into the school and volunteers run library sessions. Head comments, 'The community of the school is a huge thing.' Lots of like-minded families who become close and go off on holiday together. Seemingly, a cohesive group of relatively unpushy parents. Emphasis on fundraising and children are expected to do their bit for charity, including getting their hands dirty. Head feels it is important for them to experience giving back, not just to be aware of it.

The last word: Very traditional school (from the berets and boaters to the emphasis on good manners and fair play) but combined with a forward-looking approach. On the day we visited, the school was awash with happy, sparky children who appeared to be thriving in this caring environment. According to one parent, 'the great thing about Norland is that it doesn't dim the flame of learning' through excessive exam focus. No wonder there is a stampede from the maternity ward.

Headmistress: Since September 2019, Sarah Knollys BA PGCE (40s), previously head of Glendower Prep, who took over on the retirement of founding head Jane Cameron. Educated at Exeter (a degree in French and Italian) and Roehampton universities. Started teaching career as SEN assistant at Finton House; rose from form teacher to maths co-ordinator, SCITT mentor, key stage 2 manager, senior management team and school governor at Allfarthing, a busy state school in Wandsworth; founding head, Maple Walk School, London (2005-2012). Married to Christopher; they have two teenage sons.

Bright and bubbly, Mrs Knollys exudes warmth and is highly accessible. She is the kind of person who rolls up her sleeves and gets on with it, whether it be teaching netball, transforming school lunches or wearing her slippersocks round the school on Red Nose day and dressing up in something crazy on Fun Friday. She gets things done – as can be seen from a previous job at Maple Walk, the pioneer New Model school which started 'out of a trunk' as she puts it, with two pupils, and had 150 pupils by the time she left. She has been on the Notting Hill Prep governing body for the past year, so has an insider's view of the school.

Entrance: Luck or an elder sibling has to be on your side to get into NHP as approximately seven names go into the scrupulously fair ballot for every place. One parent, whose offspring squeaked in, said it was a great relief as it is 'definitely the right place for us'. Siblings are always accepted and although it is not automatic for children from the Acorn Nursery (still attached to the school) to get in, it is certainly no disadvantage. Recently moved to three form entry but demand still far exceeds supply.

Exit: Almost all move on to independent secondary schools with the occasional leaver to Holland Park or Cardinal Vaughan. Leavers in 2020 to St Paul's, Wycombe Abbey, Eton, Westminster, Godolphin & Latymer, Latymer Upper, Putney, Francis Holland (north and south), Wellington, Rugby, Bradfield, Marlborough and Harrodian. If any of the 'secure, cushion or stretch schools' turn down one of the pupils, school banishes any sense of failure by saying that it's just the same as a restaurant telling you 'we'd love to fit you in but we just don't have enough tables'.

Our view: Turn left at the bottom of Portobello (still an unlikely mix of market stalls, genuine and fake French bakeries, shops selling incense and Poundland), and you find yourself in the less exotic Lancaster Road. A typical Victorian schoolhouse, overshadowed by the rather solemn Serbian Church next door, houses the lower school, with years 3 to 6 filling a purpose-built (2011) building on the other side of the road. Yards away, round the colourful corner of Ladbroke Grove, they have squeezed a new block for years 7 and 8, also including massive spaces for music and art. The architectural styles are something of a hotchpotch and the outside space is not exactly state of the art although, to their credit, they have managed to squeeze in the unlikely duo of hens and an adventure playground. The only drawback: it takes smart timetabling to avoid children having to be endlessly escorted from A to B.

School's determination to maintain original ethos is immediately apparent on meeting everyone, from the very small people sitting on the floor, right up to the confident, friendly, amusing, only just children like the head boy and girl. This is a Thinking School and the evidence is everywhere, with hands shooting up when asked which habit was being studied this week. We sat in on a fascinating year 6 philosophy for children (P4C) class and wanted to vote ourselves when it came to choosing the question for discussion; in fact we would have paid big money to stay and listen to the intelligent arguments raised.

Leavers' results show that the system works and there is no need for parents to worry that philosophy is going to stop their children learning the basic building blocks. The ethos of the school is easily absorbed, particularly that learning how to learn is, at this stage, more important than anything else. Not a school that believes in offering a huge language choice (no Mandarin here): French all the way up, together with Latin from year 5 and Greek (optional) in years 7 and 8. Apart from the four founding teachers, there are another 15 who have been here for more than 10 years, but the average age is only 35 and the school says they lose very few, unless they are Antipodean, with quite a high percentage returning to the fold later in life.

Music is huge at NHP and there are several choirs. In fact being unable to sing is not considered an option here and you are encouraged to play an instrument even if 'you can't play for toffee'

The lower school head of SEN (who has been here since the school opened) is an articulate enthusiast for early intervention, and the children being given extra help responded happily to questions. One parent told us that when her son was diagnosed with ADHD 'they were really wonderful at supporting him', and we were convinced that the large SEN department was well on top of any problems.

Music is huge at NHP; there are several choirs, including a chamber choir which you have to audition for, as well as ones for the less sonorous. In fact being unable to sing is not considered an option here and you are encouraged to play an instrument even if 'you can't play for toffee'.

The vast new art room (plenty of room for the next Anish Kapoor) should give the subject much more visibility. Reception and year 1 take to the stage at Christmas with a sometimes slightly unorthodox nativity play which, last year, featured an angel joined on her way to Bethlehem by sundry others including cowboys/girls and footballers. Year 8s are given the task of writing and staging their own play in a week, whilst years 3 and 6 produce plays in the spring and summer terms.

Differing opinions on the amount of sport available, from both parents and pupils, some claiming that it was a bit light on the ground – 'they could definitely do more' – and others saying that 'they were brilliant getting him into sport'. At the moment the girls are confined to hockey as a team game, but apparently some are petitioning to play rugby with the boys. Not surprisingly for a Thinking School they have been told to go ahead, provided they can get enough mates to sign up. All in all, we felt that the consensus from the pupils was that they weren't missing out and there were plenty of after-school opportunities if you wanted to do more, including martial arts in year 1 and Boxclever higher up. 'There really is something to interest every type of child,' said one parent about non-sporting alternatives, including chess and coding.

Outwardly, NHP may appear a laid back school but discipline is key albeit, hopefully, self-imposed. Messing around lands you with an orange card and 'culpas' are handed out for more serious or repeated offences. These can involve a spell of community service or a detention at breaktime, luckily a rare occurrence. The modern terror of online bullying plus the perils of the internet are areas that the school is extremely aware of, running talks for parents as well as strict monitoring throughout.

The last word: On our asking founder Jane Cameron what she was proudest of, she answered, 'This may sound fluffy, but it is having created a community where everyone is happy.' Not a bit fluffy in our view, this judgement backed by a pupil telling us, with a huge smile, that coming here was 'the best decision she'd ever made'. Loud applause from parents, which carries weight, as this a collection of sophisticated, worldly individuals used to having their voices heard.

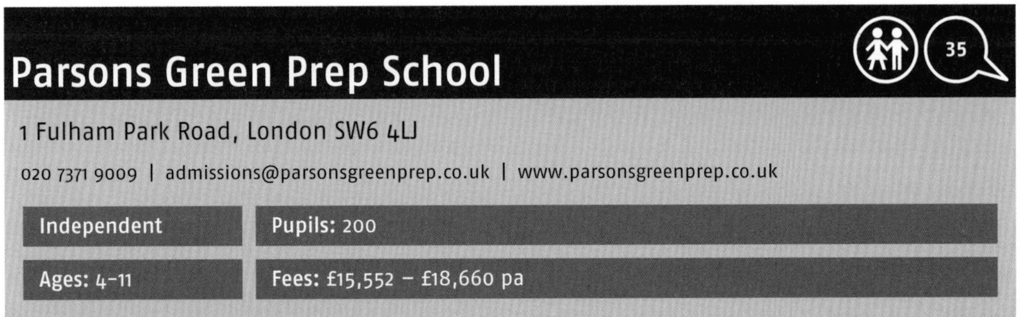

Headmaster: Since 2019, Matthew Faulkner MA (Oxon) (40s). After Eton, Oxford (French and Spanish), and a stint as a family lawyer – 'it was quite a good training' – he decided his spare-time activity taking children to France was more interesting than the day job – 'I found I loved being in shorts with a whistle' – and made a career volte-face. Started out at Sussex House, followed by a traineeship at Notting Hill Prep, then to Dorset prep Port Regis and on to deputy headship of all-boys boarding prep Summer Fields in Oxford. After four years, however, he decided he wanted to 'have ideas and make decisions', and Parsons Green felt the right place to do so. 'Even though it was a much smaller school than I was used to, I knew as soon as I walked in, this was a school I wanted to lead.' Despite his relatively brief time at the helm, parents are overwhelmingly positive. 'He's slipped into Parsons Green, but brought this cool edge to it,' said one. 'He has a really good sense of fun and seems to be able to cope with anything; we're fortunate to have him,' said another. Energetic – on our visit he bounded down the stairs – and articulate, he's considered an excellent communicator. 'He writes beautifully, and sends short, snappy personal newsletters every week.' Married – to a potter – with three teenage+ children, his weekends are spent at his family home in Dorset, and spare moments in playing the piano, sport, travelling, creative writing and cooking.

Entrance: Register from birth for one of 36 reception places. Entrance is via pre-entry 'checks' (academic report from nursery, plus 'taster day'). Selective 'socially' – so probably not ideal if your child chooses to have a tantrum on the day – but the school looks for a range of personalities and abilities, with preference given to siblings and 'like-minded' families. Applicants for occasional vacancies from year 1 and above are admitted through school report and morning activity session.

Exit: School has traditionally seen some leakage in the higher years from those looking for a larger scale and/or more ruthless 11+ preparation, but there's really no need. Head sees all parents in year 5 to discuss future plans – and pupils, after careful interview and testing preparation, proceed to the full range of local options (St Paul's Girls', Godolphin & Latymer, Queen's Gate, Harrodian, Ibstock Place, St James, etc), some with scholarships. Head now introducing the idea that boarding may be an option.

Our view: Founded as Eridge House in 2001 by Lucinda Waring, who remains the MD, majority shareholder and guiding light, overseeing her vision of an environment where children can thrive without undue pressure. The school is housed in an expansive Victorian villa, now thoroughly renovated, updated and extended to provide all the expected mod cons from new classrooms to a large assembly hall (used for lunch and whole-school productions).

In 2014, the school changed its name to Parsons Green Prep, but continues to operate very much on its original family scale with a maximum capacity of 180 and class size never exceeding 20. National curriculum provides 'the spine' of teaching, and many of the teachers – mostly under 30 – have been thoroughly grounded in its requirements. Mr Faulkner, however, has attempted to introduce some creative chaos. 'The staff have a wonderful can-do attitude, but I try to encourage them to go beyond "learning objectives" and talk about things that are interesting.' He leads by example, reading fairy tales, Greek myths and a novel (Treasure Island) to years 3, 4 and 5. 'They appreciate being spoken to like adults and older children are mad about the Odyssey. It teaches them about archetypes of good and evil, critical thinking, philosophy. I want them to have a love of learning, everything else feeds into that.'

The school's USP is its atmosphere. 'The academics are amazing, but that's almost secondary,' said one parent. 'What I love is that there's such a strong community feel'

The school has always been good at instilling the basics with English and maths – taught in small ability groups – enriched by music, French, and art (from reception), but Mr Faulkner is making the most of existing expertise to introduce specialist teaching in history, geography and STEM (in its own dedicated lab with small white coats for all) taught weekly to every class. 'Science develops teamwork, co-operation, persistence – it's very much to the fore in terms of skills.' Excellent teacher-pupil ratio – plus a teaching assistant in each early-years classroom – means plenty of attention for all. 'It's small enough for everyone to be well known, so there's no chance of slipping through the cracks,' said one mother, and parents also praise teachers' accessibility. 'You can always get hold of them by email.' 'Sensible' levels of homework, with a homework session offered at school.

Full-time SENCo assesses every child at the beginning and end of each year, tracking progress and furnishing teachers with tailor-made learning plans. 'My daughter is learning totally at her level,' said one mother. 'She feels happy and super confident.' School copes comfortably with cognitive issues and moderate autism, with a dedicated SEN room and small-group intervention, and, despite the multitude of stairs, those with physical difficulties can also manage, due to an in-school lift. The most able are given extension work. 'When I asked for more stretch for my son, he immediately came home with notably harder work,' said one parent. Those looking towards a French secondary education are also unusually well catered for, with a specialist programme guaranteeing appropriate standards in language, French history, and the French maths curriculum.

This is a small school and if competitive team games are a top priority, it will probably not be your first choice, but sport is, nonetheless, thoughtfully addressed – with one hour of games indoors, and one out. The school's large surrounding gardens house a mini tennis court and various Astroturfed play areas (with chess tables and an outdoor stage), and netball, football and rugby (with teams and some inter-school competition) played by older children at Hurlingham Park, a ten-minute walk away. Mixed hockey has also recently been introduced – 'It's naturally unisex with no baggage,' says the head. Tennis, too, offered throughout the year, and a coach from Chelsea FC runs three weekly after-school clubs.

New music programme, led by an opera singer, introduces theory and notation from reception, with skills put into practice in orchestra and choir. Many take private lessons. Art a strength – 'It's my children's favourite lesson' – with its own dedicated space. LAMDA qualifications also popular, and a classroom is soon to be repurposed as a music and drama space.

Good range of clubs – before and after school and in the lunch hour – encompass the academic, creative and just plain fun, with everything from stage fighting and film animation to parlour games, coding and engineering. Chess is major, with a daily morning session for years 3 to 6 – 'It encourages pupils to develop logical thinking' – and achievement recognized in bronze, silver and gold awards. Parents benefit from the sibling club and wraparound care. School makes the most of London with regular outings to local landmarks (eg the Thames, Science Museum) and residential trips from year 3.

Pastoral care a clear strength – 'It's all about the children's experience,' said one parent – and behaviour is immaculate. 'I've never even had to look at the sanctions,' says the head. 'Secular humanist' assemblies held twice a week instil universal morals and aspirations, with certificates for 'doing great things', and pupils can get actively involved in fighting the good fight in the school council and eco committee.

Ultimately, however, the school's USP is its atmosphere. 'The academics are amazing, but that's almost secondary,' said one parent. 'What I love about it is that there's such a strong community feel.' Something also noted by new arrivals from foreign lands. 'It was such a welcoming, normal school, in an area not rife with normal schools,' said one parent landing with three children in tow. Home-school communication also considered unusually responsive – 'You always get an answer straight away; there's nothing too much to ask,' said one mother. 'If you do have an idea, they always take it on board. Parents asked for more mindfulness, for example, and, hey presto, there was a mindfulness guru,' said another.

Money matters: Ten per cent fee reduction for siblings.

The last word: A happy, nurturing and small school, with a strong head, providing a holistic approach and producing confident all-rounders. Not as pushy as some in the neighbourhood and perhaps not the most sporty, but providing a very solid all-round education.

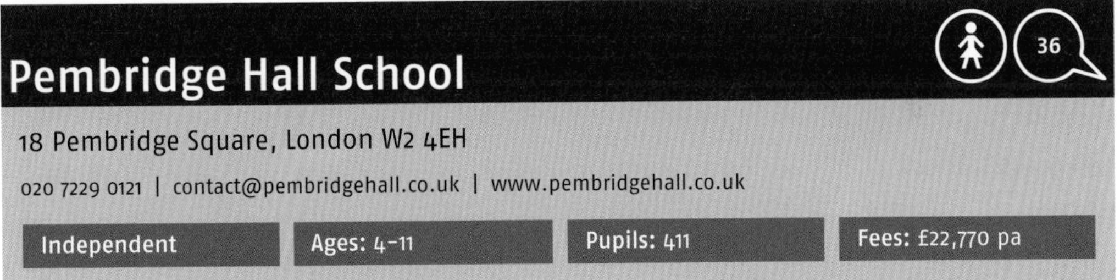

Headmaster: Since 2012, Henry Keighley-Elstub BA PGCE (late 40s), previously deputy head for three years at Wetherby Prep, also owned by the Alpha Plus group. Educated at Eton and Leeds University, where he read classical civilisation. Fully cogniscant of independent schools, he has taught history at Ludgrove, Cothill and Chesham Prep, where he was head of department and also senior master. Married to Sarah, with two young daughters.

Pupils like to see their athletic headmaster (think 'Keighley') pass by in full running gear and re-emerge smartly suited, shaking hands at the school's red front door. He clearly keeps a close eye on all that is going on, including parents parking in the wrong areas. Slight of build, he has an immediately warm, engaging personality, combining being obviously in charge without, as he puts it, 'taking myself too seriously'. In pursuit of ensuring pupils receive a well-rounded education, he champions all departments. He visits reception to learn names and teaches years 5 and 6 current affairs and PHSE, as well as taking a lunch-time years 4-6 running club. He enjoys introducing topics such as the evolution of democracy and parliament, getting to know girls well before giving senior school advice. Several parents commented on how he recalls specific details about their daughters and, whilst providing discipline, is warmly cheered in assemblies. One parent remarked, 'Mr K-E really cares and makes each and every one feel special.' Described by parents as 'an energiser', he shows no signs of moving on.

He enjoys the challenges of an international school – '61 per cent have English as a second language,' he comments – and wants to enable more to access Pembridge by developing the bursary programme. He appreciates the freedom he is given to run the school by the governing body and the wealth of excellent resources, from legal to financial. He stresses the importance of fulfilling the school's mission of preparing girls to move on fully ready to their senior schools, both boarding and day, with which he maintains close links. Parents find him supportive and value his 'practical, sensible advice'. Prior to our visit, year 6 lobbied him in writing to allow them to participate in IAPS netball finals which clashed with their school production, and persuaded him to change his decision.

Entrance: Non-selective for 66 highly sought after reception places, so names down as soon as possible after birth, but not before. Siblings prioritised as long as registered early. Places allocated randomly by calendar month divided into thirds. The year before a girl is due to start in reception, those with confirmed places are invited to an open morning, which includes a tour of the school. Parents then offered a subsequent meeting with

The Cardinal Vaughan Memorial School

the head to ask any questions and to ensure that the school's ethos matches their approach to education. At this point they are asked for a deposit to ensure a place, with a term's fees due the following March, but most affluent parents take this in their stride. Occasional places from year 1 up involve an assessment in reading, writing and maths as well as a half day visit to see whether the child will manage the pace and rigour of the curriculum. Five to 10 places are awarded each year from 7+, following an assessment day in the spring term of year 2. Parents are overwhelmingly successful professionals, many European bankers, lawyers, consultants, long-term residents and Brits of similar backgrounds from Notting Hill, Bayswater and Kensington with the odd sprinkle of celebrities.

Exit: Very impressive exit results to diverse academically selective secondaries are a key factor for parents choosing this school. Main destinations are Francis Holland Regent's Park, Francis Holland Sloane Square, Godolphin & Latymer, Queen's College, St Paul's Girls' School. Undoubtedly the many are attracted by the spacious grounds and facilities of many boarding schools after the compact London site. Mr Keighley-Elstub advises accordingly along with a dedicated transition member of staff. Plenty of scholarships each year, academic and sporting as well as musical and artistic (17 in 2020) and fine boards in the upper school hall commemorate them. Some leave at 7+ for Bute House.

Our view: Two tall, white stuccoed buildings on leafy Pembridge Square, a quiet haven off Notting Hill Gate, separated by Wetherby pre-prep, the boys' equivalent but 'a very different establishment,' affirms Mr K-E. The girls enjoy roaming through Pembridge Square gardens and are bussed to Paddington Recreation Ground with its extensive facilities for organised games, or Porchester Baths for swimming. Our visit was timely as whole school had been attractively refurbished, uniting the feel of the two buildings with the same freshly decorated white walls enhanced with photographs and pupils' imaginative artwork, and plush fitted light turquoise carpets throughout.

Both buildings have large halls which double as dining rooms at lunch time. Wide choice of healthy, tasty, cooked lunches praised by staff and pupils, with girls seated properly at tables supervised in a civilised fashion. Classrooms are uniformly spacious, bright and airy with high ceilings, tall windows, plus digital display screens and visualisers along with tablets. Parents have welcomed evident investment in digital resources and we learnt of the impending reconfiguration of 'no. 10 annexe' to provide rooms for music and drama plus play spaces outside. The science laboratory was also due for an upgrade.

Weekly whole school assemblies, with parents invited, take place round the corner in St Matthew's Church. Mr K-E described the ethos as 'lightly Anglican'. The infants have nativity plays and there's a traditional nine lesson carol service. 'Don't be surprised to find something different,' affirms Mr K-E with a smile on his lips, 'for example a rock band playing in the service.' A great lover of music himself, head plays acoustic guitar whilst his wife plays the violin. The Tabernacle Theatre hosts productions and there's a wealth of colourful, imaginative costumes and hats in the drama space in the basement. Girls – polite and well-spoken – can gain confidence performing in class assemblies, tea time concerts, full-blown productions and drama club and LAMDA exams. They are encouraged to give presentations about topics they have researched independently, and enjoy poetry competitions. They carry out responsibilities as 'green' girls, elected school council representatives or house prefects.

Caters for an international parent body; reflects London life, improves languages and cultural awareness, whilst providing a distinct, English education, appreciated by all

Mr K-E aims to ensure girls get a rounded education with plenty of fun alongside academic rigour. He reassures us, 'We can do both.' He has created a strong, collaborative senior leadership team, promoting longstanding staff, who – parents tell us – have been 'tried and tested', such as the popular deputy head, and appointing new specialists of both sexes. He has introduced setting from year 3 in maths and English, so three classes become groups of four, with heads of department working alongside class teachers. The curriculum now includes philosophy, mind mapping and cross-curricular topics. Impressive lanterns on display in the stunning art studio involved science, IT and art ('STE(A)M'). One father spoke of his delight seeing his reception daughter enjoying muddy puddles during a forest school session in Kensington Gardens. Others appreciate the upper school residential trips and in particular the team-building and outdoor activities of the exploration society.

There are various mechanisms to support those international girls who need extra help with English. Parents with dyslexic daughters commented on impressive improvements in provision and supportive ongoing discussions. We saw pupils happily engaged in learning right from reception, concentrating in a carousel of well-organised literacy activities. We witnessed year 1s exploring capacity, estimating and experimenting with beakers, working collaboratively and purposefully.

Girls are encouraged to try everything. A multiplicity of clubs include kitchen sink science, Lego and Latin. The head is proud that three-quarters of the girls take instrumental music lessons. There are baroque chamber ensembles with a harpsicord, an orchestra and three choirs: the auditioned chamber choir has biannual tours to eg Venice. Sports include football and cricket, with fixtures against local primary schools, as well as the traditional netball and rounders. The PE department has an inclusive ethos: 180 girls in years 3-6 played in matches in one week. They encounter stiff competition from schools such as Bute House and Glendower, but their efforts are clearly paying off as the U11 girls proudly told us they were playing in the IAPS netball finals.

Parents are made welcome and when we visited were busily counting money raised from a reading marathon for local community charities. Each class had designed word trees to record individual efforts. Parents we spoke to felt they had easy access to any of the staff, including the headmaster, and there's a supportive parents' association. The school has maintained its reputation for excellent pastoral care: girls see their teachers as fair and encouraging.

Pembridge caters for an international parent body; the school reflects London life, improves languages and cultural awareness, whilst providing a distinct, English education, appreciated by all. The girls seem relaxed, enjoying everything on offer, despite limited outdoor space, which might not suit a very active girl. With excellent pastoral care, happy, modest girls and good advice on senior schools, this non-selective school could be a great choice for a local clientele. Parents agree it is 'not precious' and like the sense of community, unusual for central London.

The last word: Those whose daughters have moved on have no regret in choosing Pembridge, praising the thoughtful preparation for the senior school life so their daughters 'have not been fazed and feel they have had a taste of everything'.

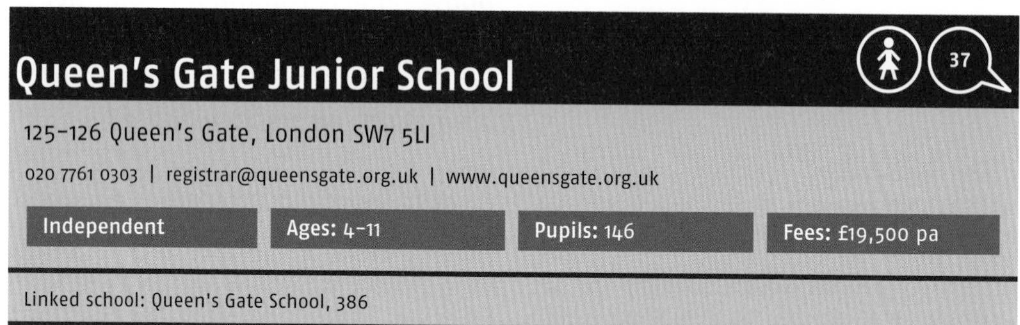

Director of the junior school: Since 2017, James Denchfield BA PGCE. English and history degree from Goldsmiths and PGCE from the Institute of Education. Brought up and educated in Norwich but escaped down the M11 to London, following in the footsteps on one of his heroes, Pip in Great Expectations. Early in his career he worked in Waterstones, just around the corner, and 'fell in love with South Ken' – so when a job at Queen's Gate School came up, he applied immediately. A stint as head of English led to him being made head of lower school and then to his appointment here.

Comes across as calm and reassuring, with a quick understanding and equally alert (just hidden) sense of humour. A very articulate man, as you'd expect from someone who admits to 'being obsessed with poetry' in his youth, he explains why he feels that he has a three-dimensional view of the school: he has worked in the senior school, had a daughter in the junior school (convincingly sad that she couldn't stay, due to the commute) and still teaches a double English lesson every week. In fact, we suspect it's hard to keep him out of the classroom as his eyes light up whenever he mentions teaching.

Claims Rosalynd Kamaryc, principal of Queen's Gate School, has 'significant presence'. But we didn't feel he's a number two type and were heartened to hear from pupils, parents and staff that 'his door really is open all the time, it's not just a cliché'. Parents feel that his changes are all positive, from subtle improvements in communication to talking to other heads and encouraging STEM subjects.

Entrance: Around 80 apply for the 40 places offered. School says it's 'looking for potential, not girls who have been taught what to say'. Important too that the whole family 'gets' the ethos of the school, echoed by parent.

There is an assessment morning at 4+ although head dislikes the term and is considering changing the way the screening is carried out too. Nevertheless, one happy candidate told her parents, 'I danced and they gave me crayons' – obviously not a frightening experience for her. A waiting list for the occasional place further up the school, caused by two or three families moving each year; normally around 10 girls for each spot.

Exit: The vast majority stays under the Queen's Gate umbrella and move on to the senior school. There are few destination surprises from the handful who go elsewhere – two or three become boarders at schools such as Downe House, Wycombe Abbey, St Mary's Ascot or Heathfield; remainder tend to go to leading London independents including Godolphin & Latymer, Wimbledon High, Channing, City of London etc. Odd few to Holland Park School, which some would class a private school in all but name.

Parents say the next step is made easier thanks to good rapport between them and school. Members of staff add that the size of the school means they grow to know each girl really well, so are confident about knowing where she might fit in best. For instance, they said that 'there are always girls who need acres and acres of green space' (presumably they meant sporty types) who might not be suited by the lack of 'outdoors' at the senior school.

Our view: Although almost next-door, this school feels different to its older sister. The ethos may be the same but the atmosphere is calmer, possibly due to more square feet per smaller child. That said, the links are many, among the most important of which is access to specialist teachers who operate across both schools – a huge plus as experts in their fields are not always available in small preps.

Recent changes in the academic structure include an increased awareness of the 'excitement of numbers' – continues at home with school now providing parents with tips on how to fan the flames of numerical curiosity. Hugely popular problem solving classes start in year 2, based on maths and also designed to develop lateral thinking. Girls are encouraged to give STEM subjects equal importance to that previously given to English and the arts – the traditional strengths of the school. Twenty-two different subjects include six languages – French all the way through; Spanish, Italian, German, Mandarin and Latin all on timetable at different stages. Fluent French speakers (several, as this corner of London is almost a Parisian arrondissement) follow an adapted programme. An extra enrichment lesson for year 5 (taught by head) covers a new topic each week taken from current issues, such as Brexit or DNA testing. Setting in maths from year 3. From year 4 onwards, some core classes are divided according to the level a particular child is at and the Albertopolis club (a great example of Victorian nomenclature, not to say immodesty, by Prince Albert) has been launched for those prepared to put in the extra work or who find the standard level not quite challenging enough. This approach chimes with a parent's view that 'the girls are encouraged to enjoy the world of academia'.

Musical talent is explored at an early stage – one girl was so won over by the music department that she asked her parent for a cello for her sixth birthday

EAL and SEN teachers operate across the junior and senior schools, but we got the impression they are not often called into play due to the small (maybe two or three at any one time) number of identified children. Head says the weekly staff meetings bring any potential problems to light. In addition, both he and the teachers say that they can almost always spot issues (either academic or pastoral) a mile off.

The preliminary classrooms on the ground floor to year 6 in the attic are bright and cheerful, although the layout means this is probably not a school for anyone finding stairs a problem. The tables in the former computer room are decorated with a certain amount of haphazard paint and there is a charming cubbyhole on a landing, labelled 'The Burrow', where one-to-one lessons can be held. The library takes up one floor and is satisfactorily full, with an enthusiastic librarian plus a popular digital interface. The school chose the winning title for the Awesome Book Awards last year and has high hopes of being on target again. 'We're rivals but we're still friends,' was the pupil comment about the scoreboard on the stairs showing the current scores in the annual battle between the two school houses and the current week's maths challenge is displayed, alongside an endearing home-made green letterbox where answers can be posted.

'There is not enough space for playing after lunch as there isn't time to go to the park,' grumbled one pupil. Indeed, the only outside space is a yard for the little ones, although the gym in the senior school and close-by Kensington and Stanhope Gardens allow more running around (there is a 50/50 split between organised sport and free time in the gardens, with head voting for 'spitfires and hurricanes', whenever he gets the chance). Plus, Hyde and Battersea Parks come into play when a larger space is called for.

Sports staff from the senior school include an ex-goalie of the England hockey team and they field teams for netball, hockey, fencing, biathlon, swimming and cricket. Fencing, taught by an Olympian coach, is enough of a draw to bring girls (and presumably their poor parents) to school at crack of dawn (well, 7am) for practice. Running has a popular programme and rowing is an option in year 6. Open to suggestion, they acted very fast when told of nearby tennis courts and that is now another games option.

The influence of the 'legendary' art teacher in the senior school has permeated down, resulting in exciting examples of work on display – 'They get to see what the senior girls can do, which is amazing,' enthused a parent. We were shown a calendar (part of a competition run by the Mayor of London) with the cover design by a Queen's Gate pupil and saw one child working towards an art scholarship.

Musical talent is explored at an early stage, with every girl given a 'music taster' on an instrument and all girls in years 3, 4 and 5 play in a strings orchestra – one girl was so won over by the music department that she asked her parent for a cello for her sixth birthday. Concerts several times a term, whether strings, woodwind, piano, choral or combinations and the Kids for Kids concert is a very big deal. Drama was enthusiastically promoted by our guides with the highpoint being an annual production by years 5 and 6 at RADA, as well as the weekly lessons on the timetable.

Once landed in year 1, girls tend to go to a club most days and even the little ones join in at lunchtime. There are some imaginative and well-subscribed arty options including papercrafts, story club, young writers and musical theatre as well as the usual sports although one parent felt they could include more languages.

The school council, made up of form captains and an elected rep from each year, feels its requests are listened to but as yet the much longed-for school pet has not arrived. PTA meets once a term and has introduced regular social outings, where parents and teachers can talk out of school. A very close-knit bunch of parents, with one remarking that when her daughter left 'the saddest thing would be moving away from the other parents'.

Money matters: Currently, only one scholarship at 7+ but they are adding another, so there will be both an external and internal offering. While not an official position, school states that attempts would be made to try and ensure that any girl affected by a change in her parents' financial circumstances could stay until a suitable break-point is reached.

The last word: There are obvious close connections but this is not just a Queen's Gate with smaller people; rather, a school with its own identity. 'That is exactly the kind of girl I want my daughter to be,' said one parent after his pupil-led tour. A traditional, genuinely friendly all-girls school, with the added bonus of access to teachers from the senior school and actively encouraged relationships between the older and younger girls. As the head says, 'We take all the best bits.'

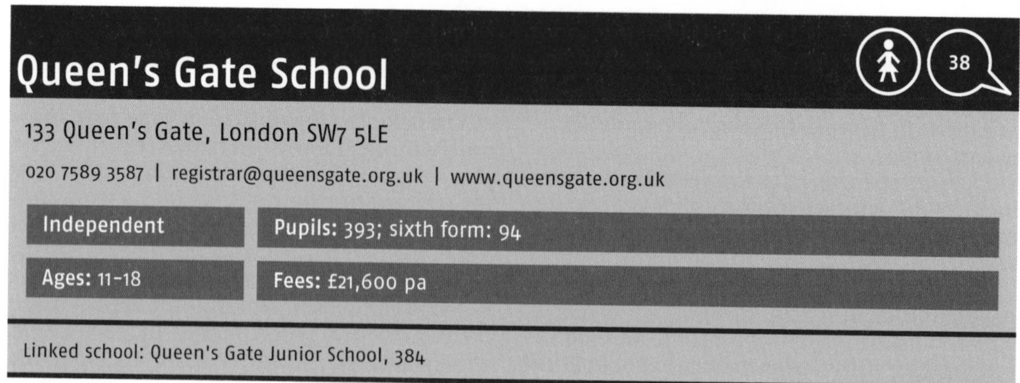

Queen's Gate School

133 Queen's Gate, London SW7 5LE

020 7589 3587 | registrar@queensgate.org.uk | www.queensgate.org.uk

Independent | **Pupils:** 393; sixth form: 94

Ages: 11–18 | **Fees:** £21,600 pa

Linked school: Queen's Gate Junior School, 384

Principal: Since 2006, Rosalynd Kamaryc BA MSc PGCE (50s). Previously did a 10 year stint as head of Wykeham House School, Fareham. Not heading for retirement any time soon but after spending over a decade ensuring that this happy, successful school became even happier and more successful, there's always the vague possibility that she might want another challenge.

Neat, confident and fit, she plays tennis seriously as often as she can and was once a keen horsewoman before she decided that tennis racquets are less trouble than horses at the end of a long day. She gave careful consideration to the questions we asked and thoughtful, if not revelatory, answers on subjects such as the change in A level choices and university destinations, showing that she has a thorough knowledge of her profession and her school.

Teachers talk of strong leadership and help when needed, while parents talk of her friendliness and willingness to communicate. It was, in other words, easy to believe this extremely capable woman wants the best outcome for her girls and her staff and that she's telling the truth when she talks of her belief in the 'Queen's Gate family'.

Entrance: Around six applicants for each place at 11+ with the same process applied to girls from the lower school as for outsiders. This means an assessment, report from their previous school and an interview, (the head always sees the candidates from the junior school but not always all external candidates). A very high proportion of the lower school applicants are accepted (usually 20+ girls). Almost always a waiting list further up the school, but occasional places due to the international background and movement of families. A very small intake for the sixth form, minimum of six 9-7s at GCSE and head states 'we are very selective'.

Exit: Tiny shrinkage after GCSEs – although the head actively encourages them to explore other options, few want to flee the cosy nest. Year 13 leavers not only aim for a wide range of universities in the UK but an increasing number want to head overseas, particularly American colleges. For example, in 2019 two girls went to Ivies in the US and one to hotel school in Lausanne. The choice of courses is equally eclectic, ranging from psychology to neuroscience, fashion design and criminology – no stereotyping here. Slightly sadly, the suggestion that they should suggest apprenticeships to their charges fell on stony ground.

Seven or eight apply to Oxbridge each year and one was accepted in 2020. There's also a high success rate among those who re-apply after taking a gap year, which head puts down to the single factor of increased maturity. No medics in 2020, but six students headed off overseas, primarily to study liberal arts – Boston College, NY University, Georgetown University, Parson's school of Design and Carnegie Mellon University all featured.

Latest results: In 2020, 75 per cent 9/7 at I/GCSE: 71 per cent A*/A at A level (89 per cent A*/B). In 2019 (the last year when exams took place), 70 per cent 9-7 at I/GCSEs; 54 per cent A*/A (79 per cent A*-B).

Teaching and learning: The head speaks of being 'always ambitious' for her girls and the academic results across the board bear witness to the school's success.

Once known as an 'arty' school, there are few academic gaps here these days and a conscious effort has been maintained to teach a wide range of subjects from year 7 onwards (unusually, you can study Latin and Mandarin for GCSE, even if it's just you). This richesse of options is particularly obvious at A level, where they offer an astonishing (for such a small school) range of 28 guaranteed subjects, even if a subject has only one or two takers, a fact the head is, rightly, very proud of.

Buzzing art rooms presided over by the 'legend' of an art teacher who was overseeing an A level project on chairs when we visited, calling for wood glue whilst wielding a drill

There has been a small swing in favour of STEM subjects at A level, with more girls taking a route which will lead them towards science or medicine, typified at the top end by one girl heading to Oxford to study engineering. Maths, art and English are still the most popular choices but biology, sociology, psychology and economics don't lag far behind.

At the moment, everyone signs up to four A levels (one of which can be dropped at any point in the lower sixth) but there is talk of reducing it to three with the option of a fourth. Head is still undecided but feels that this would probably end them up in the same place (as far as numbers of exams taken) but that it might make for a better journey on the way.

Teacher turnover is low (unless retirement beckons) and some have been here for more than 20 years. However, the head seems well aware of keeping the balance between young NQTs and familiar faces and the pupils and parents love the continuity.

Learning support and SEN: They are very careful to state that they can only cope with a certain level of SEN (which really means mild dyslexia), but there is a full-time SEN teacher and girls felt that there is always help on hand. Definitely not a wheelchair friendly school as you are constantly faced with steps and stairs.

The arts and extracurricular: Buzzing art rooms at the top of the houses, presided over by the 'legend' of an art teacher who was overseeing an A level project on chairs when we visited, calling for the wood glue whilst wielding a drill. Imagination, enthusiasm and stimulation on show among all the different classes working under the roof. 'We are so lucky to have all this – it was one of the main reasons I wanted to come here,' said one student.

Music not quite so much in evidence but a substantial percentage learn instruments in school. Cosy drama teacher was recapping the important bits of the '39 Steps' in a slightly chaotic space next to the small studio stage, the size of which does not appear to deter the girls.

Clubs are ubiquitous from astronomy to book club – 'absolutely everything you want,' enthused one mother. The location is an added boon and has led to exciting outings behind the scenes at their near-neighbour, the Natural History Museum – the chance of being up close and personal with dinosaurs makes the average school outing seem very dreary.

Sport: For a school with two small roof terraces and two other tiny outside spaces, they do well to offer any sport at all beyond basic PE in the basement gym. However, they try and overcome the practical problems and even field netball, hockey and basketball teams and can boast of a potential international rower and a 'brilliant' fencer. Perhaps not a school for a noticeably sporty girl, but encouragement is handed out liberally to anyone who has a go.

Ethos and heritage: At the end of Victoria's reign, when Miss Eleanor Wyatt opened her door in nearby Stanhope Gardens, her aim was to help well-brought up girls turn into educated young ladies. The ethos remains the same over a century later, the only difference being that Oxbridge rather than marriage is now the goal.

The facades of the adjoining houses have recently been embellished with discreet dark blue banners. Inside, the Queen hangs on the stairs next to a pupil's drawing of a screaming girl, seemingly heavily influenced by Munch. The entrance we came through was narrow and unglamorous, decorated with photographs of visits by their startlingly recognisable alumnae (think HRH the Duchess of Cornwall) and staff members (ex-chief spy, Eliza Manningham Buller) but there is a much grander hall and staircase next door.

Inside, the Queen hangs on the stairs next to a pupil's drawing of a screaming girl, seemingly heavily influenced by Munch

A stranger would need a map to negotiate the maze that consists of classrooms, libraries and staff cubby holes but it appears to be zero problem for its daily inhabitants who think it adds to the 'homeyness' of the school. The basement (apart from the gym and kitchen) is basically all about science, the top floor is all about art and the rest is squashed in-between. Fairly bonkers but it works.

Pastoral care, inclusivity and discipline: The praise (as well as fondness) for the staff and the pastoral care was unanimous and close to fulsome, if it hadn't been so obviously genuine. School appears not only to help with problems but are aware of them before the student has realised that she should be worried. Everyone seems involved, with form teachers, heads of year and the subject director all coming in for plaudits. Particular mention of the relationship and care taken by older girls for younger ones, fostered by a buddy system set up on induction day, and a residential outing for the year group at the beginning of year 7.

When asked about the existence of eating disorders or other psychological and emotional problems causing distress, honest soul-searching went on amongst sixth-formers, concluding that they could only remember one girl in trouble and that it wasn't a worry here unlike in some of the schools that their friends went to. Detention and late detention for offenders but the crimes appear minor and no evidence that serious problems are more than very occasional, or indeed are not dealt with before they manifest themselves.

Pupils and parents: Kensington has always been the respectable half of the borough alliance with raffish Chelsea to the south but nowadays the girls tend to come from both sides of the Fulham Road. The mix of backgrounds and nationalities appears not to have changed that much recently, with a cohort that includes Americans and Europeans, and Brexit has not made any significant difference, as yet. Strong links with old girls are actively encouraged by the head – not only do they come back visiting but regularly send their daughters.

An English family told us that despite the variety of nationalities, it was really easy to make friends, both for the children and the parents. She was really pleased by this as she had wondered whether this would be the case among families who often have dual nationality and two, if not three, passports.

Money matters: Automatic scholarship candidacy for 11+ entrants with the prize of a 25 per cent remission on the fees; also scholarships at sixth form entry. More money being channelled into bursaries (current sum around £500,000) and if parents are struggling, attempts are made to help existing pupils stay until they reach a suitable break-point.

Ravenscourt Park Preparatory School

39

16 Ravenscourt Avenue, London W6 0SL

020 8846 9153 | secretary@rpps.co.uk | www.rpps.co.uk

Independent	Ages: 4–11	Pupils: 220	Fees: £18,360 pa

Head: Since 2015, Carl Howes MA (Cantab) natural sciences, PGCE St Luke's Exeter, previously deputy head at St Paul's Juniors, following head of maths and second master at King's House School, Richmond. His wife is a primary teacher; son, 20s, and teenage daughter. First RPPS head to come from outside, Mr Howes is committed to the school's ethos: 'I very much appreciated the thriving, happy community I inherited.' Seen most days in the playground, smartly attired, welcoming all; parents we spoke to describe him as 'highly approachable', 'a good listener, quiet but straight talking'. Mr Howes comments, 'I enjoy the connection with the children and as a head you have to make an effort': he clearly does, as prior to our visit, he accompanied year 5's Devon residential trip. He takes assemblies, debating club, teaches year 4 and 5 mathematics sets, some sport to younger pupils. He has introduced Headmaster's Awards which acknowledge pupils' effort and attitude. Pupils describe him as 'kind, generous with his time, turning up at weekend tournaments'. 'He's a perfect adult: he understands children and what they find interesting and funny.' We found him charming, measured in approach, with a fascination for educational matters, coupled with intelligent discernment to ensure RPPS equips pupils for, as he puts it, 'the challenges of an unknown world'.

Two terms into his tenure, inspectors judged RPPS 'excellent in all areas'. He appreciates staff are 'forward-looking' and 'responsive' adding, 'I am not a micro-manager.' Parents we spoke to recognise his ' light touch' which 'empowers the teachers', whilst upholding high expectations and 'sifting out what really matters'. To relax, Mr Howes cycles to work, runs five kilometres on Saturdays and plays the saxophone. When asked about his future ambitions, he has no wish to lead an empire, enjoying the holistic education and size of RPPS.

Entrance: Children can be registered to enter the ballot from birth up to their first birthday for one of 60 non-selective reception places, with siblings prioritised. Later applicants join waiting list with a few occasional places arising each year when families relocate. All are expected to stay until the end of year 6 in gender balanced classes of 20.

Exit: The wide range of popular destinations include Kew House and Maida Vale School (linked senior schools), Francis Holland Sloane Square, Francis Holland Regent's Park, Godolphin & Latymer, Lady Eleanor Holles, Notting Hill & Ealing High School, Queen's Gate, St Paul's Girls', City of London, Hampton, KCS Wimbledon, King's College Canterbury, St James Boys', Arts Educational, Fulham, Harrodian, Ibstock Place School, Kew House, Latymer, St Benedict's, the Green School for Girls and West London Free. Mr Howes has good relationships with senior schools and can advise accordingly. The school caters for a range of ability with impressive results, including 12 to 15 scholarships every year. 'If I could, I would like to abolish 11+,' summed up one parent, disenchanted with the process but pleased with how RPPS strives to address the stresses and strains, whilst others agreed how extremely well the teachers and headmaster know each child's ability and personality.

Our view: Maria and Ted Gardener, former teachers, founded the school in 1991. The school now consists of four separate buildings on one site, close to Ravenscourt Park where most PE and games lessons take place. Some parents are nostalgic about when the school was smaller, believing the parent body was more cohesive, but acknowledge more families have benefited and are pleased 'it has kept its heart'. Part of the Gardener School Group Ltd with Kew House and Kew Green Prep, RPPS benefits from shared resources, expertise and fixtures. Some parents we spoke to talked about it being a business, especially the fact that 'the fees go up every year at the higher end'. Others bemoan the lack of bursary places, which they believe 'makes the school less diverse, to its detriment'.

The homely Old Vicarage building houses early years and year 1 in well-equipped classrooms with outside play area for supervised groups. Spacious science lab ensures pupils can carry out experiments. They are encouraged to solve problems and create models; we saw a sophisticated Galileo-inspired pendulum. Some parents criticised half termly homework projects as too demanding and questioned whether models were produced by other competitive parents. Homework and costume provision for theme days can cause difficulties for working parents but the 8am–6pm school day and after-school clubs are much appreciated. Children appear relaxed and enthusiastic, politely greeting us with 'good morning' in every class, and readily explained what they were doing. They were clearly absorbed in the task at hand, from year 5s in an English class reflecting on the plight of refugees, to year 1s explaining how to access and record work on their PCs in the IT suite. All classrooms have interactive whiteboards and iPads are used throughout. Pupils enjoy fun ways of learning to do computer coding, creating animations, games and stories collaboratively, and all are made aware of e-safety.

Pupils are encouraged to solve problems and create models in science lab; we saw a sophisticated Galileo-inspired pendulum

Fantastic facilities include a light, spacious art room with kiln. We saw high quality art work in different media on display, including a recreation of a Van Gogh-inspired painting made by classes using coloured curled card. Parents value the creativity on offer but some wish 'more of the artwork could come home'. Overlooking the playground, conveniently situated on the ground floor, is the excellent library. Librarians ensure it is accessible in break times and we saw pupils

We saw the head joining colleagues in street dancing at an assembly as part of the school's commitment to growth mindsets

thoroughly enjoying the wide range of materials on offer. There is an attractive dining room where tasty, fresh food is prepared, monitored by a food committee including some parents.

All buildings contain cheerful rooms for learning support or small group work. The SEND register is reviewed after standardised assessments termly during pupil progress meetings and 25 were on the register when we visited. The department is well regarded. Parents find the SENCo and her team 'really responsive' and praise the school as being 'inclusive'. 'They cope very well with pupils with pre-identified minor learning difficulties.' There are withdrawal lessons and provision made in the classroom to cater for individual learning difficulties at no extra charge.

Staff are energetic and dedicated. As one parent explained, 'They tick all the boxes', and best of all, 'they really know their pupils'. Pupils describe RPPS as 'a friendly community' where 'everyone is made to feel the same, equally valued' and teachers as 'encouraging', 'very fair' and 'kind'. We saw Mr Howes in a new guise joining colleagues in street dancing at an assembly. This was part of the school's commitment to growth mindsets, an educational strategy introduced to encourage pupils to make mistakes and develop resilience, so they will try something new and persevere. Year 2s had no problem explaining this approach to us with a helpful visual chart in their classroom A two year cycle of values is shared in assemblies including intellectual humility, respect and tolerance, part of the school's holistic ethos.

Parents unanimously endorsed the staff's open door policy, which ensures prompt responses to their concerns whether small or great, and agreed they are never made 'to feel a nuisance'. Communication is 'excellent', ranging from website with parent portal and Parkside newsletter to weekly 'onthefridgedoor' which encapsulates the week's events and pupil achievements. Parents commented on 'the solid system' for pastoral care with clear guidelines. Pupils we spoke to happily explained 'reminder notes' alongside the RPPS Code of Conduct. 'There is always someone to share your concerns with and plenty of opportunities for responsibility.'

At KS1, boys and girls have games lessons together; at KS2, the boys do football, rugby and cricket while girls do netball, hockey and rounders. Regular fixtures and 18 sports-related clubs are on offer. Recently, the girls' netball team qualified for the IAPS finals and year 5 had its first football and netball tour to Jersey. 'Music is fantastic,' parents agree and approximately 230 individual instrumental lessons take place in school weekly with 15 peripatetic teachers. All praised the wide variety on offer: three choirs, two orchestras, music theory club, chamber music ensembles, rock bands, an a cappella singing group and recorder, guitar and brass ensembles. Children can take graded examinations in school and many are involved in outside orchestras. A recent year 6 pupil achieved grade 8 with distinction in the violin. Specialist facilities include a 160 seat performance hall with sound and lighting, music suite and teaching rooms.

RPPS follows a full primary curriculum, making use of specialist subject teachers and classroom assistants. Parents believe the pace is 'spot on' with increased homework and more emphasis on English and mathematics from the summer term in year 5. Parents praise the life skills RPPS develops, and how staff encourage pupils' independence, dealing with homework and 'organisational skills like packing for a residential trip, which sets them up for senior school so well'. After the examinations, children enjoy themed topics and a diverse range of activities, home and away. Year 6s we chatted to were very excited about their forthcoming production and there is an annual ski trip to Austria as well as a biennial music tour, recently to Tuscany. The curriculum is enhanced by theme weeks and staff take advantage of nearby galleries, theatres and exhibitions as well as parents sharing their interesting careers. French is taught throughout with Spanish as one of the many extracurricular clubs.

This popular school caters for families with children of different needs and abilities, most living within two miles. The pupil body reflects the area, most being of British origin and a quarter from European backgrounds, often bilingual. Parents in varied professions, including marketing, law and banking. 'You can get involved as much or as little as you like,' they told us. Many participate, attending concerts, listening to readers or involved in the Parents' Association of Friends.

Parents agree the school 'is nurturing, inclusive, welcoming and truly caters for all-rounders', unlike schools 'with greater emphasis on the academics where pupils need to be more robust and confident'. Not the right school for parents obsessed with their children obtaining top grades in everything or those seeking a traditional, highly competitive environment. Even teams are colour coded rather than A, B, C, D, emphasising participation and lack of labelling. With mixed ability there is a balanced atmosphere which does not stop the very able from flying, but does mean all are encouraged.

The last word: As one parent remarked, 'RPPS is a really fun, positive and nurturing environment for the kids, who become so confident and happy about their place in life.' Others said, 'This dynamic school caters for all sorts, any character; that is one of its strengths.' The 11+ preparation is a 'well-oiled machine' with 'loads of opportunities for different characters to learn and flourish', as recent results demonstrate.

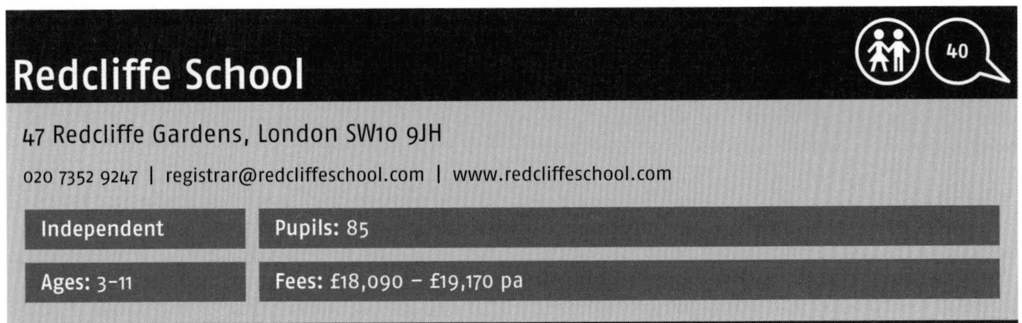

Redcliffe School

40

47 Redcliffe Gardens, London SW10 9JH

020 7352 9247 | registrar@redcliffeschool.com | www.redcliffeschool.com

Independent	Pupils: 85
Ages: 3-11	Fees: £18,090 – £19,170 pa

Headmistress: Since September 2017, Sarah Lemmon (40s). SL is so happy in her work that she leaves her husband and son (an ex-Redcliffe pupil) outside Bath and commutes to London every week. Raised in Co Wicklow until she was 17, she has spent all her post-school life in London, not because it is the dull filling in a green sandwich but because she genuinely loves the city. Once graduated from Froebel College, she tested her natural instinct to become a teacher by doing a stint in the outside world but is clearly delighted that she made the choice to switch to education.

She started teaching here 12 years ago and has climbed the ladder to the top, via the headship of the pre-prep, a CV that makes parents comfortable that she knows the school from the bottom up and, judging by their comments, certain that she is doing a great job.

Entrance: Approximately three children put down per nursery place but there is a lot of natural attrition due to some London parents' habit of applying piecemeal to keep their options open. It's a first come, first served, non-selective school with a front of the queue policy for siblings and the registrar says that she 'can't think of a time when there has been a problem with this'. All children are assessed for entry to the main school via a gently selective process and for the occasional places available further up. The vast majority of children in the nursery move up to reception, although a few go abroad or to the local Ofsted 'outstanding' primary.

Meals are no problem here as apparently the food is 'brilliant', and a parent told us that her candidate for the 'world's fussiest eater' wolfed it all down

Since COVID, school is unable to offer tours to parents but the head is happy to talk to parents via a Zoom meeting and is offering places following this and a report from a child's current school. As of 1 September 2020, Redcliffe School joined the Godolphin and Latymer Foundation.

Exit: Leavers to Dartford Grammar School for Girls, Lady Margaret, Singapore American School, Francis Holland Regent's Park, More House, St Philip's, Fulham School, Queen's College, Sussex House, Hurlingham Academy, Queen's Gate, Kensington Park School (academic scholarship), St James's, Kent Grammar School and St George's Ascot in 2020.

Redcliffe is becoming co-ed throughout but boys have tended to transfer at 7+ or 8+ to conventional preps – Sussex House, Wetherby Prep or St Philip's – with the occasional parent choosing the country boarding option. The trend for senior London schools to take boys at 11+ is increasing but, just in case, the head is already sounding out schools like Thomas's Battersea and Eaton House, who will take in boys aiming at 13+ schools. She also brings in senior heads at an annual event for parents. Girls at 11+ mainly join the old favourite London day schools but the excellent results allow them to aim at the schools for high achievers such as Godolphin & Latymer (whose foundation now also runs this school, but with no automatic entry), JAGS, City of London Girls, St Paul's and Putney High as well as Francis Holland, Harrodian and Queen's College. An impressive proportion of academic scholarships, considering the size of the school, with the odd one for sport (including ballet) or music.

Our view: The pre-prep hides in what was once an undercroft, below an uninspiring example of ecclesiastical architecture. It is now a surprisingly light and airy space, with a multi-purpose hall on one side and a cheerful passage leading to the nursery and classrooms for reception and year 1. The nursery is much praised by parents, one knowledgeable mother commenting that not only had they managed to persuade her son to sit on the carpet quietly for 'a decent length of time' but also that he came home burbling about the fun projects and activities that had filled his day. Meals, quite often a trying time at this stage for both small and large people, are no problem here as apparently the food is 'brilliant', and a parent told us that her candidate for the 'world's fussiest eater' wolfed it all down.

The pre-prep is not just about play, judging from some extremely neat writing and maths displayed on the walls, with an obvious emphasis on building confidence as well as academic skills. The most quoted example is how they successfully encourage every child (from reception onwards) to take turns at presenting work in assembly. We were told by parents that in some cases 'this was a minor miracle', persuading an acutely shy child to happily stand up in front of 150 people and start talking. SL, who believes in making sure that you never ask children to do what you would not do yourself, makes sure that the teachers lead the way by all taking assembly themselves.

The main school lives behind the modest facade of a late Victorian building on a London artery. This was originally the home of the school's founder, Lady Daphne Edwards, about whom little is known except that she left her house plus enough cash for a charitable trust, enabling the school to flourish and reach its 70th birthday. The trust funds have been well looked after and SL says that they have the wherewithal for expanding their space to match their co-ed ambitions, aiming to grow the school gradually from one to two forms.

With only 100 children, the common hustle and bustle of most junior schools feels muted and the housekeeping, despite the challenge of a cageful of fluffy chicks, is well on top of the dust bunnies. The sense of calm is apparent all the way up from the semi-basement, with its hall, tiny Maurice Sendak kitchen squeezed into the corner and classroom at the back, to the attic with its new, purpose-built music rooms and cosy staff room under the eaves. Children move about with purposeful expressions and an obvious certainty about their next destination, so this is definitely a well-orchestrated operation, although rather charmingly relaxed on the surface.

Despite this cool, rather than hothouse, atmosphere Redcliffe children leave with the full academic package: they may not have been offered the exotic curriculum options available in the larger local preps but they have no trouble in passing the 7+, 8+ and 11+ and succeeding in the ferocious competition for places at demanding senior schools. Naturally, there is some concern that the different requirements for boys (online pre-tests) will mean some additions to the current curriculum, but as English, maths, verbal and non-verbal reasoning are already on the timetable, SL believes that she is on top of this. They will certainly all be well taught at maths as the teacher of years 5 and 6 is apparently 'amazing'.

Unable to take children with anything beyond mild dyslexia; there used to be murmurings that the SEN provision was possibly a little stretched and problems were not picked up fast enough, but the evidence is that this has changed. SL and her new SENCo are much more aware of where help may be needed, and the genuine family atmosphere of the school is a huge advantage.

Knowing that she is going to have older boys in her charge, one of SL's new initiatives is to increase the opportunity for the children to enjoy sport. Friday afternoons are for games in the form of optional clubs, rather than lessons, and an extended school day on Friday will allow them to ramp up the sporting provision. The new sports facility is only a few hops, skips and jumps away and there are beaming faces at the mention of the summer sports day. Redcliffe might not be the perfect spot for a football fiend looking for the rough and tumble of team games but, having said this, they have a potential international swimmer in their ranks, so an awareness of sporting potential is certainly there.

London parents are looking beyond academics, even in a tiny school, and pupils can join clubs for budding artists or chefs, practise for a parliamentary career in debating or aim at LAMDA exams. A new programme includes science clubs, coding and Lego as well as short tennis; there's a sustainable fashion club and a plogging one (jogging whilst picking up litter) to encourage social responsibility – all encouraged by the new deputy head. Trying to ensure that her charges do not lead too cloistered a life, the head casts a termly fly into the parental talent pool and lands a willing soul to talk to them about the world outside, as well as posting a weekly blog herself.

Enthusiastic comments on the standard of pastoral care from parents – 'it's like leaving your child with a relation rather than a babysitter' – and from older girls, who appreciate the new flowery summer frocks – 'I might even wear it after I've left' – show that the head is sensitive about making changes.

The last word: The current head is well aware that finding the correct balance between remaining a small traditional London prep school and being a forward thinking modern co-ed establishment is no easy task. We left feeling confident that she would crack it.

Sacred Heart High School (Hammersmith)

212 Hammersmith Road, London W6 7DG

020 8748 7600 | info@sacredh.lbhf.sch.uk | www.sacredhearthigh.org.uk

State | Ages: 11–18 | Pupils: 1,133; sixth form: 152

Headteacher: Since 2014, Marian Doyle MA NPQH (50s). Previously deputy head since 1997. Before that she taught English and RE at Haggerston School, Hackney, Phoenix High School, Hammersmith and latterly Holland Park School, Notting Hill Gate. Mrs Doyle has brought a fresher, more contemporary style of leadership to the school. Not only does she look smart (she was impeccably dressed when we met her), the school does too. Walls are adorned with colourful canvases of the girls at work and many inspirational quotes. School systems (from admin through to bullying policies) also had an overhaul, thanks to the head's key vision of the school being run seamlessly. A parent herself, she is big on boundaries and 'tough love', but is also approachable and smiley, and is regularly seen around the school, popping into lessons and talking to the girls at break times. 'She is very keen to make sure that we like it here,' said one girl.

Entrance: Parents keep an extremely beady eye on the admissions policy of this heavily oversubscribed school, and many are unswerving in their commitment to find some way for their daughter to become one of the approximately 198 pupils to enter year 7. But you'll need to start early, as all girls need to have been baptised before they were 6 months old (although we did to talk to one parent who did it slightly later due to illness in the family) and to have attended one of 11 feeder schools, all named on the website. If you meet all the criteria, you won't need to sweat so much about how close you are to the school. Be warned that siblings don't automatically gain entry and are sometimes turned away. Separate admissions procedures for girls with an EHC plan. Parents praise the transition from primary school. Up to places for 40 external applicants to sixth form, for which you'll need eight 9-4s at GCSE, including subject-specific requirements.

Exit: Clear expectation to remain at the school to do A levels, and the majority do so. Others commonly go onto Cardinal Vaughan or the London Oratory, with a handful going into the independent sector, including UCS, St Benedict's and Latymer Upper. Recent leavers off to do courses ranging from aeronautical engineering at Imperial to anthropology at Exeter to fashion communication at Condé Nast College.

Latest results: In 2020, no GCSE results available but 36 per cent A*/A at A level (70 per cent A*-B). In 2019 (the last year when exams took place), 52 per cent 9-7 grades at GCSE; 65 per cent got 5+ 9-5s including both English and maths. At A level, 58 per cent A*-B in 2019.

Teaching and learning: Pupils' academic progress is impressive, as are their exam results. Maths the strongest subject, followed by English. RE, history and geography also stand out. In terms of languages, Spanish and French are on offer, and a group of around 15 girls are put forward for Latin GCSE, which they study at St Paul's. Science highly promoted, with 60 per cent doing science and maths post-16.

Each year group has five form groups, with setting across all subjects from year 7 into five or six groups, depending on the subject, with plenty of flexibility to move about as necessary. Class sizes vary, with many as large as 35.

Expectation for all pupils to do at least two after-school clubs (which they call enrichment), which has been accommodated by changes to the school day (which now comprises five 60 minute lessons and finishes at 3.05pm) and an expectation that staff stay longer to run these clubs on Tuesdays and Wednesdays. Outside facilitators brought in too. Subjects include all the usual suspects such as choir, sport, maths challenge, science clubs, drama etc as well as more unusual offerings including yoga and gardening.

Girls are regularly reminded of a quote from one of the founders: 'For the sake of one child, I would have founded the society,' after which they're told, 'You are the one child'

School is designated as a national teaching school, leading the West London Teaching School Alliance, which means working closely with 28 other primary and secondary schools in west London to improve standards of teaching and share best practice on issues including initial teacher training, professional development, research and development, succession planning and mentoring. Head says it's her vision for the school to become known for its drive for excellence. 'I put the same level of effort into training and development for the staff as I do teaching the girls, because I believe the two are inextricably linked,' she says.

Although the teaching staff we saw were a pretty glum-looking lot (particularly unwelcoming when we went near their classrooms), girls are clearly impressed with their level of commitment. 'Lessons are really engaging,' said one. 'They make sure nobody gets missed,' added another. Indeed, girls are regularly reminded of a quote from one of the founders: 'For the sake of one child, I would have founded the society,' after which they're told, 'You are the one child.'

Learning support and SEN: One full-time staff member (qualified teacher, as well as a dyslexic specialist; has the national SENCo leadership award) is responsible for SEN, although no special unit. She puts in place three tiered levels of support – firstly, qualified teachers' support in mainstream, with the aim that specialist subject teachers can support in their areas of expertise; second (if necessary) additional support before and after school; finally (again if necessary) involvement of school counsellor or outside services, such as speech and language and occupational therapy. Difficulties catered for include dyslexia and other needs that are physical, such as hearing loss or severe long-term conditions, communication and language difficulties, ADD, ADHD. School also claims there are some serious mental health concerns. School reckoned there were 65 in total with SEN when we visited, five of whom have an EHC plan. Very rarely, if a child's needs cannot be fully met, the school works closely with parents and the local authority to find alternatives. Help for gifted and talented through a range of enrichment and additional opportunities.

'The help my daughter has received for her dyslexia has been second to none, including trying out a range of different techniques, and the communication with us has been excellent too,' said one parent. 'Her self-confidence has rocketed and she's doing really well in exams.'

The arts and extracurricular: No shortage of peripatetic teachers for musical instruments including piano, flute, trombone, drums etc. There are junior and senior choirs, various ensembles, and the girls talk highly of the general music classes, as well as about the annual Battle of the Bands. 'Music is really good fun here,' one girl told us. We particularly like the random pianos in the corridors, all of which girls say get played regularly for practice, making for a lovely ambience when walking through the corridors.

Links to various theatres, including the Donmar, and the drama school LAMDA, give a flavour of how seriously drama is taken here, with annual all-school productions such as Hairspray and Annie. Art and DT studios are spacious, with state-of-the-art equipment and some extremely talented artwork produced by the girls. No cookery on offer when we visited, but this is being re-examined.

Sport: For a small inner-city site, they certainly pack in the sports facilities, all of which are utilised to the max, with the girls doing at least two hours of PE per week and with the option of PE as both a GCSE and A level subject. In addition to the two tennis/netball courts (which double up as rounders pitches), there's a gym and activity studio for the likes of dance, pilates and yoga. The £8m sports and science block is home to a massive sports hall that can facilitate three teaching groups simultaneously. 'It's four times the size of our gym,' enthused one girl. Also new is a running track and outdoor gym of the ilk you see in parks, all of which means the longstanding link with Hammersmith and Fulham Health and Fitness Centre has diminished. Rowing, softball, basketball and volleyball on offer, along with all the usual suspects, and after-school clubs include street dance, yoga, cheerleading, fencing, trampolining and football, among others. Plenty of inter-house sports competitions, the highlight of which is the annual sports day held at St Paul's fields (originally owned by Sacred Heart but sadly they sold it off years ago), and the school has increasing success in the borough in hockey, rounders, netball and athletics.

Ethos and heritage: The school, or 'convent of the Sacred Heart', is built on a site steeped in Catholic history dating back to the early 17th century. During its 330 year history, four different orders of nuns have taught here. Today's Tudor-style, red-brick buildings were built in the late 19th century and there's no shortage of religious reminders inside, notably the huge, austere-looking religious murals all the way along the wide, spacious corridors of the cloisters, as well as the chapel, which doubles up as the main school hall. 'We have daily morning prayers,' said one girl, 'but apart from that, the presence of Catholicism in our everyday life is through the school's ethos and values.' 'The school provides a good moral compass, but there's no hard-line religion,' agreed a parent, who added that there's a sensible and modern approach to sex education too, within the context of the Catholic Church teaching.

In 1948 the convent school was reorganised as a secondary grammar school, continuing as a grammar school until 1976, when it received its first comprehensive intake. The school then took on academy status in 2012.

The random pianos in the corridors, all of which girls say get played regularly for practice, make for a lovely ambience when walking through the corridors

Most pupils use the entrance on Bute Gardens, whilst sixth form and visitors use the main entrance on Hammersmith Road, where you'll be greeted by a single receptionist behind an oak veneer desk and a couple of rows of cream leather chairs. The hum of traffic is loud, but it doesn't take many more steps into the school to feel as if you're in an oasis of calm – not at all what you'd expect from an inner-city comp. Even during class switch-over times, when the extra-wide corridors are packed with animated girls, it somehow manages to avoid the feeling of chaos that many other schools have (probably helped by the very strictly policed one-way walking system).

A steep stone staircase leads down to the converted basement, which forms the buzzy social space and café for sixth formers. The rest of the girls eat in the dining room which, head admits, 'could be more funky' and where the food is 'okay'. Those who have packed lunch eat at temporary tables that are laid out daily in the wide corridors.

Asked what they'd improve, girls told us they could do with more quiet study space, especially in sixth form. 'We are allowed to use the library,' said one, 'but it's not ideal.' Indeed, when we visited, the library was being used by an entire class and was by no means quiet, although in fairness it is two-storey, with doors shutting out such sound on the top level. Well-stocked and imaginatively designed, it is also very light and inviting. Classrooms are bog-standard, with stand-out facilities for drama and music. Great excitement about the new science block, which is transforming provision.

Even during class switch-over times, it somehow manages to avoid the feeling of chaos that many other schools have (probably helped by the very strictly policed one-way walking system in the corridors)

Girls encouraged to be proactive, rather than spoon fed, with lots of emphasis on them doing things, rather than talking about things. When we visited, a group of girls had gone to Mexico to rebuild houses for those in poverty. A further group of six girls went to Lourdes with the Handicapped Children Pilgrimage Trust. Impressive amounts of charitable work overall, including £10,500 raised for a sister school in Kenya for disabled children via activities including sponging teachers, making teachers eat chilli, sponsored walks and rowing the distance of the Channel in the gym. School is also part of a worldwide network of schools in 45 countries which creates opportunities such as a head girls' meet-up to discuss leadership ideas and pupil exchanges across different countries.

Plenty of school trips to universities, BBC, Houses of Parliament, businesses including JP Morgan and all the usual museums and art galleries. Residential trips largely music-related, including to places such as Austria and Paris, whilst whole school European ski trips take place each year.

Strong student voice, with elected student members having requested that the science garden become more appealing, as well as having offered responses to the school's Equality Plan.

Pastoral care, inclusivity and discipline: Most recent Ofsted report rated pastoral care as 'outstanding'. High expectations for behaviour – late arrivals mean detention, even if a pupil rushes in five seconds after the bell goes. 'The point is that in professional life, if you had a meeting at 10am, you wouldn't arrive just after 10am,' head explains. 'We also want a calm start to the day.' It clearly works – there are few detentions in reality, with the girls we talked to never having been late in their entire six years. Other zero-tolerance aspects of school life include school uniform (especially length of skirts) and good behaviour, although pastoral care is highly praised here, with all the parents we talked to calling it 'very nurturing and caring'. Pupils are frequently reminded they can talk to form teachers, non-teaching pastoral support managers, the chaplain or two full-time school counsellors. In addition, there are strong links with Child and Adolescent Mental Health Services (CAMHS) and the charity Mind. 'One of my daughters went off the rails and had some counselling, which promptly nipped it in the bud,' said one parent. Head is by no means resting on her laurels, though. 'Like most schools,' she says, 'we have seen an increase in mental health issues and are very aware we need to talk about it in a more real and open way.' Peer mentoring scheme between year 7s and year 11s encourages cross-year relationships and older girls to take a leadership role.

Pupils and parents: This is top of the state school list for many families, not only in west London, but as far as Islington. Although it's non-selective and fully comprehensive, the majority of families are middle class and with English as a first language. That said, there is genuine poverty among some of the girls, with head reporting that this is increasingly the case. 'We have 14 per cent identified as having free school meals and many others with an income only just above the threshold where parents struggle to make ends meet,' she says.

Strong PA and links between parents generally. 'It's unusually sociable among parents for an inner-city comprehensive, with lots of mums' nights out, quiz nights and family-focused activities,' said one parent. Good communications between school and parents, although some parents think the annual parents' evening, which falls in the summer term, is far too late in the academic year.

The last word: An exceptional and relatively small inner-city state school that provides girls who are prepared to behave impeccably with a traditional education and sense of community that will set them up for life.

St Charles Catholic Sixth Form College

74 St Charles Square, London W10 6EY

020 8968 7755 | enquiries@stcharles.ac.uk | www.stcharles.ac.uk

State	Ages: 16-19	Pupils: 1,200; sixth form: 1200

Principal: Since 2019, Martin Twist. Previously deputy head of St Peter's Catholic School in Guildford, he studied philosophy and ethics and has extensive teaching experience.

Entrance: College is non-selective and places are offered based on a successful interview and reference from previous school. Interviews over 2,000 students a year. Priority given to disabled and looked after children, followed by pupils from Catholic partner secondary schools, then Catholic students from other secondary schools and finally non-Catholics. In reality, not many are turned down, but acceptance is dependent upon reference and interview. 'We want to recruit as many students as possible, though there has to be some integrity about who we take.' Some start but do not last long – about 100 students are lost during the year. Prepared to take some from pupil referral units, in line with its inclusive policy, 'though we won't take them all'. If a pupil's reference is poor in terms of attendance or punctuality then unlikely they would be accepted.

For A level route, minimum six GCSEs at 9-4, including English language. Minimum five GCSEs at 4 or above for level 3 BTec vocational study. For intermediate route, four grade 3s or above at GCSE. Foundation level is suitable for pupils with GCSEs below grade 3.

Exit: Of the level 3 pupils, about 85 per cent go on to university. Some to Russell Group, with London a firm favourite, as students can save money by living at home. Increasing numbers are deferring as they are not sure that they can afford it, and others not even applying as they are put off by student debt. Popular subjects include business, sociology, psychology, Arabic studies and international relations. Just a trickle choose history or English.

Many opt for art foundation courses and college has good links with Central St Martins. Others head for the London College of Fashion. One artistic past pupil is currently using his considerable creative skills in a tattoo parlour.

Some proceed straight to the world of work, particularly into retail, with increasing numbers opting for apprenticeships in business, IT or administration.

Latest results: Hasn't released 2020 A level results, and all they would tell us about 2019 results is that the average grade was D+.

Teaching and learning: College offers a variety of courses at levels 1, 2 and 3. Pupils can take A levels or vocational qualifications or a combination of both at level 3. School offers three levels of study – advanced (A levels and vocational level 3), intermediate (GCSEs and BTec level 2) and foundation (BTec level 1 and functional skills in English and maths). Two per cent of pupils make up level 1. College explains, 'Level 1 students are those who have done very badly in their GCSEs at their old school, or students who have not been in the country very long and need to develop their numeracy and literacy skills.' Level 2 pupil numbers have grown to around 150. 'They are usually students who have not done very well in their GCSEs either, but not atrociously, gaining mostly 4 and 3s.' Limited numbers of GCSEs offered and level 2 pupils tend to take maths and English GCSEs, alongside level 2 BTec programme. In recent years, the proportion of A level students has been declining in favour of those choosing the BTec route. Nearly 30 different A levels offered, including ICT, Italian and photography; newly introduced BTecs include media and music. 'We might cultivate the combined pathway a little more, as it gives pupils greater flexibility.' Possible to start at level 1 and move on up to level 2 then 3. 'Some stay with us for four years and end up at university. We support them along the way.'

Around 40 level 3 pupils take the EPQ. College is very enthusiastic about this qualification: 'We are trying to develop it, as nearly all our students take three rather than four A levels now, and the EPQ will be a good differentiating tool when applying to universities. They all start off enthusiastically but a 6,000-word dissertation can be quite hard work!' Subjects range from whether the African elephant can survive to debates on the influence of gender on crime.

Over 30 teachers have been here for more than a decade, and a sizeable number were pupils here themselves. Pressure on staff has become worse than ever and tighter budgets have led to staff cuts. Every member of staff is now up to their full complement of teaching and staff development has been curtailed.

Learning support and SEN: Well-resourced learning support centre, providing support for 10 per cent of pupils. College currently has 4.5 learning support teachers and three learning assistants who support the small number of pupils with EHC plans. One parent raved about the support her SEN son received: 'They really understood him and worked with his strengths.' Her son was given an individual tour of the school before arrival, so he would not have to deal with the hurly-burly of the regular show-round. Roughly 130 pupils qualify as having some sort of SEN, ranging from those who just need a bit of extra help with structuring essays to those who require a full-time assistant in every lesson. A fair number with dyslexia, Asperger's and autism. Help given to those who have English as an additional language but pupils need to be able to fully access the curriculum.

The arts and extracurricular: 'We don't force students to do enrichment but we really try to encourage them to do so.' College has own dance and theatre studio. Drama is offered at A level and performing arts at BTec. Annual musical, open to all, considered to be a highlight of the year. No students play instruments at school, no orchestra and no choirs. Not the place for your child if they are desperate to be part of a music ensembles. Art is very popular, with notably strong department.

Basketball team has recently won the national finals. 'We are like the Leicester football team: we came from nothing and won the trophy.' Successful at football too

College is outward-looking. Other enrichment opportunities include pupils teaching computer skills to local senior citizens one afternoon a week – so popular, there is a waiting list. Others work for charities or Young Enterprise and help with regeneration of local area. Regular outside speakers range from chief executives from Mastercard to religious leaders of all faiths. Lots of work experience organised.

Trips tend to be subject-related, including a cultural trip to New York every year for psychology and sociology students; a geography trip to Sicily where pupils visit Mount Etna; travel and tourism trips to Lanzarote. Getting harder to subsidise pupils who cannot afford it. Lots of visits closer to home, including to theatres and art galleries.

Sport: Basketball team has recently won the national finals. 'We are like the Leicester football team: we came from nothing and won the trophy.' Successful at football too. Fully equipped fitness gym is well-used, including female-only afternoon. Indoor and outdoor multifunction sports area allows some sport to take place on site but footballers trek to Westway to practise.

Ethos and heritage: Just off Ladbroke Grove. Tucked between a Catholic church, a Catholic girls' secondary, the Catholic Children's Society and a convent. Named after St Charles Borromeo, 16th century Italian archbishop who believed in the redeeming power of education. Founded by Cardinal Basil Hume in 1990.

Accepts all faiths and none but Catholic ethos pervades, though in terms of numbers only about 35 per cent Catholic, 30 per cent other Christians and 22 per cent Muslim. Compulsory RE programme, comprising one hour lesson a week. 'It is important to have a general religion programme. It is an opportunity for students to mix with students of other religions, to discuss a range of issues and to hear what others believe. It's good preparation for the world outside.'

Very inclusive, defined by Catholic values, with Christ at its centre. An explicitly Christian set of values from the Gospels, with a focus on inclusivity and service to others. A banner above the entrance proclaims, 'Show mercy to others as God shows mercy to you.' Voluntary mass every Friday and a daily morning prayer. Christmas and Easter services. On-site chapel. Annual trip to Lourdes to help the sick, organised by the full-time chaplain who also acts as an unofficial counsellor. Pupils find him approachable and he can often be spotted deep in a game of chess with one or other of them. One parent assured us that religion was 'not overwhelming'.

Pastoral care, inclusivity and discipline: Everyone is in a tutor group which meets daily, under one of the pastoral managers. 'This daily contact just keeps them on track.' External counsellors visit the school weekly. Even though this is a sixth form college, many school-like structures are in place. Ex-pupils say how much they miss the pastoral care once they go to university.

Zero tolerance of any form of physical violence or drug related incidents, both within the college grounds or in the vicinity. Immediate expulsion for these offences with suspension

An explicitly Christian set of values from the Gospels, with a focus on inclusivity and service to others. A banner above the entrance proclaims, 'Show mercy to others as God shows mercy to you'

for lesser transgressions. 'Discipline is a headache,' according to one mother, though probably no more so than in some other London schools. Security guards at the gate are strict about checking for ID and no-one allowed in without it. Giving your ID card to another student results in suspension for three days. Pupils initially surprised how strict the college is, but college believes that 'the safety of the students is the most important thing. Some have challenging lives outside and it is part of the mission to encourage them to take the right path.' Knife tunnels erected sporadically, in liaison with police, so pupils 'know that we are monitoring them'. If pupils are late to lessons then they are not allowed in. One mother divulged that her son was worried he would be bullied as 'it's a rough place, but the college handled his needs well.' Staff disagree that the college is rough, telling us 'this is simply not the case.'

The issues that pupils face are becoming more complex. 'We have many students who have mental health issues. More and more young people are coming to us who are already in the CAHMS [Child and Adolescent Mental Health services] system.' There have been incidents with suicidal pupils in the past. 'This often occurs on a Friday, with the thought of the weekend ahead.' Others have suffered historical abuse. Social media often the source of arguments. 'The exam competition is worse now – everything has to be an A. We put so much pressure on the young.' College is often a haven for those with complicated domestic lives and staff believe it is their job to provide stability for those who are troubled.

Pupils and parents: Diverse, international set of pupils who come from 165 different schools. Pupils trek in from far and wide. Wide ethnic mix, with African students making up the majority. Over 40 per cent are on free school meals, most from low-income backgrounds. Lots of siblings and cousins. 'People hear about us very much through word of mouth.'

Parents are kept in the loop regarding their child's attendance, punctuality and behaviour via the parent portal and communication with tutors and pastoral managers. Two parents' evenings a year, so most feel as though they know what is going on.

Money matters: Bursary payments made to nearly 40 per cent of pupils – grants for those in financial hardship studying full time. All charged a one-off resources fee when they start, to cover costs such as photocopying.

The last word: 'We want every student, no matter what their starting point, to do the best they can. Everyone these days is measured by their exam results but education is so much more. We are trying to do something a little bit different to others. We take on students that sometimes need a second chance, because sometimes life does not go according to plan.' For those prepared to play by the rules, this college can and does turn lives around.

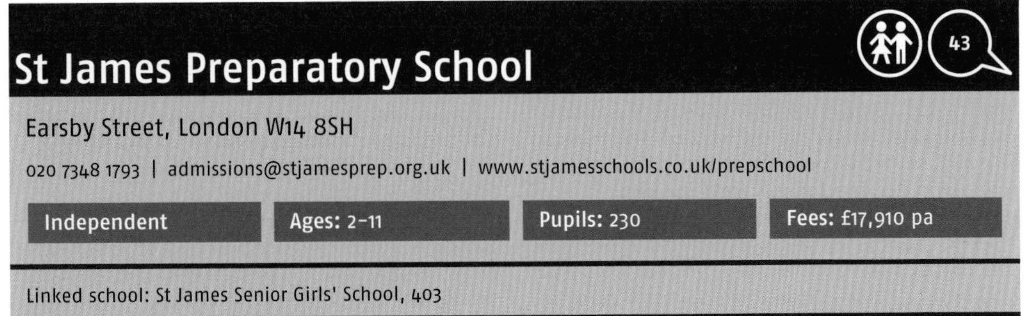

St James Preparatory School

Earsby Street, London W14 8SH

020 7348 1793 | admissions@stjamesprep.org.uk | www.stjamesschools.co.uk/prepschool

Independent	Ages: 2-11	Pupils: 230	Fees: £17,910 pa

Linked school: St James Senior Girls' School, 403

Head: Since September 2020, Kris Spencer BSc (geography). Did his PGCE in geography at Hull and postgraduate research at Jesus College, Oxford. Previously deputy head at Notting Hill Prep and before that, worked at schools including Westminster, St Paul's Girls (head of geography), Abingdon (head of geography/day housemaster) and Latymer Upper (assistant head).

Entrance: Now from age 2, thanks to new nursery. From age 4, there's no assessment as such, but a meeting with parents while children get a taster of reception, plus a report from child's nursery where applicable. Priority to nursery children and siblings. School looks for 'children and families who value what we value'. Places higher up the school often available, and children who apply aged 7+ take assessments in reading, writing and mathematics to ensure they can keep up.

Exit: Fewer than in the past move onto St James Senior Girls' (located on the same site, with some shared facilities) and St James Senior Boys' (now out in Ashford, comprehensive coach service provided by St James Schools), but it's still the majority, fluctuating between 50-70 per cent. Other recent school destinations include City Academy, Francis Holland Regent's Park, Godolphin & Latymer, Harrodian, Holland Park School, Ibstock Place, Kew House, Latymer Upper, Notting Hill & Ealing High School, St Benedict's, St Paul's Girls', Waldegrave and Wimbledon High School. Since becoming a standalone prep (as opposed to the junior school of the girls' and boys' senior schools), there is greater emphasis on 11+ and recommendations for secondary schools.

Our view: 'Isn't that the hippie school where they learn Sanskrit and only eat vegetarian food?' If St James parents had a pound for every time they heard that, they'd probably get a hefty chunk off their school fees. At least the public perception gets two out of three for accuracy – 'it's the hippie bit that's wrong,' insist most parents, although one did say, 'It all comes down to your definition of hippiedom, I suppose – there's certainly a lot that's unconventional and spiritual about this school.' Every lesson begins and ends with a 'moment of stillness' to 'give you that sense of ease and reflection', for example, and the school teaches a Socratic method of dialogue and questioning, with the children taught to develop open-ended questions and to debate as a class ('No putting-down of others' opinions is allowed,' says head firmly). Even the school's origins are alternative – it was founded by the School of Economic Science, seen by some as a cult, although the school has no associations with the organisation now.

The result is an unusual and admirable little school that's pervaded by an air of gentle wisdom and where their ethos of generosity, mutual respect and 'being the best human beings we can be' isn't just a case of paying lip-service to try to get the punters in – it permeates everything. While other schools introduced mindfulness as an add-on in recent years, St James practically invented the concept. Parents love the school and children love it more.

The school nestles quietly within residential streets, the outside resembling a monastery, with its high walls and expanse of sheer red brick, but the tableau through the security gate isn't in the least forbidding. Children play cheerfully in a pretty, cloistered courtyard (they also have a larger playground, complete with edible garden), while the preponderance of surrounding glass gives a modern, clean balance to the Victorian charm of the original building. 'The peacefulness and calmness of the school are tangible,' parents told us in advance of our visit, so we were surprised to arrive to loud screams (of delight) from a reception gym class. But that's the thing about St James – the overall atmosphere of serenity is not at the expense of vibrancy and good old-fashioned childish excitement. And it is this combo that wins most parents over as soon as they step foot inside. 'We looked at every school in this part of London but as soon as I did the tour here I knew it was right, there's something about the energy,' summed up one.

There's a lot that's unconventional and spiritual about this school. Every lesson begins and ends with a 'moment of stillness' to 'give you that sense of ease and reflection'

The 'pause', as it's known, at the start and end of lessons, 'gives you a chance to be still and turn any stress you might have into a little ball you can literally throw away,' according to one year 6 child, whose demeanour was composed beyond her years, while a younger one said, 'it calms me down after break or a more lively lesson if I'm still pumped up.' When thinking about secondary schools, one parent told us, children can find other schools totally chaotic initially, while another said that it can sometimes feel that other children are far more streetwise, 'like they're in the fast-lane while mine live in the moment – I like that, but that's not for all families.'

All the children, even the little ones, learn Sanskrit, in accordance with the school's belief that the Eastern philosophies have much to teach us – children love it because 'it feels special that only we learn it' and parents because 'it's a beautiful language, they even get to sing it.' St James describes itself as 'multi-religious', and philosophy itself is a very important part of the curriculum.

Queen's Gate Junior School

Academic performance is stronger than ever since becoming a prep, with verbal and non-verbal reasoning a focus from year 3 and interventions in English and maths from year 4, then setting in English and maths in years 5 and 6. Standards are high – all the more impressive, given that the school's intake is not academically selective. But it's the way it's taught that stands out, say parents – 'unlike a lot of preps round here that cram children with facts, they get children thinking independently,' said one. 'The curriculum is structured in such a way that it ensures the children are nurturing both sides of their brain all the time,' said another. Teachers, who do increasing amounts of tracking and monitoring of each pupil, embody what the school professes to be, with a recent influx of younger teachers, 'which has given a breath of fresh air to the school,' according to one parent. St James's policy of teaching boys and girls separately, then bringing them together for social activities, gets mixed views from parents and children, but newbies are in luck – the school trialling co-ed teaching in every subject for the 2018 reception cohort (so far, so good) and the houses are also now mixed.

Food here is vegetarian, so that all the children can eat together. 'I love everything,' more than one child told us, gobbling happily. Jamie Oliver once held up the school as a shining star when it comes to school dinners

SEN provision is good. 'One of my children is dyslexic and they flagged it up as early as in year 2 and supported her all the way through,' said one parent, although a few mentioned that 'until recently, there was a feeling of parents having to forge their way with SEN – I'm glad it's moved on.' Thirty-three EAL children when we visited, but most are fluent so don't need support. We applaud the emphasis on using Shakespeare as a teaching resource at all levels, more so than in any other school we've visited, complete with annual Shakespeare festival. 'I couldn't believe it the other day when my son, who's in reception, was quoting Shakespeare's Winter Poem word for word at breakfast,' said one parent.

All children are involved in at least one performance (though no whole-school ones here) and a poetry recital every year. Music is everywhere, with 80 children taking instrumental lessons and there are regular concerts, often featuring the school's orchestra, as well as weekly music lessons and daily singing in assembly – repertoire by Mozart, Purcell and Vivaldi is popular. Year 6 girls belted out a carol in Latin for us so beautifully it made the hairs on our neck stand on end. The attractive art room is jam-packed with astonishingly good work – everything from silk screen to kiln work to print making. Big on fine arts, cross-curricular (some lovely year 2 Roman ceramics on show and a gasp-worthy model of WW1 trenches from year 6s) and turning their 2D work into a 3D equivalent.

Games or sport for all on most days be it gym, swimming or handball (they do particularly well at this), and the upper juniors (years 3-6) go off-site once a week to Barn Elms to hone their skills at netball, rugby, cricket, athletics, cross-country and the like. Lots of inter-school competitions – two boys we met were rushing off to a big rugby match. Swimming is held in nearby Fulham Pools – some success at national level among the pupils.

There's forest school and oodles of trips to Minstead Study Centre in the New Forest, plus a varied programme of outings closer to home, the usual London fare. Excellent range of clubs includes yoga, robotics and coding, chess, karate, young engineers, cookery, model-making, archery and fencing. Wraparound care now includes drop-off from 7.45am (free), ready for registration at 8.15am, and until 6pm (for an extra fee) after school. Use of ICT has increased, although actual ICT lessons are still for year 5 and 6 only; some parents would like it to be sooner.

Pastorally as good as it gets. 'Kindness is underrated,' says school. 'Children need to feel special and loved. These are difficult words in a school but if children feel their teachers have totally got their back, the sky's the limit.'

Food here is vegetarian, so that all the children can eat together, and is included in the fees. 'I love everything,' more than one child told us, gobbling happily. We certainly went back for seconds and were not surprised to hear Jamie Oliver once held up the school as a shining star when it comes to school dinners.

The last word: This school impressed us as such a kind and enlightened medium in which to culture young minds, that we occasionally had to remind ourselves that this was a school we'd stepped into and not a Botticelli painting. It was almost a relief to hear one boy admit to talking too much in class and meet a teacher who was clearly knackered from her morning's work. But these tiny wrinkles only served to throw into greater focus the sweetness and calm of this remarkable community. Not a school for budding Piers Morgans, we suspect. But who cares?

St James Senior Girls' School

Earsby Street, London W14 8SH

020 7348 1777 | admissions@sjsg.org.uk | www.stjamesschools.co.uk/seniorgirls

Independent | Pupils: 269; sixth form: 60

Ages: 11–18 | Fees: £20,880 pa

Linked school: St James Preparatory School, 399

Headmistress: Since 2014, Sarah Labram BA (classics, King's College) (50s). As a former pupil and head girl, she was privy to the growth of the school from its inception in 1975 as part of the School of Economic Science's (SES) philosophical approach to a fixture on the London private school circuit, successful in academic league tables. Sent both her own daughters to the junior and senior schools and has worked there herself for nearly a quarter of a century, rising through the ranks from classics teacher to head of department then deputy head. Totally imbued, then, with the St James' ethos.

More gentle Kanga than a Tigger, with a mission to build self-awareness and self-management in the girls by promulgating life skills like mindfulness, compassion and citizenship. A moderniser too – she has improved the school's IT offer, as well as building a new library, lab and sixth form centre.

Parents like her, with some saying she had a big impact on their decision to choose the school. One turned down a well-known academic school for St James as 'we knew as soon as we heard Mrs Labram speak that the school was a good fit'. 'She is extraordinary, running a school with demanding professional parents – she keeps her cool, is straightforward, sensible and intelligent,' said another. But the parental praise is not without cracks – some remark on a lack of direct contact: 'there's a tier of management between us and her, but I think she's no nonsense, she seems quite firm and the girls respect her,' says one, while another questioned her long involvement with the school and whether there is 'enough oxygen' in the leadership.

Has a keen awareness of the possible 'perfect storm' that can come from an uncertain political climate, pressure from social media and the 'scope for getting it wrong', so spends a great deal of time supporting and educating the girls to make 'wise choices' which is perhaps more important now than ever before.

Enjoys spending time with her family (she's married to another head), with hobbies largely cultural – music, theatre, ballet etc, as well as cooking.

Entrance: There are 170 applicants for 30 places; the remaining 18 places tend to go to girls from the prep school (NB now at year 7 rather than year 6). These applicants come from a mix of preps and state primaries (around half each). These include Bute House, Chiswick and Bedford Park, Fulham Prep, Heathfield House, Hurlingham, Kew Green Prep, Larmenier & Sacred Heart Primary School, Pembridge Hall, Notting Hill Prep, Ravenscourt Park Prep, Redcliffe School and the Falcons School for Girls. Main northwest feeders include Maple Walk and St Mary's School Hampstead. School is part of the London 11+ Consortium, which sets a cognitive ability test (maths, verbal and non-verbal reasoning) and has a common reference form. Odd spaces higher up. Entry criteria for sixth formers is at least five GCSEs at 9-4 and a minimum of a 7 for subjects to be taken.

Exit: Up to a quarter leave after GCSEs, often for larger or co-ed schools, both state and boarding. Popular recent destinations after sixth form include Durham, Edinburgh, Nottingham, Bristol and King's College London. None to Oxbridge in 2020, but two the previous year. Strong showing in art recently, with girls going to Central St Martins, Camberwell College of Arts, the Royal Drawing School and the Art Academy.

Latest results: In 2020, 72 per cent 9-7 or equivalent at GCSE; 63 per cent A*/A at A level (87 per cent A*-B). In 2019 (the last year when exams took place), 76 per cent 9-7 at GCSE; 56 per cent A*/A at A level (79 per cent A*-B).

Teaching and learning: The head's love of classics (she still teaches) is reflected both in the syllabus and in an outstanding classics department with

Greek, Latin and classical civilisation all taught, as well as – more unusually – Sanskrit, which is available at GCSE but no longer A level (although some go on to study it at university – especially popular for Oxbridge applicants). Girls from the prep take it until the end of year 9; those who join from year 7 take it in the first term, after which it is optional. The root of many eastern and western languages, the head feels it's great for grammar and offers a wealth of metaphysical thought. Plus, say some of the girls, it marks you out as interesting. One parent whose eyebrows disappeared into her hairline at the thought of Sanskrit on the syllabus now speaks of the merits for girls in learning a different philosophical system.

These unusual 'extras' can lift excellent teaching into something inspiring. Philosophy and spirituality are imbued in the day to day, with girls meditating for five minutes at the beginning and end of each class (with inevitable reports of scuffles and giggles), and some sophisticated ontological teaching – especially from the history, RE and English departments. While one parent observed it was 'a bit of a hodge-podge what with Anglican hymnbooks, Sanskrit and various religious things,' girls report fascinating ethical discussions, and being given tools to question moral issues.

One parent whose eyebrows disappeared into her hairline at the thought of Sanskrit now speaks of the merits for girls in learning a different philosophical system

Academically, the school achieves strong results. 'We expect to get a grade to a grade and half higher than the predictive data,' says one head of department. IGCEs in chemistry, physics, Sanskrit, biology, chemistry, history and mathematics (these departments say they prefer the syllabus, which they believe offers a wider scope of learning than the current GCSE syllabus). The rest – art and design, classical Greek, Latin, music, PE, drama, religious studies, English language and literature, French, Spanish and geography – are GCSEs. There is an option to do a BTech in applied IT, which is popular. Small sixth form – just 23 when we visited, with 19 subjects offered including classical Greek, Latin, Hinduism, RS and psychology offered, alongside art, biology, chemistry, mathematics /further mathematics, physics, history, history of art, English literature, Spanish and French. Classes are small, particularly in sixth form, where there can be as few as two or three girls per subject.

The staff–pupil ration is high – 41 teachers, 14 of whom are men, to 261 pupils when we visited, although we did hear criticisms from parents about a higher turnover of staff than they'd have liked and certainly some stalwarts have left recently. On the other hand, the teachers are known for their commitment which chimes with the assiduous attention to pastoral care. Teachers take on a variety of roles, pastoral and mentoring as well as educative.

We were impressed by some of the girls' analytic abilities over and above schoolwork. A year 7 girl gave an insightful breakdown into the technical aspects of a Disney film, including its storyboard and animation. Another's passion for the Percy Jackson stories was a tonic. 'If you join at the junior school, your time is even more beneficial because you really understand Sanskrit, and the ethos of the school,' a former pupil told us.

Learning support and SEN: Around a quarter of the girls have mild to moderate learning difficulties – which is a high percentage – and the school feels that the size of class and level of academic support, including extra teaching and clinics, provides significant assistance. One parent estimated that 50 per cent of her daughter's class had extra time in exams, and 'academic results are really good, considering they take so many kids that are SEN.' School says the figure across the school for SEN is 25 per cent.

The arts and extracurricular: Art is popular. The department produces accomplished work – exquisite oils and pen and inks were on display – and a number of girls go on to foundation courses or university degrees in the subject.

Girls flex their thespian muscles with annual musicals; Mary Poppins was a recent vibrant offering, as was the school decamping to Leighton House to stage Purcell's Dido and Aeneas. The girls' and boys' schools join together for a leavers' ball (and a joint musical fundraiser to finance it), concerts and a biennial musical. One parent, a professional in the music world, said the summer concerts where both schools performed together were 'fantastic and unusual, and had real heart and soul'.

Choirs are the backbone of the musical offering, with a junior and a senior choir, orchestra, grade 5 music theory and, of course, private instrument lessons available.

The school has recently refurbished its home economics kitchen, and the girls regularly cook meals and serve them to residents from a local nursing home.

Popular extracurricular trips include a geography trip to Iceland and a history trip to Berlin.

One parent reports a girl joining in sixth form: 'It was like going home for her. She won an award for being an all-round good egg'

Sport: Despite being cloistered in Olympia, the school does surprisingly well on the sports front – all praise to the very hard work of the PE department. As such, has no problem catering for sporty girls, with an outstanding lacrosse team, ISA netball, excellent results in cross country and a successful football team, as well as the usual sports of athletics, rounders, gymnastics, cricket, handball and volleyball. The lacrosse team recently won the county lacrosse tournament (four lacrosse players were on the England talent pathway and a year 9 girl had been selected to trial for the U19 England team when we visited), and two girls represented Wales and Scotland in lacrosse at the home internationals. The school also won the ISA regional cross country competition for years 7/8 and 9/10. The U15 football team recently won the Queen's College tournament and the U18 football team won the St Paul's Girls' indoor tournament. Self-defence, karate, kickboxing, yoga and dance also available, albeit extracurricular. Athletic girls will be recognised and stretched here, says a parent of one star pupil, 'even though the school doesn't promote itself as a sporty school'.

There's a sports hall on campus and outdoor netball court, and girls from year 10 upwards can pay to use a local gym nearby. Otherwise sports days and outdoor events go to King's House sports grounds in Chiswick or Barn Elms in Barnes. Professional sportswomen come and speak to the girls, with recent speakers including Jess Grimson, Team England's top female beach volleyball player, and Jasmine Joyce, a Team GB and Wales international rugby player.

Ethos and heritage: Located down a quiet road in the shadows of Olympia, the main gate leads into an attractive gated courtyard. Up until year 12, the seniors share this site with the prep school, with senior girls turning left rather than right on entry. Classrooms smack of the Victorian (building opened as a school in 1874 then was rebuilt in 1936) with wooden desks, although of course there are whiteboards too now. Labs are well equipped and modern, there's an excellent art studio, and well-appointed hall. It is light and pleasant, but some parents have concerns about a lack of outdoor space, although there is a netball court and the girls use the playground during breaks.

The sixth form building is a couple of streets away in a large terraced house filled with classrooms, breakout rooms, study spaces and a good-size common room. Here, girls are largely autonomous, although they return to the main school for assemblies, certain classes and meals – and clearly love their independent life a few streets from the main school.

When the school was founded in the 1970s, it was very much part of the School of Economic Science movement that had built up momentum since its origins in 1937. The idea behind SES was an exploration of the world's great religions and philosophies and what it is to be fully human in a spiritual way. Although the school has actively distanced itself from the SES, the legacy of this ethos lives on through the school, albeit evolved.

Food has always been vegetarian (originally due to the SES links, although now the main benefit is 'a huge saving in CO_2 emissions,' says head) which appeals to many parents. It is simple and nourishing – with pizza a popular option.

We found girls to be articulate, reasonable and supportive of one another. Especially suited to quieter academic types that respond to a gentler approach and who embrace the meditation time at the beginning and end of each class. Such girls, say parents, 'blossom' here. One parent reports a girl joining in sixth form and finding 'it was like going home for her. She won an award for being an all-round good egg.' Phones are handed in daily for years 7 to 11, although the head is 'cheered by the sanguine attitude' of the girls to social media, observing 'different generations respond in different ways'. Sixth formers can keep their phones.

Alumnae include actor Emily Watson OBE, Emma Mulqueeny OBE, Sahana Gero MBE, interior designers Anna Jacobs and Anna Glover, writer Lucy Crehan and Natasha Tomalin-Hall, creative director of You Magazine.

Pastoral care, inclusivity and discipline: Particularly strong on mental health, with school adept at spotting signs of disturbance and involving parents and support teams. School has a network of professional support from art therapists to SEN advisors, a mental health training mentoring scheme between older and younger girls, and even a dog, Huxley, 'for emotional support' that the girls love. Head is proud of the work the school does in supporting the girls' emotional wellbeing – all part of day-to-day conversation for the girls – and has led the school in its membership of the Girls on Board scheme, with a focus on navigating the waters of girls' friendships. Parents speak of friendship groups as 'thoughtful, caring, clever and confident'. The mantra used by these staff of 'is it true, is it necessary, is it kind?' is a good one for girls who might be tempted to gang up on each other. One parent reported that 'she had never seen teachers with such a high level of commitment' to the girls. It's worth noting, though, that one parent reported more girls with problems than you might hope for, but perhaps this is simply because the girls' problems are being recognised.

Pupils and parents: Over 40 languages spoken at the school, with families from Europe, Asia and the Middle East. They find it 'easy to settle in,' says the head, with St James a 'refreshingly different space to be themselves'. Vegans, yogis and life coaches are represented in the parent body, alongside the more usual private school coterie of bankers, accountants and lawyers. Parents are invited to a 'back to school' evening when they are 'taught' by the staff, which is a hugely popular event, as is the Christmas Fair when the courtyard and school are transformed into a glorious grotto, filled with trees, cakes and goodwill. One parent felt it's a shame the school is sometimes overlooked – like others, she encourages her friends to visit the school as well as 'the Godolphin and Latymers' because her daughters are so happy there.

Money matters: Means-tested bursaries awarded to 10 per cent of current pupils. All current and future parents may apply.

The last word: St James has a special place in the panoply of west London private schools. It offers exceptional pastoral support and many girls benefit from the school's holistic and nurturing approach. For some, the emphasis on care, compassion and classical education may make it feel slightly staid, but for others it offers an excellent crack of the academic whip in a supportive intellectual environment.

St Joseph's Catholic Primary School

RC 48

Cadogan Street, London SW3 2QT

020 7589 2438 | info@stjosephs.rbkc.sch.uk | www.stjosephs.rbkc.sch.uk

State | Ages: 3-11 | Pupils: 223

Executive Head: Since 2013, Karen Wyatt (40s) BSc, PGCE, NPQH. Educated at the Ursuline Convent in Ilford, then at Roehampton University, where she studied business and sport, 'taking the plunge' into teaching with a PGCE at Digby Stuart College. Worked for more than a decade at a St Helen's Catholic Primary in Brixton, rising from student teacher to acting head, before taking over at St Joseph's from an interim head who'd stepped in to smooth over a difficult patch. Has since fully cemented positive change, lauded by both Ofsted and the Diocese of Westminster for her exceptional leadership. Now splits her working week between St Joseph's and St Thomas of Canterbury RC Primary in Fulham. With a young daughter at the school, she still manages to squeeze in twice weekly netball and an annual pilgrimage to Lourdes. Considered by parents to be approachable, focused and down to earth. 'She's very humble and straightforward,' said one. 'She's always willing to listen to parents' suggestions,' said another. 'Firm but fair.'

Head of school since 2016, James Stacey (40s), BSc, GTP. Mr Stacey's relationship with St Joseph's dates back to his own schooldays and, after studying English and sports science at Surrey University, he returned to the school under the graduate training programme, advancing through the ranks. Heavily involved in the parish (where his early participation was as an altar boy) as well as a passionate advocate of the school, he's married to a fellow head and has two young children, one at St Joseph's. Parents and pupils like his empathy and sense of humour. 'He's very understanding,' said one mother. 'The children really warm to him.'

Entrance: Around 50-60 apply for 26 nursery places; 130 for 30 spots in reception. Attending neighbouring St Mary's Church is the surest way through the gates. After that, it's other Catholics, then other Christians, then other faiths; almost all families, however, are practising Catholics. Heavily oversubscribed at the outset, places do arise further up the school, when latecomers are selected from the school's own waiting list.

Exit: Largely to RC secondaries: Cardinal Vaughan, London Oratory, Sacred Heart Hammersmith, Ursuline High School, Wimbledon, and adjoining

St Thomas More Language College. Some, too, to the independent sector, again largely to Catholic day and boarding schools (the Laurels, St Mary's Ascot), but also to St Paul's, Emanuel School and the Knightsbridge. All families given one-to-one guidance in the run-up to transfer, and those looking to selective schools, independent or state, offered specialist support in an 11+ club.

Our view: In 2012, the school received a less-than-desirable 'satisfactory' from Ofsted. Since then, things have seen a dramatic upwards trajectory and recent key stage 2 Sats (with 88 per cent of pupils reaching the expected standard in reading, writing and maths and many soaring above) put St Joseph's comfortably in the top tranche of primaries in an area known for its high-achieving outcomes. The turnaround has been achieved by purposeful leadership and teachers who, like the head, have a can-do fervour. 'When you challenge the staff, they say, "how high?" not, "I can't do that",' says Mrs Wyatt.

'Creative and inspiring teaching' (says Ofsted) delivered in calm, orderly classrooms. 'The academic standard is exceptional,' said one mother. 'The teachers know every child, understand what they're capable of and make them feel they can achieve it.' All pupils given 'robust' initial assessment, followed by rigorous tracking and well-planned support thereafter. SENCo attends three days a week providing individual attention for those who need support or stretch. The most able challenged to work well above the expected. 'My son goes up to the next year one day a week; they really push him along,' said one parent. All, however, encouraged to try, try, and try again under the inspiration of the growth mindset philosophy – 'helps them see things they can't do as a challenge and never give up,' claims school. One parent, whose son started reception with little English and is now finishing his schooldays in top sets, says, 'For several years, his work was well below average, but they put so many resources into him and really helped him achieve the goals he'd set himself.'

Broad-ranging curriculum includes science, history, geography, IT (with dedicated classroom and recently purchased iPads) and Spanish, but RE remains at its core. 'It's so open,' says Mrs Wyatt. 'It really builds in philosophy and ethical debate and allows them to address big questions.'

The arts a priority. Weekly music lessons and hymn practice included in the curriculum, and all taught recorder, ukulele and drums. Instrumental specialists provide individual lessons to about a third and the sufficiently proficient participate in the school orchestra. Two main school choirs and three smaller choirs get plenty of opportunities to display their talents, singing carols at Peter Jones and the Royal Hospital, alongside the Bach Choir at St John's Smith Square and other venues. Drama firmly woven into the classroom experience, with performance opportunities in the annual nativity and year 6 musical. Chess, too, has become central, taught in class as a mind-stretching exercise from year 3, and coached by an expert in an after-school club, which has triumphed in local competitions.

Religion very visibly at the heart of the school – stations of the cross adorn the classrooms and communal space – and children are encouraged to live their faith

PE twice weekly taught by a specialist coach. Swimming at nearby Chelsea Baths in years 3-5; football on offer as an afternoon club, with a school team competing against other local schools. Some suggest a wider range of sporting opportunities might benefit those whose talents/interests lie elsewhere. Broad out-of-hours offering, with clubs for Spanish and French, arts and crafts, yoga, ballet and Flamenco, as well as – a boon to working parents – before and after-school care. 'The wrap-around care is one of the reasons we chose the school, and it's amazing,' said one mother. 'They do loads of arts and crafts and reading, and my daughter has really bonded with the staff.' Regular visits to local cultural hotspots such as the House of Commons, the National Army Museum and the Royal Albert Hall.

Doubly blessed in its site and building, with the listed 1844 Pugin-ascribed Victorian-Tudor schoolhouse now supplemented by an expansive modern addition, providing bright, spacious and immaculately maintained classrooms (each with its own welcoming 'book corner'). Ample outdoor space, too, with older years enjoying a weather-friendly Astroturf surface: nursery and reception benefit from a sensory-focused forest school approach, with their own mud kitchen and vegetable patch.

School divided into four houses named after saints (Paul, Francis, Bernadette, Helen), and pupils compete for house points, cups and the privilege of parties (with popcorn). Pupil voice encouraged with peer-elected representatives delegated to weekly school council. All given the chance to take on positions of responsibility. 'My son, who's in year 2, has been made a friendship ambassador, which has helped make him much more socially attuned and articulate,' said one mother. Pupils confident and polite – chorusing 'good afternoon' as visitors enter.

Religion very visibly at the heart of the school – stations of the cross adorn the classrooms and communal space – and children are encouraged to live their faith. 'We like them to be practical in their Christianity,' says Mr Stacey. 'The idea that you make a contribution to society is very much to the forefront.' As well as donations to a range of Catholic charities, pupils regularly visit Chelsea pensioners and raise money for others, such as the victims of the Grenfell fire. Historic association with the Royal Hospital Chapel and neighbouring St Mary's Church, which pupils attend regularly for Mass, St Joseph's Feast Days, and occasional Sundays (in uniform).

A high percentage of families derive from central London's ethnically diverse, peripatetic professional middle class, with parents working in embassies, finance and universities. Three-quarters speak English as an additional language. 'Pupils are often trilingual and families generally very well educated,' says the head. Most are looking for a strong Catholic education. 'Quite a lot of parents who could afford to pay have chosen St Joseph's over the independent sector,' said one. 'They don't want their children to live in the "Chelsea bubble"; they want them to be socially articulate, global citizens with a strong local conscience.' About 15 per cent, however, are significantly less affluent, and the school is a member of the London Mayor's Gold Club for achieving consistently good results for children attracting the pupil premium. Home-school relationship unusually tight, with parents supplementing in-class provision in a holistic approach. (Parent mentors, for example, help 'de-risk' maths for year 6 girls by demonstrating its practical application.) Energetic parents' association raises money through summer fair, international food festival etc, while a recently established knights' fund encourages those who feel able to contribute to bridge funding shortfalls.

The last word: An exceptionally warm and caring place, providing a secure, supportive community, high aspirations and high achievement for all. 'They don't just care about the most gifted; every child here feels safe and valued,' said one happy parent.

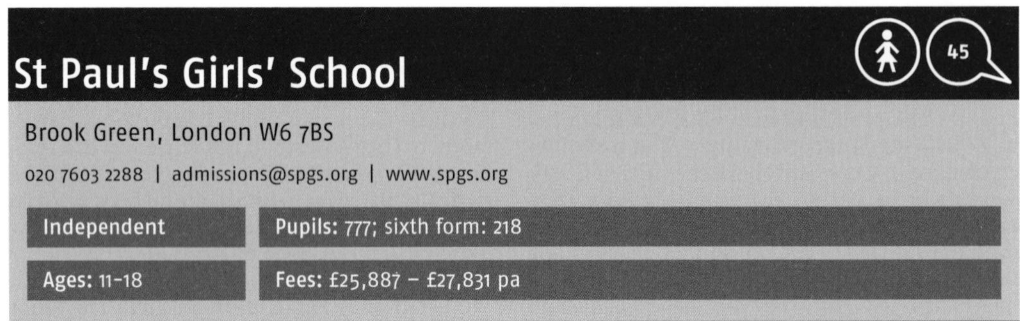

St Paul's Girls' School

Brook Green, London W6 7BS

020 7603 2288 | admissions@spgs.org | www.spgs.org

Independent | Pupils: 777; sixth form: 218

Ages: 11–18 | Fees: £25,887 – £27,831 pa

High mistress: Since September 2017, Oxford historian Sarah Fletcher MA PGCE NPQH (50s). A lady who doesn't shrink from a challenge: she was previously head of City of London School, the first woman to captain that ship in its august history. Other posts have included Wycombe Abbey, St George's Montreux, Habs Girls' ('I loved the intellectual buzz there'), Lawrence Sheriff Boys' Grammar and Kingston Grammar, where she had her first headship. Relishes scholarship and her credentials for promoting independent learning are impressive: she was involved with the development and launch of the Pre-U and the EPQ.

Attended King Alfred's School in Wantage, where she was in the first mixed comprehensive cohort of what had been a boys' grammar. It wasn't an easy ride. 'The majority of my peers were not academically minded,' she reflects. 'They cleared out a broom cupboard for me to sit my Oxford entrance exams, and the good luck card said Mind The Drips.' She did her PGCE at Exeter in history with a subsidiary in special needs.

Parents are nervous of changes she has made so far eg in the senior management, which by September 2018 had only three people remaining from the previous team, but admire her energy, drive and 'light managerial touch'. 'She certainly is more approachable and down-to-earth than we've been used to,' was one mother's verdict.

Married with two grown-up sons. Her interests are music – she plays clarinet in the school's concert band – and theatre. Having arrived at the top job in girls' independent education, she has no wish to move on. 'I love it, I really love it here – I feel as if I've come home.'

Entrance: At 11+, up to 110 places in five classes, with a maximum of 22 per class. Pre-test taken in the autumn term of year 6 weeds out those who'll never make it. Those who pass sit a further test in January, designed to reveal how much girls really think: maths, English and a paper on problem-solving. Those who do well are invited for interview. School is looking for girls who can 'reason, articulate and show quality of thought.' Largest single cohort is from Bute House, which regularly sends up to 20 girls here; the rest from a wide range of preps and primaries across London and beyond. Applicants for any occasional places that arise higher up the school are subject to the same stringent assessment procedures and should already be studying at least two modern languages.

At 16+, about 20 join each year. Applicants are tested on their A level subjects and invited to interview if they do well.

Not a particularly local intake, but parents have to declare on the application form how their daughter will travel to school, and for years 7-11 the journey cannot be longer than an hour.

Exit: A handful leave after GCSEs to try co-ed or boarding, but the great majority stay on and gain places at top-flight universities at home and abroad. Around half go to Oxbridge (43 in 2020). The rest mostly to Durham, Edinburgh, Bristol and the London colleges. Increasing numbers to leading US universities: 12 in 2020 including Brown, Columbia, NYU, Princeton and Stanford; Europe is also becoming popular eg Bocconi in Italy. Fifteen medics and one vet in 2020.

Latest results: In 2020, 64 per cent A*/A at A level and Pre-U. In 2019 (the last year when exams took place), 99 per cent 9-7 at GCSE; 85 per cent A*/A at A level and Pre-U.

Teaching and learning: A rollercoaster of cerebral activity, where the stellar exam results are a by-product of the joyful intellectual leaping and diving that make up the days here.

'You very much go beyond the syllabus,' the head girl told us. 'The entire cohort is exceptional, and the teaching really stretches them,' confirmed a mother. 'It's less about the facts and much more about analysis, thinking and going beyond the boundaries.' Parents full of praise for the way that intellectual stimulation extends to all parts of the curriculum. 'I have never met a child so enthused about Latin as my daughter!' 'My daughter thought she was a scientist. Now she loves the arts.' Lessons here are teacher-led but 'all the teachers are interesting people in their own right' so the results are great fun. We dropped in on a zestful English lesson where year 7s were lapping up Twelfth Night under the guidance of a cheerful young prof with a knack for making scholarship exciting. Questions from the girls poured in, and were handled with kindly energy and superb subject knowledge. Lessons we saw with older year groups were relaxed and seminar-like.

'Her teachers have been absolutely superb, unbeatable, and there's a tremendous respect for real intellectual curiosity and academia rather than exam results'

Wide-ranging curriculum is still quite traditional, and we loved the emphasis on languages. On arriving in year 7 the girls do Latin and have a course on Introduction to Languages. They then start whichever modern language their languages teacher specialises in. In year 8 they choose two further modern languages and continue with Latin, which remains compulsory until they start their GCSEs. In year 10 they can opt to do Greek. A feature of SPGS is the number of school-directed courses where the school itself is the awarding body, validated by an external examining board. Art, art history, music and drama are all taught this way and have enjoyed a great deal of success. 'Our qualifications are taken very seriously by universities, and they give the girls more freedom to follow what fascinates them.' Similarly, there's no EPQ here: long before it was introduced, Paulinas took the school's own Senior Scholarship programme, which involves writing an essay on 'anything you like – it's about pursuing a scholarly interest'. Our tour guide was doing hers on personalised medicine.

Despite the A level reforms, girls here still take four subjects and drop one at the end of year 12, which here is called the VII. The Pre-U is taught in some subjects eg English lit, French, history of art, but there are no plans to introduce the IB. 'There's no distinction here between hard and soft subjects,' claims head proudly. Nonetheless, she would like to introduce more engineering, and is looking at how to improve the provision of computer studies. DT is taught as part of the art curriculum, and our impression as we walked about was that the arts, humanities and languages still rule the waves here. It may be no coincidence that none of the high mistresses to date have had a degree in science.

Work is rarely graded, and there are few internal academic competitions to pit the girls against each other. 'There's very little for them to compete about, and hand on heart, my daughter has never experienced any meanness from the other girls,' said one mother. Another wrote, 'Her teachers have been absolutely superb, unbeatable, and there's a tremendous respect for real intellectual curiosity and academia rather than exam results.'

Learning support and SEN: Full-time learning support coordinator handles the small number of girls with eg dyslexia and organisational issues, but this is a school where girls with even mild difficulties can find themselves bumping along the bottom. We spoke to one parent who took her dyslexic daughter away after hearing her observe sadly that she was never going to be top of the class in anything. But the school works to create as stress-free an atmosphere as possible around academic attainment.

The arts and extracurricular: The art rooms frame the main hall, and in a very literal sense therefore are central to the school and its ethos. Artwork of an astonishing standard and creativity is everywhere. We lost count of the number of pieces that amazed us, but a Chagall-inspired painting and a wonderful leaf sculpture particularly stayed in the memory. We loved the year 8 art class making 'hybrids' – joining two or three animals together in clay sculptures, like something from a medieval bestiary. School still has its own dark room; we're always overjoyed to see these surviving in this digital age. And in 2021, building will start on a new centre for design & innovation.

We loved the year 8 art class making 'hybrids' – joining two or three animals together in clay sculptures, like something from a medieval bestiary

The music has been deservedly famous since Gustav Holst took up his post as director of music here in 1905. The music department was built in 1913 under his direction and a beautiful stained glass ceiling panel celebrates his suite The Planets. The Singing Hall has a lovely acoustic and holds about 250: orchestras rehearse here, and we saw a lively group composition session in progress. An exquisite harp concerto was being rehearsed when we visited, but the school also stages musicals eg Grease, Les Misérables, The Sound of Music, often in collaboration with the boys' school. The Endangered Musical Instruments Fair is held every year in the Great Hall, and girls are offered free taster sessions offered on the ones that have caught their fancy – saxophone, bassoon, viola, etc. Wonderful range of ensembles, some inclusive, some by audition only, that play to an extremely high standard. Drama, once something of an also-ran, is now strong and diverse, and taught in its own well-equipped black box theatre. Recent productions include an all-girls' Lord of the Flies. Students have lots of opportunities to get involved – one sixth former set up a club for set design – although murmurs persist that it isn't as inclusive as it could be.

Wide-ranging and enticing range of clubs on offer – dissecting, medieval society, art history, IT workshop – and the girls are always encouraged to run their own: we loved the secondhand clothes shop, Re-Store, set up by students to raise money for local charities. With so many activities to choose from, some girls can feel a little overwhelmed, especially as they move up through the school and choirs, sports, productions, etc become more selective. 'One of my very few gripes about the school is that there's so much to do, but nobody pushes the girls very much,' was one comment. 'Extracurricular activities are abundant and inclusive of all abilities in the younger years, less so in the senior school,' wrote another.

Sport: Lacrosse continues to be the main sport, but netball is also extremely popular – the school had to create an H team recently because so many girls signed up for it. School aims for and achieves excellence in sports as you'd expect, with students frequently picked to play at county level, but there are plenty of opportunities for everyone to get involved for fun. Other offerings include fencing, basketball, rowing, cross-country, swimming, gym club, kick boxing – the list goes on. Dance is offered as part of the PE provision.

Huge numbers of trips abroad, including an exchange with the National Cathedral School in Washington DC, language trips to Siena, Montpelier and the like, history trips to Paris and Dublin, and so forth. 'We're mindful of not offering too many expensive trips,' observed the school's director of communications, 'but girls on bursaries can apply for up to 100 per cent assistance.'

Ethos and heritage: Founded in 1904 to complement the boys' school after the latter had been around some 400 years, St Paul's Girls' quickly climbed the academic heights and is now widely regarded as the parthenon of girls' selective independent education in England. The building, designed by Gerald Horsley, is a handsome but imposing red-brick in the Queen Anne Revival architectural style. When we arrived the great wooden doors were shut and, on our ringing the bell, swung silently open without any accompanying words of welcome, adding to the school's air of slightly forbidding quietude. Indeed, for a community that prizes intellectual freedom, our visit had a curiously constrained feel to it. We were given no opportunity to speak to any students other than the head girl and deputy head girl, and were watched warily wherever we went, leaving us with an impression that the school's busy schedule left little room (or wish) for visitors. However, the lovely traditional old entrance hall, affectionately known as the Marble, soon warmed up at break times as girls poured out of lessons to chat and recharge their batteries. 'The atmosphere is one of considerable freedom – few rules and much humour,' observed a grateful parent.

When we arrived the great wooden doors were shut and, on our ringing the bell, swung silently open without any accompanying words of welcome

From the outside, SPGS nestles cosily in amongst what must be some of the best kept residential streets in London, quirkily suggestive of the school itself in their individuality and mix of classic charm and modern innovation. Inside, it's much bigger than it looks. New building, built over some former netball courts, offers superb accommodation for the senior school, including lounge areas, work stations, quiet study areas and some inviting seminar rooms.

From many windows, the view of exquisitely pretty back gardens in the surrounding houses gives a feeling of peace and normality amidst the scintillating academics, and as we walked away at 4pm we were touched to see a young Paulina buying an ice cream from the Tonibell van that had pulled up outside the school.

Glittering roll of alumni includes Celia Johnson, Rosalind Franklin, Victoria Coren Mitchell, Imogen Stubbs, Clemency Burton-Hill and Harriet Harman.

Pastoral care, inclusivity and discipline: Since the 1960s, no uniform, as befits a free and open-minded culture. Girls are trusted to dress sensibly, and they usually do. 'When I go to other schools, it's weird to see everyone looking the same,' commented one of our tour guides. Amazing canteen (it served as an air raid shelter during the war), decorated with photo exhibition of SPGS history, and the food was simply awesome – we had one of the best school lunches we'd ever been offered, and the girls we saw ate with gusto. Girls can arrive from 8am for breakfast, and must be here by 8.30am. Day finishes at 4pm, and long lunch break gives lots of time for clubs and societies. After school, girls are generally off site by 6pm.

Endearingly, some year 7 girls were given detentions for gatecrashing a senior school lecture, but otherwise there are few sanctions. 'Generally, we can deal with most things by talking. There are very few rules, so it's hard to break them.' Small tutor groups ensure the staff get to know the girls well. School denies the presence of drugs, eating disorders and self-harming, but several parents we spoke to were adamant that they can be found here, inevitably perhaps at such a selective school where some of the girls will be very highly-strung.

The school hit the headlines in November 2017, when an email from the drama department to Old Paulinas, soliciting stories of sexual abuse for a documentary-style drama inspired by the MeToo campaign, drew a furious response and resulted in a teacher resigning. The parents we spoke to, however, had nothing but praise for how Mrs Fletcher had handled the crisis, and emphasised how happy they were with the pastoral care provided. 'Both my daughters have been happy throughout their time at the school, and felt fully supported by the staff; the pastoral care was exemplary.' 'The pastoral care has been very good and the girls aren't stressed – my daughter has made some lovely friends.' 'I wish I had known before my daughter started at SPGS that all the rumours were untrue. I haven't seen any bitchiness, competitiveness, or a single eating disorder.'

Communication between school and parents is 'prompt, reliable and efficient', according to several sources.

Pupils and parents: Intake is 'increasingly international'. Many girls here speak more than one language and we heard a number of north Atlantic accents as we moved around the school. Families of Paulinas are typically highly-educated, professional, successful and very supportive of the school, giving generously of their time, money, expertise and connections. Parents' Guild works to raise funds, but has no input into the running of the school.

School is quite 'stratified', claimed one parent, 'between the cool girls and the geeks, but you can be who you want there and everyone mixes with everyone else.'

Money matters: One of the nation's most expensive day schools, but about 15 per cent of girls are on bursaries of between 85 and 100 per cent. School is working to increase access to these and to become 'as needs-blind as possible'.

The last word: For very bright, academically minded, hard-working, grounded and motivated girls, this is the best start in life imaginable. As one mother typically put it, 'For both my daughters it has been a truly wonderful experience and one that they feel lucky to have had.'

St Philip's School

6 Wetherby Place, London SW7 4NE

020 7373 3944 | office@stpschool.co.uk | www.stpschool.co.uk

Independent | Ages: 7–13 | Pupils: 110 | Fees: £17,475 pa

Headmaster: Since 2016, Alexander Wulffen-Thomas BA PGCE (30s). The suit, tie and polished shoes are neat, tidy and conservative but the first impression is that he might be happier outside (runs up the stairs at speed). Born in the wilds of West Yorkshire, one away from the tail end of a large family, brought up in Cheshire and schooled at St Ambrose Prep, St Ambrose College and then Stonyhurst. Read Russian – 'it's a country with a soul' – at Durham, then used his languages to find a job in the City. Left in his late 20s as it involved too much time in front of a computer screen dealing with dreary problems such as money laundering regulations and went to work at Westminster Cathedral Choir School, initially in an Evelyn Waugh-type role as a teaching all-rounder of history and games. Obviously more successful than the original as he landed the post of deputy head and then applied for the job at St Philip's, seeing it as a natural progression for someone with Catholic values and a leaning towards traditional teaching.

Married to Olivia; one dog – attends the school; no children as yet.

Entrance: The main intakes are at 7 (approximately 10 boys) and at 8 (another 10 boys). Usually three to four applicants for each place and mainly from local pre-prep and state schools as most of the boys live nearby. They are oversubscribed but make their choices based on teacher's impressions as well as academic potential; this is definitely not a hothouse school and they take in boys with minor learning difficulties as long as they can cope with the mainstream curriculum and routines. St Philip's does not hide the importance of its religious roots and the majority of boys are from Catholic families, often children or relations of previous pupils. However, the school is also catholic with a small c and about 10 per cent of the boys follow different faiths. When we asked some Catholic pupils whether this was ever awkward they responded convincingly in the negative, although possibly with a hint that the others might be missing out.

Exit: A minnow compared to some of its competitors in London, St Philip's rightly holds its head up high in the academic stakes, although its leader is emphatic that this is not a 'show-off school and the pupils' work does the talking'. Parents are helped to make the choice of 'where next' by an excellent app produced by the head, and most boys move on to their first-choice school. Of the 2020 leavers, half went to either Eton or City of London, with scholarships awarded at Bradfield (drama), City of London (sport) and Worth (music). Other popular destinations include Dulwich College, Harrow, KCS Wimbledon, Radley, St Paul's and Winchester.

Our view: Housed in a tall red-brick building in South Kensington, the only advertisement is a charming plaque depicting a very blue St Philip Neri, and you could easily miss the word underneath announcing that it is a school. The spiritual aspect remains very important and assembly in the morning tends to be RE with sporting analysis sandwiched between the opening prayer and the collect for the day (presumably when their horse was in training it also included prayers for the creature's chances in the 2.30 at Kempton).

On a hot day, the blazers hung neatly on the back of chairs and the old-fashioned desks were bare, lids firmly down

It is a logistical triumph that they fit 100+ boys into this space, but it may help the pupils to organise themselves as there is literally no room for discarded items of clothing or belongings. On a hot day, the blazers hung neatly on the back of chairs and the old-fashioned desks were bare, lids firmly down. We did look inside a few, with the head's permission, but nevertheless feeling rather guilty due to the Keep Out notice in one, and found the usual variety of orderliness but absolutely no sign of any illicit items. Outside, there is a communal garden, which ticks the fresh air box but results in sighs from all concerned as it comes with major drawbacks, such as a noise cap, which is not ideal for small boys wanting to let off steam.

An individual school from day one; not many of its rivals can boast having owned a racehorse or having had a headmaster who doubled up teaching the boys with acting as chauffeur at the beginning and end of the day. Mr Tibbits – the name in itself a joy – started the school as the result of a complaint by a priest at the Brompton Oratory about the sad lack of education for Catholics in the neighbourhood. He was an exceptional teacher but may have been helped by fortifying himself for the task with a glass of sherry before lunch and a glass of red wine with the cheese whilst the boys unhappily chewed their way through Spam and mash, followed by blancmange. Nowadays, this miserable experience – no-one was allowed to leave until the last plate was clean – has been superseded by packed lunches, but the very mildly eccentric atmosphere remains. Only two more headmasters bridged the gap between his death in 1967 and Alexander Wulffen-Thomas's arrival in 2016, and maybe for this reason the 21st century is slightly less in evidence than at some of its rivals.

A high proportion of the teachers have been here for a long time but there is young blood, the head intends to move from one to two 'gappies' next year and there's a new multi-talented deputy head. Parents and children speak very highly of the teachers, not only about their competence but also about their kindness, one small boy taking a great deal of trouble to explain – vocally and by mime – how one teacher gave you a minus mark but was 'really kind' whilst she was doing it. They believe in ensuring that the basic building blocks are carefully laid and regularly checked, with daily spelling and twice weekly maths tests in lower forms, and also encourage learning by heart through poetry competitions. Higher in the school all the teaching is praised but maths and Latin are exceptionally strong, and science may well benefit further when they are able to provide the intended new lab. There are 'no mountains of homework', but parents are relaxed and confident that their boys will do well.

Art is hugely popular, taught in a surprisingly bright and airy basement with one parent saying that her 'totally talentless' child kept returning with 'frankly miraculous' objects. Not afraid of the big time, pupils are entered in Royal College of Art competitions and 12 students had their work displayed recently. Music is an intrinsic part of life, from playing the piano at assembly to singing in the Schola, and all pupils are encouraged to play an instrument or sing, with up to half of them performing at the school concert.

Sport is important; possibly to compensate for the lack of space back at base, they have invested in acres of well-manicured games fields in Barnes where the whole school decamps on two afternoons a week, leading to boys having 'smiling faces when you pick them up after a games day'. Despite their tiny numbers they field teams that are not frightened of taking on larger boys from much larger schools and quite often succeed in beating them. Swimming is a weekly lesson and the boys have recently organised squash teams that play in tournaments at Queen's club. Most importantly, neither the boys or their parents seem worried that they will be at a disadvantage on the games pitch when they move on. On a daily basis, table tennis is played in the garden with a staggering number of boys whizzing round the table at any one time, and logically they are bound to turn out a champion at some point.

The spiritual aspect is important and morning assembly tends to be RE with sporting analysis sandwiched between the opening prayer and the collect for the day

Homework clubs take place every day with some of the choices being languages, judo, art and fencing, but Airfix was definitely the favoured option of both one very enthusiastic boy and the head. There is no impression that this is a 'strict' school but the boys jump to their feet when the head walks into a class with a crisp 'Morning, sir' and shake your hand, looking you straight in the eye. One parent, on being asked how they dealt with the inevitable small boy playing up, said that whilst discipline was not obvious, there were 'no hiding places; it's a tiny school in a tiny place'. When asked, the head told us that this was an advantage as every member of staff knew every child, which meant you could spot trouble and deal with it even before the boy was aware of it himself.

Lots of expeditions and a school skiing trip every year. On asking one boy whether he had learnt the history of Canterbury Cathedral at school before the impending visit, he replied,

'Well, it would be silly if we hadn't,' then 'St Thomas a Becket' accompanied by an excellent 'being stabbed' routine.

The SENCo is a form teacher who co-ordinates any help needed and specialists are called in from outside when parents and teachers have planned a course of action, one parent confirming that they 'get it' when you have a child who might have social problems.

The fees are low by London prep school standards, partly because of the no frills approach – boys bring their own packed lunches – and partly because they have not invested in a shiny new look. Current parents seem very laid back about this, feeling that the whole nature of the school might change if it presented a more polished exterior, a sentiment echoed by the head's wish to keep this as a 'discreet school that speaks for itself'.

Money matters: A bursary fund can accommodate discounts up to 100 per cent of the fees, with an independent financial auditor assessing all applications.

The last word: At somewhere both as small and individual as this it could be easy to overestimate the importance of the teaching staff, but St Philip would be proud of this lot and the boys they turn out – shiny halos all round.

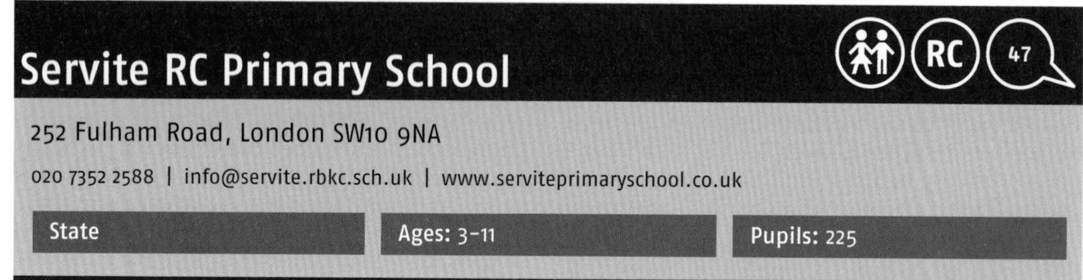

Servite RC Primary School

252 Fulham Road, London SW10 9NA

020 7352 2588 | info@servite.rbkc.sch.uk | www.serviteprimaryschool.co.uk

State | Ages: 3-11 | Pupils: 225

Executive head teacher: Since 2002, Kathleen Williams BEd NPQH (40s). Has spent all her teaching career in borough of Kensington and Chelsea. Previously deputy head of St Mary's Primary, Ladbroke Grove. Married with a young child, who (she hopes) will soon be a pupil here. 'I couldn't think of my son going anywhere else. I want him to have the grounded education which Servite provides,' she says. Loves theatre, opera and all things musical. Friendly, capable and calm; an experienced pair of hands. Servite works in partnership with less serene local schools, to help raise standards and strengthen leadership. Head is ably supported by associate head teacher, Claude Gauci, who takes over the reins when she is out nurturing other schools. They make a robust team. Head admits that teaching is a demanding profession, but 'we're lucky. It's a privilege to be part of this happy school.'

Entrance: At 3 to nursery but a separate application is required for entry into reception. If they don't meet the strict criteria, then nursery children don't make it through. Oversubscribed: approximately 60-80 apply for 30 places in nursery and 170-200 vie for 30 places in reception. Ever-decreasing catchment area (currently about half a mile). Pupils come predominantly from World's End estate and Earls Court. Priority given to baptised, practising Catholics who worship next door at Our Lady of Dolours. Occasional places further up school, though pretty rare due to low pupil mobility. V few non-Catholics. School currently at full capacity with 30 pupils per class.

Exit: Not a feeder for one particular school. Vast majority go to local Catholic state schools, including Cardinal Vaughan, Sacred Heart, St Thomas More and London Oratory, as well as a handful each year to Chelsea Academy. One or two go down the independent path, usually to Queen's Gate on bursaries. No special preparation given for 11+ and school seems to have escaped fanatical tutoring which goes on elsewhere in final years. A breath of fresh air.

Our view: This successful school is tucked away behind an unprepossessing façade on the Fulham Road, opposite Chelsea and Westminster Hospital. Surprisingly spacious once inside with large, light classrooms and three playgrounds for different year groups (the one for the smallest children particularly colourful and welcoming). Impressively large hall which transforms into a dining room, gym and theatre and boasts sophisticated lighting and sound equipment.

Head believes Servite offers a broad education, which encourages self-confidence and independence. Children are well prepared for life at secondary school by the time they leave.

'Servite gave my daughter the firm foundations on which to build,' said one grateful parent. Parents value the close association with the church that backs onto the playground. Pupils visit on holy days and every week one class celebrates mass there. Only three school rules – follow instructions; use kind and helpful words; keep hands, feet and objects to yourself. Pupils seemed to be adhering to these when we visited, though last rule appeared hardest to uphold.

Significant proportion of male teachers now. Staff consists of dedicated long-servers whose average age is 40. Appear devoted to the school and appreciate its family feel. 'They go the extra mile,' says head, 'and attend events at weekends such as school family mass with parents. No matter where the teachers live, they come to these events and the parents really appreciate it.' New teachers aren't taken on if they won't make a strong commitment to the school, beyond the classroom basics. Palpably strong relationships between teachers, parents and pupils. 'We have an open-door policy,' says head, 'but within a structure. Not mayhem! Boundaries are set in a respectful way and issues are dealt with quickly.' One parent said, 'The school is professional but understanding.' Problems tend not to fester for too long.

Academic standard has been raised and school now boasts impressive results. Able children are extended through creative writing groups and extra maths support. Some bright sparks achieve high levels in maths. Links fostered with Imperial College and Royal Institution to extend knowledge and develop scientific understanding. Spanish, music, dance and art taught by specialist teachers. Daily homework from the beginning. Project work given to older children to encourage effective time management and independent learning. School has pupils with a range of special needs, including autism, cerebral palsy and moderate specific learning difficulties. Behaviour support, learning support and pupil referral units offer considerable help to those in need. Currently five children with EHC plans.

School reflects the international, mixed community in which it finds itself. Head comments that many pupils come from 'poor, working families, where parents are often in domestic service.' Many families struggling but tend not to be on benefits. One in five pupils is entitled to free school meals. Roughly 60 per cent have English as a second language. Many pupils hail from Philippines, South America, East Africa and Western Europe. Main languages spoken at home are Spanish and Tagalog. Extra language support catered for through small targeted group work and some one-to-one support on offer. Parents happy with speedy progress made by those with limited English on arrival. 'Now you wouldn't know which ones were behind with English when they started,' commented one.

Fantastic, flexible wrap-around care on offer but school admits it's hard to sustain at a competitive price. Includes breakfast at start of day as well as tea, activities and opportunities to do homework at the end of the day. Children can be looked after from 8am-6pm. Parents aware they are lucky and are the envy of other schools nearby which don't have extended care on-site.

Only three school rules – follow instructions; use kind and helpful words; keep hands, feet and objects to yourself. Pupils seemed to be adhering to these when we visited

Impressive range of sport that is offered as taster sessions. Netball, football, athletics and swimming taught either on site, in Battersea Park or Chelsea baths. Dance and gym compulsory. A wide assortment of clubs including taekwondo, yoga, zumba and street dance. Football, drama and cooking currently very popular. Parents pay for these. Good use made of the local community and has strong links with neighbouring Chelsea Football Club. School participates in Educate through Sport initiative and an English reading programme offered by the club. Paul Canoville, first black player for Chelsea, regularly visits the school as part of its programme to promote positive attitudes towards racial diversity.

Excellent use made of its central London location. 'You name it, we've been there!' says associate head. From designing apparatus for Cirque du Soleil acrobats to jump over in the Albert Hall to PGL visits to Weymouth, the pupils have fun here. Parents pay for school trips, but school helps those who are genuinely struggling to meet the cost. School payment plan in operation and parents encouraged to save for trips on a weekly basis.

Impressive art, drama and music. Annual art show to which parents are invited. Fantastic, carved Viking longboats on display and amusing portraits done by pupils of the staff line the stairs. Christmas nativity put on by youngest children and year 5 performs the Passion at Easter. Two nights in July are devoted to a musical production, generally led by year 6 leavers, and about which parents rave. Years 1-6 learn a class instrument, including ocarina, violin and ukulele. Currently 75 taking one-to-one lessons in piano, violin or guitar.

Effective communication between school and parents via weekly newsletter. Parent council discusses initiatives such as school meals and uniform. Money raised by PTA tends to be spent on travel expenses for school trips, restocking library and equipment for playground.

The last word: School lives by its motto: 'Learning to love and loving to learn.' Family feel to the place. Children skip in each morning, excited about the day ahead. On the day we visited, ambulance sirens blared incessantly on the road outside while the children danced around merrily in the playground, totally oblivious to the noise and fumes engulfing them. Above all, a welcoming school. No wonder head won't be considering anywhere else for her son.

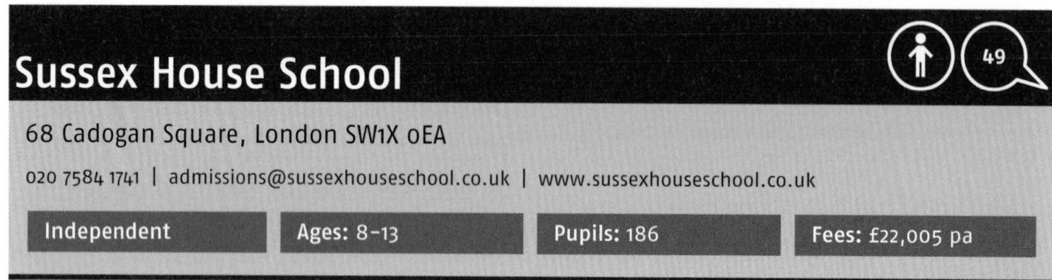

Sussex House School

68 Cadogan Square, London SW1X 0EA

020 7584 1741 | admissions@sussexhouseschool.co.uk | www.sussexhouseschool.co.uk

Independent | Ages: 8–13 | Pupils: 186 | Fees: £22,005 pa

Headmaster: Since 1994, Nicholas Kaye, MA Cantab FCOT, who was deputy head before that. As a founding trustee of Sussex House, he has more freedom than most heads to form the vision and direction of the school. Erudite and fun, he is a Cambridge graduate in English followed by music research. These passions are apparent in the school. He describes SH as a 'creative project', a non-profit-making charitable trust, with funds channelled into the school. 'If I am determined to have something, I can usually get it sorted by the end of the week,' he says.

Certain headmasters change pupils' lives, and Mr Kaye is one of them. He loves to educate, teaching the top year group English, where they explore Conrad, Dickens, Shakespeare and Graham Greene. A parent tells of a moment when, discussing how Dickens uses description in Great Expectations, he jumped up, put the boys in a taxi, and took them to a cobbled street in London so they could hear how noisy cobbles were. 'Children are not a separate species,' says Mr Kaye in the school magazine, 'they are adults writ small and, as such, it is our duty not to patronise them with limited expectations.'

Parents speak of his 'deep humanity', and his ability to understand the boys. They love the 'bespoke education' that the school provides. One boy, gifted musically but academically behind, was given a place after the head heard him play. Kaye said, 'If you can do that, I can educate you.' The boy went on to Eton, as so many SH boys do.

Mr Kaye presides from a study crammed with comfortable sofas, a pianoforte, a portrait of a St Bernard, a carved parrot and many books. He has created an idiosyncratic and personalised Arcadia where excellence is expected in all areas. He lectures on architecture, offers 'unfussy' bursaries for those that need them ('we look for the best pupil and honour them'), and negotiates a path between privilege and merit with grace and élan.

Entrance: There are 36 places at 8+, and approximately 160 boys sit the entry test which includes reasoning and perception papers that cannot be prepared for. All boys interviewed. They come from Wetherby, Garden House, Eaton House, Norland Place, Chelsea Christ Church and St Peter's Eaton Square. Getting in is 'not for faint-hearted', said one parent.

Exit: 'Easily our most popular boarding school is Eton and day school is Westminster (six in 2020), followed by Winchester, KCS and St Paul's – and Wellington for those who want co-ed,' says school. Fifteen to Eton, six to Westminster in 2020. Rest to eg City of London and Charterhouse. Frequent scholarships, often in music.

Our view: With only 184 pupils, Sussex House has a sharp classical syllabus, using music, art, and literature to achieve academic excellence at common entrance.

'Nothing is spared on the artistic or creative side,' declares Mr Kaye, and this is true. Music here is exceptional – international violin soloist Nicola Benedetti gave a masterclass recently – and boys perform annually with a professional orchestra at Cadogan Hall. Many have grade 8 distinctions – recently one achieved an ABRSM diploma – and 95 per cent play musical instruments or sing. There are 12 music staff, full-time and visiting.

As well as the Cadogan Hall concert, there are six annual concerts in the 'ballroom' and a host of other events, including regular church services (the school has a chaplain, and boys are churchwardens for St Simon Zelotes Church, which was transformed into a forest for last year's school production of A Midsummer Night's Dream). The boys perform Gilbert and Sullivan operas at the Fortune Theatre in Covent Garden and have an annual production of a Molière play in French. In 2019, they put on an original work written by the director of studies about the last meeting between Puccini and Toscanini, and a verse play called The Death and Life of Viscount Ballybunion – contributed by the head.

There is an annual exhibition of building models; the theme this year was West End, A Night on the Town. Each year group contributes (the younger boys did Chinatown, the older ones focused on Piccadilly and its environs) and creating some 30 detailed models of West End buildings, which were admired by visiting architect Quinlan Terry. The school is also strong in other areas of art, to judge by an exhibition of portraits in oils that hangs in one of the corridors.

The spirits of William Morris and John Ruskin hover over the Norman Shaw building redolent with arts and crafts and Pugin wallpaper (the original blocks were reconstituted to produce the Pugin wallpaper in the staffroom). The school is on two sites, 68 Cadogan Square and the Nicholls Hall, a converted mission hall in Cadogan Street, where a vaulted room houses a sports hall, and there are music practice rooms. The school is allowed to use Cadogan Square gardens for tennis and foot volley.

While outside space is limited, every boy spends two afternoons a week at Battersea sports fields, where football, tennis, cricket and fencing are all available, with an optional football club on Saturday. 'They can handle sports to county level,' said a parent. They have three fencing coaches, win both national and international awards, and claim to have produced more national champions than any other school in Britain in the last 25 years.

'There can be a lot of crossover between boys who are talented in both sports and arts,' observes the head; 'it's not unusual to find your best football player is also your best flautist.' However it is perhaps not the school for boisterous rugby types.

There is a good science lab, and a well-kitted-out computer room. The head says their highest recent CE marks were in maths and science, although when walking round the school we had the impression of more emphasis on the arts than on STEM.

'Teaching can't be faulted,' says one parent. Staff are chosen for 'talent and energy, and also something off-beat', and include poets, artists and musicians. They are also selected for the flow of talent among current boys. SH develops by evolution and fine tuning – they have a special niche and they stick to what works.

The atmosphere is intimate, with two classes of 18 boys for each year. In the final year the forms are split into three classes of 12, which include a scholarship group. Most pastoral matters are dealt with by the deputy head, and there is a part-time SENCo lead. All boys are screened for dyslexia, and about 14 boys are currently being supported for this.

'Nobody leaves at 11,' says the head. The main modern language is French, and there is a renaissance in Latin and Greek ('it's better taught now and the textbooks are better'). There are also Spanish and Mandarin clubs.

Mr Kaye presides from a study crammed with comfortable sofas, a pianoforte, a portrait of a St Bernard, a carved parrot and many books

There is no outside space for breaks, or a dining hall. Boys eat lunch brought from home at their desks. 'Not a problem,' says one parent, although others find it a fag.

The school fundraises for and has close links with the Asra Hawariat School in Addis Ababa, where the head is a trustee, and he also taught there briefly.

Parents tend to be very alpha, 'but it's not an oligarch school,' said one, although another spoke of the many 'smooth black cars at the school gate.'

Old boys include two runners-up for the Booker, and a host of actors, directors and musicians. Remarkably, some old boys return to the school just before sitting A levels for brush up sessions with their teachers. 'It's not a school you grow out of,' says the head.

Timetabling, described as 'subtle', is designed to give all boys the chance to do as much as possible, and to have opportunities to shine. 'I like to think there's room for everyone to star. We don't just showcase the same little group,' says the head, adding, 'Anyway, the boys know what is good.'

The last word: The boys seem engaged, and are very busy. One teacher observed that many of the boys were producing work at a level that would be expected of a year 12 or 13. In a typically SH appreciation of individuals, teachers recognise the disconnect between the boys' abilities and their ages and emotional understanding, and adapt the teaching.

Thomas Jones Primary School

St Mark's Road, London W11 1RQ

020 7727 1423 | info@tj.rbkc.sch.uk | www.thomasjonesschool.org

State | Ages: 3-11 | Pupils: 235

Head: Since 2001, Mr David Sellens OBE (for services to education), BA English, Goldsmiths (40s). Cut his teeth in teaching at New End Primary School in Hampstead, where he worked for five years as the youngest member of staff; 'I had a lot of energy, and the head at the time afforded me the luxury of opportunity.' His energy and enthusiasm swiftly saw him on the leadership team, at a time when the national curriculum was being implemented. However, feeling slightly constrained and wanting to do things his way, he started looking for a post where, he says, 'I could make a difference.' The role of deputy head came up at Ashburnham school and the young, enterprising Sellens, bursting with ideas, hotfooted it straight from artistic and aspirational Hampstead to a school south of the river in dire straits; 'I was suddenly thrust into an environment where results and aspirations were very low.' He and the new head, working closely together for sometimes up to 80 hour weeks, turned the school around over the next four years into Ofsted outstanding and awarded beacon status. Shortly afterwards, he was alerted to the fact that nearby Thomas Jones Primary School was on the verge of closure and, keen to become a head teacher, he applied for the post and promptly set about changing the fortunes of the school. Fourteen years on, he has exceeded the expectations of even the most optimistic.

In his second decade of tenure, Mr Sellens still appears like an enthusiastic and irrepressible newbie to the post. He is a hard man to pin down and his boundless energy sees him flit from one room to another, starting with the 8.45am meet and greet of all pupils and parents at the school gates; 'You'll like this,' he assures us; 'apologies if it gets a bit loud with the bell.' He describes his approach as radical rather than traditional. He teaches year 6 pupils English and says he doesn't pay 'too much attention' to the national curriculum. When asked if he sees himself as a bit of a maverick (after all, this is a head who walks into assembly eating a bowl of porridge and banana extolling the virtues of having a healthy breakfast, a head who ditches the traditional end of year musical, opting instead for Under Milk Wood), he says that although this comment has been levelled at him many times, he sees himself more as an individual who occasionally likes to 'buck the trend'.

Mr Sellens admits that he is 'incredibly fussy' about a lot of things. 'I'm fussy about [the state of] buildings, pupils' attire, their demeanour.' He also insists that pupils make eye contact with people and greet visitors with a handshake: 'He has meticulous attention to detail,' one parent told us. This head is also big on homework – year 6 pupils can do up to two hours a night. Even with this 'bossy' approach, he says that he doesn't face much protest from pupils or parents, as there is a sense that 'it is being done for all the right reasons and the outcome is extremely strong.' One pupil said he was 'controlling – but in a good way.'

Brought up on the south coast, Mr Sellens says he was the typical story of an 'industrious' child from a humble background who won a place at grammar school and worked hard to better his situation. He always carried with him a strong sense of social justice which is what motivates him daily; 'I want to give every pupil the opportunity to shine, to look back and think they don't have regrets and it doesn't matter what they do, as long as they enjoy doing it.' When asked if he has any children of his own, he replies 'no', then pauses, has a think and says, 'yes, 235 of them!'

Entrance: The catchment is so small for this one form primary school that you virtually have to live in the grounds to get in (we kid you not – one pupil who lives two doors away last year didn't qualify: such was the outcry, she eventually managed to secure a place). The head says he is sometimes overwhelmed by the number of prospective parents, 'some with children who have yet to be born'. Distance from the school is now measured from the centre of the school outwards (mostly therefore to those in the nearby housing estate and their siblings).

Exit: Mainly to the local comprehensives – Holland Park or new Kensington Aldridge Academy; some try to gain bursaries or scholarships to independent schools. In 2020, destinations included Notting Hill Prep and West London Free School.

Our view: There are primary schools, and then there's Thomas Jones Primary school. Former secretary of state for education Michael Gove has waxed lyrical about this school on many occasions, claiming in one speech that it offers a better education than nearby £20,000+ pa prep school which taught the heirs to the throne. He said: 'There are state primary schools every bit as ambitious, as supportive, as exciting, as the smartest of private prep schools – like for example, Thomas Jones Primary in west London.'

Named after Thomas Jones of North Carolina – a passionate crusader against the evils of slavery in the early part of the 19th century – this state primary in the borough of Kensington and Chelsea (a short walk from bustling Ladbroke Grove) is as true to its ideological namesake as it is to his inspirational work. By any stretch of the imagination it is a major achievement for a primary school serving a deprived inner city area to secure a rolling five-year average of over 99 per cent of children achieving level 4 and above in maths and English – about three-quarters achieving grade 5+ and a few achieving level 6 in maths (often top in the borough for both subjects). What makes Thomas Jones's achievement even more remarkable is that barely any pupils who sit the tests come from an indigenous English-speaking background, with one in three speaking Arabic as their first language. Moreover, 30 per cent of last year's cohort were on the SEN register.

Nowhere is London's diversity of culture or chasm of social inequality better highlighted than at this school. One side of the school (Lancaster Road) is flanked by grand period properties where a three bedroom maisonette can set you back a mere £2m. The other side (St Mark's Road entrance) is a stone's throw away from a large, austere housing estate, 'not fit for purpose' we are told, which accounts for roughly 70 per cent of the school's intake. More than half of the pupils live in difficult circumstances and are entitled to free school meals; some of them, we are told, 'don't own a desk and do their homework on an upturned tray or in the local library.' One parent we spoke to told us that the strength of the school is its diversity, 'and that it caters for all'.

There is nothing ordinary about this school – certainly not if one compares it to other inner city state primaries. The interior is so immaculate and shiny we could see our own reflection in the wooden parquet flooring and the walls looked as if they had been freshly painted; 'we keep them white so it's easy to match and cover any dirt marks.' When asked how they manage to keep a primary school of 230 children so unbelievably pristine, Mr Sellens tells us that the pupils demonstrate real pride in the school and often ask to be on the 'cleaning rota'. For a bog standard (architecturally speaking) 1970s prefab, as this school is from the outside, the inside came as quite a revelation. Light and bright 'to create an illusion of space', the open plan and organic design is quite remarkable both in terms of its functionality and aesthetics.

The artwork which adorned the walls had been carefully selected and beautifully displayed, and we were particularly struck by some stunningly creative models of castles made from toilet rolls and other household objects, displayed outside the year 3 classroom. We also liked a large, colourful mosaic of Elmer the elephant with a large caption reading 'It's good to be different.'

And then there are the candles! This most certainly was a first for us and we wondered whether this was part school and part holistic retreat. Large (glass-encased) scented candles, wafting scents of vanilla or lavender, flickered on teachers' desks in all classrooms bar the ones with the youngest pupils. The result was a calm, almost hypnotic ambience, 'the antithesis of what some students get at home,' the head told us. We even heard classical music (from Schindler's List) emanate from the year 6 classroom as they were in deep discussion about their current literature book. As Ofsted remarked, 'Immersion in the plays of Shakespeare and high quality literature, such as Lord of the Flies, has instilled in pupils a love of literature and has enabled them to reflect with confidence.'

We liked a large, colourful mosaic of Elmer the elephant with a large caption reading 'It's good to be different'

No doubt the school's recruitment policy has played some part in its outstanding achievement. Many teachers are recruited straight from university and stay for a few years before moving on, possibly to jobs outside London where they can more easily afford a home. 'Some of them are very talented, they are enthusiastic and idealistic… they want to teach in this type of environment – even if sometimes they don't stop for very long.' It is now a teaching school and can train its own. Sellens attributes the quality of what is afforded to pupils to his skilled and deft team and especially the deputy Lindsay Johnson, who exudes gravitas and energy. She has worked at the school for 20 years and is, in Sellens' words, 'the lynchpin of the school's success'.

We were taken on a tour of the school by six well-mannered, extremely articulate and very lovely pupils of varying ages, who each in turn solemnly shook our hands, looked us directly in the eye and said 'welcome to Thomas Jones primary school.' This editor couldn't have felt more revered if she were the Duchess of Cambridge. Pupils were as pristinely turned out as the school they inhabited. Hairclips and bobbles matched their uniform and we were hard pushed to find a strand of anything out of place. The head told us it is extremely important to him that all students look exactly the same and 'exquisite in their uniform, so there is no way of telling their background'. Those from deprived backgrounds can get help with the cost of the uniform.

Future plans for the school include a beehive, which the school says is its modest way of contributing to the ecosystem and 'teaching the pupils to care for something'. This will add to the existing mini outdoor nature reserve set amongst pretty, manicured gardens and (slightly sparse) play areas. Indeed, dare we say it, our one criticism of the school would be the lack of outdoor facilities (although we appreciate this is an inner city school) or much time given over to sports, which seems to be a criticism echoed by a couple of parents we spoke to. One told us: 'There's not much in the way of drama or sports at this school which is probably indicative of most state schools nowadays. Sadly, when schools are monitored so closely, something has to give.' However, netball, football and athletics teams, training after school, sometimes with professional coaches, have enjoyed significant successes in borough leagues in recent years.

Ofsted – which regularly rates the school as outstanding – has praised it for high aspirations: 'Year 6 pupils don white coats for science lessons and eagerly respond to the school's expectation that they are preparing for university.' We also noticed that pupils called their smart navy blue school bags their 'briefcases' and year 6 pupils are expected to pick up a daily newspaper, because as one former student told us, 'pupils need to experience language they don't normally use.' It is not unusual, according to Mr Sellens, to hear the children talking about going to university or becoming barristers or doctors when they leave school.

The last word: Everything about this school is aspirational. You won't find a 'home corner' filled with dolls, cookers or microwaves in the gorgeous and colourful nursery. Instead there is a medical corner filled with realistic medical apparatus and costumes. Similarly, we loved the weekly interchangeable corner in reception which encouraged playing various professional roles such as doctor or teacher. It has a gold healthy schools award and year 4 children were recently treated to a trip to a Jamie Oliver restaurant and have been learning how to make sushi wraps using healthy ingredients – and fish fingers and baked beans are banned from the school menu because 'we want to afford them food they wouldn't get at home.'

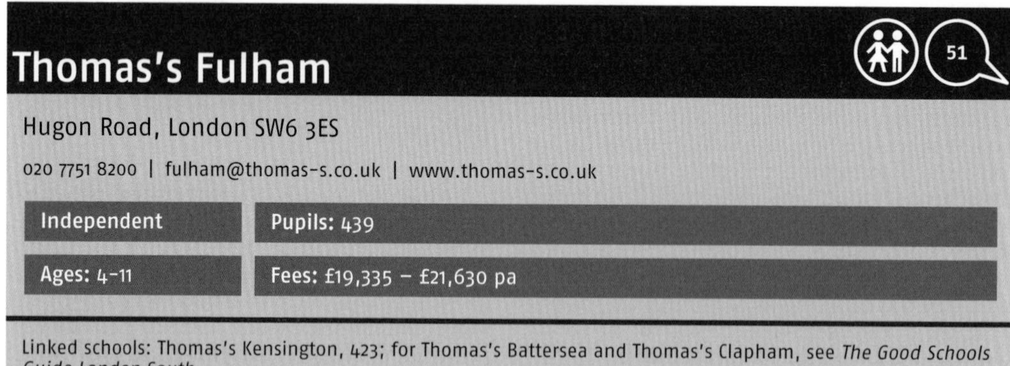

Thomas's Fulham

51

Hugon Road, London SW6 3ES

020 7751 8200 | fulham@thomas-s.co.uk | www.thomas-s.co.uk

Independent	Pupils: 439
Ages: 4–11	Fees: £19,335 – £21,630 pa

Linked schools: Thomas's Kensington, 423; for Thomas's Battersea and Thomas's Clapham, see *The Good Schools Guide London South*

Headmistress: Annette Dobson, 40s, opened the school in 2005. A slightly low key dresser with a laugh that reaches her eyes, one only has to look at her feet to see that snappy shoes and clear-headed dedication are not the sole preserve of Theresa May. Wanting to be a teacher from the get-go (maybe influenced by her mother's voice teaching in an adjacent classroom), she swam into the professional A stream by graduating from Homerton College, Cambridge. After a spell at North Bridge House, she crossed London to Thomas's Clapham, heading up the lower school, collecting a postgraduate degree and completing a study in phonics.

Thoroughly aware of the need to keep abreast of the numerous practical and technological changes in her world, she still keeps her feet firmly in the playground by maintaining a close, personal involvement with each child. On Monday mornings she stands by the door and shakes them all by the hand and, far more amazingly, remembers their names, a nice touch that illustrates the emphasis she puts on manners as well as her commitment to approaching her charges as individuals. Genuinely passionate about improving her school, she even spent her sabbatical visiting educational establishments around the world, although luckily she shows her human side by admitting to having eaten pretty well along the way.

Entrance: It's no longer necessary to have the admissions office on speed dial from the delivery room – registration now takes place when the child is between one and two years old, three years prior to entry. At 4+, a non-academic assessment takes place in January for September entry. Eleven years of experience makes the head fairly certain about the kind of child that would or would not relish the opportunity of beginning their education here. She is tactful but clear that it is potential team players as well as bright individuals she is looking out for. There is a strong sibling policy (on average about half the slots go to siblings), which usually leaves a minimum of two children applying for each remaining place. Parents can feel very pressurised; one observer said that a 'parent was completely manic to get child in', but the process is fair with advance information for parents, and one child came out saying, 'I like this big school.' Places do become available further up the school, mainly due to the constant whirling merry-go-round that lands London parents anywhere from Manhattan to Moscow at the drop of a city chapeau. At this stage, children spend half a day at the school to make sure they will fit in and also need a letter from their previous school.

All change for 2021 entry, though, due to COVID, when school will operate a ballot system for reception (not a permanent change).

Exit: As you would expect from such a professional outfit, detailed practical information and knowledgeable help on the which, when and how of senior schools is handed out to help parents navigate this educational minefield. In 2020, over a third of pupils moved at the end of year 6 to Thomas's Clapham to prepare for the 13+. Others to a variety of schools, including Thomas's Battersea, King's College School, Putney High, Emanuel, Francis Holland, Wimbledon High School, Harrodian, St Paul's Boys', Latymer, Ibstock, Epsom College, Benenden, Ardingly, Lady Margaret's, Fulham Boys' School.

Scholarships are won but head confirms that there are not many available at 11+, and this is not an academic hothouse, a point echoed by one parent who felt that a very clever child might not get as far here as in a more competitive environment. Parents seem pleased with the advice given on senior schools and the head's statement that they 'aim to work in tandem with parents to find the best fit for a pupil' is backed up by the results. Thomas's Senior School is opening in September 2021.

Our view: This youngest outpost of Thomas's private empire has settled in a handsome Victorian school building, gazing out over the top of a smart new asphalt athletics field at the green park beyond. Nineteenth century it may be, but with sparkling two-tone brick, huge windows and a tidy colour-coded interior, this is definitely not a modern version of Dotheboys Hall and there is absolutely no air of laissez-aller neglect: in fact the energy and enthusiasm of the school is almost instantly apparent.

Nineteenth century it may be, but this is definitely not a modern version of Dotheboys Hall and there is absolutely no air of laissez-aller neglect

With walls covered in pictures from an exceptionally imaginative art department housed in a large beamed outbuilding and neat, well-conceived timetables for music and games on the stairs, the atmosphere is vibrant. Happy, eager children look you straight in the eye and teachers appear to be enjoying themselves as much as their pupils. Judging by the cheerful munching of buns at break and excellent reports from the head girl, the food served on primary coloured plates (matching the house colours) keeps the energy levels up through a satisfyingly full school day.

Particular praise is handed out by parents of reception teachers, one commenting that her child coming into the school with zero skills did 'really well in her first year' and others saying that almost all the class are pretty independent, at least at the laces tying end of the scale, by the end of the year. All the way up reading is heavily encouraged, with pupils taking home a daily diary including a book page that parents have to sign off. A library complete with cheerful librarian is nestled under the roof. Maths is taught imaginatively, not just as learning numbers but as a link to other subjects, and science appears to be popular, apparently due to explosion experiments, luckily under control in two purpose-built labs.

French is introduced in reception and croissants and conversation feature in a biennial French day in Fulham and a week's trip to France for year 6. History and geography are both taught with the emphasis on connections to the outside world, and with classics added in years 5 and 6, round out the rest of the curriculum. Like most schools with an ecumenical viewpoint, RE is taught from a moral guideline and historical angle.

The arts – particularly music and drama – form a central part of life, over half the children learn an instrument and nearly three-quarters sing in a choir. Very popular plays are put on in the school's own theatre by all year groups, and after-school or lunch time clubs encourage would-be gymnasts, thespians, musicians and ballet dancers to go further and take external exams, such as LAMDA and the Royal Ballet School. All children, including those whose idea of art is to splash a lot of paint about (actively encouraged last year by a gigantic Jackson Pollock themed bonanza) are able to learn the fun that can be had out of being creative.

'We love off-piste children here, they are so often better at problem solving.' The head reckons that it is part of her job to help find the solution to each child's difficulties

Despite the practical problems of operating on a small campus set in bricked over West London, the head (a fresh air fiend) runs the full mile to bring the outdoors into the pupil's daily routine. Little ones do PE and ballet, in the lower school they have general games and later on they can pick from a wide offering of conventional single sex sports. Some take place in the park opposite, which is regularly filled with small people jauntily dressed in the school's red and blue uniform complete with stripey socks. Otherwise they walk or are bussed to nearby facilities, a necessary evil for London schools and which makes the head look longingly at the space available to her peers in the country. Despite the logistical problems, there is enthusiasm all round about games, both competitive and recreational, and particular pleasure when a team beats other schools in the group. Sporty children can choose further exposure by joining popular extracurricular clubs for gym or judo, golf or tennis, while swimming, sailing and kayaking are available if they want to get wet. Classroom themes regularly incorporate outside expeditions, both in London and further afield, often with the help of the Exploration Society to give them a more adventurous time away from the tarmac. Recently launched 'Thomas's Outdoors Programme', includes week-long visits in Lent term for year 5 and 6 children from all the schools to Thomas's Daheim, school's new 'mountain outpost' in Upper Austria.

Takes an early warning approach, starting in reception, to spotting any learning problems, which are jumped on quickly by full-time staff, backed up by specialist help from the outside. The head, who used to teach in this field, reckons that it is part of her job – 'we love off-piste children here, they are so often better at problem solving' – to help find the solution to each child's difficulties. Equally, she feels that tutors should only be employed to mend a particular gap in the wall rather than act as structural engineers, a policy which can be hard to get across in a city full of aspirational parents. Rules clearly exist but are wisely enough applied to make for few confrontations and the vice-head is on standby to have words with the inevitable, occasional small child trying it on. All of year 6 are encouraged to take a responsible role and show particular pride in overseeing the playground, although they sensibly admitted that they grabbed a teacher pretty quickly if anyone looked in need of first aid.

Twenty-first century technology connects parents, described as cosmopolitan, via a Twitter feed, and a newly updated portal allows them to follow their child's every move. Most of the content is popular (particularly the photographs), but one parent remarked that she preferred talking to the teacher rather than looking at her boy's exploits on an iPad. The head, however, convincingly counters this by saying that she will never allow face-to-face contact between teachers and parents to be lost. In another minor quibble a mother said that she was probably old fashioned but found receiving online reports irritating, as she likes to keep the real thing. An unsurprisingly lively PTA backs up the school and works its socks off to raise money for charity with the Bake Sale streaking home in the popularity stakes. Thomas's ethos to 'give not take' seems to have sunk in well as children often donate a book to the library to mark their birthdays and sometimes turn up with money for charity that they have raised off their own bat. Outreach programme now includes regular intergenerational activities for reception classes with local Age UK groups.

The last word: Promoting the Thomas's motto Be Kind quite so prominently could have backfired, but the evidence of the success of the strategy is everywhere. From the top ('fabulous, fantastic head') to the bottom (smiley children leaving the assessment clutching balloons), this is a school that really does succeed in doing what it says on the shiny tin.

Thomas's Kensington

17-19 Cottesmore Gardens, London W8 5PR

020 7361 6500 | kenregistrar@thomas-s.co.uk | www.thomas-s.co.uk

Independent | Pupils: 397

Ages: 4-11 | Fees: £22,185 - £23,550 pa

Linked schools: Thomas's Fulham, 420; for Thomas's Battersea and Thomas's Clapham, see *The Good Schools Guide London South*

Headmistress: Since 2012, Jo Ebner BEd MA PG Dip Couns Cert FT NPQH (late 40s), previously head of the Royal School, Hampstead (now absorbed by North Bridge House and owned by Cognita); 'I got the school to a place where it was worth buying,' she says. Educated at North London Collegiate (where both her mother and her daughters were at school too) and Homerton, Cambridge, she also trained at the Tavistock Clinic as a school counsellor and completed her MA at the Institute of Education, London. Tall and statuesque, Miss Ebner has long brown, lustrous hair, is highly emotionally intelligent, with a self-deprecating sense of humour. She has three children – now in or approaching their 20s – and shares her comfortable office with her adoring golden retriever, Maddie.

Her first teaching job was at Primrose Hill primary school ('from the age of 7, I was determined to be a teacher,' she avers). She set up the first counselling service when she was at South Hampstead High School. She also taught at a primary school in Willesden and at the North West London Jewish Day School as well as a successful stint as deputy head of The Hall junior school in Hampstead. A deeply committed educationalist, she is heavily involved with the GSA (Girls' Schools Association), serves as a governor of several schools, including St Mary's Ascot, and has written several articles on parenting.

One of the first things Miss Ebner did here was to remove the position of lower school head. She is very much in charge of the whole school. While she operates an open door policy and parents praise her direct approach when dealing one to one, her reputation at the moment is that she can be distant, 'certainly not cuddly,' observed one, but 'very cheerful, involved and approachable,' said another. She teaches religious studies to year 2, and set up a mindfulness course for parents, staff and pupils – 'it is really helpful in the run up to exams,' she confides. She regards communication as being vital, 'the bottom line, as with any relationship, is that it's about trust.' A transparent approach will nip things in the bud so she makes herself available – parents can drop in to discuss any issues with her. However, she doesn't cosy up to them – avoiding the dinner party circuit so that she can remain objective about what is in the best interests of their children.

Passionate about investing in her staff and striving for the highest quality of teaching, whether through further professional development or promotion, she is regarded by parents as having made shrewd recruitments as well as keeping good teachers and teaching assistants who mature and develop under her leadership. Her teachers value her big picture approach to their futures and the encouragement she gives for them to seize opportunities. She set up a bespoke masters programme for all Thomas's staff, in conjunction with Roehampton University. At the time of our visit a few teachers doing this masters programme were enthusing about their research on, eg, the pros and cons of setting.

Entrance: Three classes of 20 (split 50:50 boys and girls), so in theory, 60 places at reception. However siblings take priority (though will only take siblings they think will thrive) so you should expect only about half that number of places. Over 100 tinies are interviewed the year before entrance. They are not looking for children who have been tutored and prepped but who are adaptable, willing to get stuck in and have plenty of initiative. The pace is fast here and your child is likely to have a number of different teachers during a typical day. Register at birth to be sure that you get on a list for assessment. Once the list reaches 180 it will close and your only chance will be a waiting list place, currently limited to 50 names. Occasional places rarely arise but there are formal assessments at 7+ and 8+, where school will consider applications from up to 10 children for each of years 3 and 4. School only ever offers a couple of places at this stage.

Exit: There is an option to continue to Thomas's Battersea from 11 to 13 and about a third choose to do this, mostly boys, and girls who are going down the boarding route – automatic transfer, subject to the head's recommendation. Some of these have been successful at the pre-test during year 6 and are armed with offers from top 13+ schools from King's Wimbledon and St Paul's to Eton and Winchester. Lots of help and preparation to ensure the transition is smooth, as despite being part of the Thomas's group, they are different schools with a different make up and transition isn't necessarily seamless. Battersea teachers come to the school to meet the children who are moving, and a number of events are organised to help with integration, from games in the park to cupcake decorating, as well as coffee mornings and drinks parties for the parents.

Children here fizz with energy that a highly dedicated team of teachers channels very successfully. Thomas's kids are exuberant, confident and very, very busy

Otherwise a range of schools as one would expect as there is a broad range of ability here. Latymer Upper and Godolphin & Latymer currently very popular, followed by the American School, Francis Holland SW1, Queen's Gate and St Paul's boys' and girls'. A cluster of academic scholarships as well as the odd music and drama scholarship each year.

Miss Ebner makes it clear that the school does not prepare pupils for 7/8+. If you want your son to apply to St Paul's Juniors, Westminster Under etc, you're on your own – the school will not do any extra preparation. Boys do still occasionally leave at 7 or 8 to go to these schools – it's not impossible – but it is not something the school will actively encourage.

Senior school opening in September 2021 – Thomas's Battersea Square.

Our view: A stimulating, creative but also nurturing school in a very fashionable corner of London, Thomas's Kensington has a cosmopolitan flavour to it without being flashy or ostentatious. Children here are privileged but not spoilt, and fizzing with energy that a highly dedicated team of teachers channels very successfully. Thomas's kids are exuberant, confident and very, very busy. Lots of drama perhaps contributes to their looking you in the eye and explaining things with an articulate awareness that belies their young age.

Situated on three sites in a leafy, salubrious triangle of elegant properties at the south west corner of Hyde Park, Thomas's Kensington was the first school in the Thomas's quadrumvirate (the others are Clapham, Battersea and Fulham). Founded by Joanna and David Thomas in the early '70s and the family members are still the proprietors. Their two sons, Ben and Tobyn, are heavily involved as joint principals. Joanna and David, who have a flat above the junior section of the school in Victoria Road, are still very present around the school. The involvement of such a charismatic family and their wholehearted dedication to the place gives it a distinctive, family feel. Joanna and David Thomas are highly respected among the parents who generously donate to the CAIRN trust, a charity they set up to educate children in Nepal.

All three buildings are elegant, spacious and well looked after. Reception children enter the junior section on Victoria Road thorough a little passageway and wooden gate into a secluded garden and play area. Lots of scooters and bikes parked inside the black wrought iron gates of the pale blue painted Georgian mansion. Most kids live close enough to walk and scoot so there is a refreshing lack of Chelsea tractors at drop off. Lots of fresh air for all; the little ones are split into small groups from each class at playtime and spill out into the little Astroturf courtyard between the reception classrooms. This is just one example of how the classes are mixed up here so that friendships can be refreshingly fluid betwixt classes. From year 1 they walk 10 minutes to Kensington Gardens for fresh air and exercise.

School is mixed ability – assessments for entry are not primarily focused on any kind of academic prowess. This, and the tendency to take siblings, makes for a broad range. Lots of focus on reading. Children are listened to four times a week and a 'mystery reader' regularly turns up at school. To one child's (and his father's) enormous delight one week the mystery reader was his grandfather reading via Skype from the USA. Any difficulties are picked up quickly by class teachers and any special educational need is coordinated by the SENCo and her team. Parents praise the school's responsiveness when support is required, and an occupational therapist as well as a speech and language therapist come regularly into school. A number of children go to the Kensington Dyslexia Teaching Centre (just around the corner). Controversially, school made the decision to teach mixed ability maths and English groups all through the school until year

5. The decision was made partly as a result of the masters research that one of the teachers is doing at Roehampton. The evidence apparently suggests that setting is not beneficial to either the less or the more able students. A number of parents of able mathematicians are not supportive, parents of children who are not at the top of the game are more open to the idea. School says the research is still ongoing. French is setted – some strong French speakers in the school. Spanish and German offered as after-school clubs (parents recently requested Italian, so this is to be introduced). Latin taster in year 4 and then taught as part of the curriculum in years 5 and 6.

The creative and performing arts and sport are all given a lot of emphasis here and the school positively hums with activity beyond the classroom. Thomas's children stand out as being sparky and articulate, and the extensive drama and dance provision must play some part in this. All children, girls and boys, do ballet during their lower school years. Chelsea Ballet comes to the school to teach pupils once a week. Each year group puts on a large-scale production in the theatre. We watched year 4's fabulous production of Aladdin – worthy of any professional production, complete with tiered seating and first class lighting as well as stunning costumes. Watched by parents, staff and pupils, but what was particularly noticeable was the warm support of fellow pupils, one year 6 boy spontaneously rising to his feet to make a congratulatory speech at the end of the show. Year 6 was due to perform Arabian Nights at Imperial College. Music also flourishes – everyone given a violin to learn in years 1 and 2. A number of groups and choirs to participate in, including a full orchestra and a chapel choir. Concerts are performed at the Cadogan Hall as well as on site. Lots of sporting fixtures – primarily against the other Thomas's schools, but others too, eg Fulham Prep. Main sports – netball, hockey and rounders for the girls, football and cricket for the boys, plus tennis for both in the summer term. Parents praise the inclusive approach – children are encouraged in music and athletics, for example, even though they might not be showing a particular talent.

Even more impressive than the wealth of opportunity within the school is how much energy is put into a community spirit and to giving something back. From the CAIRN charity – Joanna and David Thomas's baby – supporting children in schools in Nepal, to various outreach programmes in local state schools, children here are busy raising money or sharing resources and thereby instilling and being instilled with a sense of public responsibility, generosity and kindness. Independent-state school partnerships have been established eg providing and teaching Latin in local state schools, collaboration between orchestras and choirs, and whole school community days when children from each year group carry out various projects in the community from reading to local nurseries to art, drama and music productions. The TSF (Thomas's Schools Foundation) is focused on working with local state schools, to widen educational opportunity and to provide bursaries. Joanna and David, together with Ben and Tobyn, are all actively involved in leading the whole school community to support the Foundation.

The last word: A remarkably cohesive and vibrant school. Bubbly children that are nevertheless polite and well behaved; 'It can be noisy,' acknowleged one parent, 'but with laughter not screaming.' Privileged, yes, but spoilt, absolutely not. These children are developing a strong sense of social responsibility and couldn't be better prepared for the complex global environment they are growing up into.

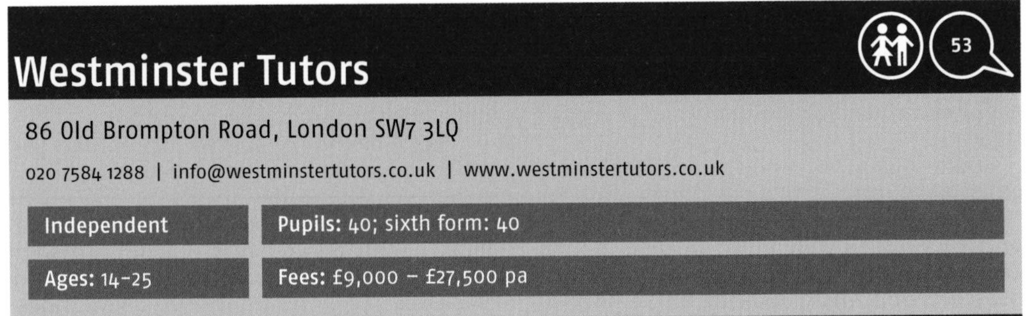

Westminster Tutors

53

86 Old Brompton Road, London SW7 3LQ

020 7584 1288 | info@westminstertutors.co.uk | www.westminstertutors.co.uk

Independent	Pupils: 40; sixth form: 40
Ages: 14–25	Fees: £9,000 – £27,500 pa

Principal: Since September 2020, former vice principal Joe Mattei. Joined Westminster Tutors in 2014 as an English tutor and SEND mentor. Recently completed a master's in special and inclusive education (Institute of Education UCL), his research project was on using a novel interventionary method (network analysis) to reduce anxiety for autistic students. Enjoys live theatre and music, cinema, literature, sports and travel.

Entrance: This is a totally non-selective school but the majority of the intake are above average academically. They may have found it difficult to succeed in the competitive world of a large, hothouse London day school or have come from another educational system. The head interviews parents and potential students and considers whether they would be suited to this very individual environment as well as their previous academic performance. They do not take students who have been expelled for serious breaches but are sympathetic to anyone who might have struggled to stay afloat in a larger pond.

Exit: The school tries to give very personalised university and career advice and is proud that they publish the destinations in full rather than just choosing the highlights. Around three-quarters to Russell Group. One student to Oxbridge in 2020, and one to study dentistry. The majority of people choose the school because they want to make a successful transition from A levels to a top university but this is not always the case, and recently one student left to do a BTec in mechanical engineering and one to a retail apprenticeship because it was agreed that this was a better route for them. Parents agree that they are 'on the money' about university choices and come up with good suggestions to add to their children's ideas.

Latest results: In 2020, 68 per cent A*/A at A level (92 per cent A*-B). In 2019 (the last year when exams took place), 64 per cent A*/A at A level (86 per cent A*-B).

Teaching and learning: There is a maximum capacity of 45 students of whom, in any given year, there are likely to be about five doing GCSEs (including retakes), about 20 taking A levels and 15-20 doing A level retakes. Occasionally, they enrol people in their 20s who need to take different or extra qualifications for career or further study.

Occasionally the students are taught in a group (three maximum) if their target levels are the same, but almost all the teaching is one-to-one. They offer a wide range of subjects from classical Greek to physics and psychology and the school prides itself on being able to cater for obscure requests. For the more obvious subjects there is a pool of tutors and the head personally makes the match between pupil and teacher. One parent asked if the tutor could be changed if the relationship didn't work and believed it when she was told that it wouldn't be a problem, although luckily the situation never arose.

The school may be diminutive in terms of pupil numbers but in the quality of its staff it rates as a Titan. The teachers tend to be stars in their fields with a level of letters after their names that would make most of their profession blush. School recruits mainly by word of mouth and from direct applications, mixing very high-powered people close to retirement or only wanting to work part-time with younger artists, musicians, writers and PhD candidates. The only rule is that they must have a 2:1 or first in their first degree; however this year, 40 per cent have Oxbridge degrees, 70 per cent masters and 35 per cent already have PhDs. The average period that they work here is three or four years but they often come back at different points in their careers.

They combat the lure of Xbox and Netflix by constant communication with parents so even potentially wayward students switch from sci-fi movies to science homework

Each student has an individual timetable and the system is immensely flexible, making it a logistics nightmare for the smiley, hugely competent college secretary, who has been struggling with spreadsheets for over 10 years. The students all praised the teaching and describe the tutors as being 'really on top of it' and one parent described it as 'brilliant across the board, all A*s'. Parents liked the 'old-fashioned, comprehensive reports that offer an accurate assessment with no false promises' and felt 'confident that we know where we are'. A pupil agreed that the report was fair and highlighted the areas where she needed to progress. One girl described a teacher as 'she knows what she's doing' (presumably a relief to her parents…) and other students talked about great personal attention such as being emailed in the holidays if they voiced a worry.

They efficiently combat the lure of Xbox and Netflix by constant communication with parents so that even potentially wayward students switch from sci-fi movies to science homework. GCSE pupils have homework diaries and if necessary A level students have study slots built into their timetables. The net result of this highly individual (in every sense) and carefully monitored approach is results that exceed those of their competitors in the tutorial field and are impressive by any measure. Recently rated outstanding in all categories by Ofsted.

The teachers tend to be stars in their fields with a quantity of letters after their names that would make most of their profession blush

The arts and extracurricular: All art, music, English and humanities students have tutorial guides who often include lessons in the real world of art galleries, concerts and stage performances.

Sport: Bearing in mind that the school is above a row of shops in central London with no outside space and that the 40 odd students are not all here on a daily basis, it will not come as a surprise that sports do not feature as a significant part of the curriculum. There is a circuit training session once a week but almost all other outdoor activities are organised by the parents or the children themselves, with a staff versus students bowling outing as the only competitive event that we found.

Ethos and heritage: Although it has the legal status of a school and has to abide by the same rules as its much larger competitors, head is happy that there is not a 'schooly atmosphere'. This is hardly surprising given the nature and appearance of its founder. Miss Freeston inhabited a smoke-filled den in Victoria, giving the distinct impression that there might be a bed hidden under either the piles of books launching an attack on the ceiling or the ancient, smelly dogs on the hairy sofa. You might have thought she was just a parody of a mid-20th century female academic, particularly as she always wore a mid-calf, much sat-in tweed skirt and layers of doubtful moth-eaten cardigans. However, you would have been foolish to underestimate her ability to understand people as well as texts. The exterior may have presented the unmistakable combination of erudition and dottiness, but under the holey woollens was a sensitive, thoughtful woman with a formidable understanding of bright, if lost, teenage girls. It was for this reason as much as her belief in the value of education that she started Westminster Tutors in 1934.

The school has kept the same ethos and atmosphere despite its move to South Kensington and the current building is still more of a rabbit warren than a conventional educational space. It might not impress parents or students looking for a polished, modern environment and it is not for teenagers needing wide open spaces. It is quite clear that the money goes on the staff and not on the classrooms: for instance, chemistry experiments take place in a galley kitchen. This slightly unusual classroom surprisingly passed an inspection from the A level boards with flying colours and without any culinary or chemical disasters. Orchids, a guitar and a chess set might not be what you expect in a tiny maths classroom but you probably would not expect a teacher who is also finishing a doctorate, either.

Pastoral care, inclusivity and discipline: The pastoral care is described by Ofsted as excellent in 'spiritual, moral, social and cultural' areas. Several parents remarked on the quick response they received if they contacted the school. The only hard and fast rules are attendance and safety, both of which are seldom a problem. The school reserves the right not to enter students for exams but says that the threat has always been sufficient so far. The only odd rule that it is enforcing at the moment is banning them from sitting on the strange red sofa outside the café opposite, presumably due to the smokey nature of its usual occupants.

There is an elected head boy and head girl but they admit that their duties are mainly social, including that 'we have enough milk for tea'.

Pupils and parents: Over 50 per cent of the enrolments are by word of mouth, including a large number of alumni who want their children to have the same experience. A parent told us that they had chosen the school over similar options because the alternatives felt like 'crammers and were run on military lines'. He also said that he was 'happy coming into a place covered in modern art, and it just felt right'.

Although it has the legal status of a school and has to abide by the rules, head is happy that there is not a 'schooly atmosphere'

The intake tends to come from a mixture of top public schools and London state schools with a fair sprinkling from abroad as the transition can be handled more easily in an operation where teaching provision is adaptable. One student told us that it suited her better than her previous school because 'you can't just hide at the back'.

There is no obvious archetypal parent although most tend to be successful in their fields or professions. It can be an option for parents of fairly modest means as some pupils only need to attend for a year to get back on track or be helped into a top university.

Money matters: Inevitably not a cheap option but compared to alternatives with larger classes it offers value for money.

The last word: Students are shoehorned into tiny classrooms, reminiscent of the dormouse being stuffed into the teapot at the Mad Hatter's Tea Party, and there is definitely an element of the unusual in the workings of this place but there is also an academic wizard at play here. Some may hanker after a swimming pool but the students lack for nothing in the level of teaching or encouragement in learning how to learn.

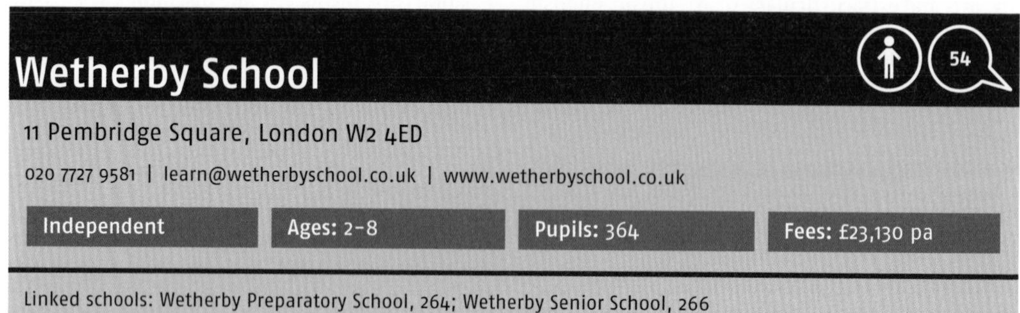

Head: Since 2009, Mark Snell BA PGCE (mid 40s). Educated at Eastbourne College, University of Westminster (a degree in business studies) and Brighton University, where he gained his teaching qualification. His first job was at Eaton House the Manor. Utterly down to earth, direct, no nonsense and unpretentious (although one parent observed that his 'oikishness verges on the pretentious given his background'). With his buzz cut hair style and his gruff manner, Mr Snell is so robust and hearty he could pass for the manager of a medium sized football club. He is also deeply committed and completely devoted to the boys and their needs. 'I enjoy life and don't give a stuff what anyone thinks of me,' he says. Most parents love him ('he still makes time to for me to discuss my son even though he's no longer at the school') though a few dissenters bemoan his encouragement of the alpha in these already uber alpha boys.

Deputy for two years before taking over as head, he is completely au fait with the ethos of the place and is hugely respected by his fellow Alpha Plus heads. ('Nick Baker is a great bloke,' he says. Nick Baker – head of Wetherby Prep – thinks the same of Mark Snell, though he put it slightly differently.) Previously head of maths at King's College Wimbledon, and prior to that he taught at Westminster Under where, he says, he really cut his teeth and learnt a lot of what he knows now ('though I'm thick as two short planks,' he repeatedly assured us). Despite his 'street' manner, he was born into prep school aristocracy and teaching is very much in the blood. He was brought up in a south coast prep school with his three siblings. His father inherited and ran Mowden School near Brighton (now a prep school to Lancing College), and the wider family are involved with Ludgrove Prep School (in Berkshire). His wife also teaches ('though she is much cleverer than me'). They have a son and a daughter, both school age.

His subject is maths, and though he kept telling us how dim he is, he had us stumped on more than one occasion as so many of his explanations were put in arithmetic form and he relishes statistics. Teaches maths to years 3 and 2, and loves it, he says. An added advantage is that he really knows each individual and can give informed advice on where next. 'If parents choose not to listen, that's fine,' he says; 'that's their prerogative, but I know the schools, understand the assessment data, and I know the boys.' Very accessible – to the boys especially, but to parents too. Many spoke of their complete confidence in him, his judgment, and his recruitment of teachers ('you feel confident that he will never employ a duff,' enthused one parent). A loyal Seagulls fan, his faux wood panelled study (a present from parents, along with most of the colourful decorations) has several Brighton and Hove flags and memorabilia and is brimming with evidence of his personality and the affection families past and present have for him.

Entrance: Non-selective. Register the month your baby is born, and ideally the day he is born. If you try to register any later than when your baby is 3 months old, you're too late. School gets approximately 35 applications a month – or about 360 a year for 88 places (four classes in each year group). Staggered entry by the month to avoid a

The Wetherby brand is currently putting even Balenciaga in the shade. It is hard to find anyone who doesn't glow about the school

preponderance of December (say) babies. You only get to see round the school if you are going to be offered a definite place. If you are on the waiting list there is still hope, but not a lot. Parents feel they have a golden ticket if their son gets a place here and are unlikely to turn it down for anything other than 'act of God'. Lots of international families and a number of children speak more than one language at home, but not much EAL support needed, as most arrive here fluent in English. No longer as local as it once was, parents prepared to travel far for the first-class education they feel their son will get here.

Exit: High numbers to the most academic prep schools. In recent years as many as 40 per cent to Westminster Under, Sussex House and St Paul's Juniors. Increasing numbers, currently 50 per cent, to Wetherby Prep, where entrance is automatic and the standards are rising, so why go through the stress of exams? The other 15 per cent elsewhere – eg locally to King's College Junior School and Latymer Prep or to board at Summer Fields, Caldicott or the Dragon.

Our view: The Wetherby brand is currently putting even Balenciaga in the shade. It is hard to find anyone, past, present or potential parent, who doesn't positively glow about the school. They single out the quality of the teaching – not only does Mr Snell recruit excellent teachers but he motivates them and makes them go the extra mile. Homework is 'innovative and thorough'. Communication with parents is 'exceptional', plus the 'school really understand boys and how to educate them.'

Lots of competitions and games inside the classroom as well as out. Learning here is fun, whether it's a project on the Romans or a fabulous end of year party, which incorporates an ice cream van and a bouncy castle. School is lucky enough to be able use the square opposite and the boys get lots of fresh air and exercise during breaks throughout the day. Reception and nursery children have their own outside playground, complete with springy tarmac and climbing wall, which is in constant use. On top of this they have several gym and swimming lessons (at Kensington Leisure Centre), as well as sport (in Hyde Park and Westway) in the afternoons. Lots of football and tag rugby in the winter, cricket in the summer. Plenty of fixtures against other schools, in swimming as well as field sports, and an annual sports day at the Wetherby sports grounds – at the Park Club in Acton. Dads' and boys' Saturday morning football is hugely popular, as are chess club, martial arts club, arts and crafts and drama. The choice of clubs is huge, from chess and cookery to Lego and French.

Plenty of music too – a choir in each of years 1, 2 and 3 as well as the wonderful Wetherby singers, created for those who couldn't make it into the choir but still love to sing. 'They make a terrible noise,' growled Mr Snell, 'but parents love it.' More than half the school learn an instrument – peripatetic teachers for guitar, violin and piano. There are instrumental concerts at the end of each term in St Matthew's church up the road as well as impromptu recitals in the hall. Drama part of the timetable as well as offered as a club. There is a performance at the end of each term, and the year 3s perform a major production (in recent years Peter Pan and The Jungle Book) at the Tabernacle Theatre.

Despite being non-selective the pace is fast here. Boys are expected to work hard right from the word go. We saw boys as young as 3 and 4 reading and writing (beautifully). Standards are high and everyone is aspirational – teachers, head and parents alike. Children who need support are usually identified early – good systems in place for spotting and diagnosing any difficulties. What is done about it next depends on the level of support required. At the more severe end – boys with moderate learning difficulties – many parents choose to take them to Emerson House in Shepherd's Bush to get that support. Others are taken out in groups for extra support – it could be the top, middle or bottom group in maths or English; others may have one-to-one support lessons. School employs one support teacher full-time and one other teacher who has half her timetable dedicated to learning support.

With his buzz cut hair style and his gruff manner, Mr Snell is so robust and hearty he could almost pass for the manager of a medium sized football club

There are 22 boys in each class, and they get lots of attention. Ratio of pupils to teacher (or teaching assistant) is high – more than one teaching assistant in every classroom as well a lot of floating teachers. Lots of differentiation

– and boys taught according to academic capability not according to syllabus. 'We teach them when they're ready to learn.' Only in the final year, year 3, are they grouped according to ability, in maths, English and reasoning. Relatively high number of male teachers (14) unusual for this age group. 'We can attract a different kind of teacher – Alpha Plus pays very well, especially at this level, and we rarely lose anyone to another school,' says Snell. Although they couldn't fault the education in the classroom, some parents boldly suggested that more attention could be paid to the importance of moral values. The idea of being 'nice' to each other, so focused on in girls' schools, is missing here, they said. These are alpha boys with alpha parents and, parents observe, there is a limited public spiritedness where writing cheques replaces baking cakes.

School is currently expanding up to 360 pupils. The new building in Pembridge Villas, once the site of Chepstow House, is already being used for reception and Little Wetherby (the nursery). New kid on the block is another pre-prep, Wetherby Kensington. Despite an increase in the number of places, we doubt there will be less pressure on them.

The last word: A busy, successful, well-run, well-resourced school, full of happy, spirited boys. For as long as this formula remains the same Wetherby is likely to remain the brand parents want.

West

Brent
Ealing
Harrow
Hillingdon
Hounslow
Richmond-upon-Thames

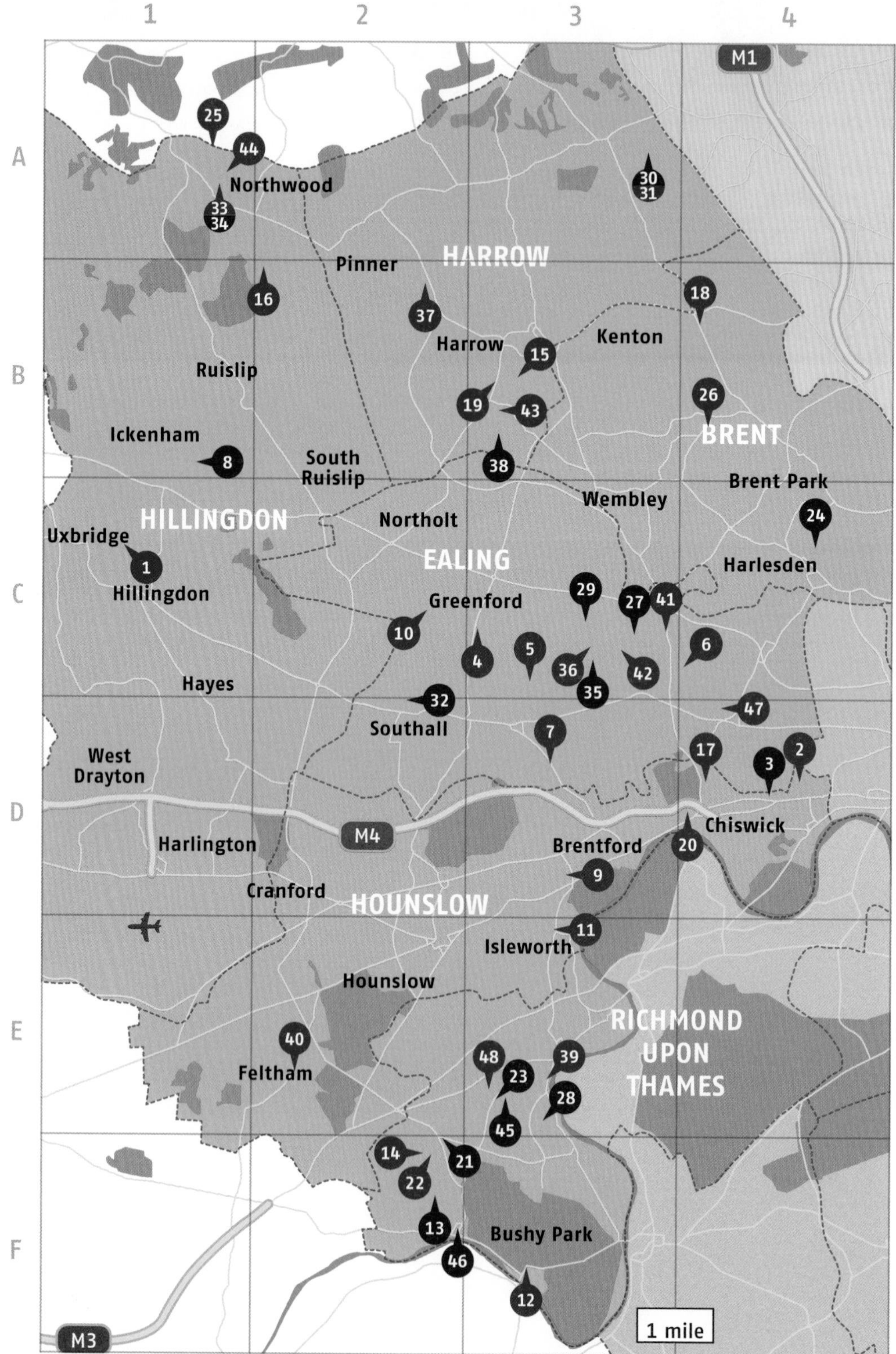
1
2
3
4
A
B
C
D
E
F
M1
Northwood
HARROW
Pinner
Kenton
Harrow
Ruislip
BRENT
Ickenham
South
Ruislip
Brent Park
Wembley
HILLINGDON
Northolt
Uxbridge
EALING
Harlesden
Hillingdon
Greenford
Hayes
Southall
West
Drayton
Chiswick
M4
Harlington
Brentford
Cranford
HOUNSLOW
Isleworth
Hounslow
RICHMOND
UPON
THAMES
Feltham
Bushy Park
M3
1 mile

WEST

West London and its state schools

Brent

Gritty Brent with its huge ethnic mix is largely famous for Wembley Stadium, whose Norman Foster designed arch can be seen from many viewpoints. Next door is Wembley Arena, the art deco building originally built to house the swimming pool for the 1934 British Empire Games, which now hosts acts from Bruce Springsteen to Beyoncé. Plenty of redevelopment is going on around, with 5,000 homes promised over the next 10 years. Wembley is classic MetroLand — the term coined by poet Sir John Betjeman for the expansion of London in the 30s along the Metropolitan line. It has lots of detached, semi-detached and terrace houses from the period.

Southern areas such as Kensal Rise and Queen's Park are rapidly acquiring a cachet amongst young arty professionals and City workers. Chamberlayne Road, with its mix of cool bars, cafés and boutiques, was even dubbed the hippest street in Europe by Vogue magazine.

The leafier northern part of the borough hosts JFS qv, the extremely popular secondary school (despite a few recent hiccups) that is the largest Jewish school in Europe. It moved from Camden to a purpose built site in Kingsbury in 2002. Islamia Girls School, in Brondesbury, is rated as outstanding. Kingsbury High and Queen's Park Community schools are good local non-faith schools. Ark Academy in Wembley is a newish all-through school. The Lycée International de Londres, which opened in 2015, and has now been upgraded to good by Ofsted, is no doubt affecting the demographics of the area. Probably the most controversial is the Michaela Community School qv, set up in 2014 by head Katharine Birbalsingh (who it is fair to say is not publicity shy) and renowned for both its discipline and excellent results.

One of the best-rated primary schools is North West London Jewish Day School. St Joseph's and Our Lady of Grace are popular Catholic primary schools, whilst

Malorees is an outstanding non-faith school, as is Oakington Manor School in Wembley, which has its own centre for children with speech and language difficulties.

Ealing

Ealing, a sprawling west London borough, comprises Acton and Ealing to the east, Greenford, Northolt and Perivale to the North and Hanwell and Southall to the west. It is the fourth most ethnically diverse borough with 55 per cent of residents coming from an ethnic minority. This is reflected in the make up of the schools.

An influx of residents (there are large Polish communities particularly in the north in Greenford, Perivale and Northolt, as well as Somali residents in Acton and Hanwell, and Indian communities in Southall) has resulted in most of the primary schools expanding from two form entry to three and in some cases four. The question many are asking is how the secondary schools are going to meet the greater demand for places.

One of the most popular secondary schools at the moment is Drayton Manor qv. Residents describe it as structured and old fashioned with good results but perhaps lacking a creative edge. The more arty child may be better suited to Brentside High, a modern site with shiny new facilities. Elthorne Park qv remains top of many parents' lists, on a spectacular site with extensive playing fields. Results here are impressive too. Cardinal Wiseman (Greenford), Greenford High (Southall) qv and Twyford CofE High School (Acton) qv come out top on the results table but Elthorne is hot on their tails. A stone's throne from Elthorne Park, also backing onto the extensive green fields close to the River Brent, is the new Ealing Fields non-denominational, co-educational free school (opened in 2016). It promises an all round education with a focus on character, resilience and life skills as well as academics. With Professor Guy Claxton as its patron, and the simple motto 'brave hearts, bold minds', it is has found a niche in the local provision. The more established and traditional Ellen Wilkinson qv in West Acton is a good choice for girls keen on science and maths.

Twyford's reputation is phenonomenal. Parents are prepared to move mountains (by which we mean dedicate themselves and their weekends to the local church) in order to get their children in here. We agree, it is good, and probably worth the sweat, particularly shining in music and languages. William Perkin CofE, part of the Twyford Church of England Academies Trust (along with Twyford), got off to a very impressive start since 2013. It's popular with parents and judged to be outstanding by Ofsted in all categories. Situated in a relatively deprived area of the borough, the main admissions criterion is proximity to school (rather than, like Twyford, years of churchgoing). Alice Hudson is unstoppable, and the third school in the Twyford CofE Academies Trust, Alice Lovelace CofE High School, opened in 2018 and is currently based at the William Perkin site. It, too, has open rather than faith-based admissions, and there are 12 places for talented linguists.

Practically all primary schools are good, some outstanding. Popular primary schools include Derwentwater, Berrymede and the new Ark Priory and Ark Byron in Acton (Ark Byron has finally moved from the premises it shared with Ark Priory into brand new premises on the edge of Acton Park), Fielding (which as its name suggests is lucky enough to have a green field rather than just the usual tarmac playground), North Ealing qv (known for good results) and Montpelier qv in Ealing, plus Hobbayne, Mayfield and Brentside in Hanwell. Southall alone has 18 primaries, including one Sikh faith school. North Primary qv and Havelock are considered to be outstanding and the rest, with one or two exceptions, good. In contrast, Perivale has only three primaries, one of which,

St John Fisher, is Catholic and outstanding. In Northolt and Greenford (19 schools between them) ones to consider are Vicar's Green and Gifford.

Harrow

The little village of Harrow-on-the-Hill was where wealthy 16th century farmer John Lyon obtained a charter from Queen Elizabeth I to found a Free Grammar School. Harrow School qv is no longer free nor a grammar, but one of the country's leading public schools.

Harrow, with Hertfordshire to its northern border, is undoubtedly one of the leafier of the London boroughs, dotted with small detached and semi-detached houses and a good proportion of garden-for-money, though the affluent areas of Harrow-on-the-Hill (with its pretty, winding high street and rows of cottages), Pinner (with its clutch of timber-framed buildings) and Stanmore contrast with more deprived areas such as Wealdstone. The Metropolitan tube line has shaped the area, with large areas of commuter suburbs being developed in the 20s and 30s. It is extremely diverse ethnically and religiously, with a large Indian population.

Nower Hill High qv and Whitmore High are the top rated secondaries along with the girls' Sacred Heart Language College. St Dominic's Catholic Sixth Form College qv has an excellent record.

Around half of its students are Catholic, nearly all the rest Hindu or Muslim. New state comprehensive Pinner High School opened in 2016 in buildings vacated by the former private Heathfield School for Girls.

Harrow has several high-performing Catholic primary schools eg St Anselm's, St Bernadette's and St John Fisher. The Moriah Jewish Day School does well too. Popular non-faith schools include Newton Farm, Grimsdyke, Pinner Park, West Lodge and Whitchurch Junior.

Hillingdon

Hillingdon sits right on the western edge of London, a mix of green belt land and residential suburbia, with the Metropolitan and Piccadilly lines providing a quick link to the centre. The M4 and the M40 run through on their way west; Heathrow airport is in the borough, as is part of the Colne Valley Park, the first real countryside to the west of London.

Uxbridge, with its fine tube station, grew up at the point where the ancient London to Oxford road crosses the River Colne. The western edge of the town has a peaceful network of rivers that once powered watermills — flour milling was its major industry for many years. The town grew in prosperity after the arrival of the Grand Union Canal in 1793, and then again after the arrival of the Tube.

Haydon School qv in Northwood is one of the most popular secondaries (specialises in languages and applied learning, with lots of BTec options), alongside Bishop Ramsay CofE in Ruislip, Douay Martyrs Catholic school and Vyners, both in Ickenham, and Queensmead in Ruislip.

Amongst the primary schools, Catholic St Swithun Wells, Sacred Heart and St Mary's all perform well. Other popular primaries are Whiteheath Junior, Hillingdon primary, Oak Farm Junior and Breakspear. Guru Nanak Sikh Primary Academy, half of whose pupils enter the school knowing little or no English, is vastly oversubscribed.

Hounslow

Hounslow, which abuts the Thames at Brentford, is a gateway to all roads west. The M4 runs more-or-less along its northern boundary. Heathrow airport, just over the border in Hillingdon, is a major employer, and the population is very diverse, with large numbers of families speaking English as an additional language.

Chiswick House, designed by Lord Burlington, is a grade 1 listed Palladian mansion with a garden of historic importance. The Griffin brewery, which has stood by the Hogarth roundabout for hundreds of years, has been churning out millions of pints of London Pride since the 1950s. Bedford Park, near Turnham Green tube, was the first garden suburb, planned in the 1880s by Arts and Crafts architect Richard Norman Shaw. Strand-on-the-Green was once a riverside fishing village, and still feels like it.

When the court sat at Kew, the rich and famous built big, ostentatious houses in Osterley and Isleworth. Though most have gone, Syon House on the Thames has been a home of the Duke of Northumberland for over 400 years. It, like fine, Tudor Osterley House, was remodelled by Robert Adam, while Capability Brown laid out their parkland. Old Isleworth is still a picturesque enclave of period houses.

Isleworth's Gumley House School qv is in a Queen Anne house surrounded by lovely grounds. The Green School qv (girls, CofE, Isleworth) and St Mark's Catholic School (co-ed, Hounslow) are other popular faith-based schools. Heathland School and Lampton School in Hounslow are high performing non-faith, co-ed schools. Cranford Community College takes large numbers of disadvantaged children, the vast majority from ethnic minorities, and is rated outstanding. Latest addition is Boulder Academy, which opened in Isleworth September 2018, though in a familiar story, building work on its permanent site won't be finished before 2021.

Belmont primary qv caters for an affluent area of Chiswick and gets some seven applicants for each place. Spring Grove, Grove Park, Blue CofE and Chatsworth are other popular primary schools, as are St Mary's RC schools in Chiswick and Isleworth.

Richmond-upon-Thames

Straddling both sides of the Thames, Richmond's borough limits can confuse even locals (just as well they don't go in for drumming strangers out of town: they'd probably never leave).

But whether cosying up to Kingston (south bank) or Hounslow (north), schools suffer from similar overcrowding. The LA has been tackling the problem, tacking on classrooms and building new schools from scratch. Meanwhile, living as close as you can to the desired school (dustbin in playground ideal if has own postcode) has never been a better idea.

Many of Richmond's comprehensives were, until recently, no better than they should be and, in many parents' eyes, rather worse, given the excellence of the local primaries. Waldegrave qv (girls only to year 11; boys in sixth form) remains the star performer, among the top non-selective schools in the UK for every measure, with pupils making progress that's 'well above average'. Long may it continue under the new headteacher. Grey Court School and Orleans Park are similar academic sizzlers.

Senior leaders of successful schools have been giving a leg up to some of the borough's outliers, Twickenham School and Hampton High, to overcome some pretty underwhelming results and go on to better things in the future. Parent feedback is increasingly positive, results ... less so, with only 26 per cent of Twickenham School's year 11 pupils achieving a 5 or above in GCSE English and maths in 2018.

Of the borough's three newest secondaries, St Richard Reynolds, a Catholic school in Twickenham (with linked primary), is the beneficiary of a recent glowing inspection report and is, it says, 'passionate about improving the life skills and chances for children created in God's image.' (Doesn't say anything about chances for those who aren't.)

Turing House, a free school for 11-18-year-olds sponsored by the Russell Education Trust (RET) missed out on the same site and is currently making do in temporary premises, an underwhelming office building in Teddington, with a much anticipated move to a permanent home – likely to be in nearby Whitton.

Newest of the lot is The Richmond upon Thames School. Though it goes only to 16 – an anomaly in a borough that has been busily bolting on sixth forms elsewhere (to mixed reviews) – the plan is for pupils to transition seamlessly to Richmond upon Thames College, on the same campus, for their post-GCSE education.

Currently, however, top sixth form destination for many Richmond families remains out-of-borough Esher College, known for consistently good A level results (60 per cent A*/B grades in 2018) and wide subject choice (not matched by the diversity of the intake, say locals).

Popular primaries north and west of the Thames are Archdeacon Cambridge's CofE and Hampton Junior (deemed 'good' by Ofsted), together with Orleans, St Mary's Church of England, both rated 'outstanding', as is Collis, one of first to be surgically enhanced, now boasting indoor facilities so good that at least one envious visiting teacher had to be coaxed to leave for own less impressive establishment. Downsides headed by danger of low-flying helicopter parents (as well as flight path noise).

Borough-wide praise for staff, whose own enthusiasms translate into impressive extracurricular activity. Hampton Hill Junior School, federated with Carlisle Infants, excels at music. It holds a Sing Up platinum award, gives all year 3 pupils the chance to learn violin, viola or cello and boasts numerous ensembles and choirs including a boys only vocal group, as well as an audition-entry chamber choir. Chase Bridge, meanwhile, also equipped with lovely new buildings, makes the most of links both with army music centre Kneller Hall and Twickenham stadium (both nearby).

At primary level, both Richmond's budding free schools have finally bloomed. Twickenham Primary Academy, meanwhile, sponsored by not-for-profit GEMS Learning Trust (a branch of the for-profit international group GEMS Education), is up and running in refurbished offices close to Twickenham Green, offering an abundance of 'laughter and delight' (measurement criteria will be interesting), as well as a longer school day (recent 'outstanding' inspection rating suggests the two are compatible).

Deer Park School (recently securing top marks in its first ever inspection) moved to permanent premises in East Twickenham in 2019, above a Lidl. Jokes about a cut price education probably won't go down well.

ACS Hillingdon International School

Hillingdon Court, 108 Vine Lane, Hillingdon UB10 0BE

01895 259771 | hillingdonadmissions@acs-schools.com | www.acs-schools.com

Independent	Pupils: 550; sixth form: 100
Ages: 4–18	Fees: £11,070 – £25,390 pa

Head of school: Since 2017, Martin Hall (50s), who hails from Aberdeen, studied economics and philosophy in Glasgow then to Worcester College of Education where he did his PGCE (secondary economics), working first at St Olave's Grammar school and then off to Tanzania for two years' voluntary service. 'It was very formative, it made me content with small things and realise that a good teacher can achieve wonderful things regardless of a school's facilities.' This tall, affable man still has an outdoor spirit and a desire to do good. He came back to the UK for more teaching jobs but then returned to Tanzania and there he met his wife. That was his first experience of IB teaching, to which he is now committed: 'more room for experiential learning'. After a further stint (six years) at the Inter-Community School of Zurich, he moved back to Tanganyika International School, overseeing two campuses and gaining a good head for business.

He was drawn to ACS Hillingdon because it allowed him to get back to the the UK, to be closer to teaching again, and he immediately liked the warmth of the school and the 'ambition and pluckiness' he felt that this small school has. Pupils are excited about him teaching economics – they 'are lucky to have him so involved, even though they like their other economics teacher'. He is aware of the challenges – a transient population, a lack of tradition, a need to provide a huge range of curricula for the pupils with so many different academic trajectories. However, his wide experience and open nature mean he may have solutions – building up a coherent curriculum and creating identity: 'Learning is not just about communicating knowledge, it must be transformational.' After several changes of head and an acting head here, everyone very much hopes he does indeed have a vision and will stay to carry it through.

He has all three of his children at ACS and his wife teaches at a local primary school. Parents say they don't see him often – most contact is with the principals of high, middle or lower school. New high school principal September 2018, middle school principal in post since 2014, lower school principal in post for more than 20 years.

Entrance: Admission at all times of the year after visits, references, school reports and questionnaires. Children accepted without English in lower school but higher up must be able to access curriculum. There is learning support department for mild learning differences. Some mobility difficulties can be accommodated but the old, listed building not suitable for wheelchairs.

Exit: Good career input – 'I have an internship this summer thanks to the school' – and school counsellors help with university choices. University applications to UK based on Measurement of Academic Progress data obtained on all students, and internal tests. Increasing numbers are staying all the way through school: 'We extended our stay in the UK so that our child can finish at ACS.' Exit to Bournemouth, Imperial, King's, SOAS, Birmingham, Warwick; or in the USA – Boston, Emerson, Florida State, Northeastern, Parsons, Syracuse. A peppering to other countries including Canada, Australia and the Netherlands.

Latest results: In 2019, average IB points of 32.

Teaching and learning: Non-selective and taking pupils at all times of the year from all different academic traditions means this school needs to be flexible and adaptable and have a good range of curricula to offer. The IB middle years programme has been dropped and the school now offers its own special blend of IB, British and American courses.

Reception and year 1 have their own spacious bungalows and playground, and the linked indoor–outdoor learning, teaching assistants and generous facilities make it a dreamy place for kids to be. 'Parents choose this over the local state schools in order to allow their children to learn through play – it matches a more international style of school where pupils don't start formal learning until after they are 6 years old.' Teachers and teaching assistants supported by specialist art, music and PE teachers.

Lower school continues the comfortable atmosphere, with a sofa in each classroom, groups of tables, teamwork, collaborative projects and thematic learning. EAL support extensive in these early years if needed, and highly differentiated reading schemes. iPads used regularly, with technology lessons ensuring they know how to upload video and recordings and photos of their work onto the intranet site to be shared with parents and saved at the end of the year in a digital file. Lower school pupils can then use their technological skills for creating, building and innovation and STEAM (science, technology, engineering, art and mathematics) integrated in all their learning. We have rarely seen so much opportunity for building and making – enough Lego, straws and cardboard to make tiny fingers itch. Native language enrichment ensures pupils keep up and develop their mother tongue, and they learn Spanish in lower school as well as having a language of the month so they are exposed to languages to match the different nationalities. Parents called the lower school 'phenomenal', with good structure and purposeful development.

Upper school students have a wood-panelled library worthy of an Oxford college, and the lower school library had sofas and hidden corners to lose yourself in a book

Middle school pupils have homerooms where they meet and have lockers, but they move to specialist teaching rooms, gaining independence and study skills. Spanish and French for all in middle years. Choice of drama, dance or visual arts each term. And again, generous lashings of designing and using technology, including building robots, in all their learning – presentations, videoing, displaying, investigations and finding solutions. 'I wish my child could have more lessons with the technology teacher – she is fantastic and they learn so much.' The school has a Genius Bar that is available to resolve problems with devices – don't we all wish we had access to that!

Teachers expect pupils to question and learn from mistakes: no rote learning happening here. 'We teach them to be ready for things we don't even know will be in their futures.' Pupils were expected 'to ask yourselves what would you have done in that situation'. Pupils going on a school visit to Apple asked designers, 'What was the worst mistake you ever made?' Realising it is from mistakes that come the most exciting developments. Parents are concerned that since abandoning the middle years programme, neither pupils nor teachers are clear about the curriculum. 'The middle years seems to have lost its way – my child doesn't have a clear idea of where they are or where they are going.' 'It is all very laid back and chilled, but that is not what I am wanting from a school.' Though in annual parent surveys, most say their children are challenged by the curriculum and some parents appreciated the flexibility of not having the MYP.

A new suite of science rooms with large light rooms dedicated to physics, chemistry and biology, with and space for experimenting. The success of the science labs can be seen in the students' extended project choices, with conference level posters of research: 'How does temperature affect the concentration of iron in fresh and frozen spinach?'; 'How do the different lengths of hydrocarbons affect the rate of combustion?'

Upper school involves more independent learning. Weekly sessions with university guidance counsellors in the first term to ensure they are on target with deadlines and that they have chosen pathways that will suit their education goals. 'My daughter enjoys the breadth the IB offers over the science A levels she would have taken in her old school.' Pupils have a choice of IB courses, American AP courses or High School Diploma courses, but they all have to be involved in CAS (creativity, activity and service). We met pupils who were following the IB diploma fully, some who were taking the odd IB course as part of acquiring the High School Diploma – plenty of choice and options to be busy and extended. Most recently, the school has added the IBCP (IB careers programme) for grades 11 and 12, and they're also the only place in the UK offering the Global Citizenship Diploma, avilalbe for all upper school pupils. Pupils seemed motivated and engaged: 'The IB course is really hard, and even though I have an unconditional place at university and don't need the grades, I owe it to myself to do as well as I can in the exams.'

Upper school students have a wood-panelled library worthy of an Oxford college, the middle school library provided a generous study space and chill out zone, and the lower school library had sofas and hidden corners to lose yourself in a book. Three full-time librarians make sure that despite the modern acceptance of iPads, technology and screens, all the pupils read and love books.

Learning support and SEN: Most of the learning support is based around EAL and language acquisition together with supporting pupils' mother

The school has a Genius Bar that is available to resolve problems with devices – don't we all wish we had access to that!

tongue languages. There is some dedicated learning support. The use of technology through the school does help to support different learning styles. Parents also liked the way that particular strengths were noted and pupils extended and challenged with extension work or put into advanced classes – especially in maths.

The arts and extracurricular: Exceptional artworks in a huge range of media cover the walls, including photography displays, with a large number of pupils choosing art at IB and achieving well above average (last year 25 per cent of pupils achieved a grade 7 out of 7 in IB art). Four dedicated art teachers going above and beyond as we saw printing, graphics, modelling, painting, mosaics, collage, displays, oil, portraiture and in-depth analysis. A pottery kiln is an added bonus – pupils were making plaster casts of their hands and using these to make sculptures based on Anthony Gormley's work – serious stuff, particularly for the lower school.

Film studies a relatively new IB course – very popular, with excellent sound, filming and editing suites as well as trips to nearby Pinewood Studios.

A large space dedicated to STEAM activities. Learning to work in teams, design and build experientially and practically develops problem-solving skills. The technology room includes a student-built 3D printer, alarms, pupil-built robots, drones and devices worthy of the most technologically advanced homes.

Music taught by specialist music teachers twice weekly from reception onwards, with middle and upper schools having use of a dedicated building, Harmony House, with individual practice rooms (plenty of peripatetic music teachers for individual lessons), music lesson rooms and generous suites of computers for composition work. 'I like it that they are able to extend their musical interest – my child is now part of a rock band.' A choir allows pupils to help complete their CAS requirement.

After-school activities included theatre, fencing, golf, cooking, eco club, street dance, kickboxing, zumba, track and field, chess and language enrichment. Older pupils involved in Duke of Edinburgh, National Honour Society and International Schools Theatre Association.

Sport: Regular PE lessons take place within the school timetable (twice weekly) but it is the after-school sport that is extensive – sports fields 10 minutes away host a range of sports and competitions against other international schools both locally and abroad. 'There is an emphasis on participating, thanks to the encouragement and the general ethos of the school,' according to one dad. Swimming at a local pool. Specialist PE teachers ensure that the cabinet of trophies is well stocked with wins by the Hawks.

One parent said 'the sport culture is excellent, there is a balance between academic development and strong sport involvement. Sport is used as a positive balance to develop a rounded person.' 'We see sport as an integral part of our child's school life': even though it takes place after school, 'they come home less stressed and fitter than if they had not done the sport between school and homework.' Parents commented, however, on the few galas and matches with other schools. And one pupil complained about mixed-sex football teams as numbers were too few for separate teams.

Ethos and heritage: Set amidst a leafy, residential suburb is the 1855 grand country home of the Mills family with their 13 children. It became a convent in 1920 and was bought by the school in 1978. Listed building status means that the fine stucco work, high ceilings and elegant windows are lovingly maintained – and now used and enjoyed by pupils and staff. A glorious red room used for recitals overlooking immaculate lawns and manicured planting. Modern buildings have been added on – slightly incongruous, but very spacious and practical gyms, classrooms, canteen, with a new science floor on top. High school uses the older buildings, lower and middle school the more modern section and the youngest classes have their own bungalow and playground space next to the learning support pavilions.

The grounds include tennis courts, a multi-sport all-weather sports field, vegetable patch looked after by the eco club and parking for the 37 school buses at drop-off and collection times. School playing fields a short bus ride away. Overall a great feeling of space – staff room enormous, wide corridors for pupils to move around, huge science labs, extra rooms for team working and studying, generous numbers of art rooms, meeting rooms, music rooms. A luxury to have so much space for learning and playing so close to London.

Parents felt that they had good access to teachers on the whole with three reports with narrative each year.

School lunches a flexible arrangement as pupils can decide each day whether they are eating school lunch or packed lunch (a fingerprint system avoids money being brought in). Large salad bar (special low salad bar for the tinies), good range of hot food, sandwiches and soups, and interesting menu from a different country each day. No pushing or shoving, things run smoothly and calmly and mealtimes chatty but not noisy.

Pastoral care, inclusivity and discipline: International pupil body very accommodating – parents grateful 'that we are family to each other' and that 'kids are kind'. Many parents mentioned the small size of the school as a positive: 'everyone knows each other' and 'teachers are really available for students and they know them well'. A 'positive peer group' and 'international mix of kids adds a real richness and creates a nice social network'.

'I haven't had to expel anyone – a short discussion with pupil and parents quite enough to right any wayward behaviour. And that is limited to some roughness in the playground or leaving premises without permission – never anything worse than that,' says the head. This is not a traditional or rigid school – kids set their own standards in the main and stick to them. There is a sense that pupils are reasoned with rather than told. And parents confirmed that they are emailed or phoned if there are any issues to avoid them escalating, though some noticed increasing amounts of 'mouthiness' going on in middle school years.

Pupils and parents: Some 70 per cent of pupils come to school on one for the 37 buses that either collect from homes or from collection points. Families around Gerrards Cross, Richmond, Chiswick and St John's Wood (known as little America). A growing number of local British families. 'Most of us have several passports and may not even have lived in the country our passport is from' – but some 35 per cent American, 17 per cent British, plus small numbers from 40 other countries.

Parents in banking, oil, film, increasingly military and diplomatic services. The school sees a change towards more 'local international families' – those that came for a short time on international placements but have stayed and are now very much local families.

Money matters: School fees do not include bussing service nor lunch nor learning support, but huge range of facilities and equipment an indication that the school is not cutting corners. Privately owned by a not-for-profit corporation with two sister schools in the UK and one in Doha. Becoming a charity so they can offer more financial assistance (scholarships previously only for two final years, but now financial awards from 20-100 per cent available at 11, 13 and 16).

The last word: This school gives a well-rounded education, humane and with priorities about the student's wellbeing rather than school's image. Not wildly competitive in any area, with the drive coming from the students rather than imposed. Music, sport and art balance the enquiry-led academic life of students in spacious and generous grounds with good facilities. 'We chose this school because it felt very relaxed and there was a happy buzz in the school with children laughing and talking,' say parents.

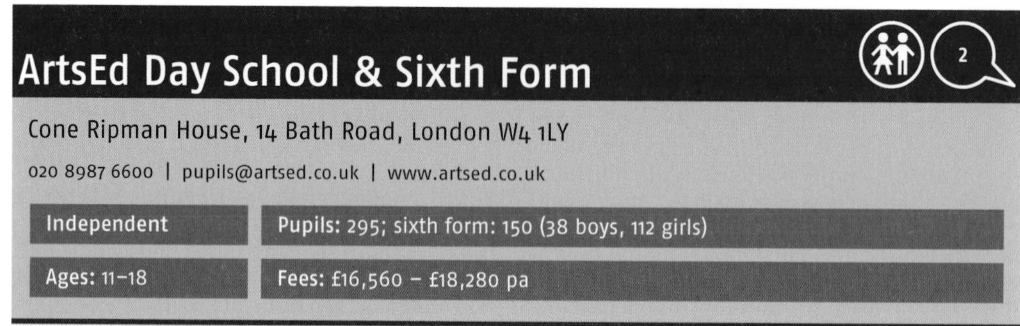

ArtsEd Day School & Sixth Form

Cone Ripman House, 14 Bath Road, London W4 1LY

020 8987 6600 | pupils@artsed.co.uk | www.artsed.co.uk

Independent	Pupils: 295; sixth form: 150 (38 boys, 112 girls)
Ages: 11–18	Fees: £16,560 – £18,280 pa

Headmaster: Since 2012, Adrian Blake (40s) BEd MAPgDip NPQH. An actor who worked professionally (and still does a bit, most recently in a B-horror movie, music videos and corporate films), who found he liked education. After a spell as lecturer in performing arts at North East Surrey College of Technology, he became director of thinking and learning and advanced skills teacher at Greenshaw High School, then moved to Lambeth Academy as assistant principal before coming to ArtsEd in 2009, initially as director of teaching and learning. Still teaches (acting for camera) for 10 periods a week. Rarely found in his office, in fact, though doesn't miss a trick when it comes to ensuring school stays ahead of the game both academically and vocationally.

A fast-talking enthusiast, he is immensely popular and – with the one exception of his fondness for education jargon – is about as far from a typical head as you can imagine. 'I thought he was the security guard when I first met him,' admitted parent and with his shaved head, trim beard, all black attire (including waistcoat) and keys jangling out of his back pocket, we're guessing she's not alone. 'He's brilliant – funny, honest, nurturing and encouraging.' 'Jolly, upbeat, caring and does great speeches.' 'Fully immersed in the school – lives and breathes it and creates this amazing environment where people are genuinely happy and want to excel.' Students are equally quick to eulogise: 'Friendly, easygoing and genuine.' 'I forget he's the head because he talks to us on our level.' 'Remembers the details – he came to see me in my primary school play and months later asked if I still had my green boots from my year 6 play. Incredible!' Goes both ways, it seems – he got more than a little misty eyed when expressing pride for students past and present.

Lives in Surrey with his wife, a deputy head at a nearby independent school, and their three-year-old daughter 'who is truly awesome'. And just to mix things up a bit, he's also executive coach to eg armed forces and a senior partner in a law firm, and runs a martial arts business with instructors across Surrey.

Entrance: Usually around 65 applications for the 24 year 7 places, but school won't take full number if there aren't 24 good enough to take (looks for potential, not polish). Another eight places become available in year 9. Odd vacancies come up in other years too so always worth checking. Entrance is by audition, with students trying out for either the dance or drama pathway (or both, in which case school picks which one they feel is best suited to the student). Written assessment in maths and English is simply to gauge academic progress – the school is academically non-selective. Biggest entry point is sixth form, when around 300 apply for the 75-ish external places. Similar entrance procedure, albeit more detailed and tougher: audition, workshops, interview. They join around 15-20 existing students, who go through the same process.

Exit: Up to a quarter leave after GCSE, most commonly for other sixth forms in order to study A levels not offered here. Not unusual for some of the more academically inclined to go on to the likes of Latymer Upper and Tiffin. After sixth form, around 80 per cent to an impressive array of prestigious conservatoires: Guildhall School of Music and Drama, Bird, Laine Theatre Arts, LAMDA, London Studio Centre, Mountview, RADA, Royal Central School of Speech and Drama etc. Some also overseas, eg Alvin Ailey New York, American Academy of Dramatic Arts. Around 15 per cent move upstairs to the highly regarded ArtsEducational degree schools in acting and musical theatre. Some go straight into professional work – students had moved on to star in the TV series Finding Alice and The Nest when we visited. A small number to university – most recently to study politics at Warwick, history at York and business at Bristol.

Latest results: In 2020, 50 per cent 9-7 at GCSE; 50 per cent A*/A at A level (89 per cent A*-B). In 2019 (the last year when exams took place), 40 per cent 9-7 at GCSE; 30 per cent A*/A at A level (78 per cent A*-B). At least triple distinction for all BTecs in both 2019 and 2020.

Teaching and learning: 'They're not just dancing around in legwarmers all the time – the academics are really serious here,' said parent. Certainly no shortage of attentive faces in the (rather cramped, but soon to be joined by bigger, airier ones) classrooms during our visit, with school in top one per cent (top five per cent for sixth form) in the UK when it comes to value added. No mean feat when you consider that several of the students we spoke to were scathing about their academic performance before arriving here.

The head is 'fully immersed in the school – lives and breathes it and creates this amazing environment where people are genuinely happy and want to excel'

It's no accident that academic and vocational teaching is interspersed throughout the day. It all helps performance related skills spill over into more academic ones (performance becomes practice, learning lines becomes revision etc). In one class, students were creating a 30-second radio commercial from scratch; in another, they were producing bang on 50 words of media copy. Before they knew it, they'd learned about questioning techniques, deadlines, persuasive writing and writing succinctly as well as they would in any English or history lesson. The mixing up of lessons has benefits on a more basic level too – 'means that if you, say, hate maths, you know you've only got 40 minutes until a lesson you love, like ballet or drama,' confided one, though most told us that even subjects they'd loathed in their last school were made bearable or even likable here because the small classes (24 maximum, but many much smaller) allow for teachers 'really getting to know your individual learning style'. 'Plus, the teaching is fun here.' It's not lost on students that many of the academic teachers have themselves dabbled in the arts (maths department is made up of an ex mime artist, stand-up comedian and Bollywood dancer, while some English teachers are published poets and playwrights) – 'Them having that appreciation of the arts is really helpful in them really understanding what makes us tick,' said student.

'You should have been there for our discussion on how Christopher Nolan writes women characters into film – made for an excellent debate,' said student

School walks the talk when it comes to the growth mindset – we lost count of the times the students added 'yet' at the end of sentences about concepts they hadn't grasped. So-called black box thinking is also in evidence: What went wrong there? Can you reflect on that? etc. The strong work ethic and a can-do attitude helps set a tone of high expectations. And the fact that no student is allowed to do professional work outside the school (more of which later) unless they're on top of the academic side of things must surely act as an incentive too.

Core of subjects covers all the basics, including humanities and French. Students take eight (occasionally nine) GCSEs, over three years starting in year 9, including double science (a few take triple) and French (though you don't have to), with native language options also available for bilingual students, eg Russian, Hebrew if requested. Arts related options, not surprisingly, get a big take up; film studies, whose results are top five per cent in the country, is huge here and it's easy to see why – we practically had to be dragged away from the riveting class discussion on the male gaze. 'You should have been there for our discussion on how Christopher Nolan writes women characters into film – made for an excellent debate,' said student. Homework is kept to reasonable levels, with academic teachers understanding the pressures of vocational claims on students' time ('Thank God,' said one).

'Intense' was the most common adjective from students about sixth form. At this stage, they choose three (occasionally four) A levels or a mixture of BTec and A levels, with options almost entirely arts-based: dance, drama, art, music, film studies, etc. That said, English, history, and French are there for the more academically minded, plus maths, which is, according to head, very popular. Biology and psychology to be added soon – a nice correlation between the latter and acting, reckons school, 'as it can help you work out why actors do certain things'. Some setting, though one student felt there should be more – 'in my French lesson, for example, there's a clear divide between the more able half of the class and less able but there's not the staff or space to facilitate two groups.'

Learning support and SEN: Two full-time SENDCos (one specifically for sixth formers) support the 30 per cent of students with mostly dyslexia but also some ('myself included,' says head) with ADHD. As with other performing arts schools, neurodiversity is a celebrated term, with school keen to recognise the correlation with the right side of the brain. 'Just a different way of learning.' Some withdrawal from lessons, depending on need. No TAs, with SENDCos both trained teachers (the sixth form one in drama – a great fit for the school).

The arts and extracurricular: The reason they come in their droves, with the mere mention of the arts lighting up these fresh faces. From years 7 to 11, pupils specialise in either dance or drama, but everyone receives classes in both disciplines; superlative teaching in both. Parents would be wise to put dinner time back – the amount of time students are required to spend in school increases as they move up: younger pupils stay until 5.30pm doing vocational work two or three days a week, in the sixth form it's every day. 'I am sometimes here until 8.30pm,' said one – 'and even then, I don't want to leave.' Lively and busy programme of shows and presentations including two major music, one major dance and one major drama productions a year, all exceptionally high standard and taking place if not in the 'as good as West End' Andrew Lloyd Webber Foundation Theatre, then in eg Stockwell Playhouse, Lyric Hammersmith, LAMDA Theatre or the Tabard Theatre (though good luck getting a ticket – one parent told us they are 'hotter than tickets to see Madonna at the Royal Albert Hall', largely because half of them are taken up by drama students going along to support the dance students and vice versa). Whole raft of smaller assessment-related productions throughout the year, including a dance one on the day we visited – 'both the assessors are ex-students,' whispered the head, who jokes that ArtsEd is like the mafia ('once in, never out').

'They're not just dancing around in legwarmers all the time – the academics are really serious here,' said a parent

Music also taught to a high standard, with many individual instrumental lessons. Several leavers go on to the Royal College of Music and one recently bagged a highly sought-after place on a jazz singers' course at Leeds. We loved hearing from a student how he'd only picked up a guitar for the first time a few months before starting at ArtsEd 'and now I'm in a band with classmates that regularly gigs.' Visual arts are also strong and creative, as evidenced by artworks in corridors – it's not unusual for ArtsEd students to jump a foundation year at prestigious art colleges.

While this isn't a stage school or agency that seeks out professional performing work for its pupils, ArtsEd isn't averse to permitting 'enhancing opportunities' for students who are willing to make up any work they miss. When we visited, one had recently taken three months out to star in Sex Education; another had a regular part in Casualty; and one played in the West End production of Matilda.

Sport: Expect your child's games kit to gather dust unless they're proactive sporty types (of which we did meet some) who are likely to be able to gather some of their mates together for eg netball, five-a-side football or cross country during the extended lunchtimes at nearby facilities (school has no outside facilities of its own). But with so much dance going on – and drama also being an active pathway – the students have no trouble keeping super-fit.

Ethos and heritage: ArtsEd's history reads like a maths challenge (just needs a 'so how many schools…?' question at the end). Originated from the Cone Ripman School, founded in 1939, which was itself the result of a merger between two previous dance schools. Originally located just off Oxford Street in Stratford Place, the outbreak of war forced a move to Tring in Hertfordshire where the school shared premises with the Rothschild Bank at Tring Park Mansion House. In 1941, the school was able to move back to Stratford Place, but kept its Tring premises as a second, boarding school. In 1947 both places were renamed The ArtsEducational School, to reflect Grace Cone's and Olive Ripman's commitment to a proper academic education for their young performers. Gradually the two schools diverged and are now good friends but completely independent of one another (in 2009, to avoid confusion with its former partner, Tring changed its name to Tring Park School for the Performing Arts). ArtsEd moved to its present premises in a leafy part of Chiswick in 1989, renaming the building Cone Ripman House in honour of its founders. Although something of an eyesore from the outside, extensive modernisation and refurbishment is improving things. Inside, we particularly liked the new mammoth walls of fame featuring larger-than-life photos of existing and old students and the new small corridor stage where students will lead their own lunchtime performances. The new facilities (which, as with the older ones, are partly shared with 'the degrees', as the ArtsEd undergraduates are known here) will double the footprint of the school and include even bigger, industry-standard studios, plus a second theatre.

The school was originally for girls only, and even today there is a 65:35 per cent split – that's not unusual for performing arts schools, though. 'Finally, I found my people' is the kind of phrase you'll hear regularly from both genders – in particular, they like the small size of the school where 'everyone knows everyone'. Uniform is a black branded track suit, while sixth formers wear their own clothes and call teachers by their first names. A strong student voice seems to nip most niggles in the bud. 'That even counts for the little things – 'I once wrote on a feedback form, "Can we have olives at lunchtime?" only to find they served them up the next week and have never stopped since,' said a student, still aghast.

Pastoral care, inclusivity and discipline: If we had a pound for every time we heard the school was 'like one big family', we'd probably have enough money to send the whole Good Schools Guide team off to see these kids in a West End show. 'Everyone is so supportive,' said a parent, while students told us teachers 'never fail to notice if you're down in the dumps and will always help.' Nobody thinks twice about popping in to see a favourite teacher about something that's bothering them, whether or not it's related to their lessons, and all students are assigned a staff mentor from year 10, which probably explains why nobody seemed bothered that there's no counsellor except for sixth-formers. Surprisingly little by way of eating disorders, even among the dancers, although school keeps a beady eye – 'I think it helps that the actors come in all shapes and sizes, and increasingly the dancers too,' says head. One parent, whose child had gone through serious mental health problems, said, 'I can't imagine she'd have survived anywhere else.' Emotional resilience and bounce-back-ability is a great source of pride of the school – vital in what can be a brutal industry. And we were suitably convinced they're fully up to speed when it comes to Black Lives Matter, LGBTQ+ etc – plenty of student groups plus regular speakers and visits from eg Stonewall.

Minimal behaviour problems – students worked hard to get here and work harder still once they're in. Also helps that boundaries are crystal clear, with a tiered sanction system starting with de-merits (there are also merits for good behaviour), going up to community service and eventually temporary exclusions (though no permanent ones in living memory). Woe betide any student who is late, and one parent told of how her child was 'hauled over the coals for chewing gum – quite right too'. Friendship issues crop up from time to time but students say most are willing to bury the hatchet quickly 'simply because you're quite likely to be sitting next to them in your next class, so you might as well move on'. Occasional temporary exclusions, however, for 'unkind moments'.

Pupils and parents: Inevitably, some families of film-makers, actors, writers and dancers. Makes for some cracking careers talks – think Trevor Nunn, David Tennant etc (we imagine the parents would pay a pretty penny to come along too, given half the chance – we know we would). But not quite as many as you might think, with the 'we've no idea where she gets it from' brigade growing. The robust academics help convince sceptical parents, eg professors from Imperial (they have more than one), that the school is worth its salt. Ethnic diversity could be better – school says it's on the case. Socio-economically, things are a little more varied – we met two students who said they wouldn't be here were it not for the means-tested help. Vast majority of families are from London, mostly local, but the school recruits from a wide radius with students travelling from as far as Surrey, Brighton and even Folkestone. In sixth form, 20 per cent live away from home and there's a growing minority coming from overseas, eg USA, Russia and Dubai (largely due to the launch of ArtsEd International in 2018).

Forget the stereotypes – the students we met were unassuming and well-mannered; nobody fought for the limelight, but equally we noticed how uninhibited they were compared to children in other schools – all were completely unfazed when we put them on the spot. 'I don't do divas in parents, staff or kids,' says head.

'Communications could be better with the parents,' was a common grumble. 'The parents who have been here longer tend to have to fill in the gaps,' said one.

ArtsEd alumni include, to name just a handful, Julie Andrews, Darcey Bussell, Martin Clunes, Nigel Havers, Bonnie Langford, Tuppence Middleton, Finn Jones, Sam Barks, Ella Balinska and Nigel Harman.

Money matters: Means-tested bursaries of up to a third of fees for pupils in years 7 to 11. In addition, 10 full-fees scholarships are available in the sixth form, and 10 headteacher's excellence awards offering £4,000 towards fees over sixth form. The school does not receive any government or local authority funding.

The last word: Whether or not your child winds up pursuing a career in performing arts (many do), this dynamic, hard-working and exciting school has nailed it when it comes to offering youngsters a first class vocational education that carries infinite benefits beyond the stage and without compromising on the academics. A happy, inclusive and supportive environment that parents, pupils – and the performing arts industry itself – can't seem to get enough of. We're not surprised.

Belmont Primary School

Belmont Road, London W4 5UL

020 8994 7677 | messages@belmont.hounslow.sch.uk | www.belmontprimaryschool.org.uk

State | Ages: 3–11 | Pupils: 472

Head: Since September 2018, Elaine Lacey, previously deputy head at the Blue School in Isleworth.

Entrance: Preference given to siblings. Next in the pecking order are those who live within the Primary Admissions Area – 'catchment' to you and me. In recent years, even living in the catchment has not guaranteed a place at the school. Children in public care and those with medical/social needs come high up in the pecking order.

After that – don't even try. Parents are known to rent property within the area just to qualify, and then...? More hope from year 2, however, as a steady trickle leave to go to prep school/move out of London.

Exit: Majority to Chiswick School and West London Free School. One or two to Hammersmith Academy, Twyford, Lady Margaret, Gunnersbury and the Green School. A few to local independents including Godolphin & Latymer, Notting Hill and Ealing High, Latymer Upper, Hampton, Ibstock Place. The occasional one to St Paul's Juniors at 8 as well as at 11. Lots of outside coaching during years 5 and 6 to prepare for independent school entrance exams. School asks for a financial contribution for the school reports required for entry into such schools.

Our view: The reluctance of the previous head and staff to welcome us to look round this super, oversubscribed, well-funded state primary (or indeed respond to our messages) bemused us – especially considering that Belmont is one of the most successful and popular state primaries in west London, with seven applications for each place.

Pupils bubbled with enthusiasm and love for their school as they showed us round. An abundance of facilities – from musical instruments, playground equipment, books and materials to the brand new stage for dramatic performances. Results are excellent, showing much higher than expected progress between key stages 1 and 2 and with a quarter getting well above expected levels in year 6.

The school caters for an affluent corner of Chiswick and the catchment area is becoming ever tighter. Families from sumptuous houses in the Bedford Park area can no longer expect to get a place. Were it not for the council accommodation on the school's doorstep, you might not get the social mix one would expect in an inner London state primary school at all. Our first impression was that there was an unusually high proportion of white middle class kids; the head was keen to give precise statistics and told us that 52 per cent of Belmont's pupils are from minority ethnic groups (in this case Eastern Europe and a few affluent UK residents from say, Canada or Sweden). This ain't your typical London primary.

School is housed in a large, three-storey brick building that benefits from the high ceilings, large windows, well-proportioned rooms and wide corridors typical of Victorian buildings of its kind. A generous refurbishment programme has resulted in shiny polished floors and child-friendly primary and pastel walls – helping the building to fall firmly on the side of happy, modern school rather than gloomy Victorian institution.

Two classes at either end of each spacious floor, each one charmingly named after fruit – apples, pears, cherries. The main hall in the middle space between classrooms is used for play (reception and year 1 – lots of dressing up and imaginary play goes on here), assemblies (years 2 and 3 on the middle floor) and drama and gym (years 5 and 6 on the top floor). Yet more rooms house musical instruments galore (drum kits, pianos, flutes, various percussion), two well-stocked libraries, two ICT suites (the juniors have the luxury of one computer each, one between two for the infants) and dedicated SEN provision. Teaching up to the end of year 2 is mixed ability; setting in maths and English from year 3. Two sets, the higher slightly larger.

Shiny floors and child-friendly primary and pastel walls help the building to fall firmly on the side of happy, modern school rather than gloomy Victorian institution

About 20 per cent of children identified as having special educational needs but a very small proportion of these have EHC plans. School has coped in the past with more severe special needs, but children must be able to climb stairs.

About a quarter of pupils don't have English as a first language (about 43 different first languages other than English recorded) but no marked difference in the performance of these children – credit to the school. Dedicated part-time EAL teacher as well as SEN coordinator with a team of teaching assistants. Those with EAL needs are seen individually or in small groups for as long as necessary. A reading recovery teacher sees individuals who, by year 1, are falling behind – with 'fantastic' results. When we visited, there had been a relatively high turnover of staff (we were assured that this is a result of career progression, maternity – no reflection on the school). Five male teachers – always a bonus. Years 3 to 6 have 40 minutes of French weekly. Everyone has two hours of physical activity a week.

All classes have class music lessons and learn singing with a specialist teacher. Many learn individually, too – often more than one instrument. Recorder is offered to the whole of year 3 and there is a choir. Swanky staging facilitates an annual production from year 6. Other year groups, sometimes working together, also put on shows each year. Photographs on display suggest a high level of dramatic productions, much supported by parents, many of whom are 'in the arts'.

Good sports provision. A school sports partnership linked to Chiswick School and an outsourced sports programme (football, netball and athletics) in addition to members of staff teaching sport. On Friday afternoons here there is 'enrichment time', when for 30 minutes children can choose from a wide variety of activities, from Glee Club to comic making. Strong after-school club provision. These include, as well as the sport and music, Big Bang Science and Doughlightful – a clay modelling activity.

The Belmont Home School Association – PTA to you and me – raises between £20,000 and £30,000 each year. This has helped make the playground ever more luxuriant, with designated spaces for quiet reflection, a wilderness garden, covered areas for performances with costume boxes, lots of bike sheds, a super climbing wall painted by parents and plenty of gardening boxes replete with flowers, herbs and plants.

The early years spill out beautifully into carefully designed outdoor play areas, secure from the rest of the large playground. The nursery is particularly spacious and attractive – three large rooms, own toilet facilities and a large kitchen area ('mummy sometimes comes in to help us cook,' said an excited 3 year old) as well as access to the hall and library. Few chic little independent nurseries provide as much as this. Everyone eats in the school canteen and the number of pupils having cooked lunches delivered by the borough increases all the time. The rest bring their own.

Ofsted hasn't done a full report since 2007, when school was judged 'outstanding' (confirmed by an interim assessment in 2011). Staff are greatly aided by a posse of 'liberal middle class' parents only too eager to help in all areas of school life, including arranging fundraising events to enable disadvantaged pupils who might not otherwise be able to afford to take part in trips etc. They are aided, too, by an excellent governing body, as well as by a good relationship with her local authority. A very small number of exclusions in previous years, but none for some time. A proper and well-understood system of sanctions. Also an established homework system with extension work on the school website for those who want to push their offspring further.

Many parents commented that they were sometimes frustrated by the blank wall that meets their follow-up questions on their child's progress and results. 'Teachers can be cagey,' remarked one parent, 'which makes me nervous. I might be surprised.'

The last word: If you can cope with minimal updates on your child's progress and a certain complacency ('we don't need publicity,' we were told at one point), then this is a no-brainer – an excellent state school with most of the advantages of an independent school but without the fees.

The Cardinal Wiseman Catholic School

RC 4

Greenford Road, Greenford, Middlesex UB6 9AW

020 8575 8222 | info@wiseman.ealing.sch.uk | www.wiseman.ealing.sch.uk

State | Ages: 11–18 | Pupils: 2,000; sixth form: 450

Head: Since 2010, Michael Kiely (50s), BEd (University of London) and MA in education (UC Berkeley). Joined the school in 1985, becoming a deputy head in 1997. Before that, he taught at alma mater Drayton Manor, as well as Chiswick Polytechnic and Featherstone High School, Ealing.

His two brothers went to Cardinal Wiseman and he was a hair's breadth from attending himself; his mum even bought the blazer. But grammar school it was to be, not that he has many fond memories of it: 'It wasn't set up for people like me who were bright but didn't know how to engage and that always stuck with me,' he says, the early seeds of his future teaching career clearly being sown (although at the time, he had his sights on becoming a footballer). Further reflecting on life-changing moments, he recalls his school sending him to an interview at Birmingham University. 'The way the public school boys, who were also waiting for an interview, spoke left me feeling totally intimidated and I totally flunked the interview, completely unable to address an audience. I don't want the children here to ever be in that position. Ever.' 'He has their back, that's for sure,' a parent confirmed, and the students – who have regular contact with him during class changeovers (he showed us the central spot where he stands for 40 minutes a day) and during lunch – agree. 'He's friendly and you can have good banter with him,' said one, while another told us, 'The way he speaks gets everyone on side – he just has a way.' We found him cheerful, savvy and sincere. Also considerate (it still haunts him that he had to exclude a student for carrying a penknife, which she most likely only had on her because she'd been fixing her bike, 'but rules are rules') and humble (he got rid of the headmaster's parking space in favour of a first-come-first-served system for the staff car park).

By his own admission, he arrived at a difficult time, following the departure of a long-term charismatic headteacher and just after one of the school's students was stabbed nearby – 'it took a couple of years for the school community to heal and confidence to be rebuilt.' It's safe to say he's seen as a bit of a legend himself now – parents like that's he's 'very down to earth', 'leads by example' and 'is not afraid to talk about the struggles of parenthood' (he has a son and daughter himself, both in full-time education). Loves football – 'well, most sports, actually,' he says, his time in the USA having given him a specific interest in American sports.

Entrance: Around 1,350 apply for 300 year 7 places. Pupils come from 40+ schools. Looked after children and those on an EHCP plan get first dibs (in that order), then it's siblings, followed by Catholic families who have a letter from their priest saying they have attended church regularly for the last five years and who have a child at one of the 11 named Catholic primary schools (the closest). If it's a tie-breaker, it goes on distance. There are no scholarships, interviews or 'banding tests' – 'we are not into cherry picking'. Entry for sixth form is more open, reflected in around 20 per cent of students being non-Catholic, but youngsters need a minimum of five 4+ GCSE grades, including English and for most academic courses they'll need a minimum grade 6 in the related GCSE subject. Around 470 applicants for 250 places.

Exit: Forty per cent leave after GCSEs, usually for more vocational qualifications or, as one year 11 student put it, 'because I just want a change'. Of those who stay on for sixth form (increasingly the highest achievers), 95 per cent to university across the UK, 30 per cent of these Russell Group. Humanities and science courses have always been popular and engineering and law are increasingly prevalent. Two to Oxbridge in 2019. Growing numbers do degree apprenticeships.

Latest results: In 2019, 22 per cent 9-7 at GCSE; 87 per cent 9-4 in both maths and English. At A level, 29 per cent A*/A (55 per cent A*-B).

Teaching and learning: Impressive, particularly given the non-selective intake; in the top five per cent of non-selective state schools nationally for academic achievement. In the top two per cent for value added between Sats and GCSEs.

School loathes the 'datafication of education' but head admits to regularly assessing students 'to check progress and to identify any who may be underachieving'

School puts it down to a combination of 'focusing our budget on teachers' (all are subject specialists and there's a huge emphasis on partnering with other schools to share best practice) and 'immediate intervention' for anyone that needs it (ranging from pastoral support to after-school or Saturday catch-up, depending on the reasons for lack of progress). Year 11s, when we visited, were living and breathing this intervention – some clinics compulsory, some not. 'You don't always love it at the time, but we know it will help get us our results,' said one. Students told us of 'interactive' and 'buzzy' lessons, and although that certainly wasn't the case in some classrooms we visited we didn't spot one inattentive student. Parents also complimentary of the teachers, although one said, 'If you don't, as my child doesn't, get on with your form tutor that can have a major impact.' Much praise (including in latest Ofsted report) for middle leaders – 'they run their ships tightly'.

French and Spanish from year 7, dropping down to one language from year 8, and 85 per cent continue it to GCSE. 'Unapologetic' setting from year 7 in English, maths, science and humanities; languages added from year 8, leaving only sports and the arts taught in mixed ability classes. Students take between eight and 10 GCSEs, with a push on EBacc subjects (English language and literature, maths, the sciences, geography or history and a language) 'as that's what employers want'. All take RE. Relatively small class sizes, given the 12 form entry – between 17 and 21 for English and maths and no bigger than 21 for other subjects. Limited vocational sixth form offerings, which leads to an inevitable mass exodus; of the 24 A levels on offer, most are traditional, with maths the most popular and sciences increasingly so, although there is photography and now film studies. Around 20 per cent (the 'Russell Group kids') take EPQ.

Homework levels on the highish side, with around an hour-and-a-half a night from year 7, building up incrementally. 'It's important fodder for independent learning but we don't want the kids to get sick of learning,' says head. School loathes the idea of the 'datafication of education' by endless testing and even refused to carry out PISA tests (tests that enable the government to compare schools in the UK to other countries) for that very reason. That said, head admits to regularly assessing students 'to check progress and to identify students who are underachieving or even coasting'.

Fabulous art department with art school feel: students working with headphones in, creating stunning, expressive pieces, many displayed tastefully throughout the school

School regularly seeks partnerships with global blue-chip companies in banking, building, TV etc to enrich the curriculum, eg a design, engineering and construction course has been introduced in collaboration with Turner Townsend.

Learning support and SEN: Forty or so languages are spoken here and eight per cent of students have SEN. Support for both (if needed) is provided in or outside the classroom on a case-by-case basis. 'My daughter is dyslexic and I'd been to see the SENCos at all the local schools, all of whom gave me an off-the-shelf reply about taking her out of languages and giving extra maths and English, but this school had a much more individualised approach, which has really paid dividends,' one parent told us. 'They even kept her doing the conversational side of French as she enjoyed that side of it so much but struggled with the written side. They are very accommodating.'

The arts and extracurricular: Musically, the school feels on a journey. Previously, we are told, it was 'rubbish', but a newish head of music has shaken things up and there are now four choirs, an orchestra and – for the first time ever – ensembles. Peripatetic teachers were also changed and consequently 100 students now learn an instrument. Whizzy facilities include a recording studio and practice rooms. Don't hold your breath for concerts (though that may change) but there are 'showcases' whereby students 'turn up and play' and there are chances to perform in church services. Around 20 do GCSE music and although they currently don't offer music A level (to the disappointment of one parent who said her son had to leave after GCSEs because of it), the school is hoping to stump up numbers – 'come back in a couple of years', we were told.

We saw GCSE drama students completely in a world of their own (in a good way) and parents are invited to watch short performances, but there hadn't been a whole-school performance for two years when we visited (last one was Grease) and it's a shame there's no LAMDA offered (though drama teacher did tell us they were 'considering it for the future'). Fabulous art (popular at both GCSE and A level) department with art school feel of students working with headphones in and creating stunning, expressive pieces, many displayed tastefully throughout the school. Cleanest, tidiest DT room we've seen – we're still trying to work out if that's a positive thing or not.

Plentiful clubs covering sports, music, drama, art, debating, film, chess and more. There's also Army cadets, Metropolitan Police cadets and DofE. Regular speakers, eg Jacob Rees-Mogg, David Dein. Lots of charitable works; in the last three years students have raised enough money to allow a primary school in Burkina Faso to expand. Some enrichment trips, including languages to France and Spain and history to the Somme battlefields, although pupils and parents feel residential trips are 'a bit thin on the ground'.

Sport: Parents speak of an 'amazing PE department' with 'dedicated staff who work tirelessly'. Everything except swimming (15 minutes' walk away) takes place on site, either on their all-weather floodlit playing field behind the school ('it was so exciting when they Astroturfed it,' a student told us), sports hall or gym, including the core winter sports of football and rugby (boys) and netball (girls), and core summer sports of cricket and athletics (boys) and rounders and athletics (girls). Rowing and basketball also offered. Gaelic football, table tennis, archery and cheerleading, among others, offered as extracurricular. School wins its fair share of silverware, especially in football (county cups in the last couple of years), netball (where girls have reached the latter stages of national competitions), rugby (development competitions, not elite) and rowing. Disappointing, though, that some year 11s we met did absolutely no PE on account of doing triple science GCSE instead (a few grumbles from students that you can't do both). Some parents told us it's hard to get in the teams, but one mused, 'I guess it's inevitable given the size of the school.'

Ethos and heritage: The school, whose namesake was the cardinal archbishop of Westminster from 1850, was originally built in 1959 to provide a secondary modern education for thousands of (mostly Irish) families who had settled in west London following WWII. In 1974, it became a comprehensive and in 1985, it expanded following a merger with the Cardinal Newman School, Acton. In 2012, the school was the last to be rebuilt under the Labour government's Building Schools for the Future programme and you won't find any complaints about the facilities here. 'They have everything they need, and more,' was a typical parental response, with students itching to show us everything. 'You have to see the science labs', 'The library is so well stocked' and 'Just look at that!' our guides proclaimed. All the study areas are named after religious places – Nazareth, Bethlehem, Galilee etc – and classrooms are large, bright and airy. We loved the ICT facility with 130 purpose-built study carrels to accommodate five classes in the event of staff absences, a facility that doubles up as a well-used homework hub during lunchtimes and before and after school – 'a definite bonus for the school,' said one parent. Besides the main four-storey building, which also hosts a modern refectory (everyone loves the food here and so did we) and a large school hall (where we saw firefighters giving a fire safety talk to year 9s), additional smaller ones at the rear mean nobody is ever short on learning space.

From its inception, the school has reflected the changing demography of west London – following the Irish, there was the Windrush generation, growing numbers of Asian and African migrants in the 1980s and 90s, and most recently economic migrants from both Western and Eastern Europe. As well as a mixture of different cultures, there is socio-economic breadth, but families are firmly united by their Roman Catholic faith. Students say the religion 'isn't in your face, it's more spiritual than that' and although we were told some decide religion isn't for them, the head says, 'I won't acknowledge that – I'd bet my bottom dollar they'll come back to their faith later on.' Parents describe the 'welcoming atmosphere' of the school – 'It's just a lovely environment and you get a warm feeling whenever you have to drop something off like a PE kit,' said one.

Former pupils include former pop band The Magic Numbers, footballers Jason Roberts, Aaron Pierre and Ruben Loftus-Cheek, actors James Forde (EastEnders) and Joe Prospero (Finding Neverland) and comedian Javone Prince.

Pastoral care, inclusivity and discipline: High standards, clear boundaries and zero tolerance (all with buy-in from students, most of whom justify just about every rule) mean behaviour is (in the main) exemplary. If a student comes through the gates with a potential object of harm, cigarettes, alcohol or drugs, it will be their last day at the school; 'I don't know why you'd risk it,' said a bemused student, although the odd few have, albeit only one in the last year and one the previous year. Typically around four per cent of students will be sanctioned through a temporary exclusion, usually for being disrespectful to staff, poor behaviour out of school and fisticuffs (although nobody can remember the last time there was a fight). Tellingly, only one student in the last 10 years has been excluded for persistent poor behaviour – 'we find a way to turn them,' claims school, eg a boy had set off the fire alarm the week we visited but once the head explained the impact on students who were 'desperate for lesson time leading up to their exams', he was suitably remorseful. Less serious offences (untidy uniform, unnatural hair colouring, chewing gum, turning on a mobile phone in school, lateness etc) lead to minus points and detentions; conversely, you get plus points for good behaviour. Get out of jail free cards for new year 7s when no student is sanctioned in relation to organisational issues.

The students were itching to show us everything. 'You have to see the science labs', 'The library is so well stocked' and 'Just look at that!' our guides proclaimed

Pastoral leads at the top of the school (all with reduced timetables), along with beady-eyed teachers, mean not much is missed here by way of mental health. A family therapist is in three times a week and there's a full-time chaplain for self-referrals. Vulnerable students are identified from the outset (those with social services intervention, for example, or those just lacking in confidence) and outside experts are brought in as necessary. Outside speakers do talks on issues such as social media and there are 'down days' dedicated to specific issues – year 7s had just had an anti-crime day when we visited, complete with judges and police and a 'carousel of activities'. Leadership opportunities include prefects, sports captains, chaplaincy reps and year leaders. One parent expressed disappointment that 'some children get more of a punishment for doing the same thing as others – they just seem to get labelled. I have a friend who is looking at another school because it's happened to her son.'

Pupils and parents: Most hail from Ealing, although some come as far as Harrow, Hillingdon, Hayes and Slough. Many of the parents didn't go to university and have higher aspirations for their own offspring. We found students equally aspirational, as well as polite, fiercely proud of their school and happy in their own skin. 'You don't really get bullying here because there's a culture of looking out for each other,' said a student (who also pointed to the effective Wiseman Spirit), although there's no pretending it's not happening and school drums it into students that 'the bully will be more scared of us than they are of you, so always report it'.

Money matters: School asks for a voluntary contribution of £25 per child per year. Most pay it, although school says 'we are not in the business of pestering.' There is a hardship fund for those on free school meals or struggling to pay, so they don't miss out on the likes of extra tutoring, trips etc.

The last word: A modern, outward looking school that really stretches young minds. We observed strong leadership, clear boundaries and a dynamic, welcoming environment in which students of all abilities feel driven to achieve yet (for most) without undue pressure. But it's not for a rebellious child.

Drayton Manor High School

Drayton Bridge Road, London W7 1EU

020 8357 1900 | adminoffice@draytonmanorhighschool.co.uk | www.draytonmanorhighschool.co.uk

State | Ages: 11–19 | Pupils: 1,532; sixth form: 313

Head: Since April 2020, Lisa Mills. She started her teaching career at Drayton Manor having read French and German at York, then a stint teaching in Japan. Worked her way through the ranks, holding positions including head of sixth form and member of the senior leadership team. Spent time as deputy head in another inner London school while studying for a masters degree in educational leadership at UCL before being appointed to take the reins here.

Entrance: Non-selective. Successful court case means that children gain a place at Drayton Manor if it is the nearest school to their home. If you live a mile from the school but it remains the nearest school to home, then you will have priority over children who live half a mile away but have other schools from which to choose. School explains, 'Roughly speaking unless you live 0.8 miles away or less, you won't get a place.' Massively oversubscribed, with roughly six applicants per place. Waiting list for all years. Generally, a grade 6 is needed at GCSE to pursue the subject in the sixth form, whether existing pupil or from outside. Fifty or more pupils join in year 12, to replace those who leave after GCSEs (they usually head for vocational courses elsewhere or employment).

Exit: Up to 50 per cent leave after GCSEs. Popular universities include Westminster, Southampton, Warwick, Reading, Portsmouth, King's College London, Imperial and University of London. Subjects range from international politics to mechanical engineering.

Interview practice for those applying to Oxbridge or for medicine, as well as shared careers workshops, at Highgate School. Oxbridge society prepares pupils for applications, including test practice. School says pupils don't always know what they are capable of so encourages those who would never have considered university to believe that they can achieve it – 'This is a seven-year programme. You can't just turn it on in year 12. Students need to learn how to crack the code. They need to learn not to be intimidated by institutions.' Four to Oxbridge in 2020, and one medic.

Latest results: In 2020, 36 per cent 9-7 at GCSE: 29 per cent A*/A at A level (54 per cent A*-B). In 2019 (the last year when exams took place), 30 per cent 9-7 at GCSE; 59 per cent 9-5 in both English and maths. At A level, 15 per cent A*/A at A level (36 per cent A*-B).

Teaching and learning: Has received awards for exceptional GCSE results and letter of congratulation on EBacc results received from minister of state for school standards.

Thirty subjects offered at A level, including media studies, sociology and psychology. Popular A levels currently maths, biology, chemistry and history. Government and politics, as well as history, recognised nationally as superb departments. BTec qualification also offered in creative media and applied general qualifications in business. Wide choice of GCSE subjects including computing and economics.

Pupils can take between five and 12 GCSEs. Modern languages offered include Spanish, French and German, though no Mandarin nor Russian. One parent we spoke to wished that her daughter could have taken two modern languages at GCSE but not possible. On average, 35 pupils learn Latin in first year with around 20 pupils taking it for GCSE in year 10. 'The students love it; the parents love it and it adds something to the character of the school. It attracts good, interesting staff and it adds an extra dimension,' says school.

Average class size is 23; maximum 31. Five one-hour lessons a day. School recognises the benefits of setting by ability – English and maths from year 7 and science, French and Spanish from year 8. School told us, 'Differentiation is a strength – all our pupils are pushed, whether very able academically or not.' Awarded 'outstanding' in last Ofsted inspection.

EPQ is embraced here, with a broad range of subjects chosen by pupils ranging from bovine TB to Jane Austen. About one third of the year end up taking it. School encourages the pupils to take it on if manageable: 'It's a conversation we have with the student and family.' Pupils were highly focused in the lessons we observed, whether being tested on GCSE biology modules or role-playing gritty scenarios in drama group. School delights in the fact that 'they enjoy being challenged. They can listen for long periods of time. They can express their opinions with confidence.'

On average, 35 pupils learn Latin in first year. School says, 'The students love it; the parents love it and it adds something to the character of the school'

School stretches the very brightest sparks. Gifted and talented pupils might be given extra lessons or be sent off on a trip. One mother we spoke to commented that her clever son 'was very well supported and extended throughout'.

Homework club in library for those who struggle to concentrate at home. The pupils we spoke to did not find amount of homework too onerous, with one even shyly confessing that she enjoys it. Booster revision sessions laid on for A level and GCSE pupils after school, in holidays and at weekends, so no-one is left to flounder in exam season.

Teachers are ambitious for their pupils and are rated highly by the parents. 'You really feel at parents' evenings that the teachers know your child inside out.' Pupils feel most teachers are 'easy to talk to'. Over 20 members of staff have been at school for more than a decade but there is a healthy balance with plenty of youthful faces too. School admits that recruitment of excellent staff 'can be challenging with teacher shortages' and it can be hard when a head of a faculty leaves but 'we are like a gyroscope. It takes a lot to knock us off our stride.'

Learning support and SEN: Over 300 pupils on the SEND register, well above the national average. School offers excellent provision for those with milder end of learning difficulties such as dyslexia, dyscalculia and autism and those with social, emotional and mental health difficulties. Staff are trained to deal with attachment and anxiety disorders as well as school phobias. Baseline assessment on arrival. Beautifully designed new inclusion centre. 'Probably the best facilities in the school for the students who need the most support,' explains school. 'They all arrive early as they love coming to this area.' Alternative curriculum in phonics, literacy and numeracy offered to those that need specialist support in the first few years. EAL pupils also withdrawn from class for extra help if needed.

The arts and extracurricular: The arts faculty is made up of art and design, drama, music and media subjects. Numerous choirs. Concerts galore, both formal and informal. Lots of opportunities to take part in musical events, from participating in national orchestra days to hearing musicians at Albert Hall. Currently 150 students learn an instrument. Music department has undergone recent refurbishment. Excellent new art, design and technology studios too. Though some impressive work on show, including sensational portfolios, art is not a popular A level. School takes part in Shakespeare Schools Festival. Annual summer showcase is highlight of school year. 'The shows are sensational,' according to one parent.

Sixth form enrichment options include chess, debating and trampoline sessions. Pupils participate in National Citizen Service and fundraisers for children's charities. School promotes learning outside the classroom including ski and snowboard trips to Maine, homestay visits in France and residential stays in Devon.

Sport: Wide array of sport offered from cricket to gymnastics and dance. Some pupils perform at national level as well as county level. School is regular winner of cups and tournaments across borough and new display cabinets are being built to house the abundant silverware. Netball, rugby and football particularly impressive. Excellent facilities. Everyone is encouraged to participate at some level, whether house dodgeball or more giddy heights.

Ethos and heritage: Opened as a grammar school in 1930, before becoming a comprehensive in 1973 and an academy in 2011. Still feels like a grammar school, with its stained-glass coats of arms in the library and its Latin motto Nec Aspera Terrent, meaning 'hardships do not deter us'. Sums up ethos of school.

Current head is only the sixth head in school's history and many of the buildings are named after her well-loved predecessors. Yellowing old school photos adorn the corridor, reflecting the changes in its history from genteel 1930s arrangements to hippy groupings from the 1970s.

Vivienne Westwood's striking Union Jack on a main corridor adds a dramatic punch to what could otherwise feel like a National Trust property

An £8 million building programme, including a new humanities faculty, outstanding new library and refurbished science labs, has transformed the school. Beautiful central piazza, complete with immaculate topiary and a total absence of grime or litter make for stunning premises. Vivienne Westwood's striking Union Jack on a main corridor adds a dramatic punch to what could otherwise feel like a National Trust property.

Pupil successes are celebrated, whether at congratulatory breakfasts, coffees, lunches or a year 13 boat trip to Craven Cottage. Prizes awarded in all year groups for effort and progress, as well as for humour and good character, and for courage.

Old Draytonians include footballer Peter Crouch, BBC business editor Kamal Ahmed and Lord Justice of Appeal Sir Michael Fox.

Pastoral care, inclusivity and discipline: Each year comprises 240 pupils, organised into nine tutor groups. Each pupil sees their tutor every day. 'I love my tutor,' smiled one boy. When head meets with heads of year, she expects to be told the key things that are going on in each year group. Has finger on the pulse, as have her deputies, we were told.

Discipline is important. Schools keeps rules to a minimum but expects them to be obeyed. Only sixth formers are allowed mobile phones and punishments for others in possession of them are no-nonsense. Third time caught with a mobile phone counts as defiance and can be met with an exclusion. 'Even for sixth formers, if they are caught doing anything iffy then the sanctions kick in. They respect that,' explains school. Strong policies in place regarding social media. 'Our values are clear on social media – it all comes down to good manners.' At risk of permanent exclusion for possession of drugs and offensive weapons. Four or five permanent exclusions annually. One mother summed it up: 'The kids respond to the discipline. There is not much wriggle room!' Another parent said, 'The children know where they stand. They know the consequences for bad behaviour and the school carries through with these. No idle threats at Drayton.' One mother commented that some boys mess around in class but that generally there is zero tolerance of larking about. School thinks it can be a relief for the pupils to have to comply with strict rules: 'They can blame us. It allows them to perform at a high level.' Over 95 per cent attendance rate.

A caring ethos is at the heart of the school. 'We insist on high standards. Being courteous and considerate comes before academic prowess. How we treat other people is the number one priority. That is our bedrock. It's the Drayton Manor way.' This sense of decency is expected not only in the classroom but between lessons, at break time and even at the bus stop. 'The whole continuum from home to school is important for us. It does not end at 3.30pm. They need to learn that this is their life now.'

School recognises that it can be hard being a teenager. 'It's important they know there is more to life than just being popular. The children feel safe here and can develop their own personalities. They can express themselves without being made fun of.' The pupils in turn say they can trust the staff and feel that if they tell the teachers about any problems, they will make it better. 'Pastoral care is not just about having the structures in place but trying to work out what it feels like to be one of the students. We think a lot about it,' says school. One girl said the school had supported her incredibly well through a bereavement and another mother expressed her gratitude for the way Drayton had built up her daughter's shaky confidence. Very few suffer with depression, anorexia or self-harming.

Ninety-five per cent of food is home-made, including breakfast for early birds from 8am. Chef worked in a Michelin-star restaurant and certainly wowed us with delectable pastries. Lots of options, including halal, gluten-free, vegan and vegetarian, though one pupil told us 'it would be easy to get away with just eating a cookie every day for lunch as no-one checks'.

Pupils and parents: Socially mixed intake, from affluent professional families to the very deprived. Pupils head in from north and west Ealing and Hanwell. One third white British with many different ethnic minority groups. Sixty-five per cent EAL and over 50 different languages spoken at home. Parenting support classes offered. Above average number of pupils on free school meals.

Excellent home-school communication. Head genuinely likes meeting people and enjoys being around at events such as parents' evenings.

Money matters: Sixth form bursary. School uses its pupil premium to fund learning support, masterclasses, mentoring, Easter revision and some subsidising of school trips. Voluntary contribution of £10 per family per year.

The last word: Pupils we spoke to were thoroughly impressive: modest, polite, caring and articulate but with a developed sense of fun. An inspiring and exciting school that provides a truly outstanding education.

The Ellen Wilkinson School for Girls

6

Queen's Drive, London W3 0HW

020 8752 1525 | office@ellenwilkinson.ealing.sch.uk | www.ellenwilkinson.ealing.sch.uk

State | Ages: 11–18 | Pupils: 1,287; sixth form: 242

Headteacher: Since 2014, Rachel Kruger (late 40s). She arrived here in 2012 as deputy head, and taught maths and music (she has a music education degree from the university of Stellenbosch and a pure maths degree and an MBA from the OU). In 2013 she became acting head and took over as permanent head in March 2014. She started her career teaching music in Stellenbosch, moving to the UK in 1999 to a post as music teacher at Uxbridge High then maths teacher and assistant head at Dormer Wells High. She now feels she has come full circle, relishing the atmosphere of this all-girls school. She is clear about the benefits of single sex education for girls. 'I love seeing the girls in year 7 playing hide and seek,' she says. 'I doubt you would find that in a mixed school.' The women in the senior leadership team all went to girls' schools.

Modelling behaviour and expectation for her pupils is key for Ms Kruger. You can immediately see why she is hugely popular with parents, staff and girls. Wreathed in smiles and generous with her warm greetings to everyone she passes, she exudes positive energy. 'Everyone respects her,' said our guide. 'The girls benefit from her warmth,' commented a dad. She combines a tough, focused approach with the soft femininity of the floral print dress she was wearing when we met. Just being in her company makes one feel that anything is possible and nothing is too much of a problem. Open and relaxed in conversation, she is easy to talk to and parents warmly appreciate her approachability and her ability to listen and deal with things quickly and effectively. They describe her as 'a good leader' and 'effective manager'.

She clearly loves her job and puts her heart into it, is active in the head teachers' group among Ealing schools, and receives lots of support through mentoring from other female leaders, as well as giving support in return. She knows the girls, and unusually for a head of a busy secondary school, still finds the time to teach maths. A love of learning is one of her defining qualities. A trained opera singer, she is currently studying for a law degree. No plans to change career, however. 'I just want to keep learning,' she twinkles, 'and it has the added bonus of setting an example to the girls: they can see my disappointment if I don't do as well as I would like and they witness me striving to do better.' Parents remarked on her gutsiness in singing a solo at a winter concert – 'if the girls are expected to do this, so should I be.'

Entrance: Always oversubscribed, with over 500 applicants for 216 places. Priority given to looked-after children, siblings, children of teachers at the school and those with specific medical or social needs. Then distance to the school is the deciding factor – currently around 1.5 miles.

About 40 girls from other schools join the sixth form each year, with a baseline of 5+ 9-4 GCSE grades for A level courses, including 6s in their A level subjects. Those who don't make the grade can take two or three BTec courses.

Exit: The majority go on to university. Large numbers to the London colleges (Queen Mary University of London, Westminster, Roehampton, Royal Holloway all popular destinations) to read a range of courses from biomedical science and chemical engineering to photography and Japanese. The maths and science specialism here is clearly effective, as most go on to study STEM-related degrees. Three to medicine, two dentists and a vet in 2020; others into optometry, nursing and pharmacy.

Around 40 per cent depart after GCSEs to sixth form colleges elsewhere (eg Harris Westminster, William Morris, St Dominic's in Harrow and Hammersmith Academy), a few to further education colleges.

Latest results: In 2020, 40 per cent 9/7 at GCSE, 84 per cent per cent got 9-4 in both maths and English; 35 per cent A*/A at A level (63 per cent A*/B). In 2019 (the last year when exams took place), 82 per cent got 9-4 in both maths and English GCSE; 14 per cent A*/A at A level (40 per cent A*-B).

Teaching and learning: English, sciences, languages (including Arabic and Latin) all strong at GCSE. RE is a noticeably popular subject at which girls do well here. A specialist maths and science college since 2002, a healthy proportion of the girls take maths, biology and chemistry A level. Further maths, psychology and philosophy are recent additions to the A level choices. Several vocational options at level 2 and 3, including business studies, and health and social care. Suggestion in some quarters that sixth form is less stimulating and a few start to look elsewhere after GCSE. Lots of setting – maths and English from year 7, science and languages from year 8. Mandarin now offered as part of the curriculum from year 8. School runs maths and science taster sessions and masterclasses for feeder primary schools, with excited pupils trying out practical experiments in real science labs.

Food tech, product design as well as textiles offered at GCSE. The latter particularly popular. We saw examples of a project on headpieces in Alice in Wonderland. One year 11 pupil won an award with the London College of Fashion and went on to work with print designers in East London. Lots of extracurricular academic clubs, including Latin.

Modelling behaviour and expectation for her pupils is key for Ms Kruger. 'Everyone respects her,' said our guide

Busy careers library, particularly well used by years 9 and 11; 'we're giving support with careers a lot, but apprenticeships too,' says the careers officer.

Learning support and SEN: A number of students need learning support and are taken out of class for one-to-one sessions. Those on EHC plans tend to be girls with a physical disability who need practical help. Lots of careful differentiation takes place in the classroom, we are assured, and careful monitoring as to who needs more support. 'We are gradually moving this support away from the just the SEND department and giving the support in the class room,' says Ms Kruger. One full-time SENCo, one deputy and one EAL teacher. Higher level teaching assistants and several other teaching assistants in both SEND and EAL departments. Some 70 per cent of students speak English as a second language, supported by a strong EAL team and school, deservedly proud that the results of the EAL students are well above national averages. Value added scores strong, among the best in the borough.

The arts and extracurricular: Frequent drama productions as well as concerts, jazz band and string quartet. All girls do drama in years 7 and 8 and a fair number continue to GCSE. The shiny polished Victorian main hall is used for annual theatrical productions as well as concerts and there is a good sized drama studio. A number of successful musicals are performed each year, including Oliver!, Little Shop of Horrors and Les Misérables, and they performed the Rocky Horror Picture Show at a local theatre. 'The standard is professional,' observed more than one parent. Music is a passion of Ms Kruger's, and she encourages lots of concerts throughout the year, the winter concert being a particular highlight, with other different kinds of opportunities for the girls to perform and develop a musical interest.

Three large and spacious art studios, bursting with industry and colour and situated around a green grassy area, are an inspiring place to explore different styles for budding creatives. Art GCSE results are good, and A level results, though less consistent, are solid.

Extracurricular clubs range from sporting and music to academic and learning support.

However, at lunchtime girls can also choose to do a variety of activities from tapestry to debating and dominoes to eco learning. It's up to the girls how much they get involved.

Sport: PE facilities have been transformed by the recent addition of a new sports hall. Successful basketball and netball teams; girls here also play football, run cross-country and our guide plays handball for Ealing. School enters teams for a number of competitions, tournaments and fixtures against other schools. Minor sports clubs too, including trampoline, badminton, and ultimate frisbee. They recently received funding from London Youth Rowing and were awarded Middlesex Education Provider of the Year for tennis. Lots of outdoor space, with grass and all weather hockey pitches as well as tennis and netball courts enabling the school to host a number of competitions across the borough. Ellen Wilkinson prides itself on being a 'sports leadership academy', one of very few schools in London to have this status and based on the fact that the school offers the Sports Leadership Award at both level 1 and 2. Perhaps more importantly, our guide confirmed that it's 'cool to be sporty'.

Ethos and heritage: Named for the Mancunian Labour MP Ellen Wilkinson, who led the Jarrow March in 1936 and became the first female Minister for Education in 1945, the school was founded in 1974 and is still the only all-girls comprehensive school in Ealing.

First impressions as you arrive in the new foyer are of a thoroughly modern, state of the art school, with clean lines, minimal decoration, and monochrome appearance punctuated with bursts of colour – a fresh bowl of flowers strategically positioned, for example. The new building, which houses senior staff offices, administration and conference rooms, as well as the entrance hall, is replete with white stone floors, glass walls and Perspex chairs. The smell of fresh paint blends in with the scent of freshly cut flowers. The library – also recently finished – is designed in the same style, and on a clear winter's day, when the trees are bare, there is a clear line of vision from one building to the other.

In between, however, there is a hotch-potch of different styles: Victorian, polished wood floors and high ceilings, lined with gold leaf embossed honours boards, and a tranquil Japanese garden surrounded by 60s two-storey blocks, where the girls can enjoy lunch in the warmer months.

The grounds feel extensive with a number of netball courts as well as 'the field' – a wonderful large green space, only spoilt, when we visited, by an unsightly amount of litter. School already on to this with plans to fence the field off. This is where the girls do athletics and can sit outside and eat lunch.

New girls in year 7 are given a map when they arrive and then packed off on a treasure hunt to acquaint themselves with the territory.

'We help everyone to find their own way through acceptance; kindness is a big word here, ultimately it's their choice whether to do the right thing,' says head

There is a distinct professionalism about everything here. A tightness. Things are done well. Crisp. Effective. Even the uniform has smartened up, with crisp white shirts beneath their maroon V-necks.

Pastoral care, inclusivity and discipline: An area that has vastly improved under Rachel Kruger's compassionate but firm leadership, confirmed by all the parents we spoke to. There was a lot of low-level disruption that needed tackling. Part of the response was to revamp the pastoral team, another to ask the students to write their own code of conduct. 'A strict but comfortable school; everyone is kept in order but we don't feel pressurised, we understand the rules are for our benefit,' confided our guides. One parent commented on how swiftly a problem between a teacher and her daughter was resolved by the head of year. There are systems in place and they seem to work. Staff work hard with parents, and communication is improving, we were told. Fathers attend workshops on sex education, all parents now want to get involved.

'We help everyone to find their own way through acceptance; kindness is a big word here, ultimately it's their choice whether to do the right thing,' says head. Politeness and good manners are essential requirements here. Swearing at a member of staff will result in exclusion. 'We will do everything we can, use as many resources as possible before permanently excluding.' Pastoral systems include peer mentoring – both internal and external – and the five-star canteen with a focus on hygiene and health is part of the campaign against any kind of food disorders. Ms Kruger acknowledges the challenge of gender identity. 'They are legally women until they are 18,' she says firmly, 'and therefore can remain in EWS, but they get fantastic support' from Gendered Intelligence – a community-based project that delivers educational programmes as well as offering advice and counselling. Ms Kruger puts safeguarding before everything, something that was reflected in the recent safeguarding audit, which was outstanding.

Pupils and parents: Most parents and daughters here made a conscious decision to choose Ellen Wilkinson above any other school. The odd pupil has chosen it because someone in her wider family has been here, many because it is a real community school with a local feel. Some teachers are former pupils. One parent said her daughter chose it 'because of the extracurricular clubs, diverse cultures and because it's sporty.' Most like the all girls atmosphere, but this is definitely not a religious school. One Muslim parent said her two priorities were that her daughter be 'happy and safe'; Ellen Wilkinson fits the bill.

A genuinely relatively balanced mix of cultures and religious groups with about 20 per cent white British, 30 per cent Asian, 20 per cent Black and 20 per cent Arabic; others include Japanese (some choose this over the local Japanese school), Chinese, Polish and other European. Sixty-six different languages are spoken in the school. Although in some families the mother might speak very limited English (though the father's English is fluent), 'all groups integrate', affirmed everyone we spoke to; there are no cliques based on race.

They all share a common interest in developing the confidence and aspirations of all the girls. 'They will be the leaders of tomorrow,' affirms Ms Kruger. Tolerant, broadminded, self-aware and thoroughly 21st century, our guides looked slightly baffled at our questions about diversity. Girls here are proud of their school and have a strong sense of giving something back and contributing to society.

The last word: A school with history, substance and a wealth of experience that is more than keeping up with the times and has a refreshingly modern and progressive outlook. Under its current leadership, a warm wind blows through its wide corridors which, together with high expectations and standards, makes for a thoroughly healthy and successful institution.

Elthorne Park High School

Westlea Road, Hanwell, London W7 2AH

020 8566 1166 | elthorne@ephs.ealing.sch.uk | www.ephs.ealing.sch.uk

State | **Ages:** 11–18 | **Pupils:** 1,200; sixth form: 220

Headteacher: Since 2012, Eliot Wong BSc PGCE Dip Ed NPQH (40s). Married with a school-age daughter, Mr Wong is a west Londoner through and through. Educated at St Peter's Primary school in Hammersmith and then Burlington Danes, he graduated with a first class degree in mathematics from King's College London before following his vocation in teaching (maths). He still finds the time to teach further maths to a class of about five who choose to do it ('it's the most enjoyable thing I do') as well as running revision classes for GCSE. Sixteen years of his career have been spent in schools in Ealing. Previously deputy head at Brentside High School, and before that assistant head at Cheam High School. He has also worked at Cardinal Wiseman (head of maths) and in Woking.

Thoughtful, determined and with a razor sharp logical mind, Mr Wong has achieved much improvement. Graphs depicting GCSE data are moving in a healthy northerly direction and the latest Ofsted inspection in 2015 graded the school as good (from a 'requires improvement' in 2013) with the proviso that it only missed an outstanding because there were only two years of available results data. Far from being disheartened by missing out on an outstanding, Mr Wong sees this as an opportunity to innovate and change continually: 'once you achieve an outstanding, there is a risk of complacency,' Mr Wong smiles. An advocate of Jim Collins' hedgehog concept, Wong believes if you focus on doing one thing really well everything else will fall into place. In his view it's the teaching that you need to concentrate on. 'If you teach really well, behaviour improves and parents are happy.' He measures the quality of teaching in a number of different ways, including regularly observing lessons and checking exercise books.

A simple but effective change he has made is to the school's mission statement: from 'achieving in a learning community' to 'achieving excellence in a learning community.' He has introduced rigour, challenge and aspiration and observes that 'most staff have responded very positively'. A regular tweeter, he celebrates his students' achievements in the public sphere as well as making sure his school remains prominent not only on social media but also in the mind of the local authority, from which he has been effective in extracting funding (for the new £14m expansion, for example). He is proud of the liberal atmosphere that is immediately noticeable, but asserts that 'we are old fashioned in some senses – in that we work hard and show a positive and respectful attitude.' However, this is achieved not by 'imposing draconian measures' but through 'trust (and verification) and expectation'. That is the Elthorne way, he says, and applies as much to the staff as to the pupils.

Excellent teachers and motivated pupils are only two legs of the three-legged stool; another focus of his is parental involvement. He has introduced the 'text challenge', challenging parents to support their children with weekly texts about particular issues, in current affairs, for example. Mr Wong is deeply conscious of having to find ways to add value not only to aspirational but also disadvantaged families. 'If you want to get the best out children you can't drag them, but you need to stimulate them with interesting, engaging lessons and the support of their parents.' This is the ACE formula – Achievement, Challenge, Excellence. It seems to be working.

Mr Wong is an advocate of Jim Collins' hedgehog concept. The head believes if you focus on doing one thing really well everything else will fall into place

Mr Wong is well respected by the pupils (they panic if they are on their phones when he appears in the playground), but parents speak of their frustration with his failure to respond to emails, and to complete references on time, and complain how difficult it is to get hold of him. An industrious and thoughtful head, however (his office is decorated with hundreds of yellow post-it notes), he is highly committed and canny.

Entrance: About 1,000 apply each year for 240 places in year 7. The four main feeder primaries are Fielding, Oaklands, Little Ealing and St Mark's – perception among parents is that Fielding dominates. As the primaries expand, so there is greater pressure on places. Proximity to the school the main criterion (after the usual criteria have been taken into account – children in public care, exceptional medical or social circumstances etc). Catchment has shrunk from a 1.5 mile to a one mile radius. Parents want their children to come here and consider it to be outstanding – regardless of what Ofsted says. Siblings given priority. To get into the sixth form you need a minimum of five 9-4s including English and maths at GCSE with at least a 6 in chosen A level subjects.

Exit: Of the upper sixth approximately 75 per cent go on to university, with about a quarter of these to Russell Group. Brighter pupils attracted elsewhere for sixth form, observed one parent. 'No NEETs for the past three years!' says head proudly. Some 93 per cent stay in education post-GCSEs, around 50 per cent stay at Elthorne to study advanced courses in the sixth form – over 70 per cent of these study A levels, but all sixth formers study advanced (level 3) courses which may include BTecs. About 20 per cent each year go on to art school and one or two each year go to the BRIT school.

Latest results: In 2019, 30 per cent 9-7 grades and 54 per cent got 9-5 in both English and maths at GCSE; at A level 22 per cent were A*/A (48 per cent A*-B).

Teaching and learning: ALPS value added rates the sixth form as 'outstanding' for teaching and learning and results. Each year five or six pupils take further maths A level.

Elthorne Park is currently the top performing school in South Ealing and Hanwell (and has held this position for the third year running), and is in the top quintile of schools nationally in terms of GCSE attainment (including English, maths and two sciences). Out of over 5,000 non-selective, co-ed schools in the country Elthorne recently ranked 91st in performance tables, putting the school in the top two per cent.

Ofsted identified particularly imaginative teaching in modern languages with high standards of marking. Over half the year takes at least one language and French, Spanish and German all get a good smattering of 9-6 grades, Polish too. A foreign exchange is organised for each language and about 50 pupils go on a language exchange each year. Elthorne's modern language results are in the top five per cent of the country. Mr Wong says he will support anyone who wants to learn Latin (and ancient Greek) but a visiting teacher will have to come in specially or the pupil will have to go elsewhere.

The quality of teaching is closely observed and monitored. 'Book looks' at least half termly to check that marking is up to standard and each teacher is observed three times a year. Each year to GCSE has six classes with about 26 pupils in each. Setting in maths from year 7, English and science also broadly set as well as modern languages. Excellent DT department, offering separate exams in food technology, textiles, resistant materials and graphic products. Music, drama and theatre studies are strong, as well as all three sciences, particularly chemistry. All departments run 'intervention sessions' to support pupils who are falling behind.

Innovative teaching includes 'flip learning'. Students are required to research a subject before a lesson. The lesson can then be conducted in a more discursive way

Some 75 per cent of students have been taking EBacc subjects for some time but 'I will no way force every student to do subjects that aren't suited them,' avers Mr Wong. BTec courses in media, business and health and social care also available as well as level 1 courses in eg motor vehicle maintenance and salon services. The ASDAN Award Scheme provides a course in basic skills, life skills and general knowledge for those students who wish to limit the number of GCSE courses they study.

Innovative style of teaching includes 'flip learning'. Students in the sixth form (and some classes lower down the school), given an iPad and required to research a subject before a lesson. The lesson can then be conducted in a more discursive way – students therefore learn to think, as well as to carry out independent research.

Enrichment lessons form part of the curriculum for years 7 to 9 – an effort to broaden the academic experience so that pupils are not confined to EBacc subjects. They might study, eg, Japanese or film. Gifted and talented pupils can used it as a springboard to enhance their skills.

One parent observed reluctantly that there remains a culture of low expectation at Elthorne, however, citing as an example the practice of basing target grades at GCSE on earlier Sats results. Parents also commented on a lack of support with regard to A level choices and the university process. There is a lack of clear communication and flexibility about options, they say. This results in a few going elsewhere for sixth form when their inclination would have been to stay. School's response to this is that the senior leadership team now interviews every year 11 student and discusses the extracurricular guarantees made to every student, which range from travel abroad to gym membership and personalised help with Oxbridge applications. Communication when a child is not reaching targets, on the other hand, is very good, observed another parent. A subject teacher will send a text, and similarly if a child gets detention, the parents are sent a text.

Learning support and SEN: The number of students with SEN is not high – less than 20 per cent – but a relatively high number of students (between two and three per cent) with EHC plans. 'They are attracted to us as we are a nurturing school, and they are well supported,' says Mr Wong. The SENCo has a team of 10. Children are supported in class as much as possible with teaching assistants attached to subjects. EAL tuition takes place outside the classroom. One parent observed how little support you get if you are a middle class kid with dyslexia – we have heard that before. A £14m expansion project, the Additionally Resourced Provision for Special Needs, opened in 2017. This is a hub of activity working to support children with speech, language and communication problems and those with specific learning needs (SLCN – speech, language and communication needs). The new development also houses facilities for all the students, including a new hall and drama studio, a life skills room and two extra ICT suites.

The arts and extracurricular: 'Expressive arts are at the heart of our community,' says Mr Wong. We were impressed with just how much goes on in here – in creative arts, drama and music.

For budding thespians there is the opportunity to perform extracts from Shakespeare plays at the annual Shakespeare Schools Festival. In addition there is an annual major whole-school production, often a musical (recently they performed Grease). Students get involved with all aspects of the production – costumes, choreography, music, set and props. Decent drama studio where lessons and rehearsals take place. Performances happen in the hall.

Gifted musicians are identified and given lots of opportunity to compete and perform. Numerous concerts and recitals plus a classical music competition and annual rock concert. Plenty of ensembles – brass and guitar as well as a chamber and whole school orchestra. Macs in music rooms where students are taught music composition. The popular summer festival and barbecue brings together performances and displays – art and DT as well as drama and music.

Lots of trips and activities including annual ski trip and Spanish, French and German exchanges (with a twin school), as well as geography field trips and visits to eg Oxford University and the theatre. Plenty of extracurricular opportunities such as public speaking competitions, DofE, bushcraft and PGL trips, the STEM challenge (EPHS were recently regional winners) and UK maths challenge. A plethora of clubs take place after school, from debating to film and volunteering in the community.

Sport: Elthorne teams have excelled in the borough in various sports including cross-country, netball, basketball, rugby, football and cricket. Girls' sports are especially strong. The current year 11 girls' netball team has been unbeaten for the past four years and the U13 girls' football team are national champions. There are regular competitions and matches – inter-form and inter-school as well as regional. An annual sports day, which includes track and field athletics as well as softball, takes place at Perivale sports ground.

Ethos and heritage: Elthorne may be in Hanwell but it stands out from other schools of its kind because it's situated on the edge of the seven and a half acres of green space that is Elthorne Park. Children can spill into this area during lunch break (supervised), and the football pitches and sports areas are a tremendous additional resource. The main buildings are positioned around a central courtyard – a mixture of low, single-storey, temporary, and two-storey buildings as well as the shiny, modern sixth form centre. Eight modern, spacious and well-equipped science labs, a suite of specialist music rooms, a purpose built drama studio, four art studios with a dark room, graphics and kiln facilities. Specialist DT including food technology, textiles and resistant materials. Plenty of Macs available for use in graphics as well as in music. Large sports hall as well as separate school hall where lunch, assemblies and drama happens. Purpose built sixth form centre. A feeling of space – no cramped corridors and a comfortable well-resourced library.

Mr Wong works hard and expects those around him to work hard. Trust is key – but trust with verification. We will trust them, he says, but we will check on them

Maroon uniform creates a somewhat dour impression and can be worn scruffily: 'they are not super strict about ties and tucking in shirts here,' said our guide with warm appreciation. This school is far from dour, however, but vibrant and buzzy. While Mr Wong clearly has a firm grip, the school has a relaxed feel; children are not deferential but their behaviour seems to fall on the right side of the line.

Pastoral care, inclusivity and discipline: Mr Wong describes the school as a healthy mix of old-fashioned and more relaxed values. While there is a finely tuned system of 'levelled' detentions (ranging between a 15 minute personal detention with a teacher to a head teacher detention on a Monday night) as well as a three strikes policy and a system of internal isolations, the key element is trust. This can't be imposed, says Wong, through draconian measures, but through example and respect. He talks about 'the Elthorne Way', an expectation of high achievement and excellence through a healthy symbiotic relationship between staff and pupils. Students appear relaxed, but that doesn't mean they aren't polite and well behaved. Mr Wong works hard and expects those around him to work hard, both staff and pupils. 'I believe in hard work and striving for excellence,' he says, 'I don't believe in excuses.' Trust is key – but trust with verification. We will trust them, he says, but we will check on them. The students have a voice – the student council have regular breakfasts and lunches with staff and there is an annual student survey. They, too, are listened to and treated with respect. When it comes to drugs and weapons, however, the line is clear and inflexible.

Parents warmly supportive – and appreciative – of the school's approach to incidents that happen outside school hours, often with the local community. They step in quickly and with tact and understanding. Behaviour – according to most parents – is 'on the whole good'.

Pupils and parents: Just under 50 per cent of families here are white British. The rest split fairly equally between black, Asian and Eastern European. Some support for EAL but most have learnt good English at primary school. Local Ealing families who, on the whole, are keen their children do well and will work hard with the school to achieve this. Relatively low number of pupils are on free school meals (25 per cent compared with a national average of 28 per cent). Stable student population.

Money matters: A local authority funded, well-resourced school – reserves, we were told, are greater than five per cent. Lower than borough average spent on supply staff, large proportion of budget spent on teachers and education support staff. Almost double spent on learning resources and ICT compared with local and national averages.

The last word: Value added – an often overlooked measure – is strong here: mid and high achievers will make significant progress, especially compared with their peers nationally. If you have a motivated child, keen to do well, this school won't hold him/her back but will inspire and work to meet that potential. A school with a genuine liberal arts and creative ethos. A precious gem in this age of emphasis on EBacc subjects. Let's hope it will preserve its arty tradition as it consolidates the academics in the face of pressure from on high.

Glebe Primary School

Sussex Road, Ickenham, Uxbridge UB10 8PH

01895 462385 | office@glebeprimary.org | www.glebe.hillingdon.sch.uk

State | Ages: 3-11 | Pupils: 639

Headteacher: Since 2017, Melanie Penney MA (special education – hearing impairment) BA (theology, religious studies, drama) PGCE, previously assistant head and deputy head. Before that, at Pinner Park, Harrow. Never in any doubt about teaching being her vocation. Originally joined Glebe in 1999 as a SENCo and class teacher. 'In 2009 I was asked to cover the deputy head who went on long-term sick leave and when that post ended a year later, they wound up creating a position for me of assistant head. In January 2017, following a staffing restructure, I became deputy head. Six months later, I became headteacher – it's been quite a rollercoaster.' Headship was never the plan – 'I love being in the classroom, so I still teach RE to year 6s, but I got swept along with management and now I love it.' Trained as a specialist teacher of the deaf.

One of the warmest heads we've come across, and highly regarded by staff, parents and pupils, who call her 'aspirational' and 'not one to let things stand still, always looking for improvement'. 'Everything at this school is done with compassion and it all comes from her,' one parent told us. 'Everything – and I mean everything – starts with the child and she provides the consideration, kindness, familiarity and humour that stops there being a "them and us" feel,' reported another. She's out on the gates every morning and afternoon, 'always smiling and approachable and she doesn't shy away from parents speaking their mind.' Pupils like her open-door policy and her hot chocolate Fridays (when two 'beacons of outstanding behaviour' from each class get a hot invitation).

Lives in Berkshire with husband, Steve, and their son and daughter, both at secondary school.

Entrance: Looked after children and SEN get priority, then it's siblings and after that it comes down to distance. Catchment area shrunk a few years back as school grew more popular, with some pupils even transferring from schools that previously had a better reputation. But as school increased to three form entry, it's expanded again, with families now hailing as far as Slough, Hillingdon, Uxbridge and beyond, 'though few come further than three miles'. There's quite a bit of movement in the area (10 per cent of pupils come from military families stationed at the local RAF base and often only stay for two years; and high house prices force many families who look to move from renting to buying out of the area) so it's worth checking places further up, although when we visited there were waiting lists for years 2, 5 and 6.

Exit: One or two go to the independent sector and a few to local grammars, but the majority head to Vyners School in Ickenham (over half) or Ruislip High School, Douay Martyrs, Bishopshalt or Oak Wood.

Our view: Set in the deepest London suburbs (Ickenham tube is near the end of the Piccadilly and Metropolitan lines), the school moved into brand new two-storey L-shaped block in 2014 which now caters for three-form entry. Apart from one remaining prefab, which is used for before- and after-school care (provision by school from 7.45am and by an outside company until 6pm; waiting lists apply) and music lessons, everything takes place in this shiny new building, with red accents everywhere you look, including in the uniform – a nice reflection of the vibrancy of the school. Everywhere is clean, bright and airy, with wide corridors and break-out areas and colourful displays of pupils' work on the walls. Good, clear (again, red) signposting at every turn means there's no chance of getting lost. Highlights include the large hall that doubles up as canteen ('the food is really good,' pupils assured us) from the pupil-named Pegasus café and homely nurturing room 'where you can go when you feel sad,' as one pupil put it. Well-stocked, if rather disorganised, library. 'Disappointing that they didn't put in any dedicated rooms for the likes of art,' admits head. Ditto for science labs, we thought – one would have been lovely, even if it doubled up as a form room.

Everything takes place in a shiny new building, with red accents everywhere you look, including in the uniform – a nice reflection of the vibrancy of the school

The school's go-getting motto is 'We can and we will!' and the strength of the academics do it justice. Sats results are above the national average and although a recent Ofsted report found that 'more able pupils have not always done as well as expected', the school is addressing this, mainly through setting. It starts in reception, with setting for phonics, then from year 2 in writing, from year 3 in maths and – depending on the cohort – in English from year 4: 'We realised those at the top needed pushing further, with things like greater depth of comprehension.' History and science are popular, showing 'it's not just a school hell bent on maths and English' (as one parent put it); French for all from year 3.

Teachers ('all of whom are effective, although one or two lack the warm touch,' said one parent) are encouraged to be constantly reflective, including via regular video observations which they go through with the head or one of the two deputy heads. Technology well integrated into lessons, with enough iPads for two classes to use at any one time and laptops aplenty. New outdoor classroom.

The caring ethos is another USP for this school. 'A happy child will learn' could just as easily be its slogan. There's a dedicated pastoral worker, who works not only with pupils but staff and parents. And there are plenty of leadership opportunities, with photos on the wall of the head boy, head girl and house captains, with other opportunities including prefects, mentors and buddies. 'Kindness is in the very bones of this school,' said one parent.

Around 10 per cent of children have SEN, 17 of whom had ECHPs when we visited. Described as 'taking a united approach', the school works closely with both families and outside agencies and 'we look at the child, diagnosis or not.' The school is a regional centre for those with impaired hearing, with two specialist teachers of the deaf (one is the head) and places for nine hearing impaired children. Every classroom has a Soundfield system, amplifying the sound of the teacher's voice, and there is an inclusion office with a speech and language area and two teaching rooms. All of the children are on the roll of their mainstream class and school aims for them to be taught in class alongside their hearing peers, with support if necessary. 'This is an incredibly inclusive school,' one parent told us.

Sports include football, netball, cross-country, athletics, cricket, hockey and tag rugby, much of it delivered by a specialist sports coach. The school takes part in inter-school competitions, with a particularly strong girls' football team, unbeaten so far – 'unusual for us, believe me,' says the head, who has historically had to do a lot of talks on 'how it's all about the taking part'. 'But while we're gracious in defeat, we are getting more focused and really giving winning a go.' All pupils do the Daily Mile three times a week, come rain or shine.

All children get the chance to study a musical instrument. This starts in year 1 with African drumming, year 2 with recorders and year 3 with the ukulele. Keyboard and guitar also on offer for all, while peripatetic teachers offer paid-for lessons in violin, cello, clarinet and flute. Surprisingly, no school orchestra, but there is an annual music concert and a choir that works its socks off at Christmas time visiting local shopping centres and old folks' homes, as well as taking part in Young Voices at the O2. Drama does not feature in stand-alone lessons, but every year group performs at least once annually, in addition to class assemblies and the likes of performance poetry. 'All children get a chance to shine on stage,' one parent told us. Clubs range from gardening to Mandarin, plus all the usuals – 'and if we suggest a new club, the school usually listens and acts,' one parent told us.

Art is 'so much more than just mixing paints', according to the school – they set regular ambitious goals such as self-portraits, 'then working back from that to ensure the pupils have the skills they need to achieve it within a set time period.' No get-out clause for less arty teachers; they're simply encouraged to learn from their colleagues or watch YouTube tutorials.

Behaviour mainly good, 'with small proportions of children who find it hard, predominantly due to SEN.' The school has 10 expectations widely displayed, plus a strong rewards system. Sanctions, where necessary, include removal of five minutes from golden time (free time on Friday afternoons) which can be earned back. Anything more serious involves missing playtime and writing letters of apology, with parents called in where necessary and around one temporary exclusion a year. Parents impressed with 'the way problems in friendship groups are taken seriously and dealt with sensitively' and the 'nuanced approach to preventing and dealing with bullying'. Staggered playtimes, friendship benches, trained year 6 play leaders, PSHE and regular assembles on kindness all help.

Families predominantly white British, reflecting the local area, with around 17 per cent Asian descent. Mainly middle class, but less so as catchment expands, and mostly dual income. Thriving Friends of Glebe. Former pupils include TV presenter Sue Cook and London 2012 athlete Julia Bleasdale.

The last word: This is a school with a strong nurturing ethos and robust (but not pushy) academics. 'Children leave here not just reaching their potential, but as really nice people,' one parent told us. 'My daughter wanted to give Easter presents to 17 different members of staff, from teachers to dinner ladies and cleaners and to me that sums up Glebe as every single person who walks through the gates is valued.'

The Green School for Girls

CofE 9

Busch Corner, London Road, Isleworth TW7 5BB

020 8321 8080 | enquiries@tgsgirls.com | www.tgsgirls.greenschoolsonline.co.uk

State	Ages: 11-18	Pupils: 952; sixth form: 159 (boys 10, 149 girls)

CEO and Executive Headteacher: Since 2015, Sally Yarrow (late 40s) BMus PGCE, educated at Aylesbury High grammar school and Hull University before completing her PGCE at Goldsmiths. Started her career as a music teacher and music remains her passion in education. Previously deputy head at St Marylebone school, a consistently high performing all-girls CofE secondary, she fits like a glove here but has nonetheless stepped out of her comfort zone, having been at St Marylebone for almost her entire career. 'I could have stayed there for the rest of my working life, I loved it and was very happy, but I was ready for a new challenge,' she confides. With two school-age boys of her own, Mrs Yarrow is approachable, youthfully girlish and enthusiastic, and deeply principled. Very popular with parents and pupils who regard her as having made a real impact. One parent described her as shrewd with a definite presence. Many of the girls see her as stern and strict, 'which is no bad thing,' affirmed another parent. On a very local level, she introduced whole-school assemblies in the capacious sports hall, a hugely popular fixture with the girls which gives the school a sense of unity and purpose. She is definite about her vision and expresses it without any fudge or waffle. Her expectations are high but her approach is entirely child centred. 'It is all about what's best for the pupils,' she says. 'We are a fully comprehensive, inclusive and diverse school and I am very proud of that.'

Her title is now CEO and executive head of the Green School Trust and she oversees both the girls' school and the new Green School for Boys. Head of school is Stephen Burns, previously deputy head, who is responsible for the day-to-day running of the school.

Entrance: As this is a Church of England school, parents are expected to be committed to the Christian ethos and give full support to the school. Girls are expected to attend Christian acts of worship and take part in the religious curriculum. A hundred of the 155 places are reserved for practising Christians, 30 places allocated to 'other world faiths' and 25 are community places. Priority to siblings (including brothers at the Green School for Boys) and those who live closest.

Sixth form admissions (boys as well as girls) according to predicted GCSE grades and proximity.

Don't be shy about making an in-year application for an occasional place. As with all areas of London there is movement and there are often new arrivals in years other than years 7 and 12.

Exit: A challenge for Mrs Yarrow is to keep as many of high performers as she can for the sixth form and encourage them to appreciate its strengths. Around 55 per cent leaves after GCSEs. After A level students go to a wide range of destinations to read an equally wide range of subjects. UCL, King's College London, Lancaster, Nottingham,

Royal Holloway and Brunel recently popular. A small number to art foundation and five per cent take gap years, including apprenticeships or internships with eg the BBC. No Oxbridge in 2020.

Latest results: In 2020, 37 per cent 9-7 at GCSE; 81 per cent 9-5 in both maths and English at GCSE. At A level, 61 per cent A*-B. In 2019 (the last year when exams took place), 36 per cent 9-7 at GCSE; 57 per cent 9-5 in both maths and English. At A level, 24 per cent A*/A (51 per cent A*-B).

Teaching and learning: Consistently impressive GCSE results. History, maths English and religious studies perform particularly well with high numbers of 9-7s. Science is also getting stronger. A level subjects include art and design, film studies, sociology and psychology as well as BTec level 3 in health and social care. High numbers choose biology, psychology and religious studies at A level. Value added scores are good (Progress 8 is a positive 0.5, placing the school in the top three per cent of schools nationally) – pupils make good progress, a valuable indicator of good teaching and a well run school. Parents comment about their daughters in the lower sets being stretched just as hard as if they were in the top sets. High expectation runs through all the layers of the school. Number of pupils with English as an additional language is very high – there is the option to take a GCSE in a native language, or indeed any language in which a pupil excels, in year 9.

A level results do not match the impressive GCSE scores – 'yet,' Mrs Yarrow intervenes. 'We lose a few of the high achievers after GCSE, and the girls for whom English is not their first language find the challenges are greater at A level – but this is something we are very much working on at the moment,' she explains, adding 'there is a huge amount of support for sixth form provision.' The school is part of a Hounslow sixth form consortium (others include Gunnersbury, Brentford, Gumley and Chiswick), so girls in the sixth form here can travel to other schools for certain lessons, which may include boys. Extended Project Qualification (EPQ) is popular and highly successful. It taps into all the skills and qualities that Mrs Yarrow is so determined to develop here: self-reliance, resilience, being able to think and stand on one's own two feet. An enrichment programme in the sixth form, 'broadening horizons', incorporates academic literacy, discussion and discourse. It is aimed at developing academic minds; their form tutors are known as 'coaches' and they coach them with their studies. Opportunities for stretching as sports leaders, in Young Enterprise and LAMDA. Sixth form mentors, or co-tutors, work with particular forms as part of their leadership development, and they assume positions of responsibility whether as prefect, head girl, or one of four deputy head girls or assistants (a mirroring of the school's staff senior leadership team).

An enrichment programme in the sixth form is aimed at developing academic minds; their form tutors are known as 'coaches'

Setting for maths from year 7, and from year 8 in English and science: 'This may change; there is a fairly broad range within the sets,' avers Mrs Yarrow, who is mindful to ensure that teaching in the lower sets doesn't create a false cap of attainment. Teaching methods, language used by staff and senior leaders' attitude all encourage the building of a growth mindset and resilience. 'This is one of our school priorities,' says Mrs Yarrow, 'along with the application of performance skills to all the subjects and to life.'

Learning support and SEN: Additional support given to those who need in it in years 7, 8 and 9 in maths and English (known as the Bridge Group). There can be as many as 15 pupils taught in a lesson of their own by the very experienced SENCo as well as a teacher and learning support assistant. Girls are taken out of language lessons to attend these classes. Less than one per cent of students have an EHCP.

The arts and extracurricular: DT GCSE options are textiles and food technology, but no electronics or resistant materials. Eighteen sewing machines as well as three embroidery machines and two overlocker machines, but only one textiles teacher. If your daughter wants to do A level textiles she will currently have lessons at one of the other schools in the Hounslow consortium. Everyone does food technology in years 7 and 8. Art is a popular A level. We saw some impressive ceramics, a very tangible pineapple in particular.

Old hall used for fashion shows (a fundraiser) and drama productions. There is also a drama studio – where we witnessed a very noisy game known as 'the splat game' designed to warm up the acting genes. Lots of productions by all year groups. Annual school productions have recently included Archie Dobson's War, Much Ado About Nothing ('slightly adapted,' we're told) and The Ash Girl. The sixth form theatre company recently produced, performed and directed The Great Gatsby.

Since the arrival of Mrs Yarrow, a huge and healthy increase in numbers wanting to join choirs and bands; music has been one of her priorities. Girls describe it, with infectious enthusiasm, as 'a really fun subject'. Music technology popular; lots of fancy equipment – Apple Macs and keyboards, and we saw a year 10 class writing a rap song. Lots of practice rooms for the large numbers who play an instrument – many play more than one, and music permeated several mainstream lessons we saw.

Debating club also very popular – open to any year group and recently, we were told, they examined issues from gay marriage to stem cell research and thrashed out the question of whether Black History Month should be abolished.

Plenty of residential trips – especially in year 9 – to Spain and France as well as ski trips to Austria. Duke of Edinburgh awards, bronze (year 10), silver and gold.

Careers advice and support strong. School awarded level 3 Investors in Careers.

Sport: Wide choice of sporting activities include rowing, netball and badminton. School participates in various borough competitions including the National Youth Rowing Competition. Plenty of facilities on or adjacent to the site – netball courts as well as rugby and football pitches. Tag rugby one of the main sports here. A large, modern and squeaky clean sports hall can accommodate volleyball, dodgeball, trampolining and self-defence as well as netball, basketball and badminton.

Ethos and heritage: Although this is a Church of England school with a Christian ethos, it is overwhelmingly multi-faith. About a third of pupils are from Muslim families. One parent explained that girls' schools are popular 'because girls won't lose the attention of their teachers to the boys, the discipline is good and they can choose science subjects without feeling overshadowed by the boys'.

A five form entry school, the Green School is on the large side but not vast. Swathes of green tartan stream into the welcoming café Sorrento opposite the school. Not shouty girls, but considerate and polite, and all different cultures and backgrounds seem to integrate well as they pile into their waffles before the start of school. They file in an orderly fashion into the vast sports hall for assembly, in time to the soothing classical music that bounces off the sporty walls, and the hall becomes a sea of green uniform.

A school steeped in history (it was originally founded in 1796), the main building is a handsome 1906 Edwardian brick and timber building situated on the busy junction at Busch Corner in Isleworth. This now houses the library and a performance hall (where the clock has always been wrong) as well as some classrooms. Linking them are long, wide corridors which smell of freshly polished wooden parquet floors. Gold leaf plated wooden merit boards from the 1950s line the walls, and cupboards stuffed with silver cups nestle in corners. A satisfyingly traditional smell of learning, scholarship and achievement. The library, despite its traditional feel, is buzzing with activity. This is where girls come to do their homework – both during and after school hours. Books here are well thumbed and there are plenty of computers.

The modern buildings are bright, filled with sunlight, with lots of space. Our guides particularly enjoyed lingering in the sociology classroom, a favourite subject here. The sixth form centre is civilised with attractive space to eat and talk as well as have meetings, perform plays and listen to talks. An area to chat and use mobiles is screened off from an area to work and use computers (we presume for work). The school canteen is comfortable, streaming with sunlight through the large windows when we visited. All the girls we met said the food was good. Many get in early to eat breakfast here at 7.30am.

Not shouty girls, but considerate and polite, and all different cultures and backgrounds seem to integrate well as they pile into their waffles before the start of school

The school is divided into five houses – named here after trees (Willows, Oaks, Beeches etc) for the purpose of competitions, whether sporting, academic, or other – there is an inter-house Christmas carol competition, for example.

The Green School for Boys, part of the same Trust, will join the girls' school to form a joint co-ed sixth form from 2020, with sixth form facilities and courses at the two schools open to students from both.

Pastoral care, inclusivity and discipline: The pastoral care here is universally acclaimed. A number of parents described how much their daughters have grown in confidence here – whether as a result of performing in plays and assemblies, playing sport or being encouraged to question and challenge their teachers during lessons. While there is respect for the staff among the pupils, it works both ways, enabling the timid types, prone to being overly deferential, to emerge from their shells and speak up for themselves. The school motto, 'Let your light shine', seems to have genuine resonance.

The very congenial school chaplain is in school three times a week and she takes part in assemblies and services. By all accounts she plays a key pastoral role for students and staff alike.

There is a clear disciplinary procedure which appears to be appreciated by pupils, parents and staff. Final step after three warnings. If a girl needs to be removed from a lesson for being disruptive, she is sent to the Improvement Area. Curriculum parking is when a student is removed from a lesson and 'sent to an appropriate parking lot' to work. Detentions here are known as 'learning meetings'. 'You don't sit around doing nothing, but discuss a solution.'

Naughty behaviour seems to boil down to disrupting lessons and occasional bullying behaviour. The girls we spoke to looked wide eyed when we asked about drugs. This is a school of predominately good girls. Any incidents of bullying are dealt with quickly through the year leader and heads of year. Response is speedy and effective. Girls seem quite confident that they would go to the teachers if they needed to.

Social media – as in all secondary schools at the moment – is causing the most sleepless nights for heads. Here mobile phones have to be stored in lockers during the school day and if they are found on a girl during a lesson they are confiscated. The strict policy is bearing fruit – fewer social media related incidents this year than in previous years. A more relaxed policy is adopted with sixth formers, however.

One girl, who said she never used to like school, now enjoys coming to school and said she 'feels safe'. Parents, too, are confident that any issues of bullying, social media abuse or self harming will be dealt with swiftly and effectively. One mother described how 'in tune' the school is with its community: there is a genuine understanding of and empathy with the issues that face teenage girls at this time.

Pupils and parents: An immensely diverse, multicultural CofE school. Many Muslim pupils, some Hindu, as well as devout Christians and some of no faith. Many parents are practising Christians but plenty are not. Pupils come from Brentford and Chiswick as well as Staines and Isleworth and a wide range of local and far flung primaries. Over 30 per cent of pupils are on pupil premium. One parent talked of it being a 'balanced community', families from all walks of life, earning a living in so many different ways, but what virtually all parents have in common is a shared belief in high standards. They are committed to supporting their daughters to reach their full potential.

The last word: We agree that this is a genuinely outstanding state secondary. The high standard of pastoral care and the attention that's paid to each individual and their needs makes this a good fit for almost any girl, but especially those who are aspirational, hard working and committed to doing their best. A tolerant, diverse school with strong Christian values – of the very best kind. Those with sons, too, keep an eye out – the new Green School for Boys is one to watch.

Greenford High School

10

Lady Margaret Road, Southall, Middlesex UB1 2GU

020 8578 9152 | office@greenford.ealing.sch.uk | www.greenford.ealing.sch.uk

State | **Ages:** 11–19 | **Pupils:** 1,802; sixth form: 500

Headteacher: Since September 2019, Mia Pye, previously deputy head of Elthorne Park High. English degree from Sheffield and and PGCE and MA in education from the Institute of Education. She joined Greenford as a student teacher in 2000, becoming head of English, faculty leader and assistant head before moving to Elthorne in 2015.

Entrance: Most oversubscribed school in Ealing. Receives more applications than any other school, with 1,500+ applications for 300 year 7 places. Siblings given priority. 'This is a family school; a family could live in Slough and get a place at the school' (many do – as many Sikhs moved to Langley and Slough). 'We don't have a catchment.' However the next criterion is proximity to the school and most live within half a mile, though 10 per cent of pupils live further away.

Exit: Around a third leave after GCSEs. Three off to Oxbridge in 2019, plus eight doing medicine or dentistry and two overseas. Lots of contact with

Oxbridge colleges to make school and students known. Approximately 230 go on to university each year but there is also a lot of investment in apprenticeships. 'You have to be realistic; university is not for everyone but it does offer the chance to lead a different life.'

Latest results: in 2019, 31 per cent 9-7 at GCSE; 64 per cent got 9-5 in both English and maths. At A level, 21 per cent A*/A (47 per cent A*-B).

Teaching and learning: A fully comprehensive, non-selective school, Greenford High has to cater for two extremes, without overlooking the middle tranche. It does an impressively good job. Japanese, GCSEs and A levels at one end of the spectrum, and a BTec in business and enterprise at the other. DT product design, fine art and photography as well as business and economics are all offered; science labs are well equipped, science teaching effective. The high expectations for academic students do not just include a university exit, Russell Group, perhaps or even Oxford and Cambridge, but Harvard and Princeton too. At the other end of the scale, some apprenticeships are harder to achieve than a university place. Some 500 students were competing for one apprenticeship with Honda; it was a Greenford boy who won it.

Years 7 and 8 now have nearly all lessons in their own 'middle school' building, and pupils graduate formally from year 8 into year 9 – they get a 'degree' to show they are ready for the GCSE course that starts from year 9. The only test is their attitude to learning. Those that are not ready continue for longer in middle school. 'This solves a number of problems, not least it stops year 8 from being a fallow year.' Setting from year 7 in maths and English (about nine sets in total), science is setted later (moderate setting in year 7, more refined at KS4). Every pupil takes RE GCSE at end of the year 9, 'a gateway GCSE', 80 per cent pass, a third achieve 9-7, and 'even if they don't do as well as they would have done had they waited until year 11, it will have motivated and challenged them'. At the end of year 10 they all take a language GCSE (which they have started in year 7 and could include Spanish, French, German or Japanese), some take two languages, some take a community language – facilitated, but not taught, by the school. A study club after school for years 10 and 11 supports their organisation, revision and individual learning. Some classes have a mixed year group – eg years 9 and 10 are mixed as are years 10 and 11 – usually for options at GCSE.

GCSE results impressive. Consistently high progress scores at GCSE and A level.

Particularly strong GCSE results in business and economics (business handily appeals to both ends of the academic spectrum and Southall has one of the highest number of small businesses), all three sciences, computing, Japanese (though small numbers take it), German and history. Most popular subject at A level, by some margin, is maths, with pleasing results. Excellent results at A level too in media, film and TV studies (best results in the country), DT product design, physics and fine art.

'As with so much of the approach at Greenford,' observed a parent, 'if the pupils show enthusiasm and drive, the school will support them and nurture any talent or interest'

Greenford used to be a language college and 60-70 per cent of students continue to take a modern language at GCSE. Japanese has always been strong – 'it's always about the personalities. We were lucky to have an outstanding Japanese teacher and we continue to attract excellent teachers.' They are proactive – whether it be inviting the wife of the Japanese prime minister to the school or beating Eton and other high achieving independent schools at the Nihongo Cup run by the Japanese embassy. The experience spills into pupils' later lives: one ex-pupil is now working for big business in Tokyo. With difficult decisions impending on funding, however, the fate of Japanese here lies in the balance – and it seems now to be an extracurricular subject.

Greenford High has pulling power, attracting high quality teachers. One of the physics teachers we met is possibly the only Somali female physics teacher in the country. The school has a partnership with Teach First, as well as with the Institute of Education, and trains 30 teachers a year – many stay on. Healthy mix of the long established, stable and experienced, some of whom form part of the senior leadership team, and the young and dynamic, bringing fresh ideas and fuelling the tangible vibrancy in the classroom.

Learning support and SEN: School is consistently in the top five per cent of the country for progress, and while the SEN progress is still above average, SEND pupils make lower progress compared with other pupils in the school. A fair number of pupils have support with their learning, but only a handful on EHC plans. School pained that these pupils make less progress than their mainstream peers despite the fact that they are still making more progress than the national average, and confirms that this is one of their targets. Recent improvements on speech and language needs.

The university style campus is not necessarily conducive to people with EHC plans – but the new block, in development, will have an ARP area to work with students who have different needs, and a capacity for 20 students.

The arts and extracurricular: Despite corrosive cuts, school manfully continues to offer excellent art, DT, textiles, cooking and photography (three art teachers have had to go as department has shrunk from five to two). Impressive display of design products – toys and automated hoovers. School is proud owner of a laser cutter as well as a 3D printer. All pupils do art in years 7 and 8, between 15 and 20 do GCSE, a few do fine art A level and about about four to six a year go on to art colleges. 'It is important that we don't forget those students.'

New buildings, opened by David Miliband in 2008, are painted in bright colours and named after key people (A for Aristotle, B for Brunel, F for Fitzgerald – Ella, not Scott)

School very supportive of Cadets, Scouts and Duke of Edinburgh Award. Some 150 trips a year, including to Lille, Berlin and Tokyo, to Cambridge, Oxford and Reading. Mixed year groups help to spread the cost – school helps as much as it can with funding. 'There is not a culture of the haves and have nots here, much to parents' relief,' pointed out one father. 'School is open to any initiative and will run with it, but the students need to be proactive,' commented a mother.

Music – very few take it to GCSE or A level (music tech only). However there have been successful barber shop quartets. Drum kit and guitars available for anyone who wants to have a go. 'As with so much of the approach at Greenford,' observed a parent, 'if the pupils show enthusiasm and drive, the school will support them and nurture any talent or interest.'

Drama is taken by everyone in years 7 and 8, and 20 or so continue to GCSE, though it is not available at A level. Small theatre where students put on comedy shows.

Sport: Sport is strong – as in other departments at Greenford, standards are high. An Olympic judge runs the gymnastics, an ex-England player coaches the basketball. Excellent facilities in relatively new building (funded by PFI). Well-equipped and well-used gym. Lots of space on site, including fleet of MUGAs as well as grass pitches (though notorious Ealing soil means they're waterlogged for much of the winter months, we were told with wry raise of the eyebrow). Football and netball strong (though there was an observation from one quarter that if you are not particularly keen you can end up not playing much sport at all). Both genders shine in gymnastics and trampolining. Boys and girls taught separately for PE.

Ethos and heritage: Founded in 1939, Greenford started life as a typical suburban grammar school, surrounded by farmland. The original 1930s buildings still stand and now form part of a new block. The school has gone through a number of different personalities since then and is now a large comprehensive with 1,800 pupils, increasing to 2,100 with the new middle school building, which houses years 7 and 8 and provides a 'small school' within the school.

The school buzzes with an atmosphere of endeavour, echoing its motto 'learning to succeed'. Modern, university campus style of the site reminiscent of Sussex and Warwick universities. The new buildings, opened by David Miliband in 2008, are constructed out of various materials, painted in bright array of colours and named alphabetically after key people (A for Aristotle, B for Brunel, F for Fitzgerald – Ella, not Scott). Each building has vibrant murals painted up the stairs, along the corridors, in the entrance halls – Penguin book covers, famous theatrical production posters and a Scrabble board, a surrealist portrait of 'the Greenford giraffe' outside Downing Street, a double helix climbing the stairs, a large map of England with university sites pinned to it. 'We wanted to make the place feel vibrant, that learning is stimulating and fun, and the students appreciate it, they respect their environment, we have very little vandalism.' The campus is surrounded by irregular grassy mounds, referred to as 'Teletubby hills', contributing to the overall sense that this place is an oasis of opportunity in the middle of its suburban setting.

The main reception, as you enter the school, resembles a busy airport – lots of people coming and going, a sense of industry and purpose. High tech gates and lanyard creations, but amidst all that security the atmosphere is human, friendly and flexible.

The canteen is café style, with a mix of round and long tables and a little tuck shop. Post-16 accommodation includes a common room with table football and a large quiet area filled with computer stations to work at and prepare for the next stage.

Pastoral care, inclusivity and discipline: Strong emphasis on an ethos of helping others – not reacting out of self-interest but for the good of the community and the good of others. Initiatives like hosting a dinner for senior citizens in the school hall – organised and run by post-16 pupils – helps to reaffirm these values. Assembly – taken in year groups, so each year gets together once a week – reflects on a range of issues from moral choices to healthy eating and child exploitation. Each assembly ends with an act of worship – relevant to all faiths.

Cyber issues addressed head on. System of cyber mentors contributes to an awareness and support system for any abuse of social media. School receives £50,000 each year from the John Lyon's Foundation towards this. E-safety talks regularly attended by all students – 'as a result, social media bullying and related issues are not a major concern here,' assures school.

'This is not a detention bound school,' commented one parent, 'but there are rules and there are standards, and they are high ones. If you want to get the best out of the school you are expected to work with them... You have to look smart, hand homework in on time, but these things are done by cooperation rather than the coercion.'

Behaviour, on the whole, is good. Teachers here earn respect and get it. There is genuine concern and care for the pupils, so that although good results are expected, it is the result that would be good for each individual. On the more contentious issues, we were assured that incidents of knives in school are rare and the school takes a sensitive approach to the government initiative Prevent. Issues relating to religious extremism are tackled in assemblies and through outside speakers who come to give talks. Homophobia more of a pressing issue than gender fluidity.

Pupils and parents: A diverse mix of different cultures and nationalities, about 40 per cent Muslim. Despite the diversity, the community is well integrated. When Pakistan play India in the test match, we were told, the school comes alive with excitement and the fault lines are more visible. Only five per cent white British. Other white communities from Eastern Europe, predominately Polish. Others come from all over, from Eritrea to Afghanistan, a fair few from Somalia. Many are very aspirational. Turnout for parents' evenings is always high, observed one parent. Lots are keen for their children to excel at the sciences. The demographic has shifted slightly in the last 10 years – mainly with the decrease in numbers from the Sikh community – and the school has now started to attract families with very able children – families who in the past might have chosen to send them to grammar or independent schools.

One parent commented, 'Kids here are not very privileged but become privileged from being at Greenford.' Pupils are politically aware, will hold mock elections during an election even if it coincides with exams, are flexible and ready to think on their feet.

The last word: If you want a school with a big heart, a diverse community which shares a desire for high standards and has high expectations, whether it be for results or attention to well-being, and if you are lucky enough to fall within the criteria for getting into this hugely oversubscribed school, you need look no further. But this is a school that gives to those who give: the more you put in the more you get out. Slouchers beware.

Headteacher: Since 2020, Stephen Byrne.

Entrance: Open mornings and evenings in the autumn term for prospective pupils. Non-selective academically in year 7, when 192 are admitted. Governing body in charge of admissions. Candidates divided according to the RC deanery in which they live, with a different percentage of places allotted to each of six deaneries. Preference to baptised, practising Catholics.

Pupils entering the school in the sixth form need English and maths level 5 and three different subjects at a minimum of level 5, with at least 6 in A level subjects. No faith requirement for those arriving for the final two years.

Exit: Around half depart after GCSEs, either to sample co-ed, or because they prefer vocational courses, or for geographical reasons. Of those who stay the overwhelming majority opt for university. Liverpool, Bristol, Kent and Royal Holloway all popular destinations, with recent courses including law, English, politics, psychology and history. One vet in 2019, plus one student heading off to study overseas (Spain). None to Oxbridge in 2019. Some choose art foundation courses. Others prefer apprenticeships, including in the civil service and in engineering, which often translate into real jobs on completion.

Latest results: In 2019, 45 per cent 9-7 grades at GCSE; 69 per cent 9-5 grades in both maths and English. At A level, 28 per cent A*/A grades (51 per cent A*-B).

Teaching and learning: Generally very decent results. Around 26 subjects offered at A level. Currently, English, maths, sociology and chemistry are popular sixth form choices. Part of a consortium with Gunnersbury and St Mark's, so those favouring less conventional subjects such as classical civilisation can study them at their sister schools. Conversely, their pupils venture over here for media studies and economics. Compulsory RE at GCSE. Parents feel that teaching is 'generally very good throughout', though one mother we spoke to felt homework 'could be more structured and meaningful.' The school disagrees with her view, telling us that 'our research and knowledge does not highlight homework as a general problem.'

Gumley has a language specialism. French, Italian, Spanish and Mandarin offered, as well as Latin for the most able. Annual language festival celebrates the diverse languages spoken by pupils. School also has partnerships with schools in Africa, China and India, reflecting its international make-up.

School feels pressure on staff is worse than ever, and that recruitment and retention of teachers is a problem here, as it is nationally. Pupils rate their teachers highly as 'they listen to us and care for us. They want us to do well.' One girl we spoke to praised her teachers' speedy responses to emails, often well into the evening. Many teachers go well beyond what is expected.

Chasing league tables is not Gumley's style. School explains that 'academic excellence is of paramount importance, but in tandem with the development of a young person's mental and emotional well-being. We do not lose sight of the person while aiming high academically. Education is not just about maths, science and so on. It's about making someone fully human and able to take their place in society.'

Annual poetry festival involves pupils writing their own poems. Gumley boasts its own poet laureate

Learning support and SEN: SEND provision considered to be excellent. Three fully qualified teachers and nine learning support assistants. Gumley can support the milder end of physical and learning difficulties, including ASD, dyslexia and speech and language needs. Everyone is screened for literacy levels at the start of year 7. Those requiring help are offered extra tuition, in-class support and reading clubs. Wheelchair access throughout.

The arts and extracurricular: Music is an integral part of Gumley life. Keen singers and instrumentalists are spoilt for choice, with numerous choirs and ensembles. Christmas and summer concerts are described by parents as 'exciting' and 'impressive'. Music department encourages pupils to try out different genres of music, one day experimenting with edgy rhythms on the drum kit, the next day performing traditional choral music. Enthusiastic staff choir.

Energetic drama productions ranging from Shakespeare to West End-style musicals. Pupils become fully immersed in the productions, including watching professional adaptations as preparation. High profile drama festival. Annual poetry festival involves pupils writing their own poems. Gumley boasts its own poet laureate. Local and national poets and artists are invited in for inspiration.

Annual art exhibition. One talented pupil won the Young Brit at Arts Award, beating off competition from over 2000 competitors. 'Our art is outstanding,' explains school, and the masterpieces adorning the walls support this. 'We are a school that allows exploration of all types of art,' she explains.

Impressive range of after-school clubs, all free of charge, including maths, STEM, eco, Latin, as well as 11 sports clubs, and music clubs including Gumley Glee. Trips abroad include annual language exchanges with schools in Europe and China; geographers head to Iceland; history and politics pupils to New York and Washington. Head joins the pilgrimage to Lourdes. For those looking to challenge themselves physically, there is skiing in Austria and a water sports week in France. Something to tempt all tastes.

School is good at encouraging the girls to think about careers from year 7 on, to look beyond the school gates and to be adventurous in their choices. Gumley also has a business and enterprise specialism and has developed close links with a range of businesses. Lots of industry workshops and work experience organised by school, including with British Airways, GSK and Merrill Lynch. Alumnae, including bankers, engineers, scientists and film directors, give career talks to pupils. They give their time for free, hoping to egg on the next generation. The phrase goes 'once a Gumley girl, always a Gumley girl.'

Sport: Sporty pupils are not short of opportunities here. Athletics, cricket, football, badminton, netball, rounders, gym and dance all offered. Excellent sports facilities, including eight tennis courts, five netball courts, a gym and dance/drama studios. Well-used Astro pitch. Athletics at park across the road. Gumley has secured numerous titles within the borough and at the London Youth Games.

Ethos and heritage: Founded in 1841 by Marie Madeleine D'Houet, an aristocrat in post-revolutionary France. Inspired by the spirit of Ignatius of Loyola, she established her own religious order – the Faithful Companions of Jesus (FCJ). In setting up Gumley, she hoped to empower local women. Part of a group of four schools in England under the trusteeship of the FCJ; the others are in the Wirral, Liverpool and London. School motto is Vive Ut Vivas ('Live that you may have life'). School sees foundress as an inspirational figure as 'she did not put a ceiling on herself. We want the pupils to realise that the power to determine their path in life is in their hands.' The school still follows the guidelines laid down by Marie Madeleine, as the head explains. 'She always said to the sisters that they should never tell a child off publicly. Take them aside and do it quietly. Never speak to a child as though their feelings do not matter'.

A Catholic school (now an academy) for girls with a handful of sixth form boys, who choose Gumley for specific subjects such as economics, government & politics, and media. Boys are fully integrated, including a deputy head boy. Some non-Catholics attend who join in fully with spiritual element of school. School believes that 'they enrich the community. Though they don't have to participate, they often want to.' Respect for different backgrounds and faiths is fundamental to the school.

Education is based on gospel and FCJ values with a focus on excellence, companionship, dignity, gentleness, justice and hope. The pupils themselves feel Gumley 'teaches us to be virtuous and hopeful'. Bethany, the chapel in the grounds, can be used for quiet reflection throughout the day, and is particularly popular in exam season, given its location bang next to the exam hall. Also used for a weekly mass (school has its own chaplain). Retreats implemented across all year groups, so pupils have time for quiet reflection away from the hustle and bustle of school life.

Gumley pupils are keen on fundraising. Substantial sums raised for variety of charities, both high-profile and local, especially those supporting children, the elderly, homelessness and Catholics. Pupils venture out into the community, visiting hospitals and offering story-telling sessions to local primaries. 'We teach them to put faith into action, through the understanding of linking charity work with the curriculum,' explains school.

Spacious campus. The central Queen Anne house is set in 10 acres of pretty grounds. Lawns are punctuated with numerous picnic tables, which are well populated in the summer term. A large canopy covering an outside eating area lends an attractive Mediterranean touch to this corner of Isleworth.

Pastoral care, inclusivity and discipline: Pupils, parents and teachers all rave about the outstanding pastoral care. 'We strive for pastoral excellence,' says school. Team is made up of two pastoral managers, two on-site counsellors and a teacher responsible for inclusion. One person oversees the smooth transition from year 6 to 7, and parents are impressed by this 'great induction and inclusion programme'. All pupils are in a tutor group. School will not economise on pastoral care and pays for staff supervision 'so they do not take difficult issues home with them'. The well-being of the whole community is central here.

Bethany, the chapel in the grounds, can be used for quiet reflection during the day, and is particularly popular in exam season, given its location bang next to the exam hall

Pupils are taught how to protect themselves, particularly online, and to consider the implications of present action on their prospects. Gumley emphasises the importance of learning to communicate with people from every walk of life: 'if you can communicate with all sorts of people, you will fly'.

Discipline taken seriously. Low truancy rates. Expulsions are rare, generally only for extreme behaviour. School does all it can to support those who are pushing the boundaries but sometimes a parting of the ways is inevitable. Forgiveness and reconciliation are part of the Gumley ethos. 'Girls and boys are not known by their failings,' says school. Success is celebrated, including through awards for achievement, progress, perseverance and contribution to school life.

Food considered to be fine and there is a choice on offer, though sizeable minority opts to bring in packed lunch from home. One parent we spoke to felt 'there could be healthier food options at the canteen'. Breakfast for early birds from 8am onwards.

Pupils and parents: School composition is predominantly Catholic. Wide mix of nationalities with over 65 languages spoken at home, notably Portuguese and Polish. Three or four pupils arrive per year with minimal English, and support is offered to those whose English is not up to scratch. Broad ethnic and social mix.

Parents feel communication from school is generally good. However, one mother commented that the school would benefit from 'a report system that better informs parents of students' grades and progress'. School says it is 'stumped' by this parental comment as monitoring reports are sent home every eight weeks.

Money matters: Gumley asks for voluntary contributions to the school development fund. Recently money has been used to help cover the upgrade of the security system, keep text books up to date, build a new roof, replace windows and make improvements to the music suite.

The last word: School wants pupils to be the best they can be. 'It's not the career, it's not the job, it's who you are that matters.' Gumley pupils are well equipped to face the challenges of the 21st century.

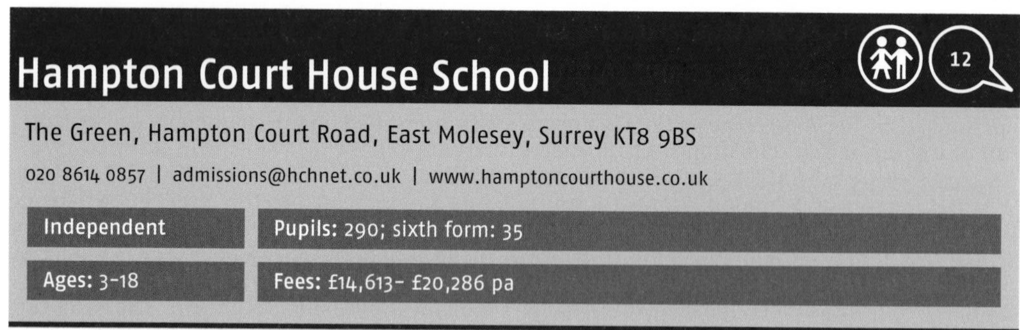

Hampton Court House School

The Green, Hampton Court Road, East Molesey, Surrey KT8 9BS

020 8614 0857 | admissions@hchnet.co.uk | www.hamptoncourthouse.co.uk

Independent | Pupils: 290; sixth form: 35

Ages: 3-18 | Fees: £14,613- £20,286 pa

Headmaster: Since 2001, Guy Holloway MA (Cantab) NPQH, known as 'Guy' to all. With his own Russian/German background, he is passionate about the importance of languages, both ancient and modern. He studied at King's College School, Wimbledon, before reading English at Peterhouse, Cambridge. He spent many years in Paris, first at the international PR firm, Burson-Marsteller, and then at the École Active Bilingue, where he was head of English in the section Britannique. For several years he was a volunteer with Save the Children UK, working with disadvantaged children. He is now patron of the children's charity Their Future Today, which supports abandoned and institutionalised children in Sri Lanka.

Part of the 1993 founding team which opened the Harrodian School, where he was director of studies, he is a co-founder of HCH. A committed educationalist, he lectures at the Institute of Education's London Centre for Leadership in Learning. He believes in giving pupils a global perspective so they have an appreciation of cultures and informed tolerance, partly borne out by the international flavour of his staff appointments, including a Spanish head of pastoral care and a German head of mathematics. He runs a weekly seminar – a comprehensive history of music course for all children in years 1 to 8 – and teaches cultural studies to years 10 and 11. He believes staff have a responsibility as role models, sharing the love of their subjects with their pupils. He acts on his beliefs, eg, he encourages all in the acquisition of vocabulary and shared his personal discovery, lustrum, in assembly on the day we visited.

Guy sees his future as 'married to HCH'. He champions creativity and is justifiably proud of the school's culture, which 'enables pupils to fulfil their passions' and nurtures individuals so that they develop quality relationships as a life skill. He is approachable and totally committed to the school's ethos: 'We believe in questioning our beliefs' and 'the primacy of the idea over the person'.

Alongside his fascination for psychology and learning, Guy has a diverse range of cultural and linguistic interests alongside languages, including foreign travel, literature, chess and concert-going, and he is an active member of the Rose Theatre Players. He enjoys directing films as well as plays (over 30) at HCH and recalled many ambitious productions to us with pride.

Entrance: Into the nursery at 3, or year 1 at 5+, following an informal interview with child and parents. During visit child will be observed by the teaching staff for both academic and social behaviour, and will meet with the head of lower and early years. If applicable, a confidential report from the child's current school will be requested. Head wishes to ensure that parents are committed to the school's ethos and approach to learning. At 10, children are tested in English and maths. More selective in recent years, but potential is still considered carefully.

Main senior school entry points at 11+ and 13+. Interview for candidate and parents plus maths and English tests. Parents are welcome to visit more than once as it is essential pupil and family believe in school's distinctive ethos and approach to education. New sixth form applicants need at least six grade 6s with 7s in subjects to be studied at A level.

Exit: Will prepare for 13+ exams and, unsurprisingly, incredibly diverse range of destinations, including lycées abroad, state schools, Eton, Wellington, Westminster, Bryanston, Kingston Grammar, Wimbledon High, Surbiton High, with some scholarships, although in recent years more are staying on. There is some turnover of children because families move abroad, but those remaining develop a widening circle of friends. Around a third leave after GCSEs. Recent university destinations include Bath, Bristol, Imperial, Queen Mary's University London, King's College London, Surrey, East Anglia, Loughborough and Exeter.

Latest results: In 2019, 78 per cent 9-7 at GCSE.; 53 per cent A*/A at A level (83 per cent A*-B).

Teaching and learning: The study and celebration of languages and the arts are integral to HCH, which is a UNESCO associate school and the only school in the UK to be granted Institut Français status by the French government for its commitment to French language and culture. In a liberal, civilised, relaxed, atmosphere where staff are addressed by first names, individuals are encouraged to pursue their passions to the full, whilst learning how to appreciate art, music and drama. The staffing reflects this, with native speakers and professional performers as role models; so important.

Very special indeed is the opportunity for all children from early years to year 4 to receive a bilingual education in English and French with fluent French speakers, so all can become at least competent and develop good accents. From age 6, pupils can also follow the French curriculum for the Centre National d'Enseignment à Distance, which we saw in practice as a year 5 group successfully completed assigned writing tasks to time. Grammar is taken seriously, along with teaching accurate use of punctuation, as seen in pupils' books. All learn Latin from year 5 and Spanish is lively and enthusiastic. Junior school language options include Mandarin and HCH is one of the leading prep schools for this in the UK. French is taught through other subjects (such as mathematics and humanities) and we saw year 1 pupils completing maths addition work happily asking questions in French and slipping back into English with ease. It all seemed perfectly natural and there was support from classmates as well as teachers.

Many nationalities are represented amongst staff and pupils and the curriculum reflects this, so children learn to appreciate and respect other cultures. We saw a year 5 English class tackling creative writing and were impressed by the articulate, confident responses to our questioning, whilst attentive year 6 pupils were appreciating Beowulf. Parents value the imaginative cross-curricular opportunities teachers take to make topics more meaningful eg Queen Victoria in history alongside Great Expectations in English. We saw year 2s, basing their designs on South American wildlife, making imaginative moulds in art, which would later be used to produce Fair Trade chocolates

The only school in the UK to be granted Institut Français status by the French government for its commitment to French language and culture

High numbers of 9/8s for languages at GCSE. Everyone takes at least one, with nearly a quarter studying French/Spanish in the first year of the sixth form.

HCH has gained the Good Schools Guide award for best performance in English independent schools by boys in both psychology and Spanish. This is not a result-driven academic school; instead, the head describes it as a 'shared intellectual environment'. Pupils are prepared for 13+ as well as GCSEs and now A levels. As one long-standing parent put it, 'Don't expect one of the local hothouses without uniform. You won't find the mechanistic, predictable, step by step approach for all at HCH, but instead a joy in the educational experience where pupils gain a rounded introduction to life, and where it's not just about passing exams.' Unavoidably, not all parents are convinced, and some question the fact that, despite degrees, teaching staff do not necessarily have teaching qualifications, whilst others praise their 'inspirational enthusiasm' and the attention and support given to each individual. Ofsted has judged that 'the mostly good or outstanding lessons enable pupils to make rapid progress' and recognised HCH as 'good and increasingly outstanding'.

The school is a lead school in the Network of Excellence in Computer Science, with an emphasis on programming. 'If a child needs to be extended and takes a subject a step further, this is acknowledged and encouraged.' Pupils do need to be motivated and exert self-discipline as this will not be imposed from above.

The sixth form has been in the spotlight with its novel late start. Lessons run from 1.30pm to 7.00pm aiming to maximise the benefit of improved sleeping patterns

In 2015 HCH opened its gates to a newly-established sixth form led by experienced, traditionalist headmaster Tristram Jones-Parry MA (Oxon), previously head of Westminster and Emanuel, and teacher of mathematics. Guy explained that the decision was made initially to offer 'heavy duty A levels as well as psychology'. We caught the end of a physics lesson with a small, predominantly male group of sixth formers in one of three new specialist science laboratories. The sixth form has been in the spotlight with its novel late start. Lessons run from 1.30pm to 7.00pm and the school is linked with Oxford University research, promoting a later start for under 20s which aims to maximise the benefit of improved sleeping patterns. Sixth formers can stay on to enjoy a diverse range of speakers, as part of the Form Seven adult education programme involving topics such as Napoleon and the Battle of Borodino, women and enlightenment science, and 18th century French art history.

Learning support and SEN: School is very accepting and inclusive of SENs. SEN department comprises a SENCo, who comes into school twice a week, plus three others: one maths specialist, one specialising in early intervention, and the other very experienced in dyslexia and dyspraxia. They work in small groups or one-to-one, as best suits the child. Seventeen per cent of pupils are on the SEN register – mostly mild to moderate dyslexia or dyscalculia, but school will support ADHD and dyspraxia. One parent commented how proud she had been of the way her daughter and friends had been deliberately protective and inclusive of a pupil with ADHD, and another commented on the positive approach staff showed, allowing the pupil to let off steam by running up and down the corridors when necessary.

The arts and extracurricular: The arts and music are superb, with imaginative use made of music composition linked with filming and animations, and pupils winning prizes for artwork and photographs. Small classes mean staff all really know the pupils. Talents are recognised and promoted and the school is sufficiently small to be flexible, a great plus if your child carries out arduous sports or music practice or has to attend rehearsals outside school. Many do, including a current ballet pupil dancing at the Royal Opera House; others attend West End show rehearsals and music performances, and there is a genuine respect for the work ethic involved. As Guy comments, 'Our current national gymnasts complete hours of training a week, and that requires real commitment and dedication.' In the lunch break we heard a young Cambridge choral scholar master successfully putting the choir through its paces, practising a Rutter anthem in the Great Hall. Many junior and senior students have one-to-one music lessons in school.

There are daily lunchtime clubs as well as after-school clubs in judo, archery, table tennis, football and athletics. One parent did suggest: 'There are lots of clubs but it would be good if they had some physical activity every day of the week, building exercise into their daily lives', although acknowledging that 'healthy eating is considered and the food is amazing'.

Sport: All sports are taken by qualified sports teachers and everyone up to year 4 has weekly swimming sessions at Imber Court Pool, a short ride away. In addition, after-school tennis lessons are on offer with tennis specialists. There is a varied sports curriculum, with fixtures against local schools in football, netball, cricket and athletics with coaching in rugby VIIs and hockey too. Sixth formers can use a gym across the road if they wish.

The school grounds are extensive and include a netball and tennis court, football pitch and a smaller five-a-side football pitch. Pupils enjoy running in Bushy Park and Hampton Court Green.

Ethos and heritage: Completed in 1757 by the Earl of Halifax, Hampton Court House was intended as an extravagant gift for his mistress Anna-Maria Donaldson and was designed by architect and astronomer Thomas Wright. He was responsible for special period features including a

Maple Walk School

heart-shaped pond and enchanting shell-lined grotto with its painted blue ceiling with gilded wooden stars, and an octagonal ice-house now used for drumming practice. Set within nine acres, the beautiful Georgian mansion has a stunning entrance hall with columns, gallery, ceiling, fireplace, conservatory, winter garden with palms and dining room, all tastefully decorated and looking out at the vista of Bushy Park. After Mrs Donaldson's death the house passed through a succession of tenants and was sold to Marmaduke Blake Sampson in 1871. He was city correspondent to The Times and Argentine consul in London, and was responsible for adding the picture gallery. Much later it passed to the tea-planting Twinings, until in the 1980s, quite extraordinarily, it was a Save the Children home for refugee Vietnamese children.

The irregularity of the classrooms, and the abundance of comfortable sofas and country house furniture, may seem quirky to those used to pristine, purpose-built establishments

Following considerable restoration and refurbishment of the house, the school started its life with a pre-prep and prep in 2001, expanding upwards until it opened its sixth form in 2015. The irregularity of the classrooms, along with the abundance of comfortable sofas and country house items of furniture, may seem quirky to those parents used to pristine, purpose-built establishments. Nevertheless, much thought has been given to light, and the ambiance is spacious; pupils are not as crammed in as they might be in some central London schools.

Early years children have their own garden, and all can freely enjoy the wonderful space for outdoor play. There are trees to climb, grounds to explore including a sizeable pond, and the stunning house itself in beautiful countryside. One parent remarked, 'HCH is not an imposing, austere place: instead, very warm and welcoming. My child has had an amazing childhood at HCH. They read books and then play outside enacting them, letting their imaginations run freely.'

This school has a palpable atmosphere and culture of kindness. As a parent explained, 'HCH is a microcosm of society based on respect and developing useful, responsible citizens ready to take their place in the world.' Parents rightly value the warm welcome and friendships made at HCH with fellow pupils and staff. We noticed the relaxed way in which ages and genders mixed happily and naturally at lunch, moving about with ease, whilst parents are delighted at the way pupils support one another, enjoying activities such as camping, chess, or performing in concerts and plays.

Former pupils include environmental campaigner and filmmaker Ayrton Cable, winner of Diana Award and nominated for the International Children's Peace Prize for his work in Malawi; two international ice skaters; many young actors and actresses, eg Rupert Sadler, Harriet Turnbull, Nell Tiger Free and Isabella Blake Thomas; not forgetting a heavy metal singer, Austin Dickinson.

Pastoral care, inclusivity and discipline: At HCH the belief in developing quality relationships is key, whilst reflecting and learning from one's mistakes in a community based on mutual respect. Guy explains, 'I may hold a door open for a pupil but expect a pupil to hold a door open for me.' First names are used throughout, but despite the non-uniform, each pupil has an almanack in which there is a clear code of conduct and dress. When we visited we were impressed by the pupils' smart appearance.

Freedom to run about in home clothes and be encouraged to gain a love of learning without the usual constraints can, in many cases, lead to happy, self-disciplined, motivated children. Undoubtedly some individuals would not thrive in such a liberal, non-hierarchical setting, and Guy admits that it is important to match the individual to the right school. Some parents flee after a while and are not assured that the ethos works in practice or that all claims are realised. This is not the right school for those conservative parents who prefer a more conventional, pedagogical approach and obvious rigid hierarchical structures and families often visit several times for reassurance. But parents tend to agree that 'the teachers know all the pupils, and because of the small nature of the school, they are often able to intervene and defuse situations'.

School actively promotes mindfulness, and nutritional advice and time management skills are included in a comprehensive well-being programme. In the past the head has expelled a boy over drugs, and is very aware of safety and security. He regularly chats with the gatekeeper, who can spot if a child is looking miserable or has a concern.

School is flexible about keeping children down a year or bumping them up one in consultation with parents. This can work exceptionally well, especially in a case of mild bullying, exceptional aptitude or slowness, but it can pose a problem if the child is destined elsewhere.

Pupils and parents: Pupils come from a 30-mile radius, with many from Kingston, Surbiton or Hampton, and there is a school minibus which collects from Chelsea, Richmond and Kingston. Not surprisingly, there are a number of international families including some French, who want their children to maintain levels of French 'whilst immersing themselves in English and English culture'. HCH attracts the unconventional, the liberal, the arty. As one parent summarised, 'We appreciate an all-through school where time is found to explore ideas and there is a conventional output but not process.'

Money matters: Up to three scholarships – academic, music, arts – each year, worth 10 per cent of fees maximum. All 11+ candidates are automatically entered.

The last word: Ideal setting for individuals who can be trusted to be responsible and will thrive on civilised, relaxed values and learn from enthusiastic, approachable teachers who share their passions for their subjects. Several parents acknowledged, 'We visited three times before making up our minds because the school offers something different.' In recent years the school has become more selective, but the head, quite rightly, remains interested in individuals and what they have to offer. As one parent remarked, 'This is a place where it is ok to be different and ask questions, and not be considered a nuisance.'

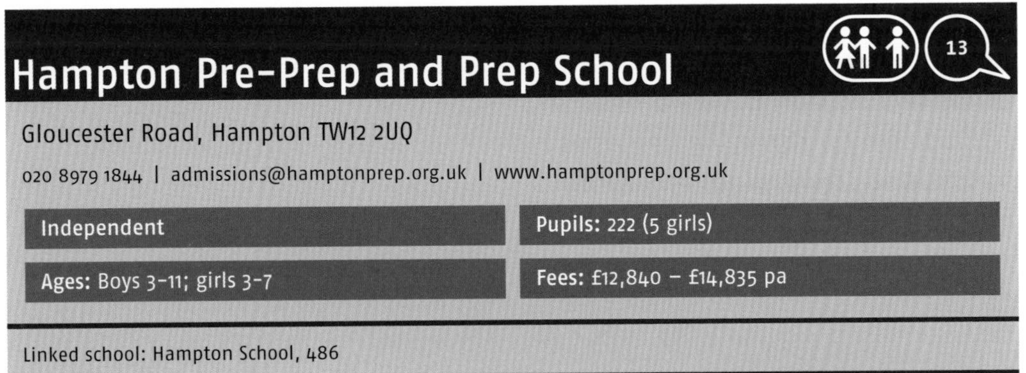

Hampton Pre-Prep and Prep School

Gloucester Road, Hampton TW12 2UQ

020 8979 1844 | admissions@hamptonprep.org.uk | www.hamptonprep.org.uk

Independent	**Pupils:** 222 (5 girls)
Ages: Boys 3-11; girls 3-7	**Fees:** £12,840 – £14,835 pa

Linked school: Hampton School, 486

Head: Since 2015, Tim Smith, BA, MBA (40s). Previously deputy head academic, The Hall School Hampstead, for five years, originally joining in 1994 as games and French teacher, becoming head of learning support and then head of middle school. Also deputy chair of governors in Camden state primary.

Full of the joys of spring. Actually, make that all seasons. 'I love coming into this wonderful place every day,' he exults on the website.

A linguist, he's arty (a regular at the Barbican; partner is head of exhibitions at the Royal Academy) but has only ever wanted to teach. 'Always wanted to play schools,' he says of childhood in New Zealand. Years of wrestling with nervy north Londoners haven't dimmed enthusiasm for career he describes as 'exciting, rewarding, engaging, motivating, joyful and hilarious'.

A shrewd operator, choice of SW London school with less toxic parental vibe – at least for now – compared with NW London is deliberate. Ditto prep finishing at 11 rather than traditional 13, as many senior schools up year 7 intake at the expense of common entrance places. Keen to avoid ivory tower complacency, an occupational hazard for preps, he thinks (state schools often do it better), and keep the innovations coming to improve quality of teaching – 'the light at the heart of school'.

His emphatic approach has come as a bit of a shock to parents though (largely) in a good way. 'Quirky' was a description we heard more than once. 'Eloquent' ditto. Felt to have made real effort to get to know pupils. 'Had the measure of our son quite quickly,' said mother. Excitement of the job? Like other heads, says no two days are the same (we're dying to find the first school where they are). Unlike them, explains how. Easy to forget you're dealing with children, he says, who 'do lots of extraordinary and enlightening and motivating things no matter how hard you try or how much you want them to… go in a certain direction.'

Doesn't pull his punches, particularly when it comes to nervy parents who tell him they only 'want the best' for their child. Do they imagine teachers 'munching on breakfast of baby seals and endangered penguins [and thinking] "I can't wait to come into school and be mean to children?"' he wonders.

Short shrift also given to their fears that strengthened links with Hampton mean school door, as one expressed it, 'no longer open for all boys'. Stresses that nothing is set in stone, academic standards largely going to be determined by intake and any change will be gradual – with no wholesale notices to quit. 'Won't be gathering children up by their ankles, and flinging them into park because they're not clever enough.' A relief all round, then.

Entrance: In a crowded part of the world where limitless parental aspiration meets finite school places, school's willingness to go extra mile a real help for parents – one family wrestling with decision was given mobile number to call during hols for extra reassurance.

Years of wrestling with nervy north Londoners haven't dimmed head's enthusiasm for career he describes as 'exciting, rewarding, engaging, motivating, joyful and hilarious'

Main intake at age 3 into co-ed nursery (20-22 places) and into boys only prep in year 3, when between 14-17 places on offer depending on how many boys leave at end of year 2 (some lured away by well-regarded state primaries). Screen for learning needs in kindergarten, then it's assessments for reception, and years 1 and 2, plus reports. Entry to prep currently automatic-ish for existing pre-prep pupils. Others have tests plus interview with head and report from previous school.

Exit: Girls at end of year 2 to local all-through schools such as Surbiton, LEH, preps (Newland House, Twickenham Prep) and state sector.

In year 6, around half to the senior school. Others to Reed's, St James Senior Boys', Halliford and Claremont Fan Court, among others. Assured places scheme available from year 2 to year 5 based on combination of assessments, teacher reports, exam results and in-depth discussions by admissions committee unsurprisingly a huge parental incentive. Other boys welcome to sit 11+ on equal footing with external candidates. Five scholarships in 2020.

Our view: Relationship with big brother Hampton School wasn't exactly a secret even before change of name (from Denmead) in early 2016. Part of Hampton School Trust since 1999, founded in 1924 by one of English masters in own dining room after own son's left-handedness made him an educational pariah.

Pre-prep, just a hop, skip and jump away across pretty public park, is where it all starts. 'The jewel in the crown,' thought one parent. Housed in original school buildings with grassed front garden and miniature lych gate entrance, home-like feel and nurturing ethos makes it a popular standalone option for daughters as well as sons.

Long-serving pre-prep head, Mrs Murphy, gets star ratings from all for ability to get the best from pupils, effortlessly wrapping up fun and learning together with cross-curricular approach felt to be particularly successful (pirates covered by coordinates in maths, on board rules in English and top marauding destinations in geography). Lots of experienced teachers who make connections but ensure pupils 'make the vital links for themselves.'

Attractive two-storey building houses eight airy classrooms, brace of IT suites, art and music rooms and efficient-looking library, all under nature and neighbour friendly living roof, angled to blend in with residential surroundings.

Plenty of greenery courtesy of allotment with raised beds and that horticultural essential, a potting shed, part of revamped outside space that also includes playing fields (shaping up nicely on day of visit) and all-weather area. Back gate on to Carlisle Park provides extra overspill games space, senior school's 27 acres and theatre also coming in handy for large scale events.

Other changes are less root and branch than nip and tuck and made only where demonstrably better than what's gone before (we liked the lesson bell, lifted from French educational system and featuring mellifluous four-note leitmotif).

'What we do is based on substantiated, evidence-based, peer reviewed, professional practice,' says Mr Smith. 'We're not pulling mad ideas out of a hat.' (Harvard University, no less, called in to help with review of pastoral care.) Far more emphasis on tracking – no doubting where your child is and what they're capable of achieving, while assessments are regular without being excessive and can't be prepared for (and don't get Mr Smith started on tutors – 'a racket'). Formal exams limited to maths and English, with verbal reasoning added to English and NVR to maths from year 4.

Team of 20 academic staff in the prep (around equal numbers of men and women), 12 in the pre-prep (all female) and just under 30 non-teaching staff, including three gap year students.

Two sets for maths and English from year 4, three in years 5 and 6. Will often double up on teachers to support and challenge (school's headline staff to pupil ratio of 1:18 doesn't reflect this) while three-strong learning support team (same again for pre-prep) help small numbers (around seven) with ADD, ADHD and mild SpLD. Their highlight is the 'ladder of success' – top rung winners who successfully complete daily tasks acknowledged in assembly with 'huge, noisy fuss...' and edible prize. Individual support for EAL pupils (around 35 across whole school) in pre-prep and in class in prep.

Ad hoc prizes (including sweets and tennis balls) are popular incentives, though discipline felt by parents to be excellent – 'Only takes a look for boys to be quiet'

Curriculum 'shouldn't be a mile wide but only inch deep,' says Mr Smith, who also comes up with own three Rs – 'richness, relevance and rigour'. Thus subject list doesn't bulge with the outré or unusual – French is only language taught, for example – but concentrates on core range done well, and given more time. Mr Smith is also bumping up recruitment of subject specialists – like parents, feels currently too many generalists, particularly in top years.

With staff training and appraisals also being revamped, teachers 'go the extra mile,' said parent, encouraged to go exploring if lesson takes a different tack. Universal praise for English, boys learning to 'critique their own work and improve it,' said approving parent. Love of books reinforced all the way through – school will set reading as only holiday homework, for example.

Maths felt to be improving, online resources used increasingly to advantage. Results in all-through confidence – year 3 boys eager to explain division by four ('divide by two and by two again'), others in year 6 yomping through hinterlands of mean and mode. 'Teachers aren't going to blow you out of the window if you get it wrong,' reported one. 'Make teaching fun.'

Exam pressure – which pupils agreed could be tough – similarly well handled, focus on preparation without panic. Boys able to rattle off practical techniques that help. 'Make the point, use a quote and explain,' said one.

Ad hoc prizes (including sweets and – from one teacher – even more popular tennis balls) are popular incentives, though discipline felt by parents to be excellent – 'Only takes a look for boys to be quiet.' Masses of reinforcement, from weekly award of courtesy cup in prep to flowers, cloth and special pud for best behaved pre-prep lunchtime table. Easily understood golden rules for younger pupils, though slightly tortuous house point system for year 4 upwards (fine detail runs to several pages) is being revamped. 'Too complex,' agrees head.

Trips range from creative writing workshops to suitably bloodthirsty Saxons vs. Viking experience – firmly linked to curriculum, while clubs span debating to cooking, changing by season. Otherwise, sport's the big thing, with three sessions a week and easily the highlight for majority of pupils. Biggest stars can, thought one parent, get the 'c-leb' treatment (the eternal problem) though another praised numbers of teams (A to D for rugby and football) and regular swapsies so Bs get at least second dibs on training and attention. Means that while truly uninterested might struggle, anyone who's keen but with a modicum of talent is felt on the whole to have a good time. Results justify the effort with frequent successes, school handicapped only by size (some larger Richmond-based opponents can choose from bigger pool of talent).

Swimming has been major casualty of timetable rejigging, axed in the prep (though still offered for years 1 and 2). Not everyone's happy about this – 'focus is on football and rugby to the detriment of any other sport,' said parent, but Mr Smith isn't budging. 'We're not going to use valuable curriculum time to teach them to splash around in some grubby pool when parents can do that themselves on a Saturday.'

Art, however, has had a reprieve. Initially pared back and rotated in 10-week blocks with drama and DT, has regained weekly slot on the timetable after fears that talented weren't getting enough time to hone work to scholarship standard.

With around 60 prep and pre-prep pupils learning instruments (beginners to grade 5), a choir, orchestra and wind band and several scholarships in recent years, performing arts are good, think parents, though anticipate better things to come. 'Don't have enough children scratching, blowing, tweeting and trumpeting,' agrees Mr Smith. Added space for more of everything – instruments, informal as well as class-based concerts plus whole school annual production all on the way, activity across the octave and decibel range should increase.

Parents very sociable, newcomers quickly brought into the fold. While the many working parents can inevitably end up missing out on coffee mornings, 'Always someone who'll scoop up your child.' Helped by before and after-school care – 7.45am start (8.00am in the pre-prep), 5.30pm finish – more activities after school would make life even easier, felt one parent.

Mr Smith stresses (and will probably have to keep on stressing) that ethos of school won't change 'simply because ... we apply tenets of the admissions policy ever more carefully as time goes by.' Some current parents have yet to be convinced. Prospective parents eye up growing numbers gaining places at Hampton and make up their own minds.

The last word: Pastorally, it's carrot, not stick. Academically, it's stimulating, not just chalk and talk. For the big exams, it's preparation without panic. This is, in other words, a school that well and truly puts the child first.

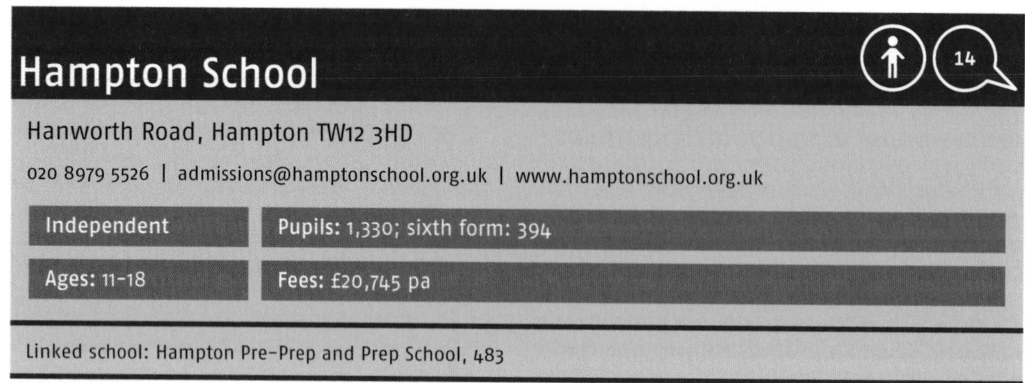

Hampton School

14

Hanworth Road, Hampton TW12 3HD

020 8979 5526 | admissions@hamptonschool.org.uk | www.hamptonschool.org.uk

Independent | Pupils: 1,330; sixth form: 394

Ages: 11-18 | Fees: £20,745 pa

Linked school: Hampton Pre-Prep and Prep School, 483

Headmaster: Since 2013, Kevin Knibbs MA (early 40s). Joined Hampton as deputy head in 2007. Previously history master, head of lower school and senior master at Bolton School Boys' Division. Educated at King Edward VI Grammar School, Chelmsford and read modern history at Oxford (gaining two football blues in the process). A career schoolmaster who still teaches history to youngest boys. 'I happen to run a big business, but that's not why I chose teaching in the first place,' he tells us. Not one to hog the limelight. At his happiest when talking about the boys, of whom he is fiercely proud.

Very visible head who can often be spotted at weekends on the touchline and towpath, supporting Hampton boys and chatting to parents. Friendly, approachable and generous spirited. 'I am lucky to lead a school that is on this trajectory and I want to keep it going. It's a privilege to be in this job. I love it. I hope that comes through.' It does.

His wife is one of the chemistry teachers. He has a weakness for off-piste skiing in Colorado.

Entrance: Highly selective; now more than six applicants per place. No sibling policy. Pupils generally enter the school at 11, 13 or 16. The 11+ route is normally for 125 boys; current batch from Hampton Prep and from 75 other feeder schools (54 per cent of them joined from state primary schools, the remainder from preps which finish at end of year 6). At 13+ a further 65 boys enter the school, from about 25 different independent prep schools. Around 10-12 boys join in sixth form though few places up for grabs at this stage.

At 11+, entry is via school's own entrance exam (maths, English and reasoning) plus interview and reference. For 13+ entry, boys must sit the pre-test at 11; from 2020 offers will not depend on common entrance scores. Entrance at sixth form is via personal statement, head teacher's report, written and online assessment and interview. Boys must also get a good clutch of GCSEs, with a minimum six 9-7 grades including English and maths. The staggered entry at 11 and 13 works well and one teacher made it clear that 'we're standing firm with the 13+'.

School council currently hotly debating whether to replace text books with ebooks

Head devotes hours to speaking to prospective parents and says he tries 'to be clear about our ethos to parents. The families we choose need to be on board. It has to be the right fit for their son.' Warns parents not to 'force the pace' but to aim to put their son in an environment where he will be happy. Looking for boys who are academically able, inquisitive and hard-working, but they also need heaps of stamina to keep up here. A willingness to join in and try new things is crucial. 'Along with appointing staff, it is the most important thing I do,' says head. He manages to make the selection process as personal as possible and sends out good luck cards to all 1,200 applicants before entrance exams. A characteristically thoughtful gesture.

Exit: School is keen to point out that 'we do not cull anyone post-GCSEs' and there is no minimum number of GCSEs that internal boys must gain to be allowed to stay into the sixth form. 'We do talk to parents and pupils openly, however, if a boy is struggling. They might choose to put in place a contingency plan.'

Up to 20 boys head for Oxbridge each year (14 in 2018) in a wide range of subjects. Head explains, 'We don't get obsessed about it. It is certainly not a case of Oxbridge or die.' Vast majority tends to head for Russell Group universities. Occasionally, boys venture to the Continent while others choose medical schools (seven medics in 2018, including one at Cambridge and one in Bulgaria), drama schools or conservatoires. Favoured universities include Warwick, Durham and Nottingham. A handful disappears off to Ivy League colleges in the US, often on sporting scholarships. Boys regularly return for career advice long after they leave.

Latest results: In 2020, 87 per cent 9/7 at GCSE. In 2019 (the last year when exams took place), 91 per cent 9/7; at A level, 78 per cent A*/A grades.

Teaching and learning: In lower years, all boys study chemistry, biology and physics as separate subjects, computer programming and coding, at least one language out of French, German, Spanish, Russian or Mandarin, and Latin which is compulsory in years 7 and 8. Setting in maths and modern languages from third year.

Currently physics, chemistry, history, philosophy, German and Mandarin (short course) offered at Pre-U. At A level, maths remains perennially popular with regularly 30 per cent taking further maths. As one teacher explained, 'maths is like a magnet for these boys.' High uptake of chemistry, physics and economics too. In sixth form, all boys follow an enrichment programme which includes six-week courses on topics including university life and finance, mindfulness and current affairs. School offers its own extended project qualification, with recent essays focusing on quantum gravity and the feasibility of time travel.

School is no slouch on the computer front, with eight different ICT suites and a new coding room. Boys bring in their own iPads and use them in every subject. School council currently hotly debating whether to replace text books with ebooks.

Hamptonians impress regularly in national competitions, including as winners of the UK Maths Trust challenge for two years running, and in winning essay and poetry prizes.

Over a third of staff have been at school for more than a decade. Each year roughly 10 per cent leave, so constant flow of fresh blood, including some sparky graduates who are grabbed straight out of university and are trained on the job. Head acknowledges that 'we are a springboard school and people want our staff. Any of my senior team could run their own school but I am clinging on to them.' Approximately 40 per cent female teachers. 'That's changed a lot. When the boys leave here they know exactly who is in charge,' smiles the head. Pupils feel their teachers are friendly. One of the younger boys explained, 'Homework got the better of me at the beginning. But if you email a teacher to say you are struggling with the work, they are more than happy to go through it the next day. You just need to give them the heads up.' All the lessons we observed were lively and led by dynamic teachers, many of whom have grammar school backgrounds and like the down-to-earth ethos of the school.

Learning support and SEN: Around 185 pupils have some kind of SEN. Support tends to be small group intervention (currently around 40 such groups) with lunchtime drop-in sessions popular, especially as exams loom. 'Some of our highest achieving boys are on our learning support register and that's how it should be,' states head. Forty pupils are classified as EAL, though none requires additional support.

The arts and extracurricular: With over 50 clubs on offer, including model aviators, debating, and photography, there does seem to be something for every taste. Over 200 boys take part in DofE scheme each year. Adventure society, open to all years, offers a heady mix of kayaking, power-boating, orienteering and sea-cliff climbing. For the more sedentary, chess is thriving: five teams regularly represent the school. One pupil was recently U18 national chess champion. Beekeeping society is the latest club on the list.

Head says he tries 'to be clear about our ethos to parents. The families we choose need to be on board. It has to be the right fit for their son'

Performing arts have taken off in the last decade and serious resources have been funnelled towards both drama and music. The Hammond theatre seats 380 and boasts a hydraulic orchestral pit, hi-tech lighting and sound systems and, one pupil told us, watching plays here 'feels like being at the West End'. Well-equipped art/DT department, and some stunning artwork lines the corridors, though surprisingly few take these subjects at A level. School produces a steady stream of Arkwright engineering scholars.

Around 400 boys have music lessons, many on more than one instrument. Significant numbers attain grade 8. Two current pupils with diplomas. Plenty of performances from rock, jazz, keyboard to strings and boys have 23 music ensembles to choose from. Celebrated male voice choir, Voices of Lions, enjoys a high profile and performs at Edinburgh Fringe. The lively rendition of Drunken Sailor in school assembly was apparently 'legendary'. Nine Hampton musicians have received organ scholarships from Oxbridge in recent years.

Sport: School is well-known for its excellent sports provision, with at least 17 different sports offered. Over 27 acres of playing fields so all facilities (bar the Millennium boathouse) are on site and head has been known to joke that he would move the Thames if he could so that it could flow closer to the school. All-weather 3G sports ground very well used, including at break time when swarms of boys congregate there and kick balls about with great gusto. 'It's good for morale and improves concentration in the classroom,' states head. One boy told us that 'my mum loves the 3G grass as I never come home muddy!' Another told us that he fell in love with Hampton the moment he saw the huge number of pitches stretching into the distance.

Celebrated male voice choir, Voices of Lions, performs at Edinburgh Fringe. The lively rendition of Drunken Sailor in school assembly was apparently 'legendary'

Sports practice mostly takes place at lunchtime to enable those travelling home by coach to participate. Boys can choose which sports they want to play and the school excels at most. As always, Hampton is competing at the highest levels in national schools' competitions and churning out some exceptional sportsmen. Deserves its reputation for being one of the top football, rugby and rowing schools in the country. No hockey offered which one parent found 'disappointing, as many boys would be keen to play it'. School stresses importance of participation for all, and multiple teams are fielded in all age groups. One mother we spoke to was not so sure, saying that 'in reality, there may be some who struggle to make a team.' Starry old boys include Olympic gold medallists Greg and Jonny Searle as well as Surrey and England all-rounder Zafar Ansari.

Head insists that school is not just for those who can perform brilliantly on the games pitches. 'There are many quiet, effective learners who find their own niche. We want to make sure that all boys get opportunities'. Boys agree that 'there is no hierarchy of worth. Being in the first XV is not seen as being any better than being in the Voices of Lions.' School has worked hard to encourage this view and head is adamant that that academic, musical and dramatic successes are now celebrated just as much as sporting triumphs.

Ethos and heritage: The school was set up over 450 years ago thanks to a bequest of property and land by local brewer and businessman, Robert Hammond. Formerly a grammar school (went independent in 1975). Not the most beautiful of schools (though a recent building project has provided new classrooms, science labs and learning support suite, plus some new outside space), but the warmth and friendliness of both staff and pupils makes up for the lack of architectural splendour.

School is outward looking and has developed links in the local community and abroad. Boys help in local primary schools and put on a Christmas party for elderly locals. School provides a Latin class for GCSE pupils from local state schools. Also has an association with a safe haven in Malawi. Hampton is proud of being a 'beacon school' for Holocaust education and raises awareness of more recent genocides. Certainly not a school that just looks after its own.

Close ties with neighbouring girls' school, the Lady Eleanor Holles School. Since the appointment of the current head there, there is 'an enhanced desire to work collaboratively, especially at sixth form level'. Schools already share much, including drama productions, language exchanges and Oxbridge interview preparation.

Pastoral care, inclusivity and discipline: School takes great care to integrate boys who arrive at 13 with the well-established 11+ cohort. Pupils are supported by a pastoral team, including their form tutor and head of year, as well as sixth form mentors, though one parent we spoke to said 'the lack of a house system and small tutor groups may mean that some boys may slip through the net, no matter what the school tells you.' Some reports of bullying in the early years, though parents felt this was generally stamped out quickly. Head runs a weekly pre-school drop-in for boys to approach him on any matter they wish and he meets with head boy and his deputies once a fortnight and jokes that 'they tell me how to run the school'. This head has his ear to the ground.

Head has helped establish Hampton as a national leader in mindfulness. 'We're one of the early pioneers of it,' he says proudly. Believes it is a useful tool for helping these boys deal with 'the ups and downs of teenage life in this high-achieving setting'. Mindfulness, life issues and well-being/resilience taught for nine weeks as part of the curriculum in fourth year, followed by a top-up session before GCSE study leave begins. One pupil we spoke to admitted that 'it can be a struggle to balance everything as there is so much going on here, but mindfulness helps.' Head believes that it is no coincidence that since it has become a mainstream part of the school, 'the academic results have improved, and the school has become a kinder, gentler and calmer place.' Head adds, with a smile, 'If it's good enough for Jonny Wilkinson…'

Pupils and parents: Diverse mix of boys. Many parents have state school backgrounds and choose it for its unpretentiousness. Increasing numbers of European parents whose sons are bi/trilingual. Many boys walk or cycle to school and older boys can drive, provided they park at a distance. Extensive coach network (run jointly with LEH) attracts families from all over west and south-west London and Surrey. Coach journeys with girls apparently awash with witty banter.

Parents are very involved with the school, often helping with careers advice and fundraising. Head admits the parents can be demanding, but 'we're better off than some schools in that respect. We seem to attract families which do not tip over the fine line between aspirational and obsessional.'

Money matters: Fifty-six boys are on full bursaries and another 127 are on substantial bursaries. Plans afoot to provide more such places and this is a matter close to the head's heart. 'In terms of the school's future, to maintain our grounded feel, and with fees going up, we need to make sure that more bursaries are available. We do not have a big endowment so have to do it through fundraising.' Academic, all-rounder, art, choral and music scholarships carry a remission of up to 25 per cent of fees. 'If there are financial issues, we do try to help,' says head.

The last word: Hampton is riding high. Though head is conscious that 'we can sometimes hide our light under a bushel here,' they would be justified in shouting their achievements from the rooftops. There is currently a real energy about the school and boys appeared to be genuinely happy.

One of the aims of the school is for Hamptonians to strive 'for personal success while supporting those around them'. If the boys who showed us around are anything to go by, they are accomplishing their goal admirably. Hampton is producing young men of integrity. No wonder the head is so proud of them.

Harrow School

5 High Street, Harrow on the Hill HA1 3HP

020 8872 8007 | admissions@harrowschool.org.uk | www.harrowschool.org.uk

Independent

Pupils: 837; sixth form: 333; Boarders: 837 full

Ages: 13–18

Fees: £40,050 pa

Head Master: Since April 2019, Alastair Land MA (Cantab) (40s), previously head of Repton after three years as deputy head here. Educated at Manchester Grammar School and Trinity College, Cambridge (first class hons in natural sciences). He comes from a lineage of skilled horticulturalists who nurtured his early interest in science. A man with a vocation to serve, he seriously considered a career in the armed forces (and hasn't closed the door on one in the church), but above all he 'always knew he wanted to teach'. His first job gave him the opportunity to combine the two and he spent nine years at Eton as biology teacher and commanding officer of CCF. Thence to Winchester College where he was master in college and senior housemaster. Father of two young sons and a daughter.

Aims to review the curriculum 'to ensure a greater focus on the skills, dispositions and attributes that Harrovians will require to thrive in the future', working more closely with parents and bolstering the pastoral side, plus developing even deeper partnerships with local organisations, eg John Lyon's Charity.

Entrance: Very competitive. Around 800 apply for the 160 places on offer at 13. Prospective pupils should ideally register by the end of year 5; supply school reference and sit pre-test in year 6; most are expected to be invited for assessment at the start of year 7, through tests and interviews. Offers are made – subject to CE or scholarship exams 18 months later. Sixty-five per cent expected at CE. 'Some weight' given to sons of OHs and boys' siblings – 'but brothers don't automatically get in,' said a parent. Boys arrive from more than 250+ junior schools. All-boys boarding preps like Caldicott and Cothill top the pack but others from a myriad of co-ed and day schools.

Total of 24 new pupils a year into the 340-strong sixth form. Candidates need at least seven or eight 9-7s at GCSE but many will have straight 9/8s. Candidates write a CV, plus letter to the head explaining why they want to come to Harrow, and take tests in their proposed A level subjects. The best attend a day of interviews and assessments.

Exit: Very few leave after GCSEs and nearly all sixth formers off to university, usually with large numbers to Oxbridge (11 in 2019. Other top destinations include Exeter, Bristol, Edinburgh and UCL. US very popular – students head for eg Brown, NYU, Chicago, Stanford and Yale – now has a guidance counsellor specifically for the 25 per cent who apply to US universities. Three medics in 2019.

Latest results: In 2019, 83 per cent 9-7 at IGCSE; 62 per cent A*/A at A level (87 per cent A*-B).

Teaching and learning: Teachers, parents and the boys themselves describe Harrow as an 'academic' school. Harrow's results don't appear in league tables – they say they're fed up with the 'one-dimensional snapshot' they deliver – but results are impressive. Everyone takes at least one MFL, with other options beyond the core subjects including ancient history, classical Greek, drama and computer science.

Thirty-one subjects on offer at A level – all the usual, plus business studies, politics, history of art, music technology, photography and theatre studies, with a range of languages. Maths is the most popular subject at A level, with nearly two-thirds taking it. Half the boys do four subjects at A level rather than the usual three (one boy recently did nine). Sixth form electives are a relatively recent innovation for sixth form pupils – a chance for boys to experience university-style teaching in specialist areas and have increased from five to eight periods a fortnight, with boys taking three one-term courses – the last relating to their chosen university course. Cerebral subjects on offer include programming, the history of western art, the greats of European philosophy, psychoanalysis and its impact on European culture, conflict and creativity in creation, post-genocide Rwanda and financial mathematics. Now offers EPQ.

Everything from the Alexander Society for boys interested in military history to the Turf Club for horse racing fans

Dazzling array of languages – French, German, Spanish, Italian, Russian, Turkish, Polish, Japanese, Arabic and Chinese. School has its own observatory with three telescopes and astronomy offered as a GCSE. Timetabled reading periods and new seminar programme for years 10 and 11. At GCSE classes range between 14 and 20 pupils while at A level the average is eight and none are greater than 12.

Embracing technology – all new joiners asked to purchase a (subsidised) laptop to be used in all lessons – but also making increased use of school's archive and private collections in lessons, eg material on notable alumni such as Churchill, Trollope and Byron as well as Greek and Roman antiquities, paintings by Gainsborough and Constable and medieval manuscripts.

Dedicated band of teachers (or 'beaks' as they are known at Harrow) includes many writers of scholarly books. Women make up some 20 per cent of staff.

Learning support and SEN: School caters for mild dyspraxia and dyslexia. One-to-one help given off-timetable, at no additional cost.

The arts and extracurricular: Head of music admits that when he arrived there was a perception among rival directors of music that Harrow was 'an old-fashioned school where little value was placed on music and the arts'. To his delight he found the reverse was true and there's a 'wealth of musical talent'. Half the boys learn musical instruments and 50 per cent of these achieve grade 8 or better by the time they leave. Practice sessions timetabled for younger boys. Loads of orchestras, choirs and strong tradition of singing. More than 100 concerts a year, with recent performances at the Royal Albert Hall and Royal Festival Hall. Steady stream of boys to top universities and conservatoires to read music too.

Excellent Ryan Theatre seats 300 and is used for school and professional productions but annual Shakespeare productions take place in the beautiful arts and crafts Speech Room. A huge, wood-panelled half-moon, it boasts authentic Globe-style staging and seats the entire school. Old sculpture studio now houses drama lessons. Wonderful art and, befittingly for a school where photography pioneer William Fox Talbot was a pupil, photography. DT, sculpture, art and photography now in a new state-of-the-art facility that also includes a new digital design suite. There's no lounging around with nothing to do at weekends either – scores of extracurricular activities to choose from, everything from the Alexander Society for boys interested in military history to the Turf Club for horse racing fans.

Sport: There's no doubt about it, Harrow is a very sporty school, with hordes of teams regularly trouncing their opponents. Sport played five afternoons a week, around 30 sports on offer and director of sport encourages even the less enthusiastic to have a go at something. Main sports are rugby, soccer, cricket and Harrow football. The latter is played with a pork-pie shaped ball which absorbs the wet and can be propelled by any part of the body. Even though it's played in the depths of winter and is a very muddy affair the boys love it and only wish more schools played it (Harrow is the only one). When we visited pupils were counting the days till their Harrow football match against an OH team. Last year lots of their fathers had played and there was even one grandfather in the side – 'but we were very careful with him.'

Vast expanse of playing fields, sports centre with indoor climbing wall, weights room, 25m pool and sports hall, courts for tennis, rackets and squash, nine-hole golf course and Olympic-sized running track. School boasts national champions in rackets, fencing, fives and judo, two boys playing rugby for England and number of cricketers playing at national and county level. The mother of a gifted sportsman was full of admiration for the way the school nurtured her son's sporting talent whilst keeping him focused on his academic studies and helping him achieve stellar grades. 'The school sees each boy as an individual and were very supportive and flexible,' she told us.

Boarding: All pupils board at Harrow. We visited two very different houses – Druries, which dates back to the 1790s and is a maze of charming nooks and crannies, and the ultra-modern Lyon's, or the Holiday Inn, as a few wags have nicknamed it. 'It's the best piece of real estate around here,' joked one boy, hugely appreciative of its light, airy, five-star rooms. 'There's room for us to move around and not cause too much havoc.'

Each house has common rooms, games rooms (kitted out with plasma TV, pool and table tennis tables), garden and 'yarder', an area where boys can run off steam and kick a ball about. Two boys sharing is the norm in the first year but by year 11 (or even earlier) they get their own room, complete with desk, shelving, computer and, occasionally, en-suite shower. All pupils' names etched on wooden house boards, with head of house's name picked out in gold. Boys can make toast and heat up soup in their houses – 'and the more ambitious make Pot Noodles,' said one boy. We trust he was joking. Meals are eaten centrally and food gets a firm thumbs-up – from us too, if the lunch we had with sixth formers was anything to go by. Boys are allowed to go out for a meal with their parents on Sundays but there's no weekly or flexi-boarding. Two weekend exeats in the autumn and spring terms and one in the summer.

Ethos and heritage: Harrow is one of only four all-boys, full-boarding schools left in the UK (along with Eton, Winchester and Radley). Boys have been educated here since the 13th century, but the school was founded in 1572 under a royal charter granted to local farmer John Lyon by Elizabeth I (Lyon's, the newest boarding house, is named after him). The aim was for the school to provide free education for 30 local scholars, a number later increased to 40 by the governors. School sits in picturesque Harrow on the Hill, surrounded by 324 acres and with panoramic views across London – of it, yet remote from it, as we said last time. On a clear day you can see Canary Wharf from the head's study and it's just 25 minutes by tube to Green Park. Visitors to the undulating school site take note – flat shoes are a must.

Harrow's results don't appear in league tables – they say they're fed up with the one-dimensional snapshot they deliver – but results are impressive

School is steeped in tradition and history. The 17th century Old Schools contain the beautiful Fourth Form room, with names carved into every inch of panelling, from Byron to Robert Peel. It's also where Professor Flitwick's charm classes were shot in the first Harry Potter film (lots of tourists gazing admiringly when we visited). The stunning Vaughan Library, designed by architect Gilbert Scott (he also created London's St Pancras Station) has chess sets on tables and stays open late during exam periods. War Memorial Building commemorates the 642 OHs who died in the First World War.

You can't help but be profoundly moved by the Alex Fitch Room, an Elizabethan wood-panelled room with stained glass windows and a Cromwellian table, given by a grieving mother in honour of her 19-year-old son after he died in the First World War. She asked that it should be used for the purpose of boys meeting their mothers and that a light should always be left on over her son's portrait. Plaques and memorials commemorating quirky events are everywhere. Charles I rested here while preparing to surrender and little inclines have memorable names like Obadiah Slope, wittily named after Trollope's unctuous Barchester Towers character.

Harrow songs are legendary. No Harrovian, either past or present, fails to mention the strength of feeling they engender and the lump in the throat they provoke

Harrow songs are legendary. No Harrovian, either past or present, fails to mention the strength of feeling they engender and the lump in the throat they provoke. Songs have been an important part of the school since 1864, when the head of music wrote the first song, and they are considered to be 'a unifying force'. In November each year the whole school assembles in Speech Room in honour of its most famous alumnus, Sir Winston Churchill, for the Churchill Songs. Like rival Eton, school has its own jargon. 'Skew' is a punishment, 'tosh' is a shower, 'tolley up' is permission to work late and so on.

Long and distinguished list of former pupils – seven former prime ministers (including Sir Robert Peel, Lord Palmerston, Stanley Baldwin and Sir Winston Churchill), 19th century philanthropist Lord Shaftesbury ('a towering figure – we refer to him a lot,' says the head), Jawaharlal Nehru, King Hussein of Jordon, Lord Cardigan (who led the charge of the Light Brigade), General Sir Peter de la Billière, plus countless other men of military renown (20 holders of the Victoria Cross and one George Cross holder). The arts and sciences are equally well represented, with a dazzling list of luminaries including Lord Byron, Richard Brinsley Sheridan, Anthony Trollope, Terence Rattigan, John Galsworthy, Cecil Beaton, Edward and William Fox, Richard Curtis, Benedict Cumberbatch and James Blunt, plus Crispin Odey (one of the UK's most successful hedge fund managers), Julian Metcalfe (founder of Pret à Manger), cricketer Nick Compton and Tim Bentinck (better known as David Archer).

Pastoral care, inclusivity and discipline: Pastoral care is meticulous, with highly structured system of resident housemasters, assistant housemasters and matrons. Harrow's 12 houses are integral to the school and boys are fiercely loyal to their own house. Some houses are regarded as stricter than others and parents we spoke to said it's important 'to pick and choose carefully'. One of the houses – West Acre – was the subject of an ITN documentary series following the life of the school for a whole year. Housemasters usually in post for 12 years and as well as doing most of the admissions assessments each gives their house its character and reputation. They also work round the clock – 'At the beginning of every term I say to my wife "see you at the end of term",' one housemaster told us with a grin.

Harrow takes a pragmatic approach to technology and social media but the boys are so busy there isn't much time to sit around and play computer games. Pupils understand that bullying is 'completely unacceptable' and school says that it has plummeted, 'not down to zero, but pretty close'. School does a bullying survey every winter and housemasters, year group tutors, matrons, two school chaplains, health education tutors and school psychologist pick up on most things. Discipline is clear and firm but the place feels pretty relaxed, with boys knowing exactly where they stand. 'You are given freedom but if you abuse the freedom you would be punished,' one boy told us. Zero tolerance on drugs and use or supply in term-time or holidays means expulsion. Anyone found with spirits suspended and warned, while smoking is handled through 'escalating sequence of sanctions imposed by housemasters'.

Smart uniform of dark blue jackets (bluers), grey flannels (greyers), white shirts and ties, plus, of course, Harrow's infamous boaters. Boys wear them or carry them and either love them or loathe them. They're allowed to write their names and draw pictures on the inner rim and spray them with varnish to protect them. Members of Philathletic Club (school's top sportsmen) get to wear bow ties. Sunday wear is black tailcoat and the whole kit and caboodle.

Pupils and parents: Pupils come from all over and school is proud of its 'broad and varied intake'. We said last time that it's the sort of place where a Yorkshire farmer's son will be sharing a room with the offspring of a City banker – and it still holds true. Between 10 and 15 per cent are progeny of OHs, while 20 per cent are from overseas (some expat, others from vast range of countries – nearly 40 at last count). Twenty-five with EAL requirements. Most boys are CofE but there's a 'significant' RC community. Small numbers of all other main faiths or none.

Harrow football is played with a pork-pie shaped ball which absorbs the wet and can be propelled by any part of the body. Even though it's played in the depths of winter and is a very muddy affair the boys love it and only wish more schools played it (Harrow is the only one)

The boys we met were engaging, appreciative of the fine education they get and very proud of their school. 'It doesn't give you a sense of entitlement, just a great responsibility to give something back,' one boy told us, while a sixth former who'd joined from a state school at 16 said that he'd been 'pushed and challenged' and that there was 'a lot more opportunity for debate' than at his previous school.

Parents reckon the school suits all-rounders who work hard and like sport. 'It's very disciplined and the boys are busy all the time so they have to be organised,' one mother said. 'There isn't any time to get up to any mischief and the boys are really tired by the end of term. There's a real camaraderie about the place and the boys make life-long friends. I can't fault it.' Another reckoned that even though it's 'strict', any boy would thrive at Harrow, as long as they can cope with being in a large school where they won't necessarily be 'king pin'.

Money matters: School has given franchises to Harrow Beijing, Harrow Bangkok, Harrow Hong Kong and Harrow Shanghai. These are all successful enterprises carefully monitored by Harrow and also fund generous bursary schemes at home.

Wide range of scholarships and bursaries at 13 or 16. School offers means-tested bursaries of up to 100 per cent of fees to pupils who win a scholarship of any sort. Up to 30 scholarships a year for academic excellence, music, art or talent in a particular area (normally worth five per cent of fees). There are also Peter Beckwith scholarships for gifted and talented boys whose parents can't afford to send them to Harrow. Two awarded each year to boys aged between 10 and 13 – these can cover fees at a private school from the age of 11 and Harrow fees from 13.

The last word: Parents looking for a top notch, blue chip, full-boarding, all-boys school will be hard-pressed to beat Harrow. This is a school on top of its game.

Haydon School

Wiltshire Lane, Eastcote, Pinner HA5 2LX

020 8429 0005 | info@haydonschool.org.uk | www.haydonschool.com

State | **Ages:** 11–18 | **Pupils:** 1790; sixth form: 409

Headteacher: Since 2011, Robert Jones (50s). Read economics at LSE (he had an amazing, passionate school economics teacher who really encouraged him), followed by his first teaching job at Holland Park School in 1990: 'I've always wanted to teach at a comprehensive school – and this was a big state comp. I think it's because I went to an all-boys comprehensive in Stockport and was the first person out of my family to go to university.'

Five years later, he was offered the opportunity to teach at an international school in Hong Kong, where he spent the next four years: 'My wife and I are both teachers and both love travelling, so it made sense to grab this opportunity when it came. We were there for the handover of Hong Kong, so it was an exciting time.' On his return he moved to Haydon School as head of department in 1999 and quickly moved up the ranks to become assistant head, deputy head, then head: 'I've always been quite ambitious.'

Some 20 years at the school – Mr Jones can barely believe it himself. Thankfully he continues to be inspired by the changes he has been a part of during his tenure. The school has grown significantly and the size of the sixth form (up to 460 students) is 'a unique selling point'. 'With so many new free schools opening up in the area, there is much more competition – but having such a large sixth form means that we can offer a huge variety of subjects.' He still teaches economics to A level students (we get the feeling he has more of a connection with the older students and is certainly more visible to them).

A Reading Football Club season ticket holder – he still plays football and coaches Ascot United U13s (his younger son plays for the team; the other is grown up). Married to a drama teacher. Still tempted to travel again later on.

Entrance: Most students live within a mile or so of the school. Admissions criteria: children in public care, then siblings, then employees' children, then children living nearest to the school. A good percentage of students join in the sixth form because of the variety of subjects on offer.

Exit: Just under half of pupils leave after GCSEs – for college, other schools, apprenticeships or employment – and up to 10 per cent after year 12. Some 80 per cent of sixth formers go to university, around 30 per cent to Russell Group universities (the largest percentage of any state school in the borough). One or two to Oxbridge most years (one in 2020, plus two medics and one vet).

Latest results: In 2020, 34 per cent 9-7 at GCSE; 86 per cent got 9-4 in both maths and English. At A level, 32 per cent A*/A at A level (58 per cent A*-B). In 2019 (the last year when exams took place), 20 per cent 9-7 at GCSE; 14 per cent A*/A (37 per cent A*-B).

Teaching and learning: Offers a broad curriculum with more than 30 GCSE and four BTec options, plus a multitude of A level subjects. 'We want to offer as broad a curriculum as possible,' explains the head.

Language provision is very good (some 90 per cent taking a language GCSE) – with students starting off with French and Italian or Spanish. Mandarin no longer offered, which saddens the head: 'We had to drop it as recruiting staff was a nightmare.'

Parents generally praise the quality of teaching, and in particular the revision lessons offered around exam time, plus the quick communication with many teachers via email as well as the odd phone call saying, 'your child has been terrific today.'

Students need six GCSEs at 9-4 (including maths and English) to study three A levels. Those who do not have a good pass in English or maths can retake these alongside.

Parents like the fact that class sizes are around 25, but some would prefer more streaming. 'At present in year 7 there is streaming just for maths,' said one parent. 'I would like to see this extended to other key subjects such as English and science, as they do in other local schools.' The school does cater well for the very able student too, we are told, with some 15-20 high achieving pupils (HAPS) in each year group given extra opportunities and extension work. One parent told us: 'Both my children have been on the HAPS programme, and both have benefited from it.'

Learning support and SEN: One SENCo and a team of learning support assistants support around 20 or so pupils with an EHCP. There is also a special centre where students can be taught in small groups.

The arts and extracurricular: Strong media department, and a significant number of pupils go off to study media at Bournemouth University. Thriving art department achieves excellent exam results. Art, textiles and photography available at A level. The art on display was some of the most impressive we've seen (including some by TV and radio presenter Fearne Cotton – a former alumna of the school). A great DT facility in the Woods building, courses including resistant material workshops and graphic design, 'a nice break from heavy academia,' one student told us.

Originally two grammar schools that merged to form one large building joined internally via various passageways – we were disorientated after five minutes

School has two orchestras, jazz band, samba band and wide variety of other music groups. Two big concerts a year as well as annual musical – and Haydon's Got Talent is a big yearly event. Lots of extracurricular offered – everything from film, poetry and philosophy clubs, to Thai boxing, trampolining and fitness clubs.

Plenty of opportunities to travel: Snowdonia in year 7, annual ski trip in year 9, watersports in the south of France – and a biennial 'life changing' sixth form expedition to a developing country – recently Uganda – for three weeks, for those who can raise £4,000 for the trip.

Sport: 'Sports at Haydon has been brilliant for my child,' one delighted parent told us. 'So much on offer here and great facilities. A brilliant head of PE, which helps.' There does seem to be something for everyone. Rugby a biggie here, so too are football, cricket, basketball (all for boys and girls) plus netball and indoor athletics. There is also an ultimate frisbee team in the sixth form. New sports hall helps facilitate this, as do the extensive grounds with several tennis courts and sports pitches. Successes at both local and county level: 'We have won the borough cricket tournament four years in a row,' one proud sixth former told us.

Ethos and heritage: School is situated on the edge of the Northwood Hills in Pinner, surrounded by spacious playing fields with the feeling of being almost in the country. Originally two grammar schools (St Mary's and St Nicholas) that merged in 1977, in a what is now one large, rather nondescript 1950s building joined together internally via various passageways and corridors – we were disorientated after five minutes. 'You get a very good induction tour when you first join and teachers spend a long time showing you around,' one pupil told us. 'They expect you to get lost in the beginning,' another said.

A stark difference between the old and the new: 'the start of the yellow part denotes the new,' we were told. First off, the new sports hall, which was very impressive. Bright with underfloor heating and well equipped with foldaway trampolines and badminton nets – soundproofed, too. Also impressive was the fairly recent sixth form block, amongst the best we have seen and simply vast. On offer were a choice of cold and hot food (so good that staff choose to eat there), a colourful chill-out area, a pool table, computer area and a couple of quiet study areas, all partly cased in a glass exterior. Worth joining the sixth form for, we thought.

School has also benefited from a £5 million art and design building and £2 million music and performing arts centre (three music rooms, drama studio and music mixing room, plus one-to-one teaching rooms). The head told us: 'We did get quite a large cash injection, but the problem is the money has now all dried up. We have to be far more enterprising about how we raise funds.' This includes letting out the site on the weekends to everyone from the Italia Conti Theatre School to local cricket and football teams.

Pupils looked well turned out in their navy and black uniforms with different coloured ties for each year group. 'It means that teachers can quickly look into the classroom from the outside and see which year is being taught.' A typical comp made up of all shapes and sizes – the handful we spoke to were a bright bunch with strong opinions and no major complaints. All seemed very happy to be there. We were particularly impressed with the two extremely eloquent and engaging sixth formers who showed us around. We chatted politics (Brexit) amongst other things.

Pastoral care, inclusivity and discipline: Most significantly, a new 'relationship charter' has recently been introduced, with everything now geared towards positive reinforcement rather than punishment. One parent said: 'Before this, pupils got a C1 (a first warning) for forgetting a pen but also for throwing a chair, which seems a bit crazy. With this new method they are doing away with detentions and actually talking to the child – finding out why they are late. Did something happen at home?' So far so good we hear, and pupils and parents are responding well: 'I for one am really happy that my children go to a school that is pro-change,' one parent told us.

Haydon school values are reinforced throughout the building: Excellence, Respect, Perseverance, Community, Kindness. 'The students get really angry if a child misbehaves, that's the sort of school it is,' one parent told us.

'Haydon has a really good reputation round here,' a student told us, 'and all my friends at other schools wish they were here'

The school also has a great relationship with the local police (Hillingdon), who sometimes drop by for spot checks, and all pupils are required to walk through a metal detection arch for knives etc, with sniffer dogs for drugs. 'It's a great unwarned deterrent,' we were told. Parents are happy with school's approach to behaviour. 'I have always found that a high level of discipline is maintained from the minute the children arrive at the school,' said one.

School also operates a positive reward system, which 'is a great motivator: my child strives to get good news notes, commendations and other rewards.' Meanwhile a year 8 student said: 'I really look forward to the awards assembly. It's a way of showing how hard we are working.'

Several exclusions a year, but only as a last resort. 'We really don't want to permanently exclude unless we really have to. We also use an offsite provision (Jubilee Academy) to work with these young people.'

The biggest change the head has seen during his 20 years of teaching is sadly, but not unsurprisingly, the rise in mental health issues: 'I do blame social media for this. Snapchat is every head's nightmare.' School has brought in extra professionals to help with mental well-being (for staff too) and there are two full-time student counsellors on board.

Bullying dealt with quickly and effectively, according to the parents we spoke to.

Pupils and parents: 'Haydon has a really good reputation round here,' a student told us, 'and all my friends at other schools wish they were here.' What is really special, we are told, is how many former pupils stay in touch: 'Quite a lot of them go into finance, and it is great when they come back to visit and tell the existing pupils how they got to where they are,' says the head.

The school offers both pupils and parents a chance to voice their opinions – parent voice group meets four times per year. Many professional parents at the school, but a real mix as reflects this area of London. Active PTA which raises money via curry nights and quizzes etc.

The last word: A friendly comprehensive that really does cater for all, with strong vocational courses as well as the more traditional A levels – all taught to a high standard. 'I would have no hesitation recommending Haydon,' said one parent. 'I feel my children are lucky to attend the school.'

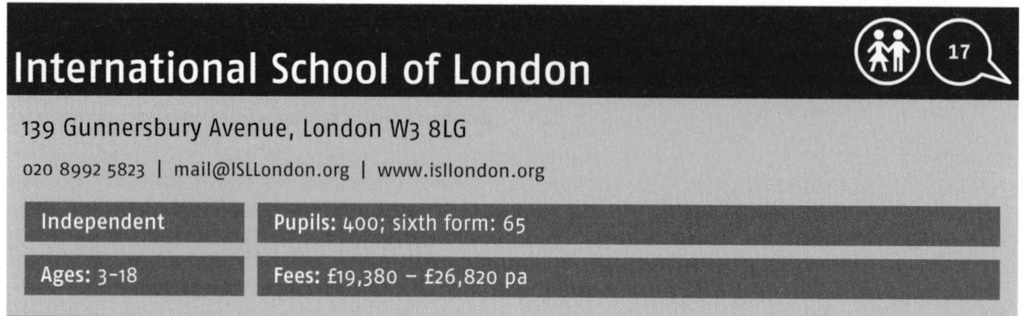

International School of London

17

139 Gunnersbury Avenue, London W3 8LG

020 8992 5823 | mail@ISLLondon.org | www.isllondon.org

Independent | Pupils: 400; sixth form: 65

Ages: 3-18 | Fees: £19,380 – £26,820 pa

Principal: Since September 2018, Richard Parker, who has been principal of ISL Surrey primary school since 2015, and was also co-principal of the London campus. Started working in a law firm in the City, which may have been the inevitable job choice for a Cambridge graduate in history, but he left law and went to the Institute of Education, London, trained as a secondary school teacher and taught at several state London schools before he and his wife moved to teach in international schools in Spain, Argentina, Hong Kong, Portugal and Brunei. Two children.

Entrance: A rolling admissions policy to match the needs of relocating families. Initial contact through admissions team who work hard to ensure that visits and questions and contact generally runs smoothly and easily, since 'parents are already stressed enough'. Interviews by Skype if needed and sight of current school reports. They don't expect kids to have fluent English, but do expect behaviour they can manage and learning needs they can support. Sensible experienced admissions staff keen to maintain non-selective mix at the school, including those with learning needs. Registered as Tier 4 sponsors for visas.

Exit: Over three-quarters stay in the UK to universities including UCL, King's College London, Queen Mary. A smaller proportion of students move to universities outside the UK including Toronto (with full scholarship), Tokyo, Leiden (Netherlands) and the Royal Technical Institute of Sweden in 2020.

Latest results: In 2020, average point score of 35 for IB. In 2019, average point score of 32. Seventy-three per cent of students graduated with bilingual diplomas.

Teaching and learning: Early childhood classes start full time from 3 years old and parents said it was a blessing to have all children at the same school with the same school hours. Long days for little ones, but the option to have a rest in the afternoon helps. Not that there was much sleeping when we visited – children were busy eating and cleaning up and playing. Lots of equipment and adults meant children were cheerful and well occupied. A very well-designed play area just for the early years with plants, wooden toys and climbing benches and even a mini amphitheatre, where story telling and plays take place. Small classes and high teacher:pupil ratio. Parents confirmed that much of the learning takes place through play.

Primary class size varies from but is never more than 22 pupils, which together with the fact that we saw a classroom assistant or extra teacher in many of the classrooms means that the high teacher:pupil ratio continues up the school, and confirms what the pupils explained to us as 'lots of support and help whenever you need it'. Parents said that the longstanding head of primary knows every child by name and is very present and responsive. The school follows the Primary Years Programme, an international curriculum leading to the International Baccalureate. Learning is done in six-week Units of Enquiry and the aim is for each topic to cover all subjects. Much of the learning is student interest based and interactive, with peer-to-peer teaching and debate. The aim is for pupils not only to acquire knowledge but to have conceptual understanding, gain skills and develop beliefs and attitudes which they can demonstrate through responsible action. This interdisciplinary learning seems to be appreciated by pupils, who told us that school was fun and they looked forward to coming to school, and parents, who appreciate that pupils 'learn how to learn' and that the school has a 'liberal approach to education'. Several spoke about the advantages of 'a fully integrated curriculum'.

The end of the Primary Years Programme is celebrated at a grade 5 exhibition. Parents we spoke to felt that since the curriculum is fairly child led, the level is well matched and work is differentiated by ability – possible with such small classes. However, some suggested that native English speakers may not be overly stretched. The language programme is a distinguishing feature of the school. Regular teaching in their mother tongue as well as intensive English lessons ensure that that pupils maintain their own language while acquiring a second or third language. Parents said that every child showed real fluency within two years. This basic tenet of ISL maintains that children will learn a second language better if they maintain and develop their first language – any language learning enhances language development as well as being good for personal and educational development. We saw pupils in tiny groups or individually learning Swahili, Finnish, Arabic, Spanish or French, and the library has an impressive selection books in 18 different languages.

The Middle Years Programme does not feel very different from the primary years. Pupils, however, felt that there was more work and more independence required. The language programme continues alongside the MYP with its emphasis on global contexts and key concepts. The aim is to acquire skills to help with learning and life. There are self-initiated personal projects, work on laptops (given by the school or supported with bring your own device initiative) and an emphasis on independent reflective learning. One student said, 'It teaches you how to work and gives you explanations', and another said, 'You are graded on how you work things out, not on the result only, and teachers mark on your critical thinking.' Clearly the message on reflective teaching and learning has got through. Facilities are not extensive, but the school is well equipped. Two science labs, plenty of laptops, a large well-stocked current library which includes newspapers and magazines, interactive whiteboards, and endless language learning rooms. The mother tongue language programme and intensive EAL continue where needed in middle years.

The language programme is a distinguishing feature of the school. Regular teaching in their mother tongue as well as intensive English lessons

The IB diploma programme is housed in a building some 10 minutes' walk from the rest of the school, and so it feels like a sixth form college with fingerprint entry registration and a spacious, bright common room overlooking the small courtyard garden. The library is at the top of the building in a quiet study zone with many students wearing headphones. Smaller classrooms cover the various IB subjects on offer – economics is very popular, as are maths and the sciences (biology perhaps even more than physics and chemistry). A huge, light art room. Languages, unsurprisingly, often taken at higher level IB as most students are multilingual.

A grade 10 foundation class (15/16-year-olds) particular to the school gives intensive English lessons and preparation for the IB curriculum. Students follow a range of subjects (English, maths, science, humanities, PE, mother tongue) and the course focuses on developing their academic English so that they can move successfully into post-16 education. Most stay on to take IB diploma at ISL.

Learning support and SEN: Learning support department consists of SENCo for both lower and upper schools who sees pupils regularly as well as coordinating speech and language therapy and outside professionals. Learning support for up to two hours if needed included in fees, and extra (for example individual classroom assistance) paid for by parents. Pupils frequently self refer to full-time counsellor, who also supports teachers and sometimes meets parents. Counsellor also gives talks on relationships and general health (though sex education left to the biology teachers).

The arts and extracurricular: Extracurricular subjects and the arts have taken on new energy recently – one parent said it was unrecognisable now with the number of clubs and non-academic subjects being taught. A new music teacher who is proving very popular and dynamic has increased the music uptake and output – all grade 3 pupils take violin now, and grand primary and middle years musical theatre productions clearly a matter of great excitement and preparation. Similarly, a new middle years drama teacher seems to be a good influence, using the large bright space at the top of the main school.

A real highlight for the pupils is the 'makers' space' where student-led technological creations can take place. James Dyson would be thrilled, as are the students

For art, classes are divided into three and students do a rota of visual art and design technology with both hard and soft materials. Laser cutters and 3D printers, sewing machines and collage, mask making and woodwork. A lively hive of activity and creativity with much emphasis on the planning and design elements.

A real highlight of the school for the pupils is the 'makers' space' where student-led technological creations can take place – either as part of a lesson or in breaks and after-school clubs. Video recording and editing, creation of a 3D printer, video game design, innovations and machines of every sort. Dyson would be thrilled, as are the students, with the possibilities to make and create. Students said to us that the school makes you want to learn more but without making it feel like work. We certainly got a sense of learning through creating in that classroom.

Sports and other after-school clubs clearly well used – Glee Club was one child's favourite for musical theatre; there's also eg journalism, badminton, chess, Lego robotics, global issues debating. Many clubs led by students from the diploma programme, presumably in order to gain points towards the IB and to fulfil the community or action side of the programme. DJ-ing taught by one student who proudly told us this had resulted in his club members getting their own equipment and setting up as part-time DJs.

Sport: Sports led by three-person PE team – dance, hockey, basketball, volleyball, football. Swimming every year in junior school with kids bussed to Brentford Sports Centre. The school has a gym and playground but uses a nearby playing field for wider sports activities. A recently signed contract means school now has access to newly built sports centre at nearby Gunnersbury Park. Sports rarely involves many inter-school competitions but some fixtures arranged with other international schools. Lots of time and clubs for tennis, yoga, basketball and football. Parents felt that kids get an excellent sports education despite paucity of on site sports facilities, partly because they are taught general skills – such as kicking or throwing – rather than a specific sport. More competitive children use local sports clubs.

Ethos and heritage: An older red-brick building with modern additions on two sides forms a U-shaped school round the playground/school bus parking area. All pupils now come in through the main reception area (fingerprint entry system as well as more usual registration in class) and there is a flow to the school despite its many additions. It was bought in the 70s and was one of the first schools to offer all three IB programmes (PYP, MYP and DP). It is one of three schools owned by a Lebanese family who are still very involved, although there is an active board of governors too. Some links and support from the conglomerate of the schools, but this school is the largest and most established, with the heads reporting directly to the board and the proprietors.

It is liberal in outlook, catering for an almost exclusively international student body. This makes it wonderfully international in values including a great openness to other cultures. It also makes it painful for pupils who stay longer and live through friends leaving regularly. This turnover is part of the reality of ISL though an effort is being made to appeal to more local families, and not a moment too soon, according to parents. There is an active alumni body and one of its aims is to ensure links between ex-students of all ages are maintained. The transitions programme supports families and students when friends leave as well as supporting families who are new to the school – with a good family mentoring system.

Pastoral care, inclusivity and discipline: Part of being an international school means that all the students have something in common, and pupils told us that was why they all got on so well and there was never any bullying, stealing or behavioural problems – they said, 'We are all different and that makes us the same.' They mentioned talks about drugs, mental health, guidance, sexting, use of the internet and alcohol, and parents felt that kids had a good education in ethics and values – words like empathy used from early years. No-one could remember incidences of discipline so we couldn't get examples of this – though a discipline policy available in writing.

Student council in evidence and clearly plenty of input from pupils and parents. Some parents felt that the school listened to parents too much – the school is very anxious to please, rather than having the confidence to state its position. But perhaps the active and eloquent PTA is hard to ignore.

Parents spoke of the a 'warm atmosphere' and in particular the 'smooth transition', with school praised for its warm welcome to the many new faces each year. Good relationships between different year groups enhanced by vertical integration – clubs, mentoring, joint drama and fundraising activities etc.

School lunches delicious and prepared in house, with limited choice. A continental school feel with everyone eating the same food together.

Pupils and parents: Large numbers of Italians, Japanese, Americans, Dutch, French and British represented in the pupil body – which is why some families choose it. Also popular is its location – mentioned by every parent we spoke to – near Kew, Chiswick and Ealing. All family friendly areas and good for parents working in town. Not much evidence of chauffeur-driven pupils or security guards for little princes and princesses, despite fairly chunky fees. Some of the classes are small lower down the school so less choice of friends for some, but 'more of a community than a school' and 'like family'.

Regular transition workshops to support parents. 'Strong' parents' association organises cookery clubs, outings, welcoming and pairing up of established families with incoming families as well as having regular meetings with school to both support and offer suggestions – and parents say school 'listens to us and is open to implementing parental suggestions'.

Door-to-door bus service is available but with growing London traffic problems school strongly recommends that families choose to live in neighbourhoods like Kew, Chiswick or Ealing.

Money matters: Privately owned by the Lebanese family who started with this International School of London and now also run the International School of London in Surrey and one in Doha, Qatar. The Makarem family are still on the board, have weekly updates and visit regularly.

Fees are substantial and often paid by employers. No extra charges for the mother tongue language programme (as long as there are at least five students), learning support, day outings, most clubs, but extras include transport, lunches, intensive English, and 'capital development fee'. No bursaries.

The last word: A perfect school for a child to get intensive English language learning whilst actively maintaining their mother tongue and ideal for families who want to remain near central London. This school seems to be changing and flourishing with new and better facilities and management, whilst having a solid background of experience in international teaching. We liked the international culture of the school and the calm, purposeful atmosphere.

JFS

The Mall, Kenton, Harrow HA3 9TE

020 8206 3100 | admin@jfs.brent.sch.uk | www.jfs.brent.sch.uk

State | Ages: 11-18 | Pupils: 2059; sixth form: 533

Headteacher: Since June 2018 Rachel Fink, previously head of Hasmonean Girls School. A chemistry graduate from UCL, she has an MA in Jewish studies from King's College London and a teaching degree from Michlalah, Jerusalem College for Women. She spent 10 years teaching science in high schools in Israel, is a graduate of Cambridge University's Co-Exist interfaith leadership programme and has been a member of Partnerships for Jewish Schools' (Pajes) working party on mental health. A former JFS student herself (and head girl), she was drawn to the post of headship at JFS after her husband saw it advertised: 'I thought wow! This is the opportunity to be head of the school that taught me so much.'

We weren't quite sure what to expect prior to our meeting this head. In her relatively short time at the school, she has already (unintentionally) sparked two controversial issues which have found their way onto to social media. 'I wish parents would speak to me rather than addressing Facebook,' she sighs. Firstly, she changed the shoe policy at the school in a bid to smarten up the uniform (causing parental outrage); more recently she took the decision to remove the main toilet doors from the girls' and boys' toilets (not cubicle doors). She says: 'They became a fire hazard and there was graffiti. The toilets are now clean and safe.' The incident even made its way to the Jewish Chronicle: 'I haven't responded – I don't feel I need to. I never make kneejerk decisions, these have all been carefully thought through.'

Mrs Fink says it's a shame that people often make an initial judgement when they meet her: 'Because I cover my hair, people sometimes make assumptions – but I am much more than my headscarf.' We couldn't agree more and we immediately warmed to this head's open and honest approach to education, as well as her vision for moving the school forward after its public descent, following the departure of the previous head. 'My main focus was to get the whole school – teachers and pupils – reading from the same page. I wanted them all to understand the ethos of the school. There seemed to be no common ground when I first started.' No easy task when one considers the vast disparity of religious observance within the school.

The head is resolute about learning Ivrit: 'Culturally it is a very important language to learn as a Jew'

There is an air of quiet confidence about Mrs Fink which comes from someone with clear convictions and a deep-rooted faith. Yet for somebody who considers themselves as 'a traditionally Orthodox Jew', she has a very modern attitude to issues that many other religious people would steer away from: 'Hosting Pride Week would be a challenge for us, but we are an inclusive school and our job is to treat everybody the same.' She's extremely popular with the pupils we spoke to, one of whom enthused, 'Oh my goodness, she is amazing and has really changed things around already.' The parents we spoke to seemed to be in agreement. 'She is the best thing about the school and has won me over totally. I like the fact that she is not reactionary, but looks at the bigger picture.'

Married to Stuart, also a schoolteacher and her 'sounding board'; they have four children, the youngest of whom has recently completed her gap year. Clearly not much spare time on her hands, and even if she had, this is one head who wouldn't sit on her laurels for long: 'My mother always said, if you want to get something done – ask a busy person.'

Entrance: Heavily oversubscribed, with around 800 applications for 300 year 7 places. Applicants must submit a certificate of religious practice; after looked after children and siblings, just 10 places for those living closest, with the rest by random ballot. Following the Court of Appeal ruling in 2009, students no longer have to have a Jewish mother. Around 35 external applicants are accepted to join the sixth form each year, on the basis of GCSE results and religious practice.

Exit: Between 10 and 20 per cent leave after GCSE to try something else. Of those who stay almost all go on to higher education, either directly or after a gap year. In 2020, 14 to Oxbridge, five into medicine and one to study in USA (Rutgers, New Jersey). Common courses include PPE, various types of engineering, psychology, maths, business etc. Most popular universities outside of Oxbridge are Nottingham, Birmingham, Bristol, Leeds. In London UCL and KCL. A few each year go to music conservatoires or drama schools.

Gap year option arranged by the school to study in Israel is always popular and the school has also developed a bespoke programme to support and guide those aiming at eg apprenticeships.

Latest results: In 2020, 56 per cent 9-7 at GCSE; 94 per cent 9-4 in both maths and English. At A level, 61 per cent A*/A (81 per cent A*-B). In 2019 (the last year when exams took place), 46 per cent 9-7 at GCSE; 72 per cent 9-4 in both maths and English. At A level, 50 per cent of A levels A*/A (76 per cent A*-B).

Teaching and learning: Consistently in the top one per cent nationally of non-selective schools, JFS continues to achieve pretty stunning results. To add to this, the school's Progress 8 score indicates that value added is well above the national average.

Year 7 pupils set for English, maths, Jewish studies, Hebrew and PE, but in mixed ability groups for other subjects.

Ofsted had commented in its most recent report that more needed to be done to support those towards the bottom of the middle, some of whom don't make such rapid progress as their peers. Parents, however, told us that the school catered well for difference. 'My children are different in every way and the school's been brilliant with both of them.' 'The school has found a way to reward each of my children for what they do well.'

School is very well-equipped, with interactive boards in every classroom, and no fewer than 14 science labs. Indeed, science was praised as a particular strength of the school. Annual science festival, and the department creates plenty of science leadership opportunities. Astronomy offered to all year 10 students as an optional extra, and Science Support Club for years 7 to

11. History and politics extremely popular subjects too, and Jewish studies widely regarded as excellent – it has won universal praise for its intellectual breadth and inclusivity. 'It's been taught in a way that's allowed my son to challenge the material, rather than trying to indoctrinate him,' said one parent.

'Hosting Pride Week would be a challenge for us, but we are an inclusive school and our job is to treat everybody the same'

However, modern languages, which had somewhat of a battering from parents in our last review, is still not the school's strongest feature: 'We have had to get a tutor for my daughter for her chosen modern language,' one parent told us. Either French or Spanish offered to all year 7s, along with Ivrit (modern Hebrew) – many dismiss the latter as the 'subject everyone intends to drop in year 10'. However, the head remains resolute about learning Ivrit: 'Culturally it is a very important language to learn as a Jew. How lovely for our students when they go to Israel to be able to communicate in their language. And if they ever visited Jewish communities in South America, it's Hebrew they'd be speaking, not English.' She dismisses the popular trend of offering Mandarin as 'very difficult to learn'.

Teaching at the school generally praised. 'The school is incredible academically'; 'The teaching is amazing'; 'I feel I'm being really stretched, especially in maths'; 'The teachers praise you so much, they really notice your achievements,' said students. While parents added, 'The teachers for the most part are either good or wonderful'; 'First class teaching in a safe environment.'

Given that this is a school so celebrated for its academic excellence, Mrs Fink believes it is very important to support more creative options too such as DT and food tech 'even at the risk of the school dipping slightly in the league tables. I am willing to take that hit if it benefits the students and their futures.' This head, who believes that a holistic approach to education is very important too, says that one of the biggest challenges as a head is to say that your exams don't define you: 'I didn't do well in my A levels, and I haven't done too badly now. No one in my family has gone to university via the normal route... People skills really matter.'

Learning support and SEN: Excellent support for both high and low ability students, and a large and well-equipped SEN department: 'The support to my child has been fantastic – staff have bent over backwards to help her,' an appreciative parent told us. Another said: 'If you would have told me in year 7 that my autistic daughter would be sitting GCSEs in year 11, I would've said you don't know my daughter. And now here she is sitting nine GCSEs in a quiet room by herself with an invigilator. The school couldn't have done more.' Plans are also underway for a sensory room and a sensory garden, as part of the development of the well-being centre.

The arts and extracurricular: Superb artwork everywhere we looked, including some really huge canvases – 'They're not short of ambition,' commented the head of art. Drama also flourishes on a big scale, with musicals such as Return to the Forbidden Planet alongside Shakespearean offerings. Music is high-quality, lively and wide-ranging. Students can learn 'any and every instrument', and there are regular concerts. Dance, too, is popular and is offered at GCSE with a 'free flow' dance performance yearly.

Sixth form newspaper held in high regard and student journalism is strong throughout the school. Student journalists' weekly reports on school events are published on the JFS website, and they can also train in creative writing for the school blog. A couple of lucky candidates are invited to visit Bloomberg or Sky where they can produce a news show. Model UN popular as well as 'loads' of student-run societies: 'Mrs Fink is very open to suggestions from us about a new society and even if it's a no, she will always hear us out and give reasons why it can't happen,' one student told us.

Many excursions on offer including to Poland (with a visit to Auschwitz) – and two 'incredible' opportunities to spend time in Israel. A Taste of Israel programme involves two weeks in Israel visiting the main sites of interest and 'developing their own relationship with the Jewish state'. And new from January 2020, the JFS LEV programme includes 12 weeks at the American High School in Israel following the British curriculum interleaved with touring the country.

Sport: Impressive array of trophies on display won in Maccabi Games (often referred to as the 'Jewish Olympics') as well as local fixtures. Students also represent JFS in Brent League swimming and years 8 and 9 boys and girls won the Brent football cup this year. Good opportunities and facilities for sport on offer: netball, football, badminton, basketball, trampolining, athletics, rounders, rugby, cricket etc. Magnificent climbing wall – very popular and much used. Yet one parent we spoke to grumbled that there was not nearly enough sport

Orley Farm School

done at the school: 'It's such a pity, they have such wonderful grounds, yet PE seems to be rather randomly taught and there is no girls' hockey team.'

Ethos and heritage: Founded in 1732 and moved to London's East End in 1832. The site was bombed during the war, and in 1958 relocated to Camden. Expanding numbers, plus the need to upgrade school facilities, led to the move in 2002 to its present purpose-built home in Kenton. The school today has around 2,000 students and is the biggest Jewish school in Europe.

Set on a 23 acre site with a sweeping driveway to get to the main school (part of their top-notch security measures,we imagine), the new school building was designed to be light and airy, to have learning at its heart, and to have the synagogue situated where it would catch visitors' eyes. This is certainly the jewel in the school's crown, with beautiful stained glass windows and a library and study area in the gallery. It's in constant use, both for services and Lunch and Learn sessions. Elsewhere the building is curvy and lightsome, with wide corridors and a progressive feel, although here and there carpets and paintwork are showing their age. The sixth form section is particularly inviting, with spacious and attractive study areas. A recent addition is the Pod, a covered outdoor area with tables and chairs and a café serving hot drinks and panini for years 10 and 11, 'to avoid the lunchtime crush,' we are told.

JFS, motto Orah Viykar (Light and Honour), is divided into four houses named after leading lights in the Anglo-Jewish community (Angel, Brodetsky, Weizmann and Zangwill), and is orthodox in the sense that its denominational authority is the Chief Rabbi. However, it admits children from a wide variety of Jewish families, both practising and secular: 'The school prepares you to mix with any background,' said a very likeable sixth former, 'and it's a great place for the secular as well as the observant.' All faiths are represented in the staff team, 60 per cent of whom are not Jewish. The head says, 'The religion of my staff is not an issue. More important is that the school is the right fit for them and vice versa. I want to know that they care about the school as much as our students do.'

It was interesting to see conservative, orthodox-looking girls alongside those with lots of glossy hair and barely visible skirts. Kippahs (skullcaps) are an obligatory part of the uniform for boys and are (supposed to be) worn at all times in the building. As we moved round the school, the students seemed cordial, purposeful, orderly and generally well-turned-out in their dark blue, light blue and white uniforms and colour-denoted house tie.

We liked the warmth of this school community – lots of energy and lively discussions (it was lunchtime). Pupils carried themselves with confidence and, we thought, joie de vivre. One student said, 'JFS is really good, really welcoming, and I settled in quickly,' and another added, 'I feel really lucky to be here. It's such a big school that there are so many opportunities.'

Pastoral care, inclusivity and discipline: In 2014 parental complaints about some students' behaviour led to an unannounced visit by Ofsted and the lowering of JFS's status from 'outstanding' to 'requires improvement'. Something of a shock, one imagines, but the school rallied, and two years later was regraded as 'good' in all areas except the 16-19 study programmes where it was graded 'outstanding'. Ofsted said: 'The most notable improvement in the school is in pupils' behaviour. Leaders have worked hard and effectively to introduce a better rewards system and to ensure that all staff implement behaviour management practices. Pupils now behave well in lessons and around the school.'

Student journalism is strong throughout the school. A couple of lucky candidates are invited to visit Bloomberg or Sky where they can produce a news show

Mrs Fink has done much to address this issue too. Not out to win the popularity vote, she scrapped the traditional pre-GCSE 'muck up day', which in the past had seen some 'terrible incidents', instead focusing on an end of year 11 'celebratory graduation'. One parent said: 'I am 100 per cent behind her. If you do bad things, you have to expect repercussions. It's a good life lesson.' Pupils, surprisingly, have responded well to her stricter measures; 'It feels a lot more stable now,' said one. In turn, hard work and good behaviour have paid off: 'Mrs Fink allowed some of us to miss school and go to the Climate Change Protest. She said we could go if we did something positive with it.'

'Everyone feels safe here' was a typical student comment, and school says, 'bullying is not tolerated.' That said, JFS is a big school and sometimes this can slip under the radar as with any school. Peer mentoring schemes for year 7s were 'second to none', according to one grateful parent, and staff were said to be approachable and contactable in the main. Safeguarding and well-being are notably well resourced. There are two full-time counsellors, a well-being practitioner and a designated social worker as well as non-teaching heads of year. Mrs

Fink says: 'If anxiety is becoming a thing in year 9, we will try and preempt it in year 8.'

The issue around drugs has also had much time and thought put into it: 'We have a zero tolerance policy to drugs at the school but we are aware what goes on outside the school. It would be naive to think it doesn't exist.' There's a joined-up approach to drugs education. The school works closely with its local authority as well as the Amy Winehouse Foundation. Indeed her father, Mitch Winehouse, recently visited the school to give a talk. The school has run programmes for parents, staff and students, including mental health first aid instruction and peer mentoring, and has a clear well-being support sign posted on its website.

Pupils and parents: A broad social mix of families, with about eight per cent on free school meals. Students are confident, articulate, 'sometimes audacious'.

The last word: Still the main school of choice for Jewish families wanting the best education for their child – both Jewish and otherwise. As one parent said, 'When my son received his place at JFS, my husband and I felt we'd won the golden ticket, and our feelings haven't changed.'

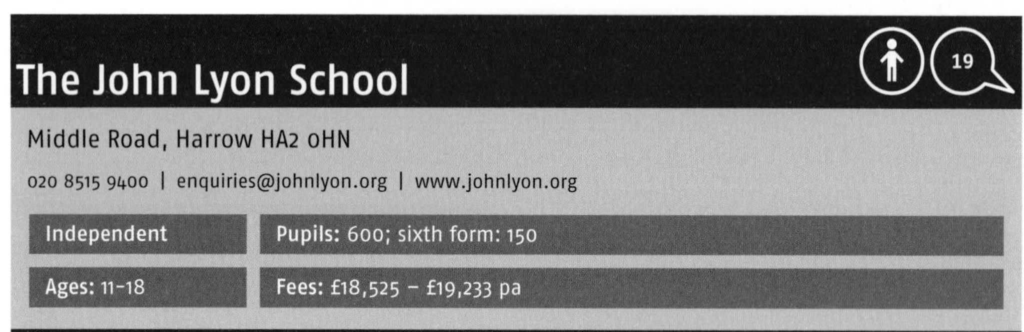

Head: Since 2009, Katherine Haynes, BA MEd NPQH (40s). Attended Oxford High School for Girls ('No doubt, that's the reason I'm driven in the way I am'), before reading maths at Warwick, followed by an MEd. Then taught in the Midlands, becoming head of maths at Edgbaston High School, followed by Warwick School, where she first started out as a school inspector and took the professional training scheme for headship. Her appointment at John Lyon made her the first woman ever to head an HMC boys' day school, but she had no hesitation in taking up the challenge. 'I felt I could provide a different perspective and saw what was possible. I wanted to make it more academic and put it on the map.' Has acted decisively on this brief, expanding the academic and extracurricular offering and polishing the pastoral care. Parents undoubtedly appreciate her approach. 'She's vibrant and dynamic, with no airs and graces, no nonsense,' said one fan. In term time she 'lives and breathes' the school, and all praise her involvement with pupils ('She really has time for the boys') and their families ('We were so impressed she invited parents of new boys to dinner at her house'). Continues to work as a school inspector, and, in her limited free time, enjoys gardening and travelling.

Entrance: At 11, 75 per cent come from local primaries (about 200 apply for 80 places, with increasing numbers making John Lyon their first choice); English and maths exams plus group activity. At 13 (when three or four forms expand to five), all from local preps, with main feeders Durston House, St Martin's, Orley Farm; English, maths, French and science exams (no pre-tests). The school is academically selective, but here the term 'potential' is not just rhetoric. All applicants are interviewed by senior staff (at 13, all by the head), with the intention of snuffling out 'those happy to be busy, active and willing to push themselves'. Applications are now open for girls into year 7. Small intake into the sixth form, plus occasional mid-year admissions. From September 2021 John Lyon will welcome girls for the first time.

Exit: Some 30 per cent leaves post-GCSE for local sixth form colleges. Of the remainder, 70-80 per cent to their first choice of university, with significant numbers to leading London colleges (LSE and King's), then Russell Group (50 per cent) countrywide. Sometimes a few to Oxbridge, though none in 2020. University advice up-to-date and thoughtfully tailored to individual needs (including STEP classes for mathematicians). 'We're ambitious for boys and see what's possible,' says the dynamic head of university applications. High proportion to professional degrees in science (one medic and one dentist in 2020), law, economics, architecture and finance.

Latest results: In 2020, 68 per cent 9-7 at GCSE; 53 per cent A*/A at A level (80 per cent A*-B). In 2019 (the last year when exams took place), 62 per cent 9-7 at GCSE; 32 per cent A*/A at A level.

Teaching and learning: Small class sizes (20-23 in years 7-9, 18-24 at GCSE, 10-16 at A level) mean that pupils are well known by staff. ('A good relationship with teachers helps with their work,' says the head.) Currently reducing GCSE numbers from 10 to nine, 'to give more scope to go beyond the curriculum'. IGCSEs in maths, English and all sciences ('The exams are harder, but they make the transition to A levels smoother'). Carousel of languages, with Mandarin taster in year 8 (including a successful exchange programme with Harrow's sister school in the Far East), Latin from year 8, classical Greek from year 10. Post-GCSE, the school remains happy with A levels, adding classical civilisation, psychology, government and politics, music technology, computer science and, soon DT, to the subject range. Also major emphasis on the EPQ, with an impressive 100 per cent achieving A*/A most years. Results overall very solid, a reflection of the effort to instil self-discipline, hard work and high expectations. Parents believe the school gets the balance just right. 'The grades are good, but you're not made to feel awful if you're not at the top of the league tables.'

Learning support and SEN: About seven per cent of pupils receive some sort of learning support (typically for dyslexia), which is provided by two specialist teachers in the learning support department. Those with English as their second language – the school does its best to accommodate families relocating mid year – also aided by a qualified EAL teacher. Gifted-and-talented programme, too, for those in need of 'enrichment'.

The arts and extracurricular: Drama a popular choice at GCSE and A level, with aspiring thespians busily practising their lines outside the two well-used drama studios on our visit. Boys also mount productions at Harrow School's Ryan Theatre and have the opportunity to work with professional companies, including the Donmar Warehouse, the Lyric Hammersmith and the Royal Shakespeare Company. Music – praised by parents as 'phenomenal' – benefits from a purpose-built recording studio.

A 'rounded' education given a firm emphasis, with a timetabled programme of 'skills-based' activities including everything from cooking to changing a tyre. Out-of-lessons options also extensive, with a particularly high take up of Duke of Edinburgh (an impressive 30 pupils successfully completed gold recently). CCF also on offer, as part of the Harrow School cadet force. Plenty of trips (football to Iceland, cricket to South Africa, joint ski trip with Harrow, Wellington and Dulwich) and societies, from computing to chess. 'It's a very broad ranging education,' commented one contented father.

Sport: Though the school overlooks some of the playing fields of Harrow, its own expansive 25 green acres are a five minute minibus-ride away. These have recently been updated with a state-of-the art MUGA (multi-use games areas) pitch, providing excellent floodlit facilities for hockey and tennis alongside football and cricket (and archery). Pupils also have access to Harrow's nine-hole golf course, squash and tennis courts (clearly made good use of, since one boy recently gained a tennis scholarship to the US). On site, there's a gym, 25m pool and fitness suite, with sporting options including basketball, judo, and badminton.

Ethos and heritage: John Lyon School – established in 1876 to 'educate local boys' – forms part (along with Harrow School) of the John Lyon's Foundation, and sits a street away from Churchill's alma mater in leafy Harrow on the Hill. The two schools have a happy, but not smothering, relationship, with heads of departments meeting for lunch, boys enjoying use of each other's more covetable facilities.

A particularly high take up of Duke of Edinburgh: an impressive 30 pupils successfully completed gold recently

One of the head's greatest achievements has been a 10-year plan to modernise the outdated buildings. First on the list was the introduction of a dining hall. 'I wanted somewhere the whole school could sit and chat.' Moving the library to a new location has provided an attractive central space, where staff and students can socialise over a hot or cold meal (though the food itself is perhaps not a highlight – 'It's OK,' said one boy politely). Other, much-appreciated, improvements include a sixth form centre, occupying the entire Victorian school house, which provides both learning and leisure space for older boys. Next on the agenda is a flagship STEAM (the sciences plus art) building where DT, computer science and maths will unite with art.

A rebrand is also in the pipeline, which, it is hoped, will put the school more prominently in the spotlight. 'People describe us as one of the best kept secrets in London,' says the head, who clearly now intends the secret to leak out. 'We want to bring across the vision of what we represent: heritage and innovation, creativity and resilience.' Other widely acknowledged USPs include 'the family atmosphere', the 'friendliness' and the attractively small scale. 'It's not too big,' said one father. 'Everyone knows my son's name, from the registrar to the guy who sits on the front desk.' Some feel the rebrand is long overdue. 'The school doesn't beat its own drum enough; it's sometimes seen as an also ran, which it definitely shouldn't be.'

Alumni include Michael Bogdanov, theatre director, Timothy West, actor, Stephen Pollard, journalist and Alastair Fraser, cricketer.

Pastoral care, inclusivity and discipline: Great praise for the care and attention boys receive, with parents united in the view that the school does its utmost to develop every inch of potential. 'My son is a bright child, but not A*, nor is he massively sporty, but John Lyon is a lovely, nurturing, comfy school, which gets the absolute best out of him.' Confidence building in the public arena very much part of the package. 'My son has really flourished here and is turning into a nice young man who is able to talk to anyone.'

Boys generally motivated and ambitious with little evidence of teenage rebellion. 'We promote a code of conduct rather than having endless rules, so it's usually possible to pull back before declaring "time's up",' says the head. Even so, if that code is broken, lines are firmly drawn.

A rebrand is in the pipeline. 'People describe us as one of the best kept secrets in London,' says the head, who clearly now intends the secret to leak out

Girl-free zone compensated for by good links with neighbouring schools, so debating with North London Collegiate and Northwood College, drama with Royal Masonic.

Pupils and parents: Primarily local, very cosmopolitan, with over 50 per cent from Asian families, whose children will often be the first in the family to go to university. 'They're aspirational and hardworking and want to do the best for their children,' says the head. Boys are positive, focused and keen.

Money matters: Good value. The John Lyon's Charity continues to help with means-tested bursaries.

The last word: A small, thriving school, with historic links to Harrow School, which provides a well-rounded, well-grounded education in a welcoming atmosphere.

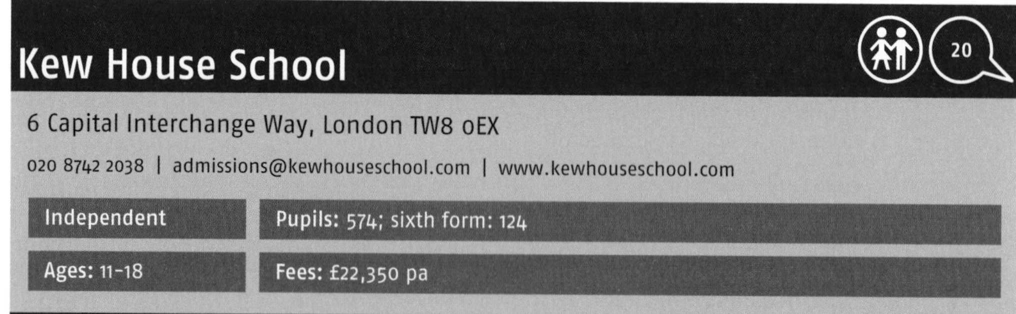

Headmaster: Since September 2020, Will Williams. Previously senior deputy head of Pangbourne College in Reading, where he was also acting headmaster in summer 2019. Has also had teaching, coaching and managerial roles at Marlborough College, Wellington College and St Paul's, the latter as director of learning. An Oxford University graduate, his initial foray into the City as a US fund manager confirmed his belief that he should follow his passion for teaching geography. He is an ISI inspector, a published author and ed-tech advisor.

Entrance: Now over 450 registrations for 88 year 7 places (four classes of 22) from almost 90 prep and primary schools, including Avenue House, Heathfield House, John Betts, Kew Green Prep, Orchard House, Prospect House and Ravenscourt

Park School. Very occasional places in other year groups (school currently completely full – except for sixth form).

Aim is for balanced cohort of 'inquisitive, intelligent students displaying a confident sense of identity and an original approach to learning, problem-solving and creativity'.

So while entrance exams (maths, literacy, but no reasoning) count, there's 'greater weighting' for reports, achievements and interests, and presentation on subject of choice. 'Currently lots on single-use plastic – the Sir David Attenborough factor,' says school. 'And cakes. We like cakes.' Staff may also visit current school. Process ensures that bright and articulate who may struggle to express themselves on paper get a fair hearing.

Exit: Have tended to lose half a dozen or so after GCSEs, many to state sector, but it's being balanced by new intake. Most to first choice universities, with around 40 per cent to Russell Group.

Latest results: In 2020, 59 per cent 9-7 at GCSE; 51 per cent A*/A at A level. In 2019 (the last year when exams took place), 38 per cent 9-7 at GCSE; 33 per cent A*/A at A level.

Teaching and learning: School, until recently the back-up choice at 11+, offers an alternative in competitive west London. Instead of super selectivity, takes students from across the ability range. 'Far more professionally satisfying to see a student come in with moderate or even limited academic prowess and see them grow into someone who can do really well.' Thus prize-giving only happens in the sixth form. 'Immensely divisive if go by results alone,' says school.

The school is also less than keen on termly/annual reports and 'speed dating' parent-teacher events – don't flag problems quickly enough, they reckon. Instead reports – shown to pupils first – are sent out every half term and parents are invited (and expected) to comment and get in touch. Works for proactive parents – welcome to drop in at any point – and have own café. 'If there's an issue, you go in,' said one. Others felt you could end up slightly disconnected from what's going on.

Average class size 22, far smaller in sixth form (maximum class size of 12) with pupil:staff ratio of around nine to one. Good choice of subjects at GCSE – options include computing, PE, food tech and four languages (including Latin). Start GCSE curriculum in year 9 – time to change option subjects if have made wrong choice.

More generous still with A levels – currently 25 including computer science and music technology, Latin, statistics, product design and business studies. Most take three subjects (plus EPQ) and occasionally four (one pupil also racing through art in a year). Most popular subjects maths, sciences, politics, economics.

Admissions policy stresses (as do we) that parents must support the school's educational approach, particularly as applied to length of lessons. Most are 90 minutes, while art, design and food tech, CAD, games and science lessons are all three hours long, joined by some GCSE option subjects higher up the school. No question of going out on an educational limb, says school. Tried and tested elsewhere, including at Thomas Telford. Adds up to a day's extra teaching time each week (and means less homework).

Benefits are manifest, says school, from easier trip planning (no complex negotiations with other subject teachers over missed lessons) to reduced time in corridors. 'Keeps the school calm,' says school. 'Ninety per cent of all pastoral issues take place when children are moving around.' Classroom time is also more productive – normal 40-minute lesson can be substantially truncated by late arrivals and packing-up time. Head not keen on shattering siren of school bells so there isn't one. No clocks in classrooms, either.

The teachers we talked to were enthusiasts. 'Love them,' said art teacher. 'Can get things done.' Food tech teacher, pointing to fab-looking deconstructed Pavlova, agreed – even enough time to make the tiny meringues on top.

Undoubtedly requires sustained razor-sharp teaching and planning to ensure that interest levels (staff as well as pupils) don't flag. Some parents query if this happens all the time. Others are full of praise. Supplementary tutoring takes place as elsewhere. If it gives a short-term boost or catch up, the school accepts the need – and invites tutors to work with the school – but shouldn't be a permanent prop.

Pupils rate help from teachers – 'focused on the individual,' said one. With no staff room, teachers are easily found either in classrooms or the café and willingly – say pupils – give up time at breaks or after school, plus holiday revision days (compulsory) in all subjects, with after-school homework club staffed by different teacher each night. No sanctions for unfinished homework. Instead, teacher and pupil will sit down and work it through. 'They're here if you struggle,' said a pupil.

All requires and largely gets strong and generally young teaching team, most reckoned by parents to be in for the long haul. Staff turnover 'modest', says school. In total, nine staff departures since launch, with six out of the seven founding team still there. In rare cases where teachers don't fit in will move on fairly quickly, think parents.

School's proud boast is that never use supply teachers – pay own staff for cover instead, better for pupils. Curricula are all written by school's teachers, nothing shop-bought. Not all homework is online but aim is to get more of it that way, making lost assignments a thing of the low tech past and ensuring that anyone who's missed school finds it easy to catch up.

Learning support and SEN: School's approach to teaching and learning felt to be particularly helpful for pupils with specific learning difficulties (generally mild to moderate) as ensures time and space for extensive differentiation. 'Would definitely think of sending dyslexic son here,' said prospective parents. Four-strong SEN team, some smaller group lessons, but focus is on effective staff training and integrated support in lessons.

'Great thing about the SEN is that it's embedded in everything they teach,' said parent. School's excellent reputation for SEN puts off some prospective parents (watch the shutters come down during open days). It shouldn't, says school, which stresses relatively small numbers involved. While 130 or so have an ed psych report, only 55 currently receive extra support in their lessons. Around 10 per cent of pupils have previously been educated overseas but vast majority of these bilingual – just one currently supported as EAL pupil.

The arts and extracurricular: Activities list impressive – 90 or so in total, changed termly. DofE, with speedy sign up, now takes the most enthusiastic through to gold ('fastest accredited school,' reckons school).

Lots of outside speakers, including parents (politicians, engineers, actors) and trips, some curriculum-linked, many local (Kew Gardens, Wetlands in Barnes), others residential, ranging from survival skills in Cornwall to art appreciation in Rome (could work vice versa, too). Older pupils may travel much further afield – one sixth former off to Great Barrier Reef: extended project topic. Good works happen locally (supports autism unit in Chiswick primary) and further afield (building eco-bungalow in resource-poor village in Laos).

Art is exciting as well as impressive – highlights on view included stunning A level project, inspired by 1970s slogans and street protests, with raw, powerful words and images reproduced clothes-pegged on a washing line. Year 9's contrasting workbooks featured technically adept delicate plant images. Currently in single (well-lit) room, a second home to the most dedicated, with handy balcony for spray painting. Additional room for A level work on department head's wish list.

Lively drama with plenty of productions (High Society the latest in list that includes Joseph, Little Shop of Horrors and Pygmalion) though sixth form currently feel they're less involved

School's proud boast is that it never uses supply teachers – pays own staff for cover instead: better for pupils

than years 7-11 (down to small numbers, not neglect). Now offered as A level and can study for LAMDA exams and pupils regularly (and successfully) enter local competitions and festivals.

Music coming along nicely – lots of Steinways round the place and plenty of ensembles, selective and otherwise, and including parent and staff choir and joint concerts with Gardener prep schools. The very enthusiastic may be home late – head doesn't care for disrupting curriculum time so all individual music lessons (around 100, beginners to diploma standard, learn in school, 50 outside) happen between 4pm and 6pm three days a week.

Sport: 'We don't have the rolling acres,' says school – a distinct understatement with just a couple of courts on site (though nicely screened with vegetation) used for informal footie sessions at break.

Not the place for athletes, think parents, though range, all within a 10-minute walk or bus ride, is extensive. Swimming and indoor sport happens closer still at local leisure centre next door. Rowing – growing fast – at picturesque Strand-on-the-Green riverside. Cricket, rugby and football all on local pitches with good complement of girls' teams. Some individual successes (year 9 Surrey netball development squad) and team wins (recent national table tennis champions in ISA competition).

Ethos and heritage: School's owners – the Gardener Schools Group – run two successful preps in the area, both relatively recent additions to the local educational scene. Opened in 2013, this is the first (and so far only) senior school in the group. Maria Gardener cited by parents as reason for looking at KHS in the first place. 'She's a special-needs teacher herself and gets it when so many other heads and owners don't,' said one. Some events (eg quiz night, occasional concert) bring prep and senior school parents together – creates nice atmosphere.

Setting takes a bit of getting used to. From the road, it's a quintessential red-brick office block, surrounded by heavy traffic and redevelopment. Inside, however, head has had a free hand (and what appears to be considerable budget) to design it as he sees fit, to excellent effect.

Space is effectively and even beautifully planned, as well as being conspicuously neat and tidy. It's super quiet, too (making crash of a couple of doors in need of soft close fittings particularly noticeable).

Areas, subjects and staircases zing through the entire colour spectrum (pupils must travel to end of the rainbow and back several times a day). Even the displays coordinate with the paintwork, striking aboriginal inspired designs in terracotta and burned yellows a perfect match with the paintwork, while the dinky but well-equipped labs are primary coloured, ditto canteen which features one of the few clocks (Swiss railway).

Lighting is just as eye-catching. Newer, second block housing sixth form independent learning centre on the ground floor notable for massive lampshades in contrast with smaller clusters twinkling away in corners, all bringing illumination where it's needed. 'Like Soho House,' say parents. Other practicalities include densely packed row of power sockets at counter top height, making laptop charging a doddle. Younger years, who use upper floors for maths and languages, must admire from a distance.

Stunning A level art project, inspired by 1970s slogans and street protests, with raw, powerful words and images reproduced clothes-pegged on a washing line

Uniform, in contrast, surprisingly preppy – blue blazers, jumpers and shirts plus brown skirts or trousers – some girls pushing to wear either. Parents seemed generally happy. 'I like it, the kids don't,' said one. Freshman-style hoodie popular with all. Parents have no problem with absence of official kitbag but one wish list would include same colour shoes for all (currently black or navy for girls, brown deck shoes for boys), particularly at concerts when 'you really notice it.'

Other sensible touches include absence of lead weight backpacks. Only sixth formers have lockers. For other years, daily textbooks (normally no more than four) come in and go home in strong plastic folder (previous iteration, in cardboard, proved too flimsy for the job). Saves back pain, time and trouble. 'They don't get lost because they go in and out all day,' said parent.

Pastoral care, inclusivity and discipline: Vertical tutor groups mean siblings can be together (if want to). Same personal tutor ensures continuity and in-depth knowledge of pupils. Generally works well – as long as long as teachers don't leave and pupils like them, say parents, though possible for pupil to request change of personal tutor if the chemistry isn't there. Rare, say pupils, and would 'need a very good reason'. Could make request a bit Beadle and Oliver-ish – off-putting for all but the most robust souls.

Worth enlisting support of head boy and head girl, current duo (nominated by staff, final choice through pupil vote) busy working through lengthy wish list.

Sixth formers want to be allowed off the premises during 45-minute lunch break (can't be done in the time, says school). School food is a work in progress though vegetarian options have improved, thought one pupil, and sixth formers can now order appetising-looking sandwiches. Not cheap – 'most expensive croissants in west London,' thought a parent, though 75p is not unreasonable, counters school.

Sanctions are unambiguous – instant exit for drugs and alcohol, only possible leeway is student who owns up to having a problem, but no guarantees. Break school's strict phone policy (allowed in school only if switched off) and it will be left in reception for parents to collect (only happens once). Forget school tie and you have to borrow one of senior teacher's cast-offs (one girl unfazed by shiny, multi-pleated number).

Some nice touches – like name tags, worn by all pupils (school reminds them to turn over when on public transport) that mean year 7s are known to all and to each other. 'Unusual but inclusive,' said parent.

CCTV throughout the building also helps, say pupils, who felt that people are 'generally nice to one another'. Parents agree.

Smartphones the perennial out-of-school issue. Opt for Nokia retro phones, urges head – with limited success, even with the nostalgic joy of playing Snake. School has upweighted resources here – onsite counsellor recently recruited – and parents feel school is getting to grips with cyberbullying. Rare that pupils asked to leave for bullying but would happen if behaviour consistently 'detrimental to others – important that parents realise you stand by your principles,' says school.

Pupils and parents: Families thought to be less anxious and more down to earth than at other schools – some very affluent, many dual income. 'Very normal, very relaxed,' thought one. 'Perhaps more comfortable because they're more experimental, so quite chilled.'

Pupils generally make own way to school. Drop offs possible but infra dig beyond initial newbie phase. Mostly families relatively local – Kew, Chiswick, Barnes, Putney, anywhere within reach of Kew Bridge station (overground) or Gunnersbury (District line – a 10-minute walk). Currently need to do bit of dogleg to dodge busy motorway feeder road – a worry to parents – though working with developers to make this safer. Some pupils bike to school (plenty of cycle paths) and helmets must be worn. 'When I forgot, teacher was on my case immediately.' The canny (or 'lazy toads,' says school) catch bus a single stop from Kew Bridge, dodging busy roads and saving their tired legs.

Money matters: No scholarships, bursaries or even sibling discounts though most SEN support included in the fees. Everyone expected to eat at school. 'School does not provide facilities for packed lunches.' On the bright side, sixth form coffee machine which charges £1 for everything, even, according to pupils, hot water for own teabag, is to be supplemented with Quooker or similar in the near future. 'Was charged for short period but now a dispenser is in place,' says school.

The last word: Inclusive, different and surprisingly beautiful. Essential to understand and commit to approach – especially those extra-long lessons. Emphatically not the place for clockwatchers.

Head of Juniors: Since 2016, Paula Mortimer BEd (40s), previously head of St Christina's school in St John's Wood. A science specialist with a degree from Oxford, she has taught in preps and all-through schools, latterly as deputy and acting head of Channing Junior School. Also has experience as SEN coordinator. Still loves teaching. 'I have no plans whatsoever to stop spending time working with children in the classroom,' she says. A hands-on head, she is known for fostering honest, open relationships not only with staff, but with pupils and parents. Very committed to pastoral care. 'For me, a role as head is all about ensuring children are secure and happy first and foremost, as that's what makes them successful learners. They're two sides of the same coin.' Particularly keen to see children take risks in the classroom. 'That's how they learn.'

Head of whole school is Mrs Heather Hanbury (see senior school entry).

Entrance: School's own entrance tests in English and maths at 7+, and top performers invited back for an activity session. About 48 places, split across two forms. Only two girls trying for every place, but don't be fooled – the older they get, the faster the ride, so best for those who seem exceptionally bright and eager to learn. That said, they do take some borderline performers. 'Some show high potential, but have not had the fire in their belly if, for example, they've been at a pre-prep that just drills facts into them. We are looking for what girls are capable of, not what they've already achieved – along with a can-do attitude.' Pupils come from a combination of primaries and many from pre-preps like Hampton Pre-Prep and Jack and Jill.

Exit: Some 80 per cent move up to the senior department – the school insists that in any one year, usually only three or four girls do not progress due to not being academically able. Thankfully, no exam separating those who get in vs those that don't – instead, girls are assessed on the basis of their classroom work and school exams and offered a guaranteed place in year 5. The few who don't make the cut get lots of support and extra help to prepare for tests to other schools and they may still sit the LEH entrance exam if they wish. Those who want to try for a scholarship also sit the entrance exams, along with the outside applicants. Those who do get a place, but decide to go elsewhere, opt for Tiffin Girls, St Paul's Girls' or Nonsuch, with others going to Kingston Grammar, Sir Williams Perkins, St James Girls' and St Catherine's.

Our view: A warmer welcome to a school you will not find, thanks to the lovely receptionists – and this really sets the tone for this surprisingly informal school where girls thrive academically, and then some. Four or five thick, bound photo albums take up the entire coffee table in the reception area, packed with pictures of the girls at carol services, on school trips, doing drama productions etc – also giving a flavour of school life here, where enrichment and extracurricular is seen as important as the demanding classroom based learning. 'My daughter recently told me she's taken up chess – I knew nothing about it. Absolutely brilliant!' said one parent. When we visited, two whole classes were absent for enrichment purposes – one practising for a big drama production in the senior school and one on a visit to the BFI, all dressed in Roald Dahl-themed costumes, complete with face-paint.

The school building started life as an attractive old house, although build-ons over the years mean that outside it is less aesthetically pleasing. However, unlike preps elsewhere, it has fabulous outside space – real space. A super garden area with excellent climbing frames and other apparatus, courts and pitches – much of it, of course, shared with the senior school.

Particularly valued by girls are the 'hedge homes' – little dens in the hedges abutting the brook separating the school from the grounds. Plus new tepee, which is used for story time and other activities as an outside classroom. The girls use pebbles for money and run these little domestic havens just as they would their brick and drainpipe equivalents.

Inside, everywhere is carpeted, which makes for quiet corridors and a civilised feel. A sense of purpose and attentiveness pervades, but it feels as if the girls are having real fun too – and their work is displayed in every corridor in witty, appealing and imaginative ways. Great cross-curricular approach too – if they learn about the ancient Greeks, they make Greek vases; if they learn about circuits, they design and make a working toy car. Arts and crafts and DT throughout are unusual and clever – girls showed us examples of 3D mazes they'd made, along with personally designed carry-bags, clever photography, moving toys and home-made slippers. Even the plastic plates they use at lunch (where food has mixed views from pupils, but mainly good) are each designed by a girl in the school. Particularly great excitement about the animated films the girls make, using their own clay and cut-out models, in year 5.

The wow-factor science lab is designed for interactive learning, with five hexagonal shaped high tables with Bunsen burners and plug sockets in the middle with six stools round each, plus state-of-the-art flatscreen Apple TV on the wall. 'We recently hatched chicks in an incubator,' girls told us. Library, which used to be small and barely adequate for this number of girls, has now been moved to a larger classroom-size space. Good traditional hall for productions, assemblies and younger girls' gym, and they use the fabulous senior school theatre. Decent ICT suite.

Weekly music lessons take place in a good-sized dedicated room, while around three-quarters have private music lessons in the senior school. Junior choir (for years 5 and 6 – you have to audition), chorus (open to anyone), orchestra and string group (which has performed in Hampton Court). 'My daughter adores her trombone classes – they really enthuse her,' said one parent.

Drama is also much loved, as we saw for ourselves during a practice session in the senior school theatre. Big singing and acting voices for girls so small – a treat to watch. The school takes part in everything from poetry recitals to debating competitions to Shakespeare festivals. Superb sports (great preparation for the legendary sporting culture of the senior school) and girls are lucky to use many of the older girls' facilities. In winter, the focus is on swimming, netball and gymnastics and in summer, on swimming, rounders, athletics and some tennis.

Great cross-curricular approach – if they learn about the ancient Greeks, they make Greek vases; if they learn about circuits, they design and make a working toy car

Back in the classroom, there's very little setting, although girls are sometimes taught in smaller, mixed-ability groups if it's felt it will aid their learning. French and extracurricular Mandarin are offered as languages, although the languages model is being reviewed. Specialist teaching in science, music, PE and computing from year 3, with everything else taught by the form teacher – then specialist teaching for everything from year 5.

Academically, this school holds a reputation of being a hothouse, which clearly infuriates staff and parents alike. 'They are just little girls who have a growth mindset.' The 'growth mindset' is a phrase you hear a lot here – with the school avoiding words like 'bright' and 'intelligent' like the plague. Homework seems fair – 20 minutes a night up to year 5, then 40 minutes. 'The school understands that if you're a working parent, you might not have time to do hours of homework – I applaud that,' said one parent.

Mild SENs only – although note it's not called that here, with them favouring LDD (learning difficulties and disabilities). Help just as likely to be for a spelling group that need short-term strategies as for anyone with dyslexia or dyscalculia, which means no stigma. Short-term bursts of intervention is the name of the game here, with a major focus on arming the girls with tools and techniques to keep up with the fast academic pace.

Pastoral care strong, with deputy head at the helm. They take a proactive approach, with lots of staff meetings to discuss, 'Did you think what X did was out of character?' 'Did you think X has been a bit distracted lately?' etc and they discuss it with girls if appropriate – and indeed parents, who they aren't afraid of calling to ask if everything is all right. Likewise, parents feel welcome to call the school. Girls praise the strong system of buddies, including coach buddy, house buddies and peer mentors, who help people out in the playground if they're sad. Lots of leadership roles (science leaders, head girl, house captains etc) and there's a term of mindfulness teaching for year 5s.

Bullying minimal, due to zero tolerance attitude, anti-bullying assemblies, golden school rules, talks about making the right choices and – perhaps most innovatively – a contract that each girl signs every year. If they break the contract, the head shows them the document and their signature and they get a firm questioning session – girls consider this deeply shameful.

Misbehaviour negligible, with little need for discipline – forgetting homework and calling someone a bad name is the worst of it, for which you get a 'sanction', three of which in a half term mean you have to stay in during a breaktime. 'You lose perspective of behavioural issues in a lovely school like this,' said previous head.

Trips to interesting places – including the National Archives at Kew to look at Victorian prison records (after which they 'used metaphors to write poems as if we'd been in prison') and the Globe theatre, plus residentials to Surrey (year 5) and France (year 6).

Parents not all super-rich, with many parents holding down a couple of jobs to pay the fees. Lively PA. Most families live within a half-hour radius and arrive either on foot, by car or via the super-efficient coach system that is shared with both the senior school and neighbouring Hampton School for boys. Juniors get a coach buddy to make the whole thing less daunting.

The last word: Overall, we found the girls to be conscientious and bubbly (the ones who showed us round didn't stop talking, such was their enthusiasm for seemingly every detail of the school) and happy learners. 'My child loves going to school,' is a phrase we heard time and time again – and we saw for ourselves the reassuring skips down the corridors and beaming smiles in the classrooms. 'Anything you'd change about the school?' is one of our common questions to parents, to which we twice got the answer, 'Only that I didn't get to go there myself.'

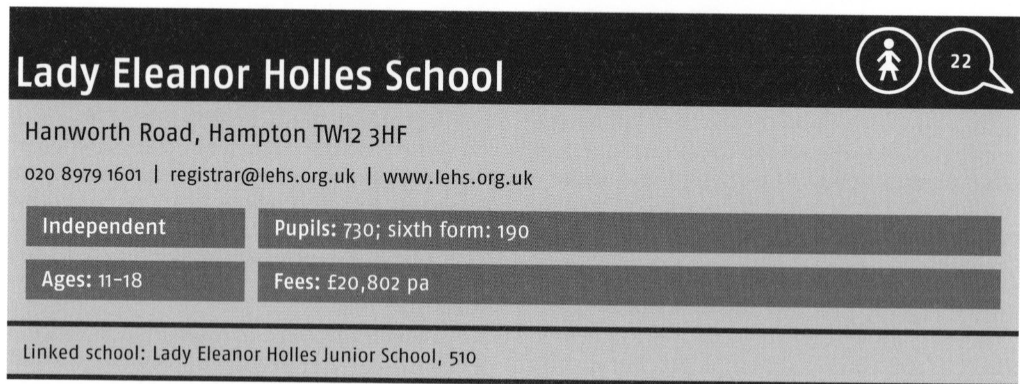

Lady Eleanor Holles School

22

Hanworth Road, Hampton TW12 3HF

020 8979 1601 | registrar@lehs.org.uk | www.lehs.org.uk

Independent

Pupils: 730; sixth form: 190

Ages: 11–18

Fees: £20,802 pa

Linked school: Lady Eleanor Holles Junior School, 510

Headmistress: Since 2014, Heather Hanbury, previously head of Wimbledon High. MA Edinburgh, MSc Cambridge in geography then land economy. Prior to teaching, she spent nine years working in various management consultancy roles in the City, then as a corporate fundraiser – 'real world' experience that both pupils and parents value. Moved into teaching because she was so frequently told she 'should' – 'but I initially resisted it because I don't like to do the expected,' she laughs. Eventually had a change of heart and took a PGCE with the express ambition of becoming a head. 'I always wanted to run things. I like making organisations efficient, effective and happy' – something that everyone agrees she's achieved, with bells on.

Began her teaching career at Blackheath High School in 1996, quickly rising through the ranks to head of sixth form, before moving on to Haberdashers' Aske's School for Girls, thence deputy head of Latymer Upper School. Teaches all year 7s for half a term each ('I get to know them, but more importantly, they get to know me – far better than helicoptering my way into sixth form teaching,' she insists). And although she does herself down when it comes to her teaching abilities ('I do the least damage,' she laughs), girls say she's actually very good. The only school where we've heard pupils describe their headteacher as 'very sweet', they gush over her assemblies ('She recently did a fantastic one on friendship and talked all about the movie Mean Girls,' enthused one) and say she is 'involved', 'interested' and 'approachable' – attending every event imaginable, even wearing sports kit to matches.

In school, she adorns glamorous suits (no staff member we met would have looked out of place at a wedding), hums with energy, has just the right amount of modesty (as is the LEH way), is quick to smile and laugh and is intent on injecting some fun into school life. Her office is among the nicest, largest and swankiest we've seen – if you replaced her desk with a bed, it could pass as a luxury boutique hotel room.

Lives with her husband in Hammersmith. Interests include bridge ('I'm not very good,' – there's that modesty again), cooking and theatre.

Entrance: Around a third of entrants come up from junior department. Of the remainder, about two-thirds come from the private and a third from the state sector – around 40 different schools in total. Private ones include Newland House, Twickenham Prep, the Study, Bute House, Holy Cross Prep, Kew College. Four to five applicants for each place. Normally, tests in maths, English, non-verbal and verbal reasoning and a problem-solving paper. But in the interests of creating a level playing field after the mixed educational experience of the summer term of 2020, the school has removed tests in maths and English for January 2021 entrance assessments. Expect the unexpected in the interview. 'We can tell a mile off if we are hearing not the girl themselves, but their parent or tutor. I'm absolutely allergic to that,' says the head, wincing. 'I don't even care if they do something silly in the interview – at least it shows they're being themselves.'

School sets its own exams for sixth form applicants, who need a 7 in subjects they want to study – and, in fact, 9-7s in pretty much everything. 'The odd 6 here and there is okay, but we want girls who can leap in with the rest and move fast,' says the head. Reports from current schools also count, along with an interview.

Exit: The school loses around 10 per cent of girls at sixth form – most to other high-level but (crucially) co-ed sixth forms. A few leave for financial reasons. Around 80 per cent to Russell Group universities. Destinations include Oxbridge (13 in 2019), Durham, Bristol, London, Exeter, Edinburgh, St Andrews and usually a few to Europe and USA. Mainly traditional degree subjects, with lots studying medicine (13 in 2019), English, history, sciences. Two overseas in 2020, both to study liberal arts in the USA – one at Oregon and the other at Cornell.

Latest results: In 2020, 95 per cent 9-7 at GCSE; 85 per cent A*/A at A level. In 2019 (the last year when exams took place), 90 per cent 9-7 at GCSE; 77 per cent A*/A at A level.

Strong links with Hampton School – just across the playing fields. 'It almost feels co-ed without having the distraction of boys in the actual classroom – what could be better?'

Teaching and learning: Few teach academia better and it's done via thrilling, not drilling. 'What's the point in boring them into submission?' says head – although she admits it's not always easy, particularly around GCSE learning, 'which can be very routine especially for bright, lively minds.' 'I really admire the school's ability to go sideways in any subject, bringing in current affairs or going cross-curricular, for instance,' said one parent. Meticulous record keeping for monitoring and targeting. Results outstanding. Staff clearly delight in what they do and all teach their own degree subject. Pupils told us teachers are always available, with the staff room practically empty at lunchtimes, as teachers run clinics or answer pupil queries from their departments. Sixth formers increasingly help the younger ones ('It's easy for them to remember the bits people find tricky in years 8 and 9,' explains the head. 'And it's good for them too – there's nothing like teaching to help you learn yourself.') Traditional subjects taken at GCSE, with computer science and PE the most recent offerings.

Committed to A levels, rather than the IB or Pre-U, with the academic offering upped via EPQ, plus an enrichment programme across every subject. Good range of subjects, including classical civilisation, psychology and economics, although maths and sciences remain the most popular. Sixth form feels quite a separate entity here – these older girls are revered and there are lots of sixth form only areas, including their smaller classrooms which cater for more tutorial style learning, in which there are no more than 12 girls in any one class.

Setting in maths during year 7, with groups reviewed annually. Languages include Latin, German and French from year 7, with the option of Spanish and ancient Greek added at GCSE (although French remains the most popular language at GCSE). Mandarin now also available from year 9. The school has one of the biggest German A level cohorts in the country, and Spanish is growing. Girls quite competitive around their learning, although they are also quick to support and praise others' achievements, with lots of patting on backs and high fives.

Learning support and SEN: Few with more than mild learning difficulties here, for whom SEN support is embedded into classes, with some one-to-ones where required – and it must work as they get the same results as everyone else. A good school to consider if you have mobility problems or are wheelchair-bound – flattish site, lifts and wide corridors, plus can-do approach – although we were surprised no girls in this situation when we visited.

The arts and extracurricular: Artistic talent evident from the walls of the new art rooms and corridors – there were several pieces we'd have gladly hung in our own homes. Beautiful ceramics displayed in a glass cabinet. Lively textiles and photography.

Music exceptional – the Holles Singers reach the finals of the BBC Youth Choir annually. We lost count of how many other choirs there were – some for which girls audition, others open to all. Orchestras and ensembles galore, with bands ranging from rock and pop to jazz. 'Unbelievably, we even have a symphony orchestra!' smiles the head, wide-eyed. Sixty per cent of girls learn an instrument with a peripatetic teacher. Brass popular, with many budding saxophonists. Plenty of space for all this in the shiny purpose-built arts block (where the arts studios are also based), with wow-factor purpose-built theatre where we heard a girl practising a solo song for the annual musical when we visited; she was amazing. Drama outstanding, with each year group performing something annually. The two big set pieces are joint musicals with Hampton School (years 11 up) and the summer musical (for years 7 and 8). 'They are something else – so professional,' said one girl.

Extracurricular life is thriving, including lively debating society, model UN and lots of charity and community work, including going into local schools. DofE and CCF take-up good. Masses of day trips to museums, theatres etc, plus residential trips from year 7 upwards – language exchanges, ski trips and battlefields, among them. Greece and Italy (classics), Berlin (history) and Iceland (geography) are other examples.

Sport: Legendary for sports and the facilities in this 23-acre plot are outstanding for a girls' day school, including three spectacular and very green lacrosse pitches (which many of the classrooms overlook – lovely, especially in summer); six outdoor courts; a massive modern sports hall; and indoor swimming pool (recently refurbished). At the front of the school are grass tennis courts and croquet lawn ('embarrassing, really, but rather fun!' laughs the head). Some parents choose the school on the strength of the sports alone. Lacrosse, not surprisingly, is the main winter game and played to win – which they do. Rowing also a speciality – a welcome rarity in a girls' school, for which boathouse facilities are shared with neighbouring Hampton School, and they also collect lots of silverware. 'It's great because if you don't like running around after a ball, you can sit in a boat instead – although many do both,' says the head. Other sports include gymnastics, netball, swimming, basketball, fencing, rounders, athletics, tennis and badminton. Some girls feel sport can be a bit elitist. 'You start out with A-E teams in year 7, but now we've got an A team and half a B team – if you're not in those, you don't get anywhere near as much attention,' one complained, although others disagreed. Sports tours to eg Barbados and America.

Ethos and heritage: The school was established in 1710 under the will of Lady Eleanor Holles, daughter of John Holles, 2nd Earl of Clare. This makes it one of the oldest girls' schools in the country. It began life in the Cripplegate Ward of the City of London, then moved to other premises in the City till 1878, thence to Mare Street in Hackney (that building now houses the London College of Fashion). The current school, purpose-built and designed in the shape of an E, opened in 1937. Such a long history is scarcely uncommon in many of our great public schools but rare in girls' schools. A palpable pride underpins the place. The staffroom has seen many distinguished names. They include Pauline Cox, former head of Tiffin Girls', Margaret Hustler, former head of Harrogate Ladies' College, Cynthia Hall, former head of Wycombe Abbey, and Frances King, former head of Roedean, who all taught here.

Very long, horizontal, featureless and functional, the two-storey main building doesn't delight the eye but then again, it doesn't offend either. Inside, the corridors are wide, the rooms are light and everywhere is well-kept. Some areas are somewhat hospital-like, with lengthy corridors and polished wood floors. Latest addition – Gateway Building in 2018 – saw refurbed sports

Music here is exceptional. 'Unbelievably, we even have a symphony orchestra!' smiles the head, wide-eyed

facilities plus new activity studio and ergo room as well as state of the art product design and computing suites. Big main library is well stocked. Lots of innovation in the cookery room – we saw girls were making their own versions of Bakewell tart. Excellent sixth form centre features small teaching rooms. The sixth form library is notable – light and overlooking the pitches – and includes more mature books and careers and university materials, with neat tables for study and rows of PCs. Nice sixth-form café and common room too.

Girls are well turned out and the sixth formers look fresh and neat in casual dress. A sense of order and high expectations pervades throughout. It's cool to be clever and cool to be sporty. Strong links with Hampton School – just across the playing fields – including in careers and university preparation and increasingly for extracurricular clubs. 'It almost feels co-ed without having the distraction of boys in the actual classroom – what could be better?' delighted one parent.

Notable old girls include Lynn Barber, Charlotte Attenborough, Carola Hicks, Annie Nightingale, Saskia Reeves, Jay Hunt and Gail (University Challenge) Trimble.

Pastoral care, inclusivity and discipline: Much praise for the pastoral care system – a clear structure and everyone knows who to go to. Teachers described as 'supportive mentors'. One parent whose daughter needed significant time off called the ongoing support from afar 'incredible'. No noteworthy sins of the drink/drugs/fags kind and minor bullying problems are dealt with swiftly. A culture of openness means that it's all right to tell someone if you're not happy. Good buddying system, plus a great cyber mentor system, which involves sixth formers being trained to go into classes without teachers to discuss any online problems. 'The training means they know when a line is crossed and they report it to us to intervene,' says the head. In fact, e-safety overall is taken very seriously here, with a dedicated e-safety officer. Two school counsellors available throughout the week. Plenty of talks on how to cope, including around exam time, and school wants to increase its offering around specific mental health issues. 'I think we're at the point we were with bullying 10 years ago – in that it's time to bring it out of the closet and admit it's okay to have issues and deal with them. It's about de-stigmatising,' says the head. Despite the school's reputation of being highly pressurised and hothousing the pupils, it's the girls who seem to be the ones putting pressure on themselves. 'It's just the culture of the school,' one girl told us. House system is a big deal here – there are even inter-house jigsaw competitions. Girls like the inter-year friendships this leads to, although some girls told us cliques can be hard to penetrate.

Low-level misbehaviour, such as forgetting homework, leads to a 'pink slip'. Three of those in a half-term and you get a strongly worded letter. But it's more carrot than stick here, with rewards of sweets if you don't get any pink slips and a class pizza lunch if your class does particularly well in something eg charity work.

Who wouldn't this school suit? Girls who aren't prepared to try new things (this matters more than whether you're good at it) or who aren't willing to work hard, said the girls we met. Food much better than it used to be, girls told us. 'There's loads of choice too – you can grab a sandwich or have a full-on hot meal.'

Pupils and parents: Parents tend to be much like the pupils here – academically brilliant, with a go-getting attitude. Not all super-rich, with many parents holding down a couple of jobs to pay the fees, something that the school values as enriching the school community. 'There aren't as many very wealthy families as I thought there'd be when I joined,' says head. Lively PA, called the Friends, is open to both senior and junior school parents. Mainly white British, although younger years are more ethnically mixed, with the second biggest ethnic group being Asian. From a wide area – Ealing, Windsor, Woking, Wimbledon and Chiswick, and all points in between. Public transport links aren't great, but an impressive coach map shows the multitude of routes they cater for (joint with Hampton boys' school) at the beginning and end of the school day (some later to cater for girls who do clubs) and which 50 per cent of the girls utilise. The rest walk, cycle or dropped off. Lots of parents have boys at Hampton.

Money matters: Drive under way to increase the number and value of bursaries. Means-tested and reviewed annually. Academic scholarships worth up to 10 per cent of fees at 11+ and sixth form level. Music scholarships up to 10 per cent. At A level, academic, music, art, drama and sport scholarships available – each worth up to 10 per cent of fees. Music exhibitions worth up to 7.5 per cent – and that's at 11+ and A level.

The last word: This is a school that bangs the drum very loudly about empowerment, constantly reminding girls they can do anything if they put their minds to it – and they excel in giving them the tools to achieve that. Not for the fainthearted, the girls work hard – and we mean hard – but they play hard too. If your daughter has the potential to be a determined, committed learner with a can-do attitude, this could be her ticket to a highly successful future.

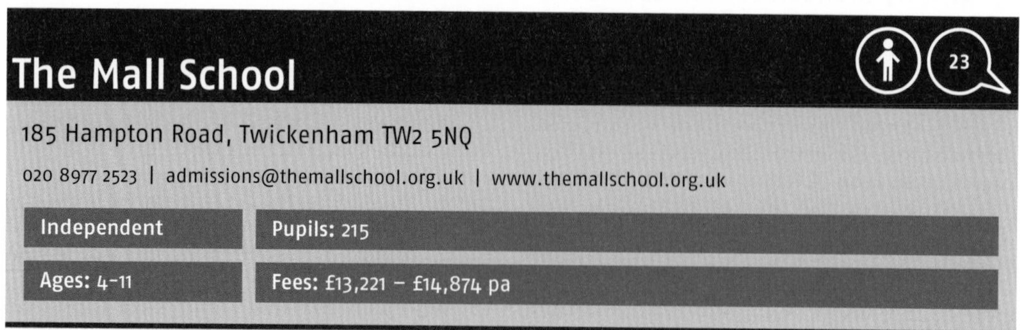

Headmaster: Since 2011, David Price BSc MA PGCE (50s), married with two children in their late teens. Brought up and educated in the Black Country, his first introduction to the western edge of London was Kingston University for his MA. After a spell as head of English at Latymer Prep he went down under to teach at Melbourne Grammar School. He says he felt a bit homesick there, so he returned to his 'pom' roots, moving on to be head of juniors and director of studies at the Mall, before becoming top dog.

Calm and understated, no fireworks, 'a mediator and negotiator', he inspires confidence that he knows exactly what the school is about and his role in its performance. Equally, the parents trust him to run a tight but friendly ship which will land their sons safely in their chosen academic port. Known to be behind his desk if needed, he also gets about a lot, often at the school gates talking to parents, invoking the comment that he uses these opportunities as 'a sounding board for new ideas'.

Entrance: The largest feeder for the first come, first served pre-prep is Jack and Jill Nursery, usefully sited on the green next door, but children also arrive from a variety of other nurseries or straight from the home version. Two forms move from pre-prep up to the main school with three from year 3 onwards, adding additional places at the existing entry point of 7+ and an occasional place at 8+. At these stages, potential pupils come to an assessment in maths and English during a day in the school where both sides have the chance to eye each other up. Unlikely to accept any new pupils after the start of year 5 as it becomes a 4-11 school.

Boys from a wide variety of backgrounds, often with two working parents, come here from all over west London, although one parent counted its proximity to their house as a huge plus. Despite tending to move on to similar schools, they can end up in very different lives, for instance Zac Goldsmith with his mayoral ambitions or the actor, Alex Pettyfer, who reverted to his schooldays by playing Tom Brown in a TV adaptation.

Exit: The move to becoming a 4-11 school is now complete, with all boys joining the school leaving at 11+. First 11+ cohort sat entrance exams in 2019. Most popular destinations are St James, St George's College, Kingston Grammar and Hampton.

Our view: The pre-prep, five minutes down the road from the prep school, has an exceptional, brand-new playground complete with a huge pirate ship and interactive games on the walls, imagination and energy equally well catered for. We badly wanted to play and boys have been known to cry on having to leave. It's small, and not so small, boy heaven. Incredibly tidy; even the smart red scooters have their own designated parking spaces inside neat white lines and a nice man was sweeping up the leaves that had dared to deface it.

Inside, the newly refurbished classrooms are equally colourful with interactive whiteboards, matching, bright plastic chairs and lots of lesson related photographs and images on the walls. We particularly liked the washing line strung with pages of handwriting on a pirate theme. 'He had a brown hat... and no legs' was our favourite description of Captain Hook.

Juliet Tovey oversees it with a practised eye, having been involved in education all her career, teaching in a variety of state and private schools as well as working as a local authority maths consultant. Not much chance that she'll get caught on the hop as she runs 20 km a week.

The two classes in reception and year 1 (maximum 18 per class) are each taught by a teacher and an assistant, the mornings being mainly for maths and English, the former prominently using the domino look-alike Numicon bricks. A reward system in each class allows all boys a daily start on the rainbow, with progress either to sunny uplands or downwards to a very unthreatening cloud. Apparently, they rarely stay in the rainy zone for long and can redeem themselves right up to the final bell.

Everyone has a hot lunch in the newly decorated basement where once a week there is a 'top table' for the four boys who have managed to avoid spag bol down their fronts and the temptation to talk with their mouths full. This innovation has worked extremely well and JT says it really does encourage good behaviour. Once the boys are fed, the afternoon is taken up with music and PE lessons and learning to swim in the pool at the main school.

One parent told us that JT had been 'fantastic over the transition from pre-prep to the big school' and the boys feel at home straight away because they are used to the feel of it, from coming swimming, on visits in year 1 and to Friday assemblies where they bravely march up to receive their commendations in front of the whole school, a sure sign of a confident small person.

The main school is nearing its 150th anniversary but has been on this slightly squeezed site since 1922, the only major interruption a fire in 1960 that wiped out all the buildings except the stable block. Possibly not a disaster, because they were able to rebuild and now have managed to cram in a 130-seater theatre, music rooms, an art studio, a DT workshop and science labs. Outside space is strictly limited but there are playgrounds, an outdoor classroom with ponds and a veggie patch, which had so impressed one leaver that he announced in the school magazine that he 'would like to become a naturalist'. There is also an indoor swimming pool, excellent for little ones as it only has a fraction of the normal chlorine levels and the temperature is more like a warm bath than an arctic lake.

The high academic standards are definitely a prime reason why parents enrol their children here: 'We wouldn't have put our boys in the school if we didn't think they could keep up with the pace.' Classes are an average of 17 (no more than 20) and will continue at this size after the top two years have been phased out. Form teachers and tutors (from year 4), about a third of whom have taught here for more than 10 years, closely monitor progress. Enthusiastic praise for the teaching – 'the academics are extraordinary' – is handed out all round, but French taught in French by Frenchwomen, 'part of the DNA of the school,' says DP, probably scores highest, swiftly followed by every other subject on the curriculum. A new science teacher has raised standards in her subject to the level that year 5 and 6 gained third place in the National Inter-School Science Quiz championship. IT which, admitted DP, had been 'a little on the back foot', has been sharpened up with speedier Wifi, more computers and an IT whizz permanently on hand to crack any problems.

The concentration in the classrooms is palpable, whether it be year 8s pouring over history textbooks or year 3s filing the edges off acrylic heart keyrings. That 'students step up to the challenge', as one parent stated, is clear when you look at the number of scholarships, including many to Hampton and several to St Paul's.

Exceptional, brand-new playground complete with a huge pirate ship was incredibly tidy; a nice man was sweeping up the leaves that had dared to deface it

Tackled on the subject of SEND provision, JT talks about the benefit of enrolling boys at reception because they can start evaluation from day one and identify any potential problems before they move up. Once in the main school, there is regular appraisal and a supported English class in years 4 to 6, taught by the SENCo; at the moment about 12 per cent of all pupils need additional support including a tiny number of EAL boys.

The new head of sport has hit the spot with both students and parents as he has brought in 'a certain level of organisation' which both felt was somewhat lacking, in particular when it came to uniforms and matches. Swimming is the big thing here, they are borough champs and amongst the top five junior schools in the country. Field sports, rugby, football and cricket are played in Bushy Park, luckily only a stone's throw away, and although this is not known as a sporty school there is a concerted effort to find an opportunity for every boy to represent the school in some form of team.

Parents talk happily – 'big, big plus' – of the extracurricular activities that take place after school and allow them to do a late pick-up (until 6pm), with one mother informing us that she had been told off by her son for arriving early. Kiddy Cook aims at catching future masterchefs whilst tennis and chess clubs are full to bursting right up the school. Although the judo master is a 'tough guy', he obviously holds no fear for the boys as his judo clubs are hugely popular.

Arty boys are successfully encouraged with three year 8 boys winning scholarships to senior schools recently. Almost three-quarters of the boys play a musical instrument and they hold a Summer Prom and inter-house music competitions as well as training junior and senior choirs. Budding thespians are well catered for in the new theatre and it was smiley faces all round when we asked boys about their acting experiences at school.

Pastorally, the overall consensus is that the 'children are happy, due to the teachers and staff, who are patient and untiring' and have a motherly approach to new boys, who are given an older buddy to run to, which goes down well with parents. The proof of the pudding came from three separate parents remarking that one of the main reasons that they had chosen the school was because they wanted their sons to turn out like the boys who had shown them round. Most parents felt the rewards system employed (points on a credit card) was an incentive to behave as well as succeed but there was a comment that the criteria on awards were not explained clearly enough. We tackled DP over this and, encouragingly, he said that he would address the subject at the coffee mornings he holds with parents.

The resolution that DP and the governors have made to close the top two years will bring about a sea change and we listened carefully to parental reaction. The dust has settled and the

Three separate parents said that one of the main reasons they had chosen the school was because they wanted their sons to turn out like the boys who had shown them round

general consensus appears to be that the move will prove to have been an intelligent, forward thinking response to the increase in entries at 11+ by local senior schools. However, the way that it was handled led someone to say that 'it was a shock we could have done without'. In our opinion, this considered decision to alter the shape of the school will not affect either its ethos or its efficiency.

Money matters: Up to 100 per cent bursaries (means tested) available at 7+ and 8+ point of entry, but hardship bursaries also available to parents who fall on hard times.

The last word: Apart from the all-singing and dancing pre-prep playground this is an unflashy, sensible, feet on the ground school. They concentrate on what they do best, giving boys a superior academic grounding in a safe environment and preparing them to succeed in senior schools.

Maple Walk School

24

62a Crownhill Road, London NW10 4EB

020 8963 3890 | admissions@maplewalkschool.co.uk | www.maplewalkschool.co.uk

Independent | Ages: 4–11 | Pupils: 180 | Fees: £10,740 pa

Headmistress: Since 2012, Sarah Gillam, BEd from Homerton College, Cambridge. Originally Dorset born, but started her career at Lyndhurst House Prep school in Hampstead. She left education for a while to 'gain some experience in the professional world' but came back to education as she missed teaching and the children. Her 30 year career includes two middle school headships and one head of junior science. Prior to her role as head of Maple Walk, Ms Gillam worked for six years at the now defunct White House Prep school in Wokingham (although during her tenure, it was an outstanding prep school, she says). She was attracted to the post of head at Maple Walk 'because of its wonderful history and story' and because she felt it was a school with great potential.

Warm and likeable (she was very concerned that we should have nice biscuits with our coffee), slightly distracted but perhaps it was nerves, so keen was she to impress. However, the parents we spoke to praised her ambition for turning 'a small villagey school' into a 'proper prep school'. One parent told us: 'Ms Gillam takes very seriously the reality of living in London and has worked hard to make sure the pupils are well placed and prepared to take exams for secondary school. She has done this with a more rigorous curriculum.'

Ms Gillam herself says that she has been very keen to work on the process of transforming this school – already an amazing galleon – into a tighter ship with more rigorous applications and monitoring of crew. She has worked at strengthening the senior leadership team and now has an excellent range of advisors. Also an ISI team inspector, Ms Gillam says this can be a great resource for the school as she gets so many ideas from other schools as well as being able to confer with specialists 'who are at the top of their game'. She still teaches RE from year 3 upwards for one lesson a week.

Described as a very visible head who is always wandering around the school, is very approachable, open to ideas and someone who 'patently cares about her job'. She has an open-door policy and as one parent said, 'is probably quite frustrated that more people don't walk through it more often.' Ms Gillam has three grown-up daughters, one of whom is also training to be a teacher: 'If you have this as a vocation, it is something I would always encourage.' Any free time she has, she enjoys cooking, travelling and spending time with her family.

Entrance: Some 200 applicants for 20 places per form. Siblings get preference, then in order of registration – waiting lists for several years ahead. The advice given is 'get them on the list as soon as possible.' For spaces higher up the school, the head meets the parents and the child has a trial day in the relevant class, 'to check that they will fit in socially and academically'.

Exit: To a wide variety of schools, including Aldenham, City of London, Emanuel, Queen's College, Latymer Upper, John Lyon, North Bridge House, Belmont Mill Hill Prep School, Wetherby Prep, Francis Holland, St James Senior Girls' and Maida Vale in the private sector, and St Marylebone, Hampstead School, Chelsea Academy, and Twyford C of E School in the state sector.

Our view: The New Model School Company (NMS) was set up by Civitas (but is now an independent entity) when research identified a gap in the market for a low-cost chain of not-for-profit independent primary schools. Maple Walk was the first NMS school, starting in a rented room in a sports centre off Ladbroke Grove in 2004 with one teacher, two pupils and school materials stored in a trunk. A year later the fledgling school of a dozen pupils moved to the upper floor of a church hall off Kensal Road. In 2009 the school – by now with classes up to year 4 – moved to its own purpose-built premises in Harlesden, which have impeccable ecological credentials: a sedum roof, solar panels, and a ground source heat pump.

Although the school has had a reputation for being a no-frills, low-fee-paying school and a decent alternative for the independent sector, parents we spoke to felt that it was now time to redress this reputation because, as one parent told us, 'it punches above its weight.' Another parent said: 'They do far more than you would expect from a school of this size and have really upped their game.' The general consensus seems to be that it delivers a great education and is a school which pushes each individual to strive.

Sport has been an area of focus for the school. For the particularly keen, an early morning (7.30am) cross-country run is offered to both pupils and their parents

The education is traditional, with reading taught by phonics, French taught from reception, history taught chronologically and Latin taught in year 6. Maths is set from as early as year 1, but there is movement between sets. The school says: 'We recognise that within each class there are pupils of widely differing mathematical aptitudes and we aim to provide suitable learning opportunities for each of them.' The school follows the increasingly popular Singapore maths scheme, although this is 'often supplemented by other resources'. English is not set, but there is differentiation within the classroom for the more able and also for those who need more assistance. One parent told us: 'One of the perks of a school of this size is the small classes and that each class has a teacher and teaching assistant, so you know your child will get a lot of individual attention.'

The teaching was praised by parents and pupils alike: 'They have really nice teachers who know the children well.' 'Teachers are absolutely on it.' The head's after-school secondary transfer club introduces exam techniques to older children, and the year 6 class teacher 'is very experienced at secondary transfers'. 'They do their absolute best to make sure they are well prepared,' said a parent. Certainly parents are happy. 'They seem to be getting a very good grounding,' said one.

The school can cope with mild SEN – 'We don't assess children coming into reception, but we do ask parents to be honest and transparent and we may talk to their nursery if we have any concerns.' One-to-one literacy and numeracy assistance at extra cost; some children get speech and language support outside school.

Sport has very much been an area of focus for the school, with a 'competitive but inclusive policy'. Whilst onsite sport facilities are pretty basic, the school has the use of nearby Roundwood Park for tag rugby, hockey, football and netball etc. For the particularly keen, an early morning (7.30am) cross-country run is offered to both pupils and their parents. We were told of an inspirational PE teacher who encourages even the most uninterested of children to give competitive sports a try, even at the cost of sacrificing a win for the school. One parent said: 'My son is not great at cricket, but this teacher put together a team of all the least talented cricket players in the school to encourage them to have a go at a competitive game against another school. They loved it.'

An emphasis on children becoming confident public performers: the annual Craigmyle poetry competition (named for the charitable trust that paid for the new site and building works) involves everyone from reception upwards reciting a poem by heart, and there are public speaking competitions, music concerts and drama performances. 'The children are very confident,' said a parent. 'They have nice manners, they can talk to adults, they look you in the eye.'

The curriculum is further enriched by a wide range of educational visits for all year groups, whether it's mudlarking on the Thames or visiting the Imperial War Museum

This is a busy, busy school. Lots going on to excite and motivate – indeed their most recent Independent Schools Inspectorate report praises the range of extracurricular activities. This includes photography, art portfolio club, Spanish, chess, dance, puzzle club, drama and football.

The curriculum is further enriched by a wide range of educational visits for all year groups, whether it's mudlarking on the Thames or visiting the Imperial War Museum. There is the year 5 residential trip, which has included a bushcraft trip where students are taught basic survival skills, and the annual year 6 week-long residential camp – which could be staying at a château in France or a PGL adventure course on the Isle of Wight. One pupil told us: 'I really like the variety of things on offer here. There's lots of great stuff to do, but it's also quite academic.'

The teaching was praised by parents and pupils alike: 'They have really nice teachers who know the children well.' 'Teachers are absolutely on it'

The school copes well with its limited premises. 'Of course that would be the one thing I'd change about the school if I could, but without physically moving the school, there's not much you can do,' said one parent. But the outdoor space still manages to squeeze in playgrounds for infants and for juniors – with a climbing frame, football/netball court with climbing wall (also funded by the PTA, Friends of Maple Walk). There are interesting-looking outdoor 'pods' for music classes with peripatetic teachers. The gardening club grows vegetables in tiered beds and a butterfly/bee-friendly area is in concept. The children learn to swim at a local pool and try out a different sport each half term.

The school has a broadly Christian ethos, with some religious assemblies and nativity plays, but all faiths are welcome and Jewish and Muslim parents come in to talk about their religions.

Despite the low fees, it is still very much a white, middle class demographic – albeit mostly journalists, artists and musicians rather than bankers and lawyers. A much larger percentage of families now live locally (previously the majority from Queens Park and Willesden Green) and the fact that it is so predominantly white and middle class probably represents how the area has changed. But as the school says, 'it doesn't stop us hoping and trying to attract a more diverse demographic.'

Money matters: School made a recent Telegraph's top Ten Value Prep Schools: 'Excellent value for money,' one parent said.

The active PTA has raised funds from auctions, casino nights and summer fairs to name but a few, for part-time specialist dance and sports teachers, and parents have donated computers, including a suite of Netbooks that travel round different classrooms.

The last word: Parents cite the 'village school' atmosphere as one of their main reasons for choosing Maple Walk. 'There's a nice, cosy, community feel,' said one. 'I liked the fact that it is small, pioneering and affordable,' said another. 'It's a really vibrant, eclectic community.' Parents emphasise how happy their children are – 'Mine will look back and feel they've been part of something really special and exciting.'

Merchant Taylors' School

Sandy Lodge, Northwood HA6 2HT

01923 845514 | admissions@mtsn.org.uk | www.mtsn.org.uk

Independent	Pupils: 930; sixth form: 280
Ages: 11-18	Fees: £21,526 pa

Head master: Since 2013, Simon Everson MA PGCE, educated at Solihull School and Cambridge (English) before completing a masters in philosophy at Nottingham. Latterly head at Skinners' School in Tunbridge Wells. Was adamant that very few schools would tempt him away but couldn't resist the lure to MTS, where he took over 'a school with wonderful tradition, but one that's vibrant and relevant now'. Still 'loves the classroom' and 'borrows classes' when time allows. Moved immediately upon appointment to reintroduce significant financial benefits to scholars, with scholarships for the brightest and most able across the board now worth at least 10 per cent of fees: 'We are determined to seek out excellence and reward it.' Enjoys walking, birdwatching and Scotland and is a qualified apiarist (beekeeper). An electric guitar sits tucked in the corner of his office – 'I wanted to put myself in the boys' shoes and remember how it feels to struggle to learn something new,' he says. Businesslike and sincere. Married to Ginny, a psychotherapist.

Entrance: Selective with two main intakes at 11+ and 13+. At 11+ around 380 boys (roughly two-thirds from state primaries) apply for 60 places. At this point, applicants tested in maths, English and a general paper with those delivering the goods on paper invited back for a one-to-one interview ('they always leave with a smile on their face,' says school).

A further 100 places available at 13+ with fewer applicants for each place but larger hurdles to clear: boys hoping for entry in 2021 or before are interviewed first in May/June of year 7 (registration by end of February) on strength of prep head's report with high flyers offered 'unconditional' places at that point in the expectation that the exam will present no problems. Those offered a 'conditional' place after interview will need to pass every paper in the CE-style exam in January (English, maths, science, humanities, MFL and optional Latin).

Potential entrants from 2022 onwards will face an entirely new process. Applications will need to be made by June of year 5, followed by an interview in the autumn of year 6. Conditional offers are made shortly after, subject to performance in examinations in January of year 6 (English, maths and a general paper). Those who accept a place will then take 'setting examinations' in almost all subjects in January of year 8. Candidates will no longer be able to try again at 13+ if not successful at 11+.

School clear that parents tutoring boys heavily for the exam 'are not doing them any favours – we're looking for intellectual curiosity, a passion for something, reasoning skills and ways in which boys can make a wider contribution to the school.'

At 16+ exams in four A level subjects; offer confirmations depend on GCSE results.

Up to 40 or 50 feeders at 11+, with preps including Radlett Prep, Manor Lodge, Buckingham College, Reddiford and Gayhurst. At 13+ large numbers from Merchant Taylors' Prep, St John's, Durston House and St Martin's, plus a few each from the Beacon, Davenies, Orley Farm, York House and St Anthony's, amongst others.

Exit: Very little fall-out after GCSE. Thirteen to Oxbridge in 2020 with vast majority of remainder to top universities. London colleges feature highly (particularly Imperial, LSE and UCL) as do Warwick, Nottingham, Durham and Bristol. Strong numbers to read medicine (four in 2020), economics and engineering but diversity across the board from sports science to English, humanities, law and the occasional one choosing film or drama school over university offers, or heading to university overseas.

Latest results: In 2020, 92 per cent 9-7 grades at GCSE; 80 per cent A*/A grades at A level (95 per cent A*-B). In 2019 (the last year when exams took place), 88 per cent 9-7 grades at GCSE; 76 per cent A*/A at A level (91 per cent A*-B).

Teaching and learning: A school populated by an intellectually curious and highly motivated cohort. Academic rigour – and ultimately success – is par for the course here but head is clear that they do not want to create a monoculture: 'We reject the philosophy of moulding children into specific types.' Boys inspired by staff who, in head's words, are 'fiercely intelligent – no school is better than the quality of its staff', and are striking to visitors either for their youth, energy and enthusiasm or wit, wisdom and worldliness. Humour and empathy pervade the classrooms, evident as much in the way staff speak to the boys as the quirky touches around the buildings – we've never seen fairy lights or a Ferrari flag in a biology lab in any other school.

Humour and empathy pervade the classrooms, evident in the quirky touches – we've never seen fairy lights or a Ferrari flag in a biology lab in any other school

Traditional curriculum – and, although one parent said that academically 'it's not for the faint-hearted,' school adamant that it's 'not merely a conveyor belt to top results'. 'Exam results are a given,' says school; 'it's about what else they leave with.' Boys take IGCSEs in majority of subjects with consistently outstanding results. Flexible setting in maths and science from year 7, with some 'banding' in English literature from year 9. 'We tend to separate out the boys who read; the ones who can handle Chaucer and Shakespeare with no problem.' Top half take maths IGCSE in year 10, with one third also taking French a year early. It's French and Latin in the languages department in years 7 and 8 with the addition of German, Spanish or Greek in year 9, all available at A level. Around 60 per cent take the EPQ. Maths, economics and the sciences top choices at A level with around half the number opting for humanities and English but with no less stellar results. Small numbers for languages – although school still timetables minority subjects such as Greek even for lone students.

School really shows its mettle in university application process and careers advice, an area which head says has reached 'Rolls Royce quality'. Parents describe the UCAS application process as 'incredibly well organised', with each sixth former assigned to the head of department of their chosen subject who acts as adviser and referee. Personal references from tutors are the cherry on top of the holistic application process. Boys encouraged to begin thinking about future careers early with a World of Work day in year 11, plus a joint careers conference with the girls of nearby St Helen's School. OMTs highly visible as mentors to current pupils, who are encouraged to use active database of over 600 old boys willing to offer work experience, and allowed time out of school to pursue such opportunities.

Learning support and SEN: Learning support (mild dyslexia, dyscalculia some ASD) viewed in the same way as educating the most able children: 'they just need a slightly different educational experience to everyone else,' although school also quick to point out that even those with individual needs 'must be able to keep up with the pace here' and there's strictly no withdrawal from classes. ESL students must be instantly able to access curriculum as are fully immersed from day one. Can accommodate pupils with mobility problems, including wheelchairs.

The arts and extracurricular: Endless opportunities to get stuck in outside of the classroom and sports field at lunch times and after school. Every sport imaginable, from sub aqua to cycling, has a society and there's chess, bridge and stamp club for those more inclined towards brain sports. Boys can flex their journalistic muscles by contributing to one of six school magazines or try their hand at societies ranging from dissection society to debating, most of these included in fees. Music and drama 'amazingly active,' says head, with ensembles and choirs galore, including Dixieland, Merchants of Groove and swing band in addition to a host of more traditional offerings. Two major theatrical productions each year in the Great Hall, in addition to smaller endeavours and a fiercely fought house drama competition. Parents rave about quality of productions. CCF (one of the largest in the UK) in conjunction with St Helen's, and DofE schemes offer super opportunities to follow outdoor pursuits and take part in trips to eg Morocco, Canada or Nepal. Huge sense of collective pride in relation to outstanding work with Phab, with funds raised throughout the year and an annual residential care week staffed by senior pupils, who consider it a great honour to be selected to take part.

Excellent standard of art and DT, which has 'outstanding' teaching, according to parents – MTS has a produced higher number of Arkwright Scholars than any other school since the scheme began in the 1990s. Atmosphere surprisingly relaxed and no sign of the macho testosterone culture that's endemic in so many boys' schools. 'We achieve results by inspiring boys,' says head. Enrichment programme for most able scholars 'turns seamlessly' into Oxbridge preparation.

Years 7 and 8 classics trip to Naples, geography to Iceland and history to Istanbul. Eleven

Twyford Church of England High School

language trips each year and six language exchange programmes across year groups.

Sport: Sport seen as a hugely important part of the MTS ethos, with sportsmanship and camaraderie as high on the agenda as winning. Part of the strong community feel comes from the whole school, including 80 per cent of the teaching staff, heading out to the (spectacular) sports fields together twice a week. Rugby, hockey and cricket are major sports and although there are varying degrees of success in the former (there was almost a hint of pride in the boy who self-effacingly told us he was in the 'least successful rugby A team on school record'), hockey and cricket are flying increasingly high, and the fixture list grows annually to encompass more top schools. School boasts over 60 county and five national sportsmen and the U17 cricket team were recently crowned national champions. This in no small part due to dedicated directors for each major sport, as well as regular visiting coaches. Sport for all – every boy competes for the school as often as is feasible with as much celebration when the Super E rugby team (unbeaten) brings home a victory as the more elite squads. Rugby and hockey tours to South Africa and Australia and cricket to Barbados.

Excellent standard of art and DT – MTS has a produced higher number of Arkwright Scholars than any other school since the scheme began in the 1990s

With over 20 minor sports, boys have no excuse not to find something they love. One or two grumbles about lack of footie until sixth form, but that doesn't stop boys having a good kick around the quad at break times, and school provides goalposts for the purpose. World class facilities include all the usual suspects plus all-weather hockey pitches ('better than the Olympic ones,' one keen player assured us), heated indoor pool, athletics track, lakes for sailing and kayaking, squash and fives courts, an assault course and fencing salle.

Ethos and heritage: Founded in the City of London in 1561 by the Worshipful Company of Merchants, then the largest school in the country. Relocated in 1933 to its current location – a 250-acre site comprising a core of listed art deco buildings plus a host of sympathetically incorporated modern additions set before endless playing fields leading down to a lake. Visitors greeted by exquisite formal gardens and a handsome fascia. School lacks dreaming spires and turrets but gives an immediate sense of purposefulness and solid endeavour.

'Civilised' a word that comes up again and again, along with a sense of a truly cohesive community spirit. Older boys mentor the younger, the whole school eats together (no exceptions, no packed lunches) and assembles together – 'invaluable', says head. 'We are a corporate body not a disparate group.' There's also a great sense of the traditional juxtaposed with gleaming new facilities – a feeling that a boy who has walked the corridors of MTS would not be remotely overwhelmed walking into an Oxford or Cambridge college for the first time.

Actor and alumnus Riz Ahmed chose MT as the backdrop for one his first movies and Grammy Award winning OMT band Nero (the lead singer read philosophy at Oxford, incidentally) recently returned as the surprise act at leavers' ball. Other famous alumni include Nobel prize-winning medic Sir John Sulston, Lord Coggan (former Archbishop of Canterbury), Sir Alan Duncan and Boris Karloff, as well as a host of others from the worlds of politics, business, sport, the military and the arts.

Pastoral care, inclusivity and discipline: Discipline 'almost always low profile due to our hugely positive culture,' says school. Boys are not 'spiky' or 'entitled', transgressions rare and bullying almost non-existent ('I couldn't believe how much friendlier it was than my prep school,' said one happy boy). Vertical tutor system praised almost unanimously by parents and boys. For the most part, parents described tutors as 'almost part of the family', and many keep in contact with former tutees way beyond the A level years. Thriving house system facilitates yet more cross-fertilisation for friendships and opportunities for boys to shine in competitions, with weekly house assemblies covering topics from 'the art of small talk' and 'how to tie a bow tie'. Plenty of chances for responsibility at the top of the school. Head boy voted in by 50 per cent student vote, supported by 10 elected monitors and a JCR of a further 30 boys. School run on Christian ethos, with services held in chapel and all faiths welcome, but there's also a Muslim prayer room and societies for all main faiths.

Pupils and parents: 'What makes a Merchant Taylors' boy?' we asked. 'Well, we don't really do posh,' came the smiling reply. Our opinion: smart, charming, self-effacing and diverse. Not a hooray Henry in sight, but a group of boys wearing their school tie with humility and an

'What makes a Merchant Taylors' boy?' we asked. 'Well, we don't really do posh,' came the smiling reply. Our opinion: smart, charming, self-effacing and diverse

awareness of privilege rather than entitlement. Fun to sit with (yes, even year 10s) in the dining room and totally at ease with adult company. Minds of staff and pupils alike on higher things than the minutiae of shiny shoes and tidy haircuts obsessed over at so many schools. Head says school is 'always hanging on the coat tails of the pupils' enthusiasm', and keenly supports pupil-led initiatives. Perhaps because around a quarter of boys receive some level of financial assistance, social awareness is a key factor in their all-round pleasantness – 'It just wouldn't be the done thing to crow about wealth or status,' said one parent. 'Many families make huge sacrifices to send their sons here.' School concurs: 'Those from affluent backgrounds wear their wealth lightly'.

A school where three worlds don't so much collide as mesh. A hybrid London/country school with appeal to local, north and west London and Herts/Bucks families. The London crowd loves the spacious campus, laid back feel and multitude of sporting options on offer, and those from the shires enjoy the slightly edgier, more worldly feel than they find in schools closer to home. Reflective of local area, around 40 per cent British-Asian, a large Jewish contingent and all other main faiths represented. Wonderfully inclusive – 'there's zero tolerance of racism or homophobia,' boys told us – and although firm friendships are formed on the tube trains and coaches that transport boys in, all reported that new friends are constantly made through tutor groups, forms which are mixed up each year, subject choices (from year 12 forms are grouped according to A level choices) and activities.

Parents maintain close contact with school, attending events and committees in droves. Head reported around 200 attendees at one of his recent termly parent forums. In turn, school has unique relationship with many OMTs well beyond the A level years, with tutors speaking with deep fondness of past tutees' achievements.

Money matters: School prides itself on staying true to the ethos on which it was founded – to offer an excellent all-round education to boys from all walks of life and offer financial aid to those who would most benefit – these days, around 200 boys at any one time. Academic scholarships awarded to boys who perform particularly well in the entrance papers, with scholars benefiting from an enrichment programme. Up to five major academic scholarships at both 11+ and 13+ worth at least 10 per cent of fees. Also sport, art, drama, DT, music and all-rounder scholarships.

The last word: A rare breed – a London school with a country feel. Sitting coolly around the top of the league tables, seemingly without trying too hard, a testament to teachers who inspire without applying undue pressure. Not the most obvious choice for macho rugby types, or for the parent hoping for their son to leave school with a public school swagger, but for those looking for an environment that actively encourages boys to 'lean in to difficult questions', get involved in enriching activities outside of the classroom, and that values the quirky and erudite, look no further.

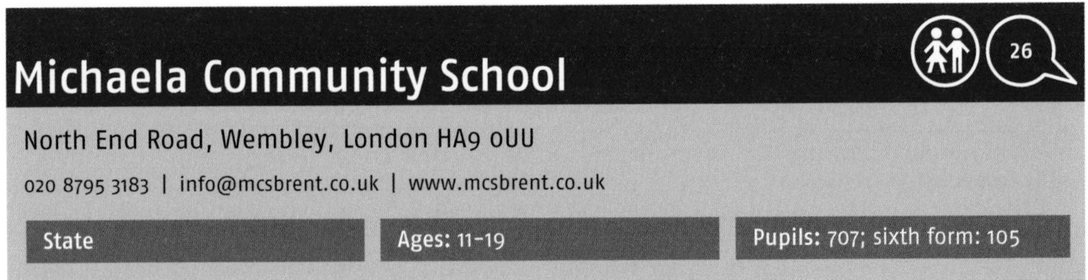

Michaela Community School

North End Road, Wembley, London HA9 0UU

020 8795 3183 | info@mcsbrent.co.uk | www.mcsbrent.co.uk

State | **Ages:** 11-19 | **Pupils:** 707; sixth form: 105

Headmistress: Founder and head since the school started in 2014, the vibrant and dramatic Katharine Birbalsingh MA Oxon NPQH (40s). A graduate of New College Oxford (French and philosophy), she did her teacher training at the Institute of Education. Previously deputy head of a south London state secondary, she spent all her years since university teaching in inner London state secondary schools, working her way through the usual channels. She has come a long way since her groundbreaking speech to the Tory party conference in 2010. Condemning the state of an education system that 'kept poor children poor' to roaring applause, Ms Birbalsingh, in her 30s at the time, looked startled at how well her speech was being received. Naïve politically, and not even a Tory, the accolade took her by surprise but she found herself without a job immediately afterwards.

She is clearly loving being in charge of this groundbreaking school ('I always planned on being a head,' she confides), and being able to fashion it according to her principles and beliefs. 'It's like being the conductor of an orchestra, but it's very important that it still works without me,' she insists. That is the beauty of systems and attention to detail. Passionate about social mobility and empowerment through knowledge, she and her team have created, in Michaela, a finely tuned collection of instruments that play beautifully in time and in sync. 'The systems here are tight and will only get tighter the more the school fills up and the older children influence and educate the younger ones.'

Pupils are told exactly where they rank among their peers, and are praised in detail about what they did right, just as they are chastised about where they have fallen short

'When they arrive in year 7 quite a lot is about damage control,' she says. 'Some don't know their times tables, their reading is limited... we need to start teaching them the right habits for learning... we also have to help some of the parents to step up... However we don't do anything that's a waste of time – I don't believe in targets, they waste time... Every decision we make is whether it's right for the kids, not whether it's right for Ofsted.' Parents warm to her straightforward approach. She sticks to her boundaries and is uncompromising about what she believes to be right. They also notice her respect for her staff and others around her, and how much she herself is respected.

Confident, articulate, determined, driven and very brave, Ms Birbalsingh is an inspirational role model for both the boys and girls at her school and they feel very fortunate to have her.

Entrance: There are 120 places in year 7. Priority given to siblings, but otherwise the main criterion is a lottery system for people living within a five mile radius of the school. As word spreads, and the school becomes increasingly oversubscribed, proximity to the school will become ever more essential.

Application is through Brent Council, and for an occasional place, ring the council to get placed on the waiting list.

Exit: In 2020, 70 per cent left after GCSEs. If Ms Birbalsingh's vision is realised, expect a number of pupils to go to top UK universities, including Oxbridge. The first sixth formers will get their A level results in 2021.

Latest results: In 2020, 53 per cent 9-7 at GCSE; 89 per cent 9-4 in maths and English. In 2019 (the last year when exams took placea and the year of the school's first GCSE results), 54 per cent 9-7 at GCSE; 85 per cent 9-5 in both maths and English.

Teaching and learning: It is already clear that the progress the students are making and the standards they achieve are remarkable. The tools are teaching from the front, silence in the classroom (until called upon to speak), repeated memorisation of facts leading to deep retention of knowledge, regular self-quizzing, testing and open competition, as well as a challenging curriculum. Everyone does all the same subjects – English, maths, French, humanities, science, music and art. A pupil who is struggling may be allowed to take a reduced number of GCSEs; most will take eight though the bright ones will do nine, having done RS early in year 10. Pupils have two group music lessons and two art lessons a week. The library is stacked to the gunwhales (just under 4,000 books) in the grey, functional office-style bookcases, with classical literature, contemporary literature, predominately fiction and plenty of poetry and plays. There are class readers, Friday readers and group readers. By year 9 all pupils will have read seven Shakespeare plays (including Macbeth, Julius Caesar and Othello) – the full versions, in the original. They will have memorised huge chunks of them and studied characterisation, plot device, pathos and humour. Reading is given great emphasis: the 'academically gifted' read over 100 classics from Homer to Orwell from the quality-controlled library. In English and maths as a whole the school's tests show pupils making double the expected level of progress.

Not all teachers at Michaela have a teaching qualification, something the school is proud of as it feels they are not all moulded from the same clay, but all are graduates from top universities including Oxbridge and Russell Group. They are motivated and enthusiastic. Ms Birbalsingh understands the pressure points on the profession only too well, so in her school (or 'their' school, she prefers – 'this is very much a collaborative effort') there is no detailed marking, and box ticking exercises are limited to a minimum. Teachers are needed to supervise on staircases during 'transition', when the pupils march quickly in silence between lessons: if they were marking each essay in minute detail they wouldn't have time for this. Staff read all essays and make comments, but give detailed feedback to a class as a whole so everyone can share understanding of where the strengths and weaknesses lie. No pupil is spared. They are told exactly where they rank among their peers, and are praised for their performance in detail about what they did right, just as they are chastised about where they have fallen short – not enough focus in class, overlooking the opportunity to catch up in support lessons after school, not being diligent enough while self-quizzing. Teachers relish the opportunity actually to teach, impart knowledge, wisdom and learning. The job here is not about classroom control. These classrooms and corridors and dining rooms are strictly controlled at all times. Teachers are respected as being the ones whose age, wisdom and experience give them a natural authority. 'This', says Ms Birbalsingh, 'allows the children to be children, and they feel safe knowing where the boundaries are and understanding the consequences if they cross those boundaries.'

The plan for A level (sixth form opened September 2019) is that the most rigorous academic subjects will be prioritised – maths, further maths, physics, chemistry, biology, English literature, French, art, music, theology and philosophy – but Ms Birbalsingh is busily visiting outstanding sixth forms to learn about what works best. She and her team will fashion the sixth form just as they created years 7-11, with meticulous attention to detail and a fundamental belief in the acquisition of knowledge imparted from specialist teachers who love their subject.

Expectations are unashamedly high. Oxbridge and other top Russell Group universities are all within reach for many and the year 9 students are being taught to appreciate that already. One year 9 girl said that she 'isn't focusing on Oxbridge' as she wants to go the LSE. Pupils are streamed in four sets but there is fluidity between the sets and they are not referred to in front of the pupils. Oxbridge hopefuls can be found even in the lower half of the year group. One girl who arrived from the Sudan started in the bottom half of the year group; now, two years later, she is in the top... 'but we never say "bright" or "able", only "are you working hard?" We celebrate the pupils who spend the most time on their homework – here there is no "bottom set mentality",' avers Ms Birbalsingh. She has been busy networking at Oxford and Cambridge colleges, preparing a strategy, paving a path.

Several parents remarked on their sons' appetite for homework. One year 9 boy works for two-and-a-half hours each evening. The incentives are there – they love to earn their merits, and as they start to see the fruits of their labour in their improved scores, a virtuous cycle is set in motion.

Ms Birbalsingh almost purrs when questioned about the quality of her teachers: 'We have the best,' she affirms, citing their quality of life as part of her pulling power

The teachers are wholeheartedly supportive of the regime at Michaela. You only have to read their book, Battle Hymn of the Tiger Teachers – the Michaela Way, to get a sense of their dedication, and total commitment to the ethos and practice here. Ms Birbalsingh almost purrs when questioned about the quality of her teachers: 'We have the best,' she affirms, citing their quality of life as part of her pulling power. Parents and pupils we spoke to agree.

Learning support and SEN: SEN is not a comfortable acronym at Michaela. Labels are seen as damaging. They would prefer to focus on the effort involved. 'Weakest pupils need more rigour, more focus and more practice,' asserts Katie Ashford, one of the deputy heads and an English teacher. Ms Birbalsingh accepts that some students need extra support – they have put on an extra lesson for those who 'are so far behind' in maths for example, but the focus is on each child.

The arts and extracurricular: The art room here is disciplined, with as clear lines and boundaries as you find everywhere else in the school. Lots of charcoal and pencil drawings adorn the walls ('it's so difficult to find an art teacher who knows how to draw these days,' observes Ms Birbalsingh.) Tasteful artwork – and carefully displayed, detailed portraits on the walls of each floor of eg Mandela, Boris Johnson and David Cameron. Clear simple lines – minimalist. Not fussy. Not messy.

Apart from performing excerpts in class from the Shakespeare plays they are studying – eg Julius Caesar – not a lot of drama. 'We don't have the facilities – this is not what we are about,' is the explanation.

There is a focus, however, on a co-curricular programme that stretches the academic and cerebral. Visitors' programme includes talks, starting from year 7, from speakers ranging from hedge fund managers to barristers and politicians: recent examples include Boris Johnson, Nick Gibb, David Lammy MP and journalist turned teacher Lucy Kellaway. A rhetoric programme from year 9 paves the path towards Oxbridge applications. A scholars' programme includes the Brilliant Club from year 10 to challenge pupils with independent research projects and essays.

Every pupil goes on two trips a year, to the Natural History Museum, the British Museum, the National Gallery, the Globe Theatre and Cambridge University. Extracurricular clubs include films (pupils watch six classic films a year including Frankenstein, Romeo and Juliet and The Imitation Game), Future Leaders (pupil prefects are selected to lead conversations at family lunch), Lizard Point (stretching online quizzes of locations and regions) and competitions (Times Table Rockstars, Poetry Declamation, Dates and Capitals). For the more athletic child there is football, table tennis and basketball and those with an interest in music can do chamber choir and flute choir.

Sport: Sport takes place one afternoon a week in a sports centre round the corner. Just football and dodgeball – not a lot of choice – but they get exercise and the opportunity to play matches against other schools as well as the chance to shine if sport is their thing. There are table tennis tables in the yard as well as basketball hoops – a chance to let off steam and be competitive between lessons.

Ethos and heritage: Founded by Katharine Birbalsingh in 2014 as a free school 'with a private school ethos', the school makes an initially forbidding impression. An office block in the heart of a very industrial part of Wembley (the tube trains roll regularly past the dining room windows). Huge iron gates and a security system more fitting of a high security prison need to be negotiated before you enter the reception area.

Once inside the austere grey walls, the remarkable thing is that there is complete silence. Even in the reception and waiting area, the silence is broken only by the occasional whirr of a photocopier and the whispered exchanges behind the desk. On arrival all guests are presented with a list of rules – including 'Do not talk in normal voices in the corridors – only a whisper please!', 'Do not demonstrate disbelief to pupils when they say they like their school', and 'Do talk to the pupils at lunch and at break.'

As you tread carefully through the corridors you observe children at their desks in rows, arms folded on the desk except when they are eagerly throwing up their hands or writing carefully in their books. In the classroom there is plenty of interaction. Teachers lead from the front but lessons are delivered not like a lecture but as a series of questions and answers. Feedback from the front (no marking policy – marking can waste too much teaching and supervising time).

Kindness is as much a part of the ethos as achievement. Children are taught to understand that the strict regime is for their own benefit

'Transition' – when the children move between classrooms at the end of a lesson – is astonishing to witness. Like clockwork the system slips into place. Teachers station themselves at key points of the staircases and the end of the corridors. Children move at a rapid pace without running or talking. There are smiles and nods of hello – this isn't a prison, after all – but the focus is on supreme efficiency. Every moment of learning time counts and movement between classes can be a drain on these precious minutes. Here at Michaela there is a determination among staff, shared by pupils (remarkably), not to waste this valuable learning time. Once in the classroom, every pupil knows their role, and books, piled at the correct place on the window sill, are retrieved and distributed quickly and quietly down the line. By the time the teacher commands 'Go!' – dot on time – they are ready to begin the lesson. Merits and demerits are distributed as an acknowledgement of this performance.

'Family lunch' is another unique feature of the school, and key to the school motto 'Work hard and be kind.' It begins with the whole school chanting a poem in time. We heard Coleridge's Kubla Khan. Everyone eats the same food, vegetarian menus carefully chosen to suit all faiths and eating requirements. Hot, freshly cooked food but no canteen. Food is served by the children on individual tables of six. Each child is given a role and they all know exactly what they are doing, whether it's pouring the water, dishing out the food or clearing up. During the course of lunch each table will discuss a topic that has already been chosen by the teacher in charge – 'Does what you're taught at Michaela affect your behaviour outside school?', for example. Once the food is eaten it is time to record 'appreciations'. Individual pupils stand up and declare their thanks to the 150 pupils, guests and teachers present, for anything they like, from the care their history teacher took to giving feedback on an essay, to the help his mother gave him in getting him to school that day. The audience applauds, with two sharp claps, merits are awarded for effective articulate speaking, a demerit for any suggestion of ridicule or lack of respect.

At break, lunch, mid-morning and afternoon, children spill out into 'the yard', or as one pupil, remarked, 'it's essentially a disused car park', but it serves its purpose – fresh(ish) air, table tennis tables, football, basketball, a chance to let off steam and above all a chance to talk. This is where friendships are formed and ideas – other than classroom ideas – can be exchanged. Pupils clearly value it a lot, as part of the system of punishment includes being 'banned from the yard'. Apart from during lunch – which is formally structured with general group conversations rather than private individual conversations – this is the chance they have to talk to each other properly.

Pastoral care, inclusivity and discipline: Everyone in year 7 attends behaviour bootcamp a week before the start of the new school year in September. This is when the system – of detention, merits/demerits, how to manage 'transition', how to walk fast but in silence through the corridors, how family lunch works, which way to walk past your chair when leaving the classroom, how to address a teacher or any other adult, and what attitude to bring with you to Michaela – is carefully, systematically taught, reinforced and embedded. It is an invaluable week for teachers too, new ones especially. By the time term starts everyone understands the systems and can row together.

Once inside the austere grey walls, the remarkable thing is that there is complete silence. Even in the reception and waiting area, the silence is broken only by the occasional whirr of a photocopier and the whispered exchanges behind the desk

One of our guides ('a girl who struggles academically,' we were later told) was articulate and polite to the nth degree, and proudly told us there was no bullying in the school. There are barely any moments to bully. The reasons pupils don't run in the corridor is that there would be an opportunity to knock into someone, for a fight to brew; for the same reason they walk in a particular direction around their chairs, and cross their arms on top of the table, to avoid surreptitious shoving, a sneaky peak at a mobile phone or anything else that may lead to demerit or detention, but ultimately being someone you don't really want to be.

Unashamedly strict, this is a 'no excuses' school. The discipline is centred on a system of merits and demerits – six detentions and you are in isolation, three demerits have you removed from a lesson. Detention is used regularly but intentionally. The time is not wasted. Each pupil is fully occupied with self-quizzing while they are in detention, and some even start to appreciate the progress they can make while being punished.

Kindness is as much a part of the ethos as achievement. Children are taught to understand that the strict regime is for their own benefit. Family lunch and appreciations, as well as everyone working to serve and clear the food, all contribute to an ethos of gratitude, kindness and empathy.

Parents need to support this approach, and it's often they who find it more of a challenge than their children. Faced with the prospect that a mobile phone would not be returned until the end of the half term, after a child had been caught using it in school, the parents have the choice of accepting it or finding another school.

Pupils and parents: Extremely diverse, pupils here come from a number of different cultures and are of different faiths, but no one dominates. Some walk to school, most take buses from all over London, but mainly from the north west, a few take the tube to Wembley Park and walk across the road to the school. One thing they do have in common, however, is that these are not pupils from highly privileged backgrounds. Half the pupils are eligible for pupil premium. Parents are told that they need to be prepared – 'Michaela', they are told at open evenings, 'will be like the personal trainer in fitness regime and that is what you are signing up to.' The occasional child leaves – not because they can't take the strain, but more often because their parents can't. However the majority of parents, pleased that their children are being taught to such high standards and that behaviour is excellent, are fully supportive of the firm line taken by the school.

The last word: A challenging and rigorous academic education with high expectations for every pupil. For the right child this is a truly extraordinary and superlative school. Not for the fainthearted, the cynical or the fragile. Strict, but with a warm heart beating below the surface, Michaela creates a safe, but stimulating environment, and the chance to fly.

Montpelier Primary School

Montpelier Road, Ealing, London W5 2QT

020 8997 5855 | admissions@montpelier.ealing.sch.uk | www.montpelierschool.net

State | Ages: 4–11 | Pupils: 682

Headteacher: Since 2003, Am Rai (50s). BA in sociology, Birmingham Poly, MA in educational management and administration at University of London, Institute of Education. Very experienced head who had already worked in seven London state primaries prior to his arrival at Montpelier. He had been twice seconded to rescue failing schools – one that was set to fail six weeks before an Ofsted inspection. It passed. However, rather than thinking of himself as some great saviour, he says with a degree of humility that 'you take with you a footfall of strategies that have proved successful.' Teaching was almost an inevitability for this head with a history of teachers in his family – both parents no less.

'A bit of a strange fish' one parent referred to him as (rather affectionately). Quite guarded and perhaps a little brusque at first, he warmed up considerably throughout the course of our meeting. Some parents thought him to be a bit of a remote figure while others say he is extremely visible much of the time. Opinions may be divided about his accessibility, but all unanimous in praising him for being a very dedicated and hard-working head, who has more than a few challenges on his hands. As one parent told us: 'There are always a few parents who want to make waves – Montpelier is a state school, with state school issues, but being in an affluent area, parents expect X,Y and Z and ultimately want a private school.'

In the course of our nearly two-hour conversation with him (including a tour around the school), we found Mr Rai to be a man of very clear vision and sound, liberal educational principles, highly articulate and straightforward. No jargon, no pseudo-academic parroting, no political posturing – so refreshing. Clearly still a dedicated head teacher even after 17 years in the role. He is concerned that we're living in a world of 'helicopter parenting', which he says 'disables our children and doesn't empower them.' He is also very focused on the rising levels of mental health issues facing young people which they, as a school, try to spot as early on as possible and support that child.

Offers an amazing amount of support to his teaching staff too, with a lot of training and empathy for the challenges they face both economically and within the line of their work: 'Our teachers know when they come to this school, we will take a pound of flesh, but in return they will get the highest level of respect and back-up from us. We are a very supportive environment. We are a teaching school – we have to get it right.'

Married, two children, still seems comfortable in the role even after all this time with no obvious itchy feet, although he did mention that 'a lot of the independent sector doesn't get it right and I would relish the opportunity to change that.'

Entrance: Oversubscribed at all levels with the most applicants per pupil place in Ealing. 'We moved to get into this school', or 'we appealed' were things we heard from a few parents. High turnover among local international community means that occasional places at all stages are not uncommon, although this has slowed down somewhat with the opening of a new high school nearby, meaning more parents are staying rooted. All managed by Ealing LA and, if you have no special circumstances, you need to live up close and personal to get a place. We hear that more than a few families swap their large homes further out for flats round the corner from this school.

Exit: A few good local secondary comprehensives on offer in the area, most popular are Drayton Manor, Ada Lovelace (although being a new school, the jury is still out), and Ellen Wilkinson HS – the local girls' comprehensive. The rest of the cohort go either to local RC or CofE high schools or to the local independents – Notting Hill and Ealing, St Benedict's, St Augustine's. Increasingly, some to the Tiffins, to Bucks, Berks or Middlesex grammars, to St Paul's Boys' or Girls', Godolphin & Latymer, John Lyon and Latymer Upper, and some parents even move house after their bright buttons gain places there or at eg Henrietta Barnett. No disaster schools in the area – another good reason for coming here.

Our view: Sited on a corner of two quiet, tree-lined roads and adjoining a pretty park. The surrounding streets are similarly well-appointed, orderly and solidly middle class – this is suburban bliss, though the North Circular grinds along only a couple of hundred yards away (fantastic access to Heathrow airport for the international contingent). The nearest schools are all independent and, not surprisingly, these are the chosen destinations for a sizeable minority of Montpelier leavers.

Magical was our first impression on entering the chocolate box, Christmassy foyer, which looked like we had walked onto the set of The Lion, the Witch and the Wardrobe and not a school off the North Circ! A projector was running silver snowflake patterns across dimly lit walls and everything was shimmery and sparkly. The effort put in by staff to make this a miraculous Christmas experience for pupils was nothing short of amazing. The head told us that none of the children were aware that this would happen and they have just been blown away 'worth it just to see the look on their faces'. He carries on. 'In this life, everybody works so hard and has so much on their plate that from time to time it is important to create something memorable.'

Aesthetically this school doesn't disappoint. It has a light and open feel and looks very well cared for with a 'regular cycle of redecoration', we are told. Three connected school buildings, the latest a clever extension housing reception and admin. Infants and reception on ground floor – makes sense. Four playgrounds with good equipment. The gazebo is a fairly recent addition for outdoor lessons. Reception classes have integral loos, so no tots trailing down corridors and no class feels overfull, despite 30 in each plus staff.

Each class is equipped with the latest interactive digital boards but these 'have not replaced teachers', the head tells us drily. When asked to elaborate he said that technology was actually slowing the class down and it became a hindrance so the upgraded screens and teachers' computers needed to 'catch up'. Learning legacy boards provide testimony to what has been learned during the term and show pupils what is expected of them by year 6. Monitoring and appraisal embedded into everything – each child has their own targets for the core skills and a list of 'I Can' statements to keep parents abreast of what has been mastered and what still needs to be done.

'Montpelier make their goals very clear,' said one parent. However, she continued by saying that if a child is not meeting those goals, an 'amazing amount of support' is given to those who need extra help. Another added: 'I have had two children on the opposite ends of the academic spectrum, both of whom have been encouraged and pushed in different ways.' A democratic learning system which doesn't buy into the whole streaming idea at an early age per se, although pupils are seated accordingly in class more to ensure that they don't fall behind or conversely get bored. The head explains: 'Why would we say to a child, you're average, so we'll take you to the average room.' He adds 'we're not a results factory, a lot of parents' focus has changed too. Much more concerned with pastoral and wider curriculum needs than before.'

Magical was our first impression on entering the chocolate box, Christmassy foyer, which looked like we had walked onto the set of The Lion, the Witch and the Wardrobe

That said, they do achieve out very good results, some of the best in the borough for state primary schools and top 20 per cent nationally. Maths in particular, teaching of which is based on the Singapore method, gets very high outcomes across all levels. We were also amazed by the stunning examples of joined-up handwriting on display from pupils as young as seven years old. SEN accounts for roughly 8 per cent of the cohort, lower than the national average but each child's case individually looked at with 'teaching strategies for that child put in place.' Organised time made to equip those who arrive with no English with key words and skills.

Lots of imaginative cross-curricular learning: displays everywhere are evidence of lively thinking and teaching. A good hall/gym, a nice little library – properly used for lending and reading – two IT suites, art room, and every class has an art week in which they can drop everything else and experience sustained and concentrated work on a project of their own. Plenty of choice for extracurricular: 20 after-school clubs on offer including Spanish, Mandarin, art, science and a good mix of sport. Heavy emphasis on performing arts with a dedicated drama teacher. Unusually strong music – 146+ learn an instrument in or after school. Big on outings and two residential trips on offer in years 5 & 6, to The Isle of Wight and France respectively.

'High schools will always know a Montpelier child,' the head told us. 'They are taught a set of skills which they carry along with them.' We had to concur. The pupils we chatted to were extremely polite and wonderfully respectful of each other. No butting in, just hands up waiting to speak (we felt like teachers). One of the first things that does strike you on an ordinary school day is how quiet it is and how in every class 30 diverse children can be seen working absorbedly and happily together. Few behavioural problems – they're jumped on smartly when they occur. Head 'will exclude if a child is spoiling the lives of other children', but hasn't had to permanently exclude anyone in his 16 years of being at the school: 'I have to work on the basis that this could be my child.'

One pupil told us: 'Teachers at this school teach with expression. They don't make the lessons boring.' Realistic staff turnover for a London school, but never because of the school itself, mostly for promotional reasons or expensive living costs, or relocation. 'The great untruths' told to parents about low teacher turnover by some schools really irks Mr Rai, who says: 'You have to be straight with parents, they are not stupid. No one can really expect that young teachers will stay more than three years in the job these days due to the cost of London living.'

As socially diverse as any school in the capital. Around 65 per cent speak a language other than English at home – huge range of languages and cultures – among which highest proportions from Japan and the Middle East, Australia, North America and various bits of Europe. While parents love this diversity and appreciate how great this is for their children, others did say that sometimes the language barriers have been an issue in forging friendships or getting parents involved in the PTFA. One parent told us: 'My bugbear is that there have always been a few very dedicated parents who have raised thousands for the school, but many don't get involved, which is often down to cultural differences.'

'High schools will always know a Montpelier child,' the head told us. 'They are taught a set of skills which they carry along with them'

The PTFA do seem like a dedicated bunch. £16,000 alone was raised through their summer fete alone and a plethora of other fundraisers are always on the go. Parents generally talked about a community feel to the school and how 'all faiths and beliefs are celebrated'. One or two spoke about 'parent politics' and how annoying it is when some parents make a fuss about their child 'not being able to wear orange Nike trainers on sports day' and oblivious of the 'really tough issues a school has to face'. No-one, however, wishes they had sent their children elsewhere.

The last word: No parent we spoke to would dispute that the head and a very stable senior team have made a stunning success of a school which, before, had been content to be good enough. 'We judge things by the happiness of our children,' asserts head wisely.

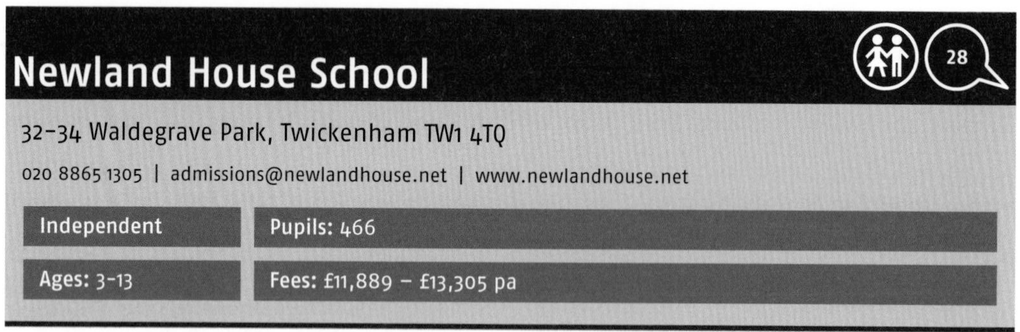

Headmaster: Since September 2019, Chris Skelton, previously academic deputy head at Newton Prep. Started his teaching career in the state sector, teaching in southeast and east London before moving to Dulwich College Junior School as the pastoral deputy in 2012. Moved with his young family to Teddington specifically for the role – spending time with them is his raison d'être outside school. His commitment to a healthy, active lifestyle means he's got the energy to keep up with them.

Entrance: All change, with term time only nursery in own building (was former pre-prep), and 7+ entry phased out. Now has 50 per cent more spaces in reception (three form entry) following recent pre-prep expansion into premises on main school site. Nursery places offered on first-come, first-served basis – but only to families who have been offered a reception place. Often oversubscribed – best register your child as soon as possible after birth. At 4+ entry is again on a first-come, first-served basis, with siblings given priority. Sixty places available at this stage and a waiting list in operation.

Exit: Predominantly to private day schools, occasional boarding. Girls leave at 11 and boys at 13. Girls can stay on to 13, but don't. 'It would be a leap of faith,' says school. Destinations at 11 include Halliford, St George's College, Kingston Grammar, Hampton, Claremont Fan Court School, St John's Leatherhead. At 13+ Wellington, St James, Reeds, Hampton, Bedales. Consistently high number of academic, sports, music and all-rounder scholarships. School puts this down to outstanding teaching and the fact that the children are in a happy environment and so want to learn.

Our view: Pre-prep is run by the approachable and calm Tracey Chong. All-female staff ('by coincidence') give it a homely air. Its building, right next door to the main school unites the two parts of the school and means additional places in reception. 'The teachers at the pre-prep are lovely and smiley and it rubs off on the children,' said one parent.

Classes at the prep are mixed ability, maximum 20 children. Lessons are lively and fast-paced with specialist teachers for PE, art, music and ICT from the start. Separate sciences taught from year 4. Children set for English, French and maths from year 5. Days are long, especially for those who start with the full cooked breakfast on offer at 7.30am.

Once the girls leave at the end of year 6, the boys are placed in two mixed ability classes and one small scholarship set; vacancies left by girls are not filled. Greek on offer to potential scholars. Parents love the fact that children get so much individual attention at the top of the school. 'A real strength,' said one. Children are well prepared for 11+, 13+ and scholarships. 'We are a preparatory school. It's our job to prepare them for the exams for entry to their next schools.' Parents report that a massive amount of coaching goes on in the final years, of which the school is critical. 'It's not necessary. We are all fighting a coaching culture but people get sucked into it.'

Classrooms are spacious and light, with traditional wooden desks arranged in neat rows. Impressive ICT suite, tablets about to be introduced but head keen this shouldn't be a gimmick. The school enters a huge number of national and international competitions with frequent success. Recently won three World Maths Day trophies, out of a total of five awarded to UK schools. DT department is the envy of other schools and recently assembled a car for the Shell Eco-Marathon that achieved a mileage of 1,000 miles per gallon. Currently a group of senior boys is investigating the effect of tyre pressure on the environment and presentations have been made to MPs.

Plenty of choirs for each year group, new pop choir for year 7/8 boys is thriving. Several hundred individual instrumental and singing lessons take place every week. Lots of bands, ensembles and orchestras. Children have taken part in performances at the Kingston Music Festival and concerts at the Barbican with the London Symphony Orchestra.

Art clubs include weekend activities where parents can become involved. Local artists exhibit and sell their work in the reception area and include a couple of inexpensive pieces so that children can buy a picture if it catches their eye.

Classrooms spacious and light, with traditional wooden desks in neat rows. Impressive ICT suite, tablets about to be introduced, but head keen this shouldn't be a gimmick

Sport is a real strength of the school. Boys play rugby, football and cricket; girls play netball, rounders and hockey. Swimming, cross-country and athletics also on offer and even more sport possible through numerous after-school clubs, including golf at neighbouring club. Main playing fields are five minutes away by minibus; two multi-purpose, all-weather courts and four cricket nets on site. Lots of tournaments and matches mean everyone gets the chance to compete.

Full-time head of SEN. School believes 'a good learning support culture enhances what you do'. Provision for mild dyslexia, dyspraxia and dyscalculia, though not the place to send a child with severe difficulties.

Many long-serving staff. One satisfied parent commented that staff were 'prepared to go the extra mile for the children'. Two gap year students help with sport and a French assistant teaches conversational French.

Parents are typically hard-working professionals. 'The school reflects the local community and lots of the children arrive at school on foot or by scooter,' says head of pre-prep. Active PTA raises substantial funds, half money raised goes to charity, the other half to the school – recently paid for a climbing wall. Activity-based wraparound club from 7.30am to 6pm.

Money matters: Academic and music bursaries available – up to 50 per cent of fees, negotiated on a yearly basis. Ten per cent discount for third sibling when all are in school together.

The last word: A competitive, purposeful and demanding school which has retained old fashioned values (the pupils call the head 'Sir' and scramble to their feet when an adult enters the room). Pupils are challenged on all fronts and, as one parent put it, 'By the time the children reach year 5, they are under pressure to perform. It's not a soft school but, for the right child, there simply isn't anywhere better in the area.' One mother felt that 'it's not for the retiring child. I think they'd get trampled underfoot.' The school disagrees and feels it caters for all personalities and abilities as there is so much on offer and so many chances to shine.

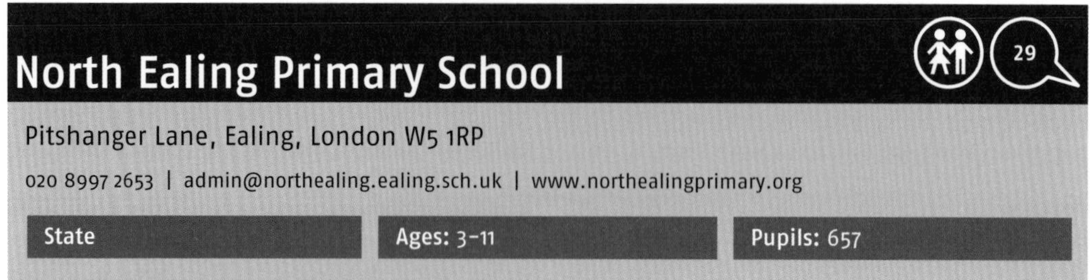

North Ealing Primary School

Pitshanger Lane, Ealing, London W5 1RP

020 8997 2653 | admin@northealing.ealing.sch.uk | www.northealingprimary.org

State | Ages: 3-11 | Pupils: 657

Head: Since 2014, Sally Flowers, previously deputy head. She joined the school as assistant head in 2011. Prior to that, she was an educational consultant for nine years and before that she taught in mainly London schools. Did a BA in anthropology and history at Kent, her PGCE at Sussex and an educational psychology degree via Open University. Particularly loved consultancy ('I love training people') but now happier being settled and making a difference in just one school.

And making a difference, she is. This head is on fire. Not afraid of taking risks, she is exacting yet laid back, forthright yet friendly and is all about the children. No ego whatsoever. 'If the children are happy and know their rights, they can learn,' she says. Parents like that's she's 'a local mum' (she has three children), describing her as 'visible', 'positive' and 'a very strong leader'. 'She's been seriously challenged by recent funding cuts, but she knows exactly what the school needs and works within her constraints to get it,' said one. Pupils say she's 'firm' but 'fun'.

Entrance: Looked after children get priority, then siblings and after that it's distance. Larger intake now due to three form entry but pupils still need to live within a mile of the school to get a place (no official catchment, admissions by distance as the crow flies). Like all Ealing schools, there's high mobility so there are often places further up the school, albeit with some waiting lists. Nursery numbers now reduced to 26 places each for morning and thirty hours places.

Exit: A massive spread. Usually most to Ada Lovelace, others to Brentside High, Ellen Wilkinson, Twyford, Cardinal Wiseman, William Perkin, Elthorne Park, Greenford, Ealing Fields, and Dormers Wells. 'Lack of places at secondary schools is a historical problem,' says head, 'but at least it's made slightly better by the opening of Ada Lovelace.' A handful each year to grammar schools, mainly Tiffin (boys and girls) and Henrietta Barnet, but some further afield. Depending on the cohort, around a third go private – St Paul's, Kew House, St Augustine's, Latymer, St Benedict's, Notting Hill & Ealing, Hampton and John Lyon.

Our view: Pitshanger (the name of the main road on which the school is located) is considered a village all of its own with a tight-knit and diverse community and this primary school is at its heart. Ask anyone in the local area (most of whom seem to be pushing a buggy) where it is and chances are they'll know – a good job as it's pretty well hidden. And woe betide you if make the mistake, as we did, of trying to enter via the back entrance as the school will make you zigzag all the way through the residential streets to the front, a good five minute walk.

This school is completely immaculate, with a clear sense of order everywhere you turn

Once inside, the community feel is palpable, with down-to-earth staff and pupils and lots of laughter. Nobody stands on ceremony here. In fact, nobody really notices you as there's so much going on – a year 6 flash mob suddenly burst into spontaneous dance at breaktime during our visit, while every classroom and hall, along with many of the corridors, was buzzing with activity during lesson time. 'Bend the knees!' for dancing in the school hall. 'Hands in the air!' for singing in the dedicated music room. 'Well done – that's a long word!' for guided reading in a corridor. 'Who's ready for a hands-on experiment?' for science. You get the picture.

Nobody denies the move to three form entry hasn't been challenging – the school was originally built for one class per year group. At times, it can feel like it's bursting at the seams, but the head has utilised every inch – even the lower staff room is now a shared teaching space. It's by no means chaotic, however – this school is immaculate, with a clear sense of order everywhere you turn.

The school is divided into three main areas. Nursery, reception and years 3 and 4 are housed in a lovely bright and airy modern building at the back of the school site. Years 1 and 2 take up the slightly older, but still bright, building in the centre of the school. And years 5 and 6 are in the old part of the school – an old Victorian building. Classes here are more cramped but corridor candy on the walls (eg Van Gogh, Spanish vocab) make them feel welcoming and warm.

Outside, children are also separated at playtime: nursery, reception and year 1 all have their own separate playgrounds. Years 2, 3 and 4 have the back playground and years 5 and 6 are at the front. We saw tiny tots planting flowers in the planting area, a World War II bomb shelter that's been turned into a sensory garden and the school has its own garden which backs on to Pitshanger Park.

Academically sound across the board. Our guides told us maths is 'easily the best subject – we love the quizzes'. 'Maths here is fun,' says head. Setting in this subject only, from year 3. Meanwhile, for English, there's a highly structured phonics programme and a big push on reading for life. Shame the library isn't more inspiring, but there's a nice touch on each classroom door – book cover images of both what the children and teacher are currently reading. Science (picked up in last Ofsted report as an area for development) is now on the up, with a more enquiry-based approach, including with hands-on experiments in everything from magnesium to light. Spanish taught from year 1, along with a Latin club for children from year 5 (exemplifying strong links with local private schools, whereby their pupils come in to volunteer). Unusually, philosophy lessons for all. Dedicated teachers get good CPD, but as with most primary schools it's a shame there aren't more males.

SEN hovers at around 10 per cent – higher than other local schools, with an excellent reputation in this area. Particularly significant numbers of children with ASD. Plenty of praise from parents about the interventions that range from SENCos working closely with class teachers to pupil passports for vulnerable children. Sixty languages spoken among pupils, with school finding every opportunity possible to celebrate their growing diversity. 'Nobody feels left out here,' pupils told us.

'It's mega,' says head about the clubs, with a list of privately run and teacher-led classes that would give any posh prep school a run for its money. 'It's almost busier after school than during school.' Coding, debating, film club, hockey, golf, netball and tag rugby are among the favourites.

Nobody stands on ceremony here, there's so much going on – a year 6 flash mob suddenly burst into spontaneous dance at breaktime during our visit

This is a creative school, with art embedded into lessons, especially in the younger years, and dedicated weekly music lessons for all. Peripatetic teachers cover a range of instruments including flute, violin, guitar and recorder. Three choirs (including choral), two orchestras and a singing club for younger ones, with plenty of opportunities to perform locally. Parents told us drama is less in the limelight than it once was, but it's still a core part of English lessons and there are all the usual end-of-year plays.

Sports are high profile, with a glass cabinet bulging with cups in the school reception, although head admits they 'don't win as much as we used to when we were two form entry.' Unfazed, she is more keen on embedding a positive sporting attitude than winning everything. All the usual suspects, plus the likes of basketball and dance. If there isn't enough room on the school site, the local Pitshanger Park is used.

This is a Place2Be school, meaning that this children's mental health charity provides school-based support and training to improve emotional well-being. Everyone raves about the counsellor – 'I go whenever I feel sad about anything and they make me feel better every time,' one girl told us – and with four additional volunteer counsellors, no pupil needs to miss out, although those with a critical need get priority over pupils who self-refer, and for parents there's a 'huge waiting list'. 'It's a powerful and fabulous service – we're very lucky,' a parent told us. Pupils have a strong voice here and the school has a Rights Respecting Schools silver award from UNICEF (they are currently working towards gold). Behaviour well managed through praise more than sanctions. 'Is it strict?' we asked our guides. 'Firm but fair,' was the response.

Two-thirds of pupils have the hot dinners which are cooked on site, the rest have packed lunches. The school has a healthy eating policy – no sweets or chocolates are allowed in children's lunch boxes and classes who eat the healthiest get prizes.

All parents must attend parents' evening – 'if they don't turn up, we relentlessly ask them to come.' Active PTA, although one parent told us 'I think they could do more.' Former pupils include Peter Crouch and Honor Blackman.

The last word: A friendly and positive school that's an integral part of the local community. Children are grounded, curious and happy and they achieve excellent results. 'I just wish they ran a secondary school too,' said one parent.

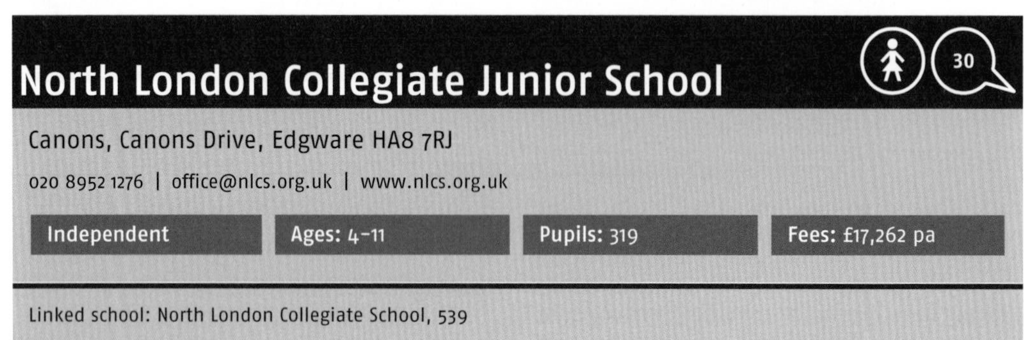

North London Collegiate Junior School

30

Canons, Canons Drive, Edgware HA8 7RJ

020 8952 1276 | office@nlcs.org.uk | www.nlcs.org.uk

Independent | **Ages:** 4–11 | **Pupils:** 319 | **Fees:** £17,262 pa

Linked school: North London Collegiate School, 539

Head of junior school: Since 2003, Mrs Joanna Newman BEd (50s). Old North Londoner, thence to Homerton College Cambridge (geography and education). Began teaching career at Haberdashers' Aske's Boys' Prep before rising to deputy head of NLCS First School then on to first headship at Channing Junior School before returning – via a brief sojourn in Spain courtesy of her husband's job – to NLCS Junior School as head. Brimming with the kind of serene confidence unique to heads secure in the knowledge that they have the cream of the crop clamouring for places at their school, yet warm, capable and hands-on – Mary Poppins meets Mary Berry. Glad recipient of hugs from pupils in all manner of locations both in and outside of the school day and described by parents as 'involved', 'present' and 'an incredible diplomat' (vital skill for a north London head). Assemblies see girls hanging on her every word (to be honest, so did we); she's clear that 'every girl is known' and that 'love is innate in our junior school teaching'. We saw it in action as she handed out awards in her office for excellent work on the week of our visit. Bright eyed misses glowed with pride and chatted with ease as she praised their achievements and duly assigned them with a good old-fashioned sticker. Lovely. Sitting pretty in what must be a serious contender for the nation's most plum head teacher seat, she's far from complacent. 'We have a tradition of not accepting the status quo,' she says. Is working closely with NLCS senior head Sarah Clark to ensure constant motion; a new library, science labs, music room and IT rooms are all on the agenda for September 2020.

Married with two adult daughters, both of whom are also ONLs (Old North Londoners); describes herself as a 'culture vulture' with a love of theatre, cooking, travel and getting her hands dirty at gardening club with the girls. Brings her experience to bear as mentor and manager – her last three directors of studies have moved on to headships elsewhere and she is involved in training staff at NLCS's outposts in Jeju, Dubai and Singapore. Says her involvement in the Prince's Teaching Institute, a charitable organisation dedicated to delivering professional development for teachers and school leaders, where she works closely with state school heads, keeps her grounded.

Entrance: Highly selective from 4+ with over 300 trying for 40 reception places. Assessments in January of year of entry. Girls are observed participating in 'relaxed activities' in groups of 10 to 12 of the same birth month. Although parents describe the mere thought of it as 'daunting to say the least', there's no requirement for advanced literacy; 'they don't need to be able to write their name,' insists head, 'but they should be able to dress themselves.' Applicants work with 'really skilled staff' on eg puzzles, cutting and sticking and listening to a story. School says at this stage it is looking for 'school readiness': potential, curiosity and processing speeds. Some 100 invited back for round two and more activities, such as singing or dancing, plus a one-to-one chat with a teacher. Head meets all parents but is firm that 'it is not an interview' but a two-way process: 'a bit like buying a Ferrari,' she says, which in school terms is exactly what

An offer from NLCS is largely considered to be akin to winning Roald Dahl's fictional golden ticket to the chocolate factory

parents are doing. Parents urged not to despair if no offer is forthcoming at this point; 'we impress upon some that if their daughter isn't ready at 4, we'd love to see her again at 7.' At that point, a further 8-10 places up for grabs, with around 120 applicants, again assessed in two rounds.

Exit: Almost all to the senior school; in 2020, 89 per cent were offered places. Others to St Paul's and Godolphin & Latymer. Parents are given an early heads-up if the 'pace' of the senior school may not be quite right for them. All sit the entrance exam, albeit in their classrooms rather than formally with external candidates ('important for them to feel they've earned the place,' says head), although there's absolutely no cramming for exams – at least not inside of school.

Our view: An offer from NLCS is largely considered to be akin to winning Roald Dahl's fictional golden ticket to the chocolate factory – and with places almost as hard to come by, we half expected Willy Wonka himself to appear as the GSG-mobile was cleared to pass the security guard to enter through the wrought iron gates at the entrance to this cradle of academic excellence. With the fearsome reputation of its big sister (not to mention legends of notoriously competitive entry) looming large in the local ether, we wondered what hotbed of tiny talent we were destined to find cultivating here. Our sighs of relief were audible, then, when our first encounter was with a host of reception-aged children – many fresh from breakfast club – dancing along to Lazy Town in the hall, smiles abundant. Parents pop in and out of classrooms at drop-off: 'we encourage it,' says head. The same happy vibe was in evidence throughout the day; from forest school for the littlest ('girls are outside as often as in,' beams teacher), via arts and crafts and on to a year 5 team building day outside on the chilly field. Although unashamedly academic, head is clear that girls are 'having so much fun they don't really know they're learning'. Could it be true? Parents concur that 'girls are allowed to be who they want to be' and uniformly describe teaching staff with strings of superlatives: 'phenomenal...sensational... amazing, warm and friendly'. One described the academic rigour as 'couched in music, art and drama – all while running at a fast pace'.

Fast paced it is – and academics, in the words of parents, 'are a given'. This helps in terms of readiness for secondary, but interestingly girls are rarely given an official mark or a rank. We approve. Parents report that the curriculum itself is traditional. The standard, however, is well above and beyond, and a gold Primary Quality Mark award has recently been awarded for geography, with history on target to follow. Pupils' 'intellectual character' is constantly stimulated not only via the curriculum but also PSHE and assemblies, and head says that risk-taking is genuinely encouraged. The academic energy around the school is palpable; 'there's something about the buzz of girls running their own race,' says head, and whether it's chess (part of curriculum in year 2; school is national U11 champion) or Lego robotics (regional winners for past four years), excellence is par for the course in most things NLCS (one parent told us that when on school trips in London, girls frequently burst into song on the tube: 'in perfect tune of course; they're North London girls'). Languages taught a year at a time to give a taster for the senior school: Spanish in year 3, German in year 4, Mandarin in year 5 and French in year 6. Latin not on curriculum but available as a club. Singapore maths has been taught since 2017, resulting in a 'dramatic effect' on the standard of maths as well as girls' enjoyment of the subject; 'they're now clamouring at our door to enter maths challenges,' laughs head. Parents say that the standard of English is 'exceptional', particularly creative writing. Homework, we are told is 'reasonable' averaging at 30 minutes per night, and school intervenes when necessary if pupils need to put less pressure on themselves. On the subject of intervention, we are reliably informed that 'tutoring is rife' at all stages. We know this to be no different to any other school in the area but always live in hope of finding one that bucks the trend. School says it actively discourages any external intervention and always aims to offer pupils support when it's needed. Focus on early identification and intervention where SEND is concerned and learning support is run by a 'fantastic' SENCo. The site itself works well for those facing physical challenges, and the school has, when required, incorporated additional aids, such as a hearing loop.

Drama thrives, with an annual play per year group – some written by staff, some classics such as Pippi Longstocking – and a major production for year 6 leavers, often values-based eg Wind in the Willows or The Wolves of Willoughby Chase. Refreshingly, school tries to discourage counting lines and tries, as far as possible, to allocate equal involvement to all. Music an extremely busy department, working closely with drama. Practically all girls take peripatetic instrumental lessons, about 80 per cent within school. Over 30 per cent learn two instruments, some three or more, providing plenty of candidates for the 11 ensembles which cater for everyone from beginners to the not insubstantial number of girls who have achieved their grade 8. Compulsory choir for years 3 and 4; auditioned Canons choir – winner of multitudinous competitions – thereafter. Suspiciously tidy art room, although super cubist portraits on display at the time of our visit – soon to be developed into masks in either clay or wood – told us that standards are high.

Parents report a 'strong community feel', with very little need for rules or discipline. Even the youngest pupils have 'invisible boundaries' in the playground that are rarely crossed – this could easily serve as a metaphor for the whole school culture

Everything present and correct in the sports department, with the added benefit of access to the senior school's facilities. Swimming from reception, often coached by senior girls, new dance squad from year 3 and myriad opportunities, in addition to the major sports (netball, hockey and athletics), such as bouldering, table tennis and badminton. Pregnant parental pauses when asked about sporting culture and achievements, however, made us wonder whether NLCS would be an obvious choice for a supremely sporty girl. Naturally, there are plenty of elite athletes in the cohort but we gather that the majority of these pursue their training outside of school, although a new elite athlete mentoring programme has recently been introduced to try to address this, along with recent partnerships with Saracens (rugby) and Mavericks (netball) which promise to up the girls' games in terms of competitive spirit and mental resilience. Competitive cries at the AGM from parents asking why school doesn't perform better in the sports leagues are met with 'we're doing our best' year after year and one father commented that on sports day he found it hard to understand who the winners were. That said, he did add that 'nobody dreads it', and that's a good thing in our book. Crucially, the culture is one of integrating physical exercise into one's life; the daily mile for years 3 to 6 is a key part of the day. The 'hidden curriculum' is the bedrock of an NLCS education and a vast array of clubs and societies (choir, languages, sports, film, street dance, cheer, gardening, chopsticks cookery, Globetrotters school magazine, to name a few) keep girls busy round the clock – and happily for parents late transport is provided to allow for after-school clubs. Frequent external speakers (engineers, animators, fine arts dealers) – often ONLs – broaden girls' career aspirations.

Pastoral care is at the heart of the school's culture – 'amazing,' say parents – and girls are actively encouraged to be kind to each other and mindful of other social classes; 'good global citizens'. Major problems, particularly those where the school counsellor is drawn in, are often addressed with the whole family to ensure a cohesive way forward. Parents report a 'strong community feel', with very little need for rules or discipline. Even the youngest pupils have 'invisible boundaries' in the playground that are rarely crossed – this could easily serve as a metaphor for the whole school culture. Parent after parent told us that this isn't a school for 'cookie cutter' girls and that individuality is embraced – although let there be no doubt that the common qualities of diligence and an eagerness to please are prerequisites. A thicker skin is also beneficial to protect those who may otherwise be daunted by their 'stratospherically bright' classmates and, as with all 'all-through' schools, we recommend carrying out thorough due diligence of the senior school too before signing on the dotted line. Small touches make a big difference: 'personal appointment time' is formalised once a term for girls to reflect on their successes and challenges with their form tutor; they can request additional 'bubble time' to have shorter one-to-ones as needed. The hugely diverse parent cohort – from the extremely wealthy to those making huge sacrifices to send their daughters to NLCS, as well as the full melting pot of races and religions reflective of modern London – add to the girls' rich educative experience. Parents, too, appreciate the fact that social events tend to be low key quiz nights or fireworks rather than pricy 'big ticket' occasions, as well as the 'postcode drinks parties' that encourage community. Fantastic full wrap-around care with breakfast club, after school clubs galore and a coach service, covering swathes of north and west London and parts of Hertfordshire, that allows girls to travel to school from reception (older pupils are 'coach pals' and take care of these little ones) are a godsend to dual income families.

The last word: NLCS parents say they feel 'in safe hands' and we have absolutely no doubt that they are; a place won here is indeed a golden ticket to a world class education.

North London Collegiate School

Canons, Canons Drive, Edgware HA8 7RJ

020 8952 0912 | office@nlcs.org.uk | www.nlcs.org.uk

Independent | Pupils: 781; sixth form: 228

Ages: 11–18 | Fees: £20,430 pa

Linked school: North London Collegiate Junior School, 536

Headmistress: Since January 2018, Sarah Clark MA PGCE (50s), formerly head of the Queen's School, Chester. Hails from Walsall and educated at state grammar, Queen Mary's High School, and Newnham College, Cambridge (history and classics). Believes in 'right pegs in holes' – as did the school's governors when they headhunted her to the role; 'as a historian, I just couldn't say no to one of the oldest academic girls' schools in the country,' she says. We must say she looks most at home in her stylish office, once the music room of the Duke of Chandos, its walls now adorned with students' artwork. Is steadily moving this most illustrious and high achieving of schools from a deeply entrenched culture of stand-offish perfection to 'a bit more rough and ready – definitely no less committed to excellence and scholarship – just on a kinder footing'.

Described by parents as 'being full of common sense', she definitely cuts an informal dash around school; statuesque with an imposing but warm presence and shock of distinctive red hair. One for the Good Schools Guide 'heads we'd most like to have dinner with' list, although some of the more seasoned parents we spoke to are still adjusting to her less formal approach to headship (will join girls unannounced for lunch in school dining room rather than inviting them over for afternoon tea like her predecessor, for example). Staff we spoke to positively glowed with praise for her, however, and she clearly reciprocates with adulation for her 'immensely bright' team: 'they have so many ideas it's like living through an episode of The West Wing'. High on to-do list is to overhaul school IT system (cheers all round from parents – although it won't be a quick win) and to update STEAM offering with an IDEAS (innovation, design, engineering, art, science) hub to bring a new inter-disciplinary approach to these subjects and replace the currently rather cramped 'drawing school'. Sport also on her radar – 'it hasn't had as great an emphasis as it should'. Most crucially, she's driving an ongoing focus on the pastoral offering – an area seen by the parent body as in need of improvement: 'We now have a robust system that takes into account the fact that young people do make mistakes.'

Lives on site with husband, a history lecturer, two young adult children, her labrador Penda (named after a bloodthirsty Mercian king), and two warring tabby cats. In snatched moments away from school (parents and pupils tell us 'she goes to absolutely everything – including all four nights of a school production'), she enjoys bell-ringing in nearby churches.

Entrance: There are 65 places at 11+ for external applicants who join around 40 moving up from the junior school. Apply by end of November the year before entry; exams in English and maths take place early January of the year of entry (school is not part of the London 11+ Consortium). Over 500 apply and just over 200 are invited back for interview, with between 120 and 130 girls offered places. No sibling policy. For girls coming from feeder preps (eg St Christopher's, Glendower), school works closely with prep heads to ensure good fit, although around 40 per cent also join from state primaries. Prior to joining, an induction programme includes meetings with the 'big six' head girl team, picnics with new forms over the summer and a letter from year 8 buddy. About 25 extra places available for entry into year 12; apply by the end of November in the year prior to entry. Exams in four chosen A level subjects and subject specific interviews with departmental staff.

Exit: No culling after GCSEs and under 20 per cent leaves at this point to either co-ed or state schools. Girls praise the university admissions process; everyone is assigned a higher education mentor in year 12, usually a departmental head. Almost all to their first choice of university; 23 to Oxbridge in 2020, with other popular universities including UCL, Durham and Warwick. US universities a growth area ('it suits some girls in terms of breadth and co-curricular'); a specific department to support admissions was set up in 2014. SAT/ACT preparation is now done in school (delivered by external tuition company) and 13 girls accepted offers in 2020 including to Harvard, Princeton, Columbia, Stanford, Chicago and UCLA. Three further students off to Canada to study at Toronto, McGill and UBC. Despite hit rate at top institutions, head says school is equally supportive of girls heading to eg Sheffield to read computer science or Newcastle-upon-Tyne for interior architecture. Twenty-two medics in 2020.

Latest results: In 2020, 99 per cent 9-7 at I/GCSE; 79 per cent A*/A at A level (99 per cent A*-B). IB average point score 41. In 2019 (the last year when exams took place), 98 per cent 9-7 at I/GCSE; 73 per cent A*/A at A level. IB average point score 41.

Teaching and learning: If you're looking for an unashamedly ambitious and academic school, look no further. NLCS consistently tops national league tables and in sixth form is one of the only London day schools to offer both the IB plus a mixture of A levels and Pre-Us as part of its commitment to 'personalisation of the curriculum'. Girls generally take 11 GCSEs and outstanding results are virtually a given. A cohort of around one quarter of students most years take the IB. Most girls start with four A levels, with some dropping to three and the majority (85 per cent) taking the EPQ. There are no plans for school to drop either either the IB or A levels, but it feels the 'international mindedness' and 'outward looking nature' of the IB is a very close fit with the aspirations of its students, as well as lending itself well to the growth area of applications to US universities. Maths, sciences and economics are most popular subjects at A level, although across the board it's a 50/50 split between sciences and arts/humanities. Girls and parents both praise school's philosophy of flexible timetabling which allows students to follow the subjects they wish rather than pick from restrictive columns.

Strong languages offering; girls start in year 7 with French and Latin, with options to pick up Spanish, German or Mandarin in year 8 plus Italian and Russian in year 10 – all available at GCSE. Greek in year 10 as a GCSE option for budding classicists. We were delighted that in such an academic powerhouse, there is plenty of take up of art and drama at GCSE (over one third of year group in both cases) and not insignificant numbers at A level either. Girls attribute their success to two main factors: 'teachers that model passion for their individual subjects' and 'inspirational teaching' were recurring themes, and the girls themselves are extremely driven. The murky issue of girls being tutored outside of school was reported by a number of parents we spoke to, although head's clear message is that 'tutoring is never a good idea and I take action when I hear about it. Staff give a huge amount of one-to-one time outside of classes and senior students are on hand to mentor younger girls.' Our sources told us that girls are burning the midnight oil by year 10, so relentlessly focused are they on their academic success. Could it be true? A show of hands, albeit from a small sample, told us it was – and even those putting in less time were still working for around two and a half hours a night. We were earnestly assured (by parents and girls as well as head) that this diligence is driven by the students ('we want to live up to the school's success'), often by parental expectations too, but not by the school.

The estate formerly belonged to the 1st Duke of Chandos and, during his time, Handel was composer in residence

Learning support and SEN: A surprising number of pupils on SEND register – currently over 80 with a diagnosis and a further 25 with identified traits. Targeted support offered to individual students, who receive an 'individual education plan', with ongoing monitoring and all staff fully briefed to ensure continuity in the classroom. Despite its extensive and complex site, school is also happy to cope with physical disabilities – 'as long as the pupil can communicate and access the curriculum' – working with parents to ensure the right support is in place.

The arts and extracurricular: School speaks constantly about girls 'finding their passion' and there's no shortage of things for them to choose from. With around 50 activities a week on offer, students are spoilt for choice and the majority are making the most of the opportunities – sometimes to the detriment of downtime. School says it is 'working hard to make sure students have time to breathe', with the introduction, for example, of relaxation club comprising nature walks, yoga, knitting and running, but industriousness is so entrenched in the school culture we wish them luck with getting the message through. Overseas trips and endless productions ('phenomenal,' according to parents) add to the buzz of the school; the super theatre can seat 340 at full capacity and hosts performances galore from musical theatre (recently Sister Act) to plays

The Cardinal Wiseman Catholic School

written and directed by either staff or students themselves. Drama on curriculum for all to year 9 and school takes a production to the Edinburgh Fringe biennially.

Newly created assistant head, enrichment takes the view that 'education is not all about exams' and has the brief to dovetail co-curricular with the academic programme. Extensive range of enrichment activities (Duke of Edinburgh, Model United Nations, debating, Young Enterprise) help develop public-speaking skills and an appreciation of the world elsewhere. An international perspective is part of school's DNA; exchange programmes take place with schools in the USA, Australia and Germany. In 2011, North London opened an overseas campus in South Korea, NLCS Jeju, and students have the opportunity to visit the campus and do internships here, with NLCS Dubai new in 2017. Charity also firmly emphasised, including raising money for and teaching at a school in Zambia and visiting a local school for severely disabled children.

Sport: 'Nobody would describe it as a sporty school,' said one long-term parent but compared to many academic London day schools we'd say NLCS is doing a pretty good job (although PE is not a GCSE or A level option); with its renewed emphasis and, according to head, a 'shift in thinking' we felt that girls of all levels of interest and ability were catered for. Good facilities including huge sports hall, indoor pool, fitness suite and dance studio, and tons of outdoor space – including a new X trail – compared to most London schools. Although head describes the act of implementing change as 'like steering a luxury ocean liner', things are looking up in the sports department with a great number of non-competitive options such as zumba, pilates, kick-boxing, self-defense and life-guarding on offer to all girls, as well as a new elite sports programme covering strength and conditioning coaching plus nutrition advice for top athletes. Plenty of sport on curriculum – although less so as the years progress and non-compulsory in sixth form – with hockey top dog, plus netball, rounders, athletics and tennis all covered in games lessons. No hockey, but there's ultimate frisbee, tag rugby, football (with a few match fixtures) and cricket on the extracurricular schedule.

Ethos and heritage: Founded in Camden Town in 1850 by the formidable Frances Mary Buss, a highly effective crusader in the cause of education for women. (She also established Camden School for Girls, with whom North London continues to share a Founder's Day.) The school bought its current spacious, 30-acre semi-rural site in 1929 to use as a sports ground, and relocated here fully in 1940. The beautiful setting was cited by many parents we spoke to as the deciding factor for families choosing the school and we can see why. With its grand fascia, leafy green surroundings and charming pond (complete with fluffy goslings on the day of our visit), the vibe is more country boarding school than London day and there's no sense of space being at a premium. The estate formerly belonged to the 1st Duke of Chandos and, during his time, Handel was composer in residence. The central core of the building is a country house of 1760, now joined by a multitude of varied later additions.

If you're looking for an unashamedly ambitious and academic school, look no further. NLCS consistently tops national league tables

The atmosphere is calm, orderly, and purposeful. Mixed reports from parents about position on the pressure scale; school describes itself as having a 'relaxed self-confidence' but there were a poorly disguised splutters from parents we spoke to regarding the word 'relaxed', indicating that regardless of who is applying it, the pressure to do well is most definitely on. Local jungle drums told us girls need to be 'tough' to survive here. We felt that with the academic bar set high and the constant buzz of activity, resilience, confidence and boundless energy would be a winning formula for applicants. Head, however, insists that school 'works very hard to build resilience in girls; a sense of confidence, integrity and commitment that enables even the quietest child to find her voice and feel that she can take on new challenges with humility and determination.' We were were thrilled to see so many smiling faces (and hugs for their neighbouring junior school pupils) as girls moved around the school at break times.

Long list of illustrious old girls includes: Anna Wintour, Judith Weir, Stella Gibbons, Susie Orbach, Marie Stopes, Stevie Smith, Myfanwy Piper, Dame Helen Gardner, Gillian Tett.

Pastoral care, inclusivity and discipline: First stop on the day of our visit was a session with the pastoral team which we think (and hope) speaks volumes about the direction of pastoral travel at NLCS. An entirely new team, appointed by Mrs Clark, is now in place to tackle the issues that are, unfortunately, so often part and parcel of high achieving female environments. Parents had very mixed views of pastoral provision, although our observation was that girls at the lower end of the school are having a very different experience to that of their older peers. Mrs Clark and her team have taken the situation in hand and the new deputy head, pastoral was described as 'outstanding' by even the most cynical parent we spoke with.

The team we met were young and oozed genuine empathy and understanding for the plight of today's teenagers. The pastoral structure 'is central to our strategic thinking and underpins everything', we were told. All staff have a pastoral responsibility, with some forms having two or three tutors to touch base with girls at morning and afternoon registration, giving them the freedom to pick up on any issues one-to-one while the other tutors take the rest of the class. Staff INSET days often have a pastoral theme and school also says it does lots of work with parents via its programme of topical talks covering issues such as perfectionism, drugs, screen dependency, resilience and consent. Staff told us of an 'informal culture of being there to listen – sometimes even in the minibus on the way to a fixture', and for issues requiring a more structured approach there's an onsite nurse, a counsellor, a mental health and well-being society with peer mentoring over cups of tea and a year 8 buddy system for incoming year 7s. Annual pastoral survey introduced in 2018 and the 'big six' head girl team meet head weekly and are her 'eyes and ears' on the ground.

Pupils and parents: Cosmopolitan, ambitious professional families – many dual-income and some extremely wealthy. Girls from every conceivable ethnic background, with over 50 languages spoken at home. High percentage of Asian and Jewish families plus increasing numbers of Europeans and Americans. One or two reports of cliques amongst some groups plus occasional grumbles from girls that there aren't as many parties as at some of their friends' schools (not seen as a bad thing in the parents' books). Some parents, of the belief that a private education automatically buys top grades, definitely driving their daughters hard to succeed; school says it intervenes when it feels that parental pressure is affecting girls' mental health or happiness. Shuttle buses whisk girls to and from Edgware and Stanmore underground stations, with a coach service covering 22 different routes across north and west London and out as far as Harpenden, St Albans and Rickmansworth. Late buses to Baker Street and Potters Bar only.

Money matters: North London has always prided itself on being affordable and accessible and offers some scholarships and bursaries. From 2020 school will no longer offer academic scholarships, preferring to recognise every student's intellectual abilities rather than single out a small number. The money formerly offered to academic scholars will be invested in greater opportunities for all students. Music scholarships at 11 and 16 (girls must pass the entrance exam as well as the audition in which grade 5 is generally the expected minimum). Means-tested bursaries (reviewed annually) range from 10-100 per cent of fees and can be awarded in conjunction with scholarships. Bursary funding is partially underwritten by the South Korean franchise, and the school is looking for other projects to further extend these opportunities.

The last word: A top drawer school for super bright, confident and resilient girls, ready to throw themselves into everything on offer.

Headteacher: Since 2015, Nicola Forster BA NPQH PGDip (mid 40s). With a personal pedigree from the best Ealing schools, Ms Forster took a degree in geography and education at Roehampton, before beginning work in the first (of eight) London primary schools. She was promoted from acting head at Hathaway Primary to head at Ryefield Primary, Uxbridge, before joining North Primary, following its troubled spell making headlines over the solar eclipse. Inspired to teach by her mother's example, 'I learnt from an early age how you could influence children's lives through teaching,' she is at ease in her trainers and sportswear ('I'll put on a dress for the town hall!') despite having just run four times round the neighbouring sports fields with the children for Sports Relief.

Parents showed guarded respect; 'We all look at results,' said one, who had had experience of four successive heads at the school, but they applauded her candour: 'Her door is open, which parents do like.' Children approached her with ease in the corridor, addressing her formally as 'Mrs Forster' but responding familiarly, 'Yeah, cool!' Divorced with two teenage girls at the local secondary school, she is a keen runner. She has introduced a new assessment system for the children and plans a shift of emphasis in the curriculum: 'We have very high attainment in literacy and numeracy; I'd like to increase the range.' She has refurbished some of the buildings, including a stylish makeover in a Victorian classroom to create a colourful office for herself and her deputy. She applauds her school's participation in the national evaluation scheme, Challenge Partners: 'it's really helpful to hear other people's points of view, to help us tighten our systems.' We forecast that, barring rare astronomical incidents, she is on course for a successful run.

Entrance: London borough of Ealing admissions criteria. Many come via the outstanding children's centre next door, Grove House. Catchment area includes the residential area west of Hanwell and north of Uxbridge Road. Oversubscribed.

Exit: Most to local secondaries: Villiers, Dormers Wells and Greenford High school are popular choices. Some go to selective state schools: Tiffin, Upton Court.

Our view: Astoundingly high Sats results have earned this school its reputation. The head attributes much of it to the expertise of the staff and good resourcing; the parents put it down to commitment of the community. Two form entry with 30 children to a class, supervised by one teacher and a teaching assistant. Despite 98 per cent EAL – 22 different tongues, mainly Indian languages, but some Somali and eastern European – the teaching is in English, and the school is proud of its EAL lead status. There is some EAL support for the 30 per cent who arrive without any English, and bilingual staff throughout the school and offices. Lower than average numbers of SEN, nurtured in individual sessions or small groups in a corner of the hall. One mum was dissatisfied with the SEN support: 'My child has had one-to-one; it has sometimes been a bit tricky.'

The classes are named after flowers (Cornflower, Poppy, etc) after the school's address in Meadow Road. No hedgerows now; the school is in one of London's more economically deprived suburbs, with twice the national average on free school meals. Drawing from an area between Hanwell and Heathrow airport, home to a large Asian community, Southall is famed for its productive and hard-working ethos. 'There are very high expectations from parents and teachers,' says the head. A dad acknowledged the pressure this puts on the staff: 'We've had an up and down period in the last few years… recently some teachers left,' but he reassured us, 'teachers do get along with the pupils; the pupils are encouraged to achieve.' The head describes the staff as a real blend of ages and genders, some home grown, some from overseas.

Visitors are greeted at the door by an appliqué wallhanging of local landmarks, from the famous Southall water tower to shops selling Asian sweets

A single-storey brick and slate schoolroom, with ornamental weather vane, is what remains of the village school. Adjoining is a Victorian arts and crafts extension, while additional low-level classrooms from the 1970s spread out into the playground at the rear. 'The premises need a revamp,' said one parent, but the high ceilings and corridors lined with pegs, lend an air of trusty tradition to the building. The reception and year 1 classes on the ground floor enjoy direct access to the playground, where there is an outdoor classroom, as well as giant number square and snakes and ladders. Indoors, classes are peppered with scarlet tables and chairs, with carpet-time nooks. Upstairs year 2 was studying the Great Fire, with a flame-ridden dolls' house in Pudding Lane.

Gym frame and ropes for PE are installed in the first floor hall, used for assemblies, as well as whole school gatherings once a week. A modern dining hall connects the old and new buildings and serves a halal menu twice a week (fish and chips with Eve's pudding on the day we visited). Beyond is a corridor resplendent with children's work (design your own Greek urn was our favourite), with a full library at one end. We peeked into a discrete sensory room, for SEN time, and an ICT room, hiding 30 computers inside tip-up desks. The upper floor classrooms are a delightful mix of modern and traditional: whiteboards displaying familiar columns of spellings and fractions, while high-ceilinged rooms are ventilated by the original telescopic winder poles. Lively year 6 classes were in session when we visited, discussing the construction of pyramids, while a pair of young boffins at higher-level learning tasks, were cracking a secret code.

Visitors are greeted at the door by a colourful montage of art, reflecting the diversity of the school, with a collage of religious symbols served up on paper plates, and an appliqué wallhanging of local landmarks, from the famous Southall water tower to shops selling Asian sweets. In the reception class exotic instruments lay ready to play at one of the many school celebrations: Eid, Easter, Diwali, Holi, Chinese new year; 'It's one big party,' laughs the head. Some take the form of shows for the parents, such as The Elves and the Shoemaker or the traditional nativity play, with contributions from their own Bollywood dance troupe. There's a diverse choice of sports, too, football, cricket, netball and golf, as well as an American football club after school. Sports day is held at the local Spikes Bridge Park. Plentiful after-schools clubs include the three Rs: reading, rugby and recorder.

Mindfulness, from year 4, prevents the myriad amusements causing sensory overload. The deputy head keeps a model brain on his desk to teach the children the mechanics of de-stressing; 'It helps them deal with test situations,' says the head, and 'The stressed child would have a specific adult to link to.' Parents were satisfied there were no serious issues with bullying: 'In the main... it's a misunderstanding more than anything serious,' said one dad, and 'The kids are all respectful to the adults.' Communication with parents was felt to be good; 'there is a system', which includes face-to-face chats with the head or class teacher; 'Morning and night, someone is on the gate,' reassured the head. Emails to the office produce a quick response; 'School is good at getting back to you,' said one mum. There is a strong parent council – 'Which helps the standards... where some parents have issues, but don't know how to voice them,' said a governor – as well as a student council. Other school trips include the Kensington museums, the RAF museum and a residential to Surrey for the older ones, while the youngest children's outings include learning to make and post a mother's day card at the post office.

Dressed in their scarlet jumpers and white polo shirts, the children we saw were both relaxed and purposeful as they prepared for a trip to the local sports field. As one dad said, 'The kids feel safe and respected and enjoy going to school.' A strong PTA funds extras, such as new playground equipment, via quiz nights, a ladies' night and the lavish Mela, or summer fête, a cornucopia of sweets. The head was astonished at the generosity of the participants. One parent said, 'Parents are quite involved and do a lot to make sure their children do well... A lot of parents bounce ideas off each other; it's an Asian thing.' Some parents are former pupils. The head is quick to recognise the parental input: 'Children are very focused, families are very supportive; families are ambitious... the parents are like private school parents.'

The last word: A fusion of traditional and progressive values makes this school special, from code-breaking science lessons to Bollywood spectaculars, from Gulab Jamun to fish and chips. The community support is palpable and the academic success skilfully orchestrated by the head and watchful governing body, who make the most of the rich diversity among the children. North Primary is clearly a rising star in Ealing's firmament.

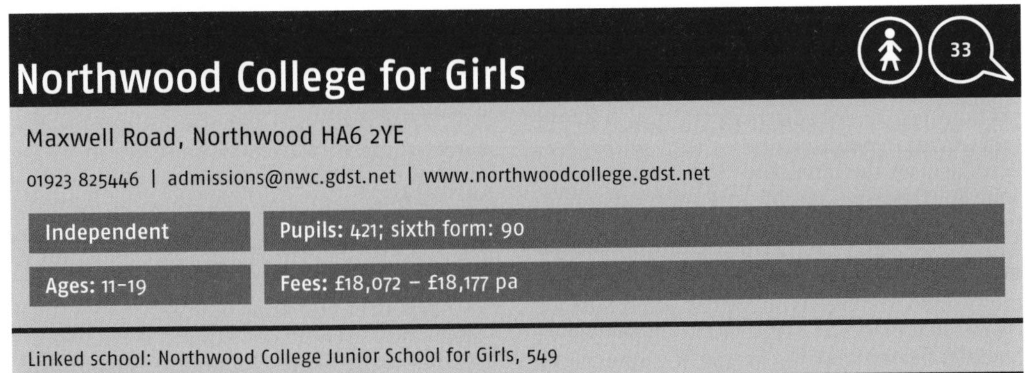

Northwood College for Girls

33

Maxwell Road, Northwood HA6 2YE

01923 825446 | admissions@nwc.gdst.net | www.northwoodcollege.gdst.net

Independent	Pupils: 421; sixth form: 90
Ages: 11–19	Fees: £18,072 – £18,177 pa

Linked school: Northwood College Junior School for Girls, 549

Head mistress: Since September 2018, Zara Hubble, previously head of Northwood College junior school since 2015. Educated at Westonbirt School and City of London Girls, after which she took a Montessori nursery teaching course then a BEd specialising in KS2 at Southbank University.

Cut teeth at St Hilda's in Bushey before joining Heathfield, where she taught year 6 and ultimately became head of year 7. Was persuaded to come to Northwood for one term post-merger with Heathfield in 2014, where she 'completely fell in love with the school because it quickly struck me that everybody is a somebody here'.

Surprised but elated when it was suggested she went for head honcho ('junior heads don't become whole school heads'), she is immensely popular and widely praised for her research-based thinking in taking the school forward and emphasis on taking an already strong pastoral offering to the next level ('I firmly believe it's the gateway to academic success – the most successful people I know have the strongest mental health'). 'It's as if she was made for the job,' said one parent; 'she's a breath of fresh air, effortlessly motivating everyone around her – you almost want to work there yourself,' cooed another, with all agreeing that her 'one of us' approach means 'she's never intimidating, always welcoming and thoroughly lovely'.

Pupils, who describe her as 'engaging' and 'empowering' and 'a real listener', say she has 'brought new energy to the school' and love that her door remains wide open at all times – 'it was a bit scary at first,' admitted one, 'but now we realise we really can just drop in with ideas whenever we want.' And what a striking office it is – flooded with light, with soft and contemporary greys, stunning pupil artwork and a large conference table instead of a desk ('everyone has something equally important to say here'), all reflecting her inclusive, welcoming temperament.

Youthful, calm poised and sociable, she lives locally with her husband ('You can never go out in your tracksuit – everyone is a parent or prospective parent,' she laughs), with whom they have two grown-up daughters, one who works in financial PR, the other studying postgrad medicine at Oxford. Keen skier and book lover.

Entrance: Girls joining senior school from other prep or junior schools take the London 11+ Consortium cognitive ability test, with great emphasis on the interview. 'But don't worry if your daughter is quite shy – we are good at finding the spark,' says school. A few join for A levels, with places conditional on GCSE results (at least five grade 9-5s in total, with 9-7s in the subjects they want to study) plus online test and interview. Occasional places in other year groups ('we've recently been inundated in year 8 – now a very popular year to join') so worth a call if you're moving into the area.

Exit: Around 10 to 20 per cent leave after GCSE, with nearly 85 per cent of those who stay moving on to Russell Group or new universities. Recently popular are Queen Mary University of London, UCL, King's College London, Cardiff, Birmingham, Southampton, Nottingham, Edinburgh, Nottingham, Leeds, Durham and Warwick.

In the ferociously academic context of this corner of north London, this school has historically favoured a more pastoral bent

Latest results: In 2020 GCSE, 77 per cent 9-7 at GCSE; 61 per cent A*/A at A level (85 per cent A*-B). In 2019 (the last year when exams took place), 74 per cent 9-7 at GCSE; 39 per cent A*/A at A level (66 per cent A*-B).

Teaching and learning: In the ferociously academic context of this corner of north London, this school has historically favoured a more pastoral bent and value added over striving to be top of the pile when it comes to results. But with pastoral provision gaining increasing recognition as an academic strength, not a 'softly-softly' add-on, it should perhaps come as no surprise that results are good.

Make no mistake, these girls work hard. Expectations are universally agreed as being higher than in the past and the Oxbridge whip is cracked harder than it was. But the broad-ish church intake and continuing pastoral emphasis means that academic superstars coexist happily alongside their more pedestrian peers, with neither group feeling undue pressure. 'Girls are supported to get better results than they thought themselves capable of, but somehow it's achieved without the hothouse, competitive and non-nurturing environments of some of the neighbouring schools,' summed up one parent. 'And they prepare us for well beyond university,' one pupil told us. 'It's also about becoming highly employable, so everything we learn is given relevance to the world of work. Why are we learning this? How will it help us in the long run? How can we make sure the learning sticks? These kinds of questions are embedded into lessons, increasingly so as you move up the school.'

Independent thinking is also in the spotlight – staff say it's the school's raison d'être, with a full-time cognitive development director ensuring consistency of message and integration across all parts of the curriculum. Even the youngest in the school evangelise about it – 'teachers don't spoon feed us', 'we are taught that mistakes in learning are good – it's how you learn' etc.

Lessons we visited bore this out and were interactive (think periodic table bingo), with open-ended questions from teachers, for which girls gave articulate, confident and considered answers. And nobody is resting on their laurels – 'If I'm being completely honest, I still want the girls to be a bit more feisty – asking more questions, challenging in more creative ways,' says head. Teachers offer extra classes and clinics not only for those who feel they're falling behind but to stretch the more able.

Girls choose one modern language from French, Spanish or Mandarin in year 7, one of which must be continued to GCSE. Latin also compulsory from year 7 (not popular with everyone). Setting currently in maths from midway through year 7 and English from year 8, plus in science at GCSE level, although head's signature evidence-based thinking means it might not stay that way ('Looking at the latest research, I'm increasingly convinced mixed ability is the way forward so we're re-evaluating'). Girls take between nine and 11 GCSEs from a traditional curriculum, with non-core options including classical civilisation, drama, music, art plus the very popular textiles. IGCSEs taken in some subjects, at the discretion of each departmental head.

Independent thinking is in the spotlight. Even the youngest in the school evangelise about it – 'we are taught that mistakes are good – it's how you learn'

Similarly broad choice of A level options, of which most girls take three, with popular choices including sciences, psychology, economics, maths and music. EPQ compulsory – 'it isn't popular with everyone and some girls in my year really didn't enjoy it, but we all felt glad we stuck it out,' said one pupil. Historically, there was a disappointingly low take-up of more 'artsy' options, reflecting the parent demographic aspiring to careers in the sciences for their daughters, but there has been an increasingly successful push from the school on both the value of doing a subject you really love and that even if you want to be a scientist, you need to be able to express yourself, for which non-science subjects can be crucial.

University application process universally praised by parents and girls. Dedicated full-time careers and UCAS adviser delivers 'loads of one-to-one advice,' say parents, plus programme to provide every opportunity for girls to build CV. Visiting advisers are frequent fixtures, eg mock university interviews with admissions staff from Imperial College or staff from nearby Merchant Taylors' and endless internship opportunities.

Learning support and SEN: Because large number of girls move through from junior school, any SEN usually identified years before arrival in senior school, with seamless transition a major benefit for girls requiring support. Most mild SENs managed in lessons, with only occasional withdrawals.

The arts and extracurricular: Performing arts centre looks newer than it is and includes an excellent drama studio, recital hall with a sprung floor plus well kitted out music tech room and a plethora of instruments from steel drums up. Plenty of opportunities for budding thespians to throw themselves into productions, most recently School of Rock and Daisy Pulls it Off, and although there's no grand theatre space for such performances, the assembly hall does the job. Parents describe music as 'amazing' – for all tastes and levels – from a 50 strong orchestra that plays everything from classical to pop, to jazz bands and chamber choir. 'My husband isn't musical at all, but I dragged him along to the latest concert, in which the head of music did an incredible version of Bohemian Rhapsody with the girls, and he absolutely loved it,' one parent told us. Singing is a biggie here, including head's popular new Monday morning singalongs – 'there's something really special and tribal about group singing that gives you a real feeling of belonging.' Art popular, with three large studios, lots of talented work on display throughout the school, and an animated head of art. Extracurricular activities mean there's something for everyone – from the active to the cerebral. School supportive of girls pursuing interests or sports to a high level outside of school.

Sport: Doesn't boast the most gleaming array of facilities we've ever seen and the field is tiny, but for what is essentially a London school, it's well enough equipped. Stand out facility is the recently refurbished 25m pool – with everyone swimming all year round and weekly lessons for years 7 to 9. Sports hall has a new climbing wall used both in PE lessons and by clubs. Gym also attractive and well equipped, apparently well used at lunchtimes by older girls. PE and games compulsory even in sixth form, with girls playing to a high level in netball, plus tons of extracurricular sports on offer to suit all tastes – hockey, badminton, football, cricket basketball, yoga, you name it. Perhaps not the most obvious choice for super sporty types, parents told us – 'it's not sports-crazy or fiercely competitive, although we are getting better in matches and the new director of sports seems to have a better vision,' said one. But for every girl that agreed, one seemed to disagree – 'Sport is my absolute love and I've never felt I've missed out here,' said one, with a number of outstanding gymnasts and swimmers attending the school.

Ethos and heritage: Founded in 1878 in Endsleigh Gardens, Bloomsbury, with around 25 boarders and a handful of day girls. Headmistress Miss Buchan-Smith, concerned about the unsavoury influence of the Euston area on her girls, moved the school to its current site in Northwood in 1893. The current front building – red-brick late arts and crafts with leaded lights – was opened for 20 boarders and just two day girls. The Briary, next door, accommodated little boys, and although they are long gone, school pays tribute to those who went on to fight and fall in the two great wars with an annual wreath laying at Ypres.

Joined Girls' Day School Trust (GDST) in 2013 as a precursor to merging with Heathfield School, already a member of the Trust, with Northwood girls now benefiting from participation in GDST music and sport competitions, and in conferences on eg Oxbridge application, as well as access to travel scholarships and to an alumnae network numbering some 75,000 members, bringing a healthy pool of work experience and internships in which to fish. Staff also benefit from additional training and development opportunities, which bears obvious fruit in the classroom.

The library is among the most attractive we've seen: a contemporary Scandi-style space, in the same muted greys and whites as the head's office

Space is at a premium and the plethora of disparate buildings wouldn't win any beauty contests, but somehow it all hangs together nicely in this urban setting to create a cosy and unintimidating atmosphere – and all aspects are highly functional. The library is among the most attractive we've seen – once the original gym, it is now a contemporary Scandi-style space, in the same mute greys and whites of the head's office (same interior designer) and lovely mezzanine level for fiction. The homely sixth form common rooms buzz with chatter, and there's plenty of seminar rooms and quiet working space for this upper end of the school who feel well looked after. The dining room, although not huge, is light and airy and we enjoyed tasty fodder and plenty of choice. Most striking to visitors is the calm – almost serene – atmosphere that pervades the school. Smiling faces are everywhere to be seen and parents and pupils report supportive behaviour between girls. New sixth form centre to open soon.

Pastoral care, inclusivity and discipline: Pastoral support has long been the backbone of this school, although some might say it's been a double-edged sword, giving it a reputation of being the softer option among local schools. The reality is, say pupils and parents, that the 'strong school community' and 'ethos of kindness' which permeates every aspect of school life has a direct impact on learning – 'I can be myself here,' said one pupil.

Behaviour-wise, there are minor transgressions only in the main, and these mainly tiny bumps in the road to adolescence, reportedly dealt with 'brilliantly and sensitively', with school focusing on discussion and resolution (including coaching), although there is a detention system. 'They hear both sides of the story and keep an eye on girls they need to,' said one parent. Older girls pick up concerns of their younger peers and head reports 'very few' eating disorders or instances of self harm – highly commendable in an academic girls' school; 'we don't value aggressiveness.' Lots of talks for parents and pupils alike on subjects such as social media and cyberbullying. There is a strong house system with competitions in anything and everything, the highlight being the house music competition in which every girl participates.

Pupils and parents: Majority from British Asian backgrounds although all cultures and religions represented (there's a multi-faith prayer room for free use by girls as and when) and a more sensible and earnest cohort you'd be hard pushed to find. No reports of cliques, and girls we met appeared to work towards their own best, not someone else's, as well as genuinely celebrating each other's achievements and thinking outwardly – 'these girls have a huge moral compass,' one parent told us. Parents, many of whom are dual income, are – as one put it – 'just normal and down-to-earth. You don't get many of the mums who have been home all day and turn up done up to the nines.' Wide-reaching coach routes transport girls from Ealing, Edgware, Kenton, Gerrards Cross and Pinner, while proximity to Northwood station on the Metropolitan line gives easy access from both directions – a good job given the 'nightmare parking' reported by parents.

Money matters: A few means-tested bursaries – up to full fees for particularly deserving cases. Scholarships for academics, art, music and sport.

The last word: If neighbouring options feel too large, aggressive or hothouse, this may be just what you've been looking for. All things pastoral are at the very heart of what they do and this, combined with a purposeful culture and vibrant and evidence-based teaching, means Northwood girls emerge as independent thinkers, confident communicators and happy all-rounders, with nobody left festering in the background.

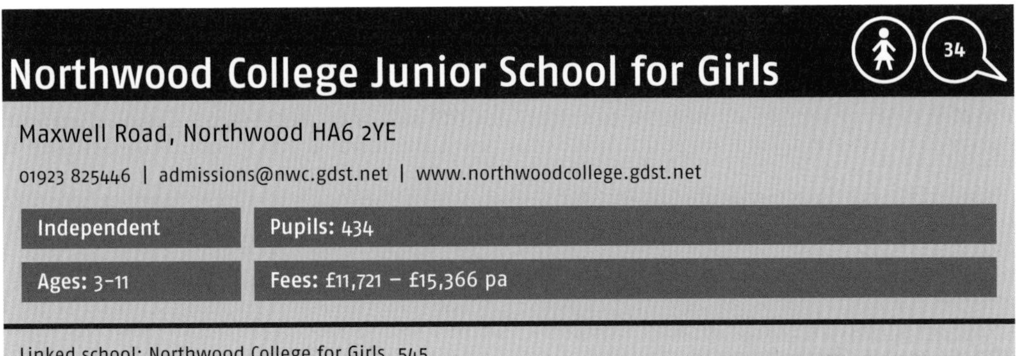

Northwood College Junior School for Girls

34

Maxwell Road, Northwood HA6 2YE

01923 825446 | admissions@nwc.gdst.net | www.northwoodcollege.gdst.net

Independent	Pupils: 434
Ages: 3-11	Fees: £11,721 – £15,366 pa

Linked school: Northwood College for Girls, 545

Acting head: Since September 2020, Zara Hubble (head of senior school).

Entrance: Oversubscribed for entry at 3+ and 4+ with three to four applicants for every place. Gently selective with nursery and reception places offered after observation in play. Head meets all parents: 'we want to see them in a sociable environment to gauge whether they will thrive in a busy school environment and with a long school day.' Up to 10 new places at 7+, when applicants are assessed in maths, English and reasoning and by interview.

Exit: Almost all to senior school at 11+ with a small handful taking up state grammar places most years.

Our view: Junior school comprises three purpose built buildings – along with Wray Lodge, which houses the headteacher's office and admin staff – all on same site and a handy hop, skip and jump from senior school, which makes the already super-smooth transition from year 6 (when a few lessons start to be taken with their soon-to-be secondary teachers) even more efficient.

Delightful Bluebelle House is home to early years girls – designed with a fabulous playground, outdoor explorer area (minibeast heaven), masses of IT and spacious, airy and inspiring classrooms where girls learn Spanish via action songs, yoga and ballet from age 3. Three reception classes of up to 20 girls also enjoy this space with life skills such as resilience already high on the educational agenda. Years 1 and 2 in Vincent House, with junior school housing years 3 to 6 – both immaculate, modern buildings, with every available space proudly adorned with colourful art and meticulous handwritten work. Benefits from sharing facilities including swimming pool, sports hall and science block with senior school – and occasionally they get access to the fabulous Scandi-style library, one of the most welcoming we've come across (a good job as one year 4 girl told us, 'I've almost read all the fiction in the junior library – it could definitely be bigger').

Parents, who are spoilt for choice for local schools, praise the 'inclusive atmosphere' and that 'it's really not pushy, yet the girls thrive'. 'You still get the results, it's just how you get there,' said one. Pastoral support isn't just prioritised – it is thoroughly embedded, insist parents, who talk about the 'personal level of care they have for each child' and the 'culture of kindness that you see in every person in the school'. Parents feel teachers take time to understand who their child is and what makes them tick – 'they capture sparks of interest, grow them and make them shine,' said one. 'If you want your child to be in a competitive environment, outwitting each other, with academic wins at every possible opportunity, go for one of the other local schools – this one teaches you that winning comes from within, how to get there without burning yourself out, and that looking after your mental health is key, even at this young age,' summed up one parent. Girls, too, talk about how they feel 'nurtured rather than pushed' and, happily, few are denied the right to move into the senior school. Head told us, 'The children's emotional literacy is incredibly powerful here – that really hit me when I arrived. There's no sense of, "here's the pastoral care and resilience model – go figure". There's a kind of built-in CBT programme, with the school constantly questioning ourselves, "how can we teach you to become emotional strategists and work out what you need and how to access it?"'

Thinking skills – pioneered by the whole school from nursery through to year 13 – taken very seriously by all with pupils able to explain the purpose of De Bono thinking hats with enthusiasm and clarity. Curriculum well-paced and not so overloaded that deep learning is missed. Setting in maths from year 3 and all girls learn Spanish from nursery upwards and Latin from year 5. Teachers are described as 'professional', 'dedicated' and 'thoughtful', with 'impressive amounts of preparation for each class'. 'They love the girls – they really look after them.' Lessons we observed were engaging and interactive – not a yawn in sight. All girls screened for SEN in year 4 and supported in small groups either within or outside the classroom – 'they've been really good with my daughter,' said one parent. A handful of girls receive EAL help.

'If you want your child to be in a competitive environment, outwitting each other, with academic wins at every possible opportunity, go for one of the other local schools'

Despite academics taking centre stage, school also works hard to ensure balance with a dazzling array of extracurricular clubs which take place either at lunch time or after school. Something for everyone, with all major sports represented, plus a wide range from ballet, martial arts, outdoor explorers and gardening to newspaper club. 'I started up a cupcake club,' one year 6 girl told us, while another had set up a movie making club.

PE lessons focus on mobility, flexibility and core strength in years 1 and 2, then there's specialist teaching from year 3, with sports including netball, rounders, athletics and tennis (other specialist teachers, including in some academic subjects, are introduced from year 3) and weekly swimming for all in the magnificent 25m swimming pool. 'It's probably not for the super sporty, but it's absolutely fine,' said one parent. Music, for which there's a dedicated teaching room, 'is in the DNA of the school', we were told, with a much-praised junior head of music who teaches the foundations of music 'almost by osmosis' and gets the girls involved in 'joyful but highly accurate performances'. 'You do get the parents who demand why their kid isn't picked for the concerts, but the school manages it in a good way,' one parent told us. Peripatetic teaching also available, and frequently taken up, by year 1 upwards. As with the senior school, communal singing is huge – 'there's a real lack of inhibition with it, which makes it very uplifting'. 'Really extraordinary' major stage production each year – practising for Joseph and the Technicolour Dreamcoat when we visited – with the whole of year 6 participating and many behind the scenes roles up for grabs for lower year groups. Art is primarily taught by form teachers, who work closely with heads of art in the senior school, often with cross-curricular themes – plenty of evidence of talented work adorns the walls.

Misbehaviour is minimal. 'Families here take education very seriously and really believe in us and support what we're doing and they share those values with their daughters, so they come to school ready to learn,' explains school. Teachers rarely have to get further than a 'quiet look'. 'It's almost as if the girls know what they want from their education and that's a lot more powerful than sanctions,' says school. You almost wonder if the girls are a bit too compliant, although there is all the usual 'scratchy sort of stuff' between the girls, says school. 'We're mainly encouraged to sort it out ourselves, which usually works, and if it doesn't a teacher advises us,' a pupil told us.

Super catering, with lunches (included in fees) freshly prepared on site. Year 2s upwards eat together in dining room. Wraparound care run by Superclubs from 7.30am (includes breakfast) and after-school care (including supper) up to 6pm – great for working parents, although the new system has had 'some teething problems', according to one parent.

Majority from British Asian backgrounds although all cultures and religions represented (there's a multi-faith prayer room for free use by girls as and when) and there's a strong parent community, with no cliques – 'I absolutely love the mums,' said one, although another told us, 'It's not in your face – there's a massive social life if you want it, but it's not frowned upon to step away.' Most come by car – 'not an easy drop-off,' admit parents about the residential street where the school is located.

The last word: Gone are the days when this school felt it almost had to apologise for itself. In fact, we spoke to parents whose original plan involved moving their daughters to other secondaries at 11+ and in some cases won places at arguably more high-flying schools. Invariably, none wanted to leave, thanks in no small part to the clever balance of nurture and academic rigour they enjoyed at Northwood. Definitely one for the list if you want an all-through, rounded education – not to mention avoiding the 11+ frenzy.

Notting Hill and Ealing High Junior School

26 St Stephen's Road, London W13 8HH

020 8799 8484 | juniorenquiries@nhehs.gdst.net | www.nhehs.gdst.net/junior-school

Independent | Ages: 4–11 | Pupils: 305 | Fees: £14,814 pa

Linked school: Notting Hill and Ealing High School, 552

Head: Since 2013, Silvana Silva BEd (50s). She arrived at the school as a year 4 class teacher in 1989 and has stayed ever since. Deputy head for 11 years before taking the top job. A north Londoner by background, she attended St Michael's Catholic Grammar School in North Finchley and did her degree at Roehampton University. She always wanted to teach and previously taught at primary schools in west London. 'But as soon as I walked in here in 1989 I thought, this is for me,' she says. 'Everything has always been new and exciting.'

A positive, energetic and sympathetic head, she is very proud that the school was named as the Sunday Times independent prep school of the year in 2018. Much liked by pupils and parents. 'We offer academic excellence in a happy and relaxed environment,' she says. 'The girls have to be happy and they are our number one priority. Pastoral care is paramount for us.'

She still teaches both reception classes once a week and says it's the best part of her job. 'It's really important to get to know all the girls and their personalities,' she says. 'They are full of life and joy and love telling me about their day.'

Married (her husband works for John Lewis), with one grown-up son. She's a great believer in 'healthy mind, healthy body' and in her spare time enjoys going to the gym, theatre and spending time with her family.

Entrance: The two main entry points are 4+ and 7+. At 4+, 100 applicants try for 40 places – two reception classes of 20 each. The girls are observed in groups of three or four doing 'nursery style activities' (playing, interacting and talking to junior school teachers). No formal reading or writing required. At 7+, 30 to 40 apply for an additional eight year 3 places. Girls are tested in maths, writing and verbal reasoning. Girls who do well in the test are invited back for a short, informal interview and a tour. The school is full but places occasionally come up in other years (mainly due to families relocating).

Exit: Virtually all (93 per cent in 2020) progress to the senior school at the end of year 6. Confirmed, unconditional offers of places for the senior school are made in the spring term of year 5. The juniors still take the senior school entrance test with outside applicants though – so they can be considered for scholarships on an even footing. A few leave at 11 for other senior schools (such at St Paul's Girls', Godolphin & Latymer and Lady Eleanor Holles) but the assumption is that once they join the junior school they're here for the duration.

Our view: The national curriculum is watched but certainly not slavishly followed. Girls do key stage 2 Sats – the head says teachers find them useful to track the girls' progress. 'It's all very low key,' she adds. 'There is a bit of preparation but no angst about them. It's just part and parcel of what we do.' Teachers focus on developing literacy and numeracy, with daily lessons in each subject. The school is rightfully proud of its integrated curriculum, introduced eight years ago. Designed 'to give meaning to humanities subjects', each year group from year 1 to year 6 is given a theme (anything from pirates to the First World War). When we visited year 6 pupils were studying the geography of the First World War battlefields and having philosophical discussions about what is worth fighting for.

'As soon as I walked in here I thought, this is for me,' says head. 'Everything has always been new and exciting'

Most subjects are taught by class teachers but science is led by a dynamic former research scientist from King's College London. She teaches girls from year 1 and enthuses them about the subject from the start – everything from snail races to learning how to purify water. 'We need to get girls passionate about science from a young age,' she says. Computing (lots of coding) and Mandarin are taught from year 1 onwards. French and German are offered as after-school clubs. Other clubs run at lunchtime and after school include computing, sewing, animation, art, touch typing and yoga.

Sensible levels of homework. Reception pupils get reading every evening, year 1s take spellings home and year 2s and up have homework – once a week in year 2, four nights a week in year 5 and every night in year 6 (but only for 30 minutes). Every so often homework is suspended and girls take part in an 'open homework' project – subjects range from hopes and dreams to heroines (choices included Mother Teresa, Rosa Parks and Malala Yousafzai; one girl nominated her granny). Girls have two PE lessons a week (gym, dance, netball, cricket), with weekly swimming from reception through to year 4.

The school is academically selective so while some have learning support for dyslexia and dyscalculia they must be able to cope with the pace of the curriculum. Support given one-to-one or in small groups. Strong links with the senior school. Girls from years 7 and 10 come and read to their junior counterparts, year 12s run a Minimus Club for year 4 girls and many pop in to say hello to their former teachers. Music, led by a former professional opera singer, is a tour de force. Girls take instrumental lessons from year 3 and there's an 80-piece orchestra. Plenty of opportunities to perform in concerts, bands and choirs too.

The junior school is located in a well-kept Victorian villa on a quiet residential road. It's on the same site as the senior school, with a green Astroturf, playground and south-facing garden at the back. Whole school assemblies are held twice a week in the junior hall but the junior girls also use the senior school's impressive hall and indoor swimming pool. The girls, in jaunty navy and red uniforms, walk across to the senior dining room for lunch. They all belong to one of four teams which compete for an annual team cup. Great emphasis placed on self-esteem, confidence and being happy at school and as girls progress through the school they take on responsibilities such as acting as 'playground pals' to younger pupils and elected reps on the school council.

Most pupils live relatively nearby. The majority have two working parents (lots of doctors, lawyers and media types) and the school runs a breakfast club from 7.30am and an after-school club till 6pm, both run by staff rather than an outside agency.

The last word: An academically excellent school that nurtures its pupils and helps them to develop into happy, confident girls. The head says that it's vital that the girls are happy – and they really are.

Notting Hill and Ealing High School

36

2 Cleveland Road, London W13 8AX

020 8799 8400 | enquiries@nhehs.gdst.net | www.nhehs.gdst.net

Independent	Pupils: 594; sixth form: 142
Ages: 11–18	Fees: £19,212 pa

Linked school: Notting Hill and Ealing High Junior School, 551

Head: Since January 2017, Matthew Shoults MA (40s). Educated at King's College School, Wimbledon, then read classics at Worcester College, Oxford. Spent two years on the civil service's graduate fast track scheme before deciding he wanted to be a teacher. After doing a PGCE at Cambridge he taught classics at King's, his old school, for four years. Moved to North London Collegiate School as head of classics, becoming deputy head and then senior deputy. After 12 years there he was appointed to the top job at Notting Hill and Ealing High School.

The first male head in the school's 145-year history, he was struck from the start by its warmth and friendliness. During his first visit one girl told him: 'It's a school of conversations,' while another said: 'The teachers trust and believe in us.' 'Yes, it's academic,' he says, 'but it's a happy place to be. It's our job to nurture the girls – and nurture their ambitions. It's incredibly easy to progress here.' Parents are impressed by his energy and dynamism and like the fact that he's very visible around the school. 'He's bringing in new ideas and is really good for the school,' one told us. Another said that the girls respected him and found him 'down-to-earth and easy to talk to'. Head has launched a drive to get as many pupils as possible involved in public speaking. We attended morning assembly during our visit and after notices about the forthcoming inter-house maths challenge and an appeal for clothes and toiletries for refugees, a group of engaging sixth form girls led a presentation about how languages affect the way we think. The head encourages pupils to come up with new ideas – girls often put their heads round his door and say 'I've had an idea'. Recent suggestions, both implemented, saw the launch of a dissection society and an origami club.

Head sees all year 11s as they decide their A level choices and all year 13s before they leave. He teaches public speaking and debating to all year 7 pupils so he can get to know them, will teach Greek to sixth formers next year and already spends time helping girls with their university applications. He often describes people as 'a good egg' and was amused when sixth formers presented him with an egg box labelled 'a pack of good eggs'. Inside were six decorated eggs, one depicting the head. In his spare time he plays the violin, sings, does cryptic crosswords and 'spoils' his three godchildren. He's also part of the way through climbing Scotland's 282 Munros.

Entrance: Very oversubscribed but doesn't give out application numbers – 'because we don't want to put parents off'. Around 45 girls move up from the junior school each year, with another 50 coming from local primaries and preps. The school is a member of the London 11+ Consortium and entry now consists of a 75-minute cognitive ability test incorporating verbal, non-verbal and maths questions. At 12+/13+, maths, English and MFL exams. All applicants to the senior school have a one-to-one interview. 'We are looking for girls with an inquiring nature,' says the head. 'We don't have a type. One of the fundamental aims of the school is for them to be themselves.'

Six or seven girls join the sixth form from other schools. They must have at least eight 9-7s at GCSE, including in all their proposed A level subjects, plus a short interview and aptitude test.

Exit: A handful leave after GCSEs, usually for co-ed independents and state schools. Some decide to head back within a few weeks and the school accommodates them if it can. Virtually all go straight to university (very few gap years), majority to Russell Group with five to Oxbridge and fourt medics in 2020. Several a year to art foundations. STEM related degrees on the up (now making up a quarter of all university courses), including mechanical engineering, architecture and cyber security and computer forensics.

Latest results: In 2020, 93 per cent 9-7 at GCSE; 70 per cent A*/A at A level (90 per cent A*-B). In 2019 (the last year when exams took place), 89 per cent 9-7 at GCSE; 55 per cent A*/A (83 per cent A*-B).

Teaching and learning: Results are impressive. Most popular A level subjects tend to be maths, biology and chemistry but arts and sciences are equally represented. Girls can take virtually any combination of subjects (luckily the assistant timetabler used to be a railway timetabler) and even if only one or two girls want to do an A level subject the school will run it. Most take three or four subjects at A level (25 subjects to choose from, including history of art, economics, psychology and politics) and 10 or 11 at GCSE. EPQ is growing in popularity for sixth formers and year 12 students take a variety of enrichment courses, choosing from an eclectic list of topics, from medieval art to the psychology of happiness.

Head often describes people as 'a good egg' and was amused when sixth formers presented him with an egg box labelled 'a pack of good eggs'

Languages are strong here. All study Mandarin in year 7, plus a carousel system of French, German or Spanish; from year 8, girls choose two from these four languages and continue with them in year 9. Most take two languages at GCSE. Excellent take-up of Mandarin at GCSE and a high proportion of top grades. There's also a biennial trip to China. Latin is taught from year 8, with classical Greek offered from year 10. Class sizes of around 24, with maths the only subject set (from year 8). 'We want to create a sense that they aren't competing against each other,' says the head. 'It's how they are doing themselves that's important.'

Learning support and SEN: Two dedicated learning support staff offer extra help where needed. Parents say the academic side of the school is 'very solid' and praise the way it helps new year 7s transition to senior school life. 'They want to them to settle in their friendship groups and develop their confidence before the work ramps up,' said one mother.

The arts and extracurricular: Music is a real strength of the school. A multitude of individual music lessons and plenty of opportunities to play in orchestras and ensembles and sing in choirs. Recent choral tours to Barcelona, Florence and

Croatia. Less experienced musicians get the chance to build their confidence by performing in atrium concerts. Parents say drama is 'fantastic' (there's a studio space as well as the main hall). School play every year, with girls designing the sets, lighting and costumes as well as performing and directing. Art department is vibrant and exciting, boasting three purpose-built studios kitted out with everything from digital scanners to a printing press. Several girls a year head to do art foundation and architecture courses.

Vast range of extracurricular clubs, many of them student led. Work experience is compulsory in year 11 and most girls find their own placements. On the day of our visit an enterprising sixth former was busy organising a fashion show at the school and had fixed for a national newspaper fashion editor and a representative from a well-known sports brand to attend.

Sport: Sport is important (at the time of our visit the new director of sport had been shortlisted for the London's sports teacher of the year award). The site is compact but clever architects have managed to fit a lot into the space. New four-court sports hall is impressive, as are the Astroturfs and 25-metre indoor pool. Sixth formers can train as lifeguards. The new extension to the school has added a stunning rooftop dance studio and fitness gym, with views across the school. All pupils take part in sport, from mainstream sports like netball, hockey, tennis and athletics to activities like cross-country, trampolining, running, badminton, cricket, football, zumba, yoga and kickboxing. Many notable local and national successes, including winning the year 7 Middlesex cricket tournament and reaching the national finals in U14 netball.

Ethos and heritage: The oldest school in the Girls' Day School Trust (GDST) portfolio, Notting Hill and Ealing High School was founded in Notting Hill in 1873 and moved to leafy Ealing in 1930. The site has been transformed in recent years – a dazzling reworking of the central core of the school retained the school's period façade and a sleek glass extension has been added at the rear, with a spacious library, ultra-modern assembly hall, music recital hall, recording studio and sports hall. The extension looks out over a tree-lined courtyard with lots of benches to sit on during the summer months. Parents like the school's size. 'It's like Goldilocks,' said one. 'Neither too hot nor too cold. Neither too big nor too small.'

Sixth formers enthuse about their sixth form centre, a former children's home a five-minute walk away from the main site and equipped with six classrooms, common room, gym and café serving sandwiches, jacket potatoes, pasta, tea and

Parents like the school's size. 'It's like Goldilocks,' said one. 'Neither too hot nor too cold. Neither too big nor too small'

coffee. Sixth form classes are small, girls don't have to wear uniform (no midriffs and no strappy tops) and they can go home in the afternoon if they don't have lessons. 'The sixth form girls like the fact that they get the support and outward-facing perspective but we aren't cocooning them,' says the head. Parents agree. One told us that her daughter had thrived in the sixth form. 'The environment is very nurturing but they are treated as adults too,' she said. Head of the sixth form reminds the girls of the importance of maintaining a healthy work-life balance – 'the vast majority are very sensible,' she says. Plenty of opportunities for leadership roles. Contenders for the role of head girl have to write a letter of application, make a speech and have an interview. All sixth formers are school reps and there's also a six-strong head girl team (including a sports captain).

Strong emphasis on helping others – girls of all ages raise money for chosen charities by running cake sales, nearly new sales, games and raffles. Strong links with the local community, including a Saturday morning Mandarin club for primary school children and a netball tournament for nearby primary schools run by year 10 girls.

Distinguished alumnae include historian Bettany Hughes, Labour MP Rupa Huq, stand-up comic Pippa Evans, London Grammar singer Hannah Reid and 2018 GDST alumna of the year Nirupa Murugaesu, the clinical lead for molecular oncology at Genomics England.

Pastoral care, inclusivity and discipline: This is a school where pastoral care is prioritised as much as academic drive. When the head arrived he was struck by how 'joined-up' the pastoral care is. It's overseen by senior deputy head (pastoral) and staff work closely with parents. Heads of year meet form tutors every week to problem-solve and discuss any concerns. Girls can also talk to the school nurse and counsellor.

New year 7s are well supported via the big sister scheme (year 12s act as big sisters to them, offering help when they need it). Other activities include a picnic with year 8s and the chance to write a letter to their future selves, expressing their hopes and ambitions. Much to their delight, they receive it back in year 11.

All the girls we met were enthusiastic about being in an all-girls school. 'It's far more relaxed without boys,' one told us. Parents say that issues and concerns are handled well – 'in a very thoughtful and individualised way'. In years 7 to 11 girls have to put their mobile phones in lockers when they arrive at school – 'if they are spotted with their phone we have a word with them,' says the head.

Pupils and parents: The pupils we met were enthusiastic, outgoing and full of charm. One parent told us that the girls were six months behind their central London counterparts when it came to social life and teenage parties – 'and we are very grateful for that,' she added. Girls predominantly come from Ealing, Chiswick, Hammersmith, Harrow, Notting Hill, Richmond and Kew. Travel links are good and 70 per cent travel in by public transport – tube, train and bus (the bus from Ealing Broadway stops right outside the school). They are a very grounded group of girls – 'in touch with reality,' says the head. Most parents work (lots of doctors, lawyers and media types).

Money matters: The GDST has been providing high-quality academic education at a reasonable cost for nearly 150 years and Notting Hill and Ealing High does exactly that. Academic scholarships worth up to 50 per cent of the fees and music scholarships worth 10 per cent of the fees are available for year 7s. For those entering the sixth form there are academic, art, music, sport and drama scholarships worth five to 10 per cent of the fees. Means-tested bursaries available too (scholarships can be supplemented by these).

The last word: A forward-looking school that provides a stimulating education in a friendly and nurturing environment. Academic achievements are excellent and these energetic, exuberant girls are definitely a force to be reckoned with.

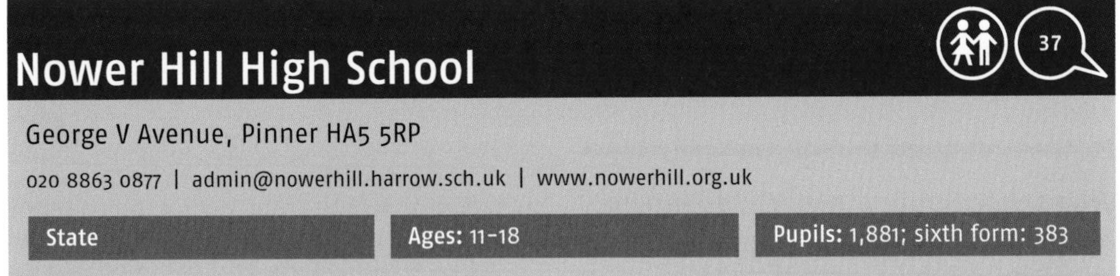

Nower Hill High School

George V Avenue, Pinner HA5 5RP

020 8863 0877 | admin@nowerhill.harrow.sch.uk | www.nowerhill.org.uk

State | **Ages:** 11-18 | **Pupils:** 1,881; sixth form: 383

Head: Since September 2019, Louise Voden, previously deputy head with a student support remit, and the school's safeguarding lead.

Entrance: Hugely oversubscribed. Approx 1,400 applications are submitted each year group for 324 places. Waiting list system is operated by the local authority. School catchment is roughly a mile, and you'll get in if you have a sibling or a looked after child. However, one unhappy parent told us: 'My only real gripe with the school is that the sibling policy stops at GCSE, so if you have a bigger age gap between your children, there is no guarantee at all that they will get in.'

Exit: Around 35 per cent leave after GCSEs, mostly to do vocational courses elsewhere. Over 90 per cent of sixth form students go on to university and over a third to Russell Group. In 2020, two to Oxbridge, and four medics. Popular courses include computer science, economics and psychology. Oxbridge admissions preparation with academic mentors who have themselves been to Oxford or Cambridge. Popular destinations also include elite art colleges and music conservatoires. The few who don't head to uni go into employment, take a gap year or get an apprenticeship at eg Google and BT.

Latest results: In 2019, 36 per cent 9-7 at GCSE; 65 per cent of students got 9-4 in both English and maths. At A level, 21 per cent A*/A (54 per cent A*-B).

Teaching and learning: This Ofsted outstanding school is well known in the area for its academic standards. One local parent told us: 'Nower Hill has always had a good reputation, now it has an excellent one.' Part of its success could be down to its class sizes of 25 pupils, spread across 12 forms in a year group, part of it could be down to the dedicated teachers 'who always have their lines of communication open to parents' to the point where one parent told us: 'I feel a bit sorry for the teachers. They work so hard during the day and then call or email us back straight away if we have a query.' Ofsted said: 'The leadership of teaching and learning is exceptional.' Staff feel that one of the reasons for the school's success is that 'we pride ourselves on working hard for all learners.'

'For a not particularly competitive school, they still get the results,' one parent told us. Another said, 'The school does very well at stretching bright children, whilst at the same time providing a round education for everyone.'

The curriculum is wide and varied with 24 optional subjects offered at GCSE level (Mandarin offered as an extracurricular language), with more able students being offered the opportunity to learn ancient Greek and astronomy. An enthusiastic parent told us: 'The options in year 8 are fantastic. Students start their GCSE course in year 9 and they are given a chance to chop and change a bit for the first term and decide if it is the right course for them.'

Each student has been given their own tablet, which they can take home and use for homework. Quite extraordinary in a school of 1,900 pupils and clearly highlights the school's priorities in terms funding. One parent told us: 'It's things like this that make this school so progressive.' The head is quick to point out that this is an educational tool only and that students don't have access to Facebook or Twitter: 'Everything they need has been put on there for them.'

This school puts a big 'C' in charity. When we were there, a dedicated area of the school hall had been given over to black bags, full of clothes and toys for Syrian refugees

Parents have also welcomed an online app called Show my Homework where students, parents and carers can access homework details and retrieve and submit work online. Students also have their own personal portfolio where they can store all their electronic documents, allowing access to them in or out of school. It is part of the school's Managed Learning Environment (MLE) for which Nower Hill won the award for secondary schools.

Learning support and SEN: Excellent facilities for students with disabilities, including ramps, improved corridor lighting, lifts, handrails on steps, widened doorways for wheelchair access and yellow lines to assist visually impaired students. Roughly 13 per cent of the school intake is registered with an SEN. For those students, a well-supported inclusion staff team is on hand to offer extra support, including a SENCo, qualified SEN teachers, inclusion manager, behaviour manager, mentor and counsellor. There is also extra support for maths and English

The arts and extracurricular: The school has a very long tradition of strength in the arts subjects, which was evident as we walked round. Astoundingly good self-portraits from GCSE students were on display as well as an interesting montage of student-designed film posters. Several of Nower Hill's art students have had their work displayed in local art galleries, national exhibitions and at the Mall Galleries. Many continue their art studies post-A level, at well-respected art colleges. Photography also strong.

Drama is popular and taken up in fair abundance. Big scale biennial musicals, which have included The Lion King and Oliver! Watford drama winners recently. The dance department offers a wide range of extracurricular dance activities including contemporary dance, tap, ballet, Bollywood, street dance and modern. There are many performance opportunities available both in and out of school; school productions, a dance showcase, summer extravaganza and a performance at the Royal Albert Hall.

Musical students have a choice of a dozen ensemble music groups and orchestras to take part in, including a soul band, and school hosts concerts several times a year. Some 400 pupils have peripatetic music classes, and groups include everything from steel pan ensemble to African drumming to a full 51 piece school orchestra. Well-equipped recording studios. One pupil told us: 'This school really caters well in all departments and has something for everyone.'

Aspiration is definitely a buzzword at Nower High, and an Aspire programme is run on Wednesday and Thursday lunchtimes for Y12 and Y13. This programme helps to develop 'interview, thinking and critical analysis skills, provides personal feedback and mentoring' to ensure students have the best possible chance at future employment. Training is also offered to become mentors for younger students and give older students the opportunity to run lower school science, sports and dance clubs as well as a variety of other leadership roles.

This school really puts a big 'C' in charity. It doesn't do things to tick boxes, or to excite an over-zealous PTA. Pupils seem to be charitable to the core. When we were there, a dedicated area of the school hall had been given over to black bags, full of clothes and toys for Syrian refugees: 'We like to instil charitable values in children of a young age.' School fundraising events have included a leavers' ball, pizza and quiz event and charity sports fixtures against staff. There is also the opportunity for sixth formers to work voluntarily in an orphanage in Romania as well as with

One parent told us: 'This school's motto should be above and beyond. They really do go the extra mile here'

elderly people in the local community. Events are planned throughout the year to raise money for their chosen charity – St Marcellin's Children's Village in Zimbabwe.

Sport: Sports play a big part in the school and there is a wide range of activities. The faculty prides itself on 'giving very generously of its time'. Sports include netball, basketball, handball, rugby, trampolining and indoor athletics. All clubs are fully inclusive. School athletes compete at borough, county and national level with 'considerable success'. Sporting facilities include a 3G Astroturf pitch, two tiered grass playing fields, six tennis courts, six netball courts a multi-purpose sports hall, fitness suite and gymnasium.

Ethos and heritage: Formerly Headstone Council School, this red-brick building on Pinner Road first opened its doors in 1929. The school's purpose was to educate 292 5-14-year-olds with an average class size of 50. The school soon expanded to meet the ever-growing number of children resident in rapidly expanding north Harrow and Pinner. Its steady expansion has withstood many a hitch including the Second World War, when many of its male teachers were called up for military service and the playing field was dug up for trenches and air raid shelters.

Redevelopment work continued throughout the 60s and 70s (when the school became Nower Hill) – continuing throughout the 90s, which saw the start of a £2.75 million development programme, including a new 13 classroom block and the Gristwood Centre, housing music, dance and drama studios, a fitness suite and the sports hall. The school added a sixth form in 2006, which a few years later moved into its £4 million sixth form extension. The site was further enhanced in 2010 by the addition of a block of five science labs and a new English teaching block hosting 13 classrooms. This is one big site.

As a result, the site is a bit of a hotchpotch of buildings, none of them particularly pretty, but functional and purposeful and very much in keeping with large comprehensives. Plus, as every parents knows, schools are much more than bricks and mortar – and this school is so much more. The pupils who showed us around were extremely articulate, warm, kind and very proud of their school. Big mix culturally and harmonious atmosphere. Room after room was explained with equal enthusiasm (even the less aesthetically pleasing ones), and each montage on colourful walls was discussed in detail – especially those of past school trips. We were taken through a labyrinth of corridors and would've lost our bearings many a time if it weren't for our guides. There were a few nice touches we spotted on our tour, most notably the 'ancient' Greek columns outside the classics department (homage, possibly, to the head, who is partial to a bit of classics).

Other things worth mentioning include the spacious library, well equipped with books and computers, and six different outlets for food and snacks, including a cold canteen for grab-and-go pastas and salads and a hot canteen. However, one parent did say that the downside of such a large school is the difficulty in accommodating everyone: 'My son finds school dinners all a bit stressful and too much of an effort to have something hot. There are just too many other kids and often nowhere to sit. I think they should stagger it more.' Sixth formers have now been offered the incentive of a £1 coffee and cookie in the common room, instead of traipsing to the local café and wasting valuable time.

Pastoral care, inclusivity and discipline: Discipline is 'bang on', one parent told us: 'For a school with this many children, you really don't hear of many incidents like bullying etc, and if there are, they are dealt with quickly and appropriately.' One parent told us: 'The teachers always walk out with the kids at the end of the day and often accompany them to the local shops. That way the shopkeepers are always reassured that a grown-up is with them.' Another said, 'You never ever see any Nower Hill pupils lighting up outside the school gates or nearby, like at other schools. The students here are very aware that they are representatives of the school and they wear their uniform proudly.'

Uniform is a very smart navy affair, with the odd splash of varying colours on the V-neck pullovers denoting the year group. All blazers have the school's crest with the motto 'service not self' emblazoned on it. Although strict on uniform, school does display a softer side, especially in relation to the assortment of hair colour that passed us by (most noticeably green), on our tour of the school: 'We won't argue with a child about their hair. It's a very happy environment here and that's the main thing.'

In a school of this size, we wondered how feasible it is to oversee the well-being of all students and to prevent the more vulnerable ones from slipping through the cracks: 'We work very hard at keeping a large school, a small school.'

And indeed Nower Hill does seem to have a pretty robust infrastructure. There is a full-time attendance officer who works with parents around punctuality and is there to pick up on any possible issues. There are two co-ordinators for every year group and a well-staffed student support team. There are also two peer mentors for new students allocated to each class.

One parent told us: 'This school's motto should be above and beyond. They really do go the extra mile here. The lines of communication are always open if you need to speak to a teacher, and somebody always gets back to you pretty promptly.' Another told us how the school bent over backwards to help facilitate her daughter's studies after a long period absent due to ill health: 'Home tutoring was arranged for my daughter as soon as we needed it and the tutor was very impressed with the excellent support material provided to her from the school.'

Recently reintroduced new house system designed to reflect the core values of the school. These six houses have been named after influential people who, together, inspire millions around the globe – Gandhi, King, Shabazz, Franklin, Bannister and Nightingale – and this reintroduction has been has been welcomed by pupils. One told us, 'It's more fun and you become loyal to your house. It also promotes a healthy competition between the houses on things like sports days.'

The school sees the qualities of being well mannered, articulate, well behaved, hard working, smart and kind as part of the DNA, and reminders are displayed throughout the school. Ofsted said in the last report that: 'Student' behaviour is excellent... the school provides an orderly, welcoming environment entirely conducive to learning.'

As with any school, particularly of this size, disruptive pupils will always be an issue. However, school says that permanent exclusions are below the national average: 'We have very high expectations here. Any poor student behaviour is dealt with in a clear and consistent manner' through what the school calls its Ladder of Consequences. This includes an inclusion centre for students temporarily excluded from lessons, which is equipped with computers and other educational resources.

Pupils and parents: Pupils and parents pretty much reflect the general demographic of the local area of Pinner and north Harrow. Roughly 30 per cent white British, nearly half Asian and the rest a mixture of other ethnicities. Parents are largely professionals, pupils aspirational.

The last word: If you live in the north Harrow area and are within catchment of this school, applying for it is a bit of a no-brainer.

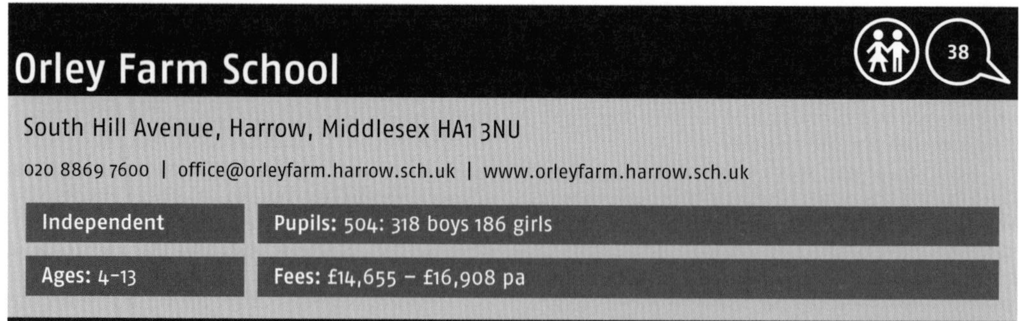

Orley Farm School

38

South Hill Avenue, Harrow, Middlesex HA1 3NU

020 8869 7600 | office@orleyfarm.harrow.sch.uk | www.orleyfarm.harrow.sch.uk

Independent	Pupils: 504: 318 boys 186 girls
Ages: 4–13	Fees: £14,655 – £16,908 pa

Headmaster: Since 2013, Tim Calvey (40s), formerly school's deputy head and art teacher. Hailing from a teaching dynasty, grew up in Zimbabwe in the boarding house run by his father. Passionate about sport and art, got his teaching degree at Christ Church University before cutting his teeth at Northbourne Park School in Kent under an inspirational head 'who pushed all the boundaries', then landing at Eagle House (Wellington College's prep) around the same time as Anthony Seldon took the helm at the senior school – spending a six-year period there that 'shaped him'. In true Seldon style, impassioned by well-being and development – 'we have to find ways to release the pressure children are under.' A challenge indeed in this most competitive of postcodes.

Shades of Gareth Malone – sharp, quirky dress sense, warm charisma, palpable energy and a real human touch. Parents uniformly comment on how informal he is compared to other local prep heads. Happily donned Willy Wonka costume at behest of parent committee at recent Christmas fair. Pupils describe him as 'effervescent' (well done that child's English teacher), 'enthusiastic' and 'funny' – the first head we have met known to wear Iron Man cufflinks. Rarely have we seen a head teacher so naturally connect with even his youngest charges, all of whom chat away to him merrily. Feels 'huge duty of care' to bright children and warns destination obsessed parents that it's about the journey and that Orley Farm is 'not for them if they just want their child tutored – we don't want to be defined by either the name of the school or our grades.'

Lives on school grounds with wife Rachel, who teaches RS and science at the school, and his three children – all of whom have attended Orley Farm.

Entrance: Vast majority enter at 4+ with places oversubscribed by about three to one. Children are observed participating in a carousel of activities and head is clear: 'don't bother tutoring your 4-year-old' – school is looking for 'sparky children' and doesn't expect them to read or write. Around 20 places come up for year 7 when many girls, and a few boys, leave for 11+ schools. Short shrift given if potential parents are looking for prep merely as springboard to top schools. 'Have I put parents off with this attitude?' muses head. 'Probably.'

Exit: Huge breadth of destination schools – most recently Merchant Taylors', Mill Hill, Northwood College, Parmiter's, Queenswood, Rugby, South Hampstead High School for Girls, St Albans School, St Bernard's Grammar, St Helen's, St Paul's School for Girls, John Lyon, Royal Masonic, Westminster, Aldenham, Haberdashers' Aske's (boys and girls), Haileybury and Harrow. Seven scholarships awarded in 2020 (academic and music).

Our view: Occupies a Tardis-like plot fronted by a Victorian school building, tucked into a leafy residential area. Having just finished an £11 million refurb programme, school boasts smart classrooms and facilities galore (barely a tatty corner in sight), plus not only the shiniest dining room for miles around but also a state of the art library designed to inspire the most reluctant of readers. Delightful grounds sprawl behind the main school building, providing space for all manner of activities – as well as the Orley Farm chickens (the box of freshly laid eggs we were given on departure, rather than the usual piles of self-promoting literature, could almost be a metaphor for how this school differs from others). Main playing fields amounting to some 40 acres are over the road, plus separate gym and sports hall, pool and Astroturf.

A holistic vibe in evidence at every turn. Recent introduction of the Creative Curriculum in pre-prep much welcomed by parents who feel it 'brings topics alive' for the school's youngest pupils, to the extent that they want to do more under their own steam when they get home. The Edge programme, which sees children participate in experiences from planning – then following unaccompanied – a route into central London on public transport to fixing a bicycle puncture or spending time with local elderly people, demonstrates that school is not just paying lip service to developing EQ as well as IQ. There is, however, a question mark over how unanimous parents are in supporting this approach – definite rumblings in evidence from those who would like school to fall into line with local academic hothouses and reports of parents demanding homework for their 5- and 6-year-olds (then setting it themselves when not forthcoming). This is explicable by school's demographic, typified by its geography. Around 70 per cent of families are Asian, with the vast majority dual income professionals, 'incredibly committed to education,' according to head. Many Harrow School and some John Lyon staff in parent cohort. Pupils, thankfully, come over as carefree, likeable and down to earth – head 'can't stand arrogance'. Teachers reportedly 'go the extra mile' and pre-prep parents are delighted with recent appointments of young staff.

The box of freshly laid eggs we were given on departure, rather than the usual piles of self-promoting literature, could be a metaphor for how this school differs from others

Curriculum broad, with majority of girls heading for 11+ and boys for 13+ exit. French and Latin in the languages department, with a taste of Greek at the top of the school. Gentle setting from summer term of year 2 and children are class taught for most subjects until year 5. Classes maxed at 21, often with smaller numbers in English and maths sets. Head says 'academic life is a given – we go a long way beyond what's expected.' Staff ratios are 'absurd', he says, with a full-time classroom assistant in every class up to year 4. Full-time SENCo plus some part-timers to assist those with additional needs. Around 30 children currently supported with anything ranging from organisational skills to mild dyslexia, with withdrawal avoided wherever possible. Open to taking children with greater needs, recently profound deafness, as long as they are able to successfully access curriculum.

DT and art in strong evidence, both with impressive studios. Head still teaches art – his lessons greeted with enthusiastic fist pumps from pupils. Drama on curriculum to year 8; dynamic teacher who has breathed life into performances. Music, though, is the jewel in Orley Farm's crown, with choirs and ensembles galore ranging from the Fab Fives which sing 'funky' hits to the chamber choir which tackles three part harmonies with reported aplomb. Compulsory recorder for all in year 2 and over 90 per cent of all pupils learn a peripatetic instrument. Unsurprisingly, given facilities, sport high on agenda with 'strong' rugby and netball, a non-compulsory Saturday morning sports academy and A to E teams fielded whenever opposing schools are big enough to match their numbers. A few grumbles from parents that school could do more to develop those with less talent, but overall sports universally praised.

Four houses encourage 'healthy competition' amongst pupils and children are given positions of responsibility right from reception. We love the playground traffic light system used for solving disputes – no teachers involved, just worldly-wise year 3 pupils to mediate spats. Each class has a form tutor as well as form teacher to monitor pastoral well-being. Psychodynamic counsellor on staff two days each week, with children able to self-refer for help with concerns related or totally unrelated to school (fears, phobias, stress). Extracurricular activities, known as 'hobbies', not as broad or varied as at some schools but solid, with all the usual suspects. Wonderful annual Expeditions Week which takes everyone from year 4 up all over the place from mountaineering in Wales to 'total immersion' in a French château. Best of all, it's included in the fees.

The last word: Going places under fabulous head. If you're looking for a school to drive your child hard towards academic superstardom and a ticket to a top academic secondary, Orley Farm probably isn't for you. If, however, you want them to skip joyously into school every day, have time to play when they come home – and quite possibly land one of those coveted top school places on the grounds of their roundedness, likeability and passion for learning – get your name on the list and cross fingers and toes (tutoring won't work).

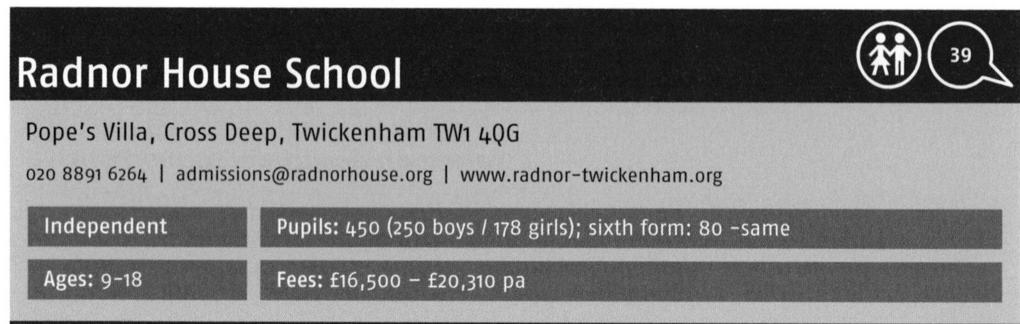

Radnor House School

39

Pope's Villa, Cross Deep, Twickenham TW1 4QG

020 8891 6264 | admissions@radnorhouse.org | www.radnor-twickenham.org

Independent	Pupils: 450 (250 boys / 178 girls); sixth form: 80 -same
Ages: 9-18	Fees: £16,500 – £20,310 pa

Head: Since September 2017, Darryl Wideman (50s). Previously head at Silcoates School in Yorkshire and taught at Millfield and Fettes. Read ancient and modern history at Oxford; still teaches a year 12 class. Grew up in Surrey and pleased to be back in the area – lives nearby with his wife and daughter, now at university. Loves reading, gardening and spending time at his house in France – 'I must sound terribly boring'. Far from it, we found him very engaging, with more of a twinkle in his eye than one might expect given his straight-talking approach. 'Perhaps I'm not fluffy enough for some,' he says, though most admire his ability to make decisions and deliver on them. 'Doesn't pander to the south-west London mums,' we were told, though he dismisses any stereotypes about this affluent part of the world: 'It's a myth that they're more demanding than elsewhere – parents are parents wherever you go.'

Refreshingly open about Radnor's changing place in the landscape: 'In the early days they sometimes came because they couldn't get anywhere else,' he says, but now 'we punch above our weight'. Proud and supportive of his staff. 'My job is to get the very best out of everybody in this organisation, children and grown-ups.' Accepts that exam results will always be regarded as a measure of a school's success but seems confident that Radnor's results will continue to improve without needing to apply more pressure.

Entrance: Main entrance points into years 5, 7 and 12. Reports and references from current school are important. Entrance to year 5 for 20 children based on English and maths tests and classroom activities, including a show and tell. Guaranteed place for them in year 7 unless there is a major issue. There are 45-50 further places available in year 7 depending on performance in written English and maths tests and an interview. Potential scholars invited back for a scholarship interview. Year 12 hopefuls submit a personal statement and are then interviewed by director of sixth form, head and head of department in each of their chosen A levels.

The intention is to gain a rounded view of every candidate while not making the process 'too gruesome', though we heard that it's getting more competitive. Applicants from other Dukes schools have an unofficial edge. Siblings are given priority but only if the school is otherwise the right fit, and more than one parent to whom we spoke was nervous that their younger son or daughter would not make the cut.

Exit: Around a third leave after GCSE mainly to bigger local sixth forms. University destinations reflect the range of the intake, with 60 per cent to Russell Group. Exeter remains popular ('south-west London on sea', one parent muses), plus Durham, Edinburgh, York, Bristol and Southampton. Oxbridge success in 2020 was school's first, though a few have a go each year. A handful to Imperial, UCL and LSE. Specialists support those on medic or Oxbridge 'pathways' from year 11. They don't push it, though: 'we're hitting the right names but not trying to bump our reputation by squeezing pupils into universities that aren't right for them,' says Mr Wideman and parents agree that 'nobody is traumatised by the UCAS process'. Growing experience with school leavers' programmes and apprenticeships at eg KPMG and Dyson.

Latest results: In 2020, 55 per cent 9-7 at GCSE; 48 per cent A*/A at A level (79 per cent A*-B). In 2019 (the last year when exams took place), 40 per cent 9-7 at GCSE; 27 per cent A*/A at A level (52 per cent A*-B).

Teaching and learning: Confidence flying high after inspectors declared the school 'excellent' across the board for the first time in February 2020 – head admits he shed a tear. Long seen as an academic back-up in a competitive area, Radnor's 'caring and compassionate' approach to results has been vindicated. 'We may not be first choice for parents who want A*s across the board', but a careful balance of encouragement and pressure seems to be working.

Indeed, we found Radnor parents to be ambitious for their children, while retaining a healthy sense of humour about it all. Many seemed relieved to have found a school where results are one part of a bigger picture – 'I know that her A*s will not come from being over pushed,' said one. There's no denial that there's a (relatively) broad range of abilities here; the emphasis is on getting the best out of every child, regardless of their starting point. The secret? Young, approachable, engaging teachers who stretch rather than push – as one biology teacher remarked to his year 11 class, 'This is way beyond GCSE, but it's interesting, right?' (Yes, it was.)

Pupils and parents gush about the teachers across the board – 'brilliant', 'sensitive', 'beyond fantastic' – nobody had a bad word to say

At A level, take-up is always strong in maths, with social sciences like economics, geography, psychology usually popular (given the small cohorts numbers vary year by year). As ever, just a few opting for languages – a handful doing French or Spanish A levels. EPQ growing in popularity. Happy to run an A level even if only one or two are taking it – individual teaching not unheard of. No doubt the refurbishment of the sixth form common room and creation of more dedicated sixth form teaching rooms will entice more year 11s to stay.

Pupils and parents gush about the teachers across the board – 'brilliant', 'sensitive', 'beyond fantastic' – nobody had a bad word to say. One, bowled over by her daughter's improvement in maths, told us, 'she has gone from saying "I can't do it" to "I can't do it yet".' Parents trust the teaching staff but are pleased nonetheless to be able to email them directly to check in on progress. Classrooms are small ('cosy', pupils told us) but immaculate, with stimulating displays everywhere; one English classroom had quotes from Shakespeare written all over the windows in whiteboard pen. Marking is meaningful and encourages children to reflect on teacher comments.

Unencumbered by 11+ exams, junior school pupils enjoy a fairly carefree existence. On a scorching September day, new year 5s were scampering around on the terrace carrying enormous numbers – learning about decimal places? Maybe. Having a lovely time? Most definitely. There's 'lots of baseline testing', though, we are assured. These children, and their parents, know just how lucky they are to have escaped the local 11+ rat-race. Funnily enough, although they are now part of a senior school one feels that these children have been allowed a couple of extra years of childhood compared with their peers at pushier local preps.

Small, welcoming library hosts outside speakers and an annual Harry Potter quiz as well as providing a quiet spot to escape with a book at lunchtime.

Learning support and SEN: Around 12 per cent of pupils have specific learning support requirements, generally mild dyslexia, dyspraxia, hypermobility. Majority are supported in-class – teachers adapt resources and use scaffolding as appropriate. Extra English and maths in a small, welcoming classroom at the top of the school for individuals or groups who would benefit from some extra tuition. No capacity for further specialist intervention in terms of space or staffing.

Those with mobility issues will struggle: set over four floors, the school has a lot of stairs and narrow corridors.

The arts and extracurricular: A packed extracurricular timetable offers something for everyone, particularly in the younger years. Wide-ranging clubs include ukulele, ornithology, chess, puzzles and gardening (run by Mr Wideman, obviously). Healthy balance of traditional with more high-tech: fashion and textiles on the one hand, robotics and coding on the other. Cookery run by the school's chef in the actual kitchen. Recent introduction of vertical houses a sign of the school's new maturity – spelling bees, creative writing, sporting competitions and debating all present chances to win house points.

Rowing is big, with regional and national regatta successes recently – unsurprising given the riverside location, though the boathouse itself is located a few minutes away

Approach to music, art and drama is characteristically inclusive. The small theatre-cum-hall hosts civilised 'soirées' a few times each term, when parents get dressed up to enjoy musical performances and canapés – we were charmed. Lots of opportunities to perform besides this, eg choir sings annually at Hampton Court Palace. School has invested in web-based music software to support those who want to work on their compositions from home. Around a quarter of pupils take individual music lessons.

Drama encourages collaboration and builds confidence. School's own small studio theatre is a good space for rehearsal and small performances. Two large-scale productions a year take place at local venues such as St Mary's University or the Waterman's Arts Centre. Senior production of Little Shop of Horrors was a box-office hit – year 7s made up the whole backstage crew. Successful LAMDA programme. Drama offered at GCSE and A level.

Ambitious art department make the most of their limited space. Much evidence of creative thinking, for instance hosting virtual exhibitions using whizzy new software to display student work online. We enjoyed colourful displays of children's work throughout the school – all quite traditional, lots of painting and felt-tips rather than anything particularly high-tech. Lots of extracurricular art for those that want it including a popular digital art club. No DT – there simply isn't the space. Art offered at GCSE and A level and photography as an A level.

Sport: Rugby and football for the boys, netball and hockey for the girls. Mixed cricket teams lower down the school. Main competition is other local co-eds – wouldn't be fair on anyone to be playing the big single sex schools. Every year 7 plays on a team at some point. It's definitely the taking part that counts, though they do win too – U12s rugby team undefeated last season.

Rowing is big, with regional and national regatta successes recently – unsurprising given the riverside location, though the boathouse itself is located a few minutes away alongside Eel Pie Island. Year 7s get to have a go on dry land and are allowed out onto the river from year 8.

Recent partnership with Teddington Cricket Club has enabled super new development a few minutes' drive away. Scandi-style pavilion is straight out of a Condé Nast feature with its pine floors and stained black wooden cladding; the café inside advertises oat milk and babychinos. Lots of nets for the children to practise in and a beautiful pitch with views beyond into Bushy Park. Mixed cricket in years 5-8 is characteristic of the 'get involved, have fun, make friends' approach. Annual parent-staff-children fixtures in both hockey and golf suggest that Radnor families really buy into it.

We encountered mixed feelings about sports provision, though. With a small, co-ed intake it's difficult to field a competitive team. Parents seemed a tad relieved that everybody gets to have a go; no first XV alpha mentality. Pupils are active and there's certainly enough sport going on to satisfy most. Meanwhile, your budding Jonny Wilkinson can get his fix elsewhere – lots seem to play at local clubs on a Saturday.

Ethos and heritage: Very clear ethos, underpinned by four core values – courage, excellence, perseverance and respect. We were pleased that everybody either referred to them or was able to recite them without batting an eyelid.

St Helen's School

Founded in 2011 by David Paton, a former teacher at nearby Harrodian School. His departure in 2016, and then a change in ownership to Dukes Education in 2019, prompted many parents and staff to question whether the school would become more businesslike, losing its core values and charm. 'Radnor parents have had a lot of change,' Wideman says, but he is now excited about building on strong foundations. New ownership has brought new opportunities and more cash, but he still has his freedom – 'there's no micromanaging'. Parents impressed that the owner of Dukes (Aatif Hassan) came to meet them early on. As an alumnus of Radnor's predecessor on its current site, Hassan seems personally invested in its success.

The school occupies an unusual and completely blissful site right on the Thames. The main building is Pope's Villa, a neo-Tudor pile built on the site of Alexander Pope's original house (demolished by a subsequent owner). The school still has access to the wonderful gardens next door which they use for science walks and quiet reading sessions.

The building's history plays a part in the school's identity today, with houses named after Pope and three of his literary contemporaries. Our tour guides were not totally au fait with Pope's work, but were far more knowledgeable on the Easter egg hunt held in Pope's (suitably spooky) grotto each year.

We could have sat on the school's sunny riverside terrace all day, surely one of the most idyllic spots around. We half expected somebody to bring us a gin and tonic; no wonder parents rave about the summer drinks parties. All are welcome at the school's café, which boasts the most impressive range of Pukka teas we have seen. Parents congregate here after drop-off or come to meet a member of staff over coffee. Younger siblings at school elsewhere are brought here for a hot chocolate before pick-up.

It may be very comfortable, but there is no sense of entitlement. Charity boards prominently positioned in the reception area show how this term's chosen charities support those within the school community, including current pupils with chronic illness. This kind of intimacy speaks buckets for the kindness and warmth that pervade the school.

Pastoral care, inclusivity and discipline: Parents, pupils and staff all sang the praises of the pastoral care and in particular how flexible the systems are. We too were impressed. A weekly bulletin to all staff highlights any individuals who are struggling, 'just so that we can all keep an eye on them'. Friendship issues are dealt with swiftly and proactively. That there are only 60 children in a year group allows for strategies that can be adapted to meet the needs of the situation or the individuals involved. A couple of parents became quite emotional in describing to us how sensitively the school had handled difficult situations. The lack of bullying and acceptance of differences suggests that the big-happy-family vibe actually works.

PSHE runs throughout the school. We met year 12s slightly hysterical after a 'horrifying' session on household finances

PSHE, known as 'reflections', runs throughout the school. The usual issues are addressed with an encouraging emphasis on life skills including self-reflection, discussion, listening etc. We met year 12s slightly hysterical after a 'horrifying' session on household finances. Good to see sixth formers actually engaging with PSHE.

Inclusivity comes naturally at a school which a remarkable number of pupils have joined from places that were too big or tough – a lot seem to have arrived in need of some TLC. We found a high level of empathy amongst pupils we spoke to, who seemed to be an emotionally intelligent bunch. There's no LGBTQ+ society, as is now the norm in a lot of schools, but we felt that there would no stigma attached to setting one up and that at Radnor it might actually be quite cool to be different.

Similarly, discipline does not seem to be a worry: 'there's simply nowhere to hide'. Staff seem to know every pupil by name, making it much easier to maintain a sense of calm and order without being draconian. Uniform goes downhill a little as pupils get older but nobody seems to mind too much. Sixth formers look smart and feel grown-up in their 'business attire'. We saw a lot of co-operative teenagers who were happy to tuck their shirts in when told.

Pupils and parents: The pupils we met were chatty and good humoured, delighted to be given the chance to talk about their school. Confident without a hint of arrogance, and charming in a down-to-earth and rather endearing way. Not growing up too quickly. Boys outnumber girls at the top end of the school but year 5 intake is now exactly half and half. Some are from wealthy backgrounds but many have parents working hard to fund private education. Around half arrive from local state primaries and many have considered Radnor alongside local comprehensive or grammar options. Minibuses bring children in from

Ealing, Wimbledon and Chelsea, though the huge majority live nearby.

Money matters: A small number receive bursary support. There are no big endowments to fund this as might be found at an older school but they are doing their best. Academic scholarships (up to 20 per cent of fees) awarded to highest performers in 11+ and 16+ entrance. 'Radnor Values' and all-rounder scholarships (10 per cent of fees) allocated to existing cohort in year 7 and year 12.

The last word: Loving and warm, less frenetic than some of its neighbour schools but no less stimulating for it. Happy children do well: a cliché now, but in reality much harder to achieve than it sounds. Competitive A*-seekers and champion goalscorers should look elsewhere – we found pupils, parents, staff and leadership working together to build a school that provides something a bit different. Radnor may not yet be a name that's dropped at dinner parties, but given the collective satisfaction of parents who have discovered it, it can only be a matter of time.

Reach Academy Feltham

53-55 High Street, Feltham, Middlesex TW13 4AB

020 8893 1099 | admissions@reachacademy.org.uk | www.reachacademyfeltham.com

State | Ages: 4-19 | Pupils: 870; sixth form: 71

Headteacher: Executive headteacher is Ed Vainker MA OBE (30s), previously principal since 2012. Following experiences as Teach First trainee in inner city schools and exposure to US Charter School movement, his burning desire to set up a school to address injustices over dismal prospects for disadvantaged pupils was born. His Eureka moment for a school where the partnership with parents isn't just about education, but everything from aspirations to parenting skills and diet, came in the US (he'd won an educational scholarship) – 'stayed up all night committing educational vision to paper.' Serendipity was the clincher: a mutual friend introduced him to Rebecca Cramer, Reach's co-founder and previously secondary head, now director of education (third co-founder, Jon McIntosh, remains a governor but doesn't have active teaching role). Had to be an all-through school, they decided, so teachers could get to know children, and their families, inside out. Chose Feltham because, although only five miles from Hampton Court Palace, it's a lot grittier and is in the bottom third of areas for education. Hugely impressive, he is idealistic but clear-sighted and everything about him oozes innovation, energy and enthusiasm. OBE in 2019. Parents, all of whom have his mobile number, can't speak highly enough of him: 'An amazing guy, with particularly good listening skills.' 'You can ask him anything.' 'He's created so many opportunities for my children that I feel like I've won the lottery when it comes to schooling.' 'Has never hesitated to make time for me at the drop of a hat, then acts instantly on what I've said.' Lives in Hampton with his wife, an environmentalist, and their two young children. Enjoys travel, sport (refereed son's football team the day before our visit) and family nature-themed activities (most recently armed with bat detectors).

While most parents and some pupils consider Ed (everyone is on first name terms here) to be headteacher, the leadership structure is actually rather more complex. In his last day in office post-Brexit, David Cameron announced the go-ahead for a second school and the plan is for Ed to oversee both. But an ongoing monetary game of tennis between DfE and MoD means they're still waiting for funding, leaving Ed 'slightly in a situation where I'm all dressed up with nowhere to go.' So, despite being a systems and strategy man with policy, curriculum etc all at the ready, for now he remains 'more present on a day-to-day basis'.

Head of secondary school is Beck Owen (30s) who has held the post since 2018. She was a founding teacher at Reach, becoming head of English and then deputy head. English degree from Cardiff and a masters in education leadership; previously taught in Birmingham. Was part of the Getting Ahead London programme, which supports leaders into headteacher roles. 'I came out of university feeling really angry about the inequalities in the system,' she told us. Good news for local families is that there's still plenty of fire in her belly. Lives in Tooting.

Head of primary school since January 2020 is Matilda (Tilly) Browne (30s). Joined as head of year 3 and moved up to literacy lead, assistant head of KS1 alongside curriculum and assessment, deputy head of culture and relationships before moving into current role. Degree in social and political science from Cambridge and she also spent time working as an educational consultant in Hong Kong prior to completing the Teach First programme in Hayes. Lives in Fulham.

Entrance: Over 1,000 families apply for 120 reception places, condemning majority to disappointment – second school can't come soon enough. After looked-after children come nursery pupils qualifying for early years pupil premium, followed by exceptional medical and social needs, siblings, others qualifying for pupil premium, staff children and those living within admissions area (chosen by electronic ballot). No official entry point at year 7 although 11 pupils left (much to disappointment of school) at the end of year 6 in 2019, all to grammars (school expects this to change over time). An additional four or five places become available from reception to year 11 in any one year, mainly due to relocation – waiting lists used to fill spaces (again with electronic ballot).

Cracking team of teachers is key. Highly qualified subject specialists. All addressed by first names, much appreciated by pupils for 'breaking down power dynamics'

Sixth form entrance threshold is five 6s minimum at GCSE with 7s required to study toughest subjects (eg maths, sciences, languages, history). Similar number of 9-4 grades will see you on to a BTec.

Exit: Around a third leave post GCSEs, mostly to Logic Studio School and sixth form colleges – it's a small sixth form so far, so doesn't always have the courses pupils want, plus some don't hit the entry criteria. School is broadening its curriculum to address this. In first first sixth form leavers of 2019, two to study medicine; none to Oxbridge, though one offer for 2020. Others to eg Nottingham, Bristol, Brighton and Durham and more locally to Royal Holloway, Imperial and UCL. Wide range of courses.

Latest results: In 2019, 35 per cent 9-7 at GCSE; 67 per cent 9-5 in both English and maths. At A level (school's first cohort), 19 per cent A*/A (53 per cent A*-B).

Teaching and learning: Impressive GCSE results, ditto for A levels. Ahead of national averages in most areas although the acid test will come in 2021 when first year 11s, home grown from reception, sit GCSEs.

Cracking team of teachers is key. Highly qualified subject specialists, including physics grads from Oxford and Imperial, a geography grad from Cambridge and a maths teacher with a Phd. A lot have done Teach First and many trained here. All addressed by first names, much appreciated by pupils for 'breaking down power dynamics', and they answer texts from early morning to late at night and over hols. A parent told us, 'The quality of relationships is amazing – teachers are expected to know pupils really well.' Mostly young – 'means my kids really relate to them,' thought a parent, while Ed told amusing story of his wife heaping praise on latest annual panto but adding, 'I really don't think you should have had a teacher as the dame' – was in fact a sixth-former. All teach a house style focused on high engagement levels, and all are observed for at least 10 minutes a week and given detailed feedback. Outward looking too, eg assistant head of primary school sits on five DfE panels, advising on curriculum development, and is regularly published. Much is expected of these teachers by way of emotional intelligence and nobody here takes piles of books home as they are constantly reminded that being tired, preoccupied, burnt out etc can affect the quality of their interaction.

Curriculum is home grown with comprehensive A4 workbooks for every lesson in most subjects (and which 110 other schools now subscribe to – great multiplier effect). Keeps everyone on their toes and a building bricks learning culture with (unusually) a seamless transition between years 6 and 7. Ambitious learning outcomes with year 9s, for example, talking effortlessly about totalitarianism – must make grasping Lord of the Flies a piece of cake.

There's role play to develop confidence for reception pupils and the involvement of senior school subject specialists (science, Spanish) from year 3 onwards. Lesson length varies according to subject, little and often for languages but longer sessions (up to two hours for seniors) in literacy and numeracy, which dominate curriculum. Competence in both areas is a non-negotiable that's well understood by parents. Sats results not great (but improving) – school claims it's because they refuse to make them the be-all-and-end-all, favouring a broader learning experience and what they deem to be 'better ways of preparing for GCSEs and beyond'. Setting only in maths from year 10 – 'really important to our culture which isn't about children knowing they are in a top or bottom group.'

Everyone is expected to take between eight and 10 GCSEs with art, music, French and Spanish among the options – most bases covered though no DT. Sixth formers have choice of 18 A levels and two BTecs (music, health and social care) and all do EPQ (well, start one at any rate) – a recent example was on the impact of technology on sleep, with the pupil surveying every child in the school on two different occasions and later producing guidance to parents. School constantly on lookout for ways to raise the bar in sixth form, eg partnership with Hampton School which sends in weekly teachers in chemistry, biology and maths; ditto with physics teachers from Lady Eleanor Holles. Additional partnerships with Eton and St Paul's, and plenty of support around Oxbridge entrance, plus help with summer schools.

Learning support and SEN: Doesn't shirk from SEN, with 3.5 per cent on EHCPs in primary and five per cent in seniors; 20 per cent on SEN register. Thoughtful, inclusive classroom strategies – has lots of ADHD, for instance, so teachers regularly reiterate to everyone what's coming up next – going through what the day will look like, letting families know if there's a different teacher etc. Highly praised TAs – Ofsted couldn't tell the difference between them and the teachers in some classes – and if, say, six children need additional support in a class, it's the teacher who will often lead the group, leaving TA to teach rest of class (reverse of what other schools do 'because those six are the ones who need more expertise,' explains school). Impressive resource centre for eg dyslexia. Maths booster sessions offered at the beginning of the day for those that need it ('works better than catch up lessons,' found school). 'We've had lots of meetings to discuss how to tackle my son's difficulties both in the classroom and at home, with master classes and mentoring offered – couldn't have asked for more,' said a parent.

The arts and extracurricular: As with everything here, learning outside the classroom plugs social as well as educational gap. Down on the farm that's a gated hop, skip and jump from the playground, pupils can volunteer to be young farmers and learn responsibility by working here after school. 'We've got 20 new chickens and we're getting rabbits too,' our guides said excitedly. Meat and eggs are sold to parents who can also sample other edibles and there's a virtuous circle, with pigs (sensibly not named) fed spare break time fruit (unlimited for all). Adjoining forest school may be more of a coppice but gets non-stop multipurpose use, especially mini-beast hotel and tyre swing hanging from tree. 'We use the farm in the summer holidays and love it,' said a parent, with other whole family holiday meet-ups including picnics on the lake and London museums.

Music 'modern, relevant and generally very good,' according to a pupil. Around 150 learn an instrument in school. Well-used recording studio. No orchestras, choirs etc but there are bands and ensembles and a sixth former wrote a Christmas song that the whole school performed. Grumbles from pupils around drama, though – no specialist teacher, not a big curriculum subject and no real clubs, although there is a show every year and school is hoping to recruit a specialist in the second school that could work across both. In the spacious art studio, we saw year 11s sketching, painting and doing multimedia work on laptops – unusually, all in silence.

Meat and eggs from the school farm are sold to parents and there's a virtuous circle, with pigs (sensibly not named) fed spare break time fruit (unlimited for all)

Wraparound care 7.30am to 6pm, taken up by around 55 pupils, while 300 or so do clubs – usual range of sports, plus debating through to yoga. Some are pupil led, eg a sixth former runs the year 6/7 football team, including organising fixtures. Six trips a year for primary pupils, with overnight stays from year 3, and uni residentials every year from year 7 to eg York, Bristol, Bath, UCL and Cambridge. Work experience for all year 11s in autumn half term to beat the post-GCSE rush. All year 9s do DofE bronze and around 12 do gold (compare that to two in the whole of the rest of Hounslow the year we visited).

Sport: Opening of second school should mean more outside space all round. In the meantime, sporting successes are coming, eg senior girls' football, cross-country, while colossus of a sports hall also goes some way to compensate, as does its rooftop Astroturf (with views of glorious sunsets over Feltham). Pupils praised 'good breadth of sports – we get to try a lot', though one wanted 'more racket sports'. Junior sports noticeboard revealed upcoming events for younger children including year 5 cross-country, boccia, tag rugby and sitting volleyball. Termly Cooper run gets children breaking their previous record. 'I worried about the lack of sporting facilities but didn't need to,' said a parent.

Ethos and heritage: Built on the principle of cradle to career, and with a special interest in whole-family support for those traditionally short on decent life chances, the school opened in 2012 and now provides everything from ante-natal classes through to belt-and-braces careers advice. From helping to carpet a family's new flat to supporting families to get their kids to bed on time, there's pretty much nothing the school will shy away from to ensure children have the best shot at a good education. Two years in, it became first all-through free school to get an outstanding (which it did in all areas) and it now educates 900 children aged two to 18 years, achieving consistently strong academic results. While the ward has traditionally seen 19 per cent of young people going into higher education, 64 per cent of the school's first GCSE cohort went on to do a degree. No wonder the school gained star status, becoming the must-see educational destination of choice for range of ambitious politicians and royalty, with pupils having been met by the likes of David Cameron, Lord Adonis, Boris Johnston, Michael Gove and – most recently – Duchess of Cambridge. All the more impressive when you consider this was a school with no proven strategy or big backer and, as such, started literally by canvassing for pupils. Those who took a leap of faith and got in early thank their lucky stars; neighbours who didn't and are on the waiting list (which moves, but at glacial speed) wish they'd done the same. The small-is-beautiful ethos (two form entry) remains key – 'means staff know everyone's names, and that even goes for the receptionist,' said a parent.

The school opened in 2012 and now provides everything from ante-natal classes through to belt-and-braces careers advice

Area, though not picturesque, is brilliantly connected for trains, automobiles and of course many, many planes. Inside, the school, designed from scratch by founders, is a well thought-out and attractive oasis of calm. Includes separate primary and secondary meet and greet areas and playgrounds, unisex toilets, no hidden corners and visible staff areas. Life centres round five phases, each with its assistant head, made up of one or more year groups in own area consisting of classrooms off a multipurpose central space (nursery, in own single long room, the only exception). 'They're here 16 years so we wanted each phase to feel distinctive,' says Ed. Unless location is key (science, music and art) it's the teachers who move – none of this 100 kids rushing through the corridors to get to a lesson. Sixth form centre (top

The small-is-beautiful ethos is key – 'means staff know everyone's names, and that even goes for the receptionist,' said a parent

floor) boasts rooftop terrace, sofa-filled room and well-stocked fitness suite. Inspirational quotes (JK Rowling, Ghandi, Martin Luther King) everywhere you look, but library could be more inspiring.

Pastoral care, inclusivity and discipline: The Hub, started by the school but now an independent charity, remains at the heart of the school. Based in a local community café, staff help with everything from practical issues such as organising visits to the job centre, optician and food bank to bigger issues such as risk of homelessness or immigration difficulties. 'A lot of people think, "Hang on, that's not the role of a school," but if a child is living in a stressful environment, how can they make the most of their learning?' explains Ed, who adds that while the Hub was originally created just for school parents, the need to broaden horizons soon became clear – now offers eg parenting programmes which are now run across eight nurseries and which eight parents have been trained up to deliver as outreach programmes. Back on the school premises, there's a Place2Be where 35 children are receiving counselling at any one time – again, with more integration with the whole family than at other schools.

Food matters. For some children it's their first encounter not just with healthy diet but also with the social rituals of mealtimes. So there's food mindfulness in primary (distraction-free silence during first mouthfuls) to minimal choice menu, family service with older pupils serving younger ones and home visits for serial non-eaters.

Incentives include payslips for good work and behaviour – exchangeable for golden time (primary) and auctions where you can buy eg a lie-in, book tokens, teacher does your homework etc (senior pupils). Lots of messages home if a child's done well. Clear and consistent boundaries, especially around disruption in class and disrespect to staff – clear three-step sanctions lead to time out of classroom, then detention, then exclusion – around 60 fixed-term a year. Managed moves to other mainstream schools replace exclusions – around two a year, with school taking pupils from other schools under similar circumstances. 'Can't eat junk food in public' and 'it's not worth being late,' pupils told us when we asked for examples of school rules. 'But all come with explanation – I think they're fair,' felt one. 'Some parents think it's too strict but speaking as someone with a boy that gets regular de-merits, I can tell you it's always fair and they work with me as I have to agree to carry on their work at home – and it's all paying off,' said a parent.

Active school council – one pupil reeled off changes they'd implemented around eg lunches, more clocks in classrooms, more sports tournaments, and they'd just proposed a school newspaper too.

Pupils and parents: Rumours of places being awarded to wealthy parents have all but disappeared – we certainly saw no evidence of posh cars at drop off. Instead, there's a diverse community socio-economically (43 per cent pupil premium) and ethnically (albeit less than so than at its inception when it was 80 per cent ethnic minority – now a third white British, a quarter Indian, Pakistani and Bangladeshi and rest a huge mix, with 55 languages spoken). Catchment stretches about a mile and a quarter, including TW13 and TW14 postcodes. PTA does the usual events although one parent felt 'there could be more commitment from families – it wound up being five of us doing everything at one point.' We found pupils friendly, sociable and articulate – they mix well across year groups too, said a parent: 'When we're walking through Feltham, I hear much older children calling out my son's name and he loves it.'

Money matters: Sixth form bursaries for everyone on free school meals. As and when hardship bursaries also available – no pupil will miss a school trip because of lack of money.

The last word: 'Shoot for the moon and even if you miss you'll land among the stars – that's the message for pupils and for a deprived area like this, it's hard to exaggerate the impact,' summed up a parent.

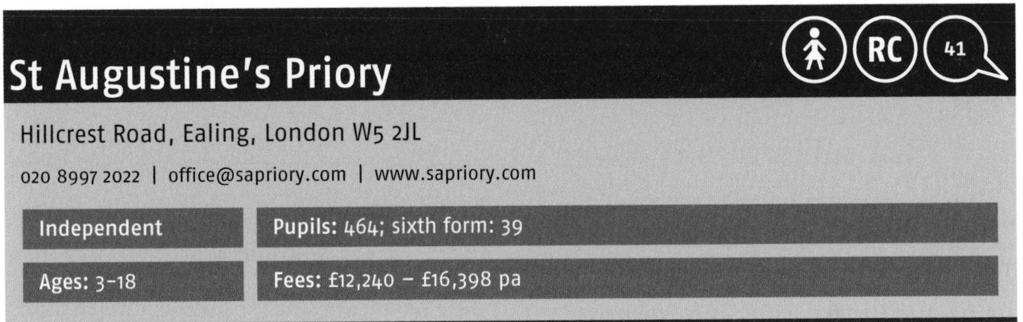

St Augustine's Priory

RC 41

Hillcrest Road, Ealing, London W5 2JL

020 8997 2022 | office@sapriory.com | www.sapriory.com

Independent | Pupils: 464; sixth form: 39

Ages: 3–18 | Fees: £12,240 – £16,398 pa

Head: Since 2012, Sarah Raffray BA (English and Latin, Manchester) MA (literature and modernity, Salford) (40s). Knows more than most about Catholic schools having taught at St Mary's Cambridge, St Bede's and St Mary's Shaftesbury, where she was deputy head; governor at Farleigh School and Stonyhurst, where her son was a pupil. 'There's something really special about Catholic education which the world struggles to articulate,' she says. 'Adores' literature and still teaches English. Believes you get to know how somebody ticks in a discussion about books. Warm but firm, funny but sensible: all the contrasts you'd want in a head. Married to Mr Raffray, who manages the school's farm.

St Augustine's was struggling when she arrived and parents claim she's been 'revolutionary', 'retaining its heart whilst taking things forward'. A constructive approach to criticism, a good listener; 'reasonable and normal'. 'Terrific' with the girls, inviting groups for cake and card games in her study. Zero pretensions or ego: 'I once had a long chat about my dogs with a really nice lady at the gate before realizing later it was Mrs Raffray', laughs one mum.

Vision is to equip girls for success in life, 'whatever that may look like'. Serious about the school's social responsibility: 'we need to level society, not create more barriers'. An 'avowed feminist' (small f); believes passionately that every girl should 'know her worth'. Wants girls to leave knowing how to have difficult conversations and talk through conflict rather than 'nourishing grievances'. Loves the school's diversity and the 'richness' that this brings; eyes twinkle as she tells us about Hindu and Sikh parents who want a Catholic education for their daughters in London having been educated by nuns in India.

A vocal advocate for rethinking how we assess teenagers ('GCSEs have got to go') and for parity between academic and vocational qualifications. Speaks eloquently on social and national media about it, though her focus is on nurturing young people rather than plugging any kind of political message or self-promotion. Supports young people 'unconditionally' – 'we've got your back', she tells them.

Laughs a lot too – 'serious moments are punctuated by absolute hilarity', she says with a knowing grin. Personal commitment to fancy dress during Book Week is legendary; recently burst into song during weekly video message to parents. Finds herself in 'hysterics' at the jokes in the nativity play. 'We're pretty unusual,' she tells us, 'we're not nutters, but we are different'. We're all for that.

Entrance: Around 15 at nursery, 12 more in reception and then 12 again in year 5. A further 25 in year 7 and a handful in year 12. Other entry points considered. Every applicant interviewed by Mrs Raffray. For nursery and reception, classroom assessment to ensure key academic and emotional milestones have been met. Prospective year 5s take exams in English, maths and reasoning alongside a taster day. School recently joined London Consortium at 11+ to avoid year 6s 'sitting a vast number of entry exams': multiple choice test in maths, comprehension and reasoning. Year 12 applicants submit school reports and mock grades before being interviewed; offers are conditional on GCSE results. Sensitive approach to admissions; extenuating circumstances considered.

The head's eyes twinkle as she tells us about Hindu and Sikh parents who want a Catholic education for their daughters in London having been educated by nuns in India

A lot from state primaries, sometimes before year 7; parents and girls recognise that making the jump before 11+ relieves the pressure. Those joining higher up often looking for something calmer than their bigger, noisier secondaries. Recent growth of year 7 numbers in part to allow for smaller class sizes – two bigger forms have become three smaller ones. An admirable alternative to the usual 'bums on seats' attitude.

Exit: A few leave for year 7, often to state schools. Just under half leave after GCSEs, usually in pursuit of a bigger setting and perhaps boys – parents commend the school's supportive approach to this. Popular university destinations include Exeter, King's College London, SOAS, Plymouth. Two to Oxbridge in 2020 – the first the school has sent but not the last, we suspect.

Latest results: In 2020, 77 per cent 9-7 at GCSE; 72 per cent A*/A at A level. In 2019 (the last year when exams took place), 69 per cent 9-7 at GCSE; 69 per cent A*/A at A level.

Teaching and learning: Sciences, modern languages and English literature successful recently, though small cohorts mean numbers vary. Good take-up of EPQ. Sets from year 9 in maths and foreign languages; choice of double or triple science at GCSE is 'effectively streaming'. Religious studies compulsory at GCSE.

Notably positive language around academic results – 'we cherish all results individually,' Mrs Raffray says, and we believe her. Adamant that nurturing does not mean fluffy – 'we produce brilliant girls who are not defined by their grades'. Staff tell heartwarming stories of girls who beat the odds or overcome a challenge – whether it's a C or an A*, the grade is less important than the individual journey. Parents feel the school 'does well with those in the middle' who may get lost elsewhere. Mrs Raffray sums it up with characteristic grace – 'While we rightly celebrate with girls who have earned the top grades, we also rejoice with all girls who have exceeded expectations at every level.'

Teachers wonderfully un-corporate – lots of personality in the classroom. Mrs Raffray is conscious of it – apparently St Augustine's first Greek teacher, 'a horrible Miss Trunchbull-type', put him off it and she's determined that won't be the case here. So, lots of Miss Honeys (and Mr Honeys too): relatable and amusing, they have a comfortable, easy rapport with the girls. We enjoyed a lesson on religious postures ('I usually demonstrate prostration, girls, but the carpet in this room's a bit thin'). Casual reference to exam questions ('who can write a 4 marker on this?') suggests an awareness of the end goal without it being rammed down anyone's throat. No danger of being picked on or caught out; an unthreatening atmosphere for those who might feel anxious elsewhere. We felt that classrooms lacked a bit of fizz, or bustle, as a result; but then again, fizz does not work for everybody. Lively trips calendar (Italy, Iceland, Paris etc) enriches it all and brings it to life.

A broad range of academic subjects; versatile teachers and flexible timetabling. Some students pointed out gaps in practical subjects – no food technology, no D&T – though this is quite common in a smaller school. Happy to run unusual GCSEs and A levels – Russian, computer science, ancient Greek, classical civilisation – though as one parent pointed out, 'it's hard to get a debate going in a class of one'.

Learning support and SEN: Just over 10 per cent on the SEN register, majority dyslexic. Can cater

We enjoyed a lesson on religious postures: 'I usually demonstrate prostration, girls, but the carpet in this room's a bit thin'

for ASD and ADHD. Lessons tailored to individual needs by experienced and sensitive teachers. Learning Support team supplement with 1:1 support and drop-in sessions. Very few receive EAL support though lots from multilingual households.

The arts and extracurricular: 'Vibrant' extracurricular offering and a sense that everybody gets involved in everything. Music prominent – choirs perform demanding pieces and tour internationally. We cooed at the display of brightly-coloured ukuleles in the prep's dedicated music room, with specialist computers and software for composition introduced in year 7. Around a third have individual music lessons. You don't have to be on the Grade 8 treadmill, though – one angelic prep student told us that what she really loves is 'DJing on the decks with my dad'. Lively collaborations with drama including major biennial at Questors Theatre in Ealing – staff and pupils alike very excited to share plans for upcoming production of Hairspray.

Drama recognised as an excellent way to build confidence and social skills. Drama Gifted Pathway offered to those who show sign of some talent. Very high take up of LAMDA throughout the school. Busy art department encourages girls to 'live and breathe their art'. Life drawing and textiles offered off curriculum. Sixth formers have been let loose on the staircase up to the art rooms, creating an awesome collage of work and interesting images that literally plaster the walls. Famous alumnae are creatives: musician Hannah Kendall, comedian Phoebe Waller-Bridge (learnt her trade in the nativity, presumably) and Valerie Hobson, actress and long-suffering wife of John Profumo. All the gallery and theatre visits that you'd expect given the school's access to central London. Drama, music, art all offered at GCSE with photography added at A level; creative teaching is 'fabulous'.

The school's real USP, though, is Priory Farm. It's what 'makes our school the best school', according to year 6. Developing organically from a chick-hatching activity in 2017, it's largely run by the girls and requires significant commitment. The benefits are myriad. Ducks quack joyfully when they see us coming (expecting lunch, according to our guide); pigs – real, grunting pigs, not a sanitised London version – snuffle and snort. It's properly muddy work (note: remember your wellies) with the girls involved at every step, from helping with lambing to selling eggs to fund chicken feed. They take it seriously – some will go on to study veterinary science having become managers on the farm. The simple, back-to-nature combination of fresh air, physical work and looking after animals is therapeutic, an enormous help to those who are struggling elsewhere. 'If you're having a bad day, the animals are always there', says one grateful mother whose daughter has benefited. A superb initiative for which the school has deservedly won recognition. While up and down the country teenagers huddle around YouTube in the common room, Augustinians are running around the orchard or digging the vegetable patch. A modern Malory Towers without the 1940s attitudes or the saltwater pool – it all seems so unlikely in west London, and yet it works.

Sport: Thirteen acres in London? 'What a winner', say parents. Sport central to the outdoorsy culture. As one parent says, 'it's all onsite, so you might as well'. An inclusive approach – everybody gets to have a go – with special sports breakfasts laid on as a treat for those who have turned up regularly. Recent addition of sports scholarships suggests the school keen to attract talented athletes too. Netball and hockey busy with lots of fixtures and regional tournaments. Training for both before and after school; shouts of 'Oggies!' at the sideline apparently drown out opposition chanting. We were pleased to hear that these otherwise gentle girls show their true mettle on court. Killer instinct doesn't always translate into victory (does it matter?); 'they win, they lose', say parents. Small intake historically made it challenging to field decent teams, but with growing numbers this will be less of an issue. 'Superb', 'inspiring' coaches spot potential and encourage girls to play for local clubs too. Other options include gymnastics and football. Team involvement drops off as girls get older (a story everywhere, really), but they stay active – zumba popular in sixth form.

Ethos and heritage: Epic foundation story kicks off in 1634 when English nuns, escaping persecution, set up a convent in Paris. They taught girls there for nearly 300 years – surviving two revolutions and hosting both Napoleon and Wellington – until in 1911 new anti-clerical laws forced them out. And where did they go? Why home, of course, to leafy Ealing. One became a full-blown, chained-to-railings suffragette, whilst the other Sisters set about building a new school as war tore Europe apart. What mighty women. As Mrs Raffray says, 'those nuns didn't just roll over and give up'. It's feisty and no-nonsense – Sound of Music meets

Les Mis – a potent blend which sets the tone for the go-get-it attitude that we see throughout the school.

Their 'think big' approach also survives – 'Spread your wings and see how far you fly', cries one classroom noticeboard, surrounded by pupils' tiny origami birds. A sixth form pressure group which campaigned against 'period poverty' recently won TES Student Initiative of the Year. Any concerns about small schools being too molly-coddling quickly dispelled: on the contrary, we found confident, brave young women.

Girls embrace the charmingly unsophisticated uniform, complete with St Augustine's tartan. Pleated skirts remain firmly knee-length: no creeping hemlines here

Weekly mass in the pretty chapel – lots have 'no idea what they're doing' the first time. A few parents wary of the Catholic ethos before they came but found it 'not nearly as Catholic as we had thought it might be'. Indeed, other than one earnest confession that 'sometimes mass can be a bit boring', we heard nothing but praise for the positive role that mass and prayer play in school life. Focus on faith rather than Catholicism per se: Eid Breakfast an annual highlight. Member of the Three Faiths Forum. Rich and varied community partnerships and a generous approach to sharing resources and expertise, particularly with local state schools.

Pebbledash buildings create a distinctly suburban look not out of keeping with the residential neighbourhood. Site feels warm and welcoming. Nice convent-y touches with original signage still in use – Rev Mother's Parlour now a cosy meeting room with traditional brown furniture that looks like it belonged to Rev Mother herself. Some classrooms could do with brightening up a bit and it all smells quite, well, school-y: none of the Farrow & Ball on the walls, Diptyque in the loos' effect that we see elsewhere. Major development set to modernise things, providing 'new academic heart' including glass atrium, new classrooms and library. Parents grumble about building work but appreciate that it's for the greater good.

Pastoral care, inclusivity and discipline: Pupils say their school is 'loving', 'caring' and 'friendly' – it's this atmosphere that draws many families in the first place. Displays remind girls who to talk to if they are worried about something, though 'you can practically talk to anybody', we are told.

Inclusivity lies at its heart. Girls comfortable coming out; school has supported a handful through gender transition. Sixth formers act as informal mentors to younger girls – we were struck by the refreshing lack of hierarchy with genuine friendships apparent between year groups. Big sister-little sister scheme encourages this culture. Older girls wave to little ones on the street at the weekend, something which would be deemed deeply uncool elsewhere.

Exceptionally non-judgmental community – everybody bumps along together. Attitudes towards socialising and friendships unusually mature and unselfconscious, particularly in sixth form. Single sex factor feels like a natural part of that – this is a safe place where girls can be themselves. Pastoral and academic teams closely interwoven – wellbeing is front and centre throughout the day, not a vague concept discussed once a week in PSHE. Dedicated wooden cabin in the grounds acts as a snug 'Sanctuary' for those needing a quiet moment.

How does the school's Catholicism sit alongside its modern values like equality and diversity? We had to ask – Catholic schools are having a rough ride at the moment. Our tentative questioning was met directly by Mrs Raffray, who is excited to 'reclaim the word Catholic from a negative semantic field' and 'talk about its modernity'. 'We would not be allowed to teach ferocious dogma. We talk about loving them'. They really do; that 'L' word seems to underpin everything.

Girls embrace the charmingly unsophisticated uniform, complete with St Augustine's tartan. Pleated skirts remain firmly knee-length: no creeping hemlines here. Juniors walk to school wearing their distinctive felt hats, ribbons tied under chins. Girls, particularly the younger ones, wear their smart PE kits with pride. Suits for sixth form with 'smart casual' Fridays. Not a scrap of make-up in sight.

Flexibility when it comes to discipline; another advantage of being small. Teachers don't seem to mind too much about the odd missed deadline or forgotten hockey stick. As a result, no dog-ate-homework culture: 'if I haven't done it I apologise and do it for next time'. School's motto is 'veritas' (truth); girls respect this and take responsibility for their actions. System straightforward: warning for minor infringement, three warnings and you're in detention. Girls 'mortified' on receiving a warning. Corridors feel calm and orderly: 'we can be understanding, because girls simply follow the rules'. Ideal.

Pupils and parents: 'None of those shouty girls', says one parent. We agree. Not all outwardly confident or particularly polished, but engaging, amusing and well-mannered to a tee. Plenty of space for those who have yet to find their voice. We met a super mish-mash of girls, all brilliant in their own ways and all very loyal to their school. Younger than their peers at racier west London day schools, though not naïve. Birthday parties are sleepovers, bowling, pizza.

Wraparound care popular with working parents. Parents are 'low key', says one gratefully: 'if they do have flashy jobs, they keep it quiet'. Lots of successful professionals: doctors, lawyers, pharmacists. Not posh, although inevitably in this area some very wealthy. Less of a drinks party scene than elsewhere – those we spoke to did not seem that interested in comparing notes over canapés – though lots of coffee mornings in the prep. Most are Ealing locals though some from Chiswick, Acton and Shepherds Bush.

Very diverse. 40 per cent Catholic including families from India, Africa, eastern Europe. France and Spain well represented. Further 20 per cent from other Christian denominations, and the rest from other faiths (lots of Muslim, Hindu, Jewish families) or none. Nearby Japanese prep school sends a few. Clearly not a place for those too squeamish about religion, but other than that it is very hard to pin down a St Augustine's 'type'. We have rarely seen such a mix of colours and creeds in a small independent school and we are delighted to report that it works beautifully.

Money matters: Means-tested bursaries offered to exceptional candidates at 11+ and 16+ who meet admissions criteria but may otherwise be unable to attend due to financial hardship. Bursaries for girls already at the senior school who experience a substantial change in circumstances.

The last word: It's not every day in London that you see year 9s leapfrogging through an orchard, bare-kneed in the chilly autumn sunshine. 'Lots of cake, lots of jollity, lots of having a really good time', as one happy mother says. Different from its neighbours, but not for the sake of it. Kind and loving – we really couldn't find a nasty bone in its body – with a commitment to getting the best out of your daughter. A quietly brilliant little school.

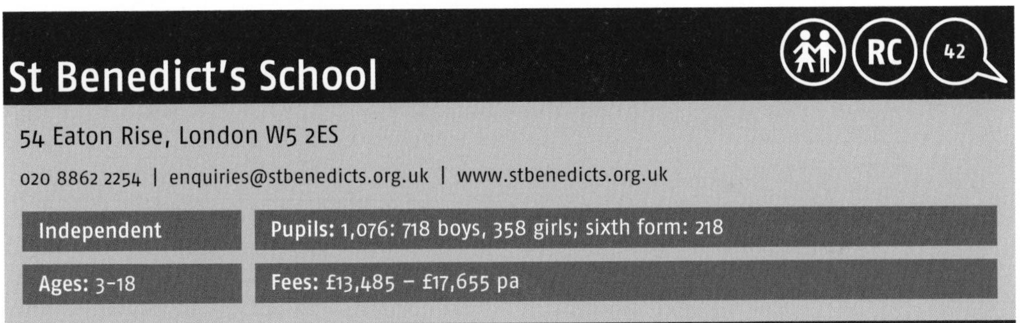

St Benedict's School

RC 42

54 Eaton Rise, London W5 2ES

020 8862 2254 | enquiries@stbenedicts.org.uk | www.stbenedicts.org.uk

Independent	Pupils: 1,076: 718 boys, 358 girls; sixth form: 218
Ages: 3–18	Fees: £13,485 – £17,655 pa

Headmaster: Since 2016, Andrew Johnson (50s), married to Dawn with two sons at university. Educated at Skinners' School in Tunbridge Wells; read modern languages at Bristol and then went straight into teaching. His degree landed him head of the subject at Winchester and then took him north, first to Birkdale School in Sheffield and then on to the top job at Stonyhurst, where he introduced the IB and embedded coeducation.

His arrival here was announced as 'a real coup' by the governors and he is definitely on a mission to try and make the world sit up and notice this school. An easy, tidy man with a controlled sense of humour, who despite describing himself as 'not an office worker' obviously has impressive management skills. He has brought in an infusion of new blood at the top, including a new deputy head, deputy head academic and bursar, and is confident that he can mesh the new with the old as far as staffing goes. Determined to get to know the pupils as well as the teachers, he tries to observe three lessons a week and cheer on as many of his vast array of rugby teams as possible.

Head of junior school: Since 2005, Rob Simmons BA MEd (40s), married with children and grandchildren. Schooled at St Benedict's; after a history degree and time abroad on voluntary service he returned to his alma mater, landing up with headship of the junior school. A trim, dapper dresser, he is not shy about his passion for aviation, planes neatly arranged on shelves and a favourite paperback, starring a Second World War aviation hero, tucked in amongst the history books. He has started Hot Chocolate (and marshmallows) Friday for one pupil from each class who has ticked all the right boxes during the week.

Entrance: Entrance at 3 is non-selective; at 4 it is more formal, with children observed doing tasks in a classroom. For entry at 7 or above children are asked to do tests in maths, English and verbal reasoning as well as an assessment.

At 11+ pupils from the junior school compete in the same exam as external candidates from local state primaries and preps, for the 120 places available. There are occasional spaces at 13+ and in the sixth form but the bar is on the rise with increasing numbers applying.

Exit: Some 70 per cent of juniors move up to the senior school, and around 85 per cent continue to the sixth form. Around 70 per cent of leavers head to Russell Group universities. Bristol, Exeter, Leeds, Birmingham, Liverpool, Manchester, Nottingham and Warwick all popular. Four to Oxbridge in 2020, and four medics. Sometimes students head overseas, including to USA.

Latest results: In 2020, 72 per cent 9-7 at GCSE; 61 per cent A*/A at A level (87 per cent A*-B). In 2019 (the last year when exams took place), 58 per cent 9-7 at GCSE; 42 per cent A*/A at A level (71 per cent A*-B).

Teaching and learning: Nursery, rescued from its Nissan hut island in the playground, is now housed in the junior school with an experienced head – 'I just love the little ones' – in charge. A full curriculum, including art, drama, music and computing alongside traditional subjects, is taught from reception onwards and in keeping with AJ's new approach to academics higher up, they have recently introduced setting in maths and English from year 5. The new building has been designed with early years children in mind and there are cosy break-out spaces (including a ribbon bedecked 'rainbow' room) and a full-time SENCo who operates on both a group and one-to-one level.

One pupil beat entrants from nine other European countries to win the Youth Debating Competition in Budapest, a project well outside their normal comfort zone

AJ's conscious decision to raise the game academically – 'we want to give a greater sense of zip to academic life' – is paying off. He states that it will be a slower process, maybe up to five years, to make the same sort of progress at A level, but results are perfectly respectable. He now monitors the school's ranking against other independents rather than all schools, and has introduced more frequent testing, so that 'we can be straightforward about a pupil's ability'. He has also expanded the tutorial system so that all pupils from year 7 onwards have access to two form tutors.

After three years of studying a wide range of subjects, including the option of Mandarin Chinese in year 7, everybody aims at a minimum of nine GCSEs. Once in the sixth form most take three A levels with 40 per cent doing an EPQ in the lower sixth on subjects as diverse as phage therapy (how to crack treating viruses) and the moral stance of Woodrow Wilson. Students' wide variety of answers on particular academic strengths implied that they were confident about the teaching across the board. A source of pride to all was the pupil who beat entrants from nine other European countries to win the Youth Debating Competition in Budapest, a project well outside their normal comfort zone.

Learning support and SEN: Some eight per cent of pupils receive SEN support from a full-time SENCo, operating alongside a new counsellor, whose brief is to listen to any problems that are brought to her by pupils or parents.

The arts and extracurricular: Extracurricular offerings in the junior school range from the head's aviation club, which has proved so absorbing that one ex-member is now in the RAF, to the more grounded chess, gymnastics, ballet, sewing and drama. Regular trips to museums and theatres and in years 5 and 6 residential outings to the Lake District for the great outdoors and to Normandy to learn about baguettes and butter. Older pupils are given over 60 options to widen their horizons, lots of DofE awards and charity work but also a massive music offering from rock groups to close-harmony singing. The cadet force is popular and the less regimented can choose from arts, drama, dance, languages, science and extra sport.

Music is a common strand, from little ones singing in their nativity play, past the juniors who all learn the violin in year 3, to the near professional spring and summer concerts by senior pupils. There is a busy, buzzy art room at the top of the junior building full of enthusiastic children and imaginative mobiles, and in the senior school there is a new art, design and technology department. We were particularly impressed by a papier-mâché tour de force, posing as a futuristic chair, and students showcase their work with two major art shows each year.

Drama is not timetabled in the junior school, although nativity and form plays are an annual event, but once in year 7 – 'we have a wealth of acting talent' – it takes regular billing. The middle school recently put on Lord of the Flies whilst the seniors staged West Side Story and Amadeus.

Sport: Nursery and reception do PE including dance, but from the age of 7 serious sport begins. Girls play hockey in the autumn and netball in spring, boys play rugby for two terms and both head to the cricket pitches in the summer. Rugby tops the bill with twice weekly fixtures, international tours and the chance to be part of a London Irish training scheme. Not to be left out, girls play tag rugby, but the emphasis is on netball and hockey and they have recently fielded teams who have successfully toured abroad. Everyone is encouraged, according to one parent, and there is a large indoor sports hall with an impressive array of fitness machines and a full complement of professional staff to help would-be stars develop. Fencing is very strong; add in athletics, football, cross-country, rounders, swimming, badminton, basketball, volley ball and jiu-jitsu and you can see why the sporting side of the school often pops up when talking to parents, one naming its 'sporty' side the reason for choosing it.

Ethos and heritage: Nearly 400 years after the Reformation, the Benedictine monks of Downside decided it was time to expand from rural Somerset to suburban London. Initially known as Ealing Priory School, the school opened in 1902 with three boys and five pounds in the kitty, was given its current name in 1948 and has been fully co-educational since 2008 (though currently two-thirds boys).

The architectural chimera lying on the summit of a gentle slope above Ealing Broadway is composed of solid Edwardian villas, rather dreary brick buildings and a lot of tarmac all sandwiched between unlikely golden doors and the 1900s abbey; fortunately, the slightly weary creature is in the midst of a massive refurbishment.

They've already finished a building for the sixth form with art studios above, a small chapel featuring primary coloured windows, designed by a pupil, and an entirely revamped junior school in a modern Scandinavian style which ticks all the right eco boxes. Inside they've brightened up the reception area and the main school hall and plans are in the pipeline to revamp the elderly classrooms. Parents' reactions are positive, one saying that the school was 'a bit tatty', but now looks 'much fresher'. AJ would like to build a performing arts centre in the medium term and there is even talk of planting an avenue of trees once the builders have finally departed – a decidedly good idea as leafy, green trees would definitely improve the present overall monochrome effect.

Alumni include Julian Clary, Peter Ackroyd and the poet/songwriter Labi Siffre as well as a sprinkling of politicians (in particular Chris Patten) and rugby players.

Pastoral care, inclusivity and discipline: Rules are here to be obeyed and AJ is not shy of suspending pupils for a few days if they consistently break them or insist on remaining academically lazy, but hopes that this can almost always be avoided by close monitoring of each pupil's academic and social progress.

Cheerful 'worry' boxes are spread round the junior school and in the senior school there are quiet rooms and the new chapel (complete with chaplain) as well as the counsellor who is always on site.

The massive refurbishment includes an entirely revamped junior school in a modern Scandinavian style which ticks all the right eco boxes

The recent conviction of a priest, ex-middle school head, for sexually assaulting pupils in the 70s and 80s, plus the departure in 2015 of the deputy head, following his arrest over indecent images (not involving any St Benedict's children), have resulted in extremely thorough measures to safeguard pupils. There is both internal and external monitoring of the internet and the last ISI inspection was passed with flying colours. Parents remark that the school is very hot on e-dangers and the modern pressures put on pupils via social media and selfies. In our opinion St Benedict's is aware of the mistakes of the past and has moved on.

Some 55 per cent of the pupils are Catholic, the remaining 45 per cent from other faiths or with no faith. The school is no longer marketed solely as a Catholic institution, but talking to students made us very aware that the Benedictine ethos is still omnipresent. The visits to Lourdes, charity fundraising, weekly mass in the abbey and the voluntary service carried out by all members of the lower sixth plus the attitude of pupils to staff and to one another, remind you that this is a school that takes faith and social behaviour seriously.

Pupils and parents: A large number of dual income parents who work extremely hard in order to pay the below-average fees charged here. In western London school terminology, St Benedict's is counted as middle of the road compared to some of its flashier rivals, but all parents that we talked to felt that it provided good value for money, very good pastoral care and that the new leadership team was pushing the academic standards to a higher level.

At the younger end of the school the children are almost all very local, but higher up the catchment area spreads significantly, and they now run regular transport from Hammersmith, Harrow and Richmond. The children who showed us round the lower school were smiley, charming and confident and all the older pupils were polite and articulate, if not appearing quite as sophisticated as some of their inner London contemporaries – not necessarily a bad thing.

Money matters: Academic, music and sports scholarships, worth up to 50 per cent of the fees, available at 11+ and sixth form for internal and external candidates. Bursaries available in the senior school are strictly means tested, but 'once a child is in, if a parent falls on hard times, we will do our best to help them'.

The last word: The 'granular scrutiny' that the ambitious headmaster is applying to all things academic and pastoral is already bearing fruit, and this school is definitely on an upward curve scholastically. If you then take into account all the new buildings and refurbishment programmes, this could soon become better known amongst the schools to the west of the city.

St Dominic's Sixth Form College

Mount Park Avenue, Harrow on the Hill HA1 3HX

020 8422 8084 | admissions@stdoms.ac.uk | www.stdoms.ac.uk

State | Ages: 16–19 | Pupils: 1330

Principal: Since 2013, Andrew Parkin (40s). Studied music at Durham and Cambridge and started his professional career in London at St Marylebone Girls' School. Went on to be deputy head at Sion Manning Girls' School in Kensington and then St Augustine's High School in Westminster. 'For 18 years, I worked in fairly tough comprehensives, which probably explains why the hottest topics for me are teaching, learning, attainment, consistency and attendance and punctuality,' he says. 'But I love the way that here, we get to combine these with informalities such as addressing each other on first name terms, as well as a greater emphasis on independent learning – the result of which is fantastic preparation for university.'

Not someone to hide away in his office, he greets students on the gate, observes lessons, teaches general RE (and occasionally some music) and regularly chats to students and staff. 'I'm not really a number cruncher – I don't believe that is what headships are about.' Clearly passionate about his role ('I absolutely love it! I feel I've got the most perfect job, with happy students that work their very hard, and no discipline issues'), he is also a keen member of several committees in the wider sector. Among the key changes he's brought to the college are a strong emphasis on teaching and learning, more peer observations, a hands-on leadership team and embedding IT into learning. Students don't have a bad word to say about him. 'He seems to know everybody's name,' said one. 'He's so approachable and easy going.' Parents similarly keen: 'He is absolutely fabulous – a supportive leader who's not afraid to get his hands dirty, rather than being just a figurehead.'

Both interested and interesting, he is keen amateur musician and is chairman of the BBC Symphony Chorus.

Entrance: About 40 per cent from its two partner schools, Salvatorian College and Sacred Heart Language College – the rest from over 100 other feeder schools, stretching as far as 1.5 hours travel away. 'I know someone who comes in from Kent,' one student told us, while one from Enfield told us it takes her 'an hour-and-10-minutes' travelling one way – and that's on a good day'. 'Most of our students live in Harrow, but if you looked at a heat map of London, we'd have dots representing students' homes all over it, and I think that's great,' says the principal. 'At 16, people are old enough to make decisions and if they recognise excellence and are prepared to make an effort to get out of bed for it, then I'm all for it.'

Students from the main two feeder schools are guaranteed a place, providing they get at least five 9-4 GCSE grades including English language. All other applicants must get at least seven 9-4s and meet the individual subject requirements. These range from a 4 in English for religious studies to an 7 in maths for further maths. Priority to Catholics, then other practising Christians, then other faiths and no faith. Applicants must acknowledge their commitment to the religious values of the school in writing. Conditional offers are made in March and are based on academic references, including predicted grades. Any remaining places offered based on subjects with spaces and highest GCSE average score. Some spaces also become available after the first year. 'Many parents round here work abroad, so there's quite a lot of movement in the area,' explains the principal.

Exit: Over 90 per cent go on to university, nearly half of those to Russell Group. London universities are very popular, as are Nottingham, Southampton and Warwick. Law and medical/biomedical subjects tend to top the tables. Fewer Oxbridge applicants than one might expect given the calibre of students (15 places in 2020), largely because so many are prospective medics (25 medics/vets/dentists in 2020).

Latest results: In 2020, 36 per cent A*/A at A level; 67 per cent A*-B. In 2019 (the last year when exams took place), 32 per cent A*/A and 62 per cent A*-B.

Teaching and learning: Some 29 subjects available in more-or-less any combination. Maths, history, the three sciences, economics and psychology are the most popular A level subjects – with strongest results in maths, chemistry, biology, history and economics (in terms of attainment) and history, classics, languages, music and art (in terms of value-added).

Option to change subjects in the first week or two if you really loathe geography or have just developed a passionate interest in Italian. Currently, students can take four subjects in year 12, dropping down to three in year 13, enabling them to keep options open. Offers level 3 BTec national and extended diplomas, ideally suited to those who don't like the sound of lots of final exams, which can be combined with one (extended course) or two (national course) A levels. 'BTecs are often undersold, but they afford our less academic students an opportunity to achieve highly and go on to the likes of York, Nottingham and London universities. The business studies one has validity and is taught well here,' claims the principal. College has also brought in a core maths programme, which enables students to keep up with maths without taking the full A level.

Class sizes range from two to 25 and teaching is largely discussion-based. 'The teachers' subject knowledge is phenomenal – some have two degrees,' one told us. 'Teachers here are so inspirational and really passionate about what they teach,' said another, although be warned they are very hot on homework, being 'very strict on both completion and deadlines'. Professional development for teachers is a strength, with all having spent time in London schools. 'It's been great for them to see what life is like elsewhere – it's got them to reflect on their own practice and raise the bar,' explains the principal.

There's a newly installed electric organ in the chapel, that is used by keyboard players. 'I've been known to pop in to play it for half an hour myself,' admits the principal

Offers the EPQ. 'They have a free choice of subject, but it makes sense to relate it to a subject they may do at university, and gives something to talk about at interview.' Large numbers of aspiring medics, so the college runs a programme of BMAT preparation and mock interviews. Excellent university and careers advice; has been awarded the Investors in Careers mark and has a designated HE and careers advisor. 'We're realistic and honest, and allow no poverty of aspiration.'

Effort and achievement grades given every six weeks. 'Our monitoring is much more frequent than they have time to do in schools. All our staff are focused on the sixth form – not on settling in year 7s or helping year 9s choose GCSE subjects, or indeed behavioural issues.'

Learning support and SEN: Good for those with physical disabilities – we met one wheelchair user, who couldn't praise the college highly enough. 'There's not one area I can't access,' she said. Students with hearing or visual impairments are equally impressed. Very few students with SEN, though. Support for them is 50 per cent classroom support, while the other half takes place in the Study Plus area, which other students access for anything from revision workshops to small project groups – all of which helps to prevent any stigma. 'Our son has Asperger's and the college has been brilliant – really going out of their way to help him on his terms and he got far better results than we thought he would,' one parent told us.

The arts and extracurricular: Music is part of everyday life – we heard the practising for the annual bands' performances when we visited. Decent numbers (around 25) do A level, while seven peripatetic teachers cover individual teaching of instruments including piano, flute, strings, guitar and drums. Choir and orchestra both popular and good, with termly concerts providing opportunities to perform. Department comprises of teaching space, recording studio and rehearsal rooms, and there's a newly installed electric organ in the chapel, that is used by keyboard players. 'I've been known to pop in to play it for half an hour myself,' admits the principal.

Top floor art studios could be bigger and better, but they do the job and are reassuringly cluttered with colourful resources and some very talented work. Three teachers cover art, art history and DT, and the sophisticated artwork and fashion creations are exhibited in the chapel annually, with several students each year going on to art and design courses. Drama studio is okay, but any lack of cutting edge practice areas doesn't put off keen thespians, who put on an annual musical production, plus various productions throughout the year. Great excitement about the devised pieces being showcased annually in the so-called 'shack' – a covered outside space for which the college hires in tiered seating. 'With the sounds of nature and the London hum in the background, and the sheer talent of the students, it's all highly dramatic,' says the principal, recalling that one performance required a pig's head having to be ordered from the butcher, then kept under health and safety conditions.

Faith is a major part of the deal here, with the principal big on the Dominican tradition. About 60 per cent of the staff is Catholic, but all buy into the ethos

Volunteering and fundraising are important parts of the ethos. 'Charity efforts spring up out of nowhere.' Students do sponsored walks and sleep outs, work in soup kitchens, volunteer on a Catholic farm, join a pilgrimage to Lourdes. 'There's a philosophy of respecting other people and helping the wider community.'

Long list of day trips and residentials. 'London is used to the max – theatres, museums, concerts, Houses of Parliament and so on.' Among the regular overseas trips are Great Wall of China (general trip, open to all), Washington DC (history and politics students) – and there's an annual exchange with a school in New Jersey. Other recent trips have included music trip to New York, art trip to Rome, general trip to Venice and classics trip to Athens. Extracurricular activities not obligatory, but widely taken up – including everything from flower arranging to sports. Guest speakers regularly invited in – including the Spectator's editor Fraser Nelson, Sir Bernard Hogan Howe, Mark Damazer and Phillip Coggan.

Sport: State-of-the-art sports hall includes a multigym and hall for badminton, table tennis and five-a-side football, with its use juggled between A level PE students and general recreation. Sport is not compulsory, but the hall 'has increased motivation and attendance. We've been pleasantly surprised that participation rates have been very high.' Indeed, the principal encourages all students to utilise the multigym, which is open from 7.30am-5.30pm. Outdoor space includes a five-a-side football/netball court and a football field set among beautiful woodland. There's at least one team for each of football, rugby, tennis, basketball, table tennis and netball – 'Football trials are particularly popular, with around 100 students applying for just 11 places,' one student told us. They do well in local leagues, and some competitions further afield, particularly for football and badminton. There's a cycling club and golf club, plus opportunities for cheerleading and street dance for those less competitively inclined.

Ethos and heritage: Opened in 1978 in what had been St Dominic's Independent Grammar School for Girls, run by Dominican nuns. Sits on a hill above a leafy, gated estate of substantial houses with large gardens that could have strayed from the Chilterns, and amazing views across London – as far as the City and Canary Wharf on a clear day. By the entrance to the 28-acre site is the chapel, a peaceful and atmospheric building with lovely stained glass, 'the heart of the college'. Assemblies (each year group gets four a year, which are supplemented by the principal's Sunday night emails on a theme for the week, such as 'What is truth?') and introductory talks take place here, as well as morning masses, and Muslim students use a side room for prayer. Four large blocks make up the key teaching areas – Hume (humanities), Catherine (maths, English, languages), Aquinas (sciences) and Siena (sports hall and psychology).

The most recently developed facility is the remodelled library – among the nicest we've seen, in which the £1m investment paid for a bright, airy space, with multicoloured seats and two glass-dominated mezzanine areas, with masses of study space and computers. 'It's well staffed and equipped – we love it,' one student told us. Indeed, it's generally packed until closing time at 4.30pm. Next up is a refurbishment of the Cardinal Hume building which will provide more teaching spaces.

Devised pieces are showcased in the 'shack' – a covered outside space; one performance required a pig's head having to be ordered from the butcher, then kept under health and safety conditions

No common room ('We don't need one – we're not a school,' says principal), with students gathering instead in the spacious canteen, library and the Shack, where an all-day coffee kiosk augments the canteen offerings.

Faith is a major part of the deal here, with the principal big on the Dominican tradition – with links with its sisters and brothers all around the country. Mass is held every week, tutor groups take it in turns to choose readings, everyone studies RE. 'We want our students to develop on an academic, personal and spiritual level. We want them to critically examine their faith, to mix with people from other faiths and hear why it is important to them. It makes a tremendous difference to what we can offer and how they develop in later life,' says principal.

About 60 per cent of the staff is Catholic, but all buy into the ethos. Prayers are said each morning and each tutor period. 'It is a moment for thinking outside oneself – a lovely sharing moment.' Very good relationships amongst staff and between staff and pupils and overall, there's a real buzz around campus – the atmosphere is relaxed, informal, yet hardworking.

Pastoral care, inclusivity and discipline: Any student problems tend to be ironed out by teachers or the college counsellor, the latter whose hourly slots over two days a week are always packed out. 'If I could afford it, I'd have her here five days,' say the principal. One parent whose family had suffered trauma was particularly impressed by the pastoral offering. 'They could not have done more for my son.' Mental health issues, particularly anxiety, on the up, reports the college – but that's no different to what any other head tells us. In the main, things tick over pretty smoothly here – and students were aghast when we asked them if there was any bullying. 'Unlike a lot of sixth form colleges, where you get cliques, this one has a really warm and friendly atmosphere,' said one. Strong student voice – changing everything from more loo rolls in the toilets and better air-con to helping organise events like the annual talent show and cultural day.

Electronic registration for every lesson means that everyone is accounted for: the pastoral team phones parent and student if the student is not in by 10am. If lateness becomes a regular occurrence, homework is late, a student shows lack of effort, or takes unauthorised absence, then they're put on warning. If they still don't pull their socks up, they are asked to attend supervised learning and teaching (detention basically – although they won't call it that). 'It's an opportunity for students who haven't worked hard enough that week to do so,' says the principal, although not many students wind up actually having to attend one. If there's still no improvement, parents are called in – again, it's very few students overall. Zero tolerance for drugs or violence, but no problems with either for many years – in fact, no temporary exclusions whatsoever in current principal's reign.

Pupils and parents: About 40 per cent Catholic, most of the rest Hindu or Muslim. Homogeneous in that all take their religious faith seriously, with the exception of one or two atheists (but no zealous ones, unsurprisingly). 'All students are serious about academic life – you need to be motivated and have a certain level of intelligence to get on here,' one student told us – indeed, the college offers virtually no vocational courses. And as there is a high level of competition for places, those who get in feel a great sense of gratitude. 'I feel really lucky to be here' is something of a mantra.

White British is certainly not the majority here. 'Harrow is one of the most diverse boroughs in the area, and we are reflective of that,' says principal. Good mix in terms of class too – with many students the first in their families to aspire to university. Parents are nearly all highly supportive, with 97 per cent attendance at the annual parents' evening – doubtless helped by the fact that parents can drop in anytime between 9am and 7.30pm and the principal stipulates that they do so. 'I insist every young person has someone to represent them because it's my experience that when young men and women get to 16, many parents take a back seat, and that's not what we want here.'

Money matters: Free if you're under 19. Excellent and enlightened system of bursaries for students and staff to fund specific projects and trips.

The last word: Greatly sought-after college in pleasant leafy location with high academic standards and a strong Catholic ethos of care for each other. 'A lovely place to work and study,' say staff and students.

St Helen's School

44

Eastbury Road, Northwood HA6 3AS

01923 843210 | admissions@sthelens.london | www.sthelens.london

Independent | Pupils: 1,163; sixth form: 168

Ages: 3-18 | Fees: £14,532 – £18,321 pa

Headmistress: Since September 2019, Alice Lucas (50s), previously vice principal at UCL Academy in Camden. She has also been head of history at St Marylebone, head of sixth form at City of London School for Girls and deputy head pastoral at South Hampstead High – a veritable feast of go-getting girls' schools. Grew up in London and was educated at St Paul's Girls before reading history at Bristol and later taking an MA in political thought at UCL.

Is really putting St Helen's on the map, say parents, all the more admirable when you consider that COVID dominated the start of her reign. 'Thank goodness we had her as she brought us on leaps and bounds with technology, which wound up making all the difference,' said one, with audible sigh of relief. 'Every lesson was online – completely seamless,' reported student.

Smiley (everyone is here), eloquent and savvy, she has breathed new life into the school and we noticed everyone seems to have loosened up a bit since our last visit too. 'I have so many ideas,' she told us excitedly (her last job involved researching best ways of learning from all around the world, then cherry picking the best of them). So what three things top her agenda? First, sixth form – 'needed to become more academic and is already a more dynamic hub of intellectual excitement, partly thanks to new sixth form leadership.' Second, stretching the most able – more mentors, challenges, competitions, speakers etc 'to develop scholarly thought'. Third, teaching and learning more generally – 'it's common for schools to teach to the middle with support for the least able and extension for the top, but I want our teaching to be aimed at the very top and then scaffold down.' None of this is lost on parents – 'She's really raising the bar, it's very noticeable.'

Lives in Camden with her husband and two teenage children and is actively involved with a number of charities (particularly those that support London children facing unequal opportunities), as well as having (mostly) fun renovating a derelict house they've bought in the Suffolk countryside.

Entrance: At 3+ and 4+ by observation and interview. Part of the London 11+ Consortium for 11+ entry – now a single cognitive ability test, plus interview, for which around 460 apply (around half each from state and independent sector) for approximately 100 places (sometimes more if it's a bulge year). Prep school girls (who make up half the senior intake) have to sit the exam too but vast majority walk it – the few who school feels 'won't be happy in seniors' are warned in year 4 and it's confirmed by year 5. Occasional places available throughout the school, so always worth asking. Interview and reference from current school required. Up to eight join at sixth form – applicants need seven 6s at GCSE, with 7s in the subjects relevant to their A level (6s pass muster for some subjects eg business studies, geography and psychology).

See website for changes for 2021 entry due to COVID.

Exit: A small number leave after prep and a quarter left after GCSEs in 2020, mostly to local state schools. Eighty per cent of sixth formers to Russell Group universities. Edinburgh, Durham, Manchester and all the big London unis all popular. Five to Oxbridge in 2020, and eight medics. Broad church of subjects: 'architecture, business, chemistry, design – I could go through the whole alphabet to zoology,' says head.

Latest results: In 2020, 90 per cent 9-7 at GCSE; 68 per cent A*/A at A level (91 per cent A*-B). In 2019 (the last year when exams took place), 85 per cent 9-7 at GCSE; 45 per cent A*/A at A level (76 per cent A*-B).

Teaching and learning: Not top of the highly competitive north London academic tree, but no slouch. 'We are more interested in value added and in the girls being happy than pure results,' says head, though all agree academics are on a steep upward trajectory, with more stretch, exploration, academic risk taking and critiquing both in prep and senior. 'I have noticed a huge difference between my older and younger daughter in terms of academic rigour,' was a typical parent comment. Lessons meticulously planned and executed, with everything crisper as they get older, but without – insist the girls – undue pressure. No stone unturned, it seems, from current focus on refining English language teaching (although there's no EAL support needed here, many of the girls don't speak English at home) through to ensuring art is more cross-curricular. Though not without its fair share of pushy parents (more of that later), some chose St Helen's precisely because they don't want to be breathing down their daughter's neck – 'I wanted a school that would do the pushing for me, so that my relationship with my daughter wasn't ruined, and that's exactly what I've got,' said one happy customer.

'I wanted a school that would do the pushing for me, so that my relationship with my daughter wasn't ruined, and that's exactly what I've got,' said one parent

The nursery, Little Gables, and key stage 1, Gables, are in converted houses on site, each with own playground. Vibe is cosy and play based, though we noticed utter dedication to learning even among these tinies, whether colouring in pictures for Diwali or practising their (impressive) handwriting. Lots of outdoor learning, as evidenced by racks of freshy muddied wellies. Year 3 to 6 move into the all-singing, all-dancing, purpose-built prep school. Fabulous, colourful, well-stocked library is at the heart, backed up by mini-libraries outside each classroom – never have we been given such long and detailed descriptions of the intricacies of library life by young students ('attitude to reading is sharper than ever,' said parent). 'What makes a good website?' was the dilemma of the day for year 5s in their computer class (the rows of computers are in the lovely library), while year 2s looked an absolute picture doing their pirouettes in their little pink cardigans in the main hall. Neater sums we've rarely seen among year 3s, while year 6s were far too busy trying to get their teacher's attention with hands up to her punchy questions to notice us at all. 'Lessons always seem imaginative and fun – my daughter is constantly coming out telling me what she's done,' said parent.

Setting is underplayed here, both in prep and senior – 'we were finding that even bottom sets were getting 9s, so what's the point?' Languages strong – French from year 1; then in year 7, girls choose two out of four languages (French, German, Spanish and Mandarin), as well as learning Latin. Italian and Japanese also available at GCSE. Class sizes capped at 22, but are often smaller; 14 at A level – a computer science class had just one student.

Most girls take 10 GCSEs (11 for the supersmart), frequently including a practical subject such as art or drama. No weak spots, but maths, sciences (most take triple) and languages (everyone takes one, unless they have an SEN 'that makes it cruel to put them through the pain') do particularly well. In sixth form, around half start with four A levels, with most dropping one along the way. Economics and Spanish top the graphs on results day. English popular. EPQ for all. High hopes from the forthcoming new STEM building and new head of physics to buck the national trend, not that they are coming from too feeble a starting point – Heath Robinson Club is already popular and there's a big interest in engineering.

Enrichment is a given, with lateral thinking embedded into these girls' psyches. Our year 9 guides were doing independent study projects on how social media affects society and the assassination of Abraham Lincoln. Perhaps not the place for girls likely to feel crushed under the pressure of testing – they can be like buses, it seems, with one year 10 girl telling us how she had seven in the next week alone. Homework favours the flip learning model – preparing, thinking and exploring for the lesson rather than more of what you've just learned in the last one. First-class careers advice and university application support.

Learning support and SEN: Not masses of SEN, as you might expect, but the SENCo and assistant support students with eg dyslexia and dyspraxia, as well as more general problems relating to processing and sequencing. Mostly takes place in the classroom. Annual screening from years 3 to 11 to make sure nothing is missed. Learning support department also on hand to help with other barriers to learning, such as anxiety. Mixed reviews from parents, though, with one reporting that 'provision can be a bit hit and miss.'

The arts and extracurricular: Extracurricular is a key reason parents pick the school and indeed why girls feel tunnel-visioned bookworms should probably stay clear – 'the opportunities outside the classroom would simply be wasted on them'. Every girl we met belonged to, or had set up, clubs and societies – the extended lunchbreak meaning nothing is rushed. Diary writing, debating, African Caribbean Society – you name it, it probably exists. CCF in collaboration with Merchant Taylors'. DofE and Young Enterprise also popular. Visits from profs, writers and theatre companies.

Waldegrave School

Particular successes in debating, maths and physics Olympiads, technology competitions. Lots of trips – Galapagos, Venice, Lake Tahoe, Ypres, Berlin, British Museum, galleries.

There's a big buzz around music, largely thanks to new director of music and whizzy new music centre which includes striking recital hall and Mac suite (great to hear our guides raving about Logic Pro and GarageBand software – girls here are expected to recognise eg Beethoven's fifth symphony, but it's not all about classical repertoire, with music tech acknowledged as having value too). Numerous orchestras, choirs and bands, again with some teaming up with Merchant Taylors'. Around 250 girls do individual music lessons.

'What she does with the girls is magical,' we were told about drama. Sheer immersion of year 10 girls in their paired role play was certainly impressive. Currently only one drama studio, but soon to be three, and young thespians, take note – head said she's happy to splash out on flashy sets and lovely costumes for the big performances (musical or play, alternates each year, again with Merchant Taylors'). 'Let's give them their moment.' The venue – the old school hall – lets the side down a bit, but a new professional performing arts space with proper orchestra space is high on the wish list. 'House arts' is a huge deal for the girls, whereby sixth formers write and direct a play that years 9-11 star in – 'it's a highlight of the year,' said student.

The two big (and one smaller, for sixth form only) art studios were sadly empty when we visited, but what a treat to see the GCSE work all laid out. 'Mastery' is the buzzword of the head of art – 'it's all about tailoring the curriculum to meet their needs,' evidenced by mixture of mediums, themes and styles. 'Even through lockdown, they had imaginative art lessons,' raved parent. Exhibition space coming soon, says school. DT well taught.

Sport: Don't be fooled by St Helen's close proximity to Northwood town centre. So vast are the playing fields, floodlit courts and pitches extending in all directions that you soon realise that most of this end of Northwood is St Helen's. Tremendous sports complex includes large indoor pool, dance studio, mammoth sports hall with climbing wall and viewing gallery. O2-esque dome with hot air pumped in from around October onwards means girls no longer have to shiver at the thought of winter play, while the floodlit Astros were in full use (mostly hockey) during our visit. Lacrosse, netball, tennis, athletics, dance, football and many others also on offer, with hockey, badminton, rugby and cross country bagging St Helen's girls the most wins, often at county level. More niche offerings, eg kickboxing and yoga, available for sixth formers, who also get to swim or use fitness suite in their free periods ('great perk,' said one). 'Could be better at including those who don't make the first team in the extracurricular,' thought parent.

Ethos and heritage: Founded at the end of the 19th century with a vision of education for the whole child, which it still holds dear. A spacious school in trim and imaginative grounds. Rolling renovation programme means you're never far from a hard hat, with the modern, glass-fronted reception area setting the tone for the professional, business-like environment. Even the prep school building – now a good few years old – feels fresh, complete with solar panels and green roof building. There's a stand-out building pretty much every way you turn, including aforementioned music building and (nearly completed) STEM centre, plus super sixth form centre. Inevitably, some parts are more tired eg the art and drama building and ditto for the warren-like corridors and classrooms in the older part of the building. Lovely, spacious zoned library, but shame it's tucked away on the third floor, though there are entrances either end. Musty-smelling chapel, once used for boarders' services, is now available for independent prayer.

Whizzy new music centre which includes striking recital hall and Mac suite (great to hear our guides raving about Logic Pro and GarageBand software)

Happy atmosphere, no bells between lessons and bright uniform (dark green up to 16, but – good news for girls' street cred – no longer with boaters and gloves). Good food too – 'the mac and cheese is to die for,' chirped a prep girl, and our fish and chips wasn't half bad either. Social media feeds could do with updating, reckoned parent – school says it's 'on it'.

Old girls' network is huge and devoted. Alumnae include Patricia Hodge, a great supporter, Vanessa Lawrence (United Nations), Lady Lowry, Luisa Baldini, Penny Marshall, Paula Nickolds (MD John Lewis) and Maria Djurkovic.

Pastoral care, inclusivity and discipline: Behaviour exemplary. Down to high expectations ('they expect a lot of the girls,' thought parent) and clear boundaries rather than long lists of rules. Most go through whole school life without a detention. Inner London problems kept at bay – certainly no drugs, although the occasional larger misdemeanour is dealt with via temporary exclusion. All done sensitively and with clean slate promised afterwards – you're allowed to slip here. Good staff/student relationships help. 'They really do care,' said student, while parents told us school 'knows your daughter individually'. Girls told us they'd have no qualms going to their teacher if something was concerning them, while houses keep vertical friendships alive and well. Counsellor available, and we noticed a healthy awareness of issues like self-harm and eating disorders. 'Couldn't have been more understanding at a traumatic time for our family,' said one parent.

Tellingly, perhaps, when we asked some year 10s about drama, they assumed we meant friendship fall outs. Caused a few chuckles all round, of course, but also led to more serious discussion around unpleasantness between girls, which girls say does happen although 'less as you get older'. Several parents brought up the subject of bullying, though more to make the point that school deals with it well (though one felt school 'could work harder to promote a sisterhood').

An inclusive school. Lots of talk of Black Lives Matter, including at prep stage – one little girl beamed with pride over their display board of Michelle Obama, and we also spotted a noticeboard in prep about an equality group, highlighting Tom Daley, Caitlyn Jenner, Ellen DeGeneres as role models for minority groups (though sadly our guides weren't actually sure what the equality group was or anyone who belonged to it). In seniors, there's a society for every religion and ethnicity represented within the school, plus LGBTQ+.

Pupils and parents: Families come from far and wide, especially in seniors, some travelling up to 50 minutes. Radius swoops out along the met line and coach routes – latter covers Beaconsfield, Elstree, Barnet, Amersham, Ealing, Hemel Hempstead and points between. Lots of dual income (grateful for the extensive wraparound care options); masses of doctors. Don't get too excited about cosying up for coffees with new found parent friends, though – we were surprised to hear St Helen's parents characterised as 'pushy', among other unflattering epithets: 'The parents argued so much about who would be chair of the PTA that the PTA itself nearly dissolved,' reported one (great fodder for a sit-com, we thought). Girls are chatty, strong-minded and personable – genuinely good company. Many stay the course – now from 3 to 18. A culturally diverse school, with Indian children making up around three-quarters of nursery and reception, dropping slightly in prep and to 40 per cent in seniors.

Tellingly, perhaps, when we asked some year 10 girls about drama, they assumed we meant friendship fall outs

Money matters: Currently supporting 76 girls on means-tested bursaries (just under half of these on 100 per cent bursaries). Hardship fund also available, plus range of scholarships.

The last word: May not soar the peak of the league tables, but plenty of ambition – academic and otherwise – with a superb extracurricular offering to boot. Inspiring head has put the foot on the gas for just about every area of the school, with girls and parents we spoke to ready for the ride.

St James's Catholic Primary School

RC 45

260 Stanley Road, Twickenham TW2 5NP

020 8898 4670 | info@st-james.richmond.sch.uk | www.st-james.richmond.sch.uk

State | **Ages:** 3–11 | **Pupils:** 675

Headteacher: Since September 2020 Ciaran Beatty is acting head, previously deputy head. BA in English and geography (Dublin), PGCE (St Mary's, Twickenham), MA Children's literature (London), NPQSL.

Entrance: At 3, 52 places in the nursery, almost 100 per cent moving up to reception. Parents say that they would be 'mad not to' and the remainder of the three form entry is filled from the four local Catholic parishes (priority is given to practising Catholics). The school is heavily oversubscribed and although the local birth rate is falling there are still too many children for the available chairs. The only hope of a spot further up the school is if the removal vans are ordered and parents have to, reluctantly, move their child to another school.

Exit: Parents who want their children to continue being educated in a Catholic environment tend to opt for St Richard Reynolds Catholic High School in Twickenham, though others to eg St Mark's Catholic Secondary School, Gumley House, Gunnersbury. Some to independents eg St Catherine's. Apparently, the school tends not to make direct recommendations on the next step with parents mainly doing the research themselves.

Our view: With a site tucked down a cul-de-sac next to a golf club and opposite a tidy housing estate, an outsider would need to see the school hoarding to be sure they had arrived in the right place. Past the gates and in through the door is a smallish reception space furnished with 'outstanding' Ofsted citations and a plaster Madonna, her mantle toning happily with the emerald sofa cushions beside her. Immediately, you realise that this is a school not shy about proclaiming the importance of its faith and the attendant ethos.

Off the hall is the nursery where small people were stuffing woollen balls – masquerading as buns – into a play oven or experimenting with manoeuvring a motley selection of chickens and black labradors over a grassy hillock on a computer screen. Outside, others were exploring the current topic of the Arctic by enthusiastically shovelling fake snow over miniature walruses and seals but ignoring the polar bear lying on his plastic back.

Past a screen featuring the four parish saints, together with their priests, the main school lies through double doors, surmounted by a plaque announcing that the block was opened by the Princess Royal. A long corridor, classroom doors interspersed with coat pegs and panels filled by pupils' work, provides the main artery and contains the lower years, with a floor above providing a home for the older children. There is an IT room, separate spaces where individual teaching can take place and an inviting library, complete with a librarian and a Narnia cupboard marked Book Shop. No secret world but plenty of books, provided by parents, which children can buy in instalments, but unlike the real world they can't take them home until they're fully paid up.

On the way to the playground outside is the George Tancred Centre for children with moderate autism, staffed by a team of six. It was nearly empty on our visit, proving the head's assertion that 'they are extremely successful at integrating them into the mainstream' to be correct. This was backed up by a parent saying that her son considered a child from the GTC as part of his class, even though she only came to some of the lessons. The teachers and assistants are all qualified and one small boy was certainly proud of his baking skills and made a good stab at pronouncing focaccia.

In contrast to the unremarkable façade, the back of the school is a glorious surprise with acres of grassy pitches and a newish PE building. Excellent use is made of this green paradise or muddy field (depending on the season), with children having at least two hours of games a week plus after-school clubs. They are borough champions in several sports ranging from swimming to tag rugby and even scooped a bronze medal in athletics at the London Youth Games, pretty good for a school where a class teacher is in charge of PE. In tune with their beliefs, there is even a contemplative spot furnished with benches and a gigantic pair of hands in prayer, sculpted by a parent.

Outside, pupils were exploring the current topic of the Arctic by enthusiastically shovelling fake snow over miniature walruses and seals but ignoring the polar bear lying on his plastic back

Sats are consistently outstanding and French mentioned by all parents as brilliantly taught, partly due to the specialist French teacher who catches them very young. The approach is so successful that one parent told us she was 'blown away' that her 9 year old already spoke better French than her father, who was apparently somewhat put out. In addition, to help the child with a linguistic bent, the school runs after-hours clubs in Latin, Polish and Mandarin. The work ethic is very strong, encouraged not only at school but also by a sizeable chunk of homework every evening and it is definitely a source of pride if your house wins the annual cup with points handed out for homework, manners and attendance as well as academic success.

Music is major here – we met the hugely enthusiastic and friendly music mistress, who proudly showed us her shelf of brand new, yellow ukuleles. Parents affirm that she is 'fantastic' and has made music great fun: 'it's more mainstream now'. The weekly music lessons can be topped up by extracurricular music technology clubs, recorder groups and private music lessons and there are several choirs.

As you might expect from a Catholic institution, 'manners maketh man' in this school and the children leaped to hold open doors and answer questions politely. School says that it cannot remember having a child sent to the head for 'making a wrong choice' and has never had to face the unpleasant task of calling in a parent over their child's behaviour. We felt their plan to introduce a 'habit of mind passport' for the exceptionally well-behaved might be a bit daunting for some.

The cerebral side is also encouraged by the accreditation of the school as a Thinking School in 2016. This strategy, based on Edward de Bono's Thinking Hats, puts controlled thinking at the core of the curriculum from day one. In practical terms this means more theme-based teaching with a new topic each half of the term, a change that children approve of, saying that it 'makes school more exciting'.

Large numbers of parents lend a hand, although the increase in numbers of working mothers means that there are fewer these days to help the mainly young (about two-thirds of the staff) teachers. There was zero evidence of this change causing a problem and the school gave the impression of running like clockwork, obviously partially due to the capable hands of the head. A larger staff turnover than one might expect but LY explains this by pointing out the cost of local housing, a serious problem for anyone on a state school wage.

The increase in working parents has led the school to organise a Breakfast Club and a Stay and Play scheme, which allow supervision from

We felt their plan to introduce a 'habit of mind passport' for the exceptionally well-behaved might be a bit daunting for some

7.30am to 5.30pm when necessary. Some of the only negative comments were around school meals: most of the children bring in packed lunches and there was not much enthusiasm for the food, particularly if you were not a meat eater.

Lots of parent involvement. School even persuaded one exciting father, who works for Virgin Galactic, to come and give a careers talk on building spaceships to an open-mouthed, goggle-eyed audience. Again as you would expect, charity fundraising is taken seriously with a different charity each week in Advent and Lent and pupils are in the thick of it.

Money matters: The fairly affluent, middle class parents (minuscule percentage on free school meals) muck in by raising money (about £30k annually), used to buy anything from pianos to iPads, or by contributing worldly knowledge to help with assemblies.

The last word: A successful, orderly school believing firmly in putting children on the right path, not only in terms of academic achievement but also in their knowledge of themselves and their attitude to others, but might not suit those with a rebellious streak.

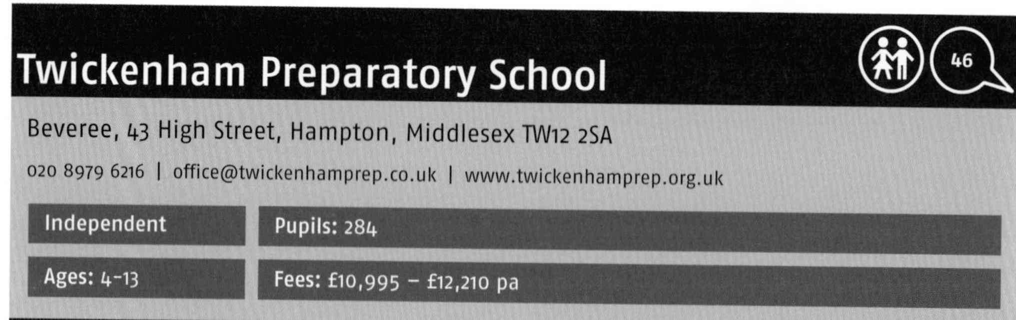

Headmaster: Since September 2020, Oliver Barrett, previously academic deputy head at St George's Junior, Weybridge. Brought up locally, he was educated at Hampton School before studying environmental studies (BA with QTS) at Roehampton, having initially contemplated a career as a zoologist during his schooldays. After realising teaching was his calling, he worked at Ashton House School in Isleworth as head of PE, games and maths, before moving to St George's in 2006 as head of year 6. Married with two daughters, both at senior school. A keen sportsman and triathlete, he competes regularly when time allows. Is also active in charity work and volunteering and currently a governor at Manby Lodge School.

Entrance: Non selective at 4+. Otherwise, occasional places only from reception onwards after assessments in English, maths and reasoning. Often take on a handful in year 6 to prepare for common entrance.

First dibs to staff children and siblings. Registered families sign acceptance form 18 months before start date. Deposit secures place – non-refundable if not taken up, deducted (with no interest) from final term's fees if it is.

Some pupils arrive at the school with undiagnosed needs, supported with, says head, 'best SEN in the area'. Parents rave about school's ability to identify barriers impeding progress – work with speech and language therapists and implement social communication programmes. 'Provision for children with dyslexia is outstanding,' said one.

Focus, however, is on pupils who will do well academically and not the right place for those who might struggle to access the curriculum. Where common entrance likely to be problematic, raised by school around year 5 though, if they want to stay, 'we would do our very best to keep them.'

Exit: Discussions about senior schools start in years 4 and 5. In 2020, year 6 girls to eg Kingston Grammar, Notre Dame, Sir William Perkins and Claremont. Years 6 and 8 boys to Hampton, St George's College, St James's Boys, Epsom etc.

Our view: So good that last full ISI inspection dates from 2012. According to parents, all that was good then (just about everything) remains so. IT – only area with a (small) question mark – is being sorted with help from ever generous parents' committee.

Name is misleading – retained after outgrew Twickenham site in the early 1990s and moved to Hampton. Not that local punters are confused. Many come from Hampton and Teddington, others from Richmond and Twickenham, a few from Sunbury, Molesey, Walton and Thames Ditton. Attracts maintained sector escapees who like school's reassuring normality. 'You don't forget where you've come from,' said one.

School's home is a pretty listed building. Modern additions including art and music block, complete with vibrant purple clock (also courtesy of parents) and matching railings. Colour also features in tasteful stripes down tracksuits, exercise in restraint that stops assembly resembling a storm at a lavender farm.

Multi-purpose hall features eye-catching wavy roof, sprung floor but variable acoustics. Older pupils must need keener hearing than ours to pick up more than the occasional word during otherwise delightfully inclusive whole-school assembly.

Open door at the back and the light, airy pre-prep kingdom is revealed. Freeflow rules outside with communal areas for all, while reception, year 1 and year 2 each have side-by-side plant-filled little gardens, with a secret leafy nature trail at the back, venue for (low) risk activities like building dens. Details-driven head of maintenance has fitted nest boxes round the pre-prep building (RSPCA occasionally called in to rescue stranded fledglings) and there's real grass over chilly perfection of artificial version (hurrah!) everywhere bar reception garden, where nature proved incompatible with over-enthusiastic scootering.

Pre-prep head Mrs Barnes, an English specialist, has been here for 15+ years and exudes warmth. Pre-prep is 'about being loved, nurtured, feeling secure and taking risks,' she says.

From year 2, testing pinwheels courtesy of teacher's hairdryer, to popular prep history teacher who performs own songs with jokes (terrible but the dates stick, say pupils), lessons are lively.

Purple also features in the tasteful stripes down tracksuits, an exercise in restraint that stops assembly resembling a storm at a lavender farm

If displays were restrained in places (art room was a bit too neat and tidy for our liking though '20 minutes ago, it would have been at a peak of messiness,' tour guide assures us), opinions aren't. Pupils have views they're keen to air, given half a chance, from reception upwards. ('We always put a chatty child by the door to talk to visitors,' says Mrs Barnes.)

Ask one child their favourite subject and you won't be allowed to leave until everyone else in the class has told you theirs, too. 'Mine is ICT, because it stands for Ice Cream Tasting,' said one impish year 4 pupil.

Considerable planning goes on behind the scenes. Pre-prep subject coordinators (specialists for music, sport, ICT) work with prep team on curriculum development to ensure seamless transition. The library is sensibly organised, with fiction and factual books in different rooms, work and play carefully separated, while do-able homework increases in upper years but so gradually you 'don't really notice,' thought pupil.

School's not very secret weapon throughout is emphasis on mind games with focus on problem solving, timetabled through the school and taught by specialists. Reception pupils might house different farm animals (where do you put the pigs if they won't talk to the sheep?); older pupils have more overt problem solving and strategy. There's even a week-long mind festival (think cerebral sports day – synapse and spoon race?).

Does wonders for exam technique – 'Helps your brain,' confirmed year 3 pupil – and boosts resilience. Just as well given the inevitable cloud on the horizon, those horribly stressful 11+ and 13+ entrance exams.

Generally, they're managed with kindness and sensitivity by the school and with grace and good humour by pupils. We did pick up a few worries at the top end of the school. 'How are you feeling about your exams?' we asked one senior boy. 'Fine... and that's the biggest lie I've ever told.'

There's competition between the four houses. Each gets an assertive website write up, headed by the surprising claim that David Garrick 'would be proud of some of our theatrical renditions of Boom-Chig-a-Boom in house assemblies'

But that's down to the system, not the school. Parents and pupils stressed (and re-stressed) the quality of staff. 'Kind and nice,' said a pupil (and umpteen mums and dads, often adding 'nurturing' by way of ringing the changes). Pressure to do well often comes from within. 'I wanted to repay my parents for the investment they've made in me,' said a scholarship winner, and clearly meant it.

Works because staff know pupils inside out (verging on over-cossetting, thought one senior pupil) with teaching and support tailored accordingly. Careful setting (maths plus small groups for English and French) avoids anyone feeling either singled out or sidelined.

Small details matter – one teacher writes end of week 'good news' note for each pupil. Rewards are all about doing better: credits and merit certificates to year 6; £5 Amazon vouchers for top years. 'Bet the teachers have never seen such good behaviour...' said year 6 girl of older boys. Demerits (for repeated transgressions – eg not handing in homework) are tactically used: 'Year 6s letting off steam after pre-tests is time to monitor everyone carefully,' says member of staff. Can result in 'sensible' detentions used, for example, to catch up with work.

Sense of being looked after is palpable. One of our guides has done 40 or so tours but insists that the 41st (ours) is a treat (we got bonus points for asking different questions). Even the fish in two tanks by the entrance – now approaching catch of the day size – seemed to exude contentment.

Rivalry does exist but is sensibly channelled. Would-be prep prefects nominate themselves, run hustings and incentivise the plebiscite with speeches and the odd song (sweets are banned). 'Odd maverick does get elected – and often surprisingly good,' says school. Otherwise, there's competition between the four houses, named for local notables. Each gets an assertive website write up, headed by surprising claim that David Garrick 'would be proud of some of our theatrical renditions of Boom-Chig-a-Boom in house assemblies.'

Presumably he'd also be impressed by the productions, mainly combining two year groups, younger as choir, older taking the main acting and singing parts, year 7 solo effort featuring cameo parts for staff. Sport was seen as less of a focus, reinforced by trophy cabinet. 'Three-quarters are for chess,' pointed out tour guide. Outdated, says Mr Malam, who reckons that sport is now on a par with other local schools and points to victories (winners of three football tournament in one term) as well as investment in good coaches and upping of fixtures.

Bar the normal girls vs boys anomalies (several girls we spoke to wouldn't mind a crack at football and cricket, though no boys were feeling the love for netball) there's masses of choice. Curriculum supplemented by numerous after-school clubs (one athletics/chess enthusiast – clearly a born multi-tasker – sprints between the two to avoid timetable clash) and extensive charity work (pupils involved in selecting deserving causes), with long-term support for Street Child African and school in Malawi.

Mind games almost essential to winkle out wish list items from these happy parents. For girls entering the school at out-of-the-ordinary times, it can be hard to break into well-established friendship groups. 'Not the same for boys – they have football,' said one, gloomily – another argument for a girls' team?

The last word: Bar a few mild gripes about slightly variable lunches (hunger damped down by break time snacks, 'some the size of a three-course meal,' said a pupil) we'd rate this a must-visit prep, which manages anxieties and aspirations of pupils (and parents) with aplomb and warmth.

Twyford Church of England High School

Twyford Crescent, London W3 9PP

020 8752 0141 | admissions@twyford.ealing.sch.uk | www.twyford.ealing.sch.uk

State | Ages: 11-18 | Pupils: 1,500; sixth form: 525

Executive head teacher: Since 2002, Dame Alice Hudson MA (Oxon). Educated at Slough Girls' High and Leighton Park, where she was the first ever head girl. Read English at St Hilda's Oxford. Taught at Central Foundation Boys' in Islington and Maria Fidelis, Camden. Deputy head at Brentside High School, Ealing before joining Twyford in 2000, where she was deputy and acting head before being appointed head. Made a dame in 2017 for services to education but, with typical modesty, at the time said she was 'taking one for the team'. Married with four children, most of whom have been educated here. Committed Christian. Loves cooking and a keen cyclist. Dynamic and inspirational. A force of nature.

Associate head teacher since 2013 is Karen Barrie, previously deputy head. Degree in maths from Manchester and still teaches one lesson a week. Softly spoken with a gentle sense of humour. Lives and breathes the school, admitting that 'Twyford has been my children.' Described by Dame Alice as 'the most brilliant headteacher the school has ever had'.

Together they make a watertight team. Highly visible at school events. One mother noted, 'They are greatly respected but are approachable, chatty and open.'

Entrance: Oversubscribed. Some 190 places in year 7, with 150 foundation (Christian) places, 21 designated as world faith places and 19 music places. Details regarding length and frequency of attendance at church are pored over with a fine-tooth comb. As one mother reflected, 'Getting a place at Twyford is the hard bit. It's a full five years of nearly weekly attendance at church.' The music scholars' places have opened things up a bit. These places are offered to those with potential, as much as to those who have had money lavished on violin lessons from an early age.

A further 130-150 new pupils (out of 650 applicants) join the sixth form each year from elsewhere. Over 500 are interviewed, so a gargantuan exercise for the school. All applicants must 'be supportive of the aims, attitudes and values, expectations and commitment of this Church of England academy'. Minimum entry requirement is eight passes at GCSE at grade 5 or better, including maths and English. Each A level course has individual entry requirements, but generally a grade 6 or 7 in related GCSE courses is expected.

Exit: Around 80 per cent stay on into the sixth form. Those leaving post-GCSE tend to opt for local colleges offering more practical BTec courses.

Roughly three-quarters of the sixth form head for university. Top destinations include Birmingham, Sussex, Leeds, Queen Mary, Nottingham, Bristol, East Anglia, King's. An exceptional 14 to Oxbridge in 2020, 13 to medical schools. Science courses most popular, followed by liberal arts, maths-related and creative arts. Seven or so take art foundation courses. Only one per cent takes on apprenticeships, in areas such as accountancy and journalism.

Latest results: In 2020, 57 per cent 9-7 at GCSE; 48 per cent A/A* at A level (78 per cent A*-B). In 2019 (the last year when exams were taken) 48 per cent 9-7 at GCSE; 76 per cent 9-5 in both maths and English. At A level, 39 per cent A*/A (71 per cent A*-B).

Teaching and learning: Superb results. Unsurprisingly for a faith school, all pupils take GCSE religious education one year early, with knock-out results. Most pupils take nine GCSEs in total, with a the most able managing 10. 'We are a high functioning academic school,' explains Dame Alice, and few would argue with her. Yet, aside from the stellar results, she also wants pupils to learn to love their subjects. It's not just about league tables.

A specialist language college. In key stage 3, half of the year group takes two languages and Latin is a core subject. Most pupils take either French, German or Spanish at GCSE, with a small proportion taking two. A minority take Latin as an additional subject. French and Latin teachers train primary teachers in the borough in their subjects. Twyford is keen to share its expertise. Starry maths and science departments too. At

GCSE, Twyford is in the top fifth percentile for progress in maths and science. Massive numbers take these at A level, some 30 of whom manage further maths too.

Strong sixth form, which has doubled in size from 250 to nearly 500. Twyford Additional Programme caters for around 50 high fliers each year who are likely to make Oxbridge or other top-notch universities, as well as those aiming to study dentistry, medicine or veterinary science. It 'aims to combine the extra skills and extended learning of the International Baccalaureate with the academic rigour and specialisation of A levels'. Focus is on developing thinking skills, presentation and honing interview techniques. Wide assortment of outside speakers wheeled in. Nearly all get A*/A for EPQ. Diverse range of essay subjects chosen including 'How far can humans travel in space?' and 'Was the English Civil War a "War of Religion"?' One parent we spoke to said, 'The school expects the children to do well and never lets up on pushing them to be the best they can. There is a very, very high level of expectation and sometimes it can feel like a bit too much pressure. But it ultimately gets the results.' Another parent agreed: 'There is no escaping the fact that if you go to Twyford, you'll work hard.' No laziness tolerated, though setting from first years ensures not everyone has to proceed at a high-octane pace. Reports of huge piles of homework from year 8 onwards.

'There is no escaping the fact that at Twyford, you'll work hard.' No laziness tolerated, though setting ensures not everyone has to proceed at a high-octane pace

Pupils assessed four times a year, so school keeps a beady eye on performance. For those slipping through the net, swift action is taken to identify the cause of the decline. 'We quickly identify whether it is lack of effort, lack of support from home or poor behaviour,' we are told. Depending upon the cause, sessions are arranged with the school counsellor or behaviour consultant, parents are contacted, or pupils are pointed in the direction of booster groups or study clubs. All hands on deck to get the faltering up and running again. No-one is left to fall by the wayside.

Despite its academic successes, there is no chance of school resting on its laurels with Dame Alice in charge. She is constantly looking at what could be done better. 'We are deeply aspirational but averse to complacency. We are a self-evaluative organisation,' she tells us.

Strong core of committed teaching staff, with 85 per cent remaining static each year. When teachers do bolt, it is usually for positive reasons such as promotion elsewhere. Teacher recruitment can be challenging in some subjects, but head remains upbeat: 'We are perpetually appointing very good graduates.' Though some opt for in-house teacher training, others come armed with a PGCE. Plenty of non-Christian teachers but they must be 'in sympathy' with the Christian ethos of the school and be happy to participate in institutional worship. New teachers are nurtured here. As Ms Barrie explains, 'Our training and support for staff has to be as tight as it is for the students.'

Learning support and SEN: Less than five per cent of pupils in years 7-11 have an EHC plan, with a further four per cent on wider SEN register. The Alternative Resource Centre (known as ARC) has a specialism in supporting those on the autistic spectrum. A wonderfully quiet haven, especially compared to the deafening Uxbridge Road outside. Attachment disorder, anxiety and ADHD as well as dyslexia, dyscalculia and dyspraxia catered for. Those on the 'nurture programme' participate in about 85 per cent of mainstream lessons, but come to ARC for support in maths and English, on an individual and small group basis. They skip some language and humanity lessons, as well as singing, to attend these sessions. Support offered includes Lego therapy, homework and lunchtime clubs. A tranquil place for the vulnerable.

The arts and extracurricular: Certainly, no lack of extracurricular opportunities and head believes that 'the students have a richness of educational experience here'.

Twyford is a specialist music college, and parents consider the music department to be extraordinary. Currently over 20 ensembles, which have performed everywhere from BBC Songs of Praise (where the gospel choir was recent finalist in Choir of the Year) to St Paul's Cathedral. High spec music rooms, including recording studios, and professional-quality performance centre. Everything on offer including a traditional orchestra, laptop orchestra, brass collective and guitar and ukulele band. Pupils encouraged to perform internally and externally at every opportunity. 'The students don't just perform for themselves, they perform for others,' explains head. Fiercely-contested music competitions. Mammoth team of instrumental peripatetic teachers give lessons to more than 350 pupils each week. Drama department also firing on all cylinders. Whole-school musical productions (eg Grease, The King and I and Hairspray) staged at the end of the summer term. Lower school also puts on a Christmas show. Huge art department too, offering textiles, photography, computer-aided design, animation, print-making and clay.

Plenty of chances for pupils to escape Acton. Trips punctuate the timetable. Language trips throughout Europe; cultural trips to Paris, Prague and Venice and sixth form historians visit St Petersburg. Active souls can ski or walk in the Alps. Closer to home, there are regular theatre and gallery trips. Parents pay for excursions, but a trip fund can be dipped into by those in need.

On top of their clutch of good grades, pupils are expected to add ballast to their CVs with work experience. Placements arranged everywhere from local primary schools and solicitors' offices to hospitals and local garages and even the Ritz kitchens. Some attend courses in hairdressing, childcare and carpentry, and others attend summer schools and workshops. Charity work also encouraged. 'We're big in the sixth form on what the students do outside of lessons,' explains Ms Barrie. Loafing around all summer would be heavily frowned upon.

Sport: Vast sports centre. Sports include rounders, netball, gymnastics, athletics, dance, football, cricket and hockey. Close links with professional coaches from QPR and Wasps to develop most talented footballers and rugby players. Takes part in multiple local leagues and tournaments. An array of trophies stretching back to the 1980s reflects its sporting prowess. Twyford also competes regularly at county level cup fixtures for football, rugby and athletics. Girls' netball particularly starry, though one parent we spoke to claimed that 'sport for girls is not perfect. It is quite old-fashioned and what's offered to them isn't great. No girls' cricket or football or hockey.' For those less keen on kicking, throwing and hitting balls around, fencing, taekwondo and parkour await. The ominously-named Cage is a fenced-off area for ball sports in the centre of the school. Though it resembles a prison compound, it is well used and ideal for teenagers with surplus energy at breaktime.

Ethos and heritage: Twyford is part of a multi-academy trust, along with William Perkin, the new Ada Lovelace and Ealing Fields, all in the same borough. 'We are stronger as a family than we were on our own. It has given us a competitive edge,' states Dame Alice. Much is shared between the schools in terms of front and back of house support, ranging from pastoral care, assessment and curriculum resources to finance and HR systems. Works brilliantly in terms of curriculum, as good lesson plans are shared on the intranet – particularly useful if one school has a weaker department. Not restrictive, however, and schools still have freedom to make own syllabus choices for themselves.

Twyford became a church school in 1981. School motto comes from St John's gospel, chapter 10 verse 10: 'I have come that you might have life, and have it to the full.' Pupils here are expected to live life to the full. This 10:10 ethos is shared by all the schools. Mostly Christian pupils, but all faiths represented. Two communions per year for each year group and the assembly we attended on epiphany was unequivocally religious. 'You need to know what you're getting into,' stated one parent.

Discipline is tight. Ms Barrie explains, 'We celebrate first. We reward positive behaviour and are not just punitive, but they need to understand the structure and rules'

The Elms, a grand Georgian building that houses reception, stands majestically at the heart of the school. Lawn in front is used by pupils to relax at break and lunch time. Jolly campus-style café serves hot food, with a canopy for those wanting a more Mediterranean experience. According to one mother, 'the real lack of variety on offer' at the café means her son is not alone in grabbing a meal deal at Tesco's instead.

Pastoral care, inclusivity and discipline: Pastoral support considered to be outstanding. Before each new cohort arrives, head of year 7 liaises with primary schools to ensure a smooth transition. Once here, year 7s have their own section of the school, as coming from a small primary to a whacking secondary presents its own challenges. Some older pupils are trained to become peer supporters to help with teething problems. One parent we spoke to commented that 'the nurturing side is strong and when my eldest had some wobbles in year 7 and in year 10, they couldn't have done more to support him. The school responds quickly to any problems and I have never felt fobbed off.' Chaplain comes in two days a week, one full-time counsellor. Seven tutor groups per year. Seven houses, named after cathedrals and abbeys: Truro, Wells, York, Fountains, Ripon, Durham and Canterbury. One mother we spoke to said that 'the school takes a lot of effort to make sure each child is prepared for the next stage in their education. In year 10, we had a one-to-one session with the head teacher to discuss our plans for A levels and university. They did this for every child in the year.'

Discipline has been tightened on Dame Alice's watch. You could hear a pin drop in assembly – not a single pupil was distracted or fidgety. Every pupil filed in past her, and each one was greeted warmly and reminded to stand up straight. Rules are strictly adhered to. Ms Barrie explains, 'We celebrate first. We reward positive behaviour and are not just punitive, but they need to understand the structure and rules.' Pupils left in no doubt about what is and is not acceptable, and one hapless boy who walked into assembly late when we visited was swiftly dispatched, with a late detention. Possession or supplying drugs, possession of an offensive weapon (including penknives), assaulting a member of staff or persistently disruptive behaviour lead to permanent exclusions. Pretty rare, though, and only a few each year are sent packing. Controversially, smartphones are banned, but 'dumb' phones (that only allow texts and calls) are allowed. Offending phones are confiscated until the end of term. 'The students know we might have to do a stop and search of their bags, if we have a good reason. If they are found with a smartphone, they know we'll confiscate it.' School not taken in by plaintive pleas of 'It's my Mum's phone and she must have dropped it in my bag by mistake this morning.' As one mother summed it up, 'The discipline if not for the faint-hearted. Zero tolerance for even minor things. You get a negative point for not having a rubber or talking in the corridor. But if you look behind the strictness you see a very kind heart, and senior management genuinely care about the children.' School runs efficiently but manages to retain the personal touch. Everyone knows where they are supposed to be at a given time and pupils scurry purposefully around the school towards their next destination. They do let off steam at certain points of the day, and breaktime can be pretty vibrant, but a sense of regimented order prevails most of the time.

Pupils and parents: Most hail from the Ealing area with large numbers from Brent, Harrow and Hillingdon and a few from Hounslow and Hammersmith & Fulham. Majority of parents are highly supportive and there's practically 100 per cent attendance rate at parents' meetings.

Around eight per cent of pupils in years 7-11 are eligible for free school meals. Just over half of the pupils are white, 31 per cent are black or mixed race. Christianity is the unifying factor. Fair amount of Polish spoken at home, as well as various other European languages and some Arabic. Not as multilingual in make-up as neighbouring schools.

Money matters: Bursaries available in sixth form for students from low income families.

The last word: A heady mixture of energetic leadership, strict discipline and high expectations. Ideal for your driven child who is keen to throw themselves into what is on offer. Not the place for the rebellious or unmotivated. Parents are full of praise and they consider their offspring to be lucky. As one mother put it, 'Twyford pupils are inspired, challenged and happy. It sets them up for life.'

Waldegrave School

Fifth Cross Road, Twickenham TW2 5LH

020 8894 3244 | info@waldegrave.org.uk | www.waldegrave.richmond.sch.uk

State | Ages: 11–18 | Pupils: 1,471; sixth form: 388 (109 boys)

Headteacher: Since January 2019, Elizabeth Tongue, previously senior deputy head at Tolworth Girls' School.

Entrance: Fully comprehensive intake. It is the only all girls' state school in Richmond so is always oversubscribed. Despite clear and rigid guidelines about admissions policies there are always appeals. Priority to those with special needs and those in public care or who are deemed by the LA to have a particular need, to siblings, daughters of staff and those living in priority areas. Most girls will have attended local primary schools in the borough. Six places are available in total in the school for those with speech and language difficulties or those on the autistic spectrum – invariably very oversubscribed.

Priority for places in the co-ed sixth form to internal applicants then looked after children, children of staff, then by distance. Five 9-4 GCSE grades needed for entry, with 6s in the subjects to be studied at A level, 7 for maths and 9/8 for further maths.

Exit: In the past students have gone to Richmond Sixth Form College, Esher College, Strodes College or to sixth forms of independent schools. This has changed as the oversubscribed co-ed sixth form enables around 50 per cent of girls to remain at the school to study for A levels. Five to Oxbridge in 2020, and five medics, one dentist and a vet.

Latest results: School won't publish 2020 results. In 2019 (the last year when exams took place), 50 per cent 9-7 at GCSE; 42 per cent A*/A at A level (71 per cent A*-B).

Teaching and learning: Consistently achieves good results in English, maths and science GCSEs. French, history, art, drama, RE always good too. The success rate in 9-4 grades is well above the regional and national average. Top of the Sunday Times Parent Power list for 11 to 16 schools for four years; now has a co-ed sixth form.

Quality of teaching is excellent. 'They're all so dedicated. I can't fault them,' said one parent. Achievements are recognised at assemblies throughout the year and at Celebration Afternoons at the end of the year. High academic standards are expected and some parents say that there is pressure on the students to get good grades. 'My daughter had to do French GSCE when she didn't want to do it as the teachers knew she would get a good grade.' But provision is made within the curriculum for all abilities, and modest acts such as helpfulness to the school or to others are duly acknowledged and rewarded.

Lessons are given in broad ability tutor groups initially, but setting for maths, science and languages occurs early on in the first years. In subsequent years, setting in other subjects if appropriate. All are entered for 6-10 GCSEs; some do up to 13 after discussion with parents and staff. Short course subjects such as ICT and PE well subscribed with good results.

A great deal is compressed into a very short 35 minute lunch break: careers advice, ICT, rehearsals for choirs and bands, puzzle club, homework clubs. Similarly, lots of before and after-school activities. A breakfast club at 8.00am every morning with badminton on offer at the same time for the more energetic. After school up until 4.00pm – choice is much more varied with a high take-up rate.

Appointed as one of the first 100 Teaching Schools, and is also a National College for School Leaders National Support School.

Learning support and SEN: Designated area in an independent learning centre for gifted and talented girls and those with other special needs. Provides 'enhanced specialist teaching provision' for six girls with speech and languages difficulties/autism. With an incredible cultural diversity (43 different languages), EAL support is strong, even offering a lunchtime club for all age groups.

The arts and extracurricular: Extra opportunities include bridge, drama (big production every alternate year and an annual joint production with Hampton Boys' School), study skills, chess, art, music theory, ICT, choirs, rock bands and full orchestra. Art and music are both strengths. Year 7s all learn the recorder and in year 8 they get the chance to play the ukulele. When we visited we were blown away by the bird sculptures made in art lessons, inspired by their sister school in Madogo, Kenya.

Lots of before and after-school activities. A breakfast club at 8.00am every morning with badminton on offer at the same time for the more energetic

After-school clubs include extra languages, eg Mandarin GCSE, and there's even an astronomy club which parents can also attend. These cost extra but the pupil premium funds places for those who qualify.

Sport: Good range of sports offered – rounders, tennis, volleyball, athletics, rugby (with the Harlequins). Classes in the fitness suite, cricket, rowing (linked in with Walbrook Rowing Club) and table-tennis. Hidden from view from the road is a huge outdoor green area with tennis courts and marked-out running track. New sixth form block features four court sports hall.

School regularly wins regional netball leagues and was recently the Middlesex hockey champion. Also borough winners at netball and rounders. Running club is popular with 40 girls doing a 5k run twice a week with four teachers before school. One of the school's aims is to improve participation in sport. Gymnastics is strong – both a multi and traditional gym on site. A dance studio was funded through the National Lottery.

Ethos and heritage: Original 1930s building has been added to over the years. Science labs are housed in newish block and brand new sixth form building opened in 2014, housing new sports hall and dining room. Outside play area transformed with money from the PTA with an outdoor theatre and landscaped surroundings. Food freshly cooked on site, and a biometric system for payment. Some girls take sandwiches. 'I don't want them having a slice of pizza and a muffin every day,' explained one parent. The girls themselves give this school a buzzy atmosphere. A former pupil remarked that 'all-girls is a positive rather than a negative.'

Pastoral care, inclusivity and discipline: No real behavioural problems. First years are invited to spend a day in the school to find their way about and practise their journey to and fro – puts a stop to later excuses about buses being late. They also start the term a bit earlier before the older ones arrive. Prefects help out with the younger ones, organise charity events, welcome visitors and play an important leadership role in the school. Each tutor group elects a representative to attend the school council, which in turn represents the school at the Richmond School Student Council. All good training ground for debating and public speaking.

School is honest about bullying and admits that, like the poor, it is always with us. However, stringent efforts made to put an end to it. Girls, staff and parents exhorted to report any incident straight away and assured that something will be done.

Pupils and parents: Although the school has no religious affiliation, the majority of the pupils are Christian. More than 25 per cent are from an ethnic minority. All come from the surrounding borough of Richmond, which is known nationally for its high level of professional parents. A local parent declares it to be the sort of school where 'decent folk will be prepared to break all sorts of rules to get their daughters in'. Co-ed sixth form is making this school even more desirable.

The last word: A really buzzy school. 'It felt more dynamic than the other schools we visited,' said one parent. This school has so much going on that you're a lucky girl if you manage to get a place here. Now with the new sixth form you're even luckier.

North

Barnet
Enfield
Haringey

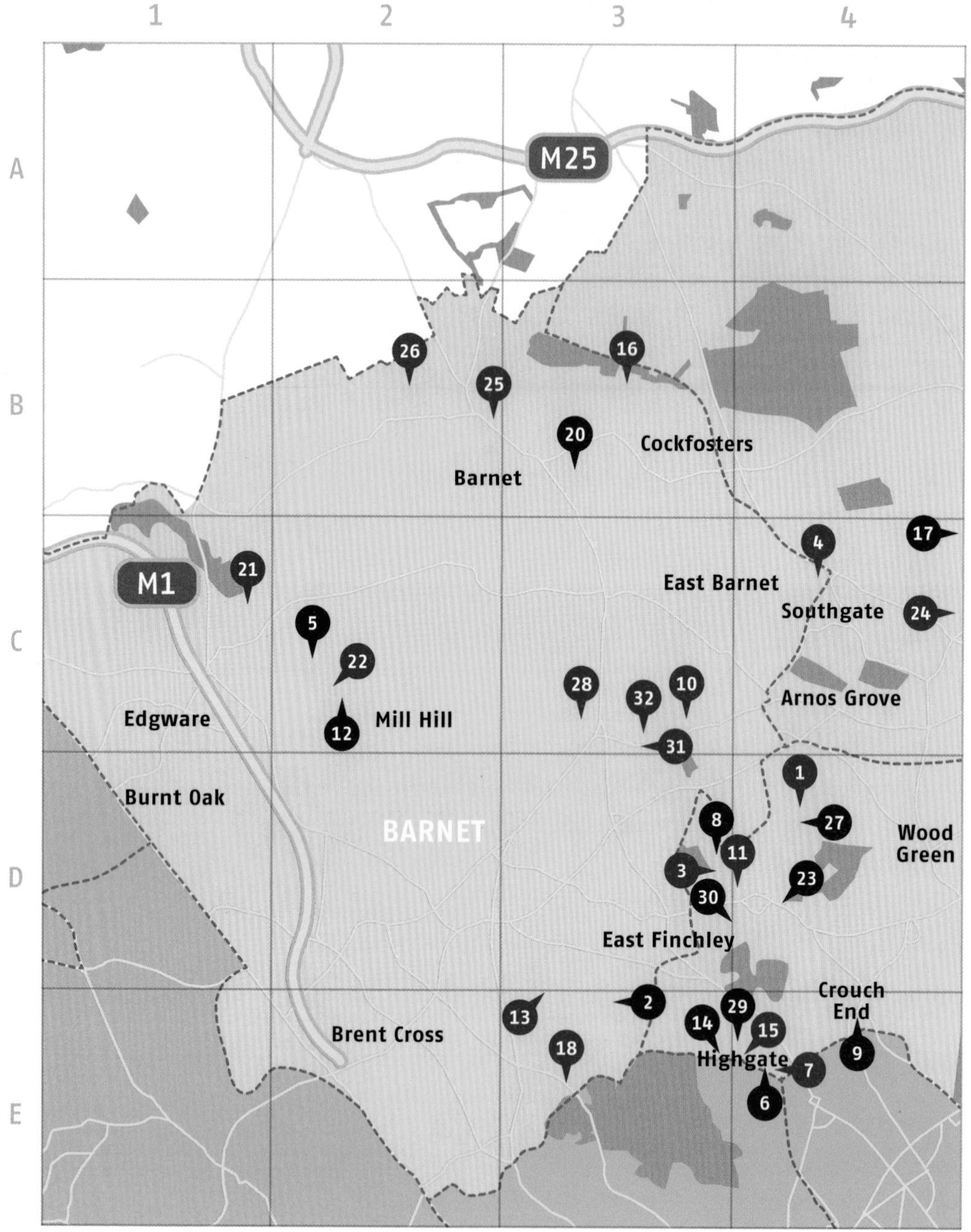
1
2
3
4
A
B
C
D
E
M25
M1
26
25
16
20
Cockfosters
Barnet
21
17
4
East Barnet
Southgate
24
5
22
28
32
10
Arnos Grove
Edgware
12
Mill Hill
31
1
Burnt Oak
BARNET
8
27
Wood
Green
11
3
23
30
East Finchley
Crouch
End
13
2
29
14
15
Brent Cross
18
Highgate
9
7
6

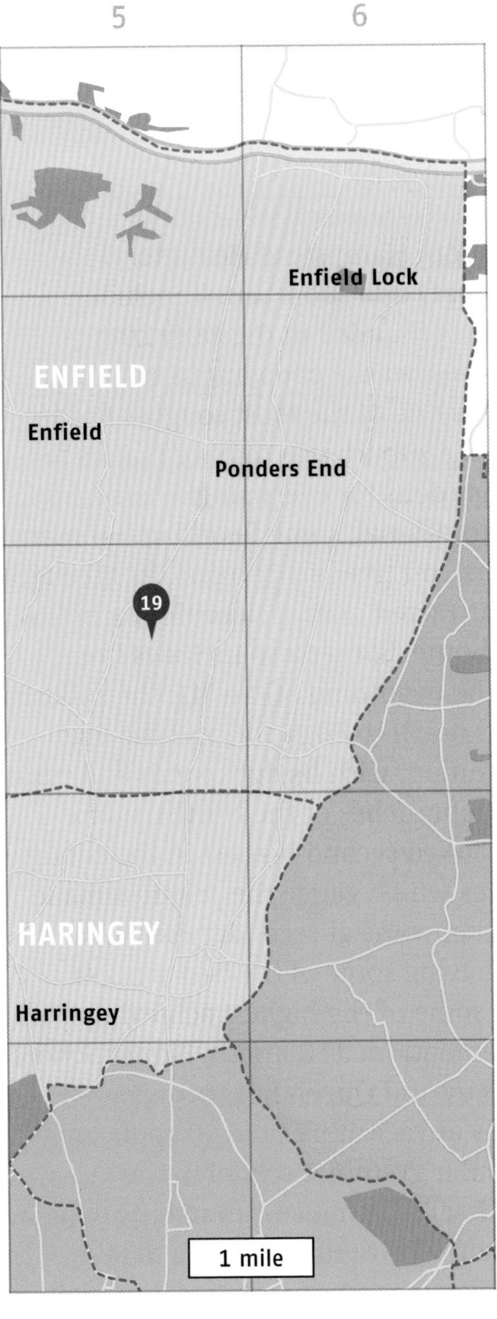
5
6
Enfield Lock
ENFIELD
Enfield
Ponders End
19
HARINGEY
Harringey
1 mile

NORTH

North London and its state schools

Barnet

Barnet, which stretches from Hampstead Heath to Hertfordshire, is mostly leafy and suburban. It includes Hampstead Garden Suburb, founded in the early 20th century by Henrietta Barnet, whose eponymous grammar school in Central Square is one of the most sought-after in the country. The idea of the suburb was to have houses for a range of incomes and gardens for every single person. So houses range from tiny to palatial, some Georgian but many Tudorbethan with flowers and tree-lined streets. Its greenery and ease into town has attracted many celebrities including Jonathan Ross to set up home. Barnet also includes Brent Cross shopping centre, the beginning of the M1, the suburbs that line the A5 as it cuts north to Edgware, and the open heathland of Hadley Common, with its duckponds and rural views. It is served by both branches of the Northern line.

Barnet was recently ranked second highest in the country based on Progress 8 scores which gauge the progress made by each student during their time at secondary school and is often talked about as having some of the best schools in London. It is home to some of the highest achieving grammar schools – aforementioned Henrietta Barnet School grammar school for girls qv and Queen Elizabeth School qv (boys), which regularly attract more than 10 applicants per place. The other popular grammar school in the neighbourhood is St Michael's Catholic Grammar qv (which is currently undergoing a major refurb expected to take just under two years to complete). Non-selective, but highly sought-after Ashmole qv, Compton, Wren Academy qv (50 per cent church places), ever popular Woodhouse sixth form college qv and Finchley Catholic High also do well. The newish Archer Academy qv is attracting increasing number of applicants including some of the bulge who previously went to Fortismere qv. Hasmonean High is for orthodox

Jewish children (boys' and girls' sections on different sites) and JCoSS qv a cross-communal Jewish school.

The new kid on the block is Saracens High School in Colindale which opened its doors in 2018 'in one of the most deprived communities within the borough of Barnet.' Although the school is part of the Saracens Multi Academy Trust, the first launched by a professional sports club in the UK, it is not a sports academy or a rugby pipeline, but an actual 'bricks and mortar' secondary school. Plans for a primary school are under way.

Another school new in 2019 is Ark Pioneer Academy – a secondary school being developed on the former Underhill Stadium site, former home of Barnet FC. The school is non-denominational and non-selective, serving the local community.

Lots of faith primaries here too, including Monken Hadley CofE, St Mary's CofE, St Theresa's and Sacred Heart Catholic schools. Wren Academy has opened a primary school on the same site as has Ashmole Academy. There are several primary schools for orthodox Jewish families, including the Independent Jewish Day School and Menorah Primary. Popular secular primaries include Brookland, Garden Suburb, and Moss Hall infant and junior schools, Foulds, Monkfrith, Martin and Northside.

Enfield

Enfield is the northernmost edge of London, with the M25 dividing it from Hertfordshire and Epping Forest to the east. It has over 100km of rivers and waterways, copious parks such as the amazingly varied Trent Park, and numerous golf clubs. It also houses the Chickenshed theatre, home to the largest youth theatre in Europe, and Crews Hill, which is one of the largest specialist garden centres in the UK.

The town of Enfield sits where the suburbs give way to Hertfordshire countryside. Lee Valley Regional Park Authority runs open spaces and sports venues along the 26 mile long, 10,000 acre park. The park was created by a unique Act of Parliament as a 'green lung' for London. Southgate has mostly 30s houses built after the arrival of the Tube (Piccadilly line) and the opening of the North Circular road in the same year. Cockfosters tends to be a favourite of north London footballers and pop stars attracted by the large new houses with electric gates and security fences.

The borough's best known school is Latymer qv, a co-ed grammar school, which attracts over 2,000 applicants for 186 year 7 places. It will generally only make offers to those in 'inner' area postcodes which includes parts of Waltham Forest, Haringey, Hackney and Islington as well as Enfield. Good non-selective secondaries in the borough include Highlands (which people are now moving home for) and Southgate Ashmole is nearby (but officially in Barnet).

Much excitement abounds for Wren Enfield, or 'Wrenfield' as it will be known – which opened its doors to 180 Year 7 students in September 2020. The school which will move to the Chase Farm Hospital site in the north west of Enfield, will be the sister school to the already hugely successful Wren Finchley and hopes to create another 'close and inclusive community with a strong Christian ethos.'

One Degree Academy, rated outstanding by Ofsted in all areas in 2019 (currently in Heron Hall in Ponders End, but also relocating to the former Chase Farm Hospital site in 2021), is a small charity-funded 30 pupil per year through school from reception to 18, which aims to give 'low performers personalised support and inspirational role models, encouraging them to believe in themselves and aim higher'.

Walker primary in Southgate is top of many local parents' primary school lists (although hugely oversubscribed and has been criticised for turning away people who live literally next door) – as are Chase Side, Monkfrith, Eversley and Firs Farm. St George's RC, St Paul's CofE and Our Lady of Lourdes are among the most popular faith schools.

Haringey

Hilly Haringey is bordered by Highgate Golf Club in the west and Lea Valley in the east. Its westerly wards include some of the most prosperous – Crouch End, Muswell Hill and Highgate – and its easterly wards some of the most deprived. Highgate village is quietly residential with a definitely country atmosphere, Highgate and Hampstead golf courses nearby and Highgate School qv occupying much of the local land and property. Many young families move to the family-friendly areas of Muswell Hill and Crouch End to take advantage of the Victorian and Edwardian houses, the arty vibe, the busy shopping streets and breathtaking views over the city (best seen from Alexandra Palace, which has recently undergone a multi-million pound revamp and has just restored the Victorian Alexandra Palace Theatre). A branch of the Northern line threads the western edge, but otherwise there are no tubes in the area, though two overground train routes make their way en route to Hertfordshire and there are good bus services. House prices have had a meteoric rise in Haringey, arguably one of the sharpest inclines of any borough in London. This is largely down to its fantastic state schools.

Fortismere qv, at the top of the liberal, intellectual and media-centric Muswell Hill, has long been the comprehensive of choice for those fortunate enough to live close enough, but Alexandra Park School (APS) qv is vying for the crown and recently achieved much media hype after scoring better in international rankings than top performers like Singapore. (Catchment in 2019 shrank to a tiny 0.48 of a mile.) Highgate Woods is increasing in popularity, so too is Heartlands High in Wood Green (near Alexandra Palace overground). It now takes much of the cohort who traditionally went to APS.

The much anticipated London Academy of Excellence Tottenham is an academically selective 16-19 free school which opened as part of the redevelopment of White Hart Lane in September 2017. The school is based on the 'phenomenally successful' model of sister school LAE Stratford – named by the Sunday Times as the State Sixth Form of the Year for 2015-16.

The more westerly areas in particular abound with excellent primary schools: Rhodes Avenue qv, Coldfall qv, Muswell Hill qv, Tetherdown qv, Coleridge, St Michael's CofE qv and St James CofE. Several have expanded in recent years to cope with huge demand, but catchments are often rather less than half a mile.

Alexandra Park School

Bidwell Gardens, London N11 2AZ

020 8826 4880 | office@alexandrapark.school | www.alexandrapark.school

State | Ages: 11–18 | Pupils: 1,787; sixth form: 635

Headteacher: Since 2008, Michael McKenzie BSc MSc PGCE. Educated at a Birmingham comp, he studied chemistry at Nottingham before qualifying as a teacher at UCL Institute of Education. Worked at various Camden schools (William Ellis, LaSWAP, Parliament Hill), then on to deputy and associate head at Beal High School in Redbridge. Immensely hard working – a 12-hour-a-day man – he no longer teaches ('There are far better chemists here than I am'), but still manages to know virtually every child by name (clearly evidenced as we walked round).

The son of a cleaner and factory worker, he waxes lyrical about the power of education to transform lives. Says this explains his early adoption of the academy model ('It allowed us to keep all the things that are special about the school'); no academic edit whatsoever in year 7; and the provision of a wide range of vocational courses. It's also influenced the decision to increase numbers in sixth form, broadening an intake that had become increasingly socially narrow as the school's popularity has grown. 'It's good to meet another range of kids,' he says.

Describes his job ironically as 'picking up litter' – and does, indeed, tidy up the few stray pieces of paper we encounter – but his main activity is orchestrating and encouraging his well-qualified and enthusiastic staff, keeping them as free as possible from modern education's tidal wave of 'initiatives'. 'There are great teachers here, and my job is to give them the time and space to perform.' That, of course, and making Alexandra Park a stimulating and happy place. 'My vision is that the kids love the school as much as I do.' His efforts are much appreciated by parents. 'He' got a vision,' said one. 'Uniform, punctuality and professional standards are all high and if a teacher's not performing, they don't last.' Chatty and engaging, he spends off-duty moments cultivating his own garden, a large London patch that would do credit to the Chelsea Flower Show.

Entrance: Now Haringey's top choice and hugely oversubscribed (1,847 applied for 232 year 7 places in 2019). Those outside the usual prioritised categories (children in care, siblings, etc), will need to live well within half a mile (0.4 in 2019) to be in with a realistic chance. The school expands in the sixth form, with about 150 new arrivals bringing numbers overall to 550 overall. Those applying to study A levels require at least five GCSES at grades 9-5, with 5s or 6s in their chosen subjects.

Exit: Just about every student that could be successful at sixth form stays on, 10-20 per cent leave post GCSE for alternative courses at colleges. Virtually all sixth formers proceed to university, about 50 per cent to Russell Group. Seven to Oxbridge in 2020 and 14 to medicine or dentistry. Other popular destinations include UCL, Exeter, Leeds, Bristol, Warwick, Manchester, Queen Mary's and King's College London, with talented musicians often proceeding to conservatoires. Good advice given, too, for those interested in apprenticeships.

Latest results: In 2020, 37 per cent 9-7 at GCSE; 72 per cent 9-5 in both English and maths. At A level, 33 per cent A*/A; 67 per cent A*-B.

Teaching and learning: A level results put Alexandra Park in the top five per cent nationally. The sixth form curriculum is broad, broad, broad, with 33 courses on offer and a range that extends from further maths and Pre-U Mandarin to vocational health and social care and applied business. Economics, English, sociology, and chemistry all achieve notably strong results. Ditto for science and maths – the school's specialist subjects, both of which are 'massively popular' and served by 17 well-qualified teachers, with pupils achieving stellar results and many continuing to STEM subject degrees. All do four subjects in year 12, and – unusually nowadays – more than half carry the fourth on to A level. 'If not, what do they do with their spare time?' asks the head.

At GCSE, the school has always believed in the fundamentals and is rock solid on core subjects. Maths particularly commendable. 'The maths is terrific,' said one parent. The school's outstanding success in PISA – the Programme for International

Student Assessment, which tests 15-year-olds from 75 developed countries in maths, science and reading – is further proof; the cohort who sat the tests from this school topped the world charts.

Most pupils take 10 GCSEs, over 40 per cent take all three sciences. 'The recent changes to exams have benefited schools like ours that are quite traditional and have never taught to the test,' says head. But, they're traditional, too, in their belief in breadth as well as depth, side-stepping the government EBacc benchmark to allow student greater subject choice. 'English, maths and science are all compulsory, then you do what you enjoy and want to study.' Other bureaucratic hurdles – such as Progress 8 – have been sailed over (top five per cent nationally), despite the more limited scope for improvement presented by its high-performing intake. 'It presents a different challenge,' says head.

This is just one of just 14 founding schools on the Mandarin Excellence Programme, the national project aimed at developing students with near native proficiency, and Mandarin is compulsory for all in year 7 ('With Mandarin everyone starts on the same level,' explains head, 'it's not down to whether your parents own a gite.') A second foreign language – either French or Spanish – also compulsory at this stage, and Turkish available at GCSE. Broad range of GCSE options, both academic (classics, music, RS) and vocational (business studies, music BTEC, hospitality and catering).

Mandarin is compulsory for all in year 7. 'With Mandarin everyone starts on the same level,' explains head, 'it's not down to whether your parents own a gite'

Teachers, generally young and enthusiastic, couldn't receive higher praise from the kids – 'The teachers are fantastic,' said one. 'Probably some of the best you could find,' said another. 'They're always here to help with anything and connect with students rather than just talking to you. They want us to do well for ourselves.' Parents, too, find most staff are willing to go the extra mile, whether that's working at weekends, seeking out opportunities for kids to benefit from or listening to parental concerns. 'When I rang for a cathartic debrief about my daughter, who'd been struggling in the sixth form,' said one, 'her teacher gave me an hour of his time and took everything I said on board.'

The school is a National Teaching School, training up debutantes in collaboration with the UCL IOE – 'I believe that teaching is a profession not a vocation,' says the head firmly, 'so we deliver through key partners.' School works collaboratively with ten local secondary schools, placing the majority of its graduates in local schools. 'We get access to bright young things, we learn from them, they learn from us and my belief is you never let a good teacher go.'

Learning support and SEN: Strong special needs, with experienced SENCo. Targeted support given in year 7 to those still facing difficulties with maths and English, and parents appreciative that the needs of the struggling middle are well attended to. 'If you look at the lower and middle end,' said one father, 'they get everyone through with good GCSE grades.' Gifted-and-talented sixth formers are identified by a dedicated member of staff. 'They're spotted and pushed forward, whether that's towards Oxbridge or Imperial,' says head. High aspirations are aided by the overall atmosphere. 'It's a school where it's cool to be clever,' said one parent. The school also copes well with specific difficulties (autism and Down's, for instance), with high praise for help given to those with more profound needs. 'Everything we were promised has been delivered without the need to chase it,' says one mother. 'My son is extremely happy and well supported and communication with his class tutor and other teachers has also been excellent.' The quality of assistance for those with EAL (about 30 per cent) was clear in a conversation with a year 10 boy, who'd arrived last year with not a word and was now able to joke about his teacher's Newcastle accent. 'Everyone here treats you the same,' he said with the broadest smile, 'they're not interested in where you come from.'

The arts and extracurricular: 'The best thing about the school is the extracurricular,' said one sixth former, 'especially the music.' Music is indeed stand-out, with a whopping 15 pupils currently taking the subject at A level and large numbers sitting the GCSE (35 the year we visited). A phenomenon the head explains by positive word of mouth. 'You get a reputation for teaching music and that reputation builds.' That reputation is rooted in a thoroughly inclusive approach, with music and drama offered in all three terms from the start, and every student expected to study both each week. Plenty of opportunities, too, outside the classroom to learn and perform, with nearly 300 studying an instrument, three choirs, orchestra and jazz band.

Drama is also offered at GCSE and A level and budding thespians are encouraged through participation in annual Shakespeare festival and

The motto of the school is 'success for all', and parents agree about its welcoming multi-cultural atmosphere and inclusiveness

large-scale productions. Art, too, flourishes – 'My favourite lesson,' said one sixth former – with a bright studio, and ample scope to test your range in exam options that include photography, art, textiles, and design technology

A myriad of clubs in lunch hours and after school – Latin, hamster and guinea pig, board games and sign language sit alongside the more mainstream. Over 120 trips a year to enlarge horizons and deepen subject knowledge, including Mandarin exchange to Beijing, social-care work placement in Portugal, classicists (with 100 students at A level and GCSE) off to Pompeii and Athens, annual orchestra tour to Europe. Scientists seem particularly blessed with visits (to CERN), activities (science week, science fair) and investment in tech (a virtual reality suite has recently been added).

Sport: Though not a school lavishly endowed with grounds, it makes the most of what it has (sports hall, fully equipped fitness centre, gym and three pitches alongside access to adjacent facilities in Durnsford Park). Wide range of sports on offer including football (boys and girls), rugby (boys and girls), athletics, cricket, basketball, tennis, volleyball, plus, for the less team-game minded, dance and keep fit. A large glass cabinet of shiny silver cups pays testimony to recent triumphs in badminton, table tennis, cricket, and volleyball, and the school won the 2019 Haringey Shield for both genders. Current pupils compete at national level in ice hockey and table tennis. Even so, not all parents are blissful about what's available. 'They are handicapped by the facilities, but I wasn't overly concerned because I felt I could plug that myself elsewhere,' said one.

Ethos and heritage: Founded originally as a technical college in the 1950s, the school was relaunched as a community comprehensive in 1990, the result of parents lobbying the local authority for a new secondary school. On a relatively restricted site – 'My only complaint is that I wish it had more outside space,' said one mother – the school is nonetheless surrounded by the greenery of Muswell Hill golf course and adjoining Durnsford Park, and clever remodelling of outdoor areas plus the purchase of some additional land now provide suitable space for lunch, play and hanging out. The inherited mix of pleasant, low-rise brick buildings, some from the 50s, some from the 80s, has been joined by some sleek modern additions, including a sixth form centre with its own cafeteria, and two new floors on top of the science block. 'I believe in adding quality,' says the head, 'not just reflecting increasing numbers.'

The motto of the school is 'success for all', and parents agree about its welcoming multi-cultural atmosphere and inclusiveness. 'They really try to be there for everybody,' said one. Its success, academic and otherwise, is attested to by the multitude of awards and accolades that plaster the website and school halls.

Pastoral care, inclusivity and discipline: A calm and orderly place where a tight, but never strangling, rein is kept on behaviour. 'Students need firm boundaries and it's important for the school to set them,' says the head. 'We expect them to be at school on time, in uniform, ready to work.' An approach appreciated by parents ('The head's very good on discipline,' said one), and on our tour of the school – where classroom doors are left open during lessons – only industrious attention was observable.

The rate of exclusions, permanent and fixed, is well below the national average – but, as the head explains, 'We use the full range of sanctions before we get to that position. We have a list of no's, and the pupils know what these are.' So, no jewellery, no fake nails, no dyed hair or make up in the lower school ('We want them to stay young as long as possible') and no mobile phones on site ('If we see them, we confiscate them – we want them to talk to each other at playtime, not text each other'). Repeat offenders of any sort are sent to The Bridge, a fully staffed, self-contained unit providing interventions for those 'who present challenges in class'. 'Where there are problems they are dealt with roundly and fairly,' thought a parent. Black and red uniform pre-GCSE is generally neatly worn, as is sixth former 'uniform' of north London casual. Pupils are friendly ('Hello, sir,' was heard repeatedly) and polite. One girl rushing to a lesson, for example, stopped to dig out her door pass from her bag to let me through. Drugs not a notable issue. Weapons, too, have fortunately been a rarity. Year 7 has its own 'transition managers' and pupils remain in the same tutor groups for five years with a director of studies for each year, learning mentors and counsellors.

Communication between parents and school unusually strong – 'All my emails, however trivial, get answered promptly,' said one. Positive reinforcement delivered through phone calls or postcards plus a commendation system of silver, bronze and gold awards. Slacking is also carefully tracked. 'They're very good at being on their case, and if they're falling behind they're immediately on to the parents.'

Pupils and parents: The school started life with an intake that stretched far into the more impoverished reaches of the borough, but its increasing popularity has meant that pre-GCSE, families are largely middle-class professionals inhabiting the broad streets and roomy period houses that encircle the gates. The large intake at sixth form introduces a broader mix – 'It's very positive, and makes pupils more aware and street smart,' said one father. Parents throughout hugely supportive, and the active PTA runs endless fundraising events and are closely involved in the day-to-day running of the school. Pupils are industrious and articulate – and most very much enjoy their time here. 'My children have all enjoyed school and have made great friends,' said a mother of three.

Money matters: A school that seems to be particularly good at tapping into broader resources, with teacher-led initiatives accessing funds from the Erasmus scheme and elsewhere. Training School and academy trust status bring in additional money and generous parents contribute to the hardship fund and facilities such as the virtual reality suite.

The last word: One of London's top performing non-selective, non-faith comprehensives, with excellent results for all, delivered through inspiring teaching, firm boundaries and positive and supportive intervention.

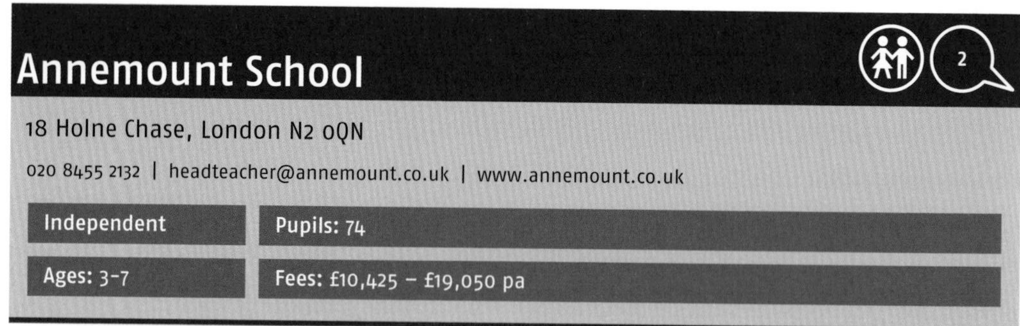

Annemount School

18 Holne Chase, London N2 0QN

020 8455 2132 | headteacher@annemount.co.uk | www.annemount.co.uk

Independent | Pupils: 74

Ages: 3-7 | Fees: £10,425 – £19,050 pa

Head teacher: Since 1993, Geraldine Maidment BA MontDip. She followed a degree in German and art history from University College London with a stint at Sotheby's. Here, she realised she preferred people to objects. 'I'd taught children as a teenager, and loved the interaction. I realised that it was a vocation.' Started her career at Bassett House, then, when her own two daughters were tiny, launched Hilltop Nursery in a local church hall. In 1993, she bought Annemount, winning out against considerable competition. ('Mine wasn't the highest offer, but they felt I would continue the style of the school.') A two-year stint in the US with her late husband, an academic at the Open University, allowed her to take a masters in early childhood education at Denver University. A talented linguist (she speaks five languages), she's also a very 'outdoorsy person', who enjoys music, the theatre and cooking. Parents undoubtedly respect and trust her. 'She cares deeply about the children and wants their happiness above all.'

Entrance: Sensible to sign up early. The school tries to keep families together, but admissions are by observation, with each child invited to a play session to ensure they're 'suited to the programme we offer and would enjoy it.' Most enter nursery at rising 3 or reception, but children considered at any point.

Exit: Most sit 7+, though a few leave before ('There's no pressure about moving if that's part of the family's plans,' said one mother). At 7, to a broad sweep of north and central London schools. Popular coed options include Highgate, North London Collegiate, Belmont, Devonshire House and Northbridge House, with girls off to St Margaret's Hampstead, Channing, City of London, South Hampstead, Haberdashers' Aske's, boys to Haberdashers', UCS, Lyndhurst, St Paul's Juniors and St Anthony's. Head's office lined with individual files on each child and 'evidence-based' discussions about future schools start in year 1. 'Sometimes it's easy to fall in love with a school and lose sight of what is best for the child. We want children to be happy and shine, grow and mature into positive learners with good life skills.' Most parents respect the head's counsel: 'We knew she'd done this a million times before, so we completely trusted her.' Children are well prepared in a fun, relaxed way, with 7+ camps (in half terms and holidays) and 7+ clubs, and head has close links with the full range of schools, ensuring transition is as smooth as possible. Not the place for those who expect hothousing.

Our view: The school follows the national curriculum, and numeracy and literacy (with one-to-one reading daily) are taught to the highest standards ('excellent,' say the inspectors) by an ample supply of well-qualified, empathetic staff. Parents particularly praise how well staff understand their pupils. 'They really get to know them academically, socially and emotionally,' said one. Another commented, 'When I go to parents' evening, I always feel teachers are describing my children, and what pleases me as much is that my children are happy and confident enough at school to behave in the same way as they do at home.'

Teaching equally successful at challenging the most able and supporting the struggling (though, perhaps, more of the former than the latter). The school has received an award from the National Association for Able Children in Education, and addresses ability largely through 'differentiation'. 'We look at who will benefit from being stretched and give them the opportunities to showcase their strengths. A singer or string player may be given performance opportunities, an able writer encouraged to enter competitions or discuss what they've been doing.' Those with difficulties are given equally seamless support, with a specialist learning support teacher, closely monitored assessment and a well-planned timetable of booster sessions worked out with teachers and, where necessary, external experts. Homework – 'manageable and achievable' – encourages independence, and parents are expected to play their part, giving children real money when shopping, measuring with them in the kitchen.

Plenty of specialist teaching, with French taught by a native speaker (in situ for 20 years), chess by a coach who supports the British junior team. Budding athletes and dancers are also aided by professional experts. Music is central, and singing given emphasis both in lessons and clubs (choir). Highly popular violin programme, with instruments passed down via the PTA. 'They like carrying the case; they think everyone plays,' says the head, who believes that learning enhances study skills and develops the academic.

Hugely popular clubs (athletics, cookery, adventure, football, science and art) from reception. 'For such a small school, the extracurricular is amazing,' said one mother, whose children participate most days. No breakfast or after-school club, however: 'It's a school, not day care,' says the head firmly. 'Umpteen school trips', too, near and far, ranging from a summer walk around the school's leafy surroundings to Verulamium (St Albans), which inspire activities such as learning Roman numerals.

Founded in 1936 as a gift to their former governess by some generous parents, the school has had only two heads (the first remained in situ till she died at the age of 93), and has something of the feel of a secret passed on from generation to generation. Housed in a low-rise private home, it makes the most of this domestic mood (with birthday teas, for example, in the head's study.) Located in leafy Hampstead Garden Suburb – 'marvellous to park and safe to walk around' – it has a large and beautifully maintained garden studded with rose bushes and apple trees. This, thoughtfully subdivided into a sensory garden, a vegetable plot (where pupils harvest their own potatoes) and a woodland garden (where children can pile up logs), acts as the school playground. More vigorous games like football – the school has its own team and strip – are played off site, while gym and swimming take place at Hendon Sports Centre. No dining hall and everyone brings their own lunch boxes.

'We make every child feel safe and loved,' says the head, who sees developing independence as a key part of her brief. 'I want pupils to greet and be greeted with a handshake, speak in full sentences, express gratitude through letter writing, and manage their belongings from an early stage.' Parents encouraged to support these goals and most are impressed by the results. 'Even my 4-year-old knows there's show-and-tell and will remember to bring something.'

School has a large and beautifully maintained garden, subdivided into a sensory garden, a vegetable plot and a woodland garden, which acts as the school playground

All pupils given responsibility, with a school council from reception debating such issues as how to improve the library and which charities to support. 'Travel ambassadors' encourage safe walking and 'rangers' ensure everything in the garden is 'ticketty boo'. All year 2s given a go as head boy and girl. Disciplinary problems are rare. 'I've never heard of any,' said one parent.

Families generally live within a four-mile radius of the school, spilling out from Hampstead Garden Suburb into West Hampstead, Highgate and Alexandra Park. Parents, from all round the world, are mainly professionals, with the rest in media, business and sport. Most choose

Annemount because they share its values ('We agree with Mrs Maidment that children should play outdoors, have time to be bored, just be children,' said one parent), and virtually all delighted with the outcome.

The last word: Parents feel their children are nurtured, encouraged and happy, as well as stretched (but never pressured) in the classroom. 'The real benefit is that they started off by loving school,' commented another. 'I give it five gold stars.'

The Archer Academy

Eagans Close, London N2 8GA

020 8365 4110 | info@thearcheracademy.org.uk | www.thearcheracademy.org.uk

State | Ages: 11-16 | Pupils: 802

Head: Since 2015, Lucy Harrison (40s). Read history at Birmingham, followed by a PGCE also at Birmingham and then a masters in educational leadership at Warwick. One could say her path was predetermined, having a head teacher for a mother and a lecturer for a father, although she says on the contrary 'my parents tried to talk me out of the profession as they know how difficult it can be, and they wanted me to consider other professions.'

Not to be dissuaded, this head dived into the deep end and started her teaching career in a 13 form entry comprehensive in Cannock in Staffordshire. Although officially hired to teach history from Y7-Y13, she was quickly promoted and took on the role as head of department for citizenship: 'It was quite a tough school in a tough area but it meant that I could start up a student council service there and also head up citizenship, which was a subject that was starting to be introduced.'

After moving to London, she took a post as head of year for primary transition at Hertswood Academy in Borehamwood, shortly afterwards becoming assistant head. Seven years later, whilst living near the Archer Academy, she saw the advert for an assistant head, which really captured her imagination. 'I had been following with interest the development of this soon-to-be school.' When the former head left to go overseas, Miss Harrison applied for the position as headteacher, alongside external candidates, and was appointed.

This is one dedicated head teacher. She virtually lives, breathes and would probably sleep at the school if she could. Pupils clearly think the world of her: 'She is amazing, we are really lucky to have her,' said one. 'Really good about being involved and cares about the school,' said another. Parents are equally glowing: 'Miss Harrison knows every single pupil by name and will do lovely gestures like send individual postcards home to pupils who have done particularly well at something.' Always available for parents to speak to we are told which, as one said, 'is pretty rare at secondary school stage. My friends at other schools can't believe it – they barely know what their heads look like.'

Understated and elegant, this head is almost a metaphor for the school, we felt. She clearly regards it as her pet project and undoubtedly feels the weight of responsibility a new school carries with it: 'This is the greatest privilege – I need to get it right.' When she has free time (which probably consists of very few hours), Ms Harrison enjoys reading, the theatre and is a dedicated gym goer.

Entrance: Heavily oversubscribed with pupils mostly living within about half a mile. No longer has a feeder school system, though most come from Martin, Brooklands, Garden Suburb and Holy Trinity primaries, which the school says 'is good for the community and developing strong relationships.' Now gives priority to those in N2 (45 per cent of places), N3 (35 per cent) and NW11 (20 per cent). Head says: 'Whilst it's wonderful to be so popular, I am also very sad that we can't offer a place to everyone who wants to come. However, I have to hold onto the fact that it was only ever meant to be a small, local school.'

Exit: Archer currently has no sixth form, so pupils leave after GCSEs. The head told us: 'I always wanted Archer to be an 11-18 school and we did put in an application, but it was rejected.' This, we understand, is largely due to space.

But every cloud... and as a result of this, the Archer has forged a partnership with neighbouring Woodhouse College, renowned for its academic excellence and difficulty in securing a place: '80 of our students went there last year and although they still have to get the same results as everyone else, they are top of the pile.' Forty or so of the students went to other high performing sixth forms including Latymer, Highgate, Henrietta Barnett, Dame Alice Owen and Fortismere. Also has links with Barnet & Southgate College, and the remaining 30 went on to do vocational courses or apprenticeships – one student went straight to Mercedes. 'Every young person went on to a post-16 placement,' the head told us proudly.

Latest results: In 2020, 43 per cent 9-7 at GCSE; 86 per cent 9-4 in both maths and English. In 2019 (the last year when exams took place), 36 per cent 9-7 at GCSE; 77 per cent 9-4 in both maths and English.

Teaching and learning: August 2020 saw the Archer Academy's third set of GCSE results and they place the school in the top 10 per cent of schools nationally. Extremely high performing subjects were Italian, art, chemistry, physics and biology. French from year 7 and Spanish from year 8; nearly everyone takes one of these to GCSE. Vocational options include a BTec in health and social care and a VCert in engineering. There is also a functional skills course instead of a foreign language, with options for higher achievers including further maths and statistics. Currently no sixth form, so pre- and post-GCSEs students get help from teachers in choosing the right A level options for them at other schools or colleges. Recently rated outstanding by Ofsted.

A dedicated head who virtually lives, breathes and would probably sleep at the school if she could. Understated and elegant, this head is almost a metaphor for the school

'Ever such a lot of assessing,' one parent told us, and said they were not sure if that was down to being a new school, or new curriculum demands. That said, the school seems to cater as well for the academic child as those who find it a bit more of a struggle. Its relatively small size (six forms per year with approx 27 per class) gives it the luxury of being able to offer extra attention to those who need it.

We loved the idea of thematic learning which, we were told, is 'unique to the Archer Academy'. Students study a variety of subjects thematically 'rather than through the lens of one particular subject'. The content is changed yearly – when we visited, Icons was the theme and students were exploring the work of artist Frida Kahlo.

Learning support and SEN: There's a well-resourced SEND department with a very involved and dedicated SENDCo. They have wheelchair facilities and are completely DDA compliant: 'We are a very inclusive school.'

The arts and extracurricular: For the artistic child, this is definitely a school to consider. Possibly the most ambitious offering we have seen for a long time. Hosts an annual week-long literary festival, which in 2019 focused on Shakespeare to tie in with his birthday, with debates around Romeo and Juliet and visiting performers.

We were also super-impressed with the beautifully presented Archer Anthology: a collection of short stories written by 23 students as part of the fundraising for Make Beaumont Brilliant campaign. So far parent power has raised over £100K towards the required £150K for a brand new upper school library. The anthology, together with other events such as a whole school Archer Adventure walk, have all helped. The school has many visiting authors, too – recently Amy Cross.

Big on drama – recently won the Welwyn Drama Youth Festival for the fourth year running and 2019 saw the first whole-school musical – Fame. Dance is also a very popular subject and seemingly done to quite an advanced standard. The school has competed successfully in dance competitions against other schools in Barnet, winning the Barnet Dance Competition three years in a row. They also won gold at the London Youth Games in both junior and senior categories recently.

Several music groups – choir, orchestra, strings and jazz – with recitals performed at the local church and occasionally in Marylebone church as well. 'Phenomenal yearly showcases,' we are told.

The excellent twice-weekly enrichment programme 'is a chance to discover new talents and passions through stimulating and fun activities'. Picasso art, woodland school, fencing, web design, taekwondo, rock climbing and environmental society are just some of the amazing subjects on offer. Year 9s spend one of their enrichment sessions on a year-long accredited activity such as DofE or sports leaders qualifications.

Plenty of opportunities to travel: French and Spanish exchanges for linguists, Berlin for historians, Iceland for geographers and a USA or Austrian ski trip for years 9-11. Year 7s go on a bonding trip at the start of the year.

Lots of exciting ways to inspire the students. We were told of the 'amazing' math-magician, the visit from writer/broadcaster Alex Bellos, the year 10 trip to Downing Street and the cultural society. One parent said: 'Ms Harrison is so unbelievably dedicated. She really tries to expose her students to as many opportunities as possible. Her cultural society is a great idea. She can take up to 20 pupils out on a first-come-first-served basis – and so far my son has been to see School of Rock and Swan Lake, at very reduced prices.'

Sport: Sports historically not the strongest subject, but that is slowly changing. Boys' football is starting to thrive with extra help from a parent who is also a professional football coach. Cricket and rugby are also slowly coming up through the ranks in local fixtures, although girls' football and netball still have a way to go. One parent told us, 'If I had any criticism of the school it would be their sport. Both my girls tried netball and football but weren't very impressed, mainly because of the apathy of the students and games getting cancelled.' Another said, 'Because the girls' sport was a bit lacklustre, my daughter started drama instead. That has been amazing for her. It has completely engaged her.'

'Inspire' and 'aspire' seem to be the two underlying themes of this school – very much in keeping with the IB philosophy. 'I'm glad you picked that up,' the head said

Good gym facilities including mirrored dance studios, trampolines and a very impressive climbing wall. Climbing is an assessed module and even offered at GCSE.

Ethos and heritage: School derives its name from a local landmark and opened its doors in 2013, following a rigorous campaign by local parents frustrated by the lack of mixed, non-selective, non-denominational secondary provision in the area. The excitement was almost tangible in East Finchley. One parent told us, 'We've waited so long for a school around here. You wait, people will be moving into the area soon to get in.'

When we first visited, the school was on one site on Beaumont Close, a small turning off the Bishops Avenue in East Finchley, formerly home to the Institute, an adult educational college. Fast forward several years and the school is now on two sites – the swanky new, larger one is a brisk 10-min walk away. This £12m development is home to students in years 7, 8 and 9. Set back from the busy East End Road, it is on Stanley Road, a small cul-de-sac accessible only by foot from this entrance.

The school premises struck us as clean and elegant. Choice artwork was meticulously and beautifully framed, as was the series of quotes on each floor by the wide staircase, by everyone from Nelson Mandela to Lao Tzu, intended to 'inspire', we were told. 'Inspire' and 'aspire' seem to be the two underlying themes of this school – very much in keeping with the IB philosophy, we thought. 'I'm glad you picked that up,' the head told us.

The students we met were respectful and articulate. Fiercely protective of their school, and when one pupil said something slightly negative another shot them a look. They presented as a dapper bunch in their grey uniforms with an injection of lime green on the V-neck pullovers and the school archer logo. Students graduate to 'blazer' status once they reach the upper school: 'it gives a sense that they are aspiring to something and moving to the next stage.'

Very much split on two sites. 'Feels like a progression to get to the other site,' one parent told us. A small graduation ceremony even takes place at the end of year 9 before moving from the Stanley Road campus to Beaumont Close. One parent said, 'I love the fact that it is on two sites. Arriving from small primaries can be so daunting, but this feels like another small school for them.' Year 9 students get to mentor the new year 7s, 'which gives them a sense of responsibility', and they in turn get mentored when they graduate to the upper building.

Pupils from Stanley Road commute to the other building for their bi-weekly enrichment classes, and the older years use the Stanley Road outdoor sports facilities. When we revisited Beaumont Close, we were a little disappointed and felt it was very much the poor relation to its newer, shinier sibling. Not much had changed since our 2014 visit, and we felt it could do with a little love and a serious injection of colour. However, the brand new library should kick-start this.

Pastoral care, inclusivity and discipline: Boundaries are firm. Smartphones or any other screens are a complete no-no anywhere on the school premises, and even if spotted in a student's bag will mean an immediate Saturday morning detention: 'This is a black and white rule, which means we have removed a lot of that issue with pupils and parents and they are fine with it,' the head says.

One parent told us: 'The school does try to embed a disciplined environment from a young age, which sometimes feels like a grammar school setting. This has suited my kids, but other parents have decided not to go down that route.'

For the artistic child, this is definitely a school to consider. The most ambitious offering we have seen for a long time

Another said: 'Lucy Harrison tries to instil quite a strong sense of respect in her pupils and make them conscious of the world around them.'

Disruption in class has been an issue, according to one or two of the parents we spoke to, who told us that sometimes they feel that the younger teachers may not be equipped to deal with it. One said, 'You get class clowns in every school and those who are not motivated to work, but I feel that because some of the teachers are not that much older than some of the pupils, it can sometimes be a problem as they don't have experience on their side.'

But other parents are more forgiving and say that the school is still growing and learning, and that whilst the teachers are a pretty young cohort, they are enthusiastic. One parent added: 'The school listens, that's the main things. I've had to go in on a couple of occasions to voice my concerns, but it doesn't fall on deaf ears – they are proactive.' We were also told of very good communication between staff and parents: 'We weren't able to have their email addresses before, but now we can.' Ofsted commented that 'staff have the highest expectations of themselves and of pupils'.

Zero tolerance approach to drugs and school organises 'drop down days' where outside agencies and specialist drug charities come to give talks and run workships. The head says: 'You can't ever think you've ticked that box – these are ongoing issues for young people. It's about accessing the right information and being continually informed.'

We were extremely impressed with the transition process for new year 7s. All prospective pupils are expected to read The Phantom Tollbooth by Norton Juster: 'It works as a bridge between schools and is a shared experience when we come to discuss the book at the start of the term,' the head told us.

Pupils and parents: Extremely dedicated set of parents, particularly for a secondary school – perhaps because many of those who are involved with the Friends' Association are the same ones who helped to set up the school. Parents have raised substantial funds through cheese and wine evenings, quiz nights, school auctions (teachers even get 'auctioned off'), 70s and 80s discos etc.

Ethnically mixed, but a predominantly professional and middle class bunch: 'Generally, a fair reflection of the school's location.'

The last word: A much-needed local school, which by many accounts is proving to be a resounding success. A great option for parents who want a smaller school for their child that doesn't shy away from discipline and high standards. Veers towards the artistic child. As a parent, be prepared to muck in.

Ashmole Academy

4

Cecil Road, London N14 5RJ

020 8361 2703 | office@ashmoleacademy.org | www.ashmoleacademy.org

State | **Ages:** 11–18 | **Pupils:** 1,717; sixth form: 412

Head teacher: Since 1997, Derrick Brown MA MBA DipEd – degree subjects psychology and business. Mid 60s but, much to the glee of parents and pupils, 'nowhere near retiring'. Previously vice principal at Leigh City Technology College in Dartford and then senior deputy at Cranford School. Originally a scientist but changed career when he realised it wasn't all about 'filling pretty liquids into tubes. It was actually quite isolating and I'm a people person.' He was advised at the time to become either a teacher or a prison governor. He opted for the former.

Indomitable, earnest and tirelessly focused, he is a seriously (and serious – we found humour quite thin on the ground in this school) successful head. It was his own 'not great' secondary school that was largely responsible for his determination in bettering the state school system – in this case, turning a bog standard local comp into one with all the academic benefits of a private school education, without the fees. Within just one year, the results were up 10 per cent and the fruits of his labour have borne ever bigger harvests in the years since. Secret lay in digging down into areas that were lacking, forming partnerships with parents, creating a new discipline system, scouting good teachers and having a football manager's mentality of never giving up on finding things to improve. Also understands education on a personal level, having two (now grown up) children of his own. One gets the feeling that he has little time or inclination for pursuing extracurricular interests and hobbies.

The head's secret lay in digging down into areas that were lacking and having a football manager's mentality of never giving up on finding things to improve

Parents and students are mainly in awe, nobody left in any doubt of his role in providing them with comprehensive education at its best. But we couldn't find anyone who claims to see much of him. Parents told us, 'He's very professional and easy to talk to, but we don't have much, if anything, to do with him'; 'We've never met him personally although I did see him in reception once'; 'Not everyone's cup of tea because he runs a tight ship and the school is run very much like a business, but I like him'. Etc. Students, who say they occasionally see him at assembly or in the corridors, struggled to describe him at all, eventually settling on 'professional' and 'business-like' – although one added that 'his addresses make it very clear how much he cares about us'.

Entrance: More than 1,500 apply for the 261 year 7 places (now nine form entry), with a recent spike in the number of places taken by siblings (140 the year we visited – the highest ever). The commitment to siblings aside, you'll get in if you have a looked-after child or live very close – otherwise no chance, with the catchment area having recently decreased from an already small 0.6km to an even tighter 0.4km. Up to 20 music aptitude places; these pupils, along with others who show talent, are placed on the music scholarship programme.

At sixth form, the school usually takes 50-60 external applications (although that figure may be on the rise – it was 100 the year we visited). Entrance criteria are a 5 in English and maths and 6 (with a few exceptions of 5) in the subjects they wish to study at A levels.

Exit: Some 40-50 per cent leave after GCSEs. With Barnet College just a hop, skip and a jump away and Southgate College not a great deal further, vocational courses lure some. Others leave because they don't get the grades to stay on – a sticking point among some parents, with one feeling it is 'unfair on those who worked hard but just missed the mark – where is the school's commitment to these students?' Around 40 per cent to top universities, but they don't get huge numbers wanting to go to Oxbridge (two went in 2019, and five medics). Others to places like Durham, Warwick, London universities, Nottingham, Leeds. Science, law and humanities are all popular.

Latest results: Excellent results for an entirely non-selective school: in 2019, 75 per cent got 9-5 in both English and maths at GSCE and 43 per cent 9-7 grades. At A level, 25 per cent A*/A and 57 per cent A*-B.

Teaching and learning: The high results are sustained year after year and knock the socks off other non-selective schools in the area. Strong on value added too. Anyone can achieve here, we were told – boys, girls, the less motivated, 'everyone does better than they think they will'.

Close monitoring and regular assessments are considered the magic ingredient, but that doesn't necessarily mean an endless stream of tests (although students say there is a lot of that too), with homework, essays and questions in class also used to spot any areas of underperformance so that staff can intervene quickly – whether via extra work, small-group work, one-to-ones etc. Teachers are also closely monitored, although some parents told us they would like to see teachers staying longer – 'The churn of teachers has been my only disappointment and it does worry us,' said one. But school says turnover is similar to most London schools and is actually healthy in preventing complacency. With the exception of a few parental niggles, teaching gets thumbs up, with students reporting that they 'really care about your results' and 'ensure they do whatever they can to ensure you achieve'. Homework levels reported as fair.

French or Spanish from year 7 (usually depending on what the student learned in primary school), with Spanish significantly more popular. A second language is added in year 8, with 90 per cent taking at least one at GCSE – 'A few years ago, parents were battling to avoid their child taking a language at GCSE and now they're battling for the opposite,' says head. Setting in maths and loosely in languages from spring term of year 7, then in English from year 8 (students are taught in the same groups for humanities,

School downplays G&T programme – one student we met said, 'I think I might be on the programme, but I'm honestly not sure'

although these are not officially set). Most do an ambitious 11 GCSEs, with English gaining the strongest results, and maths and sciences not far behind. At A level, students usually take three (sometimes starting with four to help them decide between two subjects), with sciences among the most popular subjects, and geography and history the shining stars in terms of results.

For the 30 to 40 per cent of students who are identified (mostly in year 7, sometimes later) as having the strongest ability across English, maths and science, there is the 'gifted and talented' programme – includes teachers challenging them further in the classroom, visiting Oxbridge, learning through Firefly (the school's virtual learning environment), GCSE mentoring etc. After a rather rocky start (at our last visit, some parents complained that it was an 'exclusive club' that made other students feel less worthy), it now has buy-in from most parents whether or not their child gets the golden ticket. School believes it's because the programme is now much less rigid, plus they offer more opportunities for those not on the G&T programme; it also downplays G&T – one student we met said, 'I think I might be on the programme, but I'm honestly not sure.'

Learning support and SEN: A third of students have EAL, 'but they often speak English quite well' so in-class intervention is adequate although additional help is there if required. Around a seventh have some kind of SEN – about one or two per cent with EHC plans, again with support provided in or out of the classroom (by TA in younger years) or smaller group or one-to-one work for more serious needs. Good progress is reported among parents of children with SEN, as well as for medical needs. 'The school promises to help every child succeed, and I'd say they live up to that promise,' said a parent.

The arts and extracurricular: Musical children are unlikely to be disappointed, with decent amenities and technology including two recording studios and an extracurricular programme to rival most comps including orchestra, jazz band, chamber string group, junior string group, brass band, senior wind ensemble, Latin rock band, two choirs and show band for the annual school musical. The school also has its own radio station. Amy Winehouse spent a few years here (although head, who was here at the same time, says: 'Amy left us quite early on to join the BRIT school'). Music scholarships available to help those with talent develop their skills, and students can also take individual music lessons with peripatetic teaching. 'My boys get an early lunch pass so they can rush off to the music lesson, where they spend most of their lunch break,' said one parent.

Rehearsal for A Christmas Carol was in full swing when we visited (there's always an annual whole-school production) and we also saw the two spacious drama studios being used for GCSE drama, with small groups of boys and girls engrossed in their scripts. Not much chance to get involved backstage, though – we wonder if parents are shooting themselves in the foot by writing, as they do, to the head saying things like, 'Great production, shame about the sound.' Light, bright art studios lure in wannabe artists, while teachers get them enthused by 'really letting you experiment' – we heard how one student was working on a project 'with only natural objects'.

Clubs aplenty, both at lunchtime and after school, including film club, debating societies, Mad for Books club, philosophy, FemSoc, homework clubs and numerous language clubs. Meanwhile, enrichment groups offer a choice of cultural, entrepreneurial and environmental activities. 'Boredom doesn't feature here,' a student told us – and if it does, they get out their 'book of choice' (head insists everyone carries one – 'there's no such thing as doing nothing').

Sport: Your sporty child will be suitably wowed by the facilities including huge floodlit Astro, playing field, tennis courts, sports hall and separate studio for dance, aerobics and net sports, but no pool. Outdoor table tennis tables prove popular, especially at lunchtime. Football is the star sport here, both for girls and boys, with netball, basketball and badminton among the other offerings. 'They are looking to win trophies and they do quite well,' said a parent, with successes widely celebrated, but this does not seem to be at the cost of wider participation with students telling us 'you don't get too many people hating PE here'.

Ethos and heritage: Quite literally unrecognisable from the Ashmole of a few decades ago. School was hanging on by the skin of its teeth when current head arrived in 1997. He organised to sell six acres of school land and began his visionary building programme with the proceeds in 2004 (at a cost of £14m). The result is a bright and spacious, well-mapped-out building, which is practically impossible to get lost in thanks to all subjects being grouped into their own sections and everything impeccably labelled. The only thing that's confusing are the different coloured named staircases, like the 'orange staircase', which in fact is blue (the plan for colour coded stairs didn't wind up being DDA complaint for partially sighted people, so everything had to be kept white and blue). Lifts are also available for students with disabilities.

The corridors are large, open and wide with CCTV cameras to deter and spot any deviant behaviour or bullying (right from the planning stage, the head insisted on no 'little cul-de-sacs' where vulnerable students could be cornered); students and parents report that there is now very little, if any, of either. If there was a Good Schools Guide prize for the quietest school, Ashmole would be a strong contender – turns out there's a school policy for lessons to be silent unless the teacher decides a discussion will keep things focused. Walking through the school as lessons were in progress we became acutely aware of how loud our softly-spoken voice sounded. Most classroom doors were closed, but we did spot one wide open, revealing students, all heads-down, quiet as church mice.

If there was a Good Schools Guide prize for the quietest school, this would be a strong contender – we became acutely aware of how loud our softly-spoken voice sounded

Newest kid on the block is the sixth-form centre (2015), kitted out with its own Starbucks (a major pull to sixth form) in the downstairs social area and silent study area upstairs, but we noticed it was full to the brim – 'We definitely need more space, but thankfully the school is working towards an extension,' said one student. That's if you don't count Ashmole primary school, which opened on the premises in 2016 (our advice: book your kids in now). All this, and there's still plenty of outdoor space left in the 28 acres of land in residential Southgate, including immaculately kept lawns and outdoor classroom and environmental area, fully equipped with wooden table and benches. Inside and out, it's spotlessly tidy – not a single piece of litter in sight.

Pastoral care, inclusivity and discipline: With 1700 children on site, there is no room for waywardness. 'If your child is not interested in behaving or working hard, this is not the school for you,' we were told time and again by parents in a myriad of ways, most of them revelling in disciplined approach to eg disruption in class, unpleasantness to other students, rudeness to staff and uniform code, as well as the zero tolerance of eg drugs, weapons and violence (on or off the premises). 'The tight discipline is the very reason I chose the school,' said one, although we found fewer votes of confidence in the mobile phone ban which applies to all except sixth formers. Even we were told no phones, please. Apparently phones are confiscated immediately if found and we didn't want to risk it (needing, as we did, Google Maps to navigate our way home). To add to the humiliation, parents have to go in to school and pick them up. But while it has long been a bone of contention with parents ('There are times I need to get hold of my child, for goodness' sake', said one), others are grateful, if for no other reason that it avoids phone thefts in the area as muggers know not to bother with Ashmole kids.

For youngsters who break the rules, it's usually a detention or community service, but never without explanation, eg sloppy conversations in class can lead to name calling and unpleasantness, a push or a shove could lead to greater violence, uncontrolled talking in class can be a breeding ground for threats that can form part of bullying. For more serious offences, students are sent to the individual learning room, where they work under supervision and have zero contact with their friends and hate it. One day usually does the trick, with the head rarely having to exclude (once in the last few years). The result is a school in which pupils feel safe and secure and feel free to express themselves and learn within those boundaries – 'it doesn't feel restrictive, although I guess it could appear like that,' was a typical student comment, although we did hear a few niggles about the 'one way system' and 'rules around boys' haircuts – so much stricter than for girls'.

There's a full-time counsellor and each key stage has its own managers and learning mentors who students told us they can approach at any time. They feel mental health is prioritised and regularly discussed, eg in the daily 'thought for the day' debating session in each form room. Students also praise the mixing of year groups, encouraged by the cultural and charitable activities such as Jeans for Genes and inviting old folk from local care homes in for a roast dinner.

Pupils and parents: Diverse ethnic mix, reflective of the Southgate area, including a traditionally high number of Cypriots – Greek and Turkish – plus a more recent increase in Eastern Europeans and those of African-Caribbean and Chinese origin. Christianity, then Islam, are the main religions. Nearly all families are dual income, but many find time to join the active PTA which makes a significant contribution to the school's development. Parents are very much on board with the school's academic, no-nonsense ethos; you'll get few, if any, marching into school to demand why their offspring have been reprimanded: 'if they get into trouble for misbehaving, bring it on,' said one. Students too are mainly loyal to the school's principles and clearly feel fortunate to be there; we found them ambitious, focused, polite and positive. Alumni includes Amy Winehouse, former S Club 7 member Rachel Stevens, musician Stephen Sidwell, goalie Mark Bunn, Oscar-winning producer Mark King, The Feeling lead vocalist Daniel Sells and Channel 5 tsar Sham Sandhu.

The last word: A highly disciplined, aspirational school with a welcoming, community feel and a culture where it's cool to want to learn. A comprehensive in the truest sense of the word with (not surprisingly) an ever-tighter catchment area. If there was ever a Southgate street where estate agents punch the air with elation when a house comes up for sale, it will be Cecil Road.

Belmont Mill Hill Preparatory School

The Ridgeway, Mill Hill Village, London NW7 4ED

020 8906 7270 | imanfredi@belmontschool.com | www.millhill.org.uk/belmont

Independent | Ages: 7-13 | Pupils: 538 | Fees: £18,822 pa

Linked schools: Grimsdell Mill Hill Pre-Preparatory School, 632; Mill Hill School, 659

Head: Since 2015, Leon Roberts MA PGCE. Taught for four years in the state sector, moved to Keble Prep as head of history for the next four years then became deputy head (academic) of Belmont in 2004 before being promoted to senior deputy head (pastoral) in 2010 and finally taking on the headmaster's role. Married with three young daughters, including twins, he enjoys cricket (playing and coaching, both boys and girls), walking and watching Nordic Noir drama.

Down-to-earth, hands-on and with an equally energetic style as the previous head, he approaches the job with the same consultative and open approach – he's building on a school which is in great shape (which he's been involved in creating) and adding his own mark.

Entrance: Automatic entry from pre-prep (Grimsdell) to prep (two-thirds of entry); a few (very rare) exceptions. For external candidates, 7+ and 11+ are the two main points of entry. Occasional places in other years. Heavily oversubscribed for external candidates; reading, creative writing and maths tests together with a reference from their previous school.

Exit: At least 95 per cent move on to Mill Hill School, although all have to sit the entrance exam (only for setting purposes). 'Children for whom Mill Hill is not the right school' leave at the end of year 6. Once in year 7, automatic place at Mill Hill at 13+ provided they don't mess up. A parent felt that going through to 13+ was a massive advantage. 'At 13 they are desperate to make the next jump and are confident to do it. They are not little 11 and 12 year olds floundering around.' Occasional transfers to boarding schools eg Harrow, Tonbridge and Stowe.

Our view: Established in 1912, following the success of its senior school Mill Hill, Belmont Prep opened its gates with one student – Harold Pearse Soundy. A year later it had 12 pupils. Originally a boarding prep for boys, it has been a day school since the 80s and co-ed since 1995. The school is in an enviable location on Mill Hill's Ridgeway – set back from the road and flanked by large houses and beautiful greenery. Hard to believe that central London is so close. Harder still, after taking in the 35 acres of parkland and the panoramic views of the Totteridge Valley. Undoubtedly the school's selling point, the grounds and its facilities are impressive for a London-based prep school.

For a sporty child, this must be nirvana; seven rugby pitches, 10 football pitches, three cricket pitches, five cricket nets, five rounders pitches, two Astro mini hockey pitches, six Astro tennis courts, six netball courts, a fully equipped gymnasium and a small dance hall. There's also a 1,500 metre woodland cross-country course known as the Oti (in memory of a former student who died of sickle cell anaemia) and new sports hall with climbing wall and space for wellbeing. Pupils also have the use of the new 25-metre indoor swimming pool at Mill Hill School. As one parent told us, 'Forget this school if your child has absolutely no interest in sport; they'll be unhappy.'

Outdoor facilities also include a large wooden adventure playground, a variety of large games including a giant chessboard and a gardening area where pupils tend seasonal plants and flowers. We spotted a little recycling area only to learn that Belmont has been awarded the much coveted Eco-Schools Green Flag Award.

The original 18th century house acts as the main entrance to the school and houses the function rooms, main reception area, staff rooms and the head's office; a slight anti-climax after the spectacular exterior. Tastefully refurbished (with the original beautiful winding staircase) but several of the classrooms on the upper level seemed on the cramped side and lacking in imagination. The science labs (in the Cloister Block) and the gymnasium, particularly, struck us as archaic and in need of a refurb. That said, the Jubilee Hall, which accommodates most of the lower school classrooms, the dining/assembly hall and the head of lower school's office, is modern and airy.

Hard to believe that central London is so close. Harder still, after taking in the 35 acres of parkland and the panoramic views of the Totteridge Valley

The school has a slightly informal, genial vibe. Colourful and interesting displays of student work adorn the corridors, and the pupils we witnessed, whilst not particularly noisy, were 'spirited'. The latest ISI inspection spoke of pupils 'with confidence, whether in a classroom discussion, reading in an assembly or conversing with adults'. This was particularly evident amongst the school's council members – a bunch of 8 and over boys and girls who were bright, articulate and bounced off each other like the future spokespeople they may one day become. They were confident, polite and hard pushed to find anything negative to say about the school. One bemoaned the fact that lunch should be better organised, whilst another commented incredulously that 'we've been to play other schools that don't even have their own cricket grounds' – which made him feel very lucky.

A Belmont child is a busy one. School opens at 7.30am for optional breakfast and, from there on in, a cascade of activities barely allows for an oxygen intake. Fifty clubs are on offer during lunchtime and after school, so if elastic or kicking a ball ain't your thing – why not try ancient Greek? Or perhaps origami, Dead Poets Society (we presume without Robin Williams), jazz band, bell plates or Bollywood dance. Popular after-school activities include chamber choir and horse riding. Fabulous trips (including a history trip to Venice) are offered from year 6.

Academic results are well above national expectations. This, we are told, is achieved through 'excellent teaching' (ISI 2012), a broad curriculum that includes French from year 3 and Latin from year 6 and smallish class sizes. Teachers have annual performance reviews and their planning is monitored termly. No sluggards allowed here. A couple of parents we spoke to said that academia across the foundation has definitely been stepped up a notch over the past few years. One parent told us: 'Belmont was always more of a nurturing school, but the goalposts seem to be constantly changing and you feel like you are kept on your toes the whole time.' In school's view, 'High academic performance is our number one target'.

Sats abolished in favour of continuous assessments from year 3. No longer follows the CE curriculum because nearly everyone goes through to the senior school. Instead, teaches a Mill Hill curriculum which aims to give the same rigour as the CE version but tailored to enable pupils to delve deeper into subject topics.

Places at Mill Hill are not unconditional, but any early problems, academically or behaviourally, are usually flagged up whilst the child is at Grimsdell (the pre-prep), so there are 'rarely any surprises'. 'If we didn't feel a child could cope, we wouldn't allow them to progress to year 7.' The school has a small learning support department and is happy to accommodate children with mild cases of dyslexia and dyspraxia. Anything more severe, and 'we're not the school for them'. Small groups of gifted and talented children are arranged across the years, and most are prepared for the 11+ and 13+ scholarship awards.

Belmont is a Christian foundation based upon the principles of 'religious freedom'. Chapel services are obligatory, because if you start pulling pupils out, 'you lose the ability to say we can work together'. However, the school's pupils represent a wide range of faiths and cultures, so chapel services and assemblies are inter-denominational.

During our tour, we noticed the school undergoing building works – six new classrooms, two science labs and an impressive hall. Shortly after our visit, we discovered that Belmont, along with the other two schools in the Mill Hill foundation, was merging with the Mount School for girls (hmmm!). The merger came as a great shock to parents who were informed by email, with no prior warning. School insisted that it was not planning a permanent expansion; pupil numbers have increased by some 55 or so, and boy-girl ratio is now more even. The Mount building now houses the Mount, Mill Hill International school.

The last word: A school that gets the best of both worlds – the rich diversity and good transport links of a London school along with the overall feel (partly because it's on the fringes) of a more rural English school, including what some call a sporting paradise. Academic? Increasingly so, but this is no hothouse, and children lap up the informal ambience that gives them room to grow into the very best version of themselves.

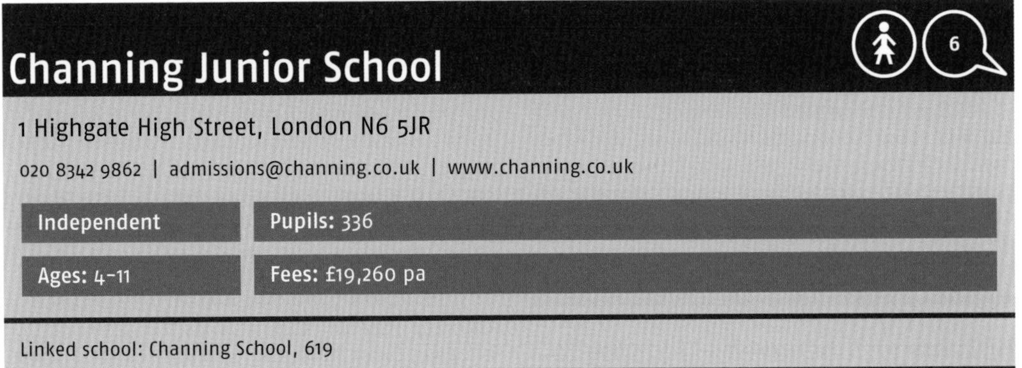

Channing Junior School

1 Highgate High Street, London N6 5JR

020 8342 9862 | admissions@channing.co.uk | www.channing.co.uk

Independent	Pupils: 336
Ages: 4–11	Fees: £19,260 pa

Linked school: Channing School, 619

Head of the Junior School: Since September 2018, Dina Hamalis, previously academic director of Sarum Hall. She has a degree in education, specialising in English and history; she spent five years at St Albans High Prep as English coordinator, moving to Highgate School (curriculum coordinator) then UCS pre-prep (SENCo, G&T and EAL coordinator) before joining Sarum Hall in 2011. She is an ISI inspector.

Entrance: Main entry at 4+. About 200 assessed (ie observed performing a range of 'nursery tasks') for 48 places (two classes of 24) in January before entry, then whittled down in a second round. 'We're looking for bright girls, who are interested, engaged and willing to have a go.' The school's increasing popularity means they're now first choice for most applicants. No 7+ entry; a smattering of vacancies higher up. Most families, however, are here for the duration.

Exit: The mode' is 'all-through', and the focus is to prepare girls well for the next stage, not for admissions elsewhere. ('We don't provide extra tutoring or practice papers.') The assumption is that all girls will proceed to the senior school without further entrance testing. ('Not having to do the 11+ is a real advantage,' said one mother. 'It enables you to have a longer term view of education, which is very appealing.') In most years, a small handful leave for other schools – 10 per cent in 2020. Some to board, some to the state sector (including highly competitive selective schools, like Henrietta Barnett), one or two to other leading independents, such as Highgate and St Paul's Girls'. Children who would really struggle at the senior school are also gently guided elsewhere. 'It isn't a question of having a bar that has to be met. We want girls to thrive. Some children find the academic pace a challenge and flourish nonetheless, but if a girl's self-confidence starts to dip, we help the family find the best alternative.'

Our view: Set opposite its senior school, behind high walls and tall gates in Highgate's traffic-packed high street, the school's rather forbidding exterior belies the pleasures within. Located in what was once Fairseat, the fine Victorian mansion of the Waterlow family, the junior school moved into its current accommodation in 1926, retaining a generous slice of the original gardens (the remainder was donated to the community to become adjoining Waterlow Park). The expansive house (with far-reaching views) now contains large, light classrooms, a performing arts studio, music rooms, a practical room for science, a specialist art and DT room and plenty of elbow room for all (even more so with recent extensive refurbishments). The gardens, with their mature trees, also house an adventure playground while three new outdoor learning areas (mud kitchen, classroom and a pavilion) are used by every class. All in all, 'it gives them a freedom rarely found in London. They can go into the bushes and make dens and still feel totally safe.'

A fundamental aspect of the school's approach is its personalised attitude to the academic; all are taught to a high standard, but not all are taught in the same way. ('One of my daughters needs – and gets – much more support than the other,' said a parent.) Bright and breezy teaching moves at a brisk, imaginative pace. (We watched girls create a 'storm' using a variety of sounds, for example, for a lesson on weather.) Specialists in ICT, modern languages. Art, DT, PE, drama and music throughout. Innovative new Spanish language programme engages all pupils from reception in 'Spanish language and culture'. French also added in year 3.

IT firmly embedded from the off, with a dedicated IT room lined with Apple Macs, and iPads used as 'learning tools'. 'Somehow they see them as something completely different from the tablets at home. Here they're used as dictionaries, for creativity and for research.'

Girls are well behaved – leaping to their feet to chorus 'Good afternoon' – but building confidence is as critical as good manners. 'My daughter used to be very shy,' said a parent, 'but performing in everything from music assemblies to poetry readings has made her much more self-assured'

Reasonably heavy homework load. ('My daughter couldn't manage more,' said the mother of a girl in year 5), but it's cool to work hard and parents, pupils and students all have high aspirations. 'The school manages a good balance between stretching them academically, while still nurturing them and treating them as individuals,' said one parent. 'I feel my daughter's pushed about the right amount,' said another.

Designated additional learning coordinator works with classroom teachers to put together appropriate learning plans. Children are sometimes withdrawn from lessons to work in a quieter space, but always follow the same work as their classmates. Gifted and talented also given additional stretch.

Attractive, well-used library with dedicated librarian, encouraging even the youngest to borrow, express opinions, and carry out research.

Music undoubtedly a strength, with enthusiastic head of music working closely with her equally energetic colleague in the senior school. Regular music lessons, plus plenty of opportunities to perform in music assemblies, orchestra, brass and wind bands, string quartet and choir. Wide range of individual music lessons, with vast majority taking classes in anything from saxophone to harp. (The school currently has four harpists.) Does its best to ensure girls find an instrument that 'fits their character' and lets parents borrow rather than buy in the early stages. Three girls recently invited to join the National Children's Orchestra, and usually several music awards to senior school. Art, with its own designated room, also vibrant.

Large sports hall on site (recently vacated by senior school, which now has its own), plus well-used netball and tennis courts. Swimming takes place elsewhere, and the school has its own playing field a brisk walk away, used for sports days and rounders matches. Pupils have competed at regional and national level in tennis, swimming and cross-country.

Has significantly boosted the extracurricular offering introducing in- and after-school clubs ranging from judo and gymnastics to fencing, ballet and chess (with one Grand-Master-in-the-making competing in the U11 World Chess Championship). Busy schedule of visits (eg Neasden Temple, Sky Studios, engineering workshop) and residential trips for older pupils.

Girls are well behaved – leaping to their feet to chorus 'Good afternoon' – but building confidence is as critical as good manners. 'My daughter used to be very shy,' said a parent, 'but performing in everything from music assemblies to poetry readings has made her much more self-assured.' The atmosphere is friendly and bustling, girls engaged and enthusiastic. 'My daughter loves the school,' said one mother. 'If we ever discuss moving, she says she doesn't want to leave. She has a wide variety of friends – the school's not cliquey at all.'

Channing used to be very much a local school, but the increased intake and improved academic reputation mean that, while there are still plenty of locals (some whose families have attended the school for generations), the pool now spreads out five miles, with plenty arriving from Islington and beyond. Families are also more international than before, though still largely made up of a solid core of affluent professionals. Active parents' association arranges regular events and recently also helped raise £17,000 or so for charity.

The last word: This traditional school has increasingly high academic standards, with tailored and imaginative learning to ensure no pupil misses out. Coupled with the fact that extracurricular also on the up, it's no wonder that families are applying from further out than ever before.

Channing School

Highgate, London N6 5HF

020 8340 2328 | admissions@channing.co.uk | www.channing.co.uk

Independent	Pupils: 633; sixth form: 142
Ages: 11–18	Fees: £21,300 pa

Linked school: Channing Junior School, 617

Headmistress: Since July 2020, Lindsey Hughes, previously deputy head of Lady Eleanor Holles. She has a history degree from Warwick and a PGCE from Roehampton; before joining LEH she was director of students at St Helen and St Katharine. She has a keen and active interest in politics and international relations and enjoys singing, theatre, watching sport (especially cricket) and walking her dog with her son.

Entrance: At 11, 300-400 sit the London 11+ Consortium exam for around 56 places, joining the 40 or so coming up from the junior school to form four forms of 24. ('Junior school pupils don't have to sit 11+ – it's a dream ticket,' says the head.) Exam consists of a cognitive ability test (rather than maths and English exams) with great emphasis on the interview. For sixth form entry, applicants are interviewed and expected to achieve nine or 10 9-7 grades at GCSEs, with a minimum of 7 in the subjects they intend to study. School says it can sometimes bend the rules for existing students 'as we know they have firm foundations, but we'd turn away someone from outside who didn't have the grades'.

Exit: A quarter leave at 16 – to board, to co-ed, to local state schools. The rest depart two years later for serious subjects at predominantly Russell Group universities. Leeds, Edinburgh, Durham and Bristol all popular. Oxbridge often features – eight in 2020. About half go on to science-related degrees (with four medics in 2020). The head takes a personal interest in all applicants, interviewing each girl.

Latest results: In 2020, 89 per cent 9/7 at GCSE; 78 per cent A*/A at A level. In 2019 (the last year when exams took place), 84 per cent 9-7 at GCSE; at A level, 69 per cent A*/A.

Teaching and learning: Channing is an academic school, but not one where academic achievement overrides all else. The intake here is slightly broader than at some of the local competition, and not every pupil will be cut out for straight A*/9s. ('Here, if a girl is outstanding at art, but not at maths, it's not the end of the world,' says school. 'Some are exceptionally bright; others exceptional at something, but, naturally, not everything.') Every girl, however, should get the best she's capable of, and often significantly more than might be expected. ('Some achieve more than you'd have ever have thought possible.')

The sixth form is not huge and nor is the subject range (19 on offer); the core is serious stuff and the conventional arts/science divide is roughly in balance, with biology and economics attracting similar numbers to history and English (though few physicists). Maths tops the popularity stakes; biology and politics take away the highest grades. Good spread of languages, with Spanish, French, German and Latin all on offer at GCSE and A level, plus Greek as a twilight GCSE subject. Adelante programme from reception upwards aims to produce girls fluent in Spanish and with a love of Hispanic culture.

Adelante programme aims to produce girls fluent in Spanish and with a love of Hispanic culture

The school prides itself on the quality of its teaching. ('Our teachers are experts in pedagogy,' claims school.) The Independent Schools inspectors found teaching 'excellent', and also waxed lyrical about the 'exceptional' quality of 'pupils' learning and achievement'. No doubt at all that value is added here – in every direction. Good take up, for example, of the research-directed Extended Project Qualification (EPQ). Technology, too, thoroughly embedded, with all girls issued with a school iPad 'to support research, investigation, creativity and communication'.

Learning support and SEN: Special needs addressed by a qualified SENCo, called on to assist a range of difficulties, from profoundly deaf pupils to 30-or-so girls with mild visual impairment, dyslexia, or processing issues. 'We carry out appropriate assessment, but it's as much about helping teachers to adapt their teaching to meet individual needs.'

The arts and extracurricular: Art and music both unusually strong. Art ('absolutely amazing,' said one pupil) is housed in roof-top studios with stunning views across London. Strong emphasis on drawing as the basis of it all, but art rooms are lined with Macs and scented by oil paint. Plenty achieve external glory, with recent prize winners in Young Art at the Royal College of Art. Student work also displayed (and sold!) at a north London gallery. Music, always strong, has undoubtedly been enhanced by the completion of the new music school, which has added 10 practice rooms, a technology room and a sound-proofed percussion studio. Record numbers now take external exams, including the first set of musical theatre awards (with 23 distinctions). Plenty of opportunity to perform in-house – annual and lunchtime concerts, plus informal recitals – and in formats that range from string quartets and guitar ensembles to a jazz band and contemporary music group. Recent finalists, too, in Voice Festival UK. Biennial international tours to eg Lisbon, Madrid, Vienna, Boston and Venice.

West End quality performing arts building recently completed and LAMDA classes very popular. Staggering range of school trips and activities, from history in Berlin and classics in Greece to a music tour to Madrid and regular theatre outings to the West End. Clubs follow prevailing interests and currently include feminist society, robotics, chemistry, classics, life drawing and creative writing.

Sport: Limited running-around space on site, so probably not a first choice for those who live for goals and glory. Though 'we have county level sportswomen, and local netball clubs train here most evenings,' says the head. But if go-fight-win is not top of the agenda, keeping fit and healthy definitely is. PE compulsory throughout and newly refurbished multi-use games area plus sports hall make this a pleasure, with vastly improved opportunities for volleyball, badminton, cricket and dance, plus recent successes in cricket, tennis and football.

Ethos and heritage: School housed in four tall and graceful Georgian buildings on Highgate Hill overlooking one of London's most beautiful and under-visited parks. Backing these, previous head did a serious job of rearrangement, making the most of a relatively small site with the addition of a new complex (containing the music school, the gym and a sixth form centre). 'If you're investing in your daughter's education you expect 21st century facilities,' says school.

Established in 1885 to educate the daughters of Unitarian ministers, the school retains the founders' values of liberalism, democracy and religious tolerance

Established in 1885 by a Unitarian minister and two members of his congregation to educate the daughters of Unitarian ministers, the school's clientele has broadened, but it retains the founders' values of liberalism, democracy and religious tolerance. There's no prize-giving, for example, and the most valued award is a Conabor Badge, bestowed on 'girls of good character' (or, as one recipient phrased it, 'for being good'). 'Girls really aspire to be awarded this badge,' says school. 'It's what most embodies the spirit of the school.'

Pupils are active and engaged, participating enthusiastically in both academic and extracurricular activities (15, for example, gained DofE gold recently, impressive numbers even for a much larger school).

Pastoral care, inclusivity and discipline: This is a calm and orderly place, but it has little to do with a system of tight rules and stern warnings, with school claiming that their 'record of serious discipline' going back 13 years takes up just two pages.

Strong emphasis on student leadership, with two officers in every form – 'they hunt in packs' – including two head girls. Older girls also apply to become 'school officers' with designated areas of responsibility. 'A lot of girls aspire to the leadership team,' says school. 'They have real influence.' As well as 'advising constructively', year 12s set up and run clubs and have recently sat on a panel interviewing a teacher for a job. 'I hadn't done this before,' says the head, 'but they were so clear in their thinking, so mature and perceptive.' The code of behaviour is also co-written by the girls. 'We live together in this community.'

School's priorities are 'integrity, independence, scholarship and altruism' – old fashioned virtues, adapted to a more complex modern setting. It acknowledges that the pressures on the students are greater than ever before – 'Not all girls sail through life without hitting stormy waters' – and the school works with parents all the way, helping minimise screen time and maximise mental and physical health. 'They believe in happy girls, rather than ones who are pushed,' said one mother.

Girls generally get on with minimal bullying and cliques. 'You know everyone here, you feel very comfortable and there is a real sense of joining together.' 'It's a very safe place,' said one parent. 'If your child is slightly quirky, you know they will still be fine.' However, we have had reports of recent less-than-sympathetic responses to teenage anxieties. School appointed a counsellor on the advice of the sixth form.

Pupils and parents: Essentially a local school, so no fleets of coaches to far-flung locations. Most pupils walk or come by public transport, from a broad sweep round the gates. 'Mainly north and west, though we do get a few from east London.' Parents are cosmopolitan (South African, European, North American, Asian), highly educated ('At careers fairs, if you shout, "Is there a doctor in the house?", there's a rush') and value education ('expectations are very high'). They're also 'tremendously supportive'. Pupils, quite often the daughters of old girls, are confident and motivated, thriving in this relatively small school.

Money matters: Not a hugely rich school, but still does its bit, with five per cent of annual income devoted to bursaries, 'supporting families who hit hard times'. Academic scholarships at 11 worth 10 per cent off the fees, but music scholarships (grade 5 with merit minimum required) are particularly good, with up to 50 per cent discounts. In the sixth form, art, music and academic scholarships (of up to 50 per cent off tuition fees) on offer to existing students ('We want to recognise their talent and potential, not find them sloping off elsewhere') as well as external ones. Bursaries also available at this point.

The last word: A cosy, vibrant, local school in a very attractive setting, with high academic standards, up-to-date facilities and happy, motivated girls.

Coldfall Primary School

8

Coldfall Avenue, London N10 1HS

020 8883 0608 | office@coldfall.haringey.sch.uk | www.coldfall.haringey.sch.uk

State | **Ages:** 3–11 | **Pupils:** 659

Head teacher: Since 1996, Evelyn Davies BEd (geography and education, Homerton College Cambridge), 50s. Her first teaching job was at Cayley Primary School in Tower Hamlets, then arts co-ordinator at a 'tough school' in Lambeth (now closed), and then deputy head at Southwold Primary school in Hackney for the next seven years. By the time she arrived at Coldfall School, this head had definitely earned her stripes.

Originally from Bournemouth, she wasn't au fait with Muswell Hill at the time and drove around first to get a feel for the area. 'Many parts of Muswell Hill weren't what they are today. I had been strongly advised against going for the job at Coldfall as it was a sink school at the time... I even found used needles in the playground.' Not to be dissuaded, she went for the job, and thankfully so.

More than 20 years on and this 'superhead' has taken a less than bog-standard primary and transformed it into a star act, with an 'outstanding' Ofsted, three-form entry and very happy parents. 'This didn't happen overnight. It took a lot of work marketing the school, hand delivering leaflets, making sure any special event we had was mentioned in the local press etc. We really wanted to raise the profile of the school.' It worked. As the school crept up the Ofsted ranks, so too did the interest of many professionals who moved into the area for the school (often favouring it over the other equally successful local primaries).

Most find this head open-minded and approachable. 'I had an idea,' commented one, 'and she immediately said "let's have a chat about it".' Hard working and well organised, she gets things done. 'She's not ticking boxes, she really gets involved in the nitty gritty.' An active opponent of testing, testing, testing and differentiating children at such a young age: 'I strongly believe in self-fulfilling prophecies, which is why at Coldfall we don't stream in years 5 and 6.' This dedicated head has even been to parliament to protest, winning the admiration of her local MP:

'If I were the minister for education I would grab Evelyn Davies and put her as a key adviser. That way our children would be well educated in every sense of the word.'

She has two grown-up sons, one who is head of art at another school. She says: 'I would never dissuade anyone from going into the education sector, as tough as it is these days. There is never a day when I feel like I don't want to go into work.'

Retiring in spring 2021.

Entrance: Places given out using the standard local authority formula: children in local authority care, followed by special educational needs, siblings and distance from the gates. Recent feasibility study was carried out for a five form entry, but was ditched due to changes in projected pupil numbers. The drop in birth rate and migration out of Haringey has meant that catchment for 2019 expanded from 0.3 to 0.5 miles.

Admission to full time nursery via the school. Offers 40 places.

Exit: A primary whose catchment fortunately straddles the borough's two highest flying comprehensives. The largest chunk of year 6 proceed to Fortismere, just next door. Sizeable (and growing) slice to Alexandra Park, down the road. Enviable success rate too, in grammar school entrance (at least two each year to Latymer) – then in dribbles to a wide range of local and distant establishments. The Compton School, Friern Barnet School, Greig City Academy and Ashmole have all featured recently.

Our view: Set adjacent to the ancient Coldfall Woods in Muswell Hill, this three-form, 90-year-old primary school is meticulously run with everything going for it. Probably the most diverse primary of the Muswell Hill schools and a huge part of what they celebrate: 'We aim to create caring, global citizens who will go on to make a difference in the world.'

A teaching school which can accommodate 25-30 trainee teachers, with many of them securing posts at Coldfall once qualified. Two-thirds of staff have trained through the school, which often means low staff turnover and good internal promotion. Also has the added benefit of having two members of staff in each class (a qualified teacher and a graduate on training or a TA): 'We haven't used a supply teacher in 15 years.' Teaching here is enthusiastic and thorough, with staff constantly looking to improve performance. Young cohort who look as if they have a thoroughly good time (and the teachers' choir has become well known in the area). Academic standards are high and virtually every child reaches the government targets, many far exceeding them.

Though the school has a significant number of children with special needs, both those who struggle and those who excel are provided with interventions and support. Not all parents, however, feel difficulties are necessarily dealt with sympathetically. 'Coldfall is a great school if your child is average or above – not so if they are on the SEN register. I have found the SEN department to be unresponsive and unreceptive,' said one. Another said: 'We were made to feel like paranoid parents. We had to get a full NHS diagnosis to be taken seriously.' School says they find this surprising and that a recent review had found the school to be 'highly inclusive', although the head admits that catering for children with complex needs can be very challenging in a primary school setting.

Pupils we met proudly showed us their (beautifully written) handwriting books, and made sure we didn't miss out on any of the wall displays, installations or trophy cabinet during our tour. A charitable bunch, who talked about their twin school in Sierra Leone, local food banks – and last year's award winners of the Get London Moving campaign.

Pupils we met proudly showed us their handwriting books, and made sure we didn't miss out on any of the wall displays, installations or trophy cabinet during our tour

Pupils have compassion embedded in them from an early age and the school says that their values programme and character development, alongside their global curriculum and eco teaching, 'are equally as important as the academic agenda'. We loved the positive re-enforcement which happens in each class weekly, where one or more child is selected because of a kind or generous action and are the focus of 'the sun shines on... because...' One parent said that 'every child gets the chance to shine at this school', although another added 'not in school productions... usual suspects.'

Facilities here can only be described as exceptional for a London primary. The original, large, low-lying Victorian schoolhouse has now been joined by a sleek, modern addition, providing extra classrooms and a new gym. Expansive grounds boast country-like playing fields, as well as two large and notably well-equipped playgrounds kitted out with basketball and netball nets, table-tennis tables and sheltered cabins. Pupils also benefit from the school's own allotments and nature trail, as well as access to nearby

Channing School

Coldfall Woods. We also loved the cute courtyard area called Pond View, which acts as a walkway between opposite sides of the building.

Sport played enthusiastically and successfully and has come a long way in the last five years. One parent said: 'The new PE teacher and sports co-ordinator have been a revelation. They have turned sports around in the school.' Two hours of PE weekly and both boys and girls triumph in borough-wide competitions, boys winning recent golf and football championships, girls excelling in football and netball. Pupils also qualified for the London Youth Games.

Plenty of enrichment, in lessons and out, including chess (with championship-winning chess teams), French (taught by a native speaker), computer programming and cooking all part of the regular mix. Excellent range of clubs and activities (33 in total), including geology and forest school. 'Music is a big thing about the school.' Successful school choir has made appearances at the O2 and Barbican and every child gets the opportunity to learn the recorder and the ukulele: the 'dedicated' music teacher taught herself how to pay the ukulele, so she could teach the pupils. Plus there is a CD made every year, with each year group contributing their own song. (This is sold to raise money for Educaid, providing education in Sierra Leone.) 'Everything is well planned and thought through,' said one parent. Regular trips beyond the school gates include at least one visit to a museum, gallery and musical event for every pupil. Plus residential trips in years 3 and 6.

In the main (though not exclusively), parents are comfortably off Muswell Hill locals, so there's a good sprinkling of designer trainers in the playground, but this is low-key prosperity. Almost a third of pupils speak a language other than English at home. Both mothers and fathers (plenty of the latter at pick-up time) involved in making the school a success. 'All parents,' said one enthusiast, 'are given an opportunity to contribute, not just non-working mums.' Many arrive at weekends to help with the gardening, and the thriving PTA organises summer and winter fairs, a Valentine disco, quiz night, fashion show and organic vegetable scheme. Sizeable sums are raised for playground, computer and PE equipment. 'There's a real feeling that everyone matters,' said one mother. 'Gives an education that is across the board,' said another.

The last word: Pupils we met were chatty, happy and totally loved their school. Ditto for parents. None of which came as a surprise to us as it ticks so many boxes – great facilities, wonderful diversity, a compassionate outlook, oodles of enrichment and fabulous teaching.

Coleridge Primary School

9

Crouch End Hill, Hornsey, London N8 8DN

020 8340 3173 | ColeridgePrimary.School@haringey.gov.uk | www.coleridgeprimary.net

State | **Ages:** 3–11 | **Pupils:** 880

Head: Since 2014, Leon Cheouke BA PGCE (40s). After a first degree in community studies at Manchester and a PGCE at Goldsmiths University of London, Mr Cheouke arrived at Coleridge in 2000 and, apart from a year teaching in New Zealand, has been there ever since, working formerly as deputy to his long-serving and popular predecessor. Continuity and growth have been his model. 'He said he wasn't going to change much and he hasn't,' said one parent. 'He's kept the best bits, really listened to what parents want and cares about all the children rather than statistics.' Keen on politics, Dr Who and vinyl.

Entrance: Coleridge is a very large school (120 each year enter four reception classes), but, sadly for aspiring parents, Crouch End is an ever-popular destination for family existence, and siblings tend to elbow newbies out of the way. Mumsnet types moan, too, about affluent applicants guying the system by renting nearby. The only advice is live as near as you can (ideally, within quarter of a mile).

Exit: The majority to a strong set of local comprehensives (eg Highgate Woods, City of London Academy, Alexandra Park School, Fortismere, Hornsey School for Girls), plus a handful to state selectives (Latymer), independents and home schooling.

Our view: Coleridge is a super primary – in both senses of the word (it's the size of many secondaries). Long one of the neighbourhood's most sought-after schools, in 2007 it expanded onto two sites, doubling the number of slots available. New arrivals now start in the original 1960s low-rise, before moving across the road to the bright, old-meets-modern addition in year 2. Parents originally worried the expansion might damage the close-knit feel, but agree the mood has been maintained. 'Because the school is on two sites, you feel you're dropping off somewhere quite small,' said one. Many feel, too, the scale equips pupils well for life afterwards.

Teaching an undoubted strength (maths, considered by Ofsted 'impressive'), with staff praised as 'bright, funny and incredibly enthusiastic'. 'The teachers are well tuned in with the children; they listen to them and treat them as individuals,' said one mother. Results excellent, with large numbers of year 6 pupils reaching well above standards expected for their age (some, it has been whispered, with the aid of tutoring). 'Standards are high, but they still make it fun,' said one mother. 'They're very aware of not putting too much pressure on the children.' Careful monitoring and target setting ensure the approach to each child is tweaked for maximum benefit. Progress equally successful for those with special educational needs or struggling on the foothills of English, who all make 'outstanding progress'.

Everything done to make the day exciting and interesting. Philosophy taught weekly to enhance critical thinking and pupils regularly involved in lively political debate (the environment, housing, teachers' salaries), while the school's de-luxe scale allows for a raft of specialists (two for art, one each for music, PE and Spanish). Homework (classified as 'home learning' and operating on a long-term timetable) is intended to develop research skills rather than become a domestic battleground. Two spacious libraries, with a dedicated librarian, are open to children in break and lunch.

The school holds the Arts Council's prestigious Artsmark Gold status for encouraging pupils to become involved with the arts, and the arts are, undoubtedly, a major strength. ('We've found that it's within the arts that children who may find the more academic areas of school life challenging are able to develop their "voice",' says the head). Art taught in a light, purpose-built studio and exhibitions held regularly, in school and out. Music excellent, with weekly singing assemblies and lively participation in choirs and competitions (Coleridge Royal Albert Hall choir, Crouch End Festival Choir, Sing Up competition). Dance and drama, too, made much of, with an annual whole-school play, dance classes (again with tailor-made space and links to the Royal Ballet), drama classes (with ties to the National Theatre) and numerous arts-related clubs held in lunch hours and before and after school. Parents love the approach. 'They do a lot of art and don't concentrate all the time on maths, English and science,' commented one. 'I moved here because I liked the creativity.'

Children tend to have names like Esme, Flora and Felix, Planet Organic features in after-school snacks, and on the noticeboard an ad announces 'half cello for sale'

Sports and games considered fundamental for healthy living and esprit de corps, as well as 'an integral part of the equal-opportunities practice' (so girls encouraged to play football, boys to dance). Gymnastics and games taught throughout, with older pupils learning netball, kwik cricket, athletics, tag rugby, tennis and football, some taught by specialist coaches. Swimming lessons at local pool. Frequent fixtures against other local primaries and sports day is a proper affair, with no dilly-dallying about all fair in love and sport, and school records recording 'x is the fastest at…' ('The teachers decided to do this to challenge the children,' comments the head.) Outdoor education also involves regular attendance at forest school in nearby woods, where, as well as practical skills like putting up shelters, pupils develop teamwork and communication.

Huge range of after-school clubs (capoeira, meditation, fencing, drumming, photography, squash, art academy, tennis, school newspaper) and visiting talks (Highgate Woods feminist group – all former pupils – on gender equality, a Google employee to launch a technology competition). Also, privately-run breakfast and after-school clubs.

Crouch End is cool and media savvy – the school's Glastonbury-themed fête gives you a clue, as does a recent outing to the Guardian newspaper (where else?) – and while pupils come from the usual metropolitan multi-stranded ethnic range, the less advantaged are not unduly well represented. (The number in receipt of the pupil premium is 'below average', states Ofsted, a relative rarity in London.) 'Now that the school is bigger, there are more people from the flats and estates, and it's bit more ethnically diverse,' commented one parent. Children, however, tend to have names like Esme, Flora and Felix, Planet Organic features in after-school snacks, and prominent on the noticeboard is an ad announcing 'half cello for sale'. Parents, on the whole, comfortably off (£13,000, for example, raised at the summer fair), but also reasonably relaxed and school is warm and friendly, with parental involvement a major part of the ethos – 'I love the community feel,' said one. Though some comments, too, about a small number of the 'vocal and opinionated' whom the school attempts to keep at polite arm's length. Pastoral care an undoubted strength (with professional, confidential counselling offered on a one-to-one basis). 'Moving towards' a house structure. No uniform.

Pupils of all ages are confident and articulate (with year 6 recent victors in the Winston Churchill Public Speaking competition, beating off considerable prep school opposition) – and happy. 'My son has really thrived here. He was quite shy before he went but he has made a lot of progress socially and really loves school.'

The last word: Now, as always, the It school in the neighbourhood.

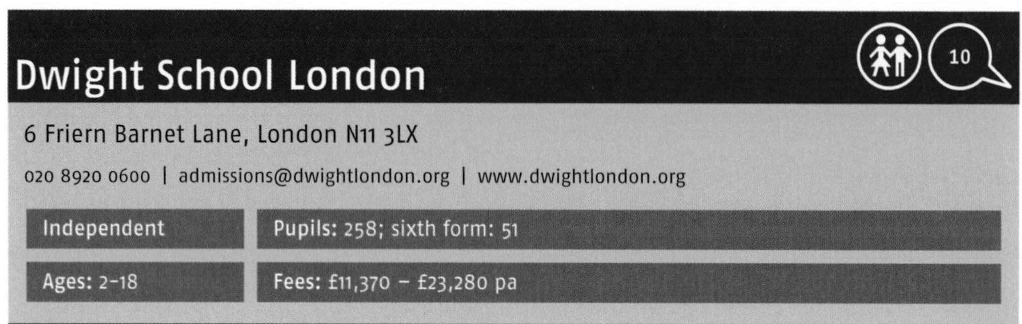

Dwight School London

6 Friern Barnet Lane, London N11 3LX

020 8920 0600 | admissions@dwightlondon.org | www.dwightlondon.org

Independent | Pupils: 258; sixth form: 51

Ages: 2–18 | Fees: £11,370 – £23,280 pa

Head of School: Since January 2016, Alison Cobbin BA Dip Ed MBA (50s). Brought up in Australia and qualified as an English and history teacher at Macquarie University in Sydney. Moved to London in 1995 with her husband and then three young daughters; after a career break, joined Dwight (then Woodside Park School) as, variously, English, games and theory of knowledge teacher, IB coordinator and upper school principal. Moved to a SE London independent school as pastoral deputy head before returning to Dwight as head of school: 'I came back because I had made a shortlist of all the things I wanted from a school, and when this job came up it ticked all the boxes.'

The boxes it ticked were: co-ed, not too big, international, non-selective, and most importantly did the IB. Alison says once you've been to a school which upholds the values of the IB, it's very hard to go back: 'The IB is built on such a different philosophy – its broad base is so different. It's more collaborative than the English education system and does more than just work towards getting into the best university.' To which the school adds: 'The IB is not subject to government changes and grade inflation – you know that if a person achieved 40 out of a maximum 45 several years ago, that would still hold true many years later with the exception of the odd curriculum change.' We were sold.

Principal of the upper school since June 2019 is Christopher Beddows, previously assistant principal at Dwight School, New York, for seven years. Brought up in York, England, he started his teaching career in Lincoln after graduating from Bishop Grosseteste Teaching College. Has worked for the IB in a range of roles.

Lower school principal Matt Parkin BEd DipEd NPQH has been at the school since 2007. He has taught in the UK, USA and Indonesia and one could say has had a pretty colourful background in education. Following a seven-year stint working in the state education sector in Devon, he was part of a start-up school in Houston, Texas. In the five years he was there he increased the school from 50-strong to 400. He was then offered a post to teach at 'one of the best schools in Asia' in Jakarta, Indonesia, which had an outdoor swimming pool, a theatre and a multi-media centre. As much of a draw as that was, he yearned for a school with an international outlook back home. 'There are not many of them around, and a job came up at Dwight, so I took it.'

Entrance: Parents describe the school as 'selectively inclusive'. In all of our conversations (with parents and staff), no one emphasised 'academic results'. Though most enter in September, since the school serves expats, there are students entering throughout the year, from abroad and from local state schools. Interview and report from previous school only real requisites, as is a commitment and understanding of the IB programme. Interviews sometimes done via Skype.

Exit: About 75 per cent of lower school pupils move on to the upper school; some leave after the

IBMYP, moving abroad or to sixth form colleges. University counselling programme in year 12, but it seems parents often start earlier, commenting they'd like to see a bit more attention to this area. Sixth formers mainly to university, a lot London based (eg King's, UCL, SOAS, Westminster) with others to eg Edinburgh and Royal Veterinary College. Four to study overseas in 2020 – two to USA, two to Japan.

Latest results: In 2020, average IB point score 35 (33 in 2019).

Teaching and learning: Runs the IB programme at all levels. Year groups in lower school divided into two parallel classes with a maximum of 20 in each. Lots of child-inspired batiks, pottery and art help create a vibrant atmosphere. IB learner profile is displayed everywhere. IB primary years programme (IBPYP) well linked with the national curriculum, which keeps inspectorates happy and ensures children are well grounded with an international mindset. All lessons in each half of term based around one aspect of the curriculum. Specialist teachers for music, art, PE, French and EAL. Homework important and can be done at after-school club.

One or two students each year opt to take a Dwight High School Diploma, earning IB course certificates rather than the full IB diploma. Average class size in upper school not normally more than 15, although we spoke to one pupil who had just three others in her geography class. 'It's great! Almost like one-to-one tuition.' Good results for IB middle years programme exams with several top students getting more than 60 points out of 70. One parent said the only downside of the IB from her point of view is that 'if you are weak in a certain area – such as maths or languages – you can't drop it, as you need to take one subject from each of the six subject groups.' However, there are choices within these.

Dwight also offers Pamoja Online courses which enable Dwight IB diploma students to take a wider range of courses while experiencing the kind of online learning that is increasingly common at university level. School says: 'These courses are fantastic. They are based in Oxford and provide a quality programme which is strictly monitored. There are over 50 different nationalities at Dwight and it's not always feasible to accommodate everyone, so these courses are a great online alternative. It is the equivalent of an IB course online.'

French is introduced in lower school, Spanish and Mandarin added as an option in upper school. Other languages considered on request at additional cost. (One Portuguese teacher does a lesson via Skype.) RE is not an IB subject, but world religion is. Photos throughout the school buildings depict many school trips, dramatic and music performances and community service activities, suggesting that a lot of learning is regularly extended out and about. After-school homework club for those who want extra help.

Teachers are international and IB-experienced. Over 60 per cent come from overseas: 'For those not from abroad, they look at their IB training as a fantastic experience'

Teachers are international and IB-experienced. Over 60 per cent come from overseas: 'London is a bit of a destination for teachers. For those not from abroad, they look at their IB training as a fantastic experience.' Parents speak enthusiastically about the teaching staff and their willingness to help and respond quickly to any parent concerns. One pupil told us: 'The teachers here are great – you can talk to them about anything, even after school.'

Learning support and SEN: Through the QUEST programme (at extra cost) the school can accommodate a range of learning needs, with the support of specialist teachers. EAL (also at extra cost) regarded as essential for children who lack English proficiency – two to five lessons a week, one to one or in a small group depending on needs. A mother tongue programme is available for Japanese pupils – the second largest group in the school (about 10 per cent) and some other languages (no extra charge is made if four or more students are in the same group and level). IB diploma students must be completely fluent in English.

A dedicated SENCo for the roughly 14 per cent on the SEN register: 'Because of the nature of this school, we're not equipped to deal with many pupils with very diverse needs.' But parents do say that what they like about Dwight is that it suits a great variety of children. 'I wanted a school where all of my children would be well served.'

The arts and extracurricular: Lots of after-school clubs and extracurricular offerings. Strong music – about 15 per cent learn an individual instrument; there are rock, jazz and chamber groups. The choir has sung at London's 02 in Young Voices, and for some lucky pupils, the 'highlight of their life' was performing with the Dwight New York choir at Carnegie Hall. Other clubs include cartoon club, sewing club, origami and magical maths.

For the last period on Tuesdays, the pupils do mixed age group activities including community service projects. This helps to develop relationships across the ages, reinforcing the 'Dwight family' concept.

Lots of outings to concerts, theatres and galleries as well as trips home and abroad. Year 6 students spend a week at the Dwight School in New York, some year groups in upper school have their activity week in Normandy (practising the French that they have been learning since they were 3) and some of them go on exchange to the Dwight School in New York. Older students are developing a community service project in Nepal. They raise funds and students and staff travel there to do volunteer work. The arts dept has been to Vietnam to study music and dance; they have also visited Hollywood, India and Cuba.

Model United Nations conference is also popular. A recent one saw the school representing Saudi Arabia.

Sport: Games obligatory once a week for each year group – the school has its own sports field 10 minutes away by minibus and uses other local sports facilities. They compete not only with local and national schools but also with international overseas schools. One pupil told us, 'I love the sports here, there are lots of options and the school is even planning a trip to Venice to play beach volleyball.' Parents say they like the variety of sports on offer – not only the traditional ones but a wider range: rugby, football, basketball, track and field, sailing, ice skating.

Ethos and heritage: The school was originally founded in 1972 by Dr Stephen Spahn, chancellor of the Dwight School in New York. Previously known as Woodside Park and North London International School, the school changed its name in a rebranding exercise to Dwight London School, to heighten awareness of its association with the Dwight family of schools that now has campuses in Seoul, Shanghai and Dubai. 'Dwight family' is a term used by staff and families alike. Dwight London has an advisory board of local parents and others who lend expertise and guidance and serve as a supportive sounding board for the principal in the strategic planning of the school.

The school is on four sites in two locations. Lower school is in Woodside Avenue. Kindergarten and reception based in their own little house, the Lodge, with its own garden for play. Part-time options are available and there's a wraparound care programme from 7.30am to 5pm for the lower school.

Years 2 to 5 in the main building here have good sized, light classrooms with washing lines displaying student work. Each child has own drawer for storage. Computers everywhere. Media resource centres, a small library collection; great gym, which doubles up as the dining hall. Healthy food served from the kitchens next to it (where meals for the kindergarten are also prepared). Photos of all the year 6 students displayed in the passage with their personal blogs. Good music room and lovely art room. Whilst we were there we saw some wonderful examples of art which had been selected for the Dwight Travelling Art Show – a yearly event where the top 20 chosen art pieces make their way around the different Dwight campuses of the world. Well-equipped library with Harry Potter translated into an assortment of languages.

The Dwight family of schools has campuses in Seoul, Shanghai and Dubai. 'Dwight family' is a term used by staff and families alike

A recent popular addition to the school is the Dwight radio station which is broadcast online: 'This is another way we feel pupils can demonstrate their learning, without it just being test test test.'

Year 6 has a separate eco-building with easy access to the specialist classrooms and playground; school has green flag eco-schools status. If we were being finickity, we would say that the interior could do with a bit of sprucing up – a new lick of paint. The red, white and blue colours of their motif (which is painted virtually everywhere) becomes a little bit wearing on the eye after a while.

Playground not huge but much use made of local park for cross-country runs and scientific experiments plus compulsory swimming once a week at a local pool. They also regularly use the school's own playing fields a short bus ride away.

The upper school is in the former Friern Barnet Boys' Grammar School and in nearby Jubilee Hall. The main building has recently been refurbished and is clean, bright and welcoming, making very good use of light throughout. The administrative offices and faculty room share the same corridors as the classrooms, which must strengthen the sense of community. Every wall is full of original and creative student art and photographs, and there are posters with quotes from Gandhi, Martin Luther King and Nelson Mandela, who we learned are the role models for the three upper school student houses.

The Jubilee Hall holds more classrooms, two science labs, the upper school library and a pleasant canteen open throughout. This looks out onto an outside playground where students engage in a bit of exercise during break or lunch, and a small world garden beyond with picnic tables and benches. The school admits that conditions are a little crowded, and they are on the lookout for new property in the area.

The individualised approach we heard so much about from parents was evident during our visit. We were shown around the school by an extremely theatrical and colourful student (who we definitely thought should be on TV) – and many others we spoke to were equally as quirky, interesting and slightly eccentric, with amazing back stories. Another seemed to be a science whizz who showed us her extraordinary end of M5 personal project (a culmination of their IB middle years) – and had created a working Enigma machine with morse coding etc.

Pastoral care, inclusivity and discipline: The IB philosophy and emphasis on tolerance and global understanding is reinforced everywhere in the school with big signs bearing the IB ethos (inquirers, reflective risk-takers, etc). Kids are divided into houses – Pioneers, Artists and Visionaries – and are awarded 'sparkies' (which refer to the IB philosophy of igniting the sparks of genius).

Kids seem happy, and although there is a uniform there are various options, so they can choose how casual or dressy they want to look. Parents love the small size of the school. 'It's a massive advantage. Everyone is known, everyone can shine and blossom.' One parent we spoke to who has home schooled her child for a while said that Dwight is the first school her son has been happy at: 'This school has literally been our saviour. I love the IB ethos in tailoring the work to your child's needs – it's so much more of a progressive approach.' The school recently introduced a vertical tutoring system, which encourages pupils to get to know other pupils from different year groups.

Parents assure us that they were not aware of any incidents of bullying. With students from so many different cultures, school says it 'comes down hard on any form of bullying.' Drugs 'not an issue' either: 'the pupils that come here from abroad are often fairly naive and not part of that London culture.'

There is an LGBT community and a 'safe room' offered to those who, for whatever reason, need to hang out alone for a while. 'For some pupils, this is the first time they have been able to express who they really are. This is often not the case in their home country.'

Pupils and parents: Dwight has a larger British student body than most other international schools in London (50 per cent in lower school; 40 per cent in upper school), which seems to make it easier for international families to integrate into the local community. The impression from parents and from our visit is that there is relatively little sense of the 'expat bubble' in this international school. Long-term families who joined the school in earlier incarnations (pre-IB) say they have been very pleased with the introduction of the full suite of IB programmes, and the interesting international experiences and friendships that Dwight's growing expat community brings. While they do see the turnover of families as a factor, many of these friendships endure and lead to exciting trips during the holidays to visit old friends who have moved on.

In recent years the Dwight community has collaborated to help families have a 'soft landing' when they arrive in London. A handy Welcome to London guide written and updated annually by the parents is found on the website with tips for families living in north London. Lots of welcome and goodbye rituals for students coming and going. There are also a variety of ways that rising year 6 students are supported as they move to the upper school. It's all part of the school's intention to give everyone a Dwight Hug. One parent told us: 'We were given a really warm welcome when we arrived and were immediately put in touch with the parents' association. The parent network at Dwight is fantastic.'

Every wall displays original and creative student art and photographs, and there are posters with quotes from Gandhi, Martin Luther King and Nelson Mandela

Door-to-door minibus service offered which collects pupils from as far afield as St John's Wood etc.

Money matters: Tuition is marginally less than other international schools in London. Extras include school trips and activities such as Model United Nations and some after-school activities. Good range of means-tested scholarships for families with an income of up to £120,000 pa (more if you have two or more children). These are awarded not for pure academic ability but for 'demonstrating the characteristics of the IB learner profile'. Also offers bursaries of 25-50 per cent for children of visiting academics and NGOs. These are all available to current as well as new families.

The last word: Dwight is a school where the education of the 'whole child' and the learning journey genuinely appear to be as important as exam results. A brave but rewarding choice for London-born children ('none of my friends had heard of Dwight before,' said one parent) – those looking for something a bit different and outside of the English curriculum. And a safe bet for international students who want the benefit of the IB in a more localised setting. The school does all it can to provide each student with opportunities to pursue their individual interests, all within the IB context. 'It's a kind school.'

Fortismere School

South Wing, Tetherdown, London N10 1NE

020 8365 4400 | office@fortismere.org.uk | www.fortismere.haringey.sch.uk

State | Ages: 11-19 | Pupils: 1,771; sixth form: 427

Co-heads: Jo Davey (40s). More-or-less an old girl, Davey, formerly deputy head, attended Creighton School, a forerunner of Fortismere. Originally joined the staff as a part-time consultant in 2013, while deputy head of Blanche Nevile School for Deaf Children. Previously, taught history and politics, acted as a school improvement consultant and senior secondary advisor. Continues to work as an Ofsted inspector. At Fortismere, her stated objective is to maintain the school's 'inclusive ethos', while focusing on academic outcome.

Zoe Judge (40s). Began her teaching career in Barking and Dagenham, before joining Fortismere in 2002 as a member of the English department. Since then, she's taught English, media and film, served as head of year, assistant head and head of sixth form, where she helped make Fortismere a hub for higher education preparation. In her spare time, plays violin with the Fortismere community orchestra.

The two were elevated to acting joint headship in 2016 and confirmed in the role in 2018. Parents feel the appointment has been a wise one. 'They've always been very present, very down-to-earth and inclusive; you feel they really care about the kids and have their best interests at heart – not always the case under previous regimes.'

Entrance: Of the 243 pupils admitted into year 7, many are from local high-performing primaries (Tetherdown, St James, Muswell Hill Primary, etc). Main criteria for entry are sibling connection and distance (usually within half a mile) from the gates (measured on an ordinance survey map from the South Wing). Competition for places is high and families have been known to rent nearby or fudge their data. (NB proof of address is required and those discovered using 'an address of convenience' can be asked to leave). Minimum 50 new pupils into its 250-strong year 12. At this juncture, those aiming for the 'academic pathway' require at least a 6 in five subjects, with a minimum of 6 in intended A levels and/or English and maths; for the 'applied pathway', the benchmark is slightly more flexible, with grade 5 in five subjects and/or 5 in English and maths.

Exit: Reasonable numbers exit at GCSE, some because they haven't made the grade, others to local state sixth forms (Woodhouse and Camden School for Girls both popular) or the independent sector. Pupils go on to a wide range of higher education with good advice available to help with selection. Leeds, Sussex, Manchester, Bristol all popular. Two to Oxbridge in 2019.

Latest results: In 2020, 72 per cent 9/7 at GCSE; 37 per cent A*/A at A level (70 per cent A*/B). In 2019 (the last year when exams took place), 80 per cent 9-4 in both maths and English at GCSE; 42 per cent A*/A at A level (71 per cent A*-B).

Teaching and learning: Fortismere is a high-achieving comprehensive with a broad curriculum and strong emphasis on traditional academic subjects. Teaching is highly rated ('The teaching is really, really good,' said one recent leaver; 'The way they teach encourages discussion and excitement about the subjects,' said a parent). Good teacher–pupil ratio throughout (one to 15) and 10 sixth form tutors focus on groups of 20-24, with an academic coach on hand to help with organisation and study skills. Relationship between staff and pupil relaxed and positive, with teachers contactable by email. Homework load manageable, some parents say too much so. ('We became

This is a large comprehensive, and students require robust inner resources to flourish. 'They're expected to be independent'

increasingly frustrated with the laissez-faire attitude to homework. The school seems better for the self-motivated and well-organised than for those who need more pushing.')

Results overall very strong and reflect not only the quality of the teaching but the profile of the intake, with entrants at 11 having better than average skills and well-to-do parents able to mop up any lapses with out-of-hours tutoring. 'Of course, it gets stellar results,' was one jaundiced view. Particularly strong A level outcome in English, maths and history. Broad sixth form offering includes Mandarin and the EPQ, and, for those looking for a more vocational focus, BTecs in sport, creative and media and performing arts.

Learning support and SEN: Wide range of in-house support for those who struggle (including learning mentors and an EAL coordinator) and extensive network of external experts on call for more specialist requirements. Ofsted happy that (the many) SEN pupils' needs are accurately identified and support well delivered, but some parents feel the approach is not always empathetic. 'As my daughter got older, she didn't want her learning support so evident in lessons; even when we asked if this could be dealt with more tactfully, nothing was done.'

The arts and extracurricular: A creative place, where the rush for qualifications has certainly not drowned out the arts. Art, music and drama are all timetabled weekly in the early years with four hours devoted to creativity. Eight arts subjects on offer at GCSE (dance, drama, art, music, music technology, DT and photography), expanded further in the sixth form to include film studies, media studies, product design and art history. Dynamic provision extended with industry-standard opportunities, including workshops with professional artists and training by West End lighting and sound designers. Music of a high standard, much conducted in the specialist music centre, which hosts events from the winter and piano concerts to the first semi-staged opera. Choir for years 9-13, but sadly no take up for music A level. Doesn't seem to have impeded the outcome and former pupils include Theo Ellis of Mercury-Prize-winning band Wolf Alice. Regular outings to theatres, galleries and concerts. Large, well-maintained and regularly updated library, with author visits, weekly creative writing workshops and a 'patron of reading'.

Huge range of extracurricular clubs cater for every possible interest (from young reporters to science masterclasses, student investor, fashion show, feminism and equality). Plenty of trips (Rome, Berlin, Madagascar), opportunities to compete (National Cipher Challenge, Foyles Young Poet) and visiting speakers from philosophers and academics (Stephen Law, Natalie Haynes) to the local butcher (for food tech).

Sport: Sport perhaps less of a strength, but girl footballers have triumphed in Haringey League and others achieved notable success in cross-country and table tennis; former pupils, too, have gone on to national glory in football (Wales U17 football and England U18 boys) and fencing. Wide range of sports on offer for lesser mortals from tag rugby to table tennis, basketball to dance, but 'go, fight, win' not necessarily the dominant mood and sportphobics will not feel under duress.

Ethos and heritage: The school has a complex history, but the first school on the current site was founded in 1879. Fortismere itself was formed in 1983 by the amalgamation of two comprehensives, Creighton School and Alexandra Park School. The school today sits on an expansive 20-acre site, subdivided into two main buildings, the North Wing (largely devoted to English, modern languages and the arts) and the South Wing (focusing on maths, science and humanities). Extensive playing fields, a sports hall, Astroturf pitches and tennis courts lie between. The secondary school of Blanche Nevile School for Deaf Children is also on the site.

Results reflect not only the quality of the teaching but the profile of the intake, with entrants having better than average skills and well-to-do parents able to mop up any lapses

This is a large comprehensive, with upwards of 1,800 pupils, and students require robust inner resources to flourish. ('They're expected to be independent – someone compared it to more of a university vibe,' said a parent.) Perhaps as a result, pupils tend to be confident, articulate and outgoing.

Rated one of London's best comprehensives by the Sunday Times, the school continues to promote the comprehensive ideals of 'non-elitism, equality and respect for diversity', with a strong culture of supporting and celebrating diversity – it is, for example, a Stonewall School Champion. Pupil voice is heard loud and clear, with peer-elected student leadership team; parental voice – perhaps understandably – somewhat more muffled. At a recent sixth form open evening, for example, no questions were allowed.

Pastoral care, inclusivity and discipline: Transition from primary to secondary carefully overseen, with primary schools visited and detailed feedback requested. Year 7s then bond over a trip away and their own common room. Four-day a week 'vertical tutoring' groups – consisting of four to five students from each year group between years 7-10 – further enhance a sense of belonging.

Atmosphere relaxed but orderly – 'I think the school works well where children thrive in a not very strict environment' – and behaviour policy consistently applied. No smartphones, for example, allowed from years 7-11 – not even in bags – and in-lesson behaviour strictly monitored. 'It's strict about the important stuff,' said a parent. Pupils generally well behaved with little in the way of fixed-term exclusions (none in 2018). No uniform, but clear guidelines on appropriate dress – nothing torn or transparent, for example. Punctuality has been an issue, but detentions have helped reduced tardiness. Mental health issues high on the agenda, with two school counsellors, mindfulness sessions, nurture groups, and all staff completing mental health first-aid training.

Pupils and parents: Fortismere serves an area of expensive property and the dominant mood is liberal, progressive and prosperous, with plenty of high-performing students to ease the way to strong results. Parents are of the involved sort, and this certainly pays dividends. Last year, the FSA (parents' association) raised £45,000 for the school through fireworks, Christmas fair, movie night, etc. Those who don't match the prevalent profile can occasionally feel isolated. 'I spent a lot of my time at Fortismere begging my mum for Converse trainers so I could "fit in",' said a recent leaver.

Money matters: Some discretionary sixth form bursaries available for maintenance and the vulnerable.

The last word: A thriving local comprehensive which suits the mature, confident and already focused. Not necessarily the ideal place for the timid or those requiring firm boundaries and push.

Grimsdell Mill Hill Pre-Preparatory School

12

Winterstoke House, Wills Grove, Mill Hill Village, London NW7 1QR

020 8959 6884 | kandrews@grimsdell.org.uk | www.millhill.org.uk/grimsdell

Independent | Pupils: 192

Ages: 3-7 | Fees: £7,125 – £15,492 pa

Linked schools: Belmont Mill Hill Preparatory School, 615; Mill Hill School, 659

Head: Since 2014, Kate Simon (40s). A Grimsdell parent, Mrs Simon is no stranger to headship. Between 2002 and 2008 she was head of the junior school of the Royal School, Hampstead (now incorporated into North Bridge Senior) and from 2008 was head of girls' upper school at Garden House School in Chelsea.

Entrance: Heavily oversubscribed, due in part to it being non-selective at age 3 or 4. 'I don't feel comfortable with failing children at that age,' says the head. Most pupils come from within a five-mile radius and there is a 'multi-cultural mix'.

Exit: The majority of pupils continue on to Belmont school. However, if the school feels that a child won't cope there, discussions about alternatives take place from year 1. 'We have to be realistic,' the school says.

Our view: Unfortunate name for a very pretty school. On a beautiful autumnal day, Grimsdell was the antithesis of 'grim'. Situated on Mill Hill's Ridgeway, but accessed via a small and very lovely private road, the school occupies the rather grand Winterstoke House. Originally a vicarage for the vicar of St Paul's and sold to Mill Hill School in

October 1923, Winterstoke House was purchased to become a school boarding house to host some 42 boys.

The school became Grimsdell in 1995 – a newcomer compared to the other two schools in the Foundation. The reason for its formation was largely due to a Mrs Grimsdell, widow of an Old Millhillian, who bequeathed a large part of her late husband's estate to Mill Hill School. Following a request from the school governors, Mrs Grimsdell agreed that the benefaction be applied to create a 'much required' pre-preparatory school, and Grimsdell opened its gates. The school is situated adjacent to Mill Hill School but has its own grounds – not quite on the scale of the other two schools, but more than adequate for a pre-prep school.

This is a cute, cosy school. Nothing grand and pretentious, despite the impression given by its exterior. We were seated in a colourful and bright reception area with a large aquarium to gaze at while we waited to meet the head. Familiar sounds of overexcited kids emanated from one or two of the classrooms (and we were particularly struck by one over-zealous music teacher doing something very strange with her arms!).

All classrooms were light, airy and well equipped – particularly the Sunshine Room, which even in its name suggests something warm and nurturing. This is where pupils who need it go for extra one-to-one learning support. Specialist on-site teachers in music, PE and French are on hand and 4- to 7-year-olds have weekly keyboard lessons with a music specialist. The swimming pool at Mill Hill School is a great addition to the PE curriculum. Pupils use the theatre at Mill Hill School for concerts and performances. Cursive handwriting is taught from the start and we were quite amazed with the standard of year 1 handwriting displayed on classroom walls.

Grimsdell has its own forest school. Each session has a theme and activities can range from mini-beast hunting to fire building and cooking outdoors

As with Belmont and Mill Hill School, Grimsdell's selling point is undoubtedly its idyllic surroundings. Pupils not only have access to 120 acres of beautiful parkland at Mill Hill school with its sports pitches, swimming pool and woodland, but they have their own great adventure playground and science garden to enjoy. A firm believer in the great outdoors, Grimsdell has its own forest school. Each session has a theme and activities can range from mini-beast hunting to fire building and cooking outdoors. With a school that states boldly in its prospectus 'there is no such thing as bad weather, just bad clothing', you had better be sure your little darlings have a healthy interest in outdoor pursuits. Forget this school otherwise – indeed discount the other two schools in the Foundation while you are at it.

The last word: Parents appreciate the expertise of the large Foundation, and the lack of pressure to take exams for future schools. One parent told us, 'Grimsdell is a secure and nurturing stepping-stone, which is illustrated by my own excited and eager children.'

Head: Since 2014, Del Cooke BSc MBA NPQH (50s), previously head of Sir William Perkins's School in Surrey. Maths graduate with MBA in educational management, her broad experience covers the comprehensive system, sixth form college, adult education and boarding at Cranleigh, where she was head of maths, housemistress and finally deputy head. She is increasingly seen as the embodiment of HBS – smart, quick-witted, friendly and empathetic. 'The girls want to hang out with her. She is like them,' summed up one parent. We found her instantly likeable, not remotely intimidating and surprisingly low-key. Made no dramatic changes so far ('It's such a fantastic school, you'd have to be pretty pompous to come in and turn it upside down,' she says), but is known as a visible head, particularly interested in getting the girls' views on various aspects of the school, and is clearly keen to focus more heavily on celebrating individual achievements. No bad thing, point out some parents, who say the girls can be 'far too modest, and need reminding how amazing they are'. Has a passion for music, playing a number of instruments, including self-taught bassoon. Married with three sons.

Entrance: It doesn't get more selective than this, with 3,000+ applying for 100 places. Verbal and non-verbal reasoning and English tests in September, then the top 300 are invited back for English and maths tests in October. Pupils come from 50-60 primaries. Priority to looked-after children and to those pupil premium who have been ranked in the top 300, then to girls who live within three miles.

Often seen as an academic hothouse, says head, 'but it's the girls who drive the pace of learning – the staff sometimes have to tell the girls to slow down!'

For sixth form, approximately 600 apply for a further 55-60 places, with six grade 7s at GCSE minimum requirement, including 7s in intended A level subjects. Girls already in the school are also expected to achieve this requirement, although in reality most far exceed it.

Exit: Up to 15 per cent leave after GCSE, mostly to sixth form colleges. In 2020, 35 to Oxbridge. Lots of medics and dentists (20 medics, dentists and vets in 2020) and a good cross-section of all other subject areas. Team of sixth form tutors provide UCAS advice, including raising expectations of what can be achieved. Alumni include Sarah Solemani (actress and television script writer), Ros Altmann (previously pensions minister), Baroness Evans of Bowes Park (leader of the House of Lords and Lord Privy Seal) and Debbie Wiseman (composer).

Latest results: In 2020, 97 per cent 9-7 at GCSE; 86 per cent A*/A at A level. In 2019 (the last year when exams took place), 94 per cent 9-7 at GCSE; 72 per cent A*/A at A level.

Teaching and learning: Consistently top or very near the top of both the GCSE and A level league tables. Most do 11 GCSEs, three or four As. Results strong across all subjects at GCSE, with a bias towards maths and sciences at A level, which around three-quarters of pupils choose, although history and English also have a healthy representation. Languages prioritised, with French, German and Latin for all in year 7, plus Spanish for all in years 8 and 9. Plus an option of ancient Greek. No setting.

Myths about this school being an academic hothouse, where girls are worked like dogs, are prolific, and even the head was initially put off the job because she thought it would be so pressurised. 'I was resistant, assuming the girls would be working in a ridiculously intensive environment. But it's the girls who drive the pace of learning and if anything, the staff sometimes have to tell the girls to slow down!' says the head. Pupils and parents agree, with one saying her daughter had just been advised to 'take some time out of her revision schedule to do something more relaxing.' Girls are encouraged to be independent, albeit well-supported, learners from day one, with many setting up their own societies and visiting universities for extra lectures. During our visit, we saw one noticeboard with pages from HB Scientist, the sixth-form produced (and very professional looking) science magazine that is sold throughout the school, whilst plenty of posters around the school advertised forthcoming speakers that pupils have organised – Zadie Smith when we visited.

Competitive learning is frowned upon, making way for a supportive atmosphere and strong sense of co-operation, which everyone agrees is a huge aid to the girls excelling academically. Teachers could hardly be considered more dedicated, although many parents say more of them are needed. 'Every one of the teachers would be a good candidate for a head of department in a private school, earning 50-100 per cent more money, but they choose to stay here because of the quality of the school and the commitment of the girls, which makes them very, very special,' said one parent. Girls love the fact that many of the teachers have had (non-teaching) careers in their subjects, also praising the informal relationships they have with them and level of responsibility the girls are given. Homework is given if and when teachers feel it's required, rather than hours every evening for the sake of it.

The arts and extracurricular: Thriving music department, with a symphony orchestra that everyone agrees is a joy to listen to, especially at concerts in the nearby ambient St Jude's Church. There are other orchestras and plenty of choirs, along with all manner of bands, including swing and rock. All pupils study music in key stage 3 and many go on to GCSE. Plenty of private tuition in a wide range of instruments, including double bass, bassoon and French horn, and there is an organ scholarship. Great excitement about the music wing built in 2011. 'Previously, we were taught music in our classroom or temporary huts, so it's a major thing,' said one pupil, who showed us the well-stocked rehearsal room and studio, with several soundproofed practice rooms. The same wing is home to drama, another lively department with strong facilities, with recent performances including Hamlet (year 9s), a play about Henrietta Barnett (year 7s) and a school-wide Our Country's Good.

'A few weeks ago, a whole class came out of art with painted-on moustaches and top hats from drama – it was so HBS,' laughed one girl

Mirroring this wing, on the other side of the main building, is the DT and art block. Downstairs, the spacious DT room is home to all kinds of interesting inventions, including a Batman-style wooden chair and scooter that changes colour when exposed to sunlight. Meanwhile, the upstairs art room is a fantastic space, with some seriously talented work on display across all media. The wrap-around balconies on both wings are both aesthetically pleasing and provide an outside space for students to work during the summer months.

Lots of extracurricular opportunities, including Mandarin, robotics (year 8 team recently got through to world championships in USA), creative writing, philosophy society, LAMDA, and many pupil-led activities. For instance, sixth formers currently teach Japanese to younger ones, as well as running a current affairs club, with speakers (invited by pupils themselves) including Melissa Benn and Lucy Holmes.

School trips, through each subject department, take every year group out once a year, with recent examples including Iceland (geography) and Greece (classics). 'It was easily the best holiday I've ever been on, just unbelievably interesting and fun,' said one pupil who went on the latter. French and German exchanges and Spanish trip to Seville. When we visited, 65 students were getting ready to head to the Rhineland for a music tour. Lots of day trips, particularly to theatres, museums and art galleries. Enrichment week, held in the summer, provides an entire week of outings. Own field study centre in Dorset, which every pupil visits for one week during her early years at the school.

Sport: Historically sports not brilliant, although improved facilities – large multi-purpose Astroturf court for netball, hockey, football and volleyball – have helped, with the school increasingly winning at both a local and borough level and holding its own against some top private schools. Facilities also include a gym, a state-of-the-art fitness suite with a good range of exercise equipment and a variety of pitches available on the nearby Hampstead Heath extension. 'Sport is very much on the up,' insists the head and there's a long list of exercise alternatives, including zumba, fencing, tang soo do, yoga, fitness, indoor rowing, cricket, badminton and dance. Rugby and athletics are also increasingly popular. No swimming pool but occasional opportunities for swimmers to take part in school events.

Ethos and heritage: Founded in 1911 by formidable social reformer Dame Henrietta Barnett, the school is housed in architecturally stunning Lutyens-designed buildings in upmarket Hampstead Garden Suburb. Not unlike the kind of buildings you'd find at Harvard or Stanford, it's also a beautifully landscaped campus. Facilities top-notch, particularly the colour-coded science labs and new swanky new wings for art, DT, music and drama, plus newly refurbished and extended library. Floors are polished parquet, classrooms are light and airy and corridors are tastefully decorated with everything from a recent photography competition to huge science-inspired pictures. Dining hall, where food is praised, and all-day café for year 10 upwards. Parts of the interiors could do with a lick of paint. But overall facilities feel spacious, with excitable students loving their environment, including after school, when something is going on pretty much every evening.

Has put in an application for the government's Selective Schools Expansion Fund, which would result in some building for expansion in 2021.

Pastoral care, inclusivity and discipline: 'No bells, no detention, no rules – it's so relaxed that if you came to school in your pyjamas no one would bat an eyelid,' wrote Tatler in its 2015 review, words that are now a source of great pride (not to mention humour) in the school 'simply because they are so true,' explained one pupil. Even a mention of the word 'discipline' will get you a blank look among pupils ('Why would you play up?' one said, genuinely bemused), whilst any occasional quirkiness that's perhaps inevitable among such an academic bunch is accepted as normal and certainly never teased. 'A few weeks ago, a whole class came out of art with painted-on moustaches and top hats from drama – it was so HBS,' laughed one girl. But this is no St Trinian's. Far from it, the girls' behaviour is impeccable and they always do their best, as well as being delightful and friendly. 'If a girl did step out of line, the teacher would just have a chat, adult-to-adult,' says the head, who believes it's the fact that the girls are treated like adults – with all the respect and trust that goes with that – that accounts for the lack of need for rules.

Bullying a non-issue, whilst part-time counsellors are on hand to deal with any problems. Currently a big push on reducing the stigma of mental health issues, with several noticeboards pointing to relevant resources. Strong student council, which is particularly strong in recruitment and raised funds for the new library, plus lunch council.

Pupils and parents: Girls are extremely bright and eager to learn, as well as both interesting and interested. Clear team spirit, where girls in different years bond naturally as well as through schemes like the student-led 'vertical families'. 'Of course, you get friendship groups, but absolutely no cliques,' said one pupil. 'It's a real community where everyone knows you and supports you,' said another. The school has always had a wide catchment area, based as it was on the vision of providing education to bright girls regardless of their means, although since the arrival of league tables, some pupils come in too far for the head's liking. ('I do question whether it's a good thing for some to travel really long distances.') Those in London mostly walk, cycle or get the bus or tube (Golders Green). There's also a parent-organised bus service to cater for those who can't easily get there by public transport.

Great ethnic mix – about a fifth Indian and a fifth white British, the rest from a variety of backgrounds. 'The school is the multicultural, meritocratic face of Britain,' said one parent, proudly. PTA provides refreshments at events, along with the odd quiz night, but not as active as some, particularly for socialising. 'It's inevitable, with families coming from such a wide area and diverse backgrounds,' said one parent, which probably also explains why after-school social life is not as vibrant as elsewhere.

Money matters: Regular fundraising via PTA, pupil-led initiatives and a parental support scheme to which many parents regularly donate.

The last word: One of the top academic state schools in the country, yet also one of the most liberal and nurturing; it's hard to exaggerate the emotional buy-in from pupils. 'The school becomes part of your DNA in a profound way,' said one. 'I don't know what happens when you get inside those four walls, but it is genuinely unique and stays with you for life.' Producing friendly, fun and delightful girls who come out with academic results that quite literally make the world their oyster, it's no wonder that top universities and employers love it too. 'My only sadness is that I can't see how it will ever be this good again,' said one pupil. A gentle and inspiring education for extremely bright girls, in a fabulous setting.

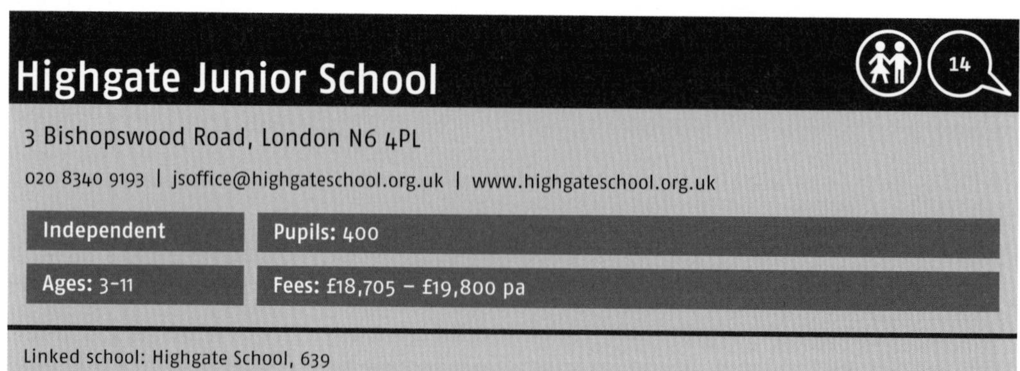

Highgate Junior School

14

3 Bishopswood Road, London N6 4PL

020 8340 9193 | jsoffice@highgateschool.org.uk | www.highgateschool.org.uk

Independent	Pupils: 400
Ages: 3–11	Fees: £18,705 – £19,800 pa

Linked school: Highgate School, 639

Principal of junior school: Since 2002, Mark James (50s). BA in theology from Nottingham University, followed by a PGCE in English from the London Institute and an MA from King's College London. Grew up in Somerset where he worked for a term at Wellington School. Started career in the state sector – Tiffin grammar in Kingston – then Emmanuel School, followed by a decade at Dulwich College and a stint at the Southport School in Queensland, prior to making the transition from secondary to primary education, becoming deputy head at King's College Wimbledon junior school. It was under his leadership that Highgate Junior was transformed from an all-boys 7-13 prep into a modern mixed 7-11 school. 'We're not a prep school,' he was swift to point out. 'Our pupils don't have to sit an entrance test for the senior school; education is a marathon, not a sprint.' In today's ferociously competitive education landscape in north London and beyond, this is a not only a unique formula but, in our opinion, a winning one.

Parents past and present unstinting in their praise for this head who is, they say, 'the heartbeat of the school'. Enormously likeable; an enthusiastic can-do character with just the right mix of gravitas and approachability to keep the (sometimes overly) ambitious parent cohort in check ('when parents challenge us on whether the maths here is advanced enough, I point them in the direction of the year 11 GCSE results') and the pupils bouncing into school every day. Seemed happy to have sacrificed his position as director of admissions for the senior school (aka THE man to know in north London) to focus solely on headship. His wife is also a teacher and they have two daughters – both of whom who have gone through Highgate School.

Head of pre-prep since 2012, Diane Hecht DCE (50s). Previously deputy head of St Columba's Junior School in Kilmacolm, she came south as two of her grown-up children had settled in London and feels that she has found a wonderfully similar school in Highgate. 'The girls here wear exactly the same tartan skirts as at St Columba's – it was meant to be!' Warm, efficient and enthusiastic.

Entrance: From September 2021 onwards, selective entry at 4+ and phasing out of the nursery (pupils already in the nursery will be able to move up automatically as before); 'we want to be more accurate with selection,' says head. Twenty places will be available in 2021 for new pupils to join the final cohort moving up from the nursery, growing to 60 in 2022, to make three forms. At 7+, an additional 50 places are available, to make five forms of 22. Unsurprisingly, places are extremely hard fought for at both entry points, with north London's finest tutors set to work to help secure an offer. Reportedly 'a bit of jostling for position' once the selected 7+ pupils make their entrance but it all settles down pretty quickly under the sensible watch of Mr James.

Exit: Almost all skip up the hill to Highgate School, delighted to have dodged the 11+ process along the way (at the time of our visit, year 6 had just taken their end of year exams – by all accounts a very low key, jolly and supportive process). A small handful depart for eg Latymer, QEB or Henrietta Barnett. Those who are unlikely to thrive in the senior school are advised by year 4 and supported throughout to find the best destination; parents we spoke to said this was handled 'incredibly sensitively'.

Our view: There are schools (and trust us, we've seen a few) and then there's Highgate Junior School. Tucked into Bishopswood Road, one of the many prestigious residential streets that line the route from Highgate to Hampstead, is – without doubt – the most impressive junior school building we've ever seen. 'I expect you see lots of schools with space like this outside of London,' mused Mr James; actually, we've never seen anything quite like it.

Without doubt, the most impressive junior school building we've ever seen. 'I'm a convert to the theory that buildings can change behaviours,' said Mr James

Opened in 2016 following a three-year build project financed by the sale of property around the village, the sandstone and glass fascia is more akin to a modern art museum than a school. 'I'm a convert to the theory that buildings can change behaviours,' said Mr James. The reception area has a beautiful feature wall by a specially commissioned artist; the first hint of what is to come. Portland fossilised stone provides the interior backdrop with a design which gently curves its way to the upper level. Reptiles and amphibians of various kinds are sculpted into the walls throughout the building to encourage children to explore and discover different surfaces and textures as part of their learning exploration. Light and space abound and from the circular central atrium you can almost see the whole school – inside and out. The hall alone, with its 360 retractable seats, would be the envy of many a secondary school we've visited. Classrooms are bright and spacious, with the luxury of having been designed for their specific purposes – art, science, DT, music etc – and many open onto the outdoor space with its small amphitheatre, adventure playground equipment and courts marked out with playground games – all surrounded by the extensive Highgate playing fields.

We're not ones to be bowled over by shiny facilities (if anything, we're suspicious of too much gloss) but Highgate Juniors is a prime example of how sometimes you can judge a book by its cover. Parents we spoke to used superlative after superlative to praise teaching staff, likening the partnership between parents and teachers to 'a long journey with two-way trust'. Pupils said their teachers are 'all just so much fun'. The staff we saw were generally young and energetic; there's an open-door observation policy with frequent feedback given plus a low staff turnover, and both the professional growth of teachers and their continuity no doubt contribute to the success of the school.

Parents past and present unstinting in their praise for this head who is, they say, 'the heartbeat of the school'. Enormously likeable; an enthusiastic can-do character with just the right mix of gravitas and approachability to keep the ambitious parent cohort in check

From year 3 onwards, classes are full at 22 and although there's 'no overt setting', according to head, there is discrete streaming within the classroom, that can vary from topic to topic. 'Happiness and safety override everything,' he says. 'We want year 6 to be a celebration of childhood with no glass ceilings, rather than a holding room for adolescence.' Hear hear. Art, music, DT, languages and sport are taught by specialists, with not 'just' French on the curriculum but a carousel of whatever specialisms lie in the staff room at any given time; at the time of our visit, Mandarin, Guajarati, Italian and Russian each on an eight-week carousel. Pupils then start languages from scratch in year 7. Teaching takes a thematic approach with threads running through all subjects, and humanities subjects such as history capture pupils' imaginations by looking at world events through eg fashion. Because of school's selective nature, numbers requiring learning support are quite small. The SENCo ('absolutely incredible; a really special person,' according to parents) takes one-to-one and small group sessions for those with mild SpLD, although time outside the classroom is kept to a minimum.

'The creative side of the school is amazing,' parents told us. More superlatives followed. Drama: 'fantastic', art department: 'amazing' and music, you guessed it: 'just fabulous'. Drama on curriculum to year 6. Plays and performances (recently Charlie and the Chocolate Factory; Verucca Salt was our guide) take place in either the studio theatre or the lovely open air drama garden, also used at playtimes for quiet chatting. Music feeds beautifully into the plethora of opportunities awaiting pupils once they reach the senior school. There's a string project in year 3 with all pupils trying the violin and brass scheme for all in year 4. Choirs and ensembles feature heavily in the extracurricular programme. Speaking of which: knitting, sock toy making, gardening, photography, Minecraft, multitudinous sports clubs and much, much more on offer. Clubs and activities tend to be activity based rather than having an academic bent: 'being interested in things is valuable without a badge or a certificate,' says head. We quite agree.

Possibly slightly less on the sporty side than more trad preps – particularly before year 4 where all sports are mixed gender, the cause of one or two grumbles from parents who would prefer to focus on competition and excellence – but it's all here and in true Highgate style is infused with enthusiasm and vigour. Fortunate to share the fabulous facilities of the senior school with the added bonus that the fields, 25m indoor pool (recently refurbished) and Mallinson Centre are right on the doorstep, pupils play football, cricket, netball, fives plus athletics and swimming and have three games lessons a week. Plenty of fixtures too – girls now pioneering matches in football and cricket – and teams often down to D or E, meaning plenty of chances for an outing and a match tea, with much success; girls' hockey team were recently placed third in Southern Regional Championships. Outdoor education is on curriculum.

Parents describe 'an incredibly caring' culture that 'feels like a family unit'. Pastorally focused, the new director of well-being from the senior school is on site once a week and pupils we spoke to were very clear on who they should go to if they weren't happy. Head spoke of a real focus on personal development and embedding character skills. As with senior school, there's a strong philanthropic emphasis; pupils from a local state primary were enjoying use of the outdoor play equipment at the time of our visit; school has partnerships with five or six primaries and shares eg early morning maths sessions, singing, science and general knowledge with them. Frequent visits too to a local care home for the elderly: 'our aim is for pupils to have a better understanding of what charity really means,' says head.

The last word: Parents commute their children from the near and far parts of north London and report them having a 'marvellous time' – we say they couldn't fail to.

Highgate School

North Road, London N6 4AY

020 8347 3564 | admissions@highgateschool.org.uk | www.highgateschool.org.uk

Independent	Pupils: 1,882; sixth form: 354
Ages: 11-18	Fees: £21,600 pa

Linked school: Highgate Junior School, 636

Head: Since 2006, Adam Pettitt MA (50s). Oxford modern and medieval linguist. Has taught French and German at Eton, Oundle and Abingdon and was second master at Norwich School under Jim Hawkins, former head of Harrow. Immaculate and clipped of tone; parents say 'visionary' and a 'driving force'. Mere mortals have to concentrate to keep up when he speaks and there's absolutely no conjecture – he is propelled by a sharply focused and incisively articulated moral and educational philosophy. Presides over quite the tidiest desk we have seen (one pen, one notebook, acres of spotless, ocean blue space). 'Employability' at the heart of his strategy: 'We have to ask firstly whether pupils enjoy themselves and secondly whether they are acquiring employable traits.' Tuned into social pressures faced by young people; aware of, and concerned about, potential for Highgate students to suffer from 'imposter syndrome' but focused on communicating that 'they don't have to prove anything – it's all about the now'. Refreshingly, not a passionate advocate for co-education but rather for good schools; 'quality is far more important than the type of school,' he says.

Created role of director of well-being in October 2018; says 'talking about mental health was the missing part of the jigsaw'. Speaks with heartfelt passion about the London Academy of Excellence in Tottenham, a state sixth form college founded under his leadership in 2017 of which Highgate is the academic sponsor. Pupils can't fail to benefit from his firm commitment to social diversity and educational values; says he is 'determined not to be beholden to exam results' – although with Highgate floating towards the top of most league tables, it's clear that top results do indeed follow where his approach leads.

Entrance: Selective and oversubscribed at all entry points. Around 100 move up from junior school and are joined at 11+ by 80 or so external candidates, around half of which are from state primary schools and 40 per cent (mainly girls) from local preps. Approximately 600 pupils apply for these places with a third interviewed. Only a handful of places available at 13+; tests and interviews currently in autumn term of year 6. At 16+, some 120 apply for between 35 and 50 places and all are invited to an assessment day comprising exams in chosen A level subjects and interviews, and up to half come from state schools.

Exit: Around 15 per cent – mainly boys – leave after GCSEs, often to Camden School for Girls, which has a mixed sixth form. Around 90 per cent of leavers gain places at their first choice university, with Edinburgh, Durham, King's College London, UCL, Imperial, Exeter, Warwick, York and Leeds among most favoured. Applications overseas are increasing – 11 went off to study in USA, Canada and Italy in 2020. Excellent Oxbridge numbers – 25 in 2020, and 14 to study medicine.

Employability core to curriculum from year 9 onwards with careers focus in PHSE plus COA testing, work experience, interview coaching workshops and heavy use of alumni as external speakers and mentors.

Latest results: In 2020, 96 per cent 9-7 at GCSE; 86 per cent A*/A at A leve/Pre-U. In 2019 (the last year when exams took place), 90 per cent 9-7 at GCSE; 76 per cent A*/A at A level/Pre-U.

Teaching and learning: School populated by a bright, energetic and intellectually curious cohort. Coupled with the fierce competition for places at 11+ and a staffroom made up of the pick of the teaching bunch (who wouldn't want to work here?) plus parents reporting favourably on the strong work ethic instilled in their children, it's no surprise that Highgate sits towards the top of the exam league tables year after year. Impressive results, although school is not an academic monoculture. 'We need to stop the hierarchy between so-called academic subjects and the rest – we tell students to do what they love,' says head. Bravo. That said, majority of pupils do follow fairly a fairly traditional academic path with relatively small numbers opting for eg theatre studies, classics or music at A level/ Pre-U and there are none of the increasingly popular 'modern' subjects such as textiles, psychology or music tech on offer. Majority of subjects now taught as IGCSEs – none taken early – and many departments opt for Pre-U as an alternative to A levels.

With John Rutter and John Tavener both former pupils, choral music is entrenched in the tradition of the school and six choirs cater for all abilities

Strong language provision; French and Latin in year 7, with Spanish, Mandarin, Russian, German and Greek on offer from year 9 to A level. Three-quarters of sixth formers take maths A level; having met one of the departmental heads we're not surprised. 'Everyone has such horror stories about how they were taught maths – our raison d'être is that none of our pupils leave with that,' she says. English teaching equally impressive, with the department boasting three published writers plus an author in residence. Creativity lies at the heart of the department and there's a focus on bringing literature alive with frequent theatre visits and tours to eg Ireland for A level students studying Joyce, Beckett and Heaney: 'we illuminate the experience so it's not fettered by exam requirements.' Ever-increasing emphasis on enhancing the school reading culture – newly appointed is a director of reading, creativity and literacy to help 'develop the reading muscle', with a view to improving not just literacy but also mental health and well-being. Super classroom facilities across the board – science taught in lecture theatre style rooms, surrounded by the prerequisite selection of exotic flora and reptilian fauna.

Learning support and SEN: Sane and sensitively individualised approach to SEN. Head of learning support covers junior and senior schools and has an expertise in autism. The support for all SpLD is individual, tailored, supportive and 'concerned with management rather than labelling'. The very few with EAL needs are usually the very bright. Those with mobility problems would struggle to navigate the main Victorian school building with its warrens of stairs.

The arts and extracurricular: Enrichment programme on Thursday lunchtimes for years 7 and 8 and after school on Tuesdays for years 9 to 11 provides a compulsory element to co-curricular participation in addition to the 80 or so clubs and societies on offer each week. There's a strong emphasis on pupil leadership and clubs include a refreshing variety of non-academic options from beekeeping or sign language to genealogy or pocket watch society as well as the usual subject related societies. Over 230 pupils were participating in DofE at the time of our visit, with seven fresh from receiving their gold award at Buckingham Palace that week and 55 working towards it.

Drama and music both thriving; one of our tour highlights was heading out of the main school building through a rather dingy concrete underpass only to pop up in the music department with its auditorium, used for concerts (drama productions are often staged at RADA), suite of practice rooms, studio used for informal chamber music performances and music technology suite, complete with fleet of gleaming Macs and new recording booth. Recent major musical productions have included West Side Story, South Pacific and Oliver! (Guys and Dolls in planning at the time of our visit), and a group of senior thespians head to the Edinburgh Fringe most years. With John Rutter and John Tavener both former pupils, choral music is entrenched in the tradition of the school and six choirs cater for all abilities range from a training choir for years 7 and 8 to the elite chapel choir; the 'huge' house singing competition in which all pupils participate takes place at Alexandra Palace and the 'massive' carol services take place in Dalston and St Michael's Church, Highgate. There are 50 peripatetic music teachers to brush pupils up for participation in one of the many orchestras and ensembles that range from the symphony orchestra to the professionally mentored hip hop collective. Superb quality of artwork on display in the Mills Centre, home to the art and DTE (design, technology and engineering) departments.

Sport: Few London schools can boast the wealth of space and facilities offered at Highgate. It may not have the campus feel of its more suburban competitors, and the walk to the pitches makes for a good 10 minute warm up, but the net outdoor space featuring fields, pavilions, hard tennis courts and Astroturfs far exceeds expectations for a London school – and that's on top of the sports hall, squash courts and indoor pool (recently fully refurbished with digital screens to share match scores). Gentle souls can breathe a sigh of relief – there's no compulsory rugby; football, netball, cricket and hockey are core sports, fives is very

Highgate Junior School

popular and strength and conditioning 'really social,' according to sixth formers. Teams, too, are 'really fun and sociable'; as with all things Highgate, there's a healthy buzz around physical activity – or SPEX as it is known here – that seems to be more about achieving individual goals and engendering a lifelong love of sport than focusing on fierce competition. On top of the more trad games, there's also an outdoor activities curriculum aimed predominantly at the younger pupils, including orienteering on Hampstead Heath, bushcraft in the outdoor classroom, climbing and sailing, as well as trips to the school's own outdoor centre in Wales.

Ethos and heritage: Founded as the Free Grammar School of Sir Roger Cholmeley, Knight at Highgate, in 1565 – former pupils still known as Old Cholmeleians. Became Highgate School in the late 19th century. The painstakingly refurbished chapel (spectacular) and main buildings are 19th century. Some impressive bits – old gothic central hall with Norman arches, leaded lights, wrought iron balcony and cantilevered ceiling and splendid new Sir Martin Gilbert library in old assembly hall; our guide told us she couldn't help but feel inspired as she climbed the Shakespearean steps to reach it – and the moment we stepped inside we couldn't help but agree: it's a real library which, unlike so many schools' learning resource centres, actually has books in it, alongside all its rows of PCs, and an atmosphere to encourage concentration and study.

Clingfilm-free ethical snacking, reusable cups for all and a 'fast fashion free February', where pupils and teachers joined forces to downscale their wardrobes

By the 1960s, the school buildings (some of which were generously described by our guide as 'brutalist') were spread over the heart of Highgate Village. The Charter Building adds new subject rooms in a five-storey glass cube. All very high tech – interactive whiteboards and PCs everywhere. The whole site is now a mix of the new, light, glass-bound, airy and stylish, and the old, rather shabby, small passages and dark areas along which school operates a clever one-way system. Much tramping up and down the hill between the main buildings and the Mills Centre, playing fields, dining hall etc, but far from grumbling, pupils say they enjoy the 'down time' these mini commutes allow. Girls joined the sixth form in

The head presides over quite the tidiest desk we have seen: one pen, one notebook, acres of spotless, ocean blue space

2004 and year 7 in 2006, and the whole school is now fully and highly successfully co-educational. A Christian foundation and an inclusive one, with multi-faith assemblies and speakers from different religions on a weekly basis.

The word on the street from local tutors and parents we spoke to was that Highgate is very much the 'school du jour' – some went so far as to describe it as 'a bit A list'. Far from feeling rarefied or entitled, however, the overall vibe is very down to earth and low key, with pupils describing themselves as 'grateful' for being there. Evidence of inclusion and philanthropy is everywhere, and volunteering is 'part of the school's DNA' said staff. Some form of community activity is compulsory in years 7 and 8, often taking place at local primary schools – Highgate has partnerships with up to 50 state-maintained schools and head is clear that involvement is 'absolutely not tokenistic'. Nowhere is this commitment more evident than with the London Academy of Excellence Tottenham, a new sixth form with Tottenham Hotspur FC and Highgate as its business and academic sponsors. This is the base for the Highgate Teaching Consultancy and eight of the school's teachers work there on a regular basis: 'Tottenham pupils are genuinely receiving a Highgate education,' says head, who himself has swapped roles with the LAE head on occasion. On a global scale, Highgate supports a school in Uganda, taking pupils there to create 'a real sense of giving back'. Another of school's leading lights is the environmental committee; 'there's a real momentum building,' said staff, 'pupils are already activists in year 7'. Clingfilm-free ethical snacking, reusable cups for all and a 'fast fashion free February', where pupils and teachers joined forces to downscale their wardrobes, are all cogs in the Highgate sustainability wheel, which is so key now that one of the school governors runs an executive sustainability committee.

OCs include Rt Hons Charles Clarke and Anthony Crosland, Michael Mansfield QC, Johnny Borrell of Razorlight, Ringo Starr's son Zak Starkey of Oasis and the Who, Orlando Weeks of the Maccabees and DJ Yoda, Phil Tufnell, Sir Clive Sinclair, Alex Comfort, Nigel Williams, Sir John Tavener, Barry Norman, Gerard Manley Hopkins and Sir John Betjeman. Doubtless, old girl Cholmeleians shortly to make their marks.

Pastoral care, inclusivity and discipline: Director of well-being, a qualified clinical psychologist, appointed October 2018 to galvanise pastoral offering. From year 9 pupils are put into one of 12 houses which encourage inter-year group friendships and permeate the whole school with a family atmosphere. Inclusivity is par for the course and sixth formers told us that the LGBT community is open and accepted and there are a number of openly gay teachers. Tolerance, however, didn't extend as far as gender neutral loos which had a very short-lived presence in the school – now only one remains. The famed gender neutral uniform (a quick Google will tell you everything you need to know) wasn't noticeably different to any other co-ed school. Discipline, according to pupils, is not dependent on the whims of individual staff but 'whole school', ie you know what is coming to you at every level should you transgress. When things do go wrong, there are counsellors on hand to help, house meetings dedicated to all matters pastoral and a culture of open dialogue between younger pupils and their older peers. Whatever they are doing seems to be working – our visit fell smack bang in the middle of exam season but year 13s were reported to be 'happy and relaxed'. 'We try to play down exam pressure,' says head, and parents we spoke to uniformly report happy, happy children.

Pupils and parents: From a wide area of north and more central London, though most live nearby, if not within walking distance. Parents are professionals, entrepreneurs or media types; 25 per cent Jewish but an overwhelmingly Caucasian majority; there's a noticeable lack of ethnic diversity. Head, however, says he is conscious of this and strategies are in place to redress the balance over time. Pupils are pleasantly self-assured, friendly and outgoing with girls and boys co-existing in sibling-like harmony. More than any other school we have visited recently, a strong whiff of social conscience permeates the place – students have placed a self-imposed ban on plastic water bottles and concerns for the environment are evident through various student-led activities (including an accompanied visit to the Climate Strike). Although parents told us that school was overzealous on enforcing micro rules such as tucking in of shirts and neatness of hair, we found a reassuringly scruffy bunch as we scanned the dining hall, with its 'massively improved' food ('we want them to be slightly angular,' says head) – delightfully boisterous and clearly happy to be there.

Money matters: Fees in line with others in area, and include lunch, books, compulsory field work and curricular day visits. Scholarships purely honorary; music and academic at all the usual entry points. Generous bursary pot allows for 10 to 12 of up to 100 per cent at 11+ and a further three at 16+ each year.

The last word: A rare and magical combination of the high-flying and the humble, delivering a first class, modern education to those lucky enough to land there.

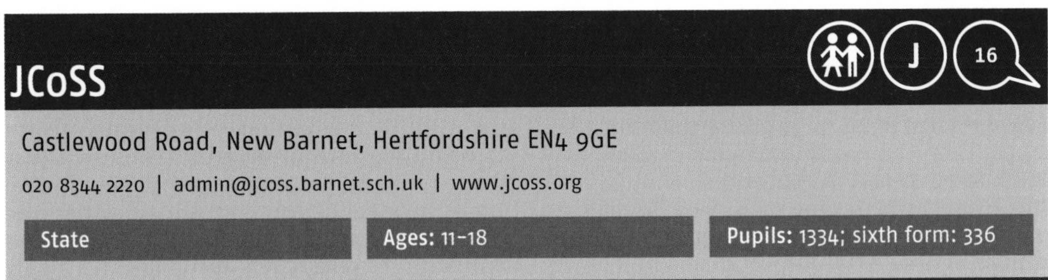

JCoSS

J 16

Castlewood Road, New Barnet, Hertfordshire EN4 9GE

020 8344 2220 | admin@jcoss.barnet.sch.uk | www.jcoss.org

State | Ages: 11–18 | Pupils: 1334; sixth form: 336

Headteacher: Since 2012, Patrick Moriarty MA Oxon MA (Ed) NPQH (early 50s.) Grew up in north London and attended Haberdashers' Aske's Boys' School, before reading philosophy and theology at Oxford, then training as a teacher at King's College, London. Taught (RE and English) at Latymer in Edmonton, Bishop Stopford's School, Enfield, and Haberderdashers' Aske's School for Girls. Arrived at JCoSS in 2010 as deputy head. 'The opportunity of a new school was very exciting and I liked the fact that it was a faith school.' Despite his unlikely background ('I told them I wasn't Jewish and I was contemplating studying for the priesthood'), he started nine months before the school opened, helping 'finesse' the curriculum.

Breathtakingly energetic, genial and thoughtful, he has undoubtedly delivered on the promise of balancing an outstanding curriculum and outstanding pastoral care. Ofsted, pupils and parents agree on his manifold virtues. 'Exceptional,' say the school inspectors. 'The best head,' said a sixth former. 'He's done an amazing job,' agreed a parent. He's also recently received recognition at the Jewish Schools Award for his 'outstanding and inspirational leadership'. Married to a musician, his out-of-school hours involve heavy-duty family responsibilities (two stepchildren at degree stage and two primary age children). He's also curate of a church in Barnet. Perhaps unsurprisingly, little time left over to play the piano and organ.

Entrance: Around 720 apply for year 7 places here, with about 400 putting it as their first or second choice. The school is mixed ability, but priority goes to Jewish children (proved by attendance at synagogue or involvement with Jewish education plus volunteering in the Jewish community). Varies between 180 and 210 places. Admissions process also changing, with less priority for feeder schools. 'We wanted to ensure there is room for children whatever primary school they have come from.' Order of acceptance is now: looked after children; siblings; 18 places on distance; staff children; then, by random ballot. The school does not expand the sixth form, merely fills the gaps. Minimum six 6s at GCSE for those considering A levels; five 4s for the vocational route. Jewish applicants are again given priority. Expansion planned to 210 intake per year, expected to start from year 7 intake in 2021 but still unconfirmed.

Exit: About 20 per cent leave after GCSEs (although only five per cent in 2020), mostly because they didn't make the grades for sixth form courses. All are swiftly replaced by external candidates. At 18, 90 per cent to university, about half to Russell Group universities (Nottingham, Leeds, Manchester particularly popular), with seven to Oxbridge in 2020, plus two medics.

Latest results: In 2020, 49 per cent 9-7 at GCSE; 93 per cent 9-4 in both maths and English. At A level, 68 per cent A*/A (92 per cent A*-B). In 2019 (the last year when exams took place), 50 per cent 9-7 at GCSE. At A level, 44 per cent A*/A (76 per cent A*-B).

Teaching and learning: High expectations of what would be achieved, and JCoSS's GCSE results certainly don't disappoint, putting the school in the top 10 per cent nationally. At A level, grades as good or better than many independents.

Largely academic curriculum with most students taking 11 or 12 GCSEs though 'set to reduce slightly in response to concerns about depth of learning and student well-being,' says school. Modern Hebrew compulsory in year 7 (alongside French). In year 8, students can opt out of Hebrew and consider Spanish or Latin. Twenty-eight subjects on offer at A level, including psychology, sociology and further maths. Good take up of religious studies, which achieves notably strong results, as do psychology, English and sociology. Six vocational courses, a mixture of BTecs and Cambridge Technicals in the sixth form (in health and social care, creative media, sport, IT and business). About 70 per cent of students do purely A levels, about 10 per cent purely vocational courses, others mix and match. 'Our aim is to break down the boundaries and get all our students successfully into university.' Energetic teachers, happy to go the extra mile, and teacher-pupil relations clearly strong. 'I feel my teachers are talented and charismatic,' said one student.

Six lessons a fortnight of Jewish education, five on Judaism, one on other faiths. 'We feel part of being Jewish is loving your neighbour and understanding their religion'

One of the distinguishing characteristics of JCoSS is the Jewish education. Students take six lessons a fortnight of Jewish education, five concentrating on Judaism, one on other faiths. 'The kids ask for it, and we feel part of being Jewish is loving your neighbour and understanding your neighbour's religion.' (At GCSE, the second faith studied is Islam.) Jewish education continues for all into the sixth form.

Learning support and SEN: Provision for SEN commended by Ofsted as 'outstanding'. The school, after consultation with the local authority, decided to create a specialist autism unit, the PSRP, with seven places a year devoted to those on the autism spectrum who can access the national curriculum (regardless of faith). The aim is to integrate these students as far as possible into the mainstream. Some spend all their time with the rest; others about half. 'It's highly personalised,' says the head. 'It's a brilliant model because it allows the maximum flexibility and enables all students to recognise and celebrate difference.' One designated SEN teacher per year group in the PSRP, plus two or three learning support assistants, all with specialist training. Others with special needs (dyslexia, dyspraxia, etc) – about three or four a year – are also well catered for, with three SEN teachers and around 30 learning support assistants, given one-to-one support where necessary. 'Able and ambitious' programme enriches the core offering for those who excel in any area.

The arts and extracurricular: Large art department with enthusiastic participants. Keen musicians enjoy chamber choir, jazz band, orchestra, guitar surgery. Good range of community involvement and social action: Duke of Edinburgh, Amnesty International, primary school volunteering, Israel club.

Sport: Sport still relatively in its infancy and limited grounds mean it's unlikely to be a big priority in the immediate future. 'We need a wider range of sport,' said one student. Some all-weather pitches and a spacious well-equipped gym, plus a multi-gym. Some 150 external recent matches in netball, football and basketball, with pleasing results. Badminton and table tennis a particular strength (recent Barnet champions). Rugby offering improving with enthusiastic encouragement from the sixth form. Elite sports programmes (with Saracens rugby coaching, Brentford and Southend football trials). Broad range of after-school sports clubs include sports leadership, table tennis, trampolining and modern Israeli dance.

Ethos and heritage: Traditionally, London has not had enough school places for Jewish families, and JCoSS was established to be a 'pluralist' Jewish secondary, where all who 'self-identified as Jewish' would be welcome. 'Religiously, we were doing something different,' says the head. 'Here, whether you're Orthodox, Masorti, Reform or Secular, we believe that's a valid expression of tradition.'

Pupils feel the approach works well. 'At other Jewish schools, you might get the feeling that one person's opinion is not as good as another's, but that's not true here,' said one sixth former. 'There are Jews from lots of different backgrounds, but I've never seen an example of bullying on the basis of people's beliefs,' said another. 'We might disagree about Israel's stance for example, but we would debate it.' 'Religion is not pushed,' said a parent. 'It's discussed philosophically.'

The school is inclusive and ecumenical, with a strong stress on inter-faith activities, including visits to temples and cathedrals. Though 99 per cent of pupils are Jewish, last summer, for example, a Ramadan tent was erected in the grounds, where Christians, Jews and Muslims formed a circle of faith.

A long time in the making, the school finally opened on a leafy site in east Barnet in 2010, with 150 pupils and 15 teachers. In 2012, a sixth form was introduced and it is now full to capacity.

Spacious (£48m) modern building, with wide corridors, large, light classrooms (more added in 2017) and excellent facilities. Calm and order reign throughout. Kosher food for all, with cool café for use of sixth formers, staff and visitors. Tight security on the gates.

Students generally mature and focused ('During my son's GCSE year everyone really settled down,' said a mother. 'I was amazed how motivated they all were.') The head boy and girl actively involved in bringing about change – getting everyone to donate blood, inviting in speakers from universities, etc. Also generous with praise for fellow students ('He's amazing at art', 'She did a wonderful job' are constant refrains.)

Pupils clearly enjoy the school. 'There's never been a day when my son has not been happy to go,' said one mother. 'When I asked him if he wanted to consider somewhere else for sixth form, he said, "Absolutely not".'

Pastoral care, inclusivity and discipline: The development of each student as a 'Mensch' – a person of integrity and honour – is the backbone of the school, and moral worth very much emphasised and rewarded (one prize, for example, for kindness, is voted on by students, another awarded for 20 hours' volunteering).

The development of each student as a 'Mensch' – a person of integrity and honour – is the backbone of the school, and moral worth very much emphasised and rewarded

Growing house system, with head boy and girl, plus deputies. 'Students put themselves forward, and are interviewed; it's a proper process,' says the head. Discipline is relaxed but clearly defined. ('Chilled,' said one parent, 'but not laissez faire.') 'It's generally a very inclusive and friendly place, good natured and human,' says the head, who has overseen a few fixed-term exclusions, but only one permanent exclusion.

Pupils and parents: From the highly observant to the not observant at all, with a reasonable sprinkling of mixed marriages. A good chunk live fairly locally, but pupils come from as far afield as St Albans and Essex, Harrow and Hackney. Many arrive by school coach, where firm bonds are formed. Parents are predominantly university-educated Jewish middle class, but a reasonable number of pupils are aided by the pupil premium and free school meals. All tend, however, to be focused on similar goals. 'The great majority of our students intend to go to university and get professional jobs in the future, and think and act in that way,' says the head.

Money matters: Parents are asked for a voluntary contribution to help underwrite unfunded Jewish education.

The last word: A school with a clear vision, which, in six busy years, has grown from a hopeful acorn to an oak of excellence. An inclusive place producing excellent results and happy, involved pupils.

Keble Prep School

Wades Hill, London N21 1BG

020 8360 3359 | office@kebleprep.co.uk | www.kebleprep.co.uk

Independent	Pupils: 160
Ages: 4-13	Fees: £12,540 – £15,990 pa

Head: Since March 2020, Perran Gill, acting headmaster. He is a familiar face at Keble, having been the deputy head since 2014.

Entrance: Register a couple of years before entry at 4 but pressure on places is not intense. For some parents this school is an informed choice and they want a small independent school – for others they have no choice as they live in a 'grey area' of schools in Palmers Green and couldn't get a place at a state primary school.

The school is non-selective, but before pupils start reception parents come for a meeting and their sons are observed doing jigsaws and playing games. 'The key thing is to ascertain that we will be a good fit for the child.' Probably not the school for a boy with a very specific or global needs, who is unlikely to be accepted. Some new entrants from the state sector at 11.

Exit: A small exodus at 11 to high-achieving local grammar schools and comprehensives, but school hopes to attract parents who understand the benefits of a school that runs to 13. 'We believe in 13+.' One parent did say, however, that her only criticism of Keble is that 'it needs to decide whether it's an 11+ or 13+ school, as many senior schools are changing their admissions policy.' However, she added that this was part of a 'bigger picture'.

At 13+, Mill Hill and St Albans are historically the two most popular choices, but horizons are expanding – 'we are sending boys to Highgate, Haberdashers, City, UCS, Westminster, Haileybury and St Columba's.' Wherever pupils go, the school does its utmost to ensure the best match between boy and school – 'we know the boys very well and recommend on personality.' A handful switch to the state sector – Ashmole, Finchley Catholic High and Highlands are popular choices, as are the Latymer and Dame Alice Owen.

Our view: Driving to this lone prep school in an affluent suburban area of north London, (along roads such as Broad Walk, which make Bishops Avenue look like social housing) we expected great things, so first impressions were slightly underwhelming, especially as we entered through the back for parking purposes. However, the minute we were ushered into the school that feeling began to dissipate, which was credit to the friendly staff who gave us coffee and plied us with delicious Fortnum and Mason biscuits.

A small school, which hovers at around 200 boys in all, so class size is reflectively intimate, ranging from 12-15 in two parallel forms. In the early years the school follows the national curriculum, with add-ons such as French, which starts in year 3. The pace is accelerated and curriculum expanded as boys get older – 'we adapt it to the boys, easing into common entrance after 11.' Specialist teaching in music and PE in first two years, then further specialisation in art, ICT and French; by year 5, all subjects taught by specialists and switch to a senior school system where classes are split for English, maths, history, Latin etc.

Enthusiastic teaching and boy-friendly approach. 'We try to make it very hands on,' said one teacher. 'We make models and castles.' Parents praise staff highly. 'My son is motivated, interested and enthused. It's a great credit to the teachers,' said a mother. 'The teachers are incredibly encouraging,' said another. In the past, the school has been criticised for not necessarily stretching the brightest, but has spent time, effort and money rebalancing that equation. A director of studies now has a clear brief and the brightest are given differentiated teaching in class and one-to-one support out of it. Boys are setted in English and maths from year 5, with informal setting in science, French and humanities.

The philosophy, however, is very much 'each child is an individual' and the struggling are equally well guided, with the full range of SEN support which includes a full-time dedicated SENCo and a team of three other assistants. Low percentage of SEN however, and whilst the school can deal fairly comfortably with dyslexia, dyspraxia, mild autism and Asperger's, they would advise a parent of a child with a more specific need to go through the state system as they just can't access the same level of support here. However, where possible, they will try and make reasonable adjustments. Parents say that the benefit of the small classes at Keble Prep is the individual attention their sons receive, and the safe and nurturing feel. As one parent told us: 'The teachers really know my child, and will flag up something immediately if there is an issue.'

This is a small site and facilities are relatively restricted but rebuild has brought more classroom space (although still fairly tight and a bit airless, which is something they are working on), a new science lab and an art room, allowing for relocation of the library, which had doubled as a music room. Limited space, too, for sports, although three new Astroturf courts have recently been put in, and a new playground area: 'The redevelopment of the reception playground splits the space into two areas to allow for free-flow indoor/outdoor play.'

Very much a traditional prep. We did feel a tad sorry for the younger boys in reception who looked so stiff in their neatly knotted ties on the floor playing with plastic farm animals

Games, played twice a week, are taken seriously. Rugby, football, cricket and tennis are the main menu and a school minibus transports players to local and distant pitches. Rugby has put the school back on the prep school circuit, and more recently too has tennis – they recently won the first north London independent schools' tournament they have entered. 'We feel we punch above our weight with other schools but would like to enter a few more national competitions.' Boys can also let off steam fairly regularly at nearby beautiful Grovelands Park, and the school is also looking into the option of a forest school.

Various lunch-time and after-school clubs on offer include puzzle club, movie club, cookery club and spy club as well as a common entrance drop-in club. Music has also been taken up several notches, with an assortment of orchestras, choirs and instruments on offer.

Has been going for 80 years and its aim now, as always, is to serve the local community, a community of small family businesses rather than City professionals. Many parents are first-time buyers. 'Our parents often want what they didn't have for themselves.' Many have Mediterranean roots (Turkish, Spanish, Greek, Italian, Cypriot) and a firm belief in family, and the school reflects those values with a strong family atmosphere. Active parents' association that puts on summer and Christmas fairs, welcome evenings, curry nights, quiz nights etc. They have managed to fund a school minibus, some IT equipment and contribute to some of the playground revamp.

Very much a traditional prep, it retains distinctive black and yellow blazers, formal good manners and neatly brushed hair (long hair is definitely frowned upon). We did feel a tad sorry for the younger boys in reception who looked so stiff in their neatly knotted ties on the floor playing with plastic farm animals. We felt they had the rest of their lives to be City bankers.

Pastoral care was more old school but now concentrates on producing grounded and well-rounded individuals: 'We need to equip these boys with the right skill set for life and cultivate a culture that is supportive of them in sometimes dealing with failure.' A new PSHE called Jigsaw is built around mindfulness and reflection, and there are now worry boxes outside the head's office and around the school, where pupils can either jot down their concerns anonymously or ask to talk to someone about them. A 'big brother, little brother' scheme matches older pupils with younger ones – evident and unaffected warmth stretching across the age divide.

Pupil seem happy and well rounded, and as a final year pupil said: 'I love the school and I'm going to miss it when I leave.' Parents are equally positive. 'We chose it because it's very friendly and has a great identity that boys can relate to.' 'We love the school. It's a home from home. My son looks forward to going to school every day.'

The last word: Keble is not a wealthy or notably well endowed place, but is undoubtedly a happy and safe haven, where all boys are treated with respect and respond in kind. A very secure place to start your school days.

King Alfred School

18

Manor Wood, 149 North End Road, London NW11 7HY

020 8457 5200 | admissions@kingalfred.org.uk | www.kingalfred.org.uk

Independent | Pupils: 660; sixth form: 110

Ages: 4-18 | Fees: £16,638 – £20,058 pa

Head: Since 2015, Robert Lobatto MA Oxon PGCE (50s), previously head of Barnhill Community High in Hayes. Married with two school-age children. Educated at the Haberdashers' Aske's boys' school in Hertfordshire before reading history at Oxford, Mr Lobatto is firmly rooted in north London and its culture. Prior to coming here he spent 25 years in state secondary schools, head of history at East Barnet school, head of humanities at Highbury Fields, deputy head at Lister Community School in Plaistow and head (at only 40 years old) at Barnhill Community High School in Hayes. The one thing all his previous schools have in common is that they are 'big, urban and ethnically diverse', he says. At Barnhill 85 per cent of the school were from ethnic minority backgrounds, 60 per cent on free school meals.

His quiet and unassuming appearance belies a man of steel and purpose. While head at Barnhill he spent eight years setting up a multi academy trust, the Barnhill Partnership Trust, taking on and turning round a primary school in its wake. He brings a wealth of experience to his current role, and despite the stark difference in demographic, says that KAS is much more similar to his previous school than he anticipated. He left the state sector disillusioned with a diet of data and performance tables – the strap had been rubbing for too long on the same spot.

He finds the supportive parental body, the resources, the small class sizes and, above all, the genuinely child-centred approach hugely refreshing. 'In the state sector we were making decisions for the school rather than for the children,' he observes. He enjoys being accountable to the governors (here known in Pullmanesque speak as Council rather than a governing board). His role here is less about admin, more about strategy. The strategy that he is particularly interested in developing is around learning – empowering the children to lead their own learning. While he believes in 'a rigorous academic education,' he says, 'real learning is about empowering the individual in the learning process.'

When challenged about what kind of child suits the liberal, relaxed ethos of the school, Robert muses, 'There genuinely is a place for everyone here as we are trying to bring out the best in each individual child. There is an alchemy about the place, they come out confident, well-balanced and articulate.' With the small numbers at King Alfred, you don't need 'heavy-handed behaviour management processes,' he suggests. He knows all the pupils, who he describes as 'delightful, easy to talk to and well behaved'. He still finds the time to teach history, which he enjoys and which gives him still greater insight into the pupils and the way the school operates. He relishes the strong ethos of working with the individual and says he is 'hugely experienced at dealing with complex behavioural issues'. There are certain goals to be achieved, however: moving forward the academics, particularly science, is one; working more with parents to help them support their children, as well as to provide inspiration to the school community, is another.

A thoughtful man, Robert Lobatto clearly commands a great deal of respect. From groundsmen to junior school pupils, everyone we passed was keen to catch his eye and receive a nod or smile of recognition.

Head of lower school since January 2018, Karen Thomas, previously head of Kowloon Junior School in Hong Kong, and before that vice principal and PYP coordinator at Peak School there.

Entrance: Not selective at 4 but put your child's name down at birth. Date of registration decides visit order and over 200 apply for 40 places in reception. Always some places in year 7 though not normally more than 10. Around 120 normally apply. 'We are looking for people who will get a lot out of King Alfred and give a lot to the school – those who are a good fit for our culture,' says Robert. Children don't just sit a few tests in maths and English but will spend a day at the school, will be asked to do group work, be interviewed in a group and will be assessed in the round. Do they have something about them? Are they sparky, confident, creative? At sixth form minimum of five 6s at GCSE – but school very flexible and inclusive, and will enable pupils to choose combinations that are individualised.

Exit: About 20-30 per cent leave after GCSEs, some to Camden School for Girls or other state sixth forms, others to UCS, Highgate or Francis Holland, for example. After A level, Nottingham, Leeds and Sussex are popular choices, with others choosing Exeter, King's College London, Manchester, UCL and Warwick. A few each year to do art foundation courses at eg Kingston or City and Guilds, and some to music colleges. Candidates choose to study a range of courses including business management, industrial design, biomedical science, history and English literature and film studies.

Latest results: In 2020, 74 per cent 9-7 at GCSE; 57 per cent A/A* at A level (87 per cent A*-B). In 2019 (the last year when exams took place), 48 per cent 9-7 at GCSE; 34 per cent A*/A at A level.

Teaching and learning: Focus here is not on exams and results, though there is a definite desire to see the pupils progress, excel and above all reach their potential. No tests, though the school keen to point out that the children's progress is monitored carefully. Barely any homework in lower school until year 5, although children take home reading books from reception onwards. 'When homework hits big time in year 10 the pupils have a massive shock,' observed one parent. Lots of projects and creative building of volcanoes and the Great Wall of China, for example, between the ages of 8 and 13. Pupils learn very much at their own pace and no one is told that they 'should' be at a certain point. 'This is fine if you are in it for the long term,' commented a parent, 'but if you decide to move your child you are likely to find s/he is way behind.' Another parent expressed it more positively: 'Bright and motivated children will do as well at King Alfred as anywhere else, but pupils who might have been crushed elsewhere do better. You must be prepared for the long haul and be patient as educational achievement is a longer process here than in other more pressurised environments.'

Relationships between pupils and teachers noticeably more personal than in most other London schools. This can lay the foundation for inspiring and motivational learning, and it is this individual approach that is at the heart of the ethos of the school and filters into every corner of school life, including the classroom.

However, a much better indicator that the school is doing something right is its value added score. Progress between GCSE and A level is among the top 10 per cent in the country – there is a broad spectrum of ability here yet the progress pupils make is impressive.

The forge, managed by a female blacksmith, is another central feature that builds into the creative, hands-on craftsmanship that the school is so adept at instilling

Deservedly known to be a school for the creative arts more than for science, popular A levels here include art and design, history, politics and English. At GCSE high numbers do art and design and photography, and a good number choose performing arts and music studies, including a BTec group. More do French than Spanish, very few choose to do Latin, and food tech is now an option. Most of the 9-8 crop at GCSE is in English literature and history.

Learning support and SEN: Additional support is available for students with mild specific learning difficulties – individually, in groups or in class. The progress of each student is monitored throughout their time at the school. Teachers build up a picture of pupils' learning profiles and identify those who might require specific intervention.

The arts and extracurricular: Music has always been popular. Trendy boys play in bands (there is a popular after-school band club). Old school Alfredian teachers with long hair in ponytails inspire a number of pupils to perform in orchestras and ensembles. Large music tech room, complete with Macs, drums and cymbals, percussion keyboards and djembes. Plenty of space for drama, including a large theatre as well as a 'black box' studio. Years 7-9 performed Emil and the Detectives, years 10 and above in Chicago and Anything Goes. However considering the number of parents in the arts, particularly the performing arts, one parent commented that the school punches well below its weight. Another parent observed that the school does not dance to the obvious 'wow' factor. What makes Alfredians stand out is not the polish of their performance but the evident joy and collaboration they bring to their performances, and that all are encouraged to join in. While other schools at a choir competition may look impeccably groomed with perfect pitch, Alfredians will be seen in a colourful jumble, singing and clapping with gusto, supporting and encouraging each other, wreathed in grins. They are not a shambles, however – the lower school has won the Watford Music Festival first prize two years in a row, and the upper school reached the national school finals.

Industrious and inspirational art room – three rooms at the top of the building that overflows with ceramics, as well as charcoal drawings of leaves and plants.

In the senior school, years 7-11 required to make their choice of co-curricular activities from a wide range, from pottery to golf; sixth form options include screenwriting for films, emotional intelligence and Mandarin. Strong commitment to volunteering throughout, with pupils helping out at the local special school and raising significant sums for international causes (including building a school after the tsunami in Sri Lanka). Good careers advice (which kicks off in year 7) helps with GCSE and A level options and UCAS applications pre- and post-A level. As one might expect, green is high on the agenda – one of the first schools to introduce solar panels and recycling bins.

Everyone we spoke to talked glowingly of 'the village project' – a week in year 8 when all the pupils set up a camp in a corner of the grounds, plan their meals, cook them over a camp fire that they have built, plan the layout of their camp, and build where they will sleep. Adults take a background facilitating role so that the children can take control of their lives and manage the fundamentals they need to survive.

The forge, managed by a female blacksmith, is another central feature of the curriculum that builds into the creative, hands-on craftsmanship that the school is so adept at instilling into its pupils. 'A wonderful outlet for those that are not so academic,' enthused one parent, who said how much the family enjoy building up a new iron poker selection around their fireplace. Children who have practical skills love being given a chance to shine at something so esoteric. The village project takes a mobile forge over to the camp to use during their week, an example of how King Alfred excels in integrating the curriculum and mixing up different opportunities that are offered here.

Sport: If you want fierce competitive sport and silverware displayed in shiny glass cabinets, look elsewhere. Matches are often mixed – in age, gender (and competence). A successful match is one which everyone enjoys. Children of all ages are out kicking a ball on the field at the heart of the school, some are climbing trees, others working in the forge.

Ethos and heritage: Founded by parents in Hampstead in 1898, original aim was to provide an education based on what was best for the child and encourage learning for its own sake. Part of the progressive movement, KAS sees its kindred schools as Bedales in Hampshire and St Christopher in Letchworth. Moved to its current site, a leafy patch of north London opposite Golders Hill Park, in 1921, and has recently expanded, with a school building for the infants across the road from the main site at Ivy Wood, once the home of Anna Pavlova. The emphasis here is for little ones to be outdoors, doing craft, and tuning into nature. Attractive grounds with a mixture of periods and styles (new fitness studio, music and drama block, lovely arts and crafts dining hall) grouped around a central village-like common. Star attractions include a wooded amphitheatre, an arbour (Squirrel Hall), formed from the sheltering branches of two ancient chestnuts, and the farm, complete with chickens, rabbits, ducks and bees. This latter forms a key part of the outdoor education – not just a quaint accessory. Design technology here is of the old-fashioned carpentry kind, preserving creativity, and forms part of the hands-on creative ethos. Pupils start design from 4 years old.

Individual approach is at the heart of the ethos of the school and filters into every corner of school life, including the classroom

The original ethos – liberal, progressive, egalitarian, child-centred – remains core to the school's values today. Parents and pupils agree that the needs of each child are foremost. 'They try to act holistically. They look at the individual and find out what makes them shine.' In many respects the school operates as a large extended family, without the rigid age divide found elsewhere. 'It's a really friendly school,' said one year 9. 'Older kids look out for younger ones and you'll see sixth formers play with year 7s.' Most children seem to enjoy their time here. 'They skip into school every day,' said one long-time parent. 'Even after the holidays, they can't wait to get back.'

New Fives Court lower school building includes auditorium, cutting-edge art technology room with kiln and multi-purpose room for food science, rural studies and general science. ICT suite, learning support area and lower school library upstairs. Dotted around the site are climbing frames, sandpits and a gypsy caravan – all wood and natural materials.

Smiling groundsmen (always a good sign), colourful array of children, a refreshing indication of individuality. Discreet and rather beautifully delicate wrought iron gates secure the entrance to this charming oasis, off the busy North End Road. Blink and you'd miss it. Staff here are all very informal – streaming in and out of the staff room in all manner of clothes, except for suits and ties. Pupils also scruffy, and sometimes it's hard to tell the difference between staff and sixth formers.

A small school, with a total of 650 pupils from reception through to the upper sixth and fewer than 50 children in each year group, together with small class sizes – between 16 and 17 – makes for an intimate school community. This is enhanced by the village green atmosphere. School provides a genuine opportunity to develop personal relationships with both teachers and the wider school community.

Pastoral care, inclusivity and discipline: King Alfred will always give your child a chance. The school's detractors comment on a lack of boundaries and leniency in the face of transgression. 'Show us a London school that doesn't have its fair share of drugs and alcohol felons,' counter its supporters.

Robert Lobatto is regarded by many as introducing some much needed tightening – automatic expulsion for bringing drugs into school or using them in school. Otherwise the approach is more about discussion, reasoning with the offender and educating them as to why they have crossed a line. There are policies of internal exclusion (taking children out of lessons) and external exclusion (removing them temporarily from school) but, as with everything here, time is taken to explain, educate and be as fair as possible. 'We would always give kids many chances and do a lot of work to support and educate children about social media – drawing clear lines.'

This is above all a nurturing school. More carrot than stick. No hierarchies, very few rules but bullies will be suspended. However, probably not the place for a child who needs strong structures. Four counsellors and strong system of peer mentoring. No uniform but pupils tend to be unkempt rather than outrageous.

Pupils and parents: A fair smattering of A-list celebrities, but 'which independent school in London doesn't have that' is the refrain. Plenty of parents who hated their school days seize the opportunity to give their children a chance to develop as individuals in a low-pressure environment. Lots are Old Alfredians themselves who relish being part of this supportive community once more. Pupils, mainly from the wealthier suburbs of north London (Hampstead, Golders Green, Highgate, Muswell Hill), are confident and articulate and expect to be given equal weight as adults. Difficult to say what kind of child suits as often it can be counterintuitive. Blue stockings are given the chance to be bold, free spirits aren't squashed. One thing is certain, the parents need to be involved and supportive to make it work. More than in any other school the relationship is triangular, and all corners need to support to create success.

Money matters: Though not particularly well endowed, attempts to keep fees as stable as possible while keeping facilities up to date. No scholarships, a small number (about four) of means-tested bursaries in year 7 and sixth form.

The last word: A wonderfully liberal education for the free spirits who balk at rigid structures and too much discipline, but KAS can also set free the souls of those children who have always been overly keen to conform. Not a school for parents obsessed with league table position, nor those who would prefer to delegate the education of their children completely. Success will depend on parents, child and school all rowing in the same direction.

The Latymer School

19

Haselbury Road, London N9 9TN

020 8807 4037 | office@latymer.co.uk | www.latymer.co.uk

State | Ages: 11–18 | Pupils: 1,385; sixth form: 425

Headteacher: Since 2015, Maureen Cobbett BA (modern languages) followed by a PGCE from Liverpool University. Originally from Birmingham, she started out as a French and German teacher – both subjects to GCSE and French to A level: 'Teachers are often inspired by that one teacher they had at school. For me it was a memorable French teacher.' Prior to her post at Latymer, Ms Cobbett was head at All Saints Catholic School in Nottinghamshire and in that time took it from an underachieving school to the 'most successful comprehensive in Nottinghamshire'. However after seven years in the post, she decided it was time to do something completely different and the right time to pursue her ambition of working and living in London: 'I wasn't initially aware of the post of head teacher at Latymer; it was my sister who lived in London who made me aware of the school. She told me about the conversations she had heard on the train from lovely, well-mannered children.'

Before meeting this head, we didn't quite know what to expect. Yes, Ms Cobbett is fairly businesslike by nature, very straighforward and definitely not concerned with winning us over – but during our meeting, we did witness a more affable and humorous side. Parents have clearly seen this side too. One told us: 'At this year's annual teachers' Christmas concert, she was there in the orchestra wearing a Christmas hat and playing the triangle.' And one pupil told us: 'She sometimes stops us in the corridor and tells us really bad jokes.' She is also popular with the teachers, we are told.

Since arriving at Latymer not all her changes have met with approval. Some parents were not happy by her immediate introduction of a stricter uniform policy. One parent told us: 'She definitely seems hung up on the uniform. It's fair enough if she wanted to change the jumper to a smarter one with a logo, but when she starts saying that girls have to wear tights, I don't think there needs to be that level of detail and it also gave the girls a little bit of choice.' However, a more satisfied parent said of her approach: 'I love what she's done with things like the school website. It's been updated and is much more professional now. Things just seem more organised.'

Only those 'deemed capable of achieving the highest grades at GCSE are considered' at this highly oversubscribed, highly selective school

Whether or not she has divided opinion, one has to admire the daunting task of heading up one of London's most high achieving schools – not to mention in an uncertain financial climate. Ms Cobbett says: 'It's quite a depressing position to be in for most headteachers – they are facing funding being slashed and yet they are being asked to make standards rise. I don't see how the two go together.' That said, she remains passionate about education born out of the values instilled in her when she was a child: 'I come from a low income Irish family, but my mum was very keen for us all to have a good education. All five siblings and myself went to grammar schools.' She adds: 'I love what I do. I never considered anything other than teaching and I love being around young people. It makes you feel young.'

Ms Cobbett has two grown-up daughters. 'I waited until they were older and doing their own thing before I moved, so I didn't have to uproot them too.' Any free time she allows herself is often spent doing sports or going to the cinema and theatre.

Entrance: Only those 'deemed capable of achieving the highest grades at GCSE are considered' at this highly oversubscribed, selective school. Selection is by the NVR test as well as literacy and numeracy. A parent said 'it used to be harder to get into', but around 2,000 typically apply for the 186 places, so many are still disappointed. Priority is given to looked-after children and those who live in designated postcode areas in the boroughs of Hackney, Islington, Waltham Forest, Haringey and Enfield. Offers also made to around 20 per cent of students who live in these areas and show 'exceptional musical talent and achievement' akin to grade 5. A further 20 places are awarded to those on pupil premium.

Around 50 external students join the sixth form. Prerequisites including living in designated postcode areas, getting at least six grade 7s at GCSE, including for proposed A level subjects, plus entrance tests for those applying to study maths and/or sciences.

Exit: Over 90 per cent go on to university or other forms of higher education in music and art. The school does not 'push Oxford or Cambridge though plenty go (19 places in 2020). Bath, Bristol, Nottingham and other Russell Group universities are also popular destinations. Very few – one or two – leave to go straight into employment.

Latest results: In 2020, 92 per cent 9-7 at GCSE; 65 per cent A*/A at A level (88 per cent A*-B). For 2019 (the last year when exams took place), 83 per cent 9-7 at GCSE; 52 per cent A*/A, and 78 per cent A*-B grades.

Teaching and learning: Excellent GCSE results, making it the top performing school in Enfield borough and within the top six per cent in London. Pupils must choose from French or German in Y7, with the choice of French, German, Russian or Latin in Y8; 'languages to get into Oxbridge with,' one parent jokingly told us.

Students study 10 GCSEs and the vast majority take the EBacc subjects. Geography is very popular as are the sciences. At sixth form, maths is the most popular subject and the school offers 'nothing apart from an unashamedly academic programme', so no vocational subjects. (Sociology has recently been scrapped due to funding cuts.) The majority stay on at sixth form – if they achieve at least six grade 7s at GCSE – but another 50 join from other schools.

Parents agree that the school is 'very good academically' and it certainly makes plenty of effort to reward academic achievement across all years. Year 13s are awarded prizes in specialist subjects too, such as mechanics, statistics and government & politics. Pupils who do not gain a subject prize have the opportunity to be awarded either a Latymer Lodge or school prize for gaining a high aggregate at A level. There are also open awards for special achievements in spoken English, creative work, instrumental performance, music composition and fieldwork, as well as prizes for service to the community, thus there is plenty of motivation to strive and to win here.

Learning support and SEN: Where pupils have a special learning need, they will find help through the learning support department which also arranges mentoring for younger students from sixth formers. EAL students are supported well and achieve equally well at GCSE and A level. One parent told us: 'At Latymer, SEN could be children who are super bright but actually need additional support for areas in social interaction which they may lack.'

The arts and extracurricular: It is important that academic success is supported by 'a life outside school' and students are encouraged to take part in the wide variety of activities on offer. Languages are supported by school journeys and exchanges through links with Russia, France and Germany; there have also been exchange visits with the Mwambisi school in Tanzania; other trips include geographers going to Iceland, classicists to Italy, artists to Barcelona, skiers to the French Alps, music to Austria, Belgium, Germany, the Czech Republic and scientists to Honduras and South Africa.

Music is extremely strong. Wonderful facilities – we counted approx 10 practice rooms and a couple of well-equipped studios. A quarter of the pupils learn a musical instrument at standards ranging from beginners to beyond grade 8. There are five orchestras (including reed and brass), a concert band and several choirs. They perform at school concerts and many are invited elsewhere, such as the National Festival for Music. 'The standard is amazing,' one parent told us, 'and what I really like is that the orchestras accept students of all abilities. It's not all about the top lot.'

Latymer had art specialism and so the subject has a strong presence outside the department, with astounding work on display around the school. Experts visit to do talks and run special workshops in oil painting and sculpture, and the department runs visits to the London Institute, Tate Modern and Tate Britain as well as European trips. As a result, examiners have commented on the good grasp pupils have of contemporary artists. Drama is supported by trips out plus the big theatre productions that take place at the school each year; a main school production in November (recently Anything Goes), a junior production in July, and the house drama competition every other year. Recent house drama offerings – one by each of the six houses – based on The Diary of Adrian Mole. One of the pupils directing it told us with a groan: 'We have to do everything – cast it, direct it and cram it all in during lunch times and after school… but it is fun.'

Music is extremely strong. 'The standard is amazing,' one parent told us. 'What I really like is that the orchestras accept students of all abilities. Not all about the top lot'

If Latymerians have any spare moment to breathe after all of this, they can enjoy a rich range of extracurricular activities that shape life at the school; over 60 different clubs and teams run before, during and after school, and at weekends. Lunchtime clubs are run by the students themselves ('a bit like freshers' week'), which include a debating society, an Afro-Caribbean society, LBGT society, gardening, chess and more. There is a Young Enterprise group, an economics society and clubs whose sole purpose is to raise funds for less fortunate people, particularly supportive of local charities such as the food bank in Edmonton.

Sport: More than 17 different sporting activities offered, which may come as a surprise to some, who know Latymer as a predominantly academic institution. One parent said: 'The school does have very good sporting facilities and outside grounds, and, whilst they may not do as well as other schools, the opportunities are there.' New long jump and athletics facilities, 'but could do with an all-weather pitch,' one pupil told us. The school encourages active lifestyles and rewards pupils' enthusiasm for sport with a number of awards that recognise outstanding achievement both in and outside school. These include rugby (played very competitively), hockey, football (for girls and boys), netball, cross-country, rounders, tennis and cricket. One pupil proudly told us: 'We have some of the top runners in the county.' Students in years 7 and 9 have the opportunity to spend a week at Ysgol Latymer, the school's outdoor sports centre in Snowdonia, for activities such as hill walking, orienteering, climbing, abseiling and canoeing.

Ethos and heritage: Tradition creates the atmosphere at Latymer. It was established in nearby Church Street in 1624 at the direction of Edward Latymer, a City merchant, who bequeathed certain property to trustees on condition that they were to clothe and educate 'eight poore boies of Edmonton'. His generosity, and the 'generosity of the many others since', are remembered each year on the school's Foundation Day. Pupils are proud of this tradition and seem enthusiastic about the events that keep it alive. The school's motto – Qui Patitur Vincit (Who Endures Wins) – aptly sums up its spirit, and is the title of the annual talk. The school moved to its present location in 1910.

Once we found the school all was pretty quiet in the snug waiting area, except for an ill student who was dealt with sympathetically and sent to the medical room. This episode added a more human side to a school whose academic reputation has become somewhat legendary. It is the first-choice school for many north London parents with an extremely clever child.

Very large, very well equipped library: 'I don't think there is anything I could need from a library that isn't here,' said a pupil

Far from the dull, intellectual conformists we expected to meet, the students who showed us around were extremely well rounded individuals – one of whom was quite possibly the biggest character we've met at any school we've visited. She was extremely entertaining, exceedingly bright and full of praise for Latymer and her six years there. The other student, also very pleasant, had just been offered a conditional place at Cambridge. They both felt very 'lucky' to have spent their secondary school years here: 'Yes, there is pressure, but nothing we can't deal with and there is a lot of support offered.'

Built on three acres of land and flanked by 12 acres of playing fields, which separate the school from the main A10 road, Latymer looks deceptively small from the front; one parent felt that planting a few more trees would help the aesthetics. Walking into the school is like walking back in time. It doesn't seem as if much would have changed since 1910, which arguably adds to its charm. We have become accustomed to sterile foyers in many other schools: the one at Latymer is a modest and cosy affair with oak panelled doors and simple but exquisite charcoal drawings adorning the walls, all by students. The lady on reception remarked: 'It's not fair is it? Not only are these kids ridiculously bright, but look how they draw!' We had to agree.

There are a number of outbuildings around the main one, added at various times over the school's life and capturing its spirit of progress: the Great Hall (1928), which seats over 1,000; the gymnasia and technical labs (1966); a performing arts centre (2000) and a sports/dining hall complex (2006). In 2010 the high-tech multi-purpose Seward Studio (performance space, auditorium, media studio, art gallery and drama theatre) was opened. The school also has a number of rooms dedicated to specialist teaching: 12 science laboratories, six fully-equipped technology rooms, and specialist ICT rooms with wireless networks. Also a very large, very well equipped library: 'I don't think there is anything I could need from a library that isn't here,' a student told us. Sixth formers now have a new modern common room equipped with a small café selling sandwiches and paninis etc (which is just as well, as the local eateries are pretty limited).

Alumnae include Dame Eileen Atkins, actor, Simone Butler, bass player with Primal Scream, and Syed Kamall, currently Conservative MEP.

Pastoral care, inclusivity and discipline: The 186 pupils in each year are organised into six form groups, and each form group belongs to one of the six house groups. They remain in these groups throughout their school lives, meeting daily for registration and form periods, including, in the lower years, PSHE lessons delivered by the form tutor. Each year group also has a head of learning (first port of contact for parents concerned about progress) who, along with the deputy head of learning, also acts as mentor. House culture is strong. Each has a senior pupil to lead, democratically elected. Senior pupils organise activities which are used to inject a sense of comradeship and teamwork across all year groups, and to make new year 7s feel fully inducted into life at Latymer. They do this via sports tournaments and various competitions such as cake-making, drama and music.

Pupils are expected to abide by the school rules and the home-school agreement they signed with their parents on joining the school, but the school views 'self discipline resulting from wanting to learn' as a more important deterrent to poor behaviour. One parent did say that students who go to Latymer are already self-motivated: 'I doubt there are many behavioural issues, but that said, clearly students are under immense pressure. However there is quite a lot of support offered to them and the school never gives up on its pupils.' Support comes by way of two counsellors who regularly visit the school, and pupils can refer themselves; a head of year and an assistant head of year who would be the first port of call for a troubled student; and a mentoring system, where students from years 12 and 13 are trained to mentor the younger students. The school has also recently introduced into the curriculum one lesson a week dedicated to 'pastoral time' – issues ranging from drugs to bullying etc.

One parent said that 'while the academic side is challenging, it is not to the exclusion of everything else.' Another said she has 'always felt comfortable emailing teachers direct if I have a concern or question.'

Pupils and parents: Anyone and everyone who is 'very clever', though the school wisely lists acceptable postcodes in its admission criteria (and suggests that no-one should apply from further than an hour's journey). Roughly 65 per cent of the school's cohort are from ethnic minorities.

Money matters: Funding cuts affect Latymer as all other state schools. Parents have been asked to make voluntary yearly contributions. The school says: 'The response from parents has been very positive and they have been very generous. They don't want the school to suffer.' The school has also been appealing to the LOSA (Latymer Old Students Association) for donations.

The last word: A peek back in time shows that some well-known former pupils like Baroness Claire Tyler (Chair of CAFCASS and president of the National Children's Bureau), footballer Johnny Haynes and Sir Bruce Forsyth CBE all did well here. Pupils clearly still do. This is a zealously traditional school with pupils who show a healthy balance between hard work and play. Ofsted has a similar attitude and in its last report described the school as outstanding.

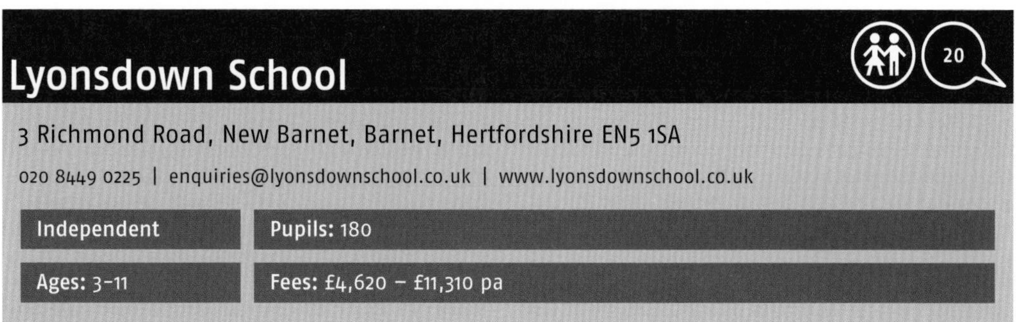

Lyonsdown School

20

3 Richmond Road, New Barnet, Barnet, Hertfordshire EN5 1SA

020 8449 0225 | enquiries@lyonsdownschool.co.uk | www.lyonsdownschool.co.uk

Independent | Pupils: 180

Ages: 3-11 | Fees: £4,620 – £11,310 pa

Head: Since July 2020, Helen Stanton-Tonner. Previously head of Holland House School in Edgware. Her first headship was at Francis House Prep and she has also been head of pre-prep and nurseries at Swanbourne House School. Was educated in Herts and did a degree in history and literature at the University of Wales. Started her teaching career within the state sector, developing a specialism for teaching and training computing in primary schools. Rose through the ranks to become coordinator for key stage 2 in a large London primary school before taking on an advisory role to support schools with their computing and technology across three London boroughs.

Entrance: Main intakes at 3+ to nursery and 4+ to reception. Non-selective; pupils and parents all interviewed by head and for entry into year 1 and up there are assessments in maths and English. A phased transition began in 2020 to all girls' education – to be complete by 2022.

Exit: Pupils leave in equal measures to the many excellent state and independent schools in close proximity. Popular state options are Henrietta Barnett, Palmers Green High School, Dame Alice Owen, Latymer, Ark Academy, St Michael's Catholic Grammar, the Jewish Community Secondary and QEG, whilst in the independent sector it's North London Collegiate, Haberdashers' Aske's, Belmont, Queenswood, St Margaret's Bushey, St Helen's, St Albans, Mount House, STAHS and Channing. Parents say girls are well prepared for their chosen route, with the school drilling them in past papers from early in year 5 onwards. Head has brought the all-important future schools conversation forward and introduced 'far more robust' interview practice to ensure girls are well prepared. Two scholarships in 2020.

Our view: There are happy schools and there are schools that make you grin from ear to ear – Lyonsdown falls firmly into the latter camp. Nestled among the leafy residential streets of New Barnet, somewhere (metaphorically and physically) between London and 'the country', the whole school fits snugly into one attractive Victorian villa, with one or two (attached) more modern additions. Not blessed with the acreage one might hope for when swapping a London postcode for EN5, but the site functions perfectly well and girls move around so smoothly that space seems magically abundant. Those we spoke to told us: 'our school isn't the biggest, but we love its cosiness'. Well, so did we. The charming nursery boasts the most inspiring outdoor space on the site (there's not a great deal of competition to be fair); large by any standards and abundantly equipped with everything imaginable to keep little ones skipping into school every day – sand, water and dinosaurs are just for starters; there's an outdoor reading den and a wonderful pirate ship where, our year 6 guide told us, she 'had made loads of memories' during her time there. In the lower school classrooms we stumbled across the reception class in the Buddha position earnestly practising their yogic breathing 'to reinstate calm after music and movement'. Once they snapped back into action they couldn't wait to tell us all about what they get up to day in and day out; between trips to care homes and visits from authors, parent cardiologists and medal-bearing grandfathers, we wondered how they found the time to practise their letters and numbers but the quality of the work that festooned the walls and adorned the charming Victorian fireplaces confirmed that they were definitely fitting it all in. Newest facilities include new library, dining hall and science lab.

We stumbled across the reception class in the Buddha position earnestly practising their yogic breathing 'to reinstate calm after music and movement'

National curriculum is a 'starting point' in most academic subjects, but 'with frills', says school. There's an added focus on problem solving and creativity, particularly in maths, where staff take children off-curriculum for problem solving sessions every week and are covering the KS3 curriculum by the end of year 5. Most subjects are team taught to enable all abilities and aptitudes to receive the necessary attention and there's no setting, 'partly to preserve pupils' self-esteem,' says school. Specialist teaching for science right from reception and by year 2 pupils are in the newly refurbished lab twice a week, following an 'investigation-led' syllabus that cleverly collaborates with maths when it comes to eg measuring and weighing. By year 6 it's all systems go with pupils testing for acids and carrying out electrical projects with circuits, buzzers and lights. Teachers, most of whom are long standing members of the staff room, told us they are frequently 'blown away' by the pupils who are 'so into learning'. 'Some take the country route, and some take the M25,' one stalwart told us, 'but we're passionate about happy children and they all get there in the end.' The part-time SENCo is supported by two teaching assistants to work with the smallish number of pupils with additional learning needs (mainly mild dyslexia or dyscalculia plus some mild ASD). Speech therapy is handled in house and school can support those with EAL needs.

Music on curriculum to year 6 and the newly appointed secondary-trained head of music has ambitious plans to breathe new musical life into the school, with the aim of 'everyone having a go'. With the snug music room home to piano, glockenspiel and a set of bongos, we wondered how on earth the choir could possibly squeeze in too. But squeeze and sing they do and a spring concert has been added to the performance calendar to supplement the gap between the carol service and school productions (recently Shakespeare Rocks) towards the end of the academic year. Parents love the music assemblies and music café performances, where performers of all abilities are invited to showcase their talents. Piano, violin, flute and voice are the limit of peripatetic lessons; there are no groups or ensembles at the time of writing other than two choirs, but they are high on the wish list, as is MTech. Art and DT are taught as one and thrive under the watch of another secondary-trained head of department. As with music, the art facility is bijoux but functional and the output interesting and of a high standard. School recently voted a finalist in the 'Excellence and Innovation in Fine Arts' awards (the only prep school to be placed); 'it's all about attitude,' said the HoD. Under the creative banner these lucky girls cover not just fine, but also digital, arts including animations ('there's loads of coding,' we were informed), textiles and cooking (no boring apple crumbles, though, it's all sushi and hearty soups). A major focus on STEAM builds on this – there's a working group of staff to drive this focus and girls code in Python and

There are happy schools and there are schools that make you grin from ear to ear – Lyonsdown falls firmly into the latter camp

enjoy robotics club. Visiting experts have recently included female engineers and theatrical make-up artists, and girls have been able to take part in workshops to hone their sculpture skills. No wonder there are frequent successes with art scholarships to eg St Margaret's and Mount House.

Not much outdoor space for sport on site so girls commute either to Woodhouse College or Barnet Athletics Club for major sports (netball, hockey, football and athletics). Despite the lack of obvious facilities, parents said the provision has 'really improved' and that the head of sport 'gets girls to believe in themselves' and 'really goes the extra mile'. Girls assured us that they get their fair share of silverware come tournament time and it was smiles all round when we asked whether team selection was fair; as with all things Lyonsdown, pupils we spoke to glowed with pride when telling us about their friends who had started out in the D team and now played for the As. The large, well-equipped sports hall plays host to PE lessons as well as dodgeball on wet days. Although nothing particularly unusual, there's something for everyone in the extracurricular programme, and the cherry on top for us on the day of our visit was watching pupils perform in their lunchtime maypole dancing club; incongruous in this multicultural urban setting but the contagious positive energy radiating from such a simple tradition was palpable. No wonder everyone we saw wore such huge smiles.

Vast majority of families are dual income professionals, comprising many ethnicities representative of the locality. Wraparound care is already a major draw for the hard-working parent cohort and set to improve with the introduction of a new homework club 'to reduce the pressure at home'.

The last word: This little school, succinctly summed up by one happy parent as 'nurturing within a structured learning environment', is one to watch. Look past the limitations of the urban site to the staff, who routinely inspire, motivate and nurture, with that ever-present Lyonsdown smile.

Mill Hill County High School

21

Worcester Crescent, London NW7 4LL

0844 477 2424 | admin@mhchs.org.uk | www.mhchs.org.uk

State | Ages: 11–19 | Pupils: 1,740; sixth form: 452

Headteacher: Since September 2019, Andy Stainton, who had been working as an independent education and school improvement consultant. Most recently, he headed Kingsbury High for nine months in 2017-18. Degree in drama and spoken language from the Central School of Speech and Drama, plus an MBA in educational management from Leicester. Senior leadership experience includes assistant head at Hertswood School, deputy head at Edmonton County, headteacher at Cheshunt and associate principal at Oasis Academy Shirley Park.

Entrance: Mill Hill has entrance criteria guaranteed to drive north London parents into a neurotic frenzy, with 243 places at 11 sliced up into small-print subsections. Lucky locals can benefit from one of the 90 guaranteed 'geography' places. But distance from the gates is frighteningly close (rather less than a mile). Siblings, too, are ensured a desk. After that children of members of the teaching staff (who have been working at the school for a minimum of two years). If there are 60 remaining places they are then awarded on aptitude and are split into: 24 for technology, 24 for music and 12 for dance. Technology is tested in two stages – a reasoning test in the summer term of year 5 whittles down about 1,500 to 240, the second round (in abstract reasoning and maths) held in September cherry-picks the rest. Music equally competitive, with up to 400 auditioning, in two sections: listening and performance. 'You can, however, play a snappy piece on the classroom xylophone and come out higher than a carefully coached grade 4 violinist.' Dance candidates are selected by audition.

The large (and heavily oversubscribed) sixth form admits a further 40 to 60 pupils out of 600 applicants, with minimum entry requirements of six grade 6s at GCSE, including English and maths. Those wishing to study science and maths need 7+s in their chosen subjects though, and most come garlanded with a string of 9-7s.

Exit: No-one is ever asked to leave (except for disciplinary matters), but a fair few (30 per cent in 2019) move on after GCSE to local sixth form colleges, independent and grammar schools. Around half to Russell Group (one of highest representations of any comprehensive in the UK) with four to Oxbridge and seven medics in 2019. Quite a number to drama and art-related degrees. Often a few to the US, though none in 2019.

Latest results: In 2019, 46 per cent 9-7 at GCSE: 73 per cent 9-5 in both maths and English. At A level, 27 per cent A*/A (54 per cent A*-B).

Teaching and learning: One of the country's highest performing comprehensives. This is a school which believes in an academic focus. Apart from a handful of vocational qualifications in ICT and media, the curriculum is traditional, with a good range of modern languages (Spanish, French, German, Latin) and a quarter of pupils taking all three sciences at GCSE. In the sixth form – the largest in the borough – the 33 subjects on offer include sociology, psychology, economics and dance. Maths and science, however, are the most popular options (with 10 groups for maths).

Teaching strong throughout (with regular awards for science, geography and maths) and most subjects provide plenty of enrichment. In English, for example, there are Shakespeare and poetry workshops; in DT, direct links with industry. An undoubted strength of the school is the focused attention it offers for all. 'Every child is taught to their own individual abilities,' commented one parent. For those at the top of the spectrum, there are two members of staff to encourage A level students to aim for A*s and Russell Group universities, while those who struggle to make the 9-4 benchmark at GCSE are offered a one-year course in which to resit. At this juncture, too, the school participates in a Barnet-wide scheme which sandwiches vocational college training with English, maths and employment skills.

Learning support and SEN: Largest number of SEN pupils in Barnet with a department reflective of their very varied needs (including provision for blind children). A raft of teaching assistants provides in-class aid and specialist staff oversee classes and support students beyond. 'It's quite an operation,' says school.

The arts and extracurricular: The school prides itself on its extracurricular offering, but there's little doubt that music is the jewel in the crown. 'There are few local schools that can hold a candle to us.' Standards throughout are exceptionally high. Recently, for the fourth year in a row, the orchestra performed a joint concert with the Royal Philharmonic ('you have to be quite good for the RPO to come and play with you'). Meanwhile the school band featured alongside that of the Royal Air Force at the Watford Colosseum. Regular lunchtime concerts, major concerts twice a term, large-scale musical in the Easter term, plus an annual European tour for concert and jazz bands. A full range of other sounds, including gospel, African drum and steel drum. Boys participate as enthusiastically as girls and one talented former pupil performs regularly at Ronnie Scott's.

The school prides itself on its extracurricular offering, but little doubt that music is the jewel in the crown. 'There are few local schools that can hold a candle to us'

Art thriving, with a weekly art club and life drawing workshop run by the Royal Academy for A level pupils. Numerous guest speakers and in-demand trips (languages to Barcelona and Normandy, politics to the US, annual ski trip) to inspire and raise aspirations. Good range of clubs run early morning and after school (which can be difficult for those who live at a distance), plus DofE, World Challenge and CCF (shared with nearby independent Mill Hill School).

Sport: In sport, the school has become a 'force to be reckoned with', particularly in boys' football and girls' netball. Basketball and rugby also on offer and table tennis played enthusiastically by all. Excellent facilities for sport include a range of pitches, three playgrounds, gym, sports hall and in summer, six-lane track and three tennis courts.

Ethos and heritage: Originally opened in 1931 as Orange Hill Boys' Grammar School, which then combined with matching girls' grammar in the 1970s. Merged again with Moat Mount School in 1984 to create Mill Hill County High School. The school, fringed by a good expanse of playing fields and forest, now sits on a hilly site with panoramic London views. There, however, the picturesque ends, with well-used buildings crammed together in an intricate hotchpotch to accommodate more students than ever. 'It is overcrowded,' said one parent. 'They're the victims of their own success.' Older parts of the fabric include some fairly basic portakabins (which house dance and drama), but recent additions have provided modern labs, a sixth form centre, computer suites, seven new classrooms and an air-conditioned assembly hall.

The lack of elbow room doesn't seem to detract from the upbeat mood, with friendly and positive staff (on the day the Guide visited a member of the office team was ringing up a local primary school to ensure a forgotten jumper was returned to its owner) and parents praise the general sense of well-being. 'The school is very good at communicating,' said one. 'They keep us informed and I have the email addresses of all my child's teachers.' Another was grateful for the empathy shown at a difficult time. 'They were understanding and supportive when we had family problems.'

Not the easiest school to get to. No tube nearby, which contributes to the mood of semi-rural calm but can be difficult for those wanting to arrive early or stay late for clubs or games. Mill Hill became an academy in 2011, but still works closely with Barnet Council, particularly in its responsibilities for Oak Hill, a successful facility for 32 emotionally and behaviourally disturbed children, four and a half miles away.

Pastoral care, inclusivity and discipline: One of the first things parents tend to mention is the uniform policy. 'They're very strict on uniform,' said one. 'Everyone looks very smart.' The school sees uniform as a means of setting the expectation bar. 'We're very clear about what we say and insist that what we say is done. We aren't repressive, but you'd be unlikely to see anyone with their shirt tails not tucked in or their ties not tied.'

The insistent focus on behaviour, attitude and good manners undoubtedly pays off. 'Most people who come across our students have positive things to say.'

Pupils and parents: About half the school's intake comes from the leafy and prosperous suburb of Mill Hill, with its high concentration of professionals and business families, but the intake is certainly not uniform. 'There are quite a lot of deprived children and the ethnic mix is huge.' It includes significant numbers of families who originate from the Indian sub-continent, Asia and Africa. Only a few, however, 'don't speak excellent English'.

Money matters: The transformation to academy status has released additional funds and these are now being used for building projects. Otherwise not rich, but not poor either.

The last word: A cheerful, well-run school producing highly motivated, high achieving students. Exceptional music.

Mill Hill School

22

The Ridgeway, Mill Hill Village, London NW7 1QS

020 8959 1176 | registrations@millhill.org.uk | www.millhill.org.uk

Independent

Pupils: 785; sixth form: 259; Boarders: 63 full, 39 weekly

Ages: 13–18

Fees: Day £21,987 pa; Boarding £29,664 – £35,067 pa

Linked schools: Belmont Mill Hill Preparatory School, 615; Grimsdell Mill Hill Pre-Preparatory School, 632

Head: Since December 2018, Jane Sanchez BA PGCE. Raised in the Midlands, she studied geography and qualified as a teacher (in geography and PE) at Sheffield University. After a stint at a community college, she taught in Argentina for four years, then, for nearly a decade, headed the PE and careers departments (while teaching geography) at top-flight girls' grammar school Henrietta Barnett. This was followed by a time as director of sport at specialist sports college Whitefield School, as school facing 'extra challenging circumstances'. 'There aren't many areas I haven't had to deal with,' she says, 'and that helps me understand what's needed is balance.'

Since her arrival at Mill Hill in 2003 as pastoral deputy head, her experience has been extended in a wide range of roles, but always with a strong emphasis on the wellbeing of pupils. Considered very down-to-earth, visible and approachable, she clearly also has a good sense of fun, starring in an April Fool's prank as a concert pianist. 'I like her a lot,' says one parent. 'She's very sensible.' Two adult children, both of whom attended the school.

Entrance: At 13+, 176 enter – including 130 moving up from the prep school, Belmont, 70 of whom join in year 7. Common Entrance no longer required for those transferring, but the 140 or so who apply for 30-40 available year 9 slots are pre-tested in year 6 (by computerised tests and interview). Most stay on for sixth form, when entrance for existing students in line with external candidates, but evaluated on a case-by-case basis. Incomers – after positive feedback from their current school – are invited for interview and expected to achieve at least two grade 7s and three grade 6s with specified grades in their intended A level subjects.

Exit: Recent destinations include Birmingham, Nottingham, Sussex, Warwick, Edinburgh, UCL and Imperial Subject choice unusually wide-ranging, from traditional professions like law and journalism to aeronautics and fashion marketing.

Latest results: In 2020, 60 per cent 9/7 at GCSE; 36 per cent A*/A at A level (77 per cent A*/B). In 2019 (the last year when exams took place), 57 per cent 9-7 at GCSE; 35 per cent A*/A at A level.

Teaching and learning: Very solid exam results throughout. No weak spots. Since her appointment, the head has rethought the timetable, reducing lessons from 50 to 40 minutes to aid concentration and allow an extra period in the day. 'It gives more time for each subject,' says the head, 'and has allowed us to make RS, very popular here, a stand-alone subject.'

'The music department is like an extension of my family,' said one pupil. 'They've supported and encouraged me in everything I've done'

At GCSE, English (lang and lit), maths and science (just under half take all three) is the compulsory core, with French, German and Spanish the language selection. After that, as well at the regular range of humanities, students can opt for classical civilisaton, computer science, PE, music, DT and ICT. At A Level, popular choices include: business, economics, geography and psychology. The EPQ is available but not widely taken as the most academically able are steered to a subject-specific Oxbridge preparation programme.

Teaching overall considered challenging and stimulating, and warm and supportive relationships between staff and pupils encourage the shy or reticent to find their voice. 'Extension' supplied by challenging in-class work, regular lectures, debates, workshops and participation in the Sir James Murray Society (where a recent student-led debate analysed the statement 'We should not be at the mercy of our emotions'). The particularly able or interested are given mentoring and regular challenges. 'There are many bright, motivated pupils and I've seen that they stretch them in the right way,' said one mother. Some parents, however, (and the last school inspectors) consider not every lesson is as exciting as it might be and marking could occasionally be more focused to maximise progress.

Learning support and SEN: SEN is a strength, with a full team including head of learning support, two part-time teachers and four assistants, who occupy four well-resourced rooms and oversee individual and small-group support as well as liaising closely with teachers to ensure they receive appropriate intervention in lessons. English language instruction for international students is supportive and positive, and those we spoke to, who'd often started out with very basic skills, had acquired a strong command of the language.

The arts and extracurricular: Music, art and drama are vibrant. Energetic participation in music at individual and group level. Singing notably strong ('Mill Hill,' says a recent magazine entry correctly, 'is a school that sings'), and there are a multitude of opportunities to give voice, from the 'Big Sing' building community spirit with an inspiring new hymn book, to the Farrow singing competition and the annual school musical. School orchestra performs significant works, such as Vivaldi's Gloria, and future maestri and maestre encouraged with annual composition prize. Instrumentalists participate in instrumental competitions, chamber groups, masterclasses, jazz soirée and twice-weekly informal coffee concerts, while school clubs extend performance opportunities with jazz band, percussion, shout band, music tech, wind band and ukulele. Music scholars – who've gone on to glory in the National Youth Orchestra, National Choir and National German Music competition – get specialist attention, with masterclasses taken at the Junior Guildhall. 'The music department is like an extension of my family,' said one. 'They've supported and encouraged me in everything I've done.'

Outstanding extracurricular offering, but sport is the jewel in the crown. As one Oxford-bound sixth former put it, 'Sport here is huge'

Drama lively, with a carousel of theatre trips, including to productions featuring Old Millhillians. Art and DT have spacious, well-equipped space, and art extends well beyond the studio with year 9's self-portrait ceramic heads – à la Antony Gormley – on show in the school chapel to become a focus for services and sixth formers' work vaunted in dedicated private view.

Creative thinking encouraged for all in the 'Big Idea', an inter-house competition to improve school life assessed by Dragon's Den-type finale. More than 150 clubs and activities cater to virtually every interest, from feminism and Model United Nations to horticulture, Hispanic theatre and touch typing. CCF particularly strong with about 150 smartly clad cadets filling the campus after lessons, and annual general inspection, chapel service, and holiday camps. Endless relay of work-related and pleasure trips – business studies to China, physics to CERN, DT to Jaguar Land Rover, ski trip to USA. Annual summer-term activities week offers a further multitude of adventures to expand the mind. 'There's so much to do here, it sometimes feels like it's hard to fit it all in,' said one year 10.

Sport: Mill Hill has a well-deserved reputation for developing the whole pupil through its outstanding extracurricular offering, but sport is the jewel in the crown. As one Oxford-bound sixth former accurately put it, 'Sport here is huge'.

The department has recently been boosted by the catch-your-breath energy of director of sport and the introduction of 11 impressive new coaches (including two professional women rugby players from Saracens Women). National aspirations abound. Until a few years ago, the school had a Saturday timetable combining lessons and sports fixtures, but the academic side is now confined to GCSE and A level workshops and weekends (including Sundays) have been freed for fixtures. Virtually all, participate in competition, with 95 per cent of year 9s involved in a school team. Main boys' sports are rugby (with national level players), hockey, football and cricket. Girls' sport as strong as the boys', and girls play hockey, netball, rounders and cricket (with old girl Sophia Dunkley recently selected for the England squad), but not football. Girls, like the boys, also excel at fives, with U14 and U15 players ranking in the top 10 in the country. Girls' aspirations and achievements recognised in girls' sports dinner, and (perhaps!) encouraged by mums' netball competition.

Talented sportsmen and women – identified through sports scholarships at 13 and 16 – are carefully nurtured (with specialist instruction in nutrition, strength and conditioning, video analysis, golf and tennis academies), and pupils participate at high competitive level in individual sports from riding (at nearby stable), shooting, golf, tennis, bouldering (GB junior team member) and sailing. Less common team sports like basketball and volleyball (in which the school recently fielded a team in the England volleyball U18 national championships) offer a broad scope for enthusiasm. Excellent facilities for everything with a multitude of pitches (including Astroturf), courts, golf centre and pool, and impressive sports trips (rugby to Japan, for example) provide exceptional opportunities, particularly for what is predominantly a day school.

Boarding: Mill Hill started life as a boarding school, but as local boarding teetered on extinction, a sustained campaign abroad led to a powerful resurgence. Now boarding houses are full again with international as well as weekly boarders. Five boarding houses (girls-only, boys-only and mixed), a short walk from the main buildings, are comfortable and up to date, furnished with triple, double and single bedrooms (depending on seniority). Meals are taken in the school dining room, but each house has a kitchen for snacks. International boarders appreciate the school's proximity to central London – 'We love going shopping on the weekends,' said one – and its cosmopolitan atmosphere. 'Before I came here, I went to a boarding school in the country where I was the only non-English pupil; I felt very uncomfortable,' commented one. 'I am much happier here.'

Ethos and heritage: Mill Hill started life as a boarding school Founded in 1807 by non-conformist reformers, the Mill Hill School Foundation now encompasses a family of schools – pre-prep (Grimsdell), prep school (Belmont), and international boarding (The Mount, Mill Hill International) – which provide a smooth transition to the senior school. Together the schools occupy 150 acres of green belt and, though only half an hour from central London, offer a semi-rural refuge of green and pleasant space and fresh country air. Now overseen by a single CEO, the foundation schools share a united mission – to produce 'a strong sense of community in which the academic and co-curricular provide a challenging and stimulating environment in which to learn the skills

King Alfred School

which play a key part in future success and happiness'. 'The modern working world is not just about exams,' says the head. 'Employers today are looking for the ability to lead, to tackle challenges, to live with integrity, honesty and fairness.'

An impressive catalogue of satellite buildings, ranging from the Basil Champneys-designed chapel with its soaring coffered ceiling to the delightful arts and crafts library

If a physical environment can contribute to these objectives, then pupils here are particularly blessed. The original school house of 1825 – by London Royal Exchange architect Sir William Tite – provides an elegant neo-classical centre, where pupils meet for meals in the tall-windowed dining hall. This is complemented by an impressive catalogue of satellite buildings, ranging from the Basil Champneys-designed chapel with its soaring coffered ceiling to the delightful arts and crafts library and thoroughly modernist humanities and modern languages building. The gardens, too, are undoubtedly 'worth a detour', containing specimens originally planted by renowned 18th-century botanist Peter Collinson, including Britain's first hydrangea.

Mill Hill originated as an all-boys boarding school, introducing the first girls into the sixth form in the 1970s; today, it's primarily a co-educational day school (with full and weekly boarding also available), but the girl-boy balance remains weighted two-thirds in favour of boys. 'You notice it, but it's never an issue,' says one girl. Some subjects (like science and history) still boy-dominated, but languages, maths and English fairly evenly split. 'It's realistic, like in the real world,' said a pupil. Both sexes feel the mix works. 'There's a really good relationship between the boys and the girls,' said one boy. 'It's a lot more relaxed, less intense in the classroom,' said a girl – 'competitive, but in a healthy way.'

Numbers continue to grow and in 2014 Mill Hill launched The Mount, Mill Hill International, its own self-contained international school, where students from nearly 30 countries (including the UK) come to sit GCSEs (in one year or two) or undertake an intensive English programme, in many instances proceeding to the main school for sixth form. Taught in their own attractive building (a former girls' school) less than half a mile away, pupils here use many of the main school facilities and boarders share boarding houses.

Still a non-conformist Christian foundation with timetabled weekly chapel, today the school welcomes all faiths and none. 'Giving back', however, remains very much part of the ethos and pupils are involved in regular fundraising activities and community action, much of it delivered through the school-wide charity committee. Strong links, too, with the London Academy of Excellence, a state sixth-form college in Tottenham, and neighbouring girls' comprehensive Copthall School, who share joint enrichment activities, and with overseas partnership schools in Tamil Nadu and Zambia.

Pupils generally happy and upbeat. 'It's a very happy place,' commented more than one parent – and few complaints even on traditional peeves. 'You're supposed to hate the food, but the food is really good here,' said one year 11, after being pressed on any dislikes.

Pastoral care, inclusivity and discipline: Eighty-five per cent of pupils arrive daily and are looked after through a day-house system, with eight mixed houses of 80-90, each with a games room, quiet study room, lockers and housemaster or mistress's office. House tutors take responsibility for the pastoral care of about 15 pupils. Wellbeing very high on the agenda, and a recently opened wellbeing wing is now its hub, home to two school counsellors, the director of PSHE, and head of pupil development, as well as the wellbeing room, a comfortably furnished, plant-filled space with soothing views of the rolling hills beyond. 'Mill Hill Minds', the student-led society formed to raise awareness of mental health, campaigned for the centre to be moved from a distant outpost. 'It used to be quite isolated, now there's a safe space where you can come at lunch, before school and after school.' Pupils very much involved in its operation, interviewing, for example, the new school counsellor. Mental health also promoted through wellbeing week and cross-school endeavours such as the Mill Hill Minds mural painted by pupils throughout the school.

Pupils generally happy and upbeat. 'You're supposed to hate the food, but the food is really good here,' said one year 11, after being pressed on any dislikes

Fairly traditional approach in other matters, so head boy and girl, heads of houses, smart uniform (business black for sixth formers, navy blue and tartan for younger years), and formal manners. ('Sorry sir,' was immediately forthcoming as we squeezed past a sixth former on a staircase.) Upper sixth given the freedom to leave at 12.30, timetable permitting, and, for those with a licence, parking is permitted.

Pupils and parents: An extensive bus route fetches and carries day pupils from affluent homes in a large swathe of north London. Eighty per cent come from no further than Hampstead, with outliers arriving from St John's Wood, Potter's Bar and Northwood. Quite a few have a long-time family link with the school, and quite a few do the full stretch from nursery to 18. Pupils are confident, articulate and poised, very much a credit to the school's holistic approach.

Money matters: Scholarships and exhibitions (academic, sports, music, drama, art and design technology), available at 13 and 16, currently limited to 10 per cent fee reduction (though this is under review), but bursaries (for new entrants and those experiencing hardship) can make this up to 100 per cent. Some extra funding, too, for non-compulsory trips, courtesy of the generous Old Millhillians Association.

The last word: A vibrant, buzzing school, with a solid academic underpinning and an outstanding extracurricular programme producing confident, articulate, mature young people, who start adult life solidly grounded, positive and well informed. 'A very happy place to be,' is the consensus of parents and pupils.

Muswell Hill Primary School

23

Top of Muswell Hill, London N10 3ST

020 8444 8488 | office@muswell-hill.haringey.sch.uk | www.muswellhillprimary.co.uk

State | Ages: 4-11 | Pupils: 420 -same

Head: Since September 2018, Mandi Howells, previously SEN support consultant for Camden Learning and deputy head of Carlton Primary School, where she had taught since 1996

Entrance: One of the most heavily oversubscribed primaries in the borough (approaching 600 applicants for 60 places). Having a sibling already at the school or living nearby are the two quickest ways through the gates, but 'near' means very, less than a quarter of mile if you want a realistic chance.

Exit: The school sits midway between two of north London's best comprehensives, so why consider anywhere else is the general parental view. Leavers to both state sector (APS, Fortismere, Highgate Wood) and private (Latymer, JQOS, Channing, Highgate).

Our view: Its last full Ofsted (2006) deemed this an outstanding primary, and there's little evidence this view should change. Results in year 6 remain rock solid. Teachers are a happy mix of experience and enthusiasm; most are in their 30s, with a healthy sprinkling of men. 'We're very happy with the teachers,' said one parent. 'They're very approachable and supportive.' The new management structure (giving responsibility for a number of year groups to three assistant heads) means classroom time is always in the hands of a qualified teacher (and parents have 'a point of contact' for concerns, gripes, etc).

Children eased gently into school life with parents allowed to stay in the early days. Good support for the basics, too, with an informative 'phonics workshop' for those unfamiliar with the jargon. French from year 3 (but 'only a little'). Good ICT, with plenty of coding. Science skills developed beyond the curriculum with final year pupils introduced to secondary school methods with classes at Fortismere. Philosophy, reasoning and 'reflection' from reception. Regular homework, with daily reading, weekly maths and spelling, plus 'the odd project'. Comprehensive special needs strategy overseen by a SENCo, aided by learning support assistants in each class and out-of-school specialists when required. Forest school recently introduced.

The visual arts important here – 'There's a lot of focus on art,' said one parent. As well as the standard fare, there's an arts week, art award, and involvement with a 'working' artist. School orchestra and choir (both provided in after-school clubs).

Sport 'huge'. Netball, rugby, dance, cricket, gymnastics, basketball, athletics and hockey all on offer, with external specialists honing skills

Generally 'millennial' in approach, so there is a clothes recycling point on site and pupils are encouraged to walk to school

to a high standard and plenty in the way of inter-school competition ('The trophy cabinet's not big enough for the trophies we've received,' says the head). But, if winning is the aim, the attitude remains inclusive. 'Football Friday' fields eight teams and eight groups of supporters (plus appropriate team shirts) and regs require three girls from each team to be on the pitch at all times. Good range of well-organised after-school clubs, from cheerleading and chess, to cooking and capoeira. (Paid-for) before- and after-school clubs extend the school day for working parents.

Formed by the merger of an infant and junior school in 2000, the school now occupies an army camp of 60s low-rise buildings. Located on the site of what was once Muswell Hill Railway Station, there's lavish outside space, with an attractive, well-equipped playground for the youngest, good-sized courts and extensive running-around space (dotted with picnic tables) for their elders, plus a delightful wooded area and wildlife garden.

'Joy, discovery and diversity' are the defining themes of schooldays here, and parents agree that this is 'a really nurturing' place. Reasonably relaxed in a north London way, so no uniform. ('It's quite liberal, but I like that,' said one mum). Generally 'millennial' in approach, so clothes recycling point on site and pupils encouraged to walk to school. Broad cross-section of ethnicity and income, but the prevailing mood solidly middle class. ('It would be lovely to go for ice cream; let's find a date.') Fundraising, too, tends to reflect the area, with a concert of Vivaldi's Four Seasons a recent moneyspinner.

Generally a friendly, upbeat place, with parents bonding in the active PTA, which raises funds through a multitude of events, from quiz evenings and cake sales to fairs and fireworks night. Also active gardening and nature groups involved in 'site development'. 'It's a very nice community and I've made some very good friends.'

The last word: Produces articulate, confident children, who enjoy their time at school. 'My son looks forward to school every day.'

Palmers Green High School

104 Hoppers Road, London N21 3LJ

020 8886 1135 | office@pghs.co.uk | www.pghs.co.uk

Independent	Pupils: 276
Ages: 3-16	Fees: £11,355 – £16,260 pa

Headmistress: Since January 2017, Wendy Kempster (50s) BSc PGCE. Originally from north Wales, Mrs Kempster studied maths at Reading University, where she went on to do her PGCE. Taught in Reading and Bristol, before moving north and taking time out when her children were young. Previously deputy head of Loughborough High, and assistant head and head of maths at Nottingham Girls' High. Attracted to PGHS because of the opportunity to know every girl: 'You can't do that in a school of 600 or 700.' Trained as an ISI inspector and an accredited advanced skills teacher, she's also been a school governor for over 15 years. Married to a fellow educator, she has three grown sons (all qualified or soon to be qualified as doctors). Enjoys singing, running, cycling, swimming, tennis – and mountains. 'I'm a country girl at heart, and every holiday I'm off to the mountains in the Lake District.' Down to earth and experienced, she appears to be keeping PGHS on a firm course and leading it to new heights.

Entrance: Selective, but not quite as intimidatingly so as some other north London options. Many join in nursery, but further official entry points at 4, 7 and 11, plus occasional places elsewhere. Younger applicants are sifted on the basis of 'ability and aptitude'; at 11, tests in English, maths, and reasoning, followed by interviews for those who perform well. All current junior pupils sit 11+ alongside outsiders, but almost all proceed seamlessly to the senior school. 'Only very occasionally do we suggest to a parent that they consider another school,' says the head. Some preference given to siblings, but entry not automatic. 'We don't want a child to be out of their depth or unhappy.'

Exit: PGHS sees itself very much as an all-through nursery-16 school. 'We view it as a journey,' says the head, 'and we're very candid that, as a through school, we don't offer specific preparation for 11+.' Nonetheless, teaching and curriculum mean girls are very well prepared and some do move on at this stage, when parents are often looking for selective state options (Latymer, Dame Alice Owen's, Henrietta Barnett, etc). In year 11, girls carefully advised and guided in their choice of sixth form, when again they tend to favour the state (Woodhouse College particularly fashionable at the moment among the usual spectrum eg St Michael's RC, Fortismere, Ashmole), but independents (North London Collegiate, Highgate, Aldenham, City of London, St Alban's High School for Girls, Haileybury, Haberdashers' Girls) also well represented.

Latest results: In 2020, 87 per cent 9-7 at I/GCSEs. In 2019 (the last year when exams took place), 81 per cent 9-7.

Teaching and learning: The Sunday Times regularly ranks Palmers Green in the top five small independent schools. Single class of about 25 in each year group ensures all girls get plenty of attention, and most make 'exceptional' progress at every stage from reception to GCSE. Parents particularly welcome specialist subject teaching (in art, DT, ICT, drama, PE and music) more-or-less from the get-go, with junior pupils sharing senior school facilities.

School values are rooted in Miss Hum's Quaker beliefs: 'By Love Serve One Another'. A recent pupil survey found an unusually harmonious and caring atmosphere

Girls currently sit a mix of GCSEs and IGCSEs, depending on which exams the schools feels will best prepare them for A levels, and perform particularly well in maths, modern languages and all three sciences (where they are encouraged to reach high with lots of in-class and external enrichment, including visits from engineers and the RAF). Plenty of extra help, too, in a wide range of academic 'surgeries'.

French introduced in year 3, and year 5s enjoy a taster of Latin, German and Russian. French and Spanish on offer at IGCSE (with the option to take one or both).

Teaching, by well-qualified staff, strong throughout. 'Everything is very well managed,' said one mother. 'Pupils are happy and enjoy what they're doing in class. The teachers are nice, too, friendly and experienced.'

Learning support and SEN: Learning difficulties tend to be mild, primarily dyslexia and a small number of autistic spectrum disorders. Support given in lessons ('Every member of staff has a teaching strategy to help girls,' says the head. 'We make sure the provision is not nebulous') with external specialists introduced as required. Extra classes before and after school and one-to-one tuition also available (sometimes at an extra charge). New push to stretch the able, gifted and talented.

The arts and extracurricular: Artwork impressive, taught by a dynamic head of art, and girls pushed to achieve in everything from monoprinting to experimental work. About half take GCSE art, and many inspired to develop skills further in after-school art club. Recently refurbished and well-equipped music room. Timetabled instrumental lessons (clarinet, saxophone, flute, piano, singing, violin and viola, plus other options if requested). Girls given plenty of opportunity to perform in junior and senior school orchestras, four choirs, instrumental groups (recorder, violin, and woodwind) and a rock band club. A highlight of the calendar is the (highly competitive) annual house choral competition. Drama a popular GCSE option and junior school (including all year 6) star in annual play. DT has its own workshop with excellent facilities (3D printers, CAD etc), where girls in the junior school are taught in half-class groups, making everything from toy cars to fairground attractions.

Over 80 weekly clubs (before and after school and at lunchtime), including book club, debating (with inter-house competitions), ICT, literary society, film skool (sic), LAMDA exams and knitting. Most take DofE bronze. Lively range of visits (Science Museum, Downing Street, the Guardian), and visitors (Onatti Spanish Theatre, author talks, professional parental insight from parents who are dentists, doctors etc), plus residential trips (skiing in Italy, year 5 to Flatford Mill, year 7 bonding at PGL). 'The school provides a really rounded education,' said one parent. Well-stocked recently refurbished library offers an inviting place to read and study. Strong careers programme from the start of senior school. 'Because girls move on in the sixth form, we have to focus on this much

Teachers operate an open-door policy and pupils feel comfortable asking for help. 'I know I can trust any teacher with my problems, however small,' said one girl in the senior school

earlier than other schools,' says the head, and all expected to undertake work experience in year 11.

Sport: Not much in the way of outside space (a decent-sized yard, and an attractive early years playground) and limited numbers mean putting B and C teams together can be a challenge, so possibly not the best home for the super sporty. That said, as the head notes, 'The advantage of a small school is that everyone gets a chance to play in a team', and the school runs competitive teams in several sports, including netball and cross-country. All study gymnastics and dance on a half-term rota in the school hall, with outdoor games (netball, football, rounders, tennis and athletics) and swimming at grounds a short coach journey away. In addition, years 10 and 11 travel enjoy the facilities of a nearby leisure centre for trampolining, basketball, volleyball, aerobics, spinning and circuits. Wide range of sports clubs (netball, gym, fitness, yoga, rounders, tennis, football, athletics), too, and support given to those who wish to pursue a talent (such as ice skating) outside of school.

Ethos and heritage: Founded in 1905, by Miss Alice Hum, with just 12 pupils, by 1918 the school had expanded to 300 and moved to its present site. New classrooms and a dining hall added in the 60s and 90s, and the Elizabeth Smith Hall more recently to provide an additional venue for assemblies, workshops and exams. Despite its age, the school seems bright, modern and well kept, and the compact site makes it girl-friendly and intimate. Purpose-built PGHS nursery housed in its own building about a mile away.

The school's values are rooted in Miss Hum's Quaker beliefs – 'By Love Serve One Another' – and a recent survey of student opinion found an unusually harmonious and caring atmosphere. ('The girls comfort you with kindness and help you if you are stuck,' said one.) Girls, educated here for a long stretch, consider it a home away from home ('PGHS is like a second family to me,' said one year 6), and make regular return visits even after they've moved on. 'They love coming back,' says the head. 'They've been here longer than anywhere else and know they'll always be a Palmers Green girl.'

Today, the school is very much multi-faith (though traditional hymn books still in use, and carol service held annually in St John's Church, Palmers Green), but making a contribution remains important. PGHS shares adventures (such as the loan of moon rocks from NASA and study skills days) with local primaries.

Lunch, freshly cooked on site, is seasonal, farm-assured and free range, and includes a vegetarian option and sandwiches.

PGHS is one of the last remaining girls-only independent secondary schools in the area and head is a firm advocate of what single-sex can offer, giving girls the confidence to be themselves and achieve. ('When I was at school, they used to say, why do you want to do maths? That's not a girls' subject.')

Former pupils include Palmers Green legend, poet Stevie Smith, and actress Dame Flora Robson; more recently, telly stars Kathryn and Megan Prescott, award-winning poet Imani Shola, Lucy Collins, the first female naval submariner, and prima ballerina Marion Tait.

Pastoral care, inclusivity and discipline: The school's small scale means there's little danger of problems getting overlooked. 'We know everyone and there's no place to hide physically or emotionally,' says the head. 'Staff quickly spot if a girl who is normally happy is looking unhappy and pass on their comments straight away.' Teachers operate an open-door policy and pupils feel comfortable asking for help. ('I know I can trust any teacher with my problems, however small,' said one girl in the senior school.) House system creates bonds across the year groups ('Unlike bigger schools, you'll often find year 10s playing with year 7s, just as you would in a family,' says the head) and senior pupils mentor younger groups and take up roles of responsibility as head girl, house captains, prefects, etc. Junior pupils also take on roles of responsibility, while the culture of 'active citizenship' means girls are canvassed on decisions, such as the choice of caterers or the new school uniform (smart navy blazer and pink shirt for seniors, blue pinafores and summer boaters for juniors).

Behaviour tends to the excellent. 'We have only very minor disciplinary problems,' says the head, 'and I haven't run a single detention since I arrived.' Mental health, on the other hand, high on her agenda. 'It has become a growing issue because of social media. We don't allow devices in school, which at least gives girls six or seven hours each day contact free.'

Parents comment favourably on the 'nurturing' environment and 'old-fashion values' (girls, for example, leap to their feet when visitors enter a classroom).

Pupils and parents: Parents, from a broad mix of cultures and backgrounds, are not super rich; mostly hardworking professionals, who have similar aspirations for their daughters.

Money matters: Fees definitely on the good-value side. Scholarships at 11 to current pupils and incomers. Limited number of bursaries of up to 100 per cent, plus music awards (minimum grade 4 required), which fund lessons on one or two instruments.

The last word: A small, friendly and nurturing school, providing a rounded education, with old-fashioned values, and an excellent academic record that prepares girls extremely well to move on at sixth form.

Queen Elizabeth's Girls' School

High Street, Barnet, Hertfordshire EN5 5RR

020 8449 2984 | office@qegschool.org.uk | www.qegschool.org.uk

State | Ages: 11-18 | Pupils: 1,043; sixth form: 142

Headteacher: Since 2015, Violet Walker BSc (UCL), MA (Brunel), NPQH (50s). When Mrs Walker arrived as head at QE Girls, she must have felt she was returning home. Not only did she attend the school as a pupil in the 70s, she spent time here as part of her training as a maths teacher in the early 2000s. Before qualifying as a teacher, however, she had a pursued a number of other routes, qualifying and practising as both an accountant and a psychotherapist. Once launched in the profession, she rose rapidly, working as assistant head at Park High School, Harrow, and, most recently, as deputy head of Northolt High School for Girls (which she helped move on from special measures). Clearly seen as a 'safe pair of hands', her aim at QE Girls has been 'to marry the sense of tradition and what might be thought the old-fashioned values of my days with the very best of the latest in education.' This ambition has already been realised in a calm and competent fashion, and, since her arrival, the school's seen a rapid turn round of its academic fortunes. Both parents and pupils acknowledge her impact. 'The head seems a lot more in control,' said one mother. 'She really has her finger on the pulse,' commented another. A firm believer in what girls-only education can offer, she acts as a coach for Women in Leadership, and her ambitions are 'for QE to be recognised as an outstanding school' and 'for girls to love school'. Mrs Walker is currently joint president of ASGS, the Association of State Girls' Schools, and works closely with other member schools.

Entrance: A non-selective comprehensive, oversubscribed by about three to one at 11, when 180 girls are admitted using Barnet's 'community' criteria (looked-after children, then siblings, then distance from the gates). Very much a local school, many parents choose it because of its 'walkability', though transport links are also excellent with the tube just a minute away. Sixth form admits a maximum of 25 new students depending on subject availability (and a GCSE point average of 5.5).

Exit: About 70 per cent of those who enter at 11 proceed to the sixth form, often declaring how comfortable and happy they feel at the school. At that point, the rest tend to float off to co-ed comps or sixth form colleges (Fortismere, Barnet College, etc). Virtually all those who remain gain entry to their first or second choice university. Majority to Russell Group, the rest to the full spectrum of higher education. Popular destinations include Nottingham, Leeds, Kings College, Sussex, Durham and Nottingham Trent. Two medics in 2020, but none to Oxbridge or overseas.

Encouragingly broad range of subject choice, too, from aerospace engineering, marine biology and mechanical engineering, to economics, law, graphic design and optometry. A few to high-level apprenticeships.

Latest results: At GCSE in 2019, 40 per cent 9-7; 66 per cent of grades 9-5 in both maths and English. At A level 15 per cent A*/A (40 per cent A*-B).

Teaching and learning: In 2014, the school experienced a major shock when standards at this traditional high-flyer were called into question by Ofsted. Since then, a new head and a new Ofsted inspection have indicated the road to recovery is fully underway. QE Girls is also now officially recognised as providing outstanding 'value added', with progress as well as achievement far above average. Teaching weaknesses (particularly of the most disadvantaged) have been resolved, with a raft of new appointments and energetic monitoring.

Girls enter year 7 from a wide range of local primaries and are quickly melded into a cohesive seven forms of 25-26. All study a largely academic curriculum, with most taking GCSEs in English, maths, science, at least one modern foreign language, history or geography plus an expressive art or technology subject. (They also study IT, RE, PE, PSHE.) Some career-oriented options, too, such as business studies and BTec in health and social care.

Teachers (including quite a few men) are enthusiastic, professional and popular. 'The teachers are really nice and you always feel comfortable going to ask for help' was a refrain heard repeatedly from girls across the age range.

Maths taught in sets from year 7 and maths and science (which came in for particularly criticism in 2014) are definitely on the up, with Ofsted praising the improvement for the middle ground. Not all parents, however, are entirely convinced by the transition arrangements. 'There has been a high turnover of maths teachers,' said one. 'My daughter finds that quite difficult as every teacher has a particular way of explaining things. Sometimes, she's just given worksheets and left to do them.' Science taught in a range of well-equipped labs, but no pressure to take all three (biology, physics, chemistry) to GCSE. 'You can go on to do medicine or science with double award,' said one teacher, 'so we generally only encourage those who really like science to do three.'

DT gets the thumbs-up from pupils. Subject matter includes food. 'I've just learnt how to cook a quiche,' said one enthusiast, 'and I'm going to make another tonight'

All start Spanish in year 7 and top-set linguists take up French in year 8 (with the option to continue with two languages to GCSE). Official praise for English, humanities and drama at GCSE, and DT gets the thumbs-up from pupils – with girls enjoying the wide-ranging subject matter, which includes food ('I've just learnt how to cook a quiche,' said one enthusiast, 'and I'm going home to make another tonight'), metalwork, textiles and woodwork. Girls seem to flourish in what is often considered masculine terrain, and, according to a teacher who has taught in both single sex and co-ed schools, comfortably take on tasks they might have shied away from elsewhere.

The fact that it is single sex is also a definite plus. 'No annoying boys,' said one pupil succinctly

Widening range of post-GCSE options (26), including business studies, DT, drama, media studies, music tech, further maths, psychology, philosophy, government and politics, photography and sociology. Also now offers a BTec in health and social care. The Extended Project Qualification (EPQ), which universities welcome for the way it fosters research skills, has also been widely embraced, with most of those taking it gaining A*/A. Sixth form class sizes are small (often under 10) and girls get close personal supervision from a 'pastoral mentor', a specialist in one of their chosen subjects. Good careers and university advice (including for Oxbridge and international options, though currently not many heading in these directions.)

Learning support and SEN: Well-resourced facilities for SEN with dedicated space and well-targeted support overseen by a SENCo and senior learning mentor. 'My daughter was struggling in English and I found the school very proactive,' said one mother. 'They identified her problem and gave her extra help, which not only improved her work but boosted her confidence.'

The arts and extracurricular: Extracurricular as well as curricular drama highly popular, with girls auditioning enthusiastically for speaking parts or stage management roles in the annual production. Art and textiles demonstrate imagination and skill, and broad range of in-lunch and after-school clubs provide additional opportunities for sports fans (netball, boot camp, hockey, yoga, football), budding intellectuals (reading the classics, Scrabble) and creatives (LAMDA, jazz band, fashion show club and film club). 'I have decided to work in film,' announced one year 9, who'd recently launched her debut work.

Variety of choirs, orchestra and bands (jazz, drumming, guitar, etc). Good range of trips and visits (PE to the Alps, English to Copenhagen, modern foreign languages to Spain) and all take part in an enrichment programme and work experience in year 12. Well-stocked library staffed by knowledgeable librarians. (Popular Accelerated Reader Scheme encourages reading more and reading more broadly.) Confidence also boosted by participation in the Jack Petchey Speak Out Challenge.

Sport: Excellent facilities for sport, with large on-site pool and gym, eight tennis courts and 29 acres of ample grounds for running around (or simply lounging). Teams and individuals compete at borough and county level, performing particularly well in athletics.

Ethos and heritage: QE Girls traces its roots back to Elizabeth I, when Robert Dudley, Earl of Leicester, requested a charter for 'the education, bringing up and instruction' of boys, and – at a future date – a school for girls. The boys' school was founded in 1573, the girls had to wait until 1888, when a small school of just 40 girls was eventually opened. Once a grammar school, the school went comprehensive in 1973.

Guidelines on behaviour are now firmer ('It's much stricter than it used to be,' commented one girl) but certainly not draconian. Pupils are keen, articulate and poised

One of the oldest girls' state schools in the country, it still enjoys the county council-funded building of 1909, but this has now been joined by a myriad of later additions (many erected in the 60s), plus general updating, replacing (after a fire), and extending to adapt to increasing numbers and new requirements. Very good facilities include an array of well-equipped science labs, technology rooms, drama studio, sixth form common room, spacious dining hall (with attractive views, outdoor snack bar and the latest thumbprint technology for cashless payment). The beautiful and extensive gardens are also a definite asset. Sixth formers have their own common room and silent study centre in the library.

Former pupils include Jane Duncan, president of the RIBA, singer Phildel, actress Stephanie Beacham and writer Anne Thwaite.

Pastoral care, inclusivity and discipline: The school's stated goals are to produce confident, independent, self-disciplined and considerate young women in an atmosphere that is calm, careful and purposeful, and they seem to be well on the way to delivering this outcome. In general, pupils are keen, articulate and poised. Though there will always be the odd disruptive force (and the odd exclusion), in general girls are well behaved and well mannered. 'I watch them going in and coming out,' said one parent. 'They always seem very well behaved, with teachers standing by to make sure they are.' Guidelines on behaviour are now firmer ('It's much stricter than it used to be,' commented one girl) but certainly not draconian. 'They let parents know if there's an issue, but they're not heavy handed about it.' Girls seem to enjoy the school very much and have excellent relationships with each other and teachers. For many parents – and girls – the fact that it is single sex is also a definite plus. 'No annoying boys,' said one pupil succinctly.

Plenty of leadership roles in the sixth form (head girl, two deputies, designated senior prefects for student council, charity, sport, library, sustainability). Sixth formers also mentor younger girls, running clubs, supporting in lessons and acting as reading mentors, which provides a strong sense of cohesion across the school. The head is also a firm believer in preparing girls for the world of work, and as well as her own involvement with Women of the Future Ambassadors programme, ensures pupils have the opportunity to attend networking events with high-achieving women.

Pupils and parents: QE Girls sits in a leafy, primarily middle-class commuter suburb, and its intake is a fair reflection of its surroundings (though it also addresses the needs of a large nearby estate). This is north London, of course, so a rich ethnic mix, with school and parents celebrating diversity. 'For me, one of its main attractions is that there are people from all walks of life,' said one mother. Parents generally attentive and involved, with an energetic PTA organising a regular calendar of quiz nights, raffles, etc.

Money matters: Funds from the original endowment still benefit the school, providing financial aid for those who could not otherwise afford it to participate in activities and support for small capital projects (such as the 2016 Upper Courtyard redevelopment). PTA-raised funds (£10 a month is politely suggested) contribute to desirable extras like school minibuses, picnic areas in the grounds and ICT equipment.

The last word: A relaxed, safe and friendly place, now with a firm hand on the tiller and rocketing results.

Queen Elizabeth's School, Barnet

Queen's Road, Barnet, Hertfordshire EN5 4DQ

020 8441 4646 | enquiries@qebarnet.co.uk | www.qebarnet.co.uk

State | **Ages:** 11–18 | **Pupils:** 1,260; sixth form: 325

Headmaster: Since 2011, Neil Enright MA (Oxon) MBA NPQH FRSA (40s). Previously deputy head, having first joined the school in 2002, rising seamlessly through the ranks. Educated at St John's College, Oxford (a geographer); MBA in 2010 from the University of London Institute of Education.

'When my son recently got into trouble and was threatened with being sent to the head, he said, "Please do because he will listen to us and is fair,"' a parent told us – and that seems to be the measure of this empathetic, even-handed head whose breezy demeanour must help put these quite serious (well, the ones we met) boys at ease. And though it is hard to believe these biddable boys could be wayward, a parent recounted 'a recent incident for which there was of course a punishment, but no marking out of the boys as the naughty ones – Mr Enright makes sure there is wobble room and I really like that about him.' But there's a backbone of authority and pupils admit to sitting up that bit straighter when he's around. Teaches geography lessons here and there, across all year groups, as well as offering bespoke tutorials.

Runs a very tight ship and his vision of where the school is going is as ordered as the school itself, with lots of talk of 'strategic plans', 're-imagined values' and 'priorities and enablers' (school is, for example, keen to make more of its location, become more adventurous with co-curricular and build more local partnerships). All appreciated by parents. As for COVID, school is reported not only to have flexed quickly and well, but learned from it too – 'the school moved forward years in weeks, not just in terms of IT but co-curricular and pastorally too,' we heard.

'You sometimes wonder if he has a life outside school because he's so involved in everything,' said a parent, and he certainly seems to enjoy a busman's holiday, spending much of his spare time governing eg a local primary school, a PRU, St Albans High and at his alma mater John Lyon School. 'Here I am conducting this amazing orchestra so to feed myself, I like to think about what we're doing in different contexts,' he explains. That said, he finds time for travel, friends, yoga and sport. Lives in Northwood, where he rarely manages a trip on the Met line without bumping into at least one current or former student or parent – 'which is actually really nice'.

Entrance: Over 3,000 boys apply for 180 places. Tests in September (register between May and mid-July), which although tough are made 'as nice an experience as possible', with year 9s brought in to lighten things up with playing hangman etc. Boys told whether or not they have met the 'standard required' before they have to make their choice of schools, so they have nothing to lose by taking the test, but 'standard required' does not guarantee a place. No preferential treatment for those on pupil premium and no catchment area. Occasional vacancies between years 7 and 10, offered to those on the waiting list. Automatic transfer to sixth form for nearly all students and no sixth form entry for external candidates – 'I see this as a seven-year education,' says head.

Exit: Barely any leave after GCSE – around seven per cent. Nearly all to Russell Group universities, with Warwick, Nottingham, Imperial, UCL, Queen Mary, Bath, Durham and Loughborough recently popular. A few off to major US colleges and Europe each year – four overseas in 2020. Forty to Oxbridge and 32 medics in 2020. Other popular subjects include economics, law, languages, history and engineering. Top-notch UCAS guidance. 'What I love about the school is that you can have a wannabe poet, banker and a politician – they encourage you to spread your wings in any way you want, although there are some parents with very set ideas for their kids,' said one parent.

Latest results: In 2019 (the last year when exams took place), 91 per cent 9-7 at GCSE; 86 per cent A*/A at A level. In 2020, 94 per cent 9-7 at GCSE; 91 per cent A*/A at A level.

Teaching and learning: Right in the top branches of the academic league table tree, rivalling most schools, independent or state, in its GCSE and A level results. And still on the up, with the percentage of A*s at A level up by 25 per cent in the last three years. Yet parents and students say the pressure is nothing compared to previous schools: 'There is no shame in wanting to do well here and nobody is teased for trying hard, whereas at primary school my son didn't feel able to admit to enjoying homework and aspiring for Oxbridge,' was a typical comment. School concurs: 'What we're offering is something niche – boys only and very selective, which means you end up with a very narrow range of ability and a common level of aspiration so the boys no longer feel the burden of being different.' In the lessons we sat in on, the pace of learning took our breath away but what impressed us even more is that how it's clearly cool to voice wacky ideas and this leads to boys feeling able to take risks in their learning. Flip learning replaces rote learning and every classroom buzzes with questioning, arguing and challenging on a wide range of intellectual topics. School goes well beyond the syllabus in every subject, stimulating these bright young minds, all backed up with the support of personal tutors, coaching, mentoring and clinics if required, although one boy felt that 'some of the extra support could be more comprehensive' and that it would be disingenuous to suggest there isn't pressure for some boys around exam time – 'If you're sitting on a two A*s offer from Imperial, even I feel the pressure on their behalf,' agrees head.

'When my son recently got into trouble and was threatened with being sent to the head, he said, "Please do because he will listen to us and is fair",' a parent told us

Setting in all subjects, including sport. Testing (about every half term) very much part of the modus operandi. All boys take French, German and Latin from year 7 and continue at least one modern language at GCSE, with Mandarin, Spanish and ancient Greek offered as extras. Economics offered at GCSE (some of these boys are already successful entrepreneurs by then). First school to become 100 per cent EBacc. Dazzling results across the board, especially in maths (typically 70 per cent at grade 9), which virtually everyone taking it at A level. This, and other A level choices (very traditional, including philosophy and Latin) are decided by tests in years 10 and 11 designed 'to tease out' aptitude. 'We don't rate GSCE results as a good enough indicator,' explains head. All do four A levels including 27 Germanists in the sixth form when we visited – again, bucking the national trend when it comes to languages. No weak departments, say students.

Boys say healthy competition pervades the classroom as much as the sports field, but there's plenty of collaborative group work too. Class sizes around 30, dropping to 15 at A level. Technology well embedded in lessons.

Teaching involves 'lots of personalisation', we heard from students. 'And while the boys are expected to call them Sir and Miss, in terms of the actual conversations, they can be informal and engage in banter,' a parent told us. 'Everyone is aware of where the boundaries lie and within that are some very good interactions,' said another.

Enrichment throughout, with extra-long lunch breaks for the wealth of clubs and student-led societies. Visiting speakers from Lord Robert Winston to Jeremy Paxman. Around a third of sixth formers do an EPQ – we just missed a mock presentation on HIV medication, and a parent told us of her son's EPQ on immigration in Europe around the time of Brexit. Big push on symposia with high-performing girls' schools, including Henrietta Barnett, St Albans High School and North London Collegiate. Competition wins (eg VEX IQ World Robotics Championships, Institute of Economic Affairs essay prize, and aspiring engineers beating professional firms at the industry's Constructing Excellence Awards) are celebrated as much as 9s at GCSE. 'If anything, we downplay exam results – given the ability, the focus needs to be on creating a fun, stimulating environment,' says head.

Learning support and SEN: Can accommodate mild ASD, ADHD dyspraxia and dyslexia. Some boys have hearing and visual impairments, including colour blindness. Tourette's and stammers also feature. All praise from parents for the new SENCo who we heard has moved the focus towards higher quality teaching rather than making it the SEN department's job to work with these students individually. 'Life isn't like that – being able to work with other students has to be the best way forward,' she told us. The upshot is teachers being trained to deliver extra help as part of the lesson without making it obvious, say parents. Plenty of links with specialist organisations eg National Dyslexia Society, and lots of nuanced work goes on here too, eg someone with organisational difficulties may be helped to negotiate the school day while those needing more emotional support might be offered peer and/or staff mentoring.

The arts and extracurricular: 'I'll be amazed if you can avoid VEX robotics as you walk round,' the head warned us, and he was right. Now something of an obsession for the school, there's even

School says: 'What we're offering is something niche – boys only and very selective, which means you end up with a very narrow range of ability and a common level of aspiration so the boys no longer feel the burden of being different'

a dedicated classroom for it, with boys barely looking up from their hi-tech creations when we popped in.

Music runs through the veins of the school, with four full-time music staff and a small army of peripatetic teachers. Over 20 different bands, ensembles and vocal groups range from symphonic wind and concert bands, to Indian ensembles, barbershop groups and Friday jazz; 160+ boys sing in the school choir. 'Very inclusive,' said a student – 'I just started learning the violin and they have already welcomed me in the junior strings.' A parent told us, 'My son started his own band – they are encouraged to follow their passions.' Facilities include a music suite where boys can study A level music technology and there's a £3.5m music school and recital hall currently under construction (completion late 2021). 'We've been to every concert since we joined the school and have never been disappointed,' said a parent.

With a member of the Bonham-Carter family heading up the drama department, it's no wonder that mere mention of the subject lights up boys' faces. Highlights include the annual autumn Shakespeare festival (a firm favourite), the annual spring school play and the house drama in summer.

Intellectual approach to art. Large, open-plan, light and airy spaces for students to discover their talents. We watched year 11s doing self portraits from mirrors and year 13s working on large abstract pieces. 'We try to push against school art – yes, it's skills based, but we want to generate a mindset of foundation for art school and avoid pastiches at any cost,' the art teacher told us, with many going on to architecture degrees. Diverse materials in use – animation, installation, sculpture, paintings etc. DT also popular, with over a third taking it at GCSE – a display box houses a complex looking drone and award-winning construction helmet that blinks when approaching danger.

Trips range from sports tours to Netherlands to German exchanges to geography breaks in Iceland.

Sport: A rugby school through and through, with everyone expected to get stuck in from the off. Fixtures list includes all major independent schools in the region and the school fields up to D teams on a regular basis, occasionally F. Next is cricket and athletics. 'Wish there was football,' we heard boys groan more than once, but don't hold your breath – that's not about to change anytime soon. Rugby 7s has been running since 1976, with school playing against 64 others, including Eton. Swimming, Eton fives, tennis, badminton, basketball and cross-country also popular, plus fencing and karate as extracurricular – boys told us they'd like to play them more competitively. Plenty of county and national representation in bridge, chess and water polo though. Eight-lane swimming pool, all-weather tennis courts, multigym and plenty of neatly trimmed green fields for team sports. No biggie if you don't like sport, though, said our guides – 'they get angry if you don't try, but it's fine if you're not much good.'

Ethos and heritage: Founded in 1573 by Robert, Earl of Leicester, with a charter from Elizabeth I. Rebuilt in 1932 by Hertfordshire County Council in a noble civic style with terrazzo flooring, parquet and panelling, all kept in spotless condition. Still well endowed with land held in perpetuity and its own Foundation Trustees, QE went comprehensive in the 1960s, reverted to grant-maintained status in 1989 and became a grammar school once more in 1994.

Behind the plentiful green fields and grand frontage lies a tightly packed campus. Among the newest additions is a spacious library and food technology facility. Café 1573 provides a Starbucks-style environment for sixth formers, whilst other years frequent the dining hall, a modern space also with its own branding and colour scheme. School even has its own (cashless) shop, selling everything from uniforms (much lower cost than in shops) to pens, with all profits ploughed back into the school.

The atmosphere is so purposeful and focused that we actually wondered if the whole school had gone AWOL when our guides led us down the silent corridors. It turned out every classroom was full to the brim and the doors were open; no low-level disruption here. Even in our discussion groups with students, nobody spoke until addressed by us or the previous person had finished their sentence – a far cry from the noisy, easy chit-chat we experience in many other schools. Those with more boisterous sons will, however, be relieved to hear breaktimes and lunchtimes are slightly more raucous. School wouldn't suit boys with a more passive approach, say students – 'if you're not prepared to work hard, you'll get drowned out.'

QE Connect is a buzzing networking portal that hooks up alumni with current students, encouraging the latter to take advantage of mock interviews, mentoring, work experience, Oxbridge buddies etc. Big programme of volunteering, with all sixth formers expected to do 40 hours over the school year (although most do much more).

Pastoral care, inclusivity and discipline: Slight mismatch between how much pastoral support the school says is available and what the boys say they experience. But there is good uptake from the part-time counsellor and all pastoral staff are mental health trained, head included. Head of year 7 is a dedicated pastoral role 'in recognition of it being a high-risk period' (pupils come from 160 different feeder schools so don't tend to come in knowing no other boys; are used to being big fish in a small pond; may have to travel quite far to school; and are probably used to being in an extreme place in terms of ability in their last school – 'not always a comfortable place to be'). And there's another team dedicated to the pastoral needs of years 8 to 10, while in sixth form smaller tutor groups are led by the same tutor all the way through. 'Because we have no new students coming in at that stage, there's no starting again in sixth form here, which helps,' says head.

The atmosphere is so focused that we wondered if the whole school had gone AWOL when our guides led us down the silent corridors

PSHE replaced by 'personal development time' – includes discussion time in tutor groups about everything from the American elections to Black Lives Matter (black alumni recently recorded videos talking about their lived experiences as young black men). Diversity of thought is valued, we were assured, and questioning of lack of diversity is encouraged, eg lack of authors of colour on the reading lists.

House points, certificates, merit stickers (for younger boys), congratulatory emails and postcards to parents all part of the reward system for extra effort and good deeds. No real misbehaviour to speak of – head puts it down to clear expectations, but sloppy uniform, bringing in a camera phone before sixth form or forgetting your text books more than once will earn you a detention. Boys feel there is some inconsistency – 'some teachers give out loads, others none.' Far from brushing bullying under the carpet, the school says it's aware that bullying can be subtle 'and sometimes even the victim doesn't recognise it for what it is' – lots of educating and monitoring as a result.

A rugby school through and through, everyone expected to get stuck in from the off. 'Wish there was football,' we heard boys groan

Pupils and parents: Over 90 per cent from ethnic minorities, mainly Asian. Around half speak English as a second language, although there's minimal need for linguistic support – these clever clogs are advanced bilingual learners who really only need help with areas like idiom and inference, which school provides. Fifteen on pupil premium in year 7 when we visited. Many of the boys who make it to Oxbridge are the first generation in their family to go to university, let alone such esteemed institutions.

Geographically, if you think of the M25 as a clock, the school caters from nine to three o'clock in a largely suburban arc. Northern line, Thames link and school coaches make the school well placed for transport links.

Students are among the most courteous we've met – they take polite to a whole new level. And, as you might expect from such brainboxes, they exude intelligence. Not exactly laugh a minute (our poor jokes were lost on them), although watching them among their peers during breaktimes suggested banter is alive and well. Parents are 'extremely supportive', according to the school – the annual Founders' Day Fete raises up to £25,000 alone, with parents taking the day off work the Friday before to help prepare.

Money matters: 'Amazing take up' for the voluntary £75 a month contribution from parents, according to head, topped up by funds from the Foundation and donations from parents, old boys and friends.

The last word: Speculating, hypothesising, synthesising – it's all part and parcel of life at QE, where they cream off the most gifted and talented boys from miles around. For hard-working, aspirational boys in the top 10 per cent ability range, it will almost certainly feel like coming home. A place where boys can expect to get carried away with the collective will to learn both in and outside the classroom, the result of which is one of the most inspiring learning environments we've ever come across. An exceptional and rounded education that even private schools would struggle to match.

Rhodes Avenue Primary School

Rhodes Avenue, London N22 7UT

020 8888 2859 | admin@rhodes.haringey.sch.uk | www.rhodesavenue.school

State | Ages: 3-11 | Pupils: 703

Headteacher: Since 2015 Adrian Hall BEd (30s). Gained his degree in primary education from Leeds University, then worked as a reception teacher at Castleton Primary School, after which he moved up the ranks to his first headship at Churchfield Primary School in Enfield, a post he had for eight years. During this time – in which he worked in a wide range of schools, some in deprived areas – he earned himself an NLE (National Leader in Education) in recognition of his work in supporting not only pupils but also teachers and leaders.

Instantly likeable, he is warm and laid back – a high-fives-in-the-corridor kind of head who wants children to feel comfortable in his presence. 'He's the best headteacher in the world,' one child told us, with others describing him as 'kind', 'funny' and 'really nice'. 'They hero worship him – and he's a brilliant teacher,' said one parent – indeed he teaches year 4s once a week. But make no mistake – he is also highly efficient and savvy about all things educational, and the policies he's brought in around discipline and punctuality have been unanimously welcomed. 'He improved an already brilliant school – that's no mean feat,' one parent told us. Meets and greets daily – 'within a week of arriving, he knew every child's name and he always chats to us. What's more, if you put forward an idea, he's on the case. He's an incredible man,' said one parent.

Loves swimming and rafting and exploring London and the world with his family. 'My son is fearless so we spend many a weekend at theme parks.'

Entrance: Admission by means of the local authority criteria – which means that, in order of priority, it's looked after children and SEN, then siblings and after that, living as near as possible. With four applications for every place, this generally means within a quarter of a mile. Local estate agents are big fans – the success of the school, and its neighbouring comprehensive, has had a significant impact on local property prices. From 2020, two nursery classes with both part- and full-time spaces for up to 60 full-time equivalent places.

Exit: The school backs directly on to Alexandra Park, one of the borough's best secondaries, and over half of pupils proceed there. Others to a range of schools including Broomfield, Greig City Academy, Heartlands, Hendon School, Henrietta Barnett, Highgate Wood, Latymer and North London Collegiate.

Our view: Undoubtedly helped by the fact that most families live within feet of the gates, this is a school with a true community feel – a vibe that parents say it has managed to retain despite moving to three-form entry of 90. And if ever there was an argument that schools benefit from great architects, this is it – the interiors meld the original 1930s building with the more recent extensions to create bright, light and modern learning spaces that are a joy to spend time in. The wide, carpeted corridors of the main split-level building are so much more than mere walkways, with private music lessons, art exhibitions etc going on throughout. The classrooms are big and airy, with huge windows – and the spongy-carpeted library is, for many children, their 'favourite place'. The art studio is well stocked; ICT suite is up-to-date; and there are two school halls – one purely for PE, while the other is also used for assemblies, lunch and performances. Nursery (now full-time) and reception are housed in a separate single-storey building, also with nice, bright classrooms. Outside, there are separate soft-ground playgrounds for different age groups. And the chickens – a relatively recent addition that give a nod to the school site's origins as a farm – are extremely popular with the children.

Children are taught mainly by class teachers, with specialist teachers enhancing areas such as French, art and PE. Parents praise the themed approach to learning – with each year group studying a single topic every half term, with a cross-curricular approach thereon, eg year 5's theme was Pole to Pole when we visited: the history aspect speaks for itself, while in geography they learned about global warming and in English, they explored Shackleton's poems etc. 'You really get to see these themes come to life in the class assemblies,' said one parent. Teaching staff – a good mix of the experienced and young – are fun. In every classroom we saw, there was a feeling of merriment, creativity, learning through doing and of getting things done with a smile and a light touch. It clearly works – the school consistently dominates the local authority league tables, with reading progress in the top 20 per cent of schools in the country, and writing and maths in the top five per cent. Ofsted can barely think of a word of criticism. Sats results are outstanding, with the majority reaching the highest levels. Though the pupils tend to be of above average ability on entry, everyone we spoke to agrees the school goes above and beyond. French taught from year 2 and 'parlez-vous' is supplemented with fun activities like a French breakfast, croissants included. Setting in years 5 and 6 for maths and English. All teachers are trained in forest school.

Academic progress is charted minutely and parents kept well informed, with three parents' evenings and three reports a year. Strong support, too, for the struggling. 'My son has a special literacy person and she's fantastic,' said one parent. An 'inclusion leader' leads SEND, with a separate SEND lead in the early years centre – both cater for not only mild and moderate, but more severe, including pre-verbal and wheelchair-using children. Their creative, child-focused support both in and outside the classroom has earned the school an Inclusion Quality Mark. 'My son has a specialist care team because of his needs and they were very impressed by how far the school was prepared to go to ensure he reached his full potential. It's just incredible,' a parent told us, while another said, 'Unlike other schools, they start with the child and adapt the school to them – rather than telling you how you have to fit in.'

The school goes above and beyond. French taught from year 2 and 'parlez-vous' is supplemented with fun activities like a French breakfast, croissants included

Sport, music, art and drama are as high up the agenda as the three Rs. In sport, there's been a push on inclusivity. 'We want every child to be able to compete, so we've introduced a squad system for football, for example, whereby 30 children get to compete, instead of the six children in the top team in the old system,' says the head. 'It's working – sport here is much more about participation than it used to be,' a parent said, although school still keen to bring home the silverware.

This is a school with a true community feel – undoubtedly helped by the fact that most families live within feet of the gates

Netball, gymnastics, athletics and rugby are at the core, plus basketball, boating, golf and handball. Onsite facilities include the two sports halls and outside cage for netball and football, and they use public parkland just behind the school. Good links with the local tennis club, and year 4s upwards go swimming at a local public pool.

Drama regularly seeps into English lessons, and there are two extracurricular acting clubs, plus a whole-school Christmas production and class assemblies. Art is popular – sculpting and printing as common as traditional art. 'We had to make a fish out of a trash can recently – I thought it would be rubbish, but it was amazing,' one child told us.

Music permeates the culture here – we saw lots of instrumental lessons in action. There's an orchestra, chamber choir, school choir and boy band – all of which publicly perform – and children sing at the local tube station to raise money for charity at Christmas. Some year groups learn instruments as a whole, with past examples including cello, clarinet, recorder, drums and violin.

Extracurricular clubs include all the usual suspects, plus the likes of street dance, coding, meditation, sewing, chess, pottery and drama. Lots of competitions entered and usually won. Breakfast club from 7.50am and after-school play centre on site 3.30-6pm, plus holiday clubs. Trips and workshops are all related to the current topic, as well as two activity-based residentials – year 5 to Wales for a weekend and year 6 to Lincolnshire for a week.

This is a nurturing school, with a strong pastoral system that includes a school counsellor (one day a week) and art therapy sessions available from the specialist art teacher. Parents, too, can get support and guidance on issues like bedtime routines and healthy eating. Huge buy-in for the no-uniform policy which, says head, 'helps children feel comfortable and that they can really be themselves.' Plenty of praise for encouraging good behaviour – 'stickers go a long way.' Children who don't follow the 'golden rules' are given 'reflection' and if that doesn't work, parents are called in. Bullying rare. Less than a handful of temporary exclusions, if any, each year. Student voice is big – the student council voted to bring in vegetable growing areas, among other things. Mixed views on the food. 'It's horrible,' more than one child told us.

Parents – a sociable and supportive bunch – are increasingly prosperous and professional, although around six per cent of pupils are on free school meals. Those with interesting jobs come in to share their expertise. Around half are white British; rest mainly other white backgrounds and Asian.

The last word: This is a friendly, upbeat and innovative local school with a fabulous learning environment, where pupils have fun, get excited about learning and have lots of opportunities around responsibility.

St Michael's Catholic Grammar School

Nether Street, London N12 7NJ

020 8446 2256 | office@st-michaels.barnet.sch.uk | www.st-michaels.barnet.sch.uk

State | **Ages:** 11–18 | **Pupils:** 816; sixth form: 274 (49 boys)

Headmaster: Since 2017, Michael Stimpson BSc MSc MA MA PGCE NPQH (40s), previously head of St Bernard's Catholic Grammar in Berkshire. Degree in natural science and teaching certificate from Durham; went straight into teaching physics and much later completed his masters in astrophysics part-time through Queen Mary, University of London. He also holds two masters degrees in educational management (one in Catholic school leadership). Has spent most of his time in selective and Catholic schools, including a spell as head of sixth form at St Michael's. Keen on the role of extracurricular education – and of the Duke of Edinburgh's Award in particular, for which he has given up many weekends. He is married with three children and enjoys literature, walks in the wild bits of Britain and listening to the music of Westminster Cathedral Choir. He is a fellow of the Royal Astronomical Society.

Entrance: Not perhaps as tricky to get into academically as some of the other north London grammar schools (some 390 apply for 128 places), simply because of its single-sex faith criteria. That said, the Catholic hurdle is not for slackers. Applicants at 11+ must provide proof of first holy communion and at least one parent must also be a Catholic with a written reference from their parish priest stating they attend mass on Sunday with the applicant. There is no catchment ('you can come from Sheffield if you want') but only girls who meet the religious criteria are allowed to sit the admissions tests (in verbal and non-verbal reasoning, English and maths). Pupil premium given preferential treatment for up to 25 per cent of places.

Sixth form applicants are not required to be Catholic (about 20 per cent come from other faiths) but 'must subscribe to the Catholic ethos'. At this stage, there are a further 30+ places (open to boys and girls with at least six GCSE passes at 9-7, with at least a 7 in the subjects they wish to study and no lower than a 6 in English and maths). Boys in this relatively large sixth form remain in the minority, with about 20 a year. 'The boys have to be quite brave,' said one parent.

Exit: Roughly 20 per cent of girls leave post-GCSE, to nearby sixth form colleges, like Woodhouse, or larger co-ed selective schools. Most sixth formers go on to the older universities. In 2020, nine to Oxbridge, plus nine to medicine/dentistry. Nottingham, Warwick and Birmingham popular. Others to Durham, Imperial, King's College, UCL, Loughborough and Bristol.

Latest results: In 2020, 97 per cent 9-7 at GCSE; 69 per cent A*/A at A level (90 per cent A*-B). In 2019 (the last year when exams took place), 80 per cent 9-7 at GCSE; 47 per cent A*/A (80 per cent A*-B).

Teaching and learning: St Michael's has won numerous awards (including Sunday Times State Secondary School of the Year) for providing an outstanding education and is now one of the country's leading secondary schools, always sitting within the top 20 grammar schools (often in the top 10) nationally at A level, usually in the top five at GCSE. Teaching is undoubtedly a strength ('There are very clever teachers who provide very good teaching,' said one parent) and the school works hard to maximize both pupils' and parents' aspirations. 'We give a great deal of time to thinking about it,' says the head.

All the girls accepted here are bright, but St Michael's still offers significant added value, with a packed, fast-paced curriculum ('You need to enjoy academic work and want to find out about things'). Almost all take 11 GCSEs, including a large compulsory core, which includes English, maths, history and/or geography, RS, a science (about a third take all three) and a modern foreign language (large numbers take two). Language offering particularly vibrant, with French, German, Spanish, Latin and Italian all on the timetable, and Japanese and Mandarin offered outside it. Italian and Spanish particularly popular A levels (as well as psychology, RS and maths). Sixth form has its own building ('St Michael's is really two schools, with two distinct regimes, a girls-only school in years 7-11, and a co-ed sixth form college').

Learning support and SEN: Only small numbers with special needs, but strugglers are provided with generous support. Homework is pushed hard. 'If you're ill you have to catch up on what you've missed,' said one mother.

The arts and extracurricular: Academic music is excellent, with dedicated practice rooms and a recording suite, though the school is pushing for higher standards of extracurricular involvement. 'Lots of girls participate in choir and orchestra, but I would like us to have greater opportunities for high quality performance.' Large, well-equipped art and DT studio (offering material technology, food technology and graphics) with plenty of enthusiastic participants.

Founded in the grounds of a convent. Attractive gardens, once the convent orchard, are graced by a monkey puzzle tree, a large redwood and a shrine to the Virgin Mary

Good range of clubs (mainly in the lunch hour rather than after school as many pupils live far away) and trips (including skiing, modern languages and faith-centred activities, such as retreats and a visit to Lourdes).

Sport: No playing fields and only a handful of courts (due for renovation), so team games not a forte (no hockey, for example), but a spacious new-ish sports hall (the largest school gym in Barnet) is used to the full to deliver high standard athletics, netball, volleyball, gymnastics, table tennis and badminton. Professional basketball and netball coaches bring out the best in nascent stars and the school is successful at local and regional level in a number of sports. The top performing school in the borough's inter-sports competitions for girls.

Ethos and heritage: Founded by the Congregation of the Sisters of the Poor Child Jesus in 1908 as a prep school in the grounds of its convent. In 1958, a girls' grammar school was launched to share the site, and eventually the prep school was closed to allow the grammar school to expand.

Still quite a compact school housed in a motley collection of periods and styles. The Grange, which now accommodates the sixth form, was once a 19th-century private house, and has the elegant proportions reflective of this history. The main 1950s school has recently been replaced. Modernisation is a constant theme (and drain on finances), with other recent additions including an air-conditioned multi-media suite and sixth form study centre. Classrooms remain a mix of old and new, but all are equipped with interactive whiteboards. Attractive gardens, once the convent orchard, are graced by a monkey puzzle tree, large redwood and shrine to the Virgin Mary.

The school, which is voluntary-aided, is conducted by its governing body as part of the Catholic church and the Catholic ethos remains fundamental. Prayers are said daily and every pupil attends a weekly religious assembly, as well as mass on feast days. But this is contemporary Catholicism. 'They go to mass, but they don't expect them to be cleaning the vestry floors,' said one parent. Attractive chapel with superior stained glass windows by Patrick Reyntiens, a master craftsman whose work also features in Liverpool and Coventry cathedrals. Girls put their faith into practice with charity work, helping in the community and giving food to homeless. Generally, the atmosphere is kind, warm and supportive. 'Academically, they push them to their limits, but they do look after them,' said one parent.'There's a very nice feeling to the school.' 'No one gets lost,' said another. 'It feels very safe.'

New school building includes new classrooms, science labs and art studios, replacing 'a tired 1950s building with a new, more spacious and modern building.'

Pastoral care, inclusivity and discipline: The primary aim here is the formation of responsible and committed Catholic citizens. 'We try to create a relaxed and happy atmosphere, but we expect high standards of behaviour, self-discipline and responsibility.' Those from bohemian families are advised to think carefully about their choice. Even those who aren't acknowledge that the regime is firm. 'There is very strong discipline, which can irritate the girls,' said a parent. 'They will stamp on anything – possibly too hard.'

The pre-GCSE years have a slightly old-fashioned air. 'There's no talk of drugs,' said one mother. 'They do go to parties, but there's no big modern teenage culture.' Girls leap to attention if the head is spotted in the corridor and pupil pressure as much as teacher pressure patrols the classroom. 'My daughter said to me in astonishment, "a new girl in the school keeps answering the teacher back. Nobody will be friends with her. We like our teachers. They're on our side; we're on theirs."'

Those from bohemian families are advised to think carefully about their choice. Even those who aren't acknowledge that the regime is firm. 'There is very strong discipline'

In the pre-GCSE years, uniform strictly enforced, with purple skirts at the knee or close to it, no jewellery or make-up. In the sixth form, mufti is permitted and the dress code becomes 'decency'.

Pupils remain accountable for what happens outside the gates if in uniform. Few problems, however. 'Most people who come here are impressed by the behaviour and friendliness of the pupils.'

Pupils and parents: Cradle Catholics from all over London and the world, with increasing numbers of Eastern Europeans, particularly Poles. Not as skewed to the professional middle classes as some other grammar schools, with more new immigrants (33 per cent do not speak English as their first language at home).

Money matters: St Michael's is a voluntary-aided school and parents are expected to contribute towards the cost of the buildings and facilities. 'The school would fall down otherwise.' An annual contribution of £275 a year is asked for and 90 per cent of parents contribute something. 'We don't go chasing the other 10 per cent.'

The last word: A happy school, with firm discipline, high expectations and outstanding results.

St Michael's CofE Primary School

CofE 29

North Road, London N6 4BG

020 8340 7441 | admin@stmichaelsn6.com | www.stmichaelsn6.com

State | Ages: 3–11 | Pupils: 450

Head teacher: Since 2013, Geraldine Gallagher (40s), BEd Liverpool University. Was NQT in a 'semi-rural' primary school with a mixed catchment, then went inner city to work in a primary school in Hackney, an experience she called 'very good although challenging at times'. She left after a year to teach at St John Evangelist School in Islington where she worked her way up to becoming deputy head. Sixteen years later she was ready to embrace the demands of becoming a head and saw the post advertised for St Michael's CofE: 'I grew up in Islington so had heard of the school and it had always had a pretty good reputation, so decided to go for it.'

Focused, 'I've wanted to be a teacher since I was 14', grounded, and knows the score. Ms Gallagher was only too aware that this was not an easy school to take on, with its prominent milieu of extremely hands-on parents (a positive in many ways but could arguably marginalise the power of a new head). She says: 'In the main the parents here are very supportive, but like most people if things go out of kilter, they will let you know.' However, judging by the feedback we've had, she need not worry. One parent told us that Ms Gallagher has already turned things around for the better in so many ways since starting: 'Parents now know where they stand with her and with the school as she has clear rules and guidelines.' Another said: 'She is a fantastic head. Before she came there was a lot of discontent and the school was in quite a bit of turmoil. The school was operating on the ethos of an old head and it became a situation of us and them between parents and teachers. Ms Gallagher has brought consistency to the school and moved it forward.'

With three of her own children at the school, this head undoubtedly has a vested interest in its success, both academically and pastorally. As one parent pointed out, 'The ethos here is very much that you get out what you put in.' Married for 14 years, any extracurricular time that Ms Gallagher has is spent with her family on days out and the odd swim or two.

Entrance: Heavily oversubscribed at nursery and reception. Around 70 apply for 52 nursery places and 100 for the 60 reception places, which are allocated on a points system, 14 points being the maximum. (Four points for church attendance at St Michael's Church, three for living in N6. Thereafter, local Christians, siblings, other faiths.) Christianity very much part of the ethos. Open days every term and, if a vacancy is available, parents are welcome to look round. Places do arise, particularly in the higher years when some pupils leave for the private sector.

Exit: On the border of three boroughs – Haringey, Islington and Camden – St Michael's sends its leavers to as many as 30 secondary schools. About half to independent schools (many with scholarships), particularly Highgate, with which the school has a close association, and City of London, but also Channing, UCS, Westminster, North London Collegiate, Haberdashers' Aske's and South Hampstead, plus top grammars Henrietta Barnett, Latymer, St Michael's Catholic Girls and Queen Elizabeth School. A considerable chunk each year to Fortismere School, the popular local comprehensive in Muswell Hill.

Our view: 'Much more academic' than it had been, one parent told us; another said, 'The school is now back on track and on its way to becoming very successful again.' The shift in the teaching structure came about following a period of upheaval at the time when Ms Gallagher was appointed head over two years ago. She says, 'I don't believe in old style leadership and pointing the finger. I knew the school had been though a difficult time, but I believe in working together to achieve the best teaching model.' This included bringing in several new members of staff and making some of the existing ones non-teaching heads of phases, which freed them up to oversee the efficient running of the year groups. While some parents were initially resistant, others feel their children are really reaping the rewards. One told us: 'There is a huge difference in what my son gets for homework to what my older daughter got at that age. It was a bit haphazard before, now it's more structured – not hothousing, just wanting each child to reach their potential.'

This is a school that doesn't rest on its laurels – which it probably could do quite comfortably by virtue of its catchment. A dedicated teacher/parent partnership ensures that even the least engaged child will derive something because of the constantly stimulating and original methods of teaching. Pupils still enthuse a year later about how 'a spaceship landed in their grounds', which they were allowed to explore – after which they were encouraged to write a story about the experience. This was courtesy of some very innovative parents, who together with the English leader spent hours creating the spaceship, and Troy, the 'legendary' school manager, who ran into each classroom shouting that a spaceship had landed, amidst loud noises and flashing lights.

Pupils still enthuse about how 'a spaceship landed in their grounds', which they were allowed to explore – they were encouraged to write a story about the experience

This year saw a campervan book bus parked in the grounds to encourage pupils to go in and read during break times (a cool spin on the old mobile library). Other stimulating learning tools include a charming open reading shed in the grounds funded by parents, a play pod with an assortment of recycled goods to encourage imaginative play and an allotment run by parent volunteers. We also loved the idea of a 'kindness wall', which we spotted in a couple of the classrooms, and which, we are told by one pupil, 'encourages us to write nice things about each other'. The pupils we chatted to were an astute bunch, happy and friendly. We even got treated to one spectacular card trick by a pupil who said he loved the school because the teachers 'let me do magic'. Another pupil told us that as a Muslim he liked how a Christian school 'embraces other cultures'.

Parents are an unusually energetic bunch – the school's parents' association (SMSA) is possibly the most committed we have come across. Last year alone they raised an astonishing £61,000 through events such as a bonfire night, battle of the bands, fun run and, the pièce de résistance, the annual parents' pantomime. This, we are told, can rival anything seen in the West End and is the highlight of the school calendar. One parent told us: 'What makes this school so special is the dedication of parents. Because we are a church school with no extra funding we can only get the extras we want if we raise the money ourselves. It does create a lovely community atmosphere, but forget it if you want a school where you can just drop your kids off and not get involved.' For a recent production of Dick Whittington, it was not unusual to see parents rehearsing or building sets until midnight, on top of the jobs they do during the day. Luckily for the school, parents include actors, musicians and set designers.

Excellent drama, with two or three plays annually, plus a nativity play and annual summer concert. A good range of sport – gymnastics, football, tag rugby, tennis, cricket, netball and basketball – taught in lesson time. Swimming, taught in years 5 and 6, is particularly strong.

Fantastic and varied extracurricular programme provides a wonderful resource for working parents. Breakfast clubs start as early as 7.45am and for the particularly energetic early bird fencing and gymnastics are offered. The quieter soul can indulge in a bit of Latin or creative writing, and an early morning maths club is also offered for 'invited pupils'. After-school activities include football, netball, dance, drama (led by the school's celebrated drama teacher, Bob Williams CBE), orchestra, French, chess and fortnightly film club (pupils have won several awards for film reviewing as part of the National Film Club).

Charity a big part of the school's ethos. On the day we visited parents were arriving with hampers to distribute to the local community and a bus-load of senior citizens arrived for their annual Christmas party. At this much anticipated event, year 6s dress up as waiters and waitresses to serve food and give out individually handmade cards and wrapped presents.

Good SEN department. Specific programmes designed for pupils who are classified as SEN or statemented (roughly 16 per cent), and access to regular sessions with art, occupational, and speech and language therapists. Each classroom has an adjoining intervention room for those who need extra help with maths, English etc.

The school is a couple of hundred yards down from pretty Highgate village – barely visible from the road, but as you approach the main gates the beauty of this building and its grounds can be appreciated. Founded in the mid-19th century as a school to train young locals to go into service, by 1852 it was on its current three-and-a-half acre site with the intention of not only providing an academic education, but also cultivating the spacious grounds as a farm. The green fields and listed Victorian buildings have since been joined by a block built in the 1970s, two large, well-equipped playgrounds and a large, new all-weather court. Both building and grounds are extensive and it is easy to lose one's bearings. The only gripe we heard from parents was about improving the concrete play area. One parent told us: 'I appreciate it is all about funding, and it's definitely better than it was previously, when it looked like a campsite, but there has been just talk for a long time.'

The last word: One of north London's most sought-after primary schools, St Michael's has high academic standards and a high proportion of pupils who reach well beyond the government's expectations at 7 and 11. This partly reflects the intake (largely middle class Highgate), but is also due to strong teaching – recently boosted by an overhaul of the teaching structure.

Tetherdown Primary School

30

Grand Avenue, London N10 3BP

020 8883 3412 | admin@tetherdownschool.org | www.tetherdownschool.org

State | Ages: 4–11 | Pupils: 420

Headteacher: Since 2013, Tony Woodward BEd (music) (40s). Started as an infant teacher in a large primary school in the Midlands before moving south in 1997, where he worked in a number of schools specialising in music, art and gymnastics, becoming head of a Surrey primary school, as well as an Ofsted inspector. In his youth was a top-ranking gymnast competing in trampolining (top 10 in the UK and contender in the European championships). A 'competent' pianist (his own words), he holds a performers' diploma from the London College of Music and also plays clarinet. 'What I like about him,' said one parent, 'is he's very nice and tries hard.' Some feel, however, he could occasionally be a bit more receptive. 'Parents just want to help and do good things,' said one.

Enjoys walking, keep fit, cinema, and theatre – and driving a car with his own personalised number plate.

Entrance: This is a community primary school and apart from the usual prioritised categories (looked after children, exceptional social and medical need, siblings), proximity is all. In 2020, you had to live within half a mile of the gates to win one of the 60 coveted desks in the admissions lottery. The school runs guided tours – led by the head and bookable in advance – in the autumn term prior to entry and late arrivals also get a chance to look around throughout the year.

Exit: Tetherdown virtually backs on to high-performing comprehensive Fortismere, and about 80 per cent of pupils have no doubt about their next destination, with many families moving to the area to ensure their children's education is sorted from the word go. But this is also a school of the prosperous, ambitious middle class and parents are also looking to north London's highly competitive grammar schools (Henrietta Barnett, Queen Elizabeth Boys, Latymer) and cut-throat independents – something recognised by the school, which advertises year 6 open events for Channing, City of London and Mill Hill.

Our view: The school sits comfortably near the top of the local league tables year after year, with over 80 per cent of pupils reaching the 'expected standard' in all three Rs (reading scores the highest Sats results in the borough). Parents are fully involved from the outset in achieving this outcome, given detailed explanations and instructions and a comprehensive breakdown of what is being studied. Well-maintained library is regularly updated with funds from the PTA (Friends of Tetherdown) and supplemented by books families donate to celebrate their child's birthday. Teaching generally strong, particularly in the early years. 'All the teachers have been a delight so far,' said one mother. 'They've made my daughter love learning.' Some, however, have reservations about a recent kaleidoscope of staff further up. 'There are some brilliant, long-serving teachers,' said one mother of three, 'but there've been a lot of changes in year 6 teaching, which has been very disruptive.'

Tetherdown was always the golden child of Muswell Hill primaries, but lost its 'outstanding' Ofsted crown in 2013 and failed to win it back again in 2017, when inspectors gave the thumbs up to improved teaching, governance and curriculum, but remained concerned about 'insufficient rigour' in monitoring pupil progress. Parents weren't entirely surprised. 'We've been told by the school that my daughter is bright, yet when she's offered three levels of difficulty and chooses the easy option, nobody encourages her to do something harder. I wish they'd stretch her a bit more.' Special needs support for those who struggle, however, comes in for praise and the SENCo works closely with classroom teachers to ensure work is tailored appropriately. Those with specific difficulties make good progress.

A lively topic-based curriculum is complemented by trips and visits. So those learning Mandarin (taught to all from year 3) also study China in geography, Chinese dance in PE, and enjoy an outing to a Chinese restaurant. Special events – Science Learning Week, Black History Month etc – punctuate the year making learning 3D through activities like orienteering and African drumming. Additional visits to eg the British Museum, the Cabinet War Rooms, a synagogue, and a care home all underline learning too, though not all parents are particularly impressed by the range. 'Trips can seem a bit by rote,' said one. Perhaps because there's a clear expectation that these will be supplemented at home, with specific recommendations on how to follow through.

'Out of school learning' given from early on, with half an hour a week in year 1 rising to two hours for those on the brink of secondary. In addition, parents here are very much of the tutor-hiring variety. 'A fair amount of learning support goes on outside the school; parents are quite driven,' said one, 'particularly those who have aspirations for their children to proceed to selective secondaries at 11.' Some, however, feel tutoring is required regardless of the end game, simply 'to keep up'.

Well-maintained library is regularly updated with funds from Friends of Tetherdown and supplemented by books families donate to celebrate their child's birthday

Sport a strength. The PE and sport premium has paid for a full-time sports coach, and all pupils have twice-weekly sessions in the large assembly hall/gym and various well-equipped outdoor spaces in the extensive grounds. Wide range of sports included as part of the curriculum (athletics, netball, squash, football, tennis, hockey, yoga, rugby and dance, plus swimming in year 6), while sports clubs (netball, girls' and boys' football, hockey, tag rugby and cross country) supplement the range, as do visits from leading sportsmen and inter-school competitions as part of the local league. 'Sport has come on by leaps and bounds,' said one father. 'The head of sport is absolutely excellent, keen to get everyone involved.'

A real village-school feel. 'I love the fact that on film night children can walk back home in their pyjamas with their teddies'

All taught to sing, play (the ocarina), read and compose music, from classical to pop, and Haringey's instrumental scheme delivers affordable tuition, timetabled during the school day. No dedicated music teacher, but opportunities to perform offered in assemblies, concerts, choir, and recently formed orchestra. Creativity highlighted by resident mural artist, author visits and encouragement to contribute to external writing competitions, while the annual short film competition (sponsored by the PTA) throws up some inventive work (not all done by parents).

Paid-for clubs – French, tennis, cookery, stitch club, mindfulness, chess and gymnastics – have something of a 'finishing school' range, but Lego, street dance and spy club break the pattern of the demure. 'The good thing is they have an extra-long lunch break of an hour and a half,' said one mother, 'so they can do a half-hour club, and still have time to eat lunch and go out to play.'

School's vision statement is to have 'a school where friendships thrive and children learn to discover a world of possibilities', and parents are overwhelmingly positive about the atmosphere. 'If you had an idea of a warm and nurturing primary school in your head, this is what it would be,' said one. Behaviour generally good, but there's nothing military in the discipline or no-uniform dress policy, and punctuality can be somewhat lackadaisical – the head gently chides, but with mixed results.

The school started life as Tollington High School for Girls in 1910 and the high-windowed, red-brick main school building is very much in the London School Board style, but the addition of an ample three-storey extension in the 2000s provided eight bright new classrooms and external teaching space.

Families in this well-to-do suburb are by and large cosmopolitan and comfortably off (the school advertises ski clothes, for example, in its winter sale) and form a tight-knit, upbeat community. 'You have to live very near, so it has a real village-school feel,' said one parent. 'I love the fact that on film night children can walk back home in their pyjamas with their teddies, and, at Christmas, you can see everyone's tree in their window.' 'My children have made really lovely, local friends,' said another, 'and so have I.'

Money matters: Hugely dynamic PA raises significant sums – as much as £50,000 some years – through an energetic cycle of activities (winter and summer fair, quiz night, silent disco, comedy night etc), helping to mop up funding shortfalls. 'We were originally paying for nice-to-haves, such as playground equipment,' said one member, 'but when the school told us they didn't have enough paper, we asked what their priorities were?' IT was the response and the resulting installation has undoubtedly been of benefit, allowing children to access their own learning space.

The last word: This is a friendly, happy school, with a strong community of professional, involved families. Not necessarily the tightest academic ship, but still providing a positive, broad-ranging education.

Woodhouse College

31

Woodhouse Road, London N12 9EY

020 8445 1210 | enquiries@woodhouse.ac.uk | www.woodhouse.ac.uk

State	Ages: 16–19	Pupils: 1,500

Principal: Since 2013, John Rubinstein BSc (50s) – read maths at Sheffield University where he achieved a first class degree. It was during his PhD that he decided teaching was his vocation: 'Part of my duties as a postgrad was to teach undergraduates, which I really enjoyed, and I realised then that this was what I wanted to do.' His first teaching job was at a comprehensive in Manchester – prior to getting his first post in London. His third teaching job was at Woodhouse College in 1994 as a maths teacher. He stayed there for the next 10 years, only leaving when he was offered the post of deputy head at a school in Haringey. He came back to Woodhouse in 2008 as deputy head, and was promoted to principal five years later.

Originally from Yorkshire, this softly spoken head seems totally devoid of any of the salesman techniques often displayed by other heads. That's not to say he's not enthusiastic about the school or his pupils – he is clearly extremely proud of both – but no doubt he feels, as we do, that Woodhouse pretty much sells itself. Students and parents alike describe him as 'very approachable' and one student told us: 'Mr Rubinstein is always wandering around the learning zones and often spends ages with pupils helping them out. You can email him anytime and he always gets back to you.' Even after nearly 30 years in the teaching profession, maths is still his passion and he still teaches four maths lessons a week which equates to a full A level week: 'It keeps me in touch with students, with the experience of colleagues, but most of all because I love it.' He even taught his own daughter, who is an ex-Woodhouse student: 'I warned her that it might be slightly strange, but it worked out fine in the end.'

'I can't say enough about the teaching. My son had no real intellectual curiosity before going there. Now all he wants to do is discuss the Russian revolution'

His wife is also a teacher and they have three children – two of whom attended Woodhouse and are now at university. Mr Rubinstein has many other strings to his bow – formerly an Ofsted inspector for 15 years: 'I gave up a year ago as the workload was getting too much and I was fed up of staying in hotel rooms'; he also enjoys running and has taken part in many half marathons and 10k runs. 'I have done the Crouch End 10k run for 13 years in a row and now train some of my students.' Recently nominated the school caretaker for a CBE for 20 years' of service to the school: 'He is the glue that keeps this community together.'

Entrance: Priority is given to applicants from one local secondary school, Friern Barnet (although that accounts for roughly 20 places and they still have the same entry requirements). After that, it's predicted grades and/or interview. Competition is ferocious (about 4,500 apply for 700 places), particularly for in-demand subjects. 'We can afford to be choosy,' says the principal, 'but we're looking for a range.' All applicants with minimum predicted grade requirements (evaluated on a points system, with specific grades for individual subjects) are given a 20-30 minute interview (with optional parental accompaniment) in the February/March prior to entry. 'We're looking for maturity,' said one teacher. 'We want them to demonstrate that they are committed to A levels and really want to work, but we also want people who will get involved on a wider basis.' The interview is frequently of as much benefit to the student as to the college. 'We often spend it giving careers advice,' says the principal.

Travel time is also taken into consideration. Students come from as far afield as Highbury, but the school 'generally considers an hour and a quarter by bus the maximum desirable distance.' Applications available from the time of the open day in November until the closing deadline in January. All candidates require a confidential report from their current school and must be between 16 and 18 when starting at the college. The college operates a waiting list for the reshuffle that often takes place after results day in August.

Exit: Over 95 per cent to university – over 60 per cent to Russell Group universities, with the most popular destinations being London universities, Warwick, Kent, Manchester and Sussex. Most popular subject choices are economics, law, engineering, business and psychology. Twenty-two to Oxbridge and 30 medics in 2020; three students got scholarships at prestigious colleges in the USA. Good advice about careers and courses, including a full time careers co-ordinator.

Latest results: In 2020, 45 per cent A*/A at A level (75 per cent A*/B). In 2019 (the last year when exams took place), 33 per cent A*/A at A level (66 per cent A*/B).

Teaching and learning: Woodhouse is one of the country's leading sixth form colleges, always in the top five nationally, usually in the top three. This is essentially an academic place, whose main focus is on A levels.

Undoubtedly a key part of the success is enthusiastic, experienced and focused teaching. One parent told us: 'I can't say enough about the teaching at Woodhouse and how they inspire students. My son had no real intellectual curiosity before going there. Now all he wants to do is discuss the Russian revolution.' Another said, 'The teachers really seem to know our children individually and their particular traits.' The consensus seems to be that 'they're excellent at monitoring and keep their finger on the pulse.' Mr Rubinstein says that close monitoring of students is vital as some students choose the wrong subjects, and

'Independent learning' is high on the agenda. Motivated students respond well to this approach. 'Teachers assume if you're interested in your subjects, you will want to read around them'

they are under so much more pressure than they used to be. 'If a student is underachieving, there will be a case conference and a discussion of perhaps reducing the number of subjects they take. They will also be offered extra supervised study.'

Results are certainly not achieved by hothousing or editing. The principal welcomed the introduction of the new A level system, which returned to the old two year study programme with no exams until the end of the second year. He says that although results have changed, 'we're not just teaching towards an end of year exam. Pupils can explore their subjects more deeply.'

A wide range of options on offer, with 27 subjects in almost any combination. Maths is the most popular A level choice (with 45 per cent taking it) and results are notably strong. One of London's largest providers of A level science, with many going on to science-related degrees. Four languages, including Italian, and an abundance of 'ologies', from sociology to music technology. The EPQ is taken by over 100 students each year and yields high grades. One parent said that 'the fantastic selection of A levels, including classical civilisation, really excited my daughter when she was looking at sixth forms, and this is what swung it for her.'

Though the majority at Woodhouse tend to favour professional courses at university, social science and arts-based studies are strong, with thriving theatre studies, economics, English literature and geography. 'Independent learning' is high on the agenda. 'We want students to prepare for lessons, so they can understand and interpret the information, using the teacher and their fellow students as a resource,' says the principal. Motivated students respond well to this approach. 'Teachers assume if you're interested in your subjects, you will want to read around them,' said one. 'They don't force you to work, but they'll give you the resources and make themselves available to you,' said another.

An enormous amount of help is offered to pupils with their UCAS forms, and extra workshops and weekly presentations are laid on nearer the deadline. A teacher is on hand every Tuesday after school to offer any extra help for university applications, and Mr Rubinstein is also very involved in the process and runs mock Oxbridge interviews.

Learning support and SEN: All students have access to two learning mentors – one for humanities, the other science and maths – to sort out any day-to-day tangles. One full-time SENCo, plus one part-time specialist providing individual support for those with dyslexia and dyspraxia and a learning mentor to help with study skills. The buildings are 99 per cent adapted for those with physical disabilities.

The arts and extracurricular: Woodhouse prides itself on providing 'a broad and civilising education' and all are expected to take part in at least two six-week courses of 'enrichment', the majority of which take place on Wednesdays afternoons, when there are no lessons. Most relish the opportunities to develop new skills in everything from observational drawing to street dance. Duke of Edinburgh and Amnesty International also on offer.

Art is strong and some of the pieces we saw on our tour were simply outstanding – something we honestly weren't expecting: 'Traditionally the more academic subjects are most popular here, and although art and drama are taken by smaller numbers, they are very successful. Several of our graduates go on to art colleges.'

Dance is also a strong curricular subject here and the college has two lovely, bright, mirrored dance studios.

Music, which was previously a 'neglected' subject, now has its own dedicated separate building outside, with a well-equipped practice room and a music studio, which works in conjunction with other Barnet schools, and offers lessons from peripatetic teachers.

Woodhouse students like to get involved and there's an active college council, which has recently helped introduce a daily loan system for netbooks. Plenty of outside speakers and activities including art trips, foreign exchanges, a ski trip and the opportunity to undertake voluntary work abroad. Debating has traditionally been strong at Woodhouse and the college takes part in the Model United Nations competition, which hosts around 40 different debates a year in various institutions, including Woodhouse.

Sport: Sports facilities are good, with a new sports hall and new floodlit 3G football pitch. Official team sports include football (girls' and boys'), netball and basketball, but individualists can also enjoy cross-country, squash, trampolining and kickboxing. 'If there isn't a club that you'd like to do,' said one student, 'the sports department are happy to try and set something up.'

Ethos and heritage: Located in a pleasant leafy suburb, Woodhouse began its educational life as Woodhouse Grammar School in 1925, but became one of the capital's rare sixth form colleges in the 1980s. Today all pupils are aged between 16 and 19 and all are studying A levels. With some 700 new pupils a year, the college is significantly larger than a traditional school sixth form, but smaller than a FE college.

The original stately Victorian façade (deriving from its former incarnation as the home of ornamental plasterer Thomas Collins) has now been joined by a motley timeline of newer buildings, leaving it today with well-equipped facilities. The bright, open plan Learning Zone is one of the most recent innovations, offering space to work in solitary silence as well as in small groups, and supervised open-access IT. In 2014 the college managed to raise two million pounds for a two-storey, purpose built mathematics facility. 'Quite a lot of students here can't work in silence at home and don't have the facility to do the "hard hours",' says the principal. 'We wanted to create learners who can work on their own.'

A strong sense of individuality. All creeds, colours, dress codes, hair colours, piercings welcome (well, maybe piercings not welcome but they're there). One student told us: 'I never feel we are judged on anything here'

To this former Woodhouse student, the college internally is barely recognisable as the Woodhouse of yesteryear. However, what still remains is the strong sense of individuality that Woodhouse was always renowned for – and is still clearly evident in the students we witnessed strolling around the grounds. All creeds, colours, dress codes, hair colours, piercings welcome (well, maybe piercings not 'welcome', but they're there). One student told us: 'I never feel we are judged on anything here. We know grades matter, but that's really it.' Another student told us: 'I've never been as happy as I am coming here. I used to loathe going to school, but now I'm worried about my time at Woodhouse going too quickly.'

The students we met were indeed a happy and likeable bunch. They all felt extremely independent and loved the free rein the college allows them. However, one student grumbled that she tends to go out for lunch in North Finchley High Road (a five-minute walk), as the canteen is too small and often can't accommodate everyone – a sentiment echoed by a parent, who suggested that perhaps the lunch hour should be extended.

Values here are traditional. 'We believe in honesty, hard work, mutual respect and taking responsibility for your own learning.' The atmosphere is generally enthusiastic, as much for work as for play. 'Here it's cool to work, cool to be involved,' said one student. 'The atmosphere is incredible,' said another. 'There's a massive sense of community. There are always things happening.'

Pastoral care, inclusivity and discipline: Not every 16-year-old is ideally suited to the self-motivation required by an academic sixth form college, but here high expectations are supported by a well-thought-out tutorial system and plenty of individual guidance. Every student has their own tutor, 'My son sees a guy two or three times a week, whom he likes and respects,' said one mother. 'When he was having trouble at home, they really kept an eye on him.'

The principal is all too aware that students these days are under a lot more pressure than previously, 'and as a result are a lot more fragile and there is more self-harming.' For this reason, they invest time in what they offer pastorally, including a pastoral manager and a counselling service. One student told us: 'The pastoral care here is excellent. There's pretty much someone you can talk to 24/7, if you needed to.' Another said, 'They accommodate for everyone and there is even an LBGT community.'

The college sees itself as a bridge between school and university, and new students are eased into this more adult world with an induction day in the summer before they start. The enrichment programme helps aid new friendships beyond the classroom. 'Everyone makes friends ridiculously fast because there are so many people in the same position,' said one boy. However, one parent did say that her child found the transition from school to college 'socially quite daunting if you don't know anyone, as pupils are always rushing off to their different classes or study period – it's unlike school where you get to know your peers over time.'

Boundaries are firm and there's zero tolerance on punctuality. 'It's an issue they have to grasp,' says the head. 'If they're not making the effort, why should other students suffer?' However, unlike most sixth forms, there is no morning registration, instead pupils go straight to their class and their ID registers them when they swipe it at the entrance turnstiles. One pupil told us: 'I much prefer it this way. It means we can go straight to our lessons and not waste time.'

One of the country's leading sixth form colleges, this is essentially an academic place, whose main focus is on A levels

In lessons, students are attentive. 'If a teacher leaves the room, people get on with their work,' said one boy. We witnessed some of the most attentive and eager students we've come across, who were happy to talk with enthusiasm about what they were learning. There is definitely a strong work ethic here. 'Issues found elsewhere are not even on the radar here,' notes the principal gratefully. Standard formula of oral and written warnings, with a code of conduct signed by all parents and pupils, but exclusion is a rarity. 'We have pupils from quite challenged backgrounds, but I have thrown out just one student,' says the principal. Parents agree that discipline is firm but reasonable. 'They run quite a tight ship, but it makes them responsible,' said one father. 'When my son's attendance was only 90 per cent, he had to see the senior tutor every week. As his attendance improved, he went less frequently.'

Pupils and parents: An eclectic mix – 'some nerdy kids, some cool kids, all sorts, colours and creeds'. The core is probably typical of the reasonably prosperous 'squeezed middle' of north London, but with a far higher ethnic intake than you'd assume from the location, and a far higher proportion of those who require some type of financial support.

Parents tend to be involved and supportive, students upbeat, mature, outgoing and energetic. They clearly enjoy the school – more than half volunteered on the annual open day held on a Saturday. 'They want to do well and they want to enjoy themselves,' says the principal. 'They're trying to get the balance right of working hard and having a good social life.' A parent agreed: 'My son is so happy. He really appreciates the fact that people are there because they want to learn, not because their parents are pushing them. Most students here are trying to better themselves and work really, really hard.' Past students include journalist Johann Hari, comedian Michael McIntyre and actress Naomie Harris.

Money matters: Parents are asked for £100 contribution for the two-year stint, enabling the college to keep up to date with books and underwrite the enrichment programme and facilities (those who can't afford it, don't pay). A £50 refundable deposit also required for text books. The college has attempted to replace some money lost through EMA cuts with bursaries.

The last word: An upbeat environment, with strong teaching and results. A firm stepping stone between school and university.

Wren Academy

C of E 32

Hilton Avenue, London N12 9HB

020 8492 6000 | firstcontact@wrenacademy.org | www.wrenacademy.org

State | Ages: 4–18 | Pupils: 1,566; sixth form: 293

Executive head: Since 2013, Gavin Smith BA PGCE, 40s. Studied geography at UCL, before teacher training at the Institute of Education. Then worked in Croydon, Islington and Barnet, leaving his job as assistant principal of East Barnet School to join Wren when it opened in 2008. 'I relished the opportunity to start a school from scratch. I liked the vision and could see it working very clearly.' Became principal of the senior school in 2013, and is now executive head, taking responsibility not only for the primary, but for a new school planned to open in Enfield.

Focused, energetic, refreshingly honest about the schools he runs, he continues to teach geography to year 9. 'You get to know 30 students really well.' Unlike many who lay claim to this achievement, Mr Smith also seems to know most pupils by name, and his high-visibility presence – he's on the gates many mornings – means they all know him. (One clearly unintimidated year 3 greeted him cheerily with: 'Hello Mr. Smith, how are you?') Ofsted is particularly positive about the school's leadership. 'Leaders work with impressive dedication, determination and vision...

relentlessly reviewing and refining all aspects of the school.'

Entrance: The most oversubscribed non-selective secondary school in Barnet, with 1,500 applying for 120 year 7 places. Siblings guaranteed a spot, the rest sorted into 'faith' (this is a church school) and 'community', with attendance at church gaining priority for those living up to about 1.3 miles from the gates; non-adherents must live significantly closer. Sixth form admittance based on academic performance (a minimum average of 5.5 in a student's best eight GCSEs, plus specific marks for individual subjects). Sixty admitted into reception.

Exit: About 40 per cent exit post-GCSE, some who have not met the sixth form entrance criteria, others to explore local sixth form colleges, grammar schools and independents. But lots stay on due to strong results at A level. Now offering a well-honed Oxbridge programme (based on partnerships with New College, Oxford, and independent Berkhamsted), although none in 2020. 'Once you get several,' says the head, 'it's not just luck and the right parents. We want to push further.' Parents appreciative of the offering. 'They demystify the process and open it as a possibility,' said one mother. 'It's a key reason I want my son to stay on into the sixth form.' Ever-improving outcome elsewhere, too, enhanced by a qualified careers adviser and UCAS specialist, with about half proceeding to Russell Group universities (Sussex, Warwick, Queen Mary and Sheffield popular). Also sends to apprenticeships (such as Jaguar Land Rover), with 'work experience week' helping all clarify their future.

Latest results: In 2020, 56 per cent 9-7 at GCSE; 93 per cent 9-4 in both maths and English at GCSE. At A level, 51 per cent A*/A (82 per cent A*-B). in 2019 (the last year when exams took place), 44 per cent 9-7 at GCSE; 25 per cent A*/A at A level (58 per cent A*-B).

Teaching and learning: From the outset, focused on progress as well as outcome – 'What we wanted was rigorous academic standards to ensure every pupil fulfilled their potential.' An ambition now fully realised, with progress at GCSE in the top two per cent nationally, as well as impressive results for all. 'Excellent' teaching is the foundation – 'Pupils are inspired and challenged by their teachers,' waxes Ofsted – combined with meticulous monitoring. Classrooms are 'calm' and 'purposeful' and high expectations produce pupils who are 'focused, diligent and mature'.

Taking their lead from sponsor school Berkhamsted, boys and girls taught separately in

Named for Christopher Wren, the school has adopted Design and the Built Environment as its specialism – 'because it's included in every subject and every subject can contribute,' says the head

English, maths and science in years 7-11. (Head believes this is why girls make up half of those taking maths A level, with good numbers of girls also going on to study science, technology and maths at university.) Broad GCSE offering includes art, design and music, plus BTecs in business and performing arts. Reading stressed at all levels, with ample, well-stocked library – staffed by a professional librarian – at the physical centre of the school.

'Rich curriculum', too, at A level with 20 subjects on offer including psychology, sociology, government and politics, and economics, plus the EPQ. A teaching partnership with nearby Compton School also allows Wren to cater for minority subjects such as further maths and modern languages. No vocational qualifications, however, post-GCSE. 'We wanted to teach an academic curriculum and what is available is too diverse,' says the head. 'We give advice in year 11 about the best place to study for those who want progress to vocational post-16 qualifications.'

Close link between primary and secondary, with senior-school specialists teaching French, art, PE and music in primary school. Seamless transition between the two stressed by placing year 6 classrooms adjacent to those of year 7 and secondary pupils making regular appearances in the primary, helping out with reading and leading assemblies. 'They're amazing role models, and it creates a family atmosphere,' says the head.

Primary achievement matches that of secondary, providing a 'superb start to children's education' (Ofsted). Over 40 per cent of year 2 achieve 'greater depth' in maths; development in reading and writing also 'especially strong', says Ofsted.

Learning support and SEN: Strong SEN with a wealth of additional support available to those who need it, including phonics catch up in year 7. Most pupils speak English as a first language, but those with more limited skills are aided outside the classroom. Gifted and talented also well supported with periods of stretch provided during weekly 'enrichment' afternoons and after school.

The arts and extracurricular: Named for Christopher Wren, the school has adopted Design and the Built Environment as its specialism – 'because it's included in every subject and every subject can contribute,' says the head. 'Focus' days illustrate this for all, with recent projects including designing an eco home, and product design included in the A level mix.

Timetabled 'enrichment' two hours a week encompasses everything from sport to chess, cookery, journalism and science. Strong drama with annual whole-school musical. Large dedicated music space shared with music education charity Da Capo, which takes responsibility for primary music. Keen jazz band and school orchestra. Art, led by a practising artist, is – according to one parent – 'inspirational'. After-school clubs (yoga, etc) offer further extension, as does Duke of Edinburgh and school trips to lectures, concerts and further afield (for example to Iceland).

Sport: Ample gym and plenty of opportunity for sport (football, netball, athletics), which is played enthusiastically and successfully (particularly trampolining and gymnastics). No swimming pool, however, and limited scope for aspiring dancers.

Ethos and heritage: The Wren Academy is the first in a multi-academy trust co-sponsored by the London Diocesan Board for Schools and the independent Berkhamsted Schools Group, which have encouraged and supported its ethos, culture and vision. Launched in 2008 with just year 7, it has gone on to achieve three outstanding Ofsted inspections.

Fundamental to the school is its Christian ethos. Faith-oriented assemblies held weekly, with bible readings and prayers taking place during tutor time. School chaplain an active member of staff and attractive school chapel allows for private worship. Though all are required to support the Christian ethos, other faiths given due deference. 'We never forget that we have a broad intake, and we give relevant Islamic or humanist examples,' says the head. 'We make it clear we value their upbringing.' Parents happy with the balance. 'They don't force it, but they encourage the kids to think about a religion and let them come to their own decision.' Parents also particularly praise the fact that the school feels 'very safe – which in London today is unfortunately unusual.'

Exciting contemporary building (by Penoyre & Prasad), designed round a large central atrium, is bright, attractive and well thought through with wide corridors, spacious classrooms and easy to supervise spaces.

Pastoral care, inclusivity and discipline: A large school, but feels intimate because of its spacious site and system of mixed-aged houses and vertical tutor groups. All pupils allocated a house (named after locations associated with Sir Christopher Wren) from day one. 'They provide new pupils with a ready-made network to help settle in.' Tutor groups (of no more than 24) are mixed age for years 7-10, with dedicated tutor group for year 11 to help prepare for GCSEs and life thereafter.

School has a reputation for strict discipline, but evidently not draconian. 'I think it has become more relaxed over time. My son, who's in year 11, didn't really enjoy it at the beginning,' said one father, 'but has now chosen to stay on in the sixth form.' Good-humoured relationships with staff and positive atmosphere throughout the school, particularly noticeable in areas like the reading steps of the open-plan library, where students sit quietly engrossed. Exclusion rate well below average. 'Students who transfer from other schools might have got into trouble elsewhere, but don't get into trouble here because of clear expectations,' says the head. Detentions known as 'reflections'. 'It avoids the punitive quality. It's more about restorative justice, learning from mistakes.' Parents welcome this approach. 'As a single parent, I really feel the school has shouldered much of the burden, and my son has blossomed into a nice young man.'

Traditional uniform – with top buttons done up – is rigorously enforced, and pupils expected to behave well not only inside but beyond the gates

Pupils notably polite ('behaviour is impeccable,' says Ofsted), greeting visitors and staff with Good Afternoon, the head as Sir. Traditional uniform – with top buttons done up – is rigorously enforced, and pupils expected to behave well not only inside but beyond the gates. 'They're ambassadors for the school in the community.' Student voice carefully listened to with year 11 prefects and 'sixth form committee' – selected by staff and students – involved in teacher recruitment and curriculum development. No staff rooms and staff eat alongside (though slightly apart from) pupils in large, light, open-plan dining room. 'The restaurant is the heart of the school with great quality food,' says the head.

Pupils and parents: What you would expect from a mixed north London suburb. So, families range from middle-class professionals to the barely managing. As news of the school's success has spread, numbers on free school meals, however, have dropped from about a third to about 20 per cent. About half white British, after that, ethnically very diverse. All mix happily. Active PTA raises large sums – nearly £50,000 last year – used to improve the school.

Money matters: Parents asked for £15 a month contribution. 'We need it to save us from more redundancies,' says the head. 'Only about half give, but it's enough to make a difference.'

The last word: A calm, orderly school with a clear vision, high expectations and excellent teaching, achieving the highest standards of behaviour and results.

East

Barking & Dagenham
Havering
Newham
Redbridge
Tower Hamlets
Waltham Forest

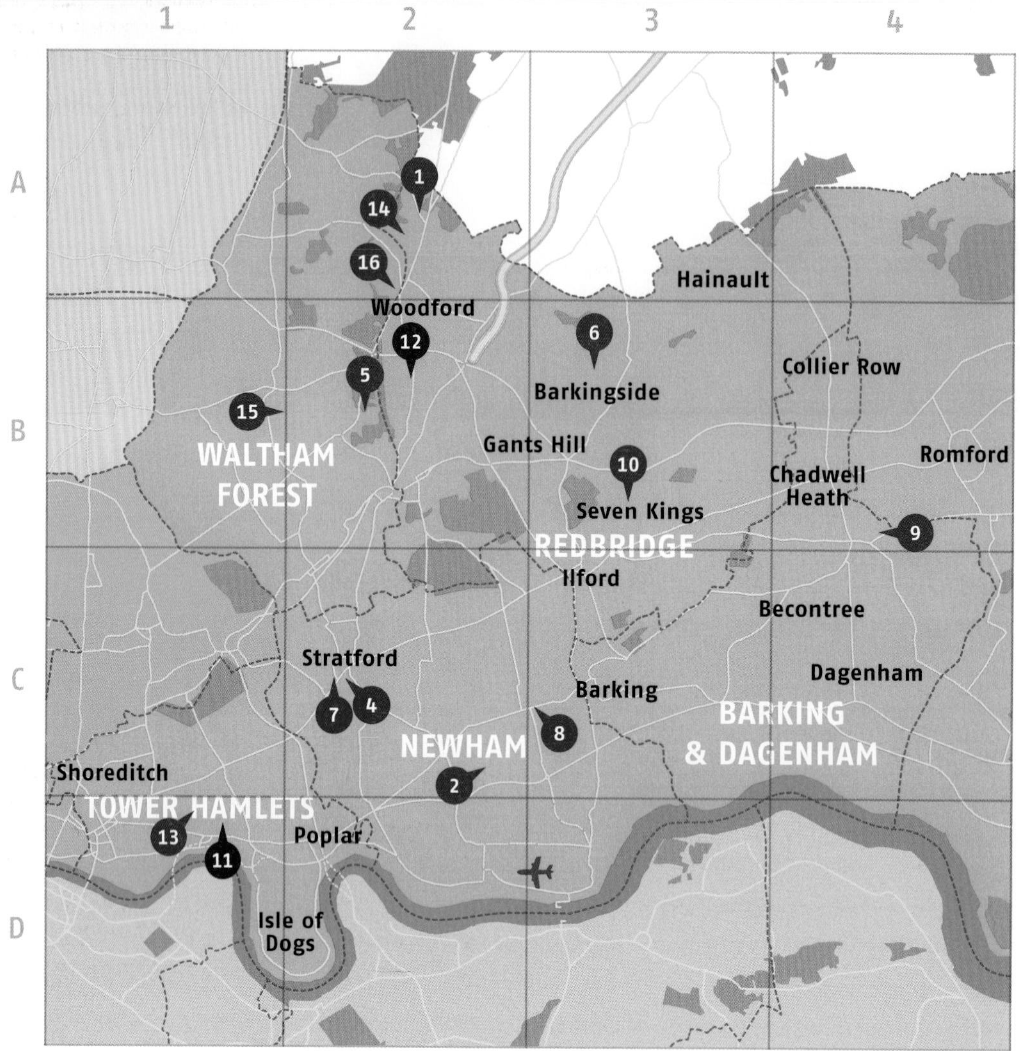
1
2
3
4
A
B
C
D
Hainault
Woodford
Collier Row
Barkingside
Gants Hill
Romford
Chadwell
Heath
Seven Kings
WALTHAM
FOREST
REDBRIDGE
Ilford
Becontree
Stratford
Dagenham
Barking
BARKING
& DAGENHAM
NEWHAM
Shoreditch
TOWER HAMLETS
Poplar
Isle of
Dogs

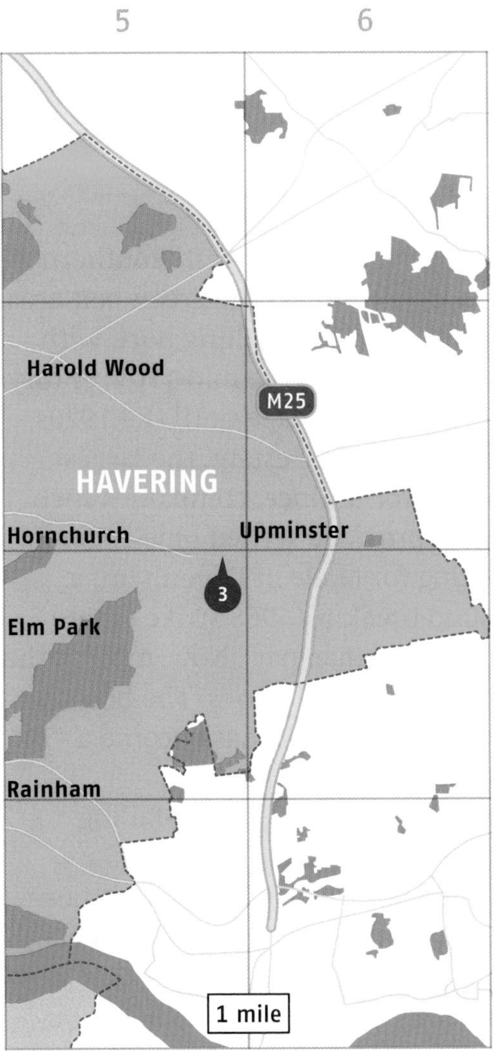
5
6
Harold Wood
M25
HAVERING
Hornchurch
Upminster
3
Elm Park
Rainham
1 mile

EAST

East London and its state schools

Barking & Dagenham

Barking and Dagenham, with the Thames as its southern boundary, stretches north to encompass the green belt area of Chadwell Heath. Barking was once a fishing port, with the country's largest fishing fleet until the mid-19th century. Dagenham was largely an agrarian village until the 1920s and the construction of the Becontree estate, the largest public housing estate in the world. Once, companies such as the Ford Motor Company provided settled blue collar employment (and the setting for Made in Dagenham, a dramatisation of the ground-breaking 1968 strike where female workers campaigned for equal pay). Now, most of the employment is in low-paid service industries. The borough has the cheapest housing in London and has become a magnet for first time buyers.

Robert Clack qv is a top secondary: this once-failing school was captained to success by the now-retired Sir Paul Grant, who took the helm in the late 90s, and is now massively oversubscribed. The huge Sydney Russell School (2,000+ pupils) – becoming an all-through school – was rated outstanding under its previous non-academy incarnation; Barking Abbey, Jo Richardson and All Saints Catholic School are all popular.

William Ford Junior School – linked with Village Infants on the same site – was founded in 1841, when Dagenham was a village surrounded by fields. Manor Infants/Manor Longbridge are also rated outstanding, as is Warren Junior School. Most Barking and Dagenham primary schools are large, with only a couple of faith schools having one form entry, and many with four or more forms in a year group.

Havering

Havering is the most easterly of the London boroughs. Its main town is Romford, a major metropolitan area, but it also includes large areas of green belt land. Romford, whose house prices are expected to rise in anticipation of Crossrail, claims to have one of the largest and longest established markets in the country, established in the 13th century. Hornchurch and Upminster are quiet commuter towns with many 20s and 30s houses and easy access to the City by train and tube. Rainham Marshes nature reserve on the banks of the Thames, closed to the public for over 100 years and used as a military firing range, is now run by the RSPB and is a haven for birds and other wildlife.

Church-goers are privileged in the search for good secondary schools. Coopers' Company and Coburn school qv in Upminster is one of the most popular secondaries and has a 'religious character': it will only consider regular worshippers from any of the major faiths. Admissions arrangements are convoluted: it gives preference to children of staff and former students; a certain percentage of places to those living in specific areas; 10 sport and nine music places. Other high performing secondary schools are both Catholic and both in Upminster: Sacred Heart of Mary girls' school and The Campion boys' school. Both give preference to practising Catholic families living in specific local parishes.

Ardleigh Green Junior and Scott's Primary, both in Hornchurch, are rated outstanding, as is Engayne primary in Upminster. Several Catholic primaries do well: St Peter's in Romford, St Joseph's in Upminster and La Salette in Rainham.

Newham

Newham – home of most of the Olympic Park, including the fabulous Zaha Hadid-designed Aquatic Centre – is also one of the most deprived boroughs in the country. It does however have rapidly improving public transport, including Stratford Station, Docklands Light Railway and – in future – several

Crossrail stations. Plus London City Airport. Stratford is undergoing huge change, with over 10,000 new homes being built around the renamed Queen Elizabeth Olympic Park over the next 20 years. And of course it has the huge Westfield shopping centre – a magnet for most visitors, and a world away from the traditional East End high street.

Plashet School in East Ham is very well thought of, as are St Bonaventure RC school for boys and St Angela's Ursuline Convent school for girls (these two have a joint sixth form). Newham Collegiate Sixth Form Centre qv, which opened in 2014, has rapidly achieved excellent results. The newish selective sixth college, the London Academy of Excellence qv, is in Stratford; it was the brainchild of the heads of the local Kingsford Community School and independent Brighton College, one of its backers. Both of these achieve Oxbridge successes that leave some independent schools floundering. School 21, set up in 2012 by Peter Hyman – once adviser to Tony Blair – is developing into an extremely popular all-through school for 4-18 year olds.

Elmhurst Primary ranks highly, as do Vicarage, Central Park, St Stephen's Primary, St Edward's Catholic Primary and Upton Cross (which has expanded to five form entry on a new site and now has some 1,200 pupils). Tollgate in Plaistow is also rated outstanding, as is St Luke's C of E in Canning Town.

Redbridge

Redbridge is one of the greenest boroughs, with plentiful parks and open spaces, and the wooded expanses of Epping Forest just to its north. The M11 extension – built after years of protest, including an occupied treehouse in a 250 year old chestnut tree – pushes its way south to join the North Circular Road, and the Central line loops round and back again. Ilford, on the main train line to Liverpool Street, developed as a commuter town. South Woodford and Woodford Green have extensive inter-war mock Tudor developments, Wanstead Victorian and Edwardian terraces. Young professionals swap flats in Hoxton and Shoreditch for houses here with gardens and nearby green space.

Woodford County High for girls qv and Ilford County High for boys qv are the local selective grammar schools, with results to match (priority to high achievers who live within the school catchment areas). But there is also a high proportion of non-selective schools rated as outstanding, including Seven Kings School qv, Loxford School, Valentines High, Beal High, Oaks Park High, Chadwell Heath Academy and Trinity Catholic High. Understandably, a large proportion of pupils go on to university.

The primary schools are good too. Christchurch Primary, a secular school in spite of its name, is one of the largest in the country with five forms in each year group. St Bede's RC primary and Our Lady of Lourdes RC primary are high-achieving, as are Redbridge, Nightingale, Churchfields and Gearies.

Tower Hamlets

Tower Hamlets, one of the oldest parts of London (tribal, pre-Roman, silted and swampy at the time), was in more recent times home to most of London's Cockney dock workers. Wapping and the areas along that length of the river were lined with docks and warehouses for the thousands of ships and workers in London's port, characterised as well by Dickensian levels of poverty and crime. Those same docks, winding streets and riverside warehouses now contain very high end flats, served by the best butcher in east London and lively cafés and trendy restaurants (one, for example, in a converted power station), but some areas still have high levels of poverty.

This is a vibrantly multi-ethnic borough – successive

waves of immigrants, including Huguenot refugees, Irish weavers, Ashkenazi Jews and most recently Bangladeshis have congregated here. As well as the largest city farm in the country – the 32 acre Mudchute Park and Farm in the middle of the Isle of Dogs – it has the oldest surviving music hall in the world, Wilton's.

In the 90s it had some of the worst performing schools in the country; now it has some of the best. It reduced absences, set ambitious targets and used its extra funding as a deprived area to attract some high quality teaching staff and heads.

The Stepney All Saints C of E Secondary School qv is one of the most popular secondary schools. Although a CofE school, only a small minority of places are for committed Christians, and the vast majority of pupils, mirroring the ethnic make-up of the area, are Bangladeshi. In 2014 it was caught up in the controversy about Islamic extremism in schools, and downgraded by Ofsted from outstanding to inadequate, primarily over segregation of boys and girls and some sixth form Facebook activity. However, an inspection in October 2015 returned it to its former outstanding status. Mulberry School for Girls, with a similar demographic, is also rated as outstanding, as are Morpeth School and Swanlea School. St Paul's Way Trust, undersubscribed and rated as 'satisfactory' a few years ago, is now, in a new building with greatly improved reports, another of the most sought-after schools in the borough. A recent arrival is ELAM, East London Arts and Music qv, a sixth form music, games design, film and TV academy that has now moved into its own new building at Bromley-by-Bow.

Amongst many popular primary schools are Sir William Burrough qv with its international primary curriculum, Old Palace, Bygrove, Bonner, Old Ford and Clara Grant – interesting that many of the top-performing primaries in this area are secular. A controversial free school, Canary Wharf College (a primary in spite of its name) hit the news for having only two per cent of pupils on free school meals in an area where most schools have 50 per cent, and limiting class sizes to 20. A second College opened in 2014, again with 50 per cent of places for Christian church-goers, and a senior school opened in 2016.

Waltham Forest

Waltham Forest is a borough of contrasts: the area south of the North Circular Road is mostly built-up and urban, with the socially and ethnically mixed population characteristic of inner cities – it includes one of the highest ethnic minority populations in Europe. The reservoirs along the western boundary are being transformed into an urban wetland nature reserve; the northern boundary blends into the edges of Epping Forest, and the area north of the North Circular is rather more suburban and leafy. At the end of the Victoria line, it is increasingly on the radar of those trying to keep ahead of the rising tide of house prices – and Walthamstow features not only the William Morris gallery but God's Own Junkyard, with its neon light creations. Walthamstow Village, the ancient heart of the town, is the site of a 12th-century church, 400-year-old almshouses and roads of highly desirable terraced houses.

Walthamstow School for Girls qv, which goes up to 16, is a flagship secondary; Highams Park is also popular. Leyton Sixth Form College has been judged the best college in London for sport.

St Mary's Catholic Primary in Chingford in the leafy northern part is highly rated, as are Henry Maynard, the massive Hillyfield Primary Academy (with seven classes in a year group and over 1,000 children on two sites), Greenleaf, Coppermill, Handsworth and Dawlish Road.

Bancroft's School

611–627 High Road, Woodford Green, Essex IG8 0RF

020 8505 4821 | stephanie.wallis@bancrofts.org | www.bancrofts.org

Independent	Pupils: 1,107; sixth form: 234
Ages: 7–18	Fees: £15,651 – £19,047 pa

Head: Since 2016, Simon Marshall (early 50s). Formerly headmaster of the English College in Prague and, before that, deputy head academic at UCS Hampstead and, in an earlier incarnation, head of English at KCS Wimbledon. A very calm and incisive communicator who has the underlying confidence to deal in nuance. He believes he has taken over a school which is already performing at a very high level, and his attention seems divided equally between maintaining all that is good, and trying to help all constituencies within the school think of themselves and their ambitions perhaps a little more laterally. No academic slouch himself, having read classics at Cambridge, where he was also a choral exhibitioner and did a PGCE. Thence to Oxford, where he took a degree in English literature and then a MPhil in 18th century studies. A keen mountaineer and runner, he enjoys gardening, music and theatre. Married to Eleanor.

One parent, steeped in the ancien régime, described him as 'a great listener, sensitive to tradition, but definitely working in his ideas. He's greatly liked, and the way he is celebrating arts and humanities is just what Bancroft's needs.'

Head of prep since 2012 Joe Layburn, previously acting head. MA in German literature from University College London, followed by a 15-year career as an investigative journalist and TV reporter, primarily for Channel 4. Retrained as a teacher and joined Bancroft's Prep in 2004. A steady pair of hands, popular with staff, children and parents. Author of a trilogy of children's books. Married with three children; two were educated at Bancroft's from prep onwards and one at a special needs school. Keen on running, cycling and West Ham United.

Entrance: At 7+ into the prep – oversubscribed by about three to one. Testing in English – reading and writing – and maths takes place on beanbags. Children seen (and offered doughnuts) in small groups with head and deputy – it's 'as informal and low key as possible'.

Some 60 pupils come up from the prep school to the senior school at 11. Around 500 apply for 65 additional places. 'It's nice to be wanted,' says the head, 'but we want to stay well away from complacency'. There are entrance tests in maths and English plus interviews – 'we need to fashion something more imaginative,' he says. 'We're working on it.' In practice around a third of those whose first choice is Bancroft's will get in. Umpteen feeders, though several from St Aubyn's, Loyola and Woodford Green Prep. Around a half from state primaries. Computer-based aptitude test added for 2021 entry in response to COVID (maths and English tests will be shorter).

Candidates for the sixth form sit the school's own entrance exam in two proposed A level subjects, need six 7s at GCSE plus the usual references. Around 20 places at this level – very few (around 10 per cent) leave.

Exit: Around 90 per cent of the prep move to the senior school. Around 10 per cent leave after GCSEs. Twelve Oxbridge places in 2020; 23 medics and dentists. Most popular current destinations are Nottingham, Bath, LSE, King's College London, Imperial, Queen Mary, Leeds, Exeter, Durham, Loughborough and Warwick.

Latest results: In 2020, 93 per cent 9-7 at GCSE; 78 per cent A*/A at A level (96 per cent A*-B). In 2019 (the last year when exams took place), 83 per cent 9-7 at GCSE; 66 per cent A*/A at A level.

Teaching and learning: Notable results across the board. Many go on to study medicine or engineering at top universities. The head is emphatic about the hard work and deep commitment of staff, but places a big emphasis too on the work ethic of pupils. Maths and physics are stellar, and all the sciences excellent. Arts, languages and humanities results are, by any standard, very good. This slight asymmetry has less to do with teaching, about which all parties wax lyrical, than with the nature of the constituency: many families here are first-generation users of independent schools, and there is an emphasis on traditional 'respectable' professions. One gets the sense the head may be keen gently to nudge pupils into believing there are more destinies for themselves than they might sometimes imagine. 'Bancroft's boys and girls have such heart and power,' he says, 'such creativity and imagination.'

No obviously weak links at GCSE but maths and science again at the heart of success; computer science now an exam option. Perhaps rather fewer taking the more obviously creative subjects – art and music, for instance, or DT. Drama is now in the curriculum, but getting real momentum behind these is less about facilities (which are good) than about winning over sceptics. It all takes time. Modern languages have been the beneficiaries of this patient dedication. German, French and Spanish are all on offer from year 8; Russian becomes available in year 9 and Mandarin in the sixth form. A particular, enlightened feature is that subjects can be chosen not, as elsewhere, from 'blocks' but from the whole curriculum. Given that Bancroft's is not a rich school, and that staff are required to teach an average 31 periods per week, this flexibility is all the more impressive.

The library, revamped with a stylish mezzanine floor beautifully integrated into the whole, is a proper scholarly resource – a place where pupils actually sit quietly and read

A terrific learning environment. The library, revamped with a stylish mezzanine floor beautifully integrated into the whole, is a proper scholarly resource – a place where pupils actually sit quietly and read. Given that library is all too often a euphemism for 'IT suite' these days, this delving among books redounds greatly to the credit of both staff and pupils. The latter evidently appreciate the librarians– 'they are fantastic – they get in anything you need'. The sixth form has a quiet study area and the Great Hall is used, amongst much else, for societies, debates and visiting speakers. IT everywhere – lots of rooms with new PCs, including a tiptop language lab.

Prep classrooms busy, not over-orderly and relaxed – we wanted to look at the displays, all of which seemed interesting and not as predictable as they so often are. We also approved some of the interesting work in progress, especially the lesson on moulds – 'We had to throw them away as they were beginning to smell,' was a rueful observation. Year 6 has critical thinking lessons – 'to expand our minds, to think out of the box, to widen our imagination,' we were told, earnestly. We were impressed by the sensible 'traffic light' system whereby pupils assess their grasp of what they have learnt and where they need help.

Learning support and SEN: Learning support department screens all at 7+ and 11+. School has a dedicated SENCo and there are two part-timers in assistance. All new staff get some training in spotting those with learning difficulties but the head is mindful that all staff need encouragement to stay alert to those with learning difficulties: these will mostly be mild dyslexics and all will be given some kind of individual support – the precise nature of which depends on need, but may well involve one-to-one time. Lower sixth get help to 'develop individual learning skills'. 'They are wonderfully flexible over special needs,' said a parent.

The arts and extracurricular: CCF is huge, very popular and enthusiastically pursued by those who surprise themselves by how much they get out of it, girls as well as boys – 'It's taught me how to get on with people I'd never mix with normally'; 'It's good that the sixth form help with it – you can have a bit of a laugh with them.' Thriving DofE. Over 200 pupils are involved in it with 30 taking gold – 'doing my gold was the hardest thing I've ever done,' said one girl, 'and the best.' Also a Sea Scout group with cubs and scouts.

Equally, steadily increased provision for arts across the school. Music and drama enthusiastic and popular – annual concert in Drapers' Hall the big annual event, with bands, solo performances and musical mix the main features. HM particularly enthused (moved, really) by the recent TAAL production – a pan-Asian body run by the Hindu, Muslim, Buddist and Sikh Society, but involving pupils of all ethnic groups – which embraced dance and music of all kinds. 'It was an explosion of energy and creativity,' he says, 'and it tells a big story.' Vast range of instruments studied, with eight classical concerts each year. Jazz, rock and other genres all celebrated in addition to the main and chamber orchestras. A suite of Apple Macs to support composition. Two big drama spaces – the Great Hall and a fine performing arts centre. A recent triumphant production of Les Misérables but also Amadeus and Sweeney Todd. All year 7s and 8s do drama as part of the curriculum, and there is house drama production as well. Productions at Edinburgh Fringe Festival.

Art, electronics and DT departments are buzzy spaces. Art is well displayed and the studios are wonderful oases of light and space, as well as excellently equipped. Excellent outcomes for the seriously committed – one recent leaver having secured a spot at Central St Martins. Pupils are given considerable latitude to be creative in design. After a period of staff turnover, DT is becoming more embedded and is now on offer for A level. Like so many schools, the cultural leap to move away from the old woodwork/metalwork shop mentality hasn't happened overnight, but the head sees an emerging synergy not merely between art, DT and electronics but extending to physics and the sciences, with big potential growth in product design.

Sport: Sports are 'big' and well resourced. Large playing fields on site plus vast sports hall with 25m pool. Five minutes' drive away is school's own West Grove with pitches, courts, tracks etc. Strong in all major sports – hockey, rugby, netball, cricket and tennis. Achievement to match – triumphs in netball, rugby and cricket as well as tours in these and hockey to, eg, Canada, Singapore/Malaysia, South Africa and Barbados. Historic complaints that sport is too elitist have become less strident but not disappeared: 'It's too often the same brilliant sportsmen getting the limelight,' said one parent. The school has taken these seriously and evolved B and C teams, along with soccer. There are practical constraints, not least finding the necessary facilities and fixtures with other schools. 'I know they're working on this,' said one parent, 'and not before time. It's our one grouse about the school.'

Like every other school, helping youngsters to make sensible use of IT is a preoccupation for teachers and parents, but as HM says, 'adults don't always find it easy either'

There is a serious wish on the part of the head that sport should reflect the values the school is trying to impart. 'We're properly proud of all the sporting success,' he says, 'but we want to create ways in which the best kind of team experience is genuinely attainable to all who seek it. Sport should offer all our pupils a medium through which they can cultivate the kinds of strength and conditioning which will sustain them throughout their lives.'

Ethos and heritage: Founded in 1737 by the Drapers' Company on behalf of Francis Bancroft as a school for poor boys; moved to Woodford from Mile End in 1889 into the present large and imposing red-brick Victorian gothic revival building – clearly designed to impress, with serious scholarly credentials by architect, Sir Arthur Blomfield, also responsible for Selwyn College, Cambridge. This is one of his more benign and attractive buildings, with towers, crenellations and oriel windows, a splendid central quad and admirably generous corridors which, though originally intended for 200 boys, still feel spacious for today's quadrupled numbers. Twisty brick staircases and leaded lights which grab eager 10-year-olds immediately – 'I chose it because it was like Hogwarts.'

Large Great Hall – typical of date and type. Excellent Courtyard Building with colonnaded atrium and sitting area, dining room (all seniors eat together, although the sixth form can exercise the option to eat in their common room). The food gets good press, too, in contrast to the dismal recollections of one old boy now a parent ('I'm pretty jealous, actually'). Some 1960s add-ons but much better later additions (such as enormous multi-purpose sports hall) and adjoining buildings, eg vast head's house now used for admin and offices too, with head's garden open to everyone for quiet time and 'well respected'. Nice new physics labs and modern language rooms and DT suite.

Integral chapel one of the best bits (complete with much-loved chaplain who is, says a parent, 'just extraordinary – you should hear what my children say about him. They leave chapel filled with fresh understanding about the need for mutual respect'). Each year group comes once weekly for an ecumenical service. Brass plaques to former heads and a vast stained glass east window set the tone for the services, which are inclusive in all ways, given the mix of pupils. Chapel also used for arts events – words and music etc, a classy extracurricular feature here.

Prep is in two conjoined, inviting-looking, modern red-brick buildings at the lower right hand side of the main school playing fields – two-storeyed and with big windows. Newish science, drama, music and DT rooms, a good-sized hall with flexible seating – lots of IT and new laptops. The library, recently refurbished, is well stocked and a good mix of fact and fiction. Outside space good and super all-weather surface for littlies with monster chess set and apparatus – not surprisingly, 'Everyone loves coming out here.'

Parental tributes to general efficiency of school and its communications. Sense of order, purposeful activity and common sense all-pervasive.

OB notables include Dennis Quilley, Sir Frederick Warner, Sir Neil McFarlane, Hari Kunzru, Adam Foulds, Yolanda Browne, Andrew Saul, Anita Anand, Lord Pannick QC, Samantha Spiro and Mike Lynch.

Pastoral care, inclusivity and discipline: Unstinting and uniform praise for pastoral care is very rare, and yet this is what our enquiries to a range of parents and pupils revealed. Tributes to the teaching staff, overall friendliness, care and attention given to individuals pour from everyone and are a delight to hear: 'My teacher is amazing – he's given me extra lessons every week'; 'They'll help with anyone – not just the Oxbridge candidates'; 'The teacher gave my daughter as much time as she needed when she was struggling.'

Staff respond especially to the wholehearted and aspirational nature of their pupils, who are so laudably devoid of a sense of entitlement. The system which facilitates such praise is based around form tutors – usually of between 13 and 17 pupils. There are also houses for competitive purposes. With 200 plus pupils in each, the heads of house and their deputies have a formidable challenge in knowing their charges.

The teachers seem also to believe pupils are overwhelmingly biddable and friendly. 'Of course,' says the head, 'teenagers can make mistakes.' Like every other school, helping youngsters to make sensible use of IT is a preoccupation for teachers and parents, but as HM says, 'adults don't always find it easy either.' He is trying to encourage a pastoral style which can be more generally proactive and – it follows on – pupils find it easy and unthreatening to volunteer fears and anxieties.

Pupils and parents: From as far away as Potter's Bar, Winchmore Hill and Cheshunt, though most from between 10 and 20 minutes' drive away. Transport from local tube station to encourage pupils to look out of town towards green space for schooling. Vast ethnic and social intake – 'very well handled by school,' say parents. Most parents first-time buyers who 'work very hard to pay fees'.

Money matters: Bancroft's has always sought to keep its fees low. There's been a hike recently which has led to some mutterings, but the HM says ruefully, 'It's always a dilemma. We don't want to change our identity, but we must be able to plan for the long term.' He feels some of the building projects of earlier times could have been better conceived had there been less of the short-termism which customarily happens when budgets are too tight.

Fifteen Drapers' scholarships offered annually at 11+ worth a quarter to a half of fees. No means-testing – based solely on performance at entrance exams. Also music scholarships worth half or quarter fees plus free tuition in one instrument. Several Francis Bancroft scholarship awards – means-tested but with a generous financial threshold, worth up to full fees, based on a sliding scale dependent on family income. Bancroft's Foundation set up in 2012 to mark 275th anniversary has raised significant amounts to increase means-tested provision – enough to fund six Foundation scholars.

The last word: An outstanding school – bright children, dedicated staff, and one of the most remarkable heads we've met. Given all its strengths, it deserves to be much more widely celebrated, although a deep part of its charm (and virtue) is that boastfulness and self-advertisement is off-limits. 'We can never repay what this school has done for our children,' said one parent. We wanted to shout it out from the rafters – this place is superb.

Brampton Manor Academy

2

Roman Road, London E6 3SQ

020 7540 0500 | info@bramptonmanor.org | www.bramptonmanor.org

State	Ages: 11–18	Pupils: 2261

Executive Principal: Since 2008, executive principal, Dr Dayon Olukoshi, OBE (50s). Nigerian by birth, he was educated at Federal Government College Sokoto and started work as a teacher in the UK in 1992. Previously deputy head of Phoenix Academy (formerly Phoenix High School) in White City, he took over at Brampton prior to its transformation into an academy. Now heads the Brampton Manor Academy Trust. A devout Christian, he is cut in the motivational-speaker mode, with a well-tailored, upbeat, energetic delivery. 'I consider every challenge I have faced as an opportunity to excel rather than an obstacle to overcome,' he says. Awarded OBE in 2016 for services to education, he regards himself and his team as 'missionaries' for education, and tells students, 'It's not about the way you look. It's not about your skin colour or whether you fit in. It's about how ambitious you are – because we are in the business of making your dreams come true.' An approach that clearly works. 'We don't see a lot of the head,' commented one student, 'but he gives a speech at the beginning of the year, which is very inspiring.' Married with young children.

Entrance: Hugely oversubscribed at every stage. In year 7, entry criteria are similar to other Newham community comprehensives, with siblings and distance from the gates given priority in the rush (about 3000 apply for 390 places). It is, however, admission to its catchment-free sixth form – some travelling for up to two hours to attend – that's really cut-throat. At this juncture, all applicants are interviewed; the successful will be predicted Grade 7 or above in their intended A level subjects, generally averaging 7-9s in the rest.

Exit: About 70 per cent of the year 7 intake leave post GCSE, generally because they don't meet sixth form entry requirements. Those who make it through, like new arrivals, are more or less guaranteed a place at a leading university. The school is celebrated for its Oxbridge success – with 41 offers (38 places) from the 130 who applied for entry in 2019. Part of this is due to the high-achieving intake (only nine Oxbridge offers went to pupils who'd been at the school throughout), but equally importantly to the culture of high aspiration. 'The secret is having the students believe in themselves,' says the head. Self-belief is not, of course, sufficient, and 'outstanding' (Ofsted) teaching (largely from Russell Group-qualified teachers) is complemented with a dedicated university access team, who devote their entire time to admissions, including preparation for interviews. Well over half the sixth form go on to Russell Group, including significant numbers to Imperial, LSE, Durham and UCL.

Latest results: Although, unusually, the school won't provide percentages of 9-7s at GCSE it is clear that results overall are fairly sparkling – in 2019, 37 students got 10 grade 9s. At A level, two thirds of all grades A*-A (with an impressive 15 students achieving three A*s or more).

Teaching and learning: A strong focus throughout on the rigorously intellectual, with a traditional academic curriculum at GCSE, including three sciences, three languages (French, German, Spanish) and computer science. In 2019, over 85 per cent sat the EBacc (the government's basket of academic subjects), and the school's added value is one of the highest in the country. The school's motto is 'success through effort and determination', and hard work is constantly underlined by staff, who share the head's zeal, but the quality of teaching sugars the pill and students clearly appreciate their efforts. 'Teachers love to help you,' said one Year 10. 'Without the teachers at Brampton, I'd never have applied to Oxford,' said a successful applicant. 'They gave me the confidence to consider it.'

The well-used study centre is open from 6am to 6pm. 'By 6.15am, there are often as many as 80 students already at their desks,' says the head

To ensure all receive the best possible support, the head overstaffs in core subjects so pupils are never taught by supply teachers.

Sixth form, housed in its own spacious (air-conditioned) building, was established in 2012 with the aim of 'transforming the progression rates of disadvantaged students to the UK's top universities'. In its first year, one pupil received an Oxbridge offer; today it's about 14 per cent. Twenty-one academic subjects on offer, including further maths, and sixth formers carefully monitored, with regular testing and half-termly tracking. Studious behaviour is encouraged by keeping all on site throughout the day, and the well-used study centre – open from 6am to 6pm – often sees the industrious glued to their seats for much of that time. 'By 6.15am, there are often as many as 80 students already at their desks,' says the head. The expected workload – 'the amount of work we get is crazy' – does not suit all, but for the ambitious undoubtedly delivers results.

Learning support and SEN: Students facing difficulties receive holistic intervention from an extensive specialist team, including bilingual and epilepsy-trained staff. Year 7s struggling with English and maths are boosted by a reading programme and smaller class sizes, and all who need it benefit from a forensic and expansive approach (differentiated curriculum, supported homework, etc). Wheelchair-friendly corridors, lifts, and a well-equipped sensory room mean a wide range of needs can be catered for.

The arts and extracurricular: The school has specialist performing arts academy status, with generous media rooms for performing, recording and dance and a good range of creative and performing arts at GCSE (fine art, graphic design, photography, design technology and music) and A level (art and design, drama, music), plus plenty of opportunities to perform and create, with steel band, band club, choir, school musical, artist in residence, and creative writing club, as well as regular cultural outings (Old Vic workshops, Frieze art fair, etc).

Extracurricular seen as part of the high-aspiring package, so pupils' engagement in after-school clubs is tracked. 'If you're called for interview at Oxford or Cambridge,' says the head, 'they know how clever you are, but they want to know how interesting you are.' Activities for younger years include everything from Christian Union, newspaper club and young philosophers to scriptwriting, beauty blogging and gardening (on the Brampton Manor farm), alongside subject-related clubs. Sixth formers devote Wednesday afternoons to 'enrichment', ranging from street dance to cooking on a budget, mock bar trials and Mandarin. Debating is major, producing regular finalists in Oxford, Cambridge and English-Speaking Union tournaments. A multitude of trips and visits, with many intended to raise academic ambitions, so year 7s tour the classics department at Cambridge, sixth formers enjoy residential stays in Bath and Warwick and outings to the Law Society and the Royal Institute of British Architects.

Sport: Sport important and wide ranging (girls' and boys' football and cricket, basketball, climbing, trampolining, fitness, netball, rugby and rowing) and teams regularly triumph in local and county competitions.

Ethos and heritage: Located in one of London's poorest boroughs, Brampton Manor is now Newham's second-largest school, which means it can be somewhat intimidating. 'It's a bit scary,' said one student, 'but you soon get used to it.' 'Sometimes I wish it were slightly smaller,' commented another, 'but the advantage is you get to meet a lot of new people.' Tracing its roots back to Brampton Girls' School (built on the current site between 1957 and 1962), it converted to an 11-16 academy in 2011. An intended intake of 420 means building work is ongoing, with the recent addition of a large sports hall, and the conversion of the original sports hall into a drama studio and theatre. Well-equipped library with 15,000 books and 80 computers.

Architecturally, the school resembles any number of 21st-century academies in its bland modernity, but its interior decoration is intended to inspire, with sixth-form walls plastered with photographs of successful students. Younger students' progress is trumpeted, too, in the annual Red Awards ceremony, where 'parents come and watch and the pupil gets a picture with the head,' according to one happy winner.

Pastoral care, inclusivity and discipline: A strong pastoral infrastructure centres on form tutors, supported by a progress leader, behaviour support manager, and personal tutors. Mental health tended to by four full-time counsellors. 'If you don't address the basic emotional needs of children, they can't learn,' says the head. 'It's just common sense.'

Discipline is tight but generally not considered oppressive. 'What you need is a discipline structure where the boundaries are clear,' says the head. An approach applied, too, to mums and dads, who can be summoned in if it is felt they're 'making excuses' for an absent or misbehaving child. 'The school challenge the parents,' said one mother, 'but most are overwhelmingly grateful they care.' Draconian policy on mobile phone use, and phones must not be seen in the school. If found, they're instantly removed – for the entire term. 'The phone is not oxygen,' says the head firmly. Bullying dealt with swiftly.

'You need a discipline structure where the boundaries are clear,' says the head. Mums and dads can be summoned in if it is felt they're 'making excuses' for their child

Behaviour is 'exemplary' (Ofsted) and to ensure it remains so, the school extends its eagle eye beyond the gates. 'It's important our students are good role models, ambassadors for the school. It matters to us the way pupils conduct themselves. This is not just an exam factory; we're about developing young people.'

Younger pupils wear smart navy blue – with 'knee-length' skirts for girls and, if desired, a Shalwar kameez with school badge. Sixth formers, boys and girls, dress in business-like black suits.

Pupils and parents: Nearly all from ethnic minority backgrounds, two-thirds speak English as a second language. Students, however, are confident and articulate. 'My confidence level grew from five per cent to 75 per cent after I came here,' said one year 8. Families generally aspirational and committed to the cause – 'We were amazed and overjoyed when our son got into Cambridge to study medicine,' said one – but where attitudes threaten to hold a student back, the school is quick to intervene. 'We have regular battles with parents who say they're not going to support their daughter moving out of London; we win most of them.'

Money matters: Two thirds of students are on free school meals, with the extra funding dedicated to additional staffing and expert support for university entrance.

The last word: An outsize modern academy, with an exceptional sixth form, producing outstanding university entrance results, and helping all students to achieve their best through hard work and high aspirations.

The Coopers' Company and Coborn School

3

St Mary's Lane, Upminster, Essex RM14 3HS

01708 250500 | info@cooperscoborn.org.uk | www.cooperscoborn.org.uk/

State | **Ages:** 11–18 | **Pupils:** 1461; sixth form: 486

Headteacher: Since March 2019, Sue Hay. A historian, she joined the school in 2013 as deputy head. Previous posts include head of history and assistant head at Greenford High and assistant head at Broadland High.

Entrance: Unusually large number of feeder schools (around 100). Admissions rules and catchment area complicated due to the school's historic links to east London and wish to preserve the principles of the Coopers' Company and Coborn Educational Foundation.

Over 1,000 applications for just 180 places and a fair number go to appeal. Ten sport and nine music places, which hundreds apply for. All other applicants must be actively connected to one of the main world faiths. Some places for children of staff and former students; others by promixity; others to those who live in specific areas including Havering, Brentwood and Billericay.

Most stay on to the sixth form after GCSE. Around 50 places for students from outside but, again, massively popular with over 700 applications. Applicants need at least eight 9-4 grades to be considered for a place, to be sympathetic to the school's Christian character and be willing to uphold its Love as Brethren ethos by giving time to serve the school. Oversubscription criteria prioritise looked after children, highest predicted grades and then availability in specific sets. 'Our sixth form is equivalent to a grammar school, in terms of offering traditional subject choices and the fact that we take the cream of the crop.'

Exit: Around half leave after GCSE for one of three reasons: to study a vocational course at college, to study different subject choices at other local schools or (a few) to take up an apprenticeship. Almost none leave to go into low-paid work. Around three-quarters of sixth formers to university, which is high for the area, of which a third go to Russell Group universities. Particularly popular are Warwick, Bristol, Durham, Birmingham, Bath, Exeter, Loughborough and Imperial. Seven to Oxbridge in 2019.

School provides a range of opportunities to prepare for post school, including careers advice from year 9, conferences, workshops, competitions and special events at universities such as Nottingham and Cambridge. Many go on to study pure science subjects or vocational courses such as medicine, veterinary science and dentistry (four medics in 2019). Other popular subjects include psychology, economics, architecture, art history, journalism, politics and theatre design.

Latest results: In 2019, 36 per cent 9-7 at GCSE; 77 per cent 9-4 in both English and maths. In 2019, 31 per cent A*/A grades (64 per cent A*-B).

Teaching and learning: There's an assumption that students will do well here ('It's built into their DNA that they will want to succeed') and they do, with the school consistently achieving near top GCSE results nationally. They are especially strong in English language, English lit, mathematics and art and design, but pupils also do exceptionally well in RS, DT, textiles technology and music. The most popular GCSE choices are history, German, geography and sport/PE, and fair numbers also choose Spanish and French.

At sixth form, there's a wide curriculum of traditional subjects plus newer courses – media studies, psychology and politics. Popular choices are the sciences, especially biology ('We buck the national trend when it comes to STEM subjects a A level,' says head), business studies, history, maths and psychology.

Spanish, French, German or Mandarin from year 7 (parents get to state a preference when they apply to the school), with a second language introduced in year 8 'Modern languages are big strength of the school,' said one parent, reflecting the views of others. Pupils are setted for maths in year 7 and there's an element of setting in languages and sciences at GSCE. Homework considered an essential part of shaping pupils' academic experience, particularly in relation to independent learning and thinking skills.

Teachers renowned for going the extra mile both inside the classroom and out. 'No teacher gets an interview until they've taught a lesson which we find to be good or outstanding.' A fair amount of emailing goes on after hours, for which both students and parents are very grateful.

Despite high results, the school is always working on improving grades and has introduced Go4Schools, an online tracking programme, enabling parents and teachers to login at any time to monitor how the student is doing, with both individual and overall grades, target grades and how they can improve, enabling all three parties to monitor progress and make any necessary interventions to keep grades on track. 'It really helps cement the three-way partnership between students, parents and teachers,' says school and parents agree. 'We have a good idea of both where our children are relative to where they need to be,' said one parent. The bottom 15 students in the year are provided with extra measures, as are the 15 at the top.

Although the school is very academic, we found it to be the antithesis of an exam factory, offering a broad and liberal education, with a major emphasis on extracurricular activities that all students are expected to get involved in. While PE accounts for the majority of the 142 clubs on offer, other subjects include music, drama, IT and all the academic subjects right through to beekeeping, chicken keeping and robot building. Many of the school teams enter national competitions – 94 of them the year we visited, reaching national finals in 33 of them and world finals in two. The debating team reached the finals at Oxford University.

Learning support and SEN: SEN has a strong team of six staff members, mainly providing classroom-based help for children with issues ranging from dyslexia to autism, although less than one per cent of these have an EHC plan. 'For major SEN issues, other schools in the borough are better equipped.'

The arts and extracurricular: Well-equipped art studios, with a studio offering individual cubicles for pupils who need a designated area in which to work. An 'open house' policy approach encourages independent work and, along with the clearly outstanding levels of work on display, creates a wonderful 'art school' atmosphere. Pupils consistently have work displayed in exhibitions around the country.

Drama standards are high, with two roomy practice areas, including a state-of-the-art renovated theatre, with retracted seating. Plenty of performances throughout the year, including one main annual performance – Singing in the Rain the year we visited.

Music also strong, with five school orchestras (including an all-ability one), two choirs and regular ensembles and concerts. Expect brass band more than rock music 'as we like to keep things traditional,' says head. Around 180 students are taught instrumental lessons in school. Students take part in music festivals and competitions, as well as playing at significant events such as the Lord Mayor's Banquet, and at a more local level within school, for example during assemblies. The inclusive and supportive ethos of the school means you never get students saying, 'I don't think I'm good enough to play in front of my friends.'

Applicants need to be sympathetic to the school's Christian character and be willing to uphold its Love as Brethren ethos by giving time to serve the school

Huge range of extracurricular choice, covering almost every conceivable area, from chess to fishing – many instigated and are run by pupils. 'The amount of opportunities is amazing – everyone tries something they never thought they would,' said one student. School trips are also big here, with around 40 domestic and 23 international ones every year. Besides the sport-based ones, there are language trips (year 8) and exchange trips (year 10) to support Spanish, German, Mandarin and French and other trips to explore interesting places such as Namibia and Botswana.

Sport: This is the number one co-ed state school for sport, if you take as the criterion the number of national-level finals reached across all sports. Also regularly enters for international events, with the triathlon team having reached the world finals, coming second mixed team, the year we visited. Students took part in the opening ceremony of the 2012 Olympics and were also involved in the handover of the Olympic Flame for the Rio Olympics. Regular competitions against leading independent schools, especially in athletics, cross-country, badminton and swimming. Not surprisingly, the students we spoke to were deeply proud of the school's exceptional achievements and aptitude.

The rich curriculum ranges from circuit gym training to trampolining, cricket and netball to indoor rowing, and PE remains compulsory throughout the school years, even at sixth form. Facilities, including a swimming pool, are impressive and sports trips are notable, including rugby tours to New Zealand and Australia, athletics training in Lanzarote and tennis training in Florida. 'The attention to detail in the coaching is second to none,' said one parent. 'Nobody is left out, with everyone given a chance to thrive,' said another.

Ethos and heritage: A rich history dating back to 1536 when it was first established as a free school for boys. Its name came in 1552 when the Coopers' Company was asked to take over the running of the school. It was then located in Stepney, Tower Hamlets. In 1891, it joined foundations with the Coborn school for boys and girls and remained at sites at Mile End and Bow until it moved to Upminster in 1971. 'Our first students would have seen Shakespeare's plays.'

Bad behaviour is simply 'uncool', students told us; the rules are so well embedded into school life that nobody really thinks of the school as that strict

Now situated a good distance from the main road amid 25 acres of greenery, and home to a pond visited by ducks and geese, the school feels spacious, exceptionally neat and tidy and well cared for. And although some of the main school buildings from the 70s are looking tired, modernisation and development have seen new buildings regularly erected since the 80s, the latest being a sixth form block.

The school motto, Love as Brethren, appears quite literally in shining lights as you walk in the school and you won't find a student who doesn't believe it's central to school life here, with many using the hashtag LasB when they sign off emails or post on social media. We found the atmosphere to be happy and thoughtful, with students displaying a healthy level of boisterousness during break times, but heads down during class.

Pastoral care, inclusivity and discipline: Students describe the school as being a 'protective cloak' and 'like a family,' with the young people looking out for each other and staff on hand to help with any issues students may have. The school buys into a student counselling service and clearly takes mental health issues seriously. A house system helps create vertical links, as well as the horizontal year groupings. Peer to peer mentoring, and around 150 sixth formers work with younger pupils.

Plenty of leadership opportunities, with a democratic process selecting school captains from year 12 pupils, who must apply for this prestigious position. The one boy and one girl selected hold office throughout their final year. School council plays a key role in the decision-making processes – including the appointment of senior staff. Pupils are given a sense of importance and are consulted on important developments. Reward system is fully utilised, including housepoints, certificates, postcards and phone calls home, letters from head and spotlight in assembly.

Not much room for making mistakes here, however, with zero tolerance of bad behaviour and very high expectations of conduct. These expectations, and the punishments for failing to adhere to them, are all outlined in both a contract that students have to sign before coming to the school, and a visually friendly charter. Staff are trained in them too, so that there is complete consistency, and parents are also expected to be on board. 'If students don't meet the standards, they can expect serious sanctions. We're quite happy to run Saturday detentions, for example, and would exclude.' Indeed, school had permanently excluded a student the week before our visit for intimidating behaviour towards a staff member, although such exclusions are rare. Talking when you should be listening, or not focusing in class, are considered as bad as writing on school walls. Other no-nos are mobile phones (except in sixth form), eating outside allocated areas and failing to adhere to uniform rules, with not a silly haircut or rolled up skirt in sight. But while it might all sound draconian, we found complete buy-in from parents and students. Bad behaviour here is simply 'uncool', students told us, with one pointing out that the rules are so well embedded into school life that in reality, nobody really thinks of the school as that strict. Bullying rare because, according to students, 'mocking just isn't what we do here.'

Pupils and parents: Most students from aspirational families. Around 80 per cent white middle class, the rest of a mixture of ethnic minorities. Although it's a Christian school, there's an eclectic mix from all recognised world religions.

Many parents are supportive of the school and help out at school events, with an active PA of about 30 members – good for a secondary state school. They arrange various fundraising events including a monthly sale of supermarket vouchers to parents and staff and they had just raised enough funds for a new minibus when we visited. We found pupils to be articulate, grounded, respectful and polite – traits for which they are known throughout the local community. They are very proud of their school, as well as extremely appreciative of having a place there. Everyone is welcoming – greeting visitors with smiles and hellos, saying thank you, holding doors open and even singing to themselves as they pass by.

Money matters: The school allocates £10k to assist pupils that need help and also provides music and sports grants of up to £500 through a bursary system from the Coopers' Company and Coborn Educational Foundation.

The last word: World class in the true sense of the word, this school is a dynamic, exciting place to learn, preparing students for successful lives. Dazzling reputation in the local community and largely responsible for increased house prices in the Upminster area. 'If you're not one of these things – academic, sporty or musical – it's probably not the school for you,' pointed out one parent, whilst students say you need to be willing to put in more time than regular school hours and more commitment than the bare minimum. 'There's no room for just plodding along here,' explained one. But for those that fit the mould, it's outstanding.

Principal: Since July 2020, Matt Sheldon. Previously at Garden International School in Malaysia for five years, where he was assistant head teacher (school culture and partnerships). Studied University of Newcastle and SOAS.

Entrance: Online application in which students' creativity and motivation is assessed. If the school is satisfied about these, applicants are invited to an assessment day. This includes a one-to-one interview and a problem-solving group activity with people they've never met before – the school here is looking for 'collaboration, integrity, communication'. Those applying to the music pathway must also do a performance. Once the day is finished, applicants are scored out of five, and only when it's identified the high scorers does the school look at their academic record and references.

Exit: Around 50 per cent to university or conservatoire: destinations have included Manchester, Newcastle, Goldsmith's, University of East London, Liverpool Institute of Performing Arts, BIMM, Leeds College of Music, the Academy of Contemporary Music. Most students on music or music-related courses. The remainder to a variety of apprenticeships or employment with companies such as BBC Radio 1 and 1Xtra, Odd Child Music, PMR Records, Sony, Warner, Universal Music, Apple and Spotify.

The school supports former trainees by allowing them access to ELAM rehearsal studios after they've left and by appointing some as ELAM 'ambassadors'. It also actively uses social media to promote the work of both current and former trainees. 'Our son feels that ELAM has provided him with an invaluable stepping stone towards his goal of being a professional performer,' wrote a grateful parent.

Occasionally students have dropped out owing to a misconception of what ELAM is about and the hard work and commitment that will be expected of them – we gathered that this had particularly applied to the Gaming pathway, perhaps unsurprisingly. School is therefore currently strengthening its initial assessment and induction process to ensure that all trainees thoroughly understand what's involved in 'turning the thing you like doing into the thing you do for work every day'.

Teaching and learning: ELAM's ethos is straightforward: to enable young people to succeed in the creative industries through offering the right skills training plus access to high quality professional opportunities. 'There's often no straightforward route into the creative industries, so we're trying to create a clearer pathway, especially for those who can't afford to work unpaid until they get their foot in the door. It's vital not just to help students get their qualifications, but to get them started on the next step.'

The school originally offered music only, but now ELAM students can opt for one of three pathways: music, games design, or film and television production. Music trainees study for the BTec level 3 extended diploma in music (now also offered at Reach Academy Feltham in a new partnership). Games and film students study for the University of Arts London level 3 extended diploma in creative media production & technology. Both are equivalent to three A levels in UCAS tariff points and teaching time.

Having the different specialisms housed within the same school 'creates a great dynamism, and the trainees collaborate with each other.'

Everything taught here is underpinned by industry demand. 'The UK's creative sector is growing at a humungous rate. Music punches well above its weight in this country. Film and TV are going through the roof, not least because a high number of American productions are made here to take advantage of generous tax breaks. And there's a huge, huge industry demand for gaming skills.' From the outset, the school's approach has been to work with industry to define the curriculum. Universal Music UK was a founding partner and still offers 'unbelievably fantastic' support. Other partners include Decca, Lovebox, Virgin EMI, Abbey Road Studios, Polydor, Machinima SBOC – and more.

Trainees are worked hard from the off, and quickly come to relish the challenge of rising to professional level standards and deadlines. 'Before I came to ELAM I knew nothing about making games,' mused a year 12 student as he showed us an impressive virtual environment he'd created set in a submarine, 'but it's hands on here, you're thrown in at the deep end, it's about constant improvement. Coming here is one of the best things that's happened to me. It's amazing.' Teaching universally praised – 'They're brilliant professionals, they don't have to be teachers!' – but students were adamant that there was nothing relaxed about it. Meeting deadlines was hectic and often stressful, we were told, but they liked the professionalism of it. 'It's like you're an intern for a job.' 'They'll tell you if your work is rubbish. They're blunt with you and honest, and I think that's the best thing.' 'The learning here is quick, they don't mess around.'

'The stuff they teach us is relevant. I have these moments when I'm using the maths I'm learning in my gaming and it's really exciting'

Understandably, perhaps, some parents need to be convinced that the school is right for their child, particularly those whose offspring are academically successful and could have joined a more conventional sixth form; but once their child is here they appear to be very much won over. A parent of a student on the music pathway told us, 'The school does everything it can to provide the very best tuition, not just in music but in every discipline involved in the professional music industry. Above all, it teaches the importance of collaboration and the necessity of taking a collaborative approach. ELAM could not provide a better grounding for somebody looking to make music a career – whether as a performer or in other aspects of the industry.'

Maths and English are compulsory here, and an intrinsic part of the school's mission to enable young people to be industry ready. 'They have to be able to express themselves clearly and be comfortable with handling data – these days, the taste makers are the ones who can analyse trends.' Students who didn't achieve at least a 4 at GCSE must retake. School has a 100 per cent success rate for English resits; maths currently at 60 per cent. Those who have already passed these GCSEs when they arrive can opt to do either A level maths and/or English, or a level 3 qualification in quantitative reasoning plus the EPQ – both are equivalent to an AS. School is unapologetic about these aspects of the provision, but readily concedes that not all trainees have full enthusiasm for them, and some of the young people admitted as much. 'I had to resit my maths, and the work for English is killing me, I'm not gonna lie,' sighed one, 'but I enjoy that I get to do the music I want to do, and get to meet industry people.' And personal reluctance notwithstanding, all the trainees agreed that the school was right to insist on it. 'The stuff they teach us, whether you like it or not, it's relevant,' said one. 'A level maths is very applicable to game design,' said another, who came to ELAM with a full crop of top grades at GCSE. 'I have these small moments when I'm using the maths I'm learning in my gaming and it's really exciting.'

Learning support and SEN: Designated SEND team offers one-to-one, group and in-class support to the small number of students – around five per cent – who need it.

The arts and extracurricular: Every student is given a mentor from their chosen industry, and additionally all trainees do two weeks' work experience every year with some pretty awesome companies. Universal Music alone offers around 40 placements, and the list of others reads like a Who's Who of hip commercial creativity: Spotify, Apple, YouTube, etc. 'For our least able kids those two weeks are transformative,' and everyone we spoke to raved about this part of the provision. 'I got to go to Red Bull Music for my work experience!' cried a young singer. Trainees soon find the confidence to set up their own projects, and these seemed to be happening everywhere we looked. We came across five personable young men who proudly gave us their business cards for the music production company they'd set up and did a good pitch to us there and then. We checked out their website afterwards – alive and banging.

School is equipped with industry standard facilities including an amazing 440-seat theatre and any number of live music rooms, recording studios and computer suites. Wherever we went, trainees were getting together to rehearse songs, practise riffs, do a spot of sequencing, or just strum a guitar and unwind. 'Everyone's basically learning from each other in this school – it's musically multicultural,' said a talented young pianist who broke off from his drumkit practice to chat to us. Everyone on the music pathway has one-to-one tuition in at least one instrument, and music theory is also taught.

Extracurricular activities not confined to the set pathways: Love of Literature week had many trainees producing poems and plays.

Lots of music and media trips to large games and film expositions, workshops at places like the Royal Albert Hall. The school often gets invited to special events such as the Mercury Prize and the BAFTA Games Awards.

Sport: Sports provision is meagre and when we asked the trainees about it we were met with perplexed silence. 'There's a football match on the 10th,' one lad finally volunteered, sending everyone else into fits of giggles. 'We're terrible at all that,' admits the school. Trainees are educated in health and fitness issues, and yoga and dance teachers apparently come in from time to time, but no details about this were forthcoming. Given the amount of time the gaming trainees in particular spend in front of a screen, we were surprised at this deficiency.

Ethos and heritage: Situated hard by the thunderingly noisy A12 and accessed from half-boarded-up Bromley-by-Bow tube via a grim-looking subway, ELAM's surroundings can't be called pretty. But that, after all, is the point: the school was founded to help young people from low income backgrounds, particularly Eastenders, and the building itself stands tall and proud, clearly signed for all to see.

Once inside, ELAM gives out an aura of calm professionalism that is very engaging. Indeed, it doesn't feel like a school at all, but like a rather glitzy recording company with a more than usually young workforce. A small but pleasing display of pop art adorns the spacious entrance hall, trainees in casual clothes with headphones and creative hair styles move about with assurance and purpose, banter and music drifts down from above. All very civilised. No sixth form common room: staff and trainees alike meet in the canteen, so that staff can be seen having working conversations. 'You can't just tell someone what is not professional, you have to model it yourself'; the aim is for ELAM to feel like a creative company rather than a school. Walls very bare at present, but high quality framed student art work is planned. Meanwhile, 'corrugated card round the edge of a noticeboard is not our vision'.

We met five personable young men who proudly gave us their business cards for the music production company they'd set up and did a good pitch to us there and then

ELAM was supposed to be a two-week summer project to 'enhance and inspire' creative youngsters in the area, but very quickly took on a powerful momentum of its own. Sir Nick Williams, former principal of the BRIT School and David Joseph, the CEO of Universal Music, urged that more was needed, for the sake of both students and the industry. The school began life up the road in Stratford as the guest of School 21, housed in their sixth form block and admitting 75 students. In April 2017 it moved to its present quarters and September 2018 saw it at its full capacity of 300, highly regarded by the community, the industry and the DfE, and '10 times oversubscribed'. By any standards, an astonishing success story.

Pastoral care, inclusivity and discipline: 'We've been super-tight with discipline,' and the behaviour we saw was exuberant but controlled and respectful. Many of ELAM's year 12 trainees are technically year 13s because of having dropped out of their first year of sixth form elsewhere; but once here, a lot of the students' previous issues seem to dissolve of their own accord. As one trainee put it, 'In secondary school, they tell you what to do. Here, you have a creative imagination and they support it.' Another confirmed, 'I hated secondary school, hated everything about it, but I want to be here. As soon as you walk in, everyone's welcoming, friendly, passionate about what they do. You get to meet other people who like what you like, so we get to build and grow together.' Teachers are, say parents, 'accessible and approachable'.

The school strives to instil professional values at all times, so punctuality and meeting homework deadlines are taught in that context, and are, according to parents, extremely effective. Likewise, dress code is relaxed but school is strict on anything too revealing, because it gives the wrong impression for work. Attendance is strictly monitored and any concerns are flagged up quickly. 'It is made clear to the trainees that opportunities such as good work placements have to be earned,' observed a parent, who rated the pastoral care as excellent. The catering looked mediocre when we visited, but they were already on it, with a new caterer appointed, and the school is looking into how this could also provide training opportunities for the students.

Perhaps the best endorsement for the school's approach comes from the trainees themselves, who take their role as creatives extremely seriously and are overjoyed to have landed at a school that does the same. 'If you're not serious, don't bother coming here,' was a comment from one year 12 lad that had everyone vigorously nodding. 'Never mind wasting your own time, you're gonna waste other people's time.' 'If you don't have passion, integrity and drive, you might as well not come here,' confirmed another trainee. The result is an atmosphere that is genuinely inspiring, according to parents. 'It is striking how students help each other and cheer on their peers at school concerts.'

Pupils and parents: A very heterogeneous cohort – some privately educated with a raft of top-grade GCSEs, some from the poorest council estates in Stratford with nothing, and 'everything in between'. Currently around 30 per cent of students on free school meals, but school is well aware of the increasing number of middle class families turning up at open evenings as the word spreads and will be 'aggressively recruiting from local comprehensives' to ensure diversity and balance.

Intake is from 22 London boroughs and beyond. A small number come from as far as eg Norwich, Wales and Newcastle. School is not registered as a boarding provider and therefore can't help with accommodation for the latter, but will put them in touch with other trainees who have done the same and who can recommend host families.

The last word: Hugely impressive, outward-looking, professional yet caring, and totally unique, this school really took our breath away. A godsend to any aspiring young creative lucky enough to come here, not least those who couldn't imagine how they would have fared anywhere else. Well on the way to becoming one of London education's hottest tickets. Apply early.

Forest School

College Place, Snaresbrook, London E17 3PY

020 8520 1744 | info@forest.org.uk | www.forest.org.uk

Independent	Pupils: 1,465; sixth form: 267
Ages: 4-18	Fees: £13,914 – £19,755 pa

Warden: Since 2016, Marcus Cliff Hodges (50s). An imposing man – looks tough and dynamic – but thoughtful, likeable and very easy to meet. A career schoolmaster in the very best sense of the word: an English degree from Cardiff plus a masters from the Institute of Education then teaching posts in Gstaad, followed by Bedford and the assistant headship at Latymer Upper. Hit the top spot (warden) at Forest after a spell as head of the boys' senior school and acting warden. No sense at all of his being overawed by the job – 'it's actually a very liberating experience' – and he is evidently devoted to a school he knows and understands intimately. A keen fisherman and mountaineer, he communicates calm dependability. Married with a teenage son (a pupil). 'Steeped in the place and a great appointment,' said one parent, adding, 'he's quite formal and old-fashioned in some ways. No bad thing.'

Entrance: Selection for the pre-prep takes the form of a morning of low-key activities for which parents are asked – perhaps more in hope than expectation? – not to coach their children for the 32 places (16 boys and 16 girls). There are further entry points at 7+, at 11+ (the start of the senior school, at which point some 120 pupils are selected from at least 750 applicants) and 16+, where the school might well take in another 20 or 30 pupils, depending on availability.

Exit: Almost all the prep school pupils move into the senior school, unless families are relocating, and the same applies to the GCSE cohort. A few leave at this point, sometimes because of families relocating, and there will be a tiny contingent who decide it's not for them or who don't cut the mustard academically for the sixth form. This is a high-octane environment: six to Oxbridge in 2019 and almost all leavers go on to Russell Group universities. The broad base of subjects studied at university testifies to the school's academic range and depth. Two students overseas in 2020 – to Maastrict University in the Netherlands and Harvard, USA. Another student won a scholarship to the Royal Northern College of Music in Manchester to study classical violin, making it the ninth year in a row for a Forest pupil to have won a scholarship to a prestigious musical conservatoire. Another student to Central Saint Martins for fashion design.

Latest results: In 2020, 83 per cent 9-7 at GCSE; 78 per cent A*-B at A level. In 2019 (the last year when exams took place), 75 per cent 9-7 at GCSE; 35 per cent A*/A at A level (66 per cent A*-B).

Teaching and learning: A highly efficient and effective feel to the teaching backed up by excellent results. Maths, science, English and history appear particularly strong. Less obvious drive to continue with modern languages – take-up at A level is slight. Masses of (trained) support for those with organisational difficulties and specific learning difficulties. The overall sense is of very capable and determined teachers plus a school packed to the gunnels with bright students and a few very high flyers. 'It's a high-achieving school,' said one parent, 'but not a hothouse. That's suited us. I really hope that it stays that way.'

Teaching was judged 'excellent' in the latest ISI report and there is no sign of anything less than ongoing commitment. 'My teachers really mind,' said one girl, 'and it makes such a difference to the way we all work'. The warden agrees: 'There is masses of good practice,' he says, 'but the real challenge is to make teaching and learning tailored around each individual pupil. Not to pander to them, but to empower them.' Forest has made a big play of 'learning characteristics' – independence and flexibility being two of them. Teachers use these to check on their charges' progress.

School has a diamond structure. Between 4 and 7, the school is fully co-ed. Between 7 and the end of GCSEs, classes are single-sex. At sixth form, they revert to co-ed

The great singularity of Forest is its diamond structure. Between the ages of 4 and 7, the school is fully co-ed. Between 7 and the end of GCSEs, classes are single-sex. Eating, recreation, sport and most other activities all take place together – it's just that boys and girls learn separately. At sixth form, they revert to co-ed. 'We haven't retained it as an historical curiosity,' says the warden. 'We believe in it. We think it's best.' As it is a one-site school, he has a valid argument that the school falls in the co-ed camp.

Learning support and SEN: Professional but pragmatic attitudes to special educational needs: basic screening tests are given to all pupils on entry and parents are told immediately if extra support is needed. A learning support department with four qualified staff lead the drive to help, whether that means specialist lessons to pupils or advising subject teachers how to contribute. There are no pupils on EHC plans, but about 80 currently have IEPs.

The arts and extracurricular: Very strong dance (musical theatre, street, ballet and tap) welds into performance. There's an annual multicultural music and dance spectacular – the so-called FUSION. Every house enters the annual house drama competition and the school theatre stages three major productions each year. The Michaelmas Play draws its cast from the whole school community. Recent productions include Oh What A Lovely War! and Dick Barton – Special Agent! They are rightly proud of old pupil Paapa Essiedu, who graduated from theatre studies here to playing Hamlet at Stratford. For the past five years at least one pupil per year has won a place at a musical conservatoire. Clear indications are appearing of the booming significance art, design and technology play in the life of the school.

Sport: Sitting on 50 green acres on the edge of Epping Forest, sporty children are in clover. The facilities are astonishing – a sports centre on site and an Olympic swimming pool. Football, in the warden's words, 'is deep in the DNA of the school', but he believes that no one sport enjoys a monopoly of prestige. 'Having sufficient alternatives is critical if people aren't going to feel excluded,' he insists. The U15 footballers have recently been in the ISFA final, and hockey is making a strong comeback, with three U15 players (two girls and one boy) in the England squad. Girls' football is also booming and the school tries to cater to all tastes and talents, taking advantage of the Olympic velodrome, West Essex golf club and local rowing clubs. All pupils have to do four games or activity periods per week, right up to their last year. 'It's simple,' said one pupil, 'they want us to have something to think about as well as our work, otherwise, you can end up fretting.'

Ethos and heritage: Began life as a proprietary grammar school in 1834. Forest's founders included the Spode industrialist, William Copeland, and the governor of the Bank of England, William Cotton. It grew sufficiently rapidly to have sacrificed some 100 old boys in the Great War but the big growth came in the last century, with girls being admitted in 1981.

The facilities are astonishing – a sports centre on site and an Olympic swimming pool. Football, in the warden's words, 'is deep in the DNA of the school'

The campus feels more like a well-ordered village rather than an institution, despite the number of pupils – modern, dynamic youngsters with an eye on what's happening next but without the brittle, jarring quality of some metropolitan children. The way in which they wear their uniforms, and interact with their teachers and each other, backs up their positive view of the school. One parent said: 'All types of pupils and all kinds of achievement are celebrated. The teachers set the example and the older pupils take their lead from them, and it seeps all the way down the school.'

The school communicates a palpable ethos of teamwork and service. DofE and CCF are both massively popular, and being linked to the Royal Green Jackets augurs a commendable degree of toughness. Civic engagement is highly prized: there is a close link to Haven House, a local children's hospice. 'We're not going to solve its funding,' says the warden, 'but our ongoing involvement is about more than money.' New initiatives are constantly springing up, most recently with pupils helping run a youth club in Chelmsford for young people with mental health issues.

The vast selection of lunchtime and after-school clubs show that Forest embraces irony as well as all that is wholesome. Warhammer and chess clubs, well-known destinations for some who are less than extrovert or athletic, enjoy prominence, as do those for Manfood and cake decoration. Alongside the medicine, engineering and law societies, those of a less squeamish disposition may enjoy time spent at the dissection society.

Distinguished alumni cover all bases: H Tubb and WJ Cutbill were founding members of the Football Association, and Paralympian equestrian Liz Stone won gold at Atlanta in 1996, whilst Ella Purnell and Nicola Walker are enjoying successful stage, TV and film careers. Less generally famous perhaps is squadron leader Geoffrey Wellum DFC, a renowned Battle of Britain Spitfire pilot. He has credited Forest with giving him the spiritual support, courtesy of his time in chapel, to fight another day in the clouds.

Pastoral care, inclusivity and discipline: Discipline is low key, but the school does not shy away from addressing occasional poor behaviour. 'We have most of the usual teenage issues to confront but I believe the safeguarding here is outstanding and that the whole ethos of pastoral care is embraced by the staff,' says the warden.

Forest is, depending on how you look at it, two schools (or even three), albeit on one campus and sharing the same ethos and genus: there's the pre-prep, the prep and the senior school – the latter divided into lower and middle schools and sixth form. Each has its own head of section who oversees pupils' academic progress.

Pupils' own tutors and housemistresses and housemasters look after pastoral care. Houses exercise a big hold on pupil identity as well as holding considerable importance in terms of school competitions (note – not just sport but also including art, dance, drama and MasterChef). There's also a chaplain (and a very beautiful school chapel) and compulsory year group services each week. It has a very Church of England feel but the susceptibilities of those of other faiths are carefully considered when it comes to hymn selection. 'I'd actually prefer it to be completely secular,' said a parent, admitting that was 'a minority view'.

Pupils and parents: Buses bring in children every day from places as far afield as Epping, Docklands and Highbury, although many pupils make their own way to school using the excellent public transport links. Liaison with parents is taken seriously: in addition to termly written reports and an annual parents' evening, there is a yearly information evening in September. 'This way parents become clued-up rapidly about what we see as important over the next 12 months, and it gives them confidence and a good reason to work with us,' says the warden. Lots of other events as well – the parental conference programme includes talks on revision, drug awareness, IT – but there is no sense that this is a school which would ever allow an 'in-crowd' of parents to emerge, and is all the better for it.

Money matters: There is a range of scholarships and exhibitions, for both academic and musical prowess, as well as bursarial assistance, depending on means.

The last word: A powerhouse with a heart. The school has an immensely purposeful feel to it – no doubt influenced by the warden, but also by skilled and serious-minded teachers and parents.

Headteacher: Since 2015, Rebecca Drysdale BSc (40s), who joined the school in 2012 as deputy and then acting headteacher. It was whilst she was doing her degree in geography at Coventry Polytechnic (now Coventry University) that she first caught the teaching bug. 'I had spent a year doing the Marks & Spencer's management training course and immediately took to the personnel side of things. This, coupled with the fact that I loved working with young people, made me realise teaching would be a great career,' she explains. Did her PGCE at Reading, then worked her way up the ranks across two comprehensives and a secondary modern (Chalfont Community College, Bucks; Copleston High School, Ipswich; Charles Darwin School, Biggin Hill), followed by a 10-year stint as assistant headteacher at Edmonton County School.

'I can be scary when I need to be,' she says (and pupils concur), but so long as everyone toes the line, she has a jolly and genial demeanour, as well as being both earnest and refreshingly unassuming – the type you feel would roll her sleeves up and get stuck in whenever needed. Staff describe her as a 'true listener,' taking on board everyone's point of views, which means that when she does make changes, everyone tends to move forward together. Teaches a little, 'but not as much as I'd like', although she regularly does lunch and break duty, and students we talked to were clearly impressed at how often she chats to them in the corridors.

Sees her role as 'helping what was already a very good school to evolve', although her attitude should not be mistaken for a lack of vision. 'I want this school to be the best grammar in the area,' she told us. 'I'd like to see people buying houses to try and get their sons into this school. I want people to move to Redbridge to come here.'

Entrance: More than 1,100 boys in the borough of Redbridge and nearby compete for the 180 places available each year by sitting the 11+ examination. The test, which has recently changed to CEM (aimed to unearth the brightest children, not the most tutored), is administered by the borough. School manages its own admissions to the sixth form, with places offered only to boys with 9-6 in their chosen subjects, plus at least eight 6s across the best of their GSCE results. 'It sounds counterintuitive, but the idea is to get breadth as well as depth,' explains the headteacher. All sixth form entrants also require grade 4 or over in English and maths. Parents of pupils who get into this school say their sense of relief is huge, which is unsurprising given that it is the only boys' grammar in the borough.

Exit: Around half stay on to sixth form. Medicine and engineering are the most popular subjects chosen at university, although others include economics, architecture, dentistry, law and physics. Majority choose to study in London at eg King's College and UCL, whilst others go to Russell

Group universities across the UK. 'If they're brave enough to go outside London, they're brave enough to pick far and wide,' says the head. Twelve medics in 2020 and three to Oxbridge.

Latest results: In 2020, 82 per cent 9-7 at GCSE; 41 per cent A*/A at A level (64 per cent A*-B). In 2019 (the last year when exams took place), 72 per cent 9-7 grades at GCSE; 40 per cent A*/A at A level (62 per cent A*-B).

Teaching and learning: At GCSE, strongest results shown in the sciences and mathematics. Everyone learns French and Spanish in years 7 and 8 and takes one language at GCSE, though few take two or continue languages to A level. No setting before GCSE and only then in maths, science and English. Besides maths and sciences, other popular GCSE subjects include geography, history and English, and every child has to take at least one creative GCSE in the likes of PE (particularly popular), art, music and technology. 'We call it EBacc Plus,' says the head, who believes it enhances UCAS forms no end.

Where possible, teaching is practical. Plenty of pongs in the science block, where one class was dissecting fish and another had their Bunsen burners all going

At A level, popular subjects include the sciences, economics, mathematics, history and government & politics. Most stick to academic rather than creative subjects, although sixth form enrichment ensures all students continue learning the arts. Subject-based reviews help to monitor each subject and data tracking to monitor pupil progress helps spot and tackle underperformance; not that there is much of that here, according to parents. Maximum class sizes, at 30 (and 26 in the sixth form), are at the higher end. The school funding crisis means that it is increasing class sizes and hasn't offered MFLs at A level for several years, but has now joined up with Valentines High School to teach French and Spanish.

Teacher profile on the older side, reflecting the low staff turnover and long-term experience. All teach their degree subject and many are examiners. Where possible, teaching is practical. Expect plenty of pongs wandering through the science block, for example, where one class was dissecting fish and another had their Bunsen burners all going when we visited. Meanwhile, a history lesson on WWII involved a mock trial for Hitler. In fact, all classrooms we visited were lively, with bright, perceptive students clearly hungry for detail and knowledge. Disappointing to walk past two classrooms with teachers shouting at their class, but maybe that's the price you pay for encouraging such energetic debate. School works on a two-week timetable.

The creative curriculum is big here, with students taken off timetable for six per cent of the time in year 7 and four per cent of the time in year 8. Mainly involves students working in small groups to build habits of mind that will stand them in good stead beyond school – leading a team, being a team player, debating, time management, structuring a piece of work etc. We saw it in action during our visit, with year 10s having created a morning of educational activities for year 7s on World Book Day. 'These students devised the plan, worked out the detail, came to me to pitch it, then carried it through,' says the head, who is loathe to call them 'soft skills' for fear of depreciating their value. Other examples include students pretending their plane has crashed on a desert island (they work out how they will survive), commemorating National Holocaust Day and committing to learning a new skill (usually off the list of activities from the Duke of Edinburgh award which, by the way, is an option from year 9 upwards). A particular favourite for students is the project that involves them researching an area of London, then taking a fellow student on a guided tour. The preparation is impressive, with students writing to the likes of Downing Street to request going through the magic gates. By the end, students have learned skills including independent research, preparing engaging speeches, navigating a map and using the tube.

Learning support and SEN: Two-thirds of pupils with EAL requirements plus 30 or so who need SEN support. When we visited, there were students with cerebral palsy, hearing difficulties (including one who was profoundly deaf and also has vision impairment), plus all the usual – dyslexia to autistic spectrum. Can and does cater for wheelchair users, although there are some struggles with the old building – this will be made easier when the new ones are up. 'If students are bright enough to study here, we'll find a way,' says head, who says individual support takes place both in and outside the classroom.

But parental views are mixed on the quality of SEN support. 'My son has a physical disability and we were initially told by people in the area that this might not be the best school for him, but they've been amazing at meeting his needs, whilst still academically challenging him,' said

A faith ambassadors scheme involves boys giving talks on what faith means to them (or not – one did a talk on atheism)

one enthusiastic parent. 'I've been particularly pleased at how they've built up his confidence. SEN support here is very nurturing and they regularly suggest things I've never even thought of.' But others reported that the school's SEND knowledge was lacking, and their child was not well supported. We'd recommend a thorough quiz of the SENCo in regards to your child's condition, and requesting a detailed outline of the support that will be given to him.

The arts and extracurricular: Oracy is new to the year 7 and 8 English/MFL curriculum and some work for LAMDA exams, but beyond that there's only student-led drama clubs – not great for aspiring thespians. Even whole school productions are rare, although you do get some smaller productions and boys enjoy the annual Speakout Challenge. Art is a different matter, with rich, bold and inspiring work on display – including drawings, paintings and sculpting. We also saw students working on some particularly impressive photography. 'Art is core to cross-curricular work here,' one pupil told us. DT also dynamic, with spirited pupils working hard.

Provision for music is also good. 'This is my absolute favourite department. There are so many chances to learn and perform and there's plenty of sophisticated equipment,' one pupil enthused as he walked us through it. All students study music in years 7, 8 and 9. Over 100 children also have extracurricular music lessons and some exceptional talent can be found here. Some lessons take place at the Redbridge Music School. Pupils have plenty of opportunity to develop their talents on piano, violin, cello, double bass, saxophone, drum, voice and more through orchestra, jazz ensemble, choirs and various bands. There are concerts and performances in London and abroad, but few pupils take art or music A level.

Extracurricular provision is largely sports-based and there's plenty of subject intervention to enable students to further and deepen knowledge in specific topics. Beyond that, there's a rich variety of clubs, groups and ensembles covering everything from astronomy to chess and gaming to debating club.

Day visits to all the usual galleries and museums (particularly for art) and fieldwork visits to the likes of Dover Castle, Epping Forest and the battlefields. Relatively thin on the ground when it comes to residential trips, however, with the exception of exchange trips (mainly to Spain, Germany and France), and sports trips have included Spain, USA and Caribbean in the past. But the school has strong partnerships with schools and colleges in Germany, Spain, Switzerland, Denmark and Iceland and has British Council International School status. 'A lot of our international work involves video conferencing,' explains the head, with examples including peer assessment with a school in Indonesia and a shared wildlife project with a school in Ghana.

Opportunities to volunteer are frequent, including sixth formers going into local primary schools to teach maths and modern foreign languages to small groups. A faith ambassadors scheme involves boys giving talks on what faith means to them (or not – one did a talk on atheism) and there's fundraising projects for local and national charities too.

Sport: Cricket and football are by far the strongest sports at this school, where on-site facilities are in no short supply. 'Cricket is the most popular and we're good at it; football is also popular, but we're not always quite so good at it,' smiled one pupil. Swimming and rugby also well-liked, whilst other options include basketball, badminton, table tennis, rowing, sailing and rock climbing. Duke of Edinburgh caters for those who prefer walking and expeditions to actual sports. 'The focus here is on fitness for life, not just elite players,' says head.

Ethos and heritage: Founded in 1901 as Park High Grade School, the school was originally co-ed and located in Balfour Road. In 1929, the boys' school split, then moved to its present location in Fremantle Road in 1935. Although smack in the middle of a built-up residential area, the school has a secluded feel. And while the building itself is traditional (think sweeping oak stairwells, large wooden boards with lists of past notables and trophy display cabinets), the fabric of the school is undergoing dramatic change. Newly opened is a science block with 10 labs and six demonstration classrooms, a sixth-form centre, DT suite and more computer areas.

The school layout resembles a figure of eight, with two storeys of classrooms organised around the two adjacent squares, with green areas in the middle that pupils can use at break times. The layout makes it easy for new pupils to find their way around.

The atmosphere here is bustling, lively and purposeful. We'd like to have seen the school corridors livened up with more displays of student work, but where they do exist, they are imaginative and intelligent.

Notable former pupils include Raymond Baxter, TV personality (Tomorrow's World), Sir Trevor Brooking, footballer, and David Miller, deputy chief inspector of Air Accidents. Lots of presentation evenings hosted by alumni, including some of these big names.

Pastoral care, inclusivity and discipline: 'You don't learn until you get stuck' is the ethos here, making for a supportive environment, which balances the healthy competition between the boys. Where possible, form tutors – who are generally responsible for pupil welfare and progress – stay with their class all the way up the school. Meanwhile, the vertical house system means all boys have a head of house looking out for them too. The system provides opportunity for the boys to develop stronger skills in leadership, mentorship and responsibility, plus opportunities to develop relationships across year groups, right to sixth form. A visiting counsellor is available; the school regularly accesses Redbridge services for young people; and there are all the usual talks on sex, drugs and rock 'n' roll through to forced marriages and knife crime. 'One charity came in to do a drama workshop on domestic violence and that was particularly powerful,' says the head.

One project involves researching an area of London, then taking a fellow student on a guided tour. By the end, skills learnt include independent research, preparing engaging speeches, navigating a map and using the tube

Year 7s receive peer mentoring from trained older pupils in year 9, 10 and sixth form. 'They're a bit of a role model for the younger ones to look up to,' one pupil told us. For one pupil, who joined at sixth form, this was 'one of the things I liked when I came, people always willing to help'. Bullying nipped in the bud. 'My child was bullied, but when I contacted the teacher, he had it sorted out within two days and he took me through all the measures he'd taken,' said one parent.

Boys are generally well-behaved – reports describe the behaviour as 'outstanding' – which is no doubt helped by the clear warning system and strict rules, for example on uniform. 'But boys will be boys and they are naughty sometimes,' acknowledges the head. Indeed, there was an incident the day we visited. No permanent exclusions, although there had been 14 temporary ones halfway through the academic year when we visited, mostly for fighting, saying mean things and bringing in banned substances.

Pupils and parents: Pupils come from a wide mix of ethnic backgrounds, with Asian (Indian, Pakistani and Tamil) the dominant group, then white British, white Eastern European and black African Caribbean. They all come from the borough of Redbridge and some surrounding areas. 'The local authority drew up the smallest circle they could to fully encompass Redbridge, which means you get a little bit of neighbouring boroughs in there too, most notably Waltham Forest and Essex,' explains the headteacher, who describes the school as one of the few grammars left that are true community schools. 'We want it to stay that way,' she says firmly.

Pupils range from bubbly, stumbling and oblivious year 7s making their way between lessons, to the year 11s who are articulate, mature, friendly and inquisitive. In fact, the older pupils who showed us round asked us almost as many questions as we asked them – both rare and refreshing.

There's no PA here, to the disappointment of some parents, but parents generally have good involvement in the school, with almost 100 per cent attendance at parents' evenings and relevant meetings – and parents say that communication is good. The school does have some anxiety about boys whose parents 'have unrealistic aspirations for them' – the 'You will be a doctor!' brigade. But staff try to ensure parents understand exactly what the career they have in mind for their son entails, and to hit home that there are other jobs out there. 'If a boy's real interest and passion is for humanities and not science, fine, as that it is where he will get real satisfaction and achievement.' Work is also done from early on to emphasise that it's about the education, not just the grades. 'The qualifications will get you to the doorway, but you need more than that to walk through it – character, resilience and so on,' says the head.

The last word: This is a school that delivers a very high standard of academic teaching and much more besides, producing young men who seem genuinely well prepared for the wider world. It's not for the faint-hearted, with firm rules and high expectations, but there's a strong support system to back it all up, with a caring head and exceptionally experienced teaching staff. We found boys well-adjusted, happy and hungry to learn.

London Academy of Excellence

Broadway House, 322 High Street, Stratford, London E15 1AJ

020 3301 1480 | office@lae.ac.uk | www.lae.ac.uk

State | **Ages:** 16-18 | **Pupils:** 485

Head Master: Since 2017, Scott Baker MA PGCE QTS. After reading history at Cambridge, he began his teaching career at Robert Clack School in Dagenham (the school he attended) in 1999. Has held senior leadership positions in a number of state schools including Sandringham School in St Albans and the Henrietta Barnett School in northwest London. He is the school's third head since it was founded in 2012.

We met him in his modern, airy, white-with-splashes-of-colour first floor office – the decorative style is continued throughout this former 80s council office block that's located a minute's walk from Stratford station. He was first in his school's 50-year history to have got to Cambridge, the first in his family to go to university at all, and the first state school appointee to head LAE. We found him unpretentious, razor-sharp and passionate about bright young sparks from all walks of life getting the educational chances they should. No wonder he calls this his 'dream job'. 'I remember reading about it opening in the Metro and thinking, "Crikey, that's a great idea – an Eton of the East End",' he said.

'He's warm, welcoming and highly intelligent,' one parent told us. Another said, 'He's dynamic, but there's no need to feel awestruck around him as he's friendly and jovial.' Keeps a hand in at the coal face by teaching politics, leading (when the students aren't) weekly assemblies, having tea with all tutor groups and organising awards dinners, among other things. 'He's not like the headteacher in my last school, who you never saw – he's always around and really friendly,' said one student.

Entrance: Minimum of five 7s at GCSE with at least 6s in maths and English, plus subject specific requirements (7-9 in most subjects, 8-9 for further maths). School gets about 3,000 applicants and will interview about 1,500 for 240 places – according to their predicted grades. Half the places are given to students from Newham, other half could come from anywhere, with over 100 secondary feeders. 'It's perfectly normal not to know anyone when you start here,' a student told us. Those on free school meals given priority, provided they meet minimum criteria.

Exit: Impressive. Ninety-five per cent get an offer to a Russell Group university. School is pushing for more to apply outside London – a road trip to St Andrews, Edinburgh and Durham paid dividends and larger numbers are going to Durham, Bristol, Bath and Exeter than in the past; Warwick is particularly popular. In 2020, 33 to Oxbridge – a higher percentage than many top independent schools. Growing numbers to USA – one or two each year. STEM subjects popular and history and geography also well represented; in 2020, 30 went off to study medicine/dentistry/veterinary. Lots of gap years, after which uni/careers advice is still available. One parent told us, 'The guidance has been as good as if she's still there.'

Latest results: In 2020, 73 per cent of A*/A grades at A level (96 per cent A*-B). In 2019 (the last year exams took place), 65 per cent A*/A (93 per cent A*-B).

Teaching and learning: Not for the faint-hearted. All year 12s embark on four A levels although three-quarters drop one by year 13 ('it still gives you a competitive edge on your UCAS form,' insists school), chosen from 14 predominantly academic subjects (what some might regard as 'proper subjects' or 'subjects favoured by the top universities'), including further maths, French and Spanish. Non-facilitating (but still strong) subjects such as government & politics, psychology and economics are also offered. Maths currently the most popular A level (70 per cent of year 12s take it) followed by sciences ('We are key providers for STEM, but not a STEM college because of our breadth'). Some students feel the humanities department gets a bit overshadowed by maths and sciences – 'It's a bit of a sticking point,' said one, 'the teachers are great, but they need more resources.' Growing numbers take modern languages, bucking the national trend, with additional languages offered outside the timetable (currently including Mandarin, Italian, Bengali, Arabic, Urdu and Japanese, but these vary year on year). Five specialist 'pathways' are specified under the curriculum (medicine, law, STEM, business, digital technologies), but students told us there is bespoke preparation for a career in any field, 'with second-to-none university application and careers advice'.

In its early days, the school was accused of kicking out students at the end of year 12 who failed to get high enough grades for entry to the most competitive universities. Head says 'the governors realised the admissions policy had flaws and no student can be asked to leave at the end of year 12 on the basis of their academic achievement.' Now 95 per cent progress successfully – something praised by Ofsted in their last inspection report. 'It's hard to fall behind here because of all the support,' one student told us, while another said, 'It's easy to switch subjects too' (eg there's a one-year politics A level in year 13). Impressive results, with LAE regularly ranked as one of the top sixth form colleges in the country and in the top one per cent for value added.

School day is long: lessons start at 8.30am, and if you take advantage (many do) of the optional subject clinics after regular classes, teaching doesn't finish until 6pm

All year 12s do a mini EPQ; a third progress onto the full EPQ, with stellar results. Exciting a thirst for learning and for academic endeavour is key here and the scholars' programme contributes incentive and prestige. Those with the top 50 scores for GCSE grades may be awarded Governors' scholarships or Merit scholarships – the prize being financial support for resources as well as more trips to Oxford and Cambridge.

School day is long – the library opens at 7.45am, lessons start at 8.30am, and if you take advantage (many do) of the optional subject clinics after regular classes, teaching doesn't finish until 6pm. Class sizes are capped at 25, with 22 for science (but most drop below 20 in year 13) and students get five hours teaching per week per A level; this, together with the extracurricular, leaves little or no downtime. 'But while there's lots to do, it doesn't feel crazy or over-pressured,' said one student. Teachers are all specialists in their field (a third have a doctorate; one biology teacher is a former doctor) and a passion for their subject make for lively, engaging lessons. Expect university-style lessons with lots of interaction – students here are taught to think, no doubt balm to admissions tutors' ears. Parents wonder at the levels of support given to their children by the teachers: from Saturday classes to making themselves available by email until 11pm ('not officially, of course,' says head). Reflecting the school's heavy focus on personal development, students also track their own progress (academic and extracurricular), taking part in a viva at the end of year 12, from which they can gain a diploma.

Although there's a more competitive landscape for academic sixth forms since the school's inception (key competitors are Brampton Manor Academy and Newham Collegiate Sixth Form Centre), LAE still regards itself as 'the strongest academic pathway to top universities for students in Newham, a claim born out by the performance tables which ranked us at the highest attaining school in Newham and the only one with an average grade of A.'

Learning support and SEN: Around 40 students are on the learning support register, although many don't have a diagnosed condition. Dedicated learning coach goes above and beyond the usual support and access arrangements with help in targeted areas. For example, some maths students are very able numerically but because more than half the students here have EAL, they may need help with academic literacy (increasingly required in the new maths A level). Results for those with SEN match those without and, in 2018, outmatched them by quite a margin. According to one student with a physical disability, the school is also 'excellent about mobility issues, including access to reliable lifts'.

The arts and extracurricular: Wednesday afternoons are dedicated to clubs and societies – 30 in total, some student led, including women in STEM, scrabble, chess, juggling, DofE, mindfulness & wellbeing, Japanese, photography, first aid, debating, Model United Nations. 'I've being doing parliamentary debating for the last two terms – it's so good,' said one student, while another told us she was setting up a new art club. A number of competitions organised against other schools. CCF now available.

Historically, the arts have been thin on the ground, no doubt because they aren't offered as A levels. The appointment of a co-ordinator of music, drama and art has helped, with piano lessons now available, plus street dance, musical theatre, rock choir, improv society, among others – although sadly still no orchestra. However, music performances do take place during assemblies and there is a music room with a speaker system, microphone and guitars.

Trips kick off with a visit to Oxford University in the first week of year 12. 'It's a great idea

Stepney All Saints Church of England Secondary School

because it raises the bar academically and is good for team building,' said a parent. All students visit Cambridge in year 13 and one other university of their choice. Students we met were buzzing about an upcoming sailing trip with Eton students, while other students go to Japan and Berlin. 'We proactively seek out opportunities for both day and residential trips, although we don't go in for the big USA type trips which need a huge lead in time for raising funds,' says head. All students do community outreach and charitable fundraising.

Sport: On Tuesday afternoons, it's sport for all – with a huge choice of 25 from girls' and boys' football, rowing, sailing and pilates to basketball, climbing, canoeing, boxercise, volleyball, yoga and zumba. Games take place at venues including the Olympic Park, Redbridge Sports Centre, University of East London and Lee Valley. One student told us she chose LAE because 'the sport looked as good as the academics – I haven't been disappointed'. Growing number of fixtures, including against independent schools, with strong results for football and netball.

Ethos and heritage: Founded in 2012, LAE was the brainchild of Richard Cairns, head of Brighton College, and Joan Deslandes, head of Kingsford Community School in Newham. They met on a bus in Beijing and found they shared a passion for Mandarin (they both introduced compulsory teaching of Mandarin in their schools) as well as rigorous academic learning and a desire for social justice. Joan Deslandes needed somewhere to send her high flyers (Kingsford is an 11-16 school). Brighton College took two sixth formers each year from Kingsford, on full scholarships. These scholarships were funded by HSBC, which still continues to support the LAE today (HSBC also has input into the school's careers programme, including networking and mentoring). However, Joan Deslandes had another 40 high attainers at Kingsford, whose academic aspirations weren't being met. With the inspirational energy of these two first class educators, the early seeds of the LAE were sown. Most agree that Richard Cairns was a driving force in gaining a groundswell of support from the independent sector, one of the innovative features of LAE.

The first sixth form only free school, it has the benefit of strong links with the independent sector. Six 'partner schools' – Brighton College, Eton College, UCS, Highgate, Forest School and Caterham – share resources, knowledge, experience and contacts and also form the names of the six houses that the students are grouped into (as a student, you get the most direct involvement with the school your house is named after). There are also links with Francis Holland and Putney High schools. Support from these schools includes seconded teaching staff, shared INSET days, coaching and support, revision workshops, academic lectures, competitions and study days, Oxbridge admissions support (including mock interviews at the schools themselves), careers events and access to facilities (eg sport). Students told us of a debating day on educational injustice at Eton, complete with keynote speakers.

Strong links with the independent sector. Students told us of a debating day on educational injustice at Eton

School is located on Stratford High Street – it's the yellow and glass building right in front of you as you walk out of Stratford station. Functional and businesslike, but the edge is taken off by the bright colours and idiosyncratic names (the large, tastefully decorated dining/study/common room area is called the agora), and walls throughout the building are adorned with wonderful large portraits of 'independent thinkers', from Coco Chanel and Elizabeth David to Srinivasa Ramanujan and Reverend William Buckland, saying profound things. All rooms are shiny, bright, light and airy; nothing feels run down. 'Shame there's no outside area – that's a real downside,' said one parent; a few students added they'd 'like more space inside, but it wouldn't have stopped me coming here'. School currently considering expanding, but not too much – the aim is 'to retain an independent school style of education'.

Pastoral care, inclusivity and discipline: The school's key values are excellence, kindness, respect, humility, independence and resilience and they underpin everything. High expectations around the everyday stuff – uniform, lanyards (zero tolerance on these not being worn), punctuality, not handing in homework. Parents are told if a child fails on any of these counts, although poor behaviour is rare; students are mature, proud of being at the school and highly motivated. One exclusion in the last two years. Mental health taken 'more seriously than it used to be', according to one parent, with a part-time counsellor, preventative workshops, relaxation room (set up by students) and talks with psychology students from Queen Mary University. Student-led networks include LGBT, mental health and feminism and gender equality.

Head of house, along with a team of five tutors in each house, is in charge of pastoral welfare.

Each student's tutor is also responsible for their UCAS reference, PSHE and monitoring their academic progress; and this tutor is the first port of call for parents. Reports are issued at the end of each term, and parents also can meet the tutor and other teachers once a term – 'the ones we've met have a very clear picture of our son and focus entirely on what they can do to help him progress,' said one parent. Schools says they've had no reports of bullying; students agree – 'There aren't cliques here, everyone's in it together.'

Pupils and parents: Unusually high proportion of first and second generation immigrant families – particularly Asian and black. Fiercely aspirational parents (many of whom haven't been to university themselves) have a positive influence on the ambition of their children. Students are dressed smartly but, apart from the blue and gold ties, not uniformly.

The students we met, a mixture of year 12 and year 13, were the kind of people you would want to represent your country – model citizens. Thoughtful, articulate, mature, curious, polite and with an ease and confidence that belied the backgrounds of many of them. 'This school makes you confident,' one student told us. There is much competition for the prestigious leadership roles, especially house captain and prefect.

Money matters: School still has the benefit of the HSBC funding that was a legacy of the Brighton scholars' funding. This is not a luxury, says school, but vital in a climate of continuing government cuts. Opportunities Fund provides financial support for trips and resources to those most in need, and the diligent few who are awarded scholarships also get financial help with resources and trips.

The last word: This school provides a rigorous academic education to bright, aspirational students who are keen to seize the many opportunities on offer. Not only do students excel academically, they also develop confidence, resilience and ambitions that set them up for life well beyond university. An inspirational school for those willing to go the extra mile.

Newham Collegiate Sixth Form Centre

8

326 Barking Road, London E6 2BB

020 3373 5000 | enquiries@ncs6.org | www.thencs.co.uk

State | Ages: 16-18 | Pupils: 620

Principal: Since 2014, when the school opened, Mouhssin Ismail (late 30s), former City banking and finance lawyer at Norton Rose Fulbright and one-time Essex cricketer. Nobody can have any reason to question Mr Ismail's deep seriousness and intensity of purpose. Very much admired and liked by all constituencies – 'There are many explanations for the school's success,' said one parent, 'but Mr Ismail is at the heart of each of them.'

Previously assistant headteacher at Seven Kings High School, with a reputation as an outstanding economics teacher (as he still is), Mr Ismail is conscious that much of his own story has resonance for his pupils: 'I am a local boy, from an ethnic minority. My parents were devoted to my interests, but they had little formal education. But they provided me with example, and they taught me the value of hard work.' He is married with a boy and girl – parenting and cricket-coaching with his young family soaks up most of his spare time.

He clearly relishes the job, but in a thoughtful and believable way. 'We've started on a journey and, yes, it's exciting. But it's still early days.' His key ambitions for the school are academic: 'We'd like 75 per cent A* and A grades, 35 places at Oxbridge annually – because, without this kind of success, too many of our kids just won't have the choices and chances.' But he is also clear that the school has an equal duty to try to make sense of the elite universities and workplaces to which he wants his pupils to aspire. 'So building up cultural and social capital to support them in their ambitions is as important and, believe me, we take it seriously.'

Entrance: Entry comes mainly from the nine 'partner' schools in Newham – most are 11-16 academies. There are a small number of students from Tower Hamlets, Tottenham and Waltham Forest, and few may have to commute for up to an hour. 'We're quite determined that this will remain a school that serves Newham and students from east London, not least because of the work demands we make,' head insists. Despite applications from some independent school pupils, the trickle of middle class intake will not become a torrent. Selection criteria is rigorously academic – you have to get a 56 points from your top eight GCSEs (including English and maths) and then score between 7 and 9 in subjects being studied at A level (or 6 in some related subjects).

One parent admitted she'd been 'sceptical' about the school when her daughter first applied. 'But as soon as she arrived, my doubts started to fade. The teachers are so engaged. They really want to understand each pupil, and take a great interest in parents as well. Very different from what I was used to.'

Exit: Over 95 per cent to Russell Group universities including UCL, LSE, Imperial and King's College London. Five students got offers on degree apprenticeships at the likes of Dyson, KPMG and PwC. Lots overseas too, including to Harvard, Princeton and MIT. A lot of time and care is expended on helping prepare pupils to make UCAS applications, to excel at interview and – in every way – to outperform the expectations that might otherwise be made of them on the basis of their postcodes. The sting in the tail is that pupils have to perform at all points to continue to year 13.

Latest results: In 2020, 95 per cent A*/B at A level. In 2019 (the last year when exams took place), 90 per cent A*-B.

Teaching and learning: This is a selective school, but virtually all of the pupils have been at non-selective state secondaries before they arrive, and the results are staggeringly good. A level results trump many of the local grammar and independent schools.

Unlike so many schools, state and independent, NCS is taking no shortcuts to get this kind of success. The A level curriculum in the core is pretty much confined to subjects recommended by leading universities: maths, further maths, English literature, economics, geography, history, psychology, religious studies, government & politics, chemistry, physics and biology are all offered. The glaring omission is the absence of foreign languages, ancient or modern. 'There just isn't the demand,' says the head, 'and we can't make it financially viable.'

Prejudice might suggest that this is a maths and science factory, but that isn't the case: 'our humanities results are also outstanding,' head explains, 'especially history and English.' In a school of some 500 pupils, overwhelmingly from ethnic minority backgrounds, this challenges many complacent assumptions. The staff (39 of them, two-thirds Oxbridge-educated themselves) are teaching right to the top end, and clearly to great effect.

How do they do it, one asks? Selection clearly plays a large part in this, and so too does academic intensity. Classes start at 8.30am five days a week, and the whole infrastructure – iPads for all, study periods instead of free periods – is unapologetically geared towards high achievement. Almost uniquely in our experience, private study periods live up to their name – the sense is that serious study is being undertaken in silence by everyone there. There's also homework, of course but, as one girl suggested, 'It's sensible homework – it ties in what we've been doing, or what we're about to do – and it's about making us think.' One parent acknowledged that there was a lot of work, but added, 'I think it's up to parents ultimately, not schools, to try to ensure our children don't get overwhelmed. If we need to restore the balance, we should do that. The school is already playing its part.'

Almost uniquely in our experience, private study periods live up to their name – the sense is that serious study is being undertaken in silence by everyone there

Another assumption might be that this makes for an examination sweatshop. That would be grossly to underplay the much richer vision of education which underpins the place. Classes end at 3pm, and the extra time this frees up allows for a massive enrichment programme, drawing off the school's super-curriculum. There are visiting lecturers (Ed Miliband, Lord Mervyn King and Professor Lord Robert Winston among many others) and pupils team up with PhD students at UCL with whom the school is partnered. There are also myriad networks with business and industry, and a range of non-examined cultural and academic courses – living testimony to the extent to which the school is embracing a tradition of liberal humanism. 'Our pupils, for all kinds of reasons, can quickly feel strangers anywhere outside London,' the head acknowledges. 'To prepare them for university and beyond, they need a great deal more than A levels.'

Learning support and SEN: Special needs are acknowledged to the extent that those pupils who have been diagnosed as qualifying for extra time in exams may receive it, but there is no in-house specialist to supplement teaching. 'Very few pupils are involved,' explains the head, 'and our staff are always happy to put in any extra effort required.'

The arts and extracurricular: The school supports students taking Duke of Edinburgh Award, and there are music and drama societies. It has had huge success in debating, with one pupil recognised for being the first state school student to be judged Best Individual Speaker in the Eton Debating Competition.

But there just aren't the resources – human, material and, above all, time – to enable its pupils to experience drama, music and sport in the ways available to those from top independent schools. On the other hand, the school is committed to facilitating these experiences – through links with partner schools, and local initiatives. In the same spirit, it supports volunteering and outreach programmes.

The school is acutely aware that it needs to help its students to confront and understand much of the world in a way which is often taken for granted by independent school pupils. 'Being in London makes that a whole lot more possible,' says the head. Trips to theatres and museums, galleries and other landmarks, easily otherwise overlooked, are an integral part of every student's experience.

The school has facilitated an all-expenses-paid work placement in Abu Dhabi with leading international law firm White & Case LLP and overseas visits to Kyoto, Japan to engage in science workshops with eminent Japanese scientists as well annual trips to Washington and New York, where students have visited the White House, Pentagon, UN headquarters and Columbia University. There is a real sense that the school is replicating many of the outstanding features of a private school education, providing its students with opportunities that would not necessarily be available in a normal state school.

Sport: The school encourages sport, but there is no specific provision for it within the timetable. The East Ham Leisure Centre is literally next door, and the fact that Friday school finishes at 2pm is an inducement for some students to go next door for a workout.

Ethos and heritage: Having started life in 2014, working in partnership with Newham Council, NCS is – and feels – like a local school. Of course, it's made distinct by being selective, and also by occupying a splendid grade 2* listed building in East Ham. At the start of 2018, it became one of the flagship schools of the City of London Academies Trust – assuring it, amongst much else, of access to a centre of wealth and influence.

The atmosphere which results is also distinct: it's utterly metropolitan, for one thing – no rolling acres here and only yards away from the bustle of east London – and multiracial and multi-ethnic.

The school replicates many of the outstanding features of a private education, providing students with opportunities that would not be available in a normal state school

When we visited the students were calm, friendly and articulate – very focused in class, but never robotic. There was lots of relaxed interchange between teachers and students, and plenty of smiles but, underneath it all, it was impossible not to recognise the deep ambition of everyone there. There's a school uniform, enforced strictly, with students looking immaculate and professional at all times, worn not so much with pride (that may well be true) but with the same sort of calm pragmatism which characterised the whole place. They are busy young men and women and, in pursuit of their ambition: striking an attitude about uniform, or indeed about many of the things which exercise some more peach-fed youngsters, would seem rather frivolous here.

Pastoral care, inclusivity and discipline: Given that competition for places at NCS is intense, with approximately 3,000 applications being received for 300 places (driven by pupils as much as by parents), and that it is a day school, discipline is hardly an issue. 'Our parents value education highly,' says the head, 'and that's a cast of mind which they communicate to their children. The school benefits from that greatly. Of course, just like any group of 16-18 year olds, issues surface, but bad behaviour isn't one of them.' Managing work pressure, social media and the claims of competing friends may each occasionally call for help. So may no longer being at the top of the class – as so many were in their old schools.

Pupils see their tutors three times each week for 20 minutes – 'long enough for the basis of good relationships to be built up'. The head insists he and all his colleagues operate an open-door policy and pupils are insistent that this really happens. 'If I need help,' said one boy, 'I know that any of my teachers will be there to help at once.' Unlike many other schools, pupils are free to email teachers on work-related questions. 'It makes all the difference,' said one girl, 'and they reply so quickly.' A particular innovation are the weekly Ignite sessions – an hour each week – based around the ambition of nurturing good 'habits of mind' and dispositions.

The values which abound feel humane and collegial. 'When one of my friends got into Cambridge,' said one girl, 'the whole school was happy.'

Pupils and parents: NCS styles itself as a local school. Most pupils come from modest backgrounds – very often they are the sons and daughters of first generation Asians in Britain, who are ambitious for their children to have opportunities not open to them. They have the dynamism of achievers, and also the tolerance one associates with those living in a global city. As one girl put it: 'We're not usually rich, but we're not all deprived either. My parents went to university, which is a bit unusual, but not very.' One parent suggested that the creed of mutual respect and tolerance is a shock to a small minority of pupils, especially those whose earlier education hasn't prepared them for it. 'I believe this is happening,' he said, 'but it takes time.' Head insists he finds the parents 'invested in the school in ways which are helpful, and a pleasure to work with.'

The last word: If NCS continues to deliver in the way in which it has begun, it will be the standard bearer for a whole new generation of schools. There are two irreducibles here: the enthusiasm and hard work of the pupils, and the way they are storming every educational citadel that confronts them. Of course, there is a concentration of talent – both of teachers and students – but that's just the start. The secret seems to owe much to unapologetically high expectations and a huge investment of time and care. That and bright children, no doubt.

The absence of rolling acres will put off some middle-class punters, of course, but they are hardly the target audience. It's a humane and imaginative society, as well as an academic powerhouse: a combination which should make a great many fee-paying schools sit up and take notice. For us, this is the real deal.

Robert Clack School

Gosfield Road, Dagenham, Essex RM8 1JU

020 8270 4200 | office@robertclack.co.uk | www.robertclack.co.uk

State | Ages: 11–18 | Pupils: 2,400; sixth form: 444

Headteacher: Since 2018, Russell Taylor BSc, previously senior deputy. He grew up in Dagenham, is a former pupil here, gained a first class degree in economics at Queen Mary and trained as a teacher at the Institute of Education. He joined Robert Clack, his fourth teaching post, in 2002. 'I didn't come back with the intention of being the head,' he says, as if he somehow surprised himself, but nevertheless rose through the ranks and became acting head in 2017 following the departure of his predecessor due to ill health.

Trim, neat, spirited and uninhibited, he is proud of his working-class roots and has a noticeable rapport with the pupils, with whom he spends a great deal of time, both teaching (economics to year 13s the year we visited) and spending much of his time 'doing the rounds' of the school. 'It means I have to do a lot of the paperwork side of things out of hours, but I don't mind as the most important thing to me is modelling the values of the school and building relationships,' he says. Is unfazed by the fact that it's spread over two sites (soon to be three) 'because I get the chance to walk between them – again relationship building, but this time with the local community.' Parents say he's 'got a way about him: 'You can see he's in awe of the school, which is what most of us feel like, to be honest,' one told us.

Lives locally with his family; his nieces and nephew attend the school. His two big passions are being with his family and dog walking. Was a torchbearer at the London 2012 Olympic Games for being a positive role model in the school and local area and uniting the community with a £50,000 fundraising campaign to support a student with osteosarcoma.

Entrance: Some 1,600 applications for the 480 places in year 7, with pupils coming from around 40 feeder schools, so pupils often arrive knowing nobody. Looked-after children get priority, as do those with special educational needs, then by distance from the upper school site – generally within just one kilometre. Around 30 pupils from other schools join the sixth form.

Exit: About 70 per cent of pupils move up to the sixth form. Nearly all A level pupils to university, around a quarter to Russell Group. Usually a couple to Oxbridge, though none in 2020. Two medics in 2020. A handful to UCL, Queen Mary's and Royal Holloway, with other high-profile universities also featuring regularly among destinations. Some 70 per cent study maths and sciences, with the remaining 30 per cent covering virtually every subject going. The remaining sixth formers go straight into work (many on apprenticeships), with significant numbers moving into the City. Plenty of careers advice and help with UCAS applications, and the school has high value partnerships with the likes of the Worshipful Company of Chartered Surveyors, the Prince's Teaching Institute, Teach First and Business in the Community, all of which provide pupils with work experience or routes into careers, as well as promoting the work of the school. Successful and expanding network of alumni, who help pupils with everything from work experience to networking.

Latest results: School says Barking and Dagenham local authority has advised them not to publish 2020 results. In 2019 (the last year when exams took place), 41 per cent of pupils got 9-5 in both maths and English GCSE, with 21 per cent of grades 9-7. At A level, 48 per cent A*-B and 26 per cent A*/A grades.

Teaching and learning: Results are way above the national standard for a school with such a big, and expanding, cohort. Used to be a specialist science college and science, maths and computing results still stand out – no mean feat in such a strongly working-class school. Pupils say the English department is also exceptional. French and Spanish from year 7, with pupils strongly encouraged to take one language at GCSE, while those who speak another language at home often take a GCSE in that too. Psychology and sociology popular GCSEs, as is the plethora of vocational options available at this level, including construction (in the impressive sponsored £30k onsite teaching area, where pupils can learn everything from bricklaying to plastering and painting), beauty therapy (in the wow-factor onsite beauty school where we'd have gladly become guinea pigs for a massage ourselves) and food and hospitality. A joy to see when so many schools are cutting back their vocational provision to focus on league tables.

The ability range is massive, from those aiming at A*s to those who joined the school with a reading age of 5 or 6. Setting in every subject in years 7 to 9, then in core subjects of English, maths and science. Pupils told us 'there's no stigma about being in a lower set – it usually just means you learn in a more visual way' and there's auditing to ensure fluidity between sets. Subject clinics and revision sessions are available throughout the year, including during some weekends and every Easter holidays; parents say it reflects 'the amazing commitment of teachers', around 16 per cent of whom attended the school themselves. 'Honestly, the teachers are so supportive and that's not just academically but emotionally too – they really want you to do well,' a pupil told us.

Plethora of vocational options at GCSE including construction and beauty therapy: we'd have gladly become guinea pigs for a massage in the wow-factor beauty school

Learning support and mentor rooms also enable children to come and catch up on literacy and numeracy – perhaps because they've been off sick or they're upset because of family problems and can't cope amongst their peers. Pupils also value the 'Robert Clack good lesson' template, which involves explaining to pupils the objective, interactive content and process of every lesson – 'you know what to expect every time you sit down in a classroom and the goals you're supposed to have reached,' said one. Homework levels on the high side, but nobody seems to mind and student planners are regularly checked by staff to ensure academic balance between pupils. Current focus on identifying and working with specific groups that are less aspirational than others, 'for example, the disaffected white British,' says head.

The sixth form is part of the North East Consortium with two other local schools, offering more than 40 courses at different levels. Many sixth formers are the first in their families to stay in education post-16. No minimum entry requirements, as courses range from a certificate in motor vehicle servicing to further maths, though students who want to take A levels must have at least five grade 4s at GCSE. 'We don't set the benchmark too high because we want to give these children a chance.' Maths and sciences are the most popular A level courses, followed closely by English, history, economics and media studies. Vocational options in business, IT, food and nutrition and sport popular, as is beauty therapy

– 'we give everyone the opportunity to be successful here'.

Learning support and SEN: SENs – which includes the whole gamut from mild dyslexia and ADHD to pupils with Asperger's, hearing and sight problems and cerebral palsy – all get plenty of support as required. We heard from one family how a girl had 'improved so much that she can now spell better than me, despite having an EHC plan'. School praised for tailoring support 'in a very personalised and caring way' and pupils reeled off long list of modifications to chairs, desks and learning equipment in their smart new year 7 block.

The arts and extracurricular: Boys', girls' and mixed school choirs go from strength to strength (we heard them in an assembly – mesmerising), including entering national song competitions and hosting musical exhibitions. Ex-pupil Sandy Shaw gets stuck in enthusing pupils when she can, including attending concerts where she has been known to throw out a tune or two herself. Impressive school orchestra and jazz group perform at Christmas and summer concerts. Individual instrumental lessons are free (although we were disappointed that none of the pupils we met had taken this up) and whole year groups learn the likes of piano (two to a keyboard – year 7), ukulele (year 8) etc. There are regular whole school performances combining music, art and drama – such as Coram Boy and the Lion, the Witch and the Wardrobe. 'My daughter was very shy when she joined the school, now she sings on the stage at Christmas – and it's all down to the music teacher using the arts to bring her out of herself,' one parent told us.

School says they see art as vital, including as an extracurricular subject, and there's some lovely artwork displayed around the school, with spacious facilities for both this and DT, both of which have reasonable take-up at GCSE. But pupils we met unanimously cited art as the weakest department, saying it is less engaging and accessible than other subjects 'and it's always the same people do well.' Good food tech facilities and plenty of opportunities to make culinary delights; one year 7 pupil we met was itching to get the theory out of the way and get their pinny on.

School trips include a French exchange, sixth form politics and history visits to Washington and New York and sports trips to Canada, Barbados, Germany and South Africa. Cultural visits to Italy and Spain; expedition visits to Egypt and Latin America. Residentials to Isle of Wight and day trips to France, among others. School sees these as critical to children's development, with regular fundraising ensuring nobody misses out on

Ex-pupil Sandy Shaw gets stuck in enthusing pupils when she can: she has been known to throw out a tune or two herself

the whole-class trips (although there was some irritation among pupils we met about how many inevitably miss out on the expensive extracurricular ones).

Sport: Rare is the comp where pupils say nobody really hates sports, everyone feels there are enough teams and they get frequent wins at high level. 'If there isn't room for someone who is interested in a sport in an existing team, they either get to be a sub or a new C or D team is created if there's enough of them,' a pupil said, with all the ones we met raving about how much they enjoy sport 'because there's something for everyone'. And they bring home the silver too. They have been 23 years borough champions in athletics and recently came third nationally. Rugby also a strength for both girls and boys ('getting in the Essex finals used to be a big deal, now it's normal'), with a rugby academy attracting talented players to the sixth form. Football, netball and cross-country all do well and individual pupils have competed nationally in a range of sports, their team shirts displayed proudly alongside photos and trophies throughout the school.

A sizeable leisure centre includes a sports hall and fitness suite, open to the local community outside school hours, and there's a new sports hall on the lower school site. Tennis and netball courts galore and no shortage of pitches, including Astroturf. 'Teachers give up a lot of their spare time to sport – the children see this and it makes them have even more respect for them,' said one parent. Another told us, 'The fact that my son gets up every Saturday morning to do rugby means he gets to know a lot of the kids in other schools – the school encourages that mingling and I really believe it stops youth on youth crime in the local area because they wind up recognising each other when they see each other in town.'

Ethos and heritage: The school is named after local legend Robert Clack, who was mayor from 1940 to 1942 and a champion of social justice. 'He was a passionate advocate for the people of Dagenham and the values he stood for – mutual respect, compassion, discipline, high expectations and aspirations, and hard work – permeate the ethos of our school,' says head. For decades, the school was considered excellent, and after a major blip in the mid-90s (kids riding bikes down corridors and even smoking in classrooms), it was brought back to its former glory in the late 1990s.

The lower school site opened in 1935, the upper school buildings, half a mile away, in 1955. A third site, for years 7-11, opened in 2020. With 360 in each year group, it is currently one of the largest schools in the borough and when it reaches full capacity of 4,000 it will be one of the largest in Britain.

It is one of the most deprived areas in the country, with the tower blocks of the Becontree Estate – one of the largest in England – casting a shadow over the playground. Yet this is one of the most ordered, neatest schools we've come across. Building works and acquisition of new land have helped eradicate pinch points and highlights include the uber modern year 7 block, zen beauty salon, good science block and stand-out sports facilities. No shortage of computers, but very few lockers, which bothers some parents. 'It's not ideal to have to keep a heavy bag with you all day,' said one.

We saw attentive pupils in every lesson we observed, looking impeccably neat in blazers and ties with plenty of pupil buy-in ('uniforms are great for equality and it's good to be smart,' said one). Pupils are also proud of their badges, reflecting the school's emphasis on praise and leadership responsibilities – we saw awards given out in assembly for 'citizen of the week' and for reading one million words. Racism issues minimal ('the worst we get is occasional silly comments,' says head), with students mixing in genuinely diverse groups outside classes. Active school council made up of 300 pupils.

Consistent behaviour policy: every positive action gets a reward and every negative action is followed with a consequence – and every student knows it

A breakfast and homework club – along with masses of extracurricular clubs in everything from cheerleading to astronomy and sports to debating – mean school is open from 7am to 6pm. Outside in the community there's little trouble, with Robert Clack kids known locally for being respectful and well-behaved – a far cry from days of old. Food could be improved, pupils told us, and some parents told us about the 'very long queues' which can make 'getting something to eat at lunchtime quite hard.'

Pastoral care, inclusivity and discipline: School has one of the most consistent behaviour policies we've come across – pupils don't even say some teachers are stricter than others. Every positive action gets a reward and every negative action is followed with a consequence – and every student knows it. Praise includes colours for sport, music and performing arts; awards during assemblies; notes home to parents; and trips to the likes of Thorpe Park. Meanwhile, the non-negotiable, tiered sanction system includes lunchtime detention, Friday after-school detention and temporary exclusion that takes place on-site rather than sending pupils home. Lateness – even by a minute – is not tolerated and there's a blanket ban on mobile phones ('social media is such an addiction and distraction'). All the big stuff – gangs, knife crime, drugs – non-issues for the most part because 'we take such a hard line that it just doesn't enter the school threshold'. One permanent exclusion in the year before our visit.

School adamant that unless children feel both safe and happy, they can't learn, with pastoral care mainly coming from teachers and school counsellors, plus an increasing emphasis on mental health. Bullying rare, which pupils put down to CCTV throughout the school and an ethos of students of looking after each other, with many friendships are formed outside their year groups (mostly through clubs).

Pupils and parents: Families largely from the surrounding estates, where there are some severe poverty issues, with many coming from several generations of unemployment – though proximity to the school puts a premium on the prices of the few houses for sale in the area. School largely reflects the fast-changing demographic, with around 35 per cent white working-class; 35 per cent Afro-Caribbean; 15 per cent Asian (mainly Bangladeshi); and the rest mixed race. We found pupils delightful – polite, resilient, articulate and hard-working. And although they are typically from underachieving backgrounds, most parents are very much on board with the school – we couldn't find a single one that wasn't thoroughly supportive. The school employs a parental adviser who visits families under stress and helps with advice and support regarding housing, clothing and food allowances. Head currently considering a scheme whereby parents who have experience around issues such as discipline, routines and study skills would help other parents struggling in these areas.

The last word: We love this true comprehensive in one of the most deprived areas of the country. All roads here lead back to high expectations and aspirations and it's all done in a context of mutual respect and compassion, albeit unashamedly strict. Staff, parents, pupils and even many of those in the local community that don't have kids attending the school seem to be bursting with pride about it. And despite the fast expansion of pupil numbers, it's managing to hold onto the values it holds so dear. No wonder parents and pupils consider a successful application a golden ticket.

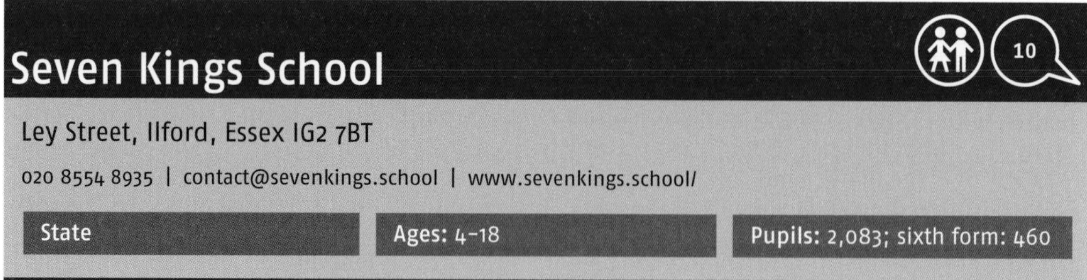

Seven Kings School

Ley Street, Ilford, Essex IG2 7BT

020 8554 8935 | contact@sevenkings.school | www.sevenkings.school/

State | Ages: 4–18 | Pupils: 2,083; sixth form: 460

Executive head: Since 2017, Jane Waters (50s), BA English from UCL, followed by a PGCE at Warwick University: 'I never really thought about teaching – I wanted to be a researcher at the BBC, but then I took a gap year to be a leader at PGL, and thought, I actually quite like young people.' Ridiculous, really, she says, given that she comes from a family of over 30 aunts and cousins 'many of whom are teachers'.

She left Wales for her first teaching job in London at Ravenscroft School where she taught English for three years, followed by a seven-year stint as literacy co-ordinator at Park High School then head of English at Loxford School. She then took a break from teaching to become a consultant and English adviser for Redbridge during the 'Blair era'. She joined Seven Kings in 2007 as assistant head, during which time she was seconded out to a couple of failing schools, which she brought up to an Ofsted 'good' rating in a matter of months. When she returned to Seven Kings it was as head, and then she became executive head of both the secondary and primary schools.

We met Ms Waters on a bleak and rainy Tuesday, but her canary yellow jacket and ebullient nature immediately warmed us up. Still enthusiastic about education even after teaching for 30 years, she says: 'Education is still the biggest lever for change there is. In my case it took me out of a pretty dysfunctional family in south Wales.' No surprise, therefore, that for the last 12 years this head has chosen to work at a school where she can really make a difference. Many of the students come from 'complex backgrounds' and the school wholly embraces children with disabilities (some severe), and currently has 93 students with a disability on the register.

However, Ms Waters has high expectations of her pupils and tells them regularly that although a grade 4 at GCSE may be the government accepted pass, she expects at least 5s from her pupils: 'The result is that the language of the pupils here is aspirational and they understand that 5 should be the minimum grade for most of them.' It is important to her that her pupils aim high and the school is very proactive with its alumni regularly coming back to give talks aimed at inspiring the next lot of graduates: 'We had one student a couple of years ago who got a job working as one of Obama's speech writers, and another very disabled student who was one of the Olympic torch bearers.'

This head is well liked and respected by parents – 'very down to earth and easy to talk to' and 'always cheery and happy' were just some of the comments we heard. She has one son who is currently doing his A levels at Woodhouse College and describes herself as a 'rugby mum', as she is often ferrying him around to his various fixtures. When she is not playing taxi service, Ms Waters is an avid reader and quite 'politically engaged in local groups'. She also enjoys travelling and visiting her family in south Wales.

Head of primary school since September 2020, Paula Murray-Mower.

Entrance: Usual primary school admissions criteria for 120 reception places, with the school reaching its full capacity in September 2021. One founding year group parent described as 'an exciting prospect' seeing the school grow as their children move up through it.

Children in the primary school are guaranteed Seven Kings secondary school places. Over 2,000 external candidates apply for the 180 year 7 places, with a waiting list well into the hundreds. As it's completely non-selective, children in the looked after system/those with an EHC plan are prioritised (following the admissions code), followed by siblings, after which it's down to distance. Around 80 per cent go through to the sixth form, with around 2,000 applying for the remaining 140 places. Successful applicants need six 5s or above at GCSE, with 6s in their chosen A level subjects (7 for science and maths).

Exit: It is expected that virtually all primary children will move up to the secondary. Some 60 per cent go on to sixth form. The rest leave after GCSEs, mostly to do vocational qualifications, other courses or apprenticeships. Of those who leave after sixth form, 90 per cent go to university – many to Russell Group, although school says 'we try not to put too much importance on Russell Group universities. Huddersfield, for example, is a great university too.' Economics, finance and science are popular courses, with 10 medical students in 2020. Oxbridge, LSE and Imperial feature among recent destinations. Some take a gap year, do an internship in the City or go into apprenticeships in the civil service, finance sector and media. Others to art college or straight into jobs.

Latest results: In 2020, 44 per cent 9-7 at GCSE; 92 per cent 9-4 in both maths and English. At A level, 33 per cent A*/A (61 per cent A*-B). In 2019 (the last year when exams took place), 42 per cent 9-7 at GCSE; 79 per cent 9-4 in both English and maths. At A level, 19 per cent A*/A (49 per cent A*-B).

Teaching and learning: If achieving top grades is your priority for your kids, then you have very little to fret about at Seven Kings. Despite its 'very average' intake, Seven Kings seems to sail effortlessly to the top of the league tables. The hugely oversubscribed sixth form produced respectable results too.

This is a school that starts with outcomes required then finds the best means of achieving them. 'This is no exam factory, but we do know the syllabus and the exam requirements, and we also know the kind of teaching that works.' Pupils concur that the teaching is both vibrant and innovative, with faces in classrooms looking hungry to learn when we visited. 'Teachers here bring subjects alive,' one pupil told us. 'There's constant encouragement to probe the teachers because they want everyone to grasp the subject really well,' said another, who added that even if you email a teacher at 8pm, you often get a reply.

High expectations for teachers too, and three-quarters of the middle leadership team trained within the school. Generally low turnover of staff 'although sadly we have lost six teachers in the last few years to Bristol, which is a bit like London, but much cheaper,' the head sighed. Parents rave about the quality of teaching and one said: 'We had the opportunity of sending our daughter to a private school, but the standard here is so good here, what would be the point?'

Monitoring, tracking and a 'can-do' culture also contribute to academic success. 'You won't find a pupil we haven't spoken to in the past three weeks about their learning'; every student receives two formal one-to-one interviews about their academic progress per year, in addition to many more informal ones. Pupils praise the marking system that means they've given comments, rather than grades. 'Understanding what you've done well and what you can do to improve is more helpful than just a mark,' explained one. Also popular is the 'passport' that all kids in KS3 get. 'The children get visas to add in for good work, eventually being made a "scholar"'; school encourages a strong triangular relationship between students, teachers and parents to ensure that everyone is on board with learning outcomes in a well-communicated way.

English and maths lead the way at this school 'and the departments are very competitive with each other,' laughs the head. Science is also one of the strongest subjects with learning for science very practical (one of the labs is university-level). Students rave about the science here and the school is a recognised centre of excellence in this subject, with some staff sitting on the boards of top science organisations.

Monitoring, tracking and a 'can-do' culture contribute to academic success. 'You won't find a pupil we haven't spoken to in the past three weeks about their learning'

Three languages on offer – French, Spanish and Mandarin – with well over two-thirds of the students studying at least one language at GCSE. Setting only in maths 'because all the evidence shows that setting doesn't work and puts a ceiling on young people's achievement'. School decided to abandon BTecs in the sixth form as they felt they couldn't be 'all things to all people'.

Around 120 out of 180 pupils continue on to the sixth form, where students get to choose from a wide range of A levels. Psychology is one of the strongest departments as is maths. One pupil who moved from another school into the sixth form told us, 'Teachers here give you a step-by-step guide to research, writing essays and getting through exams, whereas at my previous school, you're just expected to get on with it yourself.'

There are 600 pupils in the primary school, most join on average a bit below the national expectations, but make very good progress. Pupils are currently not set in maths and English, but they are in phonics: 'We'll see, going forward.' Key stage 2 pupils learn French, and younger ones have received taster sessions in a number of different languages, including Mandarin Chinese.

Learning support and SEN: Seven Kings has a national reputation as a centre of excellence for disabled children. There is a specially adapted entrance and well-equipped medical centre, plus the classrooms are accessible by wheelchair. They have a motto which is 'our ability, not disability'. One parent of a disabled child said that 'the school is fantastic. They have bent over backwards for my son and are so well equipped with lifts and hoists. We will all miss it so much when he leaves in the summer.' In addition, there's a well-staffed highly-skilled SEN department (16 per cent SEN when we visited, 65 with EHC plans), providing exemplary provision.

The arts and extracurricular: Music highly valued, with spacious and well-equipped practice areas. Years 7 and 8 are on a scheme whereby the whole class learns a particular instrument together, with past examples including recorder, clarinet and trumpet. There's a school orchestra, rock band, jazz band, ensembles (including strings), as well as student led bands. The school recently won an award to buy steel drums.

This is a place which, once visited, will resonate with you for a long time afterwards – not least because it is a school with a massive heart and social conscience

Spectacular art. We were privileged on our tour to grab a sneaky peak at the A level showcase. There were some truly astounding self portraits and innovative pieces of art. Indeed many of their graduates go on to art school or to study architecture.

Plenty on offer for aspiring performers, including an extra period for drama in years 7 and 8: 'We think it's is a great way of developing confidence and oral skills.' KS4s put on an annual community play, focusing on issues relevant to them – this year they concentrated on mental health. West End theatre groups regularly invited into school to do workshops, with students also being invited on trips to theatre performances, and there are whole school performances annually too.

School day trips to museums and galleries, as well PGL in year 8 and other residentials including Belgium (history), Austria (skiing) and Iceland (geography). Plenty of after-school and lunchtime clubs, including a home learning club which offers a quiet place to study for those who are unable to do so at home. Other clubs for sport, arts, dance, radio, Amnesty International, Model UN, rocket club, chess, model aircraft, astronomy, film and more.

Like the secondary, the primary is all about the wealth of opportunity. Music is a speciality and the younger pupils learn to play African drums, with weekly music assemblies. Specialist PE and art teachers come over from the secondary, and some PE lessons are held on the secondary school site. 'This is one of the biggest benefits of being attached to a senior school,' school says.

The primary also offers the opportunity to visit central London museums and art galleries as well as having trips to Greenwich and local sights. Extracurricular options are wide and varied too, and include everything from karate, football and street dance to cooking, sewing and gardening in the school's own lovely little allotment. Excellent before and after school provision in the school hall by external Shine Club.

Sport: Two hours a week of PE, with very few complaints from pupils. Football, cricket, netball, rugby, long-distance running and athletics all core to the curriculum, with notable successes in cricket, football and long-distance running. Judo and fencing recently added to the growing list of sports. Facilities include an Astroturf pitch, front field, sports hall and gym, along with table tennis tables dotted throughout the outside areas.

Ethos and heritage: The school started life in the 1930s as a girls' grammar school. After several changes and a merger, Seven Kings was created in 1974, to serve the community as a co-educational secondary school. Some remaining original features give a feel of the inter-war years – an expansive spread of low-rise brick buildings and evocative assembly hall. One parent said: 'I love the oldy worldy look of this school. It's a school that actually still looks like a school.' However, the reception area has had somewhat of a facelift and is bright, tastefully decorated, and at the time of our visit had some wonderful costume installations on display.

Modern additions also include the lecture theatre, glass entrance hall and shiny new science labs. Stand-out facilities include the spacious and well-used library; the DT facilities with impressive window displays of students' work; the well-resourced sixth form private study areas (which

School has a national reputation as a centre of excellence for disabled children. They have a motto: 'our ability, not disability'

you have to pre-book) and the sixth form common room, a great space with its own canteen.

This is a place which, once visited, will resonate with you for a long time afterwards – not least because it is a school with a massive heart and social conscience. As a result, there is a lot of love and respect and it has often been used as a benchmark to demonstrate what a state school in a deprived area is capable of achieving. We could tell that in the main parents are a respectful bunch and as a result have produced children with respect and a strong work ethos. 'Pupils at Seven Kings definitely stand out compared to the other local schools. There is no scruffiness and there is a real sense of pride', one parent said.

No shortage of leadership opportunities and student voice, with a vast array of headship roles for students, as well as plenty of pupil involvement in everything from designing the new primary school and its uniform to observing and feeding back on lessons. Peer mentoring also popular. One parent enthused about the hard work put in by the school: 'My daughter was very shy and highly reserved when she first started at Seven Kings. The school immediately recognised this and responded very quickly. Within weeks she was actively taking part in school life and was so excited to go to school every day.'

The school's mantra is that 'a quiet student isn't a good learner.' Innovative courses and workshops help, including a day of circus skills in year 7, which takes pupils out of their comfort zone and reminds them that if you put your mind to it, you can often do things you never thought you could.

On the day of our visit to Seven Kings, it was Mexican food day in the canteen and after a very yummy burrito meal, we decided that the head chef should be cloned – every school should have one. Not only was he a very cheery soul, but his catering team offer the most unbelievable incentives for healthy eating we have ever heard of. Last month a pupil won a bike for getting the most ticks on the healthy eating chart – other incentives can include Amazon vouchers.

The primary opened in 2015. Located in a former bus depot, it is a two minute walk from the secondary. But its modern and sleek exterior, with vibrant and bright cladding, is in stark contrast to its older sibling, and quite frankly doesn't look as if you're about to enter into a school at all. However, once you walk through the main reception area into the long and bright corridors with colourful wall displays, and hear the echoes of happy children in the playground at lunch break, it very much springs to life. We felt, though, as we walked around this pristine building with still many unused areas, that the school will gain largely from a full cohort of students (from 2021). Currently it is a bit too stark and quiet in many areas. That said, the current lucky students can benefit from everything being shiny and new and pretty much state-of-the-art.

Brand new facilities include a landscaped inner courtyard, a rooftop Astroturf playing area and wall to ceiling vertical windows on the upper floors looking down into the courtyard (handy for teachers to spot any misdemeanours, of which we are certain there would be few). Lovingly painted art installations by teachers dotted around the school and beautiful new books in the colourful library for the children to read. We also noticed a pleasant fresh smell. (Very unschool-like, we thought.)

Pastoral care, inclusivity and discipline: Seven Kings serves a neighbourhood that has social problems and deprivation typical of many parts of urban London. But despite its relatively stark surrounding streets – and the fact that many students come from difficult backgrounds – the school itself is an oasis of purposeful calm. Discipline is assumed, corridors are quiet, classes orderly. That's not to say there's no bad behaviour. As the head says, 'we do exclude students, but it is extremely rare. We have a good relationship with the PRU (pupil referral unit) which is really the last chance saloon. Nine out of 10 cases are really successful.' However, the school acknowledges that sometimes, hard as they may try, the odd pupil slips through the net.

What helps the most, according to the school, is if they can get to know each child on an individual basis: 'You have to take each child on their own merit and at the end of the day if they can't make a mistake in school and learn from it, where can they?' the head explains. There is also a big thrust towards teaching good manners: 'We make sure the students say good morning on the gates every morning as it is important that children learn their discourse at a young age.'

Pastoral care and well-being are high on the agenda of every member of staff at this school, with particular attention from form tutors, year leaders, staff mentors and the full-time student counsellor. The secondary offers yoga and meditation sessions and occasional 'drop down days' when the timetable is collapsed to focus on issues such as how to revise and stress management.

Bullying happens, but is rare. Pupils value diversity here – ethnically and in terms of disability, among other things – which students say helps in promoting a culture that values difference. No-one from years 7-11 is let off-site at breaks or lunchtimes. Lots of talks around drugs, drinking and smoking, sex, eating disorders and cyberbullying as part of the CPHSE curriculum.

Diversity is much celebrated at the primary school too, with assembles and performances about different religious festivals, but 'we also do a lot of work too on British values and learning to be tolerant of other people's beliefs'.

Pupils and parents: This is a neighbourhood comprehensive, with students mainly living within a one-mile radius (some years, it's just half a mile) and previously coming from around 40 feeder schools – now first priority to the recently opened Seven Kings Primary School. More than three-quarters come from Indian, Pakistani or Bangladeshi backgrounds with 61 per cent of the Muslim faith, 'very much a reflection of the local demographic'. Roughly 19 per cent (23 per cent of secondary pupils) are on free school meals.

Primary school pupils looked smart and happy and those who had been given special playground duties were proudly showing off their orange hi-viz jackets to us. We noticed how all the children were interacting with each other in the playground, including those with obvious disabilities. One parent said: 'There is a mix of everything here. My daughter recently had a disabled work experience teacher from the secondary school and that night she said to me, "Mummy when I grow up, I want a lovely wheelchair like my teacher's." Kids just aren't fazed by disability.' SEN accounts for around seven per cent of the school intake, with lot of large, empty areas for children who need extra support.

In the main, parents are very involved in their children's education. They aren't, however, a cake-baking, raffle-holding crowd and, to the disappointment of some parents we spoke to, there is no PTA at the secondary. The kids themselves work hard and, and on the whole, behave well. 'They are bright and ambitious and absolutely gorgeous.'

The last word: The school motto of 'Friendship, Excellence, Opportunity' is what the school is about on every level. It is a school with high aspirations, and the academic rigour can be tough because of the pursuit of excellence. But the results prove it's achievable, with a wide range of strategies ensuring that every student is pushed to reach their full potential. But there's fun to be had here too, with students clearly enjoying school life. 'Places are like gold dust', and parents who send their offspring here can be confident they will reach or exceed expectations, as well as coming out well-rounded individuals.

Sir William Burrough Primary School

Salmon Lane, London E14 7PQ

020 7987 2147 | admin@sirwilliamburrough.towerhamlets.sch.uk | www.sirwilliamburrough.info/

State | Ages: 3–11 | Pupils: 345

Headteacher: Since 1995 Avril Newman (60s) BEd, first class honours from Goldmith's, who has spent her whole teaching career in Tower Hamlets. A national leader of education, a JP and has been honoured with a Freedom of the City award. She cited her greatest achievement as integrating rigorous attention to academic standards with high emotional intelligence; qualities she noted 'don't always go together' but, in this case, are evidently modelled from the top. A warm, positive and articulate woman whose delicate stature belies a strong and dynamic force. She believes that every child should aspire to the highest possible standards in reading, writing and maths regardless of social or cultural background; the testimony of which lies in the reputation and success of the school and the low turnover of staff. One parent remarked: 'She is amazing, she really listens', and another described her as 'very accessible' and 'very good at dealing with a problem'.

She has an open door policy, literally (during our visit the lively community toddler group was in full swing just outside her office), and encourages parents to come in and talk face to face with her about any problem. Communication between the school and parents includes monthly Cup of Tea Mornings, described by one parent as 'Avril meetings', providing a forum where parents make suggestions for inmprovements. A lover of theatre, books and travel, she is married with two grown-up children.

Entrance: A highly oversubscribed school in a highly populated area means that the appetite for places is fierce: recently 180 applications for the 45 places on offer in reception. Customary priority is given to looked-after children, siblings, then proximity – and last year you needed to live very close indeed (within 260m). The recent changes to the welfare system have resulted in some local families moving away so places in the later years do crop up.

Exit: Mostly a spread of local secondary schools with the occasional child attending an out of borough independent or grammar. Most to Sir John Cass Foundation and Redcoat Church of England School, St Paul's Way Trust School, Stepney Green Mathematics and Computing College or Bow School.

Our view: In a densely urban area with the entrance tucked up a dreary back street, there is something quite magical about stepping through the gate into the friendly and colourful atmosphere. For a Victorian building spanning three floors, it is surprisingly light and airy with windows open and homely curtains billowing against a soft breeze. Children's artwork adorns all surfaces, proudly including some deft pencil drawings depicting, as one articulate boy observed, 'sociality in the city', as well as a net suspended from a classroom ceiling decorated with sumptuous rainforest paintings; a project complemented by a trip to Kew Gardens, one of many trips to take full advantage of the city's resources.

The classrooms are roomy and colourful, all with interactive whiteboards, and the library is calm and attractive. Unusually for a state primary, there is a dedicated and fully-equipped computer room backed up by widespread use of iPads. The recently refurbished reception classrooms are calm and comfortable with integrated toilets and a separate outdoor play space. The indoor gyms are a bit on the small side but there are two of them, and a series of outdoor spaces surrounds the school building, including a dedicated 'dance space' where children can dance to music outdoors during lunchtime; two multi-sport pitches; a netted cricket area; and a vast array of play equipment including a trampoline. When we visited, during playtime all children were busy climbing, skipping, playing table football or foraging in the wooded area making 'camps'. An advantage of reigning for 25 years, Mrs Newman has overseen the planting and maturing of the lush trees that encircle the playground, adding an abundance of green to this urban oasis.

Sats-wise, some 95 per cent of pupils achieve at least the expected standard in the three Rs, well above the national average, and it's ranked in the top two per cent of schools nationally. A National Support School, SWB is amongst the 200 top-performing primary schools and in the top eight per cent for the progress of all children, regardless of background, the hard data testimony to the school's academic approach. All children, apart from those with particular special needs, have learnt to read and write (in cursive!) by the end of reception, when they partake in a graduation ceremony complete with mortar boards and gowns. Once the basics are established, the Accelerated Reader and Accelerated Maths schemes kick in: online, personalised programmes which motivate through quizzes, prizes and international competitions. Families are able to win what amounts to a small library between them once they have read a million words: 'our way of ensuring children have books at home'. Other incentives include a maths Olympics, where children win rosettes for knowing their times tables, and a spelling bee.

Children's artwork adorns all surfaces, proudly including some deft pencil drawings depicting, as one articulate boy observed, 'sociality in the city'

All this takes place in the mornings, with the afternoons dedicated to the creative, experiential learning of the International Primary Curriculum (IPC). Sir William Burrough was one of the first primary schools in the country to introduce the IPC, which adopts a global perspective alongside a thematic, topic-based approach to learning. In a project on the Romans, children traced each other's bodies to create a life-size collage and went on to act out the Battle of Marathon. The children make their own movies and animations using iPads and, if the plot demands it, a green screen.

An energetic and effective use of partnerships brings in professional coaching in fencing, judo, rugby, hockey and handball alongside reading, number and chess partners from City firms. A recently established link with the Worshipful Company of Musicians complements the already lively musical culture in the school, including a 60-strong choir and a ukulele ensemble. They even have a choreographer-in-residence who ensures that every child in the school gets moving, appreciated particularly by one parent who felt that 'dance is fantastic' at the school. After-school clubs include film and animation, Spanish, sailing and debating. Years 3 to 5 build up their independence on residential trips offering challenge and outdoor adventure. Year 5s and 6s get to learn Latin. There is a breakfast club from 8.30am and a teatime club that runs until 4.30pm, facilities that were much appreciated by many of the working parents we met.

The school's You Can Do It programme 'keeps levels of confidence and resilience high, and is deeply woven into relationships of respect, tolerance, kindness and courtesy'. We saw this in action as children held open doors, enquired about the welfare of others and remarked that 'we all comfort each other'. There is an emphasis on continual practice and one pupil commented that 'if you are unsure, there is always a teacher next to you'. A caring infrastructure is evident throughout: there is a room dedicated to part-time and summer-born reception children and year 6s were helped to feel calm before their Sats through afternoon yoga sessions. There is also a system of peer support via year 6 school monitors, who look out for the younger children, and year 4s, who help the reception classes learn to read.

All SEN support is offered in the classroom by teachers and TAs 'in the moment of learning' rather than in separate sessions or groups. This is a genuinely inclusive school with an expansive cultural mix. A small majority of pupils are from Bangladeshi heritage, others are of Somalian, Eastern European, Chinese and white British backgrounds. Some 75 per cent of pupils speak English as an additional language, though most are London-born and speak English when they arrive: the school's mastery of words proclaimed by repeatedly finishing as runners up in the English Speaking Union's Pan London Debating Tournament. Parents describe it as 'like a family', 'creative, friendly, inclusive' and one pupil commented 'they accept everybody who comes here'. When faced with the question of what the school might be able to do better, the pupils understandably struggled: 'I would change the sausages into hot dogs' and 'get a bigger trampoline' were about it.

Verbal mastery proclaimed by repeatedly finishing as runners up in the English Speaking Union's Pan London Debating Tournament

The last word: Over her 25 years as headteacher, Avril Newman has been inspired by the words of John Tomsett: 'A truly great school grows like an oak tree over many years.' Under the talented and passionate guidance of its head, Sir William Burrough has matured well like the trees in the playground. A happy, inclusive and high-achieving urban primary.

Snaresbrook Preparatory School

12

75 Woodford Road, South Woodford, London E18 2EA

020 8989 2394 | office@snaresbrookprep.org | www.snaresbrookprep.org

Independent	Pupils: 168
Ages: 3–11	Fees: £9,781 – £13,084 pa

Head: Since 2018, Ralph Dalton LLB (Hertfordshire) (late 30s). Studied law, before making the leap from legal auditing to teaching via a school-based teacher training scheme, cutting his classroom teeth in state schools in Southend and Basildon. Then spent 10 years at Woodford Green Prep, rising to senior deputy head and taking responsibility for pastoral care and secondary school applications as well as teaching philosophy and maths. A kindly and sympathetic man with a co-operative and caring approach, his main objective at Snaresbrook is to ensure every child gets the focussed, individual attention the school is known for. 'I was attracted to the post because it was clear that everyone really did know everyone here.' On the gates morning and afternoon, he seems to have successfully managed an unusually smooth change in leadership, pupils welcoming minor alterations he's introduced. 'The house points system is much fairer now,' one confided. Married to a teacher, with a young son and daughter.

Entrance: Twenty-four enter nursery at 3 rising 4. The school is oversubscribed but not academically selective. Instead, the cut is made by identifying parents who share the school's values. Unsuccessful hopefuls are put on a waiting list and returned to if vacancies arise. Class size largest in the early years, reducing naturally as some leave at 7 and 8. 'We like to keep it to 16-18 in the higher years, though we do occasionally take someone if we feel we can help.' At that stage, applicants spend a morning at the school to establish whether they fit the class chemistry.

Exit: Small exodus at 7+ for larger scale or all-through schools, but most leave at 11, to a wide range of schools in the state and private sector. The majority aiming for local independents – Forest, Chigwell and Bancroft's – but good numbers, too, to City of London (boys' and girls'), commutable grammars (Ilford, Woodford County High, Chelmsford) and (faith) comprehensives. North London Collegiate features too. Head is also encouraging parents to think further afield, including boarding. Guidance given from year 4 (if not earlier). 'I try to encourage them to consider not only who their child is now, but what they'll be like as a teenager.' Thorough but not pressured preparation ('We're not pushing it in every lesson') includes mock interviews and timed practice papers. Vast majority get their first choice, many with scholarships.

Our view: Founded as a private enterprise in the 1930s, the school has now been owned and managed by the same family for 50 years, with a separate executive governing body responsible for day-to-day administration.

Main school building, situated on a leafy thoroughfare, is a large double-fronted Victorian villa, once a family home, which retains a sense of its original purpose in being not overly spic and span. Later additions include separate space for nursery and reception and a free-standing assembly hall-cum-gym.

Academically strong. Largely follows the national curriculum, but in an accelerated and enriched manner, with part-time specialists in languages (with French from nursery, Latin from year 3) and IT supplementing well-qualified classroom teachers. The overall objective is to finish the primary school curriculum by the end of year 5. 'That means we can use year 6 to provide a broader education,' says the head. Curriculum balanced between 'discovery' learning and formal knowledge 'We want pupils to leave as scientists, geographers, and historians, for which you need a core body of knowledge.' Teachers clearly well liked. 'The teachers are very nice,' said one pupil. 'They never make you feel embarrassed if you ask for help.' No setting, but school carefully monitors progress to ensure all get appropriate support.

Two out of eight classroom teachers qualified SENCos, (one of whom the school sponsored to train) so a reasonably wide range of difficulties (from speech and language to Asperger's) can be addressed in house. External experts then called upon when required. Not the ideal site for those with mobility issues due to its abundance of stairs.

'Parents tell us they want happy and confident children, who do the best they can,' says the head. It would be fair to say they get what they're looking for

Despite its small scale, the school provides well beyond the basics. Music strong, with a dedicated part-time head of music. All study the penny whistle in year 1 (a recent initiative), recorder in year 2; most take instrumental lessons (woodwind, strings, guitar, clarinet, saxophone) from visiting staff. Plenty of opportunities to make (and compose) music, with a school orchestra, assembly band (to accompany hymn singing), spring concert, choir for years 5 and 6. Decent-sized playground and gym allow for twice-weekly sport/PE on site in the younger years; older pupils travel to nearby sports centre for netball, football, tag rugby, hockey, athletics. Swimming taught weekly to all in year 3, half the year to years 4-6. Annual sports day – held at proper track – is a highlight. Team sports more problematic, but school fields football and netball squads competing in local competitions with mixed-age teams. 'The positive side is it allows younger pupils to get early experience,' says the head. Professional football coach from Chelsea visits once a week teaching all. Art and drama both lively, with performance opportunities for pupils of all ages, and broader horizons encouraged in external events such as the ISA art competition. 'Our aim is to give every child the chance to shine,' says the head, 'whether in trampolining or knowledge of Dark Matter'.

Wide variety of clubs before and after school – from weaving to Spanish, country dancing to mindfulness – taught by teachers. Good range of trips, too, with annual jaunts to France, Haworth in Yorkshire (to study the Brontës, Victorian sanitation and the landscape), camping and year 6 outdoor pursuits.

Pastoral care undoubtedly a core strength and the term 'family' atmosphere justifiably applied.

'To "look after" pupils means something special here,' says the head. 'I've seen children in bigger environments really struggle; here they're able to jump in and gain in self-esteem.' The two (delightful) year 6 pupils who showed us round clearly knew everyone and everything about the place and loved the school – even the discipline. 'You do get told off for running in the corridor; they're strict when they need to be,' said one girl. In-class behaviour exemplary with attentive, enthusiastic faces in every classroom we visited.

A Christian school with hymns sung and Lord's Prayer recited daily. Non-Christians and non-believers, however, are fully included. 'We welcome all faiths,' says the head, 'and a lot of parents like the moral compass we provide; they know we're not going to push or proselytise.' Active PTA raises money for annual charity in popular summer fête, sleepover, etc. Strong sense of community, too, encouraged in three school houses (in which families are kept together). House points gained for those who shine in delivering the school's values (respect, excellence, sharing, perseverance, enjoyment, confidence, thoughtfulness, friendship, unity, learning) and competition encouraged with a myriad of silver trophies awarded at annual prize giving. School council for years 1-6, elected by each form, choose annual charity and consult on school's development plan. Broader democracy brought into play for annual events like film night, when everyone gets their say.

Basement dining hall, where pupils eat in relays. Menus regularly rotated, with vegetarian option and salad bar, but food possibly not Michelin starred. (Our guide observed, 'Sometimes the food is not so good', though head ripostes, 'We've worked hard to improve the food this year; it's healthy and well balanced, and the school's chef takes a keen interest in what children eat.')

Families from a wide range of ethnic backgrounds; most have two working parents, many are first-time buyers. All are looking for an academic education, in a structured, caring environment. 'They say they want happy and confident children, who do the best they can,' says the head. It would be fair to say they get what they're looking for.

The last word: This is a school that produces positive, articulate, young people, well equipped to go on to future schools and future educational success. 'Having had children educated here for many years,' said one parent, 'all my experience has been positive. Snaresbrook is a well-run school where the teachers are both friendly and professional and my children's development has been aided by the excellent pastoral care.'

Stepney All Saints Church of England Secondary School

CofE 13

Stepney Way, London E1 0RH

020 7790 6712 | info@sjcr.net | www.sjcr.net

State | **Ages:** 11-19 | **Pupils:** 1,445; sixth form: 415

Headteacher: Since 2016, Paul Woods BA PGCE (40s). Originally from Enniskillen in Northern Ireland, he studied French and politics at Kingston University and did his teacher training at the University of North London. Previously head of Bishop Stopford's CofE School in Enfield. Lives in north London, where he began his career as a French and Spanish teacher, moving up the ranks to deputy head, after which he moved to Barking 'because I wanted to work in a more challenging location'. Later moved into his first headship at Bishop Stopford where, in his first week, the school was told by Ofsted that it 'required improvement' and he set to work getting it up to a 'good' status two years (to the day) later.

Students say his office door is always open 'except for meetings', which encourages an informal drop-in approach. 'And he's nearly always in the corridors at class changeover and break times, when any one of us can chat to him – and we really do,' said one. With his easy, gregarious, one-of-us manner, it's easy to believe. 'This is a social institution, so what would be the point in sitting in an ivory tower or diarising everything?' he asks, adding that most things students talk to him about take all of 30 seconds. 'Then the issue is off their mind and they can get on with their studies.' Parents, in the main, have little to do with him. 'There's always someone to help you as a parent at the school – it's just not usually the head,' commented one, although there are obvious exceptions.

Teaches French (to year 10 the year we visited), while back in his office he is clearly a man with a plan, listing a lot of exciting proposals for the school from ensuring closer links between the different levels of leadership to a greater focus on the whole child – all with an infectious enthusiasm. 'One of my plans is a cultural entitlement programme because I want to be able to say to every single student, "You can expect this number of theatre trips, this number of day trips and this number of clubs to join".'

Entrance: Some 1,200 applicants for 208 places. Everyone is placed in one of four ability bands, assessed by the standard Tower Hamlets numeracy and literacy tests in year 5, with equal numbers of places offered from each band. This is a CofE school, so it does allocate a minority of places to committed Christians, with 40 places going to worshippers in a recognised Christian church, with looked-after children, social and medical needs, living in one of the listed parishes and then siblings in order of priority. The other 152 places have a similar priority order, but 20 are offered to first-born children. Families in the area tend to be large and siblings would otherwise monopolise the intake. Distance from the school is the tie-break. Sixteen places (four per band) are also allocated to those who score highest in the school's language aptitude test.

The sixth form is also highly oversubscribed, with over 1,000 applicants for 300 outside places. Most A level courses require five or more 9-4 grades at GCSE including English and maths, with some higher stipulations, eg grade 8 in maths for maths or further maths A level (whereas with other subjects, including English, they'll consider a grade 6). But those with lesser qualifications can take lower level courses, and the majority of pupils from year 11 go through to the sixth form.

Exit: Around a third leave after GCSEs – usually to another sixth form or straight into a job. More go after year 12 but almost all who go through to year 13 go to university, while others go into apprenticeships, voluntary work or employment. Of those who go down the university route, around 40 per cent go to Russell Group universities, the vast majority (for social and cultural reasons) choosing London universities, with Kings, UCL, Imperial and Queen Mary proving particularly popular. Has had several successful Oxbridge candidates. While there's quite a range of courses studied, these do tend to be heavily dominated by sciences and maths.

Latest results: School won't release 2020 results. In 2019 (the last year when exams took place), 29 per cent 9-7 at GCSE; 53 per cent got 9-5 in both English and maths. In 2019, 16 per cent A*/A (44 per cent A*-B grades).

Teaching and learning: Consistently near the top of the value-added tables and has three times been ranked the most improved school in the country. Most students come in with lower than average achievement. At GCSE, good results in RE (all students take this), English, maths and science. Students come from over 50 primaries (most feeling like the cat that got the cream when they get a place), but many have difficult home lives. 'Our first focus is on behaviour, on creating a climate for learning. Then we engage them with exciting teaching.'

There's an impressive emphasis on business and enterprise here, including strong links with Canary Wharf and City firms, with some offering work placements

Indeed, Ofsted's latest report (outstanding) talks of 'high quality and energetic teaching' – something the students also rave about. 'You're never bored and teachers give their all to make sure you both keep up and that you're kept enthused – they have very high aspirations for us,' said one. Monitoring of student progress is meticulous, with school targeting those who need extra help in a range of ways, from one-to-one help to subject clinics for small groups. 'I'm a big fan of their marking system too – there's always such detailed feedback,' one parent told us.

Setting for maths, English, science and RE from year 7, but with plenty of scope to move up or down according to individual needs. As a specialist language college, it is perhaps surprising that students only study one language for the first three years (it used to be two) from a choice of French, Spanish and Bengali, continuing at least one to GCSE. That said, many take more, with a wide choice of languages in twilight classes (for parents as well as pupils) including in Arabic, Japanese, Korean, Mandarin, Italian and Turkish – and many pupils take a GCSE in their own native language in KS4. Many go on French or Spanish exchanges and there are many international links and partnerships which have involved students visiting Poland, Italy and the Czech Republic.

There are vocational as well as academic courses at KS4, for example in food tech and business studies. In fact, there's an impressive emphasis on business and enterprise here, including strong links with Canary Wharf and City firms, with some offering work placements, scholarships to cover university fees and jobs after graduation to talented students. Sixth form business studies students can have mentoring from business partners, visits and seminars, lectures and summer internships.

The large sixth form, with some 500 pupils, has its own centre, including a library, IT suite, common rooms and a popular café. But students say this can be a double-edged sword ('Great for sixth formers to essentially get their own school, but we rarely see them,' explained one student), so is something the head is addressing. A level subjects offered alongside a variety of vocational courses and GCSE retakes – with most popular and successful subjects including maths, science and English, with wide take-up for psychology, RE and sociology too. Many students come in from elsewhere to join those moving up, and quite a few have relatively low qualifications. Some start with intermediate level courses then move up to higher levels en route to university.

The head has just recruited a new physics teacher with a first class degree. 'It's unheard of in London,' he says, as if still incredulous at his find

Teachers seem to be as keen to work here as young people are to study here, with large numbers of applications for most teaching posts. 'We are high profile and attract high quality applicants,' explains head, pointing out that he just recruited a new physics teacher, with a first class degree. 'It's unheard of in London,' he says, as if still incredulous at his find, adding that many past students come back to teach – 'something we're extremely proud of.'

Learning support and SEN: Around 10 per cent of pupils have SEN and the school has a large learning support team dedicated to supporting them. Learning mentors and assistants work through teachers and directly with pupils, helping to track their progress and ensure they know what they need to do to improve – and there are regular extension and catch-up classes. 'They're really good on SEN – I couldn't fault it,' one parent told us. Gifted and talented students are also identified for extra support.

The arts and extracurricular: Visual arts no great shakes, but drama is hugely popular (including at A level – a joy to see), with a particularly dedicated and popular head of department, who ensures GCSE students get access to at least four operas and/or musicals, which they use to reflect on their own work. Actors regularly perform at the Half Moon Theatre – and we were impressed how drama is used to address certain pastoral themes that come up in school, with students writing and performing plays on these subjects.

Lively (and noticeably experimental, when we visited) music department, with over 100 students in every year group having individual music lessons. The steel band has played at the Albert Hall, the Mansion House and for the Lord Mayor's Show, and have won various awards. There's also a gospel choir, orchestra and various string ensembles.

Clubs are mainly focused on sports, but there's also Equality Group ('which deals with everything from homophobia to sexism' – Ian McKellen having recently been invited to the school to talk on LGBT issues when we visited), Amnesty International, Whitechapel Mission, plus charity club, debating club and Christian and Muslim unions, among others. Student-led clubs are disappointingly thin on the ground, but head plans to address this. Residentials have historically not taken place during term-time, but again this is set to change – with access to the Hampshire Cass Mountain Centre in Wales making whole year group residentials a possibility.

Sport: Among the most successful schools in Tower Hamlets when it comes to competitive sports – 'a tremendous achievement when you look at the limitations of the site,' says head – and we agree. Indeed, outside sports facilities consist of a less than a handful of courts that double up as the playground – and although there's an indoor swimming pool (everyone learns to swim by the end of their first term), it's pretty shoddy, as is the indoor fitness suite currently housed in a portacabin. Decent sports hall, however, while the likes of running and football take place at offsite at nearby Spider Park (which has tracks and Astroturf) and annual sports day is at Mile End Stadium. Table tennis, boxing and fencing are also on the agenda. 'They try to get you enthused about some kind of exercise, although it doesn't work for everyone,' one student told us, and parents agree.

Ethos and heritage: Formed in 1964 by the governing body of Red Coat School (established in 1714 for boys born within Mile End Old Town) and the governors of the Sir John Cass Foundation (a charity set up in 1710 by Sir John Cass for poor children in the East End of London). The school is owned by the Foundation, one of London's oldest educational charities, and Founder's Day in St Botolph-without-Aldgate church is one of the highlights of the school year. Its present site dates from 1965 and has been refurbished over the years since to include up-to-date science labs and learning centres stocked with computers – as well as an attractive glass-fronted main building. Classrooms vary in both age and size and while most are light and airy, some were exceptionally hot on the summer's day we visited (to be fair, school is trying to secure aircon – 'it's all a matter of funding'). Although it's in the middle of the East End, the school boasts a deceptively rural-seeming setting with a city farm opposite, a park next door and the school church and its tranquil graveyard beyond.

The library is open before and after school and on Saturday mornings, with learning mentors around to help. 'Many students have no computer at home, nor quiet space in which to do homework.' The great hall with stage and balcony doubles as a lecture theatre and can accommodate large (although sadly not quite the whole school) assemblies. 'These are important for setting the behaviour tone for the school.' Uniform is traditional, including a blazer, and while sixth formers wear their own clothes, they are expected to dress smartly. Although this is a CofE school, around 90 per cent of students are Muslims and two multi-faith rooms (one male, one female) cater for both. Cashless cafeteria serves hot food, while cold food is served from a hatch on the playground; sixth formers have their own indoor café. 'Food is good here, although we're pleased the head is on the case about getting more variety,' one student told us.

An orderly atmosphere pervades, with a high level of attentiveness during lessons. But kids will be kids and, refreshingly, that's allowed too – apparent in the corridors between lessons, albeit with classical background music and a strict one-way system (and certain routes for certain year groups) encouraging an overall sense of calm.

Pastoral care, inclusivity and discipline: The emphasis on security is palpable, with tall black, alarmed fences surrounding the school and quite a rigmarole to go through when arriving as a visitor at reception, along with CCTV cameras throughout the school and staff checking on destinations of those wandering the corridors between lessons – all of which, say staff and students, discourage vandalism and help students feel protected. Equally noticeable (many visitors comment on it) is the mutual respect. 'First of all we make them feel secure and safe, then we start to cultivate respect for all,' explains head, who describes the school as 'strict but not punitive'. Students concur, saying many of them go through school without a detention (most are given for lateness or failure to hand in homework). Students praise the fact that they (and their parents) are each assigned a named adult, whom they can approach about any personal problems – 'and heads of year are very approachable too.' There's also one full-time qualified counsellor.

In the middle of the East End, the school boasts a deceptively rural setting with a city farm opposite, a park next door and the school church and its graveyard beyond

Head insists that 'the high standards and quality of teaching, along with the consistent approach by staff' are relevant pastorally too. 'It means everyone is focused on why they're here and is the reason I believe we have to do very little firefighting pastorally.' 'The children are happy here,' concludes one parent. 'They know what's expected of them and they get down to work.' A lively school council makes regular suggestions for change – all the usual issues, including getting more playground equipment.

By all accounts, very little racial tension and very few exclusions – with only one temporary (and no permanent) exclusions in the last three years. Drugs very rarely a problem; carrying weapons even less so – both prolific problems in the local area. 'We do very occasionally have some challenging behaviour, but it does not threaten the learning environment. We try hard not to exclude if we can possibly avoid it.'

Pupils and parents: About two-thirds of the students are Bangladeshi, the rest from a variety of ethnic minorities, including many Somali refugees. Around 70 per cent receive free school meals. Although there's no formal parents' association, parents are mostly very supportive of the school and its high expectations for their children. Good communications between school and parents – 'I've always had quick responses from them,' said one. Students form strong peer groups. 'There's a very strong ethos of care for one another,' said a parent.

The last word: A beacon of excellence in one of the most deprived areas of the capital (and indeed the country), which takes in students with low levels of attainment and sends most of them off to university where they get laudable results. If your child is prepared to behave well and knuckle down to work, the expert teaching and high aspirations here will almost certainly see their grades go from strength to strength (and that goes for those who enter from one of the higher bands too).

Trinity Catholic High School

RC 14

Mornington Road, Woodford Green, Essex IG8 0TP

020 8504 3419 | schoolmanager@tchs.uk.net | www.tchs.uk.net/

State | Ages: 11-18 | Pupils: 1,663; sixth form: 464

Headteacher: Since 1981, Dr Paul Doherty OBE BA DPhil (Oxon) FRSA (70s). Middlesbrough born and bred, he originally studied for the priesthood at Ushaw College in Durham. After gaining a history degree at Liverpool University, he won a state scholarship to Exeter College, Oxford, where he met his wife with whom he had seven children. Having decided the academic world was not for him either, he became a secondary school teacher, working in Ascot, Newark and Crawley before being appointed as headmaster to Trinity.

'An inspiration' is the phrase you'll hear more than any other about this larger-than-life character and despite him being in his 70s, pupils, parents and staff alike seem terrified at the mere thought of him leaving. We found him solid and commanding, yet friendly and open-minded – a winning combo that helped lead him to getting an OBE in 2012 for services to education and that helped lead the school to gaining five consecutive outstanding reviews from Ofsted. Doesn't teach, but very much part of the furniture across both school sites, where he eats with pupils in the dining room, holds regular question-and-answer sessions and invites every child to see him on their birthday, presenting them with a card, sweets and £1 coin. 'He's always reminding us that we should treat every child here as our own,' one staff member told us. 'Perhaps not the most politically correct of heads, but I rather like that,' commented a parent, while others also praise the 'strong management team' he has around him.

Also a novelist and writer of non-fiction, with over 100 books to his name, some translated into 20 languages. Has written under various pseudonyms including CL Grace, Paul Harding, Michael Clynes, Ann Dukhas and Anna Apostolou – although he now writes only under his real name. His seven grown-up children were all educated at Trinity.

Entrance: The four main feeder primary schools are St Antony's Woodford, St Mary's Chingford, St John Fisher Loughton and Our Lady of Lourdes Wanstead – although pupils come from around 50 in total. Looked after children get priority, then it comes down to Catholicity and distance of Catholic primary school. Over 1,000 applications for the 240 places and many go to appeal, with long waiting lists further up the school.

Over three-quarters stay on to the sixth form after GCSE, for which the entrance criteria is 9-6s at GCSE for the subject they want to study. Around 50 more join from outside (depending on numbers staying on), although that figure has dipped recently as some local schools have introduced sixth forms. 'It's a shame as we could accommodate more than 50,' says school. Unlike the rest of the school, sixth formers don't have to be Catholic, but they must be willing to uphold the school's religious ethos.

Exit: Around 20 per cent leave after GCSE – usually to study a vocational course at college or different subject choices at other local schools. A few do apprenticeships. Approximately 80 per cent of sixth formers to university, around half of whom go to Russell Group universities, notably Imperial and LSE, although others head all over the country. As for subjects, school says, 'there's such a range, from law to technical theatre.' Three medics and dentists in 2020, plus one student to Oxbridge. Pupils praise the university and careers advice service – 'There's nothing they can't help you with.'

Latest results: In 2020, 39 per cent 9-7 at GCSE; 89 per cent 9-4 in both English and maths. At A level, 24 per cent A*/A (50 per cent A*-B). In 2019 (the last year when exams took place), 38 per cent 9-4 in both English and maths. At A level, 18 per cent A*/A (39 per cent A*-B).

Teaching and learning: Setting in maths from year 7, but in no other subject. 'Mixed ability classes work,' insists the head – and they have the results to prove it. Strong results across the board, particularly in the core subjects of English, maths and sciences, with pupils also doing exceptionally well in art, computer science, child development, English literature, dance, drama and food tech. Popular GCSE choices include history, computer science, languages and triple science.

At sixth form, 28 A levels are offered – mainly traditional subjects 'due to Russell Group demands' – although media studies, psychology and sociology also available, all with decent take-up. At A level, strongest results in chemistry, French, Spanish, English language and literature.

Spanish and French from year 7, with Latin available in years 8 and 9 as a 'twilight course'. They don't hold back on homework which, perhaps inevitably, isn't to everyone's liking. 'I think they should give less in years 7 and 8 so that the children have more time to develop outside interests,' said one parent, while another commented, 'My child had to drop an A level due to the workload he was expected to get through at home.' Tracking of students is meticulously detailed and well communicated to both pupils and parents, and the school's monitoring and evaluation of this system is widely chronicled (including by Ofsted) as being second-to-none. 'We all know exactly where we should be in every subject – it's incredibly thorough,' one student told us. Meanwhile, a teacher said, 'It's very fluid so that we can raise standards where we need to and likewise, add in interventions where students aren't reaching their targets' – the likes of which include subject clinics and Saturday school.

In short, a highly academic school – but an exam factory this is not, with several parents reporting that their multiple offspring's different academic levels were all catered for. 'One of my children found studying a breeze; the other really didn't, and the school managed both perfectly, finding their full potential but never making them feel over-pressured,' said one.

Learning support and SEN: The school's approach to SEN (110 on SEN register, including 30 EHC plans when we visited) is no less painstaking, with one parent praising the 'systematic approach to ensuring children get help both inside and outside the classroom – I couldn't fault it.' Adapting the curriculum is not uncommon – for example, so that a student can take six GCSEs instead of the more usual nine, with a bespoke curriculum and booster classes where needed. 'They've supported my daughter thoroughly without ever making a big deal of her special needs, and it's all coupled with clear expectations that she has to work as hard as she can. It's a great philosophy and has worked wonders for her.'

The arts and extracurricular: The art suite – which includes three art studios, plus a smaller workroom – produces some striking artwork, which is displayed throughout the school. Visits to galleries often involve mixed year groups 'so they can learn from each other' and visiting artists are regularly invited to work in the workroom, with students observing them in small groups. This approach is extended to pupils too, with younger ones frequently invited to watch and critique older ones producing their masterpieces. Meanwhile, teachers are encouraged to inspire students through their particular area of specialism.

The focus on drama tends to be more academic than extracurricular, with no all-school productions. But there's plenty to shout about when it comes to value added, with very successful results at GCSE, although this attracts relatively small numbers, usually around 20 a year.

Tracking of students is meticulously detailed. 'We all know exactly where we should be in every subject – it's incredibly thorough,' one student told us

Parents itching to watch their little cherubs perform have more joy when it comes to music, however, with the Christmas carol concert and rock and pop concerts among the popular annual events. There are also plenty of one-off performances from the various school orchestras, choirs, ensembles and school bands – plus regular music festivals and competitions. Around 60 students from every year group from years 7 to 9 are taught instrumental lessons by a peripatetic teacher (some in groups), with numbers starting to trail off after that. The annual music tour, which involves a different European destination each year, is well attended. 'Trinity really feels like a musical school – you often see pupils performing, sometimes as a background at lunchtimes while you eat,' one pupil told us.

There's a comprehensive extracurricular timetable, resulting in many pupils staying on until 5pm at least a couple of times a week. Clubs focus on sport, music, IT and all the academic subjects right through to war gaming and chess (popular with the quieter pupils). This is a lead school in outdoor education, with a greater take-up of DofE (bronze, silver and gold) within the school than across the rest of Redbridge as a whole. At least one or two school trips every week to theatres, museums etc and some residentials too, including a recent ski trip to Austria, film and media studies visit to LA and regular teambuilding trips to Wales.

Sport: All the usual suspects are on offer, including hockey, netball, football and rugby, and frequently wins competitions. Less traditional options include cycling (the school has bought in bikes), sailing (at Fairlop sailing lake), badminton and dance (to GCSE), and some parents told us the school was good at 'encouraging fitness – essential in the current climate.' Only a sports hall on site, however, with other facilities a 10 minute coach ride away; parents we spoke to either told us their children weren't interested in sport (telling in itself?) or that their very sporty child had been 'disappointed'.

Ethos and heritage: The school is split between two sites, with the upper site (main site) on Mornington Road and the lower site on Sydney Road, a five to 10 minute walk away. The lower site (originally the local secondary modern school, St Paul's) is home to years 7, 8 and 9, while the upper site (originally Holy Family Convent School, the local girls' grammar – which merged with St Paul's in 1976) is home to year 10 upwards. 'It makes starting at this vast school much less daunting for year 7s,' one parent told us – pupils concur. That said, due to specialist facilities being split across the two sites (music is based in lower school, while most science labs are mainly in the upper school, for example), all pupils access both sites, with older ones often walking between them two or three times a day. 'We used to move the teachers around, but now we move the pupils – much better for fitness.'

The upper site is made up of nine buildings, dating between 150 and two years old: Trinity House, Keswick House, Rackham House, Monteluce House, Pelham House, Grainger House, St Joseph's House, Vincent House and Becket House – each home to a different subject area ranging from humanities to food tech. Meanwhile, the lower site is made up of a single 1960s building, with a remote science laboratory in the playground called the Padua Centre (named after St Anthony of Padua). 'This is where the snakes and geckos are kept – you can borrow these over the holidays,' a pupil told us excitedly.

Inside, much of the school looks tired and in need of a lick of paint, and everyone agrees they are limited by space – there's no dedicated canteen, for instance, and the library doesn't look anywhere near big enough for 1,750 pupils. 'The school was designed for six form entry – we're now eight form entry.' We felt it in the lower site during wet play, with every single pupil crammed in the corridors and main hall. That said, the facilities are good and some areas, such as common rooms, are surprisingly roomy, albeit unimaginatively designed with a sea of conference-style blue chairs and magnolia paint.

You will be in no doubt that your child is at a Catholic school, with daily mass at 8.30am and prayers in the morning, at midday, at 3pm and before all meals

You will be in no doubt that your child is a at Catholic school, with daily mass at 8.30am and prayers in the morning, at midday, at 3pm and before all meals. There's a chapel on both sites, plus a chaplain who puts a Catholic slant on any counsel provided to the pupils, while pictures of the pope adorn several noticeboards. But that doesn't mean pupils are spoon-fed religion – in fact, they are actively encouraged to question their faith. 'Some students wind up atheist and that's not seen as a problem – all views are welcomed,' one pupil told us. Overall, there's a culture of learning – when we visited, all classroom doors were firmly closed, all desks faced forward and all pupils looked engaged. Once the bell goes, though, there's all the noise and excitement you'd expect when hundreds of tweens and teens are able to let their hair down, if only for a few minutes between lessons.

Alumni include Tamzin Outhwaite (EastEnders actress), Kele Okereke (musician), Matt Ward (record producer/songwriter), Gary Lucy (actor), Christine Ohuruogu MBE (Olympic, world and commonwealth athletics champion), Catherine Dalton, Dan Lawrence and Nicholas Browne (cricketers).

Pastoral care, inclusivity and discipline: 'Firm but fair' is how most pupils and parents describe discipline here and it clearly does the job – pupils are well behaved and there have been no temporary or permanent exclusions for at least three years. 'All the students know the rules and that there are clear consequences if you break them,' explained a parent – notably detention (lunchtime or after school), community service (litter picking etc) or Saturday school, albeit with a warning system first. The most heinous crime, it seems, is distracting others in lessons, although pupils told us the school is also particularly hot on uniform and giving in homework on time. 'We have zero tolerance for lessons being interrupted – teachers are here to teach and pupils are here to learn,' the school told us – and a daily logbook is sent round to all classes so that teachers can record any misbehaviour, even if it's only a warning. 'It means teachers know they are well supported and students know the teachers talk to each other.'

Pastorally sound. 'Teachers are approachable, with most regularly reminding us that they are available if you are struggling either emotionally or practically,' said one pupil. In addition, each year group has a head and assistant head, who – together with the school chaplain – encourage any pupils to come and see them if they want to. There's also a big prevention strategy to help stop issues ranging from bullying to radicalisation becoming a problem in the first place. Plus, there's plenty of leadership and peer mentoring type opportunities, including a prefect system and Guardian Angels (whereby sixth formers look out for younger ones).

Excellent communications between school and parents all helps, say parents. 'There has never been a time when I haven't known what's going on with my child – they tell you when they're doing really well, when they're struggling and when they really play up,' one parent told us. 'When things go wrong, they get you involved quickly so they can resolve it and move on,' said another.

Pupils and parents: A great diversity of backgrounds and ethnicity, with 47 per cent minority ethnic (predominantly Black Caribbean), with the common denominator being – surprise, surprise – Catholicism (93 per cent). Although there's no PA, parents feel involved and there's almost full attendance at parents' evenings and a good turnout at events such as cheese and wine evening. We found pupils to be chatty, grounded, community minded and well mannered, with a real pride for their school.

Money matters: Parents are generous in their financial support, with a Gift Aid scheme in place for those who donate either via standing order or one off donation. Trinity holds funds to support those in need and parents/guardians are encouraged to contact the head if financial support is required. Strong links with local community groups also ensure that families are well supported.

The last word: A strict, disciplined Catholic school with a strong pastoral system to ensure young people stay on the straight and narrow. This, together with the excellent teaching and monitoring, makes this a place where young people of all abilities thrive academically. Standards haven't slipped here in decades and it doesn't look like they're about to start any time soon.

Walthamstow School for Girls

15

Church Hill, Walthamstow, London E17 9RZ

020 8509 9446 | info@wsfg.waltham.sch.uk | www.wsfg.waltham.sch.uk/

State | **Ages:** 11–16 | **Pupils:** 900

Head: Since 2012, Meryl Davies BA (50s). Easy-going, enthusiastic and energised, she is prepared to go against the grain if it's in the best interests of the school – which staff, parents and students unanimously admire. Having studied French and linguistics at Sheffield University, she stayed on to do her PGCE as 'teaching was a long-time ambition.' Immediately attracted to some of the more radical teaching techniques of the 1980s and the more gritty comprehensives of inner London, she found the reality was quite an eye-opener, but one she nonetheless embraced, with one of her earlier jobs working on a London barge with school refusers to get them back into mainstream schooling. 'Working at the raw edge of education is an experience I think all teachers should have – you get to really understand what makes young people tick,' she says.

After moving on to Graveney School, Tooting, she moved up the ranks to assistant head, then took up a deputy headship in Elliott School, Putney, one of the biggest London comps at the time (where she was seconded briefly to take on a headship of a school on special measures). She then moved to Cator Park School for Girls, Bromley, before coming to Walthamstow in 2012. Disappointingly, results dropped a whopping 14 per cent after just a few months later, but it's widely acknowledged this was largely down to an earlier decision to get all year 11s to do a pilot course of double maths. Results are now the best the school has ever had. Seen by staff as an enabling, empowering leader, she regularly encourages others to front meetings. Teaches French to the lower school, runs a Monday surgery for parents and answers emails at weekends, seeing her job as 24/7.

Lives in south London with her partner and has three grown-up children.

Left at the end of 2020, new head is Helen Marriott.

Entrance: Heavily oversubscribed, with some 700 applying for 180 year 7 places. Non-selective, the school follows the borough's entrance criteria, which favours girls in the looked after system/ those with an EHC plan, followed by siblings, then it's down to distance. Those who get in mainly live less than a one mile radius. Occasional places further up the school when families move out of the area.

Exit: Vast majority of girls go on to sixth form college or local school sixth forms. 'They clammer to have our girls,' says head. The two main local colleges are Sir George Monoux Sixth Form College and Leyton Sixth Form college, whilst schools include Highams Park, Heathcote, City and Islington, Latymer, City of Westminster and Forest School. Most go on to study for A levels, with a heavy emphasis on sciences, whilst a few do BTecs. 'They are career savvy and know exactly what they want to study and why,' says head. Those after more specialist courses are prepared to travel, with some commuting up to a couple of hours every day.

Latest results: In 2020, 35 per cent 9-7 at GCSE; 83 per cent 9-4 in both maths and English. In 2019 (the last year when exams took place), 32 per cent 9-7 at GCSE: 54 per cent 9-4 in both maths and English.

Teaching and learning: Excellent results across the board, with the school consistently among the top performing non-selective schools in the country. 'There are no specialist subjects at this school – we aim to do well in everything,' explains head, although the school has a specialist status in maths and computing, which has done no harm to results in these areas. Head attributes results to a combination of high expectations, inspirational teaching, regular monitoring and target setting and a broad approach to learning experiences.

No setting, except in maths from year 7. 'Historically, the school has never done it,' says head, 'and this works for us.' French or Spanish from year 7, with a taster in Urdu, and Latin also available at GCSE. At the end of year 8, students take part in the Languages Festival, a celebration of all languages spoken or studied in the school and the girls perform in a foreign language in front of their year. Latin offered as an additional language at GSCE.

Targeting and monitoring are huge, with personalisation of study plans meticulous in detail – one of the key reasons no student seems to get left behind. 'It's forensic,' smiles the head, who can talk at length at how girls are identified for different types and levels of help, depending on their individual needs and the way they learn. Peer mentoring is also a focus, with older pupils trained to work regularly with younger ones around student support.

A tour of the classrooms revealed engaged students contributing animatedly. Lessons, they say, are 'engaging,' 'interactive' and 'never dull.' 'Teachers want to see that everyone is on board and thriving in their subject,' said one student. The head points to the growing focus on sharing good techniques around teaching and learning, which she hopes will improve consistency of teaching methods across the school (something they've been criticised for in the past). Low staff turnover.

The school motto, 'Neglect not the gift that is in thee,' resonates here, according to staff and students, who add that school is, in the main, fun

Phrases like 'That's not good enough' are not part of school life here, where the emphasis is on enabling and encouraging effort in much more positive ways. 'We pride ourselves on having a healthy atmosphere where we make people feel confident, not self-doubting.' The school motto, 'Neglect not the gift that is in thee,' resonates here, according to staff and students, who add that school is, in the main, fun.

Recent increase in use of iPads by years 7 and 8 to enhance learning.

Learning support and SEN: School doesn't claim to stand out in terms of SEN, but around 15 per cent require SEN support and 25 per cent speak English as a second language. No wonder the language and learning department has a 16-strong team (some of whom are teaching staff), catering for the usual remit, including mobility problems (there's good wheelchair access here). 'I've been massively impressed by how much effort the department puts into my daughter's needs and

Targeting and monitoring are huge, with personalisation of study plans meticulous in detail. 'It's forensic,' smiles the head

how well they communicate with us about it,' one parent told us. 'The school is incredibly personalised and inclusive.'

The arts and extracurricular: Impressive art facilities, consisting of two main studios; students' creations in everything from ceramics to textiles and graphics to portrait work are exhibited throughout the school. 'We all have a great sense of pride when our artwork is displayed – there's a feeling of "I did that and my school appreciates it",' one student said. A particularly attractive year 8 Grayson Perry vase project, displayed in glass cabinets in one major corridor, caught our eye. Lots of cross-curricular projects, such as maths through art, plus plenty of visits to galleries and exhibitions. The school runs an annual exhibition of self-portraits by year 7s, which appears as part of the Walthamstow Arts Trail, attended by celebs and general public, and which raises money for their link school in Pakistan.

Drama popular and seen as a key part of increasing the girls' confidence and ability to speak out, with lots of performances by individual year groups and whole-school performances every other year, such as The Wizard of Oz. Strong links with the Unicorn Theatre in London Bridge. School also involved with Shakespeare Schools Festival.

Music department is understandably proud of their highly acclaimed steel pan bands, which regularly perform in public spaces, including the Royal Albert Hall. It's been a tradition at the school for decades, with a steel band ensemble in every year group, rehearsing every morning. There's an orchestra, choir, ensembles and bands, some student led. Four peripatetic teachers. The annual Modern Languages Festival involves each class in year 8 learning a song in the language they study and performing with their class in front of the entire year group. Dance is valued and seen as key to team-building.

Food tech is innovative, with plenty of competitions and links with outside organisations – ranging from an annual project with foodbanks, in which students learn to make dishes with very limited resources, right through to trips to fine dining restaurants in top hotels.

Extensive enrichment, including trips (eg Black history month trips), workshops (eg in STEM, and also for young lawyers and for young doctors), events (eg Girls Can Crafting and Coding Event), entry to competitions (eg WSFG Cycle Planning Awards, Jack Petchey Speak Out Challenge) and links with other schools (eg primary schools are invited to the school for science days). The girls even run their own bank, through a longstanding link with MyBnk.

Extracurricular clubs include multimedia, origami, languages, sport, gardening, engineering and debating. 'Whilst these clubs are not compulsory, they are actively encouraged,' says the head. We attended a meeting of the International Club, where a group of students were busy planning all kinds of exciting initiatives, particularly schools they have strong links with overseas – including the Goodwill Secondary School in Roseau, Dominica and Read Foundation School, Ambore, Pakistan. Plenty of fundraising for the school in Ambore (over £15k to date), while teachers have travelled there to officially open the school and deliver lessons. A group has just returned after being the first volunteer 'teachers' at a school in Zanzibar. School also has live penpal links with schools in France and Spain and holds the British Council International School Award (for outstanding development of the international dimension in the curriculum).

Sport: No shortage of sporting options – cricket, basketball, tag rugby, football, rock climbing, netball, trampolining, dance, self-defence and more – which mainly take place in the sports hall or so-called MUGA (multi-use games area), a large, hard-surfaced area of courts. Sadly, no school field, although there is some outside green space, including a landscaped woodland area, which is sometimes used for PE. The local YMCA, which is in easy walking distance, is used for swimming and fitness classes. Regular competitions against other schools, and some representation at regional level and occasionally national, with one former student having made the Olympic squad for volleyball, and another for athletics. School is also involved in the NEC Wheelchair Tennis Masters. 'Some other schools around here don't seem to value sport, but this one really gets that link between physical exercise and learning well in the classroom,' one parent told us.

Ethos and heritage: Main building – with the classic grade 2, red-brick grammar school look – was built in 1911, although the school itself dates back to 1890, when it was opened as a private school in West Avenue, which later moved to nearby Church Hill House. In 1911, the school was taken over by Essex County Council and in 1913 moved to its present site on land originally part of the Vicars Glebe. The school has since been enlarged in 1918, 1928, 1962, 1974 and 2010 and the resulting combination of new and old builds works seamlessly, with no need to even leave one building to enter the next. After a period in the late 20th century as a grammar school, then as a senior high school for 14-18 year-olds, in 1986 the school once again became a school for girls aged 11-16.

In the old part of the school, expect oodles of original features, from the parquet flooring and wall tiles to traditional radiators, with the oak panelled school hall forming the centrepiece. At the other end of the spectrum is the 2010 building, which includes the new Norris Hall, providing an impressive theatre-style auditorium. Spacious classrooms and labs boast masses of natural light, and there are some attractive break-out areas, including one with brightly coloured orange and black sofas, known by the girls as the EasyJet Lounge. A vast dining hall has mixed reviews of the food from students and the library is a good size. Everywhere – and we mean everywhere – is scrupulously clean and tidy.

Break-out areas include one with brightly coloured orange and black sofas, known by the girls as the EasyJet Lounge. Everywhere is scrupulously clean and tidy

Outside, the stand-out feature is the Greek theatre, built in the 1920s, which has a circular arena with steps up to a stage on one side and pillared portico on the other. There's a reasonably sized green space surrounding the theatre, plus a rooftop area (to the 2010 building), accessible from ground level, with plenty of chairs and tables. Students also use the MUGA area at break times. Overall, there's a rural, village feel, even though they're only five minutes from the Victoria line. The only rude interruption to all this is the hideous end-of-lesson 'bell' that sounds like some kind of nuclear alert.

Breakfast is served from 8.00am and extra-curricular activities run after school daily, with girls also given the opportunity to stay on to do work after school if, for example, they struggle with finding the space and quiet to do so at home.

Former pupils include Baroness Scotland, Jacqui Harper (BBC news) and Jeanette Kwakye (Olympic sprinter).

Pastoral care, inclusivity and discipline: Pastoral care primarily comes from form tutors, and girls clearly feel safe and nurtured. Peer support is strong, and even without the formal mechanisms you get the feeling that students instinctively looking out for one another, especially lower down the school. There's a part-time counsellor, and emphasis on exploring issues that others school shy away from – from female genital mutilation to forced marriages. The school is Stonewall approved and multicultural events and projects ensure everyone's background feels valued. Transition for year 7s is notable, with a highly successful summer school giving a head-start on team-building. There's a mindfulness course for year 11s.

Strong student council and plenty of leadership opportunities, including interviewing staff. Although there are school rules, you're more likely to hear talk of rights and responsibilities, with girls very much feeling a sense of ownership in this school. 'We feel trusted,' said one girl.

Occasional bullying, although there are plenty of anti-bullying policies and the fact that this is a 'telling' school means students are quick to speak out not just about themselves, but any friends in trouble. 'Our staff are trained to notice signs,' adds the head, 'and when it happens, we involve parents quickly.' No permanent exclusions as long as anyone can remember, with fixed-term exclusions well below the national average, usually given out for very rare instances of aggressive behaviour.

Pupils and parents: Multi-ethnic population, with students from over 50 countries – a great source of pride for the school, which celebrates this rich diversity in everything from assemblies to individual projects. Majority of students from Pakistani origin, followed by white (not just British), then black Caribbean and black African, with the fourth largest group being Indian. 'Mind you, this changes all the time,' points out the head. Girls seem confident, articulate, aspirational and optimistic. 'I could take any of my daughter's friends and they'd have a very clear idea of where they want to be in two or three years' time,' said a parent of a year 10 student.

Parents equally, if not more, aspirational, expecting a lot from their girls, with almost 100 per cent attendance at parents' evenings, consultations about subject options etc. Parents are also regularly invited to take part in questionnaires and parent forums and they are consulted about policy. No PTA, however, which is a disappointment to some parents.

The last word: This is a relaxed and happy school, yet it's purposeful, vibrant and aspirational. The strong academic atmosphere, which is backed up by a great pastoral system, means there's no reason any girl should get left behind. We were particularly encouraged by the extent to which girls are encouraged to express themselves and to challenge stereotypes and indeed the status quo where appropriate. A true community school that believes passionately in the research that a single-sex environment empowers girls to realise their potential, this is a place that proves with the right teaching and school culture, anyone can thrive.

Woodford County High School

16

High Road, Woodford Green, Essex IG8 9LA

020 8504 0611 | head@woodford.redbridge.sch.uk | www.woodford.redbridge.sch.uk/

State | Ages: 11–18 | Pupils: 1,214; sixth form: 314

Headteacher: Since 2010, Jo Pomeroy (mid 50s), MA in English language and literature (St Andrews), MEd (Open), NPQH. Spent two years in a comprehensive in rural Scotland before going to work in France for three years. It was at this high achieving international school that she became aware of 'what bright students are capable of if they are given enough challenge'. Back in the UK she spent another three years working in a comprehensive school with strong languages bias and at that point 'got interested in management, in getting into position where you could make a bigger change'. Sure enough, at her next appointment at a girls' grammar in Surrey, where she spent 16 years, she eventually became deputy head.

Students seem to be in awe of her. 'She has an open door policy and is really nice, but it's definitely next level on the respect side,' a sixth former told us; and a year 8 girl, whom she asked to tell us about the working music box she was creating in DT, exclaimed, 'How embarrassing – I can't believe she picked me!' Parents impressed with how 'she's always grateful for any help from parents', 'is always pushing boundaries to get the best for the girls' and 'even though she finds it hard, as do all heads, to recruit good teachers, she won't compromise, waiting months to get the right one if that's what it takes.' We found her surprisingly mellow, soon realising that's probably her secret weapon; quietly driven and thoroughly unflustered, she has a way of making grand plans for the school sound like it's all in a day's work. Keen 'for students always to be working just beyond what they are comfortable with', this high-performing grammar is surely her nirvana.

Entrance: Massively oversubscribed for year 7 places, even though the school has expanded to six form entry (180 girls). CEM entrance tests, apparently tutor-proof, but head aware that many families now (as at other schools) see tutoring as part of the application process. 'We would obviously rather it wasn't that way – familiarity with the nature of the test is great, but tutoring is definitely not necessary and we applaud those brave enough not to put their children through that,' she says. Up to 10 per cent of places given to girls eligible for pupil premium who score above the pass mark. It is one of just three all-girls schools in the area (the other two are independent and Catholic). Common catchment area with boys' grammar school. Nearly all girls stay on to the sixth form, joined by 50 or so from other schools.

Exit: Around 15-20 per cent leave post-GCSE (although there's always a few who try to return within weeks of sixth form starting, sadly not always successfully if places are taken). Nearly all that stay go to university, primarily Russell Group. Nine Oxbridge places in 2020. Other destinations include Imperial, King's College London, Queen Mary, UCL, Nottingham and Warwick. While medicine, dentistry and optometry are always popular (27 medics in 2020), the school is also working hard to encourage students to study pure science, with increasing success; ditto with STEM and engineering. School is beginning to see girls going into computing and AI. Small numbers study classics and Latin; humanities also appear. Increasingly, girls go overseas and school also encourages degree apprenticeships, with girls increasingly going down this route – for example in big financial firms.

Latest results: In 2020, 84 per cent 9-7 at GCSE; 52 per cent A*/A at A level (77 per cent A*-B). In 2019 (the last year when exams took place), 77 per cent 9-7 at GCSE; 40 per cent A*/A at A level (67 per cent A*-B).

Teaching and learning: Named London state school of the year 2019 by the Sunday Times, this school gets the best results in Redbridge. School maintains an outstanding record of achievement. Also strong on value added. All the more impressive when you consider that many of the students speak a different language at home, with over 40 languages spoken between these bilingual (and often multilingual) girls.

All teachers are subject specialists, whom girls say 'can't do enough for you'. 'The staff, from those in the office right up to the headteacher, really care about the girls and it's that – more than any targets or pressure – that I think helps them succeed,' said one parent. Peer support also helps – it's in the very bones of the school, with older students regularly mentoring younger ones. Literacy mentors, for example, provide targeted additional support for year 7s, and this 'sustained focus on academic literacy across the curriculum' has been highly successful; other students are accredited digital leaders. Homework levels reported to be 'manageable', with a growing amount of flipped learning in sixth form ('good preparation for uni,' say students).

Setting only in science and only at GCSE. 'We used to set in maths, but we found confidence levels are actually higher in mixed ability classes,' says head. Students take two languages from year 7 (French and either German or Latin), one of which must be taken at GCSE (girls do 10 in total). English, languages and science all strong here and girls take triple science GCSE 'unless there's a very good reason not to.' Lots of information and support provided to students and parents on choosing options.

When current head joined, she asked if there was any possibility of a swing band. 'Not enough people play brass,' she was told; now all year 8s learn a brass instrument

In the sixth form, where roughly a quarter of students come from other schools, girls either take four A levels or, more usually, three plus the EPQ (other smaller research projects are also widely taken up in the younger years; and research is also a growing focus for teachers because, says head, 'educators should do research, it helps keep education dynamic'). Some subjects (eg Latin and music) only attract small numbers, but school ensures they remain on offer. At A level, many go on to medical careers (girls' uptake of maths and science is exceptionally high). University preparation is second-to-none, with 'UCAS fortnight' in full swing when we visited.

Learning support and SEN: 'Not a huge number of SEN,' admits head. Two with EHCPs being processed when we visited. Most supported in the classroom – 'students don't like to be taken out of class; we focus more on sharing what works between SENCo and teachers.'

The arts and extracurricular: DofE available, although National Citizenship Service has taken over in popularity (taken in summer of year 11); in fact, take-up so big that David Cameron recently came to do a congratulatory talk on it to the girls.

Sport features highly as part of extracurricular, with other options ranging from self-defence to film making and from hairdressing to sign language, with students presiding over many of the clubs, as well as the many talks and charity events; and there is a society for everything – even to discuss current affairs. Parents are grateful for the breakfast club from 7.45am and homework club until 5pm. Sixth form enrichment programme includes dance, cookery, computing, art, sports and an extended period of voluntary service.

Art block regrettably tatty on the outside (due to be renovated summer 2020), but that doesn't seem to put the girls off, with the two roomy art studios something of a haven and open most evenings after school (plus, students on pupil premium can borrow equipment). Good connections with organisations such as RIBA and annual art exhibition curated by the students themselves. Visits galore to London galleries and museums, plus further afield from St Ives to Berlin, and the Royal Academy organises an annual life drawing session for A level students ('we warn everyone else to stay clear,' laughs head). Sewing machines in full use by sixth formers during our visit, apparently something of a rarity. DT (which makes up the third room in this block) increasingly popular.

Drama not a taught subject, although it does feature as part of English and extracurricular. The house drama competition is also a big deal – a half-hour musical written, composed, directed and performed by each house (Footloose, Moana, Grease and Mama Mia when we visited – with spectacular posters created by the girls, complete with flashing lights) and judged by outside experts. 'It's incredibly competitive,' says head.

When current head joined, she asked the then head of music if there was any possibility of a swing band. 'Not enough people play brass,' she was informed; now all year 8s learn a brass instrument and there's just about every kind of ensemble you can think of, plus a band and different choirs including folk group and staff choir. Individual instrumental and vocal lessons at all levels also on offer, although many girls do their learning outside of school. Girls also participate in the biennial Redbridge Choral Festival at the Royal Albert Hall. Winners of the Mayor of London Music Excellence Awards, this is a school that gets the balance spot on between being inclusive while also enabling top talent to really shine. 'The concerts are extraordinary,' a parent told us.

Expeditions to eg Ghana, Morocco, Indonesia, China, Cambodia and recently Belize and Guatemala, plus a list of topic-related trips as long as your arm. 'Most students go on at least one and they're amazing,' said one girl.

Sport: Core sports are badminton (which we saw in action in the snazzy sports hall; girls regularly reach the UK badminton national finals), athletics, netball, rounders, gymnastics, cross-country and dance – and girls can pursue multicultural dance options such as Bhangra, African and street dance. 'Honestly, there's more dance going on here than on a West End stage,' we were told. Outside, the school field and tennis courts are regularly utilised – not only for sports but a variety of co-curricular day activities (recently team puzzle challenge days, circus skills etc). One parent told us, 'My daughter has always hated sport, but three months at this school and she's taking up things like running in a big way.' Determined to avoid the predictable drop-out rate of older girls, a lot of thought goes into keeping up engagement, with the likes of boxercise and aerobics a staple part of PE. Sports leadership qualification offered in years 10 and 11.

Ethos and heritage: Main, listed building dates from 1768 when it was built as the private family home of the Highams; later it became a military hospital, with wooden honours boards still displaying the names of some of the state registered nurses, including Ina Bucket (an inevitable source of hilarity for the girls). The school opened here in 1919, with every September birthday celebrated – one of the highlights of the year for the school, when they do a big parade with banners (banners are big here – all intricately sewn and displayed on walls), then a formal service, followed by 'lots of cake' and fun activities both on and off site. Such venerable features and rituals lend an atmosphere of tradition.

With its small upstairs classrooms, narrow stairwells and warren-like corridors, much of the main school building has an intimate, homely feel. Particularly welcoming library, once a bedroom, and which has one of the most progressive librarians we've come across, with regular video conferencing with other schools and universities as far away as New York; the pupils even watched a live operation just before we visited. That said, the ground floor corridor is home to larger, revamped and more modern-looking classrooms, refurbished new food and nutrition rooms and – drum roll please – an Innovation Lab, of the likes we've never seen. Looking as though it's been plucked straight out of Silicon Valley, this vibrant, colourful, wow-factor room, complete with two robots and oodles of other hi-tech equipment including drones, is part of the creative technologies department used to harness computing in innovative ways. School also boasts large new Centenary Centre with science labs ('with telescopes and other tech equipment well beyond the reach of most schools'), computer facilities, airy classrooms, break-out and event areas and even an outdoor learning area on the roof, complete with greenhouse and astronomy dome. Outdoor Greek theatre also worth a mention – used for busking Fridays (girls eat lunch while pupils play instruments or sing) and annual Greek play.

The Innovation Lab looks as though it's straight out of Silicon Valley: a colourful, wow-factor room, complete with two robots and oodles of other hi-tech equipment

Former pupils here include Lucy Kirkwood, playwright (RSC, National Theatre), Sarah Winman, best-selling novelist (When God Was a Rabbit) and Peggy Reynolds, Radio 4 arts broadcaster.

Pastoral care, inclusivity and discipline: Peer support service run by older pupils seen as an integral part of pastoral set up here. 'It's a very supportive community – we look out for each other,' one girl told us. Plenty of other leadership opportunities. Terrifically active house system. For more serious issues, there are two part-time school counsellors and a welfare officer. Students told us they knew of no eating disorders, self-harm etc, but said that for some girls, 'the pressure can turn to stress if they're that way inclined.' School currently planning staff training to help students who suffer from panic attacks.

Behaviour, on the whole, excellent, with the consequence that students are trusted to do more student-led activities than might be the case at other schools. Temporary exclusions rare, with no more than two in any one year, 'usually due to misguided use of social media'. Pupils describe the school as 'strict, especially in the lower years'; head and senior colleagues, for example, take turns to be out on the gate every morning checking uniform – 'you see them tying their hair back when they reach the traffic island; they know the score.' Surprisingly, trousers only came to Woodford in its 99th year (as part of a consultation with students, which also resulted in the design of a new hijab).

There is a university success board to inspire the girls and former students are generous with their time, providing inspirational role models at careers events and prize givings, as well as getting involved in organising work experience and networking opportunities. Year 12s spend two hours a week in voluntary service, often working with children or elderly or disabled people. Students adept at applying for (often successfully) grants, eg for 10 bikes so students can learn cycling proficiency.

Pupils and parents: Multi-ethnic population, with a significant Tamil and Indian student body. Mainly middle-class professional families, but by no means exclusively, with pupil premium usually hovering around eight per cent. Catchment circle incorporates Redbridge and neighbouring boroughs, although some come from further afield in the sixth form ('We do discuss distance with prospective students, though – we don't want them to spend too much time travelling,' says head). Most travel in by bus or tube 'although rather more than I would like get delivered to the door, which isn't good for the environment,' says head. Parents support the PFTA as an opportunity to solve many of the school's cash problems (£25,000 raised for the Innovation Lab; has previously funded a digital language lab, a minibus and external lighting).

Girls have an air of being confident, resilient and creative.

The last word: This is a highly selective school with a strong sense of community, second-to-none peer support and an enormous amount of pupil pride in the school. Coupled with the top-notch teaching, it's no wonder the academics – not to mention the extracurricular – go from strength to strength. Where other schools try and fail to marry tradition and innovation, this one seems to achieve it superbly and there's a heavy focus on female empowerment, with girls not only coming out with flying colours scholastically but gaining a good dose of confidence and leadership skills along the way.

Schools for special educational needs

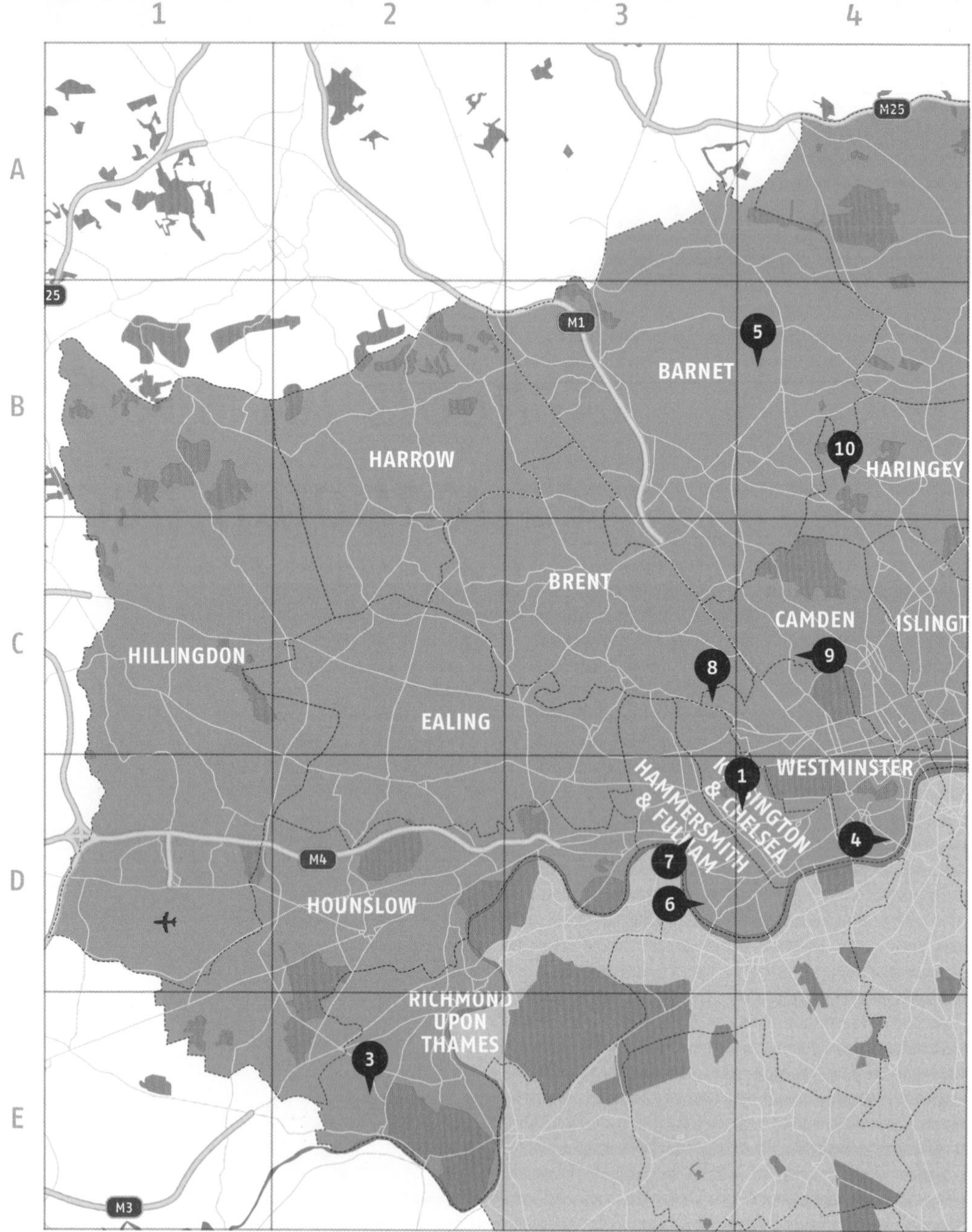

SCHOOLS FOR SPECIAL EDUCATIONAL NEEDS

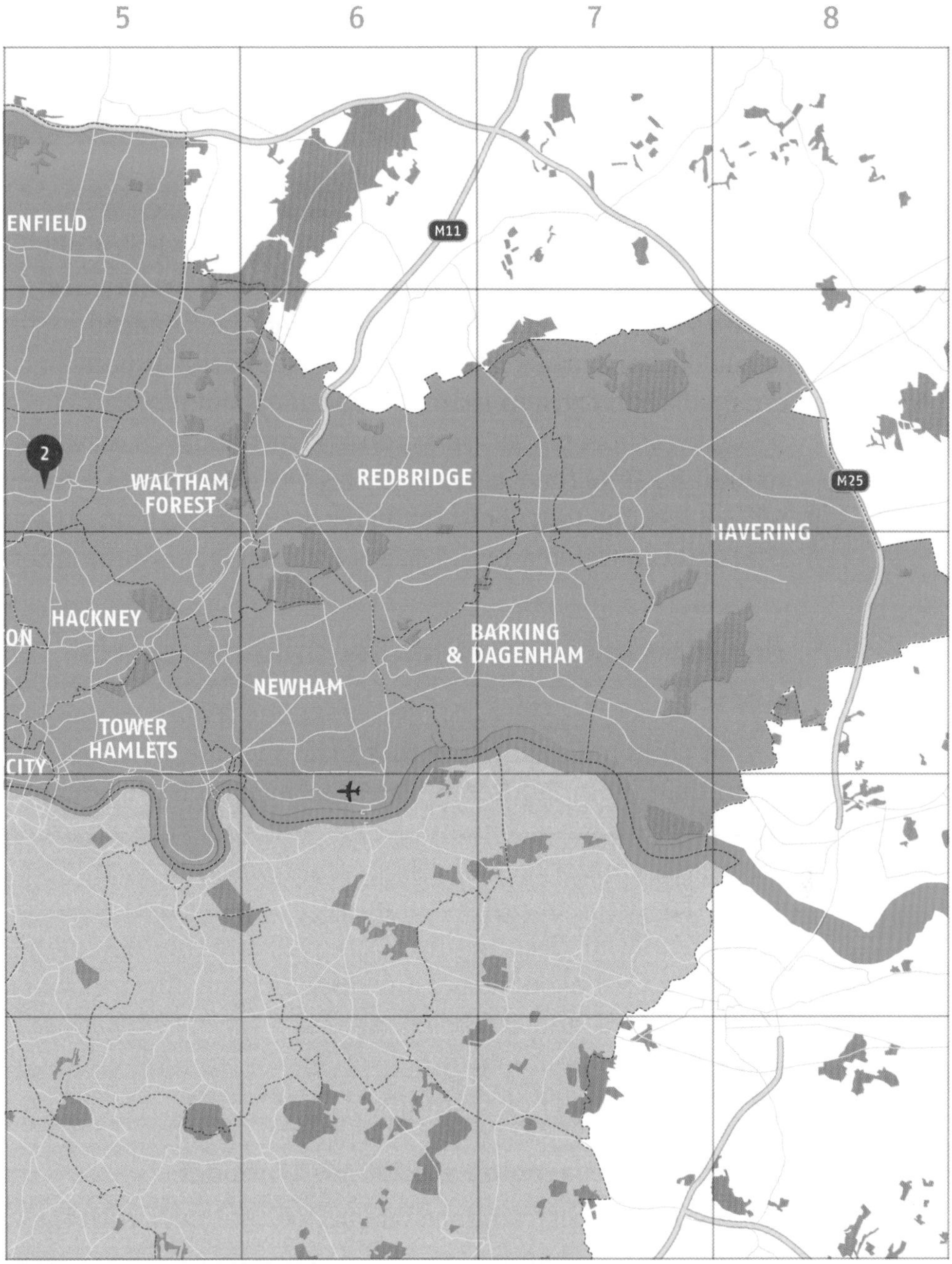

5
6
7
8
M11
ENFIELD
2
WALTHAM FOREST
REDBRIDGE
M25
HAVERING
HACKNEY
BARKING & DAGENHAM
NEWHAM
TOWER HAMLETS
CITY

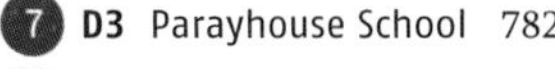

- 7 **D3** Parayhouse School 782
- 8 **C3** The St Marylebone Church of England Bridge School 785
- 9 **C4** Swiss Cottage School 788
- 10 **B4** TreeHouse School 791

Schooling for children with special educational needs

The scramble for London places has an extra layer of complexity when your child has additional needs. It's not just the decision between state and independent, but also between mainstream and specialist. And the financial considerations are greater – learning support is usually charged as an extra in mainstream independents, and specialist school places are expensive, meaning you may have to fight for state funding. And while state mainstream schools will all talk the talk about inclusive education, finding those that truly do well by special needs children is another matter.

How do I know whether my child has special needs?

If your child has a difficulty that makes learning harder for them than most children of the same age, then they may have a special need. Sometimes the difficulties are apparent from early childhood, but other conditions such as mild autism spectrum disorders, auditory processing difficulties or dyslexia may not become clear until well into their schooling. And other factors outside of any disability can affect a child's ability to learn, and can be counted as a special educational need – such as mental health disorders, or the after-effects of early trauma in adopted children.

Signs of an undiagnosed special need include:

- poor school performance which does not tally with the child's general ability
- frequent reports of misbehaviour or failing to pay attention in class
- a dislike of going to school, or onsets of headaches/tummy aches when it is time to go to school
- refusal to put pen to paper, even though articulate
- regular clashes over homework

- poor handwriting, presentation and pencil grip
- difficulties in understanding the nuance in language, social expectations, or making friends
- clumsiness or lack of spatial awareness
- and feelings of frustration or anxiety which may manifest as angry outbursts.

A common problem

If your child needs extra help at school they will be far from alone. Between 15 and 20 per cent of all children have some form of additional need. Around three per cent have more significant needs, and this is the group that qualifies for an Education, Health and Care plan (EHCP), which can provide the funding for a special school place or additional help within a mainstream school, and priority in school admissions. Those who do not qualify for an EHCP receive support from the school's own resources under a system known as SEN Support, and they are subject to the same admissions criteria as other children.

Where do I go for help?

For a young child, your GP or health visitor can advise on specialist assessments, for example from a speech therapist where there are possible issues with speech and language, or an occupational therapist for concerns over co-ordination. Waiting times to see NHS therapists are lengthy, and if you can possibly afford it, it will be worth organising one privately.

For a school age child, your first port of call should be the class teacher or the school's special educational needs co-ordinator (SENCo). Outline your concerns, and ask what they can do to help. If they dismiss your concerns, start to keep a record of instances which demonstrate your child is struggling – things your child tells you about their school day, occasions when the child has been upset and reluctant to go to school, any times the class teacher calls you in to report some problem that day. Then demand a meeting with the headteacher, and present your documentary evidence. We hear of too many occasions when parents are fobbed off – stick to your guns if you suspect things are not right.

Schools may then suggest organising an educational psychologist's (EP) report which will be able to identify any difficulties. However with current cutbacks and the shortage of EPs, we hear that schools are becoming increasingly reluctant to pay for these, while the wait to see a local authority EP can now be up to two years. Again, if you can possibly pay, it's worth commissioning one privately (our SEN team can provide details of EPs in your area).

State or independent?

You have a right to name any state school for your child with an EHCP (although for a selective school, they would still need to pass the entrance exam) in conjunction with your local authority. The LA is likely to be less receptive to naming one outside your own borough, as this is more costly for them. All schools are required by law to make any necessary adjustments, or to supply extra provision, that your child may need. The only grounds on which they can refuse a place to your child is where this would interfere with the efficient education of other children, or would not be an efficient use of resources. The schools' application of this premise varies hugely, from those who just toe the legal line, to those where the head truly embraces the idea of inclusive education, and is supported by a well-qualified and enthusiastic SENCo. Winkling out these gems is no easy task, and schools that aren't welcoming will use subtle ploys such as having no

SENCo available at an open day, or generally making you feel so unwelcome that you won't bother applying.

Independent schools have more freedom to select pupils. If they don't want to accept your child there is little you can do – even if you have grounds to challenge this decision under equality law, you are likely to be disinclined to do so when a school has taken this attitude. A few are genuinely welcoming to children with special needs, but they tend to have a quota on how many they admit in order not to overwhelm the special needs staff, and any such London places are usually snapped up at reception entry. Others will look at each child on merit, but the reality is there is little chance of a place for anything beyond mild needs.

It is possible, but rarely achieved, to get state funding for an independent school. Parents have successfully argued for this on grounds of school size/class size/peer group.

Mainstream or special school?

Most parents start with an inbuilt reluctance to contemplate a special school; but equally they can feel a huge sense of relief when their child has been placed in a specialist setting.

The right option for your child will depend very much on their individual circumstances. The biggest misconception is that a special school will somehow quash any potential – in fact a child who has floundered in mainstream can suddenly make huge leaps when the teaching is properly tailored to their needs, or when their self-esteem is restored. And behavioural problems can disappear overnight when children find themselves in a setting which understands their frustration and has the means to break through. It is possible to take a full range of GCSEs in a special school; they should enable a pupil to work to the best of their ability.

Any additional therapies needed will be more readily available in a specialist school, and it can make all the difference that staff at these schools have specifically opted for special needs teaching. The downside is that these places are more costly, so you need to ready yourself for a fight, and may need to take the LA to Tribunal.

Conversely, some children with milder or transient needs will be better within a mainstream school. But the quality of support available can be extremely variable, so it is important to do your homework about exactly what provision there will be, and how inclusive it is. At primary school in particular, inclusion can mean the child spends their days working separately in the corner with a teaching assistant. Therapy provision will be delivered by external agencies, can be patchy, and will be an add-on, instead of infused through every part of the day as in a specialist school.

Be sure to have an individual meeting with the head and SENCo – are these people you will be able to deal with readily if there is an issue? Are they enthusiastic about the idea of taking your child, do they have knowledge and experience of their condition? Look for evidence of understanding across all teaching and support staff, rather than an attitude that this is a matter for the learning support department. And beware the well-meaning but inexperienced – it can become wearing when you have to keep close tabs on everything.

Can we help?

The Good Schools Guide website has informative features covering the various types of special needs, your legal rights, how to get an EHCP, family issues plus reviews of special schools across the country. See www.goodschoolsguide.co.uk/advice-service/special-educational-needs-service for individual help.

Abingdon House School and College

Broadley Terrace, London NW1 6LG

0203 750 5526 | office@abingdonhouseschool.co.uk | www.abingdonhouseschool.co.uk/

Independent | Ages: 5-19 | Pupils: 90 | Fees: £32,250 pa

Headteacher: Since January 2018, Tanya Moran (40s), maths and science graduate from Canada. She taught in New Zealand for six years then came to London where she taught at the Harrodian for 11 years including six years as deputy head, when she also got involved in setting up an academy. She then set up the Independent School which was subsequently taken over and closed by the Cavendish Group who then asked her to head Abingdon House School following the sudden departures of previous head, Roy English, and the deputy head.

Moran brought her deputy head from the Independent School and all the rest of the 'excellent and very competent staff' stayed on. Recognising the value of stable staff and staff development is apparent as eight teachers are undertaking dyslexia level 5 training, and five staff (including the head) are training for a post-graduate degree in autism.

Originally the school only went to KS3 but since Moran's arrival KS4 has opened and she has brought in more sports; more wellbeing and mental health in the curriculum; and worked to create links with other schools for sports fixtures and sharing good practice, including working with Trinity College of Music to bring in musical opportunities. Enthusiastic and dynamic, she gives parents and teachers 'a feeling of confidence' and 'she is a really safe pair of hands' and 'a good leader', we were told.

Entrance: Children join at all times of the year, 'though ideally at the beginning of a term or half term or even better at the beginning of the year'. The first stage is to send in specialist reports. If school feels they can meet the needs, child attends for a few days' acquaintance in a potentially suitable class for observations. School make it clear that they do not take pupils with primary behavioural issues or those unable to follow the national curriculum. Nor is the building suitable for wheelchair users or those unable to manage the several staircases.

Exit: When pupils make good progress they move on to mainstream maintained or gentle independent schools. However, parents and teachers are aware that the transition is a worry and everyone is hoping that 16+ provision might be developed. For the moment, pupils go on to further education colleges – Westminster City College, Hampstead Fine Arts or Ealing, Hammersmith and West London College – and the often unwelcome move from five structured days to the three short days available at an FE college.

Teaching and learning: All pupils have a range of comorbid difficulties – some 65 per cent have autism listed within their diagnoses and half of the children have a specific learning difficulty – dyslexia, dyspraxia or ADHD. Some with social communication difficulties, but currently none are non-verbal. The top ability pupils are expected to take one or two GCSEs in the core subjects with preparation for these from year 7. Other qualifications on offer are ASDAN, functional skills, Arts Award, entry level qualifications and vocational, personal and social development qualifications. One parent told us: 'The school works for both my children as it accommodates their different abilities.'

Classes (mostly around 10) mixed by cognitive ability (including a 'nurture class' for learners who need more time). 'The small classes allow my child to focus better. His voice is heard unlike in the large classes of mainstream school,' a parent said. The school follows the national curriculum. 'When we visited we saw projects on Egyptians and plants growing. It makes it feel like a mainstream school,' explained one parent. Seven lessons to a day (with five-minute transition time) with visual timetable in each classroom, maths and English in the mornings (streamed across age groups to match ability). Maths skills made as applied as possible so that maths looks to practical skills like choosing, calculating and buying. 'The school identified my son's strength in maths and so he takes maths with older kids and gets awards – they are playing to his strengths.' English supported with small library with both group readers and individual reading books – helps with 'accelerated reader programme' which includes 15 minutes in form time for reading as well as timetabled reading lessons. Google Classroom has been brought in which allows parents to see work that has been done, pupils to see what has happened if lessons missed, to see progress in work, and allows sharing between all staff and pupils.

There are specialist teachers for English, maths, science and ICT, as well as art, music, drama and PE. Touch typing from the youngest classes and technology used to enhance communication and produce work. Science lab also has kitchen equipment and laundry facilities so it can be used for life skills. Classrooms adapted for pupils with tables adjustable for height, wedged cushions, ear defenders and use of sensory boxes.

We heard good reports on the teaching: 'There is continuity of staff which is important to our children – it means they know my son very well and what makes him tick.'

'Staff are intelligent and thoughtful and respond within the hour if I message them.'

The arts and extracurricular: Arty activities are notable according to one parent, who said: 'One of the strengths of the school for my son is the quality art and music and drama teaching that goes on and was not available at other schools we visited.' They have started the Arts Award qualification and we heard from parents that 'the art is particularly well taught and not just used as therapy'. We watched a music lesson with four pupils to prepare music for the end of term show – listening, counting, making sounds – and working together. There are also individual music lessons by peripatetic teachers – piano, guitar, singing, violin and flute currently being taught.

We watched a music lesson with four pupils to prepare music for the end of term show – listening, counting, making sounds – and working together

As well as two timetabled sessions of art and music and sport each week, enrichment for 45 minutes at the end of each day allows pupils to choose an extra club or activity – more music, drama, art, sport, chess, cooking, yoga, bicycle maintenance or working towards an additional qualification (Art Award for example).

Being in central London allows for regular outings to museums, concerts, shows – 'We go on public transport – more life skills training.'

Sport: Two tiny playgrounds and a gym useful for short break times or sensory circuits, but for sport pupils either go to Regent's Park or use the local play area. 'Just the walk to the park is good exercise for my son,' one parent said. Many on the autism spectrum don't manage team sports but like the running club. 'Marathon club is the best thing ever to release tension and get him moving – it is absolutely brilliant. They go to the park and do laps around the lake and get a band for each lap. It makes him proud and gives him a sense of accomplishment.' A strong partnership has also grown with local Fourth Feathers youth club which has a 'cool, street vibe feeling which my son likes. They have ping pong tables, murals and a terrace that the boys go on to wave at the trains going into Marylebone Station.' Fixtures arranged for football with other schools including Fairley House, the Moat School and the Bridge.

Ethos and heritage: Abingdon House opened in 2005, initially just providing interventions for pupils who were in other schools. It moved to its current site in 2011 as a primary school, then extended first to KS3 then KS4 – but it is no longer taking the youngest pupils, now only open from year 2. It fits well in the Cavendish Group of special need schools with a range of needs met in different schools. 'It means we can support each other for training and share good practice.' The Cavendish Group is a for-profit organisation: 'that is problematic and they are not popular with many of us parents due to poor communication,' we heard. But while there were some comments about the ownership of the school, parents spoke well of leadership in the school – saying it is well managed and has a well-oiled staff team. 'There is a strong sense of community and shared purpose,' and 'Staff are well trained, calm and thoughtful about children,' parents said.

The school is hoping to find a way of providing for 16-25-year-olds and all parents we spoke to expressed concern about where their child would move on to.

Lunch made on site with plenty of fruit and vegetables in a three-week rolling menu. A few pupils bring their own food in but eating very much part of skills to learn and teachers and therapists supervising tightly at lunchtime. Signs on walls encouraging pupils to 'try every type of food'.

Pastoral care, inclusivity and discipline: Each morning starts either with a wellbeing session – where they do a joint activity to transition from home to school (walking the school dog, mindfulness, sensory circuit) – or with twice-weekly PATHS (Promoting Alternative Thinking Strategies) developing resilience and mental health. School uses system called 'zones of regulation' which is aimed at helping pupils recognise what their

'The small classes allow my child to focus better. His voice is heard unlike in the large classes of mainstream school,' a parent said

feelings are and where they are at emotionally – in the blue, green, yellow or red zones. We saw a group talking about appropriate feelings and reactions to responsibility. Therapists give parents feedback so they can follow up and reinforce activities at home.

Therapy and staffing: Speech and language therapists (two part-time and one full-time), three occupational therapists and one physiotherapist all based at the school and are able to integrate therapies within the pupils' day either by seeing them individually or in groups, or working within the classroom. CBT therapy used but no ABA. Sessions in draw and talk therapy and mindfulness are held both at the beginning and at the end of the day, specifically for taking time to be grounded, to reflect and to have an opportunity to be aware of feelings. Some behavioural issues can be accommodated if they are about settling into a more suitable school environment and so higher support initially possible. A few pupils have one-to-one support but this is very much the exception. There is a sensory room with lighting, tents and beanbags for pupils, either for regular sessions or as needed.

Pupils and parents: Three-quarters of pupils have an ECHP, the rest are privately funded. The mix should help create a diverse demographic but some parents joined the school funding privately and then applied for the EHCP which supported the child staying at the school – this creates a largely self-selecting group of middle class parents. Self-financing families tend to live more locally (and proximity to the American School seems to bring in quite a few American families). Usual problems of building a close parent body when pupils live far away exist. 'We have created a Facebook page for us parents so we can share tips and ideas.' The school works hard to develop the parents' association, give social and information events and sends out weekly newsletters. Again, typically boy-heavy – 5:1 boys to girls. One parent commented that the school is not intimidating: 'Pupils are calm and well behaved mostly – there is no swearing or shouting.'

Money matters: Support from the Cavendish Group provides a buffer as Abingdon House grows to full capacity and it also gives parents a sense of financial security. Expensive fees not necessarily apparent in the building or facilities but include all therapies and interventions and seem to ensure plenty of staffing support for individual needs and to allow pupils access to activities that would normally be too demanding on resources – outings, sports, art and music, and in-house therapeutic support which is not at an extra cost.

The last word: A small and calm environment which parents call 'happy, warm and supportive' with experienced and SEN-qualified teachers allowing the pupils, who are mostly fairly high functioning with few behavioural issues, to learn well. Mental health and emotional wellbeing a priority with daily embedded exercises and teaching. Not as much space as everyone would like but good systems ensure that pupils move easily around the school and go for regular outside exercise and other activities.

Ambitious College

2

Clyde Road, Tottenham, London N15 4FY

020 3870 8775 | admin@ambitiousaboutautism.org.uk | www.ambitiouscollege.org.uk/

Independent | **Ages:** 16–25 | **Pupils:** 85 (on two campuses)

Executive Principal: From Sept 2020, Linda Looney. Joined Ambitious about Autism in August 2013, having perviously worked as a post-16 SEN lecturer – she spent the first five years of her career working in FE colleges, after which she moved into the charity sector and set up and managed a number of services to develop the skills of people with autism and learning disabilities. These services included independent travel training, supported employment and a variety of lifelong learning and social enterprise schemes. A passionate believer in furthering the abilities of people with learning disabilities.

Each campus has own principal – Lee Helyer for Tottenham and Linda Looney for Isleworth.

Entrance: Pupils must have an autism diagnosis, many are non-verbal, many have occupational therapy needs and most have learning disabilities. They do support pupils with personal care support needs and on medication (but none on a peg feed or needing injections). Depending on the intensity and frequency of challenging behaviours, they may decline a place if the pupil needs access to individual space for large parts of the day or a positive handling approach. 'This wouldn't suit a student that needed their own space or couldn't be around others,' according to staff, who work hard to get pupils integrated into the college and wider community at every opportunity. Pupils come from Ambitious about Autism school, Treehouse, and from residential units and special schools. Assessments are usually undertaken in the young person's current placement. If the college believes it can match the pupil's needs, an application for funding is made to the local authority and the pupil can attend the college for trial days once funding is agreed.

Exit: The college is working hard to organise supported internships for each pupil and the aim is to build up relationships with local employers so that there can be mentors at work who carve up parts of their job and give it to mentees. An employment specialist ensures that each pupil has access to work experience. These internships are a way for employers to train and recruit for entry level jobs which are not always easy to fill and to retain staff. Some pupils go on to residential care or supported living, though the majority stay living at home.

Teaching and learning: Parents spoke about 'high expectation of progress' which can be seen in focused teaching. 'They listen and take on board things we would like him to do, as well as being proactive about challenging him to move his levels up and not leaving room for coasting.'

Pupils follow one of four pathways. Those at the earliest stages of learning (milestones 3-5) work in the discovery and sensory exploration group; the developing independence skills group is for learners at the next level (say milestones 6-8); and then the preparing for employment group is for those working at entry levels 1-3. An additional few learners attend vocational studies at the co-located college, whilst still gaining living and social skills through Ambitious College teachers.

There is an artist in residence to inspire pupils. We saw a pupil in the art room looking at how colours make him feel

Recently these pupils have achieved BTec diplomas in ICT, art and design, and music technology.

Each pupil has at least one assistant/support staff who ensures that they join in classes of up to eight pupils with a teacher. Functional skills are taught within a framework of four 'preparing for adulthood' pathways, covering employment, relationships and community inclusion, health and wellbeing, and independent living.

All teaching is aimed at being of practical use and integrated in general learning – filling in forms, working with money, writing invitations to parents. Each pupil has a termly set individual learning plan developed through the outcomes set out in their ECHP and through discussion with parents and learners, which helps to match current knowledge to longer-term goals. One parent spoke of the way 'they use his own loves and interests to develop him and his learning'.

Social enterprises help to ensure pupils' learning is made practical and given value. A collaboration with the Gate Restaurant gave pupils training in chocolate making and thus chocolate is made at college and sold at the theatre. A Friday staff café is run and managed by pupils – taking orders for staff lunches and cooking and selling them.

Achievements are celebrated at an end of year awards ceremony attended by learners, families, staff and governors.

The arts and extracurricular: Art includes a range of media and the music room is well equipped to enable pupils to use both art and music in a therapeutic manner. There is an artist in residence to inspire pupils, and Nordoff Robbins attend to present music workshops with pupils. We saw a pupil in the art room looking at how colours make him feel, as well as smells that made him feel particular things.

Food preparation and eating is of high importance to pupils – 'lunch is the best part of the day,' according to one student. A large food-prep area is made up of several small home-sized kitchens where pupils learn to read recipes and prepare food they have bought. They cook and clean up and then eat the food they made. 'My son can't manage the journey to the shops, so he shops online, other pupils collect it, and then he can be part of the group when they prepare the meal and eat it together. That is how the college is flexible'.

Sport: The local sports centre is used for swimming and pupils are taken to join in community pilates and spinning classes. One pupil chooses to go to the pool every day for the exercise and sensory stimulation. Another can't manage the journey to the pool, so has a car take him and collect him so he can get to the pool with two assistants and participate. The ability to adapt to each pupil's needs is a real highlight of the college. And as with the academic studies, physical exercise is integrated wherever possible – walking to the gym, collecting their own medication from the meds room. 'They encourage physical development in a meaningful way – making them walk to the shops to buy food for cooking for example,' said one parent.

Ethos and heritage: Currently the college has two campuses – co-located with the College of North East London and West Thames College – and plans for a third campus are underway.

The Pears Campus, based at the College of Haringey, Enfield and North East London (CONEL), is situated in a solid old town hall building with high-ceilinged classrooms and corridors. The aim of Ambitious College is to create as mainstream an environment as possible, and the co-located site means that there is opportunity for pupils to use the adjacent college wherever possible. This means that the college is only part of a larger building, though it has its own entrance and facilities. A largely urban part of north London means that there is very limited outside space but community access is encouraged. We saw groups of pupils setting off with assistants to a local park and to the coffee shop in the nearby community centre. The little outdoor space there is contains a small raised vegetable garden, some outside gym equipment and a little space for bicycles. Generous sized classrooms for these young people and their assistants, cooking area, art room, small 'quiet rooms', accessible showers, admin rooms.

These facilities are mirrored in the Pears Campus at West Thames College in Isleworth, which has the bonus of being near Osterley Park.

Pastoral care, inclusivity and discipline: A common problem of staff turnover and burnout is addressed at Ambitious College with excellent training, continuous professional development and even support with the costs of masters degrees. This is symptomatic of a college that looks after the wellbeing of the people in it – both staff and pupils. It is not only the pupils who get physiotherapist and counselling support but staff as well. Each pupil has several assistants whom they are used to working with and this means pupils don't become too reliant on one person and learn to manage change, as well as keeping the team of staff engaged. Much work with parents as well as pupils to help with transitions and to encourage communication. Daily notes are sent to parents and these are used by parents also to report back to staff on any issues or matters that might affect behaviour or a pupil's mood. Some parents wish these were sent by email instead of on paper but all were appreciative of good, regular communication. 'They are excellent at identifying things going wrong or our concerns and are quick at stepping in to change.'

Behaviour can get extreme if a student is upset, but staff are plentiful and well trained, and there are no rooms for pupils to be excluded or take time out, though there are two quiet rooms for individual therapies or talking. Behaviour analysts create goals, track behaviour support plan and look at what needs to change, using positive behaviour support (PBS) to overcome challenging or socially isolating behaviour. Staff are all trained in physical intervention techniques when needed, using PBS to use the least restrictive approaches.

Social enterprises help to ensure pupils' learning is made practical and given value: a collaboration with the Gate Restaurant gave pupils training in chocolate making

Pupils are encouraged to have a voice, and the student council meets regularly from both campuses. Following these meetings, pupils are given feedback and a review – 'We said... and the college said...' – so that they know they have been heard and what action has been taken as a result.

Therapy and staffing: There is a full-time occupational therapist and full-time speech and language therapist on each campus as well as two behavioural analysts. Parent said: 'We really appreciate that all the support staff are on site and no lengthy referrals are needed.' As with all learning at Ambitious College, training is integrated into the day and into regular routines rather than only at special times. All learning is seen to be part of day-to-day life rather than like school lessons. Learning to shower, for example, was integrated into the pupils' lives by expecting them to have a shower after exercise, rather than being taught personal hygiene as a special topic.

Where appropriate, each pupil has a personal care support plan, a behaviour support plan and medical support plan. A communication passport is used to integrate speech therapy goals into everyday expectations of communication. One parent explained how hard they had worked to put together a programme of language, waiting for her child to speak rather than speaking for him. 'They will wait forever for him to speak, and so now he has started to speak and you can have a conversation with him for the first time.'

Pupils and parents: Pupils come from a wide geographic area. Not ideal in terms of travel for both pupils and parents, and parents said 'it means friends are far apart and it is quite hard to involve parents'. Local authorities can be reluctant to fund students sent out of borough, and many parents experienced a battle to get funding.

Money matters: The college is supported by Ambitious about Autism charity which raises huge amounts of money to help develop education for people with autism. The college is paid by local authority funded places but the extra money it raises can be felt in high staff ratio.

Parents get local authority funding for places at Ambitious College: 'The college really helps us with the annual review and completing the forms properly so we can get funding.'

The last word: Dedicated staff and focused but flexible learning opportunities make this college an example of good practice and a place for students to continue to learn and grow. The constant aim for practical independent skills is what parents find invaluable and the only complaint we heard was that 'the college should go on forever!'

Clarendon School

c/o Clarendon School Secondary Centre, Egerton Road, Twickenham TW2 7SL

020 3146 1441 | jkipps@clarendon.richmond.sch.uk | www.clarendon.richmond.sch.uk

State | Ages: 4–16 | **Pupils:** 165 (50 primary, 90 secondary); two-thirds boys

Executive head: Since 2006, John Kipps (50s). Two grown-up daughters, one a teacher, one a zookeeper. Originally joined the school in 1993 as a year 7 teacher, becoming key stage 3 team leader in 1995 and acting deputy head in 1997, made permanent a year later.

A local boy (born in Hounslow), his original plan, aged four, was to be a vicar – felt any job where you only worked on Sundays had to be a good bet. He was won over to teaching after encountering PGCE students during a post-uni temp job as a lab technician at the West London Institute (he's a geography and biological sciences graduate). After training at St Mary's Twickenham, he worked at St Mary's and St Peter's CE primary school in Teddington for four years, where he met Clarendon pupils as part of an inclusion project and found his vocation.

A kind and effective leader, he's presided over the school's expansion from 90 to 140 and its move from run-down site in Hanworth ('the school used to be a good sell but the building wasn't') into new buildings in 2018. Secondary centre is now in Twickenham, primary three miles away in Hampton.

Parents are delighted. 'Made it his dream to open this amazing site – the building is incredible,' said one. In the face of all this change, Ofsted ratings have remained consistently outstanding.

Since 2016, school has been part of an educational trust, Auriga, which also runs other special schools in the area. Newest, Capella House, opened September 2019, senior pupils occupying another chunk of the same new Twickenham site, Capella House primary pupils on revamped listed premises close by. Mr Kipps is also in charge of these, managing total staff team of close to 90 including those at the Gateway Centre (secondary school provision for 20 pupils aged 11-16 with ASD, co-located adjacent to a Richmond mainstream school).

Also – somehow – continues to teach (takes GCSE science class). Important to show colleagues 'that can walk the walk – won't ask them to do something I wouldn't be prepared to do myself. Also keeps me fired up and in love with my profession – heads too often lose sight with what they're doing it for.'

Very popular with pupils. 'Going round the school [every child] wanted to show him their work,' said parent. Primary school parents who don't know him as well praise leadership that makes school as effective as it is. 'No organisation like this would run if he wasn't doing his job, so assume he's excellent,' said parent.

Here for the duration. Will stay until retirement, he promises (to the relief, no doubt, of everyone).

Head of Secondary Centre: Since 2001, Rosemary Clarke. Has had a range of roles, teaching primary and secondary year groups before becoming KS3 team leader, then assistant headteacher and deputy head. Music specialist with a 'warm, positive relationship with the secondary pupils,' says Mr Kipps.

Head of Primary Centre: Since 2002, Angela Mason. First teacher in the family – had wanted to be a nurse but changed her mind when she helped out at a local school. This is her third time at the school after assorted promotions elsewhere. 'I really like it here – the children are wonderful.'

Particularly good at reassuring new parent, who describe her as supportive and lovely. 'She made a big impression when we first saw her.' 'What you want as a parent is just a normal teacher. She's incredibly reasonable and likeable – there to do her job,' said one.

Entrance: School caters for moderate learning difficulties. Has 140 places, 50 in primary, 90 secondary. All pupils will have significant global developmental delay though some (particularly those in reception and year 1 with early diagnosis) have more severe difficulties. Other learning needs vary from Down's Syndrome to ASD (growing numbers, currently around 60). All pupils have an EHCP.

Vast majority are verbal, some highly articulate, though will normally be some primary pupils who are non-verbal. Most a key stage behind mainstream peers. Have three classes for those with borderline severe difficulties who are further behind cognitively but a good fit socially. May move out into other classes if make greater progress than envisaged; others will move in if start to slip further behind.

Pupils joining in reception and year 1 tend to have the most significant level of need. Significant cohort joins in or after year 6 – have coped in supportive primary schools but would be lost in mainstream secondaries. Otherwise will take in any year group where have spaces and they are a good fit – one pupil, who had previously not been attending school, joined in year 11, during which reading age improved by over four years.

Wouldn't take if, say, had only specific learning difficulty or ASD – MLD diagnosis is key. Do have some pupils who previously had challenging behaviour – will judge whether it's the result of needs not being met or a primary need in its own right.

Always visit the child in current setting as paperwork 'doesn't always match the child'. Will sometimes invite child in for a day at the school but only if judged not to be too disruptive to the pupil, particularly if not offered a place.

Some parents have predictable battle to get LA to fund (but one worth fighting). 'Loved it the moment I saw it,' said one.

Exit: Pupils stay until 16. Link with Richmond College – year 11s study there for a day each week as preparation for moving there in year 12. SEN Connexions officer supports and mentors year 10 and 11 pupils.

The head is a local boy (born in Hounslow): his original plan, aged four, was to be a vicar – felt any job where you only worked on Sundays had to be a good bet

For many pupils, progress made in English will hamper likelihood of going on to higher education – just four have gone on to university over the past 25 years. Great success in moving into further education, however, with the vast majority of pupils moving on either to Richmond College (next door) or others. Usually a few needing more specialist environment move either to Strathmore or St Philip's School in Chessington.

As so often, the issue is what happens post-education. Between a third and half are in some form of employment but 'nowhere near high enough,' says Mr Kipps, whose pre-retirement goal is to find solutions, particularly for the most and least able pupils who tend to struggle most. In process of launching Independent Citizens' Award. Designed to recognise efforts of pupils in going out into their community, from scouts to voluntary work, so lives don't grind to halt after school or college.

Teaching and learning: School aims high. Website talks of creating a centre of excellence, support and challenge, with pupils achieving full potential, academically, socially, creatively and morally, gaining confidence and making a contribution to society. Ambitious, yes, but as long as pupils are here, school will make sure that as many of those boxes as possible are ticked, pushing (gently) when they feel it will yield results.

Starting here can require a slight leap of faith as school doesn't generally offer one-to-one support. Often comes as a shock especially when have battled to get it specified in EHCP in other settings. 'Can be a difficult message... but we're highly staffed and able to respond,' says Mr Kipps. Stay with it, agree parents, because it's replaced by a greater focus on independent learning, with a teacher and TAs in each class who have 'a much more realistic idea of how child is working and what they can do,' confirmed one.

Teaching is excellent and heavily tailored to individual pupils. For one primary age boy, highly incentivised by public transport, 'we even had a bus rather than a donkey taking Mary to Bethlehem at Christmas,' says Mr Kipps. Highly effective. 'Suddenly he's starting to communicate – before, he wasn't responding at all,' said another primary school parent.

Primary day starts with breakfast for all staff and pupils at 8.30am then runs to 3pm, with three learning periods of between 75 and 90 minutes, interspersed with break and lunch.

Teachers know when to ease back if, for example, it has been a tricky start to the day. 'Really care about the children in their class,' said parent.

School aims high. Website talks of a centre of excellence, support and challenge, with pupils achieving full potential, academically, socially, creatively and morally

Teach full curriculum in KS2 (years 3-6) – English and maths plus science, ICT, RE, humanities and DT. Specialist classes (one primary, two secondary) of around 6-7 pupils. Otherwise around 12 in a class though can be six or seven differentiated activities going on. Music plays a big part in life here – have junior pupils' signing choir using Makaton (tactically used throughout the school – some classes need it, others don't).

Senior school subjects are English, maths, humanities, art, food technology, PSHE, French, music, drama, DT and PE. Secondary Centre follows a primary teaching model with some curriculum areas taught by subject specialist staff. Every senior school pupil gets a Chromebook – ensures that on a par with mainstream peers next door school. Much valued, very exciting. Classrooms named for famous and long-dead Richmond residents, eg Sir Joshua Reynolds (no chance of tabloid exposés...).

Lifeskills curriculum has immediate practical benefits – own room with range of hobs so similar to what pupils have at home, plus washing machine/dryer. 'If PE kit is dirty – or their home chaotic – can bring and wash here,' says Mr Kipps.

Will do whatever they can to get pupils where they need to go, say parents. 'If there's a chance that child could do a GCSE, they will do it – am so surprised at the quality and standard.' (English likely to be the exception – if able to pass at GCSE, would normally need a mainstream environment.) Final decision always based on cohort – currently have able year 8 group working towards double science GCSE over three years. Also offer range of other qualifications, ASDAN, in eg maths, DT and adult numeracy – entry level, and level 1 – eg BTecs.

Almost no quibbles from parents. Generally respond quickly to emails and communicate well, though a little more advance information about events would be welcome, and some parents would like more formal homework, eg maths topics worksheets. Mr Kipps feels that generally (apart from reading and spellings) it's not needed. Ground is covered during the school day and children are frequently exhausted at the end of it, though happy to consider, eg when homework is part of the routine for siblings in mainstream schools.

For parents who worry that there's not enough formal learning time, other families stress that every activity or outing is beneficial. 'My child is learning more than he did when he was behind a desk for six hours a day and learned nothing,' said primary parent. 'You can't compare the progress made here compared within a mainstream school.'

Whether on primary or secondary site, non-verbal or highly articulate, pupils have an unmissable rapport with staff. Tend to be long stayers (many a decade or more), average age mid-40s. 'I'm blessed to have such strong staff team,' says Mr Kipps.

Pupils' work can be very impressive. Art is outstanding by any measure – borne out by results. In 2018, 11 took art GCSE and all got 7s and 8s. Current KS3 pupils appear just as talented, judging by the galleons, intricate to last detail, in full sail (they're painted on to photographs) and the group of Keith Haring inspired figurines – plaster on wire frames, brightly painted, in assorted poses – determined karate expert, gold-bodied, pink-belted, kicking out into space.

Corridor display of love letters produced by some year 9 pupils studying Romeo and Juliet were both moving – 'you turn my rain into sun and clouds into stars at night' – and quirky. Who could resist being wooed with: 'The light reflected on your blond hair reminds me of the sand of a golden beach located in a suburban area of Spain,' or 'Your eyes are as pretty as a kiwi bird'?

The arts and extracurricular: Notable for unusually large range of clubs offered. Fewer in primary – some, like football, at lunchtime – because of travel logistics and sheer exhaustion. Include cookery (very popular). Big range at senior level, from cross-country to dance, life skills, kayaking and canoeing (at Young Mariners nearby), yoga (very popular) and gardening. After-school transport a barrier (a reason clubs are such a rarity in other special day schools). Mr Kipps is keen to encourage independent travel. Happens with some year 7s; goal is for all year 10s and 11s to use public transport if they're able.

Display of love letters produced by some year 9 pupils studying Romeo and Juliet were both moving – 'you turn my rain into sun and clouds into stars at night' – and quirky

Gardens on both sites are packed with impressive greenery, nothing grown that isn't edible, own produce picked, cooked and served, with pupils' help. Secondary Centre also has chickens (confined to own area after decimating young plants when allowed to roam free) as well as an elevated pond – hoping for newts or frogs, whirligig beetles and water boatman in the meantime.

Cycle maintenance, one of the school's biggest endeavours, has led to paid employment (one former pupil is now managing a team of five). Fix all school bikes and trikes and do running repairs for Richmond College students (have corner room for easy drop off and pick up), while police pass on all unclaimed stolen bikes for restoration or spare parts.

Similarly extensive range of residential trips, starting in year 6 with overnight camping and again in year 7, who also get a longer trip. For pupils in years 8-11 there's opportunity to study performing arts in Suffolk for a week, courtesy of Pro Corda (high powered youth music organisation – celebrity visitors include eg Julian Lloyd-Webber). Outdoor pursuits offered to year 11, with an activity week for pupils who might not be able to access residential trip – comes with assorted challenges and qualification.

Saturday club in Hampton for pupils and siblings (originally for young carers), Wednesday evening youth clubs, one for 14 to 19 year-olds, another for 18 to 25 year-olds.

Sport: Impressively good at sport – trophy cabinets in both senior and primary schools worth a look. Some highly talented individuals, including senior school girl who's achieved gold and silver in London Youth Games Swimming Gala Sport despite VI; also tend to do well in cross-country. As with academics, aim for difficult balance of encouragement without overstressing. One parent reported that her child, who'd previously needed step by step instructions, had participated in sports day here on his own.

Ethos and heritage: Secondary Centre – which moved from single deteriorating site in 2018 – is one of three occupying a brand new building in Twickenham, SW London. The new Richmond upon Thames secondary free school (mainstream) will be the largest – so takes the lion's share of the space (though there's plenty to go round) while Clarendon occupies same spot on each of the building's three floors. A second special school, Capella House, for cognitively able pupils with SCL, opened September 2019 (also all-through, with primary pupils on a different site).

Auriga's sensible, joined-up approach (all too rare) is that schools will provide what Mr Kipps describes as a continuum of provision. 'Where there's clear daylight between needs accommodated in different schools, there will be pupils who fall down the cracks. Here we try to make sure there's some overlap between the provision so we can see where children will fit best,' he says. Clarendon suits those somewhere in the middle, with Capella House supporting pupils of average cognitive ability, and a third school in the borough, Strathmore, taking those with more severe needs.

Two Clarendon sites were eight years in the planning – time well spent, given well thought through designs they've ended up with.

Clarendon's primary age pupils are next to (but separate from) Buckingham Primary School in Hampton in a single-storey building, previously another special school (now closed) which has had a top to bottom refurbishment. Primary school is beautifully done, from the colour-coded doors (blue for classrooms, red for 'don't enter', green for shared spaces) to low-noise environment. Inside, spaces include busy but calm classrooms, a multipurpose hall (assemblies, PE – even has vaulting horse) and small, unintimidating dining hall (also have breakfast here).

Outside, in addition to allotment, there's a path divided into 'road' and pavement and attractive play areas. Reception and year 1 have own playground and free flow experiential learning – with diggers for moving sand, mud kitchen and board mounted with range of light switches, door handles, phone and tap.

On the senior site, there are few shared spaces; classrooms for all three schools are entirely separate, though Clarendon and Capella House share smart specialist teaching areas – science, DT, food tech, art and drama and dining area.

There's some territorial ambivalence in areas shared with the mainstream school, most marked in the playground. Though in theory there are no physical divisions, the two sets of pupils observe an invisible boundary line and stick to their own patch. Even the glorious zipwire (Clarendon side) doesn't lure mainstream pupils across. 'Could use it, but don't,' says Mr Kipps.

The senior site is based round block configuration, with classrooms round the outside – 'Only way to make it financially viable,' says Mr Kipps. Little touches are numerous and sensitive, including some height adjustable tables and worktops, noise reduction (even the biggest rooms are low-echo), lighting (frequencies chosen to minimise risk for 10 or so pupils with photosensitive epilepsy) and calming grey paint tones with colour coding for different floors. (Other schools are starting to pop in and note down the Pantone shades.) Even the dining area (its boundary again shared with mainstream school) offers a pleasant mix of booths (most sought after), conventional long tables and counter seating.

There are few hand dryers and mirrors in the senior school (and none in the primary) because of the potential for sensory overload and power to distract. Seniors also have individual toilets 'so not a focus for bullying'.

The senior school science lab is close to its mainstream equivalent so there's extra support available if needed, while the larger of the two smart sports halls, complete with sprung floor, projector and screen and tiered seats (automatically tuck themselves up when not needed) – offers potential for extra revenue – could even host film screenings. (The second, smaller, can is used for anyone who needs a less intimidating environment, as well as for other sports such as yoga.)

Primary school has Crosbie, a fully trained therapy schnoodle (poodle/schnauzer cross), with a nice line in helping pupils to overcome dog phobias

Similarly thoughtful approach extends to parents, with short, humorous descriptions of non-teaching staff on office doors ('puts parents at ease if don't come across them very often') to location of family partnership office close to the entrance (lower stress for visiting children who are phobic about school, minimal disruption for current pupils when parents attend a meeting without them). Website even features a jargon-busting guide to acronyms – 13 pages of useful decoding, from ADD/ADHD to WLSSG.

For families reeling after the news that mainstream education isn't the best option, school's new premises can at least soften the blow. 'We had very mixed thoughts about a special school and didn't know what to expect,' said parent. 'We went to the open day and were absolutely amazed.'

Pastoral care, inclusivity and discipline: School's approach is all about valuing the individual and taking at their own pace so 'can learn and move forward,' said parent. Essential, given that pupils' backgrounds can be less than ideal. Some, despite having learning disability, are also carers for parents or siblings, sometimes both, with more severe needs. 'Have some families who have been represented here since I've been at the school.'

Mr Kipps is particularly keen that parents 'should have high aspirations for their children and not just choose the school because of family history.' Also working on getting parents (sometimes the first in several generations) into employment, with some success. Plans more direct action – coffee shop is on Mr Kipps's wish list to provide employment and work experience to pupils and their families.

Some staff have expertise in mental health – some pupils at risk of self-harm – and both primary and secondary sites have dedicated health and well-being leads, driving mental health agenda and dealing with any medical issues.

Parents praise teachers' knowledge of the pupils – 'those I have never seen before say "hello, how are you?" to my child,' said one. Nothing left to chance – transition to new buildings was carefully planned, with lots of visits and updates to reduce anxiety. Only one senior pupil found it hard to cope. Staff, a tight-knit community, have also had to adjust to being on two sites – easier for some than others.

Reward achievement in favour of sanctions wherever possible – house points, special mentions book – day trip for winning house each year.

Expectation is that pupils will behave appropriately. When they don't – 'Will sometimes have a pupil kicking off,' says Mr Kipps – it's dealt with, but with dignity. 'Behaviour is communication,' he says. When they have difficult home lives, they can be doing well to make it into school at all.

Restorative justice 'to help pupils learn from their experiences' – reported by Ofsted as 'helping pupils make sense of their behaviour and the impact it has on others' – has been introduced, but works only when everyone buys in, including staff, though do receive training. Also Team

Teach trained in positive behaviour management strategies. Behaviour generally excellent – school had had just one 1.5 fixed day exclusion during the school year – a historic low.

Approach comes across as both flexible and highly effective – quick de-escalation during visit when senior pupil's description of hurt finger came with some choice four-letter words. If approach comes as a shock to prospective members of staff, used to a more punitive regime, it won't be the right place for them.

Therapy and staffing: Hot and cold running therapy, as and when you need it and tailored to each child. A huge contrast with mainstream experience, say parents – provision of SALT and OT 'is fantastic'. Instead of seeing an OT only once a term (if you're lucky), here it might be provided twice a week. 'You feel as a parent, "I don't need to worry. If you say can you look at this, the school will do it".' Also offer behaviour support, music therapy, counselling and art therapy. Primary school also has Crosbie, a fully trained therapy schnoodle (poodle/schnauzer cross), with a nice line in helping pupils to overcome dog phobias.

Approach extends to the whole family. Family workers provide 'an impartial shoulder to cry on or simply a friendly ear' (and very possibly both). Also offer family therapy – so generations (parents, siblings, grandparents) can 'work through issues and for their children to understand themselves a bit more'. Mainly primary based – funding permitting, hope to extend to secondary pupils.

Academy status means can contract own therapists (provision of OT in particular was previously poor). Now have full-time OT with two part-time assistants, one on each site, being recruited. Means can offer to all pupils, whether or not specified on EHCP. Physio provided by LA; goal is to bring SALT in house as well. Also provide art therapy, counselling and EP (none currently full-time).

Pupils and parents: 'These are not children who are backwards in coming forwards,' says Mr Kipps. In every class and corridor, pupils hurry forward to share their views. Non-verbal children in primary specialist class notable for desire to interact. Another primary pupil asks about this reviewer's voice recorder – 'is it because you forget things?' In secondary school they admire Mr K's outfit – 'Nice tie!' – and commend his leadership. 'If he ever leaves the school, think they should have a statue,' says effervescent year 9 pupil.

Unusually have excellent boy/girl mix – currently around 60:40 – partly down to better identification of SEN in girls at an earlier age in the borough.

Majority live in Richmond with about 10 per cent from Hounslow, same again for Kingston and small number from Surrey. Despite the affluence of the area, many of these pupils, though local, are from difficult backgrounds – while there's a core of prosperous, professional families, others here are struggling – about 45 per cent receive pupil premium. School also more diverse than most with about 50 per cent other than white British.

In every class and corridor, pupils hurry forward to share their views. One asks about this reviewer's voice recorder – 'is it because you forget things?'

Though travel distances between families can be a barrier, there's a strong sense of community among the parents. 'We're in the same boat… here it's like people understand.'

Some school events take place, eg bingo night, and recent appointment of new family partnership worker (based across two school sites – does everything from helping with DLA to liaising with support services) should lead to more, thought parent.

Heartwarming parent-made video (has made national television) features primary pupils movingly talking about themselves. Taking child out of mainstream and moving in a different direction from all other families can be a lonely time and pupils, not just parents, can be acutely aware of the differences. One senior school pupil request was for uniforms to change from blue to green and include a formal blazer – worn with pride. Pupils 'didn't want to be different,' says Mr Kipps.

While special school 'is not what anybody wants… these are lovely kids who are going to take longer on their journey,' said father.

The last word: As one parent pointed out, nobody wakes up thinking that they hope their child will go to a special school. Ending up here, with a leader whose calm, humanitarian approach shines through and staff who'll work tirelessly to make every pupil achieve everything they're capable of (and sometimes rather more), won't make things better but will make them as good as they can possibly be. If only – as so often – they could do the same for their life chances once they've left, there'd be even greater grounds for hope.

Fairley House School

4

30 Causton Street, London SW1P 4AU

020 7976 5456 | ps@fairleyhouse.org.uk | www.fairleyhouse.org.uk

Independent	Pupils: 212: 143 boys, 69 girls
Ages: 5–16	Fees: £33,600 pa

Headmaster: Since 2013, Mr Michael Taylor (40s). Prior to Fairley House spent a year as deputy head, joining the school originally in 2008 as head of the senior school. After university took a job as a transport engineer but it was never going to stick and, with employer's full backing, moved into teaching in 1998. Started off as a year 9 tutor at Malory Comprehensive in Lewisham, moving into independent sector in 2000 when he spent two years at St Martin's Prep in Northwood as a geography and history teacher (and basketball and rugby coach). More importantly, success in identifying and helping dyslexic and dyspraxic pupils made him realise that this was where his future lay.

Moved to the Elms in Colwall in 2002 (teacher and sports coach) before rejoining the maintained sector in 2003 as a geography, leisure and tourism teacher at the Malling School in Kent. His move to specialist teaching came about when he joined More House School, Frensham, in 2004, as deputy head of boarding and English, history, geography and PE teacher to a range of ages.

Still finds time to teach – good for credibility with staff, he feels. 'Nice to be able to sit and sympathise.' Attends as many school matches as possible. 'Even if we didn't win he's still happy,' says pupil. In his spare time he's pretty outdoorsy. Cites interests as keeping fit, travelling and whitewater rafting, plus conversation and animal behaviour (clue provided by presence of live chameleons Misty and Fog in his office).

'Fantastic', 'Approachable', 'Kids love him,' say parents, who speak of delighted juniors being given piggybacks at end of year picnic. 'He's always coming around and cheering people on,' confirms pupil. 'I have never seen him have a frowny face.' Travel round the school with him and it's like accompanying a fantastically approachable celeb, he's instantly mobbed by senior school pupils. 'Sir, is it mufti day on Friday?'; 'Sir, I love assembly.'

Children appear in his office, most of which is now taken up with sundry items including desks, whiteboard, two chameleons and CCTV monitors (head says children particularly enjoy a spot of ad hoc spying), to chat and let off steam if they have a problem with other staff and pupils. 'In here they can shout and swear at me but it stays in here,' he says. He's a big personality with the happy knack of achieving right balance between fun and gravitas – deliberately so. 'Here it's a special place – we can't just be teachers, we must be a little bit more,' he remarks. Watching a celebration assembly where each award was greeted with a drum roll (performed by series of pupils), jokes (by the head) and a real sense of shared joy, it was hard to disagree.

Pupils always know just who's in charge. 'It's respectful but the gap is different from regular school in a good way – you learn the most from the teacher you love best,' says parent. Dyslexic himself, he vividly remembers how it felt: singled out but never in a good way; 'classed as being this awful thing' and compelled to walk to a 'dusty room' for extra lessons. 'Would walk very slowly there and sprint back.' Determination to ensure that no pupil here ever feels like that shines through everything he does.

Entrance: Start with tour of the school and meeting with the head. Most children have primary diagnosis of either dyslexia or dyspraxia and at least average cognitive ability. Stick closely to this – won't admit children with social, emotional or behavioural difficulties (includes ADHD) and not registered to accept children with ASD. Anyone with EAL needs to be sufficiently proficient to access the curriculum. About a third of junior and 45 per cent of senior pupils have EHCPs.

If paperwork adds up, child will have three-day multidisciplinary assessment at the school, including time in class and in the playground, followed by feedback session where school outlines support. Can ask for written reports from OT, EP and SALT (there's a charge for this).

Exit: Goal is that as many pupils as possible return to a mainstream school so most stay for two to three years – though with growing pressure on independent school places, no longer as easy as it used to be. 'Harder to get schools to take into account pupils' personalities outside the written [entrance] paper,' says head. Very occasional departure because of behavioural issues – though only happens when all other measures have failed. 'We try not to get to that point,' says head. Otherwise, good links with local sixth form and tutorial colleges, state and independent, where can work towards additional qualifications with appropriate support.

Teaching and learning: For many it can feel like school of last resort. 'Some of the parents are in a bit of a desperate situation,' says parent. 'Feel their child cannot be taught anywhere else.' 'If they can't learn the way we teach, we have to teach the way they learn,' says the school. Simple, yet devastatingly effective, particularly for children who've previously learned in an often hostile environment, with teachers who make no concessions for anyone who doesn't fit the mould.

School starts with an assessment to find out 'how children tick' followed by IEP, collaboratively produced by OT, SALT, Ed Psych and teachers and used as the yardstick to monitor progress of pupils. Most children are at least of average ability, some way ahead. While inspectors felt tracking could be improved (a tiny detail in a very positive report), numbers of pupils joining or leaving mid-year makes it logistically tricky. School has all the top-notch benchmarking systems in place, while parents get a termly update of the child's progress, eg their reading age.

We watched an endlessly calm teacher getting junior pupils on side. 'I'd like everyone sitting in five... four...three... two...[long pause for the stragglers] one.' It works

Small size and range of needs makes progress highly individual to each child. For some, it's about arriving unable to count and mastering times tables or learning to write in full sentences; for others, acquiring the strategies that will secure a place in selective senior school. One parent cited all the things school had done for her child, 'structuring what has to be retained and not retained, helping 200 per cent'.

Achieved by seamless, integrated support. 'Impossible to divide the two.' Plenty of experienced members of staff undoubtedly help. Average age of staff is 40, 18 have been at the school for ten years or longer, many either with, or working towards, an SpLD qualification. Can take teachers a while to adjust to this very different way of working; 'Normally takes them two years to settle completely,' confirms head. All are praised to the eyeballs by parents. 'They have a quirkiness children can relate to,' says one. 'It's not "I'm a teacher and am going to tell you what to do." I wish I'd had a school like that.' We watched an endlessly calm and brilliantly effective teacher getting junior pupils on side. 'I'd like everyone sitting on the carpet in five... four... three... two... [long pause for the stragglers] one.' It works.

Classes, average just over eight children, maximum 12, aren't necessarily based on chronological age but ability. Teaching covers all national curriculum subjects but with own schemes of work, therapists are involved in teaching and learning process (get own training). Inspiring, sometimes off the wall, approaches are the norm.

English naturally takes up considerable share on the timetable and is approached with much inventiveness and confidence boosting, essential given just how fragile children here can be. 'I don't know what an adjective is,' says junior pupil, sounding panicked, but they are quickly reassured.

Multisensory word study sessions hone every useful technique going, way beyond phonics and spelling rules. Here, children will also study word meanings, structure, origins – it's all about making connections that will help with unfamiliar words.

Learning to write fluently, at length, with interesting and well punctuated sentences can be extremely hard, so work with SALT and OTs cover useful strategies. Results can be impressive; a year 11's review of a recent theatre trip urged readers to 'forget your work. Forget your existence and travel into a world of insanity, melancholy and pure chaos...'

Maths is similarly thorough. Multisensory approach includes motor maths in the gym and uses OT and PE equipment to give maths concepts a physicality. Children use bodies while learning a maths concept which helps with understanding and recall. Parents describe lessons that involve children whizzing through the hall on a skateboard to collect the answer to a times table question, or making a human clock as a way of learning to tell the time. Developed by OT and teachers working together to commit key words and concepts to memory. 'Must be something behind it to ensure that it works,' says head.

Similar care and attention elsewhere. Computing uses dyslexia-friendly drag and drop apps (rather than programming languages). In science, masses of hands-on stuff, from experiments to interactive online games that make lessons memorable and fun. History and geography work with SALT on memory strategies to help learn new vocabulary or dates. One former pupil, reported inspectors, learned about ancient Egyptians through the medium of brightly coloured pottery.

A blend of reassurance and motivation was evident in every class we saw. 'How are we feeling?' asks teacher before a year 5 maths test. One pupil is worried because 'I went to bed at 7 for the last two nights.' 'Good self-reflection,' is the encouraging response. Even the furniture is well thought through, featuring untippable wobble seats – ideal for pupils who need to keep on the move during lessons.

Decisions on options occur in year 8 (some courses are taken over three years). Goal is for everyone to aspire to GCSE English, maths and science, though can all be switched for a functional qualification if works better. Students also study two additional subjects, including child development, citizenship and iMedia as well as humanities and DT.

School celebrates all GCSE grades achieved, though that 'magic 4... is what parents and individuals look for' and head lets pupils who haven't quite made it come back for retakes. Pupils, especially seniors, are understandably enthusiastic about the approach. 'At my old school they would just expect you to know,' said one. 'Here, if you don't understand, they won't just continue.'

Parents shouldn't ever be in any doubt as to what children have been doing. Newsletters are a lesson recap all on their own, complete with illustrations – recent example included word of the week ('character', 'mature'); revision on quadrilaterals (photographs of teams creating shapes) and emotional Zones of Regulation with strategies for achieving 'green' (calm state of alertness), avoiding 'blue' ('down feelings... sad, tired, sick, bored') or 'red' ('elation, anger, explosive behaviour'). Frequent trips all over London from the Globe to the Lyric Theatre to Tate Britain as well as residential trips (e.g. to Cumbria). Underlying all is school's ability to turn miserable children with sense of failure into happy ones. 'Confidence and support is what drives the learning.'

The arts and extracurricular: Clubs run on Tuesdays and Thursdays, current range from taekwondo to sewing (juniors), DT and singing for seniors, and vary through the year. Yoga, Lego and photography also on offer and bouldering (indoor rock climbing) for everyone.

Highly creative arts: individual music lessons – piano, guitar and drumming on offer, with wonderful performances (slightly hit and miss in the juniors but breathtakingly good in the senior school, say parents). Staff write both music and the script. Everyone has weekly timetabled music and drama with several productions each year, latest including 'Spelbownd' (year 7) and Julius Caesar (year 8).

'Kids love him,' say parents of the headmaster, and speak of delighted juniors being given piggybacks at end of year picnic

Some very able pupils could be encouraged to do even more, thought one parent, to harness the creative 'superpower' that can come hand in hand with specific learning difficulties. 'Could be phenomenal; children should be down getting greasy and making go karts and building stuff and cooking to realise that creativity.' Head is listening, however, with resources being bumped up and more pupils building portfolios, some working towards formal exams (13 timetabled hours for English and maths has inevitable impact on other subjects) so it's a question of watch this space!

At the senior school, bright classrooms (art, food tech, DT) have recently been added, complete (say our tour guides) with a 'secret fire exit'. DT, a particular favourite, has staff who appear to live for their subject with a devoted following, so we heard. The big attraction was the prototype skateboards, each constructed from a different mix of veneers to achieve ideal union of strength and flexibility. For the DT teacher, who is also dyslexic, pride of place went to the manuals he had put together, ('show Miss – they're really cool'). Each colossal tome, loosely bound, was a labour of love with instructions for every project broken down into the tiniest of tiny steps, one to a laminated page, words at a minimum, illustrations copious.

Sport: School does its best with sport though its focus on literacy and numeracy eats away at remaining time. More PE lessons on several wish lists (two for seniors, would love three). Range offered includes football, netball, rugby, cricket, athletics, swimming and dance. Some fixtures against other schools with varying results, and though unlikely to nab any awards for a win-at-all-costs culture, the school does better than you might think; squash team recently recorded victories and a near miss from netball team. While not the place to dream of high-profile team glory, school is remarkably effective in arranging matches against some serious opposition and ensuring that chances to represent the school are evenly distributed. 'Lots of children with dyspraxia can't catch a ball but still play. I wish other schools could see the way they treat children here,' says parent. For the head, it doesn't matter if team loses 30–nil, it's all about the experience. 'The kids come back and love the fact they've done it. It feels normal having a fixture.'

Ethos and heritage: School was founded in 1982 by Daphne Hamilton-Fairley, a speech and language therapist whose own children were also dyslexic, in memory of her husband, Professor Gordon Hamilton-Fairley, the UK's first oncology professor. She is still very involved with the school. After several moves, school finally settled on current sites, Lambeth for the juniors (years 2-5) and SW1 (just a mile away) for senior pupils (years 6-11). Juniors have two historic buildings close to Lambeth Palace (even the stairs are listed) where not an inch of space is wasted. High-end decor largely provided by the artwork, from motivating posters to attractive butterflies with googly eyes, taking flight from watercolour backgrounds, on the walls. Seniors have a compact-looking site: smallish classrooms off narrow corridors (lesson changeovers can be a bit of a squeeze) though, like juniors, miraculously packed in a good-sized, and well-used, hall.

Both sites are mainly landlocked with limited outside space, inevitable given the location, but hard for energetic pupils who need to run round wildly at breaktime to let off steam. Juniors have delightful courtyard garden, brick paving, palms and espalier trees, shortly to be Astroturfed over, a practical and sensible decision if a lot less scenic. Also have Archbishop and Battersea Parks, both close by. Seniors have their own densely planted garden and 'The Cage' public games area just across the road.

Pastoral care, inclusivity and discipline: Pupils' previous experiences can cast a long shadow. One junior pupil described school as 'really fun because the teachers aren't angry... they joke and understand how it is to be dyslexic.'

Understandably mega emphasis on confidence building – school aims to get them to the point where they can cope when things don't work out, now and later in life. Prize giving every term, honour rolls with awards for range of attributes, including kindness. Regular focus on perseverance and growth mindset – children's understanding impressive. 'Is it when you work harder, your mind gets stronger?' ask junior pupils. 'You don't know all the answers straight away, and you're not meant to,' explains teacher.

Pupils are in small tutor groups with additional support and mentoring if they struggle either in lessons or during unstructured time, eg in break. Regular PSHE – to government-decreed specs but tailored, wherever possible, so tutors can use to address particular issues.

Occasional issues linked to such small class sizes if big personality starts to dominate. 'In a class of seven or eight students, can be hard if you're not getting on with one particular child,' says parent. 'Have to learn how to deal with each other.' Inevitably some behaviour issues but felt by parents to be well managed. 'Effective and clear – and that's what children need,' says parent. School uses yellow behaviour cards, employs behaviour management expert and problems are often temporary and resolvable. 'Primary goal is that we prevent and support, and guide them back,' says the head.

Home/school diary, signed daily, is the bread and butter of parent communication but emails and phone calls also welcome. School felt to do a good job in keeping parents up to date and personal data is sensitively handled.

Therapy and staffing: Collaboration between teaching and therapists colours many of lessons and helps staff to share skills. Also offer individual and small group therapy. Overall staff to pupil ratio of 1:3.5.

Maths lessons can involve children whizzing around on a skateboard to collect the answer to a times table question, or making a human clock as a way of learning to tell the time

While OT does have own areas (well-lit top floor space in junior school), the focus is on integration. 'They do maths while doing OT and are taught literacy by qualified speech therapists,' says parent. Nobody needs to be pulled out or made to feel different and everything happens in small, well-matched groups. Pupils will have other needs on top of SpLD. School felt to be brilliant at making everything work; 'Have all sorts of difficulties so they spend a lot of time thinking how can they fit and how can we help them,' says a parent. Support extends to families, eg for those caught up in the EHCP process or needing a bit of expert clout at annual reviews, they will attend meetings and back up parents. If they can help, they will.

Expertise recognised by others, and there's a growing outreach programme. Have recently worked with GOSH to give advice on teaching dyslexic children and are just about to launch own accredited teacher training programme run by one of school's former heads.

Pupils and parents: As only 60 or so pupils have EHCPs, majority self-fund, some struggling to pay the fees. Parents' association organises regular events, including Christmas Fair, cake sale, a secondhand uniform sale and wine and cheese evening, as well as raffle with chance to win great prizes including being head for a day or doling out yellow behaviour cards to a teacher (surely a highlight). Similarly jolly sports day. 'Of all those I've been to, theirs wins hands down,' says parent. 'If someone's sister or brother wants to join in they don't tell them to get off the track but invite them to join in. There's a real inclusive vibe to it.' Head's cunning plan is to ensure that fastest runners 'only come across each other in the 100 metres or they're going to win everything – so everyone walks away with a first or second.'

Boys in the majority all the way through with girls making up between a third and a half of pupils in most classes (though in year 11 when we visited there was only one girl out of eight pupils). Year groups start low (12 in year 3) and peak in years 6-9.

Pupils come mainly from London – all points of the compass but from beyond the M25 too – (Gerrards Cross, Walton on Thames and Bromley all feature). Can make for a really early start – some pupils are up at 5.30am. No wonder 'a later start to the school day' was on one junior child's wishlist.

Most parents are positive about the education they're getting though inevitably some can find it hard to adjust to the more specialist approach that can seem worlds away from traditional environment. Children, too, can find move initially challenging though one child who was 'devastated' to leave friends told parents after the first few weeks that they'd done the right thing, to all-round relief.

Tiny numbers of girls less problematic than it might be. Perhaps surprisingly, junior and senior girls felt that friendships had in fact been strengthened because of the necessity of getting on with each other. 'It can be a bit lonely but we know that we've all got each other's back... maybe we all are very different but we all get on,' said one

For some families, school is seen as a quick fix – in, job done, and out again into mainstream. For others, it's a school for life, or at least to 16. High turnover means inevitably transient friendships – 'lose friends every couple of years – that's the sad thing,' says one parent, though there is a trade-off, thought another – 'the opportunity to make lots of friends – which is a positive as well as a slight negative'.

Means parents can feel like two tribes, with quite different aspirations. Generally co-exist peacefully, though not always – one family overheard describing 'permanent' pupils in very disparaging terms. Wide range of nationalities currently includes American, Dutch and Russian pupils.

Money matters: Many parents self-fund – costs are 'eye-watering' is one online comment – when LAs won't cough up. School is fundraising so other children who are 'only' in the bottom ten per cent and a mere two to three years adrift from peers can be helped through outreach programme.

The last word: Inclusive, fun, intertwining therapy with lessons ('lerapy?'), all delivered by fabulous staff and a universally popular head... we could go on. If any school can erase the damage caused by previous school experiences, this one can.

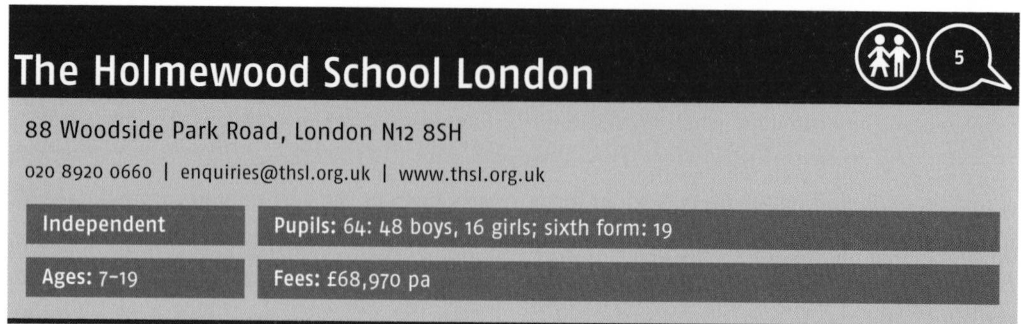

Head: Executive head: since April 2016, Lisa Camilleri BA QTS PGDip autism PGCert educational leadership, former deputy principal of NAS Radlett Lodge School, full of bright ideas and bringing wide experience. Keen on building community links and establishing an outreach and inclusion programme including training for autism teaching leaders.

Head of school: Bridget Young, BEd. Bridget was previously assistant head. She holds the national award for SEN coordination at level 4 and is a Stonewall ambassador, supporting students in SEN and safeguarding.

Entrance: Via local authorities and direct parent referrals. Admissions enquiries are handled deftly. Many children arriving have 'failed' at other schools. Taster sessions for potential pupils which can last one day, one week, even half a term. Assessment based around whether THSL can meet needs, whether child fits current profile of the class etc. The real question is whether the whole THSL experience would be right for the child. School has supported parents through tribunals, and developed positive relationships with LAs. School is clearly not afraid of the behaviours that come with often co-morbid diagnoses including anxiety, oppositional defiant disorder, ADHD and challenging behaviour. The real issue is space (current capacity is 70), 'There are only so many safe spaces when someone is kicking off.'

Exit: Majority of 19-year-old leavers continue into some form of further education. Recent leavers went to LaSWAP sixth form in Camden, Coulson College – to do A Level maths and BTec in engineering – and to a residential college in Somerset. Careers fair every year and THSL actively cultivates local employers to provide work experience for older pupils. Careers notices and ideas well displayed in school hall and impressive expectations to prepare all pupils for employment.

Teaching and learning: Range of pupils is quite wide academically as you would expect in a school for high functioning autism, Asperger's, SLCN, SpLD and 50 per cent with ADHD. Some pupils deemed unteachable before coming here and many have had multiple school failures.

Pupils work towards five GCSEs but approximately 20-30 per cent take pre-GCSE entry level certificates in English and maths instead if academic levels or anxieties preclude GCSEs. Individualised approaches help each pupil to achieve to their best level. Those taking GCSEs do so in subjects where they feel most confident. Current choices are from English, maths, ICT, science, art and design, drama and languages where relevant and suitable. Sensibly, teaching is across ability not age levels. Some very bright ones go on to A levels. In a typical sixth form, one will be doing two AS levels, one doing one AS level, and others resitting GCSEs to improve grades in maths or English. Others follow functional life skills and social skills programmes. Some are based at Holmewood (THSL) where they study functional literacy and numeracy, and access college with a TA (popular choices are a BTec in gaming and a BTec in childcare).

The school focuses on being positive about what students can do and one sixth former did work experience with Sega. Really small class sizes of three to six pupils plus subject teacher and two TAs. Average staff to pupil is one-to-two. Certain pupils have one-to-one or two-to-one.

Ninety-minute morning lessons with movement breaks as needed: run, jump, or do something OT based. Pupils are calmer, quieter and more focused as a result

Standard lessons in the morning are double at 90 minutes with breaks as needed. Most often they are movement breaks: run, jump, or do something OT based. Pupils are calmer, quieter and more focused as a result. Much work goes into encouraging self-regulation. Different systems in place for each pupil to identify that they need to take a break or to respond positively to a suggestion that they might need a break.

An almost paperless school. Pupils work on Google Chromebooks and with Google Classroom. Suggestions from parent partnership led to homework being done online, and marked online. Parents can log in and see what is going on. Real understanding that THSL pupils often need to separate home and school, and homework leads to anxiety and meltdowns. There is an after-school homework club.

The arts and extracurricular: THSL has a qualified forest school teacher on staff who develops skills such as how to light a fire with flints, cook sausages outside etc. Regular trips to a forest school on a farm near Mill Hill are highly sought after. Secondary pupils and sixth formers go on school journey week in the Isle of Wight to develop their life skills and independence, and have a chance to live away from home. Pupils are minutely prepared for the trip and know exactly what is going to happen and when. They go in small groups with high staff ratios, and staff do all the activities with them. A recent trip included surfing, tree climbing and cycling.

After-school activities are not possible due to diverse age range, local authority transport and general logistics, but once a week they have the choices of art, football, music and coding club. All the parents we spoke to wished there was more after-school life for their children.

Sport: School hall is used for indoor sports like dance and yoga and a recent visit from a golf pro. Most school sport takes place off site and is generally individual sports like badminton, kayaking, ice skating, horse riding and golf, using local parks and leisure centres.

Ethos and heritage: Upper school on a new site in Muswell Hill, with private forest and extensive outdoor space for extending the curriculum. Lower school is tucked away in Woodside Park, with a newly refurbished playground, accommodating, among other things, four therapy rabbits. The administration team sit cheek by jowl and are friendly and knowledgeable. The atmosphere is calm and friendly and you hear a lot of laughter from staff and students alike – you can see staff members getting stuck in playing alongside the children and modelling social skills and interaction. Parents feel that this works and 'the kids all get on really well'. Five minute warning before the end of break understands the need for predictability and consistency and anxiety around transitions.

We were struck by some original approaches. We particularly liked the 'conversation menus' which pupils pick up at lunchtime along with their cooked lunch, in order to provide a framework for chat and social interaction with peers and staff. As a result we didn't see any of the usual problems of unstructured time. The food looked and smelled good and not a whiff of overcooked cabbage anywhere.

We liked the 'conversation menus' which pupils pick up at lunchtime along with their cooked lunch, in order to provide a framework for chat and social interaction

Owned by the Cavendish Group, and has an additional site at the Sternberg Centre on East End Road in Finchley. The sixth form is currently based there, and pupils are gradually increasing in number.

School runs for 35 weeks a year with one holiday week of daily forest school where they build dens, make fires and have outdoor adventures. For parents the long holidays can be incredibly hard.

Pastoral care, inclusivity and discipline: Strong emphasis on self-esteem and well-being. Behaviour management based on commitment to consistency, training, having clear policy and guidelines. Collaborative approach with pupils to help them to understand and communicate how they are feeling. Behaviour management plans regularly updated, and focus on working out what is really happening for a child who might be kicking off. Acceptance that conventional consequences rarely work for ASD children but their peers need to see a consequence. Discipline involves anger management programmes, and talking to on-site psychotherapist. Other flexible options including contracts, mediation and scales of justice approach, said to be very effective.

Therapy and staffing: Therapy is timetabled but speech and language therapy is integral and aims to be functional and practical and includes a girls' group and Lego therapy. Therapies are a key part of the school's approach, seen as fundamental tools to access learning and teach students the experience of being calm (many do calming yoga). It's a committed approach and it seems to work. Experienced therapy team all on site includes one full-time SLT, part-time SLT, full-time OT/sensory integration specialist plus assistant, and a child and adolescent psychotherapist on site four days a week. There's also a part-time drama therapist, music therapist and reflexologist.

Fifty per cent of pupils have ADHD as well as ASD. Interestingly, only a few are medicated, as the school environment and therapies seem to work for them.

Full staff training weekly, and induction training for new staff takes a whole term and includes instruction from all the specialists on site. Most TAs have level 3 NVQ in teaching assistance, and they all attend every staff meeting.

Pupils and parents: For pupils aged 7-19 with high functioning autism, Asperger's Syndrome, language, communication and social pragmatic difficulties and those associated with ADHD and specific learning difficulties. Many with co-morbid diagnoses: ADHD (50 per cent), challenging behaviours (40 per cent), anxiety and ODD. Many with a late diagnosis of autism and/or history of multiple school failures. Pupils come from 13 different local authorities, as far south as Southwark and as far west as Heathrow. Some 25 per cent are picked up by parents, many have LA transport and a handful travel to school independently after six months' travel training.

Active parent partnership group works together to solve homework issues and to get other parents involved. Run a bit like a governing body. Parents report 'everyone has their say' and there is a supportive focus on helping parents to engage better with their children.

Money matters: Fee includes all therapies but cost for any one-to-one is extra. International students often self-fund, as do a few other UK students, but about 95 per cent of the pupils receive LA funding.

The last word: THSL is best suited for pupils with average to above average academic ability, although it will consider those working just below average where they can aim to close that gap. Pupils need to be verbal, but high anxieties, low self-esteem and multiple diagnoses are par for the course.

We like the fact that this school is definitely not fazed by challenging behaviour – the only thing that stands in their way is the limitations on managing it owing to space in the current building.

We saw a judicious balance of tough love combined with a deep understanding of pupils' vulnerabilities, and a determination to enable its pupils, however complex their presentation. A clear level of understanding of their pupils who may have 'the body of a 15-year-old and the social and emotional functioning level of a 5 year old'. Parents feel 'supported for the first time in years' and confident that the school will 'never give up on them'.

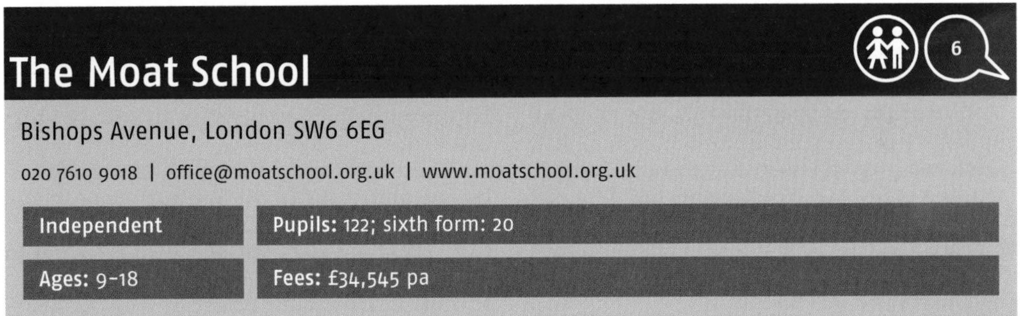

Headteacher: Since September 2019, Koen Claeys. He moved from another school in the Cavendish Education stable, Bredon School, where he had been head since April 2017. Prior to this he worked through various roles up to senior deputy headteacher at St James Senior Boys' School.

Entrance: The biggest entry point is at year 7 'when preps are weeding out'. New year 5 and 6 classes were opened in 2016, taught as a joint class, currently with only five children in it, so it would be canny to grab a place ahead of secondary transfer rather than waiting for all the competition at year 7. School hopes to eventually take year 4 pupils as well; another wish is to move to three form entry for the bursting years 7, 8 and 9.

Get the ball rolling by sending in paperwork (EHCP, school reports, etc). If your child looks a good fit on paper, they will have a two-day trial where they will join a class and meet therapy teams and the SENCo. 'I get feedback from every member of staff on how they interacted at breaktime, in class, how they get on socially. I won't take them if we can't meet need, or the dynamics of the class mean it's not going to work,' says head. Red lines? 'An absolute no to behavioural problems.' Other situations which might result in disappointment are where a child requires more therapy than the school can provide, or has high levels of anxiety resulting from a mental health condition (but it has taken school refusers where it has taken a term to get them into school).

Exit: By popular demand the school now extends to a sixth form college.

Teaching and learning: Dyslexia is the school's specialism, but it's rare for a child to have the single diagnosis – there is often dyspraxia and dyscalculia too, and about 20 per cent of the pupils have high functioning autism (it's a ratio which the school does not like to exceed, which can mean some disappointed parents).

It will also only take children who are expected to do GCSEs, and to go on to a sixth form. The core curriculum involves sitting six GCSEs, and potential students need to be able to manage that. Most do the dual award in science, but those with a particular aptitude for science can do all three. All students take English language, while candidates with stronger literacy can take English literature as well. There is an option to take entry levels in English and maths for those that cannot manage a GCSE, and there's also a BTec course in Jamie Oliver home cooking.

It has two form entry, but pupils are split into three groups by ability for English, maths and science. Class sizes are a maximum of 10 (five for practical lessons such as DT and food tech), with a 1:5 staff ratio. Lessons are one hour, with movement breaks and brain gym built in. There are all manner of fiddles on the desks. Some children are in trackpants and sweatshirts rather than school uniform – a simple solution to avoid dyspraxic tangles on PE days: they just come in wearing their PE kit.

On an end of term visit, we saw reams of lively quizzing going on as pupils reviewed what they had learned over the term. Year 11s were revising waves and the universe – 'I'm winning,' a boy told the head triumphantly.

We saw several examples of this buoyed-up self-esteem. 'My story is amazing,' said a boy in a year 8 literacy class. Not something you might expect to hear in a class of dyslexics – nor, 'Can Michael Rosen come to our school?' from another pupil.

Teaching is excellent, parents said. 'A quiet, supportive learning environment, where staff chunk and present lessons suited to each pupil, meaning many exceed expectations,' was one description. A poor teacher was swiftly removed, as a parent told us: 'One teacher I was concerned about was quickly gone, it was clear it wasn't a good match and was dealt with.'

Performing arts are embraced with gusto. They regularly roll out the greasepaint, including for their own version of a classic – Charlotte and the Chocolate Factory

Homework quantities and targets 'are sensibly arranged so as not to be overwhelming or dismaying to children and also parents', and often with a practical bent, as a parent described: 'For food tech [my daughter] needed to write out the steps to doing the washing up. This was inspired, as she certainly learns from both visual as well as practical. We did the washing up together and then she was able to write the steps involved.'

All pupils have timetabled 'skills for learning' groups which incorporate therapy and work on individual targets. They are taught for this in mixed year groups, according to their main need. 'It helps us with talking and reading', and to 'get better at stuff', pupils told us.

'The Moat seems good at making a lesson achieve several targets at once: for example, a "social" session was framed as a touch-typing lesson which offered the opportunity to engage with texts about social encounters, and provide the basis for group discussion,' said a parent.

The arts and extracurricular: There's plenty to engage the creative child. We heard some very good reports on the art teaching which has resulted in children winning national awards. 'He loves photography and was allowed to bring home a very expensive camera to take pictures over the weekend. This support is wonderful for my son and makes him feel valued,' reported a parent.

Performing arts are embraced with gusto. The school panto was 'a triumph', we heard, and they regularly roll out the greasepaint – Hamlet, Julius Caesar, The Lion, the Witch and the Wardrobe among their recent productions, as well as their own version of a classic – Charlotte and the Chocolate Factory. A couple of pupils have their sights set on the BRIT School (performing arts), but everyone gets involved in tickets, lighting and so on.

There's peripatetic singing, drums, guitar; bronze and silver DofE. 'We're a small school but we try to give as many opportunities as we can.' There are even out of school activities in the school holidays organised by teachers, such as cooking and cycling.

After-school clubs have been ditched as unworkable with pupils arriving from 21 different boroughs, often with a long journey and a rigid taxi time. Instead the last lesson of the day is known as enrichment, and there's a choice of creative, sporting, and community activities, all underpinned with social communication work.

Sport: It's idyllically set for a London school, bounded by the greenery of Fulham's Bishop's Park, but outdoor sports facilities are limited and of the public variety. 'Parents with very sporting/athletic children should bear this in mind,' warned one. But they use the public tennis courts opposite the school, play football in the park, and go out to a climbing wall and to row on the river. There are school skiing trips too.

Ethos and heritage: It's palpably cheerful inside. The potion, as a parent described it, 'is an acceptance of others, celebration of your talents (which they will find), joyful eccentricity and a low anxiety environment. Resulting in happy, achieving children.'

Parents are impassioned about the school, and are surely the most contented bunch we've yet met on our reviewing travels. One even described it as 'an educational paradise in Fulham'.

To alleviate the increased numbers in the senior school, the Cavendish Education Group has added a new sixth form college, which provides a mainstream educational setting in sparkling new facilities for A level and BTec options. As well as a focus on academics, there are opportunities for work experience for all pupils, alongside specialist therapies built into the curriculum, occupational and speech & language.

Some lively quizzing going on. Year 11s were revising waves and the universe – 'I'm winning,' a boy told the head triumphantly

Parental views on the changes are mixed – some are hopeful it will mean additional resources and greater security for the school, others are concerned by the immediate impacts – 'a negative one for many children. In two areas – teaching/disruption – and social/anxiety. Children with more challenging issues and a very different profile have arrived. The school and new children need time to adjust, but it has been painful at a deeper level than expected,' we were told.

Pastoral care, inclusivity and discipline: There has been a key recruitment in the form of Arly, the 'wonderful' school therapy dog. He joins two human counsellors – we saw one at work in a lamplit room, a boy with his hands in a sandpit working through his problems.

We heard tale upon tale of children miserable in mainstream brought back to life here. 'When she started in year 7 [my daughter] could barely read or write and had rock bottom confidence. The Moat taught her to believe in herself and she now reads and writes to a level which is beyond my initial hopes for her. They provide wonderful personal development and support,' said one. The slight downside, she added, is that it shelters you from everyday life, and leaving this environment fills both parent and child with fear.

Parents said the school also supports them to manage issues in the home with their child. 'They never give me, as her parent, a difficult time. We work together for my child's benefit. I feel very much part of their team,' one said.

There's a great air of letting children be, and no sticking to rigid school rules which don't really matter. 'My son has long hair to the middle of his back. He asked the head if his hair would be a problem as he likes to have it different colours but he ties it back. The reply was, "You may have your hair whatever colour you like just as long as you wear full uniform from the neck down." So he has worn full uniform with blue, blonde and purple hair.'

There are children wearing headphones because the noise bothers them, or because they are allowed to listen to music at times. Another goes shoeless when he wants to. 'In his previous school he would just take his shoes off and get very distressed as teachers would be trying to get them back on, as he couldn't tell them he needed them off,' his parent said.

Bad behaviour is dealt with in the 'responsible thinking classroom' (RTC) – through a combination of discipline and support. If a behavioural matter is not quickly resolved in the classroom, the teacher will send them to the RTC. They might only be there for 10 minutes, longer if need be. But it allows the lesson to continue, and the pupil to feel listened to.

No phones are allowed throughout school day, and they have screen-free Wednesday, when laptops are banned from morning and afternoon breaks to encourage conversation.

Therapy and staffing: There are three in-house speech therapists, two OTs, and two school counsellors. The TAs are all graduates, and they are required to take a SpLD level 3 qualification in their first year, and several are also going through teacher training. There is one TA to a class to enable the 1:5 ratio, but there is no one-to-one; children must be able to operate independently. Teachers are required to do a masters in SpLD within two years of joining.

The occupational therapist has worked wonders on her child's independent skills, one mother told us. 'She can tie her own shoelaces, is learning to tell the time, getting herself dressed in the morning, buttering her bread and wanting to be more involved at home with setting the table etc. We really like the fact the school promotes the children developing their life skills.'

Pupils and parents: There's a broad socio-economic mix, from children living in deprivation to around one-third whose parents can pay the not inconsiderable fees. The latter group contributes to a better than average crop of work experience opportunities for the year 10s – the Houses of Parliament, and restaurateur Ottolenghi among them.

The parents' association is healthy, and there's warm support offered to battle-weary new parents, as well as long-termers, we're told. 'Parents are incredibly supportive of each other. There is a real sense amongst staff and parents of wanting the school to work for everyone. At the prize giving earlier this year, there was an atmosphere of pride for every young person who had achieved,' one said.

If you are seeking a place for a daughter, the girl ratio is particularly notable for a specialist school – across the school they make up one-third of pupils, in itself unusually high, but in year 7 there are even numbers of boys and girls.

Relations between parents and teachers are good. 'I feel that I am listened to and the views of my son are listened to. I don't feel that I am fighting for answers from the school when I ask questions. I feel valued as a parent, and know that nothing would be too much trouble to help myself or my son,' said a parent.

They are promised an email turnaround in 24 hours, and parents confirm they get this. They have direct email contacts for their child's form teacher, pastoral contact and support for learning contact. They are updated at least weekly, and one said, 'We feel really engaged because they are so proactive and we get regular feedback.' Everyone has an annual review, regardless of whether or not they have an EHCP.

Because pupils come from far and wide, it can make managing friendships more difficult. 'It is important to ensure your child has interests and opportunities to develop friendships in their local area and that you are happy to put in the effort and time to support developing school friendships,' cautioned a parent.

Money matters: Some 70 per cent of pupils are local authority funded, but there's a good core of self-funders. The school is able to provide Tier 4 and 2 sponsorship for non-UK nationals. Therapy is included in a flat fee price.

The last word: Sits like a pot of gold at the end of the weary path trodden by parents of a child with special needs. But like the pot at the end of the rainbow, it might prove elusive. Currently crammed to the rafters, so unless it finds a way to expand, you'll have a job finding a place.

Immensely popular and likeable previous head had got the blueprint for the school bang on by being clear and unwavering about the intake. So we have to be concerned about how it is changing under Cavendish ownership; early days, we'll be keeping a beady eye.

Headteacher: Since 2019 Holly Bristow and Verity Carnevale share the role as Co-Headteachers, having both worked at the school for over nine years, first as teachers and then assistant headteachers. Both are passionate about improving outcomes for students with speech, language and communication needs.

Entrance: Pupils can enter the school at any stage provided there is a vacancy. Most come at the secondary transfer stage as 'many can just about hang on in a mainstream school through the primary years, with one-to-one support'. Some, usually those with most extreme difficulties, arrive at 7. Can be referred by parents, LA or education professionals. Parents tour the school and meet head, initially without their child in tow. This is followed by minimum two days of observation ('as opposed to assessment') of the pupil in their potential year group. This is flexible, so could just be an hour or two at a time. 'We need to unpack the needs of the child,' explains head. 'We must be certain that we can support them.' Medical and psychological reports required and every child has an EHCP 'though we have never accepted a child just on paper'. Pupils turned away if school cannot provide sufficient support or if child does not require this level of care and would be better off placed elsewhere. School admits it can be heartbreaking to turn down a child and some parents become distressed if school won't accept their child, 'but we have to be realistic'.

Exit: At 16, the school aims to return the pupils to their borough, as they begin to start their adult life. They move on to a range of further education opportunities. Some opt for non-vocational or academic courses, others prefer vocational training, while a minority move on to residential provision. Recent leavers' destinations include Westminster Kingsway College, Oaklands, Paddock and Highshore.

Teaching and learning: A non-maintained special school that caters for pupils with moderate to severe learning difficulties. All pupils have speech, language and communication needs identified as a significant part of their EHCPs. Can support children with epilepsy, visual and hearing impairment, ASD, Fragile X and Prader-Willi syndrome. Specialism in Down's syndrome, and more than 30 per cent of pupils here have the condition, but rarely as their sole difficulty. 'Nobody here has just one issue going on,' explains head. Unable to meet social, emotional and behavioural difficulties or autism as the sole difficulty.

'It's important that we're seen as a school and not as a unit or an offshoot. We do everything that is done in a mainstream school, including parents' evenings, sport, uniform and so on,' states head. Specialised and individualised curriculum tailored to the differing needs of every pupil. As one parent commented, 'All special schools pay lip service to this, but Parayhouse really delivers.' Support offered on one-to-one and small group basis throughout. Speech and language at the heart of everything.

Three possible pathways: a life-skills based curriculum working in small steps within the P scales; an adapted national curriculum, generally key stage 1, focusing on English, maths and PE; the more able follow a key stage 2-3 national curriculum in English, maths, science, PE, art, food studies and history, up to level 1 in maths GCSE.

Five classes. Groupings by age, ability and language skills. Can be as much as five-year age span within a class. Three forms cover primary type timetables, including earlier lunch and more breaks within lessons, and the other two classes cover a more demanding secondary timetable. Head explains that morning break is called fitness because 'we keep them on the move'. Afternoon break is more relaxed, because 'otherwise we are on their backs the whole time. If they just want to flap a leaf in the corner then that's fine.'

In the afternoon, foundation subjects feature heavily including sport, drama and life skills. Food studies for older pupils take place in the swish kitchen next door in the Inclusive Learning block. 'Very functional, such as making drinks, snacks and hot meals. Baking fairy cakes is fun but it's not going to be part of their everyday life beyond,' states head. Pupils also learn social and practical life skills such as how to do laundry, attend to personal hygiene, take public transport, read menus and ensure personal safety. In-house course offered on sex education. ICT is taught throughout the school with an emphasis on real life application. Online safety is the priority.

On arrival, baseline attainment is assessed in areas such as speech and listening, reading and writing. School has developed its own bespoke curriculum and assessment system. 'It's not just day care here,' explained one mother. Another parent we spoke to commented, 'At Parayhouse, they try to delve into your child and what will unlock your child's learning.'

The arts and extracurricular: Art, drama and music all taken seriously because 'we are always on the look-out for ways for these children with speech and language difficulties to express themselves non-verbally'. More able can take entry-level art, creative masterpieces exhibited in the art room. 'Drama is massive,' says head. When we visited, the pupils were madly rehearsing Romeo and Juliet for the Shakespeare Schools Festival. Staff and parents watch the performance at a professional theatre and pupils relish being in the limelight. Whole-school production at Christmas, when music comes into its own, with all songs in sign language. Everyone joins in and has an absolute ball.

Pupils feel safe and secure, both emotionally and physically. Many arrive in a fragile state with low self-esteem but are nurtured and succeed here

Tiny number of clubs offered. A girls' group takes place one lunchtime, where they enjoy 'female grooming' such as nail painting, applying face creams and hair styling; they also play music and learn to make polite conversation. Helps with bonding of girls across the year groups, as they are in a minority. Thursday club offered after school at an external location and revolves around cooking, arts and crafts, gym, pool, table tennis and playing with train sets. Transport there arranged by school but parents pick up. 'We would like to do more after school but shared transport makes this difficult. It is a big sadness to me that the Thursday club is still exclusive,' states head.

Annual residential trips for all pupils in the summer term. Mostly funded by fees but parents asked to contribute. Some happily stump up large amounts but equally many cannot give a penny. On-site activities offered. Occasionally a pupil might give it a miss but head explains residential trips are 'not an optional extra, they are very much a case of putting into practice what has been learnt in the lifestyle curriculum'.

Sport: Annual sailing day for the whole school is one of the highlights of the year. The pupils love every minute, especially when they end up splashing away in the water. Pupils take part in sport within the community including panathlon challenge (football and athletics), West London Swimming Gala and Special School Athletics. Yoga is popular, especially for those with cerebral palsy or anxiety who need 'a tool to dial themselves down'.

Ethos and heritage: Housed in an unglamorous 1970s red brick building off the noisy Talgarth Road. Occupies the ground floor of Hammersmith College, bang next door to their Inclusive Learning division which offers provision to 16-25-year-olds with special needs. Not the most beautiful school we have visited, with some gloomy windowless rooms, and the much-used hall could do with a lick of paint, but classrooms are bright and spacious. Though security of pupils is vital, the high fences, with multiple doors and gates to negotiate, feel intimidating. A new build is proposed – watch this space.

Food studies very functional: making drinks, snacks and hot meals. 'Baking fairy cakes is fun but it's not going to be part of their everyday life beyond,' states head

School is good at celebrating achievement in the weekly assembly, whether for good behaviour, academic success or effort. All pupils receive a record of achievement on leaving. Pupils and their families have fun, too, either outside at the school birthday party, where stalls are festooned with bunting, or dancing energetically at the Christmas disco. Staff love getting to know siblings on these occasions and parents agree the whole family is welcomed in by the school.

Pastoral care, inclusivity and discipline: Pupils feel safe and secure, both emotionally and physically. Many arrive in a fragile state with low self-esteem but are nurtured and succeed here. One parent commented that her child has proper friends for the first time here. The school is good at telling parents about blossoming friendships within the classroom and encourages play dates. 'Parayhouse cares for the whole child, including once the school day has finished. The staff really like the kids and genuinely want them to be happy,' said one parent.

Breakfast is provided, and enthusiastically devoured by those who have trekked across London to get here. Usually toast and cereal though pupils were going through a porridge phase when we visited. They munch in their classrooms and are expected to wash up afterwards, just as they would at home. No wraparound care offered. Head admits that summer holidays are long and that parents and pupils alike could benefit from extra provision.

Therapy and staffing: Staff is made up of teachers, occupational therapists, an art therapist and five speech, language and communication therapists, as well as learning support assistants. Art therapy occurs on an individual basis. High staff to pupil ratio. First three classes boast a teacher, three learning support assistants and speech therapist in the morning, with two learning support assistants in the afternoon. Top two classes have their own teacher as well as two assistants and share a speech therapist.

Family support manager is rated highly by head and parents: 'She even does visits in the evenings, at weekends or in the holidays.' She carries out home sessions before the child starts at the school. Also smooths the transition to the next stage of schooling, helping with interviews and arranging work experience placements for the oldest pupils. School explains, 'We try to give parents the support that they need while also helping their children become independent. That is our goal.'

Long-serving staff. More than 60 per cent have been here for more than three years. 'There are certainly some old timers!' mentioned one parent. 'They know what they're doing,' said another. 'The teachers are firm, fair and fun.' School is realistic about staff leaving: 'As a small school we do expect shift. We are a stepping stone and take a pride in that. We cannot offer head of department to everyone, so cannot lure them to stay that way.' Lots of young male teachers, from different ethnic backgrounds, who act as positive role models to the boys.

Pupils and parents: Wide range of social and economic backgrounds represented here. Forty-two per cent on free school meals but some from affluent middle-class homes. Broad ethnic mix, and 45 per cent have EAL. Largest single group is white British but sizeable contingents from Somalia and the Caribbean, as well as refugees from war-torn parts of the globe.

Pupils come from more than 12 local education authorities, right across the capital. Pupils travel from as far afield as the Isle of Dogs, Brent and Richmond. Most pupils are ferried here by local authority transport. Sharing daily transport means that friendships develop across the age range; the downside is the lack of school gate contact with other parents.

Good relationships between staff and parents. Weekly newsletter keeps families well-informed. Open evenings and parents' meetings twice a year and the parents we spoke to felt they were kept fully in the loop. Friday assemblies open to all. Most parents are supportive and come out in droves at school events. Parents usually actively want Parayhouse as their child's school, so tend to be on-side from the start. Those that are less smitten initially are quickly won round.

Money matters: Not-for-profit organisation. Became a registered charity in 2000. Pupils' fees are usually agreed and funded by local authority. Some parents work for companies who pay the fees and occasionally an embassy foots the bill. All therapy is included.

The last word: As one parent commented, 'There might be glitzier facilities elsewhere but I can't fault the school.' For the right child, this school is nothing short of a godsend.

The St Marylebone Church of England Bridge School

17-23 Third Avenue, London W10 4RS

020 3693 4752 | office@stmarylebonebridgeschool.com | www.stmarylebonebridgeschool.com

State | Ages: 11-16 | Pupils: 60

Head of school: Since 2018, Kate Miller, a drama specialist with a diploma in SpLD. Taught from 2008 at the parent school St Marylebone CE, starting in drama then training as a dyslexia teacher and assessor. Working with the many children there with speech and language needs led to her running the summer school at Bridge, which evolved into running this school. Efficient, friendly and positive, energetically creating opportunities for her pupils.

Entrance: Run by the London Borough of Westminster in conjunction with Kensington & Chelsea, there has not, yet, been a year when the annual intake capacity of 12 has been reached by referrals from these two boroughs alone so those with EHCPs from other local authorities can apply. Although the main intake is to year 7, entry is possible at any time; some years have waiting lists but as pupils transfer to mainstream, places can arise. Show-arounds are normally on Thursdays and Fridays, followed by paperwork, a current-setting observation and an assessment by school of a child's fit with the possible cohort. The ethos of the school is Church of England but the admission process is secular. The school cannot cater for pupils with severe learning difficulties or behavioural difficulties as primary diagnoses, or severe physical needs (although it is wheelchair accessible).

Exit: Bridge supports transition to mainstream schools, eg a student who joined in year 7 left in year 9 after much work on emotional resilience, mindfulness and with a 'toolbox' of coping strategies; ditto another who left in year 10 to join a Camden school. Miller sums up with a heartfelt, 'It's so important that each leaves articulate and confident, knowing their own needs,' and reports that in the first year of leavers there were no NEETS (Not in Education, Employment or Training), as students moved to courses in food, computing, drama and sports, special provision, or mainstream college. Those students are now returning to give feedback to school and current students.

The only negative feedback, voiced by several parents, was the lack of a sixth form and the wish that school would extend to cover these years.

Teaching and learning: Caters for pupils with speech, language and communication needs (SLCN) in years 7-11; 12 in a year group. Students function within modified national curriculum levels, most are verbal and some have dyspraxia and dyslexia. One or two in each year have a diagnosis of high functioning autism but Miller says the S&L techniques used don't necessarily work for children on the spectrum.

The first cohort of students completed year 11 in 2018, gaining a mix of English and maths GCSEs; functional skills, entry level and ASDAN certificates; and Prince's Trust and Jamie Oliver's home cooking qualifications.

All have EHCPs and Miller comments that as getting one now seems to require having more complex needs, so her year 7s and 8s are tending towards functional-level skills and entry-level courses rather than GCSEs, with the more able one or two transitioning to mainstream schools.

Teachers are qualified or in training and are encouraged to choose a specialism, eg dyslexia or dyspraxia, in order to develop expertise in students' secondary needs, as their primary S&L needs are so well covered. TAs receive S&L training, also attended by the head.

School opens at 8.15am for breakfast (or, if missed, a snack at breaktime) then lessons from 8.45am until 3.15pm with more focus on academic learning in the morning. There is a cooked lunch for all and a large language board on the canteen wall entitled 'Who we are'.

Embedded in teaching throughout the school is the 'shape coding' system, devised by Susan Ebbels and in use at Moor House School, taking shapes and colours to teach grammar and support students learning rules about how words and sentences fit together.

In a year 7 science class, 12 enthusiastic and engaged students were working with a teacher and learning support assistant using shape coding, to understand friction. Three iPads were in shared use and children had returned from finding, touching and taking images of examples of friction to answer questions, which each did, all being verbal, and a casual observer wouldn't necessarily realise this is not a mainstream school.

The 'shape coding' system is embedded in teaching: shapes and colours are used to teach grammar and support students learning about how sentences fit together

An English GCSE class of four students seated with their teacher around a single table going through a mock paper was highly participatory. Miller explained that students also take English functional skills so that if anything goes wrong with their GCSE they will still have a qualification. We saw handwritten work produced to a good standard. We also saw a functional skills English class, whose students had already passed entry level courses 1, 2 and 3 and Miller explained, 'We follow the national curriculum as much as possible – we want students to learn vocabulary which is needed for employment or when visiting their GP.' A functional intervention used is 'strategies and measurable interaction in Live English' (smiLE therapy) where students learn the skills required to communicate effectively in specific social situations, such as in a shop, at work experience, etc. They are filmed before therapy then, post-therapy, filmed again to see that the new skills have been learned.

We were completely charmed by a year 9 art lesson with five happy, involved and knowledgeable students, a teacher and a LSA where two (impeccably uniformed) boys gave a joint presentation on Matisse entitled 'What is collage?', proficiently using a whiteboard and slides then, following their teacher's example, questioning their classmates' understanding of the topic. It was an inclusive lesson and each created a version of Matisse's famous Icarus collage.

The arts and extracurricular: Given the head is a drama teacher, school is understandably strong in this area with performances including The Tempest and Brecht. A music teacher from the parent school also teaches here and traffic goes both ways, with two Bridge students using their recording studio.

Clubs run with the help of creative mentors, dyspraxic or dyslexic themselves, engaging students in small group work – one mentor is a jeweller and runs a jewellery club. 'It exposes our students to new people and experiences' says the head. Termly enrichment across year groups is another opportunity to develop social skills while enjoying riding, coding, football or music.

Sport: The outside space has Astroturf for football and there are daily trips to the park, useful for its larger spaces 'especially for our students,' says Miller. A parent praised the sports as 'excellent', citing a fantastic teacher who organises meets with other schools for swimming, basketball and football, engendering a great sense of pride – 'the emphasis here is on speech and language, rather than special needs'.

Ethos and heritage: Adapted from buildings which started life as terraced housing before metamorphosing into a community centre, school feels friendly and small-scale; despite its restrictions there is a lift enabling access for wheelchair users. Visual timetables are everywhere, a sign that communication is at the heart of everything. Plans to move a new purpose built school in April 2022.

Pastoral care, inclusivity and discipline: If a student is experiencing difficulties they are given a team to help, including a S&L therapist and the head or the mindfulness teacher (the child can choose). There have been no permanent exclusions. With regard to temporary exclusions, Miller's policy is 'to look at what will change behaviour, so we explain an issue, perhaps with comic strip conversations or Social Stories, and then its

'They unpeeled the mess he was in and brought back our son,' said a parent. 'He was studying Shakespeare in the first term!'

consequences'. One student was seen smoking in the playground which led to him being sent home, then the year group's next PSHE class was on the effect of drugs – eight pupils were given relevant information then asked to consider and contribute to a discussion; that temporarily excluded student is now doing well. One parent whose child had a couple of disciplinary problems on starting and was consequently given two one-day exclusions was delighted: 'I wouldn't tolerate that behaviour at home and now his attitude at school has improved.'

Although there are only 10 girls on the roll of 58, there are girls' clubs and three weekly girls-only tutor groups.

Therapy and staffing: Three full-time speech and language therapists whose work is ever-present throughout school for students, while working with and training staff. Students present not only with classic speech problems but also social and emotional communication needs, a range of developmental language disorders – some arising from autistic spectrum conditions, others from ADHD – as well as physical issues and hearing loss. Therefore work also includes emotional regulation, social awareness, input from the Child and Adolescent Mental Health Service (CAMHS), art therapy, a behaviour therapist and therapeutic horseriding.

Much S&L work is with the teachers, each having a weekly planning slot in the timetable; then there is small group work – in classes of no more than six, a S&L therapist and a LSA, described as 'intensive and challenging' – plus individual therapy if necessary. One therapist, who followed the less usual route of teaching first then training in speech and language, said, 'The main thing is, Are they happy and are they participating?' He also told with satisfaction of a student saying, 'I have a speech and language condition but I'm not going to let it hold me back'; another therapist started at school as a LSA, became inspired, left to train and returned qualified.

Three times a year progress is tracked using Therapy Outcome Measures (TOMs), for example in participation, activity and wellbeing. Drawing upon elements of TEACCH lessons (Treatment and Education of Autistic and Communication-related Handicapped Children), school uses strengths in visual processing while dealing with difficulties in attention and executive function.

We saw a year 9 communication lesson for seven students (half the year), led by a S&L therapist and a LSA, about passive-aggressive language and collective nouns – using animals, something year 9s are interested in, to aid learning, with much participation. Another communications lesson, this time preparing the year 11s for their functional skills English exam, focused on writing presentations, again letting students choose from their own interests, this time examples included persuading people to donate to ICAN (a charity supporting children with SLCN) and Ferraris.

Parents unanimously spoke of the difficulty in finding schools specifically for speech and language and so were thrilled with Bridge. One said, 'My daughter had no English in year 7 and now, in year 11, her language is perfect.' Another, whose child tried a special school for predominantly autistic children, said, 'St Marylebone CE Bridge is a school foremost with speech therapy – the children learn here. They unpeeled the mess he was in and brought back our son – he was studying Shakespeare in the first term!' Another praised the individual tailoring that enabled her child to access the national curriculum while learning practical skills, so the family looks forward to Friday evenings of spaghetti bolognese or baking, the results of learning independence and healthy-eating skills at school.

All have mental health and mindfulness in their timetable plus occasional music and drama therapy. Occupational therapy (OT) provision is from the local authority – one of the few negatives perceived by parents, especially one who says her son needs 'bucketloads' of OT which, in an ideal world, would be available in-house.

Several staff, including the head, two teachers, a S&L therapist and a LSA, have left for training or maternity leave and returned so commitment is high and turnover low.

Pupils and parents: Termly newsletters are prepared by the head boy and head girl from contributions written by the students. Three 'data drops' per year report on a child's progress, there are the usual parents' evenings, communication books, advice sent home – for example on e-safety – and a daytime parent-pupil conference, fondly remembered by a parent whose son showed with pride his achievements at school. One parent voiced a general view, her son having learned practical skills, 'Now he'll be able to cope in life.' Another, waxing lyrical, drew an image of their child previously under a dark cloud now in a ray of sunshine, while a third described her child skipping in from school. In the 'good' Ofsted report there was, surprisingly, an absence of any parent comment.

Money matters: All funded by their local authority.

The last word: Such an impressive school with its positive atmosphere – quiet and polite yet engaged and lively – a great place to work and learn. For a student with speech, language and communication needs, here is a chance to thrive in education with the curriculum adapted to their needs.

Swiss Cottage School

80 Avenue Road, London NW8 6HX

020 7681 8080 | admin@swisscottage.camden.sch.uk | www.swisscottage.camden.sch.uk

State | Ages: 2-19 | Pupils: 260

Principal: Since 2016, Vijita Patel (40s), previously deputy head since 2012; hails from the States, where she took her first degree initially in maths and sciences, though converted to primary education after meeting a child with autism at risk of exclusion. Her dissertation on legislation and barriers to schooling for children has been a constant interest and may explain her involvement in London Leadership Strategy and input in the DfE SEND policy, which has given her a chance to visit other schools and look at priorities and good practice. She did her teaching practice in Brent and then worked for nine years at Woodfield School, where she grew from class teacher to head of English and maths, eventually becoming assistant head. Having taken her NPQH, she came to Swiss Cottage School as deputy head and worked on staff training and professional learning.

Parents say that although she had large shoes to fill after last head, who was here for more than 20 years, the change has been smooth and they 'feel in good, safe hands'. She is a theoretician and administrator, and her original maths interest is standing her in good stead as the school works towards having better systems for monitoring progress in special needs schools. The fact that Swiss Cottage School is also a Teaching School and has a very active Development and Research Centre requires particularly scientific and organised thinking, and this diminutive, young-looking head clearly communicates well and has a vision that draws her senior management team tightly behind her. Presumably she delegates well as she also spends considerable time working with outside agencies and looking at wider educational policy changes. Parents call her 'exceptionally bright, an amazing head' and say she is 'dynamic and approachable and warm'. 'She is brilliant' and 'she really listens well'. She has one daughter and is married to another school head.

Entrance: Great demand for places and continuously oversubscribed (not surprising after six successive 'outstanding' Ofsted reports). Camden allocates places and pays fees. Admissions policy cites desire for pupils to be local with parental commitment and states it is a school for complex learning difficulties and disabilities. School believes that early intervention is ideal and so prefers early referrals, only taking children in the last two years of school in exceptional circumstances.

Exit: A few are able to progress to local colleges at 16; those with profound learning difficulties stay on and work towards transitioning, ideally to employment, with work skills and supported internships a major part of those last two or three years. Others stay on to 19 and then move to residential care.

Teaching and learning: All pupils have EHCPs, about half relating to autism spectrum disorder. A quarter have severe learning difficulties, with the rest having complex and multiple learning difficulties. Many children are pre-verbal and many have physical disabilities – profound and complex syndromes supported by in-house nurse and at least two teaching assistants per class, often more. For those with challenging behaviour there is positive behaviour therapy and risk assessment, not only to protect students but also to look for trends and work out solutions. Cerebral palsy, Angelman syndrome, Fragile X, autism spectrum disorder – this school has experience of all and more.

Classes are mixed in various ways – according to both physical and academic needs and social interaction as well as by age. This flexibility means that learning can be appropriate to the group, though each child has an individual learning programme. Small classrooms, each with outside space and an area for withdrawing children for some quiet or for individual therapies or learning – bright and full of displays of children's work. There are 186 staff (including 96 teaching assistants), which means the staff to pupil ratio is good (though no 2:1 assistant to pupil in evidence). We saw creativity in teaching strategies – history taught via experiences of people in another era: the smells, for example, or a home lit by candles. Goals and progress are set and recorded in the Evidence of Learning online record, which then sets next goals and timings to match child's progress.

The younger children have their own playgrounds and lower school areas; pupils are given more space and freedom as they move up the school, with 16+ having their own roof terrace. Many 'pre-verbal' ('we think that most have the potential to speak and so prefer that term to non-verbal') and so language and communication is a large part of the learning here. Three separate curricular pathways according to ability of the child, with formative assessment fortnightly to 'celebrate successes'. Efforts made to 'assess without levels', finding a way to quantitatively assess qualitative improvements in pupils. By 16 and 18 years pupils take qualifications where appropriate in life and living skills, and maths and English at AQA entry level, and attain awards such as arts award, horticulture awards, languages, and even GCSE.

Older pupils use the vocational room to learn cooking and hairdressing and life skills. There is a flat for respite for parents and to practise independent living skills

Parents were appreciative that pupils are encouraged to become independent and not reliant on a teaching assistant. 'There is actual learning here, they are learning to read and write,' said one parent. 'My child likes the activities and has friends and is very happy and wants to come to school each day – even in the holidays!' Older pupils (those who do not go on to colleges) are able to stay on and continue having therapeutic input, as well as learn and get work experience – either in school working on newsletters and pamphleting, helping in office duties or chores, or, where possible, on sheltered work placements. These older pupils also use the vocational room to learn cooking and hairdressing and life skills. There is a three room flat at the top of the school for respite for parents and to practise independent living skills. Parents appreciate emphasis on real life skills – 'shower class, shopping, dressing, chopping and cutting, how to use the toilet – these are skills that my daughter will need forever'.

The school works to an extraordinary degree with a range of related partners in a child's education – parents, therapists, social workers, who are encouraged to come to the school whenever possible. This linked-up way of working for children's wider welfare is supported by a team of family support workers with an inclusion teacher, who can help in a myriad of ways – chasing benefit claims, respite care, helping with housing and medical appointments, ensuring the parents are supported so the child can flourish. 'This school gives more than necessary, it goes over and above its role as a school and makes things work for the whole family,' head says.

The communication is critical as parents often don't hear from their children what was learned at school, but parents said that they could look at the website and see the weekly newsletter, read the daily home/school diary, see the teachers at any time and attend progress meetings. Of particular interest is the new Evidence for Learning online app, which is accessible to parents and gives a running record including videos, pictures and notes of what their child has been doing, and progress both in their work and their personal development. This degree of team working is a rare and precious strength. 'My child can't say what she has done at school but I can read what teachers have said and so my child knows we are communicating. And every Sunday I write what we have done at the weekend so teachers can use this in school.'

The arts and extracurricular: Art a good feature in the school with mixed media and plenty of colour – displays abound, not only in classrooms but also in shared corridor and dining room areas. Plenty to stimulate and inspire. Dance and drama in dedicated studio with dressing up and face paint encouraged. Music room for lessons and instrument learning – piano, guitar and drums. Music teacher goes into classrooms; we saw the guitar being used as a marker for a transition to another activity. Music, drama and sports clubs at lunch time and at weekends and holidays. School trips, not only in London but also venturing to the countryside or seaside on residential stays for horse riding, rock climbing and sailing. No mollycoddling of these children, who are encouraged to be resilient and independent. Pupils higher up the school are developing attitude and confidence from interactions and responsibilities – 'I serve drinks and cakes to parents. I am good at welcoming and being friendly.'

Parents are thrilled with the after-school clubs that have started: 'They make it feel like the children have choices and outside interests.' There's yoga, ballet, sports, paid for by parents.

Sport: This is central London so little outdoor space, but what they have has been landscaped and is used effectively, if a little worn at the edges. Each classroom has its own outside space which, particularly in the lower school, is used as part of the classroom. There are swings and slides and bikes and we liked the road skills area for learning road safety. A running track winds round a well-used horticultural area and there's greenhouse for growing vegetables and plants. Plenty of small, safe areas for being outside. Training on an all-weather terrain for five-a-side football, basketball and athletics prepare pupils for Panathlon Challenge as well as building good health and confidence. The cricket club is popular and plays fixtures. The warm, clean swimming pool is used for timetabled therapeutic lessons. Three school buses for taking pupils to local Primrose Hill or elsewhere for outings.

Ethos and heritage: The current building was completed in 2014 after a £25 million refurbishment under a PFI scheme. Wide corridors, airy practical classrooms with large windows, both to playground and to internal corridors so the (many) visitors can see activities in class. Fairly full and chaotic classrooms. There are separate areas for lower, middle and upper school, allowing the pupils a sense of progression through the school. And there are well planned, if small, outdoor spaces. State of the art facilities and practical spaces for pupils' wheelchairs, eating, changing and moving around make this a pleasurable place to be and presumably for the pupils to learn in, and staff seem well catered for with spacious staff rooms and outside areas.

Parents said it 'is a happy environment and my child is doing well here'. This school feels purposeful, effective and serious and the good practice is spread far as it is a Teaching School providing initial teacher training courses for inclusive education, acting as a National Support School (supporting other schools requiring improvement), and running conferences and training for practitioners as part of continuing professional development and learning. This is an inspiring and proactive hub for spreading the message of good, inclusive special needs education. Teachers spoke of their school and their individual areas of responsibility with pride and high aspirations, and the learning doesn't stop when training is finished as there is a policy of peer coaching and 'reflective dialogue', which is ideal for a new trainee and allows staff to feel positive and supported. A busy, upbeat mood pervades – no room for slacking here by anyone.

Three separate curricular pathways according to ability of the child, with formative assessment fortnightly to 'celebrate successes'

Pastoral care, inclusivity and discipline: The school works to ensure that these vulnerable children are given the skills to keep safe – talking about relationships, use of social media and mobile phones, keeping safe online and how to watch for potential dangers and minimise and resolve risks. In these practical ways they educate the whole child in collaboration with parents and other caregivers. We spoke to pupils who knew how to introduce themselves and ask appropriate questions, they showed us the work experience they felt they were good at – real life skills in action. Sensory Stories for Children are used to promote mental well-being for pupils with learning disabilities, so it is not only the physical and educational needs that are met at this school. 'We built a social story for my daughter to help her understand about getting her periods.'

Therapy and staffing: Part of the school building houses a small NHS department for the therapists to work from – speech and language therapists, occupational therapists, dietitians and nutrition experts, psychotherapists, psychologists and medical staff. There are sensory rooms, soft play rooms and a warm hydrotherapy pool. NHS staff not only work with pupils, but also engage with parents so that the therapies can continue in school, in the classroom and at home. We saw a speech and language therapist who had managed to get funding to allow her to teach Makaton to a group of parents who were preparing to present Who's Going on A Bear Hunt to a class – this brought parents into school, making their child's education a real partnership, and was also chance to support parents and give them tools to use at home with their children. All way beyond the limitations of the therapies prescribed in the pupils' EHC plans. As well as excellent facilities and staffing, the school makes the most of technology – with pupils using iPads to speak if necessary – 'it gives my daughter a voice as she presses the button and a voice expresses her choice' – and for increased interactivity.

Pupils and parents: Pupils virtually all from Camden, a mix of white British, Somali, Bangladeshi, and well over half the families with English as a second language, reflecting the cultural diversity of the borough. Camden places pupils here mostly from mainstream, but as places are scarce inevitably the school sees itself taking children with more extreme needs.

A parent forum meets together and with the teachers. There is a family learning week each half term when parents can attend the class, observe the teaching and share good practice and good communication methods used at school, so they can be mirrored and practised at home. Family workshops take place each week and are a chance for parents to learn Makaton, English as a second language, gardening club, knitting – anything that will help include them despite the fact that often their children are brought into school by bus or taxi. We saw parents doing communication training, which was also used as a chance to get parents into school. 'Many parents do not speak English and women are often reluctant to attend without their husbands, but we use the chance to show what we have been doing in school so that it can carry on at home.' One parent said: 'I was given training to use the iPad so my child can use the same communication method at home and at school.' Another said: 'It works as a big family and support system for me and other parents like me who might otherwise feel isolated with a special needs child.'

Money matters: Active trustees and a Swiss Cottage School Charity that holds events and works with local businesses to raise funds for extras. The research centre and conferences are the real earners, raising money from training and expertise.

The last word: Swiss Cottage School is a centre of excellence with fantastic resources, focus and interdisciplinary teamwork. The result of this success means that it is oversubscribed and pupils have increasingly complex needs. A child with moderate or profound learning difficulties will be really well looked after, given individual goals and taught here with new trainees and teachers using the latest methodologies in a safe, if well used, environment.

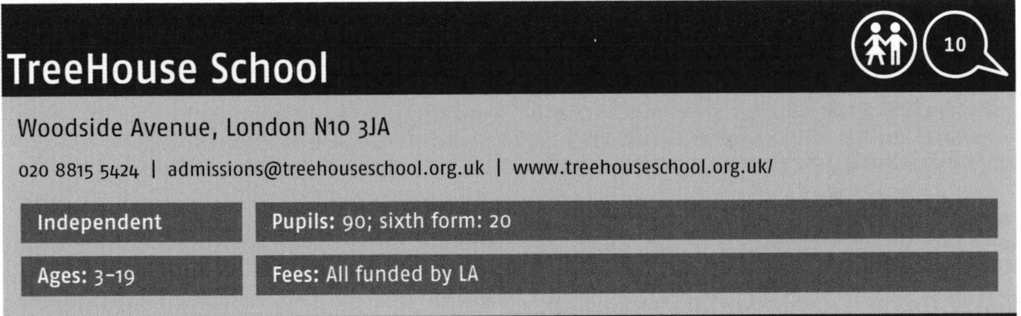

Headteacher: Since 2020, Tracey Capstick

Entrance: Transparent admission policy – all pupils have a diagnosis of autism or related communication disorder, and all have an EHCP. The school reviews reports to see if they would be able to meet needs, followed by detailed assessment at home or present school and an equally detailed assessment at TreeHouse. Then they need to agree LA funding. TreeHouse suits those with complex autism and learning difficulties. The school looks to see whether any current difficult behaviour is due to distress and would improve at TreeHouse, and whether the pupil could benefit from the teaching available. Careful matching of pupils to classes and current population to ensure good balance and integration in each class. A parent said, 'The admission process was extremely supportive and not at all stressful for us as parents, which was very different from what we experienced at some other schools. The admissions officers were clear and prompt, and a very courteous team of teachers and behaviour analysts did his assessment very quickly, while keeping me informed about progress.'

Exit: Most pupils go on to some post-school placement – some to the new Ambitious College run by the same charity that supports TreeHouse. Parents said, 'transition help was excellent, with discussions about placement and help with taster days at colleges'.

Teaching and learning: Small classes with pupils grouped in both age and ability levels – class sizes of around seven. Pupils sometimes arrive pre-verbal with about 65 per cent eventually able to use language to communicate. Some need up to two-to-one to support their behaviour needs initially. All pupils have significant learning difficulties, many are years behind their peers, and there is an emphasis on behaviour management and reducing barriers to learning rather than academics, however pupils make evidential progress. 'Not the school if you expect calm all the time; many pupils have challenging behaviour,' said one parent. Bright classrooms, with interactive whiteboards – we saw young pupils waiting patiently (a skill for some) to get onto the board, where they focused and worked to develop hand-eye coordination and fine motor skills. Every pupil has at least one-to-one support and individually planned goals.

The curriculum is based on academic as well as social and functional skills, whilst following the national curriculum as far as possible, which allows some pupils to gain entry level qualifications in maths and English. The curriculum up to 14 years is aimed at developing communication and independence and in, key stages 4 and 5, to preparing for adulthood. There may be more emphasis on behavioural issues than academic, parents saying, 'sometimes we are concerned that not much is demanded of our child academically: we see him sitting on a sofa, looking out of the window and hiding behind poor language skills.' Another parent said, however, 'We have been in contact with teachers asking for homework as we would like our child to be stretched academically, and the teachers have responded promptly.'

Pupils taken on open days to workplaces and colleges. 'They are enterprising in how they support pupils for transition,' said parent

There are daily lessons in English with language and communication seen as critical for accessing the curriculum and taking a place in society. Similarly, daily maths planned by specialist head of maths, with emphasis on using maths to develop logic, establish connections and patterns and life skills. This can then be used in practical ways to help with money, time and space, and older students are involved in the school shop to enhance life skills and prepare for independence. Early interventions take place if any pupils need extra input in their learning. TreeHouse has daily personal, social and health education (PSHE) lessons to work specifically on educating pupils to lead healthy lives, including relationships education, staying safe, understanding others and making responsible choices. ICT is inevitably hugely relevant for these pupils because they tend to gravitate to the safety of a screen for interaction, and so whilst they are at school, screens are used primarily to develop communication (for literacy, communicating with others, as well as using technology for art and creativity). No use of iPads while eating, for example: 'We want children to look around them rather than at a screen.' However, parents felt that 'technology could be used more creatively, especially since pupils may end up using ICT in work'.

By key stages 4 and 5, daily activities include meal preparation, enterprise and work-related experiences which 'use work as a context for learning', including horticulture, working in the school shop, office skills and learning about money and dealing with people. This emphasis on preparing for independence is furthered in the sixth form with pupils going on supported community placements wherever possible (charity shops, sports clubs, allotments, local church) with daily maths and English lessons being about functionality. Parents praised work on transition, including taking pupils on open days and taster days to workplaces and colleges. 'They are enterprising in the way they support pupils for transition.' Vocational skills in areas such as catering, performing arts, sports, retail experience and horticulture. Pupils leave with foundation level qualifications and OCN at entry level for English and maths. Parents appreciate the way 'life skills are incorporated in the curriculum – self care, road safety, money, health'.

The arts and extracurricular: They do art in school as well as outings in the school bus to exhibitions at the Tate and Royal Academy. Wide-ranging materials for sensory and therapeutic input – silk painting, mosaics, watercolours, acrylic paints, ceramics. There is an artist in residence whose remit is to engage with students and who is developing a 'pupil voice canvas' with huge bold paintings that can be seen round the school. An art therapist works to ensure art is used proactively to improve pupils' well-being.

Music lessons aid pupils' self-expression. Weekly music classes with specialist teacher for those up to 14 years and then weekly 'expressive arts' class which is wider and includes music composition and musical theatre. Some music making – drums, brass band. End of term performance gives pupils an audience for their musical skills.

Interesting pods within the school, one that functions as a shop and one that works as an office and provides a space for work experience for students, who laminate and photocopy and sell snacks.

There's a healthy living emphasis within PE curriculum. A yoga teacher is a popular presence, giving classes for all 4–14-year-olds

As many enrichment activities as possible take place, inside and outside school. Cross-curricular day trips to a café, to a museum, to the park, to the leisure centre, and the opportunity for residential visits of increasing length as pupils develop confidence. Some clubs at lunchtime – board games, sports, art and music – to give pupils a voice and a choice of activity, as well as providing structured leisure time. They also have links with mainstream local schools, who visit and share time with TreeHouse pupils in 'reverse inclusion'.

Sport: A wall with sporting trophies is a new addition to the school as it develops its sporting presence and prowess. Pride of place was the trophy for coming third in recent Panathlon Challenge. Full-time head of PE as well as supporting teachers to ensure pupils get as much time moving as possible – football, bowling, horse riding, bouncy castle, swimming, fitness. They take part in in Sports Relief Day, Jack Petchey competitions and Duke of Edinburgh. Trips to local woods as part of 'healthy living' emphasis within PE curriculum. A yoga teacher is a popular presence, giving classes for all 4-14-year-olds. Parents like the fact that pupils are regularly taken out and the school is not restricted by the need for safety precautions and labour-intensive support. 'My son has started to enjoy swimming and horse riding as well at school,' one parent said.

Ethos and heritage: Originally set up by parents of children with autism to ensure a safe and pleasant learning environment, this school has some celebrity status within the autism world: it was one of the early specialist autism schools with its mission to 'make the ordinary possible for young people with autism'. Lots of emphasis on Applied Behaviour Analysis (ABA). However, the leadership has worked hard to make it 'feel more like a school'. A wonderful light, purpose-built space with the charity (Ambitious about Autism) and staff rooms on one floor, the lower school filling the ground floor and older pupils' classrooms above. Despite lockable doors separating areas and small breakout rooms, the school feels very open, thanks to large glass doors and huge windows. It is not a state school so has control over how it is run and which pupils to accept. Large grounds and good facilities, from the lunch room to the office pod. More use could be made of the extensive outdoor space, though a planted sensory garden is being developed, there is a cycle path route for road safety training and some equipment – trampolines and table tennis tables – for use in the playgrounds. The front area seems underused and parents felt 'there is not enough variation in outside activities to engage in'.

Pastoral care, inclusivity and discipline: There are six-weekly review meetings to check individual goals and progress for new pupils, termly target monitoring and the annual reviews of EHC plans. Tight reviews and communication between staff and parents help to keep pupil behaviour monitored and supported. Pupils do get agitated but 'we can deal with challenging behaviour based on distress or disruption' thanks to sufficient well-trained staff and good systems. Distressed pupils supported whilst other pupils kept separate and calm to avoid spread of anxiety. We saw pupils bouncing from space to space exploring while a support teacher alongside ensured safety. We also saw an overwhelmed pupil surrounded gently by support staff until ready to resume activities. Parents say, 'shouting and aggressive behaviour is managed very well, but that is part of what a substantial number of the pupils display.' Interventions kept to a minimum since pupils are constantly watched over. The consistent behaviour management systems seem to give pupils the security they need to become open to learning. 'I like school – everything, especially break time,' commented one pupil. When break times can be very worrying in mainstream schools, that is indeed good news. Parents all said that they felt there were 'extremely good procedures in place for the challenging population and safety is paramount'. They felt that their children were kept safe in a respectful and sensitive manner.

Therapy and staffing: The 144 staff keep the 86 pupils well supported. There are efforts to recruit more male staff and older staff as well as the good supply of young psychology students. This, together with concerted efforts at staff development and well-being (staff breakfasts, trusting staff more, encouraging them to leave school early on Fridays), is helping to improve staff retention – 'it is a challenging job and there is burnout'. Parents say that 'the school attracts the more extreme end of challenging behaviour, accepting pupils who have been rejected by other schools'. Seven behaviour analysts work with pupils to ensure their openness to learning. Gradual move towards Positive Behaviour Support (PBS), underpinned by Applied Behaviour Analysis (ABA) programmes.

Two full-time speech and language therapists and one full-time occupational therapist (all school based) have time with pupils both in individual spaces and within the class to ensure therapy is carried through. There are also art and yoga therapists. Communication systems include PECS and Makaton. No school nurse but qualified first aid trained staff look after pupils who have medical needs.

Pupils and parents: Pupils come from ridiculously far away – up to an hour and a quarter journey time each way, from all London boroughs – as there is so little provision elsewhere. As a result, it is often hard to get parents to be involved, so they are all called prior to the three annual parents' evenings to encourage good turnout, which seems to be working. The parents' evenings are also used as information sharing on topics such as reading, residential trips etc. Ethnically diverse pupil group, but predominance of boys (85 per cent). About a quarter of pupils on pupil premium. A family liaison officer helps support parents with matters such as transport and transition, and encourages family engagement.

Money matters: Close link between Ambitious about Autism charity in the same building and the school. The charity supports the school as well as having a large team that raises funds and awareness about autism, and works to influence national policy. Aims to have TreeHouse as a centre of excellence for autism teaching as well as a centre to teach others. Twelve governors for three-year terms include an ex-special school head, parent governors, community, LA and staff governors. No shortage of money for facilities and teaching – this is a well-resourced school.

The last word: Staff are engaged and valued and as a result pupils are sure of support, and feel safe enough to be able to learn and develop in this exciting building. Pupils achieve more than parents could ever have imagined thanks to well-thought-through curriculum and individually set goals.

City slippers – boarding schools for Londoners

Boarding, like sheep herding, polytunnelling and muck spreading, is something many Londoners assume to be a predominantly rural activity. Whether this adds to or detracts from its appeal is down to the individual but boarding, especially weekly boarding, is now an increasingly popular option for London parents.

It's hardly surprising that families who have never before considered the idea of boarding might question whether the bracing two-hour trek across London to and from that excellent day school (and in the dark both ways during winter) really is as character forming as they'd hoped. For such families, boarding can begin to look like a life-enhancing option, making it possible for their children to start early and stay late with food and friends provided – and without a punitive journey at the beginning and end of the day.

For some London parents, day places will always be the educational black, the only goal worth pursuing, with boarding the reserve choice when all other options have been exhausted. Others, relishing the out of hours opportunities, from extra tuition to drama, debate, music and sport, feel very differently. Costs permitting (and boarding is, undeniably, costly) it could well be worth taking a look at both.

Weekly and flexi boarding

Weekly boarding is growing in popularity, particularly for children who live too far away to be day pupils or whose parents work long hours and/or frequently travel abroad. Weekly boarders either go home on Friday evenings or Saturday afternoons and return to school on Sunday evenings or Monday mornings. For many children, this offers the best of both worlds: they can enjoy school during the week, work hard and spend lots of time with their

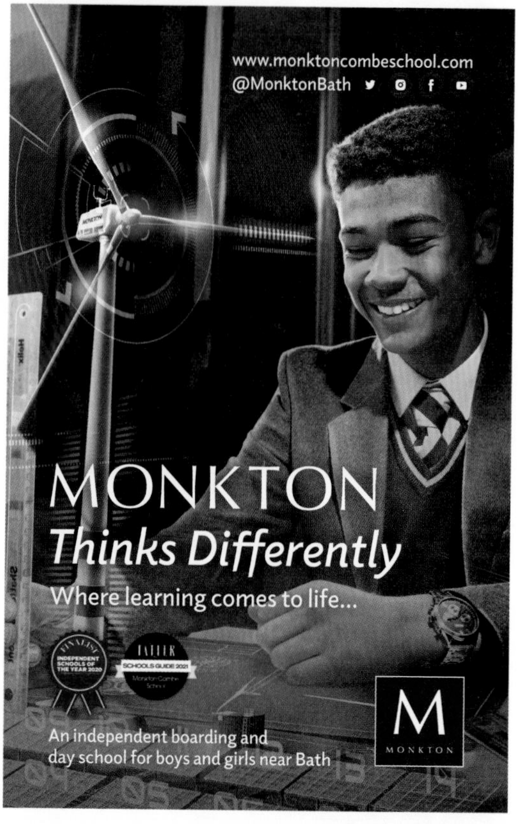

friends, then relax at home with their parents on Saturdays and Sundays. Parents are keen on weekly boarding too. They like the fact that they don't have to nag about homework or getting up on time in the morning and feel that home time is 'quality time'. Many opt for boarding schools within an hour's drive so they can still turn up for sports matches, concerts and drama productions during the term.

Flexi boarding gets a mixed press; parents are generally in favour but for some schools it's a step too far. One prep headmaster describes it as 'a bit of a nightmare, like glorified hotel management'. Unlike full and weekly boarding, one school's definition of 'flexi' may not be the same as another's. It's certainly never going to be bed and breakfast at the drop of a hat. Most schools require parents to book boarding nights at the beginning of each term, with Thursdays and Fridays being the most popular. Not surprising if it means parents can enjoy a night out without having to find a babysitter (and not have to get up for the Saturday morning school run). While it can be complicated for schools to manage, flexi boarding could be just the ticket if your child has to stay at school late for sport, music or drama one or two nights a week, or if you want to dip your toe in the water and see if boarding suits your family. Schools that offer flexi boarding will inevitably have some spare beds and many told us that they will always do their best to accommodate a pupil at short notice if there's a family emergency.

There are quite a few schools that offer weekly and flexi boarding places within or close to the M25. Girls only schools include Woldingham and Prior's Field in Surrey, Marymount in Kingston-upon-Thames and St George's Ascot to the south and south west. North of the river the Royal Masonic School for Girls in Chorleywood and

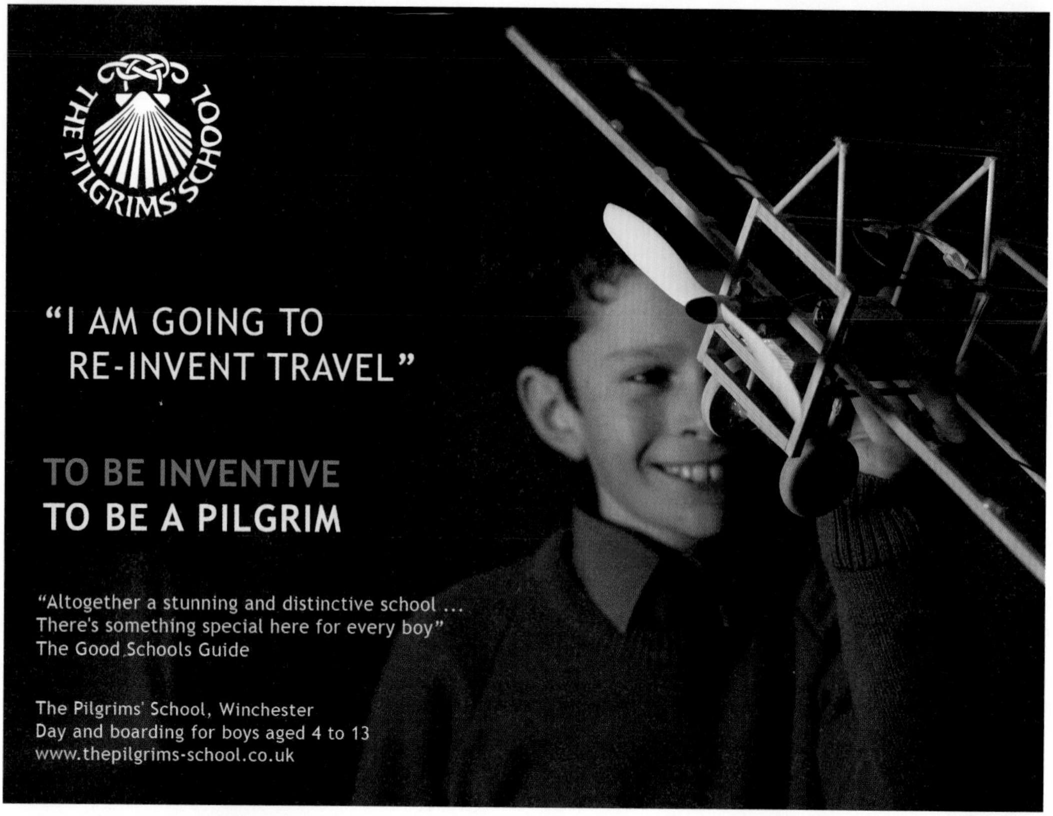
THE PILGRIMS' SCHOOL
"I AM GOING TO RE-INVENT TRAVEL"
TO BE INVENTIVE
TO BE A PILGRIM
"Altogether a stunning and distinctive school ... There's something special here for every boy"
The Good Schools Guide
The Pilgrims' School, Winchester
Day and boarding for boys aged 4 to 13
www.thepilgrims-school.co.uk

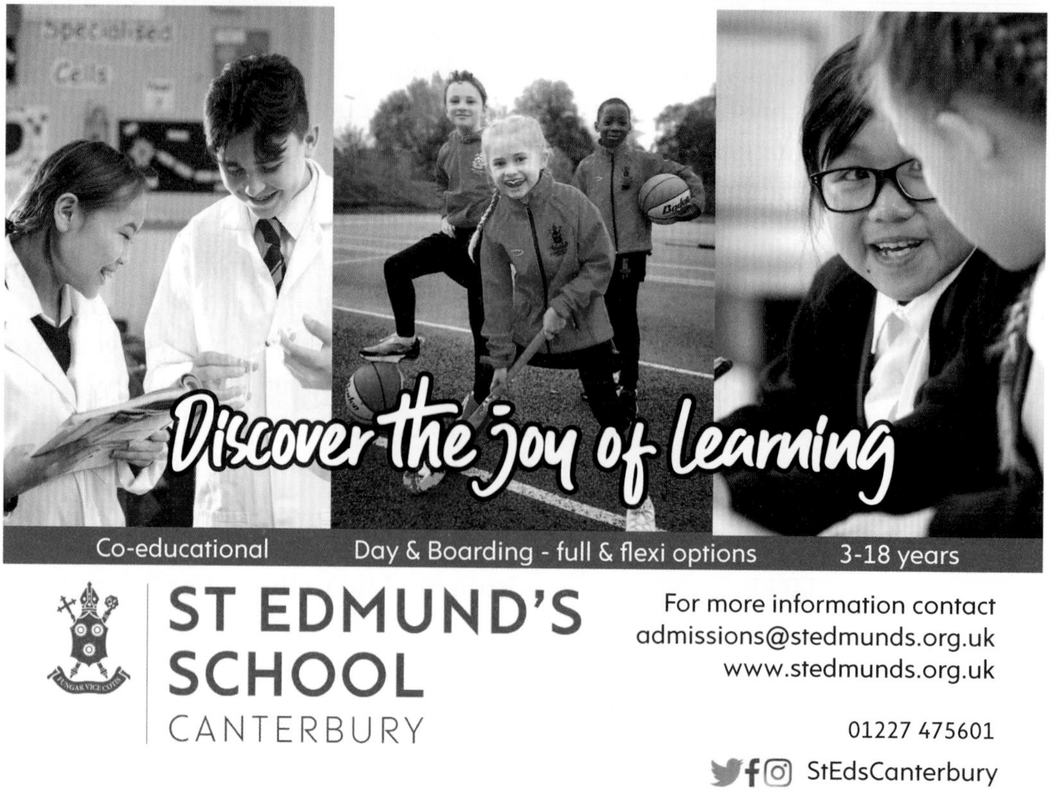
Discover the joy of learning
Co-educational
Day & Boarding - full & flexi options
3-18 years
ST EDMUND'S SCHOOL
CANTERBURY
For more information contact
admissions@stedmunds.org.uk
www.stedmunds.org.uk
01227 475601
StEdsCanterbury

Queenswood in Hatfield fill a similar niche. For boys there's Whitgift and Dulwich College. Co-ed boarding is provided by Mill Hill School in north London and, further afield, Royal Russell School (Croydon) Aldenham and Haileybury in Herts, Sevenoaks in Kent and Epsom College and City of London Freemen's School in Surrey, among others.

Full boarding schools

Most famous are for the boys: Eton, Harrow and Radley. This trio used to be a quartet but in 2021 Winchester College announced plans to take girls in the sixth form – starting with day girls until a girls' boarding house has been completed. At these schools all pupils board and may go home only for exeats, usually two per term, Saturday pm to Sunday pm. However, parents are more involved with school life than formerly; those who live close enough attend matches, concerts and plays and technology enables much closer contact over long distances too. Full boarding boys' preps in the home counties include Cothill House and Horris Hill. Preps where boarding is compulsory for all in the last two years (7 and 8) such as Caldicott and Papplewick are particularly popular with London parents.

Benenden is one of the very few remaining full boarding schools for girls, but boarders can opt to go home for weekends to some extent if they wish to. Downe House, Heathfield, Wycombe Abbey, Sherborne Girls and Tudor Hall are essentially full boarding (no flexi/weekly) but also take a few local day pupils. Hanford School in Dorset and Sunny Hill in Somerset are two of a tiny handful of girls only boarding preps.

If you want your sons and daughters to attend a full boarding school together there are quite a few co-ed choices including Oundle, Uppingham, The King's School

Canterbury, Charterhouse and Marlborough College. Because of its proximity to London, Wellington College is de facto weekly boarding since so many pupils go home for Saturday night, nevertheless all boarders must spend two Saturday nights in school per term. All these schools also take some day pupils but don't offer weekly or flexi boarding options. Girls and boys live in separate boarding accommodation with clear rules about what is out of bounds to visitors of the opposite sex. Some schools have co-ed sixth form boarding houses, but boundaries are in place.

Other options

At specialist schools – such as the Purcell School (music) and Tring Park (performing arts) – boarding helps the super-talented to hone their skills in and out of hours, free from tube strike blues and similar aesthetic lows. There are even some state boarding schools close to London where parents pay for accommodation only and teaching comes courtesy of the ever-generous taxpayer; these include Cranbook (selective), St George's Harpenden (church-goers) or Gordon's (all-comers).

For any dyed in the wool Londoners who come over all faint at the prospect of breathing air outside the congestion zone, it's hard to beat boarding, literally, on your doorstep. Westminster School, with 185 or so boarders (including girls, admitted in the sixth form), is pretty much as close as you can get to total immersion in the beating heart of the city without squatting in Big Ben. 'You get that sense of community,' says a former Westminster parent. 'You have more time to get involved and people tend to stay late anyway.'

For detailed information and reviews of the UK's best independent and state boarding schools, including those outside London, see Good Schools Guide Boarding Schools or visit our website (www.goodschoolsguide.co.uk).

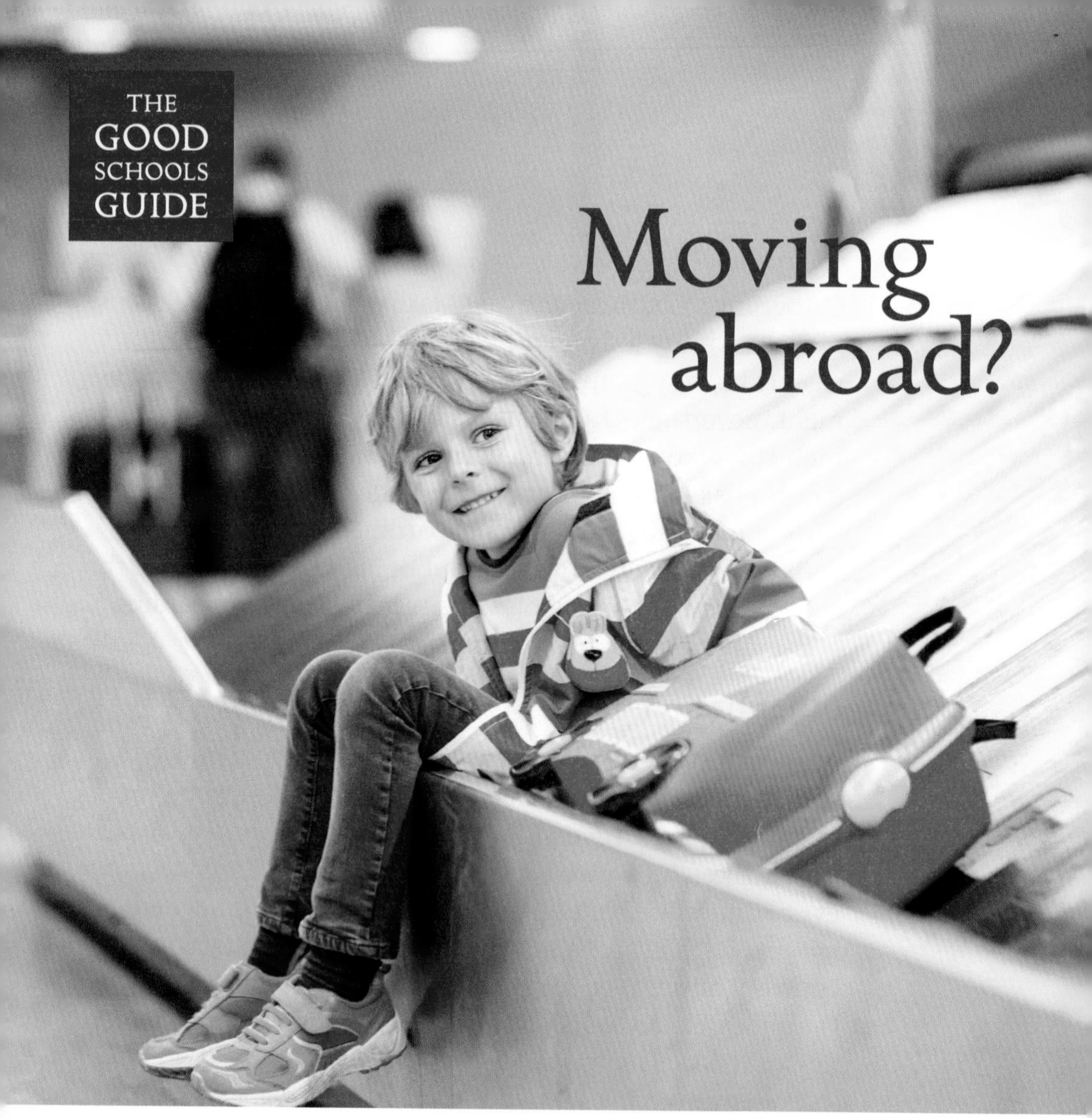
THE GOOD SCHOOLS GUIDE
Moving abroad?

Tutors and tutoring – a Londoner's view

Tutoring is endemic in the UK these days, and nowhere more so than in the capital, where the top agencies have parents queuing up to pay £80+ an hour to buy their child an advantage. They'd have you believe that without a tutor your toddler will miss the academic boat, but keep your head – there's still plenty of time.

Two is too early

Seriously, there are folks out there offering to tutor children as young as 2, but don't be taken in. Spend the money at one of London's wonderful bookshops and read to your child instead. What pre-school-age children need is not tutoring and angst, but time and love from the grown-ups who care for them. If you're reading this article, you are by default an educated, thinking parent who wants the best for your child, so give her the treasures of your mind, your vocabulary, your tastes; they will far out-class anything a tutor can provide.

A clear reason

When do you need a tutor? Put simply, when there is a clear and specific reason for using one. Your child may need help with the 11+ or 13+ entry to an academically selective senior school, particularly from a state school. Or perhaps he's struggling with a particular GCSE/A level subject. Or she may be falling behind at school. Or he may have missed school through illness or some other crisis. Where there is a known goal to work towards, or a genuine problem to address, tutoring comes into its own.

For a shy child who's underperforming, a friendly tutor can be a godsend. Free from the distractions of the classroom and other pupils, he or she can sit quietly with your child and concentrate solely on whatever's confusing her, filling in gaps in her knowledge and building up her confidence. Grades start to improve, and the child becomes a happier learner, keener to put her hand up in class and more relaxed about going to school. For a teenager who's struggling with maths, demoralised by always coming last in his set and stressed about approaching exams, quality one-to-one teaching from someone with no preconceptions about him can make the difference between failure and success; between giving up and keeping on.

Or it could be that you're putting your child through the state system to begin with while you save up for the independent senior school you hope he'll attend. But an over-stretched primary school teacher, with 30 children to get ready for their Sats, will have no interest in helping Harry prepare for independent school entrance, and even mention of the local grammar school is unlikely to get a sympathetic response. After all, from her perspective, selective education isn't what school's about. No matter how bright your child is, he'll be up against other children who have been intensively coached so tutoring is pretty much essential unless you are confident about your ability to fill in gaps.

A real need

Perhaps you feel your child needs a tutor even though he's already at a good preparatory school. Well, maybe. Be very sure, though, that the need is real. You are already paying a fair whack for his education at a school whose job it is to prepare him for secondary school exams. Depending on where he is, a year's tutoring in the run-up to Common Entrance may make sense, if only because it'll bring you peace of mind. But to have your tutored 7-year-old win a place at a high-achieving prep, and then immediately start having him tutored some more just because everyone else is doing it, will only exhaust him and your bank account. Wave him off to St Brainiac's with a proud smile, and let the school do its work.

On the other hand, if you've just relocated to the UK from overseas, using a tutor is an excellent way to get your kids up to speed with the English system and help them to feel more assured and comfortable in lessons. This in turn will help them to make friends, and the whole settling-in process will be smoother. For a child in a new country, confidence is key.

Where to look

If you want a tutor for your child, how do you find one? The best way should be word of mouth, of course. However, tutoring is one of those things parents usually do in secret, either because they don't choose to tell it around that their child struggles at school, or because they've no wish to increase the opposition's chances in the race for places. Try asking a friend with an older child, who won't begrudge your using what they no longer need. If this doesn't bring results, don't worry. This is London, and you have plenty of options.

Tutor companies

The first of these is to approach a tutor company. We review many of the best of these on The Good Schools Guide website, and using them has a number of benefits. They'll be skilled at matching your child to the right person, and will give you redress if you're not happy. The work of looking will be taken off your hands, and, since the tutors usually come to you, the whole process becomes very straightforward. This is the most expensive way of employing a tutor, however. Almost all companies will charge you a registration fee, which can be anything from a few quid to a hair-raising £180, and the hourly rate for tuition will be high (be prepared for at least £45), because the company will take a cut before paying the teacher.

Some of the really big tutorial companies cover too wide a geographical area to interview all their tutors in person, but they will have interviewed them by phone, and checked their references and DBS record.

Online search

A cheaper option is finding a tutor online. There are a number of websites on which tutors can advertise, and whose contact details you buy, usually for around £20, after you've had an exchange of messages with your selected tutor to see if they're the right fit. Tuition rates vary from around £16 ph – probably an undergraduate trying to earn a bit of extra cash – to £45+ ph for an experienced and qualified teacher. The website companies run checks to ascertain whether the tutor advertising is who they claim to be, but otherwise it's down to you to judge people's suitability. Use your common sense. If a person's replies to your messages are semi-literate, don't engage them as an English tutor.

Do your homework

Whether you're paying top whack for Kensington's finest hand-picked Oxbridge scholars, or searching through the online jungle with only your five wits to guide you, there are some measures it's sensible to take. After all, this is your child. Self-employed individuals are unlikely to be DBS-checked, because the law prevents them from running a check on themselves, so ask to see references or to speak to previous clients. In fact, do this even if they are DBS-checked. Interview the tutor on the phone before fixing a first date, and don't feel pressured into accepting someone who doesn't sound right. Don't be afraid to sit in on the first lesson, and afterwards ask your child what she thought. If the tutor is travelling to you, check that they can get there easily. Don't believe them when they say they can get from Wood Green to Putney in half an hour; they absolutely can't. Lastly – and this wisdom comes from years of weary experience – insist on punctuality. A tutor who is routinely late will soon drive you up the wall.

In short, if you do your homework your child's tutoring experiences should be happy, productive and affordable. Good luck.

A word on child protection

If you are preparing to entrust your child to a school – whether day or boarding – you will most likely assume that your child will be safe and that all members of the school's staff will take the greatest care to ensure that this is always the case. The chances are that your expectations will be fulfilled, but unfortunately in a sad minority of cases that is not what happens.

A flood of historical allegations against schools, court cases, mobile phones, flexi-boarding, more parental involvement, the internet, sex education and heightened awareness have together helped usher in some sunlight and fresh air. Schools are now a less than perfect setting for paedophiles and bullies. Child protection policies, found on every school website, usefully make plain the possibility of abuse at schools – something rarely contemplated a generation ago.

Abuse can occur at any school, anywhere. Fame is no protection, and nor is obscurity. Do not think less of a school because a case of abuse has been brought to light there. Tabloid coverage can be the price the school has to pay for handling a case of abuse or bullying openly. It is inevitable that abuse will occur somewhere. What matters is how well the school deals with it, how well it performs in bringing the abuse to light and how open it is on the subject with current and future parents.

What can you do?

Parents do well to warn their children – gently but seriously – of the dangers, however remote these may be, so they feel that it is easy to speak to you should they meet them. It is worth pointing out that abuse can come from anyone – including a teacher or an adult they know well, or from another child at the school.

Raise your own antennae at any school you may be

considering. You can inquire about the steps taken to safeguard children in the same way you might ask about bullying or learning support. As always, much can be gleaned from the head's attitude when questions about child protection are asked. Is he or she ill at ease? Defensive? Or happy to engage, and proud of the steps their school has taken? Openness is what you're looking for.

How easy is it for a child, or a parent for that matter, to report an incident? Schools make this possible in a variety of ways; what matters is that passing on concerns is a routine thing (children and parents do it about lots of things all the time), and is welcomed by the school, and is low-stakes. The person registering the concern should not feel that they are putting their relationships within the school at risk, let alone threatening someone's place. That may seem an odd thing to say, but if you fear to report, say, careless management of a museum trip because it will harm an otherwise much-loved teacher, you probably choose to stay mum. Your concerns have to cross a high threshold before you communicate them, so you never pass on those troubling observations that may be the outward indication of serious problems. To be safe, schools need to hear the little voices, not just the shouting.

Further reading

The Good Schools Guide

Features independent and unbiased views of over 1,200 state and independent schools throughout Britain, written by parents for parents.

The Good Schools Guide Boarding Schools

Reviews 350+ boarding schools across Britain, independent and state, with advice on when to start boarding, applying from abroad, sex and drugs and homesickness, boarding for a child with SEN.

The Good Schools Guide online subscription

All the reviews plus details of every school in Britain, with exam data, catchment maps, university entrance information. Advice on choosing a school, SEN, tutors, talented children and much more.

Uni in the USA

Written by students who have been through the US system, features in-depth descriptions of 65 US universities, plus the inside track on getting in and preparing for life across the pond.

Uni in the USA and Beyond online subscription and ebook

Also includes unis in Europe and the East, from Alberta to Abu Dhabi, and advice from SATS to visas.

The Good Schools Guide International online subscription

The one-stop educational shop for expats, it reviews the best state and independent schools round the globe, plus insider knowledge on life overseas.

All available via www.goodschoolsguide.co.uk/shop-online

London North school index

School	Section	Page

List of advertisers

House ads

Notes

Notes